Advocate for the Doomed

Portrait photo of James G. McDonald, 1933. USHMM/McDonald Family.

Advocate for the Doomed

The Diaries and Papers of James G. McDonald 1932–1935

EDITED BY

Richard Breitman,
Barbara McDonald Stewart,
and Severin Hochberg

INDIANA UNIVERSITY PRESS
BLOOMINGTON AND INDIANAPOLIS

PUBLISHED IN ASSOCIATION WITH THE
UNITED STATES HOLOCAUST MEMORIAL MUSEUM
WASHINGTON, D.C.

The assertions, arguments, and conclusions contained herein are those of the author and the volume editors. They do not necessarily reflect the opinions of the United States Holocaust Memorial Museum or the United States Holocaust Memorial Council.

This book is a publication of

Indiana University Press
601 North Morton Street
Bloomington, IN 47404-3797 USA

http://iupress.indiana.edu

Telephone orders 800-842-6796
Fax orders 812-855-7931
Orders by e-mail iuporder@indiana.edu

©2007 by the United States Holocaust Memorial Museum
All rights reserved

No part of this book may be reproduced or utilized in any form or by any means, electronic or mechanical, including photocopying and recording, or by any information storage and retrieval system, without permission in writing from the publisher. The Association of American University Presses' Resolution on Permissions constitutes the only exception to this prohibition.

The paper used in this publication meets the minimum requirements of American National Standard for Information Sciences—Permanence of Paper for Printed Library Materials, ANSI Z39.48-1984.

Manufactured in the United States of America

Library of Congress Cataloging-in-Publication Data

McDonald, James G. (James Grover), 1886–1964.
Advocate for the doomed / James G. McDonald ; edited by Richard Breitman, Barbara McDonald Stewart, and Severin Hochberg.
v. cm.
"Published in association with the United States Holocaust Memorial Museum, Washington, D.C."
Includes bibliographical references and index.
Contents: v. 1. The diaries and papers of James G. McDonald, 1932–1935.
ISBN-13: 978-0-253-34862-3 (cloth : alk. paper)
ISBN-10: 0-253-34862-5 (cloth : alk. paper) 1. McDonald, James G. (James Grover), 1886–1964—Diaries. 2. McDonald, James G. (James Grover), 1886–1964—Archives. 3. Diplomats—United States—Diaries. 4. Diplomats—United States—Archives. 5. High Commission for Refugees (Jewish and Other) Coming from Germany—Biography. 6. Humanitarianism—History—20th century—Sources. 7. World War, 1939–1945—Refugees—Sources 8. Antisemitism—History—20th century—Sources. 9. Germany—History—1933–1945—Sources. 10. National socialism—Germany—History—20th century—Sources. I. Breitman, Richard, date II. Stewart, Barbara McDonald, date III. Hochberg, Severin. IV. United States Holocaust Memorial Museum. V. Title.
E748.M1475A3 2007
327.2092—dc22

2006029729

1 2 3 4 5 12 11 10 09 08 07

To Robert Derosier, William E. Leuchtenburg, and Robert J. Scally

CONTENTS

ACKNOWLEDGMENTS | ix

Introduction: Young Man from Indiana
by Barbara McDonald Stewart | 1

1. Summer–Fall 1932: Foreshadowing | 10
2. Winter 1932–Spring 1933: The Nazi Revolution | 22
3. Late April–May 1933: American Reactions | 54
4. June–August 1933: Alerting Others | 73
5. September 1933: Lobbying for League Action | 96
6. October 1933: High Commissioner | 121
7. November 1933: A Bridge from Lausanne to Berlin | 138
8. December 1933: Proposal for a Corporation | 198
9. January 1934: Washington's Views | 240
10. February 1934: Testing Germany/Family Crisis | 280
11. March 1934: Raising Funds | 308
12. April 1934: The "Jewish Question" in Europe | 342
13. May 1934: Emigration Options? | 380
14. June 1934: Turn for the Worse | 402
15. July 1934: Visit to the Saar | 415
16. August 1934: The League Keeps Its Distance | 448
17. September 1934: The Climate in Geneva | 467
18. October 1934: Criticism Is Easy | 489
19. November 1934: Grand Tour | 536
20. December 1934: A Request to the President | 572
21. January 1935: The Catholic Connection | 592

22. February 1935: A Diplomatic Maneuver | 615
23. March 1935: Brazil | 632
24. April 1935: South American Survey | 665
25. May 1935: Regret and Relief | 707
26. June 1935: Downsizing | 764
27. July 1935: Liquidation Plans | 776

Conclusion by Richard Breitman | 790

INDEX | 807

ACKNOWLEDGMENTS

Even with three active co-editors, a project this big and this complicated needed the assistance of many other brains, hands, and eyes. None of those who helped us are responsible for errors or remaining difficulties, but they certainly deserve much of the credit for the positive elements.

Stephen Mize made this diary materialize in potentially publishable form. Having tracked down its component parts and, just as important, brought the McDonald families into the effort, fortunately he did not relinquish his role. He served as an essential member of our research group, showing discernment about what would or would not work in the way of annotations and additions. He helped with the editing, and he also took particular responsibility for photographs. We could not have managed without him. Benton Arnovitz, director of Academic Publications at the United States Holocaust Memorial Museum (USHMM), steered this effort from the stage of idea all the way to publication, offering judicious advice, nuggets from his experience, and occasional editing along the way. Janet Rabinowitch at Indiana University Press expressed enthusiasm for this diary from the beginning and fortunately did not let its size deter her or the press from publishing it in proper form.

Janet McDonald Barrett, Vale Barrett, Halsey V. Barrett, and Patricia Sugrue Ketchum provided invaluable information resolving many historical mysteries, culminating in the donation of the McDonald diary to the USHMM.

Sara Bloomfield, director of the USHMM, had the vision to see the importance of James G. McDonald to the USHMM, and she made this diary a museum priority. Paul Shapiro, director of the Center for Advanced Holocaust Studies, arranged for resources for this project and gave us valuable advice. One of the most important resources was Ohio State University graduate student Amanda Rothey, who served as our research assistant as a Dorot Fellow in the summer of 2005.

Others at the museum who gave their time and assistance generously include Sharon Muller, Judith Cohen, Maren Read, Henry Mayer, Rebecca Erbelding, Mark Ziomek, Alice Greenwald, Diane Saltzman, Aleisa Fishman, Suzanne Brown-Fleming, Beth Aronson, Jordan Tannenbaum, Laura Heymer, Arthur Berger, Dara Goldberg, Andrew Hollinger, George Hellman, Jürgen

Matthäus, Peter Black, Celeste Maier, Julie Hock, Shelley Binder, Nancy Hartman, Aleksandra Borecka, Ferenc Katona, Michlean Amir, Sara Sirman, Anne Marigza, Emily Jacobson, Teresa Pollin, Stephen Feinberg, Peter Fredlake, Ann Richman, David Stolte, Peter Bonta, Duane Brant, Christine Brown, Heather Duckworth, Kristy Brosius, Katie Swangin, Linda Lazar, Robert Garber, Bruce Tapper, Victoria Barnett, Jill Weinberg, Max Reid, Curtis Millay, Steven Kanaley, Ronald Coleman, Steven Luckert, Ann Millin, and Amanda Noyes.

Drawing on her expert knowledge of the context of British events, Anne Rush helped with annotations and proofreading. Ada Rousso performed the absolutely essential task of entering repeated stylistic corrections into the first rough computer copy of the manuscript. She saved us hundreds of hours and much frustration.

Harold Miller, archivist of the Foreign Policy Association (FPA), and Robert Nolan, also at the FPA, supplied information about McDonald's years at the FPA. Stacey Lynn Sell, National Gallery, did research on McDonald's professional associations. Pamela Wasmer, Monroe County (Indiana) Public Library, tracked down information about McDonald's genealogy and early years.

Tamar Evangelistia-Dougherty, curator at the Lehman Suite, Columbia University Libraries, was extraordinarily generous. At the Joint Distribution Committee Archives, Misha Mitsel, Sherry Hyman, and Shelley Helfand were all very helpful. We are grateful to the staff of the Houghton Library at Harvard University and to the staff of the Franklin D. Roosevelt Presidential Library, especially Robert Parks.

During 2005–2006 Richard Breitman was the Ina Levine Invitational Scholar at the Center for Advanced Holocaust Studies. This fellowship, the result of the generosity of William S. Levine, allowed him to spend most of his time on *Advocate for the Doomed*.

We are greatly indebted to all of them.

Advocate for the Doomed

Introduction: Young Man from Indiana

Barbara McDonald Stewart

In 1939 American Commander Victor "Pug" Henry was appointed naval attaché in Berlin. His attractive German-speaking wife Rhoda happened to catch Adolf Hitler's eye at a reception shortly after their arrival. Using his connections and his shrewd judgment, Henry soon deduced that the Nazis were planning to sign a treaty with the Soviet Union and then go to war against Poland. His intelligence report on the subject landed in the Oval Office, and after events proved him right, President Franklin D. Roosevelt soon summoned him home for a face-to-face meeting.

Skeptics dismissed Henry, the fictional hero of Herman Wouk's 1971 novel *The Winds of War,* as the stuff of melodrama, not history. No real person could find himself at the center of the action so consistently and talk directly and frankly to world leaders at so many critical moments.

In reality, one American did manage to secure a private meeting with Hitler and to deduce something of the Führer's future plans. His encounters with Hitler and other high Nazi officials began in 1933—shortly after the establishment of the Nazi regime and in the midst of the Nazi revolution. His focus of interest was not Germany's military ambitions, which he nonetheless sensed in a broad way, but Hitler's policy toward the Jews. This same American reported his conversation with Hitler and his concerns about Nazi Germany to President Roosevelt on a number of occasions. Not a man of action, but a man of diplomatic initiatives, committees, and organizations, he nonetheless spent much of the next six years trying to prevent or reduce the scale of the catastrophes he saw looming from the beginning.

The man was James G. McDonald, who in 1933 became High Commissioner for Refugees (Jewish and Other) Coming from Germany under the League of Nations. He was also my father, and he wrote down all the efforts in which he was involved.

Well, that is not quite accurate. My father's diary was actually dictated to stenographers and secretaries. He composed it often, usually daily, but when time or secretarial support was lacking, he left it to later, sometimes recapitulating events and conversations a week or two old. In one extreme case he admitted in the diary to reconstructing day-by-day events almost a month later. He had an incredible memory.

His diary was written in the midst of events (and in the heat of them) in order to keep track of everything that was happening. It contains an amazing range of candid contemporary comments by world leaders and public figures. In addition to small numbers of meetings with Hitler and Roosevelt, in the 1930s my father consulted with Chaim Weizmann and Stephen Wise, Felix Warburg and Vladimir Jabotinsky, Cardinal Eugenio Pacelli (the future Pope Pius XII), and the archbishop of Canterbury. And with many hundreds more—Jewish refugees and German political figures in exile and Jewish notables still in Nazi Germany. Those readers curious about how this diary casts new light on historical interpretations of the Nazi revolution, disputes between Zionists and non-Zionists, the refugee policies of the Roosevelt administration, and more will find detailed analysis in the conclusion written by co-editor Richard Breitman.

Although my father stopped keeping a diary in early 1936 (or this portion of his diary has been lost), he resumed his entries in the postwar period, when, in 1946, he participated in a new and quite different chapter in world history as a member of the Anglo-American Committee of Inquiry on Palestine, and then as the first American ambassador to the State of Israel. For the period in between—when he was on the editorial staff of the *New York Times,* and as adviser, attended the now famous Evian Conference in July 1938, served as chairman of President Roosevelt's Advisory Committee on Political Refugees, and had a weekly radio program on foreign policy—we have been able to draw from his correspondence and private papers, as well as from government records and a number of private collections of other key individuals, but not from his own diary.

My father's diary and related papers have been accepted as authentic and important by the United States Holocaust Memorial Museum, which is collaborating in the publication of this planned series of three volumes by Indiana University Press.

The Indiana publication seems appropriate for our family. James Grover McDonald was born in 1886 in Coldwater, a small town in western Ohio. At some point, his family moved to St. Mary's, Ohio, and then, perhaps around 1898, to another small town, Albany, Indiana. Grover, as he was called, was the third of five boys. In Albany the McDonalds owned and ran a small hotel, maybe twenty rooms in all. After the oldest boy had gone to work as a telegraph operator and the next ones were ready for college, the whole family moved to Bloomington, Indiana, so that the boys could all go to Indiana University, live at home, and work their way through school.

His father, Kenneth, had been born in Glengarry, Ontario, Canada, and had come to the United States to find a job. He married a woman named Anna Diederick, born in Ohio of German immigrant parents. I never knew my grandfather, but my grandmother was a dour woman, with whom I had almost no contact, even when we went on a visit to Bloomington, where she lived. She died when I was about ten.

I know almost nothing about my father's early years, what his family life was like, or how he got along with his brothers, because he told us virtually nothing. There are a few stories: one, because my grandmother wanted a girl after two boys, she kept my father in long curls until he was three or four. When they were cut off, my father said he ran away from home and stole a banana at the railroad station. The only thing sure about this story is the long curls—there are photographs to prove it. My father said he and his brothers tended bar at the hotel (my father was a teetotaler for a good portion of his life), and when they went to college, they all waited tables. At Albany High School he joined the chorus, and he said they threw out the only boy who could carry a tune. I never did hear him sing. The education in Albany must have been better than one would expect, though he did say that his Latin teacher was so poor that his Latin was inadequate for his graduate studies. His graduating class, of which he was valedictorian, had all of ten members.

My mother, Ruth Stafford, also grew up in Albany, just a block away from the hotel. The McDonalds were Catholic, while the Staffords were strict Methodists, which posed a serious problem. Wednesday night was prayer meeting night for the Methodists, so when Ruth's parents had gone to church, she would go over to the hotel. A younger brother, Lee, was assigned to stand on the corner and watch for the church meeting letting out, then notify Ruth, so that she could run home.

My mother went to DePauw College, and according to family lore, she and Grover became engaged in 1908, while she was there and Grover at Indiana University. He graduated from Indiana in 1909, majoring in history, and went on to do an M.A. there the following year. Then he went off to do further (doctoral) work at Harvard. He came back to Indiana to teach history and political science in the fall of 1914. It was not until 1915 that Ruth and Grover were married—a remarkably long engagement. Then a Catholic priest performed the ceremony in Bloomington with the McDonald family present, and later that day Albany's Methodist minister performed a second ceremony for Stafford friends and family.

The couple immediately left for a six-month honeymoon in Spain, because Grover, in his capacity as a graduate student at Harvard, had received a fellowship to conduct research in France and Spain. The trip, in the middle of World War I, raised some family anxieties. Ruth's father took his new son-in-law aside after the wedding and said, "If something happens to Ruth, please send the body back."

Grover had yet to write his dissertation. In Spain he was to study an obscure sect of Spanish monks. (He later explained that he never finished his Ph.D. dissertation because he came to realize that no one, including himself, was interested in these monks. He was left with a shoebox full of notes, which my mother, the only one who could read his handwriting, had transcribed.) The trans-Atlantic crossings were uneventful, and they evidently had a wonderful time in Spain.

Even though Spain did not participate in the First World War, Grover was close enough to the battlefield to follow events closely. A few years later he wrote that during the war he had begun an active study of the methods and aims of German propaganda, both in this country and abroad.[1] The anti-German thrust of this comment obscured a more complex reality: at the start of the war, my father apparently felt that Germany was unfairly singled out as the prime originator. He definitely objected to some of the Allied claims about German atrocities in Belgium. As a result, he took an action that soon got him labeled as a German sympathizer—and almost two decades later sweetened his initial reception in Nazi Germany.

He wrote a short pamphlet entitled *German "Atrocities" and International Law,* in which he argued that most (though not all) of the charges made by Belgium and others about German atrocities were false or exaggerated, or that Germany's behavior fell roughly within the confines of modern warfare. He also essentially accepted that Germany's invasion of Belgium and violation of Belgian neutrality were justified by the extent of the threat Germany faced and its need for self-preservation.

> In her present struggle Germany faces overwhelming numbers. Her position as a great world power is certainly at stake. Her culture and civilization, she believes to be endangered. Is it strange that, under these circumstances, she chose to follow not the dictates of idealism but rather the demands of what seemed to her an absolute necessity? Only by violating Belgium's neutrality did she feel able to meet the crushing odds arrayed against her.[2]

One can see how such statements might have appealed to Nazi officials, who themselves felt threatened without and within, and who wanted to use all measures necessary to deal with their enemies.

His pamphlet, eagerly put out by the Germanistic Society of Chicago to counteract anti-German feeling early in World War I, explains why his name was found in a German agent's list of American academics, journalists, and other prominent professionals considered pro-German prior to the American declaration of war against Germany in 1917.[3] By that time, however, my father's thinking had shifted substantially.

As Germany's expansionist aims became more visible during the war, my father became more critical. If there was a decisive event for him, it may have been the sinking of the luxurious passenger and cargo liner *Lusitania* by German submarines on May 7, 1915. Having just crossed the Atlantic himself, my father must have felt keenly what it meant for Germany to kill large numbers of passengers (1,201 died) just to deny unidentified cargo to its enemies.

1. McDonald to Hon. Lee S. Overman, Chairman of Senate Investigating Committee, December 11, 1918. Copy in Indiana University Archives.

2. James G. McDonald, *German "Atrocities" and International Law* (Chicago: Germanistic Society of Chicago, 1914), 8.

3. "These Men Called Pro-German in Book of German Agent," *New York Times,* December 7, 1918.

This incident severely strained relations between Germany and the United States. For a while afterward, German submarines held off. But as the war stretched out, the German military gained even greater influence over the government. In 1917 Germany's adoption of unrestricted submarine warfare in the Atlantic drove President Wilson to join Britain, France, and Russia in the war against the Central Powers.

During his course lectures at Indiana, McDonald strongly advocated American entrance into the war. During 1917–1918, in a course on the causes of the war, McDonald focused on Germany's efforts to prevent U.S. involvement and then to neutralize its effects.[4] Yet he was not happy with the terms of the Treaty of Versailles, later believing that it had placed a terrible burden upon the new German republic, which had brought about Weimar's political collapse.[5]

In 1917 a baby daughter, Janet, arrived. The budget at Indiana was tight. Grover could not get a raise, so he accepted a job with the National Civil Service Reform League in New York, taking a leave of absence from Indiana. This shift in the fall of 1918 raised his salary from $2,000 to $3,000. I don't know what happened to him at the Civil Service Reform League, but in January 1919 he was named chairman of the League of Free Nations Association, founded in 1918, which campaigned heavily and unsuccessfully for the United States to join the new international organization, the League of Nations, championed by President Wilson to secure the peace. Afterward, the organization changed its name to the Foreign Policy Association (FPA). Grover stayed as chairman and president until 1933.

The declared aim of the FPA was to promote education in international affairs, and for Grover, it was an education also. He conferred regularly with knowledgeable and influential people such as Joseph P. Chamberlain, Lillian D. Wald, Felix Frankfurter, Felix Warburg, and Paul Kellogg. All of them, participants in liberal internationalist currents of the 1920s and early 1930s, remained important contacts later, when he was dealing with refugees and those persecuted in Germany. My father also developed good connections with conservative American businessmen active internationally, such as John D. Rockefeller, Jr. (one of the largest contributors to the FPA), and international lawyers, such as John Foster Dulles. And there was a double link with the Roosevelts—Franklin spoke at an FPA luncheon in March 1919, and Eleanor served on the FPA nominating committee during 1927–1929. These contacts facilitated my father's access to President Roosevelt in 1933.

Almost every summer he traveled to Europe for the FPA, in essence as a reporter, gathering information about what was going on in various countries. He came to know many key foreign politicians, American diplomats, officials of the League of Nations, and members of the press stationed in Europe. During most of Grover's summer trips to Europe my mother, sister, and I drove to Albany, In-

4. McDonald to Overman, December 11, 1918. Copy in Indiana University Archives.
5. See, for example, entry of May 19, 1935.

diana, to visit my mother's parents. At the time, it seemed perfectly natural for us to do so. My father sent me postcards of Princesses Elizabeth and Margaret Rose and Queen Mary with her neck encased in pearls. Later, after he became League High Commissioner, we got to make some trips with him. Later still, I went to Israel and stayed with him, but that part of the story is for the third volume of this series.

What motivated him? He was brought up in a Catholic home, with an undoubtedly clear distinction between right and wrong—and, I would expect, no-nonsense discipline. In college he would have learned that hard work and study brought opportunities. The study of history certainly taught him of the sufferings of the downtrodden and supplied examples of those who sought to help. I do not think that formal or doctrinal religion meant very much to my father as an adult. We attended a variety of Protestant services. The determining factor seemed to be the minister's sermons. Even after we moved out of the city, we often went back to the Riverside Church to hear my father's favorite preacher, Harry Emerson Fosdick, whose message was liberal and inclusive. Over time, my father became more interested in the Bible, but I think more from a historical point of view. He admired the Jewish people through the ages and became interested in Judaism in its different forms. Again, it was more a question of intellectual and ethical curiosity. I am not sure that all this explains my father's concern for others, but perhaps it sheds some light.

All his life my father was involved in educating or helping others, pursuing humanitarian causes, particularly Jewish ones. His idealism in the 1920s and hope for a strong League of Nations brought him into contact with many like-minded men and women who would have reinforced his belief in the necessity of striving for a better future. Many of these men and women were Jewish—if he had earlier been exposed to stereotypes of Jews, he got plenty of experience to contradict them. He had from the beginning or developed over time a strong antipathy to prejudice. With increasing anti-Semitism in Germany and elsewhere, he saw vivid examples of discrimination and persecution—prejudice translated into vicious practice. For him, religion brought an obligation. Over and over, he spoke of the Christian responsibility to combat anti-Semitism; again, an emphasis on right and wrong.

I knew that my father had little or no interest in a career in business, although he had plenty of connections with wealthy and prominent businessmen. If he had not succeeded in finding his niche in public service, he would have stayed in journalism (his radio broadcasts, later work for the *New York Times*) or gone back to academia—and his diary shows when and how he explored these alternatives.

As a child and even later as an adult, I did not know how my father managed financially—except that my mother was extremely frugal, and this frugality had a lasting impact upon me. My father's diary, however, supplies a good number of clues about financial arrangements for his work as League High Commissioner. At the time he was being considered for the position, he discussed his financial situation with a number of patrons and prominent figures in the American Jewish Committee and the Joint Distribution Committee—Felix Warburg, Henry Ittleson, James Rosenberg, Paul Baerwald, and Lewis Strauss. They agreed that whatever arrangements came out of the League, he would not have to receive less than he was getting as head of the FPA. They also regarded the job as so important that he should not have to hold back for financial reasons: he should go wherever he thought necessary.[6] Their funding of his expenses helps to explain how he was able to travel so frequently and widely in an age when globe-trotting was both time-consuming and expensive. Much of the time his work took him away from the family: reading his diary many decades later, I realize that he was almost never home.

Yet, amazingly, I still have vivid memories of time spent with my father; walking to school, listening to music, having him read me *Back to Treasure Island* as I got ready for bed. I was completely at ease with him, he was a central part of my life, and he was fun to be with. We must have spent together what now would be called "quality time."

After I had children of my own, I wondered how he had such complete authority. He never yelled or spoke harshly, he certainly didn't spank, yet my sister and I did what he wanted. We wanted most to please him, and the greatest possible punishment was his disappointment with us.

People used to comment that we must have had such interesting dinner table conversations with our father. While they were interesting, they were not concerned with foreign affairs. Instead, they were usually about what had happened that day and plans for the next day—the usual fare in most households.

Only once do I remember international news taking over. My father had come out to Indiana to pick us up, and we were driving home. The date was September 1, 1939. All day long we listened to the radio, to reports of German troops marching into Poland and of the new word *blitzkrieg*. For that day there was no thought of anything besides the fact that the long-dreaded Second World War had begun.

One of the reasons for my rapport with my father, I think, was that whenever we were alone together I was the most important person there. I was not necessarily treated as an adult, but as if what I did or said was of primary importance to him. Perhaps this was the key to his success in talking to anyone from presidents to elevator operators—he listened, cared, and was involved enough to ask the questions that encouraged conversation. He was genuinely interested in people and in many other aspects of life as well—international affairs, local politics, books, art, classical music, history, travel, and golf.

If I had to sum up my father's gift to me, I think I would say it was a "love of life." For him, life was full of so many wonderful things that boredom was not possible. Despite the horrors he saw and the tragedies he witnessed, he still believed in the fundamental goodness of man and the endless possibilities of edu-

6. See particularly, entries of October 14, 1933 (chap. 6), and February 23, 1935 (chap. 22).

cation. Whether he was a teacher at Indiana University, an educator with the FPA, or a Cassandra trying to make people understand the menace of Hitler and the need to help refugees, it was worthwhile as long as one believed in a brighter future, in man's generosity and ability to learn—even from the worst. Perhaps publication of this diary can help educate a whole new generation, teaching people what it was really like "back then," before anyone knew anything about gas chambers.

After my father died on September 26, 1964, I found components of the diary scattered on the floor of the little room in Bronxville he used as his study. Some sections were in envelopes, some not, some were even water-damaged, and they were incomplete. He had started keeping a diary in 1922—I am not sure why he kept such a detailed account of his activities. It may be because he never took notes at interviews and conferences, except perhaps to jot down the names of those whom he did not know. Afterward, he may have wanted to make sense of, and impose order on, what he had experienced. There were also times where he wanted to give some key associates elsewhere a better sense of what was going on and sent them copies of diary entries.

My father's habit of sending out portions of his diary, continued later in his life, led first to the loss of a significant portion of it, and then, through a series of fortuitous events, to the restoration and publication of the diary.

In the middle of 2003 the Holocaust Museum received an unsolicited donation of a portion of my father's diary from 1933 to 1936. The donor, Patricia Sugrue Ketchum, found the diary fragments in her Washington, D.C., home while cleaning house. Her father, Thomas Sugrue, had assisted my father in the writing of his memoir, *My Mission in Israel.* Apparently, Thomas Sugrue wanted a sample of my father's writing at the beginning of their collaboration. My father obliged him with a portion of his diary. Some sixty years on, Mrs. Ketchum discovered that portion interspersed with her father's papers and gave it to the Holocaust Museum after she was unable to locate my family. On receiving the fragment, museum archivist Stephen Mize read a 1935 entry concerning the Saar plebiscite and Eugenio Cardinal Paccelli. Intrigued, he went in pursuit of the remainder of the diary.

Stephen found his way to my home not by pursuing my father or me, but my sister Janet's husband, Halsey V. Barrett. He discovered that Janet had married Halsey by examining my father's correspondence at the Columbia University School of International Affairs Archives. Halsey had distinguished himself in combat during the Allied landing at Normandy. By tracing Halsey's military and professional career forward from D-day, Stephen found my sister and eventually found me in Virginia. It was very exciting to learn of our mutual delight at the discovery. The Holocaust Museum then became extremely enthusiastic about the diaries and their uniqueness in the history of the Holocaust.

Let me note a few things about the editing. My father's regular secretary, Olive Sawyer, was knowledgeable and meticulous, but many of those whom he employed in other locations were not fluent in English or familiar with the subject matter. I, and my co-editors Richard Breitman and Severin Hochberg, have felt free to correct spellings and punctuation, because they came from secretaries and stenographers, not from my father. Our version is easier to read than the originals, which are available for inspection in the archives of the Holocaust Museum. We have not, however, altered grammar, let alone substance. Inevitably, we had to make a selection, or this volume would be even longer than it is. Yet we have tried to include everything that we believe is historically significant.

One not-so-obvious decision we made was to include some outside materials that help readers make sense of what is in the diary. Although we relegated most biographical information to footnotes, we had to make insertions in the text in brackets where the meaning of a passage would otherwise be unclear. For those who are not intimately familiar with the history of the 1930s, we also decided to include capsule descriptions (in italicized inserts into the text) of major historical events to which my father alluded but did not explain. Finally, where my father went to a meeting and wrote up his account in his diary, and where we knew of another participant's account (in a diary or letter) that was substantially different, we included excerpts of the alternative version, again in italics. So what follows in standard type is from my father, and whatever is in italics comes from the diary editors or from other individuals who appear in the diary.

For me, working on these diaries has been like spending time again with my father. This effort has given me great pleasure and satisfaction, for despite the fact that he died over forty years ago, I miss him still.

1. Summer–Fall 1932: Foreshadowing

James G. McDonald's trip to Germany in late summer 1932 gave him a chance to observe German political developments at a key moment. The National Socialist German Workers' Party (Nazi Party) had just obtained its highest vote yet in national parliamentary elections—more than 37 percent—making it the largest party in parliament and across the country. But the German political situation was still very murky.

Until September 1930, when the Nazis had their first electoral breakthrough, many political opponents and observers had thought of the Nazis mainly as a movement of roughnecks and alienated elements seeking to overthrow the republic by force. Hitler had tried and failed to do this in Munich in November 1923. Beginning in the mid-1920s, Nazi Party officials and local activists built an increasingly effective organization throughout much of the country and devised ways to appeal to different social strata. During the Great Depression the Nazis gained much greater popular support, aided by massive unemployment, middle- and upper-class fears of communism or socialism, and Hitler's charisma.

At every opportunity both Nazis and the Communist Party tried to prevent passage of government bills, while their paramilitary forces—and those of the Social Democratic–oriented Reichsbanner organization—did battle with each other in streets and beer halls in towns and cities throughout the country. Economic misery, political paralysis, and a breakdown of law and order all seemed to reinforce each other. Widespread doubts about Germany's parliamentary system, fostered by Germany's illiberal nineteenth-century political traditions, grew stronger.

Hitler's racial ideology (visible to all in his memoir and political tract, Mein Kampf*), his 1924 conviction for treason, his late acquisition of German citizenship, and his personal and political rigidity all placed him well outside the normal range of national politics. But he was able to connect with a significant segment of German voters. In the presidential election of March 1932, Hitler obtained more than thirteen million votes (to incumbent President Hindenburg's nineteen million).*

From the spring of 1930 until January 1933, three successive chancellors maneuvered around paralyzed parliaments with the use of presidential emergency powers (to issue laws by decree) and the calling of new elections. Through mid-1932, when the economy reached its nadir, each new election only strengthened the extremes.

In August 1932 Hitler's path to power still seemed blocked, partly by President Hindenburg's unwillingness to appoint him as chancellor, partly by the Nazis' lack of a majority or coalition partners. But as McDonald quickly began to sense, these barriers were not secure. Nor was the current government likely to last very long.

Berlin, Monday, August 29, 1932

To the Kaiserhof [Hotel]. Learned to my delight that Hitler was making his headquarters there and that also the Stahlhelm[1] would be there. After getting settled, went directly to the Warburg office. Called Erich[2] on the long distance telephone. Found that he was home in bed, but able to talk. He said that I should study the von Papen[3] economic program, which he in general approved, though he was skeptical of some of its financial provisions. He urged me to come to Hamburg before I sailed. . . .

. . . . . .

Tuesday, August 30, 1932

Lunch with Elliot[4] of the *Tribune.* Then over to the Reichstag Building, where members were assembling. Spent most of the afternoon watching the crowd and the police, demonstrations for the fascist [Nazi] members as they arrived.

Over to the American Commercial Attaché's office. Conference with [Attaché] Douglas Miller,[5] who seemed to be unusually well informed. This is one of the men upon whom Knickerbocker[6] relies most heavily. He said that many Germans still considered that they had to pay a reparations bill of nearly a million dollars a day. By this they mean the Young and Dawes Plan[7] annuities, and the interest on some of their commercial obligations, many of which would not have had to be contracted, had it not been for reparations.

Then with Miller over to one of the hotels to meet Knickerbocker. There was much talk about German autarky. Knickerbocker urged me to help popularize the word here. Then with Knickerbocker over to the Kaiserhof, where we sat and had something more to drink and awaited Hitler with a group of his confreres waiting on the reports from the Reichstag. . . .

1. Stahlhelm, the large veterans' association. Politically very conservative.

2. Erich Warburg, son of Max M. Warburg, reluctant heir to his father's leading position in the M. M. Warburg bank of Hamburg. Highly assimilated Jew and thoroughly German.

3. Franz von Papen, very conservative Catholic aristocrat who was then chancellor. Formerly a member of the Center Party, but by this time closer to the National People's Party.

4. Charles Elliot, correspondent for the *New York Herald Tribune* since 1926.

5. Douglas P. Miller, acting commercial attaché, who believed that the Nazis were intrinsically aggressive. Later wrote a book entitled *You Can't Do Business with Hitler.*

6. Hubert R. Knickerbocker, International News Service correspondent in Berlin, 1925–1927; in Europe, 1928–1933.

7. Young and Dawes Plans, revised plans for German World War I reparations payments established originally by the Treaty of Versailles and set in 1921 at more than thirty billion dollars payable over many decades. The German public and most political parties resented reparations obligations, which proved a constant source of political and economic trouble for the new republic. Following near political collapse and a German hyperinflation of unimaginable proportions in late 1923, Britain, France, and Belgium agreed to renegotiate the obligation. American banker Charles Dawes worked out a new lower payment schedule in 1924. The Young Plan of 1930 represented a second reduction of reparations.

Wednesday, August 31, 1932

To see Dieckhoff[8] of the Foreign Office. Talked about disarmament and then about the American position in the Far East.[9] He urged me to see von Bülow[10] on that subject.

Lunch with Nathan.[11] Found him in a very disappointed state, first because he was not at all well, and second because of the way in which the Socialists were being ridden over roughshod by the government. I asked him why they had not resisted the Prussian coup d'etat.[12] He said that after all, it was legal, since the President had signed the decree, and probably they could not have effectively resisted it, had they chosen to do so through a general strike or otherwise. He promised to try to arrange an interview with Luther[13] for me.

Had arranged earlier with Hanfstaengl[14] for a ticket to the Hitler meeting the next night. . . .

Thursday, September 1, 1932

To see Geheimrat Kastl,[15] who is one of the leaders of the Manufacturers' Association. He did not deny that he and his group had had a great deal to do with the economic program [of the Papen government]. . . . He was frankly reactionary in his point of view. He seemed confident that the new program had a good chance of success, especially if a business turn for the better occurred soon.

Had a luncheon date with Breitscheid,[16] but it was cancelled.

At four o'clock went to see Dr. Schacht[17] at his club. He was friendly as ever. He took out an FPA [Foreign Policy Association] Bulletin from his pocket and said, "Look at this! This is all wrong," referring to Miss Wertheimer's analysis of the June 30 [actually July 31, 1932] election. "The writer," he said, "does not understand the Hitler movement and belittles it." He himself was critical of

8. Hans Heinrich von Dieckhoff, German Foreign Office specialist on the United States and Britain.

9. Following Japan's attack on China, Secretary of State Henry Stimson stated, on January 7, 1932, that the United States would not recognize any change in the status quo and reaffirmed the "open-door policy" in China. President Hoover, however, refused to use sanctions against Japan.

10. Bernhard Wilhelm von Bülow, state secretary in the German Foreign Ministry.

11. Otto Nathan, economics professor and former adviser to the Economics Ministry. A close friend of Albert Einstein.

12. On July 20, 1932, Franz von Papen's national government got President Hindenburg to declare a state of siege and used emergency powers to oust the coalition government of the large state of Prussia, headed by a Social Democrat. That step removed what had been the strongest protector of the republic.

13. Hans Luther, chancellor (1925–1926), and former minister of finance. Head of the Reichsbank since 1930.

14. See textbox on Hanfstaengl in this chapter.

15. Ludwig Kastl, managing director of the *Reichsverband der deutschen Industrie,* the large association of heavy industry.

16. Rudolf Breitscheid, one of the leading parliamentarians and speakers of the Social Democratic Party, the main supporter of the republic.

17. Hjalmar Horace Greeley Schacht, economist and former head of the Reichsbank. Originally a member of the German Democratic Party, Schacht had migrated to the political right. Not a member of the Nazi Party, but on better terms with Hitler than most knew. See also chapter 2, note 43.

Mildred Wertheimer

Mildred S. Wertheimer was one of James G. McDonald's advisers and a key figure in the creation of the League of Nations High Commission for Refugees. A graduate of Vassar, she studied at the University of Berlin, and she received her Ph.D. from Columbia in 1924. In the peace negotiations after World War I she worked under Colonel Edward House, and she later interviewed many foreign statesmen. Her academic background—she wrote a book on the Pan-German League and later substantial reports on Germany under Hitler—and practical foreign policy experience and contacts gave her unusual breadth of experience—all the more striking for a woman in the 1920s and 1930s. A friend described her as "no blue-stocking, no grind, no pedant, but rather a gay and happy 'good companion' always seeking, ever radiating the joy of life."[1]

In 1924 she began work at the Foreign Policy Association, becoming its resident expert on Germany. By the early 1930s she became concerned about the possibility of the Nazi Party coming to power, and she tried to give a picture of what influences accounted for its political strength. Her reports on German rearmament after 1933 received substantial press coverage.[2]

She and Dr. Ernst Feilchenfeld were probably the originators of the idea to elicit League of Nations interest in an organization to assist refugees from Germany. Wertheimer convinced American diplomat Arthur Sweetser and Professor Joseph Chamberlain to join a lobbying effort, while Feilchenfeld worked to win the support of American Jewish organizations. Once that backing was obtained, British Jewish leaders joined in. Wertheimer later wrote (at McDonald's request) that "my part in this whole business was that of 'pusher behind the scenes.' "[3]

McDonald later found Wertheimer too willing to consider economic concessions to the Nazi regime. Her early death in 1937 at the age of forty-one nonetheless deprived him of a friend and trusted colleague.

1. Mary Townsend's letter to the editor, *New York Times,* May 13, 1937.
2. "German Arms Seen Far Beyond Limits," *New York Times,* April 2, 1934.
3. Wertheimer to McDonald, December 20, 1933, McDonald Papers, USHMM.

the von Papen economic program, doubted that it would work, and seemed sure that the Hitler group would force von Papen to terms.

At five went to see Dr. Melchior[18] at Warburg's office. He wondered if it were possible to have a more centralized and effective German representation in the United States vis-à-vis Germany's creditors. Unfortunately, we did not have a very long time to talk because I had to go to see Dr. Nathan and Dr. Hertz.[19] Breitscheid was to be there, but he sent word that I could see him at the Reichstag the next day if I wanted to come over. Again I got the same impression of Socialist futility in the face of the determined program of the reactionaries.

Before seven o'clock I stopped to pick up Mrs. Reed,[20] and we went to the Hitler meeting. We arrived in the neighborhood of the sport palace about seven o'clock but were stopped several blocks away by the police lines and were told the building was packed and we could not go through. We showed our press cards and were permitted to pass on. Finally arrived at the building, found it packed, except for places reserved for members and Hitler party on the platform. Perhaps 25,000 people were in the audience. The aisles, stairways, and entrances were guarded by massed groups of Hitler's shock troops. The band was playing stirring music, and the audience joined in the singing.

At 8:30 Hitler arrived. His reception was the most extraordinary I have ever seen given a public man. There was something almost startling in the passionate response of the crowd. Similar response was given to the parade of the banners, as these standards were advanced to the platform. Each had attached to it a small symbol of some fascist martyr killed in a brawl with Communists or Socialists.

Hitler began to speak at 8:50 and talked until 10:35. He was followed with the most intense interest. Occasionally there were many outbursts of personal feeling on the part of members of the audience. His type of speech showed much more variety than I had expected. He not only could build up his climax, but very strikingly utilized satire and humor.

Among the large streamers carrying slogans in the hall were the following:

"Gebt Hitler die Macht" [Give Hitler power]

"Deutschland Erwacht" [Germany arise]

"Sagt [*sic,* should be Jagt] die Bonzen aus des Gesellen" [Drive the bosses out—the last word is garbled][21]

After the meeting went to one of the restaurants in the neighborhood and there met one of Erich's [Warburg] relatives with his wife and continued our discussion of Hitler. Despite their tendency to belittle Hitler's power, the experience of the evening had given me a new picture of him and his movement.

18. Carl Melchior, former diplomat, legal adviser, and partner of Max Warburg in the banking firm M. M. Warburg and Company of Hamburg.

19. Paul Hertz, prominent Social Democratic representative in the Reichstag.

20. Mrs. David Aiken Reed (Adele Wilcox), wife of the Republican senator from Pennsylvania, 1922–1935.

21. The thrust of this is an attack on the Social Democratic trade union and party leaders.

Friday, September 2, 1932

Went to see Dr. Oberregierungsrat Thomsen,[22] one of the close associates of von Papen.

Lunch with Hanfstaengl. He is an extraordinary person, a graduate of Harvard in 1909, German family and German sympathy during the war. He was alienated from most of his old friends in the States. The last ten or twelve years he has been a close associate of Hitler. He talked to us at length about the Hitler movement, about Hitler, and his own relations to the Nazi leader. He denied most of the current charges about Hitler and his followers, laughed at the idea that the party was short of funds, said that their great meetings were self-supporting, and that Hitler himself made large sums of money through his phonograph records, receiving as high as $20,000 for a single record. Throughout all of this talk he was reasonable and convincing.

Then I asked him about the Hitlerites and the Jews. Immediately his eyes lighted up, took on a fanatical look, and he launched into a tirade against the Jews. He would not admit that any Jew could be a good patriot in Germany. He attributed to them the fact that Germany was forced to sign the peace treaty[23] and charged that the Jewish bankers were profiting from Germany's reparations payments. I tried to argue with him, citing cases of several of my Jewish friends like the Warburgs, but made no progress at all. It was clear that he and, I presume, many of the other leaders of the Nazis really believe all these charges against the Jews.

At five o'clock went to the Foreign Office press conference. There seemed to be nearly a hundred journalists there. The government officials were von Papen, von Neurath,[24] and another cabinet member, and Mr. Marks, the chief of the press. It was a pleasant meeting, but one got very little from the questions or answers, so I left before the meeting broke up to keep my appointment with von Bülow at the Foreign Office at six o'clock. He was cordial as usual and just as interesting. He talked to me for more than an hour. Most of the conversation was about the German demand for technical equality of armaments, which he explained in detail and, of course, defended vigorously. He insisted that Germany did not wish to build up to France, but merely to establish the principle of equality; that it had now become intolerable that a great power should indefinitely remain in a secondary position. Germany was willing to give guarantees that the freedom of action it requested would not be abused, but it would have to insist

22. Hans Thomsen, an official in the Reich Chancellery.

23. The Treaty of Versailles that formally ended World War I. The Allies determined the terms unilaterally, then threatened to resume the war if Germany did not sign. The German government, then headed by Philipp Scheidemann, a Social Democrat, resigned; a new coalition government headed by Gustav Bauer, another Social Democrat, reluctantly signed under duress. Neither Scheidemann nor Bauer was Jewish or of Jewish origin, but right-wing extremists closely associated Marxists with Jews. They also blamed the loss of the war on the November 9, 1918, revolution—the revolutionaries were accused of stabbing the German army in the back—even though that event actually followed Germany's recognition that it had lost militarily.

24. Konstantin von Neurath, German foreign minister, 1932–1938. A nationalist, but not in sympathy with Hitler's vast expansionist objectives.

Ernst Hanfstaengl

Ernst "Putzi" Hanfstaengl was perhaps the most colorful and eccentric figure in Hitler's inner circle in the 1920s and early 1930s. Raised in Munich, he attended the *Gymnasium* in which Heinrich Himmler's father taught—proximity not bringing with it admiration for either the father or the son, later to become the head of the SS. Hanfstaengl's German father and American mother (a member of the well-known Sedgwick family of New England) equipped him to move back and forth between the two countries. After Harvard, where he was a marginal student but a well-known figure on campus, he ran the New York branch of the family art business based in Munich. His first period in the United States was marked by a Bohemian lifestyle and an affinity for boisterous piano playing. The latter benefited him after he became transfixed by Hitler in the early 1920s. One biographer called him "Hitler's piano player."[1]

Hanfstaengl earned Hitler's good will in other ways. He introduced the would-be Führer both to potential German patrons and to foreign diplomats and observers. For someone as provincial as Hitler, Hanfstaengl represented exposure to the world beyond Germany and Austria. He became, first unofficially and in 1930 formally, Hitler's foreign press chief. He decided which foreign correspondents got interviews with Hitler, and he monitored the foreign press for the party.

This was not a secure base in the Nazi hierarchy, and to make matters chancier, he intrigued—and feuded regularly with key Nazi officials such as Joseph Goebbels and Alfred Rosenberg. Still, in the early 1930s Hanfstaengl enjoyed the advantage of frequent informal contact with both Hitler and Hermann Göring, which enabled him to give James G. McDonald extraordinary access during his visits in 1932 and in March–April 1933. McDonald's diary contains Hanfstaengl's account of how Göring reacted to the first news of the Reichstag fire on the night of February 27–28, 1933.

Hanfstaengl fell into disgrace in late 1934 by criticizing Hitler directly (McDonald's diary entry of August 22, 1935, in volume 2 has an account of how this happened) over his choice of associates—Kurt Lüdecke in particular. After a number of threatening signs, Hanfstaengl fled to Switzerland and then England in 1937. At the start of World War II the British interned him as an enemy alien, then sent him to a camp in Canada. In 1942 good fortune intervened when Franklin Roosevelt and one of his advisers decided that Hanfstaengl might offer useful perspectives on the Nazi leaders and on German propaganda broadcasts. He was kept isolated but comfortable at a farmhouse at Bush Hill, Virginia, where, into 1944, he supplied information to the Office of Strategic Services in an operation called the S-Project (S for Sedgwick). After publishing unreliable memoirs and a work about Hitler, he died in 1975.

1. Peter Conradi, *Hitler's Piano Player: The Rise and Fall of Ernst Hanfstaengl, Confidant of Hitler, Ally of FDR* (New York: Carroll & Graf, 2004); also David Marwell, "Unwonted Exile: A Biography of Ernst 'Putzi' Hanfstaengl," Ph.D. dissertation, SUNY Binghamton, 1988.

on a definite pledge of a second conference, at which time their adjustments would have to be considered.

He insisted that the German demand could not be interpreted fairly as in any sense endangering the French and that the French military men knew it, but that the government was unwilling to take the responsibility for following the military advice. When I asked him if the permission to be given to Germany to have a few tanks and large guns, etc., would not permit them to lay the basis for manufacture of these in quantity, he did not answer. Later on in the talk I referred to the American Far Eastern position and urged that Germany support that. He assented in principle, but was in fact not encouraging.

. . . .

Saturday, September 3, 1932

. . . .

At 11:30 went to see François-Poncet,[25] French ambassador. He talked to me about disarmament, nearly as long as von Bülow, but, of course, from a quite different angle. He said the difficulty with the Germans was if you made them a very great concession, they swallowed it at one gulp, and then their mouths were wide open demanding a second. He spoke of the power of the reactionaries and of their ability to throw out Brüning[26] as one would dismiss a lackey.

I spoke to him of the American attitude on the Far East and of France's stake in supporting that attitude. He was much interested and said that I ought to see Herriot.[27] I explained that I did not intend to go to Paris, but that I would see if I could change my plans so that I could do it. Later that day I wrote him a note to the effect that I could go and said that I would do so if an appointment could be made with the French prime minister Tuesday afternoon or Wednesday. . . .

About 6:30 Mrs. Reed and I started out to the Stadion to see the Stahlhelm demonstration. . . . We arrived . . . about seven o'clock. Fortunately, through Mowrer[28] I had an excellent seat in a box near the reviewing stand, and Mrs Reed was similarly fortunate. First were the gymnastics of some thousands of young men in the center of the field. Then a relay race followed by some military exercises, scaling of barriers, wriggling through entanglements, etc. About eight o'clock began the most notable event of the evening for me, the march of the Music Corps. There were many, many bands playing martial music and accompanied by the regimental banners. After they had encircled the field, they massed back in the center. Six or eight hundred instruments played classic music

25. André François-Poncet, French ambassador to Germany, 1931–1938. One of the more perceptive foreign diplomats in Berlin.

26. Heinrich Brüning, a leader of the (Catholic) Center Party and chancellor, 1930–1932.

27. Edouard Herriot, then prime minister of France. After his government collapsed, became president of the Foreign Affairs committee in the Chamber of Deputies.

28. Edgar Ansel Mowrer, chief of the Berlin bureau of the *Chicago Daily News,* 1923–1933. President of the Association of Foreign Correspondents, author of *Germany Puts the Clock Back* (1933).

beautifully for an hour. Then began the parade of the banners, three or four thousand Stahlhelm banners carried by the regimental flag bearers about the field and maneuvering in the center. It was a thrilling spectacle, with the floodlights playing on the flags.

Meanwhile, through four hours of the demonstration, the thousands of Germans in the Stadion sat in religious silence, except that now and then they cheered a passing contingent. At the end of the evening were gigantic fireworks. On the reviewing stand were the officers of the Stahlhelm, officers of the Reichswehr,[29] heads of the government and some of the old regime. Here was the old Germany reorganizing. It left one with a feeling of marked uneasiness. The greetings of the Stahlhelm leaders to the government and to the Reichswehr was in marked contrast with the parade a few weeks earlier, when the Stahlhelm was in disfavor with the government.

After the meeting to a restaurant to talk it over.

Sunday, September 4, 1932

Out to the Tempelhof to see the even more military demonstration of the Stahlhelm. This time I profited from Mrs. Reed's company, because I had only a press ticket, while she had what turned out to be an admission to the *Ehrenplatz*, that is, the place of honor. I therefore got in with her to the place reserved for the Hohenzollerns[30] and others of high rank. It was the balcony of the Lufthansa headquarters. There during the day we saw the Hohenzollerns, the Crown Prince[31] and two of his brothers, their wives and children. Unfortunately, I did not myself see the Crown Prince because he left before I had been told he was there, but his two brothers remained in evidence throughout the day. Von Papen, von Neurath, General von Schleicher,[32] and other high officials joined the group. Also came generals of the old regime, von Mackensen[33] being the most picturesque. These older generals were all wearing their imperial decorations and, of course, their imperial uniforms.

The so-called "march by" of the Stahlhelm troops began at about eleven and continued until dusk, and that was until 160,000 or 180,000 men had passed in parade before the reviewing stand, all of them breaking into the goose step as they passed their reviewing officers. Of the thousands of banners carried by these forces, not a single one was of the republic. It was a martial, nationalist, and reactionary demonstration.

....

29. Reichswehr, the military, generally used to mean the army at this time. Under the peace treaty Germany was limited to a small navy and was forbidden to have an air force.

30. Until November 9, 1918, the German imperial family. Former Kaiser Wilhelm II was in exile in the Netherlands, but some of his sons and grandsons remained in Germany.

31. Former Crown Prince Friedrich Wilhelm. The reception given to the Hohenzollerns was a symptom of the political climate.

32. Kurt von Schleicher, retired general, political intriguer, and defense minister in Papen's cabinet.

33. Field Marshal August von Mackensen, eighty-three years old. Veteran of the Franco-Prussian War and highly decorated World War I general.

Monday, September 5, 1932

. . . .

I went to see Luther, head of the Reichsbank, and was with him for about forty-five minutes. He stressed the virtual impossibility of Germany's meeting her financial obligations, unless the interest was reduced on the private debts.[34] . . . He explained in some detail the von Papen scheme for encouragement of business, denied that it was inflation, and compared it to the work of the Reconstruction Finance Corporation[35] at home. . . .

. . . .

After his return to the United States on September 13, McDonald tried in various ways to discern how the presidential campaign was affecting and would affect American foreign policy. The two highlights are printed here.

Tuesday, September 27, 1932

. . . .

At seven to the dinner with some of the members of Roosevelt's "brain trust" at the Roosevelt Hotel. Those present besides Buell[36] and myself, who were guests, and Shotwell,[37] who was also a guest, were Tugwell,[38] Adolph Berle,[39] General Johnson,[40] more or less representing Baruch,[41] and Bob Straus.[42] As we began discussion of question as to whether Roosevelt should make a speech on foreign affairs, I was much discouraged by what seemed to me hard-boiled attitude of his regular advisers, but as discussion developed, I was encouraged. No decisions, of course, were arrived at. One got the impression that if the [Hoover] administration sought to capitalize [on] its foreign record for political purposes, Roosevelt would probably make a speech on foreign affairs.

. . . .

34. That is, private loans to Germany from abroad, mostly from American banks, as distinct from Germany's reparations obligations.

35. Established by President Herbert Hoover in February 1932 to make emergency loans to banks and railroads in danger of default during the Great Depression.

36. Raymond Leslie Buell, FPA research director since 1927 and president (after McDonald resigned), 1933–1939.

37. James T. Shotwell, professor of the history of international relations at Columbia University. Historian of the American delegation at Versailles, associated with the Carnegie Endowment. A member of Roosevelt's "brains trust" in 1933. Author of *At the Paris Peace Conference* (1937).

38. Rexford G. Tugwell, Columbia professor and another member of the brains trust, who helped Roosevelt with planning on economic and social issues.

39. Adolph A. Berle, corporate lawyer and law professor at Columbia. Author of *The Modern Corporation and Private Property* (1932). Economic expert in Roosevelt's brains trust, 1933–1938. Later assistant secretary of state.

40. Brigadier General Hugh Samuel Johnson, who drafted the Selective Service Act during World War I. In 1933 became administrator of the National Recovery Administration.

41. Bernard Mannes Baruch, South Carolina–born financier who served as an adviser to presidents from Woodrow Wilson to John F. Kennedy. A member of Roosevelt's brains trust.

42. Robert Kenneth Straus, grandson of Isidor Straus (co-founder of Macy's), New York City politician, business executive, and deputy director of the National Recovery Administration in 1933.

McDonald was able to arrange a meeting with New York Governor Franklin Roosevelt, the Democratic presidential candidate, about three weeks before the presidential election. Polls indicated that Roosevelt would win easily, and McDonald hoped to give him some sense of the foreign policy challenges he would face.

Sunday, October 16, 1932

Drove up to Hyde Park alone. Interview with Governor Roosevelt at twelve o'clock.

I was shown into one of the governor's studies. While waiting for him Moley[43] came in to chat with me for a few minutes and also Tugwell. Promptly at twelve the governor was pushed into the room in a wheelchair. He slid himself off of the wheelchair into an armchair. As he sat there and swung his legs back and forth, one would never have guessed that these would not bear his weight. He seemed extremely well, looked as though he were just back from a vacation, instead of from an intensive campaign tour.

He started in by reading me and those that he assumed I represented a sort of a lecture. He said in effect, "You people see only one small part of the prob lem. You do not see the picture whole. Some of you are more concerned in the League [of Nations] than you are in peace, and more concerned that we cooperate with the League than that we further the ends for which the League exists."

I vigorously dissented from this generalization. I said that I was not one of those to whom he referred and added that it did seem to me that it was important that he take the curse off of his recent statement about the League,[44] which had caused many people to think that Hearst[45] and McAdoo[46] would have great influence in the shaping of his foreign policy.

In reply the governor indicated that there need be no fear on that score, though he was not very specific or definite.

I then raised the question of intergovernmental debts and told him that while I was much more interested in what he did as president than in what he said as candidate, nonetheless I was much concerned that he should not make his own work more difficult by committing himself in the campaign to a program which in fact he would have to reverse. He replied, "You need not worry. I

43. Raymond Moley, member of Roosevelt's brains trust, professor of public law at Columbia University. Soon to become assistant secretary of state.

44. In response to a letter by W. R. Hearst asking him to clarify his position on the League, Governor Roosevelt spoke before the New York State Grange on February 2, 1932, and declared his opposition to American participation in the League of Nations. "The League has not developed through these years along the course contemplated by its founder, nor have the principal members shown a disposition to divert the huge sums spent on armament into the channels of legitimate trade, balanced budgets and payment obligations." *New York Times,* February 3, 1932.

45. William Randolph Hearst (1863–1951), self-made multi-millionaire and media baron known for sensationalism (inspired the term "yellow journalism"). Starting with the *San Francisco Examiner,* his newspaper empire in the 1930s consisted of twenty-eight newspapers. A nationalist who had a benign view of Nazism.

46. William Gibbs McAdoo, Democratic candidate for the Senate in California (elected shortly). Formerly secretary of the treasury 1913–1918 (under Woodrow Wilson). Senator, 1933–38.

am not going to say anything about debts in the campaign, though perhaps I may ask the President [Herbert Hoover] how he intends to help the farmer through his handling of the debts."

On the whole, I got the impression that he, having made up his mind that it would be inadvisable to speak about foreign affairs in the campaign, was paying very little attention to them, but I was disappointed not to get any assurance from him as to any particular line of policy. He struck me as being almost 100 percent politically minded.

As I was driving out of the Roosevelt place, Mrs. Roosevelt, the governor's mother, had drawn up to the entrance. Though I obviously had the right of way, she imperiously waved me to back up. She was such a grand old lady that I did it with pleasure, though I was rather amused at her manner.

. . . .

After Roosevelt's sweeping victory in the presidential election, McDonald considered whether he might play a foreign policy role in the new administration.

New York, Monday, November 14, 1932

Over to Ambassador Morgenthau's[47] for tea. . . . In the course of this discussion Ambassador Morgenthau said, "What would you really like to do, looking at the thing in the large for the next ten or fifteen years?" It was in this connection that he raised the question about the chancellorship of New York University, which had never occurred to me. . . .

We also discussed diplomacy. I told him that I could not afford a diplomatic post and was not enamored of the glamor of diplomacy; that there was one post I should like to have, if and when it were created, that is, diplomatic representative of the United States at Geneva [i.e., to the League of Nations].[48] He thought this a good idea, but said what was obvious; it was not now available and might not be for some time. He raised the question of a post in the Department of State. I said that, of course, the undersecretaryship would be excellent, but I did not know whether I ought to take anything else. It was in this connection that he suggested I ought to see Colonel House.

. . . .

47. Henry Morgenthau, Sr., lawyer, adviser to Woodrow Wilson, ambassador to the Ottoman Empire, 1913–1916 (where he was one of the first to denounce genocide carried out against Armenians), and to Mexico, 1920. Expert at the 1933 London Economic Conference.

48. The United States was not a member of the League.

2. Winter 1932–Spring 1933: The Nazi Revolution

In the November 1932 Reichstag elections the Nazis obtained about two million fewer votes than they had won in July. They were the strongest party, but they lacked a majority in parliament, which remained paralyzed by the extremes. Ideas of dismissing parliament temporarily or permanently or restoring the monarchy circulated behind closed doors but failed to win President Hindenburg's support. Although a monarchist at heart, the aged World War I hero felt obliged to respect the republican constitution and feared the civil unrest that a coup might trigger.

General Kurt von Schleicher replaced Papen as chancellor. Schleicher nourished hopes of recruiting some trade union support with government measures to stimulate employment, and of splitting the Nazi movement.

Resentful of Schleicher, in mid-January 1933 Papen brokered a deal behind the scenes—Hitler would become chancellor; Papen, vice chancellor. Papen helped assemble a cabinet of ministers acceptable both to Hitler and to President Hindenburg, who up to now had resisted the idea of making Hitler the head of government. Lacking any base of support in the newly elected Reichstag, which was set to convene, Chancellor Schleicher acknowledged defeat and resigned. On January 30, 1933, Hitler was legally appointed chancellor.

In full command of his own party, the new chancellor also had an alliance with the traditionally conservative German National People's Party, which supplied him with a base of just over 40 percent of the seats in the Reichstag. Hitler's cabinet had only three Nazis out of eleven members; the rest were conservative nationalists or non-party experts. Vice Chancellor Papen thought that through this arrangement (and through his own close ties with President Hindenburg) he could contain Hitler, who served the purpose of mobilizing the masses for nationalist goals.

The Nazi revolution came after Hitler was already in office. He and his inner circle freed themselves of the political and constitutional constraints that had shackled his predecessors. Establishing a dictatorship in stages, they used its powers to realize a significant portion of their racial and geopolitical agenda, which was anything but conservative.

On Saturday evening, February 4, McDonald devoted his broadcast to the significance of Hitler's accession to power.[1] *His next diary reference to Germany comes ten days later.*

1. Since April 23, 1928, McDonald had been giving fifteen-minute weekly broadcasts about foreign affairs on NBC. The program, *The World Today,* usually ran from October to May and was a pioneering effort in public radio. There are no surviving copies or transcripts of this broadcast of February 4.

New York, Wednesday, February 15, 1933

Conference with Henry Goldman.[2] He is fairly optimistic about German conditions. Thinks that anti-Semitism there is merely a different manifestation of a nearly universal feeling of anti-Semitism. He does not think it is worse than here, though different in its form. He anticipates a continued swing towards the right in Germany.

Monday, February 20, 1933

Night train to Pittsburgh. . . . Then over to the Twentieth Century Club. . . . I talked about the international situation much as I have done since I came home [in September 1932], little realizing that, I was to learn later, . . . I had shocked and frightened my audience.[3] I knew, of course, at the time that I was telling them a story which would jar them, but I did not think it would have the ramifications it did.

On the evening of February 27 the Reichstag building was set afire. The arsonist, arrested on the spot, was Marinus van der Lubbe, a young Dutch Communist of questionable sanity. High Nazi officials immediately jumped to the conclusion that there was a Communist conspiracy to bring down the government. Nazi Minister of the Interior Wilhelm Frick drafted an Emergency Decree for the Protection of the German People and State, which was issued the next day by President Hindenburg. The government suspended constitutional protection of free speech, freedom of the press, the right of assembly and association, and mail and telephone privacy. The government also had a more or less legal basis to arrest and hold individuals without trial. This decree was never lifted during Hitler's reign.

The national parliamentary elections of March 5 gave the Nazi Party 43.9 percent of the vote and 288 seats in the Reichstag. With their coalition partner, the German National People's Party, they now held a slim majority. Even with the aid of state-sponsored terror, intimidation, and propaganda, the Nazis as yet were unable to obtain a majority by themselves.

Over the next weeks Nazi officials used violent incidents as an excuse for the national government to assume control of some state police forces. This was but one variant of a process of "coordination," in which the Nazis extended their control of the national government into other spheres of influence.

2. During World War I Henry Goldman was forced out of the investment banking firm of Goldman Sachs because of his pro-German attitude. When he returned to Germany later in 1933, he was searched and seized and came back to New York totally humiliated and disillusioned about the Nazis.

3. Based on what McDonald said a week later to a different group, he apparently warned that the United States had only two choices: One, do nothing now, and wait until the conflict comes, and disaster is upon us or, two, help strengthen the institutions of peace, because if conflict came there would be no way for the United States to stay out. McDonald's speech to the Rhode Island Bar Association, reported in *Providence Journal,* February 28, 1933.

New York, Saturday, March 11, 1933

Chatted with Mendelssohn-Bartholdy,[4] who had just arrived from Germany. He had not heard of the election figures for Bavaria. When I told him that the Nazis had outvoted the Catholics, he said that that was the most significant fact of the election.

Tuesday, March 14, 1933

In the evening Ruth and I went to dinner at the Henry Morgenthaus. It was a large party. After dinner Morgenthau insisted that I talk somewhat about Germany, which I did, also about the Central European situation.[5] The dinner was really given for Professor Monroe, who was going back to the Far East, but interests seemed to be so much more intense in the results of the Hitler election, etc., that the Far East never had a fair chance.

Monday, March 20, 1933

Talks with Baerwald,[6] Sulzberger,[7] and Rosenberg[8] about Hitler and the Jewish situation. Told Van Kirk[9] I thought the Federal Council [of Churches] ought to take some action.

Tuesday, March 21, 1933

On my way back to the office at three o'clock the thought occurred to me, why should I not go to Germany tomorrow night on the *Europa*? At first it seemed a mad idea, but the more I thought of it, the more it fascinated me. I asked Miss Wertheimer what she would think if I were to sail on the *Europa* the next night? She said, "I would think you were a lucky bum!" I asked Miss Ogden[10] if she thought it would be all right if I would do it without hurting the FPA budget. She said, "Yes." Buell took the same view. The executive committee was meeting at the office that afternoon. I explained to them my anxiety to go to Germany. They gave their assent. I then called Rosenberg and asked him

4. Albrecht Mendelssohn-Bartholdy, grandson of the composer, Felix Mendelssohn. In October 1933 he would be dismissed from his post as professor of international law at the University of Hamburg where he had taught since 1920, and from the Hamburg Institute of Foreign Affairs, which he had founded.

5. On March 15 McDonald, in a speech at the Cosmopolitan Club, said, "the world is nearer today to a catastrophe of major proportions than at any time since the World War." Reported in the *New York Times,* March 16, 1933, p. 20.

6. Paul Baerwald, chairman of the American Jewish Joint Distribution Committee (JDC), the organization for overseas relief, partner in the Lazard Freres investment firm.

7. Arthur Hays Sulzberger, acting publisher of the *New York Times,* president and publisher from 1935 to 1961.

8. James Naumburg Rosenberg, a lawyer with the firm of Rosenman, Goldmark, Colin, and Kaye. On the executive boards of the JDC and the American Jewish Committee, one of the founders of the JDC and vice chairman in 1934. McDonald often said that he was a man of a hundred ideas, at least one of them brilliant.

9. Walter W. Van Kirk, secretary of the Department of International Justice and Goodwill of the Federal Council of Churches of Christ in America.

10. Esther G. Ogden, FPA executive secretary 1928–1937. A woman of unfailing sound judgment combined with a sense of humor.

what he thought. He said he thought it would be fine. I asked him if he would call Felix Warburg[11] to inquire if he would approve. He did, then said Felix would be very grateful.

About 5:30 called up Ruth and asked her what she would think if I said I would go to Washington that night and sail for Europe the next night. She replied that she thought I had better come home and have supper to talk it over. This I did, packed and left for Washington on the ten o'clock train from Bronxville.

Washington, Wednesday, March 22, 1933

Long talk with Phillips.[12] He asked me if I would come and report to him when I came back. Then chatted with Moffat,[13] Moley, and Feis.[14]

On March 21 Moffat wrote in his own journal:

The situation concerning the Jews in Germany is causing the utmost alarm to the race here. There have been a series of meetings held far and wide over the country and a huge mass meeting is scheduled for Monday next. The reports of outrages reaching the Jews here from their co-religionists who have left Germany are alarming to a degree. Thus far, nothing we have received from the Embassy tends to bear this out. We drew up a telegram, however, telling the Embassy that it was important for us to have the exact facts and requesting them to telegraph a full report after consultation by telephone if necessary with the [American] consulates in the principal cities.[15]

Over to see the German ambassador. Prittwitz[16] was out, but Leitner arranged for my laissez-passer and my visa. Back to the State Department, where I ran into Prittwitz, who seemed very sad at the prospect of leaving. Back to New York about six. Worked at the office from six until nearly nine.

Reached President Butler[17] on long distance telephone, told him of my plans. He approved them. Another talk with Rosenberg, who asked me to get in touch with some of his friends in Berlin.

About half past nine went out to have a bite of supper with Ruth and Mr.

11. Felix Warburg, born into the leading German Jewish banking family. Emigrated to the United States, married the daughter of Jacob Schiff, head of the banking firm of Kuhn, Loeb, and became a partner. Chairman of the JDC when it was founded in 1914. By 1933 considered the elder statesman of Jewish philanthropy, serving as a link between the Zionists and non-Zionists. McDonald had known him since the early days of the FPA.

12. William Phillips, undersecretary of state, 1933–1936. Had started his diplomatic career in 1903 and retired in 1929, but returned at Roosevelt's request.

13. Jay Pierrepont Moffat, chief of the Western European Division of the State Department. Like Roosevelt, a graduate of Groton and Harvard and a friend of the President.

14. Herbert Feis, State Department adviser on International Economic Affairs and chief technical adviser to the American delegation to the World Economic Conference in London, 1933.

15. Moffat Journal, vol. 33, Moffat Papers, call number MS Am 1407, Houghton Library, Harvard University. By permission of the Houghton Library, Harvard University.

16. Friedrich Wilhelm von Prittwitz had just resigned as German ambassador in Washington.

17. Nicholas Murray Butler, president of Columbia University.

Deane.[18] Shortly after ten when they started back home I took a taxi and went to the boat alone.

Earlier I had called Mr. Lamont[19] and told him I was going to Germany.

Thursday, March 23–Tuesday, March 28, 1933

At sea.

On March 23 the Reichstag, reduced by the arrest or flight of some leftist deputies, gave the Hitler government formidable new powers under the Enabling Act. This law modified the constitution, offering a simpler process to make laws—the chancellor would prepare them, the cabinet would enact them, and the official gazette would publish them. Only the Social Democrats voted against passage.

On March 28 the Nazi Party announced a boycott of Jewish businesses in Germany. After President Hindenburg expressed reservations and after it became clear that foreign countries did not support an economic boycott of Germany, the Nazi action was confined to April 1.

The diary March 29–April 3 is written as a letter to the FPA.

Berlin, Monday, April 3, 1933

Dear FPA:

This is a mad world, or I am mad from the effects of the past five days—hectic, tense, tragic. This frank summary of my impressions is, of course, not for publication, but for your information and use as you see fit. It is going forward to you in the diplomatic pouch, through the courtesy of Consul General Messersmith.[20]

On the *Europa* the attitude of the Captain, who received frequent wireless messages from Germany and at whose table I sat, was that all the reports from abroad were lies—propaganda to discredit Germany. This seemed to be borne out by the superficial appearance of Bremen and Berlin. But I was very soon disillusioned.

I arrived in Berlin March 29 at 4:48 in the afternoon. I was met at the station by Dr. Bertling.[21] He was concerned at reports reaching America and showed me a copy of his reassuring cable. He stressed moderation of government as compared with its campaign threats.

18. Albert Lytle Deane, president of General Motors Holding Corporation. A family friend, FPA Board member since 1926, and treasurer since 1928.

19. Thomas W. Lamont, chairman of the firm of J. P. Morgan and member of the FPA Board since 1926. Both he and Mrs. Lamont (Board member 1926–1950) were strong financial supporters of the FPA.

20. George S. Messersmith, U.S. consul general in Berlin. Strong and knowledgeable anti-Nazi, whom McDonald frequently conferred with.

21. Dr. Karl-Otto Bertling, director of the Amerika-Institut in Berlin, who had sent McDonald a telegram saying, "Shocked at gross misrepresentation of recent German events. . . . Present [Nazi] movement is against Bolshevism not Judaism." Bertling to McDonald, March 24, 1933, Felix Warburg Papers, Box 299, American Jewish Archives, Cincinnati.

At 5:30 went to see Gordon[22] at the Embassy. He painted a different picture—much personal violence against the Communists, Socialists, and Jews. Terror, he said, was undoubtedly practiced in many sections. Moreover, espionage, censorship of mails, telegraph, and telephone were current. He could not be sure even of his official code. Economy at Washington deprived him of sufficient courier service. He urged me to come to see him the next day.

On the way home from the Embassy stopped at 2a Tiergartenstrasse [Siegmund Warburg's home]. Saw Siegmund[23] and Dr. Melchior. They were obviously much worried and concerned for themselves, their business, and their people. I told them I was to dine later with Hanfstaengl. They said I might tell him that their people were considering a public statement signed by a hundred prominent Jews pleading for the rest of the world to leave the [solution of the] problem to Germany.

I called Hanfstaengl immediately on arrival in Berlin. He had just returned from Munich with Hitler. He said he had a cold, but would dine with me. I called for him at 8:30 at 30 Friedrich Ebert Strasse, opposite the Reichstag, where he lives with Göring.[24] While waiting, saw Hanfstaengl's famous march[25] (written for Hitler) on the piano and much of his other music.

He greeted me as an old friend. As usual, he talked of himself as exhausted, day and night on the move with Hitler. The latter could stand the strain better because he never abused himself, never drank or smoked, etc.

At Horchers we settled down for the evening. He spoke almost poetically of the new regime, Hitler, the chancellor, standing side by side with Hindenburg, an unbeatable combination. What a victory! he exclaimed. "How different from only six months ago, when you were here last! And each day the Leader's strength grows. He is supreme!"

Eventually we reached the subject of the Jews, especially the decree just announced for Monday's [April 1] boycott. He defended it unqualifiedly, saying: "When I told Hitler of the agitation and boycott abroad, Hitler beat his fists and exclaimed, 'Now we shall show them that we are not afraid of international Jewry. The Jews must be crushed. Their fellows abroad have played into our hands.'"

I assured Hanfstaengl that the agitation abroad was not instigated by German Jews, indeed that powerful conservative Jews in New York, like Warburg and the American Jewish Committee, had opposed Jewish agitation. He said he was glad to know that some Jews in Germany had not been "traitors." Then he

22. George Gordon, chargé d'affaires at the U.S. Embassy. The post of ambassador was then vacant.

23. Siegmund Warburg, from another branch of the Hamburg Warburgs, who because of his ability became a partner in the banking firm of M. M. Warburg and Co. of Hamburg and then head of the London branch.

24. Hermann Göring (often spelled Goering), then minister without portfolio in the national government and placed in charge of the Prussian state government. The best-known Nazi official after Hitler.

25. March played by the SA band at the Brandenburg Gate on January 30, 1933, supposedly adapted from Harvard's "Rah, Rah, Rah."

launched into a terrifying account of Nazi plans: The boycott is only a beginning. It can be made to strangle all Jewish business. Slowly, implacably it can be extended with ruthless and unshakable discipline. Our plans go much further. During the war we had 1,500,000 prisoners. 600,000 Jews would be simple. Each Jew has his SA [storm trooper]. In a single night it could be finished. (He did not explain, but I assume he meant nothing more than wholesale arrests and imprisonments.[26]) He added that the Reichswehr is not good against civilians, but the SS[27] and the SA[28] are perfect instruments for such purposes.

I protested the danger to Germany's economic life. He laughed: "The Jews are the vampire sucking German blood. We shall not be strong until we have freed ourselves of them." I protested the patriotism of such German Jews as I knew best. He answered, "Maybe some Jews are not like the others, but we cannot trust them. They are not, they cannot be Germans. They must never be trusted with high or low government positions again. They must be cleared out of all the government services at home and abroad." (This occurring now here—it will be followed soon abroad. Our friend Kiep[29] is not likely to be exempt.)

Hanfstaengl told me of his discovery of fire in the Reichstag opposite his window. His call by telephone to Göring, the latter's refusal to believe, the excitement of the moment, the order for the Communist arrest, etc. Hanfstaengl was furious when I suggested that abroad it was suggested that the government had set the fire. Hanfstaengl exclaimed: "If that is being said, then the Communist [van der Lubbe] must die. Your story lost him his life. We must end the vile rumor that we started the fire."[30]

And so, for two hours or more Hanfstaengl talked and I listened. About Mowrer[31] he said, "Of course, he is a Jew and so is his wife. So also Knickerbocker." "What of Enderis[32] and Birchall?"[33] I asked. He answered, "You know what hand feeds them." He asked me about the next ambassador to Berlin. He

26. McDonald was trying to convince himself of this interpretation, but see his entry of May 16, 1933 (chap. 3).

27. The *Schutzstaffel* or elite Nazi protection guard. Organization, headed by Heinrich Himmler since 1929, that became the center of activities directed at Nazi Germany's perceived enemies.

28. The *Sturmabteilung,* the large Nazi paramilitary force, founded in 1923 and headed by Ernst Röhm and composed of elements prone to political violence.

29. Otto Karl Kiep, German consul general in New York City, dismissed for attending a public luncheon for Albert Einstein. Later reinstated in the foreign service.

30. Many inside and outside Germany suspected that the Nazis set the Reichstag Building afire in order to issue emergency decrees and consolidate their power. Most recent studies have concluded that Marinus van der Lubbe was the real arsonist. Although hardly conclusive, Hanfstaengl's comments to McDonald add to the weight of evidence against a Nazi conspiracy.

31. In August 1933 Mowrer resigned from his post in Germany and was transferred to Tokyo, presumably in a bargain with the Nazis, who freed Dr. P. Goldman from prison.

32. Guido Enderis, Berlin bureau chief of the *New York Times,* 1933–1941. Swiss born and thought to be sympathetic to Germany. "Enderis . . . had limited journalistic abilities and excessive German sympathies, as even his editors admitted." Laurel Leff, *Buried by the Times* (Cambridge: Cambridge University Press, 2005), 55.

33. Frederick T. Birchall, correspondent for the *New York Times.* Birchall had gone to Berlin in 1932 as the *Times* chief European correspondent. He won the Pulitzer Prize for foreign correspondents in 1933.

denounced the idea of sending a Jew like Herbert Swope[34] or Ira Nelson Morris.[35] Then looking at me critically, he said, "Why don't they name you? You are an Aryan—a pure Anglo-Saxon—not an enemy of Germany. Let me organize pressure for your appointment. I could get Hitler, Göring, Goebbels[36] to demand you." I replied, "My dear Hanfstaengl, that would be the surest way to defeat your purpose. The American ambassador must represent the United States, not your regime."

Finally we drove home together, Hanfstaengl rapturously singing the praises of the Chief [Hitler]. But I said, "Revolutions eat their children." "Yes," he replied, "I am ready, but no force can overthrow us. The Stahlhelm is more than 50 percent Nazi. The Reichswehr [the army] is loyal. We have a vast secret police of our own. We are awake to every intrigue and we can do what may be necessary to scotch counter-revolution. We are on the march."

I reached my hotel before midnight. But there could be no thought of going to bed. So I walked alone to the Unter den Linden and the Tiergarten—a beautiful night, spring-like, bright stars, many lovers in the park, a world seemingly at peace and yet these ghastly hatreds breeding such shocking plans for heartless oppression of a whole section of the people. I almost thought that I had experienced a nightmare. But it was all the enthusiastic exposition from a man who called himself my friend and promised to do his utmost to arrange for me to meet his idol—the Chief.

Long uncertainty, whether to cable or what to cable. Then did cable and to bed but not to sleep.

Thursday, March 30, 1933

Went first to 2a Tiergartenstrasse. Walked in the garden with Siegmund [Warburg]. Told him of Hanfstaengl. Siegmund thought the Reichswehr might be counted upon for defense. But I replied that it was unthinkable that the Reichswehr could be used against the Nazis and public opinion to defend the Jews. Later everyone to whom I talked expressed the same views. (I should add perhaps that I never wrote or telephoned the Warburgs. Going to 2a seemed safer, since Hanfstaengl and others in the regime knew that the Warburgs are my friends.) Promised to return later to see Siegmund before he left for the States.

Then to see Gordon at the Embassy. He was intensely interested in my report of talk with Hanfstaengl, especially in: (1) Hitler initiative in boycott; (2) plans for imprisonment; (3) disregard of economics; (4) welcome of opportunity against Jews supplied by foreign agitation. Gordon agreed continuation of foreign efforts would intensify persecution here.

34. Herbert Bayard Swope, journalist, editor of the *New York World,* and first recipient of the Pulitzer Prize for reporting, assistant to American financier Bernard Baruch during World War I.

35. Ira Nelson Morris, had been American minister to Sweden in the Wilson administration and later in April was appointed ambassador to Turkey.

36. Paul Joseph Goebbels, newly appointed minister of people's enlightenment and propaganda.

Lunch with Max Jordan, NBC representative. He offered to permit me to broadcast to the States whenever I chose. I answered that now I did not want to speak because: (1) I could not tell the truth and I did not want to be a party to the distortion of the situation; (2) it seemed much more important to continue in a position to be useful in other ways. Max Jordan agreed.

Jordan's analysis of the situation was that since fall complete change had taken place:

(1) The [Roman Catholic] bishops' peace with Hitler meant decay of Centrum [Catholic Center Party].[37] Brüning is a shadow of his old self.
(2) Socialists weakened and powerless. *Vossische Zeitung*[38] now *Völkischer Beobachter.*[39] No leader, no program, no fire, *done.*
(3) Only alternative to present regime is Communism or chaos. This is general belief.
(4) Reichswehr increasingly fascist. There were two contradictory rumors, however:
    (a) Hindenburg to declare [a] state of siege and Reichswehr to take charge.
    (b) Hugenberg[40] to be assisted by Nazis.

In any case it seems certain that Nazis will oust their Nationalist [German National People's Party] colleagues.

Max Jordan told several tales of treatment of Jews. This one must suffice to illustrate. Scheffer, chief engineer of the German Broadcasting Company, a Jew, and his wife committed suicide because of the shock of the brutal dismissal along with all other Jews immediately after Goebbels took charge.

In the evening to dinner with Edgar Mowrer and his wife. Found both of them highly overwrought. I have never seen him so tense. He could talk of little but terror and atrocities. He stigmatized the leaders of the regime as brutes, sadists, vile, etc., recognizes that they are extremely intelligent. He thought the movement was out of hand, Hitler no longer in complete control and the local leaders daring to ignore the party chief. Socialists are ruined, the Centrum discredited, the bishops duped. Country on road to fascist dictatorship. Undoubtedly Reichstag building burned by Göring.

Unfortunately, we could not talk very freely at Horchers because a German waiter insisted on remaining within earshot. In any case, Mowrer was too excited and too bitter to give his usual brilliant analysis of a complicated situation. I should add he thought a moderate foreign policy probable.

37. After wrenching debate the Center delegation in the Reichstag had voted in favor of the Enabling Act on March 23.

38. *Vossische Zeitung,* perhaps the most prestigious and literary of German newspapers, with its origins in the eighteenth century. Formerly left-liberal political orientation. Ceased publication in 1934.

39. *Völkischer Beobachter,* the central newspaper of the Nazi Party.

40. Alfred Hugenberg, leader of the right-wing German National People's Party, which was the junior partner in Hitler's government.

On the way back to the hotel I stopped to show Siegmund the text of my telephone call to New York. He approved cordially. Then he told me he had sent his family to Stockholm and that he was leaving on the *Europa.* So it was "goodbye"—he to his boat and I to the Kaiserhof.

Back to the hotel to telephone. I was at fault not to have asked the office to have two stenographers to take the message down, in alternate sentences, thus saving much time.[41]

Friday, March 31, 1933

....

To see Consul General Messersmith. He is spoken of in the highest terms by everyone for his courage, his indefatigable industry, and his willingness to defend his people against the Nazi abuses. He read my telephone message and approved it cordially. His account of present conditions was extremely illuminating. He feels

(1) SS and SA are out of hand at least in some instances. He cited four—Königsberg, Breslau, Halle, and in one case in Berlin;
(2) told of many cases of beatings;
(3) thought possibility of declaration of state of siege, but doubted Reichswehr would act itself;
(4) boycott abroad[42] is *excuse* for boycott here. He promised to keep closely in touch with me.

Then went directly to Gordon's. He, too, approved my telephone message enthusiastically. When I told him I expected to see Schacht,[43] he asked if I would try to find out if the latter had any plan about ready in connection with the German short-term and long-term obligations. He is anxious to keep ahead of the news. I promised to let him know if I learned anything.

I asked him if there was any possibility of Roosevelt's personal intervention to forestall the boycott being put into effect Saturday. He admitted the matter had been frequently telephoned about between his office and Washington.

Lunch with Otto Nathan. He is a broken man. Had to resign his position

41. McDonald spoke to James N. Rosenberg, telling him of the fear and tension in Berlin and asking if President Roosevelt might appeal to Hindenburg or Hitler personally. He stated that the boycott was called for one day only and then would be suspended to see what the foreign reaction would be. He urged calm in the United States, and Rosenberg reassured him that all important and responsible people were doing everything possible for peace and quiet. Transcript of phone conversation, McDonald Papers, USHMM.

42. In order to put pressure on Hitler to stop his persecution of the Jews, many individuals were boycotting German goods and were advocating a general boycott. The American Jewish Congress was one of the leading organizations in this effort.

43. Hjalmar Schacht, newly appointed president of the German Reichsbank.

immediately after the election. Sadly he said, "I am a Jew and a Socialist. There is no place for me in Germany." This despite his record as a brilliant, creative economist. He asked if I would give him a letter to expedite his receiving a visa. I said yes.

As to the future, Nathan thought there was a possibility of Reichswehr intervention, but only if and when conditions became much worse. He offered to be of any help he could be to me, even though being seen with me might end in his imprisonment for two years.

Had tea with Dr. [George] Norlin, president of Colorado University, the visiting Roosevelt Professor,[44] in his room with his wife. Found him tense and disheartened. All his colleagues in the university [in Berlin] either supported or tolerated the new regime. Impossible to talk with them. Thought thousands of political prisoners were being held. Work at the university now impossible. He was fighting each day to resist pressure to issue a statement clearing Germans of atrocity charges. Would go home if that would not be interpreted as a breach of intellectual relations between the two countries.

Then over to 2a [Tiergartenstrasse] to offer my services as liaison in case the next few hours brought grave developments. Dr. Melchior, though obviously suffering from overwork and prolonged worry, greeted me with his friendly smile and marvelous courtesy, inviting me to have tea. I told him I was at his service. He seemed almost pathetically grateful. What a situation! He finally said, "I remain, no matter what happens." How ungrateful is his country!

Telephoned Calvin Hoover[45] to invite him for dinner. He accepted. Earlier had tried to get Knickerbocker. He too accepted, but asked to bring his lady friend, the same one as last September. Finally he brought also another couple as well. So we were six for dinner.

Before the others arrived Hoover and I talked of Russia and Germany. Hoover thinks Russia faces conditions like 1921, largely because of the pressure on the peasants. As to Germany, he is amazed by the change during his six months here. During recent weeks it has been like a flood. The probability of Reichswehr interference with the Nazis is very slight.

Knickerbocker is confident that the regime is holding more than 40,000 political prisoners. Confident Hitler's popular following greatly increased recently. The Germans present disagreed. Knickerbocker detailed cases of atrocities.

During dinner there was a report that the boycott had been suspended. Later, however, the more accurate news was received, just before I telephoned New York. After talking to Jimmy Rosenberg, walked for a while with Hoover, unable to go to bed and sleep.

44. Roosevelt Professor, probably an endowed visiting professorship at the University of Berlin.

45. Calvin Hoover, professor of economics at Duke University.

Saturday, April 1, 1933

April Fool's Day. The boycott in effect. After working with papers, called up Gordon, but he had little that was new. About 11:30 out on the streets to see the boycott in action. Walked past Wertheim, down past 2a Tiergartenstrasse, Unter den Linden, and Leipzigerstrasse. The SA were orderly and so, for the most part, were the crowds, though these showed hostility if anyone ventured to enter a Jewish shop. The posting of the yellow circles on a black background was most shocking. These medieval signs of Jewish ostracism were used to cover the signs of Jewish doctors, lawyers, etc. One or two incidents I shall never forget—an old Jew facing alone a great crowd; another place the laughing, jeering children making sport of a national shame. No doubt the boycott was effective. It showed that Jewish trade could be completely stifled. No hand was raised against the SA. But the boycott is only the outward visible sign of an equally destructive discrimination against all Jews in law, medicine, school, civil service, shops, and industry, which continues unabated despite the suspension of the boycott itself.

Lunched again with Max Jordan, who left that night for Basle. He stressed the responsibility of France for the development of Hitlerism.

Just as Jordan and I finished lunch, Schacht's office called from the Reichsbank. I went at once. He greeted me in a very friendly fashion. I thanked him for setting me straight on German affairs last September and the year previous. He liked my recognition of his prevision and said, "Since we could not change the financial policy, we had to change the government. At first I gave my sympathy to the movement, later my support. Now it is triumphant."

I said, "Dr. Schacht, the eyes of the world are upon you. You alone in the regime are known abroad in financial and business circles." He did not object to this assertion.

Then we gossiped about affairs at home, the banking investigation, the make-up of the Federal Reserve Board, etc. He asked especially about [John Foster] Dulles,[46] who, by the way, I think might have real influence on Schacht.

I, of course, told Schacht how seriously the boycott was regarded abroad. I stressed the attitude of the conservative Jews in New York and in Germany. He replied, "Yes, not all Jews are unpatriotic. But why should those-----in the East End of London dictate to us. We do not so much attack Jews as we do Socialists and Communists. Anyhow, after a week or two, nothing more will be heard of it."

We then talked of Germany's financial short-term and long-term obligations. Schacht insisted that he would stand by Germany's contracts. It is not for him to suggest lowering of interest, etc. Germany would pay as long as possible;

46. John Foster Dulles, son of a Presbyterian minister. Both his grandfather (John Foster) and uncle (Robert Lansing) were secretaries of state. Legal counsel to the American delegation at Versailles and partner at Sullivan & Cromwell specializing in international law. In addition to his law practice, Dulles, who was deeply religious, attended many international conferences of churchmen during the 1920s and 1930s. Became secretary of state under President Eisenhower.

when and if transfer were no longer possible, then payments would be made in Marks. The two problems, payment and transfer, should never have been confused; the one is private, the other is governmental. Of course, if Germany could find, borrow 2,000,000,000 Marks, it would then very advantageously be able to convert its short-term indebtedness. But where to find the funds?

After about forty minutes of talk, and as I was leaving, Schacht asked me to come back again the following week after I had seen other people. I should, he said, report to him what was being said. (Remember Schacht is very, very close to the Leader.)

Incidentally, you may be interested to know that Schacht has not been very well—severe case of grippe. Now he looks thin and pale, but is obviously thrilled with a new sense of power. Now he stands next to the throne and all the other German financiers, Jewish and Gentile, are as dirt under his feet. Those who would bring Germany back into the Society of Nations from the economic and financial viewpoint must concentrate on Schacht.

Out late to tea with Colonel von Herwarth von Bittenfeld,[47] whom Hanfstaengl had asked to call upon me. He was military attaché in Washington before von Papen [during World War I]. He knows our country very well. What a Nazi he is! He becomes absolutely lyrical in his panegyrics on racial purity, conquest of the blood, return to primitive German culture, the Nordic racial supremacy, the idealism of the Nazi leaders and rank and file, the omnipotence of the Leader, the uniqueness of this national revolution, unparalleled in the history of the world. At last Germany is ready to declare itself free of foreign dictation. Soon it will say to the outside world—"No, no, no!" And yet this man knows the world, is a scholar and a courteous gentleman. His manners would do credit to an Englishman at his best. But to him Jews are not Germans—they cannot be treated as such, they are always foreigners or worse. They must be driven from all government positions of every sort and in the professions must be limited to the percent they constitute of the population as a whole. Even after hours and hours of this, he would not let me go until I promised to bring Hanfstaengl and a group of like souls to spend a gemütlich evening.

Sunday, April 2, 1933

After working with the papers in the morning, drove to the country for the day with Mr. and Mrs. Messersmith. Lunched at the golf club and then visited Potsdam, my first trip to San Souci[48] and the new palace. I much enjoyed it all.

During the afternoon Messersmith elaborated his views of the situation. But since these have all been set forth by him in his reports to the Department, which I assume Stone[49] has access to, I refrain from reporting on them further.

47. Hans Wolfgang Herwarth von Bittenfeld, press official in the Nazi government.
48. The mid-eighteenth-century palace of Prussia's King Frederick II.
49. William T. Stone, a former newspaper man. Joined the staff of the FPA in 1924. In 1927, when the Washington bureau was set up, became its head.

When we were having tea, some reference was made to Einstein and to Lippmann's[50] attack on Messersmith for the visa incident. Mr. Messersmith is very unforgiving, for, of course, neither the Consulate nor Messersmith were the least to blame. Walter Lippmann's apology Messersmith thought worse than his attack.

Back to Berlin in time to have dinner with one of my informants who must even here be nameless. During the evening was much interested in

(1) number and prominence of Jews who had supported Hitler even up to March 10 of this year. They expected and hoped Papen and Hugenberg would control the Nazis;
(2) stories of individual cases of cruel hardship suffered by Jews;
(3) estimates of effect of boycott and racial discrimination upon Jewish banking houses.

I forgot to mention that on Friday afternoon I went to the American Jewish [Joint] Distribution Committee office to see Mr. Schweitzer.[51] He and his associates were in a state of active tension. His associate, Bernhard Kahn,[52] had been unable to stand conditions longer and had gone to Switzerland. Mr. Schweitzer was debating whether or not to send his foreign people home. He himself considered moving to a hotel with his family for safety. Two days earlier he would have laughed at such precautions.

Monday, April 3, 1933

[Otto] Nathan came to see me again with more tales of cruelties. He reported too on his experiences with the boycott. He had entered three shops against the will of the owners in each case, who were fearful of riots. He wished never to go through with such humiliating moments again—the jeering, the hatred of the crowds.

I had to walk out with Nathan before the Nazi press representative in the United States, Kurt G. W. Lüdecke,[53] came to see me. Later with Bouton,[54] the Nazi-sympathetic correspondent. We all three lunched together, Lüdecke lecturing us on racial purity, the international danger of the Jews, the menace they are even in America, the rising tide of opposition to them that is likely to sweep away

50. Walter Lippmann, *New York Herald Tribune* columnist. His attack on Messersmith arose from a delay in issuing an American visa to Albert Einstein. American Consul Raymond Geist was forced to ask Einstein whether he was a Communist. Messersmith was not even in Berlin when the incident occurred and he himself blamed it on "stupidity in the Visa Division." Lippmann issued an apology.

51. Probably David J. Schweitzer, who held a number of posts in Europe for the JDC.

52. Bernhard Kahn, European chairman of the JDC, who had been in the Berlin office. Also general European chairman of the Hilfsverein der Deutschen Juden [Aid for German Jews]. One of the best informed social workers on the continent.

53. Kurt Lüdecke, an anti-Semite who had joined Hitler in 1922 and had represented him in early foreign contacts (Mussolini and others). Later arrested and fled Germany to the United States. Author of *I Knew Hitler.*

54. S. Miles Bouton, Berlin correspondent for the *Baltimore Sun.*

all bounds soon. Lüdecke intends to look after my education. Lüdecke and Bouton agree that the establishment of the foreign office under Rosenberg[55] in the National Socialist German Workers' Party is the beginning of the end of von Neurath and the first step in the purification of the Foreign Office and the Foreign Service. Prittwitz here is Nittwitz. Kiep's absence from his office the two weeks before the March election is not likely to be forgiven. These people do not forgive those who would play safe. I tried to explain that Kiep was ill, but it did not go down. This *is* a revolution and only the revolutionary temper is acceptable.

Amusing tales are circulating about Hindenburg.[56] A typical one is this: A man went to call on Meissner, the President's secretary. The visitor was carrying his lunch in a paper and while waiting started to eat his sandwich, leaving the wrapping paper on the table. Meissner exclaimed in alarm, "Don't leave that paper around, the Old Man might come out and sign it!"

Short chat in the afternoon with Birchall and Enderis, but had to hurry off to see Bergmann,[57] Reich representative in the Dresdner Bank. Found him depressed and hopeless. He sees no future in this regime for Germany. All gains are jeopardized. Ignorant young men in charge, agitators who know nothing of affairs and who are unwilling to learn. Schacht he considers a wild man, now most dangerous. Bergmann for one refuses to go to humble himself before Schacht. Bergmann much interested in my interview with Schacht. He asked me to be sure to come back after I see Schacht again.

Illustrative of changes here, Bergmann was told that the *Berliner Tageblatt* was now a government organ (speaking normally for the Jews) and was being aided by the state to secure financing. Nazis demanding the Dresdner Bank extend loans and new credits to the *Berliner Tageblatt.*

Returned to the hotel to have a second tea with Hans W. Priwin, radio newspaper man. Being a Jew, he had lost all right to work with the German Broadcasting Company and German papers. His tale is just one more.

A few minutes ago Lüdecke, the fascist interested in my education, called to say that he hoped to arrange for me to see Goebbels soon—he of the fiery tongue. You see thus far my Nazi friends believe that I am not completely lost. My long head, light hair and complexion, my Scotch name—these may save me yet from the darkness of Jewish influence!

I hope you can read this. If not, call on my wife. She has read much worse.

You told me to get a rest. This is a revolution in full speed—no rest cure, but I would not miss it for the world. Cable me when you receive this, please.

Good luck.

JGM

55. Alfred Rosenberg, a Baltic German who was an early intellectual influence on Hitler. Author of *The Myth of the Twentieth Century* and an early editor of the Nazi newspaper, the *Völkischer Beobachter.* In January 1933 appointed leader of the department of foreign affairs of the Nazi Party.

56. Hindenburg was then eighty-four years old and was showing some difficulties of age.

57. Carl Bergmann, financial expert, formerly German reparations adviser in Paris, and then on the board of directors of the state railway system. Although known as an opponent of Schacht, he hung onto his railway post until his death in 1935.

P.S. After midnight each day I refresh myself by a brisk walk up the Wilhelmstrasse, guarded by police with carbines and assisted by Nazi SA. This revolution may eventually be civil war!

Tuesday, April 4, 1933

Finished my letter or nearly finished it, at two o'clock in the morning. I was writing many things which the regime would have bitterly resented. I had a sort of spooky feeling that perhaps I was being spied upon. Left a call for six o'clock.

After breakfast worked on my letter until time to go over to the Consulate.

At the Consulate made corrections until Messersmith came in about nine. I gave him the letter. He said he would attend to it personally. Then he talked about some of the problems which were worrying him. He told me of the case of three American firms which were being discriminated against during the present wave of intense economic nationalism. He had arranged to see Göring informally and unofficially. He would report later on that conference.

He said that Bücher[58] of the German General Electric had gone to see Hitler the previous Friday, determined to tell the Chancellor the truth about Nazi excesses. Apparently he did so, but when Bücher returned to his office the next morning, he found two Nazi representatives there to begin a process of purification and he, Bücher, feeling it was unsafe to communicate, at least with his foreign friends, by telephone. Purification in this sense, of course, meant elimination of the Jews first of all. The significance of this action against Bücher becomes clearer when we remember that the General Electric in Germany is relatively more important than is the General Electric here. Indeed, it is probably the foremost German industry.

At 10:30 I worked for a time with Margrave, my German secretary.

At twelve over to see Luther[59] at the Wilhelmstrasse. He was very cordial. We talked for nearly an hour and a half. Much of our conversation was in figurative language because it was obvious to me that Luther dared not say about recent developments many of the things he would like to say. He expressed perfunctory regret at the retirement of Prittwitz. Spoke highly of Kiep. We discussed the importance of his mission in the States and the difficulties which he would encounter. Said he recognized some of these; that he would not have accepted the mission [as ambassador], had not his long interview with Hitler convinced him that the Chancellor was essentially conciliatory.

Further along in our discussion of the party and its possible program Luther said, "You yourself, I think I am right in saying, have used the word 'indoctrination' in speaking of the party's teachings on the Jewish question." This was an evident reference to my long cable of three nights before to the FPA of-

58. Hermann Bücher, chairman of Allgemeine Elektrizitäts-Gesellschaft (AEG), the huge electrical firm once run by Walter Rathenau, Germany's first Jewish foreign minister (assassinated in 1922). AEG was founded by his father, Emil Rathenau.

59. Just appointed to replace Prittwitz as ambassador to the United States.

fice. I had believed that cables and telephones were all listened into, but had not previously had a confirmation of this. Luther continued, "You see, therefore, there is need for time to permit the regime gradually to moderate in practice its announced program. Fundamental relations between the United States and Germany have not changed. The basic points of common interests are permanent. So soon as the first phase of the revolution is completed, the revolutionary tempo will lessen, and there will be opportunity for reconciliation within Germany."

Luther's reference to Schacht, though careful, indicated that he considered that Schacht was not averse to great power.

I outlined to Luther the new set-up in the State Department, the special position of Moley, etc. He inquired about Lippmann, and I explained the latter's unique place as a journalist.

Luther was surprised when I told him that the feeling in the States was so intense that he might be faced with a hostile demonstration on his arrival. Luther's attitude was so much more conciliatory than that of typical members of the party as to be almost startling. Men like Lüdecke, Hanfstaengl, and Daitz, the latter one of the leading Nazi economists, never spoke in such conciliatory terms. Instead, Daitz one night, when showing me the pictures of his children, said, "It is for these that we fight," meaning fight against racial contamination, as well as attacks from abroad.

Lunch with Elliot, the *Tribune* correspondent. He, though a very quiet and retiring individual, expressed intense feeling about the regime. Spoke of the leaders in as uncomplimentary terms as had Mowrer or Knickerbocker. To him the degree of violence and intolerance was unprecedented in Western Europe. He was not inclined to blame Brüning for policies that brought on the Nazis. Rather, he attributed the Hitler success to von Papen's withdrawal from the Center and his foolish thought that he could take the Nazis "into camp" when the new cabinet was set up at the end of January.

Elliot was confident that the Nazis could even then have been checked. I was not convinced by his analysis. It seemed to me, as I talked to Elliot, as when I talked to Knickerbocker and Mowrer, that because of his preconceptions about the weakness of Hitler, he continued to underestimate the veritable groundswell of public opinion in support of Nazi ideas.

Over to see Erich Warburg. How he has changed! No longer is he the carefree, optimistic young man who was so sure of his own future and that of his people in the Reich. The developments since March 5 had been a great shock to him. He asked me what I thought of the prospect for business of the Jews in Germany. I told him that, of course, I had no adequate basis for judgment, but that personally I would sell such business short. Erich asked me what I would think of a direct appeal to President Hindenburg by three prominent Jews. I replied that I thought it would probably be futile and very dangerous to the individual Jews. Whether it was tried, I do not know. Erich thought that appeals might be directed, too, to the Vatican and to Mussolini. I agreed to the desirability of such efforts, but questioned the expedience of the Jews themselves making them.

We then talked about the possibility of my staying in Germany for some time. I told Erich I should like to do so, but I had not been able to convince my office by cable or telephone. Evidently, my committee felt that I was more needed at home, perhaps even that I had been so stirred by my German experiences that I had lost a sense of proportion. Erich argues, however, that he was sure that the FPA would not lose by my staying. He indicated in detail why. I replied that of course the FPA was an American institution and should not be dependent upon any except American sources. He did not think this an insuperable obstacle. He stressed again and again that my position in Germany was unique. I had come there year after year on business of the Association [FPA]. No one could doubt my right to remain. He added, "Your physical characteristics would seem to the Nazis to stamp you a perfect Nordic type and would give you much more influence."

We then discussed my earlier idea that John Foster Dulles, one of the few Americans of whom Schacht is really very fond, might be useful if he came to Germany, on some business of his own, but while there available for informal friendly conferences with the head of the Reichsbank. Erich seemed to anticipate great damage from Schacht, who is no friend of the Warburgs. Max, however, is still on the Board of the Reichsbank and has no intention of resigning unless forced to do so.

As I prepared to leave, Erich stressed again his desire and what he felt was also the desire of his family that I should stay.

Then over to the Embassy for a few minutes. Chatted downstairs with Mrs. Levine, sister of Herbert and Gerard Swope.[60] As usual, she seemed so relieved to see me, to have someone to whom she could talk to very frankly. She has been living almost in a state of terror, not for fear of what might happen to her, but because of her friends.

Gordon, counsellor at the Embassy, was delighted to have another example of the regime's interference with cables. He said he would note down the Luther disclosure in his report to the [State] Department.

On the way back to the hotel stopped in at the residence of the Reichstag to see Hanfstaengl. He was again very critical of Lüdecke, said that he could not trust that man. He had connections which were not easily accounted for. He was self-seeking and on the whole a man who should not be given power by the party. Hanfstaengl admitted, of course, that Lüdecke is influential with [Alfred] Rosenberg, but deplored it.

As to American opinion, Hanfstaengl again expressed a view that it would change as soon as the first reaction had died down. He spoke of Lippmann as one of those whose views were, of course, controlled by his Jewish background. I arranged to see Hanfstaengl again next day.

60. Gerard Swope, president of General Electric Company.

After a very light supper, went alone to the opera to see *Elektra*.[61] It was an excellent performance, sung without intermission, but was not what you would call a comic relief to my very depressing day.

After the opera I had an engagement at eleven o'clock with Lüdecke and a Nazi economist, Werner Daitz. We met in the lobby of my hotel, the Kaiserhof, talked for nearly an hour. Daitz is a member of the committee that is preparing to reorganize the trade unions more or less on the Italian model.

I had looked forward to an informing analysis of the Nazi economic program. Instead, after we had discussed it for ten or fifteen minutes, both Daitz and Lüdecke drifted back to the subject of the Jews, which seems to be an obsession with so many of the Nazis. Each of them stressed the fundamental Nazi tenets about racial purity, the incompatibility of the Aryan and Jewish races, the necessity of racial purification, etc. Their discourse, a sort of dialogue, reminded me of nothing so much as conferences I had in Moscow with militant Communists. In each case the discussion was completely dogmatic. The answers to every inquiry were definite and final, as though issued by an infallible authority. The casual expressions used by both men in speaking of the Jews were such as to make one cringe, because one would not speak so of even a most degenerate people.

When I indicated my disbelief in their racial theories, they said what other Nazis had said, "But surely you, a perfect type of Aryan, could not be unsympathetic with our views." Of course, I realized that they may have been attempting to flatter me, but I had the impression that they really do set unbelievable store by such physical characteristics as long heads and light hair. They are in this respect very young. Both men spoke of the necessity of choosing between Germany becoming a mongrel race or re-establishing racial purity.[62] In its struggle for the latter, Germany is fighting, they said, the battle for the world, the battle of the white race. The French are in decay; they are becoming negroid. This is a danger which the United States also faces. The Germans were determined not to be ruled by 600,000 or a million Jews. They were stressing the biological elements. They think in centuries and in continents! We, too, according to them must be purified. The Jewish and oriental elements must be eliminated. There must be established a real Germany, Nation, Christian, etc. The Catholic Church is really incompatible with the regime!

"If one wished to sense," they said, "where real spiritual leadership lies, one should attend a Nazi funeral. The minister or the priest drools through the rit-

61. Opera by Richard Strauss, who was in good favor with the Nazi government. Strauss soon became head of the Reich Chamber of Music.

62. Such views came directly from Hitler's *Mein Kampf*: "Every racial crossing leads inevitably to the decline of the hybrid product as long as the higher element of this crossing is itself still existent in any kind of racial unity. The danger for the hybrid product is eliminated only at the moment when the last higher racial element is bastardized. Regeneration . . . [may take place] which gradually eliminates racial poisonings as long as a basic stock of racially pure elements is still present. . . ." *Mein Kampf*, tr. Ralph Manheim (Boston: Houghton Mifflin, 1971), 401.

ual, but no one pays attention. It is as dead as the corpse, but when the Nazi leader snaps to attention, salutes and speaks, then a thrill runs through the crowd. There is the spiritual leadership."

Germany is seeking to remake her people by return to the primitive, simple national German qualities. In this development, there is need for the strongest discipline. People must be molded for their own good. The objective is not aggression, but purification.

As to foreign policy, the two men were very frank and perhaps extreme. Fundamentally, the United States, Great Britain, and Germany have common interests. These three working together could achieve their will in the world. Germany's future is in the East. The immediate danger is in the Polish corridor. Some day, however, Germany will be able to rectify that.

Both Lüdecke and Daitz agreed that the Stahlhelm is soft; it must be dominated by the storm troopers. Hugenberg, who is a fat bourgeois, understands neither the purpose of the revolution, nor its technique. Luther, too, is bourgeois, not a part of the movement. He can represent it only for a short time.

Speaking of Schacht, both men agreed that he is 100 percent with the regime. They regard him highly. He is evidently in the very intimate circle on all economic, financial matters.

Long after midnight Daitz left, and Lüdecke and I talked for a while alone. He asked me about Hanfstaengl. He seemed anxious to know whether Hanfstaengl was critical of him. I naturally did not make myself a tale-bearer.

Long cable home, urging that Ruth join me if I were to stay.[63] The situation had gotten on my nerves to the point that I did not wish to remain alone, for there was no one in Germany whom I could talk to with complete frankness.

Wednesday, April 5, 1933

Lüdecke called and said that Daitz had been very much interested in our talk and hoped we might talk later again.

Cable from home asked me how long I would want to stay if the committee authorized me to prolong my visit. The tone indicated that they did not want me to stay.

At 11:30 over to see Hanfstaengl. He talked at considerable length about Lüdecke, again expressing his lack of confidence in him. We discussed Rosenberg. Hanfstaengl is critical of him, too, though only on the ground of difference of view. Rosenberg, according to Hanfstaengl, sees only one side, his anti-Polish and anti-Russian program. He cannot see the forest for the trees. He fails to realize that a new orientation of foreign policy is possible.

Hanfstaengl then suggested the possibility of a Polish-German alliance, while I suggested advantages which would come from a conciliatory démarche

63. On April 12 McDonald also wrote a letter to this effect. Ruth replied she did not feel she could leave. McDonald Papers, USHMM.

by the regime. Hanfstaengl intimated that he himself might go into the Foreign Office. He told me that Messersmith had had a long and, he thought, satisfactory interview with Göring.

Lunch at the Rotary. Chatted for a moment with Luther and Dr. Eckener.[64] Told Messersmith that I had heard he had had his interview with Göring. He was surprised that this was known by anybody except Göring.

Long cables home. Office replied by urging me not to stay.

In the evening to the Philharmonic concert conducted by Monteaux. It was a thrilling performance. I was struck by the incongruity of an audience of Germans, with their theories of degeneracy of the French, applauding wildly a French conductor who did not possess the slightest Nordic physical trait.[65]

During the intermission and afterwards I chatted with Klieforth[66] of the Embassy. He knows his Germany extremely well. He told me of instances which convinced him that the President is not "ga-ga." Said that his children play with the Hindenburg grandchildren, that the old man knows all the children by name, remembers from week to week which ones were going to certain parties and asks them whether they had a good time and whether they saw so-and-so. Kliefoth, of course, admitted that the old man had gradually surrendered one post of advantage after another until he was no longer in a position to stand out against the regime.

Thursday, April 6, 1933

Called Mr. Stolper,[67] editor of one of the technical economic journals that had been suppressed, and inquired from him about Siegfried Salz, a friend of Miss Wertheimer's. Stolper said that Salz was well, but very sorrowful.

During the afternoon went over to see [André] François-Poncet, French ambassador, with whom I had had long talks before in Berlin and Geneva. Poncet, as usual, talked extremely well. Leaders of the regime, he said, were living through a whole series of fantastic nightmares. The Jews, of course, were suffering intense humiliation and worse. There could be no doubt that the regime's foreign program was intensely aggressive, once they had the power. It was amazing that the German people did not realize that the greatness of their nation had never been really in the German army. Instead, the army had brought humiliation and defeat. The real greatness was in the spiritual qualities of the folk, which were now so much sneered at by the Nazis.

Late in the afternoon called at the Foreign Office to see my friend Hans von Dieckhoff, who was also a close friend of Miss Wertheimer's. He is in

64. Hugo Eckener, commander of the Graf Zeppelin, the famous trans-Atlantic airship.

65. Pierre Monteaux, at various times conductor of the Boston, San Francisco, and London Symphony orchestras, premiered works by Stravinsky, Ravel, and Prokofiev. Of (Alsatian) Jewish descent and McDonald probably knew this.

66. Alfred W. Klieforth, first secretary, American Embassy, Berlin.

67. Gustav Stolper, economist, member of the Reichstag for Hamburg (German State Party). Later in 1933 came to the United States as a refugee.

charge of English and American relations and is not a member of the Nazi Party. He talked with a frankness which amazed me. He argued at first, however, that the Foreign Office was still a spokesman for the regime; that Hitler's speeches had all been written in the Foreign Office; that there was a chance that the clean sweep which had been made in every department might not be made in his. He argued that the fascists who had thrown out the officials in other departments had left the Foreign Office intact. He admitted, of course, that already a few Nazis had been put in the Wilhelmstrasse.

Dieckhoff said that one must recognize that there had been some gains from the regime:

(1) the unity of the Reich;
(2) restoration of the imperial flag, which should never have been dispensed with; and
(3) elimination of much of the corruption which had crept in during the republic.

He did not deny the obvious abuses of the regime. He admitted that the Jewish persecutions were mistakes and that they would have serious repercussions abroad. He recognized, too, that there were many individual excesses committed by individuals in the regime, especially by the shock troopers. He told me a number of incidents of such abuses.

He confirmed what I had heard from other sources: that it had been the influence of Hindenburg that had checked the boycott and limited it to one day. According to him, Hindenburg had considered resigning, but had been dissuaded. He thought that there was at least a chance that the anti-Jewish excesses and the Jewish program would be gradually modified. He admitted that Rosenberg might have an increasing degree of power in determining the foreign policy and of course thought that this would be very dangerous. He admitted, too, that Hitler and Blomberg[68] would probably come to have, or already had, a good deal of respect for one another.

As to his own future, he said that, of course, he could not be sure; that he felt that he might not be touched. I carried away, however, the fear that his days as an important official were numbered.

Late in the afternoon I ran into Knickerbocker at the Adlon. He greeted me with his usual cordiality and indicated that he had something very confidential he wished to take up with me. He explained that a very close friend of his, a Dr. Schlessinger in the Foreign Office, and his wife (Jewish) were in danger of their lives and wished me to cooperate in getting them out of the country. I promised to meet him later when he could outline specifically what he wished me to do.

Dinner with Miss Biermann, a woman thirty-five years old who had been a

68. General Werner von Blomberg, head of the Reichswehr and minister of defense.

student at Indiana shortly after I graduated. She is now working in the Reichsfinanzministerium. She is typical of the large section of middle-class Germans who had lost most of their savings in the war. She is not Nazi, but had become more and more sympathetic with their regime. She saw nothing to complain about in their Jewish policy. Indeed, she herself is a member of one of the Nazi cells in her department, though not as yet a member of the party. When I asked her why she was pro-Nazi, I received no very satisfactory reply. She seemed to feel that they had established order and discipline and unity and that through them the lot of the average German might be better. She told me of the shift in the headship of her department, with the Nazis replacing the old regime officials. Apparently this has been done almost everywhere except in the Foreign Office.

Friday, April 7, 1933

The April 7, 1933, Law for the Restoration of the Professional Civil Service was cast as a means to create a more efficient and professional administration. But in actuality, this measure defined non-Aryans (primarily Jews, those descended from even one Jewish grandparent, and those married to Jews) as immediately unqualified. One exception, Jewish war veterans, was made at President Hindenburg's request. The law also stripped all civil service protection from those whose prior political activity the Nazis considered illegitimate, and it allowed the government to force anyone into retirement, even if he or she was not judged unfit, simply to streamline the administration. The law had almost immediate effects on the composition of the corps of teachers and professors who in Germany were government employees.

I called up Miss Gaedicke at Warburg's office. She told me she had bad news for me; that Max, though he was in town, thought it better that we not meet. Miss Gaedicke and I arranged to chat in the Tiergarten. She there explained to me that Max thought he was being followed and that it would be embarrassing to both of us if I called.

Then over to the Embassy. Mrs. Levine made me promise that I would certainly call up her two brothers as soon as I reached New York.

Long talk with Kliefoth. He told me the same story about the old man [Hindenburg] and the boycott as that Dieckhoff had related. Klieforth seemed to feel that the old man would still declare himself against Hitler if he thought the welfare of Germany demanded it.

Conference with Hanfstaengl. He told me that he had suggested that Eckener make a national broadcast expressing Germany's sympathy with the *Akron* victims[69] at the hour of the funeral in Washington. He indicated again that Hitler, not Neurath, was the real minister of foreign affairs.

69. The airship *Akron* crashed at sea in a storm April third. In the disaster seventy-three officers and men were lost, including Rear Admiral Moffett, chief of the U.S. Bureau of Aeronautics; three survived.

Over to Mowrer's office. Found him in with Knickerbocker engaged in checking and double-checking case stories of Jewish atrocities they were preparing to send to their papers.

Then lunch with Mowrer. He seemed to me even more tense and nervous than when I dined with him a week or ten days earlier. He could not speak too scathingly of the regime, its objectives, and its personnel. To him the leaders are thugs, perverts, and sadists. One reason for the present intense feeling against the Jews is that the orgy of hate and slaughter had been stopped halfway. The revolution had been too bloodless to satisfy the urge of the leaders for blood.

In reality, he felt that fascism is one of the weakest forms of government. He reached this conclusion after years in Italy and years in Germany. Yet he did not see any chance of the regime being overthrown at present.

As to himself, he is going on with his work. He is not sure whether he will resign from the Press Association or not. In any case, he is not going to yield his principles of sending back to his papers news which he thinks most important, irrespective of the reaction of the regime.

Earlier I had a talk with Klieforth about Schlessinger. He confirmed what Knickerbocker had said. He considers him one of his best friends and one of the highest authorities in the world on Russia. He did not consider that Schlessinger was in immediate danger; perhaps he might be in the future. He could not confirm Knickerbocker's statement about Schlessinger having independent means, but he would deeply appreciate anything which could be done to get Schlessinger out of the country.

He talked again about the old man, the latter's vivid memories at receptions, said that Hindenburg had remembered him after a year and a half. The Reichswehr, if called into action by Hindenburg, was still capable of crushing the SS and the SA. The Reichswehr, he felt, would still be loyal to the old man. It is a great force for moderation.

According to Deutsch of the U.P., Hitler had told him of the previous Sunday when Hindenburg had said he would resign if the boycott was to be continued and that he would then stand for re-election.

After lunch with Mowrer, which he would willingly have continued until tea-time, I went to see the Italian ambassador. He, though comparatively new in Berlin, seemed to me very well informed. He stressed the amazing order and discipline in the Reich, admitted that the Jewish program was a serious mistake. He had been much impressed by Hitler as chancellor, his dignity and restraint. The future of the Foreign Office he considered to be in doubt.

The Italian ambassador told me a story of the difference of opinion between Hitler and von Papen on January 30, when Schleicher was thrown out of office. Von Papen is said to have gone to the President to urge that Schleicher be given something so that he might not use his influence with the Reichswehr against the regime. Hitler, hearing of this, went to the President, protested, said, "No, we need not do anything for von Schleicher. I can answer for the Reichswehr." If that story be true, then the Reichswehr is surely by this time in the hands of the regime.

As to the movement in general, the Italian ambassador confirmed my feeling that it is still in the full tilt, or, as Dieckhoff put it, the first phase of the revolution and not yet been completed. The seizure of power has not yet been made 100 percent. Nonetheless, there are many signs that the present tempo will be maintained unabated until the last remnant of authority has been seized by the regime. Dieckhoff earlier seemed to me to take the same view.

Late in the afternoon, after an hour or so with the Italian ambassador, I called on Sir Horace Rumbold,[70] the British ambassador. He is very critical of the regime, almost as much, so it seemed to me, as Knickerbocker or Mowrer. He stressed what he considered to be the many foolish mistakes which were alienating gradually world public opinion. I could see that he was tired of his post.

Earlier in the day when I was at the Embassy, I overheard Jäckh[71] speaking to someone there and I asked if I might speak to him. I did. He was very cordial, said he would come to see me at the hotel that afternoon, but he did not. Nor was I surprised. His own position is so precarious that seeing a foreigner might have been dangerous.

Back to the hotel to dress for dinner. Mr. Knickerbocker came to my room and there started to talk about Schlessinger. I told him that I thought it would be better if he would write out a draft of the telegrams that he wanted me to send from the States.

Just then Otto Nathan called up from outside, suggested that I meet him on the street, rather than he come to the hotel, so while Knickerbocker wrote his telegrams, I went out and walked up and down in back of the hotel with Nathan. I told him I had spoken to Messersmith about his visa and would speak again. He said with deep feeling, "No, there is no place here for me, for I am a Jew and a Socialist. Nor will there be any work for me. I am especially anxious to get an immigrant visa so that I can go to the States to stay."

Back to the hotel. Finished with Knickerbocker. Then off to the Herrenklub[72] for dinner. It was a party of perhaps twenty or twenty-four men gathered to hear a technical paper of transportation within Germany. I sat between my host von Gleichen and the director of the *Deutsche Allgemeine Zeitung*, who happens also to be the head of the German Press Association. We talked first about the Far East, of which he knows much. He thinks the Russians are in a parlous state. We talked, too, about Germany. Naturally he was very guarded in what he said. He evidenced great interest in the FPA, said he hoped they might have similar organizations in Germany. I did not say it to him, but I don't see how an FPA type of discussion could flourish in fascist Germany.

Back late. Long cable to the office.

70. Sir Horace George Montagu Rumbold, British diplomat since 1891, ambassador to Turkey and since 1928 ambassador to Germany. Retired later in 1933.

71. Ernst Jäckh, from the German Hochschule, friend of Hjalmar Schacht.

72. An aristocratic (male), right-wing club in which Franz von Papen was a key member.

Saturday, April 8, 1933

Received a message that the Chancellor would see me at 12:30.

At 11:30 had an appointment with Henry Goldman at the Adlon. As I greeted him I saw that he was a broken old man, was different from the vibrant, confident person I had talked to in New York two months before. Then I had gone to ask him if he did not feel that intense anti-Semitism in Germany was an evidence of something wrong with the German people. He had replied to my question brusquely and dogmatically, "No, there is no more anti-Semitism in Germany than in the United States. The difference is not in amount, but in form." Now when I sat down, he asked me what I thought of Germany. Before telling him, I inquired if he was sure there were no listening machines about. Then I gave him my interpretation and asked for his opinion.

"Mr. McDonald," he said, "I never would have believed that the worst of the fifteenth and sixteenth century would return in this the twentieth century and of all places in Germany." I asked him how long he had intended to stay. He replied, "Just as long as I can bear it."

After an hour, as I was leaving, I said, "Mr. Goldman, because of my desire to return to Germany I am not sure what I shall say in public about the situation." He flared up and said, "One thing is certain. You dare not condone or excuse the regime. You may leave some things unsaid, but you dare not be an apologist or else you will lose the respect of those whom you regard most highly." I was at first inclined to resent this, but then I remembered how cruelly the old man had suffered, he who for twenty years had been an apologist for Germany, with the certainty of loss of friends, position, and a considerable part of his fortune, and now he was lecturing me against becoming an apologist.

He gave me a note to Miss Wertheimer and said I should tell her not to write to him.

I was at the Chancellery at 12:30 to keep my appointment with Hitler. The halls and doors were lined with shock troopers. I was ushered into the waiting room, where I was greeted by Hanfstaengl. An officer of the Reichswehr was also waiting. He was Blomberg's aide. He knew the United States well. Presently we were joined by Mr. Thomsen, Hitler's liaison man with the outside world. Thomsen had been with von Papen and had continued with Hitler, though, of course, not the confidant of the latter that he had been of the former. He said that Hitler received hundreds of letters from abroad and that a great many of these cordially praised his regime.

Finally, after one o'clock, I was shown into Hitler's office. He came forward to greet me. He is not as small as his pictures indicate. I should judge he was five feet nine or ten, rather stocky, though by no means stout. As Hanfstaengl was introducing me, Hitler sized me up from head to foot with glances obviously half suspicious. I had intended to talk about certain aspects of foreign policy first, but Hanfstaengl thought that it would be better to discuss the Jewish question directly. This I did. Immediately Hitler replied, "We are not primarily attacking the Jews, rather the Socialists and Communists. The United States has shut out such people. We did not do so. Therefore, we cannot be blamed if we now take measures against them. Besides, as to Jews, why should there be such a fuss when they are thrown out of places, when hundreds of thousands of Aryan Germans are on the streets? No, the world has no just ground for complaint. Germany is not fighting merely the battle of Germany. It is fighting the battle of the world, etc."

After McDonald returned to the United States, he spoke about his meeting with Hitler and gave additional details of what Hitler said: "His [Hitler's] word to me [McDonald] was, 'I will do the thing that the rest of the world would like to do. It doesn't know how to get rid of the Jews. I will show them.'"[73]

The man does have, as I thought when I saw him first last September, the eyes of a fanatic, but he has in addition, I think, much more reserve and control and intelligence than most fanatics.

As Hanfstaengl and I left the Chancellor's office, Hanfstaengl again raised the question of the German Embassy. I laughed and said, "Of course, it is impossible for many reasons," but he said, "Don't think that it is too expensive, for there is very little society now in Berlin. We are too busy to indulge in it. Your friend Mr. Rockefeller could arrange the finances." I scoffed at this and said "goodbye."

I jumped into a taxi and rushed off to the luncheon which was being given by the Foreign Office for Norman Davis[74] and his party. I, of course, was not a member of that group, but since the Foreign Office knew I was in town, they had invited me.

Present besides the Davis party, which included Norman and Mrs. Davis, John Foster Dulles and Pell,[75] the members of the American Embassy, Gordon and Kliefoth, the ranking officers of the Foreign Office, von Neurath, von Bülow, Dieckhoff, and Blomberg, head of the Reichswehr, Krosigk,[76] minister of finance, and Ritter.[77] There was no general conversation at luncheon nor afterwards. During the informal talks after the meal von Bülow came up to me and said, "Mr. McDonald, you have not been to see me." I said, "No, you have been very busy and I did not wish to bother you." Then I added what might have been better left unsaid: "And you see, Dr. von Bülow, I have been interested this time to find out what is the foreign policy of the party." Von Bülow smiled and seemed not to resent my unintended intimation that he and von Neurath might soon be mere figureheads. During the whole luncheon I had the impression that

73. McDonald quoted by Rabbi Stephen S. Wise in Wise to George A. Kohut, April 26, 1933, Wise Papers, Box 112, Correspondence—Zionism, American Jewish Historical Society, New York.

74. Norman H. Davis, U.S. ambassador at large, chairman of the American delegation to the Disarmament Conference, 1933.

75. Herbert C. Pell, former congressman.

76. Lutz Graf Schwerin von Krosigk.

77. Karl Ritter, director of the economic department of the German Foreign Ministry.

the men there were for the most part on their way out, as it were, from their places of power.

Chatted for a moment with Davis and arranged to see him at the Hotel Bristol in Paris the following Tuesday.

Tea with Messersmith at his house. He told me more of the troubles he was having with the economic nationalism of the Nazis, which was leading to discrimination against American as well as other foreign firms. He added, if I were interested in these cases, the State Department would doubtless let me see the official reports from Washington.

I asked him about his interview with Göring. He told me of it at some length. Göring seems to have very naive ideas about economic matters. He is, of course, against the big department stores and thinks that their capital can be jeopardized without involving foreign complications, though much of the capital of these stores had been borrowed from American bankers. Göring appeared rather to regret that the revolution had been so bloodless. He said, "We had two alternatives. We chose the bloodless one. Now whenever an individual is hurt, there is an international sensation. Had we let the blood run for a few days during the revolution, that would have been finished, and the world would have soon forgotten it."[78]

As Messersmith talked, he gave me the impression that he is so stirred by the violence and injustices of the regime that he sometimes feels that it would be better if no compromises were made with it and if it were forced to fail, even though in the failure scores of the Jewish population were sacrificed.

Back to the hotel to do my packing, for I had to leave that night at ten o'clock for Basle. While packing, I called up Lüdecke to ask if he would come up and chat with me before I left. He came. We first talked about Jäckh. He expressed the greatest contempt for Jäckh. He said, "Do you know what he has had the audacity to do?" I said "No." "He has come back here and dared to go and see the Leader." I could not at first understand why that was such a crime. Lüdecke went on to explain. He said, "You know what Jäckh has been saying in the States, how he has attacked Hitler, telling audiences that they would have to choose for Germany between Hitlerism and Bolshevism. Yet, despite this, he had the effrontery to ask and to obtain an interview with Hitler. For this he will not be forgiven. He deserves at least to be beaten up, and I am inclined to urge that we talk then about Kiep," of whom Lüdecke is also very suspicious. He,

78. Air Ministry State Secretary Milch arranged this meeting, which was supposed to be private, unofficial, and unpublicized. Although scheduled to take twenty minutes, it lasted two hours. Messersmith's lengthy account of this meeting, written on April 5, 1933, is to be found in the George S. Messersmith Papers, Box 1, calendar no. 135. University of Delaware Library, Newark, Delaware.

For present purposes, perhaps the most important thing is that McDonald accurately reproduced one segment of the Göring-Messersmith conversation. Messersmith also told Göring that American public opinion reacted negatively to what appeared to be a wholesale persecution of the Jews. Göring believed that American mobs had attacked Germans in the United States and that the American government had the capacity to crack down on newspapers publishing "horror stories" about what was taking place in Germany.

Lüdecke, talked at length about Hitler. He was unqualified in his praise. Hitler was the spotless one, the man who with uncanny intuition knew what was right to do, the Leader who harmonized and caused to work together their different sorts of lieutenants. He was like the leader of a great orchestra, who kept all of the instruments in harmony. The party was absolutely 100 percent loyal to him. There can be no thought of a secondary loyalty.

The Foreign Office was scheduled for a house cleaning. It would not be long until von Neurath and von Bülow were displaced by men in whom the regime could have confidence. Rosenberg was a future leader in foreign affairs. Schwarz, that fat Jew, was soon to be thrown out of his office in New York, and Kiep would not long survive him. It was on that note that I said "goodbye" to Lüdecke.

As I was paying my bill, I met Dr. von Schubert, formerly undersecretary of state for foreign affairs and later ambassador in London. I asked him what was going on. He said he did not know, which is doubtless the truth. He, being of the pre-fascist regime, is quite out of touch with developments.

Just before I left the hotel, Professor Norlin came up and asked if I would take a message to Dr. Butler. I said, "Of course." Dr. Butler is responsible for his appointment as a Roosevelt Professor. The message was, "Tell Dr. Butler I will stay as long as I can stand it, but I cannot be sure of remaining during the whole period."

Paid my bill and loaded up in a taxi and went to meet Miss Gaedicke. We had a bit of supper together and she reported to me from the Warburgs. She said that Max, as Erich, was anxious for my early return.

Then to the station. Train for Basle. As the train pulled out, I felt a sense of relief on leaving, but nonetheless regretted that I had to go before the first period, that of seizure of power, had ended.

Basle, Sunday, April 9, 1933

Shared my compartment with a German who looked as though he might be a traveling salesman. After breakfast we fell into a conversation. I asked if he was a Nazi. He said, "No." He felt, however, he had underestimated Hitler, who was much stronger than he had thought. I asked, "Don't you think that the Nazi Jewish attitude is unfair?" He answered me with an emphatic "No!" "We must remember," he said, "that the Jew is the bacillus corrupting the German blood and race; that once a Jew, always a Jew. He cannot pass from one kind of animal to another. The Jews are but 1 percent of the German population, but they have dominated our culture. That cannot be tolerated. They are not so serious in their effect on the Latin races as on the Germans." In short, he was wholeheartedly in support of the Nazi Jewish program.

Arrived at Basle about ten o'clock. Went first to the hotel, then over to the Bank [Bank for International Settlements]. Was met by Fraser's secretary, who explained that the president-elect was in New York, as I knew when Mr. Mc-

Garrah[79] had arranged for me to talk with Mr. Jacobson. McGarrah himself would have had me come for lunch, but that day was the first directors' meeting attended by Schacht. The directors were lunching together.

At the Bank met Schacht. He asked me if I had had my interview with Hitler, was it satisfactory? He added that he had arranged it and in conclusion said, "Now tell the U.S. the truth."

Chatted with Jacobson, a Swede who has been in the Bank from the beginning. Later lunched with a French-Greek, Mitszakis. Both Jacobson and Mitszakis stressed the danger to Germany of the silent boycott.

Took a late afternoon train. Reached Geneva in time for a very late dinner.

Geneva, Monday, April 10, 1933

....

Over to the Consulate. . . . In to talk to Gilbert,[80] who looked fagged and discouraged. Was glad, however, of the ratification of the opium convention.

Then to the Secretariat. Chatted with Pasvolsky,[81] who compared the present German situation to that of the Bolsheviks.

Out to lunch with Arthur Sweetser.[82] He listened with intense interest to my story of Germany. For the first time he was inclined to be pessimistic about the League.

In the afternoon conference with Carter.[83] He thought there was a chance for peace if Germany would only hold off. Carter was rather critical of the League atmosphere and of the work of the Graduate Institute there.

In the evening dinner at the Sweetsers. . . . Talked about Germany and about the School.[84]

Night train for Paris.

Paris, Tuesday, April 11, 1933

Arrived in Paris early in the morning. Over to the Hotel Durant. . . . [Then to the Chamber of Deputies.] Much talk about the Herriot mission,[85] etc. The political atmosphere in the Chamber was wholly different from that in Berlin.

79. Gates W. McGarrah, president of the Bank for International Settlements, 1930–1933.

80. Prentiss Gilbert, U.S. consul general in Geneva, 1930–1937. Acted as a liaison with the League of Nations and was involved in intelligence gathering. A shrewd reporter and much admired by journalists.

81. Leo Pasvolsky, economist, director of international studies, Brookings Institution.

82. Arthur Sweetser, in the League of Nations' Secretariat information section and, during the existence of the League, its highest-ranking American. Also important because of his close relations with the Rockefellers and Washington foreign policy-makers.

83. Edward Clark Carter, secretary general of the Institute of Pacific Relations.

84. Presumably the New School founded in 1919, later New School for Social Research. Its University in Exile, founded 1933, utilized the talents of refugee professors.

85. Edouard Herriot, president of the Foreign Affairs Committee of the Chamber of Deputies. Went to the United States as the French delegate to the Washington economic talks on debts and disarmament.

Over to see Norman Davis. Chatted with him and Pell. Compared notes with Davis about Hitler. He said that he had talked to the Chancellor frankly on the Jewish question, but that the latter had not replied. I asked him who was the interpreter, and he said Hanfstaengl. That caused me to doubt whether Hanfstaengl had correctly interpreted what Davis had said. We also compared notes on von Neurath and von Bülow.

Then out to meet Raymond Patenotre. . . . Patenotre is the undersecretary of state for national economy. We talked about the United States on our way over to the Ministry of War.

While waiting to see Daladier[86] we met and chatted with Pierre Cot, minister of air. . . .

Daladier received us cordially. We talked first about Germany. Daladier remarked rather grimly, "You can always count on the Germans doing us a good turn." We talked about the Herriot mission. I said that I had understood that Herriot could have paid the debt without asking the Chamber. Daladier said yes, but Herriot did not discover that until he was out office. Daladier added that the French objection to paying the debt was not at all financial. It was moral.

We spoke also of Laval.[87] Daladier was rather contemptuous in his comments. On the whole, Daladier is much less expansive and attractive than Herriot, and plays his cards close to the cushion.

. . . .

Wednesday, April 12, 1933

. . . Over to talk to [John Foster] Dulles about the Four-Power Pact, also about disarmament and the possibility of his going to Germany.

Then lunch with Paul Scott Mowrer, brother of Edgar. He thought he saw a new balance of power in Europe similar to that before the war. After lunch met one of his associates, Epstein of the *Chicago Daily News,* and a German lawyer.

Called the Spanish Embassy and Madariaga[88] invited me to dinner. Went to the Embassy about 7:30. Found it a magnificent establishment. It is perhaps the finest embassy in Europe, more like a palace than an embassy. We talked about Germany and then about armaments. Madariaga thought that war might be put off for three or four years, but probably no longer. Is pessimistic about the League, he thought that possibly there might be an agreement on a measure of disarmament, but that was all that could be hoped for.

86. Edouard Daladier, French prime minister.

87. Pierre Laval, prime minister, January–February 1932, subsequently June 7, 1935–January 22, 1936.

88. Salvador de Madariaga, Spanish ambassador to France, formerly a member of the League Secretariat at its inception, then Spanish ambassador to the United States and Spanish representative to the League. Brilliant and charming, a noted Spanish writer and historian.

Thursday, April 13, 1933

... In the evening to the theater to see Josephine Baker, but before that had tea with Leland Stowe,[89] who stressed the prevailing fear in France of war.

Friday, April 14, 1933

Over to Herriot's hotel. Met Sinclair[90] there and Stallforth,[91] who said he had just been talking to Schacht. The latter appeared to me to be nervous about his relations to the regime and the possibility of keeping the Mark stable. Stallforth took me up to Herriot's floor. Met Bauzin[92] and then Herriot. I talked about Germany and then about FPA's invitation [to speak]. He said he would like to accept and referred me to his associate, LaBonne, minister to Mexico. I talked with LaBonne, and it was agreed that I was to wireless him from the steamer.

....

Saturday, April 15, 1933

On the boat train met again Mr. and Mrs. Goldwyn.[93] After embarking on the *Berengaria* met Carlisle MacDonald.[94] Had tea with him and his wife.

The voyage was uneventful. The weather was fine. Usual routine. Saw a good deal of the MacDonald[95] delegation. . . . Chatted frequently also with the Goldwyns and a Captain Maud, who made me seem short. He is nearly seven feet.

89. Leland Stowe, head of Paris bureau of the *New York Herald Tribune,* Pulitzer Prize–winning correspondent, author of the book *Nazi Germany Means War.*

90. Sinclair, probably Harry F. Sinclair of the Sinclair Oil Company.

91. Federico Stallforth, born in Mexico, son of the German consul there. A well-to-do German-American businessman.

92. Lucien Bauzin, solicitor general for the National Supreme Court and undersecretary of state to the prime minister in charge of economic planning.

93. Samuel Goldwyn, formerly of Metro Goldwyn Mayer, then of Sam Goldwyn, Inc., an independent movie production company.

94. Carlisle MacDonald, *New York Times* European correspondent.

95. British Prime Minister James Ramsay MacDonald was traveling to the United States to discuss world economic recovery with President Roosevelt. In his party were his daughter, Ishbel; Sir Ronald Lindsay, the British ambassador in Washington; and British Permanent Under-Secretary of State for Foreign Affairs Sir Robert Vansittart.

3. Late April–May 1933: American Reactions

New York, Friday, April 21, 1933

Landed. Met by Ruth.

At the office for an hour, then to the Mays.[1]

At Mr. May's I gave a brief account of my impressions and then on to an early supper at Morgenthau's. In the course of the talk there the question came up of the Berlin post [McDonald as U.S. ambassador]. Morgenthau indicated that he would support me, but it was left for later to have a fuller discussion. He suggested the possibility of coming over with me to Mr. Warburg's, but I said that there were some family matters that I wished to talk to Mr. Felix about, so Ruth and I went there alone.

Felix and I discussed the situation in detail. I talked to him very frankly and found that he already had sized up the situation with extraordinary fairness. I told him of Erich's anxiety to have me return. Felix took the view that he did not see what one could do there, especially if he were to stay for a long time. He agreed that occasional trips might be valuable, but did not commit himself to nearly the extent that Erich had. As to special financing for the FPA in connection with such an enterprise, he was also non-committal.

He spoke almost bitterly of Siegmund, said that the latter had been able to tell them nothing new, and I seemed to sense in his attitude something of resentment at Siegmund's and Erich's assimilationist views.

Throughout our talk Felix was most cordial, and as I left, said that this was to be merely an hors d'oeuvre to a fuller and less pleasant meal, meaning a more detailed discussion of conditions in Germany.

. . . .

Saturday, April 22, 1933

In the evening Ruth and I had dinner with President and Mrs. Butler. We had scarcely sat down before President Butler began to ask me questions about Germany. I talked to him at length and with complete frankness. Throughout the dinner and afterwards he continued to ask questions and limited himself to these and to ejaculations. His comments indicated surprise and strong disapproval verging on horror at some of my accounts of the Nazi methods and excesses.

1. Herbert L. May, a lawyer and businessman who retired at forty-five and devoted his life to humanitarian causes. In 1933 appointed to the World Opium Supervisory Board. On the FPA Board from 1932 to 1952.

Felix Warburg

Felix Warburg. USHMM/ Helen Hamlin.

One of the most important American Jewish leaders of the twentieth century, Felix Moritz Warburg was born in Hamburg, Germany, on January 14, 1871, one of seven children of the banker Moritz Warburg and his wife, Charlotte Oppenheim. His father was a partner in M. M. Warburg and Sons, one of Germany's most important and influential private banks. In March 1895 he married Frieda Schiff, the daughter of the American-Jewish banker Jacob H. Schiff. Moving to New York, he became a partner in Kuhn Loeb & Co., a Wall Street investment bank with close Warburg connections (in which Warburg's father-in-law was senior partner).

Felix Warburg spent much time in philanthropic activities. Unlike his brothers Max (the preeminent private banker in Germany), and Paul, (the creator of the U.S. Federal Reserve Board), Felix had little patience for business or finance per se and much preferred charitable work. In Hamburg he used to see emigrants who were fleeing from other countries to America because of persecution, and on the Lower East Side of Manhattan he met similar immigrants and was moved to help them through the Educational Alliance, the Henry Street Settlement, and his membership on the New York City Board of Education.

Felix Warburg had little use for what he called "the silly layer cake" of class difference and snobbery that separated "uptown" German Jews from the Eastern European immigrants. He led or made major contributions to numerous Jewish and non-Jewish organizations and charities. He helped create the Federation of Jewish Charities, was chairman of the American Jewish Joint Distribution Committee from its establishment in 1914 until 1932, was a major contributor to the American Society for Jewish Farm Settlement in Russia, and helped create the United Jewish Appeal and the Palestine Economic Corporation. Despite the divisions within the Jewish community, Felix Warburg was to some extent able to unite German and Eastern European, including Orthodox, Socialist, and Zionist Jews, at least in support of the organizations he headed.

In June 1933 uncle Moritz and aunt Käthie Oppenheim in Frankfurt committed suicide as a result of the Nazi takeover of power. Although at heart Felix supported the American Jewish-led boycott of German goods, he bowed to the wishes of his brother Max and nephew Erich and opposed a formal boycott. The *New Republic* accused Felix of appeasement, accusations Walter Winchell repeated in his column. In fact, he had few illusions about the Nazi regime and pleaded with his relatives to leave Germany. The plight of German Jewish refugees became a major preoccupation for him.

Felix Warburg backed McDonald for the position of League of Nations High Commissioner for Refugees. The Commission was privately funded, and Felix per-

(*continued*)

suaded the JDC to contribute generously. When McDonald became discouraged, Felix attempted to raise his spirits, as when he wrote him on August 28, 1934. *"I am exceedingly sorry that you feel so discouraged about the achievements of your office. I do not think you are justified in feeling as blue as you did when your letter was written . . . You have been an outstanding figure in illustrating that Christian idealism is not dead."*[1] Warburg mentioned several achievements of the High Commission, including *"the very fact that for the first time in history . . . governments . . . have taken an interest in the well-being of refugees."*

The refugee crisis caused him to redouble his efforts to promote Jewish immigration to Palestine. During the 1920s he had become a non-Zionist member of the Jewish Agency Executive, whose administrative committee he chaired, resigning in October 1930, together with Chaim Weizmann, in protest against the Passfield White Paper's restrictions on Jewish immigration. Although personally sympathetic to Palestinian Arabs, he was sufficiently disturbed by Arab rioting as to suggest their transfer to Transjordan.

Despite major political differences, Felix and Weizmann admired each other. In his autobiography, *Trial and Error,* Weizmann described Felix as "a man of sterling character, charitable to a degree, a pivotal figure in the American Jewish community, if not in very close touch with the rank and file. There was something of *le bon prince* about him. . . . I found (at a luncheon at Kuhn Loeb's) an extremely affable and charming gentleman, very much the *grand seigneur,* but all kindness."[2] Yet the relationship between the two men grew increasingly turbulent. Warburg somewhat naively believed that immigration, sufficient economic development, and a rise in the standard of living could overcome nationalist and religious differences and allow Arabs and Jews to live together in Palestine. At the Zionist meeting in Zurich during the summer of 1937, Warburg and Weizmann clashed bitterly when the latter accepted the Peel Commission's plan for the partition of Palestine, and Warburg felt betrayed. His altercation with Weizmann may have precipitated his death of heart failure, at the age of sixty-six, on October 20, 1937.

1. Felix Warburg to McDonald, August 28, 1934, McDonald Papers, Columbia, Special File—Felix Warburg.
2. Chaim Weizmann, *Trial and Error* (New York: Harper and Brothers, 1949), 309.

During the evening I took occasion to sound him out on the rumor that he was being considered for the Berlin post [U.S. ambassador].[2] Neither he nor Mrs. Butler would deny that they would accept it.

There was no occasion to talk about the FPA or organizational coordination. This I thought better be left until some other time, but on the whole it was clear that he was pleased at my report and that I had gone to Germany.

. . . .

Monday, April 24, 1933

Lunch with Raymond Fosdick.[3] I told him at length my German experiences, stressing especially the international implications of the policies of the new regime. He was intensely interested. I mentioned to him the possibilities of the ambassadorship. He offered to be helpful.

. . . .

Dinner at Felix Warburg's. Frederick [Felix's son] joined us before dinner. I was talking to the group made up of Frederick and his father and mother without reserve. Frederick was inclined to minimize the conditions in Germany, and as he was leaving to go to dinner elsewhere, he whispered to me, "Don't frighten them." I discovered, however, during dinner that that was a needless warning, because both his father and mother were already much better informed about conditions than he, and both were quite willing to face the realities.

The talk covered somewhat the same ground as the few evenings before, though more attention was given to family matters. Late in the evening, Felix took me aside and we discussed the possibility of my returning. He clung to the view he expressed earlier that a long stay might be futile, that frequent trips might be valuable. Nothing definite was decided about plans or about means. Nor was it clear from his remarks that evening or the previous evening that he felt that he ought to make any special contribution to the FPA in connection with my March trip. There was considerable talk about the Embassy, Felix explaining why he had suggested the three persons, Butler, Guthrie,[4] and myself.

Tuesday, April 25, 1933

Meeting for nearly two hours in the morning with Henry Morgenthau. Discussion about the situation in Germany and the Embassy. Morgenthau reiterated his doubts whether I should undertake it, from my own point of view.

2. Because McDonald was very much interested in the post of ambassador to Germany, he had a problem in reporting on his visit. In private, he was completely frank about the situation, but in public speeches he refrained from spelling out all the facts and was circumspect in criticisms of the German government. If he were to be appointed, he would have to be acceptable to Hitler.

3. Raymond Fosdick, director of the Rockefeller Foundation and president of the League of Nations Association of the United States. At the start of the League had been undersecretary general. Also active in the FPA. Brother of Harry Emerson Fosdick, a writer and famous preacher at the Gothic-style Riverside Church built by the Rockefellers on upper Riverside Drive.

4. William D. Guthrie, president of the French-American Society, counsel to the Roman Catholic hierarchy in the United States.

The probabilities of failure he thought were so great as to make it questionable whether one ought to undertake it. But he said that, if I wished to try it, he would do everything he could for me in Washington, that he was going down soon.

At a quarter past twelve I attended a meeting at the headquarters of the Lutheran Church. In addition to some representatives of the Federal Council of Churches and Lutherans, were present Rabbi Wise and John Haynes Holmes.[5] I spoke briefly of my impressions in Germany. My account of the Jewish situation brought tears to Rabbi Wise's eyes.[6]

Downtown to lunch with John Rockefeller, 3rd. He was deeply interested in the German situation and the Jewish persecution. During the latter part of lunch and afterwards we talked about the possibility of the Embassy. He seemed to be very anxious to have me secure it.

In the late afternoon up to Dr. Harry Fosdick's[7] office at the Riverside Church. I gave him my interpretation of the Jewish situation in Germany and answered his questions about it. He repeatedly expressed his gratitude at my willingness to come up.

Wednesday, April 26, 1933

Over to see Colonel House[8] in the morning. After talking briefly about the German situation, we discussed the question of the Embassy. He evidently was surprised that I had been suggested. He said that he was sorry he had not thought of me; that he had already recommended President Butler; that now, as he thought it over, he concluded that I would do the job better, but he did not commit himself to helping me definitely. Nonetheless, I had the impression that he would be friendly.

At 11:30 to see Sulzberger at his office. I went over with him much the same ground I had covered with others. He was repeatedly interrupted by the telephone, but in nearly every case he asked the person to call back again. I have never seen him so intensely interested. He said that one of the worst things from his point of view was that Hitler's attacks had made him for the first time race conscious. He spoke with pride of the *Times* initiative in launching the first of the stories about persecutions. He is evidently deeply troubled by the problems created by the Hitler attacks. I told him of the Embassy suggestion. His response was favorable. I doubt, however, that the *Times* could take any move on their own initiative, though they would doubtless give a friendly editorial comment if my name were sent in.

5. Rabbi Stephen S. Wise, leader of the American Jewish Congress and strong advocate of a boycott against Hitler, and Wise's friend, John Haynes Holmes, pastor of the Community Church of New York, director of the American Civil Liberties Union.

6. See inserted commentary in chapter 2, April 8, 1933.

7. Brother of Raymond Fosdick (see n. 3).

8. Edward M. House, elder statesman who had been a close adviser to President Woodrow Wilson.

Spoke at FPA research conference in the afternoon. I thought that I made very clear my attitude, but so strong was the emotional reaction of some of the members of the staff that they seemed to feel that I was apologizing for the Hitler regime. That was to be only one of many experiences of a similar sort.

. . . .

Friday, April 28, 1933

Back to the office and found a telegram from the White House from Mrs. Roosevelt's[9] secretary saying, "Can you spend next Monday night at the White House: President most anxious hear your impressions." I, of course, accepted.

I called Swope and told him that perhaps his initiative had already secured this result. He said he thought no. As a matter of fact, I think the invitation came because of the letter I had written Mrs. Roosevelt the previous day. In it I had said nothing about going down, but had told her briefly of my experiences and my concern about peace and the excellent reception of the initial moves the President had made in Europe.

Telephoned Colonel House to tell him of the invitation to the White House. He said that he had just been reading an editorial from the *Boston Herald* in which the importance of the Berlin post had been strongly stressed. He felt that either Butler or I would meet the conditions necessary for that important place.

. . . .

Washington, Monday, May 1, 1933

Reached Washington about three o'clock. Went to the office. Learned there that I was expected at the White House about five. Reached there just at that time. Was shown to my room, the famous Lincoln Room which had been occupied by Ramsay [MacDonald] and, I suppose, also by Herriot. I had scarcely entered the room when I heard Mrs. Roosevelt's voice and she came and said, "Mr. McDonald come on, you are just in time for tea," so I went out with her and found Miss Cook and one of the secretaries and a couple of Puerto Ricans discussing with Mrs. Roosevelt Puerto Rican problems. Later Anne O'Hare McCormick[10] and her husband came in and a couple of family friends of the Roosevelts from Boston.

About six, the President came with the Argentine delegation. As the President came in, everybody rose. He, during the next hour, carried on his conference with the Argentineans and then with several other members of the group at tea. The President's military aides helped serve the tea.

9. Eleanor Roosevelt had been on the board of the FPA from 1927 to 1929. She and McDonald were well acquainted.

10. Anne O'Hare McCormick, *New York Times* writer on international affairs who, by sheer brilliance as a reporter and writer, surmounted discriminatory attitudes and eventually became the first female member of the editorial staff.

Moley came in about a quarter past six, and as the crowd thinned out, he and I sat off in the corner and talked about Germany. He seemed very much disturbed about the Jewish situation and the international aspects of the problem. He was generous enough to say that it was good of me to come down to help them to work out the problem. I stressed with him the importance of naming someone to Berlin for reasons which I later elaborated with the President, but, of course, nothing was said about myself.

As the tea party was breaking up, the President said to me, "McDonald, after dinner you and I will talk about Germany." I replied, "Mr. President, what I have to say is not a bed-time story." He said, "Well, I guess I will be able to stand it." Earlier Mrs. Roosevelt had explained that when the invitation was sent to me, it was expected that I would dine quietly with the family, but since then, it had been arranged that there would be a state dinner for the Argentineans,[11] so I was dining with the men, and the ladies were going out with her.

After tea there was just time for a brief walk and then to dress. I was sharing the bathroom with Louis Howe.[12] I met him first in the bathroom. He was certainly not a communicative person, at least with those whom he does not know well. I had trouble tying my own white tie and so was forced to borrow one from him.

At eight o'clock we were all downstairs, about twenty of us waiting for the President and the Argentine representative. Included in the group were the secretary of state and the undersecretary of state, Samuel McReynolds, chairman of the House Committee of Foreign Affairs, Key Pittman, chairman of the Senate Committee of Foreign Relations, young Morgenthau,[13] Jimmy Warburg,[14] the President's two military aides, one of whom urged me to speak at the War College. A few minutes after eight, the President of the Argentine came in. We all then filed past and were presented by the President to his guests. We sat down at a long table, not, of course, in the large dining hall, but in the smaller one, but it would have seated many more people.

The dinner was not unusually elaborate, though the plate and china were impressive. During the dinner the President told informally a story of his relations with the Argentineans during the war, but there was no formal speaking.

About 9:30 we adjourned to the upper floor, where we saw the movies, first Mickey Mouse in a very amusing skit, then a newsreel. At about ten or a little after that the guests left, except some of the secretaries. The President said that he and I would talk in his study. We went into the so-called "Oval Room," which he has had fitted up with his own furniture and the walls covered with pictures of ships and many models of ships about. He sat at his desk and I on

11. The delegation had come for commercial talks on the balance of trade between the two countries.

12. Louis Howe, Roosevelt's confidant and close friend, living at the White House.

13. Henry Morgenthau, Jr., appointed secretary of the Treasury in 1934.

14. James Warburg, son of Paul Warburg, banker, writer on economic and foreign affairs. Financial adviser, London Economic Conference, 1933.

one side. He started the discussion by outlining at considerable length and in detail and with what seemed to me complete frankness his picture of the international situation. First he spoke of the Far East. He thought it probable that Japan would go on and on, that nothing could forestall the seizure of Tientsin and Peking if the military desired to take it; that perhaps the Japanese authority would be extended further. At last he said the British are really frightened. They don't feel that they could defend either Hong Kong or Singapore. In other words, the Japanese fleet is supreme in Chinese waters.

The President then told me of an experience he had had as a student. One of his best friends was a Japanese with intimate connections in high and official quarters. One day after a student party the Japanese was very drunk. It was late at night. In a period of unguarded indiscretion, he spoke at length of Japan's plans for the Far East. As the President told the story, it seemed to me that the program outlined by the student was not so very different from that indicated in the so-called Tanaka Memorial.[15] The President did not say so, but I had the impression that he felt that the student's disclosure was a fairly accurate picture of the underlying program of Japan. It, of course, is not a program for a day, but for generations.

It was against this somber Far Eastern background that the President then turned to discuss the situation in Western Europe. To him it appeared that Germany was the very center of the problem. Upon German concessions at Geneva depended the success of the Disarmament Conference. Upon that in turn depended the possibility of any program of security for France, and upon that in turn depended the possibility of having a chance for success at the Economic Conference.[16]

The President outlined clearly what he had in mind to offer to the French. He was willing to promise to sit in with a jury of the powers to discuss the question of the aggressor, but he would not be bound by the decision of the jury. The United States would reserve freedom of decision. If we agreed with the jury, the President would then declare that he would not enforce American neutral rights against those who were seeking to punish the aggressor. American citizens would have to trade at their own risk with the aggressor. Furthermore, he indicated that he would use the arms embargo against the aggressor. All of these measures he said could be put into effect by executive action and would not require senatorial consent.

This outline as he presented it took nearly a half hour. Then he asked me to talk about Germany. I did for perhaps an hour. During the course of my discus-

15. A plan for Japanese world conquest, allegedly written by Prime Minister Tanaka in 1927. Regarded by scholars as a fake of mysterious origins.

16. International Economic Conference, June 12–July 27, 1933, London. Met under League of Nations auspices to negotiate an agreement on currency stabilization while ignoring the problems of war debts and reparations. FDR (who took the United States off the gold standard) did not support a currency stabilization program, and American delegates were ordered to limit negotiations to bilateral tariff treaties. After FDR condemned the conference in a radio address, the conference collapsed.

sion the President asked many questions, showing a very real grasp of the situation. He was deeply interested in Schacht, wanted to know what sort of a person he was. I told him that Schacht was a man ambitious almost to an extremity, that he was very close to Hitler and in the confidence of the regime, that he could, I thought, be used better as a medium of communication with Hitler than Luther, who is not in the confidence of the regime. I expressed the view that it would be desirable if some very frank speaking could be done to Hitler through Schacht. The President did not commit himself, but left me the impression that he intended to use Schacht for just that purpose. He also intimated, though I did not at the time get the full implications of it, that he had a plan in mind to appeal over the head of Hitler to the German people and over the heads of other governments to their people. I ventured to express a doubt as to whether such an appeal would be carried in the German press. He said he thought he could present it in such a way that it would have to be carried.[17] I had forgotten whether he then indicated that he was addressing the heads of the governments, rather than the prime ministers or chancellors. In any case, it was clear that he was considering, through Schacht and otherwise, telling the German government how seriously he considered their general policies.

In the course of my remarks about the danger of a Franco-Polish occupation of Germany, the President intimated that Herriot had suggested that the French might have to move.[18] The President told a story that he had told Herriot, which Clemenceau had told him. It was to the effect that Clemenceau's ambition was to see to it that one French generation might live its life without a German invasion. The President seemed to feel that Herriot was pacific, but was the more impressed, therefore, by his fatalism. The President did not quote [Ramsey] MacDonald, but I got the impression that the prime minister had said that he would not oppose a Franco-Polish move.

The President asked me whether I thought the government ought to send an ambassador to Germany. I replied with an unequivocal "yes" for the following reasons:

(1) There is no advantage in not sending one. The effect of not being represented by an ambassador in Germany is too minor a slight to impress the Nazis.
(2) At any time something might occur which would make it embarrassing to name an ambassador and more embarrassing not to have named him.
(3) In the event of a Franco-Polish movement, the United States might be one of the few neutral powers represented in Berlin.

17. On May 13, 1933, FDR conferred with Secretary of State Hull and Undersecretary Phillips about sending a message to the heads of government, in which "he could convey a few necessary home truths." Moffat Journal, vol. 33, Moffat Papers, May 13, 1933, call number MS Am 1407, Houghton Library, Harvard University. By permission of the Houghton Library, Harvard University.

18. Because of the fear of Germany's intentions, France had strengthened her alliance with Poland.

(4) While it is, of course, important to have the views of the French and the British, it is more important that the United States should make up its mind on the basis of its own information and on the basis of its own national interest.
(5) No one can be sure what can be done with this regime, but there is at least a chance that when it reaches the end of its first period, the seizure of power, a period which will close soon, America may be able to exercise considerable influence. At any rate, the effort ought to be made.

To these arguments the President did not reply. Instead, he went on to ask me what sort of a person should be chosen as ambassador. I suggested among others the following specifications: a person who knew his Germany thoroughly, who knew also the European scene, someone who is really sympathetic with the German people and who could have a fair chance of gaining the confidence of the regime. Moreover, it should be a man who would not be afraid to fail. The chances of failure would be great. Therefore, a career man might be disadvantaged. Besides, it would be necessary to consider dealing in unconventional ways, for the regime is not the usual one. It is a revolutionary government. I added that in any case, I hoped it would not be a political appointment.

The President's only comment was that I should be sure that it would not be that. There was no one on the political list who was up to it. He gave no indication, however, as to when a nomination would be made. He told me that he had offered the place to Cox[19] and then to Baker,[20] but both refused. As to the latter, the President said there might have been some doubt anyhow because of the report that his wife was a Jewess.

As the clock moved on towards midnight, I became more and more ready to leave, because I had been warned by Phillips not to keep the President up too late, but since he gave no indication of wishing me to go, I, of course, stayed. We were interrupted three times during our approximately two hours. Once one of the secretaries came in to ask if he might deny again the rumor that the President was going to the Economic Conference. The President said "yes." The other interruption was when the secretary came to ask if one of the other house guests should wait to see the President that night. The answer was "no." There was still another time when a secretary came to check with the President on his program [for the] next day. But none of these interruptions took more than a minute or two.

Just after the clock struck midnight, I was on my feet to go. I said to the President, "I hope that despite my story of conditions in Germany, you will sleep well." He said he thought he would. I then referred to what his wife and mother had said of him about his not worrying and told him the story just current that

19. James M. Cox, 1920 Democratic presidential candidate.
20. Newton D. Baker, secretary of war under Woodrow Wilson.

in Soviet Russia the regime there had abolished worry by edict. This seemed to him very amusing. He laughed heartily.

My impressions of the President were extremely favorable. Naturally I was pleased by his evidence of confidence in talking to me so frankly. I was encouraged by his obvious grasp of the world situation and by his program to deal with it. Moreover, he gave no signs of being tired, though it was at the end of what for him was a very long day. On the contrary, he appeared to enjoy the discussion and showed the keenest interest throughout.

Tuesday, May 2, 1933

I was up about seven. As I was going into the bathroom, met Mrs. Roosevelt going out for her morning ride. She had asked me the evening before if nine o'clock would not be too late for breakfast. Later met Louis Howe, he very much in informal attire. Certainly in his more intimate life he puts on no more show than he does in public.

About nine Mrs. Roosevelt came and said that breakfast was ready. She went into Louis Howe's room and called out, "Louis, are you ready for breakfast?" We sat down in the same room-like hall where tea had been served. Mrs. Roosevelt sat at one end of the table and Mrs. Cook at the other end. I and one of the secretaries were on one side and Louis Howe and one of the other of Mrs. Roosevelt's secretaries on the other. The talk was quite informal. Mrs. Roosevelt read a letter from one of her sons giving plans he wished to make for the summer. She commented upon them as any mother would do, anxious about the friends that he was going to be with.

Louis Howe talked of his love of thrillers, was rather sarcastic about Senator Carraway for continuing to refer to the bite which the White House dog had given him. As a matter of fact, Mrs. Roosevelt said, it had been a bare scratch.

As we were having breakfast Farley[21] came in, and I was presented to him. The secretaries of the President came in and out from his bedroom.

About ten o'clock I went over to the State Department to keep my appointment with Mr. Phillips. He called in Mr. Moffat. I talked to them for about forty-five minutes. They asked a number of questions. I got the impression that Phillips, though knowing most of the facts, did not really sense the situation. Urged on them, as I had on the President, the desirability of naming an ambassador promptly.

I asked Phillips about the possibility of seeing the secretary [Cordell Hull]. He looked in at the secretary's office, said he was then dictating a speech. He took me into McBride, the secretary's secretary. The latter said he would try to arrange something for that day or the next.

....

21. James Aloysius Farley, FDR's campaign manager and closest political adviser. Chairman of the Democratic Party, later, postmaster general.

Moffat wrote in his journal on May 2:

James G. MacDonald [sic] of the Foreign Policy [sic] explained at great length his opinions on the German situation. He was one of the few observers who returned from Germany last summer reporting that the Hitler movement, in spite of seeming reverses, was nonetheless gaining. He had talked with the President for approximately two hours last night. In his opinion the President has an admirable chance to talk with brutal frankness to Schacht, who is close to Hitler and is a medium whose opinions and recommendations would be trusted, whereas Luther does not belong to the "gang" with the result that his recommendations would undoubtedly be discounted.[22]

Back to the White House. My bags were packed and I was sent over to the club in a White House car, a Chevrolet.

Called Raymond Fosdick, gave him the gist of the President's talk. Telephoned also to President Butler along the same lines and asked him if there was anything he could do with Schacht to influence the Germans to be more conciliatory and avoid a crisis.

Lunch with Jimmie Warburg at Carlton Hotel. He was deeply stirred by what I had to say.[23] We then talked about the Embassy. He promised to sound Moley out that night.

Wednesday, May 3, 1933

I called Jimmie Warburg to ask him what reaction he had from Moley. He said he had spoken to Moley. Latter was non-committal and seemed to leave the impression that it was better not to press the matter actively now.

. . . .

Back to the State Department to keep 2:30 appointment with Moley. Found he had been called to the White House, so talked instead to Miss Gaddell, his associate. We had a longish interview. She was much concerned about the Jewish situation.

Up to the Hill, spoke for a moment with Borah[24] and with Senator Pittman.[25]

22. Moffat Journal, vol. 33, Moffat Papers, May 2, 1933, call number MS Am 1407, Houghton Library, Harvard University. By permission of the Houghton Library, Harvard University.

23. Warburg said that McDonald was horrified by his talk with Hitler, who told him, "I've got my heel on the necks of the Jews and will soon have them so they can't move." McDonald predicted that German Jews would retrogress to medieval ghetto status and that Hitler would trigger a European war. "All in all, the picture he paints is far worse than anything I have heard yet." Quotes in Herbert Feis, *1933: Characters in Crisis* (Boston: Little Brown, 1966), 137, and James P. Warburg, Columbia Oral History Collection, 644.

24. William E. Borah, Democratic senator from Idaho, chairman of the Foreign Relations Committee since 1924, a personality of force and influence.

25. Key Pittman, Democratic senator from Nevada, 1912–1941, member of the Senate Committee on Foreign Relations.

Four o'clock train home. Had a long talk with Deutsch.[26] I told him I hoped that his group would not heckle me as they had the speaker at the Town Hall shortly before. He said there was no danger of that; that the previous speaker was a well-known anti-Semite.[27] We then discussed the situation in Washington and in Germany. We did not differ particularly, except in his attitude to members of the American Jewish Committee. He said that in his view the members of that group would willingly sacrifice all Eastern Jews in Germany if they could save their own friends and relatives. This seemed to me a very harsh judgment. I told him I thought it was quite unfair.

Thursday, May 4, 1933

Busy at the office and outlined my speech for the evening.

....

The Town Hall was packed. It was really an excellent audience. My interview with the President had increased my anxiety about the European situation and also my desire to avoid making a faux pas. The atmosphere of the audience too was tense. I spoke almost exactly as I had planned, except for my reference to the so-called "left-wing" Jews. The question period I should have left to Kellogg[28] and particularly should not have myself decided when the meeting should end and should have let Kellogg handle my friend Kelsey.

The reception of the talk was mixed. I have never been more extravagantly praised and I suspect never more harshly criticized. But given all the circumstances, I doubt if anyone could have pleased everybody. In any event, the major objective was accomplished. There was no open display of opposition and no news in the press.

After the meeting Mr. May spoke enthusiastically as did many others, but I could sense from the reaction of people like the Jonases that there was deep disappointment.[29] I was to hear much more of this during the ensuing days. Nonetheless, I was glad that it was over.

Friday, May 5, 1933

I learned that one of the persons at the meeting the night before who had criticized me for being pro-Jewish was a Dr. A. Scheurer of the Hamburg-American Line, who was there with Mr. Julius T. Meyer.

26. Bernard S. Deutsch, president of the Board of Aldermen of New York City and active in the American Jewish Congress.

27. Ellery Walter, writer and lecturer, had spoken on "Hitler and Germany." Walter said, with reference to Nazi anti-Semitism, "There is persecution, but there is a whole lot more smoke than fire" and added that "Germany is a charming place; I say in defense of Germany." *New York Times*, May 3, 1933, p. 11.

28. Paul U. Kellogg, one of the founders of the American Civil Liberties Union in 1920. Editor of *Survey Associate* (later *Survey Midmonthly*) and *Survey Graphic*, publications for social workers. Served on the FPA Board from 1918 to 1949.

29. Disappointment at McDonald's failure to denounce the Nazis in harsh terms. For the reasons, see following diary entry of May 5, 1933.

Mr. Charles Crane came into the office to congratulate me on what he had heard of my speech, but his congratulations frightened me, because he showed a very strong anti-Jewish feeling. He tends to justify the whole Nazi program. A few days later when I met him on the street, I asked him what he thought about the Japanese advance. He said, "Well, this is a fine world, the Japanese seizing control of the East and the Jews in control of the West."[30]

Lunch with Mr. Ittleson.[31] He had been hurt by some of the things I had left unsaid at my meeting. He asked me if there was any reason why I had not spoken with complete frankness. I explained the situation exactly [the possibility of the Embassy appointment]. He not only was satisfied, but offered to help me in any way he could. In particular, he said that he would get in touch with Swope and see what he could do to induce Swope to act with special vigor.

. . . .

After I came home I called Mrs. Lehman to ask her if she would speak to the governor[32] about the possibility of his using his influence in Washington. She said she would be glad to. I said that perhaps the governor would like to speak to Felix Warburg first. She said she would ask him to do that. The governor then called Felix Warburg, and later Mr. Warburg called me to say that the governor had been in touch with Washington.

A few days earlier there had been a mix-up about Felix Warburg and Felix Frankfurter. Mr. Herbert Swope had misunderstood my reference to Felix Warburg as meaning Felix Frankfurter. Moreover, he had gone ahead to speak to Felix Frankfurter and the latter, not having heard anything from me, was naturally a little put out. But by telephoning Frankfurter I was able to straighten up the misunderstanding.

Saturday, May 6, 1933

. . . .

Four o'clock tea with Mr. Filene,[33] who was deeply affected by what I had to say about Germany. He offered to help me in any way he could at the Embassy and asked me if I cared to go as his guest to the Economic Conference. He showed more personal interest in my career than he ever had in the past. I thanked him heartily, said I would let him know how my plans developed.

. . . .

30. On June 4 the *New York Times* published a letter from Charles Crane in which he equated Communists and Jews.

31. Henry Ittleson, founder and chairman of the board of Commercial Investment Trust. A leading Jewish philanthropist and strong supporter of McDonald.

32. Herbert H. Lehman, Democratic governor of New York and first Jew to hold the office.

33. Edward A. Filene, prominent Boston retailer and founder of the Twentieth Century Fund, of which McDonald had been a director from the beginning.

Thursday, May 11, 1933

At 4:00 went to the Jewish-Christian meeting on the invitation of Roger Straus. . . . [34]

After the meeting rode up with Judge Proskauer[35] to Felix Warburg's house. Proskauer outlined the plan of action he had in mind. It was two-fold: (1) continuation of the quiet boycott; (2) encouragement of non-Jewish protests throughout the country. He said nothing about having approached Justice Dowling.[36] I heard later that he could not do it.

Friday, May 12, 1933

Over to the special meeting of the Administrative Committee of the American Jewish Congress. It was a meeting of perhaps fifty to one hundred persons. Deutsch presided. Rabbi Wise was the only person who spoke at length following my statement. . . . I gave my impressions of the Jewish problem in Germany and also here. I stressed the danger of rising anti-Semitism in the United States and urged a large degree of tolerance among Jewish groups. I recognized, of course, that the chief responsibility for curbing anti-Semitism should be on the Gentiles, but that in all likelihood they would not assume this responsibility; that, therefore, it was doubly necessary that differences among the Jews themselves should not be permitted to stimulate anti-Semitic feeling.

Saturday, May 13, 1933

. . . .

Then Ruth and I drove to the Sherry Netherland, where I had an engagement with Schacht at 6:30. He received me immediately. I found him with Professor Lichtenstein. Schacht, at first without any suggestion on my part, said the Jewish policy is a mistake. Apparently he had been much impressed by the dinner the night before, about which Judge Proskauer had spoken to him and about what he had heard in Washington.

I said to Schacht, "As a friend of Germany, I have been very much startled by a phrase which has recurred in a number of conferences that I had since I left him in Berlin and Basle. You know perhaps that I have been in Paris and in Washington. The phrase is 'the dismemberment of Germany.'" I had earlier explained that, of course, no one of the men with whom I had talked had necessarily approved such a program, but nonetheless it was being seriously considered at least in some places. When the meaning of this phrase had become clear to Schacht, he literally exploded, marched up and down the room and was talking in a very

34. Roger Straus, American Smelting and Refining executive, later chairman and president of the board, philanthropist, active in the American Jewish Committee.

35. Joseph M. Proskauer, justice of the Supreme Court of New York 1923–1930, president of the American Jewish Committee.

36. Victor J. Dowling, retired associate justice of the Appellate Division of the New York Supreme Court 1st Department; a prominent Catholic layman.

loud voice declaring that Germany would not be frightened by such a threat, that if an attempt were made to carry it out, it would lead to Bolshevism and grave disorders throughout Europe, etc. I explained that I had mentioned this merely as preliminary to my desire to express my hope that Hitler would make a conciliatory statement on Wednesday. Schacht said, "What sort of a statement?" I said, "Conciliatory in reference to disarmament and thus confute his enemies." Schacht said, "Exactly what should he say?" I said, "Well, it should be conciliatory." He replied, "Write out exactly what you think the Chancellor should say on disarmament and I will cable it to him." I retorted that, of course, it was not my job to write the Chancellor's speech, that at most I could only venture to express a general point of view. Then I continued to argue how Germany would be greatly advantaged by a conciliatory démarche, but Schacht would not admit it, but kept insisting that if he were making the speech he would say to the Allies, "You have broken your word, now goodbye." He added, however, that he would, of course, send on the substance of my suggestions.

Then Luther came in. He and I talked about the situation along somewhat the same lines. He was, of course, much less explosive than Schacht.

Later Schacht came back in a more moderate frame of mind. As I was leaving, I took him aside and told him that I hoped he would not be misled by any reports which he might have had of what I was supposed to have said about Germany.

....

Tuesday, May 16, 1933

Lunch with Walter Lippmann at the Century Club. Usual discussion about Germany. Towards the end of lunch Coudert[37] came up and joined us. He said to me, "What do you think would happen if there were a Franco-Polish occupation of Germany?" I replied, "Of course, I don't know, but my guess is that the first thing would be a wholesale slaughter of the Jews." This seemed to startle Lippmann. Later we spoke about the Berlin Embassy. I mentioned Butler as a possibility and that my own name had been mentioned. Lippmann said nothing definite, but I gathered that he would not make any move to support me; rather, he might help Butler. We walked together back to his office and I went in to see Geoffrey Parsons. He called in Walter Millis.[38] We discussed the President's statement that day.[39] Millis and I thought he offered Hitler a way out. Parsons did not agree. In other respects Millis and I interpreted the statement in much the same way. The question of the Berlin Embassy came up. I had the impression that I could be assured of favorable comment from the *Tribune* if the nomination were made.

37. Frederick René Coudert, former congressman, lawyer with Coudert Brothers, vice president of the Comité France Amerique and director of the French Alliance in the United States.

38. Parsons and Millis were also *New York Herald Tribune* writers.

39. President Roosevelt made a personal appeal to the heads of fifty-four governments to resume their attacks on the twin problems: the economics of world depression and disarmament. He proposed international cooperation in the event of aggression and linked the two issues in an effort to limit the dangers of war. Roosevelt's speech was timed to put pressure on Hitler, who was due to make a major speech to the Reichstag the following day.

Wednesday, May 17, 1933

At home to wait for Mrs. Paul Warburg[40] to pick me up to go to Miss Wald's.[41] She came about half past ten. We drove about two hours to Miss Wald's. I discovered what did not surprise me, that Mrs. Warburg is a woman of extraordinary intelligence and breadth of culture. She is not an Orthodox Jew, but understands Jewish literature and religion intimately. She has a singularly clear grasp of the Jewish situation in Germany and is fatalistic about the way it will work out there and here.

Found Miss Wald cheerful and showing none of the signs of facial paralysis about which I had heard. We talked about Germany, then after lunch I talked with Miss Wald alone. She said that if she had an opportunity she would be glad to speak to Eleanor Roosevelt or to the President.

On the way back Mrs. Warburg and I talked about the families, especially about Bettina and Jimmy. She asked me if I would like to go to Berlin. I told her yes, I thought I would. She was rather insistent in her question, and I am not sure whether there was anything back of her inquiry or not.

. . . .

Washington, Thursday, May 18, 1933

Over to the State Department promptly at 9:35. Was kept waiting by a series of rather confusing unexpected engagements of the secretary, including a long distance telephone call from Sumner Welles.[42] Afterward had a very pleasant chat with Hull, mostly about his economic theories. He urged me to stress with the organizations the need of reiterating the basic importance of certain elementary truths about freer trade.

. . . .

To lunch at the German Embassy alone with Luther. I congratulated him on the Hitler speech.[43] We talked about the Jewish situation in Germany. There was very little that was new.

. . . .

40. Nina Loeb Warburg, wife of Felix Warburg's brother, Paul.

41. Lillian Wald, founder and organizer of public health nursing and the Henry Street settlement house in New York City, also active in the peace movement and on the FPA board, 1919–1935.

42. Sumner Welles, then assistant secretary of state for Latin American affairs. State Department official closest to President Roosevelt.

43. Hitler's speech of May 17 to the German Reichstag was, on the surface, conciliatory. He claimed that Germany wanted peace, but it had to be a peace based on equality and dignity. Playing upon feelings that the Treaty of Versailles had treated his country unfairly, Hitler claimed that since then 224,000 Germans had committed suicide, almost all of them because of the ensuing disgrace and misery. He warned others against threatening Germany and mentioned the possibility of withdrawing from the League of Nations. The *New York Times* article on the speech (by Birchall) highlighted Hitler's denial that he wanted war and claimed that Hitler had dropped his truculent tone. *New York Times,* May 18, 1933.

New York, Sunday, May 21, 1933

Lunched with the Sulzbergers in the home of Mr. Ochs[44] at White Plains, a magnificent colonial establishment. Besides Mr. and Mrs. Ochs and Mr. and Mrs. Sulzberger, Ruth and I, were the Sulzberger children, four of them, Mr. and Mrs. Merz,[45] and about four other guests.

We had some general talk about the Jewish situation at lunch. After lunch Mrs. Ochs showed me a very interesting group of family portraits. Especially striking was the picture of her mother. Then Mr. Ochs and I had a long talk about Germany, but more especially about the Jewish situation in this country. He is a very broad-minded person, and I sympathize completely with his desire to be known as the owner of the *Times*, the world's foremost newspaper, rather than to have that journal stigmatized as a Jewish organ. I could understand, too, his refusal to be associated with the different Jewish committees. The question of the Embassy came up. While he was friendly, he was non-committal.

. . . .

Saturday, May 27, 1933

. . . .

About six drove into town for my broadcast and then to dinner at the Necarsulmers. Among those there besides Mr. and Mrs. Necarsulmer and Ruth and I were Mr. and Mrs. Schwarz,[46] the former German consul. There was no particular general talk at table. After dinner Schwarz took me aside to say that he thought I would be interested to know that not all of the members of the Foreign Office in Berlin were enthusiastic about the possibility of my being named ambassador. He said [Hans] Dieckhoff was for me, but not all the others. The same thing was true in the Embassy in Washington. But he did not indicate to me which members were for or against me. I thanked him for his information and said that I was very doubtful about the appointment in any case.

. . . .

Wednesday, May 31, 1933

. . . .

Long conference during the day with Dr. Mattfeld, correspondent of the *Frankfurter Zeitung*, in reference to his article in the May 15 number, attributing to me a statement made by Buell, urging the outlawry of Germany if it contin-

44. Adolph Ochs, publisher and controlling owner of the *New York Times*, father-in-law of Arthur Hays Sulzberger.

45. Charles Merz, previously a well-known writer, hired in 1931 by the *Times* as an editorial writer. In 1938 he replaced Finley as editor of the editorial page, a position he filled until 1961. Close socially to the Arthur Hays Sulzbergers.

46. Paul Schwarz, who stayed in the United States and became a strong anti-Nazi.

ued to be non-cooperative.[47] I wanted Mattfeld to write me a brief note saying that he had been mistaken, that I had not said it. He was willing to do that, but he insisted on adding that it had been Buell who had said it, in other words, that instead of it being the chairman, it had been the director of the research department. This obviously was much less usable for me. It was left that he would write a letter, and we would see if it were satisfactory. I called in Mr. May during our discussion.

47. McDonald and Buell's speeches were summarized on June 15 and June 20, 1933, *New York Times*, p. 9 and p. 12, respectively.

4. June–August 1933: Alerting Others

On June 10 William E. Dodd was appointed U.S. ambassador to Germany. He had earned his Ph.D. at the University of Leipzig in Germany and was a professor of history at the University of Chicago.[1] *Although McDonald must have been disappointed that he did not get this post, he was now freer to express his views of the Nazi regime.*

Catching up on work at the FPA and continuing his weekly radio broadcasts, McDonald also spent a great deal of time in June and July speaking to various groups on his visit to Germany—the Lincoln School, which his older daughter attended, Harvard Business School, Wellesley College commencement, the American Jewish Joint Distribution Committee, and others. He constantly emphasized that the Nazi movement in Germany threatened not just Jews, but civilization and world peace. "Anti-Semitic persecution, practiced by Christians in the name of Christianity, is a non-Jewish problem. It is a challenge to civilized men."[2]

New York, Tuesday, June 20, 1933

Up to White Plains to see Felix Warburg. Reached there promptly at five. First had a cup of tea with Mrs. Warburg and Mr. and Mrs. Lewis and Mrs. Hellman.[3] The latter proceeded at once to attack me for my Town Hall speech, with which attack the Lewises were sympathetic. Then I explained the matter of the American Embassy in Berlin, and all three of my assailants seemed willing to forgive me.

Mr. Warburg and I then went into his study and talked for more than an hour. I explained my feeling of unrest and desire to make somewhat more adequate provisions for my family and said that I would like to have his very frank advice as to my future. We then discussed the matter in detail. He was of the opinion that a business connection would be a mistake, that I should keep a public or semi-public position where I would be free to utilize as fully as possible my abilities in reaching public opinion. Said that he had thought of me in connection with Eugene Meyer's purchase of the *Washington Post.*[4] Thought I might be a logical New York representative of that paper, with a

1. There is some analysis of Dodd as ambassador and as diarist in the conclusion.
2. "Drive to Aid Jews Opened by Lehman," *New York Times,* June 15, 1933.
3. Probably the wife of Maurice Hellmann, of the Farmer's and Merchants Bank of Los Angeles.
4. Eugene Meyer, former chairman of the Federal Reserve Board, bought the *Washington Post* in June 1933. Father of Katharine Graham, subsequent longtime owner of the *Post.*

broad, free-lance commission. He asked whether I would be interested to be mentioned in this connection. I said I would, though I was not sure it was just what I should do.

As to the FPA, he thought there were many advantages to my continuing as the head of that organization, but I ought to be relieved of financial responsibility. He stressed, however, that my wife and I probably underrated the way we were regarded by our richer friends; that those among them who were really intelligent were most grateful for the opportunity to bring into their homes people who were other than mere checkbooks.

I then told him about our tentative plans to buy a house. He was inclined to discourage me on the ground that an intellectual should not be burdened with things. I told him that we had no ambition to ape our rich friends with town houses and country houses, etc., but that we did feel the need of having some roots somewhere, especially with the children growing up. He admitted the force of this but on the whole stuck to his earlier view.

We then drifted into a discussion of a number of other more personal matters, in the course of which he said in advising me he was thinking solely of what would be best for me. I had about this time told him that whatever I did, I hoped I might be in a position to break a lance in the Jewish cause. It seemed to be so vital for the whole of human relations, and I was inclined to make it secondary only to my major interest in international relations. As the talk developed, he said that he was advising me much as he would a brother, that indeed, he felt towards me in much more that way.

We then joined Mrs. Warburg and chatted for a long time about conditions in Germany and the Warburg relatives there. I found myself in the rather anomalous position of defending Max and Erich against Mrs. Warburg's criticisms. She is almost bitter against such Jews as Erich, who had become almost assimilated, and of men like Max, who were unwilling to break with Nazi Germany altogether.

After nearly two hours Felix walked out with me to the car and he said to me as I was getting in, "If you decide to buy the house and need any help, I should be glad to carry the mortgage, so that you would never need to be afraid of being pressed in connection with it." I frankly told him we were still quite uncertain.

. . . .

Wednesday, June 21, 1933

After dinner over to Dr. Kiep's house for a *Bierabend* with Dr. Luther. As I met Luther, I had the feeling that he was cooler than before, presumably because of my recent talks. Kiep was as cordial as ever. I had no opportunity to find out whether the German Embassy had seen Drew Pearson's[5] distortion. While I was

5. Drew Pearson, one of the most widely syndicated political columnists/reporters. Known for breaking stories stylized to be sensational in his "Washington Merry-Go-Round" column.

chatting with Arthur Draper, Bernard Ridder[6] came up and said, in effect, that nothing had happened in Germany to the Jews. I was so incensed that I could not bear to argue the matter with him.

Sat down at a small table with Senator Wagner.[7] Chatted with him about the Industrial Recovery Bill and individual members of the Senate, especially Robinson of Indiana. Then hurried off to catch the train for home.

Thursday, June 22, 1933

Lunch with Michael Williams[8] at Players Club. . . . Williams shared my view about further dangers to Jews and Catholics in Germany, but he thought that the Nazis might be seriously weakened from either one or two sources: (1) dissension within through dissatisfaction among left-wing Nazis with the mildness of Hitler's regime; or (2) from the Junkers acting through the Reichswehr and Hindenburg. I expressed great pessimism on both these scores.

. . . .

Tuesday, June 27, 1933

Down to see Mr. R. J. Cudahay.[9] Talked for nearly an hour, but was unable to sell him the Rosenberg proposition (concerning Catholic-Jewish cooperation vis-à-vis Germany). He thought the Catholics were not yet in danger and that so far as his obligations to the Jews were concerned, this was being met through his contribution to the Jewish Christian Committee. We got on to the subject of Herbert L. Hoover, and he gave me from personal experiences very disquieting interpretation of the latter's selfishness and self-seeking. The more I learn of Hoover, the less I feel that he is the great man that he was so commonly believed to be.

To lunch at Frank Altschul's[10] office. Before I went in to lunch, Frank Altschul said he would like to talk to me. He began by reporting certain criticisms he had heard of my Town Hall talk. I resented this from him and replied that my observation was that most of those who had criticized me were Jews who had only within the last few months discovered that they were Jews; that the older, more faithful Jews much more nearly understood what I was getting at, but in any case the consideration of the Embassy had made it impossible for me to say everything that I might otherwise have said, but I had no apology to make either for what I said or had left unsaid. He seemed to grasp this interpre-

6. Bernard Ridder, owner and publisher of the *Staatszeitung*, a German-language newspaper in New York City. Later, head of Ridder Publications.

7. Robert F. Wagner, Democratic senator from New York.

8. Michael Williams, editor of the Catholic journal *Commonweal*. In 1933 he investigated religious persecution in Germany for the *New York Herald-Tribune*.

9. R. J. Cudahay, probably former American diplomat John Cudahy, who worked closely with Herbert Hoover in relief supplies for Europe after World War I. Became ambassador to Poland, 1933–1937.

10. Frank Altschul, chairman of General American Investors Co. His wife, Edith, was the sister of Herbert and Irving Lehman.

tation. At any rate, I had the feeling that he respected me more for standing up to him.

July 10–15, 1933

During the week of July 10 McDonald gave the morning current affairs lectures at the Chautauqua, New York, summer program, discussing particularly Germany and the problems of Nazi persecution. He emphasized the following points:

(1) Hitler's significance must not be underrated. Hitler is a man of "terrific power and tremendous faith in himself" and a great orator and organizer. He can "see into the hearts of the German people" and appeals to prejudice and humiliation resulting from the war. He has centralized and unified Germany more completely than ever before in its history.
(2) "The Jewish problem under the Nazi regime in Germany is not primarily a Jewish problem at all; the Jews are just the victims. It is a Christian problem, because the persecution is carried on in the name of Christianity. The Christians are the persecutors, and they are violating every principle of Christianity."
(3) "The Nazi denials of cruelty to the Jews are an insult to the intelligence. . . . The Nazis believe the myth of the supremacy of the Aryan race, and are determined to crush Jewish economic life. . . . No Jew can feel sure of police protection on streets, justice in courts, or of his place in the state or schools."[11]

In a July 24 letter to Eleanor Roosevelt, McDonald summed up his fears and concerns.

[Dear Mrs. Roosevelt:

I wish I might have now an opportunity to sit down and talk with you. Not since my visit to Germany in March and April, 1933—about which I told you and the President on my return home—have I had as deep a sense of impending tragedy as now. Unless present tendencies are sharply reversed, the world will be faced in the near future with the problem of another great exodus of refugees from Germany. And in that event the percentage of non-Jews will be higher than in the first exodus. That problem would be literally overwhelming, and would fall—as the problem of the refugees so far has fallen—upon the countries of refuge and upon the generosity of the citizens of those countries.

It is my conviction that the party leaders in the Reich have set for themselves a program of forcing gradually the Jews from Germany by creating condi-

11. "Cruelty of Nazis to Jews Asserted," *New York Times,* July 11, 1933, p. 12; July 12, 1933, p. 6.

tions there which make life unbearable. Many of us closely in touch with German affairs have feared this for some time. The news of the last few weeks brings confirmation.

There is also another phase of the Reich's program, even broader in its scope. This is the determination, openly avowed in high party quarters, to establish a State church, loyalty to which, particularly of the children and the younger people, would take priority over loyalty to any of the established religions—Catholic, Protestant or Jewish. These extreme forms of statism must have repercussions far beyond the German frontier.[12]

Under these circumstances I wonder how long the governments of the world can continue to act on the assumption that everything which is taking place in Germany and the threat implicit in present developments, are matters purely of German domestic concern? Is that not merely to evade for a time an issue which must sooner or later be faced? And is not the refusal to face it now, giving aid and encouragement to the extremist forces within the Reich?

In short, I am raising a question whether the time has not come when, in harmony with many precedents in American history, the American government should take the initiative in protesting against the prevailing violations of elementary civil and religious rights in Germany. Such a protest would, I anticipate, evoke enthusiastic and grateful response from millions of Americans.[13]]

In August those concerned with the continuing stream of refugees turned for help to the League of Nations. Dr. Ernst Feilchenfeld,[14] Professor Joseph P. Chamberlain,[15] and James Rosenberg of the JDC initiated a draft petition to the League to reestablish the office of a High Commission for Refugees.[16] They approached Mildred Wertheimer of the FPA and Arthur Sweetser, the American official on the Secretariat of the League.

Mildred Wertheimer and Esther Ogden, both key officials in the FPA, worked with Jewish groups to urge swift action. The League could not act without a formal proposal from one or more member states. McDonald and Herbert May became the

12. The ideas of the "German Christian" movement for a state church dated back to the 1920s, but formal guidelines were issued in 1932. They called for a struggle against Marxism, pacifism, internationalism, and Freemasonry. Hitler initially supported the German Christians and appointed one if its key figures, Ludwig Müller, as Reich bishop, but later, Hitler distanced himself.

13. McDonald Papers, Columbia School of International Affairs, Correspondence Eleanor Roosevelt.

14. Dr. Ernst Feilchenfeld, German born, instructor in international law at Harvard, member of the American Jewish Congress. Author of the draft petition discussed here.

15. Joseph P. Chamberlain, professor of public law at Columbia University, 1923–1950, active in migration questions. Served on the FPA Board since 1919 and in November 1933 became its chairman.

16. In 1921 the League had created a High Commission to deal with the problem of Russian refugees. Dr. Fridtjof Nansen of Norway, a heroic Arctic explorer, pioneered passports for stateless people and used his Nobel Peace Prize (1923) to help refugees. His task as High Commissioner was expected to last until 1938, but he had died in 1930, and the office had subsequently languished. Technically, the Nansen office dealt with stateless persons, who were granted "Nansen" passports.

promoters whose job it was to find a way to gain entrée to European governments, winning their support and sponsorship. McDonald, with his wife, Ruth, and Herbert May sailed for Europe on August 2.

At sea, August 2–10, 1933

The voyage was pleasant but uneventful. I had an interesting chat one day with John Schiff[17] about the German situation and the attitude of young Jews towards it. He said that he and Erich Warburg were of course at a disadvantage as compared with their fathers. The elder Schiff had been much nearer to his rabbinical forefathers, and besides, he had not had the disadvantage of having a rich father. But young Schiff added: there is little that one can do, thus as it seemed to me, rationalizing his desire not to be involved in the attempt to save his fellow religionists. The young man is, to my mind, a good deal of a snob.

....

Hamburg, Thursday, August 10, 1933

We reached Hamburg late on the afternoon of the tenth. I went directly to the Hotel Atlantic and telephoned Erich Warburg. He happened to be telephoning me at the same moment. He drove by and took Ruth and me out to Blankensee to spend the day. For hours that evening and the next day we talked about Germany. Erich said that one factor in the situation which had been much overlooked abroad had been the increasing proletariatization of the masses of the people and of the middle class during the later years of the republic. Hitlerism was in a very real sense a movement of resistance against this process. It is also the result of terrific pressure from the outside, the peace treaty, and the policy of the Allies since the war. Help from outside had always come too late.

He felt that the position of the Jews in Germany was being made worse by the divisions among themselves. He especially resented the attitude of the extreme Zionists, who, from his view, were aiding and abetting the Nazis. Moreover, the recently arrived Jews having Polish passports in effect occupied a special position and were more fully protected than the Jews who had been in Germany for centuries. There should be a discrimination as between the two groups of Jews. Personally he is determined never to leave Germany. When I asked him what could be done, he said: "Tell these people the truth as did Eddy, and continue the economic pressure." Throughout much of his talk he stressed the place of the *Frontsoldaten* Jews[18] and deplored that their leadership was not accepted by the other Jews in Germany. He told me of a number of instances where apparent concessions to the Jews were in fact vitiated by administrative interpretations, e.g., the case of the Jewish surgeon who had lost his arm in the front-line hospital at Verdun and yet was declared not to be a front-line soldier.

One of Erich's friends, a member of a prominent Junker family, told me in-

17. John Schiff, Jacob Schiff's grandson and later chief partner at Kuhn Loeb.
18. German Jews who had served on the front lines during World War I.

teresting tales about the Junker weaknesses. She stressed especially the inadequacy of their education. To her mind, therefore, it was not surprising that this class had been forced to yield so easily to the Nazi domination.

Hamburg-Berlin, Friday, August 11, 1933

I spent the morning in the country seeing something of Hamburg. Lunched with Eric and Mr. Brinkmann[19] of his firm. In the afternoon took the Flying Hamburger to Berlin. It is a fantastic train. Most of the time we traveled 140 km an hour. The vibration was so marked that one could scarcely read. It was an interesting experience for once, but I should not take the train again.

When we arrived in Berlin we went to the Kaiserhof. It was too late to go to the Embassy so I called up Erich's sister Lola,[20] and arranged to go out there after supper. I was shocked to see how much older she had become. It was obvious that the strain under which she lives is telling heavily. Two of her Jewish friends were there. We discussed the present situation in Germany, especially the divisions among the Jews. It was all terribly depressing, particularly since there were no indications at all of lessening of anti-Jewish persecution.

Saturday, August 12, 1933

Over to the Embassy to see Mr. Dodd. He was very cordial. He told me of Aldrich's[21] visit to Hitler and of the hopes of Schmitt[22] and Schacht. He thought there were some encouraging signs of moderation in the regime.

Lunched with Sheffer at the Bristol. He would not say a word about Germany but denounced Duranty[23] as a shocking propagandist [i.e., pro–Soviet Union]. Only when he returned to our rooms would he venture to comment on the German situation, and then he whispered in such a low tone that Ruth, who sat across the table from him, could scarcely hear a word. He seemed frightened of his own future and even more fearful of the future of his country.

Long talk with Knickerbocker, who furiously denounced Cooper and the others who had been unwilling to aid in bringing his Jewish friend to the States. He also attacked Isaiah Bowman and Finley[24] of the American Geographical Society for their failure to help under similar circumstances. As to the regime, he felt that it was more moderate and that it would [rather] yield on foreign matters than risk a crisis. Hitler, to his mind, was growing with his job. He told me

19. Rudolph Brinkmann, became co-head of M. M. Warburg when it was "Aryanized" in 1938.

20. Lola Hahn, oldest daughter of Max Warburg. Active in social causes. Had an affair with Chaim Weizmann over several years. At this time her husband had been taken to a concentration camp, and her son had come down with polio.

21. Winthrop Aldrich, president of the Chase Bank.

22. Minister of Economics Dr. Kurt Schmitt, also director general of Allianz, Germany's largest insurance company.

23. Walter Duranty, foreign correspondent of the *New York Times,* 1913–1939, also correspondent for the North American Newspaper Alliance in Europe, 1934–1939.

24. John H. Finley, president of the American Geographical Society, 1925–1934. Also had a position with the *New York Times.*

of Lüdecke's fall. As to the Jewish policy of the party, he said there was no possibility of moderation.

Sunday, August 13, 1933

Talked with Duranty, who admitted that he had been mistaken about the Russian agricultural experiment. Rykov had been justified in his criticisms. Nonetheless, Duranty insisted that perhaps the Russians had gotten over the worst hurdle.

Then out to the Stadium to see the demonstration of the SS from Eastern Germany. It was a good show but not so large or so appealing as earlier ones I had seen.

To tea with Messersmith. He traced three significant steps since I had been in Berlin in April marking the swing towards the right, but he added that there was no chance of moderation for the Jews. He developed his thesis of the possibility of a monarchy under Louis Ferdinand [Hohenzollern], but he was not convincing on this point. He told me of a number of instances of difficulties with the Nazis and their treatment of American businesses. On the whole, he was pessimistic about the economic future and saw possibilities of disaster. He thought he could discern the beginnings of discontent among the workers and the beginning of disillusion among the Nazis. On the whole, he thought that the revolution, when seen in perspective, might be shown to have been shallow except for anti-Semitism.

Monday, August 14, 1933

Over to the Warburgs to talk to Miss Gaedecke, then later to the Embassy to talk to O'Donoghue and Flack. They stressed the swing to the right and were certain that the unemployment figures given out by the Nazis were misleading.

Lunched with Sherman.[25] He confirmed the economic moderation of the regime but added, as had all the others, that the Jewish situation was worse. Only outside pressure could help.

A long talk in the late afternoon with Siegmund Warburg. He admitted the moderate tendency in economic matters but looks forward to a swing to the left. Schmitt is excellent and a friend of the Jews. Less immediate danger of personal violence but no softening in the regime's attitude. The need is plain speaking and continued and increased pressure. He still thought it possible to use a joint committee with a view to working out an economic concordat.

. . . .

25. Probably Irving Sherman, vice president of A. G. Becker of Chicago and head of its Berlin office, 1930–1939. Of Jewish background. During World War II served in the Office of Strategic Services.

Tuesday, August 15, 1933

Over to the Embassy and then to see Dieckhoff. He discussed the situation quite frankly and admitted that party excesses made foreign relations very difficult, and he did not deny that the international situation was very grave. I told him frankly of my talk with the President about the situation in Germany and of the misquotation by the Washington colleagues. He said that from the German point of view the chief difficulties were Austria, disarmament, and the Jews, the last the most difficult of all. On this point there would be no yielding by Hitler. The latter's speech of May 17[26] was his own. Neurath was gaining in strength, but Kiep was leading.

Lunch with Sherman and Tietz,[27] the latter impressing me very favorably. He has a comprehensive grasp of the situation and knows how to move about, but he shows dreadful signs of the pressure under which he is laboring. He told at length how the condition of the Jews becomes progressively worse. There is imperative need for a long-range program of relief and of emigration, financed by world Jewry.

Chatted at the cocktail hour with Bouton and Neal Dowdecker at the Hotel Adlon. Fortunately, I had to return to my own hotel promptly or I might have gotten into trouble as I came out of the Adlon. Just at that time they were preparing to film the last part of the Horst Wessel picture in front of the hotel. It was in that crowd that an American was that evening beaten for his failure to salute the flag. Had I not had to return to the Kaiserhof, I might have been that victim.

Dinner with Miss Gaedecke. She is a friend of a number of young SA and SS men, told us of their attitude towards the regime. She thought that the people as a whole were satisfied. Her picture was much more reassuring from the Nazi point of view than that given by Messersmith.

Erich [Warburg] joined us after dinner. He expressed the opinion that there must be no surrender, or if the program were made to succeed in Germany, it would inevitably spread elsewhere. His talk of his experiences in Portland was pathetic.

Wednesday, August 16, 1933

Long and interesting conversation with Consul Respondek[28]—an intimate friend of Brüning. Mowrer had prepared the way. Respondek was most pessimistic. He foresaw the disintegration in the Reich from outside dangers and from those inside. He characterized von Papen as a Judas. Lunch with Knickerbocker and his friend. Later joined by Mowrer.

26. See chapter 3, note 43

27. Ludwig Tietz, vice president of the Centralverein deutscher Staatsbürger jüdischen Glaubens, a large German-Jewish organization that had fought anti-Semitism.

28. Erwin Respondek, former professor of economics, strong anti-Nazi. Later gave wartime intelligence, including a warning of Germany's plan to invade the Soviet Union, to the United States through Switzerland.

In the afternoon tea with Bertling. Dinner that night at the Embassy. Other guests besides Ruth and myself were the Mowrers and the Messersmiths. During the dinner most of the talk was about university life, a welcome relief from talks of Jewish persecution. I was especially interested in the ambassador's account of how the President had telephoned to him in May to ask him if he would accept the Berlin post. After dinner, we drifted back to the inevitable subject of Jewish persecution. Tales were told of wives divorcing their husbands, so that the husband, thus freed of a Jewish taint, could hold an academic post. It was all very saddening.

Thursday, August 17, 1933

Over to see Brüning in his cell-like room in the hospital where he lives. To my surprise, he looked very well. He is not at all sick but stays in the hospital as an added measure of precaution and because he has a very simple personality. He received me most cordially and talked with marked frankness for about half an hour. He is evidently pessimistic about the future but counts upon the leader of the Reichswehr, von Hammerstein, to be a moderating influence in foreign affairs. The future is very grave. Hitler is more concerned about Austria than other leaders. On the other issues Hitler is likely to yield but remains adamant on the Jews. Brüning had tried vainly to change that attitude.

Brüning is obviously a very intellectual type with sensitive feelings. After talking to him, I can understand how difficult it has been for him to compete with Hitler in appeals to the masses.

Lunch with Leverkuehn[29] and Fritz Salm. The latter a young man of about thirty-five, with broad international contacts and liberal in his leanings, gave a complete defense of the Nazi programs. Its Jewish feature must be carried through even if it resulted in a lowering of the standard of living. The prohibition of intermarriage should be made legal, this despite the fact that he himself is in love with a Jewish girl and therefore cannot marry her. It is necessary, he added, for the present generation to sacrifice itself to the future. The Third Reich must be reborn no matter what the cost. It was all very disconcerting—this intelligent young man so fanatically prepared to sacrifice himself.

In the afternoon tea with Bergmann. Nothing very new.

In the evening with Ruth to the opera.

Friday, August 18, 1933

Conference with Dr. Schacht. As usual he was very cordial, not seeming to hold against me our recent talk in New York. Speaking of the prestige lost by most financiers, he said that he alone among this group in Germany retained his prestige. He told me of Aldrich's visit to Hitler. Apparently Aldrich had no opportunity to say anything about the Jewish problem. Hitler forestalled him by

29. Probably Paul Leverkuehn, lawyer, former German diplomat and financial expert. Headed the Abwehr (military intelligence) office in Istanbul during World War II.

what Schacht said was an overwhelmingly convincing argument. First, that there had been no protest by the world when the Rhineland was occupied by Negro troops.[30] Second, that if the other powers were so anxious to help the Jews, why did they not open their doors to them? Third, Germany not having restricted its emigration in the East, had to take these special measures now. It should not be blamed for doing perhaps somewhat belatedly what, in effect, the United States and other countries had done more effectively earlier. I had definitely the impression that Schacht had not made Aldrich's job any easier.

On the economic side, Schacht did not deny that the situation was serious or that Germany's need for foreign trade was perhaps greater than that of any other of the larger powers. He stressed also the importance of good relations with the United States.

Over to the Embassy to see Gordon, but there was nothing of importance to report.

Lunch with Max Jordan. What a change there was in him since I last saw him in April and how different was his manner of speaking. He whispered as though he were in acute fear. He told me that the charge just made against Brüning that the latter had intrigued against the Concordat was based on the fact that a letter had been written by someone else embodying Brüning's ideas and carried by special messenger to the Vatican. Jordan saw three present weaknesses in the regime: (1) economic; (2) the discontent of the women; and (3) an increasing disillusionment. He felt that instances of personal violence were increasing, not diminishing. He anticipated serious danger during the winter.

Over to the Italian Chamber of Commerce but the man in charge who was said to be an intimate friend of Mussolini's was not in. Talked with a young man who, on the whole, was completely apologetic for the Nazi regime.

Arranged with Mr. Sherman to buy 800 Marks (212 dollars). Met Jordan again for a moment as we were dining just before taking the train.

At the train saw Bill Tilden, the tennis professional. How he has aged since I saw him in action at Garden City.

Geneva, Saturday, August 19, 1933

Reached the frontier early in the morning and Geneva that afternoon. Met at the station by Mr. May. We spent the next few hours discussing the cable he had received from New York in reference to the refugee problem.

Mr. Lyall came to dinner, and in a discussion on disarmament he tended to take the German view, but it was up to the Allies to make the next move.

30. From 1919 to 1930 France and Belgium occupied the Rhineland under terms of the Treaty of Versailles. Perhaps as many as thirty to forty thousand African colonial troops were used, although by 1929 there were probably no more than a thousand left. The children of bi-racial unions between these troops and German women were subject to compulsory sterilization under a law of July 14, 1933. About four hundred were sterilized by 1937. See Tina Campt, *Other Germans: Black Germans and the Policy of Race, Gender, and Memory* (Ann Arbor: University of Michigan Press, 2004), 30–36.

Sunday, August 20, 1933

Lovely day—golf at Onex. I played fairly well, an 86. At dinner at Mr. May's. He had invited the Walters, the Streits, and Mrs. Sweetser. Streit[31] developed the most optimistic interpretation of the international situation that I have heard from an intelligent interpreter for many days. He saw progress at the Disarmament Conference, the cause of the substitution by the French of the idea of control for that of security. He interpreted favorably the Franco-Russian rapprochement and thought that the strengthening of Hull at the Economic Conference would in the long run bring the United States into closer European cooperation.

Captain Walters was rather encouraging about League action on the refugees, provided Italy and Germany did not oppose and finances could be cared for.

Monday, August 21, 1933

Talked with Abraham about the refugee matter. He was discouraging and, I thought, rather fearful.

Then over to see Phelen at the B.I.T. [*sic,* undoubtedly the Bank for International Settlements]. He explained their interest in the project and urged that it be carried out through the Nansen Committee for reasons of economy chiefly.

Long talk with Miss Ginsberg about the work of her committee. Lunch with Mr. May and Mr. Zilliacus. The latter took much the same view that had been taken by Captain Walters.

Talked with Johnson of the Nansen Committee. He was optimistic that his group could handle the problem with little or no outside assistance. He suggested the desirability of an advisory committee but would I think oppose a change in the leadership of his committee.

Chatted with Steinberg and Rassinsky with reference to possible invocation of Article 11 of the German letter in connection with the Treaty of Versailles.[32]

Late in the afternoon, had a long conference with Avenol.[33] The Secretary General was much interested, took much the same line as had Walters, stressing the importance of Germany's attitude. As I was leaving, he asked me if, since I

31. Clarence K. Streit, reporter for the *New York Times.*

32. Article 11 of the Versailles Treaty of June 28, 1919:

> Any war or threat of war, whether immediately affecting any of the Members of the League or not, is hereby declared a matter of concern to the whole League, and the League shall take any action that may be deemed wise and effectual to safeguard the peace of nations. In case any such emergency should arise the Secretary General shall on the request of any Member of the League forthwith summon a meeting of the Council. It is also declared to be the friendly right of each Member of the League to bring to the attention of the Assembly or of the Council any circumstance whatever affecting international relations which threatens to disturb international peace or the good understanding between nations upon which peace depends.

Presumably the refugee crisis caused by the Germans was such a "circumstance."

33. Joseph Avenol, French, secretary general of the League of Nations, July 1, 1933–1940, assistant secretary general for the previous ten years.

was going back to Germany, and [I] found out anything there about the attitude of the regime that might interest him, would I let him know. I said yes.

Tuesday, August 22, 1933

Dictated a long letter for the office summing up Mr. May's and my interpretation of the situation here. Chatted with Hudson, Miss Shaw, and Ginsberg and left on the mid-day train for Rome. It was a lovely day, and I enjoyed the trip through the mountains. We reached Italy early in the evening; we had an hour or two in Milan before taking the night train to Rome.

McDonald reviewed the events and discussions of the past few days in an August 22 letter to Mildred Wertheimer. Although there is some repetition of the diary, the letter gives greater depth, and it also clarifies what he thought the League might do. (Spelling and punctuation here have been standardized with that in the diary entries.)

[Dear M.S.W.

This letter will not cover, except incidentally, my impressions of Germany during this last week and the week before. Instead, I am merely trying to set down hastily, for I must take the train for Rome in a few hours, the feelings which Mr. May and I have about the possibilities of utilizing the League effectively for the purposes about which you cabled and wrote.

In Germany today there are many indications that in several important respects the Nazi regime is becoming more moderate. This is especially clear in the economic sphere. The appointment of Mr. Schmitt to succeed Hugenberg and the continued large influence of Dr. Schacht have resulted in the withdrawal of the Nazi commissars from most of the large businesses, the curbing of the radical activities of the shop committees in the factories, and in general, in the shelving of the regime's socialist program. Moreover, as you of course know, the Polish Danzig settlement involves considerable concessions by Hitler.[34] In other ways, too, he is showing the influence of responsibility. But in the one field in which you are especially interested, the Jewish question, he has repeatedly shown himself even within the last few days absolutely irreconcilable. I know that Winthrop Aldrich failed to shake Hitler's conviction that the Jewish program must be adhered to irrespective of its adverse economic effects on Germany. I was told too, on excellent authority, that Schmitt also failed to shake the Chancellor's fanatical determination. As to Schacht, I doubt that he any longer seriously tries to influence the leader on this issue. The Chancellor insists that no matter what the cost, the Third Reich must be built on the basis of an Aryan race unimpeded by the foreign influence of Jews in governmental, cultural, or

34. The agreement concerned the permission given by Poland for German airplanes and hundreds of cars to cross the Polish corridor to East Prussia for a loyalty festival in September.

high professional and financial posts. I doubt, therefore, that anything save the most direct and telling pressure can modify his unqualified intransigency.

Meantime, though the extent of personal violence has diminished and the danger of open or extensive outbreaks against individual Jews or groups of Jews has become less, the situation of the Jewish population steadily worsens. There is a marked tendency to interpret the existing restrictive and discriminatory decrees in harsher and harsher ways. In fact, therefore, the difficulties of the Jewish lawyers, doctors, and other professional men and women increase, while the silent boycott against Jewish business and Jewish workers is maintained with its cumulatively heavy toll.

Here in Geneva I was fortunate to find many more members of the Secretariat available than would ordinarily be the case at this time of the year. In my conferences I discussed not merely the question of possible League action on behalf of refugees, but also the possibility of action which might influence German policy towards the Jews in Germany. On this latter point I have to report that the conviction of all the members of the Secretariat and most emphatically the conviction of Avenol is that nothing can be done to bring pressure to bear upon Germany to change its domestic policy. Indeed, the Secretary General went so far as to say that in his opinion it would be dangerous to try to use the League for that purpose, that to do so would almost certainly fail and would probably endanger any League program for the refugees. I know, of course, that this attitude of the League officials will be disappointing to many Jews and others who have hoped that through Geneva official and public opinion might be marshaled in such a way as to force material concessions by the Nazi regime. Personally, I am convinced that that cannot be done, and that it would be unwise to try it.

Nonetheless, I intend during my conversations in the next few days in Rome, Vienna, and Prague to sound out the governmental authorities on the question of political pressure. I shall do this not with much hope of discovering any willingness on the part of the foreign offices to act, but because I do not want to leave any method untried. Moreover, long experience with civil servants and especially with members of the Secretariat has convinced me that they are almost invariably conservative. There were, of course, notable exceptions during the Sino-Japanese crisis.[35] But in general, permanent officials incline to play safe. Undoubtedly they are doing so in this case. Therefore, I wish to canvass for myself the possibilities of direct political action in reference to German internal policy. I will, of course, keep you informed of the results of my talks.

On the problem which directly concerns you and your associates—that of relief for the refugees now outside Germany—the responses from the Secretariat were almost unanimously encouraging. It is true that few of the persons

35. Probably a reference to the April 30, 1932, resolution by the League Assembly declaring that the Japanese occupation of Manchuria was illegal and that the territory was part of China. Japan quickly announced its intention of leaving the League, which it did in 1934.

with whom I talked had thought very seriously about the question, and none of them had envisioned the enormous possibilities for service which lie before the League, nor for that matter the great opportunities to make the League respected more highly in many parts of the world where it sadly needs to recoup its prestige. But, when the issue was put squarely before such leading members of the Secretariat as Walters[36] and Avenol, their response was, within the limited field which they considered practicable for the League's activities, very satisfactory.

The Secretary General said that he would be glad to see the League take on the refugee responsibility provided two essential prerequisites could be secured. The first of these is the tacit assent, if not the whole-hearted cooperation, of Germany. He felt that, unless this could be secured, it would be impossible to get League action, particularly because if Germany opposed, then Italy, for reasons which you, of course, know, would support the German opposition. The Italians have always opposed the League's assumption of responsibility over anti-Fascist émigrés, so Mussolini would not require much encouragement, probably, to take a stand against any League action which might be a precedent for later actions that might embarrass Italy.

The second prerequisite which the Secretary General stressed may seem strange to you. It is that the approach to Germany should be made in such a way as to make sure that Hitler would not reply: "Of course we are delighted to have the League take charge of Jewish refugees. We accept this proposal enthusiastically, but we must ask that the League agree to take charge of all the Jews." In other words, the Secretary General seems to be fearful that Germany would wish to embarrass the League by making this impossible condition. Personally, it seems to me unlikely that even the Nazis would go so far as that, but in any inquiries which I make in Berlin I shall, of course, keep in mind the Secretary General's fears on this point.

There is a third prerequisite for League action on relief which, though not mentioned by the Secretary General, was stressed by all the other members of the Secretariat with whom I spoke. It is that adequate financial resources must in some way or other be guaranteed before the Assembly would be likely to act favorably. It was emphasized that in view of the League's own financial difficulties and the pressure under which most of the governments of the League are now laboring, the Assembly would not be likely to assume new obligations unless the financial side were taken care of. I do not mean to indicate that the possibility of an international loan under League auspices was thrown out as unthinkable, but it would be very difficult to arrange and would certainly require much more time than is available between now and the time the Assembly could take action.

Provided these three prerequisites were met, the question then arises, in what form could the League intervention on behalf of the refugees most effec-

36. Captain Frank Walters, Dutch.

tively be organized? The suggestion you make of a League High Commissioner was not rejected—it was recognized that there would be considerable advantages in securing the leadership of a world figure. I must add, however, parenthetically, that the enthusiasm for Herbert Hoover was by no mean unmixed. Several persons doubted that his prestige is sufficient to counter-balance the bad taste left here in the mouths of many of the important persons with whom he worked during and immediately after the war. Moreover, they doubted whether he possesses the tact necessary to deal with this situation, where he would not have the enormous advantage of war psychology. But I do not wish to indicate that he would be unacceptable.

On the whole, however, the impression here is that it would be both easier and more effective for the League to broaden the mandate of the Nansen Committee, rather than set up a wholly new organization. It was admitted, of course, that the Nansen Committee without Nansen has become less and less well known and that indeed in some quarters it has made enemies. The present president, a Dr. Werner (of Switzerland), is in no sense a world-figure. On the other hand, the committee does exist. It still has a large personnel, trained in the work of placing refugees (mostly agricultural, it is true). It receives from the League annually a sum large enough to care for administrative expenses and could, therefore, take on the Jewish refugees much more economically than could be done otherwise. Mr. Johnson,[37] the executive secretary of the committee, assured me that not much additional money would be required so far as overhead is concerned. He stressed also the saving in time which would come through using an existing organization, especially in view of the extremely complicated nature of the job of placing a large number of emigrants in different parts of the world. He agreed with what some of the members of the Secretariat had said to the effect that so long as there is an existing agency, the Assembly might well hesitate to create something new.

The Nansen Committee itself probably would prefer that in case it were given the suggested additional responsibilities, some one or two distinguished Jews such as Lord Reading[38] be added to the Governing Board. There are two other possibilities, however. The first of these, the creation of an Advisory Council to be attached to the Nansen Committee, could, of course, very easily be arranged. It would be wholly satisfactory to the Nansen Committee. There is a second suggestion which would require very diplomatic handling. It is that the Swiss president of the Nansen Committee be induced, perhaps through the Swiss government, to resign in order to make place for a much better-known leader. It was thought that such a change would be possible if a man of the

37. Major T. F. Johnson, who had succeeded Nansen as head of the Nansen Committee. Controversial because of his membership in Militia Christi, a militant Christian organization.

38. Lord Reading (Rufus Isaacs), appointed 1913, the first Jewish Lord Chief Justice of England. Also served as viceroy of India and ambassador to the United States. An outstanding British political personality, foreign secretary in Ramsay McDonald's government of 1931. President of the Central British Fund for Refugees.

standing of Herbert Hoover were available to take on the job. Obviously, this suggestion is one which must not be permitted to reach the ears of the Nansen Committee at this stage.

Whatever form the League cooperation may take, it is essential that much preliminary work be done before the Assembly meets. This work is necessary in Geneva, but even more necessary in the capitals of such of the countries as might be expected to support the move, and, as we cabled, most of all in Germany and Italy. I shall be able to do something in Rome, where I am scheduled to arrive tomorrow the twenty-third. I shall also make inquiries in Vienna and Prague and Warsaw. As we cabled, the Secretary General asked me to let him know if I found out in Berlin anything significant about the attitude of the regime there. This, of course, I shall try to do just as soon as I return to Berlin the first week in September. Meantime, I suggest that those with whom you are working do everything they can in London, Paris, and Scandinavian countries and of course also in the countries to which I am going.

This letter might be continued indefinitely, but my train leaves within a couple of hours, so I shall have to leave the rest to your imagination.[39]]

Rome, Wednesday, August 23, 1933

Arriving in Rome about eight o'clock A.M., we went directly to the Hotel de Russie and called up Galeazzi,[40] Mrs. Brady's[41] representative. He came over shortly, and we made plans for our brief stay in Rome. Went over almost immediately to see the American ambassador, Breckinridge Long.[42] Though he has not been in Rome more than two months, he talked interestingly and frankly. He stressed the continuation in Italy of an absolute dictatorship, including a drastic censorship of the press, but he added that he thought the people were reconciled to it. On the Austrian issue he was of the opinion that Mussolini would consider a Nazi Austria as tantamount to the Anschluss and would act accordingly to prevent it.[43]

Lunched with Morgan of the U.P. He stressed the enormous success of the Fascist regime and said that though he was personally a democrat, he had diffi-

39. McDonald to Wertheimer, August 22, 1933. Copy in McDonald Papers, USHMM.

40. Enrico Galeazzi, Rome-born architect who became a close friend of Pacelli and accompanied him on vacation trips to Switzerland and on his 1936 trip to the U.S. Architect of the Sacred Apostolic Palace, the new residence of the Pontifical North American College in Rome, and the Saint Eugenio Basilica in Rome.

41. Mrs. Nicholas F. (Anna) Brady, papal duchess, a liberal Catholic activist and journalist who lived in Rome much of the year. Her deceased husband had been a wealthy New York businessman.

42. Breckinridge Long, born in Missouri, of aristocratic Southern ancestry. Assistant secretary of state in the Wilson administration. FDR's floor manager at the Democratic presidential convention in 1932. In 1939 assistant secretary of state for Emergency War Matters (later Special War Problems), a job that included refugees. A controversial figure in the historiography of American responses to the Holocaust. See, among others, Richard Breitman and Alan M. Kraut, *American Refugee Policy and European Jewry, 1933–45* (Bloomington: Indiana University Press, 1987), 126–145.

43. Anschluss, an incorporation of Austria into Germany.

culty in restraining his enthusiasm for the Fascist accomplishments in the material sphere. In the afternoon Ruth and I visited the new excavations and were much impressed by them. We then drove out to Ostia for supper along the autostrade. It was a lovely trip.

Thursday, August 24, 1933

Galleazzi fortunately had been able to arrange an interview with Pacelli, the papal secretary of state.[44] The room in which he received me was gorgeous in its hangings and furniture. His dress was rich, and the ring he wore was so beautiful that intensely interested as I was in what he had to say, I could not take my eyes off his finger. I think it is almost the first time that I have ever really envied anyone the possession of a jewel.

Pacelli first asked my positive re-assurance that I would not quote him. He then began a long discussion of the German Concordat.

The often divided national governments of the Weimar Republic had been unable to reach agreement with German Catholic officials and the Vatican over the appropriate terms for a relationship between Germany and a powerful international Church that served roughly one-third of the German population. Hitler's government not only broke through the obstacles but also figured out ways to lure the Catholic Church into at least implicit support of some of its goals, including the elimination of the Center Party. Hitler's government had negotiated a formal agreement, a Concordat, with the Vatican and high German Catholic officials.

Among other things, this Concordat protected freedom of religion and the Church's control of ecclesiastical activities, but required all Catholic clergy in Germany to be German citizens. Catholic bishops had to swear loyalty to the Reich, and Catholic schools were to inculcate patriotism.

In the cabinet meeting of July 14, 1933, Hitler indicated that this agreement bolstered the regime, giving it a boost in the fight against international Jewry. (Hitler likely meant that the Vatican would not support efforts to sanction or restrict Germany—efforts that he automatically blamed on international Jewry.) Despite Catholic complaints about anti-Christian elements in the Nazi movement, the Vatican was willing to have a formal relationship and to commit Catholic bishops to support the Nazi state. On the same day the Nazi Party was declared the only legitimate party.

Pacelli's comments to McDonald about the Concordat came just over five weeks later.

He was, I thought, distinctly on the defensive. His argument was as follows: The Hitler regime was undoubtedly in power; it had received an absolute majority in the Reichstag. The Church in its dealings did not pick and choose with whom it would negotiate; it dealt with those in power, as it had earlier in Ger-

44. Eugenio Cardinal Pacelli, papal secretary of state. Papal nuncio to Bavaria and to Germany, 1917–1930. In February 1939 he became Pope Pius XII. Longstanding controversy about his attitude and behavior toward Nazi Germany makes McDonald's diary entry here of unusual interest.

many with a Catholic Bavaria, a Protestant Prussia, and a radical Saxony. In answer to my intonation that the Concordat was a letting-down of Brüning and the Center Party, Pacelli replied in effect: Brüning had failed, the Center Party had lost its influence, the Church could not tie itself to a single party, it had to protect the interests of its parishioners, it could not make these secondary to the interests of any individual or party. Moreover, he pointed out that many Catholics, such as von Papen, had worked earnestly for the Concordat.

We talked briefly about the Church's relations with Russia, with Mexico, and with Spain. Little or no progress is being made in these countries. I tried to sound him out on the question of the Church's attitude towards the Jews in Germany. He expressed a feeling of Christian charity, but his reply, both the tone and the contents, convinced me that there could be no help expected from that source.[45]

I later met Galleazzi and Ruth. He intimated that the interpretation of the Concordat by the authorities in Germany was causing the Church lively concern.

In the afternoon Galleazzi lent us his car and we made the trip out to Villa d'Este, a beautiful spot. On the way back had just time to stop at the Fascist tenth anniversary exhibition. It is most impressive.

Took the night train for Vienna.

Vienna, Friday, August 25, 1933

Reached the Austrian frontier in the morning, and Vienna that night. We went directly to the Grand Hotel.

Saturday, August 26, 1933

Went over to the Legation to see Klieforth. He arranged for me to see Funder. That morning I also visited the office of Dollfuss.[46] Had a long and interesting talk there with one of the Chancellor's associates.

Lunched with Mr. and Mrs. Fleming. They had just come from Denmark, where they were much impressed by the Danish resentment of Pan-German agitation. They told us of their plans to go to Nuremberg. In the afternoon Ruth and I spent an hour or so with a group of foreign press at the Café de Louvre. The most vocal of the newspaper men was Mr. Best of the U.P. He was very critical of Dollfuss, charges corruption, and anticipates the rapid development of anti-Semitic agitation.

45. Later in describing this meeting, McDonald wrote to Felix Warburg on September 14, "I was deeply disappointed by the attitude of the papal secretary of state. I talked with Cardinal Pacelli for nearly an hour. In the course of the conversation I brought up the question of the treatment of the Jews in Germany; the response was noncommittal but left me with the definite impression that no vigorous cooperation would be expected from that direction. Therefore I do not take seriously the press reports of the last few days to the effect that the Vatican has intervened vigorously on behalf of German Jews. The Church is so on the defensive in the Reich that it is hard pressed to define its own essential interests." McDonald Papers, USHMM.

46. Engelbert Dollfuss, Austrian chancellor who resisted the influence of the Austrian Nazi Party.

That evening I went to see Dr. Friedrich Funder, of the *Reichspost.* I was struck by the huge crucifixes which were hung in the halls of this office building. Funder told me the story of the rise of Dollfuss to power and of his struggle against socialism and communism. When I told him of my interview with Brüning, tears came to his eyes.

Sunday, August 27, 1933

Our chief occupation was a visit to the Imperial Picture Gallery which remains one of the richest in the whole world. About five o'clock we took the train for Prague, reaching our hotel there about nine or ten o'clock that evening.

Prague, Monday, August 28, 1933

In the afternoon had a long conference with Rabbi Wise, his associate Goldmann,[47] and Mr. Neville Laski.[48] They all agreed on a common policy about the refugees in Geneva. During our long conference, Rabbi Wise, who apparently had been working day and night, dropped into a deep sleep every few minutes. Laski struck me as a very dynamic personality.

Late in the afternoon received a wire that my office would call me that night from New York. While waiting on the telephone call, I decided that it was absurd to continue to try to get things done through cables and telephone communications from three or four centers, and that, therefore, I would suggest to New York that I go as soon as possible to London to confer there with the English group. The telephone connection was very unsatisfactory, but we were able to come to an understanding, first that the office would let the State Department know that I was going to speak to the American ambassador [to Germany], and that I would go to London, trying to arrive the following Monday.

A partial transcript of McDonald's August 28 telephone conversation from Prague with William T. Stone (of the FPA) in the United States gives additional evidence of his efforts and their limited results.

[WTS: You still plan to go to Berlin, do you?

JGM: I shall stay here tomorrow and then go to Berlin or to Warsaw and then Berlin. I could be in Berlin Thursday or Friday.

WTS: Well, we wanted to inform the German Embassy in Washington that leading Americans are deeply interested in German relief and that as you happened to be in Europe you are sounding out Berlin. Is that all right? We also want to inform [the] State Department of this step before an inquiry can come through to them from Embassy. Is that all right?

47. Nahum Goldmann, president and co-founder, with Rabbi Stephen S. Wise, of the World Jewish Congress.

48. Neville J. Laski, president of the Board of Deputies of British Jews, official spokesman of the British Jewish community in foreign affairs.

JGM: Yes. I shall tell Dodd and Dieckhoff. Dodd is very friendly. I think it better not to mention it in Washington. If you like, tell the State Department, but I do not think I would tell the [German] Embassy. I shall be here until Wednesday and after that you can get me care of the American Embassy in Berlin.

WTS: Well then, did you accomplish anything in Rome?

JGM: The papal secretary can do nothing.

WTS: Did you have a conference with Breckinridge Long?

JGM: Yes.

WTS: And did you see the papal secretary?

JGM: Long interview with the papal secretary, which was discouraging.

WTS: We didn't understand why the conference in Rome was discouraging.

JGM: The papal secretary indicated that the Church would not do anything about the matter. All the Fascist officials are away for some time. . . .

JGM: My idea is this: I ought to see the London group and together plan out what is to be done. You cannot possibly do it by long distance telephone and cable. We must decide which governments should be approached and by whom.

WTS: How do things stand with Laski and Wise?

JGM: I have talked today with Laski and Wise in Prague, and Wise is perfectly agreeable for these forms of relief, and so is Laski, but the man who is going to handle the Geneva end for the British group is Bentwich.[49] He will not go back to Geneva until September 10th. My suggestion is that the first part of next week I should sit down in London and map out the campaign if the London group is willing. They can agree on the principles by long distance telephone, and I can go to London any time. . . .

WTS: But you want to go to Berlin first?

JGM: I shall go to Germany tomorrow night and be in Berlin on Wednesday and spend the rest of that week trying to learn how things are. Arriving in London on Monday the 4th of September. I shall learn everything I can in Germany, and then we can plan the thing out in London. Jewish Congress has consented, they will go with us 100 percent. I will only sound them [the German government] out very tentatively and then as a friend of Germany, making my own suggestions without any connection outside. I shall ask them what they would think if it were done. I do not want to represent anybody, and it would be bad for them too.

WTS: You think we had better not tell the Embassy?

JGM: I think it just as well not to.[50]]

49. Norman Bentwich, professor of international law at the Hebrew University in Jerusalem since 1932, formerly attorney general of Palestine, active in League work, most recently on the question of minorities.

50. Transcript of telephone conversation between McDonald and Stone, August 28, 1933, McDonald Papers, USHMM.

Tuesday, August 29, 1933

Over to the Legation—brief talk with White. Telephoned to Jan Masaryk, who promised to make a date for me with Benes, who was still out in the country, but for reasons which have not yet been explained, this date did not materialize. Decided therefore to go directly to Berlin and took the night train.

Berlin, Wednesday, August 30, 1933

Went directly to see Dieckhoff. He said no at once to my inquiry about League action. There was, he said, no problem. There were only some 30,000 *staatenlos,* the others could have recourse to their consuls or diplomatic representatives. This, he said, was of course his personal view, and he would inquire further, but he thought it would likely be the official view. Over to the Embassy. The ambassador had just been received by the President [Hindenburg]. He was in a very serious mood; economic conditions were worse; on the Jewish question there was no yielding nor would there be any while outside pressure continued unabated. The combination of these factors might result in graver conditions during the winter and were commonly anticipated. I told him frankly of my talks in Geneva, Rome, and Prague, and with Dieckhoff.

Over to see Messersmith. He apparently is having the same difficulties as before with the regime. He emphasized the difficulty of working with it because of the mendacity of people like Goebbels. He emphasized that economic conditions were worse. He told how the Academy of Medicine had recently excluded Jewish doctors though [it] admitted Gentile dentists.

Siegmund [Warburg] . . . said that Schacht, Schmitt, and Neurath were working to ameliorate the Jewish conditions but so far had little success. Illustrative of present conditions was, he said, the arrest of a partner of Wassermann's for calling Göring "a green boy." He was freed from the concentration camp after some days but with a broken nose. Siegmund's recommendations for action were (1) accumulation of pressure; (2) Article 11;[51] (3) emigration; (4) committee to arrange economic concordat.

Thursday, August 31, 1933

Long walk with Gaedecke. She told me of party pressure which had deprived her sister of a scholarship in a Salz school.

Lunch with Tietz and Sherman. The former stressed the desirability of Liebman's coming to Berlin. His presence would have a helpful morale effect. In this statement there was an implied criticism of Kahn in Paris.

Sherman was sure that the unemployment figures given by the regime were inaccurate. According to the official account, since 1932, the unemployed had been reduced by a million or two, but the significant fact is that during that period the amount paid by wage-earners as their contributions to the unemploy-

51. Article 11 of the Treaty of Versailles (see n. 30).

ment fund had considerably diminished, thus proving that the amount actually spent in wages was less.

After lunch went to see François-Poncet. He spoke of the state of exaltation in the Reich as though the people were fed on cocaine, of the brutality of its methods, of its stupidity in bringing Poland and France and Russia closer together. To his mind, the best in Germany could only be saved through the maintenance of an independent and democratic Austria. On the subject of the Concordat, Poncet was most emphatic. It was, he said, an absolute surrender and a state of panic by the Vatican.

Took the night train for Bamberg.

5. September 1933: Lobbying for League Action

Bamberg, Friday, September 1, 1933

Reached Bamberg at four or five in the morning. Went directly to the Bamberger Hof and to bed. Saw something of the beautiful old town later in the morning and took the eleven o'clock train to Nuremberg.

Went directly to the Württemberger Hof where, to our surprise, a reservation had been made for us by Hanfstaengl. The town was crowded with Nazis and gaily decorated with innumerable swastikas. From the Württemberger Hof we went to the Deutscher Hof, where Hitler was staying. We were told that we could see Hanfstaengl there. It was quite impossible to get into the lobby, every entrance to which was guarded by SS troopers. Talking to one of these, formerly a hotel clerk who spoke perfect English, I explained that I had a date with Hanfstaengl. The guard promised to let me know as soon as Hanfstaengl came in. While waiting, Ruth and I and Lochner had a bit of lunch. Lochner talked more frankly than at any previous time to me. He said that Hitler's technique was to balance one leader against the other, Göring versus Goebbels, Schmitt v. Schacht, Neurath v. von Papen. Hindenburg was finished. When he passed out of the picture, there would perhaps be a Regency. Lochner anticipated a turning towards the left after the right had had its opportunity.

Finally, Hanfstaengl came along, and we managed to get hold of him for a few minutes. He immediately arranged for Ruth to have the necessary tickets by telling Hoffmann, one of his adjutants, to do whatever was essential.

We had tickets for the Hitler appearance that afternoon. It was quite impossible to get into the building. We went back to the hotel, where we met the Flemings and Mrs. Reed. There Hoffmann and I worked out a telegram to the chief of police in Munich[1] which we hoped would secure us admission to Dachau the next day. Hanfstaengl had earlier given Hoffmann instructions to arrange my Dachau visit. After the telegram was dispatched, Ruth and I returned to Bamberg, having decided to move into the Württemberger Hof the next morning. We reached our hotel in Bamberg in time for a very late dinner and to bed.

While sitting with the Flemings, I saw Viereck[2] in the lobby and went over and chatted with him. As we were talking, Neurath came into the lobby towards

1. Heinrich Himmler, also head of the SS, which was in charge of the concentration camps.
2. George Sylvester Viereck, friend of the former Kaiser. He returned to the United States in October full of praise for Hitler.

us. I went up and spoke to him. The conversation was amusing. I told him that I had been glad to learn in Berlin that he and his colleagues were stronger. He replied with rather a grim smile, "Yes, but you, last April, did not seem to expect that we would still be in power." I replied that I had had no such view, but that it had been expressed to me by some people in Berlin. I then asked him about the refugee League action. He promptly replied, "No, we cannot have it; there is no problem," etc., etc., as had Dieckhoff. Evidently, the matter had been discussed in the Wilhelmstrasse after my visit. After this talk I introduced von Neurath to Viereck. The foreign minister insisted that there was not going to be an international crisis, that conditions were much better.

Munich, Saturday, September 2, 1933

This section was written a couple of weeks later; it refers to other documents that have been inserted in brackets.

Ruth and I went together as far as Munich [*sic,* actually Nuremberg], where she took the luggage and herself to the Württemberger Hof, while I stayed on the train. I arrived in Munich at one o'clock, went at once to the police headquarters. Hoffmann's telegram had done the trick. After a brief talk, I was escorted in one of the official cars by two officials from the office to the camp at Dachau.[3] I have described this visit in my letter to Felix Warburg and in my broadcast from London, so I omit any general account here.

From McDonald's broadcast from London, September 10:

[The site is an abandoned factory. The grounds are surrounded by a high wall, capped by an electrified barbed wire fence. On the corners are mounted machine guns that command the whole length of the walls. Within the enclosure the guards are armed with rifles. There I walked among the more than 2,000 political prisoners who, according to the Nazi jailers, are being "educated" to repudiate their heretical political creeds of communism, socialism, or democracy.

The camp was clean, the prisoners seemingly decently fed and housed. It was a Saturday afternoon—a rest period. The prisoners were standing about in groups or playing cards, or reading. I saw no signs of physical violence but, as we passed groups of men, each individual prisoner snapped to attention, military fashion. I was thus enabled to look into their eyes. What I read there I shall not forget. Fear, haunting fear, a sense of utter subjection to an arbitrary ruthless will.

The Nazis are proud of the concentration camps. To any suggestion of criticism about the camps they are apt to reply: "This is a revolution. In revolutions

3. At the time this concentration camp, fifteen kilometers northwest of Munich, contained about 3,400 political prisoners.

elsewhere political prisoners have been shot. We try to reform them. Our camps cannot be given up."

In his September 14 letter to Felix Warburg, McDonald added one point about Dachau:

In the hall where the prisoners eat, the walls are whitewashed. Against this white background have been drawn a series of caricature portraits which reach around all four walls. Here are portrayed for the edification of the prisoners the outstanding "betrayers of Germany." Included in this gallery are Rathenau, Stresemann, Ebert, Breitscheid, Scheidemann, and Max Warburg.[4]]

McDonald's diary entry continues:

Suffice to say that when the inspection of the camp was finished, I was delighted that the Munich Picture Gallery was still open, thus enabling me to get the taste of the terror of the camp out of my mouth by enjoying the treasures of the gallery. I left Munich about six o'clock and returned to the Württemberger Hof to find that my wife had gone to the gigantic fireworks display outside the town. I took a taxi and after many detours reached the show. The explosions were so terrific at times that I thought the whole dock had blown up, but later I was told that this was merely a mild representation of what trench warfare was like.

Sunday, September 3, 1933

I should have added above that after we returned from the fireworks, the Flemings, Ruth, and I with a couple of Nazis went to the Grand Hotel, where the high officials, except Hitler, were dining. It was all a very military affair, what with uniforms and clicking of heels and the constant salutes.

Immediately after breakfast on Sunday morning, we were taken in one of the press cars to the flying field. The picture of those massed troops and flags is unforgettable, as is the solemn religious note which was maintained throughout. As always in these affairs, Hitler was the unique Führer.

As soon as Hitler left, we returned to our press car and were driven for two or three miles down the line of march. The sidewalks lined with storm troopers and the populace. The Hauptplatz, with its decorations and crowds of people, was like a scene from the *Meistersingers.* The arrival of the leaders, Goebbels, Göring, Streicher, and finally of Hitler, preceded the arrival of the troops. Among the spectators in the square, seated in places of honor were the foreign diplomats, the oldest members of the party, and what we would call the Gold Star Mothers, the mothers of the martyrs of the party.

4. McDonald to Felix Warburg, September 14, 1933, McDonald Papers, Columbia, Geneva Correspondence.

Hitler's greeting to his associates showed the charm and the political sagacity of the man. His taking of the salute was dignified and impressive. After a couple of hours watching seemingly endless masses of men pass in review, the Flemings, Ruth, and I walked out along the lines of march, through the crowds. It was difficult to resist the effect of the martial music and the singing marching men. From time to time, women dashed out from the curb to present bouquets to the leaders. Finally, later in the afternoon we returned to our hotel to look out from the window at the oncoming columns of SS and SA as they marched in time with the music—they seemed like waves of the sea.

I had a longish talk with Birchall. He is fatalistic about the Jews in Germany and, for that matter, in Austria. Talked also for a few minutes with Whiting Williams.[5] We then took the train for London.

In the compartment, as we left Nuremberg, were a group of Nazi men and women. One of these—a man apparently acquainted with some of the Nazi officials—was very glad to talk. I asked him questions about the Jews and the Socialists. His answers were interspaced with such words as "Schwein," "traitors," etc. No doubt the anti-Semitism has gone very deep.

London, Monday, September 4, 1933

We reached Ostend just before lunch; had a quiet crossing to Dover, arrived at the Stafford Hotel in London in time for dinner. In the evening we went to see Fay Compton in *Prociniem,* a most delightful play.

. . . .

Wednesday, September 6, 1933

Conference with Mr. Feilchenfeld's brother. Lunch at the Café Royal with Sir Frederick Ross and two of his associates. In the afternoon long conference with Bentwich, Montefiore,[6] and Laski at the office. Later spoke to the Joint Foreign Committee, on the membership of which is included the chief rabbi and Melchett. (Of this conference I spoke in my letter to Felix Warburg.)

From McDonald's letter to Felix Warburg on September 14:

[I had very hopeful conferences in London. I talked several times with Neville Laski, Bentwich, and Montefiore. One day I was asked to speak to the Joint Foreign Committee. The comments of the chief rabbi and of the other members of the committee almost without exception showed that they had not yet been willing to face the realities of the situation. Laski sees it, and so do his two col-

5. Whiting Williams, whose family owned Cleveland Hydraulic Pressed Steel Company. A social progressive and believer in the "social gospel," he traveled around the world assessing the plight of workers and refugees. Among the first to visit the Soviet Union to report on the famine in Ukraine.

6. Leonard G. Montefiore, president of the Anglo-Jewish Association, son of Claude Montefiore. An English aristocratic assimilationist.

leagues, but the older men had not yet brought themselves to believe that such things could be.

I lunched or dined two or three times with Mr. Liebman[7] and Mr. Baerwald. Neither of these men is of course taking any part in the present negotiations, but of course they are intensely interested in what is being proposed. I repeatedly urged Mr. Liebman to go to Berlin and to stay in Germany for several weeks. I did this not only because Mr. Tietz asked me to do so, but also because I am sure the (Jewish) leaders in Germany need sorely the moral support which the presence of an American representative would give them."][8]

McDonald's diary entry of September 6 continues:

Then directly to tea with Mr. Liebman at the Dorchester House. We were joined by his wife and Mr. and Mrs. Baerwald. As we sat chatting, I was suddenly struck by the contrast between these carefree Jews in London and [the] state of terror in which their co-religionists live in Germany.

After dinner at the hotel, Ruth and I went to see the Irish Players in an amusing farce.

Thursday, September 7, 1933

A longish conference with Vansittart at the Foreign Office. He is clearly critical of Germany, but he was non-committal on the Jews.

Pleasant luncheon with Mrs. Davis, Sarah and Mr. Raeber.

Friday, September 8, 1933

An hour's conference with the American ambassador.[9] He was most cordial, finally sending us home in his own car, but to my taste, he talked too much of honor, integrity, patriotism, and high moral principles, and the like.

Ruth and I lunched with the Liebmans at the Savoy. After lunch met Otto Schiff.[10]

In the afternoon went to see the consul general, Frazer,[11] in reference to young Feilchenfeld. I think I was of some use though I was emphatic in my statement that I had no desire to interfere with the normal consular procedure.

Then over to Woburn House for another conference with Bentwich and

7. Charles J. Liebman, later executive director of the Refugee Economic Corporation, close associate of Felix Warburg and James N. Rosenberg.

8. McDonald to Felix Warburg, September 14, 1933, McDonald Papers, Columbia, Geneva Correspondence.

9. Robert W. Bingham, American ambassador to Great Britain, wealthy publisher of the *Louisville Courier-Journal.*

10. Otto Schiff, president of the Jews' Temporary Shelter in London since World War I, organizer of the Jewish Refugee Committee, partner in the merchant banking firm of Bourke, Schiff & Co., cousin of Frieda Warburg.

11. Robert Frazer, U.S. consul general in London.

Laski, at which were present Liebman and Baerwald. Most of the time was taken up by listening to Laski dictate a long letter to Cyrus Adler[12] about Rabbi Wise. That night stayed at home and worked on my broadcast.

Saturday, September 9, 1933

Lunched with Miss Cummings. In the afternoon dictated my speech, dined that night with the Baerwalds. I was especially interested in what Mr. Baerwald's brother from Frankfurt had to say about conditions in the Reich. He suggested that one of the reasons that the Jewish minority had been so rigorously attacked now was that all other minorities had been eliminated by the peace treaties and that therefore the German urge to Germanize its minorities was all being taken out on the Jews.

On this same day Secretary of State Hull met with Jay Pierrepont Moffat, the chief of the Division of Western European affairs in the State Department. Moffat had prepared a draft of a statement that FDR or Hull could make generally rejecting religious and cultural persecution, but without giving Germany grounds to take offense. Moffat wrote:

The Secretary then asked if I would see if we could work out some sort of statement approving the settling of Jews in other parts of the world than Germany. I urged him against such a course on the ground that it would be illogical for us to urge that when we were unwilling to admit more than a small percentage under our quota law. He replied that it might be possible to make up a selective list and admit those who had no Communistic tendency. Again I urged him against such a course, partly because it would reverse the policy which we have fought for twelve years [restrictionist immigration legislation that began in 1921] and partly because any German Jew who could give proof that he would not become a public charge may enter now[,] as the quota for Germany is far from filled. Congressman Sabath had evidently made a strong impression the day before[,] and I am much concerned over the trend of the Secretary's mind on this point."[13]

Sunday, September 10, 1933

Revised my broadcast and had it retyped during the morning, then out with Ruth for luncheon at the Piccadilly Café, over to the BBC a little before seven o'clock, broadcast at 7:15, under what I learnt later were ideal conditions.[14] We waited for a few moments to get the report from New York. They said that it

12. Cyrus Adler, president of the American Jewish Committee, professor at Dropsie College, and later president of the Jewish Theological Seminary.

13. Moffat Journal, vol. 33, Moffat Papers, September 9, 1933, call number MS Am 1407, Houghton Library, Harvard University. By permission of the Houghton Library, Harvard University.

14. The title of the talk was "Encircled Germany," and the central theme was that the events in Germany were creating such animosity in the surrounding countries that there was danger of international conflagration. McDonald urged the United States to play a part in order to help prevent this war. McDonald Papers, USHMM.

had been heard perfectly and therefore was available throughout the whole country. Afterwards dinner with the Baerwalds.

....

Dublin, Tuesday, September 12, 1933

Took the morning train to Dublin, via Holyhead, arrived at the Shelbourne Hotel in time for dinner. To my dismay I found there two cables which made it practically impossible for me to sail with Ruth, and which required my return to Geneva. The cables were not quite clear but after some hours of discussion, we saw the picture as it was. There was nothing to do but accept it.

McDonald had to return to Geneva for further lobbying in connection with the establishment of a High Commissioner for Refugees. He went via Paris, arriving on September 22.

....

Friday, September 15, 1933

In the morning took the bus to Cobh. Met at the dock by the first secretary of the Legation, Mr. Denby, and Mr. Woods, the consul at Cork. It was a beautiful day for embarkation. I was terribly sorry to have to leave the boat and turn back to Ireland.[15] When the tender reached the dock, I was met by Woods, who drove me to Cork, where we had tea and dinner together. Later we went to visit Mr. Horgan, a severe critic of [Irish Free State Prime Minister Éamon] de Valera. He criticized him as impractical and fanatical. Told two stories about de Valera's belief that he had a divine mission and the report that he had seriously proposed to bring in the American fleet in connection with the arms scare a year or so ago.

Saturday, September 16, 1933

Golf with Woods on the extremely interesting island course. The sixth hole—Death Valley—is one of the more forbidding and yet one of the most interesting I have ever played.

Back to Dublin that evening to find at the hotel an invitation from Denby to come in after dinner. I was glad to go. I met there McDermott, the politician, and Mr. Guinness, a member of the well-known brewer family. Unfortunately, the talk was mostly about the U.S.A.

....

15. Ruth had to return to the States as planned because of a closing on a Bronxville, New York, house, into which they were to move immediately.

Monday, September 18, 1933

Conference with Cosgrave.[16] He is a mild professor-like person. He spoke mostly in statistical terms, showing how de Valera is injuring the country, but he recognized that the British issue gave a great advantage to his opponent.

Lunch with Guinness at one of the oldest clubs in Dublin, a former center of landowner Toryism, now in decay.

In the afternoon long conference with de Valera. He was very moderate, showed little of his fanatical side, stressed the difficulties in his program of self-sufficiency, and admitted that there was no chance of union in the near future between North and South. He rather embarrassed me at first by remembering an occasion a year or two ago when he had been at one of our meetings, but which I did not remember.[17]

....

Instead of writing a diary for the dates September 19–27, McDonald sent in essence two diary letters to Miss Ogden.

Tuesday, September 19, 1933

After six hours' sleep I joined Miss Wertheimer at lunch. She was so surprised to see me that I thought, as she put it, "she would pass out." During the afternoon and evening she brought me up-to-date on developments in New York. Most of my time on the boat, however, was taken up by the continuation of my education in Irish affairs. The Irish are a most charming people.

Paris, Wednesday, September 20, 1933

We reached Havre on Wednesday morning. On the train to Paris I fell in with Secretary McAdoo and his wife and daughter. We talked about many things including the work of Norman Davis, about the efficacy of which he was skeptical, and the adherence of the United States to the World Court. On this issue the senator from California insisted on remaining non-committal. Incidentally, he told me that he was going to Russia. Just before we reached Paris, he came to where Miss Wertheimer and I were sitting and asked me if I would go along with him on the Russian trip. I begged off.

Wednesday afternoon I went to see Commert.[18] We talked about Franco-German relations and disarmament. On neither of these issues, however, was Commert very illuminating, for he insisted on saying many things which I am sure he did not in the least believe. But between the lines one could read that the French are delighted by the way in which Germany is steadily alienating the rest of the world, thus leaving France to play the pleasant role of moderation and re-

16. William Thomas Cosgrave, first president of the Irish Free State, 1922–1932.

17. Éamon de Valera was to speak at an FPA meeting at the Astor Hotel and no one noticed that, left over from a previous function, was a large British flag hanging behind the dais. De Valera refused to speak until it had been removed.

18. Pierre Commert, in the French Foreign Office, one of the former "greats" of the League, with thirteen years of service.

straint. Underneath this French policy of calm is the hard determination that the international purposes of the Third Reich shall not be fulfilled.

That evening, Miss Wertheimer and I had dinner with Bentwich and Laski. They had both flown to Paris that day. We went over the whole situation very carefully. It is a pleasure to work with these two men. They are both so intelligent and move with such quickness and decisiveness. It was agreed that Laski would cable from London the message which I drafted, urging the importance of support by Washington of the refugee problem. Moreover, we blocked out tentatively the division of labors in Geneva. It seemed clear that the sooner we got to work on the spot the better, so it was agreed that Bentwich, Miss Wertheimer, and I should all go to Geneva the next day; Laski is to be available to fly down if needed. Montefiore is also coming.

Thursday, September, 21, 1933

The day when I had hoped to be at home I went to see Marriner[19] at the Embassy. I asked him the same question I had been asking a number of French people: "Why is France so calm and restrained?" His answer was identical with that which the French had given me. France is satisfied to have Germany put itself more and more in the wrong. The French are working more and more successfully to build up a solid front on the disarmament issue. If this unity can be achieved and Germany refuses to accept the terms which seem to Great Britain, France, Italy, and the United States reasonable, France will almost certainly take either at once or in the near future direct action against the Reich. The French are particularly anxious, however, not to make any move of this sort unless it can be done, as it were, in response to the overwhelming opinion of the non-German world.

Thursday afternoon I had a long and interesting discussion with our friend de Maud'hui. He gave me the same interpretation of the French program. He stressed what is so very true. The French become excited and voluble at small things, but when the issues are grave and the danger imminent, they become calm. So in the present circumstances. They are acutely aware of the gravity of the situation created by Hitlerism in Germany, but they are satisfied to allow the extremists in the Reich to continue to weaken Germany's foreign position and to strengthen outside opinion in its support of the French program. According to de Maud'hui, there is almost no one in France who today would consent to the scrapping of a single gun or the cutting down of a single battalion.

At dinner Miss Wertheimer and I were joined by Mr. William Friedheim, a German banker. He had just come from two or three years in the Reich. His interpretation of conditions there agreed in almost every particular with the impressions I had gained in Berlin and Nuremberg. On one important point he differed, however, with most of the persons with whom I talked in Germany. He thinks that the effect of the boycott on German goods is being exaggerated and doubts that the economic condition during the winter in Germany will be as se-

19. Theodore Marriner, counselor of the U.S. Embassy in Paris since 1931.

rious as was commonly expected by the critics of the Hitler regime. Friedheim was kind enough to say, after our three hours' talk, that he had not met any foreigner who seemed to him to understand better present tendencies in the Reich than I. He asked me to let him have a copy of my London broadcast so that he might show it to the German ambassador in Paris and send a copy by messenger to certain important bankers in Berlin.

At the Gare de Lyons we watched with interest and amusement the elaborate farewell tendered to the Polish minister of foreign affairs, who was on his way to Geneva. The French are missing no opportunity to show their great devotion to Poland. Indeed, for that matter, as de Maud'hui said to me, "France, faced by the German danger, will make peace at any price with Russia and Italy."

Geneva, Friday, September 22, 1933

We arrived in Geneva in time for breakfast.

At the Secretariat Miss Wertheimer and I talked with Arthur Sweetser and Gerig[20] at some length about the refugee matter. Sweetser made the interesting suggestion that the best possible auspices for the initiation of this project would be the group of eight powers that had worked together during the Sino-Japanese dispute. These were Norway, Sweden, Denmark, Holland, Belgium, Spain, Switzerland, and Czechoslovakia. Obviously, this would be better than the initiative by a single power, but as Osusky[21] of the Czechoslovak Delegation said to me the next day, "It is asking a great deal to expect eight countries to agree on the exact form on which such a matter would be brought to the attention of the League." Sweetser didn't seem to be discouraged by what I had to say to him about the attitude of the Reich.

Incidentally, you may be interested to know that Sweetser is very much concerned about the story which appeared in the *New York Herald Tribune* two weeks ago to the effect that there was to be a fundamental change in the relationship between the United States and the League. He fears that this story will be attributed to him, though he denies that he in any sense "leaked." In the afternoon I ran into Whitaker[22] of the *Herald Tribune.* He told me that he had just heard through a Czech source that Holland had notified Germany, France, but I think no other country of its intention to raise the refugee question in the Sixth Committee. You may wonder why the Sixth Committee (dealing with minority rights and mandates) would be considered, rather than the Fifth which deals with humanitarian questions. I am told the reason is that the Nansen refugee problems have been under the auspices of the Sixth.

Fortunately, just after leaving Whitaker I ran into Osusky, with whom, as you know, I have been acquainted for many years. He said, "Yes, the problem is

20. Ben Gerig, a member of the Information Section of the League of Nations Secretariat, also attached to League Mandates section. Later became a professor.

21. Stephan Osusky, Czech minister to France and delegate to the League. Educated in Chicago and practiced law there.

22. Probably John T. Whitaker, who later wrote for the *Chicago Daily News.*

being considered. We are now trying to find a basis in principle for action by the League, so that what is done will not be directed merely against Germany." I seized the occasion of our talk to ask him about the attitude of France vis-à-vis Germany on the issue of armaments. He gave precisely the same interpretation that I had received so frequently before. Moreover, he said that I was absolutely right in my feeling that, just because France and Czechoslovakia have such vital issues at stake in the relations with Germany, that they will hesitate to take the initiative in the refugee matter for fear of seeming to be indulging in a program of pinpricks. Nonetheless, they will, I am sure, support the refugee proposal once it is launched. (Perhaps I should put a question mark in this respect as to the attitude of France, for I have no real basis yet for saying that France will approve the refugee suggestion.)

As I was leaving Osusky, I ran into Sharkey, correspondent of the U.P., Streit of the *New York Times,* and Butler[23] of the International Labor Organization, but I learned nothing of special importance from them. A little later I again met Whitaker, who said that he had in the meantime received confirmation of the Dutch initiative. After consulting Bentwich and Miss Wertheimer on this matter, I decided to cable New York, urging action from Washington indicating our government's approval.

....

Saturday, September 23, 1933

Saturday, immediately after breakfast, Bentwich, Montefiore, Miss Wertheimer, and I compared notes and blocked out our plans for the day. I then sent another cable to New York in reference to action by Washington.[24]

Then Langes, editor of one of the left papers in Paris, and Jean Dupuy of the Society for Action by the League of Nations' Groups, came in to see me. They both gave the same interpretation of French policy as that which I have described above.

Passing through the Secretariat, I again ran into Osusky, whose only additional comment to what he had said to me earlier was, "Something will be done."

In Malcolm Davis's[25] office, I had an hour's conference with Davis, Eichelberger[26] of the League of Nations Association in Chicago, and Railey,[27] new director of the League of Nations office in New York.

I lunched with Mrs. Bullard and a group of her English friends. The talk

23. Harold Beresford Butler, director of the International Labor Organization.

24. The response in Washington was that since they had not been officially advised, there was nothing they could say, especially as it was a League matter. Stone got the impression from Moffat that there would be a favorable response if officially asked.

25. Malcolm Davis, director of the Geneva Research Center of the Carnegie Endowment for International Peace.

26. Clark M. Eichelberger, director of the Midwest office of the League of Nations Association and in 1935 appointed director of the League of Nations Association. Also wrote *Headline* books published by the FPA.

27. Captain H. H. Railey, director of the League of Nations Association, previously general manager of the Byrd Expedition to the South Pole.

was mostly about Germany. After a couple of hours of discussion, I was shocked to have one of the Englishmen begin an elaborate explanation of how the Jews had been a demoralizing influence in music and in civilization generally. I restrained myself but could not resist telling him that his doctrine was the purest form of Nazi dogma. But what are you to do with people like this?

In the late afternoon Miss Wertheimer did me the enormous favor of taking me with her to the Salève. Though I have been in Geneva for longer or shorter periods during fourteen or fifteen summers, I had never had the gumption to take the afternoon off and see the glorious view from that height. The new Téléferique (aerial cable railway) takes one up in about six-and-a-half minutes. The sensation is much like that of going up in an airplane.

I dined with young Woodward, whom you and the members of the staff will, of course, remember. He has been here in Geneva ever since the beginning of the Disarmament Conference in February last year. He is representing Cecil[28] and is working also for Reuters. He is most pessimistic. He thinks that the Disarmament Conference has already failed and that Europe faces the probability of a new war within three or four years. I wish he had been less impressive.

I started home with the firm intention to go to bed early, but stopped at the Bavaria for a few minutes. The result was two hours more of talk.

Sunday, September 24, 1933

On Sunday morning Bentwich and Miss Wertheimer came in for our usual conference. We agreed upon a summary draft of the functions of the proposed High Commission, copy attached. This is to be used merely as a means of explaining the primary purposes of the High Commissioner. It in no sense takes the place of the Feilchenfeld memorandum. This is going to be of the greatest value. We also discussed what action should be taken in the light of Stone's telegram received this morning, in which he asks that Washington be approached for its opinion by London or The Hague. This afternoon and tomorrow it is hoped that something can be started along this line. Tomorrow I also hope to see Madariaga and several other members of the Assembly, whose interest and support at this initial but vital stage would be helpful.

Please do not be too critical about the phraseology of this letter. It has been dictated hurriedly after a full morning of work. I am sending along two extra copies, one of which you may wish to send to Stone, and the other to Felix Warburg.

Since Ruth has covered so much of the ground with me on the German issue, I should be glad if you would arrange that she sees my letters and cables when she comes into the office.

I was deeply appreciative of your personal cable. I knew, of course, that the committee and you had taken into account my personal desire to return.

28. Lord Robert Cecil of Chelwood, one of the "fathers" of the League of Nations, who had helped draft the League Covenant. McDonald had known him since the early 1920s.

Nonetheless, it was nice to have your assurance on this point as well as your encouraging remarks about my broadcast.

This ends the first letter to Miss Ogden.

Sunday, September 24, 1933

My dear Miss Ogden,

When you receive this second long letter by the *Bremen,* you will think that some sort of a revolution has been worked in me that I have suddenly become so voluble. The explanation is two-fold: firstly, a number of interesting developments day by day here, and second, the importance of these developments being known as soon as possible by you and your colleagues.

After dictating my letter of yesterday, I went out to Arthur Sweetser's for their annual American tea. I drove out with Mrs. Bullard and the Jerome Greens.[29] There were more than a hundred Americans and members of the Secretariat at the party during the course of the late afternoon and evening. I shall summarize here only those of my conversations which may have some immediate interest for you.

I was very fortunate to have an opportunity to talk at some length with Mr. Pelt,[30] a Dutch member of the Secretariat, and in close touch with the Dutch delegation. He explained more fully than I had been able to learn previously the plans of the Dutch in reference to the refugees. His government has already raised the question of League action on behalf of these refugees with all of the countries bordering on Germany, except Austria, which have a number of the refugees in their territory, i.e., Denmark, Belgium, France, Switzerland, Czechoslovakia, and Poland. Germany has also been notified of the Dutch intention.

The basis on which the issue is being raised is that it constitutes an *economic, financial,* and *social* problem. Please note these three words. The Dutch have deliberately refrained from putting the question on a political or even a humanitarian basis. They are anxious to make acceptance as easy as possible for Germany. There is an added significance in the choice of the three words. It is that the Dutch are anxious not to include within the purview of their scheme the Socialist and Communist refugees, that is, they would prefer to limit it to Jewish refugees.

On this particular point of limitation, Mr. Bentwich, who was interviewing Mr. Limburg, one of the leading members of the Dutch delegation, at the same time I was seeing Pelt, suggested that the Dutch might phrase their appeal to include *racial* and *religious* refugees. This would avoid the invidiousness of selecting only the Jews. Limburg seemed to think this a good idea. He, like Pelt, argued that it would be easier for Germany to accept if this narrower basis were

29. Jerome Green, professor at Harvard.
30. Adrianus Pelt, director of the Information Section of the League Secretariat.

adopted, because the German government could explain to its people that the High Commissioner would make less likely the return of Jewish refugees to Germany and would expedite the emigration of other Jews. Obviously, there is a danger inherent in this possibility that Berlin might use the League machinery to force emigration. And it seemed to some of us that there is a second danger that German Jews might feel that the naming of a commissioner for them alone would assure their reception abroad. But this danger could doubtless be guarded against.

Mr. Pelt gave me the impression that the initial responses to the Dutch initiative had been favorable and that even Germany did not seem as intransigent as Dieckhoff and von Neurath had appeared to me to be. But only developments in the next week or two will tell whether this attitude of apparent cooperation is real.

Towards the end of our discussion Pelt said that even if it were found impossible to move through the League, another way could be found. Unfortunately, just as he was about to explain to me what he had in mind, we were interrupted by the first of the flood of guests arriving for tea. However, we agreed to get together soon to discuss the matter further. In any event, at the moment there is no advantage in discussing what we should do if we failed to secure League action.

Bentwich and Limburg discussed the element of finance. It appears that the Dutch do not think that this is as serious a matter as the Secretariat gave me the impression two weeks ago when I discussed it with them. Limburg said that provision could be made in the Fourth Committee for the necessary financing and that the League could be reimbursed later.

I talked with Avenol, the secretary general, and reported to him the attitude of the German government as expressed to me by Dieckoff and von Neurath. The Secretary General did not seem surprised nor discouraged. He was much interested in the Dutch idea of avoiding political implication. In my talk earlier that afternoon with Pelt, I had explained that the New York group was just as anxious as his government to save Germany's face. I asked him if he would be interested to study the memorandum you sent us. He said he would be, so I supplied him with a copy that afternoon.

During the course of the party, I chatted with Hugh Wilson,[31] who, as you know, is a sort of resident American minister in Geneva, and head of the American arms delegation in Norman Davis's absence. He shared my view that the relations between Germany and France and Poland have reached an acute crisis, that if the Disarmament Conference fails, as it now seems likely to do, there will be a great danger of troop movements in the near future. I urged upon him the desirability of dealing as much as possible directly with Hitler on the theory that

31. Hugh R. Wilson, U.S. minister to Switzerland, who handled official communications with the League. Between Wilson in Bern and Gilbert as consul in Geneva there was a certain amount of rivalry, and their roles vis-à-vis the League were not clear.

the Führer can and is more likely to make more concessions than any other German spokesman. Wilson thought this a sound suggestion but pointed out the difficulty and danger of going over von Neurath's head. He asked me what I would think of a meeting of the four heads of state, MacDonald, Daladier, Hitler, and Mussolini. I told him I thought it would be excellent provided an adequate basis could be prepared in advance. Incidentally, you may be interested to know that Uncle Arthur[32] was told by Hitler that he would be willing to meet Daladier provided there were a reasonable chance of tangible results from such a conference.

Just as most of the guests were leaving the party, Norman Davis arrived. I spoke to him for a few minutes and later found him surrounded by a group of eight or ten men, including Streit, Sharkey, and one or two other correspondents. As I came up to join the group, Davis was talking about the danger and the unfairness of presenting Germany with a united front on a basis which made few or no concessions to German opinion. The Allies, he said, after being responsible for resentment in Germany which has helped to make Hitlerism possible, now propose (at least France does) that because of Hitler no disarmament can be considered. Then turning to me, he said, "What else could you expect from the French when people keep coming back from Germany telling the authorities in Paris that the Nazis are incorrigible!" I ventured to reply that I hoped I had not given exactly that impression.

I drove home from the party with Prentiss Gilbert. He is in excellent form. He says he is anxious to show me the system by which he keeps the State Department informed of League developments.

Monday, September 25, 1933

At the Assembly this morning nothing occurred of special interest. Goebbels sat at von Neurath's right in the very front row. As you know, the seating is arranged alphabetically, this bringing Allemagne immediately in front of the tribune. Goebbels looked, from the balcony, like a schoolboy sitting in the front row to receive instruction from his teachers. I wish that it were in that spirit that he had come. The gossip is that von Neurath urged Goebbels to come with a view to his education. It is not expected that Goebbels will speak unless, as one person put it, Germany is attacked, and he feels called upon to reply.

I lunched today with a German, Schwartz, formerly of the *Vorwärts,*[33] but now a Nazi apologist. Happily, however, he knew me well enough not to use any of the more obvious forms of propaganda. I also talked during the morning with Dr. Schmidt, a member of the German delegation. He admitted that Germany's isolation was almost complete and was obviously worried about it.

32. Apparently a reference to Arthur Henderson, one of the organizers of the Labour Party and British foreign secretary, 1929–1931. He met with Hitler in July 1933 in a vain effort to promote disarmament.

33. The central newspaper of the Social Democratic Party of Germany, outlawed at that time.

Just as I was finishing dictating this letter, Mr. Bentwich came in in high spirits to report that the mention of Hoover's name had, he hoped, elicited enthusiastic responses from Rappard[34] on behalf of the Swiss, and Abraham of the Secretariat, and also from such of the Jews to whom he had mentioned the matter.

Tuesday, September 26, 1933

In the light of these talks with Pelt and Limburg, Bentwich, Montefiore, Miss Wertheimer, and I reviewed the situation this morning. It seemed to us that developments were much more hopeful than we had believed possible. Indeed, we were all convinced that we must at once consider another aspect of the problem, possible suggestions for the High Commissionership. We, of course, are not assuming that the fight has been won, but we think that if it is won, the results may be lost unless the Council names a commissioner capable of commanding the enthusiastic support of Jews throughout the world. We therefore thought it desirable to canvass the situation here in reference to the possibility of naming a well-known gentleman from Palo Alto [former president Herbert Hoover]. It did not seem to me fair that we should ask you in New York to sound out this American unless we could be assured here in advance that he would be persona grata.

I talked during the course of the day with Gerig, Sweetser, Lange[35] of Norway, Osusky of Czechoslovakia, and Madariaga of Spain. Only one of these—Madariaga—raised a serious objection. He said that Hoover had "let the League down," and therefore he thought it inappropriate that the League should offer him an opportunity for service that would help him to recoup his prestige. However, when I pressed Madariaga, he said that he would not oppose Hoover's nomination if the others wanted him. Sweetser raised the question whether the Germans might not feel that Hoover's nomination would be too reminiscent of the war to be palatable. Lange said he would sound out other members of the Assembly, while Osusky seemed to think the suggestion splendid but wanted time to talk with his colleagues. If within a week or so you receive a night letter asking you to inquire informally whether H. would accept, that will mean that there is no likelihood that his nomination would be opposed.

Next to H., the most likely person from this angle is Lange himself. Cecil is not strong enough nor is Reading. Others that have occurred to us do not seem to have sufficient "box office appeal." But perhaps long before you have received this, we shall have had some brilliant ideas. Certainly any that you may have will be welcome.

I was encouraged by the fact that both Lange and Madariaga favored League action. Miss Wertheimer and I are lunching with Lange on Wednesday

34. William E. Rappard, Swiss economist and specialist in international labor. Director of the Graduate Institute of International Studies of the University of Geneva since 1928.

35. Dr. Christian L. Lange, Norwegian delegate to the League, a member of the International Committee to Aid Refugee Intellectuals, an organization headed by Marie Ginsberg.

and will discuss the whole matter with him in detail. He, as you know, is one of the oldest members of the Assembly and carries large influence, especially in social and humanitarian matters. Madariaga said that he would certainly support the proposal. He was unwilling, however, to take an initiative in the matter because, he said, "That belongs properly to the countries which, because of their nearness to Germany, have numbers of refugees within their borders." For Spain to lead in such a movement would appear to be a gratuitous attack on Germany.

I started down the Quai Wilson to keep an appointment with Norman Davis at eleven. On the way I passed Mr. Limburg of the Dutch delegation, having a cup of coffee at a sidewalk café. I sat down and chatted with him for a moment, telling him we considered important that the Dutch government should inquire informally of our government as to their attitude on the refugee matter, and I suggested that this might most conveniently be done through Wilson. Limburg seemed to think this a good idea.

In Norman Davis's apartment, I found him and Wilson just parting. I asked Wilson to stay a moment while I explained to both of them the refugee project in order that they might be au courant if and when the Dutch raised the question, and as I spoke to them, I told them frankly of my position in the matter. They both seemed sympathetic, though of course neither one can move without specific instructions from Washington. After Wilson left, Davis said that he would of course leave this matter to the minister.

Mr. Davis and I then talked for more than an hour and a half. He was very frank and covered a great variety of subjects, mostly concerned with disarmament but some of them having little or no connection with that problem. . . .

Leaving Mr. Davis just before lunch, I went back to the Secretariat where I had an opportunity of speaking again for a moment to M. Osusky. He confirmed what Mr. Limburg had told me in the morning, that the matter was being actively discussed. I should have said earlier that Mr. Limburg told me that the Dutch were meeting this afternoon with the heads of the delegations of the states bordering on Germany.

I lunched with Mr. and Mrs. Habicht.[36] You will remember her as Elizabeth Peterson and he as one of the members of the Social Section of the Secretariat. We had a pleasant visit together, but to my surprise during the latter part of lunch, and for nearly an hour afterwards, Habicht delivered a lecture on the possibilities of dictatorship as illustrated in Nazi Germany in effecting a reorganization of Europe on a peace basis. I shall not here undertake even to summarize his arguments. Suffice it to say that he accepts the Nazi thesis that democracy has failed to bring peace to Europe, that constitutional regimes cannot make the necessary sacrifices to effect a stable reorganization of Europe, that

36. Theo Habicht, member of the Social Section of the Secretariat, whose wife Elizabeth Peterson had worked at the FPA. In charge of a Nazi propaganda campaign to undermine the Austrian government. Gerhard L. Weinberg, *The Foreign Policy of Hitler's Germany: Diplomatic Revolution in Europe, 1933–1936* (Chicago: University of Chicago Press, 1970), 92.

this can only be brought about through governments which control public opinion and are not controlled by it. He seriously argued that the Nazi leaders, now that they have convinced the German people that the individual must not serve himself but work only for the common good of the whole Reich, would be prepared to go further and tell the German people that the good of Germany must be made secondary to the good of the whole of Europe and of humanity. The moral he drew from all of this was that we ought to consider seriously whether it would not be better to scrap the remaining democratic institutions than to risk the danger of democracy destroying itself and masses of people through war. I shall not burden you with more of his rationalizing.

After lunch I talked with Arthur Sweetser, who had been discussing the matter of the refugees with the German undersecretary general. The latter argued exactly as Dieckoff argued in Berlin: there is no problem, only thirty-three Germans are "heimatlos," the others have the protection of their consuls or diplomatic representatives; it would be absurd for the League to take up such a matter, especially at a time like this just when the Nazis, by sending Dr. Goebbels, had indicated their increasing interest in and regard for the League. In any case, it should not be forgotten that this whole question of the refugees is a Socialist ramp.

You see, of course, that the job here is not going to be an easy one all the more since it is always easier to block a specific proposal than to put it through. Just a few minutes ago, Gerig of the Secretariat, who at my suggestion had talked this afternoon to one of his German colleagues, reported that the Reich was going to oppose vigorously the Dutch initiative. The German view is that it is an attack on the honor of their country to suggest that there are German refugees. Then followed the usual arguments.

Tomorrow I may write further about the attitude of the Germans, when I have an opportunity of talking to Gerig more fully. But there can be no doubt that, if any effective League action is taken, it will be in the face of stubborn German resistance.

On Tuesday night, I attended what has become an institution in Geneva, a cocktail party. It has some advantages for it brings very many people together, but it also has serious disadvantages for a person who insists on limiting himself to citron pressé. After two and a half hours of talk and refreshments, most of the guests had left, but the two-thirds who remained were in need of friendly attention from the one or two of us who had remained sober. I am assured, however, that one is not to conclude that these cocktail parties always end so successfully.

Wednesday, September 27, 1933

On Wednesday I began my day as usual with a brief conference with Bentwich, Montefiore, and Mildred Wertheimer. Then I went to the office of the Consulate and talked for nearly two hours with Prentiss Gilbert. I was greatly impressed by the system which he has built up here to follow and report to the State Department on League activities. Moreover, he himself has grown, it seems to me, in intellectual grasp during the years that he has been here. You will be amused to learn that he had heard the report that I had come back to Geneva with a view to displacing him as American representative accredited to the League. In order that he might have no more illusions on that point, I told him frankly why I had returned.

Mildred and I then lunched with Lange of the Norwegian delegation. We discussed many topics including that of possible League action on the refugee question. Lange is decidedly sympathetic and will help where he can, but it is not to be expected that his delegation will take an active part openly. He seemed to think that the chances were about even that the League could be induced to move.

In the afternoon at the meeting of the Assembly I ran into Gerig, who told me more of what was being planned by the Germans in their defensive operations against League refugee action. It appears that they are studying the Italian precedent—when Mussolini successfully objected to similar action on behalf of Italian refugees. It is clear that they are going to make a hard fight.

The opening speech on the report of the Council on the work of the League was by Simon.[37] It was of no particular consequence, indifferent in form and content. Its only merit was that it did open the debate.

The outstanding event in the afternoon was the appearance of Dollfuss. His speech was brief and, in a certain sense, a challenge to the Germans. But more important than the address was the reception which he received. Except for the Germans, apparently nearly all the delegations joined in very hearty applause before and after he spoke. The faces of the Germans were a study. Goebbels, it seemed, wished to reply, but he was dissuaded by von Neurath and his other colleagues.

Goebbels's exit from the Assembly Hall was worth watching. He was preceded by one or two plain-clothes men and surrounded on both sides and the rear by a solid semi-circle of six other detectives with guns bulging from their pockets. A close-up does not increase one's love for this extraordinary personality.

Incidentally, you may be interested in a conversation which I had only a few minutes ago with Derso and Kelen,[38] the two famous cartoonists, who had just returned from a first conference where Goebbels spoke. Both artists were agreed that Goebbels is much more Latin than German in his temperament, and that his infirmity and suffering early in life [he had a clubfoot] had developed a hypersensitiveness and cruelty that are his outstanding characteristics. They compared him to Snowden,[39] except that in the latter's case the tendency towards

37. Sir John Simon, British foreign secretary 1931–1935, vice president of the Assembly of the League of Nations.

38. Alois Derso and Emery Kelen. Kelen later wrote *Peace in Their Time: Men Who Led Us In and Out of War, 1914–1945.*

39. Viscount Snowden of Ickornshaw, chancellor of the Exchequer under Ramsay MacDonald, who turned against his former close friend in attacks in Parliament.

cruelty issued merely in cutting and sarcastic comments on his fellows and their work.

After the Assembly yesterday, I chatted for a moment with Madame Forschammer about the probable attitude of her delegation on the refugee issue. She said that just because Denmark was so seriously disturbed by Pan-German agitation in the Southern Province, the government would hesitate to seem to be a leader in the refugee agitation.

I went out to dinner with Mlle. Weiss, and for two hours we talked about FPA personalities and about her future. She wished, of course, to be remembered to you and Mrs. Moorhead especially. At 10:15 we were joined by Mme. Tabouis, a frail slip of a French woman who, in my judgment, is one of the most intelligent of all the Geneva correspondents. The three of us talked about European politics until one o'clock. The French are gravely concerned about the failure, as they see it, of the United States and the British to support the French program. Both women were quite without hope of success at the Disarmament Conference. They looked forward with foreboding to the day when France must take military action.

Thursday, September 28, 1933

This morning Mildred Wertheimer and I, through her initiative, managed to have an interview with Dollfuss. He was very cordial, chatting with her quite freely. There was little new in what he said, but the talk gave both of us an opportunity to study him at close range. He is certainly the least dictatorial of dictators, has a charming smile, and looks rather like a chubby schoolboy. When he stands up, he reaches just about to Mildred's chin, so you can imagine how I towered over him.

The following is Mildred Wertheimer's summary of the interview:

(1) Dollfuss made an excellent impression, quite undictatorial, but of a man absolutely sure of himself and knowing his own mind. He is charming and gay and was obviously in high spirits this morning because of the great ovation which he received yesterday in the Assembly. He seems a man still close to the soil and I felt, during the entire interview, much more representative of provincial Austria than of Vienna without regard to the Socialist question.

(2) I conducted the interview in German since he speaks neither English nor French. His Austrian accent is terrific. After the usual polite preliminaries, I asked him how he envisaged the new Austrian state. He talked at length about a state on a corporate basis, a guild state. In reality this means a Fascist state although he did not once use the term nor did he refer to a totalitarian or a Ständestaat by name. He spoke, however, of the "anti-parliamentarianism" of the Austrians and of the unending party politics which had made the situation absolutely impossible—much the same line as the Nazis use but without rancor on his part. He said nevertheless that the new state

would have two bodies representing the people and although he was very vague at this point about the electoral basis, I gathered that the higher chamber will deal with politics and cultural questions while the lower will represent the corporations on which the state will be based.

(3) In answer to a question re the Social Democrats, he said that in the provinces, many of the Socialists were tacitly with him. He seemed in no sense violently anti-Socialist although that is probably just his Austrian temperament. In regard to the Viennese Socialists, however, he said that they were all wound up in their party bureaucracy and would never support him.

(4) Dollfuss was very definite in stating that in Austria they would never resort to the methods used in Germany in order to realize the new state. He said categorically in this connection that Austria was a civilized country and made it quite clear that he did not so regard "Prussianized Germany."

(5) I asked him about the rumors of a putsch in the Salzburg region and he poopoohed the idea, said that he had the situation well in hand, that they were ready for anything and generally seemed very sure of himself.

(6) Finally, at JGM's suggestion, I asked him what we in the USA could do to help Austria and he said promptly "buy from Austria" and come to visit the country. As we were leaving, I remarked that I was coming to Vienna after the Assembly and he was delighted and said he would see me then—a graceful gesture.[40]

After lunch at the Butler's of the ILO, the other guests were all English except Hammarskjold[41] of the World Court and a woman member of the Spanish delegation. As always happens, the talk drifted to Germany. Only Hammarskjold was even moderate in his characterization of the Nazis; the others were vehement. I was surprised that Butler went so far in denouncing the German attitude at the recent meeting of the ILO. He said that the chief German governmental representative, [Robert] Ley, a director of the Labor Front in the new regime, was inefficient, drunken, and corrupt. The Swede, who is an unusually acute observer, was of the opinion that the regime would gradually be accepted by the rest of the world and was even more confident that the League would not risk alienating Germany by taking action on the refugees.

In the late afternoon I went over to the meeting of the Council. The proceedings were dull, so I spent the next hour or two in the lobby, where, as you know, the world passes by you if you will only wait. My most interesting conversations were with Derso and Kelen, which I have already referred to, and with Roehm, the representative of the Russian newspaper agency. He and I talked about the growing rapprochement between France and Russia and what he thinks are gathering war clouds in the Far East. He criticizes our government

40. McDonald Papers, Columbia, D366 H1, 1933.
41. Hjalmar Hammarskjold, prime minister of Sweden during World War I.

for defeating its own purposes by failing to recognize the Soviets in time to strengthen them against the Japanese aggressions in Manchuria. He is of the opinion that the present naval rivalry between Japan and the United States marks the beginning of an acute stage in the relations between ourselves and the Japanese. He adds that the common opinion here is that '36 or '37 will see the conflict. This is indeed a cheerful Assembly!

The rumors—and they are little more than that—which we have been hearing all day about the progress of the refugee matter are not encouraging, but we have not given up hope, if only the Dutch will make a fight. . . .

I hope I shall have better news for you tomorrow. Perhaps I should merely add that Bentwich came in this afternoon to say that he had had a most wearing day yesterday trying to reach agreement with his Jewish colleagues here representing the American Jewish Congress, the Zionist Organization, and the Comité des Délégations Juives. I, of course, am staying out of all such inter-Jewish conferences.

Friday, September 29, 1933

On Friday morning I went directly to the Assembly. It was a notable occasion. The Swedish delegate made a courageous defense of civil liberties and even ventured to criticize German concentration camps. But what was of greatest importance was, of course, the introduction by the Dutch of their refugee resolution. The method of doing this could not have been improved upon. Every possible danger that had been foreseen in New York was so far as possible guarded against.

The most amazing factor in the whole situation has been the change of front of the Germans. During the whole week, von Neurath and the other Germans have been saying that they would not accept, that they would oppose any such action. Yet the night before the Swedes introduced their resolution, von Neurath went to the head of the Swedish delegation and said, "We have changed our minds: we are completely indifferent to the action you propose." But that there has been a real change of opinion as to the undesirability of the League action, I doubt. Apparently, the Germans decided either to seem to accept the proposal, planning to defeat it later, or they are convinced that opposition would only make the proposal front-page news, whereas if it were unopposed, nothing much will be said about it and perhaps nothing effectively done. In any event, one cannot yet be sure that the German apparent attitude is the real policy.

As was to have been expected, the North European countries and those bordering on Germany are all expected to favor the proposal. The surprising country is Italy which, instead of opposing, is said to be ready to support the proposal. But there is one danger from the Italian direction. It is that they may try to limit the scope of the effort to Jewish refugees. The Dutch would deprecate this or at least they say they would. Certainly from our point of view, such limitation would be undesirable.

This morning after the Assembly, a Dutch member of the Secretariat told me that his government had finally moved to ask Washington its view. This was done through the chief Dutch delegate speaking to Wilson. The Dutch hope that some public statement will be made indicating the attitude of the United States.

At the same time I told the Dutchman of our cable of last night containing the Rockefeller suggestion (of funds for administration). He was very much interested in this and thought it an excellent way of meeting a possible serious danger later. However, he preferred that the administrative expenses of the office should be borne by the League itself. But if in the Fourth or Finance Committee, some objection to the project were raised on the ground of expense, it would be absolutely decisive if the Dutch were in a position to announce that the League would not be out of pocket at all. He was in complete agreement with the view expressed that Rockefeller funds would be more acceptable than any others.

Before going to the Assembly this morning, I talked to Arthur Sweetser about the Rockefeller matter. We had deliberately refrained from consulting him in advance. Our idea was that either he might disagree and therefore make it embarrassing for us to pass the suggestion to you, or he might feel that he would be embarrassed to have been a party to the initiative in this matter. When I explained to him, he seemed pleased that we had handled it as we had. He will therefore, I think, support it when the Rockefellers inquire of him.

Now returning to yesterday, I lunched with Allen Dulles.[42] We talked about many matters but chiefly about Germany. He said that his own estimate of the chances of securing a [disarmament] convention had increased from 20–40 percent. He outlined to me the basis on which he thought such an agreement could be reached: a convention for an eight-year period. During the first four years, when the system of control was being tried out, France would not be called upon to make substantial reductions, nor would the Germans be allowed increases beyond the enlarged force in the militia to replace the Reichswehr and possibly permission to have the prototypes of such of the forbidden weapons which might be classified as defensive. He thought that the French and Germans were pretty close together on this basis. As to the Italians and the French, they seemed to have agreed to let their naval differences rest until 1935. The chief danger he saw, from the United States's point of view, was that the convention would not be universal, e.g., that Japan would not be a party to it. But he saw no way out of this difficulty.

During the course of the afternoon, the lobby in the disarmament building literally buzzed with rumors and counter-rumors of agreement and disagree-

42. Allen Welsh Dulles, at the time State Department legal adviser to the American delegation to the German Disarmament Conference at Geneva, 1932–1933. Younger brother of John Foster Dulles.

ment between the Germans and the powers recently consulted in Paris. On the whole, the prevailing opinion was that von Neurath was returning to Germany to secure permission to make certain political concessions to France, in return for which the latter would concede what might in Germany be interpreted as the right to a measure of rearmament.

A group of Americans including Streit fell in with a discussion of the technique of Norman Davis. Everybody agreed that his characteristic optimism was a very material factor in making possible ultimate success, but there was criticism by some that he failed adequately to prepare his technical position from time to time. For example, Streit emphasized that the decisive factor in the question of control was the supervision of aerial and poison gas preparations, and he added that on both these points the position of the United States was from the European point of view very unsatisfactory. . . .

Quite late, after ten o'clock, I went out to a party given by the Tiranas.[43] There I met and chatted with a number of Americans and many members of the Secretariat. I saw again Derso and Kelen, the cartoonists. They are delightful personalities. The latter told an interesting tale of Goebbels's statement that nowadays when he feels weakening in his purpose, he turns back to his newspaper clipping files and reads his enemies' accounts of his physical infirmities. Then he is heartened to go on with his struggles.

Saturday, September 30, 1933

On Saturday morning, I went to the Assembly and discussed the refugee matter with the Dutch as I have described above. There I ran into Whitaker of the *Tribune,* whom I took to task for his mentioning my name in connection with the Hoover proposal. He excused himself on the ground that he had misunderstood that when I had told him to keep my name out of the whole discussion, he had thought that I meant only until the news had broken from other sources. Well, I had to accept his explanation although it by no means satisfied me.

Out to lunch with Rappard—the only other guest was Sarah Wambaugh.[44] We talked about conditions in Germany and about Roosevelt's attitude in regard to international questions. But from my point of view, the most interesting part of the discussion was Rappard's account of his nearly three-hour conversation with Goebbels when he sat by him [at] dinner given for the Germans by the Swiss a few nights ago. Rappard reports that he talked with Goebbels with the greatest frankness. His account of Goebbels's retorts was revealing and amusing.

. . . .

43. Rifat Tirana, Albanian economist on the staff of the League Secretariat.

44. Sarah Wambaugh, specialist in international affairs, teacher, consultant, and writer, one of the three experts to draft the regulations for the Saar plebiscite in 1935, later technical adviser to the Saar Plebiscite Commission.

It is now eight o'clock but I have tonight decided to continue my dictation instead of going out, in the hopes that I shall be permitted to sail next week and I want to have my work finished up as much as possible before taking the boat.
P.S. The Dutch have asked Wilson to sound out Washington. They hope for a public statement of the American view of the refugee matter.

6. October 1933: High Commissioner

Geneva, Sunday, October 1, 1933

Worked until one o'clock, lunched with Miss Wertheimer and Miss Wambaugh. Then out to Annecey with Miss Bartlett. It was a lovely day and, tired as I was, I enjoyed it hugely.

Monday, October 2, 1933

Down to change my sailing arrangements, then to the Secretariat. I had a long chat with the Russian correspondent, Roehm, who is quite skeptical about the possibility of success of the Disarmament Conference, largely because Japan's attitude will permit neither Russia nor the United States to disarm. Of course, he is cynical too about the European aspects of the problem. While we were talking, we were joined by Rappard. He put it: "The optimists may hope for a formula which solves nothing but avoids an open break; the pessimists can hope that war can be avoided for the immediate present."

Longish conference with Pelt. He was emphatic that if funds for the administrative expenses of the commissioner must come from the outside, it must be from a non-Jewish source. The Rockefeller source would be perfect. He thought that, in view of my sailing on Thursday, it was desirable that I get Avenol's ideas personally about the finances. He thought the Roosevelt name a good one. As to other action in case the League effort failed, he visualized an organization set up by the states bordering on Germany. He seemed confident that Great Britain would support the League project once it was definitely lodged. The Belgians were somewhat more cool, having at the moment a series of questions under negotiation with the Reichsbank.

Ran into Butler of the B.I.T. [*sic,* should be B.I.S.—for Bank for International Settlements]. He agreed on almost every particular with Pelt, especially on the matter of financing and the desirability of my seeing Avenol personally.

Talked to Arthur [Sweetser]. He said he would arrange the Avenol matter. He liked the Roosevelt name. He is still much concerned by the *Tribune* article, which, when he saw it, was worse than he had anticipated.

To lunch at the Bergues, as guest of Madame Tabuis. Others there were Politis,[1] Coudenhove-Kalergi,[2] Miss Thompson of little-lamented memory, and an unusually intelligent person whose name I do not remember. The talk wan-

1. Nikolaos Sokratis Politis, three-time Greek foreign minister.
2. Richard Coudenhove-Kalergi, writer and early proponent of a Pan-European union.

dered from subject to subject but always returned to the condition of Europe. All these Europeans were obviously terribly frightened of the future. To them, Hitler and the Nazis are a frightful nightmare that portends war and disaster. Coudenhove-Kalergi has become an ardent Francophile. He said, "What Europe needs is a Lincoln who prefers war to slavery." There was some discussion of French opinion, but all agreed with Politis that if the Disarmament Conference failed, the French Parliament would immediately vote two billions of supplementary military credits and that unanimously.

After lunch saw Mme. de Jouvenel, whom I hope to be able to escape from during the rest of my few hours in Geneva. Chatted for a moment with Bérenger[3] about the refugee matter and am to see him tomorrow morning.

Back to the hotel, where I met the Johnsons of the Nansen Committee talking with Bentwich.

Tuesday, October 3, 1933

Up early in order to keep an appointment with Bérenger, president of the French Senatorial Committee on Foreign Affairs. He is much interested in the refugee matter. He said that the administrative expenses would be relatively unimportant because the plan was to utilize, as far as possible, existing League machinery. He said that you had a superfluity of stenographers about the League which could be grouped in such a way as not [to] add materially to the existing budget. As to the Nansen Office, he expressed the strong conviction that it should be allowed to liquidate itself and not be revived through having new work put under it. He was critical of French Jews for what he termed their niggardliness in dealing with their own people. He listened attentively to my suggestion of the possibility of Rockefeller help and of large sums that might be made available from Jewish sources. We then talked about personalities for High Commissioner. He said that the consideration of the subject was rather premature but nonetheless expressed views about various possibilities. He is not enthusiastic about Hoover, rather the reverse. He put it on the ground that the latter has been defeated only recently, but I suspect that there are other considerations which affect his judgment. As to Lange, he showed no interest. De Brouckère he recognized as a man of force and of influence not only in Belgium, but in labor circles throughout Europe. Cecil he spoke of as "the plume knight" who had played his part. Teddy Roosevelt, Jr., seemed to appeal to him more than any of the others. He did not know young Roosevelt well though he had met him a few years ago.

About procedure, he thought that actions would be taken in the Second Committee this week and did not seem to anticipate that consideration in the Fourth Committee would long delay action.

3. Henri Bérenger, president of the Committee for Foreign Affairs in the French Senate and later French delegate to the Governing Body of the High Commission. Previously ambassador to the United States. Also a close friend of Secretary General Avenol.

As I was leaving, I told him of my desire to see the Secretary General before sailing. He agreed that this was important.

....

Back to the Secretariat where I heard that Bérenger had made an open attack on the Germans, in the Sixth Committee. I was sorry to have missed it.

At eleven o'clock Miss Wertheimer and I went to see Hugh Wilson. I told him of her work and that she would carry on after I left. He indicated his willingness to cooperate closely with her. I asked him what the Dutch had said to him. He replied that they had, through the chief of the delegation, simply told him of what had been done for the information of Washington. He said not only was no action on Washington's part asked for, but that there was no information that any was expected. Moreover, he thought it unlikely that our government would indicate any point of view at this time while the matter is being debated in the Second Committee and before the Assembly. As to the High Commissioner, Wilson thought there was no chance at all of Hoover's acceptance, but that young Teddy Roosevelt might be interested.

We talked at some length about conditions in Germany. Wilson said that it was remarkable how many of the former pacifists and liberals were now in effect urging the United States to go to war against Germany.

Out to lunch with de Lanuk. We discussed problems relating to Germany. He felt that the differences between Great Britain, the United States, and France were those of form, rather than substance, and that if only the leaders had enough imagination, they would see that the national points of view were easily reconcilable, and that a united front vis-à-vis Germany could be established which would be at once firm and yet permit of a generous policy towards the Reich. He refused to accept either horn of the dilemma, the sacrifice of peace or the loss of freedom. Both could, he argues, be maintained if a sufficient number really wished them to be. I left with the feeling that he is unusually suggestive and fruitful intellectually. His analysis of the weakness of pacifism in general and especially of that of Einstein was particularly telling.

Conference at 6:30 with Mr. Bentwich and the other members of the Jewish organizations here.

Wednesday, October 4, 1933

Over to the Secretariat to attend the Second Committee. Heard the head of the Dutch delegation make an excellent presentation of his plea for the naming of a refugee High Commissioner. He was followed by Ritter, who half-heartedly made the German protest against the League auspices for such action.

Was unable to hear the rest of the speeches because of my engagement with Avenol at 11:30. I told him that I would be returning to the States immediately, would be in touch with the groups there who would have to help largely in financing the refugee project; that, therefore, I was anxious to have from him as clear a picture as possible of the way in which he thought the administrative machinery would be set up. He expressed the view that in the last analysis, the Germans would not accept League auspices; that, therefore, the best that could be expected would be League initiative, the work to be carried on outside. I urged the importance, from the League point of view, of effective action, for through it might be enlisted strong support for the League in many parts of the world. He recognized this, but seemed to feel that Germany would block the most desirable form of organization.

Back to the lobby of the disarmament building, chatted with a number of persons.

Out late to lunch at Arthur Sweetser's. My talk there was mostly with Cadogan,[4] the recently appointed British minister to Peking, and the French head of the Committee on Intellectual Cooperation.[5] Drove back to the Secretariat with Arthur and Sarah Wambaugh.

Finally talked with Arthur about the Jewish refugee project, but he came back again to the question of Whitaker's news story about the U.S. relations to the League.

At tea-time met and said goodbye to several of the men at the disarmament building.

Final conference with Miss Wertheimer and Bentwich and saw him off to the train.

Thursday, October 5, 1933

Arrived at Ville Franche about eight o'clock in the morning. Had time for a few hours in Nice. Took the tender at two o'clock to the *Rex.* Was greatly relieved to get on board to have a chance for a real rest.

The *Rex,* October 5–12, 1933

The *Rex* was beautiful. Had a quiet crossing and much excellent company. Among those whom I saw the most were Mr. and Mrs. Wallace Beery[6] and their delightful adopted three-year-old daughter, Martinelli, Tito Coro, Mrs. Harris and her daughter Betty, Tony Sissa, Mr. and Mrs. Kelly, Miss Tinker, who was my deck tennis companion with whom I won a cup, Mr. and Mrs. Hodges, he of the *Evening Sun,* Mr. S ? of the Fox Movietone.

Docked early, about nine o'clock. Met by Ruth, her father and mother and Bobby.

4. Sir Alexander Cadogan, British ambassador to China, 1933–1935.

5. The second man was Henri Bonnet. The proper name of the organization was the International Institute on Intellectual Cooperation, which was funded by the French government. Henri Bergson, Marie Curie, Sigmund Freud, and Albert Einstein were all associated with it. It was transformed into UNESCO in 1946.

6. Wallace Beery, famous movie actor in silent films 1915–1929 and sound movies until 1948. Movies included *Grand Hotel, Tugboat Annie,* and *Treasure Island.*

German pressure in Geneva resulted in weakening the proposed High Commission in several significant ways. The newly established body would (1) be an autonomous organization; (2) deal only with refugees already outside Germany; (3) receive no financial support from the League; and (4) not report to the League but only to the Commission's Governing Body, which in turn would deal directly with the individual governments involved. Furthermore, there would be no criticism of the German government or any discussion of the cause of the refugee problem and, finally, the German government would have nothing to do with the High Commission.

This resolution establishing the High Commission for Refugees (Jewish and Other) Coming from Germany was passed by the Second Committee on October 10 and approved by the League Assembly on the twelfth. Those who had fought so hard for the resolution considered that they had won a victory, probably the best that was possible under the circumstances. Nonetheless, they realized that the weakened High Commission would have a much harder time achieving its goals.

The Council instructed the Secretary General to appoint the High Commissioner in consultation with the representatives of the governments of Britain, Czechoslovakia, France, Italy, the Netherlands, and Spain. The immediate issue then became the choice of a High Commissioner. In August James Rosenberg had suggested McDonald for the post, but he had asked not to be considered, as it would appear that he was being self-serving in working for the establishment of the High Commission. Events forced him to change his mind.

New York, Friday, October 13, 1933

Mr. Feilchenfeld came in. He brought me up to date on the work in connection with the Jewish refugees. Professor Chamberlain came in. We talked over some technical aspects of the League proposal, but there was no opportunity for a full discussion, because I had to hurry up to see President Butler. He was very cordial. This time he was more inclined to express his own views about Germany than to listen to any opinions I might have. He was very critical of the regime, declaring that the leaders were mad; that their government would blow up because of three forces that would not tolerate indefinitely such a situation: (1) the Catholic Church; (2) the trade unions; and (3) the intellectuals. I was not convinced by this argument. He suggested too the desirability of perhaps organizing the Society of Friends of True Germany, but I did not get the impression that he really meant to do anything about it.

As I was leaving, Moley's name came up. President Butler said, "There has been much mystery about why Moley left Washington [the position of assistant secretary of state]. The plain reason is that I told him that he would have to fish or cut bait, that is, he would either have to give up his university salary and stay in Washington or give up the Washington post and come back to the university." Butler added that he had told Moley months before that the danger he ran was that he would not be able to stand the publicity pressure.

Saturday, October 14, 1933

Up to Felix Warburg's apartment at ten o'clock. Mr. Baerwald was there. We did not discuss the general German situation, but got down immediately to the issue of the refugee commissioner. I traced briefly the development of the project and explained the present status. There was a general exchange of views as to personalities. I urged [Raymond] Fosdick and Theodore Roosevelt strongly.

Our talk was interrupted by word from Fosdick's office that I was expected there at eleven o'clock. It was arranged for me to see him at 11:30. Nonetheless, I had to hurry away from Mr. Warburg's house at once. As I was leaving, Mr. Warburg followed me out of the room and said, "Would you take the commissionership? You would be my choice if you were willing to do it. See how Fosdick feels about it." I replied that I thought it would be an excessively difficult job, that I was not at all sure that I was the best person to do it, that I would think it over, that I appreciated very much his suggestion.

As I was going down the steps, Mr. Baerwald called to say that the news had just come that Germany had withdrawn from the Disarmament Conference and from the League. I was rash enough to call back and say that I thought it could not be true.[7]

As I entered Fosdick's office, I threw on his table the early edition of the afternoon paper with its huge headlines about Germany's action. He was as shocked as I had been. We talked at some length about the general situation and were in agreement that we were back in a time comparable to 1914.

I urged that he be willing to be considered for the refugee commissionership. He said that he realized it was an important job, but that he thought he could not do it for various reasons, especially because if Mr. Rockefeller put up a considerable portion of the money needed for administrative purposes, he himself would not be willing to take the commissionership. It would be too much of a Rockefeller proposition in the public eye. He then in turn urged that I do the job. He argued that my training and background fitted me for the post. I then asked him this question: "Do you think that from my own personal point of view it would be desirable for me to do so?" He replied that he did not know enough about my financial affairs to answer definitely, but he then proceeded to argue that, in all probability, one would increase his stature by such an undertaking. He gave me the impression that he would communicate with Avenol on this matter any time it was felt desirable.

As to the Rockefeller financing of the administrative expenses, he said he was sure that Mr. Rockefeller would not do the whole thing, but that he might be willing to go along with others. He had discussed the matter with John D. informally. He had told him that I was on the water [en route from Europe] and that later the situation would be much more fully presented.

7. Germany shocked the world with its withdrawals. The *New York Times* called them the senseless actions of a megalomaniac.

At six o'clock I called at Mr. Warburg's house, and we drove up together to Mr. Rosenberg's, stopping on the way to pick up Ruth. Mr. Warburg's talk and mine in the car was mostly about the situation in Germany.

At Rosenberg's, besides the three of us, were Mr. and Mrs. Rosenberg and Mr. Roger Straus. During dinner we talked about German conditions. After dinner the subject of the High Commissioner was brought up by Mr. Rosenberg, who developed his argument in favor of my acceptance of the post.[8] I demurred and urged Fosdick and Theodore Roosevelt. There was a consensus that Fosdick would be excellent if he would accept. Mr. Straus and Mr. Warburg supported Mr. Rosenberg's point of view about me. I told them that I did not know whether I could afford to accept the position, but that if I were tempted to do so, it would be because of the challenge the place offered from the point of view of larger strategy and broader policy, [rather] than mere relief. They were completely of this mind, saying that the technical relief aspects of the problem could be handled by an assistant, the commissioner to be left free to consider the broader aspects of the problem, such as Palestine, Trans-Jordania, Uganda, etc.

On the financial side, Mr. Rosenberg stressed that I ought to be put in a position where I would have no worry about my house or obligations here. To this Felix agreed. I received the impression that I need not further let this problem stand in the way.[9] Mr. Rosenberg also emphasized the importance of being able to take my wife with me. He cited his own experience twelve years ago when, at Felix's request, he went abroad for a year for the Joint Distribution Committee.

The group seemed to be confident that since the Joint Distribution Committee would supply most of the American funds, their voice would be listened to in London. Mr. Warburg said he would speak to Fosdick and suggest that the latter communicate with Avenol, since Warburg had been asked by Proskauer to do so.

It was agreed that I would communicate to Mr. Rosenberg any new developments which might occur in Washington.

Sunday, October 15, 1933

Mr. Rosenberg called me up to say that Proskauer had talked to Felix, and that Proskauer had agreed as to my availability, and that Felix was, therefore, ready to talk to Fosdick. Later, Felix called me and I promised to try to get him Fosdick's private telephone number.

8. Cyrus Adler had written to Warburg: "but I think it is a fact that none of our European friends, including Doctor Kahn, are favorable to McDonald. This is partly due to the fact that some of them like to hold the limelight and particularly due to the fact that he is an American, and we are not popular, and partially due to the fact of his own vagueness. On the other hand I believe the entire question of the international refugees now depends upon McDonald. If this particular administration is not supported I do not believe the League of Nations will bother to appoint anybody else, so that I feel, as I am sure you do, that everything should be done to support him, as I know you will do." Letter of October 3, 1933, Felix Warburg Papers, Box 315, Adler (b), American Jewish Archives, Cincinnati.

9. This comment McDonald recalled later—see entry of February 23, 1935 (chap. 22).

Family luncheon party.

Left at 5:30 for Washington. On arrival there called up Fosdick and asked him if he would telephone Felix yet that night. He said he would.

On October 16 Felix Warburg telegraphed Otto Schiff in London:

"After considering question of commissioner for German refugees with Fosdick of Rockefeller and leaders American Jewish Committee and JDC[,] feel that appointment should go to American because large amounts to be raised here and such party should by nationality be independent of pressure government which has mandate of Palestine[.] Also should be young and not afraid of hard work and not of type who will stand on dignity too much. Among candidates suggested Theodore Roosevelt not considered well fitted temperamentally[,] Raymond Fosdick well thought of but Rockefeller group would not want him selected[,] but latter suggests James McDonald who well known in Geneva and has shown remarkable ability in helping bring appointment commissioner action, together with Bentwich whom he admires much. Good reason to believe that McDonald would accept if offer endorsed by Washington government and English Jewry. . . ."[10]

Washington, Monday, October 16, 1933

At 10:30 had an appointment with William Phillips. As before, he seemed intelligently interested in what I had to say about Germany, but he was non-committal on the question of the personality of the refugee commissioner. He was inclined to argue against an American for the post, on the ground that such a commissioner would be used as a means of "prying open" the floodgates for Jewish immigration into this country.[11] I argued that this need not be so, but on the contrary the American government perhaps would deal more frankly with an American commissioner than with one of another nationality. As to the individuals for the post, he was very cautious, but indicated no disapproval of me.

Long conference with Jay Pierrepont Moffat. He knows the situation intimately, is inclined to favor speedy action, but the first step of the government must wait on the receipt of a formal invitation. This was expected hourly. He did not seem to be opposed to an American commissioner and was very friendly to me personally. I urged that if the invitation was received, it be accepted

10. Warburg to Schiff, October 15, 1933, Louis D. Brandeis Papers, Louisville Microfilm Series, VI, Roll 100, Z/P 57-2, Library of Congress. British Jewish leaders responded that they preferred Robert Cecil, that McDonald was not trusted in Jewish circles in London and was considered untrustworthy and perhaps too close to the Nazis. Barbara McDonald Stewart, *United States Government Policy on Refugees from Nazism, 1933–1940* (New York: Garland, 1982), 110–111; American Jewish Committee, executive committee minutes, October 18, 1933, Record Group 347, vol. 6, p. 206, Center for Jewish History, New York.

11. McDonald later told Judge Julian Mack that Phillips had been "very unfavorable to Jews." Mack memo, October 17, 1933, Stephen S. Wise Papers, Box 105, Correspondence Zionism (Brandeis), American Jewish Historical Society, New York.

promptly, at least in principle, and that the government not postpone such action while waiting on replies to any detailed questions that it might have. He seemed to favor this course. In general, he thought the way it should be handled was first the American answer to the invitation. If this were an acceptance, then Avenol should ask Wilson if the United States were willing to have an American commissioner, and if so, would they be favorable or at least friendly to X, Y, or Z for the post.[12]

3:30 to see Hull. He was very cordial. He asked me about conditions in Germany and my impression of the reasons for German action. He said he was beginning his study of seventeen months of documents on the Disarmament Conference, with a view to deciding why Germany had left. After we discussed Germany's internal situation, I came to the question of the commissioner. The secretary was not informed in detail on the project, but seemed inclined to cooperate. As to an American, he made no commitment, said that, of course, everybody in the department was very friendly to me personally. He added that this was the sort of matter which he always took up with the President, because it had political implications. He made a memorandum to ask Phillips to keep him informed promptly when action would be called for.

As I was leaving, I told him of some of the kind things I had heard said about him in Europe. He reciprocated by asking me to come and see him any time I was in town.

At 6:15 to Justice Brandeis's[13] apartment. We talked for nearly an hour. He is intensely interested in the refugee project. Positively of the opinion that the commissioner should not be an American, because our government had done so little to help that a commissioner of this nationality would be disadvantaged in all his approaches to other individuals. I told him that Phillips had argued the matter just the other way around, but he was not impressed. He is convinced that Palestine could hold as many people as Massachusetts—four or five million.

I called Rosenberg and told him of developments during the day. He had no additional advice, except of course if I could see the President, it would be to the good.

Tuesday, October 17, 1933

Called up Moffat to see whether he had heard yet from Geneva. He had not.

12. Moffat's diary report of the meeting has a different flavor: "Long talk with James G. McDonald of the Foreign Policy Association, who is extremely anxious to be made High Commissioner of the League for German Refugees. He saw the Secretary and Bill Phillips as well, and tried to prevail upon them to agree in principle to participation in the governing body before knowing exactly what its functions were to be." Moffat Journal, vol. 33, Moffat Papers, October 16, 1933, call number MS Am 1407, Houghton Library, Harvard University. By permission of the Houghton Library, Harvard University.

13. Louis D. Brandeis, first Jewish Supreme Court Justice, leader and elder statesman of American Zionism.

Lunch at the White House with Mrs. Roosevelt. Those at the table were Mrs. Roosevelt, her daughter, Miss LeHand,[14] another secretary, and two other family friends, and a Mr. Newbold from Boston, a Mr. Robinson, the son of Corinne Robinson. Before the conversation became general, I told Mrs. Roosevelt about the refugee project and the necessity for action by the President in a few days.

Mrs. Roosevelt asked me if I had seen the President. I told her no, that no appointment had been arranged. She turned to Miss LeHand and asked her why. The reply was that he had not had a moment free. I am confident Mrs. Roosevelt's interest will make the appointment easier.[15] Then the conversation became general, I giving my impressions of the German situation. I judged from the responses of Mrs. Roosevelt and Miss LeHand that the White House was filled with a real apprehension of what new developments in Germany meant.

Robinson, who was a classmate of Hanfstaengl's, could not curb his indignation at what I reported.

As usual at White House informal luncheons, the food was adequate, but not too generous or rich.

Went from the White House to see Bill Bullitt[16] at the State Department. We had a pleasant chat together. He is very fatalistic about what he considers inevitable conflict in Europe. Said that he hoped we might have a meal together the next time I came down.

Four o'clock train to New York.

After dinner chatted with John W. Davis,[17] who seems to feel that not only in the international field, but in that of private rights we are turning the hands of the clock back rapidly.

Home late and very tired.

New York, Wednesday, October 18, 1933

Mr. Feilchenfeld called up to ask if there were any new developments. I told him I was going to be seeing Rabbi Wise and Mr. Deutsch, but he rather intimated that this might be crossing wires and that perhaps I should go to him, since he was supposed to be a kind of clearing house. I told him this was a mat-

14. Marguerite "Missy" LeHand, the president's personal secretary, 1933–1941. Had a longstanding personal and professional relationship with FDR.

15. In a letter the following day McDonald summarized what he had said at the luncheon: "I am anxious to see the President in reference to three specific questions connected with the United States' cooperation in the setting up of the High Commission for German Refugees. . . . The U.S. is being asked to name a member on the Governing Board of fifteen and will also, I think, informally be asked two other questions: whether an American commissioner would be acceptable and as to the availability of certain persons. What I should like to say to the President in reference to these three points would not take more than ten or fifteen minutes of his time." The meeting did not take place. McDonald to Missy LeHand, November 1, 1933, McDonald Papers, USHMM.

16. William C. Bullitt, special assistant to the secretary of state, soon to be ambassador to Russia, 1934–1936.

17. John W. Davis, leading New York lawyer with the firm of Davis, Polk, Wardwell, Gardner and Reed, Democratic presidential candidate 1924.

ter I would have to take up with the two gentlemen directly, and I would let him know if there were any new developments of striking importance.

....

At two o'clock to the Paramount Building for conference with Deutsch and Rabbi Wise. I told them of my visit to Washington. They agreed that if there were an American commissioner, he ought to be the nominee of no particular group, certainly not of the Jewish group; that he should be persona grata to all of them; that he should have the support of his government; that he should be really interested in the Jews as a people and not in making use of the present crisis for his own advancement; that he should be persona grata also to the official group.

They both said that they would like to have me do the job. We discussed the broad outlines of what the commissioner's task should be. They agreed that the immediate relief problem was only the smaller part of his total opportunities.

As I was leaving, Rabbi Wise asked if I would be willing to meet with members of the Joint Committee. I said I would put myself at their service.

In the evening meeting of the [FPA] board. I gave a brief resume of my European impressions, and of the work done at Geneva.

Thursday, October 19, 1933

Lunched with Capt. Railey at the Harvard Club. He told me of his plan to urge the secretary of state to consider announcing at once the United States's establishment of a new relationship with the League, in order to counteract the discouraging effect of the German withdrawal from Geneva. He promised to call me up and let me know how he got on with the secretary.

Saturday, October 21, 1933

Long conference in the office with Professor Chamberlain, chiefly about technical aspects of the new office in Geneva.

Sunday, October 22, 1933

Had lunch at the Sam Lewisohn's[18] in the country. Besides Sam and Margaret and Ruth and I were the Feises, the Ordway Teads, and the Lilienthals.[19] I was impressed again by the large emotional element in the Jewish outlook on the German situation. Herbert Feis showed intense emotion when any aspect of this problem was talked about.

18. Sam Lewisohn, heir to mining interests, banker, philanthropist. His wife, Margaret Seligman Lewisohn, was active in many educational and art projects.

19. David E. Lilienthal, director of the Tennessee Valley Authority, 1933–1941, later chairman of the Atomic Energy Commission.

Monday, October 23, 1933

....

Capt. Railey called me on the phone to say that at a conference which included Fosdick, Shotwell,[20] and others, it was decided before he went to Washington that he should not present to the secretary of state the plan which he had talked to me about a few days previous. He reported that the secretary was personally very cordial and that, as far as he was concerned, the Geneva leak about the Department's plans was no longer held against him. He intimated, however, that the Department was still resentful at Sweetser.

In the afternoon over to the National Peace Conference, where I spoke for about twenty minutes and answered questions for a somewhat longer period.

In his speech and in an article published the next day in the Christian Science Monitor, *McDonald saw the adamant stand of Germany's neighbors and the hardening of alliances as strengthening Hitler's hold over the German people.*

["Largely because of their hatred of the 'dictated' Treaty of Versailles . . . [and perceived treatment of Germany] as a second-class power, the great majority of the German people have gladly, even exultantly accepted the Nazi program— . . . and the regimentation of the nation until it has become a completely responsive instrument in the hands of an absolute leader."]

He concluded that only bold steps in Europe supported by the United States could avert an impending disaster.[21]

Tuesday, October 24, 1933

Lunch with Mrs. Kahn.[22] Afterwards conferred with Felix Warburg.

In the evening spoke at the FPA meeting at the Town Hall with Mrs. Dean,[23] Buell presiding. I thought Mrs. Dean spoke well, but with considerably less originality of material than I had come to expect from her. Moreover, I think her hands are beginning to play too prominent a part. The question period was draggy for various reasons.

The State Department refused to become involved in discussions of the High Commissioner. In response to a letter from Henry Morgenthau recommending Mc-

20. James T. Shotwell, professor of international relations at Columbia University, 1906–1942.

21. *Christian Science Monitor,* October 24, 1933.

22. Mrs. Otto Kahn, active in the FPA, wife of a Kuhn Loeb partner and daughter of Abraham Wolff, one of Kuhn Loeb's original investors. Otto Kahn was the first Jewish board member of the Metropolitan Opera, and he owned most of its stock.

23. Vera Micheles Dean, editor of the FPA research publications, 1931–1938, later research director and editor of the FPA *Headline* series, 1938–1961.

Donald, Secretary of State Hull wrote only that he "had known Mr. McDonald for many years and had a high regard for him."[24]

Wednesday, October 25, 1933

Found at the office on arrival there, a night letter from Mr. May indicating that the Committee of the Council was meeting on the twenty-sixth to elect the High Commissioner. I called up Warburg and Rosenberg and learned that nothing effective had been done. Since it was thus evident that I had to move, I communicated with the following persons and secured the results described.

I telephoned to Mrs. Otto Kahn, who said she would be glad to cable Count de Maud'hui, who communicated with the QD [possibly Quai d'Orsay—French Foreign Office]. More significant in that direction probably was the prompt action taken by A.B. At my request he telephoned to D. in Paris, who, as I was told later, communicated at once with Avenol. Mrs. M. [May?] cabled to her friend M., presumably then in Geneva. She also cabled her friend J. M. in London. Towards the same end N [Novak?] cabled to Oungre[25] in Geneva. Mr. May, I assumed, communicated with Mr. P. Stone, to whom I talked on the telephone several times, saw Ambassador R., who cabled at once. Thus action was initiated to five centers. Nothing was done, however, directly or indirectly in reference to Great Britain. I felt strongly that since there was another person being pressed from that quarter, it would be unwise and unfair to attempt to influence the Foreign Office.

. . . .

The British government, like some others, reluctantly yielded to the argument that an American high commissioner would facilitate U.S. involvement and make it easier to get funds from the United States. The League Secretariat, happy to have U.S. participation in some form, supported McDonald. The committee then appointed him.

In the evening spoke at the Young Men's Hebrew Association in Mt. Vernon, where I was introduced as the "next High Commissioner for German refugees." I disclaimed any such honor. The chairman's information had come apparently only from the dispatch in the *Baltimore Sun* a week or so earlier.

. . . .

Thursday, October 26, 1933

When I reached the office, I was greeted by Miss Martin and Miss Miller, who rather tearfully congratulated me. I am afraid they both felt that I was unresponsive. As I read the cables from Avenol and May and Sweetser, I felt no particular exaltation—rather, a deep sense of the many things which had to be done at once.

24. Hull to Morgenthau, Felix Warburg Papers, Box 303, JDCb, American Jewish Archives, Cincinnati.
25. Louis Oungre, head of the Jewish Colonization Association (ICA).

I called Felix Warburg, and he expressed great delight, and I arranged to see him at two o'clock.

Miss Miner called to say that Fosdick had had similar news from Geneva.

Very satisfactory conferences with Miss Ogden and Miss Pratt about cancellation of my speaking engagements. Both women were completely willing to put first my needs. It was decided to send someone else to Providence, and later it was decided to cancel or substitute other speakers for all my engagements.

Mr. Novak called to congratulate me and to suggest that, since he was going to return to the Foreign Office, he would like to be assigned to Geneva on my staff, presumably remaining on the payroll of his own government. I thanked him for the suggestion but made no commitment.

Long talk with Rosenberg about plans and about Samuel Untermyer.[26] During the day Dr. Nathan called up and David Hyman telephoned to say that anything he could do would be done, and Prof. Chamberlain and I talked about plans. I later had a considerable discussion with Rosenberg about the formal statement I should issue, and decided not to issue any that day or until I had decided definitely to accept.

Lunched with John D. Rockefeller III at the Harvard Club. Our talk was all about whether I should accept or not. John argued in the negative, on the ground that work was needed here at home, that the FPA was doing a unique job, and that I was essential to make that work most effective. I argued that the new possibility would continue my education in a different but closely related field, and that the opportunity for service was large. He was not really impressed by the latter argument, but conceded that if I wished to take the place for the sake of its effect on me, I would feel that his objections were outweighed. He evidently was impressed by the invitation, but being instinctively rather anti-Semitic, he had difficulty in realizing that the job to be done was one of potentially large scope. As we walked up the avenue after lunch, he invited me to come in and see their new offices, but I had no time, but had to hurry up to Warburg's.

Felix and I had a long talk. He again emphasized his great pleasure that I was to undertake the task. He spoke of young Parkes[27] as a possible associate, but without urging him. He mentioned also a Mrs. Seltzer, formerly a secretary of Mrs. Warburg. . . .

While I was at Warburg's house, Judge Proskauer called up to express his pleasure at my appointment.

In the evening I went up to Fosdick's church to attend the dinner of the Federal Council of Churches. It was a mistake to have done so, or at least I thought so when the evening was over. I was very tired when I arrived, and of course did not feel free to speak on the subject for which I was announced—"Political and Economic Trends in Germany." Instead, I spoke in very general

26. Samuel Untermyer, corporate lawyer, government adviser, ardent Zionist, and leader of the American Jewish boycott of German goods.

27. Dr. James Parkes, worked with the International Students' Movement and was later involved in scholarly research on relations between Jews and Christians.

terms and in a way which was not at all satisfactory to me, but what was worse, I had to listen to a fifty-minute speech by Dr. Richter and three shorter talks which lasted until after ten. I hardly survived.

After the meeting several of my friends in the audience congratulated me on the new appointment. I drove home with the Caverts[28] and Miss Warren.[29]

The press reported enthusiastically on McDonald's appointment, saying that the choice "was well received in League circles, where he is widely and favorably known." U.S. newspapers commented on his wide experience in Europe and in Germany in particular and his successful efforts to bring about the creation of the High Commission. The British, however, were disappointed in the appointment. They had hoped for a world leader and thought that the appointment had been made with undue haste.[30]

Friday, October 27, 1933

Richard Waldo called me on the telephone to say that he had had from a source very close to the conservative Jews in New York the report that I had almost lost the office because of my insistence to a personal salary larger than that of my whole Secretariat; that the Kuhn Loeb hesitated in their support of me because of my demands. I was amazed at this information because there had been at no time any discussion of a figure for my salary with anyone, and the people at Nassau and Williams[31] would in all likelihood have been the last to raise an objection of this sort. I asked Waldo if he wouldn't do me the favor in the near future of letting me hear any other rumors which might come to his ears about my job. He said he would.

Mrs. Kahn telephoned to tell me that she had heard from de Maud'hui. . . .

Downtown to see Jerome Hess,[32] then over to Mr. Warburg's office. I told him of the Richard Waldo report and of the possibility that there might be someone in his group who was not discreet and who made a good story out of whole cloth. He assured me that I need not have any concern about this in the future.

When I left his office, I chatted for a while with Freddie Warburg and then with James Warburg. Had a bite of very late lunch with Frank Davis and talked with Mr. Liebman for a few minutes afterwards.

In the late afternoon the [FPA] executive committee met at the office. The prevailing view was that I should be asked to accept a leave of absence, but I

28. Samuel McCrae Cavert, general secretary of the Federal Council of Churches of Christ in America, close personal friend of McDonald.

29. Constance Warren, president of Sarah Lawrence College, 1929–1945.

30. "McDonald Named as Refugee Chief," *New York Times,* October 27, 1933, p. 1. "Jewish Refugee Aid Appointed," *Philadelphia Bulletin,* October 26, 1933. "James M'Donald Accepts High Commissionership," *Kansas City Star,* October 26, 1933. "Admirable Choice," *Northampton* (Mass.) *Gazette,* October 27, 1933. "James G. McDonald's Job," *Holyoke* (Mass.) *Transcript,* October 28, 1933. "To Aid German Refugees," *Waterbury* (Conn.) *Republican,* October 28, 1933. Barbara McDonald Stewart, *United States Government Policy on Refugees from Nazism 1933–1940* (New York: Garland, 1982), 110–111.

31. Kuhn Loeb's offices were at Nassau and Williams streets, near Wall Street.

32. Jerome Hess, lawyer, counsel to Hardin, Hess, Eder and Rashap, active in the FPA and in international law.

urged that there be a clean break, that Buell be asked to assume responsibility, and that he not be left with a feeling that he was warming a chair for someone else. This view was finally accepted. The question as to when my resignation should become effective was left for later consideration. . . .

Saturday, October 28, 1933

Conference with Henry Morgenthau at his house. Later lunch with Felix Warburg, Baerwald, and Liebman. Long discussion about Jewish personalities in France, England, Belgium, and Holland. The chief names mentioned were Prof. Oualid, André Meyer, Theodore Rousseau, Prof. Speyer, and several others. There was a good deal of discussion, too, as to ways in which the ICA could be brought in. There was the feeling that so far as the governing board was concerned, there should be only two or three Jewish governmental representatives. In general, I had the very definite impression that the group these men represented would go along in almost any program which I helped to work out. That evening dined alone with Rosenberg. He outlined fully his concept of the work, stressing that it would be viewed in very large terms. On the financial side he gave the same assurance as had been given by Warburg.

Sunday, October 29, 1933

In the evening attended and presided over the dinner of the Friends of Turkey on the tenth anniversary of the establishment of the Turkish Republic. I had a pleasant chat during the dinner with the Turkish Ambassador and the Greek Minister; otherwise the occasion for me was uneventful, except that I nearly introduced Mrs. Elkus as the widow of the former ambassador, though her husband sat only three places from me on my right, quite alive.

Monday, October 30, 1933

Talked to Fosdick about Mr. Rockefeller's possible contribution to the administrative expenses of the High Commission's office.[33] He was encouraging and suggested that I write a letter stressing the strategic advantage of non-Jewish money at the beginning.

Interesting conference with Dr. Gustav Stolper, who impressed me most favorably again as he had some years ago in Berlin.

. . . .

Long talk with Eustace Seligman on the phone about the FPA. He urged that I reconsider my resignation and take a leave of absence, but I was not persuaded.

Luncheon with David Schweitzer. He talked with great frankness about

33. On November 1 McDonald wrote John D. Rockefeller, Jr., asking for a contribution of $25,000, urging that "nothing less is involved than principles vital to civilization itself." He pointed out the strategic advantage of having one-half of the sum, $50,000, pledged by non-Jews since "not all refugees were Jews and the Jews, after all, are only the victims." McDonald Papers, USHMM. There is no evidence that Rockefeller ever gave any money to the High Commission.

Jewish personalities and the whole problem to be faced by the High Commission office.

After lunch up to see Patterson[34] at the NBC. He was so cordial that I realized for the first time that I had become something of a personality in the eyes of the broadcasting authorities. During our chat we were joined by Dave Lawrence. Patterson called up Royal[35] and gave orders that I was to be seen just as soon as our return. Moreover, Patterson said that the NBC services would be at my disposal at any time from Europe or in the States.

While waiting to see Royal, chatted for a few minutes with Max Jordan, who had just come to the States on the Zeppelin. Royal was extremely cordial, stressed my great contribution to broadcasting, the exceptional quality of my voice, personality, etc. We then talked about the FPA and agreed upon a basis for carrying on. The substance of this dictated in a memorandum which is on file at the FPA office.

Talked again to Fosdick in the later afternoon, and to David Heyman, with whom I stressed the importance of a contribution from the New York Foundation to the FPA to clear the deficit in the radio fund and to make funds available for me to draw on until official funds were at my disposal. He was friendly to the proposal.

Tuesday, October 31, 1933

Talked to Harry Fosdick again. Arranged for Dr. Kohn[36] to speak at his church a week from the following Wednesday, thus freeing Raymond Fosdick, who agreed to take my date in December.

. . . .

Talked to Rosenberg about the desirability of quick action by the New York Foundation. He said he would help.

Lunch with Kohn and Professor Duggan at the Rockefeller Institute. Cohn presented a very suggestive outline of the work of the High Commission. It was, I imagine, very much like that which Mr. May would present. Duggan spoke about the professorial problem.[37]

. . . .

Over to Mr. Filene's at the Commodore for a talk before going home. He said that he would help in any way he could, but I began to think he is getting old because he spoke more of the past than of the future.

34. Richard Patterson, vice president NBC, 1935.

35. John F. Royal, NBC vice president for programs, 1938–1953.

36. Hans Kohn, German refugee who came to the United States from Prague in 1933. Writer and professor of history at Smith College, 1934–1941.

37. Stephen Duggan, director of the International Institute of Education (IIE), 1919–1946. On October 31 Duggan established the Emergency Committee in Aid of Foreign Scholars, a separate body from the IIE. The professorial problem involved finding positions for German academics in the United States and raising money to pay their salaries.

7. November 1933: A Bridge from Lausanne to Berlin

New York, Wednesday, November 1, 1933

Parkes came in, and we made tentative arrangements for him to go on this first trip. . . .

David Heyman called to say that the New York Foundation had voted the FPA $5,000.

Talked to Mrs. Leach[1] for the third time during recent days about an approach to Roosevelt in reference to seeing me before I sailed. After our talk I shared her view that it would be a mistake to make the effort unless, as was not practicable, she could see Mrs. Roosevelt personally.

Arranged with Cavert to have a group of Jews and non-Jews meet me before I sailed.

Lunch with Judge Mack.[2] He told me in detail of his interviews in Washington on the immigration problem. These are embodied in a memorandum which he sent me to the boat. He stressed the importance of an early conference with Frankfurter.

Mack was at the center of efforts to work out an arrangement by which German Jews could qualify for immigration visas to the United States without being barred as potential "public charges." This regulation barring anyone who might not be self-supporting, not the size of the immigration quota for Germany, was the main obstacle to German Jewish immigration to the United States at this time.

In the afternoon gave interviews to the *World Telegram* and the Jewish Telegraphic Agency, but refused to talk about my plans for the new job.

Conference with Feilchenfeld at my request. He promised to send me data on his ideas of the way in which the office might be organized and as to how it might work.

1. Agnes Brown Leach (Mrs. Henry Goddard Leach), civic leader, on the board of the FPA, active in public health and in the Democratic Party.

2. Judge Julian Mack, U.S. Circuit Court judge, previously head of the Zionist Organization of America, a close associate of Justice Brandeis in Zionist affairs, and a friend of President Roosevelt.

Thursday, November 2, 1933

Nine o'clock appointment at the office at my request with Rabbi Wise, Deutsch, and three other members of the American Jewish Congress Executive. We had a completely harmonious meeting.

A little later talked with Bernard Richards and then went over to see Henry Goldman. He should be helpful later.

Long talk on the telephone with Rosenberg. He urged me to press for an appointment with the President, but I told him that I had decided not to do so, but instead would talk with Phillips. I reminded him of his promise to keep Miss Jaffe in mind. He urged that I should think of the passport problem very early. And incidentally, he suggested that I ask Max Kohler for data on the immigration question.

Lunch with Henry Ittleson. I explained at length the genesis of the High Commission and my conception of its work. Before we had finished, he had, I think, lost any sense of injustice which he had felt because of my reticence at the first Town Hall meeting and because of my use of the cockroach illustration in my talk at his house. He gave the same assurance on the financial matter as had Warburg and Rosenberg. He said that I might be completely at ease on that score.

Down to Mr. Lamont's office. We had a friendly chat about my new job in which he expressed much interest, and then in my new capacity as a member of the "finance committee," I asked him for $3,500 for the FPA. I left with the impression that he would give it.

Mr. Wainhouse[3] and one of his associates from the International Migration Service came in, but we had very little time to talk. They told me, however, of a meeting in Geneva very soon of an international committee on the problem of immigration, which seemed to relate itself closely to my work. I should inquire into this at Geneva.

Up to see Mr. Untermyer at his apartment. We talked for more than an hour, he stressing the importance of the boycott movement, but even more his present efforts to ferret out and destroy the Nazi anti-American propaganda in the States. He was most cordial personally and will, I think, refrain from any open attacks even if he later disagrees on policies adopted by the High Commission.

Then over to Arthur Sulzberger's house. I ran into a family party just about ready to sit down to dinner. I was invited to join by Mrs. Sulzberger, but having another date, I declined. Talked with Arthur first in the study, and then later with the family at the table. He stressed his resentment at the activities of Untermyer and the American Jewish Congress and pledged his support to me in any way that he could help.

Then over to Mrs. Kahn's to dinner with Ruth. At ten o'clock we were joined by Mr. Kahn, and shortly before eleven we started for home, I completely exhausted.

3. David W. Wainhouse, international lawyer, lecturer on political science at Fordham University, 1932–1934, assistant U.S. attorney 1934–1941.

Friday, November 3, 1933

Talked during this morning with Van Kirk and again with Felix Warburg and Henry Morgenthau. Spoke with Stone on the telephone, as I had done several times during the previous days. From what he said and from my talk with Phillips the day before, I received the impression that the administration might be considering Houghton[4] as the American member of the Governing Body. This seemed to me to offer many disadvantages.

Yesterday I talked to Phillips on the telephone. He was extremely cordial, extended warm congratulations and best wishes. We then talked about the type of American representative on the Governing Body. He did not, however, mention names. He asked me what I would think of an ex-ambassador, and I said it would all depend on the individual.

Lunch at the *New York Times*. Went first to Wylie's office. I told him frankly what I thought about the possibility of Houghton serving on the board and suggested that he might, in the interest of the President himself, telephone to Washington, of course without in any way involving me.

At luncheon were present besides Wylie and myself, Mr. Ogden, Mr. Finley, Mr. Adler and his father,[5] and Bernard Gimbel.[6] The talk was mostly about my work and possible American members on the Governing Body. Baker, Cox, and Fosdick were considered admirable. As I had to hurry off in order to attend the Federal Council meeting, Dr. Finley walked out with me and assured me that Wylie would move.

Down to the Federal Council. The attendance was much better than I could have hoped for. There were perhaps twelve or fifteen Jewish representative from the right to the left, and an excellent group of non-Jews. I spoke briefly. The substance of my remarks was taken down by Miss Jaffe, but nothing was released to the press.[7] From Van Kirk's introductory remarks and from what was said to me by many of those present, I had every reason to feel assured of generous support.

Walked up the street with Horace Kallen,[8] who stressed the danger of anti-

4. Alanson B. Houghton, U.S. ambassador to Germany, 1922–1925, ambassador to Great Britain 1925–1928.

5. Julius Ochs Adler, president and publisher of the *Chattanooga Times*. General manager of the *New York Times* 1935–1965. Nephew of Adolph Ochs.

6. Bernard Gimbel, president of Gimbel Brothers Department Stores, 1927–1953.

7. In addition to explaining the scope and mission of the High Commission, McDonald emphasized that the refugee problem was not only a Jewish problem but Christian in the sense that many refugees were not Jewish and so-called Christians had created the problem. He concluded: "My hope is that indirectly, through this office, I may play some role in seeing to it that Christians throughout the world—nominal Christians—adopt and maintain towards non-Christians something more of a semblance of a Christian attitude." Transcript of remarks made by McDonald at the November 3, 1933, meeting of the Federal Council of Churches, McDonald Papers, USHMM.

8. Horace Kallen, born in Germany, professor of philosophy and psychology in several universities and at the New School for Social Research. Also involved in the FPA when it was the League of Free Nations Association. Kallen's warning was probably a reference to an anti-immigrant tendency in the French press during October and November, by which time there were between ten thousand and fourteen thousand refugees in France. See Vicki Caron, *Uneasy Asylum* (Stanford: Stanford University Press, 1999), 13–42.

Semitism among the refugees in Paris and suggested that I look into this matter just as soon as possible.

At five o'clock to the dentist, and afterwards rode up town with Felix Warburg, who took me home. He came into the house in order, as he said to Ruth, to tell her that if there was anything she needed during my absence, that she should call him up at any hour, day or night. He assured me again of his great happiness in my acceptance of the post.

The night before McDonald left for Europe, he gave a talk to a group of people called together by Mr. Van Kirk of the Federal Council of Churches expressing his sense of mission and outlining how he envisioned his job. As he was speaking to a Christian group, he first emphasized that the problem of refugees was as much a non-Jewish problem as a Jewish one since Hitler put labor leaders, socialists, potential political opponents, and anyone who did not please him into concentration camps. He continued:

[The job of the High Commissioner will not be to displace what is being done by other organizations, but to try to supplement and make more effective what is being done. Second, his job will be, as I see it, to formulate programs or a program on which there can be more general agreement than now appears to be the case in reference to most of the programs that are being proposed. That it will be easy to reach agreement on a program or a series of programs I do not believe. I know human beings too well to believe that even in a matter so vital as this, men easily merge their differences, preconceptions, and prejudices in the forming of a varied program. Nevertheless, the job of the High Commissioner will be to do what he and his associates can to ward off that difficulty. Third is negotiations with the governments concerned. The High Commissioner will have the duty and responsibility to carry on negotiations on specific questions: what these governments might be willing to do toward receiving refugees or in other ways cooperating. The High Commissioner will sooner or latter carry on, directly or indirectly, officially or unofficially, negotiations with the German government. It is my impression that technically the duties of the High Commissioner's office do not take him beyond the frontiers of Germany. But everybody knows that, if the High Commissioner's office is to function effectively, sooner or later, in practice if not in theory, that limitation will have to be broken down. It will not be the least difficult of the High Commissioner's job to find a way toward building a bridge between the outside and the inside. Presumably, a part of the negotiations with the German government will be the question of passports. . . . Then there will be the question of the funds of the refugees within Germany. This is a very vital matter. Most of the refugees have left Germany with virtually nothing. The official indication is 200 Marks. But even with the dollar at its present valuation, 200 Marks ($60 or $70) is not very much. I have read various estimates of the total of the capital left behind. It runs into very large figures, possibly two or three billions of Marks. One of the jobs of the High Commissioner, through his own office or through some other agency, will be to find a way to withdraw as substantial a portion as possible of these funds to be made available to those to whom they belong and to the people that need them.

As to the methods of the work to be undertaken, I know little more than you. The machinery is quite simple. The Council of the League of Nations has named a High Commissioner and a Governing Board to be composed of fifteen countries, including all of the countries bordering on Germany except Austria, each of the countries to name one member to the board.

You have, then, a High Commissioner and you have a Governing Board. These two have been created by the League and set afloat on the uncharted waters of the future. There are no precise precedents for this task. The Nansen Commission was not the same, nor was the situation of the Greek refugees.[9] Both of those were directly under the League, and, in both, the men were responsible to the Council and had the advice of the League and the benefit of the Secretariat and reported regularly and directly to the Council. In the present case I think it is quite different: the League creates the instrumentality and leaves it to sink or swim.

At the moment there is available immediately to the High Commissioner no money at all. I am going to Germany with two associates on funds borrowed from my own association. They show great faith in me by being willing to advance me the necessary funds. The League, it is true, has voted 25,000 Swiss francs [to be repaid later]. That, if one had it here today, is not a munificent sum. It will be sufficient to set up the skeleton of an organization, but the problem of setting up the organization will have to be met at once. I hasten to say that the money matter in this concerns me less than anything else. I am convinced that the administrative expenses will be met generously by the people who believe in its work; that the essential funds, no matter how large they may be, whether five or ten million dollars or more, will be found.

I said at the beginning that this is not primarily a Jewish problem—not in the beginning, and not technically—but in certain broad aspects it is a Jewish problem. What is happening in Germany is something so terrible, so shocking, that it is difficult to give to any one who has not been there an adequate sense of it. . . . You must use brutal, cold, contemptuous language to show what the Nazis feel toward the Jew. . . . But what is important is that what is happening today in Germany may happen next week or next month in Austria. And if this thing becomes the rule in Germany and Austria and on the whole succeeds in its policy, then I think life for the Jews anywhere on the continent between France and Russia may become impossible. Even in our own country we see from time

9. In 1922 the Nansen International Office for Refugees began to settle Greeks displaced from Asia Minor by the Greco-Turkish War of 1919–1922. Its work lasted ten years, demonstrating to Norman Bentwich that the League of Nations could be effective in humanitarian matters under the right circumstances. See Norman Bentwich, *My 77 Years* (Philadelphia: Jewish Publication Society, 1961), 130–131.

to time evidences of prejudice that may disquiet the most conservative among us.][10]

Saturday, November 4, 1933

Did not go to the office, but instead went directly to the boat. Found Miss Wertheimer there in something of a state. She was worried about the British attitude, but nothing she told me surprised me or caused me much uneasiness. She left me detailed memoranda.

On the boat there was a conference with the press and a talk before the motion picture camera. I hope I avoided indiscretions. I tried to stress the fact that the question was not primarily a Jewish one.

Was pleased that several members of the outer office staff came to say goodbye. Mr. Ittleson was also there. As usual, I urged my own family to go on home and not to wait for the boat to go out.

***Ile de France,* Saturday, November 4–Friday, November 10, 1933**

The voyage has been uneventful but pleasant. M. Villar, the purser, was most kind in transferring me to a deluxe suite. Miss Sawyer and I have managed to get up most of the back work, and there have been frequent conferences with Hyman, Schweitzer, and Parkes. The other persons I have seen most of during the voyage include Mme. Goldet, who should be helpful in Paris; Mr. Charles Donahue, a French Canadian; Miss Camac; the Hertelindys of the Hungarian Foreign Office; M. Arthur, secretary of the Line; and a very few others. Lunched one day with Emil Ludwig.[11] He is anxious to be of service, and I have promised to communicate with him later. My only regret in connection with the voyage is that there was no deck tournament, and that, therefore, I had no opportunity to win another cup.

Mr. Bentwich came on in Plymouth and joined me in my sitting room a little after 8:30. We had two hours of frank and friendly talk. I told him that I was surprised at the Geneva election, and he told me that they had supported Cecil to the end, and had been surprised by the quickness of the decision.[12] With that out of the way, we talked about representation on the Governing Body. I pointed out some of the difficulties, but did not commit myself. I outlined my conception of the work of the High Commission, both in its more immediate problem of helping to coordinate the planning and the raising of funds and carrying on negotiations with the governments and the longer-range, less tangible task of helping to humanize Jewish and non-Jewish relationships.

10. Transcript of remarks of James Grover McDonald at meeting called by Mr. Van Kirk, Federal Council of Churches, McDonald Papers, Barbara McDonald Stewart's research notes, USHMM.

11. Emil Ludwig (Emil Cohen), well-known popular biographer of Goethe, Bismarck, Napoleon, and others. A Swiss citizen.

12. These comments refer to the election of McDonald as High Commissioner.

Norman Bentwich

Norman Bentwich, Zionist, lawyer, scholar, and deputy to James G. McDonald on the High Commission for Refugees. Central Zionist Archives, Jerusalem.

Norman de Mattos Bentwich (1883–1971) was born in London into an accomplished Anglo-Jewish family of lawyers and scholars. His father, Herbert Bentwich, was a distinguished solicitor and a leading Zionist who had Theodor Herzl visit his home. After attending Cambridge, Bentwich was called to the bar in 1908 and in 1912 entered the Egyptian Ministry of Justice as inspector of native courts. From 1915 to 1918 he served in the British Army (Camel Transport Corps) and took part in General Allenby's conquest of Jerusalem.

After the establishment of the British mandate in Palestine in 1922, Bentwich was named attorney general of Palestine, a post in which he served until 1929. During the 1920s Bentwich increasingly became an advocate of Arab-Jewish rapprochement and a bi-national state. In 1932 he was appointed professor of international relations at the Hebrew University, a position he held until his retirement in 1951.

After Hitler came to power, Bentwich became interested in the plight of Jewish refugees. In 1933 he accepted the position as McDonald's deputy. In this capacity he traveled to many European countries, working with local Jewish communities and refugee organizations in an effort to coordinate relief and seek prospects for the admission of refugees. McDonald's diary shows him to be a man of real talent and energy, but without great pretence or ego.

Bentwich became the chairman of the Council for German Jewry (1936–1939), and during World War II he headed the Jewish Committee for Refugee Aid. From 1943 to 1946 he was an adviser to the Ethiopian emperor and attended the Paris peace conference in 1946 as a member of the Ethiopian delegation. During the postwar period he was chairman of Britain's National Peace Council and played a major role in securing restitution and compensation for victims of Nazi persecution.

Bentwich was the author of nearly thirty books, ranging in subject from international law to refugees to Judeo-Greek civilization. He was married to Helen Franklin, a politically active member of another well-known Anglo-Jewish family. He died in London on April 8, 1971, and, according to his wish, was buried on Mount Scopus in Jerusalem.

Lunched with Bentwich after finishing dictating to Miss Sawyer. Bentwich and I continued our discussion of plans. I told him that I was surprised at the statement attributed to Dr. Weizmann[13] to the effect that Palestine was outside of the jurisdiction of the High Commission. He explained that this had been said because Simon and the British Foreign Office had declared that they did not want to have another agency to deal with on the matter of certificates for the mandated territory. I replied that, of course, I could understand that, and that I had never had any intention of intervening in such a technical matter, but it did seem to me that, from the point of view of the Jews themselves, it was a serious mistake to accept the contention without a struggle that the High Commission was not concerned with Palestine. I explained that if that contention were maintained, obviously it would be impossible for the High Commissioner to give his moral support to a financial program, half or approximately that amount of which was intended for Palestine. Bentwich recognized this difficulty and seemed to feel that in the sense in which I meant it, Palestine was not outside the jurisdiction of the High Commission.

The question came up of his own plans. He said, "I suppose you have been flooded with applications." I said, of course, we have had a great many. I then explained my conception of the High Commission's Secretariat, that I did not see how it could be made up of organizational representatives or nominees; that, on the contrary, there would have to be a central loyalty and that the High Commissioner would have to be free to choose his associates on the basis of that consideration and of his opinion as [to] how each individual might be fitted into an organized whole. As this talk developed, I had sort of a sense that Bentwich might be thinking of himself, but I did not realize at all until I was told the next day in Geneva that his name had formally been presented by Weizmann to Avenol. Weizmann called Bentwich's appointment to a responsible position in the High Commission "of the utmost importance."[14]

We talked about the financial situation in the States, especially about how this might affect a money raising campaign.

After lunch I completed plans for disembarkation, said goodbye to M. Villar and M. Artur, the Line officials, and expressed the hope that I might be with them on the sixth of December. They certainly had done everything they could to make the voyage pleasant.

On the dock we were met by a representative of the American Express, who reassured us of our transportation to Geneva. On the train I sat with Bentwich most of the time, but before the train left I had my first experience with the European press, but I had nothing to say which interested them, for obviously I

13. Dr. Chaim Weizmann, British Zionist leader who helped convince the British in 1917 to issue the Balfour Declaration supporting a homeland for the Jews in Palestine. A brilliant scientist, he later became the first president of the State of Israel.

14. Weizmann to Avenol, November 2, 1933, in *The Letters and Papers of Chaim Weizmann*, ed. Barnett Litvinoff, vol.16—series A, June 1933–Aug. 1935 (Rutgers University Press Transaction Books, 1978), pp. 10–11.

could tell them nothing about my plans and certainly could not comment as they desired, on the situation in Germany, or the effects of my plans upon the attitude of Hitler towards the Jews.

On the train Bentwich and I continued our discussion on the general work of the High Commission, its relations to the organizations, etc. I told him with considerable emphasis that I could not visualize the High Commissioner as an agent of the organizations; that instead, he must be more than that or he would be nothing. I also stressed the importance of Bentwich and Weizmann in Paris the next day attempting to iron out some of the differences between the English and the JDC, which became apparent as soon as Schweitzer and Hyman had read the report of the London conference. Bentwich recognized that this would be important.

Occasionally during the trip to Paris I talked for brief periods with Schweitzer and Hyman. With the latter I made arrangements to telephone him in Paris after my morning conferences with Avenol, with a view to his transmitting to Felix Warburg the substance of my report.

As we approached Paris, Bentwich emphasized his pleasure at having had such a good opportunity to talk, and I told him with complete sincerity that I was delighted that he had come on at Plymouth instead of waiting for Havre, though I suspect that he was disappointed in some of my attitudes. I had the impression that, on the whole, he was convinced that I took my job seriously, and that fundamentally I desired the same objectives as did he.

McDonald soon appointed Bentwich as his deputy.[15]

Schweitzer, Hyman, Parkes, Miss Sawyer, and I went direct to the Hotel du Rhin, where, to our disappointment, the papers we expected from the States about the London conference were not available. Apparently, he must have left them at Morgans.

Dr. Kahn had come along to the hotel, so I suggested that all of us have a bite to eat before going on to the Gare de Lyons. During the forty-five minutes that we were at the table, Dr. Kahn explained briefly his conception of the refugee problem as it now exists. He seemed to feel that only a few thousand might properly be considered as subjects for colonization in France. He belittled the fund-raising capacity of the British, stressed that almost none of the effective relief organizations had been officially represented at London, that even ICA was not there officially. He impressed me as a man of great ability, much

15. In his autobiography, *My 77 Years* (Philadelphia: Jewish Publication Society, 1961), pp. 130–131, Bentwich nicely summed up his two years as McDonald's deputy: "My two years association with McDonald was altogether happy, although the office of the High Commission belied the hopes, exaggerated hopes, which were entertained about it by a part of the Jewish public. For the second time I worked with a High Commissioner who was expected to be a messiah, and circumstance was less propitious this time. McDonald was physically impressive and mentally courageous. He was single-minded in his work, direct in his approach to a problem, had a ready gift of speech, and was prepared to talk in undiplomatic language."

sobered by heavy responsibilities over a long period, and not unnaturally annoyed at the cavalier fashion in which amateurs in relief had mapped out a gigantic program at the London conference. I was a little disquieted by his estimate of the Oungre brothers, whom he characterized as very ambitious, each one thinking to achieve a personal distinction as great as the other. Moreover, he doubted if ICA was prepared to do more than settle a few hundred families in some of the areas where they were specially integrated. Nonetheless, I asked Dr. Kahn if he would be good enough to tell the Oungres that I was looking forward to the honor of meeting and conferring with them.

Talked with Parkes a little while in my compartment and then to bed.

Geneva, Saturday, November 11, 1933

Woke up to find unmistakable signs of a heavy frost and even snow as we approached Geneva.

Armistice Day—this has not been what I consider a perfect vacation.

I was met at the station by Mr. May, with whom I breakfasted alone at the Bellevue. He told me of my engagements for the day. These began with an interview with Sweetser at his office, which was merely preliminary to the long and very important conference with Avenol and Krno,[16] the Slovak member of the Secretariat, who has been handling the technical phases of this question.

Avenol received us at once, and was most cordial. I began by telling him, after the first opening remarks, that I hoped he would outline to me with complete frankness what he conceived to be the relations of the High Commissioner, first to the League, and second to the private organizations, third to the governments, and fourth the probable site of the High Commission. Then Avenol replied unequivocally to all my questions.

The League, he said, has created this institution, has named you, has invited the governments to participate, has advanced a small sum, and there its official relationship terminates. Officially, he said, we are through, but privately and wholly unofficially we as individuals shall be happy to do anything we can to expedite your work. I thanked him.

As to the High Commissioner's relations with the private organizations, he was in no doubt whatsoever. He said that the Council's action clearly envisaged a purely intergovernmental organization, that the relations of the private organizations to the High Commission . . . must be merely advisory. I asked him if it would be possible to have a memorandum of this interpretation; he suggested that Krno secure such a memorandum from the legal section of the League. The Secretary General then went ahead to explain why, for the sake of the success of the High Commission, this must be the relationship. "Yours cannot," he said, "be a Jewish organization if ever you wish to establish a useful relationship with Germany. Your only chance to do so is as an intergovernmental official, repre-

16. Ivan Krno, Czechoslovak diplomat, later political director of its Foreign Ministry.

senting governments officially, and not as representing private organizations." "This," he stressed repeatedly, "is the sine qua non of success."

As to the site of the High Commission, he said, "perhaps we had better begin by a process of elimination. It cannot be at The Hague because the Dutch government prefers that it should not be. It cannot be in London because the French government prefers that it not be there. It cannot be in Geneva." He did not say why, but he implied that it could not be in Paris, and he left the impression that the probably the best site would be Lausanne. I assumed that the Swiss government has no objection, but on this point I think further sounding will have to be made.

We then talked about the first meeting of the Governing Body.[17] I said that I was somewhat concerned at the slowness of the governments designating their representatives. He said, "This will be speeded up just as soon as you send word that you have fixed upon a time for the first meeting of the Governing Body." We thereupon tentatively agreed that we might try for the first meeting on the twenty-fifth of November. At my request he agreed that either he or Krno would telephone the British, French, Dutch, the Belgian, and the Italian governmental representatives with a view to making this date possible.

I asked the Secretary General what would be my official status as High Commissioner. He said there is no doubt that you are an international official engaged on intergovernmental business, and that therefore you have the right to the diplomatic privileges and immunities. I asked him what sort of papers I would have to indicate my status. He smiled and said, "Of course, you are not a League official, and therefore we cannot supply you with papers. Your Governing Board should supply these for you. Actually, you as High Commissioner will probably do, as I do as Secretary General, sign your own certificate of your official character." I did not say so, but I think probably such a signature would be better if it were that of the chairman of the Governing Body.[18]

We then talked about possible nominees by different governments. He assumed that the French had already named a former ambassador to Germany. He said he thought it would be difficult for the British to refuse to name Cecil, though the latter was, of course, not popular with the government.[19]

Having cleared up all the points which I felt could be properly discussed with the Secretary General, I thanked him most heartily for his helpfulness and then went with Krno to the latter's office. There we continued the discussion on technical points; together we went over the draft of a statute for the Governing Body, which Krno had drawn up. It seemed to me excellent, though perhaps re-

17. Fifteen nations had been invited to become members of the Governing Body—all those bordering on Germany, as well as those involved in setting up the High Commission.

18. McDonald later wrote that Joseph Avenol, whom he called a cautious bureaucrat, had a "tender regard for Germany's feelings." As a result, the High Commission was politically as well as financially divorced from the League.

19. Unhappy with the British government's policy (of distance) toward the League of Nations, Cecil resigned his cabinet post in 1927. He again crossed the Conservative Party in 1931, when he urged strong sanctions against Japan following its invasion of Manchuria.

quiring some modifications in detail. He promised me that he would proceed at once to carry out the communications to the various governments about the possibility of a meeting of the Governing Body on the date suggested. He spoke to me about Wurfbain,[20] praised him highly, and said that his designation would be considered as a distinct compliment to the Dutch government. He also, I think, spoke to me about Horace de Portales. As I was leaving, he told me that the League had put at my disposal 25,000 Swiss francs, and that these were available at any time, even before the setting up of the Governing Body. He then turned over to me two or three complete dossiers, together with a long batch of correspondence which had been addressed to me in care of the League. I told him how deeply I appreciated his helpfulness, and we agreed to talk together again on Monday, he saying that he would of course be glad to continue, in a wholly unofficial way, to help me to prepare for the first meeting of the Governing Body.

I should perhaps add that the Secretary General in his talk about my official status said, "You, of course, have been passed by the League, but until the Governing Body meets and organizes there is no institution in existence." Krno, in my talk with him, agreed with me that the chief purposes of the first meeting of the Governing Body would be to organize, name a chairman, treasurer, and other appropriate officials, of course, after adopting the statutes. Then the Governing Body would expect to outline, preferably in general terms, the scope of the initial efforts of the High Commissioner.

By the time I had finished with Krno, there were just a few minutes left to talk with Sweetser before I had to go out to lunch with Mr. May. When I arrived at the Mays' apartment, I telephoned to Hyman in Paris outlining the main points of the morning's discussion, for the information of [Felix] Warburg.

At lunch at Mr. May's[21] were Mr. and Mrs. May, Miss Ginsberg,[22] Mr. Parkes, Miss Sawyer, and myself. The talk was general. Miss Ginsberg, however, asked me if I would tell her what my plans were so that Mr. Hirsch [*sic,* actually Paul Hertz],[23] secretary of the Social Democratic Party, now in Prague, might come to see me. I told her that I did not think that I ought to make any normal arrangement to meet Mr. Hirsch [Hertz], but that, of course, if he learned where I was to be, I would be glad to talk with him.

Hurried back to the hotel to try to get a few minutes nap before my afternoon appointments.

20. André Wurfbain, Dutch, quite experienced with similar League commissions, good language skills, recommended by the Dutch government.

21. May had offered to host lunch or dinner for anyone McDonald would like invited. McDonald later wrote: "Mrs. May has been the perfect hostess . . . and the saving on my nerves and energy of this hospitality is inestimable." McDonald to Ogden, December 12, 1933. Copy in McDonald Papers, USHMM.

22. Marie Ginsberg, League Secretariat, economic expert in the League library, head of the International Committee for the Placement of Intellectual Refugees, and friend of Mildred Wertheimer. Experienced and creative on refugee matters.

23. Paul Hertz, on the executive committee of the German Social Democratic Party in exile.

I had telephoned Hugh Wilson on my arrival and went to see him at 3:30. I told him frankly of the morning's conversations, and we then discussed the question of an American representative for an early meeting of the Governing Body. He thought it possible that the administration had in mind Sackett, rather than Houghton. I told him that the former would seem to me satisfactory, but that there would be undoubted advantages in a person technically equipped as would be Chamberlain, Wardwell, or Fosdick. He was much interested, said that he would write Moffat a letter. I pointed out that that would be too slow to effect action in time for the twenty-fifth, and he replied that he did not feel strongly enough about any one of the individuals to wire. He added that, of course, he would be willing to sit as the American representative at the first meeting, if instructed to do so, but he thought it would be very undesirable to have this a permanent arrangement. On the whole, he thought that it was desirable to have a representative who would go back home between meetings. He was very cordial throughout, and I think can be counted on to help.

Then over to Arthur Sweetser's office. He told me in some detail of the steps by which my election had been determined upon. Apparently there had been no opposition. Mr. May's initial telegram had been worked out in Sweetser's office and submitted to the Secretary General before being sent by May. Fosdick's cable had been well received by the Secretary General, and on that basis a statement of my qualifications had been prepared, a copy of which Sweetser gave to me. The Czech representative at the meeting had said that Benes knew me and that Novak had cabled an enthusiastic endorsement. Madariaga said he knew me and approved. The Italians and the English also approved, and the vote was unanimous.

....

Discussing my new work, Arthur said he sometimes wondered if it were not time for him to make a change also.

Arthur drove me over to Prentiss Gilbert's, where I spent nearly an hour and a half with the consul general and his wife at tea. I outlined fully and frankly to Gilbert the morning talks. He took notes with a view to sending a long despatch to Washington on Monday. We agreed that I would come to his office Monday about 11:30 or 12:00 to go over the telegram with him before he filed it. I had definitely the impression that Gilbert would do everything he could to expedite my work here. After our talk he drove me back to my hotel about a quarter of seven.

....

Drove out to Avenol's with the Gilberts in their Ford. Those at dinner included the Secretary General, the Mays, the Gilberts, Professor Werner and his wife (he is president of the Nansen Committee), the Horace de Portales (he, by the way, had been recommended to me earlier during the day by Wilson who knows him intimately and likes him very much), the Krnos, and the Sweetsers.

During dinner I talked with Mrs. Krno about education and the care of children, with Mrs. Sweetser about schools and houses. After dinner Werner and I had a long talk about co-education and relief, and I asked him to tell Mr. Johnson that I was looking forward to a long talk with him. Werner said he doubted if their office could be very helpful because the problems were so very different. He asked me how many of the refugees I thought would be willing to be moved. I, of course, had no idea. I had a longish talk with the Secretary General in which we covered again in somewhat different form some of the points of the morning. I asked him whether the setting up of this office by the Assembly had really had a considerable influence in causing the Germans to leave the League, as Wilson and Gilbert both told me they were confident was the case. The Secretary General replied that it might have had some effect, but that it was not a large factor. He thought that it was really a coup d'etat, similar to, but on a larger scale than, the German withdrawal from the Disarmament Conference the previous summer. He added that one receives the most conflicting accounts of what is taking place in Germany and of what may be expected.

. . . .

During the course of the day I sounded out various people on the suggestion of my going to Germany very soon. The consensus of opinion was that this would be unwise until after the meeting of the Governing Body and after initial soundings had been made.

Sunday, November 12, 1933

Worked during the morning—dictating my diary to Miss Sawyer. Called Dr. Weizmann at his hotel. He was out, but later called me back, and I invited him to dinner with me at the Bellevue in my room. Dr. [Nahum] Goldmann called, and I begged off from an appointment today, reminding him that I had told him in Paris that Sunday was already fully occupied, so arranged to lunch with him on Monday. Herbert May came in about eleven, and at my request read my diary of the previous days, the draft statute, and other pertinent data.

Mr. Wurfbain came in to see me. He chatted for a little while with Miss Sawyer and Mr. May, and then he and I went out for a walk. I asked him a number of questions to test his general point of view about the problem, and also about his relations to the Dutch government. He seemed to be inclined to understate rather than overstate and to have an intelligent grasp of the situation. After our walk I suggested that he join us on our trip to Paris, London, and The Hague; that it would be a trial period for both of us. He very properly raised a question which had not occurred to me, which was that we would not quite be on equal terms on such a trial period, because if he went along and it was decided later that he would not stay with me, it might injure his chances elsewhere. I suggested that he might avoid the danger by announcing simply that he was going for this trip and that nothing further than that was contemplated. He said that he would call me Monday and let me know.

We met Dr. Weizmann as he was coming into the hotel, and also the representative of the Soviet press here. Dr. Weizmann met Mr. May and Miss Sawyer, and then the two of us had lunch together.

The conversation was begun by my telling him at some length of my general approach to the whole problem. I reported my impressions in Germany in the spring and fall, my sense of horror at the Nazi attitude, and my fear that this example might be followed elsewhere, and my conviction that there was perhaps no work where I could serve more usefully than in the general effort to humanize, or if one might put it, Christianize the relations between Jews and non-Jews. Dr. Weizmann responded by telling me that he was convinced that the danger to world Jewry was fully as grave as I thought; that there was immediate danger in Poland the instant [Polish leader Józef] Pilsudski was removed from the scene, and that in Austria and Hungary and Romania the danger was also imminent. Even in Great Britain, the United States, and France there could be no real assurance of the future. The Jews had always survived through the remnants of the race, and they might have to do so again. Despite these evident dangers, the bulk of the well-to-do Jews in the West failed completely to sense the realities of the situation.

In the course of our early discussion Palestine was mentioned. I took advantage of this to say that I was a little surprised that the English Jews had so unreservedly accepted the view that Palestine was outside the jurisdiction of the High Commission. Dr. Weizmann explained that this had not been on his initiative, but on the contrary it had been Simon and later Cunliffe-Lister[24] of the Colonial Office who had been insistent that the High Commission should not come between the British government and the Jewish agency concerned with applying for certificates. Dr. Weizmann had said that of course the High Commission would not want to be involved in that technical question, that he could do all the yelling necessary in the matter of certification, that the High Commission would be concerned only with more general considerations. He thought it important, he added, that the first person I see in England should be Cecil, who would tell me how to move on this issue with Cunliffe-Lister and perhaps other members of the government.

Later in our talk Weizmann developed his plans for Palestine, Syria, and Trans-Jordania, and it became quite clear that he envisages the High Commission as playing a large role there.

On the subject of the private organizations and their relations to the High Commission I explained that Avenol was sure that legally their status must be merely advisory, and that from the point of view of the effectiveness of the High Commission, especially in its relations with Germany, the High Commissioner had to be representative merely of governments and not in any legal or technical sense of Jewish organizations. Weizmann replied that he, of course, had understood that the relationship would be advisory, and he stressed that he agreed that

24. Philip Cunliffe-Lister, first Earl of Swinton, colonial secretary.

the organization must not be a Jewish one, either in fact or in the public eye. He seemed to realize fully that there were great advantages in maintaining the essential governmental character of the High Commission. Naturally, it was a great relief to have him take this line.

I anticipated any question of Bentwich's relationship to me by telling Dr. Weizmann frankly of Warburg's offer of H. [Hyman] and my reply. I added that naturally I should have to take the same line in reference to Mr. Bentwich though I had the highest regard for his intelligence and for his ability to work with other individuals and groups. Then I suggested the formula that both Bentwich and H., and perhaps one or two other persons, might be associated with me, giving all their time to the work but not as members of my staff. I said that I felt sure that if Mr. Bentwich could be relieved of his university work for the year, he could be extremely helpful. Dr. Weizmann did not commit himself definitely on this point, but I think it will probably be worked out along those lines.

Dr. Weizmann was extremely interesting in his discussion of his Palestinian program. At the moment he is especially anxious to secure a substantial tract of land in Syria at the corner where it joins Trans-Jordania and Palestine. He is now negotiating with the French government to buy the land. If this "bridgehead in the Jordan valley" could be secured and occupied with 5,000 families sufficiently armed to protect themselves against marauding Bedouins, the way would have been opened for mass colonization in Trans-Jordania. On that basis he could foresee the possibility of a cohesive Jewish community of as many as 5,000,000. That is his ultimate goal. In the meantime, he is looked upon as a minimalist by such impractical theorists as Rabbi Wise, who is never troubled by facts.

We discussed the question of persons whom I should see in London and Paris. He said [that] I, of course, should see Louis Oungre, a vain person, Mr. Levi,[25] the old president of the Alliance,[26] and Baron Rothchild. In England, in addition to Cecil whom I should see first, I should of course see Sir Leonard Cohen, d'Avigdor Goldsmid, the Rothschilds, and in Paris Professor Oualid.[27] He said that he hoped to see me in Paris or London.

Towards the end of our more than two hours' talk we gossiped together about personalities, the Warburgs, the Louis Marshalls,[28] Frankfurter, and others. I went with Dr. Weizmann downstairs and out into the street. As he left, I felt that we had had a most useful conference and that on all fundamental issues

25. Dr. Sylvain Levi, president of the Alliance Universelle Israelite, orientalist and anti-Zionist. "The doyen of Jewish scholars in France, and the heart and sun of a committee of savants which helped German academic exiles." Norman Bentwich, *My 77 Years* (Philadelphia: Jewish Publication Society, 1961), 134.

26. Alliance Israelite Universelle, Paris-based, international organization focused on protecting the rights of Jews as citizens and promoting assimilation to French culture, especially among Jews of North Africa and the Middle East.

27. William Oualid, a law professor specializing in immigration issues.

28. Louis Marshall, constitutional lawyer. One of the founders of the American Jewish Committee, president 1912–1929.

we were in essential agreement, at least so far as the High Commission was concerned, and that we should be able to work together harmoniously.

Out for a walk with Parkes. We talked about the possibility of a liaison person for Germany, but it seemed clear after our conversation that he would not be best for that purpose. It was left, therefore, that we would discuss later what if any should be his relationship to the High Commission.

Tea with Miss Ginsberg. Later we were joined by her secretary, Mrs. Wagner. Miss Ginsberg and I talked about several aspects of the High Commission's work, but I was non-committal on nearly all points. She wished to know among other things when the Governing Body would meet, where the headquarters would be, and whether her committee could be expected to be a liaison here. On the last point I said that I hoped that it might be one of the contacts with the League. On the other points I was vague, but she was, I think, able to draw fairly accurate conclusions.

Over to dinner at Mr. May's. Those present besides the Mays and myself were the Straits, Alvin Johnson,[29] the Browns, Whitakers, Tiranes, Sweetsers, and several other younger people. I talked with Major Abraham about some aspects of my work. He seemed to think that Germany might be ready to make a conciliatory démarche after the election had given an overwhelming support to the regime.[30] The rest of the evening there was light conversation and good dancing.

Monday, November 13, 1933

Over to the Secretariat to talk to Krno about the statute and other matters connected with the organization. In particular, we agreed that I would address formal communications both to the governments that had accepted and those from whom no formal replies had been received, telling them of the first meeting of the Governing Body at Lausanne on November 28. At the same time he handed me a detailed memorandum of the démarches he had made the previous Saturday with several of the governments. He agreed that he would draft the letters for my signature and that the Secretariat would type them. We then discussed enclosures. We agreed tentatively on a draft of an agenda and on the draft of the statutes which he had prepared.

I hurried off to see Prentiss Gilbert, who went over with me in detail the draft of a long telegram which he was sending to the State Department outlining the steps I had taken here. He showed eager willingness to cooperate.

Lunched with Dr. Goldmann of the World Jewish Congress. I went over much the same ground with him that I had with Dr. Weizmann. He presented much the same viewpoint as had Dr. Weizmann on such questions as the rela-

29. Alvin Johnson, president of the New School.

30. A plebiscite on November 12, 1933, had given overwhelming approval to government policies and to Hitler's decision to withdraw from the League of Nations.

tions of the Jewish organizations to the High Commission and to the latter's Secretariat. He seemed to me to be satisfied that the essential interests of his group would be protected. It was agreed that I would see him again in Paris or London.

During the morning Krno had been in conference with the Secretary General and Weizmann. Krno gave me a resumé of Weizmann's talk with the Secretary General. Apparently Dr. Weizmann took up again some of the same questions such as the organizations' relations to the High Commission and to the latter's Secretariat as he had discussed with me. On the whole, however, I got the impression that Dr. Weizmann had been fairly well satisfied.

In the middle of the afternoon Mr. May and Mr. Wurfbain came in, and we went over the draft of the statute again. So many questions were raised that I called up Krno to ask him if we might come over to talk to him about the whole matter. This we did for nearly two hours. The result was several changes in the draft, chiefly in the direction of strengthening the High Commissioner's position vis-à-vis the Governing Body and assuring that the essential character of the Commissioner would be maintained. Krno was really most helpful throughout, as, of course, was Mr. May. I also received a favorable impression of Wurfbain.

Unfortunately, in the midst of the work of the statute I completely forgot an appointment with Sweetser. Earlier in the afternoon Rappard came to see me. Speaking of de Portales, he said he could not conceive of the latter doing a substantial, hard piece of work, though he was, of course, most charming and presentable. Still earlier in the day Prentiss Gilbert had strongly urged de Portales because of the qualities which other people had stressed and also because of his having been a member of the Imperial Guard of Honor in Germany before the war. Gilbert also seemed to think that de Portales was close to the Swiss government. This Rappard, who should know, denied.

....

Tuesday, November 14, 1933

....

Mr. May, Wurfbain, and I went again to Krno's for a final revision of the draft statute. The net result was to add a final paragraph further safeguarding the Assembly's and Council's interpretation of the High Commissioner and the Commission.

Then Mr. May and I went to see Mr. Bialer about making available the funds advanced by the League. I was to write a formal letter asking for the deposit of the 25,000 Swiss francs to my credit as the High Commissioner.[31]

31. This money was a loan, repayable in six months. The League of Nations gave no funds to the High Commission.

We then returned to Mr. Krno's office and discussed with him a tentative draft of by-laws and rules of procedure. He is to have a clean draft ready for us on our return.

I then went up and talked to Arthur Sweetser about the nature of a communiqué which might be issued before I left. He thought the League could properly issue this first statement. It was agreed that I would submit him a draft after lunch, and he would discuss the matter with Avenol. This was done, Avenol very materially improving up my draft.

....

During the course of the day, I suggested tentatively to Mr. May the possibility of his being named a counselor of the High Commission, this to be a highly confidential position, but giving him entree into whatever conferences it might seem to me desirable that he should participate. He would, I think, accept such a post.

During the morning I talked to Mr. Kahane, a Zionist representative and a Jewish journalist. He stressed the importance of Jewish representation in connection with the High Commission if the rank and file of Jewry, especially Eastern, were enthusiastically to support the High Commission's work. I thanked him for his information and told him that I hoped that we should be of real use to one another especially if we found that we could trust each other fully.

Opened an account at the American Express Co. on the recommendation of Mr. May.

Called Prentiss Gilbert to ask him whether my formal letter to the secretary of state should be sent to Bern or handed to him. He said I could do as I liked, but that the latter procedure would save a day or two in having the substance of the communication telegraphed to Washington. I asked him whether I should send a copy to Wilson; he said that was not necessary for he always supplied Wilson with copies of everything he sent to the [State] Department. I told him that Wurfbain would hand him the material tomorrow.

Professor Montoux[32] came and we had a longish and very satisfactory conference. I explained, as I had to the other Jewish representatives, my general point of view and in particular my attitude towards the representation of the private organizations and on the makeup of my Secretariat. Montoux not only agreed in principle, but enthusiastically endorsed each point. He said he, of course, realized that in the minds of many English Jews and some Americans French Jewry was recreant in its attitude on Jewish questions, but if this could seem to be true, it was only because the French Jews considered themselves Frenchmen and Jews only as one might think of himself as a Norman or a Basque. He added that few outsiders realized the political difficulty involved in the German refugees, for many of the German Jews now refugees are intensely

32. Professor Paul Montoux, Alliance Israelite, chairman of the French committee of the International Student Service.

nationalistic and are still looked upon with suspicion by their French hosts. He assured me that I would have enthusiastic support of the French groups, and offered himself to be of whatever service he could be either in Paris or in his frequent visits to Geneva. He might be an excellent liaison to set over against one of our friends from London.

Parkes came in, and we chatted about the general situation, and I said that I would talk to him fully about our relationship on my return.

Mr. Wurfbain, Miss Sawyer, and I dined together and made last-minute arrangements, including a telephone conversation with Malcolm Davis, as a result of which the latter agreed to open my correspondence during my absence and to forward matters needing urgent attention.

Mrs. May and Mrs. Stepanoff came to the station with Mr. May to say goodbye to us.

Paris, Wednesday, November 15, 1933

Arrived in Paris at seven o'clock and went directly to the Hotel Continental, where Mr. May arranged excellent accommodations for us. The first few hours we spent in getting off letters and other means of communications with persons we wanted to see here. I sent a telegram to Krno calling attention to the discrepancy in the French and English texts of the draft statutes, and suggesting that the correction be made.

Mr. Hyman and some of his associates were slow in putting in their appearance, because they had gone to meet the wrong train. Mr. Hyman was helpful in putting Miss Sawyer in touch with various groups here.

Miss Rothbarth[33] came in. She suggested the possibility of our visiting the Bastion together; she also suggested that she would like to bring Mr. Breitscheid to see me. I made no decision on either of these points.

Over to the annex of the Foreign Office to see M. Fouques-Duparc, who is the League of Nations man in the Foreign Office. We talked together for more than an hour. I outlined in some detail my conception of the organization of the Commission, the relation of the Governing Body to the private organizations, of the High Commission to the governments, and of the Secretariat of the High Commission. I also sketched my present ideas of the first meeting of the Governing Body, the election of a temporary chairman, consideration and adoption of a statute, the rules of procedure and the financial regulations; then the election of the chairman. After that the statement by the High Commissioner setting forth in detail the present situation of the refugees, what is being done in their behalf, and enumerating possibilities of action to increase the effectiveness of the relief measures. A portion of this statement should be designed for the public; the other for the Governing Body only. Then the High Commissioner should lay before the Governing Body a draft of three or more general lines of

33. Dr. Margarete Rothbarth, worked at the International Institute of Intellectual Co-operation, which was concerned with political refugees.

policy within which he would be expected to carry on his work until the next meeting of the Governing Body. The Governing Body would, of course, also set up an advisory committee, a permanent committee, and perhaps a large finance committee outside of an internal finance committee.

M. Fouques-Duparc agreed in principle with all of these suggestions. We then discussed a number of specific matters. He asked me in particular when the first meeting would be held, more about the nature of the agenda, and then asked the rather surprising question: would refugees with Polish and Czech passports be regarded as German refugees? I did not commit myself. Fouques-Duparc stressed that he thought the government would, of course, favor the interpretation that the Governing Body is a governmental institution. He agreed too that an attempt should be made to open negotiations with the Germans, but that probably the Governing Body would prefer to have this done on the High Commissioner's own responsibility.

He suggested that I see Léger,[34] the permanent undersecretary, that afternoon and perhaps later the foreign minister. I left with the impression that Fouques Duparc would be good to work with.

Back to the hotel. Late for luncheon with the JDC group. This included Hyman, Schweitzer, Dr. Rosen, Dr. Kahn, and Mr. May. We discussed a number of questions. Dr. Rosen gave his interpretation of the possibilities of France for colonization. He thought there was room for a considerable number of immigrants but not anything like the quantity suggested by Liebman. He stressed that in the country and in the small towns the danger of intensifying anti-Semitism, despite contrary opinions, was not great. Dr. Schweitzer agreed with this general point of view and then outlined in some detail the present refugee situation. I asked each of the men if they would not supply me with written memoranda. They agreed to do so.

Dr. Schweitzer discussed the immediate situation in Paris, the work of the French National Committee, the imperative need for reorganization and for the French to take a broader point of view. I somehow got the impression that Kahn and the other Americans were a little high-hat, that, because the French were not fitting more nearly into the JDC general concept, my table companions were not doing French efforts justice. However, the group agreed on the necessity of working at once to clear up the present situation so that more constructive efforts would be undertaken.

I was awakened from a brief nap by the arrival of Edouard Oungre[35] of HICEM[36] and Dr. Bernstein of HIAS.[37] They said that they had come to offer

34. Alexis Saint-Léger, *chef de cabinet* at the French Foreign Ministry 1925–1932.

35. Edouard Oungre, manager of HICEM and younger brother of Louis Oungre, who was the director general.

36. HICEM, based in Paris, founded in 1927 by the Hebrew Immigrant Aid Society (HIAS) to raise funds for the relief and settlement of Jews in central, eastern, and southeastern Europe. HICEM is an acronym for three emigration organizations: HIAS (United States), ICA (Paris), and Emigdirect (Berlin).

37. See previous note.

me their fullest cooperation and to explain the facilities that they would make available. Edouard Oungre launched into a long and not wholly convincing account of the scope and usefulness of his organization. I got the impression of a personality smaller in proportions than Oungre realizes. I asked him whether the HICEM had been able to enlarge its work sufficiently to care for the exceptional necessities of the present situation. He stressed the difficulties growing out of the crisis—unemployment and the currency lack of balance. He would not admit that there was any inadequacy in his organization. This was a very different impression from that which the group at lunch had given me.

. . . .

Saw Miss Berg[38] for a moment. Was much impressed not merely with her technical qualifications, but also with her personality and character.

Late afternoon over to the Quai d'Orsay to see Léger, permanent undersecretary for foreign affairs. While waiting, chatted with Coudenhove-Kalergi. He is a pessimist about the League; said that it had never brought good luck to anybody; that Lausanne, as contrasted to Geneva, had been the site of two successful conferences, and that perhaps this would be a good omen for my work. On the general situation he is as pessimistic as ever, but feels that once the French franc goes off gold, which he believes to be inevitable, the beginning of the end of the economic crisis will be in sight. He spoke of a Mme. Ernest Mercier, the wife of one of the richest electrical magnates in France, as deeply interested in the refugee problem.[39]

Léger was most apologetic for keeping me waiting and said that something unexpected had come up at the last moment. I then explained to him more briefly than I had to Fouques-Duparc my general approach to the problem and my angle on the moot questions. On each point Léger enthusiastically agreed, reserving of course the final opinion by including the phrase "au principle" or something similar. But there seemed to me no doubt of his essential agreement. He said to me repeatedly, "Yes, that is the only practical way to do it." He agreed that abstract question of competence, organization, of relationships between the various organizations and between the High Commission and the governments should be avoided as far as possible, and that the chief concern be to secure tangible results. In particular, he agreed that the High Commission should have direct access to the governments. His unqualified endorsement of this was typical of his general attitude. On the matter of the relation of private organizations he indicated that he saw great dangers in formal membership on the Governing Body, that all of the practical advantages of close cooperation could be secured on an advisory basis. Similarly on the question of the makeup of my Secretariat,

38. Marie Louise Berg, Belgian. Became secretary for the High Commission office.

39. Her husband, the "electrical magnate," was the main financier behind the Croix de Feu, a fascist veterans organization founded in 1927! Her "deep interest in the refugee problem" was, therefore, surprising.

he agreed that it must have a central loyalty and a degree of cohesiveness which would be impossible on any representative basis.

As I was preparing to leave, he asked when I would be coming back through Paris. I asked him if he had anything special in mind; he said that the Foreign Office had not yet had an opportunity to study the whole problem fully and that they might wish to consult me again. I told him that, of course, I would be at his disposition, and that I could stop off either Tuesday or Wednesday of next week on my way back from The Hague. It was left that I was to telephone Fouques-Duparc to inquire whether Léger wished me to come back. As to the French nominee, I get the impression that he had not yet finally been named. I left with a feeling that Léger would really endeavor to be cooperative.

Miss Rothbarth came in for late tea. We talked about a number of matters. Through her I sent word to Breitscheid that I would, of course, be glad to see him at any time, but that I thought it essential that he commit himself not to reporting or commenting in his press on our talk; in other words, that I could not be put in a position of being used as a platform for émigré political propaganda. In the meantime, I suggested that Wurfbain might see Breitscheid quite personally.

Miss Rothbarth told me her own rather pathetic story about her relations with the German government. She, like all the other German nationals employed on League or related bodies, has been asked to resign. If she says yes, she returns to Germany to what she can not tell. If she says no, she keeps her job for three years but will never be able to return to Germany. If she resigned and went back, she could hold no government post, could not write or teach, or do anything of which she is capable. She had had a terrible struggle to decide, but had finally made up her mind to say no unless the German government agreed to pay the whole of her three years salary if she said yes.

To dinner at the Baron Robert de Rothschild's.[40] Instead of taking [me] out to dinner, he called up at 8:30 to say that he and his wife were improvising a meal at their house; that he had tried to secure as other guests Boncour, Bérenger, Siegfried, and several others, but they were all engaged, though each expressed his deep regret.

Those at dinner were besides the two hosts and myself, the twenty-three-year-old son, Mme , the son of Captain Dreyfus,[41] and [*sic*].

40. Baron Robert de Rothschild, chairman of the French National Committee to Aid German Refugees. Most influential personality of the French National Central Committee seeking to harness efforts of the half-dozen or more refugee aid committees that sprang up after the first influx of German Jews to France. Complained bitterly, privately and in public, of the alleged indifference of the American and British Jews.

41. Pierre Dreyfus, son of Captain Alfred Dreyfus. The latter, born in (French) Alsace in a Jewish family, kept French citizenship after Germany took over Alsace in 1871. Became a French army officer. Arrested in 1894 on suspicion of passing military secrets to Germany, convicted and sentenced to life despite the lack of evidence. His cause taken up by novelist/journalist Emile Zola and many others, Dreyfus became the center of a national controversy between republicans and traditional or right-wing forces that dragged on for nearly a decade. Pardoned in 1899, exonerated in 1906, Dreyfus died in 1935.

The dinner had none of the appearances of improvisation—soup, soufflé, fish, pheasant, grouse, vegetables, marvelous ice cream and fruit do not constitute what one calls a pick-up meal. My host was deeply disappointed that I was unable to enjoy his family Burgundy and other vintages from the famous cav.[42]

During much of dinner the discussion was about conditions in Germany, I telling of some of my experiences with the Nazis, Nuremberg, Dachau, etc. I gave them, I think, a new sense of the acuteness of the situation.

After dinner the talk was all about the refugee problem. The French stressed their hospitality in opening their doors, their expenditure of 10,000,000 francs, their desire to continue to carry on, but the impossibility of doing so without foreign aid. As to the reorganization of the National Committee discussed that late afternoon, Rothschild was very pessimistic. He said the meeting had been a failure; it had not been fully representative, and there had been few volunteers for the different committees. He felt very pessimistic. Their funds were exhausted; they were already in debt and needed very considerable sums at once, to carry on. All of which I listened to as sympathetically as I could, but, of course, made no promises or commitments of any kind. How could I?

The other part of the discussion was less technical but more interesting. It concerned the French attitude towards the refugees and the French Jews' general outlook; as to the first, even French Jews think of the German refugee Jews as Germans, rather than Jews, as Boches, former hated enemies and possibly enemies of the future. This is the feeling which will not die down. On the second point, the French Jews are French first, and Jews second. This they admitted quite freely, and it is this which makes them suspect in England and among Eastern Jews.

How deep this difference runs I am only beginning to realize. Certainly these French spokesmen indicated that they were in no sense unified with the English, either in general outlook or on a specific or comprehensive program.

As I was leaving, we chatted about different forms of amusement and the question of dancing came up. The result was an urgent and apparently sincere invitation from Mme. for me to let them know when I am next in Paris so that a party can be arranged.

Walked home along the Champs d'Elysées and to bed.

Paris, November 15, 1933

My dear Miss Ogden:

This is a hurried note written after a most hectic but on the whole very satisfactory four days in Geneva. We are here in Paris now for a day and a half, and then go to London for the rest of the week.

In Geneva Mr. May, as you would have expected, has been most helpful, and he is to be with me on this present tour.

The Secretariat, from the Secretary General on down, have been perfectly

42. McDonald was a teetotaler for much of his life.

splendid. They would not possibly have been expected to do more than they have done or are prepared to do. Without their unofficial but always cordial co-operation it would have been quite impossible for us to have prepared within four days all the material necessary to enable me to issue an official call for the first meeting of the Governing Body. This has now been done, and with the call has gone a draft of an agenda and a draft statute. The latter will, if adopted, constitute our constitution. You will realize how important it has been to draft this along proper lines.

I am going very slowly in building up my staff. In addition to Miss Sawyer I have chosen more or less definitely only one other person—a Dutchman, André Wurfbain. He has had considerable experience on different League commissions in similar work, knows the League machinery and methods perfectly, is competent in the necessary languages, and has, I think, many of the qualities valuable to supplement my own. Moreover, I am sure that the choice of a Dutchman is strategically advantageous. Moreover, Mr. Wurfbain was officially recommended by the Dutch government. . . .

The matter of building a staff is not made easier by the pressure from many directions to have included nominees of various interests. I am rigidly resisting all such endeavors to make me in any sense the agent of any group or group of groups. My office must be much more than that, or it will be nothing. Happily, none of the Jewish groups at home have urged their own nominees. This freedom from pressure from the home front has strengthened me enormously here, and I am proportionately grateful.

I have not made up my mind definitely about Mr. Parkes' relationship to the work. He has many admirable qualities, but his forte is not organization. Therefore, I had to turn to Wurfbain. There is at least an even chance, however, that once we get under way, Parkes will prove of great value in outside contacts.

In addition to pressure in reference to personalities on my staff, there has been heavy pressure from some of the organizations to be recognized as more of an integral part of the High Commission than either the Secretariat or I think is either legally possible or strategically desirable. In my talks with Dr. Weizmann and Dr. Goldmann, which were very friendly throughout, I have been quite definite in my statement that the private organizations can have only an advisory relationship to the Governing Body. Both Dr. Weizmann and Dr. Goldmann assented to this in principle, and even agreed that I would be much stronger as the representative of fifteen governments than as a representative of private organizations. Nonetheless, I anticipate that in practice I shall have to resist steadily a more or less continuous pressure to grant to the private organizations a measure of participation which seems to be inconsistent with the success of the enterprise.

My plan for the private organizations is that they shall be grouped in an Advisory Committee with which both the Governing Body and I shall keep in the closest contact. Perhaps it will be desirable to have the Advisory Committee meet from time to time simultaneously with the meetings of the Governing Body. This, however, will obviously not be possible or desirable at the time of the first meeting of the Governing Body. That meeting will be concerned with problems or organization, which must be settled before the advisory body can be set up. . . . I am assuming that the five or eight Jewish bodies suggested by the London conference will be included on the Advisory Committee.

Just as it is planned that the Governing Body should set up a permanent committee with which I could consult frequently and which in the absence of the full body will have the essential powers of the latter, I hope that the Advisory Committee will also appoint a permanent committee of its own, with which I could similarly keep in touch.

Another form of liaison between the official body and the non-official organizations which I am suggesting is this: instead of permitting organizations to designate members of my staff, I should be glad if certain of the more important groups designated representatives who might be associated with me, but not as members of the staff. For example, it would be helpful if Mr. Bentwich, on behalf of the British groups, Mr. Hyman, on behalf of the American [Jewish] Committee and the JDC, and Professor Mantoux, on behalf of the French groups (if he is acceptable to the ICA), and certain other persons representing other groups, could be asked to give all their time to this work.

In addition to the general Advisory Committee I am thinking of a powerful financial committee on which one might group the outstanding financial figures among the Jews and so far as possible among the non-Jews. It is obvious that such a committee might wield great influence.

Please do not conclude from my emphasis on the necessity of resisting certain pressures from some of the groups that I anticipate any serious difficulties in the way of successful cooperation with all the important groups. On the contrary, my long and frank talks with Dr. Weizmann, Dr. Goldmann, and Mr. Bentwich convince me that in all fundamental matters we are in essential agreement. Indeed, I was delighted with the general attitude of all these men, most of all perhaps by that of Dr. Weizmann himself. As to Professor Mantoux, who came to see me in Geneva last night from the Alliance Israelite, he enthusiastically accepted my interpretation of the relationship between the official and non-official bodies.

Thursday, November 16, 1933

Wurfbain came in while I was having breakfast, and together we arranged for a number of interviews during the morning. I called Miss Rothbarth to say that Wurfbain would get in touch with her. The day before she had told me that Pierre Diernet, the author of a book *Uncertain Germany*, was very much interested in this question, and that I should try to see him on my next visit to Paris. She had also urged me to see Hans Simons, formerly the head of Jäckh's school, who is in London and who probably knows as much about non-Jewish needs and organizations as any other one person.

Mme. Daniel Vavasseur[43] and Mme. Brunschwieg came in. They told me of the work of Miss Ginsberg's committee in Paris and offered their cooperation, and suggested that we use them as a liaison in Paris. Mme. Brunschwieg added that she could tell me now what she couldn't last night, that while one department of the French government expressed great willingness to aid the refugees to find places to work in France, the other department immediately concerned made the greatest difficulties. In other words, it was excessively difficult to secure a *carte de travail* [work permit].

Professor Sylvain Levi, president of the Alliance, came in. We had a long and to me very satisfactory talk. We discussed the general problem of scope and of organization. He gave every appearance of being in essential agreement to the views I expressed. He seems to me a singularly sensitive and intellectual person. He expressed the hope that the other French groups would accept Professor Mantoux as their common representative in Lausanne. I am not optimistic on this point.

Over to the bank, where I introduced Wurfbain and found a very cheering letter from home.

Baron Robert de Rothschild came in to leave some documents illustrating the needs of the French committee. He said that, of course, he would be delighted to see Wurfbain at any time.

Conference with Professor William Oualid. He is much more of a dapper gentleman than Levi, but I doubt if he is as direct or perhaps as sincere. We covered much the same ground that had been covered with other French spokesmen, and while Oualid seemed to assent on most of the points, I suspect that this assent was not as wholehearted as from the other representatives.

Just before going off to the train, I had an opportunity to talk to Hyman alone for a few minutes. He gave me a confidential report of his interview with Dr. Weizmann a day or two previous. It appears from Hyman's statement either that Weizmann greatly misinterpreted what I said or seriously misunderstood what I said. I do not think it was the latter. The chief points were the following: that I was naively optimistic in my expectations of securing large funds from personal friends among the Jews who happened to be rich. What I had said was not that I expected, but that I had an ambitious hope that some of these men who under normal circumstances were hardly what you would call "good" Jews might, in the face of the present crisis, be induced to make substantial sacrifices. Second: that I was indulging in a fantasy in my expectation that France could absorb German colonists. It is this misinterpretation which is fantastic; all that I said was that the suggestion of such large-scale colonization had been made and that I wondered what Dr. Weizmann's view of it was. Thirdly: that I was unwise and naive to contemplate immediate negotiations with Germany in the hope that through personal acquaintance I would be able to secure material conces-

43. Mme. Vavasseur, in charge of the Paris office of the International Committee for Securing Employment to Professional Workers, with first-rate connections with various government departments.

sions by the German government. Here again there was great misunderstanding or gross misinterpretation. What I said was that one of the most serious problems was the question of the refugees' property in Germany, and that if the Governing Board did not formally object, I would consider that one of my early duties would be to take soundings with a view to discovering whether or not a bridge could be built from Lausanne to Berlin. Fourth: that unless the private organizations were given a larger scope than I appeared to contemplate, their cordial support could not be obtained. This, of course, refers to my point of view that formal representation on the Governing Body would probably as a matter of law and as a matter of making the institution more effective, be limited to representatives of the governments. Dr. Weizmann either forgot or neglected to mention that I had reiterated my earnest desire that there should be in fact the closest cooperation between the private organizations and the Governing Body and the High Commission. I had emphasized that my concern in the matter of organization was only so to build the machine that the governments might the better be induced to permit it to be used effectively. Five: that Mr. Bentwich would probably not accept my suggestion of an advisory or liaison association with my staff. To this I can only comment that I shall discuss the matter more fully with Dr. Bentwich, explaining that I would expect him to be in most frequent consultation with members of the Governing Body and with me, and that my only reservation is that the members of my staff in the technical sense must be independent of either governmental or organizational connections.

As Mr. Hyman reported these comments to me, I know I was at first somewhat shocked that I could have been so completely misunderstood or misinterpreted, but later I realized that Dr. Weizmann might have had a definite purpose in putting those statements into my mouth. This purpose might have been either to bring pressure to bear upon me through the expectation that Hyman might repeat them to me, or with the purpose of weakening me at home through the expectation that Hyman would repeat them to Felix Warburg. I have confidence if either purpose were intended, it will be not be achieved.

During the morning and long before Mr. Hyman spoke to me I called Dr. Weizmann on the phone to express the hope that we should have an opportunity to talk again in London. He invited me to lunch at his home on Saturday. I accepted. I shall look forward to that interview with considerable interest. But I have made up my mind not be bludgeoned, bluffed, or cajoled into acceptance of principles either as to the organization of the Commission or as to the makeup of my own staff which seem to me to be inconsistent with the effectiveness of the former and the independence of the latter.

Off to the train for London with my staff, Herbert May and Olive Sawyer, Wurfbain going as far as the train. On the way to Calais Miss Sawyer and I got part of the diary out of the way, and with Herbert May we discussed various problems. Now in the train to London I am finishing this dictation.

I forgot, in dictating about the dinner at the de Rothschilds, to record that I went out of my way to deliver something of a lecture on the general attitude of

French Jewry toward the Jewish question as a whole. I pointed out that while it would be difficult perhaps for them to realize the extent to which their interests are really common with those of the less fortunate Jews in Central and Eastern Europe, the leaders of French Jewry ought to fight against the prevailing tendency of their fellow French Jews to put always the interest of their own group or even that of France so far above the common interests of Jews everywhere. In short, mine was an appeal against what to many Jews in England and Eastern Europe appears to be the exaggerated nationalism of the French Jews.

Arrived in London after seven and finally established ourselves in Brown's Hotel.

London, Friday, November 17, 1933

. . . .

At 11:15 went over to the Foreign Office to see Mr. Sargent.[44] He called in Mr. Propero(?)—Vansittart was on his vacation, and Simon and Eden were just leaving for Geneva. I outlined my plan of organization; Mr. Sargent seemed to be in hearty sympathy. On the specific points of the relations of the private organizations he was not as unqualified as had been Léger. Evidently the Foreign Office had felt the influence of the Jewish organizations. As to the point about direct access by the High Commissioner to the governments, he assented. I brought up specifically the question of a possible formal British resolution seeking to eliminate Palestine from the scope of the High Commission. I urged that this not be done, but, of course, I had no intention of interfering as between the Jewish Agency and the High Commission in Palestine on the question of certificates; that I would, of course, be punctilious not to make Britain's position as between the Jews and the Arabs more difficult; that, however, it would be an unfortunate precedent if one of the countries formally reserved a definite territory from the Commission's jurisdiction. I added that I hoped that the British government would be satisfied to leave the record as it exists. Sargent replied that he felt sure the Foreign Office would agree, that he does not think they had any intention of making a formal reservation.

We then discussed the scope of the Commission's work. On these points as outlined by me Sargent seemed to be in agreement. In particular, he recognized that the High Commissioner should be permitted to do what he can to build the bridge from Lausanne to Berlin, though of course he, not the Commission, would have to assume the responsibility for any unfortunate results.

I brought up the name of Cecil, saying that if the British government decided to name him, it would give me great pleasure; that, personally, I hope he might be selected as chairman. Sargent replied that they hoped to make an announcement in a day or two.

44. Sir Orme G. Sargent, assistant undersecretary at the British Foreign Office.

Viscount Cecil of Chelwood

Viscount Cecil of Chelwood, official Nobel Peace Prize photograph, 1937. Nobel Foundation.

Edgar Algernon Robert Gascoyne-Cecil was born in 1864 in London into a renowned and illustrious English family. He was the third son of the third Marquess of Salisbury, a dominant figure in British politics and foreign affairs, who had served as prime minister three times. Cecil received a religious upbringing, attended Eton and Oxford, became a barrister, and was elected to Parliament as a Conservative in 1906. As a free trader and supporter of women's suffrage, Cecil felt uncomfortable within his own party. He broke with it in 1910 to run as an independent. During World War I he held various posts in the Foreign Office, serving under his cousin Arthur Balfour, the foreign secretary.

Cecil was stunned by the horror and bloodshed of the war. He later wrote: "Like most people, I had very little idea of what modern war was like. . . . I could not think that the statesmen of a highly civilized Europe would plunge their countries into the 'orgy of lust and cruelty' which such a war must mean. However, I was quite wrong."[1] As early as 1916 he had circulated to the Cabinet a memorandum containing proposals for the avoidance of future wars. This proposal eventually led to the formation of a committee, under Lord Phillimore, that produced the first draft of the Covenant of the League of Nations. The League, collective security, and disarmament absorbed virtually all of Cecil's time and energy. He played a major role at Versailles in the adoption of the Covenant and in persuading neutral nations to join the League.

In 1933 Anglo-Jewish leaders pushed Cecil as their candidate for League High Commissioner. Cecil, however, showed no resentment toward McDonald, and actually became chair of the High Commision's Governing Body and an informal adviser to the commissioner too. He gave McDonald essential insight into the British political scene, even if his attitude toward Zionists (and Jews generally) was less positive than McDonald's.

From the League's creation until its demise in 1946, Cecil's public life was devoted to it. He traveled the world explaining the League to the public. At the same time he held various cabinet posts in British governments during the 1920s until he made a final break with the British Cabinet due to his dissatisfaction with its attitude toward the League. Cecil subsequently worked independently on behalf of the League. He headed the British League of Nations Union from 1923 to 1945 and was a founder of the International Peace Campaign. Among many other honors, he was awarded the Nobel Peace Prize in 1937. In the spring of 1946, at the final meeting of the League in Geneva, he ended his speech with the sentence, "The League is dead: long live the United Nations!"

1. Viscount Cecil, *A Great Experiment* (New York: Oxford University Press, 1941), 38.

When I returned to the hotel, I found Bentwich, Laski,[45] and Montefiore waiting for me. We went at once to the heart of the matter. I cleared up any misunderstandings that there may have been about my attitude towards Germany and the Liebman suggestion of colonization in France. Then I began a comprehensive and frank outline of the principles on which I thought the organization should be set up. First and primarily, efficiency should be the objective. Second, this could be secured by considering the governmental character; that by fortunate chance we had the backing of the governments; that it was imperative not to give them an excuse or reason for withdrawal. Third, that in fact and practice there should be the closest possible cooperation with the private organizations; otherwise the active power would be absent.

I then suggested that the Advisory Body name its permanent executive of five—three Jews and two non-Jews—who would be invited by the Governing Body to sit virtually as members in an advisory capacity without vote. I stressed that voting in an organization of this sort would not be important, and that the character, knowledge, and greater interest of the private members would give them a very large influence.

Bentwich was still inclined to stress the importance of status for the organizations if popular support were to be secured. Montefiore inclined to support my position, as did Laski, though the latter tentatively outlined the idea of a congress within which the Governing Body would be the directing organization. This idea won no support.

The other points discussed were of less consequence and brought out no important differences of opinion. In the course of the discussion I stressed my interest in having Cecil named and my hope that Bentwich would associate himself with me in the work.

After Montefiore and Bentwich left, Laski stayed behind saying that he wished to warn me of one or two matters. Then he characterized some of his associates: Bentwich is a dear, almost a saint, but not always practical; Weizmann is a prima donna and likes to be treated as such, etc.

Lunched with Cecil at his house. The only other person present was Lady Cecil. During the meal we talked about conditions in Germany. Lady Cecil expressed herself strongly to the effect that the treaty[46] and the actions of the Allies had brought on Hitlerism. Cecil said that France would have to make some terms with Germany on armaments because they dared not go against the opinion of England, Italy, and the United States. His own government, he thought, had been lamentably weak, showing neither intelligence [n]or courage.

After lunch Cecil and I went over the whole problem of the Commission. He told me first that Simon had asked him to serve, that he had written a con-

45. Laski wrote to Cyrus Adler that he would cooperate with McDonald despite earlier questions as to his suitability and that he had persuaded him to appoint Bentwich as his right-hand man. Laski to Adler, December 4, 1933, McDonald Papers, USHMM.

46. Treaty of Versailles.

ditional acceptance, the condition being that he would not be able to attend a meeting on November 28. I told him that I hoped that would not be permitted to stand in the way, that I would much rather have a substitute for the first meeting than to have him decline. He suggested that perhaps if the Foreign Office decided to name a substitute, that person, he, and I might get together in advance of the meeting. I agreed. I also told him that I would send my dossier of material for his study.

On points of organization Cecil was, from my point of view, satisfactory. He recognized the importance of keeping the official character, but thought there would be no real difficulty in giving the private organizations effective participation. He agreed that the High Commission should have direct access to the governments.

We talked of Weizmann, with whom Cecil has frequently been associated. He said that Weizmann, when he first met him during the war, appeared to him to be the most impressive personality he had ever met. He recognized certain difficulties in dealing with Weizmann, but added: "After all, you must remember he is a Russian Jew with a background very different from ours."

As I was leaving, I told Cecil how helpful I was sure his cooperation would be, how much I should enjoy working with him, and he was kind enough to reciprocate these sentiments, adding that since we had worked together so long without any difficulties, we should not be likely to have any now.

Back to the hotel just in time to meet Louis Oungre, who had arrived a few minutes earlier. We talked for more than an hour, covering a very wide range of subjects. He was sympathetic with my scheme of organization, but most of our time was given over to talk by him on the problem of colonization as he saw it. I asked him if he would not prepare for me for my use in getting up my opening statement at the meeting of the Governing Body a kind of sketch of the emigration possibilities, economic and political, throughout the world. He gave me such a sketch in a brief statement then, and promised to amplify it for me in a memorandum.

When he left, I felt that we had made a good beginning together. He is less vain than his brother, more intelligent and able. I told him that I expected to lean heavily upon him; this did not displease him.

Bentwich came in a few minutes after Oungre left, and we talked for nearly two hours about Jewish personalities and organizations, and about possible ways of bringing in non-Jewish groups more effectively and caring better for the non-Jewish refugees. At the end I told him that I was anxious that he give his whole time to this job, and that I was confident that we could find a mutually satisfactory basis.

Before I finished dressing, Otto Schiff was announced. We went out together for dinner at the Savoy and talked until nearly midnight. On organizational matters Mr. Schiff was completely satisfactory, taking a view very similar to that of Felix Warburg and Jimmy Rosenberg at home. He was critical of Dr. Weizmann on the ground that Weizmann was difficult to work with because of

Weizmann's obsession by a single idea and because of Weizmann's tortuousness in strategy. Nonetheless, Schiff stressed the fundamental devotion of Weizmann, his unselfishness during the war, etc. It seemed to me, therefore, that one could conclude that Weizmann was fundamentally loyal but ungenerous in his attitude toward those who did not agree 100 percent with him, and Machiavellian in methods.

Schiff explained to me the new organization, Anglo-HICEM, as a device to take the management of German immigration out of the inefficient hands of Edouard Oungre and place them in the more efficient hands of an English committee.

On the larger questions of program, financing, etc., Schiff seemed to me to be very sound. Also in his estimates of leading personalities in the United States and in England, his judgments were convincing. It was a great pleasure to talk with him so frankly.

After dinner we walked back to the hotel, he without an overcoat though there was considerable mist. He is a singularly unselfish, kindly, devoted personality.

Saturday, November 18, 1933

....

Fritz Simon, formerly of the Deutsche Hochschule fur Politik, came at 9:30. We talked about the non-Jewish aspects of the problem. He made some helpful suggestions, and I was very favorably impressed by him. If later there were an opportunity to add a first-rate German to the staff, he might be the man. I would trust him much more than Jäckh. He seems more straightforward, less the opportunist; but his capacities would have to be compared with those of Demuth, now in Zurich, and of Simon from Düsseldorf, about whom Limburg wrote us.

At 10:30 went over to Sir Leonard Cohen's[47] house, where I found Louis Oungre with Sir Leonard. We talked for more than two hours. I began by sketching the history of the Commission and my part in it. I did not intend to discuss the organization problems in detail, but Sir Leonard asked me to, so I covered the same ground that I had with the Laski group the day before. His attitude was satisfactory to me. He did not seem concerned with status as such, but only anxious that an efficient machine be set up. We then talked about program. I told him as I had Laski et al. that there was no use assuming that the London program had general support, that the Americans or the French group were really in accord. I stressed the necessity of a new approach, building on what had been done. He agreed. He said that he had hoped that the American [Jewish] Committee and the JDC would have in Europe an authorized repre-

47. Sir Leonard Cohen, chairman of the law and parliamentary committee of the Board of Deputies of British Jews. Railroad magnate.

sentative with power. I told him I did not know of their plans, but I did not think he could count on this.

As to finance, he asked whether I thought it was possible to envisage a worldwide common appeal. I replied that I hoped that there might be a program which could be pressed either as a whole or in sections, thus permitting a general or a special appeal. I offered no opinion as to the possibility of a central pool from which the funds could be allocated.

As I was leaving, Sir Leonard said that he and his associates in ICA (and this Oungre endorsed) were anxious to help in every way they could; that, of course, their work was primarily colonization and they must keep in mind their fundamental objectives. I thanked him for his offer of cooperation and added that I trusted that he and his colleagues, in view of the present tragic and in modern times unprecedented crisis, would not interpret narrowly or technically ICA's functions. He and Oungre seemed sympathetic to this view.

Earlier we had discussed the situation in Paris. They were inclined to agree that a new American personality would be helpful in that situation. They felt that Dr. Kahn, as a German, would always be disadvantaged in dealing with the French about French problems. Moreover, Sir Leonard thought that Kahn was not the same man he had been before the shock of his experiences under the Nazis. Sir Leonard hoped that either Lewis Strauss or someone like him might be brought into the picture.

Sir Leonard took me to the door and was really touching in his attitude of appreciation at my taking on this job and in his own willingness to do his utmost. He only regretted, he said, that he was an old man. I replied that he did not seem old to me, and that world Jewry was fortunate in the number of young English Jews who were showing great power of leadership and great devotion.

When I returned to the hotel, Miss Sawyer met me with the news that the Foreign Office had called to say that Cecil would be able to attend a meeting on December 1 or any time between then and December 9. The implication was that the Foreign Office would be pleased if I consented to a postponement. I called Sargent to say that I was so delighted with Cecil's nomination that I should be happy to consider the postponement and hoped that it could be arranged for the fifth; that there would probably be an official communication to this effect within a few days. He thanked me.

I then cabled to Washington, inquiring if postponement would please the State Department. The prompt answer was that it would.

Out to Dr. Weizmann's house near the Olympia for lunch. Besides Dr. Weizmann and his wife and me there were his two sons, about twenty-four and seventeen, Lola Hahn, and a woman of uncertain age of a type that one finds so frequently in English houses, to whom one is usually not introduced and who appears to occupy no particular position. At luncheon the talk was general, covering such subjects as relations between parents and children, are dancing and bridge intellectual pursuits (Dr. Weizmann taking strongly the negative, and Mrs. Weizmann and I the affirmative). Dr. Weizmann talked at length and, I thought, with almost terrible harshness, especially in the presence of Lola, about the German Jews, whom he criticized as leaders in the worst form of assimilation, as persons who cringed and whimpered when the test came, and who in general could not be admired. Mrs. Weizmann and I intervened on behalf of the condemned, but carried no conviction to Dr. Weizmann. What a pity that he is so uncompromisingly bitter towards those, especially among the Jews, who disagree with him.

After lunch Dr. Weizmann and I had half an hour or forty-five minutes together. I took occasion to correct any misunderstanding that he may have had about our previous talk, especially on the points about my going into Germany, the Liebman French scheme, and my financial expectations in reference to men like John Schiff and Bernard Baruch. He than asked me what my present ideas were in reference to organization. I outlined to him the scheme I had suggested to Laski et al. Dr. Weizmann said that seemed to him a satisfactory compromise. In this connection I asked him if he would not suggest to me a panel of five or six Jews outstanding in the world, from which might be chosen two to be associated with him on the Governing Body in an advisory capacity. He mentioned I think Professor Cohen of Amsterdam, but was not very satisfactory with other suggestions. The second point he asked about was staff. I told him that I was so convinced of Bentwich's sincerity, utter selflessness, and the wide confidence that he commanded among Jews everywhere that I hoped he would be associated with me directly in an important capacity. This seemed to suit Weizmann. The third point was funds: did I, he asked, have in mind a universal appeal? If so, he would like to be a party to it provided, of course, the interests of Palestine were adequately safeguarded; if not, he would have to make a separate appeal. I told him much the same as I had told Sir Leonard—my hope that there might be a general appeal, but with provisions for appeals on specific projects so that one might have the advantage of the broader scope and of the narrower objectives. This too seemed to suit him. During lunch and afterwards he told me something of the fund which he was raising himself directly for Palestine, and gave me the impression that funds to be received from the Allocations Committee would be proportionately reduced as he raised his own funds.

As to the High Commission and Palestine, I took the initiative in telling him of my talk with the Foreign Office, and I added with a special purpose that of course it must be obvious that the Commission and the High Commissioner could not endorse a general appeal or work for it if it included Palestine unless the Commission and especially the High Commissioner could make up their own minds about the Palestine part of the program; that, therefore, the theory that Palestine is outside the scope of the High Commissioner is clearly inconsistent with the desire to have the High Commissioner help on the general financial appeal. Dr. Weizmann acquiesced in this view, though I am sure he still has strong mental reservations about my part in Palestine.

As I was leaving, I said goodbye to Mrs. Weizmann, who said that she hoped they might see me in their house again soon. Dr. Weizmann took me to the street to show me my way. As we parted I said, "Dr. Weizmann, you can of course be of great help to me, and I perhaps of some use to you." I implied that such mutual usefulness would of course be dependent upon mutual confidence and trust. His parting words were, "I shall, of course, not always agree with you, but you may be absolutely certain of my loyalty." I, of course, accepted that at its face value. I left with a feeling that there is at least an even chance that Dr. Weizmann and I can really work together effectively. Certainly I have every intention to do my utmost towards this end.[48]

At four o'clock Mr. Joseph L. Cohen[49] came to the hotel. He is an economist now working with Marks & Spencer as a consultant. He had been lent by them to prepare a general survey of the situation on the continent for the London Refugee Conference. Obviously it was impossible to talk about the situation everywhere, so we centered on the problem in Paris. Cohen evidently is well informed, but is inclined to be dogmatic and is certainly unsympathetic towards the French. He felt that there should be a date fixed in the near future at which time all direct relief, except of course to those such as women, children, and invalids who could not be expected to work, should cease and that funds should be available only for reconstructive purposes. About this time we were joined by Otto Schiff and Louis Oungre, and they, with Wurfbain, Mr. May, and I, continued the discussion of the Paris situation until nearly seven o'clock. Out of it all certain points seemed clearly established.

First, the French must continue to have financial help.

Second, they need just as badly help in reorganization of their relief and in their plans to begin constructive work.

Third, Dr. Kahn, despite his great record of achievement and devotion, is not the man to work effectively with the French: (a) he is a German and remains very German in his accent, his approach to problems, and his manner; (b) according to those who know him best, he is not the same man he was before the shock of his experiences under the Nazis; (c) his very experience with large enterprises, where he was given a relatively free hand, makes him less suitable to effect the many readjustments essential in the local situation in Paris.

Fourth, from the above the conclusion seems inescapable that a new American personality, not of the agent type, but a man of high standing and the capacity to deal sympathetically but as an equal with the members of the French committee, should be injected into the situation.

48. On November 21 Weizmann wrote: "Last week I spoke to McDonald in person in Paris and again in the last few days here in London. . . . [He] is extremely ambitious and this alone will make him do his best so as to be able to show success in his activity. He aims much higher and intends to use this matter as a stepping stone for his future political career. . . . His election was very energetically supported by the American Jews under the leadership of Felix Warburg together with the Rockefeller Foundation. . . . I am convinced that McDonald will be forced by circumstances to pay a great deal of attention to Palestine and will . . . come into closer contact with us." Letter to Arthur Ruppin, *The Letters and Papers of Chaim Weizmann*, 137–139.

49. Joseph L. Cohen, also British member of the advisory committee on social insurance of the International Labor Organization.

Fifth, the suggestion that there be set up in Paris a committee of five, three Frenchmen, an Englishman (Frank Goldsmith, already on the job), and an American, this committee to have supervisory power. It of course was understood that everything should be done to save Dr. Kahn's sensibilities; moreover, nothing suggested would have reflected on his relations with the JDC.

It was agreed that it would be best if I should telephone Felix Warburg frankly the prevailing view.

I asked Schiff to remain for a moment after the others left. I told him that while, as I had said earlier, I was prepared to take off my coat and help raise the large funds needed for an agreed program, I did not feel that it was up to me to raise the budget for my office, that I thought this was a problem for New York and London, perhaps with some help from Holland and Paris, to solve; that I estimated roughly an expenditure for the office of $100,000 the first year. I got the impression that he approved my suggestions.

Olive Sawyer had scarcely left when d'Avigdor-Goldsmid[50] arrived. Previously I had slipped out from the conference about the Paris situation to talk downstairs with Charles Roden Buxton, who asked about possible representation on the Advisory Body of the Second International[51] and of the Save the Children Fund. I said that we should certainly consider both, that my reservation as to the former was twofold: (a) would not the representation of the trade unions international serve the same purpose better, because the trade unions might be more able and willing to help with actual relief? (b) the trade union affiliation, though not welcome to the Germans, would be less offensive than that of the Second International. I told Buxton that I hoped on my return I should have an opportunity to talk with his brother, Lord Noel-Buxton, about further cooperation.

D'Avigdor-Goldsmid brought with him the secretary of the Allocations Committee, Stephany. The latter had told me that he would be in the hotel when d'Avigdor-Goldsmid arrived, and I had said that I would, of course, be glad to have him come with his chief if the latter desired it.

I was delighted with d'Avigdor-Goldsmid. He is so simple and unaffected and kindly. He made me feel that he thought I had really done him a great honor to ask to see him. And also what is a high merit in a deaf person, he uses a machine which avoids any necessity of raising one's voice.

I outlined to him the background, the organizational scheme, and the program as I had done for Sir Leonard. D'Avigdor-Goldsmid seemed to be enthusiastically favorable to these ideas. I told him what I had said to Sir Leonard about the ICA. D'Avidgor-Goldsmid laughed and said, "Well, you know I am also on the ICA Board." I think he will be sympathetic to a broad interpretation of ICA's work.

50. Sir Osmond Elim d'Avigdor-Goldsmid, president of the Board of Deputies of British Jews and chairman of the Jewish Agency for Palestine in London. Also president of ICA. A member of the Jewish elite respected by both Zionists and non-Zionists.

51. The international association of Socialist and Social Democratic parties. Dominated by European parties, some of which were now suppressed in their own countries (e.g., Germany, Italy).

Towards the end of our talk d'Avigdor-Goldsmid said, and I think with complete sincerity, "If at any time anything bothers you in the situation and one which I might be of some help, please feel free to write me with complete frankness. I am, as my friends will tell you, discreet." I thanked him and said I would take advantage of his offer when the occasion arose. I also told him what I had said to Schiff about the administrative budget of the office as contrasted with the budget for constructive work, towards the raising of which I would welcome an opportunity to do my part. He remarked that my view about the Commission's budget was sound.

Earlier I had asked Cohen if he had any objection to my reading his reports to the London Conference. He said no, provided the Allocations Committee was willing. D'Avigdor-Goldsmid naturally gave his permission at once when I asked, and Stephany promised that they would be delivered the next day at the hotel.

During the talk with d'Avigdor-Goldsmid the telephone call came through from Felix Warburg in New York. I had earlier told Lola Hahn that I was going to speak to her uncle and that I should be glad if she said a word, so she joined me when the connection was made.

I told Felix Warburg of the Paris situation as I saw it, and urged the interjection of a new American personality. I was careful to explain that this should not be taken as in any sense a reflection on Dr. Kahn, but that through no fault of his own he seemed to me unable to work with the French in the way that was imperatively necessary. Warburg asked what I thought about Mr. Liebman coming back. I had to reply that I did not think he would be the ideal person. Warburg then asked about Mr. Hyman; my reply was the same. I added: "What you need is a man of the type of Lewis Strauss." Warburg said he could not come, and asked what I thought of Professor Goodhart.[52] I agreed that he would be excellent, but wondered whether he could spend the necessary time in Paris. It was left that Warburg would study the situation.

I had barely finished my talk with d'Avigdor-Goldsmid when Neville Laski and his wife arrived to take me out to dinner at the home of Mr. and Mrs. Frank Lazarus. Others who were either at dinner or later included Herbert May, Professor Goodhart, and one or two others. Earlier in the day I had telephoned Frankfurter and tentatively arranged to go up to Oxford Sunday afternoon after returning from Chichester, where I was to have lunch with the bishop. My friends, however, told me that this would be next to impossible.

During dinner and after there was general conversation about the refugee problem. The only point which needs recording was an incident that occurred after the dinner group had broken up. Neville Laski stood me in a corner and proceeded to argue that if there were three Jews on the Advisory Body, one

52. Arthur Lehman Goodhart, of the Lehman banking family, professor of jurisprudence at Oxford University and later Master of University College, thus the first Jew and the first American to head an Oxford college.

Weizmann and one an American, the other should be himself. His contention was that since the London conference he had become, next to Weizmann, the best known Jew in Europe; that Weizmann was not really an Englishman; that he would be able to function effectively; that he was suggesting this not in a spirit of ambition but of sacrifice, because his professional career would suffer. I naturally was a little nonplussed, but I refused to commit myself at all. On the contrary, I told him that I could not see how it would be possible for the third person to be an Englishman in view of the proposed set-up. Later Laski buttonholed Herbert May for the same purpose.

Sunday, November 19, 1933

Telephoned Professor Frankfurter to ask if he could come to London in view of the difficulty of my keeping both engagements. He explained that he would like to do so, but that he had a luncheon party at his own house, and had accepted to go to a college dinner that night, so that he could not make it. I left it with him then that I would come to Oxford if I returned from Chichester in time.

Had breakfast in my room, and was joined by Lola Hahn, Wilfrid Israel,[53] Lubinsky, and Sherman. We talked for an hour. They were chiefly concerned by two matters: first, the danger that the Reich would within a few weeks, possibly by the first of the year, decree formally a second-class citizenship for Jews. This they looked upon as a threat so ominous that they could not express their feelings adequately. I agreed that this blow would be terrible, not only for the Jews in Germany but also outside of Germany, and that it might suddenly increase the proportions of the refugee problem to such an extent as to make it wholly unmanageable.

Later during the day I telephoned Frankfurter and told him what I had learned and asked his advice.[54]

Another matter related to the question of possible second-class status was my friends' pitiful anxiety that what they called an armistice might be arranged between them and their government. At present, as they pointed out, they never know from day to day when they are committing an act of "treason," such, for example, in this conference with me. Moreover, unless and until they can know what are the plans of their government, it is and will continue to be impossible

53. Wilfrid Israel, close friend and co-worker in Jewish causes in Germany with Lola Hahn, helped found Youth Aliyah. Born in England, he was able in the 1930s to serve as Max Warburg's secret envoy to the British Jews. See Naomi Shephard, *A Refuge from Darkness: Wilfrid Israel and the Rescue of the Jews* (New York: Pantheon, 1984).

54. McDonald wrote that he had reliable information that the German government was contemplating the issuance in the near future of a decree or decrees establishing formally a second-class citizenship for German Jews. Describing the terrible consequences of such "retrogressing to the inhumane and un-Christian practices of an earlier age should, I think, be forestalled if there is any conceivable way of doing so." He also stressed the danger to world peace if the refugee exodus should become a flood as a result of these decrees. On November 23 Frankfurter wrote to President Roosevelt, enclosing the letter from McDonald with the comment, "I dare say that Dodd has informed you of these matters directly, but since McDonald writes me with great perturbation, you might like to see the letter." *Roosevelt and Frankfurter: Their Correspondence, 1928–1945,* annotated by Max Freedman (Boston: Little Brown, 1967), pp. 173–174.

for them to work out a program of organized emigration, and meanwhile, so long as the danger of the government's attitude becoming worse remains, there is the possibility of panicky exodus which would be disastrous.

I agreed with their analysis and with the conclusion which follows logically from it, that nothing in the whole of the present situation is as vitally important as building a bridge from Lausanne to Berlin. I told them that they could be assured that I would make every effort which seemed to give any hope of securing this result.

The second point which they wished specifically to discuss was the relationship between German Jewry and the Commission and the High Commissioner. They said it is impossible that any individual or individuals or group of individuals outside of Germany should represent German Jewry. How well I realized this after listening to Dr. Weizmann's denunciation of German Jewry the day previous! My guests, therefore, said that they hoped a way could be found by which they, if not represented on my staff or in the Governing Body, would at any rate be in constant and close touch. I agreed that this certainly should be striven for. I pointed out, however, that there were two difficulties preventing an immediate decision as to the method of such contact: (a) they could not be sure what their government would permit or what would be possible without their government's permission; (b) I could not be sure what form of contact to accept until I had had an opportunity to confer with my Governing Body and to sound out German authorities on the possibility of direct approaches to Berlin. It was left that they would inquire when they got back to Berlin to find out, if possible, what the government would be willing to have them do. I, on my side, would study the problem, and that they would get in touch with me as soon as possible in Geneva or Lausanne.

As Wilfrid Israel and Lola Hahn and the others talked to me, I had a sense of participating in a terrible human tragedy, these young persons so poignantly represented the suffering of their people.

A little after ten Mrs. Lazarus in her car, Bentwich and his wife, and I left for Chichester. It was a lovely drive. We arrived about 12:30. The Cathedral and the Episcopal Palace go back to the thirteenth, fourteenth, and sixteenth centuries. They are as beautiful as they are interesting. Unfortunately, we had so little time that there were only a few minutes to glance at the grounds and the buildings.

At luncheon besides the bishop[55] and his wife and ourselves were the bishop's chaplain, meek and white as a chaplain would be, [and] the bishop's wife's sister. After lunch Bentwich and I went to the bishop's study, a room which made me much more envious than was suitable for a lovely Sunday. Our

55. The Right Reverend George Kennedy Allen Bell, bishop of Chichester, 1929–1958, a forward-looking man who supported the German Confessional Church in its struggle with Hitler. In 1936 he sponsored the National Christian Appeal for Refugees from Germany, which resulted in the formation of the International Christian Committee for German Refugees.

talk was mostly about the possibility of a general appeal, especially through the Christian churches of the world, during the Christmas season on behalf of the refugees. The bishop had already secured from the archbishop of Canterbury a statement to the effect that he would gladly lead such an appeal in Britain. We then talked about how such an appeal could be made most effectively. I said that I thought through the Federal Council of Churches it might be broadcast in the States.[56] The bishop said that through Dr. Keller, the Federal Council representative in Geneva, or through the office of Life and Work, which was in the same building in Geneva, the European churches might be brought in. He thought that it would be best if the High Commission or the High Commissioner issued an appeal which would then be supported by the church groups and other organizations in the different countries.

The question was raised as to whom contributions might be sent, and for what if any specific purpose they should be allocated. It seemed to me that logically the contributions should go to the organizations in the different countries making the appeal, and then be forwarded to a central point, presumably the Commission. Bentwich thought that perhaps the funds should go to the existing organizations. I said that, of course, one could not be sure what amount would be raised, but probably it would not be larger than would be needed for urgent situations. It was left that Bentwich and I would follow up the matter and communicate with the bishop as soon as there had been an opportunity for consultation in Geneva.

. . . .

As I was leaving Bentwich at the hotel, we agreed that he would work with me, the exact arrangement to be settled later. He indicated, however, that he would not expect compensation larger than that necessary to make up what he would have received at the university. We also agreed that he would go into Germany, perhaps Tuesday night, and join me at Geneva later in the week. I have every confidence that his connection will be of great value.[57]

Back to the hotel to find Miss Sawyer anxiously waiting my return because Mr. Anthony de Rothschild[58] had telephoned earlier and had come to tea at the time when I was expected back, and was now waiting for me at his house. Meantime, Neville Laski had called to say that I was expected at his house for dinner. I told Miss Sawyer to tell him that that would be impossible unless Frankfurter was coming up, which I was sure he was not.

56. The Federal Council's response seemed to McDonald to indicate, as he wrote to Miss Ogden November 27, "that they would favor an appeal only if it emphasized the need of the non-Jewish refugees. . . . It seemed to me that unless the appeal could be made to Christians for the support of all refugees alike, it would lose its chief raison d'etre. When will the Church leaders at home come to the realization that they have a moral responsibility in this matter?" Letter to Miss Ogden. Copy in McDonald Papers, USHMM.

57. See inserted commentary in the entry of November 22, 1933.

58. Anthony de Rothschild, president of Norwood Home for Jewish Children.

I went over to de Rothschild's house about six and gave him the background of the situation as I saw it. While in his room, I telephoned Frankfurter while Anthony de Rothschild listened, and told Frankfurter of the danger referred to before and the arrangement I spoke of earlier was made. Anthony de Rothschild asked me if I was free for dinner, would I mind if he tried to get hold of Lionel Cohen, son of Sir Leonard? I told him I should be delighted to join him, and, of course, talk to Lionel Cohen.

At dinner at Anthony de Rothschild's were Mr. & Mrs., a friend of Madame, and later Lionel Cohen came in. The talk during dinner was all about the situation in Germany and what might be done. Madame Rothschild showed singular understanding and deep emotional concerns. Repeatedly she would interrupt me because she was unable to restrain her feelings. Obviously added to her feelings as a Jewess are her feelings as a Frenchwoman towards the Germans. All of us talked together until about 10:30; then the ladies left, and we three men continued the conversation. It turned then mostly on Weizmann and his relations to other Jewish personalities and the problem with which we were all concerned. I soon learned that both men had had sharp differences of opinion as to policy with Weizmann, and that they too had doubts as to Weizmann's straightforwardness in negotiations. Their view did not seem to be very different from mine, that fundamentally Weizmann is deeply in earnest and an idealist, but that in his strategy he is tortuous.

We also talked about the French situation. The two men shared a view similar to mine about Dr. Kahn and as to the desirability of a change there.

As I was leaving, both men expressed the wish to keep in touch with me. Lionel Cohen asked with whom did I keep in contact in London? I replied that I hoped to have the benefit of the counsel of Sir Leonard, d'Avigdor Goldsmid, Neville Laski, and M., and Otto Schiff, and of course themselves. Mrs. Rothschild asked when I was coming back to see them, and I replied at the earliest opportunity.

Home late and struggled alone with a last minute cable to New York.

Amsterdam, Monday, November 20, 1933

Herbert May had gone off the previous day to Paris and Geneva to take care of the telegrams announcing the postponement of the Governing Body meeting to December 5. Wurfbain and Miss Sawyer had deserted me by taking the night boat to Amsterdam. I took the early plane for Amsterdam. It was a foggy morning, but the sun broke through as we reached Croyden. It was a most pleasant flight above the clouds and over the sea, but to my discomfiture, about half an hour before we were scheduled to arrive, the pilot announced that we were going to Rotterdam, not Amsterdam. A dense fog at the latter place made landing there impossible or hazardous. Sent word from Rotterdam that I would arrive about 1:30. Arriving at the hotel I found André Wurfbain in conference with a Dutch Social Democrat. After a hurried lunch together we met the following members of the Dutch community: Professor D. Cohen,[59] Professor Fryda, Mr. A. Asscher,[60] and Mrs. Van Tyn.[61] There was time only for a brief exchange of views and to plan to meet the next day.

At 4:30 Wurfbain and I called on Professor François at the Ministry of Foreign Affairs at The Hague, and later we went to see de Graeff, and after that returned again to talk with François. With both men I was in complete agreement. Their attitude on such questions as the relations of the private organizations, the matter of direct access by the High Commissioner to the governments, the relations of the High Commissioner to Germany and on the general program, was almost identical with that which I had hitherto been urging. De Graeff made plain that he would not like to have the Commission located in The Hague, but that in any other respect he and his government would be glad to give the fullest cooperation, and I think he meant what he said. He stressed the question of passports, saying that he thought something like the Nansen passports would have to be devised to meet the exigencies of the immediate situation. Later, I asked François for his opinion on this problem, and intimated that I might lean on him for further help.

Back to the hotel and worked with Wurfbain and Miss Sawyer on various matters until the three of us went out to a late and full dinner at the Restaurant Royale.

Returning to the hotel, delighted to find a cable from Joseph Chamberlain announcing his appointment.[62] I immediately cabled him to say how pleased I was and that I hoped he might come directly to Geneva in order to help with the preparatory work for the first meeting of the Governing Body.

Tuesday, November 21, 1933

Finished up odds and ends before the arrival of Max Warburg at 10:30. I had told him that I would place myself unreservedly at his disposal. Therefore, we were together uninterruptedly until three o'clock. At least from my point of view it was a notable conference.

It began by my setting forth in detail and at length the background of the problem, the way in which the machinery was set up, my plans for its use, and my own fundamental philosophy on the relationship between Jews and non-Jews. Mr. Warburg listened with closest attention and apparent approval. He then began by outlining the reasons which in his judgment made it so impera-

59. Dr. David Cohen, professor of ancient history at Amsterdam University. As secretary of the Comité voor Bijzondere Joodse Belangen, he directed the work for Jewish refugees.

60. Abraham Asscher, chairman of the Dutch Committee for Jewish Special Needs. In 1941 named co-chairman of the Jewish Council of Amsterdam, which carried out various tasks under Nazi occupation in the hope that compliance might bring protection. Asscher was deported to Westerbork in 1943. Condemned after the war by a Jewish Honor Council.

61. Gertrude Van Tyn, social worker of independent means, co-worker with Dr. Cohen for Jewish refugees, born in Germany.

62. Appointment as American representative on the Governing Body of the High Commission.

Max Warburg

Max Warburg was a true German patriot and a highly visible member of the German-Jewish financial elite in both the German Empire and the Weimar Republic. Senior partner in the private bank M. M. Warburg of Hamburg, he supported his country without reserve during World War I and helped to finance the war effort—although two of his brothers in the United States helped the American cause. Despite growing evidence of official anti-Semitism, he remained loyal to Kaiser Wilhelm and the Hohenzollern monarchy until it collapsed under the weight of military defeat and revolt from below. No liberal, he joined the right-of-center German People's Party in the republic.

In 1933 he found himself in the impossible position of reconciling his economic and social position—and his desire to serve his country—with that of a Jew in Nazi Germany. He retreated by stages from positions of influence—he lost his position on the Advisory Council of the Reichsbank in October 1933. Still, his longstanding personal and professional ties with Hjalmar Schacht gave him some influence and a little inside information. Max Warburg initially hoped that his family and the bank might outlast the Nazi regime. His friend and partner Carl Melchior, also a Jew, counteracted his tendency to hope for the best and diagnosed the Nazi regime for what it was. Over time, Warburg concluded that the situation of German Jews was untenable, and he worked to devise arrangements for substantial numbers to emigrate. Such efforts made him a natural contact for McDonald, who had been particularly friendly with Warburg's son Erich. McDonald's repeated meetings with Max Warburg, recorded in this diary, reveal the path of Warburg's retreat and hint at the psychic toll his experiences exacted. Shaken by the intensity of Nazi anti-Semitism and at the level of popular support for it, Warburg hoped that the training of a new generation of Jews for a wider range of occupations might make Jews less vulnerable to criticism. Ultimately, he recognized that he could not maintain his family in Germany, and he emigrated to the United States in 1938. He died there in 1946.

tive that a close relationship be established as quickly as possible between Jewry in Germany and the High Commissioner. He said that Dr. Hirsch[63] could, for the time being, speak on behalf of the German communities. He thought it desirable that some representative German be associated with me and also, if possible, on the Governing Body. He recognized that this could not be done at once, because the way would first have to be cleared with the German government. I told him, as I had the group Sunday morning, that I would cooperate in every practicable way.

63. Dr. Otto Hirsch, a lawyer from Stuttgart, served as chairman of the Reichsvertretung der deutschen Juden, 1933–1939. Died at Mauthausen concentration camp in 1941.

As to the danger of a declaration of a second-class citizenship for German Jews, he said that it might happen. Then he surprised me by adding with great seriousness that if it did occur, he would be unable to remain in Germany. That gave me a fuller sense than I had had before about the tragedy that such a degradation would involve.

This led him then into a philosophical discussion of the place of the Jew in a non-Jewish world. He admitted the great merits of Dr. Weizmann, but had obviously been deeply hurt by Dr. Weizmann's unrestrained strictures against German Jews and for that matter against all Jews save those who held the same view of the Jews' relation to the national state as does Dr. Weizmann himself. Mr. Warburg then spoke feelingly of the necessity of Jewish committees everywhere deliberately redirecting the education of their children, so that in the course of time their professional, industrial, and agricultural occupations might be so varied as to avoid giving the sort of excuse which had been so ruthlessly capitalized by the Nazis. He emphasized that to him, the only basis for a feeling of oneness among Jews is religious. He was diametrically opposed to the Dr. Weizmann thesis about racial Judaism and Jewish political nationality. He felt sure that only on the religious and cultural basis could the Jews avoid recurrent and more terrible tragedies.

As to the situation in Germany, he agreed that it might be necessary to evacuate over a period of years tens of thousands of young Jews, but expressed the view that there could be no hope of accomplishing this save through some sort of an armistice such as my friends had spoken of Sunday morning. He suggested that, as a practical matter, there might be some differentiation between Jews who had been in Germany for a long period and those who had come more recently. I pointed out the criticism which would be inevitable from Eastern Jewry to any such differentiation, but he replied, "That is the only basis on which it can be done."

Before lunch we walked out together continuing our talk. We stopped in to see Jacobus H. Kann,[64] but he was out so we talked for a time with his son. Then we lunched together at the Royale. During the meal we talked mostly of personalities and especially about the possibility of some of the younger Jews in the States carrying on the leadership which their fathers had borne so long.

After lunch we walked back to the hotel and said goodbye, I with the feeling that Max Warburg would gladly do his utmost to make my work a success, all the more because he interpreted it not primarily as an immediate relief job, but rather as a long-range opportunity to play a statesmanlike role in humanizing the relations between Jews and non-Jews, and as he had urged, perhaps even helping the Jews as a whole so to reorient their lives as to fit more harmoniously into the life about them.

Though I felt quite tired, I wanted much to see Jacobus Kann, so I went back to the bank. He is a wonderful type of man—almost patriarchal in his mien and manner. After we had talked about the situation a while, he told me of his

64. Jacobus H. Kann, banker (Bank Lissa and Kann) and Dutch Zionist leader.

experiences a generation ago with Zionism and of his more recent differences with Dr. Weizmann. At the end of our talk he offered unreservedly to do whatever he could.

Back to the hotel just in time to change to go in to Amsterdam with André Wurfbain and Olive Sawyer to the Hotel Amstel where Mr. Asscher was giving a dinner. Among those there besides ourselves and the host were Professors Cohen, Fryda, Justice Visser, Mrs. Van Tyn, Dr. Van den Bergh and Dr. Jacobsen, and Mr. Hertzberger. . . .

After dinner Mrs. Van Tyn spoke to me about the problem of contacts between the High Commissioner and Germans within Germany. She told me that Dr. Tietz only a week before his death had mentioned the name of Dr. Olendorf as the person he would like to see in my office. She described Olendorf as most unattractive physically, but brilliant with a perfect knowledge of languages and the very soul of loyalty. I told her to pass on the word that I should be delighted to talk with him.

Professor Cohen told me that he had had a report from a usually reliable source to the effect that there was going to be an amelioration of the Jews' condition in Germany. His informant had within the last day or two gone back to Germany and would bring him further and, if possible, documentary details. He promised to pass on to me in Geneva this word if it seemed to be important.

Mr. Asscher, as we were leaving, pledged his wholehearted support and in a way which indicated that he meant it.

Home late and tired. I had earlier tried to telephone to Lewis Einstein in London at the request of Hyman, but failed to reach him. Therefore, I sent him a telegram asking him to call me the next morning.

Early in the morning Hyman telephoned me from London as I had suggested. First, I told him that the meeting had been postponed in order to permit Cecil to be present and also because the U.S. government preferred it; that Professor Chamberlain was to be the American member of the Governing Body and would be here several days before the meeting.

I then told him that I had discussed the general plan of organization both in Paris and in London, and that my present hope is to have an advisory body of representatives of the organizations (beginning with the eight mentioned at the London conference), and in addition, a group of perhaps five outstanding personalities who would be present in an advisory capacity; that while this did not mean that these two groups would have votes, they would for all practical purposes have a great deal of influence, and would be present during most of the discussions of the Governing Body; that the votes did not matter very much, because this would not be a group where decisions would be taken by eight to seven votes; that, of course, all of this was still tentative, because the Governing Body itself must make the final decision. I then told him that apparently my discussion of this possible form of organization had been misunderstood in some quarters, and read him Mildred Wertheimer's cable received this morning, reporting that Dr. Goldmann had cabled to Dr. Wise that I was asking that the

Americans name two representatives to the Advisory Body, and that my "American friends" were surprised not to have been notified, and suggested that I consult him (Hyman). I further explained that all of my proposed plans for organization were described in a letter to Miss Ogden, which was mailed on the *Ile de France* November 15 and should therefore be in New York today or tomorrow; that this letter contained the draft statute with the notation that it was to be shown only to Professor Chamberlain, Mr. Warburg, and Mr. Rosenberg and that he (Hyman) must make it clear to those gentlemen that under no circumstances was this draft to be shown to anyone else, or should anyone else know that they had seen it.

I asked Hyman whether, in his opinion, if one member of the group of five were an American, Ittleson or Rosenberg would be more acceptable to both groups. I explained that while Jimmy Rosenberg would perhaps be more useful on the committee, I was anxious to bring in Mr. Ittleson and tie him closely to the work for other reasons.

Turning to staff plans, I told Hyman frankly that I expected to take on Mr. Bentwich, who is going to Germany today and joining me in Geneva later in the week; that he seemed to be on good terms with all the groups in England, and I felt could be very useful to me under the circumstances; that I wished that he [Hyman] occupied the same position in relation to the American groups and that I could in that case have asked him to join me, but in any case I hoped he would be available as liaison and for special jobs from time to time.

I told him that I now feared we could not plan to sail until December 15 on either the *Empress of Britain* or the *Manhattan* sailing that day, and that I expected to make a reservation on the *Empress* at once; that if it suited his plans, we hoped that he might return on the same boat.

Brussels, Wednesday, November 22, 1933

Finished up some last minute letters and took the train for Brussels. On the way Miss Sawyer and I worked on the diary. We arrived promptly, just before 1:00, and went to the Palace Hotel. Wurfbain's arrangements worked out very well. Max Gottschalk joined us while we were at luncheon and explained the plans for the afternoon and evening. His look of astonishment was amazing when I told him that two of the persons the de Rothschilds had asked me to see were Jules Philippson[65] and Mme. de Becker Remy.[66] Not until late that afternoon was I to understand the reason for his surprise.

After a much needed nap, Wurfbain and I went over to pay our respects to M. J. Malot, director of the League of Nations section of the Ministry of Foreign Affairs. He is a typical official, precise, cautious, but intelligent. He agreed

65. Jules Philippson, member of the family banking house Philippson. His father was president of the ICA for many years.

66. Mme. de Becker Remy, wife of Baron Marc de Becker Remy, Belgian banker and politician.

in general on the status of private organizations vis-à-vis the Governing Body though he seemed inclined to narrow their scope more than had the other governmental representatives with whom I had spoken. On the issue of direct representation, or rather direct contact by the High Commissioner with the various governmental officers of the different countries, he agreed in principle but perhaps will have to be handled somewhat gingerly when one comes to deal with the different departments in Brussels.

He then took us to the room where the interdepartmental meeting on the subject of refugees was being held. This commission was presided over by Mr. Oustermans of the Ministry of Foreign Affairs, its other members being Mr. Gottschalk, de Foy of the Ministry of Justice, and Mr. Selvais of the Ministry of Labor. Mr. de Foy explained the position of the Belgian government towards the refugee problem. The government had no objection to the refugees staying in Belgium, provided they did not work there and that their stay would be only temporary, emigration to foreign countries being the ultimate objective. He also explained the working of the Interdepartmental Commission at which we were present. I said I found this an extremely useful idea and asked whether at the first meeting of the Governing Body the Belgian representative would not explain the working together of the different departments. Mr. Conternams said he would consider this suggestion.

Mr. de Foy proceeded to explain that the present situation could not continue indefinitely, and that if a great mass of refugees should leave Germany, the Belgian government would be obliged to close its frontier altogether, whereas up till now it had followed a policy based on the lines of liberal hospitality. Mr. Gottschalk remarked that it might be necessary in that case to institute methodical emigration from Germany, that is to say, that no refugee would be allowed to leave that country before assurance had been obtained that he could establish himself more or less definitely in another country. Gottschalk stressed the roles which he felt the Jewish organizations outside and the High Commission would have to play in making this sort of arrangement possible.

I replied that, of course, I considered it my duty to cooperate in any practicable way, but that obviously any such plan to work effectively would have to have the full cooperation of the German government, and as to this possibility one could at the moment only guess.

After this conference Wurfbain went off to the Maison de People, and I to see Jules Philippson. We talked for about an hour. Gradually he lost some of his reticence and showed more and more feeling, especially when I stressed what I think to be the danger to Jews outside of Germany. He was very warm in his appreciation of my interest in the whole problem, but he warned me very emphatically against permitting Dr. Weizmann or the group he called "the political Zionists" to play a disproportionate role. If, he said, you want the support of the ICA and similar groups, you must make clear that yours is a non-political effort. I let him know that I was aware of this danger; that I knew a good deal about the political aspects of Zionism and the political leaders. This seemed to relieve his mind considerably, for as we were joined by his brother, he repeated to the latter what I had said on the Zionist political question.

We then talked about ICA, of which Jules Philippson is one of the directors. I told him what I had said to Sir Leonard and the others. He gave me the impression that he would favor interpreting ICA's mandate broadly. I left him with the feeling that I could get much more from him than Gottschalk had seemed to think.

Then over to see Mme. de Becker Remy at the home of her sister-in-law, the Baroness Lambert. Mme. de Becker asked if I would like to talk in the presence of her sister. I said it would give me the liveliest pleasure. We found the Baroness Lambert reclining on an elaborate divan, and with her were two other ladies, Mme. Errea, a sister of Mme. de Becker and __________. The ladies were all about the same age, young, attractive, smart, and deeply interested. I outlined the way in which the Commission had been set up, what I hoped to do, and how. Then we talked about conditions in Germany. They were seemingly deeply stirred by my account, particularly by the possibility of the establishment of second-class citizenship. Several times I indicated that my next engagement required me to leave, but it was difficult to get away. As I was leaving, Mme. de Becker Remy followed me to the door. She said that she thought she ought to warn me that Mr. Gottschalk is a person who is out for himself, that he is not an individual of background or culture, that he would like to be the Belgian representative on the Governing Body, whereas she and her friends hope it would be someone else much more distinguished, a M. Bouffon (?); that worst of all, he has a tendency to intrigue. I said, of course, I was always glad to get all the information possible about the personalities with whom one works, but I had the impression that Mr. Gottschalk was very earnest and influential with the Belgian government.

About this time we were joined by Mme. de Becker Remy's sister. There was then a discussion about Mr. Philippson. I said I assumed that nothing they had said about Mr. Gottschalk would apply to Mr. Philippson. They said no, but obviously they had many mental reservations about Philippson. In particular, they were cynical when I quoted him as saying that he had regretted not being able to be at the front, but had had to stay at home. They intimated that he had welcomed the opportunity not to go to the front, and that his firm had been the first to resume business with the Germans. But, they added, we don't really know you well enough to tell you everything.

Back to the hotel and out with Wurfbain and Miss Sawyer to Mr. Gottschalk's dinner. The only others at dinner besides ourselves and our hosts were Mr. and Mrs. H. Speyer, he a cousin of Jimmie Speyer,[67] and she a sister of Mrs. Gottschalk. I spoke to Mr. Speyer about his cousin Sir Edgar, but he replied that he did not recognize him as such.

During dinner there was general talk. After dinner we were joined by four

67. James Joseph Speyer, international banker and philanthropist.

members of the Brussels committee. The men of the party then adjourned to another part of the house, where we discussed technical matters. They were all strongly of the opinion that there could not be an Englishman in addition to Weizmann in the group of three. Speyer intimated that Gottschalk was the logical man. Later, however, in a letter he urged that a Frenchman should be chosen. There is a strong feeling that it was very important to establish as quickly as possible relations between the High Commissioner and Germany. I explained the difficulties, the lack of technical status, the danger of being misled, etc. Speyer then made the interesting comparison with the situation when Hoover was relief administrator in Belgium. Then the Belgians, as now the German Jews, did not know from day to day when they were committing treason. Hoover then had no official status vis-à-vis the German government. Nonetheless, he was of incalculable service in acting as a liaison between the Belgians and the occupying forces. In somewhat the same way, Speyer thought I could and should act as [go-between] between German Jewry and the Berlin authorities.

Norman Bentwich had prepared the groundwork for McDonald. Already in Berlin, Bentwich reported to McDonald that he had seen Ambassador Dodd, Consul General Messersmith, British diplomatic officials, and German Jewish leaders. "All agreed no substantial improvement in the Jewish position was to be expected and that the economic pressure to drive Jews from business and professions was to be intensified in winter." Dodd did not believe that a new citizenship law giving German Jews second-class status would happen in the near future since the German government was anxious to conciliate foreign opinion. Messersmith opposed raising the question of admitting refugees with the U.S. government, saying that his own consulate was issuing 250–300 immigration visas per month, mostly to Jews, plus more from the consulates at Hamburg and Stuttgart. Messersmith did his best to discourage older middle-class persons from emigrating, but helped young people in every possible way. He was going to the United States to raise funds and felt it was essential to keep public opinion "alive to the methodical degradation of Jews in Germany." He believed in a quiet boycott of German trade but opposed any public agitation. Public opinion and economic pressure would tell in the end, Messersmith believed. Leo Baeck,[68] Hirsch, Melchior, and others told Bentwich that more German Jews, especially the young, wanted to emigrate than there were places for them in other countries. All were anxious to be in touch with the High Commission and wanted one or two German Jews appointed to High Commission office. Melchior suggested that McDonald write a letter to Baeck, which could be shown to the German government in order for them to meet with him with the government's approval. They asked that McDonald take up economic questions, particularly as regards the property of those leaving Germany. Melchior also suggested discus-

68. Dr. Leo Baeck, Reform rabbi and religious philosopher. Became the president of the representative body of German Jews (the Reichsvertretung der deutschen Juden) in 1933. After refusing to leave Germany despite many opportunities, he was deported to Theresienstadt in 1943 yet managed to survive.

sions with the German government for the establishment of a liquidation bank for the property of those leaving.[69]

Late in the evening the men all suddenly turned to me and asked what had been the result of my visit with Jules Philippson. I told them of the conference and that if later they wished me to ask Philippson for money, I should be glad to do so. They seemed greatly relieved that I had been able to break down the wall which had divided them from Philippson.

Then the group asked me if I would be willing to help them in their national drive. I said of course, added that the only consideration would have to be whether such action was consistent with general plan and with my other duties.

Back to the hotel, packed and took the night train for Basle.

Bern, Thursday, November 23, 1933

Worked with Miss Sawyer on the diary until we arrived at Basle about noon. Then we transferred to the Bern train, and Miss Sawyer and I continued our labors until we reached the Swiss capital.

Miss Sawyer went on to Geneva with all the luggage, while Wurfbain and I went to lunch. We discussed his relationship to me and to the Commission. He told me that Lester,[70] League of Nations High Commissioner for Danzig, had asked to see him again. I told him that I thought our work would be much more interesting and from the point of view of his career more valuable. He agreed. One reservation he appeared to have had was the possibility that the Commission might be in one form or another used for anti-German purposes. I convinced him that this would not be so. We concluded with the understanding that I would probably offer him the position of Secretary General and with a salary comparable to that which he had been receiving, approximately, in terms of Swiss francs, $350 gold a month.

At four o'clock we went to see Motta.[71] He was very cordial, much interested in the work. I asked him the same sort of questions that I had asked other foreign ministers. His replies were reassuring. I did not ask him specifically if the office might be permanently established in Lausanne, but I had the impression that there would be no objection to this.

Motta was most pessimistic about the disarmament problem and about the League. He said that if the meeting of the Bureau the day before had not been adjourned at the end of six minutes with no opportunity for discussion, the whole thing would have exploded. As to Germany's relations to the League, he

69. Abstract of the confidential report, November 22–23, 1933, of Mr. Norman Bentwich to the High Commissioner. Archives of the American Jewish Joint Distribution Committee. High Commission file 1, 1933.

70. Sean Lester, Irish diplomat and representative to the League. High Commissioner for Danzig in 1933, and in 1940 secretary general of the League.

71. Guiseppe Motta, member of the Federal Council of Switzerland, four times president of Switzerland, and in December 1935 chosen vice president.

feels that the principles of the Nazis, like those of the Fascists in Italy, are fundamentally in conflict with the democratic principles and practices at Geneva. Therefore, he does not anticipate Germany's return and seemed to fear Italy's withdrawal.

He told us that Dr. Rothmund[72] was probably in the building, and gave me an opportunity to say I should be glad to see him. We were received promptly by the ranking police officer of Switzerland. He is a tall, fair, extremely well built man of forty-five or so. He was cordial. We discussed some of the technical aspects of the work of the Commission. He told me that he was also a member of a committee meeting in Lausanne under League auspices to deal with indigent foreigners; that, therefore, he might not be able to attend all of our meetings, but would certainly come the first day and as frequently thereafter as possible. As we parted, he said something about the Nordic type of which he is a striking example.

Wurfbain and I took the six o'clock train, arriving in Geneva tired and late. Herbert May was very considerate to meet us with his car.

Geneva, Friday, November 24, 1933

Most of the morning was spent in a detailed and very useful, frank conference with Hyman. He reported that in Paris I had made an extremely favorable impression, especially with the Robert de Rothschilds; that in London the judgment was more measured, but that except as expressed by Dr. Weizmann, the attitude was wholly friendly and cooperative. Even Dr. Weizmann had refrained from open criticism, but apparently had indicated to his intimates considerable reservations as to the real usefulness of my probable activities. It was evident from this report that I need to come to know the men who are working with and supporting Dr. Weizmann, particularly Simon Marks,[73] Israel Sieff,[74] Harry Sacher,[75] and Brodetsky.[76]

I gathered the impression from what Hyman said that the financial leaders in London, Paris, and New York were considering supporting the administrative budget on the basis of one quarter for each group; that ICA and the JDC had in principle agreed, subject only to the British Central Fund agreeing similarly. Probably d'Avigdor-Goldsmid and Otto Schiff will continue to work on this project.

72. Dr. Henrich Rothmund, chief of police in the Federal Department of Justice and Police. One of the most powerful men in the government. Had strong views about the dangers Jews posed to Switzerland.

73. Lord Simon Marks, chairman, Marks & Spencer department store chain.

74. Lord Israel Sieff, vice-chairman of Marks & Spencer department store chain.

75. Harry Sacher, brother-in-law of Marks, executive with Marks & Spencer. With Marks and Sieff, a leader of the "Manchester Group" of Zionists and major financial supporters of Weizmann and the movement.

76. Selig Brodetsky, Ukrainian-born distinguished mathematician (professor of mathematics at Leeds University), president of the Zionist Federation of Great Britain, and in 1939 the first foreign Jew and first Zionist to become president of the Board of Deputies of British Jews.

Hyman told me of the project to have Dr. Weizmann and Captain Montagu go to New York for conferences during the holidays. This seemed to me excellent, particularly if Simon Marks and Sieff could be induced to go along, and if Max Warburg could be induced to stay. I asked Hyman to pass on this word to New York.

We then turned to the perennial question of representation of private organizations. At this point we were joined by Bentwich. Hyman explained why, from the point of view of JDC and ICA, it was impossible to sit down on a basis of equality with political and irresponsible bodies like La Comité [des] Delegations[77] and the American [Jewish] Congress. Bentwich and I urged that in practice, of course, the large financial organizations would probably always have their way, and would be effectively represented on the Governing Body, but Hyman remained unconvinced that these bodies would consent to representation on the Advisory Committee on a basis of equality with the others. Finally, we agreed tentatively to recommend to the Governing Body the following procedure: representation of the JDC, the ICA, and the British Central Fund and of the five or six Jewish communities.[78]

At twelve o'clock Parkes came in, and we discussed the possible basis of his cooperation with me. We tentatively agreed on an honorarium for part-time work; no amount was mentioned.

Lunch at Herbert Mays with Hyman and Olive Sawyer. Again the discussion centered on the relations of the private organizations to the Governing Body. Hyman suggested a questionnaire to all organizations interested, thus testing their willingness and their ability to serve in this crisis and automatically eliminating many of them as candidates for representation on the Advisory Committee. Asked Herbert May and Hyman if they would not draft such a suggested questionnaire. This they did, but as they were doing it later in the day, they realized that the time was too short to secure replies before December 5.

Stopped at the bank with Olive Sawyer to open an account with the League funds.

Hyman had suggested at lunch what I think is an excellent idea—the setting up of a committee of technical advisers; in this way many more personalities can be brought in and excellent advice be secured on a volunteer basis.

At five o'clock Bentwich, Hyman, Wurfbain, and Miss Sawyer and I dis-

77. Comité des Delegations Juives. Established at Versailles at the initiative of the Zionist Organization and comprising all the Jewish national delegations except the British and the French. Its main aims were to safeguard the rights of the Jewish minorities in Eastern Europe and encourage the settling of Palestine. In 1936 it became the World Jewish Congress.

78. The Governing Body drew up a list of the principal relief and other organizations that should be invited to nominate a representative to the Advisory Council. They chose originally nine Jewish and nine international or large denominational bodies. "The Jewish bodies comprised groups of organizations dealing with refugees in five principal communities: England, France, the U.S., Holland and Poland. . . . In addition the Comité National for the assistance of refugees in France was included, as well as the French Jewish community, because of the dimensions and gravity of the refugee problem in France. . . ." Norman Bentwich, *Refugees from Germany,* p. 81.

cussed again the problem of private organizations and the Commission. The consensus of opinion was that at the first meeting of the Commission the groups referred to above be invited to form the Jewish part of the Advisory Committee, and a comparable number of non-Jewish bodies be invited also, but that the question of the ultimate composition of the Advisory Committee be left for consideration at the next meeting of the Governing Body. It was my idea that the Advisory Committee, as set up, should be called to meet perhaps for four or five days before the second meeting of the Governing Body. I stressed with Hyman and urged that he stress with New York the importance of giving the left wing a predominant share in the choice of the representative of the American Jewish community in the light of the proposed representation of the JDC.

Dinner at Mr. May's. Those present besides the Mays, Miss Sawyer, and I were Mr. Pickard, Mr. Bentwich, Parks, Henroid, and ________. The discussion turned on the possibility and desirability of a Christmas appeal. This seemed to me desirable, if at all, not because of the prospect, at least in America, of any considerable financial return, but because of its educational effect if made on a sufficiently broad basis. After many exchanges of views cables were sent to New York, London, and Upsala, signed by Henroid and Bentwich.

Saturday, November 25, 1933

Lunch with Malcolm Davis.[79] We discussed the state of the world; he very generously offered to be of what assistance he could in unofficial ways. Especially he said he would be glad to serve for me as he had from time to time for Norman Davis and Wilson—that is, report things that he would hear which would be of interest, but which I might not myself hear. As we were saying goodbye, he said he hoped to talk with me soon about an address he had to make in London at the Institute of International Relations about an American view of the European situation.

In the late afternoon over to Mrs. Morgan's tea. Schwarz tried to sound me out on the attitude of the Commission towards Germany and would I think have welcomed being invited to be an intermediary. I declined his tentative offer.

Came back to the hotel with the Mays. Tried to get Hyman on the telephone but was unable to do so. Therefore, had the following message telephoned to him: Inquire from American Ambassador William Dodd whether he would be willing under appropriate circumstances consider acting liaison [to] German government. Second, a letter is being sent to Dr. Baeck along the lines agreed upon between Bentwich and the group in Berlin.[80] Please indicate that if German government willing would like to have both Olendorf and Is-

79. Malcolm W. Davis, Geneva-based author.
80. See inserted commentary in entry for November 22, 1933, entry.

rael present before and during meeting. Will attempt no direct communication with Hyman while in Germany. Anxious to see Hyman back here before meeting.

Sunday, November 26, 1933

Conference at Mr. May's house with Paul Hertz from Prague. Present . . . besides Hertz and myself were Bentwich, May, Wurfbain. It was made clear at the very beginning by me that this was a wholly personal and private conversation, was on no account to be made public, or was the fact that it had been held to be made public. Hertz agreed, stressed that he was concerned not at all with the political aspects of the problem. He said he realized that the number of political refugees was small in proportion to the others, perhaps only 3,000 in all. He then raised three questions: first, possible representation of the Second International or the Trade Union International on the Advisory Body; second, the possible issuance of passports on the basis suggested a few years ago; third, the property, both real and intangible, such as insurance against old age and the invalidism of the refugee. His fuller statement is summarized in a memorandum prepared by Wurfbain. I replied that I thought it better to postpone an answer to his questions until later in the day, but I suggested the possibility of the Trade Union International being a better form of representation than the Second International.

Off with the Mays for the day to Caux. It was a lovely trip, well above the snow line.

Returning, we met Hertz at the May's house, where I gave him replies to his three questions. First, I again suggested my personal preference for the representation of the Trade Union International because both for reasons of expedience and practicality; second, I thought the passport suggestion deserved careful study; third, ditto. I asked him whether Breitscheid was in accord with him as to the necessity of having only economic relationships with the Commission—in other words, that political considerations were not to enter. He answered that he assumed that Breitscheid would agree, but that if he did not he would not be in any way representative of the Social Democratic Party.

Back to the Mays for dinner, with Mlle. Ferriere, Bieler,[81] Mr. and Mrs. Pelt. There was a very profitable discussion about possible lines of organization, titles for staff members, etc. Both Bieler and Pelt showed much interest. Mlle. Ferriere was also helpful in the private discussion I had with her about her own work and that of the Nansen Committee.

Monday, November 27, 1933

Brief conference with Dr. [Nahum] Goldmann, in which I tried more or less to prepare him for the non-inclusion of the Comité Delegation in the Ad-

81. Jean Henri Bieler, a Canadian working in the League treasurer's office. Helpful in preparing the High Commission's budget.

visory Body. Lunch with Prentiss Gilbert. We discussed in detail possible relations with Germany. He strongly urged delay until the meeting of the Governing Body. Then one of the governments might be useful in making the first approach, this to be followed up by a conference with the German Minister in Bern. He thought I should go only if I were assured of conference with the highest officials. Joseph Chamberlain, he said, would have the use of government code in any way desired with Dodd and with Washington. Gilbert appreciated, I think, my coming to him before I went to see Wilson.

Wurfbain came in to report that he and Parkes thought it might be necessary for the latter to go to Paris to study the situation of the non-Jewish organizations. I rejected this suggestion and telephoned Bernard Kahn in Paris to get the information for us.

At tea-time William Borberg,[82] the Danish permanent delegate [to the League], came in. I explained my general ideas about the work because he wished to have this data before telephoning his government about possible Danish representation. He will, I think, be a useful but conservative member of the Governing Body. He did not disagree with my suggestion that perhaps the Danish government might be a link with Germany in the initial stages.

Conference with Wilson. He took much the same line as had Prentiss Gilbert, but was less emphatic that I should not approach the German government before the meeting of the Governing Body. He added, however, that since the latter was only a week off, perhaps it was best to wait. Then he would favor direct approach to Bern, possibly utilizing Motta only to make sure that the démarche toward the German minister would be properly received.

Back to the hotel to work with Miss Sawyer until nearly ten o'clock. Then to the Bavaria with her for dinner. We ran into Robert Dell and had an amusing evening.

Tuesday, November 28, 1933

Conference with Hugo Simons of Düsseldorf. Told him that I would welcome a memorandum from him on the question of refugee property, but that I could not make any commitment in reference to his association with me in any way until after the meeting of the Governing Body. I promised, however, to telegraph him from Lausanne whether or not I could arrange to meet him.

Conference with Ginsberg on a number of matters, particularly representation of the intellectual groups on the Advisory Body. She thought Rappard might be a possible delegate for the three groups. I said that would be for themselves to decide.

Conference on the Christmas appeal suggestion with Henroid, Pickard, Mr. May, Mr. Bentwich, Mr. Parkes, and Wurfbain. It was finally agreed to limit the appeal outside England to educational aspects in view of the appar-

82. Dr. William Borberg, since 1928 the Danish permanent delegate to the League. Quiet but very efficient person, liberal by tradition.

ent unwillingness of the Americans to put the appeal on the broadest grounds. Chichester, however, was to be urged to make a universal educational appeal and to carry through on his own financial appeal in England. Henroid was to write the States, and I to support his point of view in a separate personal letter.

Lunch with Krno. He thought that Cecil was clearly marked as chairman; though Henri Bérenger is also a real personality, he would not feel offended to be outranked by Cecil. Perhaps he might be named vice-chairman. Krno disclosed that Bérenger had not been the first choice of the Quai d'Orsay. On the question of relations with the Reich, Krno's view was much the same as that of Prentiss Gilbert and Wilson. He was also in general agreement with my plan as I outlined it to him for the first meeting. As to a further démarche toward the three countries from which replies have not been received, he said he would consider it. We talked for a time too about financial matters, he explaining that in the League the Secretary General's representative allowance made a substantial addition to his salary.

Long conference at tea-time with Rappard on the question of relations with the Reich. He was in agreement with the others with whom I had discussed it, except that he thought I ought to move before the meeting and to give them an opportunity to make informal observations. He offered to be the intermediary with the German consul. I said I would let him know. Then followed a long rambling discussion of the Advisory Body's relation to the Governing Body and the possibility of Rappard's representing the intellectual groups on the Governing Body. He will, I think, do it if we insist.

Before going out to dinner, cleared up two matters which had been bothering Wurfbain. One [was] what he thought was my tendency to make snap decisions and the possibility that he might be too slow and methodical to work satisfactorily with me. I told him that precisely the opposite was the case, that just because he was different, he was especially useful, and that if he worked with me more, he would probably find that my judgments were not as suddenly arrived at as might appear. Second, he was concerned about two of the ranking officials being Jewish. After we discussed the matter, he was satisfied that this would not mean that the usefulness of the Secretariat would be impaired by too much of a Jewish slant. At the end I felt that it had been useful for us to have our frank talk.

....

Before sitting down to dinner, I telephoned Professor Cohen in Amsterdam. He said that for the moment there was nothing doing on the new citizenship classification, but that on unreliable data he was told that something of this sort would be done. He felt that the truth was that radical members of the Nazi party were urging it, but that the Leader [Hitler] was not convinced, indeed, was opposing it.

As to von Baumhauer, he had a good reputation at the Bar and for public spirit, but was vain and in that lay a danger.

Wednesday, November 29, 1933

. . . .

At eleven, May, Bentwich, Wurfbain, and Parkes and I began the study of statute and related documents. Bentwich objected strongly to some of the articles in reference to the relation of the private bodies to the Governing Body. In particular, he thought that Article VI and perhaps some of the other articles should be modified. I defended the articles and suggested that May and Bentwich study further possible modifications, which might perhaps be indicated in italics in parentheses in the mimeographed drafts to be presented to the Governing Body.

I explained to the group why I thought the draft financial regulations were too involved, since I did not think that the Commission or the High Commissioner should receive or distribute substantive funds.

Over to see Wilson for a few minutes to check on the suggestion made by Rappard. He thought it a good one, but that I should be careful not to put myself in a position where the German government might make suggestions which it would be embarrassing for me to either carry out or refuse to carry out. He thought that if I limited myself to the following, I would be safe: Suggest to the German consul that if his government wished me to convey informally and unofficially any point of view to the Governing Body, I should be delighted to do so. All questions of going into Germany, etc., should be left for later conference with the German minister in Bern, to be arranged perhaps through Motta.

Came back to the hotel and telephoned Rappard that if he cared to invite me to lunch tomorrow or next day I should be happy to go.

Dr. Kahn telephoned from Paris to say:

(1) That Ambassador Dodd would be glad to have me write, telegraph, or telephone him; that he was to be in Munich till December 10, and if I wished to write him, I should send it in the French diplomatic pouch, or if I wished to telephone I could do so through his secretary, Mr. Ogletree, Lutzzow 9711.

(2) He had received a copy of Rosenberg's cable. He thought the suggestion rather fantastic in view of the fact that there could not be more than 13,000 or 14,000 of the total number of refugees who were non-Jews. He is sending us today by special mail a statement on the Jewish organizations, and will send in a day or so a statement on the non-Jewish organizations.

(3) He had received a cable from New York suggesting the possible desirability of postponing the coming of the English group, and perhaps some from the

continent, until after my return to New York, or at any rate until after the meeting of the Governing Body. I said that I saw no advantages in delay; on the contrary, that I considered it absolutely vital that the proposed conferences be held in New York while Chamberlain, Messersmith, and I could be present. Dr. Kahn replied that he wondered whether it was desirable to have the English group come to New York to propagate their special Zionist views, with the emphasis on the need for 50/50 distribution of funds. I replied that while that would be the purpose of the British group, the Americans ought to take the opportunity to try to carry their own point of view. However, so far as I was concerned, I was not at this moment taking any sides, but was emphasizing what I considered to be the absolute necessity of a common front if it can possibly be achieved. Dr. Kahn said he would pass this word on.

Wurfbain and I lunched with Mr. Bieler. He suggested that perhaps the simplest way to handle the budget would be to have one statement of expenses actually incurred and expected up to January 1, and in addition to draft a budget for the calendar year 1934. He thought Cecil might be, from my point of view, a better chairman of the finance committee than an intimate friend of mine like Chamberlain. He recognized that I could not be expected to take a smaller compensation than I had relinquished at home, that on the contrary, keeping up two establishments would justify a larger amount. As to traveling expenses, one could either have a system like the League of a per diem scale varying according to the rank of the official, or compensation for actual amount expended. As to financial forms, he said that if Wurfbain and Miss Berg would come to his office he would give them a complete set.

Afternoon spent in conference with May, Bentwich, Wurfbain re revision of statutes and related documents.

....

Thursday, November 30, 1933

Thanksgiving Day. For the first time had an opportunity to begin the study of the documents of the London conference and other material.

Lunch at Herbert May's.

At 3:30 Paderewski[83] came to urge the claims of his friend, Alfred Nossig, to a staff position. After we had discussed this matter, we had a very interesting talk about conditions in Germany. At the end Paderewski asked me to remember him to his friends, Colonel House and the Morgenthaus, and invited Ruth and I and the children to visit him at Morges.

With Olive Sawyer to the Thanksgiving Tea at the American Church. Chatted with a number of old friends, and met Maier of the American delega-

83. Ignace Jan Paderewski, world renowned Polish pianist and statesman, fighter for Poland's national independence.

tion, Mrs. Goetz, the wife of another member of the delegation, and a few other persons.

At 6:15 met the American press,[84] and explained to them why it was difficult for me to deal with them in any special way distinct from the press of other states. Streit was late in arriving, and I talked with him while in my bath and shaving.

Dinner at the Mays. Present the hosts and myself, Miss Sawyer, Wurfbain, Bentwich, Mr. Wertheimer, Mrs. Askew, Professor and Mrs. Jacob Viner. It was a delightful party.

84. McDonald letter of December 3 to Miss Ogden: "and also talked to Mr. Kahane of the Jewish Telegraphic Agency. He told me of the absurd story, which I had already heard about, sent from the JTA in London, to the effect that I had quarreled with the British government about Palestine. Of course there is not a shred of truth in it. I am bothered, however, by two considerations: first, that this canard may have been inspired for ulterior purposes; second, and more serious, that the JTA ought at least to see to it that the stories about the High Commissioner's office should be checked by conference with the H.C. before they are broadcast." The British government, as a precondition of their participation, stipulated that Palestine as a British mandate would not come under the jurisdiction of the High Commission. The report implied that McDonald had not known of this stipulation and said he was now demanding that the British government admit refugees into Palestine under a separate quota. Copy in McDonald Papers, USHMM.

8. December 1933: Proposal for a Corporation

Geneva, Friday, December 1, 1933

Talked with Parkes and arranged that he was to be definitely on part-time basis, to be given definite work to do, and paid him 1,000 Swiss francs on account, the exact terms of future employment to be discussed. He wished me to intervene directly with Felix Warburg in the matter of the New York Foundation grant to the ISS,[1] but I said that this would have to be done through Hyman.

At twelve o'clock Professor Chamberlain came in. He and Herbert May and I talked until lunch, and then Chamberlain and I continued until nearly three. It was the greatest comfort to talk with him.

In the later afternoon Dr. Paul Frei, sent by Dr Werner, came in. I was impressed with him as a possible member of the staff, and asked him to prepare a memorandum on the legal status of the High Commission and the High Commissioner in Switzerland, and also in reference to diplomatic privileges and immunities. We arranged for him to be in Lausanne during the meeting as a volunteer.

Telephoned Otto Schiff in London to ask him if he would not please try to find the source of the Jewish Telegraphic Agency rumor that I had had a row with the British government on the issue of Palestine. Schiff said that he thought the British authorities would pay no attention to the rumor, but nevertheless he would see what he could learn.

Worked until after midnight getting a start on my opening address.

Saturday, December 2, 1933

Over to see Wilson about the possibility of his suggesting to Bingham a dinner on the fourteenth for Chamberlain and me, to which would be invited leading Jewish and non-Jewish figures. Wilson said that he had never asked anybody to give a dinner, and he couldn't begin now. I replied that I had asked many people to give dinners. But he then volunteered to telegraph Bingham to the effect that Chamberlain and I would be in London on the fourteenth, and were anxious to meet certain persons through the ambassador. This seemed to me to be wholly satisfactory.

1. International Student Service.

Lunch at Harold Butler's house. Besides the hosts those present were Professor Chamberlain, Mr. and Mrs. Arthur Henderson,[2] Phelan, and possibly one or two others. Butler was most enthusiastic about the NRA and Roosevelt. As to the Scientific Management Institute, he said it was being wound up, and denied that there was any ground for Urwick's suggestion that E. A. Filene or the TC [Twentieth Century] Filene Trustees were welshing on their contract.[3] He agreed that the argument Urwick was using, to the effect that it would be bad under present circumstances for the fact to be spread that a Jew had gone back on his word, was an unfair method of pressure.

Arthur Henderson was most interesting when we talked after lunch. He is extremely pessimistic about both the League and the Disarmament Conference. He thinks that the governments have always moved too slowly; that had they kept their pledge to Germany and gotten on with the job, there would have been no breach.

The late afternoon and up to the time I dressed for dinner, dictated my opening address to Miss Sawyer. Great relief to have the first draft finished.

Dinner at Herbert May's for Professor Chamberlain. Besides the hosts and Professor Chamberlain and I were present the Krnos, the Prentiss Gilberts, the Sweetsers, Mrs. Wilson, Mme. Gallapin, and the Ascarates. It was one of the most delicious dinners I have ever eaten. After dinner I talked with Krno about the Czech delegate. He was formerly in the diplomatic service in London, is a prince, though ordinarily the title is not used.[4] He knows Jan Masaryk very well.

When it was time for everybody to go home, Arthur Sweetser raised with me the question of relations with Germany. I explained to him my talks with Gilbert, Wilson, and Rappard, and that the absence of the German consul from Geneva had prevented a first approach. In order that we might discuss the matter further, I asked Chamberlain and Gilbert and Arthur if they would remain with May and me after the others had left. We then talked on until well after midnight. Sweetser argued the necessity of a prompt move on my part, and suggested that Chamberlain might ask Washington for permission to communicate in code with Dodd to the effect that he (JDC) [Chamberlain's initials, not the organization] would be glad to transmit any communication from the German government. This was voted impracticable. I argued, and I think most of those present agreed, that Germany would make up its mind about our work not on the basis of any diplomatic maneuver, but on what it thought to be the purpose of our endeavors. Moreover, there was general agreement that the danger of being outmaneuvered would be very great; that, therefore, I should not move until after receiving the informal assent at least of Cecil and preferably of most of the members of the Governing Body.

2. Arthur Henderson, 1863–1935; leader of the British Labour Party; president of the Disarmament Conference, 1932–1933; winner of the Nobel Peace Prize, 1934.

3. Lyndall Urwick, influential British business consultant. Director of the Geneva-based International Management Institute, 1928–1933.

4. Czech delegate, Dr. Maximilian de Lobkowicz.

Sunday, December 3, 1933

The whole morning, from ten until 1:30, was devoted to an intensive study of the text of my draft address. I was greatly relieved that there were so few suggestions of radical changes. Most of the discussion was about phrasing, though the major debate was on the inclusion of the reference, in the early portion, to the possibility of the problem becoming of such proportions as to become unmanageable. Those who took part in this discussion were May, Bentwich, Wurfbain, Parkes, and later Chamberlain, and, of course, Miss Sawyer.

Early in the morning Krno had called me to OK the text, and late in the afternoon Sweetser called to suggest the toning down of the first part and one or two other changes of language which had in effect already been done.

Lunched with Mr. Hyman, who gave me a moving account of his impressions of the German situation. These were very like my own two months ago. He stressed the conviction of the German Jews, first, that they should have a close and, if possible, official relationship to the High Commissioner's office, and second, that the problem is at the moment only in its beginning stages; that we must anticipate either the regulated emigration on a large scale or a panicky exodus on an even more tragic scale. I told him of the necessity of having ample guarantee of the administrative budget thru 1934 before the matter came up at the Governing Body. He asked me what I would think of his being assigned to Europe. I told him that I thought it would be excellent; that he would be invaluable to me, perhaps even more so if he were not formally attached to my office.

Out to tea at Wurfbain's house. Met his father and mother—charming people.

Another brief conference with Wurfbain, Parkes, Bentwich, and Hyman in reference to draft of my address. In the meantime, Hyman had reached an agreement in reference to the phrasing of the references to Palestine and the London conference.

Sharkey called to say that he had arranged with his New York office to be in Lausanne during our meeting. This I think is indicative of the interest at home.

Worked until after nine o'clock dictating diary and preparing long letters for the office and final touches on the opening statement.

Lausanne, Monday, December 4, 1933

Busy with odds and ends until time for the eleven o'clock train to Lausanne, which Olive Sawyer and I caught by half a minute's margin. The others and the luggage went on by car and truck.

Began series of conferences immediately on arrival. The first was with Hyman and Kahn. With them began what was later to seem to me to be the interminable and racking debate about the Comité des Delegations and the form of the Consultative Body. Kahn was rigid and seemed to me wholly unreasonable.

Lunch with Cecil in my sitting room. We covered much ground. He told me that he would be unable to accept the chairmanship. I replied that this would be a bitter disappointment to me and to everybody interested in the work, and especially the English Jews who were counting so heavily on his acceptance. He said that he had written definitely to Dr. Weizmann to say that he could not accept, and suggesting that I be chairman. This, I told him, would never do. I pointed out to him the danger of having a chairman from one of the great powers who had recently been associated with a direct verbal attack on the Reich.

We discussed at length the program of the conference. We thought it appropriate that I should make an extended opening statement, as it were setting the problem in its framework, and that we then proceed to formal organization. It would be only necessary to precede this by the naming of the chairman. This, he thought, we could manage to accomplish through private talks, thus reaching an agreement before the actual opening session.

As to the relation between the High Commissioner and Palestine, he agreed that nothing need be said additional to what had been indicated in the correspondence.

His views on the relations between Jews and non-Jews shocked me. Speaking of the Nazi policy he said, "I should not be surprised if they did declare the Jews to be foreigners; indeed, if they were going to do anything against the Jews, I should have thought that was what should have been done at the beginning. After all, the Jews throughout the world cannot continue indefinitely to have it both ways. They cannot remain apart and still a part of the communities in which they live. It is really too much that men like Samuel and Reading should be leaders in English political life and at the same time remain outstanding Jews." I did not argue the matter with him, nor ask what would become of the Jews if his view were widely held and acted upon, nor did I ask him what was the difference between being a leader in the Episcopal Church and a prominent member of the Jewish religious community. As he explained his position, I began to understand why both extremes in the Jewish world think so highly of Lord Cecil. To the assimilationists and the nationalist Jews, he is in complete agreement as one alternative for the people. But similarly, he is in complete agreement with the nationalists and the Zionists Jews to the precisely opposite alternative. And presumably, when Weizmann talks with him, only the Zionist side is stressed, and vice-versa with the others.

I left with him the drafts of the documents so far as these had been prepared—the statute, the rules of procedure, and the financial regulations. We made a date to go over them together at six o'clock.

I forgot above to add that Cecil made a very positive suggestion as to the best approach towards Germany. He agreed that the very heart of the problem lay in Germany's attitude and that, therefore, I should move towards establishing practical relations as soon as possible. He expressed himself strongly, however, as opposed to the procedure which, after many conferences, had previously been agreed upon—that is, through Motta and the German minister at Bern. Lord Cecil suggested that it would be much better to move more directly. When I told him that I knew Schacht, Lord Cecil said it would be preferable to communicate directly to the latter, setting forth frankly that I desired to offer to lay before the Chancellor [Hitler] the scope and methods of work being undertaken. I told him that I thought this would be preferable, and that I probably would act on his advice after checking with certain other persons.

At 4:30 another longish conference with Hyman and Kahn.

Dr. Mark Wischnitzer[5] came in and explained his work.

Just after five someone from the International News Service in Paris called to ask if we had any figures about the non-Jewish refugees. Herbert May, who happened to be in the room, reminded me that it would be a mistake to give out any data at that hour because it would undercut the news value of my opening statement the next day. I therefore told the Paris man that he would have to send someone to Lausanne.

Over to see Cecil. He suggested one or two minor changes in the text of my opening statement and also in the other draft documents. I was distinctly encouraged that he seemed to think the opening statement was so satisfactory.

On the way down from his room I met and chatted with the Czech delegate, Prince Lobkowicz. He was most cordial. He raised only one question about the draft statute; this had to do with the elimination of the phrase that the High Commissioner is responsible to the Governing Body.

I noticed that Larsons was talking to Lobkowicz as I entered the hotel. Lobkowicz told me that Larsons had been urging his own candidacy as a member of the staff.

As soon as I had been told by Cecil at lunch that he could not accept the chairmanship, I reported this to Bentwich and urged the latter to tell Dr. Weizmann and the other British Jewish leaders that it was up to them to make Lord Cecil reconsider. I also told Hyman to bring what influence to bear he could from New York.

Staff dinner in the sitting room, including besides Olive Sawyer and I, May, Wurfbain, Miss Berg, and Bentwich, re final draft of speech before it was turned over for mimeographing and translation.

Dr. Kahn was helpful in one final phrasing, to meet a suggestion by Chamberlain. The stenographers worked until nearly two o'clock that night on the stencils. At our conference we also discussed the broad outlines of the budget.

To bed late.

Tuesday, December 5, 1933

Conferences at breakfast with various members of the staff. Telephone message from the American delegation at Geneva to the effect that Samuel would

5. Dr. Mark Wischnitzer, author of *To Dwell in Safety* (Philadephia: Jewish Publication Society, 1948), a study of Jewish migrations since 1800.

see Chamberlain and me and that Reading would give a dinner. Miss Sawyer tried to get me to take some action, but didn't try hard enough, so nothing was done that day—to our disconcertment later.

Downstairs in the lobby on the way to the Palais de Rumine I ran into Senator Bérenger. We chatted together for a little while. Then over to the university.

Before the meeting there were informal exchanges of views about the chairman; Bérenger told me that he wished to name Cecil, but I told him that the latter had said that he could not accept. Bérenger nonetheless insisted that he wished to present Lord Cecil's name. I talked to Lord Cecil, and he said that wouldn't do; that it was preferable to have the Swede, Mr. Westman. I talked to the latter; he said that he was most sorry, but his government had instructed him not to accept membership on the Permanent Committee; hence it was quite impossible for him to accept the chairmanship. Meantime, Bérenger had had a long talk with Lord Cecil. The result of it was that the latter said he would accept the chairmanship for this meeting. This was a great relief to me, for it got us over the first serious hazard.

Before the meeting began I had an opportunity to talk for a few minutes with all the other delegates: Borberg for Denmark, Van Troostwick for Holland, Chodzko for Poland,[6] Spocci (?) for Italy, Rothmund for Switzerland, and Guani[7] for Uruguay.[8]

The Palais de Rumine was comfortably filled. It is an ideal room for our sort of gathering, especially if, as I had decided the moment I saw it early that morning, one did not use the dais. The American press was fully represented—Sharkey, Brown, Whitaker, Streit, and several others. A number of leading Jews, including Weizmann, were there. I called the meeting to order with a few words of thanks to Switzerland, to which the Swiss delegate made an appropriate response. Then I asked for the election of a chairman, and Bérenger placed Cecil in nomination with words of commendation, which Chamberlain supported, and also Chodzko. The election was by acclamation.

Cecil took the chair and spoke briefly; then I delivered my formal address.[9] It had been previously distributed in French to the delegates, so there was no translation. The response seemed to me cordial. The meeting ended immedi-

6. Dr. Withold Chodzko, Polish representative on the Governing Body, former minister of Health in Poland. An old friend of May's.

7. Dr. Alberto Guani, Uruguayan minister in Paris, president of the Council and Assembly of the League.

8. Others attending were Prince Lobkowicz from Czechoslovakia; Mr. Westman, the Swedish minister at Bern; M. Bourquin; and the Italian member, Senator G. C. Majoni, recently retired from the Italian Foreign Office after thirty-five years. The Spanish, Argentineans, and Brazilians did not send representatives, the last saying that they were too busy to have someone from their legation attend the meeting. Minutes of the meeting of the Governing Body of the High Commission for Refugees . . . , December 5–8, 1933, McDonald Papers, USHMM.

9. McDonald stated that sixty thousand persons had fled Germany since Hitler came to power; 86 percent were Jewish, half of the refugees were in France. Palestine was a distant second, and the rest were in the countries surrounding Germany or in the United States. The functions of the High Commission would be coordination of private agencies and negotiation with governments. *New York Times,* December 6, 1933.

ately following the announcement that there would be a private session for organization purposes that afternoon at 4:30.

Before the meeting began, as we stood around talking, the whole affair seemed to me a good deal like an FPA meeting. Indeed, throughout all the sessions that followed, except on the few moments when there threatened to be a more or less serious difference of opinion, I continued to feel that what we were doing was much in the FPA tradition.

Staff luncheon with Chamberlain, May, Berg, Parkes, Wurfbain, Sawyer, and I. We discussed plans for the following sessions. Chamberlain, as one would expect, very helpful.

Bentwich reported to me the extreme difficulty he was having finding a basis of agreement with Hyman and Kahn.

Last minute work with May on the rules of procedure, etc.

The second session began promptly at 4:30 at the Palais de Rumine. The draft statute was read article by article. When changes had been suggested in the revised draft, I explained why each had been put forward. There was little discussion on any of the articles until we came to that from which had been suggested the elimination of the phrase "The High Commissioner shall be responsible to the Governing Body." The discussion on this point was intelligently conducted. Bérenger, on this matter as on the other questions with drafting of the basic documents, was very helpful.

Finally, it was unanimously agreed to accept the revised draft. We then proceeded to discuss the rules of procedure. Work on this went forward smoothly under the very skilled chairmanship of Lord Cecil. I admired the way in which he pushed everything along, sometimes rather arbitrarily but never with the least appearance of exerting undue pressure. By the end of the session we had completed the rules of procedure down to the point where we had to decide on the relations of the private organizations. It was then decided to leave this to the Permanent Committee later to be named, and the budget to a small finance committee made up of Professor Chamberlain, Chodzko, and Lobkowicz (this decision may have been taken the next day, but the exact time is of no importance). The meeting adjourned about 7:30.

After the meeting I chatted for a little while with some of the press in my sitting room; there was, however, very little news to give out.

Staff dinner—Wurfbain, Sawyer, Berg, and I, joined later by Bentwich. Talked mostly about the broad lines of the budget.

Again worked until nearly midnight, Miss Sawyer and the other members of the staff doing likewise.

Wednesday, December 6, 1933

Breakfast conference with Chamberlain, May, Wurfbain, and later Bentwich and Parkes about the presentation of the budget to the Finance Committee, the telegram to Schacht, etc. I drafted the following telegram:

SOON AFTER CONCLUSION THIS INITIAL MEETING GOVERNING BODY OF HIGH COMMISSION FOR REFUGEES COMING FROM GERMANY I EXPECT CONFER GOVERNMENTAL REPRESENTATIVES AND OTHERS PARIS LONDON WASHINGTON STOP COULD VISIT BERLIN BEFORE THEN STOP ALTHOUGH YOUR GOVERNMENT IS NOT OFFICIALLY CONCERNED WITH WORK NOW BEING UNDERTAKEN I SHOULD BE GLAD OUTLINE TO CHANCELLOR SCOPE AND METHODS OF ACTIVITIES STOP I AM MAKING THIS PERSONAL SUGGESTION THROUGHOUT BECAUSE OF NON-POLITICAL CHARACTER OF MY OFFICE STOP SAILING FROM ENGLAND FOR NEW YORK DECEMBER FOURTEENTH STOP ADDRESS PALACE LAUSANNE.[10]

Took this text with me to the morning session at the Palais de Rumine, but did not send it until after Cecil had read and approved it.

Cecil opened the session by a brief and general but excellent statement. This was followed by the presentation of statements by the organizations. Hyman read a telegram from the JDC, Oungre spoke on behalf of ICA, Bernstein[11] made a terrible statement about HICEM, I read a cable from the American Jewish Committee, Rappard spoke on behalf of the intellectuals, excellently, and finally, Weizmann made a very statesmanlike and moving address. He did not read his paper, but followed it closely. He made a real impression. His manner was that of a man sure of himself and deeply experienced in handling similar situations.

The meeting lasted until half past one. There were personal conferences afterwards, and I did not get back to the hotel until two o'clock. Then conference with Oungre at lunch. We talked first about organizational relationships. He stressed again the danger of the Comité des Delegations, but was much less obstinate than was Dr. Kahn. While we were discussing this matter, Hyman and Kahn came in. Oungre then made a new suggestion to the effect that we set up a small operating committee to which the larger group would be advisory. This at first seemed to be possible, but later I saw that it wouldn't work. Meantime Hyman and Kahn had been futilely debating with Bentwich, continuing the prolonged discussion of the night before. After Oungre left and later in the afternoon when Hyman and Kahn come back I, not having had either a nap or tea, flared up at them and told them that I thought they, and in so far as they represented the New York attitude accurately, were childishly fearful. Hyman read me a draft of a cable he proposed to send to Felix Warburg. After he had eliminated his reference to Oungre's suggestion, which no longer seemed to me

10. Schacht responded the same day, "I do not feel authorized in my capacity to approach authorities mentioned in your telegram about subject in question. I am feeling personally that it would not be appropriate at present to ask for suggested interview." McDonald Papers, Columbia, High Commission Confidential File, 1933.

11. Dr. James Bernstein, European director of HICEM in Paris.

at all practicable, I told Hyman that I thought his communicating would do good, especially if it gave New York a more vivid sense of the danger of an open break in the ranks of the Jews and a world-wide attack among the conservatives. I added that I was myself going to send a cable asking Felix Warburg to telephone me that night.

I reiterated with emphasis that I would not be the agent of the rich and conservative Jews, and that if refusing to be that meant a break with them, I should regret it but would not yield. I added, "I feel all the more right on this point because if I did yield I would by that very yielding make success of this enterprise impossible. I must, no matter what the price, do what I think right, and I am sure that whatever one may feel about Goldmann, his claims[12] must be taken into account."

Just about this time, when things seemed blackest, Miss Ginsberg came into Miss Sawyer's office. When I saw her, I irritably exclaimed, "I almost feel as if I wished each half of the Jews would destroy the other half. They are impossible."

Fortunately, I managed to steal a few minutes of nap and then had tea, and by six o'clock was more nearly normal.

During the morning and afternoon Chamberlain and May as adviser and Olive Sawyer were working avidly to get figures in shape for Finance Committee meeting at six o'clock; it had been postponed from five. I was in and out of the meeting, having had to explain at the beginning some of the general principles underlying the salary schedule and the reasonable expectations. Chamberlain and May were invaluable.

At seven o'clock conference with Demuth. He told me of the organization and scope of the German self-help organizations. He is an impressive personality.

About nine o'clock down with May to dine with Weizmann. Weizmann, to illustrate the difficulty of dealing with the Jews, told of one of his experiences in Russia thirty-five years ago. A Russian policeman who had arrested him and later released him, had given him this advice, "Don't ever try to do anything for the Jews, because if you succeed they will destroy you." So he had never expected peace. He then went on to explain in a half-humorous but what seemed to be a wholly reasonable way his ideas about the inclusion of the Comité des Delegations. As he was talking, Goldmann walked by us to another table. Dr. Weizmann said, "Look at Goldmann; he is not as innocent as he looks, but he is not nearly so dangerous as Felix thinks. He has a great nuisance value. Why then alienate him and permit him to raise scornful protest throughout the eastern world and among the eastern Jews in the United States?" Later in the conversation Dr. Weizmann reverted to his rather bitter and not unusual manner when he said, "What's the matter with Felix? Some-

12. Goldmann's claims, presumably, as a leader of the Comité des Delegations (the future World Jewish Congress) and a Zionist, to represent the Jewish masses, as opposed to the elite.

one must have gotten at him. It is a mad policy that the New York group is seeking to impose." As I was leaving, I told him that I expected that Warburg would telephone me that night. Dr. Weizmann's last words were, "Be sure to give Felix my love."

Disunity among the organizations that claimed to represent Jews long preceded the Nazi takeover in 1933, although it was severely aggravated by the crises of the 1930s and inability to change either German policy or the immigration policies of Western nations. Those organizations that McDonald had to deal with in 1933–1936 may roughly be divided into three categories:

The "establishment" organizations *included the Consistoire Central and the Alliance Israelite in France, the Board of Deputies and the Anglo-Jewish Association in Britain, and the American Jewish Committee and B'nai B'rith in the United States. They were (to a greater or lesser extent) opposed to political Zionism and believed that Jews should be defined in religious, rather than ethnic or national, terms. They opposed overt boycotts of Nazi Germany as well as large-scale immigration into their own countries. They believed in quiet, behind-the-scenes negotiations with governments. They drew their support from the Jewish middle and upper-middle classes and were generally led by some of the wealthiest members of the community.*

The Zionist organizations *included international bodies such as the Comité des Delegations/WJC, the World Zionist Organization and a large number of ideological movements ranging from the leftist Hashomer Hatzair to the right-wing Revisionists. There were also important national bodies in the United States, Britain, and Palestine (Jewish Agency). The Zionists opposed what they called the "self-appointed elite" of the establishment organizations. They claimed democratic authority and popular support, and advocated immigration to Palestine and a Jewish national homeland there. They were deeply divided, however, on the basis of ideology and strategy. These divisions were exacerbated by the charismatic personalities of Zionist leaders such Weizmann, Goldmann, Ben-Gurion, Wise, and Jabotinsky.*

The relief and emigration organizations, *such as the Joint Distribution Committee, ORT,[13] HICEM, Central British Fund, and the ICA, were generally less political and directed on a day-to-day basis by middle-class professionals. While they were sympathetic to refugees and Eastern European Jews generally, their donor base was made up of many of the same people who led the establishment organizations and thus had influence over their policies. The relief organizations often favored settling Jewish emigrants in non-Western parts of the world.*

I went over again with Bentwich and Hyman the draft regulations for the private organizations which they and May had been working on. It was agreed

13. ORT, Russian acronym for Society for Trades and Agricultural Labor, founded in 1880 to provide vocational training for Jews. Transferred to Berlin in 1921, to Paris in 1933.

that I should preside over the meetings of the Advisory Council and that I should name the members of the small committee from "among those organizations which in my judgment were best suited to help most effectively in the work." I explained painstakingly to Hyman how this would guarantee every essential thing necessary to the JDC. But in answer to this argument, Dr. Kahn earlier in the day had exclaimed: "If you allow the Delegations and such groups to be on the Council, then if the smaller committee does not do what they want done, they will call the Jewish organizations together separately and denounce the smaller group." I replied to him that he seemed to me just as difficult as could conceivably be the persons he criticized, that he did not realize that I, as chairman of the Advisory Council, could have some influence. To the end Kahn remained unconvinced though Hyman was much more willing to accept the proposed compromise.

While I was waiting for the telephone call from New York, I asked Louis Oungre to come up. I told him what I had planned as a compromise. He thought it would be all right if the larger body met rarely and if the smaller body were made up as I intended to constitute it. I then asked his advice as to what I should do if I went to Germany, in particular the line I should take with Hitler. Oungre's suggestions were extremely interesting, but since the German trip was not arranged, it would not be worthwhile to write down these suggestions.

Last minute conferences with Hyman, Bentwich, and May about the proposed compromise. Chamberlain came in to talk about the budget with Miss Sawyer, so I invited him and May to be present when the telephone call came through from New York. This occurred shortly after eleven.

Warburg's voice was clearly heard. I told him that May and Chamberlain were present in the room, thus indicating to him that I was strongly backed in the proposal that I was going to make.

However, I talked first about non-controversial matters, telling him that I might go into Germany and the way in which the inquiry had been made. Then I told him that the governments had so far been excellent, with the result that considerable progress had been made. With this preliminary I explained carefully the proposed compromise; the inclusion of the Comité des Delegations in the larger group; its meeting infrequently, perhaps not more than three times a year; I was to preside over it; I to name the members of the smaller committee on which would be named the three large organizations. I said nothing about the danger of a failure to agree, this having been sufficiently discussed in Hyman's cable. After one or two of his questions had been satisfactorily answered, Warburg said he was satisfied. So that was that. We then talked about other matters, particularly the subjects to be discussed in Germany. I also explained why I hoped we could have some really fruitful conferences in New York while Messersmith, Chamberlain, and I were there. He suggested that I issue invitations. I said I would.

I asked him what the press response had been. He said the *New York Times* account was very full and friendly, and was kind enough to add that "they were very proud of you." He was also so considerate that at the very beginning of the talk he told me that he had called up Ruth to ask her if she cared to be present and speak to me. He then told me that Janet and Bobby had recovered from their colds.

I called up Hyman to tell him the result of the interview. I think he was greatly relieved. Certainly I, at any rate, was going to bed with the feeling that the worst crisis had been passed. But unhappily, the excitement of the day left me sleepless for much longer than is my habit.

Thursday, December 7, 1933

Disaster burst on Miss Sawyer and me. Telephone message from Geneva that Reading had fixed his dinner for December 15, on which we had planned to sail. I asked Miss Sawyer why she hadn't insisted that I reply to the telephone message of Tuesday, and she replied that she had told me of it emphatically, but that I waived it aside. Anyway, there was nothing to do but cancel the sailing of the fifteenth, and take the *Manhattan* on the seventeenth. The Reading dinner, to which he is inviting leading Jewish notables, gave me the best opportunity I could hope for to consolidate my position with that group. Therefore, much as I had looked forward to the three days before Christmas at home, I had to give it up.

Before the Permanent Committee met in my sitting room the Italian delegate, Senator Majoni, who had arrived the day previous, took me into our smaller sitting room and whispered to me that his government "could not take a single one more of the refugees; there were already 500 in Italy. Moreover, I cannot sit on the Permanent Committee." We discussed the matter, but he had instructions, so there was nothing to do. During the previous day the Dane had, like the Swede, reported that his government would not allow him to sit on the Permanent Committee. It began to look, therefore, as though there would be difficulty in making up the Permanent Committee unless one included on it a Czech or a Pole, which for political reasons would be undesirable, and that the choice of chairman and vice-chairman might be even more difficult.

The Permanent Committee discussion of the rules of procedure for the private organizations went along swiftly until Bérenger burst his bombshell about the National Committee being included on the list of non-Jewish organizations. Before the meeting Bérenger had protested to me most vigorously against the non-inclusion of the French Jewish organizations on the Advisory Council. I had Bentwich explain to him the point of view expressed at the London conference, according to which the French organizations should name a single representative. This, according to Bentwich, Bérenger accepted. But he was not so easily defeated, for if the National Committee could not be included among the Jewish organizations, then he would perform the miracle of making it into a non-Jewish organization and insist that it be included in the other group. This was accepted to keep the peace, but only after Cecil had made the record that any other national organization could be accepted on similar terms.

The only other difficult matter about the internal regulations was on the point about the smaller committee. I did not want it to be called a subcommittee but had the greatest difficulty explaining why. Even Cecil was obtuse in his failure to see that from the point of view of the larger organizations, the name of the subcommittee would mean a great deal. It was not until the afternoon that someone in the larger meeting had the inspiration to call the subcommittee the "Bureau."

After the conclusion of the private meeting we went to the private meeting of the whole Governing Body downstairs. There we adopted the program agreed upon upstairs, but not without some objections from Bérenger. At the last minute he tried to induce me to accept the inclusion of the National Committee in the Bureau. I told him that I did not see how I could possibly do it, and he, smiling slyly, let the matter drop. During the meeting I had real difficulty making the delegates understand why I did not wish that the smaller committee of the Advisory Council should be called a subcommittee. It was perfectly obvious to me that the JDC and the other two organizations would prefer a name which indicated less clearly that they were a creature of the larger body. Since, however, in French there is no satisfactory word it was only through the hitting upon the word "Bureau" that a satisfactory compromise was reached.

Off to lunch with Cecil. He had invited a group of his friends from the Secretariat—the Sweetsers, the Gordons, the Walters, and Dr. Weizmann. I sat next to Arthur Sweetser, who told me that he had very encouraging reports about the progress at Lausanne. Cecil, as usual, was very amusing during the meal.

After lunch I told Weizmann that Chamberlain was anxious to go over the budget figures with him. I had earlier suggested that Chamberlain do this with Hyman and Oungre.

Meeting of the Governing Body at four o'clock (private). First was taken up the regulations in reference to the private organizations. These were disposed of without much difficulty. Much more time, however, was spent on the question of passports, which had been raised by Bentwich's memorandum. There appeared to be three distinct points of view. First, that the 1927 arrangement[14] should be extended; to this the Italian objected, thus maintaining his government's opposition to a document which might be used for political refugees. Second, that the High Commissioner issue a special document of "identification and travel" or at any rate stamp existing valid documents to indicate that the holder is a German refugee; this was urged strongly by Bérenger and the Italian; it was opposed on practical grounds as imposing a burden upon the High Commissioner for which no adequate machinery existed. Third, that the High Commission issue a paper to be attached to passports which had ceased to be valid, or to stamp such pass-

14. Actually, an agreement of July 5, 1926, by the League of Nations to extend the documents commonly known as "Nansen Passports" to other refugees in Europe beyond the Russians and Armenians.

ports in a way to make them usable as travel and identification papers; to this Cecil and some of the other delegates were definitely opposed.

On broad lines the issue was really between the countries which wanted to improvise some documents which would expedite their task of getting rid of the refugees, and the countries like the United States and Uruguay which did not wish to receive the refugees. Finally, the matter was referred to a subcommittee which met immediately after the meeting, but failed to reach an agreement, except to refer the matter to the High Commissioner for further study and report to the next meeting of the Permanent Committee.

After this discussion it was already late, but I urged Cecil to go ahead and take up the budget, but first the financial regulations. He did. He put the financial regulations through in record time.

Before Professor Chamberlain presented the budget, I spoke briefly, making the following points:

(1) That approximately three-fourths of the estimated expenditures would probably be covered by receipts from the three large organizations, JDC, ICA, and the British Central Fund, and the fourth from non-Jewish sources;
(2) As to my own salary, I had had to choose between accepting it from private sources and thereby risking the charge of being controlled by a certain group, or putting it in the budget on the basis of my income in the States; the latter seemed to me franker and therefore preferable;
(3) That I did not think it accurate to say, as had been mentioned by one or two of the delegates earlier, that "every cent spent on administration was taken from the refugees." On the contrary, if this office functioned efficiently, it would add very materially to the funds available for the refugees.

Bérenger opened the discussion by attacking vigorously the heading "Budget," saying, in effect, that it was absurd to call this a budget because there were not receipts set down against expenditures. Others supported him in his contention. He and several of the other delegates also stressed the fact that no money could be expected from the governments and no governmental responsibility could be expected. I had previously stressed that I did not count at all upon governmental receipts in my reasonable expectations.

Finally, after much discussion, it was voted to change the heading to the following: "Estimated expenditures for the year 1934 provided funds are available from other than governmental sources."

Then the Czech moved that the Governing Body approve the estimated expenditures as "very reasonable." This phrase made many of the delegates gasp, but since most of them had just finished disavowing the slightest responsibility for securing the funds, they had the good grace not to quibble about the amounts. Throughout the whole discussion Cecil was excellent. The vote was finally unanimous.

After the meeting May met the press.

Dinner with May, Chamberlain, and Miss Sawyer. We discussed procedure for the next day, and finished work by a little after eleven.

Friday, December 8, 1933

Conferred with members of the staff during breakfast, and then dictated my concluding speech, the text of which was improved by suggestions from Herbert May, Miss Sawyer, and Hyman.

A day or so previous I had telephoned Goldmann, telling him that I would gladly read a letter from him at the Friday meeting if he cared to present it, and to distribute it to the press.

The private meeting of the Governing Body began at 10:30. Before it opened, Cecil told me the cheering news that he had decided to accept the election as chairman, provided the meetings of the Governing Body would for the most part be held in London. I was delighted to agree to that.

The first business of the meeting was the presentation of the reports of the subcommittees on passports. Cecil's comment was that it was not a very glorious result. Bérenger countered by the reply that sometimes one made the largest advance by standing still or moving very slowly.

Then came the incident of the morning. Bérenger reading from a copy of that day's *"Le Moment"* announced that there had been an indiscretion, and in such a tone as would have indicated a grave crisis had been precipitated. According to the paper, "Herbert May had told the press that a budget had been discussed during the session." Bérenger then went on to lecture the assembled group on the serious impropriety of any mention to outsiders of anything that had gone on in a private meeting. He wished to have it clearly understood that in the future the most rigid silence must been maintained. Everybody assented to this. Cecil, however, saying that this is the sort of thing which always happened when there was a private meeting, and that he was opposed to such meetings on principle, but that since a budget had been mentioned in the press, we should probably have to publish the figures agreed upon.

I protested vigorously against this latest suggestion, in a whispered conversation with Cecil, on the ground that it would be misunderstood and serve no useful purpose. I also spoke up to the Governing Body and suggested that since May's name had been brought up, he should be given the right to be heard. He then said briefly to the Governing Body that he and Chamberlain had met the press, that one of them asked him if the budget had been discussed and that he had replied "yes," and that was all. He added that he had had many years of experience with international organizations and therefore had frequently dealt with the press. Chamberlain supported May's report. I then in a few words told of my complete confidence in May and of our long association together. Bérenger countered by saying in effect, "It is quite proper that the High Commissioner should pay this homage to his associate, but nonetheless he must insist that in the future private sessions remain private." In the meantime May whispered to me that one of the newspaper men had said, "Is it true, as we learn from Bérenger, that a budget was discussed." I whispered this item to Cecil. Finally, Cecil brought peace to the troubled waters by outlining what he expected to say at the public meeting: he would report briefly on the decisions of the days before, the adoption of the statute, the rules of procedure, the financial regulations, passing lightly over the estimated expenditures, and announce that he had agreed to continue as chairman and name the other members of the Permanent Committee. He assented to Bérenger's insistence that his statement would refer to "estimated expenditures" and not mention the censored word "budget." At the end it was quite clear that Bérenger had overplayed his hand by making a mountain out of a molehill. Nonetheless, it was to me amusing that May, the soul of discretion, rather than I, should have been the first to be indicted of a major indiscretion.

Bérenger then raised the question about the paper which had been distributed on the placement of refugees. He objected to some of the references to France, and said that he would have to discuss it further either in private or public session. Chodzko insisted also on the elimination of references to Poland.

The public meeting began at about 11:30. Chamberlain spoke first in a friendly but non-committal way. He was followed by the Czech, then Bérenger delivered his speech for home consumption, ending with a direct appeal to the High Commission and the United States. The Dutchman and the Pole made brief statements, the Uruguayan urged that Argentina and Brazil be brought in. During these discussions Cecil whispered to me that he would speak briefly and that I should close the discussion. I replied, "How about Bérenger's desire to discuss the placement problem further?" Cecil indicated that it would not be done. I first read Goldmann's letter and then my own statement of thanks, and Cecil, smiling at Bérenger but making it quite impossible for the latter to insist on further discussion, closed the meeting.[15]

Following the meeting there was a brief period of leave-taking. Guani urged me to follow up with Argentina and Brazil; Bérenger asked if I would be in Paris for his report to the National Committee on Monday; Chodzko apologized for his reservation during the budget discussion, saying that he had to do it as a matter of record; the Czech made a similar statement; Borberg told me of his plan for stamps to be issued by the High Commission.

Staff luncheon to make follow-up plans. I arranged with Parkes to talk with him on the train.

Long conference with Weizmann. He outlined to me for more than an

15. The next day's *New York Times* headlined a summary report of the meetings: "America Is Chided on Reich Refugees." The article went on to say that the meetings ended "in an inconclusive argument indicating only that countries having a few of these refugees want no more and those having many want to lighten their burden. . . . A general impression of disappointment with the session was given, though no discouragement was voiced." *New York Times*, December 9, 1933, p. 8.

hour his plans for colonization in Palestine and the adjoining region of Lebanon.[16] He said that the number of people who might be allowed to go would fundamentally be determined by the absorptive capacity of the regions; that this, in turn, really depended up the amount of money available. I pressed him as to the political problems involved. He denied that these were insurmountable obstacles. He gave me permission, however, to check his impressions on these points by my own conversations with French and British officials, particularly Cunliffe-Lister.

He developed his thesis that by doubling the number of Jews in Palestine and the country to the north, such a substantial beginning would have to be made that the future would take care of itself; he could die content. He said that for every one thousand colonists on the land, an equal or twice as large a number of colonists would be attracted to serve the needs of the first group. Moreover, if once the Jews can be firmly planted along the coast, they will inevitably penetrate inland with their industry, energy, and thrift, as water runs downhill. In the hinterland, where the chief business is for one man to steal another man's cow, Jewish enterprise would develop a territory to the profit of all.

We did not discuss organization matters, nor speak more than briefly about financial problems in the States, but he reiterated his desire for a common front if that could be secured on a satisfactory basis. This, he suggested, should be 50/50, but he was not adamant on that point.

A rather frantic rush to get the 5:42 train with Miss Sawyer.

To Mr. May's for supper. Worked afterwards with Miss Sawyer until about 11:30.

Saturday, December 9, 1933

Conference with Mlle. Melon,[17] secretary of the Entr'aide on the Paris situation. She urged the immediate need of assistance. I told her I would talk to her associates in Paris and with the National Committee, and later with the people in New York and London, to see if a way can be found to meet the exigencies.

Worked with Miss Sawyer. Lunched at the Mays. Miss Sawyer and I continued work until about 7:30. Dinner at the Mays; the Malcolm Davises were the only other guests. After dinner Davis told me in some detail of the message which von Hahn had been asked by Major Urwick to deliver to me. The gist of it was that for the Twentieth Century Fund, headed by a Jew,[18] to fail to meet its obligations might jeopardize American cooperation abroad and prejudice my work. I told Davis that this seemed to me an outrageous attempt at coercion and should be treated as such.

16. Lebanon was under French control at that time.
17. Mlle. Melon, probably Germaine Melon-Hollard of the Quaker refugee committee.
18. The Twentieth Century Fund, headed by Edward A. Filene.

Sunday, December 10, 1933

Took up with Miss Sawyer the answer to Parkes's letter received the night before. In the light of my explanations to Parkes on the train Friday evening to the effect first, that my salary at present proposed was only the equivalent of what I had received; second, that I had had to choose between frankness as to my needs and accepting from private individuals the amount of my salary, thus endangering my reputation for independence, and that, therefore, I had chosen the former course; that I hope still to find a way through which my salary would not, in effect, be a charge on the budget. He did not seem to be convinced, reiterating his expression of feeling that mine and other salaries, including Miss Sawyer's, were indefensibly large. We then discussed the question of his relationship to me in the future. I told him I thought he would be happier working as a freelance rather than as a member of an organization, and urged him to go to Palestine if the Rogers offer were made. I discouraged his suggestion about a speaking tour in the States. I told him that I thought we had better sever our official relationship so that each side would be free, and that on my return we could both consider de novo what our relationship might be. I had the impression that this was satisfactory to him, but he said not a word at that time about any formal resignation.

In view of this conversation his letter struck me as being offensively self-righteous. It seemed so also to the Mays and to Miss Sawyer. I replied to it in a relatively detached manner, without attempting to reply to either his arguments or innuendoes.

Later during the day I took occasion to discuss the matter frankly with both Wurfbain and Bentwich. The former, in a splendid spirit, said that he had decided the day previous to offer to give back half of his salary; that he had wished to receive what he had received previously in order to maintain his status, but that since he had a small income of his own and since we were doing the kind of work we were, he was making his offer.

Bentwich was very reasonable in his attitude. He said of course American salaries were large, even compared with English ones, but recognized that the main point was to get on with the job. I explained to him my hope of reducing the amount which my salary really weighs in the budget.

About eleven M. de Navailles, of the Ministry of Foreign Affairs (sub-director), came to see me. He had been presiding during the week over the League committee dealing with indigent foreigners. He said that the men working under Bérenger were inclined to look at the problem of the refugees from not only a technical view, but a very narrow technical viewpoint. He offered to put me in touch with some of the more representative refugees and invited me to come to see him.

The day previous at Malcolm Davis's tea I had a chat with Prentiss Gilbert. I told him of the result of the German flirtations. He agreed that the effort through Schacht was wiser than would have been an attempt through Bern. He reverted to Arthur Sweetser's suggestion of the week previous that I move in this matter before the meeting of the Governing Body. Prentiss Gilbert rarely misses an opportunity to show that Sweetser has been wrong.

....

At 4:30 staff conference. First, I talked with Bentwich, then we all had tea with Mrs. May, followed by a very useful discussion of plans for work during our absence, particularly financial arrangements. It was made quite clear that Herbert May would be consulted on all important matters and be, in effect, my alter ego.

During the day Hyman called me to say that he had word that $10,000 had been forwarded from New York by cable to my credit at the Bank in Geneva, and that efforts were being made to improve the accommodations on the *Manhattan.*

Leon Fraser[19] called me on the telephone from Basle. He reported his conversation with Dr. Schacht. The latter thought it better that we not meet. He emphasized that this was not because of any personal attitude towards me, whom he had met several times and of whom he spoke favorably; his attitude grew out of the extreme difficulty of making any headway with the Leader on this matter. This was the one subject which had gotten Dr. Schacht into trouble when he raised it with Hitler. Therefore, in view of the present tense feeling he thought it would be inadvisable for him to meet me outside of Germany, just as he had thought it undesirable that he take the initiative in arranging an interview with Hitler. I told Fraser that I had heard something of Schacht's difficulties with Hitler on this matter. Fraser replied, "Yes, but you probably have not heard it so directly before." I thanked Fraser for his good offices, and it was arranged that we would confer again on my return.

Dinner at the Mays, Bentwich and Miss Sawyer. It was a pleasant dinner, Bentwich telling amusingly of English legal traditions.

Monday, December 11, 1933

Up early so that May and I could arrange at the bank for transfer of funds to Lausanne and for advances to me for the trip to the States. May carried everything through with his usual quiet dispatch.

10:26 train to Lausanne with May and Miss Sawyer. Upon arrival there May, Wurfbain, and I went to the bank and made arrangements for handling of finances during my absence. In this matter, as in other matters, May is to have the deciding voice.

Final conferences with the staff, and then luncheon together, and off to the 3:26 train for Paris and home. Worked on the train with Miss Sawyer on diary, etc.

19. Leon Fraser, American banker and attorney, president of the Bank for International Settlements.

I forgot to say earlier that during one of the days at Lausanne I saw Mr. Aage Friis, professor of history at the University of Copenhagen and a member of the Danish Committee for Intellectual Emigres.

At luncheon at Lausanne [I] opened the cable from the Town Hall announcing that I had been awarded this year's Honor Award.

Miss Sawyer and I reached Paris about 10:30, but had to continue to work until nearly midnight.

Paris, Tuesday, December 12, 1933

Dr. Rothbarth come in early and acted as a sort of secretary for us during much of the morning. She is a splendid person.

At 10:30 Mlle. Barlow of the Quakers and Dr. Walters came in. I arranged to see other members of that group and of the Entr'aide the next morning.

At eleven o'clock Leo Simon, a German resident in Paris, came. He seemed to me to be accurately analyzed in my confidential Who's Who of Jewish personalities. Undoubtedly he is well acquainted in Paris, knowing many of the political leaders, and has continued to have some contacts in Germany, but I doubt if his judgment is specially sound or that his influence is very great.

A little later Dr. Bernstein of HIAS came to urge that HICEM be included in the Advisory Council, chiefly on the ground that the inclusion of the latter might increase the chances of the former to raise funds in the States. I suggested that this question be presented to me in writing, and that I would present the matter to the first meeting of the Permanent Committee. He said he would ask the HIAS people in New York to get in touch with me.

Lunch with Dr. Rosen.[20] We talked about a number of matters including

(1) Lord Marley's scheme to settle Jewish refugees in the Amur region.[21] Dr. Rosen thinks this is a fantastic scheme, and my first impression is similar. Nonetheless, I shall discuss this matter with Marley when he calls to see me in London.
(2) JDC representation in Europe and the role of Dr. Kahn, Hyman, et al.
(3) Dr. Weizmann and Palestine. Dr. Rosen thinks the doctor is much too optimistic about the possibilities of Palestine, and that the reports on that subject are apt to be influenced more by feelings and wishes than by realities.
(4) Dr. Rosen asked if I would like to have him raise with Litvinov[22] the question of Russia's becoming a member of the Governing Body. I told him that I was sure that he would be an excellent person to raise this issue, provided

20. Dr. Joseph A. Rosen, director of the Agro-Joint, the American Jewish Joint Agricultural Corporation, which conducted large scale colonization projects in the Crimea and the Ukraine. An American citizen, Russian by birth, a man of fine personal charm and outspoken frankness.

21. Region of nearly four hundred thousand square miles in the far eastern portion of the Soviet Union, on the Chinese border.

22. Maxim Litvinov, Soviet commissar for Foreign Affairs, 1930–1939. Of Jewish descent.

it were to be raised at all at this time, but that I could not give him an answer until I had talked to Bérenger and Cecil. After that I promised to send him word, either through Kahn or Hyman.

In the early afternoon Miss Ginsburg came in. As usual, she was full of ideas. One that concerned her especially was the question of Polish refugees in France being repatriated. She wanted to know if I could not authorize her to say something to the Polish government on this point, or if perhaps May might not have a visa. I replied that this seemed to be a matter beyond our competence. She also raised a number of questions about various organizations. In particular, she expressed the hope that I would speak favorably of her work to the JDC. I said I certainly would do so.

At 6:30 Professor Chamberlain and I started over to the Senate Office Building where we were to have a conference with Senator Bérenger and his French colleagues. We met in the senator's office as president of the Committee on Foreign Affairs of the Senate. Present were, besides Bérenger and the two Americans, Baron Robert de Rothschild, Minister Pletrie, a friend of Siekler and a prominent Corsican, Mr. Helbronner, Professor Oulid, Mr. Stern, and perhaps one other. Bérenger was amiability itself. Each of the Frenchmen made a longish statement addressed to me as Haute Commissaire. There is no need to repeat them individually. The general purport of all of them was the same: (1) France has done not only its full duty but has done it handsomely. It is imperative that it be relieved from the outside. (2) The High Commissioner should at once do what can be done to bring this relief needed at once. (3) In the meantime, plans should be made for the sending of the refugees out of France. It is absurd to think that any number of German refugees can be colonized on French soil; the land available is poor and would not be fruitful; moreover, the danger of intensifying anti-Semitism and creating xenophobia would be great.

In reply, I admitted in principle the validity of many of the arguments advanced, saying that I would do my utmost to encourage some relief for the immediate situation while planning help on the more fundamental problem. After the conference Professor Chamberlain and I were shown through the Senate building; we were served with tea in the refreshment room and were bowed out most courageously. On the way I met and chatted for a few minutes with Laval.

Worked until time for late dinner with Miss Sawyer and then over with her to Dr. Rothbarth's soirée. There I had a most interesting talk with Mme. Viennet, the wife of a leading electrical manufacturer, who is interesting herself actively and intelligently. She has some striking ideas about passports and cards of identity. I have asked Bentwich to confer with her when he is in Paris. She knows the whole matter from the practical point of view.

Back to the hotel and worked with Miss Sawyer until after eleven while waiting on a telephone call from Hyman from London. He told me a rather lugubrious tale of disquietude in ICA and Central Fund circles growing out of the fear that I had allowed myself to be pocketed by Dr. Weizmann. He urged that I see d'Avigdor Goldsmid and Sir Lionel Cohen as soon as possible. He also reported that the Reading dinner had become hopelessly confused, that Neville Laski was terribly hurt at not being invited, and that, in general, it was a mess. I thanked Hyman, but at the same time felt that he might have saved the more depressing items of news until he saw me, or at any rate only give me such of it as I could act upon before arriving in London.

....

Wednesday, December 13, 1933

Up early in order to keep an appointment with Miss Ginsberg and Mme. Vavasseur to go to the Bastion.[23] The first one we visited was occupied by a considerable number of families, as well as by single men. The impression created was extremely depressing, but did not reflect as much as I had thought it would upon the French management. The rabbi who showed us about, Dr. Hertz, was a kindly and intelligent director. We talked to the mothers in two or three of the rooms set aside for families. One was the mother of six children, living with her husband in a single room somewhat larger than the space required for the cots. There was some heat, but very inadequate bedding and no electric lights. Nonetheless, she was making a strenuous effort to keep the family in order. Most of the persons with whom I talked were of Polish nationality or stateless, that is, without any definite nationality or with inadequate papers. One of the families I was especially interested in was made up of a mother, father, and four children. One of these, a girl of thirteen, reminded me strikingly of a Warburg child. I took the name and address and hope that something may be done to give this particular family a new opportunity. It was pitiful to see the few family belongings which the refugees had brought with them, in some cases family portraits, but nearly always a few Hebrew religious books.

The second Bastion we visited for a shorter period was that at the Port d'Italie. It was occupied mostly by young men, including only a very few intellectuals.

Back to the hotel to find that in my absence a delegation of the Entr'aide had arrived. In this group were Mme. Jean Brany, Comité d'Entr'aide Europeanne et Service Social Comité National.

Mme. Barlow—Comité d'Entr'aide Europeanne
M. Friedlander—Comité d'Entr'aide Europeanne, Ligue des Droits de l'Homme Centre Triage du Comité National
M. Mallon Harvey—Comité d'Entr'aide Europeanne at Society des Amis Americains

23. Bastion, collective name for four unused barracks and military buildings made available to refugee relief organizations by the French government in 1933. On the outskirts of Paris. Housed as many as two thousand refugees in the summer of 1933.

We at once began a discussion of the situation in Paris. Fortunately, during the midst of it, Robert de Rothschild was announced, and I asked him to come up and join us. A few minutes later Dr. Sylvain Levi came in, and then Professor Chamberlain, so we had a very full house in our small sitting room. Out of the conference emerged, I hope, an increased chance of better coordination of the work in Paris.

After the others left I talked to Sylvain Levi and Rothschild about the former's complaints as to the setup of the Advisory Council. I agreed that I would recommend that the Alliance be added, but I told him that I could not make any promises about a Frenchman "aupres de moi" unless a volunteer A.D.C. could be found; that already I had two Jews in my immediate entourage—Mr. May, not because he is a Jew but because he is my intimate friend and adviser, and Mr. Bentwich, because he seemed to me the best liaison with English and other Jewry that could be found. Levi seemed to be satisfied.

When he had left, Rothschild and Chamberlain and I continued our conversation about the Paris situation. Rothschild agreed to send to the boat the data which I requested.

Meantime, time had been passing, and there was no opportunity for me to pack, so I accepted gladly the volunteer offer of Mme. Else Thulin, the Swedish authoress, to pack for me. During this operation in the other room Miss Sawyer supplied her with data for an interview with me, and Miss Ginsberg support material about my "Who's Who." I promised her that I would do my best to attend a meeting of her committee in Sweden to raise funds. She explained that those who were signing the appeal, other than the two princes, were of the academic and intellectual group in Sweden, and only three of them were Jews.

Antonia of the American Express had taken our luggage to the station, so that Miss Sawyer and I moved along more or less leisurely and arrived at the train well before the time.

On the trip to Calais I was too tired to work; as we were drawing into the Calais station, there was some delay, owing, as we were soon to learn, to the late arrival of the steamer, which had been held up by a channel gale. The reports given by the incoming passengers were so disquieting that Wilberforce and his wife, who were on the train with us, decided not to cross, so Miss Sawyer and I took their compartment. The less said about the trip over, the better, but both of us were rather cheered when, on arriving in London, we found the evening papers announcing "terrible gale in the channel—transchannel shipping discontinued," etc. Nonetheless, I was a wilted rag and welcomed the unexpected situation that I had no appointment for that night. As it was, Miss Sawyer and I worked until after eleven.

London, Thursday, December 14, 1933

Early morning taken up with arranging engagements. Hyman came in and continued his report of the disturbed state of respectable Jewish opinion.

At twelve o'clock Frank Goldsmith came. I liked him very much. He takes a broad view, not only of the Paris situation, but of organizational Jewish matters. What a relief to find someone who isn't concerned about prestige or status for himself or an organization. I told him of some of my difficulties with the larger organizations, and he promised to use his good offices, and I have faith that he will be helpful. He told us to communicate with him at any time we needed him, care of the Hotel Scribe, Paris.

At one o'clock Laski came to lunch. As compared with the horrific tales I had heard from Hyman of Laski's state of mind, he was as gentle as a lamb. When we arranged to lunch together alone, he asked me whether the conference could be "in confidence and without prejudice." Without the faintest idea what he meant by the latter part of the phrase, I assented heartily. I reassured him on the Weizmann matter,[24] but could be of little help to him about the Reading dinner, but when he read Reading's letter to Montefiore, he concluded the mistake was due to the former's cutting out of Bentwich's telegram to Jewish personalities and insisted on carrying off the Reading letter, but I consented to his doing so only after he pledged me his word of honor he would not raise the question again with Reading. Laski did not speak of representation on the Bureau directly, but I have no doubt he had it in mind. During the course of our discussion he showed me the draft of a statement which he and his associates, not including the Zionists, were considering presenting to the Colonial Office, urging more generous allocation of certificates.

After lunch had a few minutes with the Bishop of Chichester at the Athenaeum. I thanked him for his initiative, especially because of the educational effect in America.

At six o'clock Mr. B. from Frankfurt came in. He was attending a meeting of an important society. He talked very frankly about conditions. One would have to conclude from his account that there had been no amelioration, nor would there be likely to be. He thought the delay in reference to a new fundamental law was because of the desire first to complete a census on a racial basis. His stories of individual cases of unfair treatment merely documented his general thesis. He is a charming and unusually intelligent person. Speaking of the effect of feared new statutes, I asked him if, like Max Warburg, he would feel that its enactment would require him to leave the country. He replied with a positive negative, saying "It is for me, not for any outside body, to decide whether or not I am a German."

Dinner with Otto Schiff. I began by reassuring him, as I had Laski and all the others with whom I had spoken, about my relations with Dr. Weizmann. I

24. According to Laski's notes of this meeting, McDonald "thought that Dr. Weizmann had a one-track mind and that his interest outside Palestine was of the slightest." Laski to J. C. Hyman, Notes of interview with Mr. McDonald, December 14, 1933. JDC Archives, High Commission file 1, 1933.

also explained the basis of the budget. As always, Schiff was very understanding. He described the present situation about the plans for the Central Fund, was very critical of Dr. Weizmann for the nature of the separate appeal in the Dominions, but was under the impression, nonetheless, that a new basis for a Central Fund here would be found.

He asked me very earnestly to urge as emphatically as I could two policies upon Felix Warburg: first, that Lewis Strauss be assigned to this side, either Paris or London. He was prepared to try to get Ranarier actively interested in this suggestion, on the basis that Lewis Strauss would be in a real sense a European figure. Schiff did not think much of Einstein as a possibility. Second, that Felix himself spend a few days in England on his way to Palestine, and to be for that short time a focal point for the whole of the leadership of Western Jewry.

I replied that I would gladly carry out these suggestions, and that perhaps we could arrange to hold the first meeting of the Permanent Committee in time to have Warburg sit on it for the JDC.

Then Schiff asked me what he could do for me, that Felix Warburg had said that he would help me in every possible way, and that he would gladly do so. I replied, "Yes, you can help on three points: (1) make clear that in my opinion Dr. Weizmann and I can work together effectively so long as Dr. Weizmann thinks I can be useful to him, and, what is just as important, only so long as he knows he cannot use me"; (2) "Help to make clear to the larger organizations my basic philosophy as to their relations to the mass organizations"; (3) "Give to the leaders of the larger organizations a better understanding of the setup of our staff." He said he would gladly do all of these things.

Friday, December 15, 1933

Professor Chamberlain came in at ten, and remained here during the interview with Sir Leon Levison.[25] The latter did not impress me with his claim that the Hebrew Christians were being discriminated against by the non-sectarian organizations. I told him this frankly and also refused to accept the implication of his contention that the Jews had any responsibility for the Hebrew Christians. This seemed to me to be clearly a responsibility of the Christian organizations themselves. I suggest that he present his case to the first meeting of the Permanent Committee. There was a brief embarrassing moment when d'Avigdor Goldsmid was shown in before Sir Leon was shown out, so I concluded with the latter our talk in the adjoining room.

In my talk with d'Avigdor Goldsmid I took the initiative at once explaining my attitude towards Dr. Weizmann, the setup of the Advisory Committee and the body, and the basis of the administrative budget. He listened attentively and I think had in part his fears quieted. Then I asked him to tell me quite frankly all he could about the present situation of the plans here for the Central Fund, for

25. Leon Levison, founder of the International Hebrew Christian Association of "Messianic" Jews.

any information in connection with conferences at home. He explained the need from his point of view for a new basis of allocation, the difficulties in arriving at an agreement, but his hope that, nonetheless, it would be achieved. He said it would be impossible for him to come to the States, but that he hoped that Felix Warburg would come here. I explained about the Reading dinner, as I had to the others. D'Avigdor Goldsmid, I think, had not been much disturbed. As to the Bureau, I told him that at the proposed London meeting I would of course expect him as chairman of the Central Fund to sit in. Towards the end of our talk he said something about expecting results from the High Commission, especially in the matter of opening the doors for emigrants. I replied that I would do my utmost, but that I needn't stress with him the greatest difficulties. He also talked about the budget submitted by Wilfrid Israel for work in Germany, and seemed sympathetic towards meeting the German request as far as possible. He recognized of course that this would involve a very serious difference of opinion with the Zionists.

The lunch at Sir Philip Cunliffe-Lister's house with three of his colleagues: one his Under-Secretary Dugdale,[26] and two others—Sir John Maffery, permanent undersecretary of the Colonial Office, formerly governor general of the Sudan, and Mr. Parkinson, assistant secretary in the Colonial Office in charge of Middle East Department, which looks after Palestine, among other countries. The discussion which began at once was, from my point of view, extremely frank and very helpful. I began as usual by explaining my relations to Dr. Weizmann, my conception of the High Commissioner's role as not to interfere in matters of certificates or to make the work of the mandatory government more difficult, etc. I stressed the importance of handling the refugee situation, including emigration to Palestine, in such a way as not to intensify anti-Semitism or embitter Jewish-Arab relations. Repeatedly after I had stressed these points of view, Sir Philip would reply, "but you are so wise in your attitude, that I am sure you will have a large measure of success, and that we shall get on together." So emphatic, indeed, was he about my wisdom that I began towards the end a little to suspect that this might be a form of speech, rather than the expression of a conviction.

Sir Philip talked in detail about his government's attitude. He admitted that Weizmann was right in saying that the test of the number of certificates to be granted was the absorptive capacity of the mandate, but, he said, "It's nonsense to stand on the letter of a document, no matter what the document is—the Balfour Declaration, the Passfield White Paper,[27] or Ramsay's letter. I, as an administrator, don't give a damn about those things if they conflict with the basic necessities or with our fundamental policy of being just to Arab and Jew alike.

26. Sir Thomas Lionel Dugdale, later chairman of the Conservative Party.

27. The Passfield White Paper of October 1930 declared that a Jewish national home in Palestine was not central to Britain's mandate there. (Colonial Secretary Lord Passfield was the former Sydney Webb.) It weakened the Balfour Declaration of November 2, 1917, in which the British War Cabinet had viewed "with favor" establishment of a Jewish national home in Palestine (named after Foreign Secretary Arthur Balfour).

Of course we shall stay in Palestine, but we shall not permit ourselves to be used to set up a Jewish hegemony in the Levant. Dr. Weizmann's ideal of establishing half a million Jews in Palestine and the Lebanon, to be used as a base from which missions of Jews could infiltrate into Trans-Jordan, Syria, and beyond, establishing themselves as a political or quasi-political power in that region is a conception which we will never support nor tolerate. For us to do so would be to invite disaster. British public opinion would never permit that British troops be sacrificed to carry out a Zionist concept of a political state. This is not merely my personal feeling, but it is the attitude of the government and would be the attitude of any succeeding government. The Jews must realize this and realize further that for them to press for impossible demands is to risk revulsion of British opinion, which might weaken all the gains the Zionists have made. It is nonsense to talk about Trans-Jordan at present. Jews could survive there only if supported by British soldiers, and there will be no such support. It is absolutely fundamental that the Jewish leaders realize that, in the long run, they can count only on cooperation with the Arabs as the basis for security. They must get away from the narrow conception of employing only Jewish labor; they must strike out a clause from the land contracts which precludes the use of Arab labor. They must, in short, subordinate Jewish nationalism to Jewish-Arab cooperation. They should use as a model some of the old Rothschild colonies in Palestine, where today after forty years of storm and stress Jew and Arab are on intimate, trustful terms."

Sir Philip urged me to visit Palestine to see for myself. He criticized Dr. Weizmann's scheme for the Lebanon as impracticable at present. So far as details of certificates are concerned, these are handled solely by the High Commissioner in Palestine, London being concerned merely with the general principles. This policy will be maintained. I asked him about the story in the *Daily Herald* of a controversy between his office and me over Palestine. He hadn't seen it, but one of his colleagues had, but had been in no wise disturbed by it, attributing it merely to a desire of the Labour press to create trouble for the National government.

On the whole, the conference seemed to me most satisfactory. It left me in a position to take up later with Sir Philip or his colleagues any particular questions which might be pertinent.

Tea with Sir Herbert Samuel.[28] Had a general talk about the setup of my office and its work.

Tea with Lord and Lady Cecil. It was difficult for me to refrain from smiling when the maid said to me, "Her Ladyship is awaiting you in the drawing room, and His Lordship will be with you presently." And as I entered the drawing room, a very simple establishment, there sat Lady Cecil, a little old woman as far removed in appearance from the story-book conception of "Her Ladyship"

28. Sir Herbert Samuel, formerly High Commissioner for Palestine, leader of the Parliamentary Liberal Party and home secretary of the British government, 1931–1932.

as could well be imagined. We were soon joined by Lord Cecil. He and I talked about a possible meeting of the Permanent Committee late in January, and he brought up a letter from Urwick and another one from Lord Marley. I forgot to ask Lord Cecil about Russia and the Governing Body. Again Lord Cecil took occasion to express his admiration for Dr. Weizmann. Before I left, I made Lady Cecil laugh with some of my stories about Janet and the children.

Six o'clock back to the hotel to find Lord Marley,[29] Miss Ellen Wilkinson,[30] and one of the officers of ORT, a Dr. Lebovitch. Lord Marley began at once to talk about the possible relations of ORT-OSE[31] and his committee for the protection of German rights, to the High Commission. I suggested that he present the case on these points to the Permanent Committee, that I was doubtful about the third of his organizations being a logical candidate for membership on the Advisory Committee. Most of Lord Marley's talk, however, was about the colonization project in the proposed autonomous Jewish republic in the Biro-Bidjan region,[32] which he had just visited. He waxed enthusiastic and refused to be discouraged by the political questions which I raised. I suggested that he present this matter too, to the Permanent Committee, but he replied that he wanted me to designate someone to investigate the possibilities of this project. I begged off, suggesting that he, Rosen, and the ICA work out some basis for such an investigation. He, which I was to learn the next day, with excellent reason, doubted that ICA would go along. Nonetheless, I promised to speak to Oungre about it the next day, and Marley was to call me up to find out the result. By the time Marley had left I felt physically and mentally exhausted, so tried to steal half an hour's nap before going to the Reading dinner.

At Reading's, besides the host and Professor Chamberlain and myself, were Reading's son, Viscount Erleigh, Lionel Cohen, Otto Schiff, Anthony de Rothschild, Sir Herbert Samuel. During dinner Reading talked to me practically the whole time very interestingly about his impressions of Wilson, Hoover, and other Americans. Then, as soon as the simple but excellent food had been disposed of, Reading asked me if I wouldn't say what I had to say, and perhaps to ask questions. I began by outlining the nature of our organization, some of the problems which had to be overcome in setting it up, especially organizational and personal difficulties, and then came to the matter of the present problem. On this basis we had an illuminating and frank discussion which lasted until

29. Lord Marley, lst Baron Dudley Leigh Aman; decorated World War I Royal Marines officer, active in the Labor Party; undersecretary of state for war, 1930; deputy speaker of the House of Lords, 1930–1941, and chief opposition whip 1931–1937; chairman of the World Committee to Aid Victims of German Fascism.

30. Ellen Wilkinson, prominent in the left wing of the Labour Party. Known as "Red Ellen" for her hair and her politics. Labour M. P. for Middlesborough East (in Manchester), 1924–1931. Lost her seat after opposing Ramsey McDonald's government. Wrote several books, including one entitled *The Terror in Germany* (1933). Reentered Parliament in 1935.

31. OSE, Children's Aid Society, founded in Russia 1912, transferred to Paris in 1933.

32. Biro-Bidjan (also Birobidzhan), a "Jewish autonomous region" of the Soviet Union, in the Far East, near the Chinese border. Regarded by Stalin and the Communist Party as an alternative to Zionism. Begun in 1928, by 1935 had only about fourteen thousand Jews.

about 11:30. At first the talk centered on the basic question of Jewish nationalism vs. the prevailing English conception. I stressed my own philosophy and what I conceived to be the danger of the extreme interpretation of the Weizmann and nationalist position. They are all greatly worried by the possible ramifications in England and elsewhere of such an absolutistic conception. They were evidently relieved that I shared their fear.

We then discussed relations with Germany. I told them of the démarche I had made and of its failure. I stressed my fear that conditions would become such that one would have to envisage a mass migration of the youth. In this connection I gave a picture of the moral degradation suffered by German Jews, which seemed to impress Reading. We then went on to a discussion of German property. There was general agreement that the utmost possible should be done at once to try to find a formula to permit the recovery by the refugees of a portion of their goods. After a full discussion it was decided, on my suggestion, that Schiff and Lionel Cohen and the German lawyer from Breslau, Cohen, should lunch together on Sunday. It was hoped that we might at such a meeting formulate a proposal which I could present to President Roosevelt if, after a talk with him, he showed any interest in the possibility of helping to establish a contact with Berlin.

A number of other matters were brought up during the evening, but I need not relate them here. I left with the impression that both Reading and Samuel had perhaps been drawn more into the center of this question than they had been previously.

Saturday, December 16, 1933

A friend came in to see me bringing the first ray of hope that a way might be found to open up conversations with ranking persons in Germany. The data, however, is so confidential that I think it would be unwise to put anything more down about it here, since I promised not to speak to anyone of it.[33]

Over to Minister Einstein's home, where we had a pleasant chat. He is a cultured gentleman, but probably not willing to interest himself actively in Jewish aspects of the present problem. In any case, he is not available because he is taking his wife to south Italy for a large part of the winter. He urged me to call him up when I came back, if he is in town and I have time. I am sure we would have a pleasant visit.

A brief chat with Hyman before going over to lunch with Sir Leonard Cohen. When I arrived at his house, I found, in addition to Oungre, whom I expected, Jules Philippson. I did not wait for them to talk about ICA and our organization, but took advantage of Sir Leonard's invitation to open the discus-

33. This possibility was fleshed out somewhat in McDonald's December 17, 1933, telephone conversation with Felix Frankfurter. Frankfurter's summary of that conversation is included following the diary entry for December 17.

sion, to raise certain general questions with a view to putting the organizational matter, when it came up later, in sounder perspective.

First, we talked about the possibility of ICA helping to study the Russian project. Oungre replied with his usual precision that the matter had been studied, that, both from the economic and political point of view, it was absurd. He agreed however that ICA's Moscow representative would present his point of view about it at the Permanent Committee meeting.

Second, I asked them what they thought about inviting Russia on the Governing Body. Phillippson and Sir Leonard thought it should be done; Oungre raised doubts. These seemed to be conclusive after I had presented the third question—this was my relations to Germany. I told them of the Lausanne démarche and that at Basle, and added that since then the first hopeful suggestion had come from beyond the Rhine. In the light of this development they all agreed that the suggestion of an invitation to Russia should be postponed.

By the time we had gotten through these questions, it was the luncheon period. During the meal we had amusing conversations about the derivation of words like OK and I discovered that both Sir Leonard and Oungre are philologists of no mean merit.

After lunch we came back directly to the problems which were worrying the ICA group. I refused to wait for the attack, and developed my attitude towards Dr. Weizmann, thus removing one of their fears. Sir Leonard then asked who was the British representative on the Bureau, not Weizmann, he said, because of considerations which I need not here recount, not ICA because it is not English. After some discussion I agreed to recommend that a representative of English Jewry and also of French Jewry be added to the Bureau. I refused, however, to be drawn into any discussion of who should be named or by whom.

Then, before Sir Leonard could raise the question of money, I made my defense of the budget, along the lines which I had explained previously to so many others. I think that I secured almost complete assent from all of them that the figures were justifiable. They were rather amusing in the admission that Felix Warburg's suggestion as to the amount ICA should contribute had been resented. Sir Leonard then said that they would contribute $15,000 or £3,000, and if more was needed toward the end of the year, they would consider an additional grant. But before this was precisely formulated, Philippson intervened to say that he thought it would be much more appropriate to grant at once the whole amount asked, and he moved that this suggestion be passed on to the other directors. Oungre assented heartily, and then so did Sir Leonard, and it was so decided.

Throughout the long conference I sensed that Oungre and Phillipson had really been as helpful as they possibly could be at the meeting of the ICA earlier this week. Moreover, Sir Leonard was himself obviously relieved that my assurances would permit him to reassure his board. As I was leaving, he said to me, "I am delighted that our meeting has been so thoroughly satisfactory." Philippson followed me to the door and asked if I were satisfied. I told him that I was delighted and most grateful to him.

Professor Chamberlain came in about four, and he and I went off together for tea at Dr. Weizmann's. We chatted first with Mrs. Weizmann and Dr. Weizmann's brother, who were awaiting a call from the latter's mother in Haifa. After tea Dr. Weizmann, Chamberlain, and I talked. It was mostly about the possibility of a united front in the States. Dr. Weizmann said he had just received a long letter from Felix Warburg, in which the latter had spoken of the necessity of maintaining the Jews in Germany. This then led to a discussion of the budget proposed by Israel and his group. Dr. Weizmann emphatically declared that he would oppose violently any attempt to pour that amount of money into Germany. The talk then turned to Palestine, the possibilities of further colonization there, the danger of a one-crop system. (On this point Dr. Weizmann said that attempts were now being made at diversification.) I then brought up some of the points which Sir Philip had made, notably the Jewish prohibition of the employment of Arab labor under certain circumstances. Dr. Weizmann defended this on the ground that, otherwise, the Jews might become mere landlords; second, that was all Jewish money; and third, that it was important to force the Jews to diversify their occupations to include manual labor. Nonetheless, Dr. Weizmann said he was working to modify that provision in the land contracts which forbade the employment of other than Jewish labor.

As I was leaving, there was some talk as to Dr. Weizmann's plans; he seemed to be uncertain still whether he would come to the States in January or later in the year, after having been first in Palestine.

Back to the hotel to find Rabbi Hertz and Bentwich waiting for me. The former seemed to me a good natured and (despite the reports I had heard to the contrary) a penetrating person. I brought up jokingly the subject of the fears felt in London that I had been put in Dr. Weizmann's pocket, and assured Rabbi Hertz that was not the case. The latter then launched into a very emphatic defense of the program to help maintain Jewish institutions in Germany. He insisted that this would be done irrespective of what Dr. Weizmann thought.

Bentwich and I then discussed the general situation. I told him of the fears in London that he inadvertently had helped to strengthen Weizmann's position vis-à-vis me unjustifiably. He thought it amusing that he should be considered the creature of Dr. Weizmann when, in fact, he could hardly be considered now to be a good Zionist. I stressed, however, that during his stay in London he should lean over backwards to reassure his associates on this point.

....

Earlier in the evening Lord Marley telephoned, and I told him that I had been unable to convince ICA that they would participate in an investigation of Biro-Bidjan and that, therefore, I thought there was nothing to do except that he could present his case at the first meeting of the Permanent Committee.

Sunday, December 17, 1933

At work all the morning from before nine until time to go to lunch on the diary and on last minute letters.

At the luncheon at Lionel Cohen's house besides Mr. and Mrs. Cohen and myself were Otto Schiff, Bentwich, and Professor Cohen, the German expert on property now practicing law in London (formerly of Breslau). We talked about a number of subjects during the early part of the meal, then concentrated on the question of the possibility of recovering portions of the refugees' property in Germany. Professor Cohen's ideas seemed so significant that I asked him if he would not dictate immediately after lunch a memorandum which I could take with me and submit to friends at home. Professor Cohen then worked out with Otto Schiff a draft analysis. Copies of this were made immediately on our return to the hotel. Meantime Lionel Cohen said that he and Anthony de Rothschild and perhaps some others would submit to me memoranda on this project.

Back to the hotel and to the station. There Mr. Laski saw us off. He and I had a pleasant and wholly friendly discussion of the general situation, and in particular of the proposed additions to the Bureau which I had worked out with the ICA group. He seemed completely satisfied.

Arranged on the steamer for a table of six, Professor Chamberlain, Mr. Warren of the International Migration Service, Hyman, Miss Harriet Camac, Miss Sawyer, and myself.

December 17, 1933

[Felix Frankfurter's] Minutes of telephone conversation with J. G. McDonald

I had a note from McDonald on Thursday announcing that he was in London for three days before sailing for New York and suggesting that I come up and see him because "the number of people I must see here threatens to crowd me sorely" so that he couldn't manage Oxford. As a matter of fact, I couldn't go to London and so notified McDonald.

Today McD. phoned, talking about ten minutes general palaver and referring with roundabout, diplomatic language to his previous information that the Reich is contemplating legislation to give a servile status to Jewish citizens. He said that his information now was that early legislation is contemplated to render all those who had been naturalized since 1918 staatenlos, leaving treatment of other classes of Jews to the results of the census, because of difficulties in determining who were the grandparents of people.

McDonald also told me of the efforts he had made through an intermediary to enlist the help of Schacht in securing mitigation for Jews, but Schacht refused to intervene, saying that he had found Hitler fierce and unresponsive on the subject and that it would only hurt his, Schacht's, position. When McDonald, through his intermediary, suggested a conference between himself and Schacht, Schacht thought it was better not to meet McDonald. I told McDonald that I thought that seeking to reach Schacht's support was like trying to ram his head through a concrete wall—that

Schacht was an incorrigible and enthusiastic anti-Semite and wholly in accord with Hitler's policy. McDonald said that that was also his information about Schacht, but on grounds of expediency he thought Schacht might help. He then added that he had had word most recently from one of the German triumvirate [Hitler, Goebbels, Göring—word could only have come through one of Göring's subordinates] indicating the first ray of hope of alleviation. I said that they are almost ready to promise anything these days, in words, because of the international game they are playing, to which McDonald replied with very vigorous accord, as though he were surprised at my prescience, "Yes, that's exactly it."

He then went on to say that he was going home and would be back in January and hoped to see me. I said I should of course be in Oxford. He said he was going home to report and see people, and surmising that he had an unexpressed desire in phoning me, relating to the President, because he had asked, "You haven't any word for me about the President," I said innocently, "I suppose you will see State Department people and the President. To which he replied, "Of course I shall be available for the President if he desires to see me, but he may have reasons of high policy for thinking it undesirable to see me. I'm not asking you to write to him suggesting that he see me. I'm not of course interested in the mere prestige gained by seeing the President, but I just wanted you to know that I am at the President's disposal if he wants to see me." To which I replied, "Well, you'll be seeing State Department people, and they will know what there is to know." I left it at that, and with a courteous exchange, the talk ended.[34]

At sea on SS *Manhattan*, Monday, December 18–Saturday, December 23, 1933

Towards the end of the voyage Hyman, Chamberlain, and I discussed Hyman's memorandum on the German situation and other related matters. On Friday afternoon received a wireless from the *New York Times* asking for a 2,000 word interview. I arranged to dictate it the morning after Miss Sawyer had finished with the hairdressers.[35] The talk at table throughout the voyage was amusing, Chamberlain, Warren, and even occasionally Hyman playing up to Miss Camac in a diverting fashion.

The last two days or so I had several conferences with Mr. James Farley and his wife. He told me many extremely interesting things about the 1932 presidential campaign, ways in which he and Colonel Howe ran it, the President's methods of work, etc. Farley does not like Al Smith, thinks he is the most selfish politician in the States. We had a long talk about the anti-prohibition campaign. Farley took my name and address and said he would send me some of his

34. Copy in Louis Brandeis Papers, Louisville Microfilm Series, VI, Roll 100, Z/P 57-2, Library of Congress.

35. On December 24 the *New York Times* published an article based on information from McDonald: At this point there were about sixty thousand refugees from Germany, and about fifty-one thousand of them were Jewish. About a thousand had come to the United States.

speeches showing the different ways in which the question was handled in different sections. I left him with the impression that we had made a beginning which could be followed up later if this seemed desirable.

Met at the dock by Mildred Wertheimer, who drove me home. Was glad to have this opportunity to exchange views with her. She gave me a memorandum which indicated that it would be desirable for me to see Felix Warburg, James Rosenberg, and Paul Baerwald as soon as possible, and preferably that I should invite them to my house.

New York, Sunday, December 24, 1933

Quiet and happy day and home. In the late afternoon over to tea at the Coopers, and then for a short time to the Bronxville Christmas pageant.

Monday, December 25, 1933

Our Christmas was interrupted at ten o'clock by the arrival of Jimmy Rosenberg, followed soon afterwards by Felix Warburg and Baerwald and Liebman. I had called Warburg the Saturday night previous and told him that I should be glad if he and Rosenberg and Baerwald would come to see me Christmas morning from ten until one. Warburg explained that he had brought also Charles J. Liebman because he had a special suggestion to make.

I explained something of the attitude of the governments, those who have refugees and are anxious to be rid of them, and those who have none, anxious not to receive any. Warburg said he was very sorry that I had had to mix up so much in Jewish politics, but that now the important thing was to find a basis on which an adequate appeal could be made. He then asked me what I thought should be the basis. I replied in rather general terms. This did not seem to Warburg sufficient to get the results needed. He said that Charles Liebman had worked out a program which seemed to the group promising. I asked that Liebman present it.

This he did by reading a brief memorandum. It proposed in effect the organization of a corporation, either English or American, with a very broad charter authorizing it to invest in any part of the world and to utilize a part of the funds for philanthropic ends. It was conceived as possibly a $50,000,000 to $100,000,000 corporation, the securities of which would be bought by Jews and non-Jews, partly as investment and partly as charity. The idea was that in this way there might be a chance of inducing large capitalists to contribute not merely from surpluses, but even from capital funds.

I told them that though the idea in this particular form was new to me, it met several of my own basic conceptions of the problem. It was vast in conception; it would provide not merely for the immediate present but for the future, and by offering capital as well as human material, there would be a chance of changing the attitudes of governments towards the refugees. I suggested that in the early stages of further discussion the British, the Dutch, and, if possible, the French and Belgians should be brought in.

After a long discussion the question was posed as to the next step. Rosenberg urged very strongly that this project should, if it appealed to me, be put forward as my own, and not that of any Jewish group. It was left, therefore, that I would confer as soon as possible with Wardwell, Fosdick, and such other non-Jewish and Jewish individuals as might seem to me to be most helpful. Meantime, I said I would study the memorandum presented, as well as the supplementary one handed me by Warburg.

As we were breaking up, each of the men assured me of their willingness to give me 100 percent support. Warburg said he would be available any time from breakfast until bedtime.

There was some discussion during the morning of the situation in France. It became clear that Cunliffe-Lister had been misquoted on the matter of the numbers of refugees that might be settled there. Nonetheless, he stuck to the view that there were still considerable possibilities in France, despite previous mishandling.

I took occasion to emphasize the value that Hyman had been to me, and in particular to underline what I felt to be his value from the point of view of judgment.

We also discussed the possibility of inducing Strauss to spend the winter in Paris. Warburg said that would be for Strauss himself to decide; the difficulty would be that his absence would inevitably weaken his position here from the business point of view. Evidently, I must have a long talk with Strauss.

After an enjoyable family Christmas dinner at which we had the Bairds and Fosters as guests, Ruth, Bobby, and I went to the Morgenthaus. After brief chats there we went to the Ittlesons. There I talked to Mr. and Mrs. Ittleson at some length. I found him still thinking chiefly in terms of protests against German action and of efforts directed at Washington to change governmental policies here. I explained to him why I thought both of these methods of approach could only have a small measure of success, that the imperative need was for affirmative action along the lines suggested that morning. I also told him of my desire to have him and Mrs. Ittleson meet the Jewish leaders in London and Paris. And at the end intimated that I wanted his help in clearing up the financial situation. He said he would be glad to do anything he could. It was left that I would see him soon again and present the thing formally.

Tuesday, December 26, 1933

Into town with the family to see *Little Women* at the Central Theatre. Afterwards to the office for brief talks with Raymond Buell and Esther Ogden and other members of the staff.

. . . .

Wednesday, December 27, 1933

To the office late. Down to the luncheon of Jewish leaders at the Lawyers' Club. This was one of the regular series of weekly get-together meetings. Those present included Felix Warburg, Paul Baerwald, Charles Liebman, Jimmie Rosenberg, who presided, Lipsky, Dr. Wise, Deutsch, Rothenberg (?),[36] Mack, Judge Proskauer, Judge Stroock, Lewis Strauss, Joseph Hyman, Bernard Flexner,[37] Jonah B. Wise,[38] and others. Immediately after the first course had been served Rosenberg said that he hoped that I would tell them anything I had in my mind, and that I could speak with complete frankness. I began by saying that it seemed to me that certain general principles should be kept in mind in any approach to the problem:

(1) The present situation is no accurate measure of the probable scope of the task ahead;
(2) There are no indications that conditions in Germany will improve; the probabilities are the reverse. Under these circumstances one must seriously consider the possibility of evacuating the younger generation;
(3) Every effort should be made to broaden the base of any appeal to be made by stimulating non-Jews as to a sense of their responsibility;
(4) There must be unity of purpose, of action, and of leadership among the Jews;
(5) The attitude of the governments within whose borders are refugees and of those governments which might be expected to receive refugees increases greatly the difficulties of success;
(6) As a result of all these factors, one ought to consider the possibility of working out a program which would turn the refugees into assets for the various countries to which they might be expected to go. On the basis of such a program it would not be inconceivable that very large sums reaching to the tens of millions might be raised from those borderline Jews to whom appeals for funds for mere relief will either be unheeded or result in relatively petty gifts. In this connection I said that, though I realized the hard work done by the American and English committees last year, I felt, nonetheless, that the amounts raised were piffling in proportion to the needs (at this point Jonah Wise spoke up and said that he had used that very phrase in his talk at the Commodore dinner during the campaign).

There was considerable discussion on different aspects of the suggestions I had made. Attention, however, was concentrated on the problems of formulating the sort of program I had envisaged. Judges Mack and Proskauer both asked whether one would be able to present specific proposals as to where refugees might be placed, for otherwise they feared that the Baruchs and the Eugene Meyers might not be impressed. I replied that there had not yet been time for

36. Judge Morris Rothenberg, American Zionist leader on the board of the Zionist Organization of America and United Palestine Appeal.

37. Bernard Flexner, lawyer and philanthropist from a prominent Louisville (Kentucky) family. President of the Palestine Economic Corporation and active on the Emergency Committee in Aid of Foreign Scholars.

38. Dr. Jonah B. Wise, chairman of the JDC's national fundraising committee.

detailed studies of the possibilities in such countries as Argentina, South West Africa, Angola, Brazil, Panama, Biro-Bidjan, etc. Moreover, that I hoped to pitch my appeal on another ground, that is, the stake which these rich American Jews themselves have in the constructive solution of the refugee problem. I cited the feeling of English Jews that nothing less than the security of their own children in England was involved, and in general, that the whole problem would have to be viewed in the largest terms and not at all as a casual charity.

During the discussion frequent references were made to Palestine, and chiefly the following points:

(1) My relation to Palestine. I explained that there was no limitation on the scope of my office in the League documents or in actions taken by the High Commission; that, so far as I know, the only suggested limitation formally set forth was in Dr. Weizmann's letter to Simon. I then recounted my talks with Dr. Weizmann on this point, and those with members of the British Foreign Office on my first trip to London, with Cecil at that time, with Cecil later at Lausanne, and finally my long luncheon discussion with Sir Philip Cunliffe-Lister; and that the net effect of all these was to assure me that the British government had no intention of making a formal reservation; that, on the contrary, Sir Philip had expressed himself in the most cordial terms, and had urged me to visit Palestine. A little to my surprise, I saw that all the Zionists at the table, in sharp contrast with Dr. Weizmann's original attitude, were anxious not that I should stay out of Palestine, but that I should come in order to help them raise larger funds and to help influence the British government. It is evident that Dr. Weizmann often speaks only for himself;
(2) My relations with Germany. I explained the Lausanne démarche,[39] and its failure, and also my reasons for not having moved earlier;
(3) I spoke of the French situation and the need for supplementing the funds for immediate relief;
(4) At the beginning of my talk I set forth as one of the basic principles of my work the necessity of my being independent. I explained the difficulty of the salary and my decision against accepting funds personally. As to organizational difficulties, I passed these over with a light touch, but not without making clear the painful labor that had been involved, and intimating that a measure of my helpfulness would be in part determined by the willingness of the organizations and leaders to subordinate their organizational interests to the common purpose.

At the end I was asked whether I would be available for a meeting the following week, perhaps to report then more fully on the suggestion I had made tentatively for a constructive program. I replied that if they were planning to

39. See entry of December 6, 1933.

meet on Thursday, January 4, I might be able to come, but I did not wish to commit myself to present a detailed scheme at that time.

As we were walking out, Rosenberg was most flattering, saying that my clarity and persuasiveness of presentation would have made me a great success at the bar. Others spoke in similar terms, and I must add that my presentation at the luncheon was clearer and more legible than my report of it in this diary.

. . . .

Thursday, December 28, 1933

. . . .

Lunched at the *Times* with Sulzberger, Finley, Adler, Strunsky,[40] and James.[41] The discussion was about conditions in Germany and the possibility of placing the refugees. Strunsky took the extraordinary line that perhaps in the long run it would be best if the refugees, or rather if the German youth, were sacrificed, rather than be evacuated. He did not carry conviction. In general, I got the impression that the whole group was more alert to the world-wide menace of Hitler's Jewish policy than they had been previously.

Down to the Zionist Organization headquarters, where I conferred with Lipsky,[42] Rabbi Wise, and Rothenberg. It was really a good move on my part to go there, rather than ask them to come here. We discussed many aspects of the general situation. They seemed to me much less intransigent on almost all points than had Dr. Weizmann. For example, they did not take any definite stand against sending funds into Germany: they seemed more realistic about the possibilities of Palestine; they were evidently very anxious to have me help out in the Palestine situation; they were anxious also for a united front in this country, and made as their one absolute condition that Felix Warburg should head it. They said that it would be impossible if a Baerwald or a Jonah Wise were the leader. They, of course, added that Palestine should be made the center of the drive in order to stimulate the mass support. They were quite reasonable, too, about the immigration question here. Wise said that he was sure that Senator Robert F. Wagner was right when he said it would be extremely dangerous to raise the immigration question in Congress.[43] What was needed was an admin-

40. Simeon Strunsky, wrote feature articles and had been on the editorial staff of the *Times* since 1924.

41. Edwin I. James, joined the *Times* in 1915 and had been managing editor since 1930.

42. Louis Lipsky, honorary president of the Zionist Organization of America, elected president of the American Jewish Congress in March 1935, a member of the Weizmann faction, as opposed to the Brandeis faction.

43. In June 1933 American Jewish leaders and some Jewish congressmen had conferred about the possibility of asking Congress to facilitate Jewish immigration. The general feeling was that the House would be hostile (Congressman Louis McFadden of Pennsylvania had openly expressed anti-Jewish sentiments in speeches). See Stephen S. Wise to Felix Frankfurter, June 1, 1933, Wise Papers, Correspondence-Zionism, Box 109, American Jewish Historical Society, New York; and Wise's memo on telephone conversation with Congressman Sabath, June 1, 1933, Brandeis Papers, Louisville Microfilm Series, VI, Roll 99.

istrative order which would undo the harm done by the Hoover memorandum two years ago.

In 1930, under the impact of the Depression, President Herbert Hoover and the State Department acted to reduce immigration. Existing immigration law barred persons likely to become public charges—a provision originally aimed at those who lacked physical or mental capacity for constructive employment. But under prevailing economic conditions, President Hoover decided that European applicants for immigration visas without independent means were likely to become public charges. So they could not qualify for visas. This new policy was announced in a press release in September 1930, and it was still in place.

Throughout our talk it was evident that the Zionists were anxious to utilize the prestige of the new office, but I also felt that they were willing to play the game with the other Jewish organizations. As I was leaving, Lipsky said he didn't understand how in so short a time I had managed to become as well acquainted with the Jewish personalities. My reply was that if you fight with people, you soon learn to know them.

Down to see Wardwell. He, as always, was very cordial. I explained to him the project for a corporation to open the doors for refugees in different parts of the world. He listened with close attention. He agreed in principle that the project was sound, but he was most concerned about the way in which it would be administered. The general setup he thought would be easy enough. The difficulties would come in the actual working out of specific projects in different countries. Who would determine the specific policies, who would direct the work, etc.? We left it that he would think the matter over, and we would talk again after the first of the year.

Friday, December 29, 1933

Feilchenfeld came in. We had a long talk about a number of matters. He has submitted to one of the members of the JDC group a memorandum along the lines which I discussed with them on Christmas Day. I showed him the Cohen memorandum. He said that it contained no points which had not been included in an earlier memorandum of his. I asked him what his relations were at the moment with the JDC—whether he was officially engaged by them or not? He answered that he had had no official connection since my election. I asked him if he would mind if I told some of the group that I thought his advice on technical matters of great value. He assented. We also talked about his brother and the possibility of the latter securing a quota [immigration visa] instead of a student visa, which he has at present. I said that I would be glad to do what I could at the Consulate at Geneva, but it was left that Feilchenfeld was to speak to me about this matter again before I sailed.

Lunched with David Heyman[44] and Sam Lewisohn. I told Heyman that there had been some misunderstanding about the New York Foundation grant of last November. He replied that that had been intended to clear up things so that I could get away, and that, therefore, he would be glad to acknowledge my letter of December 29 in such a way as to indicate unmistakably what had been the intent of the foundation.

We talked about the situation in Germany, and I outlined in general terms the project which is now being considered. They were somewhat skeptical but did not reject the project as impracticable. I said we would talk about it again later.

Stepped in at the Bank to see Erich Warburg for a few minutes. He told me of an extremely interesting scheme by which large sums could be made available for relief purposes within Germany, provided four-sixths of such amounts were provided outside of Germany to be used for the education abroad of the children of the Germans contributing within Germany. Erich said the scheme was absolutely sound, would not be objected to by the German government, but needed to be pressed promptly.

On up to Professor Chamberlain's, where I found Liebman, but was much disappointed to be told that Bernard Flexner would be unable to come because of the illness of his sister. We discussed briefly the general project, and Liebman made the point which seemed to me sound, that before one reaches the blueprint stage, it would be desirable to bring the British and perhaps the Belgians, Dutch, and French into the picture. I then suggested that if Felix Warburg were willing, he and I and perhaps one or two technicians might sail early in January for a week or ten days in London, and then return to the States to put the plan into operation. I inclined also to agree with Liebman and Chamberlain that London might be a better site for the corporation than New York because of the greater knowledge there of world affairs and the greater experience of the British in dealing with these matters.

....

Saturday, December 30, 1933

....

I spoke to Paul and Felix Warburg about the *New Yorker* and the possibility of forestalling the printing now of an article prepared some months ago. He said that he knows Raoul Fleischman[n] (the owner) very well, but he hesitated to raise the question with him for fear of increasing, rather than lessening, the chances of the material being used. It was left that if he saw Fleischman[n], he would, if the occasion seemed opportune, raise the question.

44. David Heyman, banker, active in the American Jewish Committee, founder of the Bureau of Jewish Social Science Research.

Long talk on the telephone with Felix Warburg about:

(1) The possibility of my going to Chicago for the sixth or seventh. It was left that I gave him an option on the afternoon and evening of the seventh, I to go if it seemed that the opportunity to meet and talk with Albert Lasker[45] and Kristein and others seemed sufficient to justify the trip;
(2) He agreed that it would be desirable to bring the London group and perhaps the other groups into the picture before the project were completed, but he thought it desirable to have some large subscriptions here first. As to the trip to London, he would not say no, provided it were necessary as a means of bringing Liebman into the picture as permanent representative abroad;
(3) As to the Paris situation, he would talk to Mrs. Warburg and ask her to check as to whether the Hadassah or some of the other groups would be helpful.

Warburg told me that Max would have to leave earlier than he had at first thought because of the sudden death of Carl Melchior and another close associate. We then spoke for a moment about the assassination of Duca[46] and its significance for our problem. He agreed that it was a shocking demonstration of the growing danger.

Off to lunch with Rabbi Wise,[47] Bernard Deutsch, and Judge Julius Julian Mack.

We talked about many topics without getting involved in any controversial matters. Judge Mack explained about the ruling of the Department of Justice in which the attitude of the Department of Labor was supported as over against that of the Department of State.

Judge Mack found a loophole in the immigration provision barring anyone "likely to become a public charge." The secretary of labor could accept a bond as guarantee that an applicant for an immigration visa would not become a public charge. Mack and others persuaded the Labor Department to support use of this procedure. The State Department had, however, claimed that American consuls abroad were initially and primarily responsible for determining and rejecting potential public charges. This interagency dispute went to Attorney General Homer Cummings, who ruled (on December 26) in favor of the Labor Department's view.

C. Paul Fletcher in the Visa Division of the State Department reacted:

45. Albert Lasker, Lord and Thomas advertising agency, part owner of the Chicago Cubs, active in the American Jewish Congress.

46. On December 29, 1933, Romanian Prime Minister Ion Duca was assassinated by a member of the Iron Guard who expressed satisfaction for having eliminated a friend of the Jews.

47. On January 11 Rabbi Wise wrote to Supreme Court Justice Brandeis, "I think that McD is going to try to do a good job. . . . I never quite get the feeling that he is perfectly trustworthy. Still one hopes that he will do his best." Wise to Brandeis, January 11, 1934. Copy in McDonald Papers, USHMM.

It now seems that only by quota reduction can the 600,000 Jews in Germany and the 60,000 in France seeking so-called religious refuge be prevented from entering the United States. . . . If ships begin to arrive in New York City laden with Jewish immigrants, the predominant Gentile population of the country will claim they have been betrayed through a "sleeping" State Department.[48]

We also talked about Weizmann, whom Mack characterized a most enticing male prostitute. Apparently their differences run pretty deep. There was some discussion of a united front here, with no indication that the [American Jewish] Congress group would present great difficulties. I took occasion to suggest to Mack my desire to see Frankfurter and our telephone conferences together, but that we had been unable to see each other because I could not possibly go to Oxford, and he had not felt that he had time to come to London.

. . . .

48. See Richard Breitman and Alan M. Kraut, *American Refugee Policy and European Jewry, 1933–1945* (Bloomington: Indiana University Press, 1987), 18–21.

9. January 1934: Washington's Views

New York, Monday, January 1, 1934

Arrived at the Lewisohn's party at the fashionable hour of 2:00 A.M., Ruth and I having gone to bed after the tea party and getting up just before midnight. At the Lewisohn's chatted with a number of old friends including the Ingersolls, the Lippmans, the Nathan Strauses, and too many others to mention. Especially interesting, however, was the opportunity I had to get better acquainted with Bernard Gimbel and his wife. They were both deeply concerned about the situation in Germany. I think they could be induced to help in a large way.

About four o'clock the Gimbels and Ruth and I went over to the Arthur Sulzbergers for a kitchen party. We remained there until about five and arrived home just as the maid was getting ready to go out for New Year's Day early mass.

Ruth and I went to dinner at Felix Warburg's house. It was a very elaborate party. Everybody except Dr. Kahn and myself were in white ties. Among those present were (besides Felix and his wife and Ruth and I) Max and Erich and Mrs. Max Warburg, the Liebmans, the Judge Lehmans,[1] the Arthur Lehmans,[2] the Baerwalds, the Rossbachs (?), the Sam Lewisohns, Mrs. Borg, and perhaps a half dozen or so others. During dinner I talked for a considerable time with Mrs. Felix Warburg; much of this was about Dr. Chaim Weizmann. She seemed to me much more devoted to him than some of her close relatives had led me to think. She was unwilling to admit any weaknesses in him and insisted that he was the biggest mind in the whole movement. Nonetheless, I told her quite frankly of my difficulties with him, explaining, however, that I had done my utmost to avoid friction, partly because I knew that it was essential to work with him and partly, too, because she herself had expressed so warmly her desire that we should get on together. We also talked about Felix and the imperative need that he be in London for a series of conferences and also that he head, at least at the beginning, the drive here. I explained what Rabbi Stephen Wise had said about the necessity of Felix's heading any united fundraising effort here. So far as Felix's plans were concerned, she refused to consider the possibility of his going to London and returning for work here. She said I would have to choose as to which I thought was the more important.

1. Irving Lehman, justice of the New York State Court of Appeals 1924–1931, chief justice 1940–1946; brother of New York Governor Herbert Lehman.

2. Arthur Lehman, partner in Lehman Brothers, director of many corporations and the New School for Social Research, brother to Irving and Herbert.

Chatted also during dinner with Mrs. Borg and with Margaret Lewisohn and before dinner had a nice talk with Mrs. Max Warburg.

After the meal Felix Warburg introduced me, and I spoke for about forty-five minutes, outlining first what had been done before and at Lausanne and presenting what seemed to me the essential principles involved in the problem, and ended with the suggestion of the large corporation, adequately financed, to deal with the various facets of the problem. There was then a general discussion. Judge Lehman emphasized the desirability of making the project as specific as possible, if one hoped to secure large funds. Arthur Lehman made the same emphasis. Both of these, moreover, were dubious of the possibility of raising such a large amount. Liebman explained that it might be possible to secure considerable sums from the governments or foundations to match dollar for dollar expenditures by the corporation. There was some criticism expressed of my emphasis of the danger of anti-Semitism here and on the necessity of a far-reaching, even world, program to combat it.

On the whole, however, I felt that no fatal flaws had been disclosed in the plan. In the discussion after dinner Judge Lehman said it was important to stress two points: one, the desirability of utilizing the existing international organization—the High Commission; and second, the necessity of finding places for the Jewish refugees, for otherwise they would be driven to extreme radicalism and by hammering vainly on the doors of the countries throughout the world, they would breed anti-Semitism.[3]

Chatted with Max Warburg and Erich. They expressed themselves warmly about my presentation. We talked about possible ways of making available to certain officials some of my writings on questions relating to Germany. It was agreed that this could not be done through Jewish hands.

Talked with Felix about plans for Chicago, and agreed that I would go out. He was to let me know after he had talked to his wife about the possibility of London.

About twelve o'clock Ruth and I started home, I feeling that it had been rather a full evening.

Tuesday, January 2, 1934

Down to see Fosdick at eleven o'clock. We spent little time on preliminaries. Instead, I presented briefly my reasons for the hope that Mr. Rockefeller would feel willing personally to make a substantial contribution towards refugee work. Fosdick replied that Mr. Rockefeller had sent the correspondence to him with the request that he discuss the matter with me on my return. Fosdick explained that it would be difficult for Rockefeller to meet my request because (1)

3. Although Nazi Germany's policies at this time permitted and even encouraged emigration of German Jews, they did not try or want to make it easy for other countries to absorb Jewish refugees. Other considerations often outweighed the goal of emigration unless it had additional benefits for Germany. Stimulation of anti-Semitism abroad was seen as in Germany's interest.

Radio City and general conditions made new ventures less easy to accept than in the good old days before 1929; (2) the Foundations had established the principle of not contributing toward relief projects; (3) the Rockefeller Foundation was already contributing on a substantial scale to relief of displaced scholars; (4) the Jews themselves could, if they would, meet the needs.

My reply in general was that the problem was not merely Jewish; on the contrary, that the Jews were merely the victims, and that there was a large responsibility on non-Jews. I stressed the importance of Mr. Rockefeller's attitude as the outstanding Christian layman. Furthermore, this is not primarily a question of relief; it is reconstruction. And it involves fundamental and far-reaching moral and ethical considerations which did not at all pertain in many of the relief projects which Fosdick had referred to. I urged, therefore, that I thought it very important that Mr. Rockefeller be presented personally and forcibly with these moral considerations.

Fosdick seemed to feel that I was putting the matter rather strongly. He suggested, however, that a little later when the program was more specifically worked out, that it might be well for Felix Warburg himself to ask Mr. Rockefeller for an interview. Felix would have more influence with Mr. Rockefeller than anyone else. I sensed that Fosdick was perhaps a little afraid that I might go too far. But he was anxious that Mr. Warburg not quote him in asking for a conference.

Fosdick suggested that I see Max Mason,[4] and said that the latter needed to know more about the general problem. I replied that, of course, I should be glad to talk to Mr. Mason if there was a possibility of something coming of it, but that I was too pressed to participate in the education of Rockefeller Foundation officials merely for its own sake. It was left indefinite, therefore, as to whether I should or should not see Mason.

Over to Kuhn, Loeb's. Saw Felix Warburg for a few minutes and asked him what he thought about Liebman and Strauss going with me to London if he himself couldn't go. This seemed to stir him; because he didn't think well of it, he felt he ought to go himself. He called Strauss over and we talked the matter out. It was left that he would try to get Mrs. Warburg's permission or go over and then come back here to help on the drive, later going to California for his vacation.

Lunched with Lewis Strauss. We talked about the London conference, about his last letter, and the general program. I asked him what he thought about taking up with Ittleson the question of the latter's making a personal contribution to enable us to return half of my own and Miss Sawyer's salaries. He said that I should forget about it, that he would see to it unless I thought it would be better to have Ittleson do it. Moreover, he would contribute himself to the general fund just as largely as he possibly could.

4. Charles Max Mason, mathematician, former president of the University of Chicago, president of the Rockefeller Foundation, 1929–1936.

I asked him about the possibility of his being in London, Paris, and Berlin during the next eight or ten months. He did not think he could do it, but suggested a young Mr. David Glick,[5] formerly of Abraham and Straus, and now with Kirstein. Later Erich Warburg also suggested him.

The whole of the conference with Strauss impressed me deeply with his sincerity and his intelligent grasp of the problem.

Stopped in for a moment to see Frank Davis. Later telephoned Strauss to inquire whether Warburg would like to have Rosenberg on the trip to London.

Wednesday, January 3, 1934

Spoke at the Town Hall on the subject "The Crisis in Geneva." There was a very friendly audience which nearly filled the hall. Mr. Ely's introduction was only two or three sentences, and was very kind. I spoke on the League until quarter of twelve, then talked for about ten minutes on my work and non-Jewish responsibility in reference to it. Afterwards many people came up to talk. Among those was Mrs. Loeb and also Mrs. Kuhn. The latter told me of the situation in Cincinnati, and added that she owned a fully equipped building capable of housing fifteen children; she would be glad to make this available for that number of German children, and would herself care for them. I said I would put her in touch with the organization which would handle this. She said that she would send me some books to help out in what I had called "my education in Jewish matters."

Luncheon with a group of church leaders at the Astor. Those present were Rabbi David DeSola Pool (Spanish and Portuguese conservative group[6] in New York); Rabbi William Rosenau (carries weight in the central South especially); Father John La Farge[7] (one of the editors of *America*—an important Catholic publication); Michael Williams (editor of the *Commonweal*); Dr. Lewis S. Mudge (former moderator of the Presbyterian Church in the United States and now Stated Clerk of the denomination and vice president of the Federal Council, Bishop Philip Cook (Bishop of Delaware—Protestant Episcopal and coadjutor with Bishop Perry); Dr. Robert A. Ashworth (formerly editor of the *Christian Century* and acting as one of the secretaries of the National Conference on Jews and Christians); Dr. John W. Langdale (book editor of the Methodist Episcopal Church and an important leader in that denomination); Cavert, Eddy Jones, Wise, and Leiper.[8]

Following my presentation there was a long discussion as to methods by which the churches could function most effectively, both to combat incipient

5. David Glick, American lawyer with JDC connections. Traveled to Germany in the fall of 1937 and negotiated (with the Gestapo) the release of 120 Jews from Dachau.

6. The oldest Jewish congregation in the country (founded 1654).

7. A Jesuit and founder of a Catholic movement to improve race relations. In 1938 asked to help draft an encyclical for Pope Pius XI condemning racism, but action was delayed, and Pius died before approving the document, entitled *Humani Generis Unitas* (Unity of the Human Race).

8. Henry Smith Leiper, executive secretary of the Department of Relations with Churches Abroad of the Federal Council of Churches of Christ in America, 1930–1945.

anti-Semitism and to aid in handling the refugees. It was finally agreed that there should be a committee of three to study the matter further and to call another meeting of the larger group. I suggested the possibility of a nationwide broadcast. This was seized upon by the whole group as the very best first step. It was left that I was to call the NBC and then communicate with Leiper, who was to act as secretary.

Stopped at David Heymann's house to dress for the Billikopf[9] dinner. This was at the Harmonie Club. The guest of honor was Messersmith. There were approximately thirty men present, including Felix Warburg, Baerwald, Liebman, Herbert Swope, Judge Lehman, Kirstein, Lowenstein, David Brown, Ittleson, Dr. Kahn, Joseph Hyman.

During dinner I chatted with Warburg, who indicated that he probably would go to London and return. He whispered to me that he and his wife had looked over their situation and had decided to subscribe a half a million dollars to the new project. He said, "You can consider this as confidential, but may use it later as advantageously as you can."

We then talked about Ittleson. Warburg thought he could do even more, being the richest man in the room, worth perhaps $40,000,000, but he needed to be educated. Albert Lasker also could do very largely, but he would have to stretch to meet the half million figure.

During dinner I went over and chatted with Ittleson for a little while, and warned him that very large amounts would be needed.

I explained to Billikopf that I had to go off to a party of my family's. It was arranged that I should speak briefly before Messersmith. I explained my general approach to the problem, and warned them that the amounts needed were much larger than those raised last year. I talked about ten minutes and had the impression that I was shocking my audience, but did not feel that the response was dangerously unsatisfactory.

On my way out I talked with Henry Morgenthau. I told him that I wanted half a million dollars from Henry Ittleson and a hundred thousand from Henry Morgenthau. I asked him if he would give me the hundred thousand if I secured five times that amount from Henry Ittleson. The ambassador refused to commit himself. I said that I was going to appeal to his wife.

Thursday, January 4, 1934

Miss Razovsky,[10] Mrs. Schonberg, and Mrs. Maurice Goldman of the National Council of Jewish Women came in. Miss Razovsky had wished to talk with me about a plan she had for work here, but I told her that I wished first to

9. Jacob Billikopf, social worker, long time worker for Jewish charities, became executive director of the National Coordinating Committee for Aid to Refugees.

10. Cecilia Razovsky, worked in the Child Labor Division of the United States Children's Bureau. Also head of the Department of Immigrant Aid of the National Council of Jewish Women and the guiding light of the National Coordinating Council for Aid to Refugees. As a child of immigrant parents, she had worked in an overall factory sewing on buttons.

talk about what I hoped she might organize. This was a plan for the adoption of 100 to 200 refugee families now in Paris. She and her associates were confident that the National Council of Jewish Women could do this promptly if I asked them to do it. I called Hyman on the phone to clear with the JDC. He raised a number of possible objections, the danger of undercutting, etc. I told him that I thought it was very important that something be done in the French matter in a way that there would be no strings attached to it and no rather superior advice. He said he would talk to Baerwald and Kahn. It was left that I would speak to the executive committee of the National Council next week.

Mr. Keith of Australia and Rabbi J. Max Wise came in. Keith was anxious to know what I thought of the German situation, with a view to studying on his return to Australia what might be done there. He is to write me when he reaches the Orient.

Lunch with John D. Rockefeller III. Pleasant chat about personal matters, and then a longer talk about my work. I had the impression that John now thinks of it as more important than he did at first. I did not speak about the possibility of a Rockefeller contribution, but explained the need in such a way that he would not be surprised if the appeal came later.

After lunch John showed me the Rockefeller offices on the fifty-sixth floor of the RCA building.

Stopped on the way to the office to talk to Dr. Sachs and Dr. Baehr[11] of the Emergency Committee in Aid of Displaced Foreign Physicians. They explained to me their plans, particularly why it seemed to them necessary that there should be a special technical committee for physicians. I thought their reasons unconvincing. No specific request was made to me, but I assumed they wished to be in a position to refer to me when asking for funds.

Then I went to the floor below for a much longer meeting with the Committee in Aid of German Scholars. Present were Murrow,[12] Bernard Flexner, Dr. Alfred Cohn, a Professor Gray (?) of the Rockefeller Foundation, and one other. Our discussion covered a wide range, but the points which need to be recorded were two: first, the desire of the Committee to have a better information service in London; second, their desire to have a better coordination of the work of the different committees dealing with intellectuals. I said that I thought on both of these points the different committees would have to take the initiative, but I suggested that perhaps Dick Simpson, the representative of the Commonwealth Fund in London, might be useful in both connections. Incidentally, I explained the setup of the Bureau and my desire that there should be an adequate representative on it of the intellectual groups. It was left that they would follow up.

11. Dr. George Baehr, secretary of the Executive Emergency Committee in Aid of Displaced Foreign Physicians.

12. Edward R. Murrow, assistant director of the Institute of International Education, 1932–1935. Assistant secretary of the Emergency Committee in Aid of Foreign Scholars, 1933–1935. From 1935–1961 he was a newscaster with CBS and became known worldwide for his wartime broadcasts from London bomb shelters.

Long conference with Carlin on the telephone. Finally settled on a time for my broadcast.

Talked to Cavert about the possibility of the Federal Council distributing postcard announcements to the ministers throughout the country. He said they would be glad to do it.

Friday, January 5, 1934

Worked out details of the radio circularization with Leiper and Cavert on the telephone, and with the publicity people of the NBC. Fixed definitely on Sunday, the fourteenth at 4:00 for a nationwide hook-up.

An hour's conference with Henry Goldman. He is opposed to attempting to bring the children or younger people out of Germany. He thinks that they must bear their cross. He did not dismiss as impossible the corporation project which I discussed with him, but stressed the necessity of making the program as specific as possible, with indications in detail of precisely how the different amounts would be spent. He added that it would be necessary to raise considerable amounts of money from non Jewish sources. He said that the strain on the Jews had been much heavier than was indicated by the figures of the official contributions: first, because of the general business conditions; second, trades in which the Jews are largely interested have been especially badly hit; and third, many Jews are already supporting a surprising number of their relatives here and abroad. Nonetheless, if their imaginations could be fired, and if there were non-Jewish support, he did not preclude the possibility of large funds being raised.

Called Hyman to say that we needed a check for $1,000 at once for the postcards. He said he would confer with Baerwald and Jonah Wise, and called back within a few minutes to say that the check was being sent.

I talked to Rosenberg on the telephone and urged him strongly to sail on the nineteenth. He said that he felt that he ought to do whatever I asked him to do, and that he would do his utmost to go if I assured him, as I did, that I considered the purpose of very high importance.

Lunched at the Harvard Club with Professor Einstein, Dr. Nathan, and Henry Ittleson. As soon as we settled down, I, in answer to Einstein's request, outlined my ideas of the problem and the methods of attacking it. Then I asked him what his view was about the potential emigrés. He was absolutely unqualified in his declaration that everything possible must be done to bring out the youth and the children. Indeed, he then developed the thesis which he and Nathan had come to urge upon me. It is this: the best work can be done not through large organizations but through personal efforts. The largest opportunity, therefore, lies in centralizing the efforts here to enable Jewish and other families to adopt financially or to care for in their homes thousands of German young men and women and children. This is being done now sporadically but should be greatly enlarged and organized. I agreed in principle, but did not commit myself to the opinion that it was my job to carry this project through. It relates, however, evidently to what Miss Razovsky was talking about.

Ittleson spoke at some length about the larger project which I had outlined. He thought it a mistake to assume that the governments would not do anything unless there were financial considerations involved. He thought that stronger appeals on behalf of humanity should be made. I met his arguments by reciting the attitudes of the governments with which I had communicated, and amplifying my earlier views. He finally said that at any rate if you made investments in a country, you must have an arrangement to permit the entrance not only of the refugees needed for that particular job, but also certain numbers extra. I said that this was precisely what we had in mind. Moreover, that for every dollar we spent, another might be secured from the government interested or from some foundation. At the end Ittleson seemed willing to continue to study the matter.

Professor Einstein expressed himself most emphatically in criticism of some of the rich German Jews and capitalist Jews elsewhere. I argued that so far as certain individuals such as Max Warburg were concerned, he was mistaken.

On the whole, I had the impression of Einstein as a man of great charm of personality, of considerable natural acuteness in worldly matters, and of great breadth of human sympathy. I told him that I was anxious that Janet might have an opportunity to meet him. He said he would be delighted to receive the family in Princeton.

Back to the office. I called Lewis Strauss to find out if he had inquired from Felix Warburg about the desirability of Henry Ittleson's joining us. He reported that Warburg had said that I should go ahead. I called up Ittleson and asked him to sail on the nineteenth. He did not say no, but the chances are probably only even that he will finally accept.

Buell called me to ask about the New York Foundation and the Keith Fund and contributions to the FPA radio work. I said that I would be glad to help where I could, but I thought the first approach to the New York Foundation should be by him personally, and that in view of their recent grant, it might be preferable to postpone action until spring. This was his decision.

Made the final check up with Miss Glover of the Federal Council re postcard circularization.

Home with Esther Ogden, Catherine Meriman, and Olive Sawyer for dinner.

The evening previous I had tea with Erich Warburg and Mildred Wertheimer. He said that his scheme for an education fund was, he thought, well under way. He urged also that popular campaign here for funds be enlivened by illustrations of specific families' experiences. So far as the material which I had discussed with him and his father was concerned, he suggested that if I would send it to Amsterdam, he would see that it was placed.

Saturday, January 6, 1934

Talked to Liebman, urging him to sail on the nineteenth. He countered by saying that he thought it dangerous for him and the others to appear on the scene until I had an opportunity to present the idea of the corporation as my own to the English and the European group. I told him that I was not sure that he was right, but that I would consider it.

Lipsky came in to inquire what had developed about the project which had been discussed with him and the others a week or so previously. I told him in considerable detail of my conferences with many of the men interested. He replied that he had decided to go ahead with the Zionist drive, that it would not in his opinion conflict with the corporation project. I expressed no view as to this, but I did not oppose his suggestion. Indeed, it seemed to me that it probably would be essential that both the Zionists' and the JDC efforts go forward, rather than wait, because our project might require months before it could be launched formally.

I told Lipsky of my hopes to enlist the support on a large scale of many of the so-called "borderline" Jews; that I intended to put the situation to them in such terms that from the point of view of their own self-interest they might be induced to make generous subscriptions. In view of this approach to the whole problem, Lipsky gave me the impression that he would be willing to forgive me if I did not go the whole way in supporting any particular project of his. He asked me if I would be able to speak at a Zionist meeting in February. I told him that I was uncertain of my date of return, and that in any case I would have to take into consideration my plans for the general campaign in making up my mind about the acceptance of any particular invitation. He seemed to agree that this was reasonable. Therefore, I remained uncommitted.

FPA luncheon, subject "Our Monetary Policy: Its International Implications." Irving Fisher, the first speaker, meandered rather than convinced. Rubey, who followed, was dogmatic and sophomoric. Leland Stowe need not have explained that it was his first speech. In the discussion Jimmy Warburg was amusing, but beyond that said very little. Vanderlip was by all odds the most effective, though he had only seven minutes. After a sort of reception at the end of the luncheon I hurried off to Miss Pratt's for tea, and then to the Pennsylvania Station to take the Broadway Ltd. to Chicago.

Chatted on the train with Felix Warburg for an hour or so before dinner. Later we dined together and talked for an hour or more afterwards.

We discussed our problem both in general and in specific terms. He seemed much pleased with developments to date. He stressed the importance of interesting Kirstein and Lasker, whom we were to meet in Chicago. We ran over a long list of names of persons who might be interested in the corporation idea. I told him what Bishop Cook had said to me about Pierre Dupont's[13] pride in his one-eighth Jewish blood, and the bishop's suggestion that Dupont might be willing to help. We also talked about Liebman's fears of too large a party going to London. It seemed to both Warburg and to me that there was no substantial ground for Liebman's concern.

13. Pierre Samuel Dupont III, Dupont Company and General Motors executive.

Chicago, Sunday, January 7, 1934

We arrived on time and went directly to the Standard Club, the large Jewish organization. During the morning there was a little time for reading before we went out to Lasker's for lunch. Those present at Lasker's house, besides the host and hostess and their daughter and son-in-law and Warburg and I, were Kirstein, a Mr. Becker,[14] and three or four other leaders in Jewish philanthropies. During the first part of the lunch the talk was mostly about controversial subjects in Chicago, whether the Jewish parochial schools and similar religious organizations could fairly continue to receive support from the Community Chest. Lasker expressed very positive views against the continuance of this practice. In his statements he showed, as he had earlier, not only strong convictions but a tendency to be something that might be termed "arrogant" in his expression of his convictions. When I first began to talk with him in the car and was telling him that I had met his son in London and that Ralph Sollett, the president of his company, was a classmate of mine in Indiana, we drifted onto the subject of Will Hays. This led Lasker to tell me how he had been responsible for the defeat of the League of Nations and of his continued pride in that accomplishment. According to him, it happened in this way: he had been persuaded that the League was a danger by a man whom he regarded as probably a charlatan, but who on this issue, he felt, was sincere, or at any rate right. He, Lasker, had then organized the movement to back Johnson, not with a view to securing his nomination, but in order to show enough isolationist strength as not to permit the Republican convention to avoid going on record definitely against the League. To accomplish this purpose he had organized a nation-wide propaganda and had succeeded. I asked him about Bill Hard's[15] role, for he also claimed the credit for defeating the League. Lasker replied that Hard had not figured in this early movement, but had come in later in his work with the men in the Senate. It is easy to imagine how much self-restraint I felt called upon to exercise in order not to tell Lasker what a damn fool he had been.

About half-way through the lunch I was asked to talk about the refugee situation. I did this briefly, coming rather quickly to the corporation project. Lasker at once accepted the idea, nor was he disturbed by the figure I had mentioned of $25,000,000. On the contrary, he at once began to analyze the problem from the practical point of view: finding the money. So far as the situation in Germany itself is concerned, he expressed the very strongest views and recognized the danger of contagion.

Since he had to leave on an early afternoon train for New York, the luncheon party broke up before two. I whispered to Warburg to ask whether he thought it would be wise if I invited Lasker to go along to London. He said, "Go

14. Benjamin Becker, Chicago lawyer and organizer of the Bank for International Settlements.

15. William Hard, NBC correspondent and commentator, who frequently broadcast from Berlin.

ahead," and suggested that I ride to the station with Lasker. This I did. En route, I asked Lasker if he would consider going to London. He countered by asking what the advantages would be. I replied that he would be helpful there in working out the plan and also because he would thereby know so much more about it he would be better able to convince other people here about it on his return. To this Lasker replied with a frankness which disarmed me. He said, "I know myself very well. I would be of no use in working out the plan. My job is to promote it. And so far as knowing more about it by being in London, all I need will be two or three hours with you or Felix Warburg; then I'll be prepared to go to the country to sell it. I would enjoy going to London with you, but it is not necessary. Moreover, my wife has not been well for many years, and is completely dependent upon me to manage the household and her. Also I have promised myself that my son should have eighteen months on his own, without any interference or suggestions from me. Therefore, I had planned not to see him."

To this formidable array of arguments I could make no adequate rejoinder. Instead, I simply expressed the view that I still hoped that he would be able to come, if after he had gone over the matter further it seemed possible. But evidently it was much less important that he go than I had at first supposed. It was left that he would talk to me or Warburg in New York later.

. . . .

The dinner was informal; perhaps three or four hundred people were present during the meal or came in afterwards. Jane Addams[16] came with some friends. I chatted with her for a little while. Warburg, who was to preside at the speaking, asked Miss Addams to say a few words. She spoke briefly of my work, and then made the suggestion that the United States open the German quota and allow the refugees to come in practically unconditionally as political refugees. Later, she was disappointed when I did not follow up this lead. Indeed, I did not mention it at all. Instead, I limited myself to a frank discussion of the situation in Germany and its implications for Jews in America and throughout the world. I closed by suggesting that much more than a generous fund for relief was absolutely essential.

Following the meeting I chatted with a number of those in the audience. As I was saying goodbye to Kirstein, he told me that he would do anything that he could. Those responsible for the meeting seemed to be pleased with the evening.

. . . .

New York, Tuesday, January 9, 1934

I woke up on the train about seven o'clock expecting to look out on the neighborhood of Princeton, for we were due in New York at 8:35. But unfor-

16. Jane Addams, founder and director of Hull House, the pioneering settlement house in Chicago, recipient of the Nobel Peace Prize in 1931.

tunately, the landscape was not the least familiar. We were still in mid-Pennsylvania. Finally, after nearly six hours' delay, we reached New York at a little after two o'clock. I went to the Harvard Club for a nap, and did not reach the office until after four, just in time to dictate a two-page press release for my appearance at the Town Hall dinner that night. Miss Sawyer and Miss Stanford working together enabled me to get it out.

The Town Hall Club party went off as well as such occasions can be expected to. Ratcliffe spoke well, but as he does frequently, too long. I was glad, however, that he paid such a fitting tribute to Paul Kellogg and that he developed his thesis about the refugees so clearly. Aside from the inevitable still ceremony of receiving the medal of award,[17] I rather enjoyed the opportunity to talk to the group, but I was relieved when it was over.

Wednesday, January 10, 1934

Hugh Grant Straus[18] came in to talk about the general situation. He had no specific suggestions to make, but was anxious to know what was going on. Lunched with Ruth Morgan. Our talk was mostly about Mrs. Elmhirst's[19] committee. She assured me that there would be no hope of any large amount, because nowadays $5,000 was a very large contribution and as much as $10,000 practically unknown. She told me also that Mrs. Elmhirst had said that Michael was to be with me. She suggested that it would be helpful if I could see personally some of the other members of the committee. I told her I was sorry that I did not think I could possibly find time for that. She then agreed that that ought to be unnecessary.

In the afternoon Mr. Schlessinger came in. He talked to Mildred Wertheimer and me, mostly about his own experiences in refugee work.

He expressed the view, which seemed to me rather dogmatic, that only in the Baltic countries was there real hope of settling any considerable number. On the whole, I was rather disappointed in him, in view of the extremely high praise that Knickerbocker had given him.

. . . .

Chatted on the phone for a little while with Leiper about the plans of their religious committee. Later on, I talked to Jonah Wise and asked him to get in

17. McDonald received the Town Hall Club's Distinguished Service Medal for 1933. In his speech he declared that about 85 percent of the current refugees were Jewish—"the Jews merely happen to be the victims of the dominant racial psychology in Central Europe." He estimated that the task of removing and rehabilitating refugees might take $25–50 million dollars. *New York Times*, January 10, 1934.

18. Hugh Grant Straus, Macy's executive, director of the National Refugee Service and the Federation of Jewish Charities.

19. Mrs. Dorothy Payne Whitney Straight, married Leonard Knight Elmhirst and moved to England, where she and her husband directed Darlington Hall, a school for experimental education. In 1935 she gave up her American citizenship in order not to have her estate taxed in both countries.

touch with Leiper, because that group needed specific suggestions of ways in which they could be most helpful.

After a visit to the dentist, I went to the FPA Board meeting. Less than half of the members were present. I met Mr. Pike there. It was, I think, his first meeting. Because I had to go to the Ittlesons later for dinner, I asked permission to speak during dinner. This was granted. Therefore, I was able to get away by a little after eight.

At the Ittlesons, besides the hosts and Ruth and I, were Mr. and Mrs. David Sarnoff,[20] Mr. and Mrs. Henry Goldman, and Professor Johnson of the New School. For me, it was an amusing and restful occasion. During the whole of dinner the talk consisted of ardent, almost violent, debate between the host and Henry Goldman on the merits of the Roosevelt program and on the demerits of the bankers. Goldman showed himself a thoroughgoing radical, while Ittleson did his utmost to attack the NRA and to defend the "money changers." How Goldman has changed in the years since he could see no good at all in America, but good only in Germany. Sarnoff tended to side with Ittleson, but Johnson and I rarely ventured, and then only timidly, to express an opinion, for the two chief protagonists had attacked each other so unreservedly that it would have been dangerous for us to have intervened.

After dinner Sarnoff, Ittleson, and I talked about the refugee problem. Sarnoff stressed the importance of putting the emphasis on the non-Jewish aspects of the question.

As we were leaving, we asked the Ittlesons when it would probably be possible for them to go abroad. They said that the doctor absolutely forbade Henry to leave at this time for abroad, but that they could go later in the spring, preferably as late as May, for they then expected to stay over for the whole summer.

Thursday, January 11, 1934

Feilchenfeld telephoned me, but I had very little to tell him. I am embarrassed by my relations with him, for I feel that he played an important, perhaps decisive role in the early stages of the development of the idea of this office, but I do not see how he can be used unless the JDC group on their own choose to use him.

Talked again with Leiper about the plans of their committee, and suggested that Jonah Wise would explain how their efforts could be fitted into the general program.

Talked on the telephone again with John Simons, a man interested in finding the means of making a study of possibilities in Southwest Africa for the refugees. I told him that I could make no recommendations about the matter, but on the basis of what I knew at present, I saw no reason why the study should not be undertaken.

20. David Sarnoff, president of the Radio Corporation of America 1930–1948, pioneer in the use of radio for entertainment and information.

Lunched with Dr. Cohn. We talked at length about the ideology that should underlie our efforts. I assured him that I, at any rate, would not be a party to the settlement of any of the refugees anywhere under conditions which might seem to indicate that trouble would arise later. In other words, I was willing to go that far in laying down the general principle. Dr. Cohn said that he was sure it was fundamentally necessary to recognize that different Jewish points of view as to the ultimate objective could not be reconciled, but that once this was admitted, then agreement might be reached on a comprehensive program with different emphases and different immediate objectives. I think I satisfied him that essentially I was in agreement with him.

We then talked about the committees dealing with intellectuals. I told him that if the groups working in that field agreed that it was necessary to have additional representation in Germany for informational purposes, I felt confident our Permanent Committee would approve the idea and that the matter of financing such a person would not then be difficult.

....

Talked to Stone about Washington. He agreed with Miss Sawyer that it would be a mistake to press for an interview with FDR through Mrs. Roosevelt or Miss LeHand, but that Chamberlain and Phillips were better channels.

Dr. Kahn came in. We talked first about the situation in Paris. He said that the JDC had voted to earmark 500,000 francs for relief purposes; 200,000 of these he had already promised Rothschild, but 300,000 were new money. In speaking to Rothschild, however, I should make clear that the 500,000 included the 200,000, so that there would be no misunderstanding.

Dr. Kahn reiterated his conviction that the bulk of the refugees in France would have to remain there, no matter how much the French wished to have them moved. He insisted that it is much more difficult to find places for those outside of Germany than for potential refugees within Germany. This, he said, was because in the case of those outside, the countries to which they might wish to go would ask why, if they were desirable emigrants, the country where they now are does not desire to keep them. We parted on the most friendly terms.

Up to Mrs. Carnegie's for the Geneva Student Union meeting. President Butler was speaking when I arrived. During the tea-time I was accosted by three different old ladies who upbraided me for saying that the Christians had a special responsibility in the refugee problem. One of these pests insisted that there must be some reason why the Jews were always persecuted—something within the Jews themselves—and that she had finally decided that her sister was right when the latter said, "It's because they are not Christian." My retort was, "It is because the Christians are not Christian."

Had a nice visit with Mrs. Carnegie and her daughter Mrs. Miller, Miss French, Miss Kerlin, and with Mrs. Laidlaw, who said she hoped to have us at the opera sometime in February.

Ruth was so late coming in that I had to go off to see Mrs. Fuld and Mr. Bamberger[21] at the Madison Hotel without having an opportunity to dress. They asked me to stay for dinner, but I could only stay for about half an hour. Among their guests were a colleague of Einstein's at the Institute at Princeton, also a distinguished refugee. He was in complete agreement with my interpretation of the situation in Germany and the problems it would probably present. Mrs. Fuld and Mr. Bamberger were intensely interested in the project I told them of. I think they will go along. She and he both kindly evinced concern about my health. The other two at dinner were Bernard and Mary Flexner.

I arrived at Liebman's about quarter of eight and found Ruth already there. We had just a family dinner. Mr. Liebman referred again to his view that it would be undesirable for me to travel with the Jewish group on the *Olympic*. I told him that if I were convinced of that, I would, of course, be glad to sail earlier on the *Washington*. It was left that the latter would be discussed again the next day.

After dinner about thirty-five or forty people came in. Among these were Mrs. Howard Cullman, the Alfred Cohns, the Alfred Liebmans, Carl Pforzheimer, Dick Schuster, the Sam Liebmans, the Fred Heimerdingers, Dr. Eliot, Miss Hirshman, Frieda Davidon, Owen Lovejoy, Mr. and Mrs. Pollak, Arthur Strasser, Percy Marks, Mr. David Metzger, Mr. Leo Oppenheimer, Mr. Sterndler, Leonard Hackstader, the Rothbarths, Sidney Blumenthal, Erlanger, Mrs. Robert Benjamin, Percy Straus, Janet and Lewis Loeb, Gertrude Stein, Walter Mayer.

I spoke for about forty-five minutes, much as I had at Felix Warburg's dinner and at Chicago. There was no doubt about the intense interest felt by the audience. At the end there were a number of questions. Afterwards, Percy Straus told me that he thought I was putting the figures—$25,000,000 to $50,000,000—too conservatively. Others indicated a readiness to help. Liebman was seemingly much pleased, and I was without doubt exhausted.

Home late.

Friday, January 12, 1934

Dentist on my way downtown. Telephoned Miss Sawyer that it would be necessary to sail three days earlier than planned. This decision was reached after I talked to Felix Warburg that morning. Liebman had convinced him. I was just as pleased to have the first opportunity to present the program in London.

Lunched with Miss Sawyer at the New Weston. Afterwards spoke briefly at the executive committee meeting of the National Council of Jewish Women, explaining why I would not now ask them to finance families in France.

21. Louis Bamberger, head of Bamberger department store, philanthropist. Together with his sister, Mrs. Fuld, he donated the initial endowment of $5 million for the establishment of the Institute for Advanced Studies at Princeton.

Miss Razovsky and I talked briefly about her plans for a clearing house in New York. I told her that I wished she would speak to Hyman and to Miss Wertheimer.

Dr. Kotschnig[22] of the International Student Service came in to see me. We chatted for a little while about Parkes and about student work in general. No suggestion, however, was made that Kotschnig work with me.

Dr. Schwarz came in. He had two things on his mind: first, a desire that the Jewish groups should find him at least a little to finance the work which he was doing privately in placing refugees. He said that he had already placed more than a hundred, was in fact acting as the consul general for the refugees. He surprised me by adding that some of the Jewish leaders looked upon him as a Hitler agent. I said that I would speak to Felix Warburg about him.

The second matter he wished to bring up was the organization of better facilities for non-Jewish refugees in the States. I agreed as to the importance of this, and suggested that he talk to Miss Wertheimer further about it.

Murrow of Dr. Duggan's office came in. I told him of my talk with Cohn. He felt confident that the different groups dealing with intellectuals would be able to work out an agreement on a common representation and on the presentation of a plan for representation in Germany.

He wished also to tell me that if he could be of any real use, he would be glad to help on the job of finding non-Jewish money. I think he could be very useful.

Tea at the Biltmore with Miss Camac. She wanted to enlist my interest in the application of a young friend of hers, Mr. Lucien Hilmer, an applicant for a place in the Solicitor's office in the Department of the Interior. I said that my connections with that Department were very poor, but I would inquire when I was in Washington.

Home on the train with Jake Broyles.[23] Met at the station by Louise. After dinner at home I had the most marvelous cards at bridge. That made excellent preparation for my work the next day, dictating my Sunday broadcast.

During the evening a representative of the *Mt. Vernon Argus* came to interview me.

Earlier during the day talked with Professor Chamberlain again about Washington, after Stone had telephoned us. He promised to write Phillips a note, urging that FDR see me.

Saturday, January 13, 1934

At work most of the day on my broadcast, "Christian Responsibility Toward German Refugees."

At 12:30 Mr. Herman and two of his colleagues on HIAS came in. They wished, they said, to get acquainted and to pay their respects. Mr. Herman,

22. Walter Kotschnig, from Austria, secretary general of the International Student Service in Geneva. Immigrated to the United States, taught at Smith and Mt. Holyoke colleges.

23. Louise and Jake Broyles, close family friends who lived in Scarsdale.

physically and in manner, very like his brother. They offered on behalf of HIAS to contribute towards the administrative expenses of my office. I thanked them, but did not accept.

Brodnitz came to see me. He explained that his work with Henry Goldman took only about half his time, and that he would be glad to do other things if he could be useful to me. No commitment was made, but I think he is an excellent man.

Lunched with Dr. Stolper and Miss Wertheimer. Dr. Stolper developed the thesis that there is imminent danger of war in central Europe because of the probability that if the Nazis come into power in Austria, the Czechs would occupy Vienna. He thinks that under such circumstances, the Jews in Germany would be the first to suffer. On the other accounts his interpretation of the situation within the Reich was strikingly like my own. However, I would have enjoyed the discussion more had I not been more or less preoccupied throughout the meal by thoughts of my unfinished broadcast.

Fortunately, Miss Stanford and Miss Jaffe were willing to work through the afternoon, so we finished up in time for me to take the 7:40 train home.

Sunday, January 14, 1934

With Ruth and Bobby to hear Dr. Fosdick. At one point during the sermon, when he was using a series of words including "polygamy, prostitution, polyandry," etc., Bobby turned to me and whispered, "What a lot of strange words." After the service Ruth and I spoke to Dr. Fosdick, and I told him I would be unable to keep my Wednesday appointment because of my earlier sailing. He offered to see me earlier, but I told him that we could talk when I returned.

Home to lunch, and then drove into the broadcasting station, arriving there at 3:30. Before I went on the air, I had a considerable audience in the studio. Besides Ruth, there were Jerome Hess and his mother, Miss Emily Hammond, Miss Peloubet, an out-of-town Jewish newspaper man sent by Stephen Wise, and Miss Camac and Mr. Hilmer. But there was no time for talks with any of these before I went on the air. Mr. Havrill was the announcer, and I finished exactly on time, twenty-five seconds before 4:15.[24]

24. In the broadcast he described his visit to a refugee camp in Paris: "They were housed in old barracks in the outskirts of the city. Some of the buildings had not been used by French troops for several years. The accommodations were primitive. I talked with several families. In one room six children and their parents were struggling to maintain the decencies of life. Three of the smaller children—ages from three to eight—were kept in bed to warm one another. In another room four children and their parents were crowded together. Despite the sordid and squalid surroundings, the mother had managed, by what miracle I do not know, to keep her children clean. . . . In those wretched rooms in the barracks, I noted the few personal possessions which the refugees had managed to bring with them. In some cases they had saved old family portraits, but more often a small shelf of religious books . . . the contents of many of the books were similar. Those refugees, Gentile and Jew, treasure as their most precious possessions books which for nearly two thousand years have been the common heritage of Christians and Jews." "Christian Responsibility Toward German Refugees," broadcast over WEAF and stations associated with the National Broadcasting Company, Sunday, January 14, 1934 (original copy), McDonald Papers, USHMM.

Immediately afterwards there were two telephone calls, one from someone who knew of a refugee who needed immediate aid, and the other from someone telling me how much they had been "moved" by the talk.

Miss Hammond told me of her project for an American committee in Berlin to help Jews and non-Jews displaced by the Nazis. She said that Mr. Turner, pastor of the American Church there, had been willing to have this done through a church committee, but that Jimmy Lee, Ivy's son,[25] had blocked this by declaring that he would not permit a church to get mixed up in this work of "political" action. According to her, Jimmy also said that none of the Jews were being hurt, except those who had engaged in political or other undesirable actions.

I could not make out precisely what she expected me to do, except perhaps to express some interest in her project. She gave me a memorandum in strictest confidence. Apparently, it outlined only the work which might be done in different countries and was not really confidential. I made no commitment to her, except to return her memorandum to her. Mildred Wertheimer, to whom I gave the memorandum after reading it, said that she maintained her earlier view that it would be better not to get mixed up with Miss Hammond.

The Jewish newspaper man wanted a copy of my speech, but I was unable to give it to him because the press department of the NBC was asking for it. They claimed that the copy sent them by messenger from our office the night previous had not been received. The press department said, however, that they would still be able to have the talk released to the press.

Mr. Hilmer told me about his hopes for Washington.

In order that I might have a chance to talk with Jerome Hess about my personal financial matters, it was arranged that he would ride up with me to the Kahns, while Ruth would go up in his car with his mother and Miss Peloubet. On the way uptown he and I talked about the possibility of short-term insurance and any other arrangement which might be desirable to make the future somewhat more secure. I promised to send him the financial regulations and the budget, so that he might see what the exact situation is, and to get in touch with him again upon my return from Washington.

Just as I arrived at the Kahns, Mr. Lipsky also arrived. Ruth and I were shown up to Mrs. Kahn's Italian room, where I found her and Mr. Kahn. They had expected me earlier, and so Mr. Kahn had made a five o'clock date with Lipsky, whom he said he could not put off any longer. However, Otto Kahn stayed for a while. Then Mrs. Kahn and we talked until nearly six o'clock. They are both deeply interested, but are anxious not to commit themselves on the financial side and are not unnaturally rather embarrassed because of their earlier withdrawal from Jewish religious and cultural affairs.

Over to Felix Warburg's shortly after six. Chatted with Mrs. Warburg.

25. Ivy Lee had a public relations firm and was employed by Otto Kahn, among others. He later admitted to working for I. G. Farben after Hitler came to power.

She said she ought to be angry with me for having persuaded her husband against her will to go to London for a short time and then return to the States before his vacation. She also was sorry that I would not be on the *Olympic* to make a fourth at bridge. She remains adamant against sailing on the *Paris,* but favors the *Majestic* on the fourteenth. Met Ambassador Morgenthau there. Asked him if he had spoken to his wife about my request for $100,000. He said that he hadn't, and that I wouldn't get it. I replied that I was not accepting his no.

Chatted with Max Warburg. Told him that I hoped there would be representatives of the German groups in London during my stay there, and that I hoped that Stephen Wise might also be there. Max and Felix and I continued our talk about various problems until Mrs. Felix Warburg interrupted and said that the head of the house would have to have some rest before dinner. I replied that we were already overdue at home, and that we must hurry because it was our last night with the children.

Ruth and I drove home in time to say goodnight to Bobby and to begin to pack. In the midst of these preparations in came the Bairds and the Fosters. The result was a most hectic scramble to make the 10:15 train to town.

Washington, Monday, January 15, 1934

....

Stone was most helpful in arranging a series of appointments; first with Moffat before lunch. The latter was not interested in the technical questions of immigration, but wanted to know what were our relations with the Germans and our plans for adding new members to the Governing Body. I gave him a full account on each of these points. He was kind enough to say that Chamberlain had reported that I had done an excellent job.[26]

Over to the Army and Navy Club to lunch with Colonel MacCormack,[27] commissioner of immigration. During a part of our luncheon we were joined by

26. Writing in his diary after that meeting with Chamberlain on January 5, Moffat summarized his understanding of the situation: "there will be no hope for the young Jew in Germany and emigration on the part of the younger element, particularly those with families, is almost certain to follow. No country in Europe is anxious to take many (refugees) in and even the South Americans are rather skittish. The Jews themselves are fearful of the growth of anti-Semitism in any country where the influx will be too great. . . . MacDonald [*sic*], the High Commissioner, has had immense difficulty in steering a course between the rival Jewish factions. In particular, those elements who wish to regard the Jews as a separate race and those who wish to play this down, seem to hate each other almost as much as they hate the Germans. MacDonald has not succeeded in making contact yet with the German Government either on the question of travel documents or on the question of the release of Jewish property in Germany. There is some scheme afoot whereby the Jews hope to canalize all Jewish relief money pouring into Germany and exchanging this for the proceeds of sale of refugee property, thus in effect being able to reimburse some of the refugees without complicating the transfer problem." Moffat Journal, vol. 33, Moffat Papers, call number MS Am 1407, Houghton Library, Harvard University. By permission of the Houghton Library, Harvard University.

27. Daniel W. MacCormack, commissioner of immigration and naturalization, 1933–1937. A liberal, but not nearly as pro-refugee as Secretary of Labor Frances Perkins.

a Mr. Hodgdon[28] of the Visa Division of the Department of State. The latter in some of his talk showed a spirit which I resented. It was as if a person by applying for a visa thereby automatically stamped himself as undesirable. But as our discussion developed, Hodgdon showed himself more reasonable. Nonetheless, I remained suspicious that his first attitude probably represents fairly accurately the attitude of his colleagues, or at least of some of them.[29]

Colonel MacCormack outlined at length the way in which this question had been handled as between the two departments. He had seen Chamberlain for only a few minutes, but was otherwise completely informed. His department is more liberal than the State Department. Miss Perkins is even less fearful of reactions from a very liberal policy than is Colonel MacCormack himself. Several months ago there was an interdepartmental conference at which were represented the two secretaries, Colonel MacCormack, and others from the Department of State. At that meeting he had suggested that two men, one a Jew and the other a distinguished 100 percent by birth American, be chosen to study the whole problem and to propose a program for the two departments. Phillips, however, had insisted that there be only one person, a Jew, and had had his way. Colonel MacCormack intimated that this action of Phillips was not motivated so much by friendship for the Jews as by the fear that if the other procedure had been followed, the report would have had to be adopted, whereas one signed by a Jew alone could be ignored. Judge Mack had been asked down, had made some investigation, but now months had passed and nothing had happened. He, Colonel MacCormack, favored a return to the procedure he had proposed earlier.

Colonel MacCormack and I then talked about some of the technical matters. The acceptance of the labor bond by his department has been established in principle, but progress has not gone beyond that stage. He thinks it important that a number should be determined and that the bonds should not be used beyond that. If there are not too many admissions by bond, the situation can be safeguarded, but if they reach several thousands this becomes impossible.[30] He seemed to feel that if later I proposed a definite figure to the departments, and if this were reasonable, it might be accepted.

Meantime, the question of the situation of those refugees which claim to be unable to secure the necessary papers from Germany remained unsettled. Hodgdon, as it seemed to me, rather casually assumed that a refugee could get these papers from Germany if he had a legal right to them. He based this opinion on reports from American consular representatives in Germany. This is a question on which Chamberlain is at present at work, and the whole matter is pending on [Assistant Secretary of State] Carr's desk.

28. A. Dana Hodgdon.

29. See inserted commentary in entry for December 30, 1933 (chap. 8).

30. This notion meant that there would have been an informal "labor bond" quota within the overall annual American immigration quota for Germany (25,957).

Colonel MacCormack seemed to feel that it would be unnecessary for me to see [Under-] Secretary Phillips, particularly since I was to see the President the next day. I did not press my request therefore.

In general, Colonel MacCormack was of the opinion that immigration matters would more and more be handled by his department, and that one could therefore count upon an increasingly liberal attitude.

In the afternoon I went to see Eugene Meyer. He was interested in the corporation project, but as usual when I talk with him, I felt unsuccessful in drawing him out. He insisted that he did not know Jewish personalities sufficiently well to be helpful in suggesting those who might be the larger subscribers. He is evidently pleased with his newspaper [the *Washington Post*], and one hears on many sides of the great improvement he has achieved.

On Stone's advice I cancelled my engagement with the Brazilian ambassador, who is said not to be a person of any importance.

At six o'clock I went over to the German Embassy to see Luther. It had been reported to me a few days earlier by Mildred Wertheimer that Luther wanted to see me. The first half hour was mostly given over to two topics: one, the general state of Europe, and second, my attitude towards the past twenty years. As to the first, Luther was very emphatic that the Austrian situation would not precipitate war; he ridiculed the prevalent view about Germany's magic power to rearm. On the second point I told him of my 1914 pamphlet and of the record of the FPA and of myself since 1918. He seemed so much interested in the 1914 pamphlet that, as I was leaving, I gave him one of my few remaining copies.[31] He read the last paragraph out loud and seemed really to be thrilled by it. I told him with some emphasis that I thought his government ought to realize that, in all probability, anyone else who might take over my work would not fundamentally be as friendly toward Germany as I. In the meantime, I had stressed that I would not be a party to the use of our office for political maneuvers against Germany and that, indeed, I had seen no inclination on the part of any of the members of the Governing Body so to use it.

It was at about this point that he said, "Speaking unofficially and personally and with complete frankness as you have spoken, I should like to raise two questions. First, your radio speech yesterday does not seem to be quite consistent with your statement that you are concerned only with the technical aspects of your problem; second, what questions would you take up with the German government, or in what way could it help you in your work?"

I said that I would reply to the second question first. I then explained the importance of the matter of the property of the refugees outside of Germany, and that this could be dealt with only through an understanding with the German government. He replied that there was, of course, the basic difficulty of the transfer of foreign exchange. I answered by outlining briefly the scheme for setting off against the Marks secured by the liquidation of property within Ger-

31. *German "Atrocities" and International Law:* see introduction, note 2.

many against dollars or pounds accumulated outside for relief expenditures within Germany. He recognized that this might be a possible solution, but he added, "If this were done in the case of the refugees, great care would have to be taken that it were not used as a general method for the transfer of other funds, thus possibly precipitating a flight from the Mark."

His first question I met squarely by handing him a copy of the complete text of my broadcast. I said, "You will probably not feel that this text really answers your question, but at any rate I want you to know precisely what I said. Moreover, I stand by everything I said." It was at this point that I also handed him the 1914 pamphlet, and he read out loud the concluding paragraph.

We parted with mutual expressions of friendliness and high regard. As I was leaving, he pointed to a picture of the signing of Locarno[32] at London. We agreed that had the Allies followed up that lead, the history of the world might have been very different.

I had as guests for dinner at the hotel the Stones, the Felix Morleys, and the Professor Woodburns. Our talk at dinner ranged over many topics. Afterwards we went out to the Stone's house and sat around the fire, where we were joined by the Feises. The talk there was for the most of the evening nearly all about the new *Washington Post,* Morley's part in it, and whether Meyer was engaged in subversive activities against the [Roosevelt] administration. Morley staunchly defended his colleagues against the Feises' attack. Only late was I asked questions about my work. I countered by asking them what would be the probable effect of a liberalization of the administrative regulations affecting German immigrants. They agreed that if it were done quietly, perhaps several additional thousands could be admitted without any serious repercussions.

Just before dinner I was told that Justice Brandeis's office had called, suggesting that I come to see the Justice at 6:00 or 6:30. But this message did not reach me in time, and I could not have gone in any case because of the Luther appointment. The next morning the Justice's secretary called suggesting an afternoon date, but I explained that I was sailing and had to leave early.

Tuesday, January 16, 1934

Over to the office, and then to see Ambassador Bullitt. He was most cordial, said that he was expecting to sail on the thirty-first, but might not get away until the fifteenth of February, so absorbed was he in organizing the Embassy and consular staff. I told him that I had two questions to ask him. One was about the possibilities of colonization of the refugees in Russia, and the other had to do with inviting the Soviets to send a representative to the Governing Body. On the first point he said he didn't know enough to be of any use, but on the second he had very definite and helpful ideas. He was emphatic that it

32. The Treaty of Locarno of 1925. Germany accepted its western borders and Germany and France pledged not to modify them by force. If an attack occurred, Britain and Italy pledged to oppose the aggressor. Marked a high point in European cooperation during the 1920s.

would be much better to raise this issue with the Russian ambassador in Washington than in London. Coming from London, it would be looked upon more with suspicion than if it were raised in the States. I assented to this view, and Bullitt at once attempted to telephone to Troyanovsky. He was unable to reach him, but did so later in the day at Bogdanov's house in New York, and fortunately was able to make an appointment for me at 9:30 the day I was to sail. I asked about his [Bullitt's] plans for his staff and spoke of Mrs. Askew. He said that she was No. 1 on the list in case they took any women secretaries to Russia, that he had been very much impressed by her, but that they had decided not to take a single woman with them in a secretarial post. The reason he gave was that life would be so difficult that there would be nothing for a woman to do for relaxation except to fall indiscreetly in love, and that while a man under those circumstances might be trusted to remain discreetly silent about governmental affairs, one could not expect that of a woman. I didn't argue this point.

From Bullitt's I went to Phillips's office. He too was very cordial. Our talk ranged over different aspects of two problems, the one semi-political and the other immigration. On the latter the undersecretary showed a better spirit than had Hodgdon. He said that they had agreed on the labor bond point, and seemed to think that the remaining technical questions would be ironed out without difficulty. I did not suggest to him a specific figure as a possible number of refugees to be admitted.

On the more general or political side, I told him exactly what I had done about Germany and what I was proposing to do in reference to Russia. He seemed sympathetic on both counts. I thanked him heartily for the designation of Chamberlain, and stressed what I believe to be an important fact, that the latter will be very helpful in keeping the Jewish leaders and organizations in line, for they have confidence that Chamberlain will do the utmost that can be done. They will be apt to take his advice also on policy. This seemed to relieve Phillips's mind.

While I was in Phillips's office, he called up Hodgdon in reference to the figures for applications for immigrants' visas from Germany, and the figures of the acceptances and rejections. Later I went to see Hodgdon, who showed me the figures. These during the last five or six months ranged with a gradual increase from about 400 to 600 applications a month, with a increasing percentage of visas granted—up to 80 or 85 percent. These statistics seemed to support the department's contention that they were in fact being very liberal in their application of the administrative regulations.

Then over to the White House. Was shown in to Secretary Early's, where Secretary McIntyre was in charge. While waiting, I chatted with Gordon, formerly of the Embassy in Berlin, and later with McIntyre. The President was behind his schedule, and finally about 12:30 McIntyre brought the message that the President would either see me then for a few minutes, or we could have a real talk at the White House at tea at five. Though the postponement was very inconvenient, I, of course, had no choice but to accept.

. . . . . .

Early that morning I had called up Miss Schain and offered to speak for ten minutes sometime during the afternoon session of the Nautical Conference on the Cause and Cure of War, if she wished me to do so. She appeared to welcome this suggestion, so it was arranged that I would speak whenever I came to the meeting. About three o'clock I went to the hall, and was introduced by Stewart, who was presiding. I spoke for about ten minutes, and afterwards sat through the rest of the session. Stewart presided well.

I had had an engagement for five o'clock with the French ambassador, but had cancelled it because of my expectation of going back to New York earlier. When my plans were changed again, I might have kept the appointment, but forgot to do so.

At five o'clock Ruth and I went to the White House, she expecting merely to wait for me downstairs while I saw the President. Meantime, we had arranged to have our luggage brought there in a taxi so that we could make a dash for the six o'clock train, though I had suspected that we might not make it. We sat around downstairs after the usher had shown Ruth the public rooms, and waited until nearly a quarter of six before the President came. Then the usher told me that he was waiting upstairs. I went up alone to the room where I had had tea the previous time. I found Mrs. Dall acting as hostess and Dr. Livingston and his mother of New York, and later a Mr. and Mrs. Mack from Poughkeepsie, and Buzzie and Sistie. When I realized that it was a family party, I told Mrs. Dall that I had left my wife downstairs, and she and the President at once insisted that she come up.

Though the President had had as usual a very heavy day, he threw himself unreservedly into the discussion of my problem. He told a number of stories to illustrate what he felt to be the situation in Germany. One had been passed on to him by Dodd. In substance it was this: An American visiting in the home, I think it was, of a German professor, was present one evening when a small child, ready for bed, kneeled down by his mother's knee to say his prayers. Included in his prayers was the request that he be permitted to die with a French bullet in his heart. The President seemed to feel that this story illustrated how deep down had gone the Nazi propaganda.

FDR said that he had dealt with Schacht without gloves, and that he thought he had made some impression on him. This reference was made in connection with my account to him of my démarche towards Germany at Lausanne. He seemed to feel that I had handled the thing properly.

At that point I explained the importance of [the High Commission's] establishing relations with Germany, the question of refugees' property, and the future policy of the Reich; and I asked FDR what he would advise me to do if the Reich continued unwilling to establish some working relationship. He replied at once that we should issue a report to the world setting forth in a factual fashion what had taken place, the plight of the refugees, and the prospects for the future. This, he said, would focus world opinion and impress Berlin.

In this connection I asked him if he had heard that Ivy Lee was supposed to be handling propaganda for the Reich. He replied:

"Oh yes, I know all about that, and I understand he is receiving $200,000 a year for it. Because of these goings-on, I have at least by failing to object encouraged [Congressman] Dickstein to go on with his investigation."[33]

Though the President did not say so, it seems altogether probable that Washington will watch Ivy's activities with interest.

I told the President of our proposed flirtation with Russia. He asked me if Bullitt had told me of his concern at the possible Polish-German rapprochement. I replied that the latter had been very helpful to me, and that I anticipated that he would do an excellent job.

Once or twice the President referred to my talk with him the previous May. He told with a laugh what I had said to him about the Nazi willingness to talk to me frankly because of my Nordic physical features.

So far as immigration of refugees was concerned, he seemed to feel that there would be no difficulty in doing what was necessary now that the labor bond idea had been accepted.[34] But he wished not to have much said about it until after Congress was "off his hands." Meantime, it was desirable to stifle Untermyer and Rabbi Wise. I assured him that the latter was on his good behavior and the former was resting in California.

About 6:20 his valet came to tell him what time it was, but he replied that he would be ready in a few minutes. His interest in this general problem is keen. As we were saying goodbye, he said, "Be sure to let me know when you come back, and come to see me."

As we reached the main floor in the elevator, we met Mrs. Roosevelt and a group of friends returning from the Kreisler concert. There was opportunity for only a brief exchange of greetings.

Hurried off just in time to catch the seven o'clock train. Reached Bronxville after one, but had to pack before going to bed. Found a message from Miss Sawyer about an important appointment for the next morning. I surmised that this was the appointment with the Russian ambassador.

Wednesday, January 17, 1934

Ruth drove the children to school and then me downtown to Bogdanov's house. I had urged her not to bother to come to the boat. We arrived at Bogdanov's a little before time, so I left my luggage downstairs and said goodbye to my wife and arranged by telephone for Jerome Hess to drive downtown with me.

33. Probably Dickstein's investigation of Nazi propaganda in the United States.

34. This statement confirms other (and earlier) information that FDR was directly involved in the plan to use public charge bonds as a way of increasing the flow of refugees. In a letter of November 20, 1933, Marvin Lowenthal had written, "Yesterday I heard that Judge Lehman had gotten a promise from F.D. that about ten thousand would be allowed to enter if adequate bond were given that they would not become public charges, but the details are still to be worked out by Philips [*sic*] of the State Department." Lowenthal to Jacob Billikopf, November 20, 1933, Lowenthal Papers, American Jewish Historical Society, Box 7, Conference on Jewish Relations, Correspondence 1933–1934.

Promptly at 9:30 Mr. Bogdanov introduced me to the ambassador and left us alone. I explained briefly the nature of our Governing Body and the scope of its work. I indicated that both Bullitt and the President knew that I was going to suggest to him that he inquire of Moscow whether the Soviet government would be willing to receive an invitation to join the Governing Body. I stressed the non-political character of our work, and explained that so far we had not yet established formal relations with Germany. I suggested that since I was going to be in London at the end of the month, it would be especially helpful if he could communicate promptly with Moscow, so that the Russian ambassador might have some word for me in advance of the meeting of our Governing Body. He said that he thought this would be possible, that indeed it was perhaps more than possible that his government might accept.

He struck me as a direct, matter-of-fact person; certainly he puts on no airs.

Picked up Jerome Hess at his house, and on the way down to 42nd St. in a taxicab we discussed various personal problems. He said he thought it would be best if I could arrange for him to see Rosenberg before the latter sailed. I said I would try to do this.

At the office I found Rabbi Wise, but Lipsky was not able to come so early, and Deutsch was not able to come so late. Under these circumstances Wise, realizing that I was terribly pressed for time, stayed only a few minutes. He said that he thought it was a good idea that I was sailing alone, and asked me if I thought the collections should be postponed until our general plan was worked out. To this question I replied in the negative, and he assented to my point of view.

Called Rosenberg and arranged that Jerome should meet him at Rosenberg's house at quarter of nine Friday morning. Then called Jerome to check with him.

Telephoned to Chamberlain and told him briefly about my Washington experiences, and he said again that he hoped we would be able to supply him with further data on the matter of the difficulty refugees were having in securing the necessary papers from Germany.

Arranged with Miss Jaffe to take care of the radio mail and with Miss Miller to handle my personal correspondence.

After a few hurried goodbyes, drove off to the boat with Mildred Wertheimer and David Heyman, while Olive Sawyer came along with part of the luggage in a taxi. On the way to the boat Heyman explained that they had set up a committee of six, two Palestinians,[35] two JDC, and two Federationists to block out a country-wide united drive for relief. They intended to use the German needs as a rallying cry, and to proceed at once with their collections, not waiting for our larger corporation project. Heyman expressed the view that this latter would take time and would have to be financed by a relatively few of the well-to-do. He was anxious that I know what was being planned, and that I be

35. Representatives of organizations raising funds for Jewish settlement in Palestine.

assured that there was no intention to undercut the larger project. I assented heartily to what was proposed.

Reached the pier in time for the Movietone people and for a word with Landau[36] of the Jewish Telegraphic Agency. The latter explained that their story about the difficulties between the British government and me over Palestine had been picked up from other papers, and that Weizmann had said that the British government did not want me to interfere in Palestine. I replied that that might be the case, but that most emphatically I wanted to say that it seemed to me the Jewish [Telegraphic] Agency ought to confer with me or my office or at least check with us before publishing anything about our work. I did not wish to impose any sort of censorship, but I considered it grossly unfair that the JTA should be a party to sensationalism on this subject. Landau said that they would be very careful, and urged me in particular to say a good word to Felix Warburg. I said I would report our conference.

We sailed about fifty minutes late.

Earlier Leiper had telephoned Olive Sawyer to say that they were setting up a permanent committee, with Dr. Ashworth as full-time secretary.

SS *Washington*, the voyage, January 17–23, 1934

Extraordinarily calm weather for January. Nothing very exciting happened on board. Concentrated on swimming lessons with Keuser. Chatted from time to time with Fred Field[37] and George Pratt, and once or twice with Hugh Wilson. Others I met included Mr. Ladds and his daughter, the Walters, Mrs. Riggs, and Mrs. Latshaw; Mr. Aronson of Newark boasted to me of his contribution of $2,500 last year. Arrived at Plymouth about nine o'clock and took the night train for London.

Dr. Oppenheimer, formerly a lawyer in Berlin, told me of his loss of position and his fears of anti-Semitism in the States.

London, January 24, 1934

Conferences during the morning with Bentwich and Wurfbain. Telephone conversations with Stephany to clear up the difficulty about what seemed to him to be a conflict between the time of the meeting of the Bureau and the Allocations Committee.

Luncheon at the Rothschilds. Those present were Lionel and Anthony de Rothschild, Lionel Cohen, Lord Erleigh,[38] Capt. Lionel Montagu, and Freddie Stern.[39] In the midst of lunch I began my explanation of the proposed corporation. I was allowed to develop my thesis almost uninterruptedly. Then followed a long discussion in which practically everyone participated. Lionel de Roth-

36. Jacob Landau, born in Vienna, head of the Jewish Telegraphic Agency and founder of the *Jewish Daily Bulletin*.
37. Frederick Vanderbilt Field, executive secretary of American Peace Mobilization.
38. Gerald Rufus Isaacs, Viscount Erleigh, the son of Rufus Isaacs, Marquis of Reading.
39. Sir Frederick Stern, banker, Stern Brothers.

schild, however, had less to say than did his brother. The latter was inclined to argue that it would be more practicable to raise funds for specific projects, that it would be difficult to find resources to honor a blank check. Lionel Cohen also inclined to share this view, at least to the extent of arguing that it was important that some indications be given of the specific ways or types of methods which would be used to care for the refugees. He did not think it would be necessary to indicate fully how this was to be done, for in any case the funds would not all be available at the very beginning. Freddie Stern and Montagu did not raise specific objections, rather limited themselves to questions.

As the discussion developed, the Rothschilds and Cohen tended more and more to discuss practical ways of accomplishing what we were after, rather than urging the difficulties. They talked about the nature of the corporation, the probability that it would be primarily a lending corporation, rather than an operating company, that therefore it ought to be able to limit its losses to 25 percent or at most 50 percent, but that it would have difficulty recouping. Therefore, they suggested two types of securities, though they could not agree as to precisely what each should be. They then discussed the possibility of finding considerable funds in England—perhaps as much as $5,000,000 or $10,000,000. They were not optimistic, nor were they defeatist. At the very end Lionel Rothschild said he would invite a group of men to talk the matter over with Felix Warburg and me at our convenience.

Among the arguments which seemed to weigh with them most were: (1) the desperate need in Germany; (2) the danger of rising anti-Semitism through the non-placement of refugees; (3) the desirability of taking advantage of the existence of the Governing Body; (4) the necessity of capitalizing [on] the present situation if large funds are to be secured; (5) the willingness of Felix Warburg and others to lead; (6) the Jewish history of care for its own. As I was leaving, Anthony de Rothschild offered to be of any help he could to me while I was here.

Conference in the afternoon with Bentwich and Wurfbain.

Tea with Lord Cecil. He and I discussed the agenda, but he had few specific suggestions. Rather, he was inclined to ask what could be done. He added that unless one could show progress, there would be signs of impatience on the part of the representatives on the Governing Body. I reminded him that the governments had thus far been wholly negative in their attitude and could scarcely, therefore, fairly demand prompt and large-scale results. He agreed to that. Nonetheless, he felt that there should be a substantial report showing what had been undertaken and what the chances were of further development. He also asked if I had discussed the medical research project of Dr. Rosenstein envisaged for Liechtenstein or Monaco. I said I would do so later. As to the German situation, Lord Cecil was as pessimistic as ever.

Dinner with the staff, including Mr. and Mrs. May, Mr. Wurfbain, and Miss Sawyer.

I should have added in my notes about my conference with President Roosevelt on January 16 the following: When we were speaking of conditions in Germany, FDR said, "Felix Frankfurter passed on to me your letter about what might happen in the Reich. I was much interested in it, but I did not see that there was anything that I could do."

Thursday, January 25, 1934

Staff conferences during the morning.

Mr. May and I went over to lunch with Sir Leonard Cohen and Lady Cohen. Louis Oungre was also there. Later we were joined by Sir Osmond.

During the meal I had a very pleasant visit with Lady Cohen. She is delightful and intelligent. As usual at Sir Leonard's lunches, there was amusing talk also about derivation of words.

After lunch we were joined by Sir Osmond. I developed at considerable length the plan for the corporation. As I mentioned the figures $25,000,000 to $50,000,000, I noticed Sir Osmond look across at Sir Leonard smilingly, but before the end they were more serious. Throughout the presentation Louis Oungre bowed or indicated his hearty approval, except when I said that I thought the suggested corporation would be separate from the Governing Body. He contended that it should be as closely as possible related to the League.

In the general discussion that followed Sir Leonard and Sir Osmond raised a number of questions, mostly having to do with the possibility of finding such large sums and the method of their use. Their questions were very similar to those raised by the bankers at Rothschilds. Louis Oungre, however, had many constructive ideas. These he elaborated with his usual precision and at considerable length.

On the whole, the response of the ICA group was not discouraging. They felt that the work for the establishment of new industries or the subvention of individual entrepreneurs would be more likely to be successful, or at any rate involve less loss. They did not, however, commit themselves as to ICA's attitude on the matter of colonization.

Herbert May and I went directly from Sir Leonard's to the American Embassy. We talked with Atherton.[40] He read Mr. Dodd's letter with interest, but couldn't make it out. He advised having Dodd make inquiries in Berlin as to whether I would be received. If the answer were favorable, then I could move through the German ambassador here. After consideration we decided to adopt this course.

....

Dinner with May at Otto Schiff's. The latter and May gave many indications of enjoying their wine and brandy as connoisseurs should. After dinner we discussed many subjects. That of greatest importance was Otto Schiff's proposal

40. Ray Atherton, official in the American Embassy, later in the State Department's Division of European Affairs.

that under the immigration committee there should be set up an international information bureau as to economic opportunities throughout the whole world. He also suggested that if I approached Vansittart, the latter might be willing to give instructions to the British consuls to cooperate in supplying pertinent information as to conditions in their parts of the world. As I was leaving, I told Schiff that I thought the British Central Fund should match ICA's contribution towards the [High] Commission's budget. He replied that Felix Warburg should take that up with Sir Osmond.

Friday, January 26, 1934

Breakfast with Wilfrid Israel. He was full of his impressions of inter-party conflicts in the Reich. He thought Göring was in opposition to the Leader and that Goebbels was uncertain. He attributed this strife to uncertainty about party policies, increased economic pressure, and conflicting personalities. As to the Jews, he felt that the situation was again becoming more critical, the boycott reappearing in the small towns, and the danger of worse measures intensified.

As to the corporation idea, of which he had heard, he thought it would be dangerous to suggest to the authorities that there was such a scheme being formulated, unless in advance some agreement could be secured from them as to their treatment of the residue in Germany. He emphasized the importance of my going to Berlin as soon as possible. Whether, if I went, I should try to get in touch with him or other leaders of the Jewish relief organization, he was not sure. Certainly I should not do so unless I first spoke to the authorities about it.

We had not finished our talk when Dr. Weizmann came in. I explained to him the corporation idea, but as I went along, I sensed, if not open hostility, at least something very akin to it. But openly he showed no hostility, indeed indicated very little interest, except to say that of course it would be desirable if one could get large sums from the "borderline" Jews.

After I had finished, he launched into a bitter attack on those to whom he attributed the pressure on me which had resulted in the enlargement of the Bureau. He characterized this as a part of the general conspiracy to "pocket" him and to hurt the Palestine cause. He said that, of course, if the English and French communities were to be represented on the Bureau, then the Polish community had an equal claim, and that Mr. Goldmann would press the claims of the Delegation. I remained non-committal, except to ask if he did not agree that Laski, the British representative, was typical of English Jewry. He replied "Yes, he is empty-headed, without intelligence or understanding of the problem. He is a perfectly appropriate representative." Dr. Weizmann continued that, under existing circumstances, he would not sit on the Bureau; that he would not engage in a cat and dog fight with a lot of insignificant persons engaged in seeking to hamper him; someone else might represent the Jewish Agency; he would not.

Of course, he said, "though I will not be able to work with you, I will not criticize you for working with the plutocrats, nor will I say you are in their pocket." I replied in effect that I, of course, accepted his assurance, but that he must know, as I knew, that others would not be as considerate.

The conference ended without my proposing any concession. Indeed, at the time none occurred to me, and as I later thought it over, it seemed to me it would have been unwise to have suggested the addition of a Polish representative. Dr. Weizmann was in such a mood that no concession would have seemed reasonable. Evidently, he was laboring under the strain of a combination of circumstances: his conflict with the British Central Fund, Felix Warburg's failure to arrange to see him at length upon their arrival in London, the idea of the corporation which he had not devised, and the purpose of which he was suspicious about. But what a spoiled child he is when he is in one of these tantrums. The next time I encounter him in one, I shall be tempted to see what would happen if I replied to him in kind. This time, as before on several occasions, he expressed his contempt for German Jews as a whole, his indifference to their fate, and for that matter, his indifference to the fate of millions of Jews elsewhere, just so long as a saving remnant could be preserved in Palestine. His theory of Jewish salvation through remnants seems to be an obsession.

Conference with Maisky,[41] the Russian ambassador, at the Embassy. He said that he had had word from Moscow that his government was interested in the problem of the refugees, but did not feel that it ought to take part officially on the Governing Body. He mentioned his government's hesitance in dealing with League organizations, except when the matters were vital. I told him of course that this was not a League organization, but this did not change his conclusion. It was agreed, therefore, that I would not urge the Permanent Committee to invite his government to join.

. . . .

Lunch at the London School of Economics as the guest of Sir William Beveridge.[42] Others present included Walter Adams,[43] Professor Bagster-Collins, Professor Bonn, Professor Freundlich, Mr. Bentwich, and three or four others. After luncheon there was a frank discussion of the problems of the different committees. There was a consensus of opinion that there was no need for a full time person to get information about conditions in Germany, but Professor Bagster-Collins thought that through frequent trips and through other means sufficient data could be gathered; that it would be desirable to constitute a general information center under the direction of Adams in the A.A.C. [Academic Assistance Council], and that to do this, only funds for the salary of one additional person would be necessary; that an international committee made up

41. Ivan Maisky, Russian ambassador to Great Britain.

42. Sir William Beveridge, director of the London School of Economics and later master of University College, Oxford. One of the most renowned civil servants in twentieth-century Britain, played a critical role in the creation of the welfare state.

43. Walter Adams, lecturer at London University, general secretary of the Academic Assistance Council, secretary of the "National Appeal" being made in England by the German Emergency Relief Committee.

of one from each of the several organizations dealing with intellectuals should be formed to meet very infrequently, but to constitute a coordinating body, the secretariat of which would be under Adams' direction. I asked Professor Bagster-Collins if he thought he could get New York's assent to such an arrangement; he said he thought this probable. It was then agreed that this procedure would be recommended to the Bureau and perhaps later to the Permanent Committee.

At five o'clock there was a press conference, preceded by a conference with Frederick Kuh.[44]

....

The questions mostly had to do with the agenda for the Permanent Committee. I answered them all as frankly as I could, but on such matters as relations with Germany, where we intended to send refugees, and relations with the British government I could say little or nothing. After the conference I had a frank talk with the representative of the JTA, first about the row between the British government and myself over Palestine, and second the more recent story which gave the impression that the United States was going to fill the quota with German refugees. He is, I think, anxious to play the game fairly. He said he would inquire from Landau about the visa story.

At six o'clock staff conference about plans for the meeting of the Bureau and the Permanent Committee.

At eight the Mays and I went over to the Ritz for dinner with the Felix Warburgs. Besides them and ourselves were present Sir Cohen Spayer and his daughter, Jimmy Rosenberg and his daughter. After dinner we were joined by the following: Warburgs—Max, Lola Hahn, Sigmund, and Erich, and also by Wilfrid Israel. The conference of the men, including Lola Hahn, lasted until after midnight. It covered a wide range:

(1) Dr. Weizmann and the corporation idea,
(2) My relations with Berlin. It was generally agreed that the sooner I went the better, but it was thought desirable that I keep in close contact with the American Embassy, perhaps be met at the frontier by someone from the Embassy. I said that, of course, I would undertake to make my appointments through that office;
(3) Conditions in Germany. There was much agreement that things were about as Israel had described them to me earlier. I was impressed by Sigmund Warburg's assent that not only were conditions becoming worse for his people, but that the prospects for the future were very dark;
(4) Program. Here Felix Warburg was very insistent that the others should supply us with definite detailed statistical data as to the numbers, ages, sorts of potential emigrés. On this point he drove very hard at Wilfrid Israel and

44. Frederick Kuh, correspondent of the *Chicago Sun Times.*

Lola. They retorted, and I thought with much reason on their side, that in advance of a definite scheme which could be announced to their people, it was quite impossible to get all of the data desired. Israel at one point said that probably one could count upon ten to twenty thousand a year available, but if the Austrian situation broke adversely, it might be a question of saving what one could.

After the general discussion I asked Felix Warburg if he would speak to Sir Osmond about the matter Otto Schiff had referred to. We agreed also on a tentative date for the conference with Lionel Rothschild for Thursday afternoon of the following week. As I was leaving, Felix Warburg again reaffirmed his confidence that Dr. Weizmann would come into line after some more exhibits of prima donna qualities. During dinner Mrs. Warburg had also seemed to take this line.

Home very late.

Saturday, January 27, 1934

Breakfast with Professor Cohen of Amsterdam. He went over a number of questions which were of particular interest to his committee. Included in these were (1) the difficulty of securing American visas in Holland, which he considers greater than in Germany. I agreed to raise this question with Chamberlain; (2) the German practice of denaturalizing, and a number of other subjects. He was interested in the corporation idea, and said that there were a number of Dutchmen who had large means, and even more, Germans resident in Holland who might be in a position to subscribe. Heineman[45] is perhaps the most important of these. He promised to let me have a list of individuals who might be most useful. He was uncertain about how long he would stay.

Künstler, representing Dr. R. of Berlin, came in for a few minutes. I was not encouraging. I told him I would be glad to talk with R. about the Liechtenstein and Monaco projects, but I did not think it worth his while to come to London, but perhaps he could meet me sometime at The Hague.

Herbert May and I went out to lunch with Sir Robert Waley-Cohen and Lady Cohen. What a beautiful estate and huge house, but how cold! A tiny fireplace in a room big enough for a battalion. Excellent food, however, was some compensation.

After lunch I elaborated the corporation idea to Sir Robert. He listened attentively. His reaction was much the same as had been that of other businessmen, and he offered to work with us. But he stressed the importance of making a world appeal against what he considered to be the menace implicit in the Nazi regime—civilization itself. He thought the Governing Body and the High

45. Dannie Heineman, electrical engineer born in North Carolina, employed by AEG to build electrical production facilities in Belgium, Germany, and Italy. Became chief of the Sofina conglomerate in Belgium. A financial supporter of Jewish refugees in Belgium. A friend of Chaim Weizmann.

Commissioner were in excellent positions to arouse world opinion. After much discussion, however, he recognized that at least for the present we must undertake to do a technical job, in cooperation, if possible, with the German government, and that only when and if it became evident that this procedure would be futile, would I be justified in considering the kind of methods he suggested. He felt that to seek to create new industries would in itself be a sort of challenge to the peace of the world. Both May and I thought this a considerable exaggeration.

I left with the impression that, while he might not himself give substantially, he would be willing to help the project forward with his moral, and probably his technical, assistance. As we were riding back to town, Lady Cohen told of the plans of her husband to go out to Palestine in connection with the projects there of his country. He is leaving in the near future.

Neville Laski came in for tea. We had a quiet chat, mostly about noncontroversial subjects. I told him that there appeared to be some objection to the enlargement of the Bureau. He replied that Weizmann had told him that if he, Laski, were to be the British representative, he, Dr. Weizmann, would not object. On the whole, however, Laski took the matter apparently rather calmly.

Over to the Royal Athletic Club to swim, and back to the hotel to dress and ran into Lord Marley talking to Miss Sawyer. It was agreed among us that the consideration of the plans of ORT and OZE [OSE] on the Advisory Council and of action in reference to Biro-Bidjan should be postponed, pending Lord Marley's speaking tour in the States.

Out to dinner with the Mays and Miss Morris, who is a leading social worker here. We went to see *Clive of India*—a poor play but very well acted, especially by the chief character.

Sunday, January 28, 1934

Breakfast with Lola Hahn. She confirmed much of what Wilfrid Israel had told me earlier about conditions inside. She too thought domestic relations in Germany were for the moment more difficult, and might become very critical.

At eleven o'clock Mr. Simon Marks came in. He stayed for fully an hour. He listened attentively to my exposition of my personal attitude towards the problem and my idea of the plan for a corporation. At the end he asked a number of questions about where and how the work would be done, showing clearly that he feels that only in Palestine can an adequate opportunity be found. Moreover, he stressed that, personally, he was interested only in Palestine; rightly or wrongly, he was determined to devote his time and energy and resources to that area. I did not argue with him about the worthwhileness of Palestinian programs. I centered my replies on the absurdity of not securing large and really adequate resources for work either in Palestine or anywhere else where facilities could be found to meet the crisis. I cited the examples of men who were giving a mere pittance in proportion to their resources, whereas for a project such as I proposed they might be induced to increase ten or twenty-fold their subscriptions.

As the talk developed, it became evident that Marks' fears were similar to those of Weizmann—that is, that the corporation would be used if not for anti-Palestinian proposals, at least for non-Palestinian ends, thus defeating projects dear to their hearts or draining off resources from them. I replied that I did not believe this would be the case—that certainly so far as I had anything to do with the enterprise, there would be no anti-Palestine spirit. He generously replied that he was sure that if I controlled the corporation or others with views as broad as mine, there would be no danger. I then added that such non-Jews as were on the board would almost certainly be of the same general point of view as I. This seemed to satisfy him, and we parted on a very cordial note.

My talk with Marks was much more encouraging to me that had been my previous efforts with Weizmann. I saw in Marks nothing of the prima donna which annoyed me so much in Dr. Weizmann. He seems a more reasonable, and at the same time a more practical, person.

Staff conference, followed by my lunching with Liebman at the R.Z.C. Our talk covered for the most part familiar ground related to the corporation. After lunch he let me read the draft of a memorandum prepared by Bernard Flexner. The principal new idea in this was the naming of groups of temporary trustees.

Dinner with Olive Sawyer and Wurfbain and then over to see Walter Pollack.

Monday, January 29, 1934

Breakfast with Felix Warburg and Herbert May at the Ritz. We talked about a number of matters to come up at the Bureau meeting. I told him of my conversation with Marks, and learned that Warburg had made no progress with Dr. Weizmann. It was agreed that Liebman would represent the JDC at the Bureau that morning with Dr. Kahn, Dr. Rosen, and Mr. S. as advisers.

The Bureau meeting began promptly at ten, Louis Oungre representing ICA, with Sir Osmond as a guest, who spoke from time to time on behalf of the Jewish Agency. The non-Jewish representatives were Rappard on behalf of the intellectuals, with Ginsberg, Adams, Schneebili, and Miss Bracey as experts, and Dr. Fox as the Bishop of Chichester's representative. There was no spokesman on behalf of the Catholics. Gottschalk of Belgium, whom I invited to stay for the meeting as a guest, took part in the discussions as if he were a member.

The morning session and afternoon session were sufficient to complete the agenda. On the whole, I felt that the discussion was businesslike, each person speaking to the point and, with rare exceptions, refraining from unnecessary oratory. On many questions the experts, particularly Kahn and Rosen, spoke more fully than did the official representatives. On such questions as methods of coordinating the efforts of retraining, settlement, etc., there were differing points of view but, in essentials, agreement. This applied also to the coordination of academic and professional activities.

After the meeting of the Bureau, we held a brief staff conference at Friends'

House, to plan the work for the next day. Then I went off to see Lord Cecil. I showed the latter the revised draft of the agenda for the Permanent Committee meeting the next day. He approved it. I reported to him the work of the Bureau, and we agreed on the lines of my opening statement the next morning.

Lunch with Gottschalk. I explained to him the idea of the corporation. He was much interested. We then discussed problems which concerned the Belgians in particular. He was anxious that they be enabled to emigrate a couple of hundred of their remaining refugees, thus liquidating their problem. He also raised a number of technical questions, having to do with passports. He asked me about the possibility of speaking at a money-raising meeting at Professor Speyer's. I said that I would be glad to do it if we could find a mutually convenient date. I suggested the middle of the following week, when I would be en route to Berlin. He doubted if it would be wise to have Jules Philippson act, for J.P. had so far not been a participant in this movement. It was left then that he would communicate with me as to Speyer's plans.

Over to the Ritz at nine o'clock for conference with Felix Warburg, Dr. Weizmann, and Charles Liebman. I do not know what they had been discussing, but Dr. Weizmann seemed far from being in a cheerful mood. I, therefore, began to ask him questions about his Palestine hopes. This revived him. He talked first of the Hula swamps, then of Trans-Jordania, of Syria, particularly the Lebanon, and of the territory towards Egypt. As he talked, he became more and more animated. On each of the subjects the other three of us showed interest and anxiety to be of use in helping Dr. Weizmann to achieve his ends. Dr. Weizmann, towards the end of this phase of the talk, outlined again, as he had to me in our first conference in Geneva, his dream of a half million Jews in the Palestine area before his death, and their gradual spread eastward until they had entrenched themselves securely.

Dr. Weizmann had just finished discussing the possible cost of reclaiming the swamp area and had admitted the high price of land when I seized the occasion to bring the talk back to the question of the corporation. I pointed out that if a corporation of the proposed size were announced and it put Palestine on its masthead, the price of the land might be measurably increased. This was not denied. Similarly, I urged that other projects would be made more difficult by ill-advised preliminary notice of them. On the other hand, by their very nature several of the projects which Dr. Weizmann had nearest his heart could be brought to fruition only through large-scale financing, and if the financial guarantees could be assured from the very beginning; in other words, that they would not be carried out in a piecemeal basis or through hand-to-mouth financing.

Dr. Weizmann recognized the force of these arguments as they were amplified by a general exchange of views. But he, in turn, argued that to get this money one must appeal to the Palestinians [Zionists], and that he at any rate could only move in a direct way, straight for his Palestinian objective. We replied that there was nothing in our proposal to prevent his carrying on his own activities; that we were not asking him to give up anything, but merely to go along with us to the extent of not, through his abstention, encouraging sabotage and open attack.

Finally after two hours' talk Dr. Weizmann was in a much more tractable mood. He seemed to recognize the advantage which was offered by the new proposal, and to be concerned only to find some way through which he could satisfy his own following that he was not betraying them if he worked with us. This was a real gain.

As we were breaking up and after Dr. Weizmann had gone, I chatted with Mrs. Warburg and with Lola Hahn and with other members of the group. Mrs. Warburg surprised me by her realistic attitude towards Dr. Weizmann and especially by her statement that he no longer had any substantial following of whose opinions he had to be chary. She seems indeed to regard him very highly still, but not in any sense to be in his pocket.

I walked home with Lola Hahn and Erich Warburg. The former told me of her efforts with Dr. Weizmann, her frank talks to him about his mistaken obstinacy, and of her pleasure at his more conciliatory attitude. Erich Warburg urged that I see Dr. H. before the latter went off to Scotland.

....

Home to bed after a very exhausting day.

Tuesday, January 30, 1934

The meeting of the Permanent Committee began promptly at 10:30. Cecil presiding. Others present were Mr. Doude van Troostwijk, Senator Bérenger, and Mr. Montere de Bustamante (in place of Mr. Guani). The Swiss representative had no substitute.

I began by making a report in about twenty minutes. I reminded the Permanent Committee that at the Lausanne meeting we had planned our work along three lines: coordination, negotiations with governments, and finance. I stated that the developments to date on each of these points would be shown in the course of the discussion on the various items on the agenda. I added that perhaps the members of the Permanent Committee would be interested in a brief resumé of the results of the High Commissioner's visit to the United States. I then outlined first the attitude of the authorities on visas, particularly the new position in reference to acceptance of labor bonds. I also told of the President's personal interest in this solution, and, indeed, in the problem as a whole. I suggested that in my talk with the authorities about the relations between the High Commission and the Reich a plan had been put forward with the idea that it might be made operative if the event should prove that there was no means of carrying forward a cooperative relationship.

I outlined my attitude towards Christian responsibility in this crisis and told of my broadcast on this subject, and of the cooperation of the Federal Council of Churches.

Finally, but in more detail, I sketched the corporation idea. I stressed its

James G. McDonald as a youngster, approximately 1890. Courtesy McDonald Family.

The family of James G. McDonald, including his parents and four siblings, approximately 1898. Pictured in the front row from left to right: Kenneth (father), William, Joseph, and Anna Diederick McDonald (mother). In the back row are John, James Grover McDonald, and Edward McDonald. USHMM/McDonald Family.

The wedding day of James and Ruth Stafford McDonald, Albany, Indiana, August 25, 1915. USHMM/McDonald Family.

Group portrait of the board of the Foreign Policy Association with Italian government officials, circa 1928. Esther G. Ogden is second from left, McDonald is third from right. USHMM/McDonald Family.

Ernst "Putzi" Hanfstaengl (1887–1975) on March 28, 1933. American born and Harvard educated, he was Adolf Hitler's piano-playing friend, supporter, and foreign press chief. © Bettman/CORBIS.

SA members block the entrance to the Wertheim department store in Rostock during the April 1, 1933, boycott of Jewish businesses in Germany. Archiv der Hansestadt Rostock.

SA in front of the Wertheim department store during the April 1, 1933, boycott of Jewish businesses. The young man is forced to wear a placard that reads: “Germans! Defend yourselves! Don’t buy from Jews!” Bundesarchiv.

President Franklin Roosevelt shakes hands with Reichsbank president Hjalmar Schacht, attending the economic conference in Washington, May 6, 1933. Second from left is the German ambassador, Hans Luther. Schacht would become economics minister in August 1934. © Bettmann/CORBIS.

Eugenio Cardinal Pacelli, Vatican secretary of state, signs the Concordat between Nazi Germany and the Vatican, July 20, 1933. To Pacelli's right is German vice-chancellor Franz von Papen, to his left the German ambassador, Dr. Rudolf Buttmann. Ullstein Bild, Granger Collection.

James G. McDonald aboard the SS *Manhattan* in November 1933, sailing to Europe to take up his post as High Commissioner. USHMM/McDonald Family.

tentative character, its non-commercial basis, and its not involving conflict with efforts to secure immediate funds for immediate relief. This explanation, as had been that in reference to the attitude of the President, was listened to with intense interest.

The first point discussed was that of the corporation. Bérenger, in an ungenerous spirit, suggested that while the French had given generously in charity, the Anglo-Americans were proposing to make an investment. He recognized, however, the need for larger funds. Bustamante showed a diplomat's fear of a business connection, as had Bérenger also. Doude said that of course the High Commission could not be associated with a promotion enterprise, but this was different and should be supported. Cecil said that something of this constructive nature was absolutely essential. Despite his support, however, the resolution as presented could not be passed, so a compromise one which he drafted was accepted.

As to relations with Germany, the consensus of opinion was that I should proceed along the lines I had indicated, but that the first trip would be exploratory and deal with technical questions, rather than attempt at this juncture to raise large questions of principle or to challenge the German authorities on major policies. Cecil would have had one go somewhat further than Bérenger, while Bustamente and Doude were for a conservative course.

Bentwich presented the passport proposals very clearly and succeeded in having them adopted without any essential modification. That action concluded the morning meeting, during which we had gotten through a really surprising amount of work.

Lunched with Kuhn of the *Times,* but gave him nothing for publication which was not available to others.

The afternoon session of the Permanent Committee was a joint one with the Bureau. I had urged Weizmann to come, so he was present on behalf of the Agency, Felix Warburg on behalf of the Joint, and the others as during the previous day on behalf of the various groups. The opening statements by Cecil, Weizmann, Warburg, Rappard, Fox, Oungre had certain value but were not very thrilling. The reports from the Bureau on behalf of the Church appeal, on migration and settlement, on retraining, were adopted with brief discussion. Then came the absurd and asinine and acrimonious debate for nearly an hour about the inclusion of the AIU[46] as part of the academic clearing house. It was a grotesque performance, and when it was disposed of, we went into a private meeting.

We disposed quickly of a number of matters, once the public and Bureau were cleared out. It was decided to invite Turkey, Yugoslavia, and South Africa to the Governing Body. I reported on my failure to bring in the Russians. Then it was decided to add the Alliance to the Advisory Body, but to adjourn the question of other additions to the Advisory Committee. On the matter of

46. Alliance Israelite Universelle.

adding a representative of both the British and the French to the Bureau, I explained why I was urging this. In fairness, I felt that I should ask Bentwich to put the other view. He did it briefly, and it seemed to me, very fairly. Cecil then spoke up, opposing the additions on the ground that it was a constitutional change which should not be made without the consultation with the Governing Body. I then attempted to argue why it seemed important to make the additions, but I was interrupted by expression of impatience by most of the members of the Permanent Committee at what seemed to them the injection of insignificant Jewish political considerations. Finally, I said that I would accept the adjournment of this question only if Lord Cecil would agree to help me explain to the interested parties. He said he would. Later tried to get him to give a tea for Sir Leonard, Oungre, and Laski to explain the situation, but he refused, saying that he would write letters which he was sure would settle the matter satisfactorily. There was nothing more I could do.

We then disposed promptly of modified resolutions dealing with apprenticeships and permits to work. I then presented the financial statement announcing the contributions of one-half of the three salaries (Wurfbain's, Miss Sawyer's, and mine). Cecil was so generous as to question whether Wurfbain should be permitted to make that sacrifice. Wurfbain explained why he wished to do it. Bérenger said not a word. My suggestion was, of course, accepted. Then was adopted the proposed schedule of travelling expenses and per diem allowances. Cecil and I were in the final resolution given authority to issue a communiqué,[47] and the meeting adjourned, all being finished up in one day to our great surprise.

Back to the hotel in time for a bite of supper with Miss Sawyer and off to see Fred Astaire in *The Gay Divorcé.*

Wednesday, January 31, 1934

The day previous Lola Hahn had called me to say that she had been refused anything more than a transit visa by the French consul. This is indicative of the tightening of the restrictions. Herbert May and I lunched with Lord Melchett[48]

47. In a January 31 press release the committee reported its decision to set up a Central Information Bureau for information about settlement and emigration, its recommendation that the High Commissioner should enter into negotiations with governments for work permits, its request to all governments represented to help in setting up facilities for the apprenticing of refugees in technical trades or placing them in technical schools, its authorization of two groups to centralize the search for placement of professors and scientific workers, and further consideration of what could be done on the urgent question of passports. Copy in McDonald Papers, USHMM.

48. Lord Melchett, Henry Ludwig Mond, second Baron Melchett, executive of the family owned Imperial Chemical Industries and banker. Melchett wrote to Weizmann: "I had lunch with McDonald yesterday. I think his scheme for a Company is very interesting but unworkable unless directed to a central objective . . . a large development scheme in a suitable territory, and the only one that can fulfill the requirement is Trans-Jordan with the possible exception of the Hooley [*sic*] Marshes. . . . Political preparations would have to be made with people like Winston Churchill and Austen Chamberlain in the Commons and Mottistone and Millbank in the Lords. . . . Then arrangements would have to be made with [Oswald] Mosley to keep Rothermere quiet and I think it could be done." Melchett to Weizmann, February 1, 1934, McDonald Papers, Columbia, D366 H2, January–June 1934.

at the Imperial Chemical Industries building, a beautiful structure in Millbank. Lord Melchett was very friendly. We chatted for half an hour or so about drugs and their uses, the value of stimulants to civilized men, etc., etc. Then I explained the corporation idea. Melchett listened, but at the end emphatically expressed the view that the suggestion would be practicable only if it were aimed at a specific project. He then outlined his idea of the development of Trans-Jordania. Later, in a letter to Dr. Weizmann, a copy of which he sent me, Lord Melchett elaborated his plan. I did not undertake to argue the Trans-Jordania project as such, but argued that it would be difficult to get the funds if Palestine were the sole objective, and then I proceeded to present the possibilities much as I had to Simon Marks. I am not sure that Lord Melchett was sympathetic to them. He stressed that it might be possible to overcome British political opposition by putting the whole matter on a basis of bold enterprise, reminiscent of the Maccabbean period; that through Mosley-Rothermere[49] they might be brought to support it, or at least not to oppose it. It was agreed that we would talk again later.

At tea time Dr H.[50] came to see me. He stressed that Hitler is the victim of his religion of unity; that this causes him to consort with the beasts in his party, and to overlook the most outrageous crimes; that if he could be cured of this religion, the really noble and splendid elements in the party would have a chance to dominate. Hitler is extraordinarily intelligent in grasp of detail and of general principles. Dr. H. feels sure of this because of the reports given by army and commercial leaders who recently had had long conferences with the Leader. Dr. H. urged that the most important thing that can be done is to show German political leaders that the actions of the beasts outrage world opinion. This can be said with complete frankness, if only it is prefaced by a declaration of faith in the Leader's sincerity of purpose in his declarations of peaceful intent, and if said by someone whose record is that of friendliness to Germany. He cited the welcome reception given to certain sermons by the bishop of Ripon, and Hanfstaengl's use of these. I listened, but made no commitment.

Earlier young Feilchenfeld had come in to talk about his visa. I promised to call up the U.S. Consulate.

Pleasant dinner with the Fred Fields at their house. Was glad to see the baby.

49. Harold Harmsworth, Baron Rothermere, publisher of the *London Daily Mail* and *Evening News*. A supporter of Sir Oswald Mosley and the British Union of Fascists.

50. Probably Dr. Otto Hirsch, longtime member of the Centralverein deutscher Staatsbürger judischen Glaubens. Number two man on the Reichsvertretung der deutschen Juden, founded in September 1933 to represent German Jews to the government and to coordinate Jewish self-help. Met frequently with Jewish leaders abroad.

10. February 1934: Testing Germany/Family Crisis

London, Thursday, February 1, 1934

. . . .

Mr. Adams of the Academic Assistance Council came in to discuss the actions of the Bureau and the Permanent Committee. I suggested that he draft a memorandum and that on the basis of that we make a formal report to the American committee.

Lunch at Lord Cecil's. Others present besides Lord and Lady Cecil and myself were a retired captain of the navy, and Lady Gladstone and Lady Violet Bonham-Carter, the daughter of Asquith,[1] who had just returned from Vienna. Most of the talk was about Vienna, the danger of the upset of Dollfuss, the timidity and hesitation of the powers, the lack of imagination of the British government, etc. Later there was some talk about Germany.

. . . .

Long talk with Mr. Callahan at the Consulate in reference to Feilchenfeld's visa.

Rennie Smith came in to talk about methods of enlisting American cooperation for the Friends of Europe. I told him that it could be done in my judgment only through persons working in the States.

At 6:30 Professor B. came in. His advice in reference to my prospective visit was much the same as that of Dr. H. the night before. I remained noncommittal. He thinks that economic conditions in the Reich are becoming worse, though he does not anticipate an immediate crisis.

Baron Robert came back to report on his conferences during the day. He was in an excited state of mind. He ended by asking me for dinner in Paris the night of Sunday, February 11, the exact time to be indicated at the Hotel Continental.

Dinner with Rosenberg and Allen Wardwell.[2] After the meal, joined by Felix Warburg. Then followed one of the most profitable and intelligently con-

1. Herbert Asquith, Earl of Oxford and Asquith, former Liberal prime minister (1908–1916). Helen Violet Bonham-Carter, Baroness Asquith, was president of the Women's Liberal Federation and later first female president of the Liberal Party. A friend and biographer of Churchill.

2. Allen Wardwell, partner in the law firm of Davis, Polk, Wardwell, Sunderland & Kiend, chairman of the Government Unemployment Relief Commission, active in Russian relief.

ducted discussions I have participated in. The first half, and the longer part, had to do with relations with Germany. I outlined the questions as follows:

First, passports and travel papers. I followed Bentwich's general outline, indicating that, so far as Germany was concerned, only two questions arose: (1) the willingness to give instructions to the German consuls[3] that a clear indication be given if there was no intention to renew an expired passport; (2) the attitude on the question of supplying necessary papers to refugees who wished to offer these as proof of their eligibility for visas.

Related, of course, to the above is another question, that of the possibilities of repatriation. Would it be possible for the German government to implement the recent declaration about the possibility of return of refugees?

Second, the matter of property, tangible and intangible, left in Germany by refugees. This, in turn, subdivides itself: (a) would the German government express any view on a question of policy about such property?; (b) if the answer to (a) is yes, then could the High Commissioner consider setting up protective committees in the various countries where there are numbers of refugees, and ask for the filing of claims?; (c) if the answer to (b) is yes, should these committees be separate institutions, should they be financed from the outside or by the beneficiaries of their activities?; (d) if there are affirmative answers to the above major points, would the Reich consent to the setting up of a consolidating, liquidating, and transferring corporation within the Reich to handle the refugees' assets?; (e) should the High Commissioner go so far as to suggest that in order to overcome the Devisen [foreign exchange] difficulty, funds outside of Germany which otherwise might have gone into the Reich could be used as offsets against the assets within?

Third, questions of general policy: (a) should the High Commissioner follow the advice he had received the two previous evenings and drive home the moral on large policies?; (b) should he seek to establish an armistice or something of the sort as between the Jewish groups and the German government?; (c) should he see Jewish leaders? Should he see newspapermen and others who could give him the "lowdown" on the situation, or should he remain strictly official, see those with whom he had official business, then leave?

Each of the subdivisions under the three above heads were [*sic*] discussed fully, and a consensus of opinion was reached. In general, it seemed clear that this first trip should be primarily to establish contacts, to explore the ground, not to reach definite agreements. Therefore, I should be strictly official, see only German officials and American officials, leaving as soon as these contacts are made.

On questions of passport and travel papers, my confreres had little to suggest. In reference to property, they doubted if one could go further than attempt to secure an expression of view on policy from the German government; to try to do more might be a serious mistake. However, it would be wise for me to use my

3. The German consuls in countries where refugees had gone.

judgment and act in the light of the initial statements by the authorities. In no case would it be advisable to mention the corporation idea. If this were brought up by the others, there should be an explanation that the whole thing is so tentative that it should not be taken into consideration.

As to the third question of general policy, everyone agreed that it would be a serious mistake to follow the advice given earlier; moreover, I should do nothing about establishing an armistice, nor should I see the Jewish leaders.

All in all, it was felt that the trip, if it did nothing more than make a bare beginning, would be worthwhile. And that, I fear, is all that it will accomplish.

The other general topic of discussion was the corporation. Felix Warburg supplemented my presentation, particularly on the more practical side as to what should be done. Wardwell asked a number of pointed questions, but seemed very much impressed. We did not ask him for specific cooperation, but suggested that after he had returned to the States we would take it up with him again.

So far as Wardwell's help in Berlin is concerned, he said he would be glad to see me whenever he is free, that he would advise where he could be helpful, and if the opportunity arose, he would indicate to Dr. Schacht that I was in town and the general nature of my purpose there. He could not, however, promise this latter, for he would be able to do it only if it came in naturally.

Friday, February 2, 1934

Long staff conference to clear up matters left over by the previous meetings and to plan for the future, especially in view of Herbert May's departure the following day. After the conference was over, Adams and Bagster-Collings came with their memorandum. It was agreed to send it to the States after it had been approved by Duggan, May to take a copy as a basis for his talk with Dr. Chamberlain, Dr. Bagster-Collins to write to his office, but we to forward the material formally.

From a few minutes after twelve until ten minutes past [I] was with Ambassador von Hoesch[4] at the German Embassy. We first talked about his reparations experiences, the mistakes at Versailles, my record in 1914 and after 1916, etc. Then we got onto the subject of the day. I explained frankly how the initiative had come from Mr. Dodd, my reply to him, his inquiry at the Foreign Office, their reply, and my move now through the Embassy here. The ambassador said he could do one of two things: assume that the arrangements had been made, and telegraph the date of my coming, or better telephone to Dieckhoff to inquire exactly what the status is and whom I might expect to see. I agreed that this latter would be preferable, and that was decided upon. He suggested that probably it would be difficult for the Chancellor to see me, because of the prin-

4. Leopold Gustav Alexander von Hoesch, German ambassador to Great Britain, 1932–1936.

ciples involved. I replied that I recognized this, but I felt that I would have to see the foreign minister. I suggested that in his talk with Dieckhoff the ambassador might incidentally remind the latter that, of course, I was going to deal while in Germany with only technical matters, and to see only the officials; nonetheless, I probably would have an opportunity on my return to the States to chat informally with the President about the general state of the world, as I had on previous occasions. Of course, such a chat, if it came, would be wholly unofficial, and in no wise cutting across the regular diplomatic channels. As to refugees returning to Germany, and in reference to classes about whose property something might be done, the ambassador said, of course, there could be no question that the issue could even be raised about the political refugees or the criminals, but as to those whom I called "the poor devils who had left in panic or fear," that might be a different matter, if, as he put it, they could prove that they had not taken part in any anti-governmental activities abroad. I replied that it would be rather difficult for anyone to prove in general that he had not been guilty of disloyalty, whereas it might be relatively easy for him to disprove any specific charge of disloyalty. It was left that he would telephone as the result of his conversation with Berlin.

Lunch at the hotel for the Laskis, Montefiores, Mr. Lazarus, Mrs. Bentwich, Miss Sawyer, and I. During the lunch I took occasion to tell Laski rather casually that the question of enlarging the Bureau had been adjourned. He took it well, saying that he supposed that Dr. Weizmann was jubilant. I replied that I did not think Dr. Weizmann knew of it, that in any event, the decision had not been made because of Dr. Weizmann's opposition.

During lunch Mrs. Laski told me of her study of the work being done in some of the countries bordering on Germany.

Over with Mrs. Laski to the Anglo-HICEM immigration committee meeting at Woburn House. As I was going into the room, I saw from Louis Oungre's face that something had happened. He said to me, "There is a frightful situation; Sir Leonard has had a letter from Lord Cecil, and Sir Leonard is about to reply." There was no opportunity for further discussion because the chairman called the meeting to order.

Sir Osmond in the chair. Others present included Louis Oungre, Schiff, Montefiore, Bentwich, Stephany, Edward Oungre, Mrs. Stern, Mrs. Lionel Cohen, and perhaps a dozen others. Among the secretaries was Miss Goldsmid, niece of Sir Osmond. I was asked if I cared to make a general statement. I suggested that we proceed directly to the agenda. The first question was as to the form in which the Anglo-HICEM committee was to set up its Information Center for all matters of migration. There was an exchange of views between Louis Oungre and Norman Bentwich as to whether this committee was to be the Anglo-HICEM committee enlarged, or to have the form of a new name. Louis Oungre was insistent on the former, and I, as a practical matter, supported him, and it was so settled. Later, Bentwich suggested the organizations which should be added to represent the non-Jewish groups—the Quakers, the Protestant churches, and the International Migration Service. Bentwich's suggestion of the addition of the Trade Union Federation was rejected on the ground that it had a political slant.

The issue whether the Anglo-HICEM, in addition to supplying information to all—Jews and non-Jews—would undertake to migrate non-Jews, was discussed pro and con. It was agreed that such service would be offered, but that it could not be continued if it involved heavy expenditure unless non-Jewish sources supplied the funds.

Bentwich explained at length about passports, and answered satisfactorily all the questions dealing with that and related questions.

In reply to the question about relations with Germany, I told briefly of my plans, and expressed the hope that I might be able to report more in detail later to the leaders of the committee.

Immediately after adjournment Louis Oungre and I continued our talk about ICA and the Bureau. I called up Felix Warburg, told him what an asinine performance I thought it was, and how, if continued, [it] might jeopardize Cecil's support. He suggested that I talk to Sir Osmond. This I did immediately in the presence of Bentwich, Oungre, and Stephany. I was brutally frank, deliberately, even a little theatrical, saying that: it was impossible to proceed if one had to go hat in hand to a group of trustees for a mere pittance; that it was grotesque to argue about £5,000 and seats on the Bureau when seriously discussing a project involving millions; that it would be utterly impossible to reopen this question with Cecil, for if I tried to explain the intricacies of Jewish politics he might be tempted to say, "If that is the actual state of internal affairs, perhaps there is no use bothering about the Jewish problem at all"; that at any rate I was through with any personal efforts to satisfy the ICA demands. However, if as a practical matter, they were willing to accept my personal assurance that the English and the French communities would in fact be asked to be represented at each meeting of the Bureau, I would gladly give that assurance. This Sir Osmond indicated he thought might be satisfactory, and the matter was left there.

....

To dinner with the Liebmans at the Hungaria. Besides Mr. and Mrs. Liebman and myself there were present Mr. and Mrs. May, Mr. and Mrs. Kuhn, and the Liebmans' son. After dinner Liebman and I discussed the next steps here. He felt strongly that it would be a mistake to go home without having something more definite to show. We agreed that every effort should be made to have the English set up, if not temporary trustees, at least a continuing committee. We both hoped that on this might be included two outstanding non-Jewish personalities. It was left that he was to press this matter on Felix Warburg the next morning.

Saturday, February 3, 1934

Talked with Feilchenfeld. Agreed to speak to the American Consulate in Berlin about the transfer of his visa application to London.

Talked on the telephone to Felix Warburg about my plans in Berlin. Told Rosenberg that I had received from Cecil the letter which he wished, and was proposing to go ahead along those lines.

Mr. Liebman called to say that Warburg had agreed to his program.

Over to the office of the North British & Mercantile Insurance Company. Filled out an application for three-year short-term policy for £20,000 ($100,000), the rate per year to be £1.6 for each £100. This arrangement would permit me to continue the insurance for three years without reexamination. He seemed to be willing to pass me; at any rate, he assured me that my heart need not cause me concern.

While in the doctor's office I had word from Miss Sawyer that the German ambassador had called. I called him back. He said, "The situation in Berlin is precisely as I thought it would be. I talked to Dieckhoff. Seeing the Chancellor is out of the question as a matter of principle. You will be received by the foreign minister, but I should add that this will be 'with reserve.' This does not apply to you personally, but to your mission. If you will have Wurfbain bring over your passport when he dines with my secretary tonight, I will arrange for a laisser-passer." There was some further exchange of remarks, but nothing significant.

From the hotel I called the American Embassy, and asked them if they would send in code a telegram to Dodd telling of my arrival.

During the afternoon worked with Miss Sawyer on diary and other matters until dinner time.

Dined with Miss Caroline Berry, a friend of Mrs. Kuhn's. Earlier in the day had wired the bishop of Chichester that I was not able to come until Sunday.

Sunday, February 4, 1934

Ten o'clock train to Chichester. Arrived about twelve. Out for a very pleasant walk with the bishop's secretary. At lunch besides the bishop and Mrs. Bell were A. E. Houseman, the poet, Mr. and Mrs. Whittemore (especially interested in the drama), and the bishop's sister.

In the afternoon another walk with the bishop and Houseman. After I had a brief talk with the bishop about our work. He agreed to send a letter to Pastor Boegner[5] in Paris.

Six o'clock train back to London, arriving in time for dinner with Miss Sawyer and Wurfbain, and we then worked until nearly midnight on accounts.

Monday, February 5, 1934

Over to the bank with Wurfbain to make arrangements.

Interview with Mr. Barnett of the *Jewish Chronicle.*

5. Marc Boegner, president of the Fédération Protestante.

Conference with Goodman and a rabbi of the Agudas.[6] Bentwich and I agreed to raise again the question of their organization's membership in the Advisory Council, and let them know.

Long conference at Lord Melchett's office with him and Lord Mottistone.[7] Mottistone told at considerable length of his relations with Hitler, his admiration for some aspects of the man, his hope that by appealing to the latter's sense of pity something could be done. He had suggested to Hitler that the status of all foreigners in Germany, including the Jews, be put on a quota basis. Hitler had been sympathetic, but remained adamant on his general racial theory. Mottistone suggested that I might mention his interest in my work when I talked to Hitler or Hanfstaengl.

During the latter part of our conference Lord Melchett adumbrated the theory that Hitler is partly Jewish; that this is proven by his essentially Jewish reactions in his book. He is a sort of inverted Hebrew prophet, who has selected for his chosen people the Germans. As Lord Melchett developed this thesis, it seemed to me to have a certain measure of plausibility. At the end Lord Melchett added, "There is no use going to New Court.[8] The men there belong to the older generation and are out of touch with today. They will help you only if they are prodded by an aroused public opinion."

Over to New Court where I found a group of fifteen or twenty men gathered in a moderate sized room. No one apparently was designated to receive any one. I chatted with a number of men while waiting for Lionel Rothschild to call the meeting to order. When he was ready to do this, there were perhaps fifty men present. I was told by someone who knows the group that many of them represented seven figures.

Rothschild's introduction of me was neither gracious nor cordial, and committed him to nothing whatsoever as far as my program was concerned. I spoke for about twenty minutes, developing my thesis about Jewish responsibility abroad. I repeated what had been told to me about the possibility that New Court might lack leadership. Throughout I felt that I was talking against a blank wall, and at the end the scattering applause did not change my impression.

Then Felix Warburg spoke along his usual line, that this was not a hair-brain[ed] scheme. It offered reasonable security of capital return, would tend to purchase the interest of one's children in Jews everywhere, and needed to be one. He was very kindly in his reference to my status at home.

After he finished there was one question from the floor, not very well put, to which I replied. Then Lionel Rothschild, with stupid abruptness, said that he

6. Agudas refers to Agudath Israel, ultra-Orthodox movement founded in Katowice in 1912. Hostile to Zionism.

7. John Edward Bernard Seely, first Baron Mottistone. Fought in the Boer War, served in Herbert Asquith's government of 1921. Opposed League of Nations sanctions against Italy for its invasion of Ethiopia in 1935.

8. New Court, name of a house in St. Swithin's Lane in the City of London. The headquarters of N. M. Rothschild & Sons, Merchant Bankers.

felt the meeting should adjourn after the designation of a committee to consider the matter further. I rose in protest, saying that from my point of view, at any rate, it would be a pity if there was not some real discussion, that I did not mind a bit complete frankness, that I was not sensitive, that I should hate to go into Germany tomorrow without knowing more what the group felt about the central problem that I had thus far been able to gather. This stimulated Salmon[9] to say that he thought I was asking for a blank check, etc., etc. To this I replied as well as I could. Then Seligman rose to say that since it was so difficult to place German doctors and lawyers abroad, where were we to get out human material for considerable emigration. This gave me an opportunity to refer to the situation of the Jewish children, and for first time I felt that there was some stir of the emotions of the group.

Simon Marks rose to say that he wondered how I had arrived at the figures of $25,000,000 to $50,000,000, and since he was interested only in Palestine and since only there money could be effectively spent, why did we not direct our attentions there? I replied that if I were in Mr. Marks' position, and felt as he does that it was only in Palestine that money could be justifiably spent, then I should welcome the creation of a corporation with large funds without any indication of the specific territory to which it is to direct its attention, for inevitably the trustees would have to center their efforts in the Palestine region.

There was some other discussion. I saw that Weizmann, to whom I had referred a number of times and to whom others had referred, was anxious to say a word. I suggested to the chairman that he recognize Weizmann, but Rothschild said, "Dr. Weizmann doesn't want to speak." But Dr. Weizmann did speak, too long and not very logically, but on the whole more sympathetically than anyone up to that time.

Earlier Warburg had said to Rothschild that he wanted to say a few words, and the chairman had replied, "I think it is time for me to call on Sir Robert Waley-Cohen to close the meeting." After Dr. Weizmann the chairman then asked Felix Warburg if he wanted to say something, and Warburg refused. At that point Robert Waley-Cohen was called upon. He said something in general terms of the desirability of seeing if the program of the High Commission could be carried through, but if it failed (and he implied that it must), then one should appeal to the governments to take appropriate action. It was a stupid speech, a repetition of what he had said earlier in our conference at his house, but took no account at all of the real situation.

Rosenberg was stirred to make a rather emotional statement about the work of the JDC and Felix Warburg, the need of Jewish support for the High Commission, etc., etc. On the whole, it was a good speech, but by that time half the crowd had left.

9. Sir Isidore Salmon, Conservative MP for Harrow from 1925 until his death in 1941. Treasurer of the United Synagogue and then vice president, later chairman of the catering firm of J. Lyons and Co. and honorary catering adviser to the British Army.

Along during this period someone had moved that the chairman name a committee. He accepted this responsibility, and Sir Osmond made a closing speech of guarded thanks, and a more guarded statement about the attitude of the ICA, and then the meeting was closed.

I turned to Lionel Rothschild and said, "Who is on the committee," and looked at his list. It included no Zionist. I said, "Why don't you put Simon Marks on?" Rothschild replied, "You can deal with him better outside." I said, "I think it would be a serious mistake not to include him." So Rothschild grudgingly wrote Marks' name down. I then slipped over to Lionel Cohen and told him the situation, and he agreed that Marks must be included. That was the end of the regular procedure.

After the meeting broke up, Bentwich told me that he thought I had done splendidly. I chatted with Dr. Weizmann and Simon Marks and Harry Sacher on the way back to the hotel. Dr. Weizmann and I were of much the same view as to the stupidity and lack of responsiveness of the group. Marks said, however, "Don't be discouraged. We will get something done." Earlier I had personally urged Marks to accept membership on the committee, and he said he would if I asked him to.

Marks told me that in their drive last year he had gone to the Rothschilds and urged that five individuals each contribute £20,000. But they were unwilling to go beyond £10,000.

Marks asked if I could come to dinner on my return here, and it was arranged that I would dine with him and a small group Wednesday, the fourteenth.

Arrived at the hotel at 7:15, and had to hurry over to Cecil's to get his signature on a number of documents. I showed him the draft of a letter which Sir Osmond had suggested that I send to the ICA to clear up the matter about the changes in the Bureau. I called Cecil's attention to the fact that neither the Permanent Committee nor the Governing Body had any authority over the Bureau, but we agreed that, nonetheless, it would be unwise to move without their approval. So it was agreed that I would sign the draft letter, changing, however, a sentence which said that modifications of the Bureau had to be approved by the Governing Body or the Permanent Committee. Cecil is not to be in London when I return next week, so I shall not see him until March.

....

Tuesday, February 6, 1934

Awakened by Rosenberg's telephone call, and his excited and emotional plea that I must let the British leaders know that I was profoundly disappointed, that they had been grossly discourteous to Felix Warburg, that I am the High Commissioner and not a suppliant, that it is for them to decide whether this instrumentality is to be used, etc., etc. I said I would think it over and later drafted a long letter embodying these ideas. Then cut out most of the part to which objection might reasonably be taken, and submitted both drafts to Felix Warburg and Jimmy Rosenberg. The response from Warburg was that he thought things were going better than they appeared, that he was working out a program with Liebman, and that he thought the two groups—the one working on the MacFadyen scheme[10] and our group—could and would work together effectively. Rosenberg, having recovered from his excitement of last night and the early morning, was emphatic that no letter at all should be sent. I agreed, therefore, with the suggestion of Warburg, that a copy of the shorter form of the letter be left with him, to be used discreetly by him.

Conferences with Bentwich about last minute details, and then spent the rest of the morning preparing to get off on the two o'clock train for Berlin.

At the station met Erich, Sigmund, and Max Warburg. Had a brief chat with the two younger men, but waited until the steamer for my talk with Max.

Had a very pleasant crossing from Dover to Calais, with bright sun and almost no sea. Max Warburg and I walked the deck, talking. He explained to me the fundamental difference between the English and American points of view on questions such as I had taken up with the New Court group. The English are much more insistent than the Americans on specifications being written into any program of work. The Americans are more willing to work on the basis of a general proposition, leaving the details to be developed by a group in whom they have confidence.

Warburg outlined again the need, as he sees it, for supplementary contributions to the relief agencies in Berlin. He saw no prospect of material improvement in the situation of the Jews. As to his own future, he was similarly pessimistic; for example, he said that on his return to Germany on that occasion he might be unmolested or he might be arrested and charged with some crime, or sent directly to a concentration camp—one never could tell.

He emphasized again, as he had at The Hague, that he conceived of my work as stretching out over a period of years; that the refugee part of it was only a first stage; that he was confident I could be of great aid to his people. As we approached Calais, we said goodbye, because it seemed desirable not to see too much of each other after landing. Yet when I went to my compartment on the train, I found by a singular coincidence his was next door.

The trip to Berlin was uneventful.

Berlin, Wednesday, February 7, 1934

Reached Friedrichstrasse on time, at 8:58, and went directly to the Kaiserhof, where I was received like an old friend.

After changing and stopping at the American Express Co. to cash our registered Marks, we went to the Embassy. I was chatting with Mrs. Levine about appointments at the Foreign Office when she laughingly handed me a cable which looked as though it might be for me though it was not my correct name.

10. Probably a notion of settling refugees on Sir Eric MacFadyen's plantations in Malaya.

I opened it casually and was startled to read of Bobby's[11] sudden and apparently desperate illness. I at once wrote out a cable indicating that I could sail on Friday, and later I sent a second saying definitely that I would sail then. There was no time, however, to communicate with London before I had to go to my appointments.

Dieckhoff received me very cordially. After our first interchanges I asked him about the interview with the foreign minister. His reply was a little evasive. I then struck out boldly, told him that I had been assured by the German ambassador in London only the day before that I would be received "with reserve" by von Neurath; that if now, after having made the trip, I was unable to see him I should, of course, have to report this failure to the governmental members of our organization, which would mean to the foreign offices of twelve governments; that I did not, of course, expect to complain, but that the record would have to be made. At this point Dieckhoff went in to the *chef de cabinet* of Neurath, and returned saying that the latter was very busy, that he was seeing the King of Sweden during the afternoon and was at that moment with the Czech Minister, etc., etc. Later, during my talk with Dieckhoff I told him frankly why I was so anxious to finish up my Berlin work that day. He was evidently touched by my distress over Bobby's illness, and called von Neurath's office again explaining the circumstances. The reply came that von Neurath would see me at once. So the two of us went in together.

Before the talk with von Neurath, Dieckhoff and I had had more than an hour alone together; then we had called in Wurfbain and one of the Foreign Office experts on passports. During our talk alone Dieckhoff and I had covered the whole range of subjects which it had been agreed in London I was to discuss in Berlin. At the beginning Dieckhoff had said, "Now since we are old friends for many years, there is no reason why we should not talk with complete frankness. Of course, you understand that, in your talk with me or with the foreign minister, we are not carrying on negotiations. You may think this is a difference without meaning, but it has a real importance for us. As you know, the institution you represent is not very popular here, and it might be embarrassing for us to be charged with carrying on formal negotiations." I assured him that this was satisfactory to me; that I had come, as I had explained to the ambassadors in London and Washington, on a purely official mission; that I had no intention to capitalize my visit for political purposes, and that as soon as I had finished my formal interviews, I intended to leave. This seemed to reassure Dieckhoff.

I began first with the technical questions of passports and related topics. I explained the action of the Permanent Committee in reference to a new form of travel and identification paper, and requested the cooperation of the German government along the following lines:

11. Barbara "Bobby" McDonald, seven years old, was critically ill with pneumonia, a bacterial infection that was often fatal before penicillin became widely used in the 1940s.

(a) the prompt satisfaction to individual refugees when a decision had been made not to renew or extend a German passport;
(b) the cooperation of the German police authorities in supplying the necessary data requested by refugees as to their possible police records;[12]
(c) possible declaration of policy as to repatriation.

The first two of these presented no difficulties, and were discussed later more fully by Wurfbain and the Foreign Office expert. How far, however, the German government will go in cooperating I did not feel sure.

The third point, however, was a different matter. On this Dieckhoff spoke at length and with considerable conviction, but he emphasized that he was doing so only personally and in no sense expressing an official view. He does not expect the regime to change its legislation or its administrative regulations so as to encourage the return of emigrés; on the contrary, he is convinced that very few will be allowed to return, perhaps some who are of no consequence, but the great bulk must remain abroad. He anticipates that the requirement of proving categorically that they have not participated in disloyal activities abroad is not likely to be rescinded. He, of course, recognized that this requirement, if unchanged, made return of the emigrés extremely unlikely.

We then moved on to the general question of refugees' property. I explained that I was concerned with four possible angles of this question:

(a) Would it be possible for the German government to clarify its position as to freeing refugee property for transfer abroad? On this Dieckhoff made no comment which was helpful;
(b) If there could be some clarification about (a), we might consider the possibility of setting up committees in the different refugee centers, through which refugees might list their property claims;
(c) A third step might be the setting up of a German corporation, to function in the consolidation and liquidation on a trusteeship basis of refugee property;
(d) The issue of transfer might be lessened in difficulty by the device of setting over against funds which would otherwise have to be transferred, comparable funds outside, which otherwise would have been sent into Germany for relief purposes. Dieckhoff replied to this suggestion that he was no expert on transfers, that this is a matter for the Treasury or rather the foreign exchange division of the Reichsbank; but he knew that the general impression was that the funds available outside would not be nearly sufficient for the purpose I had indicated. He said that the largest sum he had heard suggested for transfer into Germany for relief purposes in any given year was

12. Individuals applying for visas to the United States (and some other countries) were required to submit proof that they had no police record. German Jews frequently found it difficult to obtain such documents from German police officials.

£500,000. I made no comment on this estimate, but had I done so, I should have had to admit that the figure he suggested was optimistic.

In general, I was not able to judge from Dieckhoff's replies how far one could hope to go in dealing with property.

Later, Wurfbain had a long discussion with the financial expert in the Foreign Office. The impression he gained there was that the government felt it had been liberal in releasing foreign exchange for refugees. It was estimated that 8,000 families had on an average taken with them each 10,000 Marks, making a total of 80,000,000 Marks, an almost disproportionate fraction of the total foreign exchange available.

We then turned to two general considerations:

(a) What might reasonably be expected to be the future policy of the regime towards Jews? On this Dieckhoff was not very informing because, I think, he does not know. He expressed the hope that there would be a gradual moderation and cited the announcement of Interior Minister Wilhelm Frick to the heads of the states that they should not go beyond the letter of the law in anti-Jewish discrimination.[13] But Dieckhoff's optimism was not convincing.

(b) The question whether if a planned emigration extending over a period of years, of ten or fifteen thousand young Jews annually could be arranged, would the government be prepared to give additional assurances about the Jews who would remain? Dieckhoff made no helpful comment, but a little later von Neurath was more illuminating.

The foreign minister seemed to me very tired when Dieckhoff and I went in to see him. Nonetheless, he was very cordial, and we spoke with considerable freedom. He first expressed his deep regret at the illness of Bobby and his hope that I might have better news. I then reiterated, as I had to Luther and Hoetsch, that my twenty-year record of friendship for Germany had not changed; that I was concerned to liquidate the refugee problem as quickly as possible; that I was inexorably opposed to the utilization of this question for propaganda against Germany; that I was now, as formerly, deeply interested that the Reich should have justice done for it; and that I was as convinced now as ever that there could be peace in Europe only through the satisfaction of Germany's just claims.

With these preliminaries out of the way, I quickly reviewed the points I had discussed with Dieckhoff. It was only on the last one that the foreign minister went beyond anything which Dieckhoff had said. Indeed, so interested did Neurath show himself in my suggestion of a possible planned migration and a truce

13. Probably a tendentious rendering of the German ordinance of February 2, 1934, under the law of January 30, 1934, subjecting state legislation to Reich approval.

arrangement between the remaining Jews and the government, that I felt called upon to retreat a little. I hastened to make clear to him that I was in no sense authorized to make a formal proposal, that obviously the difficulties from the financial point of view were enormous, and the task of finding places for these thousands even more discouraging. I got the impression that von Neurath might consider it worthwhile to raise with the governmental authorities this question. He did not say he would do so, but he evidently thought it contained real possibilities.

Dieckhoff and I then retired to his office and continued the discussion of some technical matters with Wurfbain and the Foreign Office experts. We also arranged for Wurfbain to carry on these technical discussions at five that afternoon.

....

At lunch with Wurfbain drafted cables to Miss Sawyer instructing her to change sailings from the SS *Manhattan* to the *Paris,* and later sent a second cable suggesting that, if possible, the conference with English leaders be advanced from the following Wednesday to the next day, February 8. I then went up to pack, while Wurfbain filed the cables, and together we went over to see Dodd.

Dodd did not seem to me a well man. He had had a cold, but I thought I saw in him more than that kind of illness. I imagined that the German atmosphere was beginning to get on his nerves.

We talked about many subjects, but the one of chief importance was the suggestion which I had made to Neurath. Dodd thought this a practicable one, and well worth pursuing further. Indeed, he seemed so confident on this point that I wondered a little whether he fully understood what was involved.

Dodd's analysis of the existing situation was not especially new, but he did not anticipate any material relief for the Jews. As I was leaving, he brought up the question of Mrs. Levine being given a post on my staff. He stressed her many excellent qualifications and suggested that she might be helpful in securing funds because of her brothers [Herbert and Gerard Swope] and other contacts. I suspect, however, that he is chiefly concerned because of his embarrassment at having at the reception desk of the Embassy a personality so obviously Jewish and so positively hostile to the regime. On the other hand, because of her relationships it would be very embarrassing for him to suggest that she retire. But I do not see where I could use her, intelligent though she is, and friendly as she has shown herself to be. I held out no hope of being able to use her.[14]

14. Dodd subsequently complained to the State Department about Mrs. Levine, alleging that she was possibly too close to the Nazis! When asked, Consul Geist told Assistant Secretary of State Wilbur Carr that Mrs. Levine was a woman of refinement and culture who performed her duties in the Embassy efficiently—she was thoroughly creditable to the United States. Carr Memorandum, June 5, 1935, Carr Papers, Box 12, Library of Congress.

In his diary Dodd gave the following account of this meeting:

McDonald impressed me again as not very much enamored of his new and difficult position, though his work as planned seems to me very important, for Hitler is never going to cease trying to ban all Jews from the Reich. McDonald told me he had raised 500,000 pounds sterling from English Jews[15] *but that the givers were not enthusiastic and did not wish many German Jews to enter England. He said that in the United States "there is much interest in limited circles but no enthusiasm for taking persecuted Jews into the country." These people must have clerical, professional or financial jobs wherever they migrate and there are few such positions available anywhere.*

He wishes to arrange with the Germans for a ten-year plan for the removal of Jews and the transfer of German property for their initial support. Von Neurath is not opposed to this plan, but unable to give any promises. To remove over 600,000 people, most of whom are fairly well to do, from any country, is no easy task. To expel them, as has been tried the last twelve months, would arouse intense hostility. Perhaps 50,000 have departed from Germany since Hitler became Chancellor in January, 1933. McDonald remained an hour talking over his difficulties.[16]

Wurfbain and I went over to the American Consulate, and had a very interesting but much too brief conference with Geist, who was sitting at Messersmith's desk.[17] Geist is convinced that there is a real revolutionary movement afoot in Germany, that even Hitler must take account of the mass feeling; that latent in the movement is a much more radical economic tendency than has yet manifested itself; that if the conservatives—Schacht, Schmitt, von Krosigk—fail to bring the return of prosperity, it will be very difficult for Hitler to resist the demand for real socialism. Those who are demanding this development are not concerned with profits for the capitalists, but only that big industries and the transportation systems contribute as largely as possible to the public good.

Unfortunately, I had gotten fixed in my mind five o'clock as the time for my train for London. Therefore cutting my interview with Geist short, Wurfbain and I hurried to the station, only to find that the train did not leave until 9:27. I checked my bags there, Wurfbain went back to the Wilhelmstrasse, and I over to the Embassy.

I chatted with O'Donoghue until it was time to go with him to his house for a cocktail party at six. I learned little that was new from O'Donoghue. He has the typical Foreign Service officer's view of a revolutionary regime. He thinks it is not succeeding; that there is a great deal of petty and even large-scale

15. Both the amount and the source are inaccurate.

16. *Ambassador Dodd's Diary, 1933–1938,* eds. William E. Dodd, Jr., and Martha Dodd (New York: Harcourt Brace and Co., 1941), 79.

17. Consul General Messersmith was then on leave in the United States. Messersmith was shortly afterward appointed minister to Austria.

graft; that the masses of the children and the younger people are everywhere drilling for the inevitable war; that sooner or later the regime will face a serious internal crisis.

....

About seven o'clock I went over to the Esplanade, where I had arranged to meet Wurfbain for a bit of supper. I was lucky to find Wardwell in his room alone, and therefore had a chance to go over with him developments of the day. He thought I had done everything which could be expected for the first visit. He had had no chance himself to speak to Schacht, but would do so later if the opportunity presented itself.

Wurfbain and I made last minute plans at supper and at the station. I told him to use his own discretion in determining what he was to take up the next day in Berlin. I told him I had complete confidence in him. He said working on this Commission is so very different from some of his experiences on other League commissions. In the other cases there was so frequently jealousy and intrigue among the members of the commission, some of whom had been placed there for political reasons. It was a relief not to feel any of that in his job.

To my surprise, I found that Jimmy Lee was returning to London on the same train. I invited him to come into my stateroom, where we chatted for an hour or two before going to bed. I encouraged him to do the talking.

Thursday, February 8, 1934

Awakened by the conductor at 2:30 in the morning with a cable which had been forwarded, as Wurfbain promised, from Berlin. It was not very reassuring, but at any rate indicated that Bobby still had a fighting chance.

During much of the day on the train and on the boat, I talked with Jimmy Lee. He was not very informing, though he doubtless has had many important contacts. I could not be certain from what he said whether or not his father Ivy Lee is representing the Reich. He did know, however, that I was coming to Berlin, because he said he happened to be in Dieckhoff's office one day when there was a telephone conversation involving my name and a mention of my coming. Lee did not indicate enthusiastic approval of the regime; on the contrary, [he] was rather critical of some aspects of it. Repeatedly he tried to draw me out about my work, but I was both too tired and too preoccupied to respond.

Had a very pleasant return crossing. Reached London a little after three. Went directly to the hotel, where I found Miss Sawyer and Bentwich waiting. I dictated a brief press communiqué to the effect that I had been in Berlin, had seen some of the officials in the Foreign Office, and had laid before them some technical matters. Actually, during the time I was in Berlin I had seen no reporters at all. Lochner of the A.P. had called up while I was at the Embassy and I spoke with him, but I asked him not to comment on my presence there unless he were asked by his people. He agreed.

A brief nap, and then over to the Grosvenor House for the tea conference. I was surprised how large an attendance Miss Sawyer had managed to gather on less than twenty-four hours' notice. Those there are listed on the next page.[18]

I had my tea before the guests began to arrive, so I had an opportunity to speak, at least for a minute or two, with practically each one as he came in. This made an excellent preparation for the conference later. After tea had been served, I began to speak at about quarter of six, continuing until five minutes past six. Then there were questions and answers for another approximately twenty minutes. I gave a frank outline of what had taken place in Germany, emphasizing of course the confidential nature of what I was telling. There was the keenest interest manifested. It seemed the general impression that a really significant beginning had been made and that it ought to be followed up. One could hardly imagine a greater contrast between that meeting and the one a few days earlier at New Court.

Afterwards the committee, made up of Sir Osmond, Simon Marks, Bentwich, and Liebman, met. Sacher,[19] who was present, also sat in.

Again at this meeting, as at New Court, I found Simon Marks and Sacher sympathetic. This time some of the others who at New Court had been cold, were also much more cordial. Perhaps this was because they had had their tea, or possibly only the result of the gradual thawing out of their English reserve. At any rate, I was decidedly pleased with the conference, and felt that it was an appropriate ending of the London visit. Naturally, too I was much touched by the genuine personal interest which so many of those present showed in Bobby's condition.

. . . .

Worked until late that night clearing up odds and ends, and also because my uneasiness about conditions at home did not permit me to relax.

Friday, February 9, 1934

Was much disturbed by the article in the *London Daily Herald* about "Secret Negotiations in Berlin." Decided to write a brief note of correction, and to see the German ambassador to explain that I had rigorously kept my promise in the matter of publicity given to the Foreign Office officials. Hoetsch was friendly,

18. Given instead in this footnote: Those Present at Tea at Grosvenor House, February 8: Mr. McDonald, Mr. Bentwich, Miss Goldsmid, Miss Sawyer, Sir Leonard Cohen, Lionel Cohen, Sir Osmond d'Avigdor-Goldsmid, Rev. Dr. J. H. Hertz, Neville Laski, Frank Lazarus, The Rt. Hon. Lord Melchett, Leonard Montefiore, Anthony de Rothschild, Harry Sacher, Otto M. Schiff, Major Fred Stern, Charles Roden Buxton, Sir Charles Seligman, The Rt. Hon. Lord Noel-Buxton, Major H. Nathan, Philip Noel-Baker, Sir Isidore Salmon, Sir Andrew McFadyen, Dr. Stephen P. Duggan, Simon Marks, Philip Guedalla, Professor Gibson, Dr. Kahn, Dr. Rosen, Mr. Schweitzer, Mr. Rosenberg, Mr. Liebman, Lord Rutherford of Nelson.

19. Harry Sacher, brother-in-law of Simon Marks, journalist, Manchester Zionist, formerly a member of the Executive of the World Zionist Organization.

thought the *Herald* story was not too bad, and that it would not be serious unless someone in the party chose to use it as the basis of an attack upon the Foreign Office. He agreed that my letter of denial could do no harm and might do good. I sent him a copy.

Some hurried last-minute shopping and arranging for the Paris tickets. Meantime, I had made an engagement to speak to Ruth on the telephone at one o'clock. Felix Warburg had very thoughtfully suggested the day previous that I do this at his expense. The connection was perfect. Ruth gave me a clear account of the situation, but I was unable to carry my end of the conversation. Nonetheless, I was greatly relieved to have had the talk.

At the station we said goodbye to a number of our Jewish friends who had come down to see the Warburgs off. We were also honored by the presence in our car of Norma Talmadge and another movie star, Mr. Grant, who played with Mae West in *I'm No Angel.*

The voyage, SS *Paris,* February 9–February 15, 1934

We were a few hours late leaving Plymouth because of the large consignment of gold which was taken on board there. It was rather amusing on the tender to walk nonchalantly over the boxes of bullion.

The voyage was the longest I have ever taken. Though I had a wireless each day, it was not until next to the last day that any of these were really reassuring. Moreover, after Sunday the weather became bad, the ship pitched, and many passengers including myself were unhappy physically. The weather did not really moderate until the day we landed.

I made few acquaintances on the voyage. A little Irish child of six did more to cheer me up than anyone else. I dined with the Warburgs and chatted with them a number of times. Most of our talks, however, were about relatives or friends. We had little real serious discussion, for I was not fit for it.

Up to noon on the day of the fifteenth we could not be certain whether or not we were to land. We were met by Miss Ogden, Leland Robinson, and by Miss Sawyer's friends, the Harrises. We were off the dock promptly and out to Bronxville by half past twelve, though we had not docked until after eleven. But because it was so late, I stayed the night at the Robinsons.

Friday, February 16, 1934

As usual during recent days, I was unable to sleep after five, so up and shaved and dressed and home for breakfast. I was startled by Bobby's looks when I saw her, so frail and pitiful.

The rest of the day was spent in anxious conferences with the doctors.

Saturday, February 17, 1934

I reached the conclusion that, before we went further, we ought to call in a new doctor simply to check with the others. I called Mr. May and asked him what he would think of my calling Dr. Cohn for advice. A few minutes later Dr. Cohn called me. It happened that as he called me, Dr. Morrill was in the living room downstairs, so I talked to both of them at once. Finally, it was agreed that Morrill would call in Dr. Chickering. In the middle of the afternoon Drs. Morrill, Chickering, Voglar, and Dr. Adie, the surgeon, met here for a conference. They simply confirmed the earlier decision that there would have to be a drainage operation, and the time was set for Monday afternoon.

Joseph Hyman came out for a couple of hours. I told him something of what had taken place in London, but most of the time was spent by his giving a report of the negotiations between the Zionists and the JDC. Despite Hyman's detailed and plausible explanation as to why there had been no agreement between the two groups, I was not convinced that the fault was wholly on the Zionist side.

In reference to a possible large mass meeting at Carnegie Hall, to be participated in by all the various groups and at which I would be one of the speakers, I expressed the view that this should be preceded by a similar conference of leaders. Moreover, I explained to Hyman why I felt it might be unwise for me to participate at all in a public meeting in view of my German negotiations.

Sunday, February 18, 1934

Sunday noon Dr. Morrill and Dr. Adie came to see Bobby. They found that her temperature had risen four points in as many hours. They decided to operate at once. Within a half an hour Bobby had been moved to the hospital where x-ray pictures were taken, and they performed the operation about 4:30. Happily, it went according to schedule, lasting only about twenty minutes, and was made easier by her courageous facing of the ordeal. We were greatly relieved when it was over, but remained anxious nonetheless.

Monday, February 19, 1934

Over to the hospital in the morning and then in to the office. Conference with May and Miss Sawyer before filing a cable to Lausanne. Talks with Jerome Hess and some others, including Paul Kellogg. The latter gave me some interesting suggestions of persons who might help in securing some funds for the Socialist refugees in Paris.

Tuesday, February 20, 1934

Despite the blizzard, in to the office in time to keep an eleven o'clock appointment with Mr. Lipsky, who brought with him Mr. Silverman. They gave me in detail their account of the negotiations with the JDC. I listened attentively, asking questions on the basis of what Hyman had told me, and at the end suggested the possibility of a joint appeal on the basis of having the minimum budgets of the organizations guaranteed, with everything above those amounts to be allocated by an impartial allocation committee. Their response was that this would be satisfactory to them, except that they had to send all of their receipts to the Weizmann Committee, and, therefore, it could not be a question of allocation.

While they were present, I talked on the telephone to their colleague, Rothenberg, about his recent interview with Felix Warburg.

At the end of the conference I had the impression that there was still a possibility of a joint effort, and I told Lipsky and Rothenberg that I would see Felix Warburg that afternoon. I also told them of my plan to have a meeting of the Jewish leaders Sunday night, and asked their cooperation in making up the list of those to be asked.

They asked me whether I would speak at a meeting that they might arrange in connection with their appeal. I told them that this would, of course, depend upon dates and on the likelihood of a joint appeal, as well as the probability of my being able to avoid being brought into a situation where Germany is made the center of direct attacks. They thought the conditions I had in mind could be met.

Luncheon with David Heyman and Sam Lewisohn. Heyman outlined his idea of an appeal, stressing the importance of having a clear program and including in the appeal all of the various causes, such as the professors, doctors, etc. I questioned whether, for the sake of symmetry, his plan might not sacrifice certain advantages of a greater degree of decentralization.

As we were separating after lunch, Sam Lewisohn said, half seriously to me, "You are a much better Jew than I am." Later when I repeated this to Felix Warburg, he commented, "That's poor praise." And Mrs. Warburg, when I told her of Heyman's interest, she replied, "Yes, but he keeps a padlock on his pockets."

At quarter of five up to Warburg's house. Met Mr. Joseph Hyman at the entrance. Later we were joined by Lewis Strauss, Sir Osmond, and Mrs. Warburg. Baerwald, with whom I had talked on the telephone at noon, said he was so sorry that he could not be at the conference, but he had to go up to dine with Governor Lehman.

We first discussed the Sunday night meeting, and the ideas we had agreed upon at the office were approved, though, since it was my initiative, I more or less assumed that I would have my way. The chief discussion centered on the question of a joint appeal. I said in Hyman's presence that he had not quite convinced me the other day that failure was inevitable, and that my talk that morning with the Zionists had left me in the same frame of mind. I could see something in their point of view. There then followed for more than an hour a frank exchange of views. Everyone except Hyman felt that there was still a chance of unity, and that it ought to be striven for. I suggested again what I had suggested in the morning. There was a general feeling that this might be the basis of agreement. I said to Hyman that I was not convinced that it would be so difficult to work with the Zionists, for it seemed to me that conditions had changed materially in the last few months. Moreover, the English example, Weizmann's assent, and my attitude were all factors which made success more likely. There was general assent to this point of view. Sir Osmond said he would be glad to be of any help he could. It was left then that informally new efforts would be made with the JDC committee, and following the Sunday night meeting a more formal attempt would be made to reopen the negotiations.

I told Warburg that I would expect him to say something about the London meetings on Sunday night, and he agreed to do so.

Home late, and unable to go to the hospital because of the blizzard.

Wednesday, February 21, 1934

Worked at home during the day with Miss Sawyer. Had much more heart for it, because Bobby seemed so much better when I saw her in the morning.

Buell telephoned, and I agreed to see Butler with Fosdick and Chamberlain on Friday.

Clarence Pickett[20] called me on the telephone to discuss two, actually, three matters: (a) the work of the Friends in Paris—was it such that I could endorse? If so, such an endorsement would aid materially in securing funds for them. I said I would write gladly; (b) He told me that he was engaged in a government enterprise to place 200,000 bituminous coal miners who would never again be needed in the industry on small homesteads. This is a work in which Mrs. Franklin Roosevelt is herself much interested. He had raised with her the question whether the President might be willing to place a certain number of German refugees on such homesteads. Did I think this a desirable gesture, for it could be hardly more than that? I replied that I was sure it would be an excellent move to make. He said that he would let me know the results of further talks with Mrs. Roosevelt as to the attitude of the President; (c) A conference is to be held this Friday by a group of non-professional peace people, including Harry Fosdick, Willis (?) Abbet, Aydelotte, Evans, Talbot, and Friday, head of the Farmers' Union of North Dakota. They are to discuss the possible adverse repercussions abroad of the intensive NRA efforts to increase prosperity here at home, and to the devaluation of the dollar. The President is said to be concerned about such possible adverse reactions, as is Mrs. Roosevelt. Pickett asked me if I would write a letter which might be used preliminary to such a conference with the group which is to see the President, or possibly at the conference itself. I said I would study his suggestion and write him.

Thursday, February 22, 1934

Worked at home with Olive Sawyer.

Arranged over the telephone to have supper with Warburg and Cyrus Adler before the Sunday night meeting.

I should perhaps include here a reference to a conference which I had with Neville Laski the day I sailed from England, February 9. Laski had just had a long conference with Joseph Wirth, former Catholic German chancellor. The

20. Clarence E. Pickett, executive secretary of the American Friends Service Committee Philadelphia, 1929–1950.

latter suggested the possibility of the Jews and the Vatican working together. Laski asked me what I thought of it. I said that it was a suggestion which would have to be handled with the greatest discretion.

Laski also asked me whether he would receive a letter similar to the one which I had written to the ICA about representation on the Bureau, and I told him yes.

Friday, February 23, 1934

Conference with Herbert May and later with Dr. Ashworth.[21] With the latter, planned the meeting of the Christian Committee the following Monday.

Lunch with Professor Chamberlain at the Century Club. The talk was mostly a report of the work done in London and my trip to Berlin. He felt that that visit had been very worthwhile. We did not have time to discuss except very briefly the Washington situation. He repeated, however, that he thought the form of paper proposed at our Permanent Committee meeting would be acceptable here, but that the Swiss suggestion of using an expired passport would not have been acceptable.[22]

Mr. Landau of the JTA [Jewish Telegraphic Agency] came in the afternoon. We discussed his reply to my criticism of the JTA report that the German quota might be filled by refugees.[23] His explanation seemed to me to be wholly unsatisfactory. He reassured me, however, that in the future his people would do their utmost to avoid embarrassing the work of the High Commission.

Fosdick and I met at the Century Club for a conference with Butler. We had almost no time to compare notes before President Butler arrived, but I did say to Fosdick that I thought it would be a mistake to start our discussion as he had suggested on the basis of J. D. Schweitzer's letter; that, on the contrary, it would be much better to begin on a note of enthusiastic approval of the president's initiative in securing the funds, assuming that there would be no difficulty in having them made available. My suggestion was followed. I began by congratulating the president on his initiative in effecting the Balkan union. This led him to expiate on his program for similar unions in the Baltic and elsewhere as a possible basis for peace throughout Europe.

As to the conditional grant made by the Carnegie Corporation,[24] Butler was extremely emphatic on the following points:

21. Dr. Robert A. Ashworth, editorial secretary of the National Conference of Christians and Jews, a member of the American Christian Committee for Refugees, former editor of a Baptist publication.

22. This discussion concerned what kind of identifying documents would be acceptable to those enforcing American visa regulations.

23. That is, that German Jews who had already left the country and were applying for American immigration visas might fill the entire American annual immigration quota for Germany (25,957). That would have prevented Jews still in Germany from emigrating to the United States. This JTA report was inaccurate.

24. Carnegie Corporation, founded 1911, dedicated to the "advancement and diffusion of knowledge." Closely related to the Carnegie Foundation for the Advancement of Teaching (1905), and the Carnegie Endowment for International Peace (1910).

(1) Conditional grants of any sort are immoral, and he, as president of Columbia, had always refused to accept any such grants. Moreover, he had told both Mr. Rockefeller and Mr. Carnegie that he considered such procedure unjustifiable;
(2) He had had nothing to do with making the corporation grant conditional—quite the reverse. He had forwarded the organizations' appeal with his endorsement, and had said nothing whatsoever about the possibility of a condition being attached to the grant. His guess was that some one of the corporation trustees, desiring either to sabotage or to block the proposal, had insisted on the condition. He thought it probably that Leffingwell[25] was this trustee; his mind worked in that way, having no interest in international affairs and believing that nothing could be done except to support bond sales;
(3) So far as he was concerned, the money would be turned over immediately when it was made available, for he is quite willing that the regular budgets of the organizations be set over against the grant. Since there is not to be a meeting of his executive committee until late in April, he is prepared to dictate a draft night letter to be sent by Mr. Haskell to the Endowment trustees, securing their assent to the transfer of the funds in advance of the meeting.

Butler, Fosdick, and I naturally expressed our great appreciation of this attitude. It was then agreed that the two of us would see Keppel[26] and undertake to expedite the transmission of the funds to the Endowment. Previously, Butler had insisted repeatedly that Scott had been unable to get from Keppel any clear definition of what was meant by the corporation resolution.

When Fosdick and I walked out together, he seemed pleased with the result of the conference. He added that, of course, Schweitzer had himself been directly responsible for the corporation reservation, or so at least Keppel had said. Fosdick is dining with Keppel next Tuesday, and if the matter is not settled at that conference, Fosdick and I will see Keppel later.

Talked to Mrs. Leach on the telephone about the Matteotti Fund. She suggested that Roger Baldwin[27] would be helpful.

Saturday, February 24, 1934

Conference with Dr. Nathan and Mildred Wertheimer. First, I asked him to report to Einstein that the project to bring over children here was in the hands of a special committee headed by Dr. Lowenstein. Then Nathan reported

25. Russell C. Leffingwell, banker, lawyer, former assistant secretary of the Treasury; partner in Cravath, Henderson, Leffingwell & de Gerndorff, on the boards of J. P. Morgan and the Carnegie Foundation.

26. Frederick Paul Keppel, president of the Carnegie Corporation.

27. Roger N. Baldwin, public law consultant, director of the New York office of the American Civil Liberties Union, 1917–1950, national director of the ACLU, 1950–1955.

that Einstein had been approached in connection with the possibility of a central committee in this country, through which all matters affecting possible incoming refugees should be cleared. I replied that I thought this was probably desirable. It was left that we would call together a group in the near future to include Razovsky, Heyman, Wertheimer, and myself.

Later I learned that the Baron de Hirsch Fund[28] would be a logical group to which to apply for funds to support this enterprise.

Sunday, February 25, 1934

At five o'clock in to see Mr. Baerwald at his house. We had a long discussion about the possibilities of a united front. I left with the impression that something might be done. He is an extremely charming person.

Over to Felix Warburg's house, where I found Mr. and Mrs. Warburg and Mr. and Mrs. Cyrus Adler.

First, the two men and I talked about Laski's suggestions of negotiations in Rome. Adler had previously heard from Laski and wished to know what was back of the latter's letter. After I had explained, Adler said that he would communicate to Laski to give his approval.

Adler told me of an Italian in Philadelphia, the head of the Sons of Italy in this country, who is very close to Mussolini, who might be helpful. I suggested I should like to see this leader when I was next in Philadelphia.

At dinner at the Warburgs besides Mr. and Mrs. were only Sir Osmond, Frederick, and Albert Lasker. The Adlers had had to go off.

During dinner the subjects of conversation were varied and need not be reported. Mrs. Warburg said she would not go along to the meeting because this was the anniversary of the death of her mother.

Warburg, Sir Osmond, and I arrived at 99 Park Avenue about 8:15. I was therefore enabled to meet various persons as they came in. Miss Razovsky, Mildred Wertheimer, and Popkin[29] helped to introduce them. There were about a hundred people present. We began the meeting at about ten minutes of nine. I spoke until about 9:25, outlining very briefly the work at London, even more briefly the idea of a corporation, but more fully my trip to Berlin. I ended with a plea for unity.

Warburg spoke very well and supported my appeal for a united front. Then I called upon Sir Osmond, who made a most effective plea. Both Warburg and Sir Osmond were more than kind in their reference to me and my work.

Then I called upon a number of people for brief statements. These included Lipsky, who at the very end interjected a combative note by calling upon the JDC to withdraw their recent letter; Rothenberg, who was more conciliatory,

28. Baron de Hirsch Fund, named after Maurice de Hirsch, German-Jewish financier, founder of the Jewish Colonization Association, and supporter of the Alliance Israelite Universelle. The fund was established in 1891 to resettle eastern European Jews as agriculturists.

29. Louis Popkin, press or public relations representative for the JDC and the United Jewish Appeal.

stressed the need of not sacrificing the principle involved in Palestine; Jonah Wise and Baerwald, who pledged themselves to work for unity; Albert Lasker, who made a stirring plea for unity and effective action; Sen. Cohen of B'nai B'rith, who indicated his approval; and the sister of Albert Lasker, who spoke on behalf of Hadassah.

I judged from the comments afterwards and from the number of people who stayed to carry on personal discussions, that the meeting had been a success. Sir Osmond whispered to me as I was going out, "I have certainly done a great deal of good for you here tonight."

Home late, very tired. I arranged with Mr. Popkin that the stenotype notes were not to be inscribed without instructions from me.

Monday, February 26, 1934

Conference with members of the Canadian community, Mr. Caiserman, Lazarus Phillips, and Mr. Belkin. I tentatively agreed to go to Ottawa to confer with Bennett, the Canadian prime minister. I was to wait, however, until I had heard again from Canada before I wrote to ask for an appointment. The Canadian Jews felt that they would be able to give adequate guarantees against refugees becoming public charges.

Luncheon of the American Christian Committee. Those present included Rev. E.J. Walsh, Rev. E.G. Wilson, Rabbi Jonah Wise, Rev. E.C. Carder, Rabbi David de Sola Pool, Mr. W.W. Porter, Mr. Henry L. Caravati, Professor Paul Tillich,[30] Reinhold Niebuhr,[31] Bayard Hedrick, R.J. Zeininger, Rev. R.A. Ashworth, Rev. H.S. Leiper, J.C. Hyman, Isidor Coons, Rev. Everett R. Clinchy.

Dr. Ashworth had planned the meeting well, and a workable program was adopted, with what seems to me an adequate organization.

During the luncheon I asked Dr. Cravati and Dr. Walsh whether they had seen the reprints of Cardinal Faulhaber's addresses.[32] I asked them what they would think of reprinting these in English in this country. They thought it a good idea, and I suggested that Mildred Wertheimer might get in touch with Cravati.

Over to see Messersmith at his apartment. We talked about a number of subjects, and only towards the end did I tell him about my visit to Germany. He was much interested, particularly in the suggestion of an ordered migration with its possible quid pro quo. He has promised to find out what he can about this possibility on his return.

30. Paul Tillich, influential German-American theologian. After 1933 professor of theology at Union Theological Seminary in New York.

31. Reinhold Niebuhr, minister in the Lutheran Evangelical Church. Of German descent, influential theologian and social activist. From 1928–1960 professor of theology at the Union Theological Seminary in New York.

32. Three Advent sermons by Michael Cardinal von Faulhaber, archbishop of Munich, attacking paganism and racism and defending the Old Testament. Faulhaber, however, tried to improve relations between the Catholic Church and the Nazi regime.

To the dentist and then home.

Tuesday, February 27, 1934

Talked to Moe on the telephone about which Guggenheim Foundation it was which had been contributing to Jewish Palestinian work. I learned that it was another Guggenheim Foundation. I spoke to a Mr. Collins there. He said that they had been contributing $200 a year to each of three Jewish organizations, but that so far as their substantive contribution to refugee work was concerned, they had decided to confer with me about it. I would probably hear from Roger W. Strauss or Harry F. Guggenheim of the Daniel & Florence Guggenheim Foundation.

Mrs. Straus called me about speaking before the National Council of Jewish Women. I told her I would perhaps not be here at the time of their meeting, and they had better not count on me. I suggested Chamberlain as a speaker.

Lunched with Warburg. We discussed the possibility of a hurried trip to Palm Beach, but more in detail the method of approaching John D. Rockefeller, Jr. I reported what Fosdick had said that it was desirable for Warburg to go alone and to ask for the interview, and that Fosdick was sure that the door would be open. Warburg said that he did not want to take the initiative, that he would like to be sent for, and that when he went he wanted me to go along so that he could talk to John D., Jr., through me by referring to my work, etc., etc. I said that I understood his feeling and would see if I could arrange it so.

I then brought up the personal matter which I had discussed earlier with Rosenberg and with Warburg. He suggested that while he wanted to talk with Rosenberg first and would do so that night, he felt that the situation could best be handled by a group mostly of women, of which Mrs. Warburg would be one. Others included in this group were Mrs. Fuld[33] and Mr. Bamberger,[34] Percy Straus, Albert Lasker, Jules Bache,[35] and Mrs. Elmhirst. It was felt that James Speyer should not be included because of his possible expectation of a quid pro quo.

On our way out Warburg and I chatted for a moment with Lewis Strauss, who told me that he was writing me a letter, presumably about his underwriting.

Soon after my return to the office I called Fosdick and told him of Warburg's desire, and asked if he could not arrange it. He said no—that would be to pass the initiative to the other side of the fence. I then asked if he could not call Warburg to say what he had said to me. Fosdick replied, "No, that would be undesirable, because Warburg in talking to John D., Jr., might very well say, 'Mr. Fosdick suggested that I call you' and then the fat would be in the fire." Fosdick laughed and said, "This may seem to you very foolish, but I am really concerned

33. Caroline Bamberger Fuld, widow of Felix Fuld, Bamberger's executive and founder of the Institute for Advanced Study.

34. Louis Bamberger, Newark department store owner who, in 1929, sold his stores to Macy's.

35. Jules Semon Bache, investment banker, Bache and Company.

that the most effective method should be followed, and I am sure that it would be best for Warburg to take the initiative as I have suggested."

Conference with Kotschnig. He wished me to speak at a soirée which they are arranging for the students' work. I told him I would not be able to do so. He then asked for a letter certifying to the role which the I.S.S. is playing in the refugee work. I told him I would study the record and write him a note. He wished also a letter of introduction to a Canadian Jew, a Mr. Berliner. I told him I did not know the gentleman, but that if I met him when in Canada, I might be able to give the letter of introduction later.

Over to the meeting at the YWCA, arranged by a group of experts in immigration matters, to meet Messersmith. Messersmith's presentation of the technical problems was illuminating, as were his answers to specific questions.

Wednesday, February 28, 1934

Spoke to Warburg on the telephone, told him of Fosdick's suggestion. He replied that he would call up John D., Jr., the next day.

Conference with Roger Baldwin with reference to the Paris Socialist situation. He told me a good deal about Marley's committee, and suggested that I enlist the cooperation of Norman Thomas,[36] but added that he would be glad to do anything further that was within his power.

Wainhouse and Warren came in to inquire about what was involved in the invitation of the International Migration Service to participate in the work of the Anglo-HICEM. I explained. They also wanted to know what would be involved if they were asked to become a member of the Advisory Council. I explained that too.

Lunch at Percy Straus's with him, Ralph, and Jonah Wise. First a general discussion about the German situation and Austrian possibilities; then Jonah Wise outlined the tentative plans for a united front between JDC and APC.[37] Straus and I were of one mind on a number of points, including (a) the desirability of reducing to the minimum budgets the initial allocations to the two organizations; (b) the desirability of avoiding any appearance of organizationalism; (c) bringing into the later plans for the corporation as large a participation of non-Jewish brains and money as possible.

I was much interested in Straus's analysis of his own conversion to the necessity of international Jewish work. He referred to what I had said at Liebman's and added that it was obvious that the German crisis transcended ordinary needs and should therefore be treated as an extraordinary claim.

36. Norman Thomas, Presbyterian pastor from Marion, Ohio, who became a leading pacifist and Socialist. Thomas opposed American entry into World War I. Co-founder of the American Civil Liberties Union in 1918, six times a presidential candidate on the Socialist Party ticket, 1928–1948, and one of the founders of the America First Committee.

37. American Palestine Committee, founded by Emmanuel Neumann in 1931 in response to the Passfield White Paper of 1930, which represented a British retreat from the promises embodied in the Balfour Declaration of 1917. Neumann, Latvian-born, became also an official of the Zionist Organization of America.

I asked him about Ivy Lee. He replied that Lee had not only denied most staunchly receiving a fee from the German government, but had insisted that his relations with the German chemical industry had enabled him to carry on a most useful propaganda with the German government.

As I was leaving, we ran into Beardsley Rummel, whom Straus introduced to me as the new treasurer of Macy's.

Telephoned to Chamberlain in the afternoon to ask him how soon he could get to Europe for a meeting of the Governing Body. He thought that he could not leave until the third week in May. I asked him what he would think of Fosdick going as his alternate. He thought it preferable to ask the government to name Fosdick as the regular representative, and then permitting him, Chamberlain, to go from time to time as alternate. This, I said, seemed to me very doubtful, and that I was unwilling to urge it without having thought about it a great deal. Long cable to the office suggesting dates for Advisory and Governing Board meetings.

11. March 1934: Raising Funds

New York, Thursday, March 1, 1934

Mrs. Lazarus called. She is returning on the *Berengaria* the twenty-first. She suggested that she might ask me to meet Herbert Fleishhacker[1] while he is here. I told her how much joy Bobby was getting from her present.

Rabbi Jung[2] came in to plead the cause of the Agudas. I told him that I would discuss the matter again with Bentwich. I was impressed by his statement.

Lord Marley came in. He told me about his tour here from coast to coast, and of the purpose to which the funds raised were to be applied. This statement followed the same lines as those indicated in the letter of February 27 from Wagenknecht to Roger Baldwin, which the latter turned over to me a few days ago.

I put up to Marley the question of his contributing to the Matteotti Fund. After some discussion he suggested an immediate draft of a thousand dollars, then he modified that by proposing to make it conditional on twice that amount being raised by the trade unions here and in England. Urged him to make it unconditional, and he seemed inclined to do so after he had conferred with his committee.

We then talked about Biro-Bidjan, a project which he defended as ardently as ever. He asked whether I expected him to be at the next meeting of the Advisory Council and Governing Body. I told him that I hoped he would there urge the Biro-Bidjan program and the claims of ORT and OZE [*sic,* OSE].

Speaking of Palestine, he asked whether it would be desirable to have questions raised in the House of Lords with a view to supporting a more liberal program of the Mandatory Power. I told him that I thought this would have to be handled very carefully, and I hesitated to make any suggestions.

Marley is planning to return for another tour next fall. He indicated that he had raised on this tour about $25,000 for his various projects.

Lunch at the *Times* with Mr. May. Present there were Finley, James, Sulzberger, and Ogden. Early in the discussion the name of Streit came up. James rather savagely accused Streit of being the mouthpiece for the Secretariat. I vigorously defended Streit as the most intelligent and hardest working journalist in Geneva, and one of the very best in the world.

Sulzberger asked me to outline my work, and I did along the general lines

1. Herbert Fleishhacker, president of the Anglo-California National Bank in San Francisco. Philanthropist and civic leader.

2. Rabbi Leo Jung, leader of Agudath Israel and its Youth Council. Active in obtaining visas for Orthodox Jewish emigrants.

that I had presented on a number of occasions before. They were much interested.

Back to the office. Interview with Livingston of the A.P.

Friday, March 2, 1934

Talked on the telephone with Mr. Felix Warburg. He asked me if we had received a letter from Mrs. Warburg, which he had sent to the house in Bronxville. I thanked him for it in advance, without knowing its contents.

I asked him how the interview with John D. Rockefeller, Jr., went. He said that the latter had been very cordial and spoke enthusiastically about the work, expressing interest in it but not committing himself as to an amount. He was to consult Fosdick before acting. Warburg expects anything from $10,000 to $25,000.

Warburg asked me to communicate with him at any time through Miss Emanuel.

Conference at Norman Thomas's house. Present besides Thomas and myself, Lord Marley and two of the trade union officials. There was much discussion, first about the famous Madison Square Garden meeting which had been broken up by the Communists, thus ending all hope of a united front between the Socialists and the Communists on behalf of refugees.[3]

Then I had a chance to explain the needs of the Paris and Prague committees. Thomas said that some money had been raised at a recent meeting addressed by one of the German leaders, and perhaps some of that money would be available. He suggested that I write to Vladeck, setting forth the need. This I did on my return to the office.

Meantime, Marley said that he had asked his Paris committee to consider the possibility of appropriating $1,000 for the immediate needs of the Matteotti Fund in Paris.

Lunch with John D. III. He was much interested in my work; indeed, he seemed to have a somewhat different attitude towards me personally since I had become the High Commissioner and was, therefore, no longer in a position of such evident dependence upon the generosity of persons like his father. He really seemed to be considerably impressed by my account of my experiences in Germany. I asked him if he knew young Sherrill, and he said that Nelson knew him well, had been on a cruise with Dr. Grenfell and Sherrill. Nelson was inclined to be critical. John asked about the members of the family and expressed great concern about Bobby.

Conference with Ashworth about the work of his committee.

Conference with the Jewish press. Those present included Parsky of the *Day,* Bernard Shelvin of the *Jewish Morning Journal,* Allen W. Levy of the *American Hebrew and Jewish Tribune,* Bernstein of the *Jewish Daily Bulletin,* Postal of *Seven Arts Syndicate,* Mr. Tarsky (connected with the *Jewish Daily For-*

3. According to the *New York Times,* on February 16, 1934, some twenty thousand people attended a rally organized by Socialists and trade unionists to "protest the slaughter of Austrian workers by the Dollfuss regime." Five thousand Communists invaded the arena, and there was much violence between the two sides. Twenty people were injured.

ward), and representatives of the *Brooklyn Examiner, Opinion,* and the *Jewish Daily Forward,* and Herbert May.

I talked confidentially to them about a number of matters, but had very little to say for publication. As usual, the question of my relations to Palestine came up. I stressed the fact that there was no conflict of view between me and the British government—and the disadvantage of Jewish journalists striving constantly to find news in a possible difference of view.

Saturday, March 3, 1934

Conference with Razovsky, Hyman, Chamberlain, Miss Wertheimer, and Miss Sawyer in reference to organization of a more effective coordinating committee to handle questions related to refugees coming to this country. It was agreed that it was desirable to set up such a body, and that Professor Chamberlain and I should join in issuing invitations to a conference to consider the proposal.

....

Washington, Monday, March 5, 1934

On arrival, went to the Cosmos Club,[4] where there was no room. They finally secured a room in one of the smaller hotels, but by that time Mrs. Moorhead had said she would be glad to put me up, so I stayed with her.

Then over to the FPA office. I met Stone coming out. He said, "I don't know whether you will be very comfortable in the office, we are so crowded." Mrs. Moorhead had said something of the same thing on the telephone. Miss Sawyer had warned me to the same effect, but the cumulative influence of three warnings didn't faze me. I had very little that had to be done in the office, and I saw no reason why I shouldn't steal Miss Goetz for as much as that. Certainly, she was glad to help, and in actual practice there was no difficulty.

At eleven o'clock over to see Mr. William Phillips at the State Department. I was kept waiting for some time while he listened to the President's speech to the NRA code conference. I profited from my wait by visiting with the two girls in the outer office.

Phillips was most cordial. I talked first about my anxiety to have Fosdick urged to go as Chamberlain's alternate to the meeting of the Governing Body. Phillips at first queried whether someone from one of the embassies or consulates in Europe might not serve the purpose. I replied emphatically that there were two reasons we hoped they would ask Mr. Fosdick: first, sending someone from this side would be an earnest show of the government's real interest; second, Fosdick is technically competent, has had a long experience in the general field in which this problem falls. Moreover, Fosdick on his return would, because the Jews here have confidence in him, help to serve, as does Chamberlain, as a shock absorber for the administration.

4. Founded in 1878 by John Wesley Powell as a club for explorers, scientists, and intellectuals. Became a social center for the Washington elite, especially public policy intellectuals.

Phillips at once admitted that he was convinced and said that he would invite Fosdick. He added that he was not sure about the financial arrangements but hoped they might be able to pay the minimum ocean fare. I said I thought this would be sufficient, that Fosdick would not insist on the whole of his expenses being covered.

I then outlined to Phillips the general nature of what we had so far undertaken. In particular, I gave him a fuller account of my visit to Germany.

There followed a discussion of the present immigration situation here, but it was only from Carr that I was to receive later a fuller statement of the State Department's views.[5]

Phillips asked me about the general state of Europe. I told him that I had really little to say, because of my absorption in my own job. However, I did talk for a little while of my impression of conditions in Germany and in Austria.

As I was leaving, I said that so far as a possible interview with the President was concerned, I would leave that to him, Phillips. I suggested that he communicate with the Executive Offices to let them know that I was in the country, and would be available if the President cared to see me. Phillips said he would do this.[6]

Lunch with Moffat at the Cosmos Club. He was my guest.[7]

We covered very much the same ground as I had already covered with Phillips. He approved of the Fosdick suggestion, adding that I should stress the importance of it with Carr so that the latter might simplify the financial arrangements.

I told Moffat, as I had Phillips, of Chamberlain's and my plan to organize in New York a central clearing house for problems concerning incoming refugees. He, like Phillips, thought this would be excellent.[8]

5. Carr's views on immigration were expressed previously in his summary of a conversation with Joseph Chamberlain, American representative on the High Commission: "He thinks there will be a great drive for placing over 200,000 Jews who are probably to be driven out of Germany. . . . Europe thinks they should, many of them, come here. . . . I fear a general onslaught on our restrictive immigration laws. So there seems trouble ahead." Carr Diary, January 5, 1934, Library of Congress.

6. Phillips wrote in his diary about McDonald: "So far I gathered he has not accomplished much. He gave me an interesting insight into the various Jewish parties of this country. . . ." Phillips Papers, Box 2, Diary of March 5, 1934, call number bMS Am 2232, Houghton Library, Harvard University. By permission of the Houghton Library, Harvard University.

7. Moffat wrote: "Lunched with James G. McDonald, the High Commissioner for Refugees, and reluctantly reached the conclusion that in spite of high sounding titles, much traveling back and forth, the actual accomplishments to date of the High Commission were perilously close to nil. The drive for funds has not been commenced, repatriation has not begun, etc. etc." Moffat Journal of March 5, 1934, vol. 34, Moffat Papers, call number MS Am 1407, Houghton Library, Harvard University. By permission of the Houghton Library, Harvard University.

8. McDonald talked to Moffat about a more active cooperation on refugee issues. Moffat sent a query to R. Walton Moore (assistant secretary of state, 1933–1937, fellow congressman and close friend of Cordell Hull), who replied that the United States could not be a party to any intergovernmental agreement, because (1) it wanted to avoid limiting its powers regarding admission or expulsion of aliens; (2) it issued no documents for travel abroad except permits of reentry; and (3) there would be problems in the fields of workmen's compensation, welfare aid, etc., where state and local laws apply. The humanitarian aspect of the problem, Moore thought, was already "handsomely served by our laws which do not discriminate against refugees, or stateless persons as such." Moore to Moffat, March 16, 1934, National Archives, Record Group 59, Central Decimal File, 548.F 1/6.

I asked him about a successor to Messersmith. He replied that the most serious consideration was being given to finding the best possible man.[9]

We discussed the political situation abroad. He seems to feel that the Nazis will permeate the Heimwehr, and that the fascism of Austria will be more German than Italian. Phillips earlier had said to me categorically that if this change were effected within Austria without the obvious interference from the outside, there was nothing that Italy could do about it.

Over to the German Embassy to see Dr. Luther. He was cordial but cautious. I gave him a report in detail of my German visit, and of the publicity attending it at the end. I expressed my real appreciation of the splendidly accurate and detailed report which he had sent to Berlin of my previous conference with him.

We then discussed general conditions in Europe. During the course of this talk, I took occasion again to underline the great interest of our government in the refugee problem. I left him with the impression that I might be expected to pass through Germany in April on my way to Poland and Czechoslovakia, and that while in Berlin I would welcome an opportunity to resume the talks which I had begun on February 7.

Dinner at home with Mrs. Moorhead, and afterwards to the movie *Carolina.*

Tuesday, March 6, 1934

Over to the Canadian Legation to see Mr. Wrong, the counselor. Told him what I would like to see Bennett[10] about. He said that he would communicate himself with Ottawa and that it would be well if I wrote also. We then gossiped in friendly fashion about a number of unrelated subjects.

Conferred with Mr. Ralph W. Close, new minister from South Africa. I went over the various documents with him, left him one set, and promised to send him another. He questioned whether membership on the Governing Body could result in placing moral obligation upon a country to accept a policy which it might disagree with. I assured him that there was no such possibility, but he, being a lawyer and not seeing any such guarantee in the Statutes, remained skeptical. I pointed to the fact that since the United States had joined the Governing Body without reservations, it would be safe for anyone else to do likewise. I emphasized that the presence of a South African representative would help very much by giving the African point of view and that the moral effect of the U.S.A.'s cooperation would be felt by all the governments concerned. It was agreed that I was to write to the minister expressing these views and sending him copies of the material, which he would forward to his government. The informal response would be sent through his government's representative in Lon-

9. Douglas Jenkins succeeded Messersmith.
10. Richard Bedford Bennett, Canadian prime minister.

don. I agreed to ask Mr. Moffat to send him a copy of the U.S. letter of acceptance of the League invitation.

Lunch at the French Embassy. Present besides the ambassador and his wife and myself were Messrs. Henry, Sauerwein, and a French commandant. Most of the discussion was about conditions here. Mrs. Laboulaye struck me as brilliant; her husband as intelligent and charming. Their son was also present, and reported that he had had a successful one-man show of his pictures in Paris.

Conference with Pickett at the office of the subsistence homesteads. We talked first about possible money from the Quakers for relief. He suggested the possibility of the Philadelphia group sending me a list of three or four thousand names which I might circularize over my own name in an appeal for funds. Earlier, I had seen Frederick Libby, who was very pessimistic about the state of the Friends' purse. Pickett was a little more optimistic.

Pickett said that he had discussed further with Mrs. Roosevelt the possibility of placing some of the refugees on subsistence homesteads here. She said that she hoped that the President would talk with him and me about it. Pickett then undertook to arrange the appointment. Two days later he reported to me that the word from the White House was that the President was terribly crowded just then, and he wondered when I was sailing.

Then I went over to the Turkish Embassy. I covered with the ambassador much the same ground as I had gone over with the minister from South Africa. But, he being a Turk and not a lawyer, was much less inquisitive, promising to pass on the data without asking any questions. I suggested that the reply might be made available to me either in London or in Paris.

Up to Justice Brandeis's house at 6:30. He was much more cordial than on any previous occasion. He asked me to tell him of our work. I outlined what we had undertaken and our plans for the future. I told him of the trip to Germany; he seemed to think this a hopeful beginning. In particular, he is interested in the possibility of evacuating the younger people on the basis I had suggested to von Neurath. As to financing this project, he thought that I was not ambitious enough in my hopes to take only half a million from a person like Ittleson. I should ask him for at least five million, and a million from Felix Warburg. I told the justice of my endeavors to get in touch with Frankfurter and expressed the hope that I might see the latter at Oxford on my next trip to London.

Out to Stone's to dinner. Others there besides Stone and his wife and I were the Canams, the Reiflers, and Mrs. May. Aside from the talk about my work most of the evening was given over to Reifler's explanation of the development of the NRA.

Wednesday, March 7, 1934

Long conference with Wilbur Carr. I found him much more cordial and liberal than I had expected. He was enthusiastic about Fosdick, and seemed to think that the financial arrangements could be made. We then discussed the immigration situation. He did not seem to me to be nearly so exclusionist as his critics say he is. He is concerned, however, lest unwarranted expectations or demands by the Jewish groups should strengthen the exclusionist tendency, and make more likely the passage of the restrictionist bills now pending before the Dickstein committee in the House of Representatives. He evidenced keen interest in our work and, I think, can be counted upon the help wherever practicable.[11]

. . . .

Conference at noon with the Yugoslav minister, which followed the lines of my talks previously with the Turkish ambassador and the South African minister.

Lunch at the Italian Embassy, alone with Rosso.[12] We had a delightful visit.

At three o'clock brief conference with the Persian minister. He seemed to know very little about what might be expected from his government [in the way of supporting refugees], said that he would like to have a list of the doctors and the scientific people available to go to Persia, and under what conditions. He would then forward this to his government for their decision. He seemed to feel that during the first two years, or what he called "the trial period," the men would receive little more than their sustenance, and that actual salaries would be fixed on the basis of experience. I promised to try to find out what was being done by other groups in reference to Persia, and to communicate with the minister.

. . . .

Dinner with Colonel and Mrs. MacCormack at their apartment. During the meal we chatted about many different sorts of things. Afterwards, the talk was all about refugees and the immigration questions, MacCormack outlined his plan for modification of the immigration law, and also his plan for the issuance of regulations in reference to labor bonds. He is unwilling to begin with this latter, however, until Judge Mack and those working on the question make a recommendation of the number of refugees to be admitted. Even then, of course, the regulations might not be publicly announced, as, of course, the suggested figure of admissions would not be announced.

Thursday, March 8, 1934

. . . .

Conference with the Brazilian minister. I simply explained that there would be no commitment involved in Brazil's acceptance to the Governing Body, and that I hoped that possibly the government might reconsider its earlier decision.

11. McDonald was generous or mistaken in his assessment of Carr. See note 5. Also Richard Breitman and Alan M. Kraut, *American Refugee Policy and European Jewry, 1933–1945* (Bloomington: Indiana University Press, 1978), 32–36.

12. Augusto Rosso, Italian ambassador to the United States.

. . . .

Over to see James Brown Scott.[13] Was with him for nearly forty-five minutes. He outlined at length his conception of a moral law of nations, his point of view about the controversy between the corporation and the foundation, and what the FPA should do to improve its chances of receiving the funds voted.

Back to New York on the *Congressional.* While I was buying the paper in Union Station, James Farley came up to me and spoke about our experiences on the *Manhattan.*

Friday, March 9, 1934

Talked to Hyman about a number of matters. Then called Fosdick. He had already heard from Phillips. I urged him strongly to accept. I got the impression that he would probably do so. We then talked about my interview with James Brown Scott. He suggested that I get in touch with both Keppel and Haskell, and I said that I would. It was agreed that we would talk again on Monday about his acceptance.

Mr. Moore of Ardmore, Pennsylvania, came in at the suggestion of Michael Francis Doyle.[14] He impressed me as a man who might be able to raise funds.

Conference with Ashworth before the luncheon meeting called by the Christian Committee. The response at the Bankers' Club seemed to me very discouraging. In the discussion Mr. Taft raised a number of relatively unimportant questions and took much time. Others seemed interested, but nobody committed himself to a definite task. Indeed, only three of the persons there could possibly be very helpful in financial matters.

Up to Mr. Packard's[15] office. He had before him an appeal from Kotschnig. He did not wish so much to have my opinion of that particular appeal as to have a general statement on the whole financial situation of the refugee problem, and any suggestion if I had one as to how Mr. Rockefeller might view the matter as a whole. This interest on his part was not a reflection of a request by Mr. Rockefeller, but purely his own preliminary inquiry. It, therefore, was not as encouraging as it would have been had it come directly from John D., Jr.

Over to the meeting called by Professor Chamberlain and me. Before the meeting began, I compared notes with Rothenberg and Hyman. They showed me the draft of the release which they had planned for Monday. It seemed satisfactory to me. I agreed to issue a statement at the same time.

Professor Chamberlain presided at the meeting, which resulted in the naming of a sub-committee to organize the new cooperative agency here. It will, I think, be a hopeful result.

13. Dean of law schools (University of Southern California and Illinois). Secretary of the Carnegie Endowment, 1910–1940.

14. Michael Francis Doyle, international lawyer.

15. Arthur W. Packard, head of Rockefeller's Davison Foundation.

Saturday, March 10, 1934

Conference with Mr. Moore of Ardmore. He arranged to send the Faulhaber material to the Paulist Press. They were to communicate with him as to whether or not the material would be accepted for publication. He was to keep in touch with Ashworth as to the possibility of his being used on the financial end by the American Christian Committee.

....

Several times during the morning Hyman, Rothenberg, and Popkin called in reference to detailed questions of phrasing in my statement. One suggestion which was eliminated was that of Rothenberg, supported by Popkin, that I change the phrase "fellow-religionists" to "fellow Jews." This I did.

Spoke to Carlin about the possibility of a good spot before I returned. He said he would let me know early next week. He finally suggested late Tuesday night, March 20, when I was to be on the train from Canada to Boston. It was therefore impossible for me.

A Mr. W. B. Cohen called in reference to the Persian government's offer to take refugees. I think he knows little that is new.

Lunched with E. A. Filene at the Commodore. Talk about this and that but no real opportunity to get down to brass tacks about the possibility of his helping in the refugee work. He seemed to me very tired and older—not surprising in view of the fact that he had just returned from a six weeks' one-night stand tour of the country. Miss Schoedler, as always, was helpful. Met Clark for a moment, but had no chance to talk.

Sunday, March 11, 1934

Ruth and I went to dinner at the Liebmans. He told me of his interviews with Heineman in Brussels (?), Baron Robert, and others re the corporation plan. He felt that Heineman was favorable, but naturally the latter had not formally committed himself. He stressed the importance of pressing forward so that I would be able to take something definite back to London. It was clear that he and Rosenberg had reached something of an impasse.

Monday, March 12, 1934

Long conference on the telephone with Hyman about plans for the opening meeting of the joint drive.[16] I promised to do what I could to secure Cadman or Harry Fosdick.

Talked with Rothenberg, and asked him if he had noticed the use of the phrase "fellow Jews" in my release. He was pleased with it. We compared notes

16. Joint drive, officially the German Jewish Relief Fund of the United Jewish Appeal. Launched by McDonald on March 23, supported by the JDC and the American-Palestine Campaign of the Jewish Agency. Felix Warburg served as chairman. Its goal was $3 million for refugees. Eventually morphed into the United Jewish Appeal (1939).

about methods of securing better publicity, particularly the possibility of a fuller account in the *Times* next Sunday.

Agreed at Tyson's and Rich's request to open the broadcast program on the Wallace pamphlet.

Talked to Raymond Fosdick. He is still uncertain about accepting the invitation to attend the Governing Body, but seems inclined to do so. I emphasized that from my point of view this appointment had nothing to do with Mr. Rockefeller, and again underlined the reasons which seemed to be compelling. He promised to let me know soon.

We also talked about the Carnegie matter. He suggested that I get in touch with Keppel myself. I agreed to do so, and said I would also see Haskell. Called Keppel and made a date for the next week, but cleared with him about my seeing Haskell.

....

Lunched with Buell. Talked mostly about the work of the High Commission.

In the middle of the day James Rosenberg called from a conference where Hyman and Rothenberg were present. During this interview we decided not to accept the Hadassah invitation, nor that of the National Council, to accept the Kaplan invitation in Boston, and for a private meeting at Rosenberg's and the public meeting here in New York of the joint group on the twenty-second.

Interview in the afternoon with Mr. Kaufman of the radio page of the *Sun.*

Hugh Moore, financial secretary of the Friends' Service Committee, came in. After further conferences the Friends had decided to use their general list to attempt to secure funds to keep their Foreign Service Organization intact, but they were willing to let me have the short list of difficult rich prospects. I said I would consider circularizing these. So far as the Paris organization is concerned, he said that if money were voted to the Friends with the understanding that suggestions from me would be made as to their disbursement, my advice would be accepted.

On this date Ambassador William Dodd, in a formal meeting with Hitler, raised the subject of McDonald's mission. "I said to him [Hitler]: 'You know there is a Jewish problem in other countries, and the State Department is lending assistance towards the solution of the problem by unofficial encouragement to an organization which James MacDonald [sic] *is setting up in Lausanne.' He [Hitler] seemed not to be acquainted with this fact, and I then described MacDonald's plans[,] as I happened to know that he had given them to von Neurath some three weeks ago. I had been informed that von Neurath had approved MacDonald's work in an entirely unofficial way. I then added that MacDonald had at his command some millions of dollars which were to be spent mostly in Germany to assist Jews to leave the country without too much suffering, and that he hoped that over a period of eight or ten years the problem might be solved in a humane way. The Chancellor then came back that nothing could come of such a movement, no matter how much money were put into it; that the Jews in Germany and outside would use the organization to attack Germany and to make endless trouble."*[17]

Tuesday, March 13, 1934

(The above conference with Moore took place this morning.)

. . . .

Lunched with Rosenberg. Chatted for a moment with Proskauer during lunch. Rosenberg talked first a good deal about the need for reform of the law in reference to bankruptcy reorganization and his part in that effort. Then he warned me about certain Jewish personalities, emphasizing particularly the danger from Weizmann (how naive Rosenberg is! He never assumes that anyone else has discovered anything before he personally has found it out).

Most of his talk, however, was about the danger of following Liebman's suggestion of setting up a committee on the corporation project unless other substantial funds comparable to Warburg's were available, or until further investigations of possible colonization programs had been made. He still favored a special fund of $100,000 from a few individuals to be used to make this investigation. This he thought, rather than an American committee on the Liebman lines, would be better for me to take back to London. I told him that I saw nothing irreconcilable between the essence of his program and that of Liebman, and that I wanted him and Liebman to thrash the thing out further.

Talked to Feilchenfeld, and agreed to speak to the American consul general in London about his brother's immigrant visa.

Talked with Murrow, who said that the memorandum about the professors would be ready soon.

Brief conference with Popkin.

Tea with Mrs. Kahn. She expressed great concern about Bobby. I could not, however, get any indication from her of her attitude on the question of refugees.

Over to dinner at Mrs. Rosenthal's, where Ruth and I were to spend the night. Among those there were the Sulzbergers, the McBains, the young Untermyers, the Rossbachs, Mrs. Rosenthal's cousin, an art dealer from Munich, and no others.

During the evening I had a chance to speak to Sulzberger about publicity on the joint drive. Also chatted with Mrs. Sulzberger about Lincoln School. Mrs Rosenthal's cousin suggested that outside funds be used to establish a mortgage bank in Germany through which German Jews could transfer portions of their capital abroad.

17. Dodd to secretary of state, March 7, 1934, National Archives and Records Administration, Record Group 59, Central Decimal File, 711.62/90.

Wednesday, March 14, 1934

Conference with Dr. Coffin. He expressed willingness to help where he could. Said he would be willing to be used as a backstop with Harkness, and suggested that I see Aldrich.

Lunched with Professor Hayes[18] at the faculty club. Hayes suggested Sheed and Ward, 63 Fifth Avenue, as possible publishers for the Faulhaber sermons. Hubert Howard is the general manager there (son of Sir Esne) and is especially interested in Germany because of his residence there.

Over to see Dr. Fosdick. He surprised me by indicating that he had never realized that others than Jews were involved in the refugee problem, and furthermore by permitting me to see that he felt no responsibility to aid the Jewish refugees other than by moral protests against the Nazi action. Indeed, he spoke in a rather deprecatory manner of "Felix Warburg trotting over to see Mr. Rockefeller about Jewish matters." I got a little feeling that in this attitude he was reflecting the point of view of his brother. This only illustrates how deep rooted and widespread is one or another form of anti-Semitism.

However, when I had explained the situation of the non-Jewish refugees, Dr. Fosdick took fire and indicated his strong desire to do whatever he could to help. He did not feel, however, that he could approach Mr. Rockefeller. He suggested that I go back again to Raymond, explaining the Christian stake in the problem. He said he would be glad to urge his brother to go to London.

Over to see Haskell. After we had chatted for a little while, he suggested that a letter be written [to] him promptly signed by representatives of the three organizations, stating that they had met the conditions of the corporation grant, and expressing the hope that the money would promptly be made available. I thanked him for his suggestion, and said that the letter would be prepared within the two days he named.

FPA Board meeting in the evening.

Thursday, March 15, 1934

Spoke to Mr. Ely on the telephone, agreeing to speak at the Town Hall on the night of March 23, on the subject "The European Scene."

Talked one after the other to Liebman and Rosenberg. Sensed a growing estrangement because of differences of view as to the next step on the corporation project. Tried to act as intermediary.

Up to see Aldrich at Harkness's office.[19] We chatted for a little while about ocean travel, kinds of steamers, etc. Then I explained the nature of our work, stressing the non-Jewish side of it. He seemed interested but said that obviously we could do nothing until Mr. Harkness had returned in a month or six weeks. Suggested that I send him a memorandum of the points covered, two or three

18. Carleton J. H. Hayes, European historian, Columbia University.

19. Edward H. Harkness, railroad financier, heir to one of the country's largest fortunes. His father was one of Rockefeller's partners in Standard Oil. Known primarily as a philanthropist. At his death was said to have given away from one hundred to several hundreds of millions of dollars.

pages. This he would take up with Mr. Harkness on the latter's return. I left with the impression that there was at least a fair chance that the latter might contribute towards the funds of the American Christian Committee.

Lunch with James Speyer. He annoyed me by inviting his partner Lindsay to join us. The latter is a nice fellow, but his presence obviously made any talk of finance much more difficult. Moreover, Speyer is in some aspects very crude, talking as he did during all the time we were ordering the meal about the cost of each dish and trying to be funny on the score of the expense of the order. His sense of humor would do little credit to a Second Avenue pushcart man.

Speyer is stirred by the German situation, but I think he will have to be dynamited if he is to be induced to give anything in a large way.

Long conference with Bernard Flexner. I told him of the differences between Rosenberg and Liebman, the former's feeling that the latter was more interested in getting the appearance of a committee than having a really substantial group. I reported, too, Rosenberg's intense interest in Trans-Jordania, and in the plan of Emmanuel Neumann in reference to that area.

Flexner then explained his own idea that there should be a group of trustees named at once with power to carry on a specific project as soon as it is approved, meantime organizing the basis of the corporation. He was delighted with my suggestions of Percy Straus and Albert Lasker as new names for such a group. Ittleson, of course, would also be logical there. I told Flexner that I thought he ought to get in touch with Rosenberg. He said he would prefer that the latter call him. So I called Rosenberg, suggested that he get in touch with Flexner.

Over to see Lewis Strauss. As usual, he was most cooperative. Said he would be glad to serve in any way he could. It was left that I would get in touch with him if it were desirable for him to take the initiative in calling Liebman, Rosenberg, and Flexner together. In any case, I felt that I should be left out of that particular conference. He assented.

Over to Colonel House's. Long conference about this and that. He is growing somewhat more inclined to reminisce about his role in the pre-1919 days. However, he still seems interested in the international situation and in my work. He asked especially that I get in touch with him again before I sail. He could, I think, still be useful with the President. He is very close to the latter's mother. And has, according to his own account, an entrée to the White House whenever he chooses to use it.

Drove with Britt Baird to open the broadcast program on the Wallace pamphlet.[20] Hard was excellent, but Wilson was difficult to follow and related his material very slightly to the Wallace pamphlet.

I perhaps should insert here that at the conference the other day with Dr. Fosdick I asked him if he would go on Kotschnig's sponsoring group. He said he

20. Wallace pamphlet, *America Must Choose,* by Secretary of Agriculture Henry Wallace (1934). Called for a middle path on tariff policy, between internationalism and protectionism.

would if I asked him. I later called up Mrs. Kotschnig and left word for her at Murrow's office to that effect.

Dr. Fosdick asked me also about Marley's committee against fascism. I told him I thought, unlike the Kotschnig suggestion, he had better not accept. But when he wished to put his refusal on the ground that he was working with me in other ways, I urged him to find a better reason, because I had to continue to deal with Marley.

Friday, March 16, 1934

Rosenberg called to say that he had had a long talk with Bernard Flexner, and he thought they were in agreement on the essential principle that it was desirable to name a group of trustees, but only if it could be made to include men like Straus, Lasker, Ittleson, Guggenheim, et al.; that if Liebman thought he could arrange it on that basis, he, Rosenberg, would attend a small conference and strongly urge that it be done.

Talked to Liebman; told him that I thought it was best that he and Rosenberg and Flexner and perhaps Lewis Strauss get together to reach an agreement, and that I not be included in such a conference.

Joseph Hyman called. Said that he thought that Mr. Hirsch, who had written me, was an irresponsible person.

Talked to Raymond Fosdick on the telephone. He said that he had already written to the secretary of state accepting the invitation to attend our Governing Body meeting. I told him I was delighted. As to Mr. Rockefeller, he thought the latter would write to Felix Warburg expressing sympathy, but at the moment not making contribution. I said that I thought it would do more harm than good if Mr. Rockefeller gave a small contribution to the joint Jewish effort, that if he gave less than $25,000 it would be more useful to give it to the American Christian Committee. To this Fosdick replied, "If Rockefeller did anything it would be as a token, indicating his disapproval of the Nazi program. He would not be interested to help merely the few Christians involved."

Lunch with Judge Mack. He gave me the address of his daughter in Vienna, and I said that I would look her up.

He favored taking as many Jews out of Germany as possible, and, therefore, approved the corporation idea, provided it was not used against Palestine. In this connection, speaking of Weizmann, he said, "Everyone sooner or later finds Dr. Weizmann out. It's too bad, because he is in some respects a truly great man." As to the meeting on Thursday night at which the judge is to preside, he said he did not intend to make a speech, so there was no occasion for my pressing the point that work outside as well as in Palestine should be stressed.

Chatted with Russell Leffingwell at his office about the state office of Europe and the NRA, the Carnegie Corporation, and the Endowment. Nothing of importance to be reported, except that everything in reference to the [Carnegie] Corporation would be decided by Fred Keppel.

Chat with Thomas Lamont. He expressed much concern about Bobby, and we talked about his new granddaughter and a little about my work. He was unwarrantedly laudatory and perhaps not wholly sincere in his comments on my part in the enterprise.

Met Emmanuel Neumann downstairs in the Morgan office. We talked a little about Trans-Jordania, reasons for Weizmann's opposition, the attitude of the British government, etc. He may get in touch with me late in April in London. I was favorably impressed with him.

Meeting of the American Christian Committee at the Federal Council offices. Father Walsh was made chairman. As usual, Ashworth had the meeting well planned. I was favorably impressed with the statements of both Pierce and Hedrick and Tamblyn and Brown. I had to leave before the committee made its decision, but before I left to meet my brother at the Pennsylvania Station, I urged that they go ahead.

Evening at home.

Saturday, March 17, 1934

Pickett came in to say that now that Mrs. Roosevelt is home, he probably could arrange for an interview with the President on the subsistence homestead proposal. I told him that I did not think in view of my heavy schedule next week, I had better try to go to Washington before I sailed. He then suggested that I write him a letter to his office in Washington, outlining the possibility of some of the refugees being available for homesteading here.

We chatted also about the cooperation of the Friends. He was surprised that the list Moore had promised me had not arrived.

Lunch with Bob Straus. He was very much interested in my story of my visit to Berlin. We talked also about his work with the NRA. He seems now to be a special assistant to General Johnson here in New York.

Sunday, March 18, 1934

Rosenberg called for me at three o'clock, to go into the meeting at his house. On the way, in his usual fashion, he "lectured" me on what I should say. In particular, he wished me to avoid having anything of the attitude of a suppliant for funds. On the contrary, I should stress that I was merely giving to the Jews an opportunity to make our international institution function effectively. Then we discussed his program about Trans-Jordania. I explained why I thought it would be a mistake to put this forward as a substitute for the corporation idea. He, however, remained insistent that Liebman's plan for a committee was worse than useless unless he secured the cooperation of a group of men who could match Mr. Warburg in the seriousness of his intentions. I agreed with this, but argued that every effort should be made to secure such a group. Rosenberg came back again to his Palestine theory, saying that he had thought it through very carefully and it was not likely that, having made up his mind, Liebman or I would be able to dissuade him. I did not press the matter further.

Arriving at his house, I had a brief opportunity to plan out what I was to say. The group numbered about thirty-five or forty. It included Jimmie Speyer, Percy Straus, Mr. Halley (the man who financed the School in Exile), Mr. Vogel, David Brown, Governor Lehman (who came in a little late), Rothenberg, Mrs. Elkus, Mr. and Mrs. Baerwald, and other officials of the JDC and the American Palestine Campaign.

In my talk I assumed that it was a family party, and spoke with direct brutality about the failure of more of the Jewish leaders to offer their cooperation. And in particular, I attacked those borderline Jews who were trying to hide from themselves the fact that they are themselves involved in this crisis.[21] I had in mind especially people like Speyer in the first category and Sam Lewisohn and Walter Lippmann in the second.

When I had finished, Rosenberg told me that he was delighted at what I had said, and the governor was called upon to speak. He thanked me for my frankness and pledged his wholehearted support. He spoke with evident sincerity and depth of feeling. He was followed by a number of others, including Mrs. Elkus, Mr. Halley, Rothenberg, Mr. Baerwald, and Rosenberg. In the discussion period David Brown asked, with an evident hidden purpose, what all this money was going to be spent for. He was obviously aiming at the Palestinians [Zionist representatives], whose type of accounting does not please him. I refused to be involved in that kind of inter-organizational fight, and expressed my assurance that the drive was fully justified from the point of view of the refugees themselves.

Home for a late supper.

Monday, March 19, 1934

Talks with Liebman and Strauss with a view to trying to get them and Rosenberg and Bernard Flexner together on a common program. Strauss promised to do whatever he could. Usually he has been very helpful. The result of this initiative was that four of them were to lunch together that day.

Rabbi Gold and another representative of the Mizrachi came in to see me.

21. Verbatim notes of McDonald's remarks: "Next Thursday night when we shall talk to as many people as can be piled into the room at the Astor I shall have to say, the Jews have shown a willingness to take care of their own. It isn't so at all. Somebody asked me this afternoon how many people have come to you on their own and said, I want to help you. I thought carefully and I said, I can name those on the fingers of one hand or two hands, and of those with real resources, on the fingers of a single hand. . . . What has happened to the Jews in Germany is something which happens to Jews everywhere in the world. The fact that a Jew is influential in business and other ways with non-Jews is no defense. . . . I want to say to some of these people that they, whether they like it or not, are in the same boat with the German Jews, no matter how much they try to hide from themselves the truth. . . . I have known Jews fairly well, but since I have undertaken this work, I have come to know more of the Jewish masses. Today my respect for the Jewish masses is comparably higher than for its foremost Jewish leaders with whom I've associated in the past. If the Jewish masses were in a position to help, our plea would not be in vain. But, it is difficult to reach them." Governor Lehman commented, "I was very much moved by what Commissioner McDonald told us. It was a frank and courageous talk which he gave us that came straight from the shoulder and heart." Meeting at Mr. James N. Rosenberg's home, Sunday, March 18, 1934. JDC Archives, High Commission File 2, 1934.

We chatted about the plan of the joint campaign. I told him of my interest in Palestine, and they explained their work in that area. Apparently they are the ultra-Orthodox.[22] They did not, however, tell me precisely why they had come to see me, but we seemed to part on very good terms.

Lunch with Mr. May. He planned out his work and mine during the next few weeks.

In the afternoon finished up some odds and ends preparatory to the trip to Canada. Was driven up to Harmon by the Bairds, where I took the train at 11:07. Ordinarily I should doubt the advantage of taking the train there, rather than at Grand Central, even though the latter does mean doubling on your tracks.

Ottawa, Tuesday, March 20, 1934

Arrived in Montreal exactly on time, a little before eight. Had time for a short walk around the square, and then took the 8:30 for Ottawa. The trip was interesting because of the signs everywhere of hard winter. I arrived on time at 11:45 and at once called up Mr. Miriam, the prime minister's secretary. He suggested that I come over right away.

I was shown into his office about twelve and remained with him until after one. My first impression of Bennett was that of a rather stolid, stout, a trifle officious person, but as our talk developed, I came to feel that he was a man of great force, real originality of mind, and essentially liberal.

I began the discussion by referring to his work in the Imperial Conferences and to the comments on him which I had heard in London, Washington, and elsewhere. We then talked about the possibility of admitting some additional numbers of refugees, I saying that I had not brought a definite program but wished merely to present the general problem and to receive from him suggestions. This led him to talk at some length about the place of Jews in Canada, their numbers, classes, etc. He called up a Mr. Blair[23] in the Immigration Department, who said that about 468 had been admitted last year. He added that there would be more opportunities for those who could settle on the land. In general, they should be immigrants who would support themselves and not be competitive in the labor market. He admitted, of course, that there were no Jews in Canada as public charges, that the Jewish communities there, as in England, had carried out literally their pledge to guarantee against such a condition. His only criticism of the Jews was that some of them were engaged in illicit liquor or narcotic traffic. He seemed to share a common prejudice that in such underground activities one usually found a Jew not directly selling, but acting as intermediary.

He finally suggested that I should have sent to the Department of Immigra-

22. Rabbi Shalom Gold, president of the World Mizrachi Movement. Although McDonald thought of the Mizrachi as ultra-Orthodox, they were closer to normative Judaism. Some were Zionists.

23. Frederick Charles Blair, director of the Immigration Branch in the Canadian Department of Mines and Resources. An influential bureaucrat.

tion lists of individuals who might wish to come to Canada, together with details as to their resources, possibilities, etc. These lists would then be acted upon as had been done with other cases during the past year, by so-called "orders in council."[24]

I spoke of the necessity of avoiding giving fuel to the exclusionists, with which to build a fire under the always ready boiler of restrictionism. I told him of some of my experiences with the Jewish press. He very warmly supported my view, and I think will be a little more ready to cooperate since he can feel that I would not capitalize any concessions that he might make.

We then went on to a discussion of NRA, Canadian problems, etc. He seems enthusiastic about Roosevelt, convinced that the latter can "buy" prosperity. In Canada, however, because of a very much larger per capita debt, a similar program is not possible though some of his political opponents seem to think so.

Early in our talk I told him of my father's coming from Glengary. This led him to try to put me in touch with some of the members of the House who were from that section, and in particular a picturesque Scotch figure, Angus Mc-something. He also had his secretary call up Mr. Jacobs and Mr. Heaps, two of the Jewish members of the House, to lunch with me. Similarly, he asked his secretary to arrange for me to meet Mr. and Mrs. Freeman, the two most prominent Jews in the capital. In short, he did everything that I could have asked him to do, save give me a carte blanche for the admission of refugees.

I showed him the letter about the possibility of establishing an insecticide plant in British Columbia. He thought the estimated number of families that could be employed was an exaggeration. However, he said he would show the letter to his colleagues and let me know what they thought of it before I left. Later, I asked him about it, but he had had no opportunity to discuss it. I will follow it up with his secretary.

Mr. Miriam took me over to meet Mr. Jacobs and Mr. Heaps in their parliamentary offices. The four of us then lunched together. We had a pleasant visit. Both Mr. Jacobs and Mr. Heaps are from Montreal; the former seemed to me more than usually interesting.

After lunch Mr. Miriam took me to meet Angus Mc— and an old Mr. McNary from my father's neighborhood in Glengary. Neither of them, however, remembered definitely my father's family, nor was this surprising in view of the fact that every third person in that region is a McDonald or a McDougall.

Earlier, the prime minister had been interesting in explaining why some of the Glengary McDonalds had remained Catholics. He thought it was because they came from the Hebrides, to which the influence of John Knox had not reached.

24. McDonald subsequently submitted lists of potential immigrants into Canada. On November 3, 1934, Bennett responded, "I have to advise you that I have carefully considered the lists which you submitted, and I am informed that at the present time it would be out of the question to permit the admission to this country of any of those named. . . . We cannot in fairness to our own population authorize the admission into Canada of a number of people who must either remain idle or take the places now filled by Canadians." Bennett to McDonald, November 3, 1934, JDC Archives, High Commission file 2.

Miriam then took me in the prime minister's car to the station, and there introduced me to the Freemans, who fortunately were going to Montreal on the three o'clock, the train which I had to take in order to keep my evening appointment in Montreal and to make my train for Boston.

Had a couple of hours with the Freemans on the train. She is the less expansive, but more attractive. As president of the Canadian Hadassah, she is very active in Palestinian affairs. He also is an ardent Zionist. She is also, according to the prime minister, very prominent in all sorts of charitable and civic work in the Dominion. I enjoyed my visit with them and with their children—two daughters. They were all going down to New York to meet a son newly engaged, returning from a Mediterranean cruise. Freeman is the largest Jewish merchant in Ottawa. A nervous, impetuous individual, he repeatedly argued against the practicability of helping the Jews in Germany, but in fact he will aid in that phase of relief.

Was met at the Windsor (not the Bonaventure) Station in Montreal by Mr. Caiserman and some of his associates. I was taken directly to the Montefiore Club for supper. About thirty-five or forty men, leaders in the community, had gathered there. Mr. Berliner was not there, but his brother-in-law, Lyon Cohen, was. Also there were Mr. Phillips, whom I had met in New York, Mr. Viner, a brother of Professor Viner, and the brother of Mrs. Lionel Cohen in London. He looks very much like her.

During the supper I was told more about the anti-Semitic agitation in the Province of Quebec. Mr. Jacobs had already given me something of a picture of the situation. Apparently certain journalists and leaders, in some cases subsidized by Nazi sympathizers, are actively stirring up prejudice among the Catholics, who make up the bulk of the population. It was charged that the Jesuits are directly parties to this propaganda. Indeed, the Jesuits are said frequently to have attacked the hierarchy itself on the grounds of lacking in sufficiently hundred percent orthodoxy. After supper I spoke from about eight o'clock until ten minutes after nine. This included the question period, and then I had to hurry off for my 9:30 train.

Two drives for Jewish funds are under way now or in preparation. The Hadassah has completed its plans and expects to complete its work within the next month. Mrs. Freeman told me that they would then turn over their machinery to the other group. She asked me if I would be willing to give a special endorsement to the Hadassah drive. I told her I would love to, but I was afraid it would interfere with the later effort. She then generously told me not to think anything more of it.

Boston, Wednesday, March 21, 1934

Before I go on with my Boston report, I should add that at the station in Montreal I had a discussion with the officials of the Jewish immigrant society. I reported to them confidentially what Bennett said, and we agreed upon a procedure for the future. In short, I would be the instrumentality for sending the list, perhaps directly to the prime minister, but sending copies to them. They then would follow up.

Was met at the North Station on arrival at 8:17. Judge Kaplan and a Mr. Stone of the Palestine office, eager about advance copy, met me. They took me directly to the Hotel Somerset, where I met Judge Cohen, who was to be the presiding officer. They asked me if I wanted anything during the day, and I said no, nothing except some stenographical assistance. This they volunteered to supply.

After breakfast set to work on my release for Boston, and had finished dictating it to a girl from the Palestine office [probably the Jewish Agency] before lunch.

Lunched alone. After a brief nap worked with another stenographer on my speech for the next day in New York. I was amused that each of the two stenographers, ardent Zionists, became a little impatient at my slowness in bringing Palestine into the picture, and asked me when I was going to arrive at that point. One of them, after the night meeting, came up to me and said, "That speech certainly sounded much better tonight than it did this morning." The other stenographer worked until eight or nine o'clock on the New York speech.

Called up President Lowell's secretary in the morning. She said yes, the president of Harvard University had had my letter, but that he wasn't interested in German refugees. I explained to the secretary that I didn't wish to talk about refugees but instead about the FPA and the World Peace Foundation plans. This didn't seem to interest him much more, because later on she called me back to say that he was tied up for the whole day, that he sent his warmest personal greetings, and was so sorry he couldn't see me. That was that.

At six o'clock a young Kahn, Harvard freshman trying for the *Crimson,* came to get an interview. I at first thought I couldn't give him anything, and then I dictated a short piece to him on the changing realignments in Europe.

Also while I was dressing, Mr. Herman of the Jewish War Veterans came to see me. He told me of an interesting letter which one of his colleagues had received from the German-Jewish War Veterans some years ago when they had been invited to participate in an international conference of Jewish war veterans. Their reply was to the effect that they were not prepared to sit down with their former enemies, and that so far as anti-Semitism was concerned, there was no danger of that in Germany whatsoever. They therefore declined to participate. I asked Mr. Berman to send me copies of this correspondence.

The dinner was attended by perhaps 150 to 175 persons. Afterwards fifty or seventy-five came in. The chairman was very brief. Judges Stone and Weiner spoke briefly. I spoke for nearly an hour. The meeting was closed by a moving but brief address by Rabbi Levy of the Temple Israel. I was struck by the enthusiastic approval of the corporation idea. It seemed clear to me that no matter what the officials of the two organizations might say, the rank and file wanted to work together. The response at the meeting seemed to me encouraging.

Afterwards, I chatted with a number of the leaders and then had a brief visit with some friends before taking the 12:30 train.

New York, Thursday, March 22, 1934

Talked on the telephone during the morning with Fromenson, Miss Emanuel, and Hyman about various matters.

At Buell's suggestion I called up James Brown Scott on the telephone to see if he would be willing to say that the organizations had met the condition of the Carnegie Corporation's grant. He said that he did not want to take the responsibility, that the Trustees existed for that purpose; formerly, when Root was president of the Endowment, the Trustees met frequently to discuss matters and sometimes to vote money. Later, they met merely to vote money. Now it is proposed that the money be voted and the Trustees meet afterwards. He begged me not to press the matter until after the executive committee had met. Indeed, he would have liked to have me ask him to delay consideration until then, but I said that I didn't care to do that, but I was sure my colleagues would not press the matter. He added that he thought the vote of the Trustees would be unanimous though President Butler had only one vote, which of course was a weighty one.

Brief lunch with Buell and Herbert May. The former was very cordial in his expressions of appreciation of what I had done about finance during my brief stay here. He said that I really ought to have a salary.

Over to see Keppel. He told me in strictest confidence that the organizations were not going to be allowed to suffer because of a family quarrel; that he was already authorized to make the payment, but was most anxious that nothing of this be known until he had completed his negotiations with the [Carnegie] Endowment. However, he emphasized that there could under no circumstances be a renewal of the grant for another year; that the [Carnegie] Corporation was determined not to be caught in the same trap again by the Endowment. The latter, when the corporation had indicated that the $65,000 was to come out of the $100,000 expected by the Endowment, had said, "We don't know why you are so keen about this cooperative project. We had merely passed it on to you."

We then spoke about the possible future of the Endowment when Butler's tenure should have ended. Keppel indicated that the Corporation under other circumstances would feel a responsibility to aid the Endowment insofar as it was doing work in this country. Moreover, he said that he was more favorable now to the possibility of my succeeding Butler than he had been when the matter was first broached. He added a significant item of gossip, saying, "Perhaps there is a possibility that Norman E. Davis might, a few years later, wish to end up in such a position. I, of course, am not expressing any preference as between you and Norman." He then went ahead to add however, quite generously: "But in any case that would merely be another job for you, whereas your present position, if it develops as you have indicated (I had referred to the possible scheme to drain off the Jewish youth in Germany), you will have something much more worthwhile."

Before I went to see Keppel, I dropped in at the Commodore to keep an appointment at two o'clock with E. A. Filene. The last time I had seen him he had asked me what he could do to help in my work, and specifically mentioned finances. I at that time had told him I was not prepared to make a suggestion. Now, however, I had scarcely begun to outline the three possibilities, the joint drive, the Quakers, or the High Commission itself, than he interrupted to say, in effect, that conditions had changed since he had seen me, that he was giving $1,000 to some form or other of the work. I had already indicated that I felt that his share was from ten to fifty thousand dollars. He went on to say that he would let the Jews do their work; they had never been willing to help him in his public activities. Anyhow, he was not primarily interested in ameliorating work, but in fundamental reform, for example, the study of the stock market by the Fund would save millions of dollars to Jewish industrialists. Then he used his favorite illustration, "If they want to know whether a man is insane or not they put him in a room with an open spigot and a mop. If he continues to try to mop up the floor, he is insane, but if he turns off the spigot, he is sane."

Both the manner and the words of the man made me furious. I told him I was not there to make a plea, that I was not interested in his fundamental propositions, that I was sick and tired of hearing about a basic and fundamental program, that I doubted if businessmen whom he was trying to reform would ever move until radicalism threatened them. In short, I left within fifteen minutes, and had I carried out my feelings of the moment I would have dictated a letter that afternoon resigning from the Twentieth Century Fund, but I did not do so because first, it is usually a mistake to move in a temper, and second, my withdrawal at this time, and especially under these circumstances, might jeopardize the FPA's chances of having its grant renewed at the April meeting. But I am through with Filene.

Down at the Astor at 8:15. Already the leaders of the two organizations had assembled in the guest of honor room, where the Paramount Movietone had set up their klieg lights and other apparatus. Then followed what seemed to me nearly a half an hour of posing and speech-making for the Movietone.

The main floor of the ballroom was comfortably filled by the time the speaking began. Hyman introduced Judge Mack, who in turn introduced Baerwald. He read a large number of telegrams, most of them addressed to me, pledging support. Among these were telegrams from Warburg and Governor Lehman. Baerwald then announced the officers of the joint campaign. It was easy for him to read the names, but back of that reading was a long story of complicated, difficult negotiations. Rothenberg was then introduced. He made a stirring [pro-]JDC speech before he said a word about Palestine. What a sharp contrast this was with Lipsky's attack on the JDC a few weeks ago! Rothenberg was also cooperative in finishing exactly on time.

The meeting went on the air at ten o'clock when Judge Mack introduced me. I followed my text closely until about twenty minutes were gone, when I could see that I was going to be a little long. Earlier, I had eliminated the list of figures, and now I had to shorten a little the description of my three Jewish friends, and managed to finish precisely with thirty seconds left over as I had promised the announcer. I had intended to go on for a few minutes after we went off the air, but when I reached that point, it seemed to me it might be an anti-climax, so I stopped.

Rabbi Jonah Wise then spoke briefly but well, and Judge Mack closed the meeting in an impassioned appeal on the note, not so much that an opportunity was being offered [to] the Jews to help, as that they should search their conscience why they were being privileged to help.

A number of people were very cordial in their expressions of opinion about my talk. The Palestinians [Zionists] seemed as pleased as the JDC adherents. The Baerwalds, Hyman, Jonah Wise, Miss Morrisson, Ruth, and I went to the Astor Grill. We sat around and danced until so late that it was one o'clock or more when we reached home.

Friday, March 23, 1934

Dr. Cohn and Murrow came in for a conference with Mr. May and me about the memorandum prepared by the former. We had a long discussion for more than an hour. The conclusions were as follows: Not to accept the precise form of the request indicated in the memorandum, that is, not to set up a separate bureau. Instead, I was to consider adding Kotschnig to the staff to deal with the whole realm of intellectuals, Cohn to inquire from Bernard Flexner how an additional $10,000, the estimated cost for this new work, could be raised. It was felt that Kotschnig's salary would be perhaps $3,300, and that the balance would be required to meet additional expenses. It seemed clear from the discussion that the Academic Assistance Council could not serve in the way the Americans desired; moreover, that there should be a first sifting place for all sorts of intellectuals. Both Cohn and Murrow felt that Kotschnig would be ideal for this position. He knows the academic world intimately, has a real intellectual grasp of the problem, and, unlike Parkes, is not an emotionalist but a good administrator.

Most of the rest of the morning was spent in blocking out with May and Miss Sawyer plans for April and May.

Over to luncheon with Percy Straus. Mr. Liebman and Ralph Straus were also there.

I was permitted to make the opening statement. I began by telling of my experience with Filene the day before, and added that I wouldn't be able to stand two such experiences. In the course of that statement I had repeated the various possibilities as to ways of helping.

We concentrated our discussion on the corporation. I explained why I thought it was important that I take back with me to London the names of a committee which would really be substantial. Percy Straus said that he recognized that this was an exceptional situation and was prepared to cooperate. At this point Liebman spoke of Felix's pledge of $500,000, and it was after that that Percy Straus said definitely that he would go on the committee, with only one condition—that he might not be able to give much time until he had freed himself from certain other obligations, but he made no reservation as to the size of his contribution.

He said that he was much impressed by the possibility of helping to liquidate on a fair basis the property of refugees in Germany. Liebman then referred to the great need also for additional credits for smaller Jewish businessmen. Percy Straus recognized this need; moreover, he assented to the larger proposal of draining off the youth if that could be arranged.

There was some talk about places to which immigrants could be sent. Percy Straus doubted the adaptability of Jews to general agriculture. In the society with which he had been working in this field, they had had success only in placing Jews on so-called "intensive" farms, such as tobacco in Connecticut.

We had a frank exchange of views about ICA. He thinks that Louis Oungre is engaged solely in keeping his trustees in a good humor. He doubts if anything can be done through Louis Oungre. I admitted that there was something in his criticism but insisted that Oungre is so intelligent, and in any event is so strategically located, that one must work with him.

We then talked about other men who might be on the corporation committee. Percy Straus was enthusiastic about Henry Ittleson, Albert Lasker, Ralph Hertz as associates for him, and Felix Warburg.

Towards the end of the luncheon Percy Straus asked about the suggested allocation committee to be set up as part of the joint drive, for, as he said, the real interest is not in the first million, but in the second and third. He recalled the discussion which Jonah Wise and he and I had had at luncheon there two weeks earlier. I tried to reach Hyman to inquire about the actual status, but he was out. He was to call Straus later.

As Liebman and I walked away from the store, the former expressed himself as highly pleased with the luncheon. We then planned to see Harry Guggenheim within the next two or three days.

Up to Mr. May's for a nap before my evening meeting. Found Mrs. May much hurt by my "neglect," not having called her or come to see her. I made the best explanations I could, but only at the end of an hour or so at tea with her, May, and her daughter, did I feel that she was beginning to forgive me. Naturally, I blamed myself, but I also blamed Miss Sawyer for not reminding me. I told Mrs. May that I had inquired about her daily, but she said that after all she was a person, and would appreciate being dealt with directly.

Dined with Ely. He wanted suggestions for some English speaker to speak on an endowment recently established at the Town Hall. He had no new thoughts himself. I suggested Lord Irwin.[25] This pleased him.

I spoke for just about an hour and answered questions for another half hour. I was pleasantly surprised by the size of the audience.

After the meeting and the "intimate" question period that followed, the lady from Berlin attacked me for not returning the paper she had given me at

25. Lord Irwin, Edward Frederick Lindley Wood, first Earl of Halifax, known as Baron Irwin, 1925–1934. Later British foreign secretary.

the NBC studio when I broadcast the time I was in this country before. I told her to go to the office and ask Miss Sawyer.

Home with the Bairds.

Saturday, March 24, 1934

Shocked to have Ruth tell me that she had learned the day before from Dr. Adie that there was the possibility of another operation. She had not told me the night before so as not to worry me. At the hospital Adie explained at length the precise situation, but said it would be some days before they would know. The x-rays the first of next week might show that the pocket which was draining intermittently was beginning to collapse. In that event an operation would not be necessary. But if the fever became excessive over a considerable period of time, they might have to go in again, but he hoped that this could be done through the original incision.

Sunday, March 25, 1934

Mostly at the hospital, in conference with the doctors.

Monday, March 26, 1934

Dr. Alfons Goldsmidt came in and told me of his wide contacts in Latin America. He evidently desires an opportunity to make a study of immigrant possibilities there. I think he would do it excellently. I asked him to send me a memorandum of his background and of what he considered the possibilities in Latin America.

Long talk with Hyman about a number of matters. He thought it undesirable to change my sailing; so also did Chamberlain. As to the JDC representative on the Advisory Council, it will probably be Kahn, with Hyman as alternate. As to telegram sent to the meeting the other night addressed to me, these will be answered in my name.

Spoke to Sulzberger. I did not complain about the Karl Brandt letter,[26] but did suggest that it was a little thick to have the letter printed two days after the *Times* had failed to carry anything from my statement at the Astor, which in substance would have given the reply to Brandt's criticism, and I suggested the possibility of an article in next Sunday's *Times*. Sulzberger said that he had thought the report of the Astor meeting inadequate, and he would talk to Markel.[27]

A few minutes later Markel called me. We decided to have an article in the Sunday *Times*. He suggested that the revision of my Thursday talk would be satisfactory, and that it could be hung on my leaving this week.

26. Karl Brandt had written criticizing McDonald for doing nothing. "We should like to ask Mr. McDonald just what he has done, what he intends to do and when. . . . By apparent inaction of its commissioner for relief . . . the League of Nations . . . seems to be losing the last scrap of prestige it still contains." *New York Times*, March 24, 1934.

27. Lester Markel, joined the *New York Times* as Sunday editor in 1924.

Lunch with Ambassador Guggenheim[28] and Liebman at the Harvard Club. Most of the lunch was given over to an explanation by Liebman, and more by me, of the corporation idea. Guggenheim asked a number of very intelligent questions, showed real interest, but did not commit himself or his uncles to large-scale participation. I think, however, he can be counted upon.

After lunch talked with Lewis Strauss. I told him I was disgusted with ICA's delay in meeting its commitment for administrative expenses; that, moreover, I felt it was a mistake for me to pass the hat to such individuals as Percy Straus and Ambassador Guggenheim for a few thousand dollars, just after talking to them about a project involving millions. Strauss agreed. I assured him that I did not expect him personally to do more than he had done, but I should be greatly relieved if he could, during the next few days, find three or four people who would make up approximately $25,000 towards the budget of the office of the High Commission. He said that he was sorry that he could not promise as categorically as he had in the other case, but he would do the best he could.

Talked to Rosenberg on the telephone. Told him of the progress being made on the corporation committee. He was generous enough to admit that this was something worthwhile. But he then proceeded in his usual fashion to tell me at some length what he thought ought to be my approach in England and at the High Commission meeting. At the close of our talk I asked him about the insurance fund. He said it would be taken care of promptly.

Tried in vain to get Ralph Sellett. Called Ambassador Dodd and found he was out. Learned that Albert Blum had had an operation, and that he might not be available, and that Ittleson definitely was not returning until the end of the week.

Little Forum[29] at the Robinsons' in the evening. Dr. Day gave an illuminating general analysis of the administration's program of recovery. This was followed by a lively discussion.

Tuesday, March 27, 1934

Long conference with David Heyman. From it certain things emerged:

(1) Promise on my part to write him from time to time personal confidential estimates of the situation, to be used by him personally in shaping his own view about the lines he will take with the federations throughout the country and the central investigating charity body in helping these groups to shape their attitudes towards various appeals for funds in the international field. I think he can be trusted;

(2) To speak to Baerwald with reference to the possibility of the JDC helping to finance the new central committee here in New York. He attaches great im-

28. Harry F. Guggenheim, U.S. ambassador to Cuba.

29. The Little Forum was started by McDonald, Robinson, Cavert, and others in Bronxville who met once a month at a member's house and listened to a prominent speaker on issues of the day, after which there were questions. The men dressed in dinner jackets and the women in long dresses.

portance to the principle that the JDC should assume some responsibility in this country. Baerwald heretofore has been unwilling to do so. As to the New York Foundation contributing to that, he thinks that they should be allowed to reserve their funds for continuing the aid of professors and doctors. But even here he is of the opinion that foundation funds should be used only to prime the pump, and that in the long run the intellectuals should be cared for from the general fund raised by popular subscription;

(3) I said I would send him the Baron de Rothschild material about Paris (English edition).

In general, Heyman stressed his desire of continuing to play his role of constructive critic, using his position in connections with the foundation and the organized charities as means of counteracting narrow organizational Jewish politics. I think that he can be helpful in this respect. I told him of my experiences with ICA, but did not ask him for any specific form of help.

Kotschnig came in at eleven. I asked him first to tell me about his own work. He explained this in some detail, indicating that he was, however, arranging to resign this spring, that he was intending to hand in his resignation at Geneva next month.

I then suggested to him the possibility of his joining our staff to have general charge of the whole field of the intellectuals. He replied that he would be very much interested in it, but since he had come to the States, he had begun to consider two other possibilities, the one a professorship of economics at Fisk University to be combined with part time work in the public forums at Des Moines; the second Butler of the B.I.T. [*sic*—B.I.S.—Bank for International Settlements] had asked him to be the assistant director of a project which Butler had asked the Rockefellers to finance. Since Kotschnig was uncertain as to the status of this project, I first called Miss Miner, who knew nothing of it, and then Dr. Day, in whose office it now rests. He told me that it was not likely to be acted upon in the near future, that he had some doubts as to the relations of the B.I.T. [B.I.S.] and the League of Nations in this field. Therefore, to both Kotschnig and me it appeared that the B.I.T. [B.I.S.] proposal would probably not be available now. Under these circumstances, Kotschnig indicated that he would be willing to accept if I were in a position to make an offer.

I asked Kotschnig what salary he would need. He replied that he is receiving 16,000 Swiss francs from the I.S.S.; that while living costs in London, where we agreed his office probably ought to be, would be somewhat less than in Geneva, there would be the necessity of covering moving costs for himself and his family. From other things he said it appeared to me that a $5,000 salary probably would be acceptable, and that with necessary competent technical assistance the office might cost in the neighborhood of $10,000.

We left the matter in this way: I am to talk to the Academic Assistance Council people and to get in touch also with the other groups interested. He is to inquire about the Butler project. If I find conditions satisfactory abroad and if the new position can be financed, I will make him a definite offer by April 7 in Geneva, the date when he is committed to letting Fisk University have his decision.

The more I talked with Kotschnig, the more I was convinced that Dr. Cohn's and Murrow's enthusiastic judgment is sound. Certainly Kotschnig's broad knowledge of the whole academic and professional field, both abroad and in the United States, and his proved competence in administration, would be factors of great value. Moreover, and this is not unimportant, his wife is helpful.

To the Town Hall to lunch with Chamberlain. Our talk covered a wide range, including

(1) The new committee to be set up in New York. I told him of David Heyman's attitude and asked that he see him;
(2) Chamberlain thinks that Kohler[30] is arousing unnecessarily opposition in Washington. Certainly, Kohler's dislike and suspicion of Carr is not a helpful element in the situation. But what can be done about it is another matter;
(3) Judge Mack has not yet made his report to the Departments of Labor and of State. Chamberlain understands that Mack will do this soon after conferring with Burlingham and Thatcher. Chamberlain agrees that Thatcher is not a liberal in his interpretation of immigration policy, but thinks Kohler is unjust in his characterization of Thatcher as an exclusionist. Certainly, Burlingham is a liberal. Chamberlain had not heard anything to the effect that the Labor Department was beginning to weaken in its labor bond policy. He thought it probable indeed that there would be difficulty in so phrasing the labor bond regulations as to execute effectively [*sic*]. Nonetheless, he had the impression that MacCormack was planning to carry through on the new regulations;

In March 1934 the House Immigration Committee held hearings on a number of bills that would have cut the immigration quotas for each country. Jewish experts such as Max Kohler and Labor Department officials were concerned that some sort of restrictionist bill might pass Congress. Partly for this reason, MacCormack delayed decision on actually making use of bonds (as financial guarantees that potential immigrants would not become public charges). McDonald apparently picked up something of the Labor Department's retreat—even though Chamberlain had not.

(4) Chamberlain is to see Fosdick and the State Department before Fosdick leaves. Chamberlain is anxious to have the drafts of the tentative agendas as soon as possible;
(5) As to the Department's attitude on the new form of paper, Chamberlain did not commit himself definitely but did not disagree with what Carr had said

30. Max J. Kohler, lawyer and chief adviser on immigration to the American Jewish Committee.

about the willingness of the government to accept for visa purposes almost any form of identification paper other than an expired passport.

Perhaps there were other items we discussed, but I do not now recall them. Certainly, Chamberlain is an admirable choice.

Samuel Rosenthal and J. M. Budish of the Amtorg came to see me in reference to a project to organize an American committee for Biro-Bidjan. Rosenthal is a real estate man. They explained their interest in Biro-Bidjan, which apparently had been reawakened by Lord Marley's visit. They promised to send me copies of a report on that region prepared for ICOR a few years ago, and also the stenographical account of the meeting recently addressed by Marley and attended by Felix Warburg. So far as I could make out neither Rosenthal nor Budish had any new data as to the attitude of the Soviet government.[31] They seemed set on an American committee to finance emigration. They consider that perhaps first it may be necessary to send an American explorative committee.

I could not make up my mind either as to the good faith of the men, particularly Rosenthal, nor as to precisely what they expected from me. As a matter of fact, they did not ask for any specific commitment. And as was inevitable, I told them that I had an open mind on the subject and could not commit myself until there was a larger measure of agreement among the experts.

Dinner at the Advertising Club arranged by Mr. Vladeck. The group consisted of perhaps thirty-five or forty Socialists, Jewish trade union leaders. Included among them were officials of the Amalgamated Clothing Workers, the head of the needle industry, and others of that kind. I found it a stimulating audience. I spoke frankly but, of course, not for publication. And as I was leaving, I said to Vladeck, so that it could be heard all over the room, that, of course, this was merely a family party.

Wednesday, March 28, 1934

Because of a consultation with Drs. Adie, Vogler, and Morrill at the hospital I was forced to cancel engagements at the office or elsewhere with Colonel House, Ambassador Morgenthau, and Mr. Bernstein. Happily, the doctors really seemed to be more cheerful than the day previous, and they all said that they thought it would be safe for me to sail.

Ruth and I arrived late at the Baerwalds for luncheon with Mrs. Baerwald's friends. Among those present were Mrs. Erdmann, Mrs. Rick, Mrs. Lazarus' sister, and Lady David, Mrs. Guggenheim, Mrs. Berg—in all twenty-eight. It was a very much dressed-up party, so I took the opportunity to stress my contempt for rich, assimilated Jews who refused to recognize responsibility in the present crisis.

Back to the office with Miss Sawyer, who told me on the way of the ap-

31. Amtorg, a Soviet-founded American firm handling most U.S.-Soviet trade at this time. ICOR, Yiddish acronym of an organization to assist Jewish colonization in Soviet Russia.

pearance in the *Vorwaerts*[32] that morning of a detailed account of what I had said the previous night, and of an inquiry made by the JTA as to whether they might use the material. Arriving at the office, I called the JTA to thank them for their inquiry and to say that nothing was to be used. I told them also that I would report to Mr. Landau[33] and to Felix Warburg my appreciation of their care in asking me about this story before they carried it.

Later spoke to Vladeck on the telephone. He gave the appearance of being even more outraged by the leak than I. His explanation was that the *Vorwaerts* writer had asked him if he might reprint what I had said, and that he, Vladeck, had replied, "You may say that Mr. McDonald met with us, and that's all." Vladeck and I then discussed what could be done about it. I said that I preferred not to make any statement. Vladeck volunteered to see that a really adequate denial or explanation appeared in the next day's *Vorwaerts.*

Talked to Liebman about the development of his committee. He seemed optimistic.

To dinner at the Town Hall with Ruth and later joined the Dennys at the Town Hall Concert—Salmon, the cellist, and Stuckgold, messo-soprano.

Home late but stayed up to talk with Ruth and Edna.

Thursday, March 29, 1934

Instead of going to the office, I spent the morning after packing with Bobby at the hospital.

While there Felix Warburg called me from Chicago. The talk on the whole was not very satisfactory. After an exchange of comments about Bobby and the families, he said that he was sorry that I was going away so soon. I explained that I had the engagement in London, and he said that was of no importance. I then reminded him that I had to get ready for the May meeting, and he replied that of course I would have to judge myself about the necessities on the other side. He added that if I left now, I would continue to be concerned about Bobby, implying that as a result, my effectiveness would be impaired. To this, I answered that Bobby's condition was such that it might continue uncertain for several weeks; that, therefore, I might not feel any easier leaving two weeks or more later; that under the circumstances I felt I must go.

We discussed the corporation. I told him I thought Percy Straus would go along. He asked if Percy had committed himself to any definite figure. I said no, nor had Guggenheim. I explained that I had not been able to get in touch with Ittleson or Lasker, but hoped he would do so soon after his return. I forgot to say anything about the desirability of pressing forward in the naming of the allocation committee for the joint drive. But I did suggest that the chances of success of this effort would be greatly increased if the large contributors made their initial subscriptions on a higher basis than last year. I did not feel

32. *Vorwaerts* [*Forvertz*] is the Yiddish-language *Jewish Daily Forward.*
33. Jacob Landau, managing director of the Jewish Telegraphic Agency.

that over the telephone I could go further in making a suggestion to him and Mrs. Warburg.

Down to lunch with Herbert May at the Pierre. While waiting for lunch, Miss Sawyer called me to report that Markel thought my article too much of a plea and therefore not usable in the *Times*. This annoyed me decidedly, and I told her to leave word with Markel that he would have to be the judge as to whether it was fit for the *Times* or not, that I was in no position to make any plea for its publication. Later May supported this view. At the same time Miss Sawyer gave a more encouraging report from Lewis Strauss to the effect that while he did not wish me to relinquish my efforts to secure ICA's participation in the budget of the High Commission, I should dismiss from my mind all worry, for the money needed would be forthcoming; and second, that if at any time I wished to anticipate further advances on account of his personal commitment, the money was available.

May and I went over a number of other subjects including

(1) The desirability of contact in this country with Dodd. I agreed to communicate with Dodd and ask him to speak to May as he would to me;
(2) The possibility and the desirability of engaging a publicity man. May thought this desirable, particularly in view of the general conditions which makes it unadvisable for me to announce many of my activities or the results of them, particularly those concerning governmental negotiations; but at the same time it is important that there should be created an impression of greater activity, and especially the next meeting of the Governing Body should be carefully handled from the publicity point of view. We discussed the possibility of part-time persons in New York and London, as compared with the desirability of a full-time individual who would travel with me. In the latter case the additional cost would probably about $10,000. It was left that I would make some inquiries, and in the meantime plan to use someone in London in preparation for and during the forthcoming meetings;
(3) May was quite firm in his opinion that I should stick to my plan to sail. He felt that the forthcoming meetings are crucial; that they could not be prepared for properly in my absence; that, of course, there would be work for me at home for the whole time if I cared to stay here, but that the prolongation of my absence from Europe could not be justified by the needs of the American Jewish groups. In the course of this discussion I put it like this, "In view of the intricate complex of personal, organizational and group conflicting interests, it is inevitable that I must from time to time dissatisfy one or even many persons or groups; that, therefore, it may be desirable, as in this case, for me to dissatisfy those who are most surely my friends, rather than those upon whom I can less certainly rely." May agreed, saying that it might not be a bad idea if this particular phrasing of one of my problems were called to Warburg's attention sometime, not by me but by someone else.

Back to the office to try to finish in a couple of hours a day or so's work.

Talked on the telephone to Mrs. de Sola Pool, who told me of her desire to help out as a volunteer, perhaps abroad. She has several languages. At the moment, however, a sick child would prevent her doing anything. It was left that she would call me upon my return.

Talked on the telephone to Bernstein of the *Jewish Daily Bulletin* and apologized for having to cancel my appointment of the previous day; expressed my interest in the Albanian project, and expressed my appreciation of his activities in that regard and my hope that he would supply me with a memorandum, and my desire to see him on my return.

Talked on the telephone to Rosenberg. Told him I had just talked to Warburg, which surprised him. Expressed my belief that Percy Strauss would do a real job, and that the others could be brought along. I said I was not going back to London in a defeatist spirit. He then in his invariable fashion proceeded to tell me that I must be optimistic in my report, but that I must not mention any general figures. He was finding it so hard to get hold of any real money that he thought it a mistake to talk in terms of $25,000,000 or $50,000,000. Like Warburg, he deprecated my leaving at this time, but to him I gave the same reply as to Warburg.

The end of our talk was interrupted by Miss Crimmins telling me that Ambassador Dodd was on the telephone, so I apologized and said goodbye to Rosenberg.

Dodd was very cordial. We asked about one another's families and plans. He is not returning to Germany until May 1. I told him of my desire that May might talk with him as my confidential representative. He said he would welcome this.

Dodd then told me that he had spoken to the President [*sic,* actually Hitler] about the matter which I had discussed with von Neurath a few weeks earlier.[34] This question he had brought up in the course of a discussion about other matters, at which no outsiders were present. The President did not commit himself, nor did he explode, as is his wont when questions of this sort are brought up. He seemed rather inclined to consider it. I asked Dodd whether it appeared that von Neurath had spoken to the President about it. Dodd thought not. On the whole, Dodd was encouraged to feel that something could be done along this line.

I then asked Dodd about the piece which had appeared three days before to the effect that pressure from outside was so adversely affecting conditions inside the Reich that serious consideration was being given to a modification of those domestic policies responsible for the adverse action outside. Apparently, this piece was based upon bits picked up here and there in the State Department and checked from sources from Berlin. Everything considered, it was a most satisfactory conference.

Henry Ittleson called me from Palm Beach in response to my telegram to him. He said that they were probably not going abroad this summer, that in-

34. The idea of an orderly planned emigration of German Jews, combined with a truce between the German government and those Jews remaining. See entries of February 7, 1934 (chap. 10) and italicized insert into March 12, 1934 (chap. 11).

stead, she might be south part of the time in connection with their plans to build "a small place" there. I told him of my anxiety that he should give Warburg the fullest possible support in the corporation idea; that his very aloofness from organizational politics would make him doubly valuable. He said he would do his utmost. He also said that Mrs. Ittleson would call up Ruth upon their return, and she would do anything she could to be helpful.

Then Ittleson put Herbert Swope on the phone. The latter asked me if I had been to see the President this trip. I replied that I had made no special effort. He then said, "The President spoke to me the other day in very approving terms of your work. He likes the way you are going about it." Swope added, "If at any time you need my help to put you in touch with anyone, just command me."

Swope said, "Do you know my sister in Berlin?" I replied, "I know her very well. I have seen her many times. She has been extremely useful to me." Then I went on to take advantage of the opportunity to tell him that I thought the strain of residence in Berlin in the midst of a tragic situation, to which she is extremely sensitive, was beginning to tell on her, as it would under similar circumstances on any one not made of sheet metal; that, therefore, I ventured as a personal friend to suggest that he and his brother ought to induce her to leave, at least for a considerable period. He thanked me most warmly for this advice, and asked me to be sure to call up his brother Gerard before I left.

Dr. Cohn, Bernard Flexner, and a little later Murrow came in for a conference about the project to engage Kotschnig and the question of finding the resources for that. I apologized to the men because of the likelihood of telephone interruptions, but explained that I had to leave in half an hour, and, therefore, these calls could not be postponed.

Flexner began by asking whether this work would be an integral part of the High Commission activities. I said yes. This led him then to ask a second question, as to why it was not a logical charge then on the budget. I admitted that it would be, but there were no funds, that moreover, we had not set up any other bureau to deal with any particular class of refugees, and that, therefore, extra funds would have to be secured. He countered by saying that the Academic Assistance Council must be made to help, and suggested that he would find one third of $10,000, A.A.C. a third, and one-third from our budget. I replied that I didn't think the A.A.C. would have any money to give, and suggested that if he would find half, I would find the other half. And so it was left. The first half of his half will be available on May 1, and the second half, I believe, August 1 (Murrow is preparing a memorandum on these details). Everybody seemed pleased by this arrangement. Cohn stressed that he thought, irrespective of what Kotschnig was to do precisely, it was more than worth what it would cost to save him for this type of work.

During the course of this conference I was interrupted several times by telephone calls. In trying to reach Mrs. Otto Kahn I was told by her secretary of the unexpected death, an hour or two earlier of Otto Kahn. I asked her to convey my condolences.

Spoke to Gerard Swope. He was reported to be in a conference, but when Miss Crimmins at my suggestion told him that his brother had asked me to call him, that I was sailing within an hour or so, he got on the wire. I said to him much what I had said to Herbert about Mrs. Levine. He replied that he had planned either to go to see her or to ask her to come to see them. I ventured to urge the latter course. He said he was going to talk the matter over with the ambassador in a day or two. I told him that of course I did not wish him to speak to his sister about my suggestion, but if he cared to mention it to the ambassador that would be all right. He was just as cordial as had been his brother.

Herbert Swope in his talk to me earlier, suggested that I ask Waldman of the American Jewish Committee to send me an advance copy of the week's issue of *Today* with its article on the Hitler menace. He also asked me what I knew about the Madison Square Garden meeting. I replied that I of course must keep rigorously aloof from any political activities. He agreed.

Called Percy Straus on the telephone, after failing to get Ralph. Percy too was in a conference, but came on the wire when he learned that I was leaving. I told him that I had called merely to stress again how important it seemed to me for him, aloof from Jewish politics and organizational jealousies, to play an active role in the corporation. He expressed his desire to help as much as he could, and again underlined his contempt for organizational politics. Incidentally, he asked me to get in touch with young Selfridge, who is sailing on the *Olympic* and had been to lunch with him Thursday.

Called Hyman, who said that they had prepared the data which had been requested by the office, that it had been forwarded to Kahn, and that the latter would represent them at the meeting. He added that if there was anything he could do at home to help Ruth, he would consider it a privilege.

Final conference with Miss Martin about personal financial matters. She had made out and was signing my personal checks covering all bills for the family or for Bobby's illness, including the hospital and all the doctors except Dr. Adie, who had not rendered his bill. I sent him, however, a check for $250 on account. Balances are owed, however, on both federal and state income tax. Of the first, only the first quarter has been paid, of the second one half of the regular tax is yet to be paid.

Brief talk with Mildred Wertheimer; then to the hospital and home to finish packing. To the train with Ruth and Janet. Made record connections, and arrived at the boat by 7:30. There gave an interview to the *City News* reporter and the representative of the J.D.B. [*Jewish Daily Bulletin*]. The latter told me that the *Vorwaerts* denial was half-hearted, saying, in effect, that I could not be held responsible for what I had said. Finished the interview just in time to telephone Ruth at the hospital before the gangplank was lifted.

To bed early.

12. April 1934:
The "Jewish Question" in Europe

Voyage, *Olympic,* March 30–April 5, 1934

Friday, beautiful sea and sun. Nonetheless, through sheer will-power, and driven by Miss Sawyer, managed to work four or five hours.

Very little of special interest. Chatted from time to time with Lady Henrietta Davis[1] and her son Philip, chiefly about her individual work with the refugees. The divorced widow of a rich Canadian, she is interesting herself in society and social work in Paris. Chatted from time to time with a few other passengers but nothing of importance came up.

In a letter written at sea to Felix Warburg, McDonald enclosed a letter to philanthropist Edward H. Harkness asking for a contribution to the Christian Committee for German Refugees because I have been led to think that he would not give elsewhere. He also wrote to Hyman that "the responses to the hundred or more letters which I wrote to leading Christians, all of whom I know personally and all of whom have contributed more or less substantially to the FPA, was almost nil."[2] There had been no reply from Rockefeller and refusals from Harkness, Curtis Bok,[3] and Mrs. Dwight Morrow.[4] The total raised was $1,240, with contributions from $10 to one of $500 from Mrs. Stephen Wise.

Landed in Southampton on the early afternoon of the fifth.

On arrival at the hotel, met by Bentwich, who proceeded to put us au courant of developments during our two months' absence.

Brief conference with Lobkowicz. Arranged to lunch with him the next day.

Mr. Gill and Miss Stanley of the Church Missions for Jews came to talk about the possibility of an appeal by the Missionary Council on behalf of the non-Jewish refugees. Bentwich and they and I went over the whole situation carefully and, considering the delicacy of various persons involved, with considerable frankness. The results were later embodied by Bentwich in a memorandum, which was

1. Lady Henrietta Davis, widow of Sir Mortimer Davis of Montreal, founder of the Imperial Tobacco Company of Canada.

2. McDonald to Felix Warburg, April 4, 1934. Copy in McDonald Papers, USHMM. McDonald to Hyman, April 7, 1934, Felix Warburg Papers, Box 316, JDC.

3. Curtis Bok, novelist and Pennsylvania Supreme Court judge.

4. Elizabeth Cutter Morrow, president of Smith College and wife of Dwight Morrow, former senator and ambassador to Mexico. Their daughter Anne married Charles Lindbergh.

sent off to Mr. Gill. In general, it was quite clear that Sir Leon Levison was not much more fully trusted by the Missionary groups than he is by the Jews.

Wurfbain arrived late. He, Miss Sawyer, Bentwich, and I went out to dinner, and continued to talk shop.

London, Friday, April 6, 1934

Young Feilchenfeld called and wished me to intervene with the consul. I told him to go ahead and make his inquiry on his own responsibility; that if he needed me later, I should be glad to help. I urged him to get out of his head the idea that the consul was prejudiced against him.

Long conference with Kotschnig and the members of the staff. I think we were all favorably impressed by Kotschnig, even though he was not able to give a very convincing or complete picture of how the job we were considering for him could be done. Perhaps, however, it is too much to expect that from someone who had not had more time to canvas the situation. We reached no definite conclusion.

Lunch with Lobkowicz at the St. James Club. We discussed many subjects, but few of them with marked definiteness. Lobkowicz did, however, make clear that Czechoslovakia was opposed to the enlargement of our organization to include Austrian refugees.[5] I assured him that no such extension was contemplated. He agreed to notify Prague of Bentwich's and my coming.

Dinner with Otto Schiff. We discussed the development of the work of the Anglo-HICEM. He assured me that irrespective of differences that might have existed earlier between HICEM and the London organization, these had been ironed out. He promised to have Ernst Kahn amplify and make more definite his report on immigration possibilities before the meeting of the Advisory Council.

After dinner Schiff and I joined three of his friends for supper. There was some opportunity to dance.

Saturday, April 7, 1934

Conference with Adams. He showed no enthusiasm for Kotschnig's appointment. He did not see how a new man could make any definite contribution. He was confident, however, that he and his colleagues would cooperate if the decision was made to name Kotschnig.

Over to the German Embassy to see Prince von Bismarck,[6] the chargé in von Hoetsch's absence. Bismarck's evident Nazism seemed to me a little amus-

5. Those leftists who had fled Austria after Dollfuss's repression in February 1934.

6. Prince Otto von Bismarck, counselor at the German Embassy 1926–1939, ambassador to Italy, 1940. McDonald subsequently described him and his comments: "B. is accused of having Jewish blood and . . . is therefore more Nazi than he otherwise would be. . . . [He declared] that no fundamental change . . . of the Nazi Jewish policy could be expected as long as Hitler is in power. The leader would go down rather than yield on this fundamental." McDonald to Felix Warburg, April 10, 1934, McDonald Papers, Columbia, Special File Felix Warburg.

ing in view of the apparently substantiated rumors that he has Jewish blood and that this fact has seriously endangered his diplomatic career.

He listened to my account of what I wished to take up with the German authorities. This was really a brief resumé of what I had said to von Hoetsch two months earlier. Von Bismarck promised to transmit my message and to indicate that I expected to reach Berlin about the twentieth of April. On the Jewish question he ventured a positive judgment that no matter what the price, Hitler would never yield, and he said this as though he shared personally the Führer's views.

Lunch with Bentwich and Miss Sawyer. Worked until nearly time to go to Chelwood. Tea with Mr. and Mrs. May, and took the six o'clock train for Hayward's Heath. Met at the station by a rather decrepit taxi, and driven to Lord Cecil's modest and very old fashioned but comfortable house. At dinner besides Lord Cecil and Lady Cecil and myself, was his sister. After dinner I went over a large number of items with Cecil. He approved the various suggestions I brought to him, and made some specific proposals in reference to modifications of the letter to the secretary of state[7] in reference to the stateless refugees. He agreed to be a member of the special committee to allocate funds to be raised by the Christian bodies for the refugees.

To bed early, by candlelight.

London-Leeds, Sunday, April 8, 1934

Up early. Breakfast alone. Then with the Cecils, drove towards the station in the same taxi, dropping them off for church while I took the 8:15 train for London where I arrived just in time to catch the ten o'clock express for Leeds. There Anthony de Rothschild, Dr. Perlzweig, and I spoke twice—at luncheon and at an evening meeting. Elsewhere in a number of provincial capitals similar meetings were being held. The London meeting had been held the week previous. (Melchett's telegram of invitation to me had not made this clear.) Nonetheless, it would have seriously hampered my work here if I had delayed my sailing by the several days which would have been necessary had I not taken the *Olympia.*

I was pleased with the meetings at Leeds. Burton,[8] the very rich owner of chain clothing stores, was not in town, but from my point of view his absence was more than compensated for by the presence of Izzy Isaacs, a relative of Lord Reading. He is one of the foremost figures in the sporting fraternity in England, a very good Jew, and a generous man. He gave our meetings the sort of flair that strengthened us with the populace.

7. That is, the British Colonial Secretary (Secretary of State for the Colonies) Sir Philip Cunliffe-Lister.

8. Sir Montague Burton, Lithuanian-born founder of the Burton clothing empire based in Leeds. Devoted Zionist.

London, Monday, April 9, 1934

Returning to London Monday morning, I completed my preparations for the swing around the circle on the continent. However, Adams and Bagster-Collins came in to talk further about Kotschnig's suggestion. They had little new to offer, and Bagster-Collins nothing at all. Adams agreed to try to get Beveridge on the telephone in time to telephone me in Paris the latter's views.

Hurried lunch with Miss Sawyer, and then off to see Cunliffe-Lister at the Colonial Office. He was most friendly. Insisted on talking for some time about Bobby's illness, and when he learned that he and she had been attacked by the same streptococcus, I had some difficulty changing the subject, and that not until he had explained that in Kenya the regular British Colonial Service had been able to supply precisely the same serum which was available only within the last six months, even in the great medical centers in New York or London.

I told him of the proposed negotiations with the Emir of Trans-Jordan, the hopes of some persons that large colonization programs could be undertaken soon in that area, and of Bentwich's and my express opposition to such a program.

Three days earlier McDonald had written James Rosenberg a lengthy letter about the British, Palestine, and Transjordania [spelled this way in the letter], excerpted here:

[. . . Undoubtedly there are large agricultural prospects in Transjordania, but it does not seem that these are twice the size of Palestine unless you include tracts of absolute desert. . . . Everbody recognizes that the economic development of Transjordan must be bound up with Palestine. . . . At the same time the British Administration in Palestine and the British Government in London have shown themselves reluctant to encourage Jewish penetration into Transjordan in spite of the undoubted willingness of a number of sheiks in Transjordan to dispose of part of their lands for the purpose of such settlement. There has been no declaration of policy, but it must be inferred that the British Administration is afraid of arousing a serious Arab movement which would affect Palestine. At the time of the riots in 1929 the Arabs in Transjordan were greatly excited; and last year when the negotiations about the sale of land in Transjordan to the Jewish Agency became public, a violent agitation was conducted. . . . It would be necessary in the first place, I think, to convince the British Government that Jewish settlement in Transjordan can be carried out in such a way as directly to help the Arab cultivators in the country. . . . But any movement for arousing public opinion in England or America in favor of Jewish settlement in Transjordan, or any publicity about schemes of colonization before the approval of the British Government is obtained, would likely to have a very adverse effect. Arab national feeling is extremely sensitive throughout the Middle East. . . ."][9]

9. McDonald to Rosenberg, April 6, 1934, copy in Brandeis Papers, Louisville Microfilm Series, VI, Roll 100, Z/P 58-1.

He [Cunliffe-Lister] then launched into a long and categorical analysis of the reasons why he would have to oppose in every possible way any such program at this time. He doubted that the so-called concession secured from the Emir for agricultural lands was seriously intended by the latter. He quoted the sheiks as saying to their followers, "It is all right for us to lease our land to the Jews; after they have settled on it, you will be free to kill them. Then we will have our money, and you will have the land back again."

He added that he had persuaded Weizmann not to continue even the most informal negotiations with the Emir, despite Dr. Weizmann's anxiety to talk with the Arabs. Similarly, he would oppose any conversations between private persons and the Emir on the occasion of the latter's proposed visit to London this summer. He reiterated what he had said to me earlier, that premature activities by the Jews across the Jordan might precipitate such a crisis in Palestine as to cost the lives of a number of English soldiers; that such a result might so arouse British public opinion as to require any British government which might then be in power to close the doors of Palestine itself for a considerable time to any Jewish immigration. Unless and until the Arabs were convinced by evident demonstrations that their interests and those of the Jews were complementary and until the Jewish population from Palestine overflowed naturally, perhaps through the Hula development, it was worse than useless to move directly towards Trans-Jordan.

I told him that I wished he would talk as frankly as this with one or two of the American Jewish leaders. He said he would consider doing so if I strongly recommended the person or persons to him.

We then discussed the situation in Palestine. He complained of the extent of illegal immigration and of the large number of Jews who, entering with a visitor's visa under false names, could later not be traced. Laski and his associates had urged the public denunciation by the government of this policy. Sir Philip hesitated to do this, and had instead insisted that the agency authorities be more severe themselves. He had already spoken to Weizmann, and the latter had promised his cooperation. My only suggestion was that he speak again to Dr. Weizmann with added emphasis.

Unfortunately, my train for the continent required me to leave the Colonial Office at the end of about forty minutes and apparently a considerable time before Sir Philip had finished his exegesis. Seemingly, he likes to talk to me and again repeatedly said, as he had at my previous conference with him, that my attitude was "so very wise." I still don't know whether this is a habitual phrase of the colonial secretary's or not.

Incidentally, the name of Dannie Heineman came up during our talk. The latter always has Sir Philip on his boards when Sir Philip is out of office. It would probably be advisable for me to meet Heineman though Sir Philip, rather than to use my letter of introduction from Liebman.

Rushed from the Colonial Office just in time to catch the boat train. Sir

Philip was so concerned about my connection that he insisted on going to the cloak room to help me on with my coat and to see me to the stairway. On the way to Paris had illuminating talks with Bentwich about different aspects of Jewish relationships; in particular, he told me about his work in Palestine.

Arrived late at the Hotel Continental.[10]

Paris, Tuesday, April 10, 1934

The first conference of the day was with the Quaker and the Entr'Aide group—Mr. Harvey, Mlle. Melon, and another woman. They stressed as before the amount of work they could do with even a small amount of money and the unlikelihood of receiving sufficient funds from the Quakers at home. Their appeal gave added point to the attempt of the Christian Committee at home to find funds.

Dr. Rothbarth[11] came in to talk about the possibility of sending some of the Jewish children from Paris to Switzerland for a three-month's period. This project was really a part of a larger Swiss Jewish project to bring Austrian children to Switzerland. This had been checked by the refusal of the Dollfuss government to permit the children to leave after the February counter-revolution. It seemed evident that until the attitude of the Swiss government was known, it would be a mistake to approach the French government formally in this matter. I promised to inquire in Switzerland.

When I saw Wurfbain two days later in Geneva, he reported that he had raised this question with Rothmund; that the latter had never heard of the proposal, did not know of the Swiss committee, was surprised that he had not been informed of it earlier, but since he was leaving for Rome, said that his colleague would give an answer later.

Miss Rothbarth's friend on the Swiss committee is Dr. Katzenstein, 140 Mühleback St., Zurich.

Called Baron Robert de Rothschild on the phone. He asked me for dinner, and I later called him back and asked if Bentwich might come too. He said yes. Mistakenly, I forgot to ask about Mrs. Bentwich, but I, for the moment, had forgotten her and in any case was under the impression that it was to be a business dinner.

Stolz, the secretary of the Matteotti Committee, came in and talked with Bentwich and me. Unfortunately, he did not seem very well informed, and Schevenels[12] was out of town. He did make clear, however, that they had not received any money from Lord Marley. The latter refused to consider the Quakers

10. McDonald wrote that on arriving in Paris, "I had lifted from me the great burden which has weighed me down for more than two months. I had cables from home telling me that Bobby had left the hospital and was feeling really cheerful." McDonald to Felix Warburg, April 10, 1934. Copy in McDonald Papers, USHMM.

11. Erwin Rothbarth, German-Jewish economist and close associate of John Maynard Keynes. Especially concerned with children.

12. Walter Schevenels, Belgian, secretary of the Socialist International.

as a non-political body, and Marley's representative in Paris wished to make it a condition of giving the funds that the individuals come to the Marley headquarters to be listed there before they received aid. In view of the fact that the Marley Committee is considered by the Matteotti group as Communist, and in view of the intense feeling between the Communists and the Socialists, this proposal was obviously unacceptable. And there the matter stands.

Later Bentwich talked with Marley's representative, who, from our point of view, gave an unsatisfactory explanation, and on the next day, when he was supposed to return for a further conference, he failed to appear, as a result of which Bentwich felt it was necessary that we put the case strongly to Lord Marley. Bentwich dictated the letter, and I sent it.

A long luncheon conference with Dr. Kahn. Among the subjects discussed with Dr. Kahn were the following:

(1) Intellectual refugee committees. Kahn thought one would either by pressure require a closer coordination through a central committee meeting frequently, or through an individual like Kotschnig. When I replied that I had no sanctions to force such cooperation, he said that neither the JDC nor the British Central Fund would aid any of the organizations if they refused to fit into a program I proposed;
(2) Biro-Bidjan. He is as much opposed as ever, except possibly for some Russian Jewish pioneers;
(3) Turkey. Dr. Weizmann had opposed sending the commission out two months ago, and now Dr. Kahn is waiting reply from the Turkish authorities redetailed program which he had proposed. He is anxious that he be assured of sufficient financial backing in the event the Turkish authorities officially approve his proposal;
(4) Morocco. Recent political developments block work there;
(5) Brazil. There are possibilities;
(6) France. The liquidation committee, meeting daily, is gradually cutting down the numbers dependent on relief. One can say that that phase of the problem is on the way towards solution. He seemed to us rather too optimistic in this analysis, particularly since many of those who were being taken off of the immediate relief lists by the French National Committee, do not appear to be adequately taken care of. Of course, underlying his whole philosophy is the basis which the French bitterly opposed whenever one ventures to present it openly, that thousands of the refugees would in one way or another have to be taken care of permanently by regular French charitable organizations. Similarly, his contention that the number of refugees acutely in need is only four or five thousand in all of the countries, seems to me to give a misleading impression;
(7) Anglo-HICEM. It is working as well as could be expected by a group of amateurs. The members of the committee are only learning their job, and may be expected later to be able to do it;

(8) Czechoslovakia. The JDC might be able to give some additional money to the Czech National Committee, but could only do it through Miss Masaryk, thus avoiding the political implications of the membership on the National Committee of political organizations. I was to ask Miss Masaryk if she would do this;

(9) Ginsberg's committee. Impossible to give her additional funds now, without giving to other committees as well;

(10) Germany. Has had long talks with the German chargé in Paris. Explained to him the adverse effect on public opinion of proposal to take young Jews out of Germany. That therefore, from Germany's point of view, it is important that at least the young Jews continue to complete their technical training in the Reich;

(11) Place of the High Commission's office. He thought Paris would be preferable to London.

In general, Dr. Kahn, as on many previous occasions, showed an extraordinary grasp of the whole situation and a complete willingness to help where he can.

Talked with Otto Schiff on the telephone. He first asked about the meeting at Leeds. I told him I thought it was reasonably successful, that Mr. Burton had not been there, but that Izzy Isaacs had come and made a substantial contribution, and that I thought the Central Fund perhaps could utilize Isaacs more than they had.

I then asked him about the meeting this afternoon of the Allocation Committee, and said that I would like to have his advice, first as to whether it would be a mistake for me to appeal to the Allocation Committee on behalf of Miss Ginsberg's work. He said that probably no money would be voted at today's meeting; that perhaps it would be a mistake to make the appeal, but that it probably would be advantageous if I sent a telegram asking the committee not to reject Miss Ginsberg's appeal, but to hold it over until there had been an opportunity to present a fuller statement about the work of the various committees dealing with intellectuals. I told him that I would probably do this.

I mentioned my talk with Cunliffe-Lister, and without going into details, simply indicated that the colonial secretary was, as he doubtless thought, vigorously opposed to any formal action beyond the Jordan at this time.

Dinner at the Baron Robert de Rothschild's. Besides the Baron and the Baroness and Bentwich and I there were present the three Rothschild daughters and the husband of one of them, the Polish minister in Paris,[13] Lady Davis, Hel-

13. Polish diplomat Anatole Muhlstein married Baron Robert's daughter Diane. Rothschild had only two daughters.

bronner,[14] and two or three others. The dinner was elaborate and good. After dinner we moved into the drawing room, filled almost to the point of being stuffed, with previous pictures, statuary, armor, etc. It seemed a little incongruous in that atmosphere to talk about the hardships of the refugees and the difficulty of finding funds to meet their needs.

The talk followed the usual line, the need of more help for the French Committee from outside, the danger stressed by Helbronner and assented to by all the others from any large scale colonization project in southern France, etc. Finally, I happened to speak of the Polish-German Treaty,[15] and I discovered that the son-in-law was the Polish minister. Then followed nearly an hour's defense, and a very able one it was, by the minister of Poland's attitude. He put the case solely on the ground of Poland's necessity of maintaining peace, and of the advantages to be gained during the interim period, such as the discontinuance of German propaganda against the Polish Corridor, and the possible gradual acceptance by the German people of the status quo.

Baron Robert said he was anxious to meet Henry Ittleson, especially if the latter had a son for his unmarried daughter. This followed after my explanation that Ittleson was probably effectively the richest Jew in the States.

Lady Davis offered to take me home, but I nobly declined and walked back with Bentwich.

Wednesday, April 11, 1934

Conference with Louis Oungre at the ICA office at 10:30. The time was too short for what we both had in mind, so I agreed to meet him later that afternoon. In these two conferences we discussed a number of current problems, but the chief importance of the meeting was the development of an idea which seemingly Oungre had been working on for some time. It can be summarized as follows: For the refugee problem in the narrow sense, there is really not enough to do to justify the High Commission. Such tasks as it can undertake, such as passports and technical discussions with the governments, could be done if necessary by the organizations. The other phase of the work must be done by the organizations. Therefore, and he put this conclusion with "due deference," the High Commission is for the immediate purpose a luxury.

However, there is a much larger problem, the one to which the High Commissioner himself had referred in his plans for the corporation. This is the gen-

14. Jacques Helbronner, counselor of state, president of the Consistoire, the central body of French Jews. In June 1933 Helbronner reportedly said, "not all the Jewish refugees from Germany are people worth keeping," and in 1936 Helbronner referred to them as "riff-raff, the rejects of society, the elements who could not possibly have been of any use to their own country." In October 1943 he and his wife were arrested and sent to Auschwitz, where they were killed. Saul Friedländer, *Nazi Germany and the Jews,* vol. I, *The Years of Persecution, 1933–1939* (New York: HarperCollins, 1997), 220–221.

15. In January 1934 Poland and Germany surprisingly signed a non-aggression pact. It gave Germany some protection against a possible "preventive war" by Poland at a time when German military strength was still limited.

eral task of directing the flow of Jewish emigration. This must be done if grave dangers are to be avoided. It cannot be done by ad hoc organizations, nor by intermittent drives. In England, after this year, probably there will not be another drive for considerable sums. The English will feel exhausted. Therefore, it is necessary to create the corporation with large funds, relate it closely to the High Commission, making the High Commissioner the chairman of the board, and thus create an institution with governmental backing and sufficient resources. He added that he thought I could do that job excellently.

Such a corporation should work closely with ICA; the two together could shape large policies and carry them through. They could work together best by contributing substantial amounts towards common projects, and he seemed to favor as a first venture the Hula swamp area, and is much opposed to the Rutenberg project[16] which I am told Sir Robert Waley-Cohen has just been convinced about, that is, the irrigation of the regions south of Tiberias.

Oungre indicated that he would like to have an invitation from the United States to talk with the Americans interested in the corporation. I expressed the hope that he might go, but did not commit myself to any attempt to wrangle an invitation.

We parted with the impression on my side that Louis Oungre is really vitally and constructively interested in the whole Jewish question. Indeed, he told me with considerable pride that it had been his idea that had created the foundation, the AMICA[17] and one or two similar bodies.

Long conference with Jesse Straus at the Embassy. There is little in it that needs to be recorded. He was extremely cordial, but our talk had little to do with Germany and less with Jewish questions. I was shocked to see how sick he looked. He explained to me that he had been suffering from the effects of a cure which he had taken for some disease, that now he was trying to undo the effects of the treatment he had received. He is able to keep in touch with affairs, but is in constant pain and obviously very far from being a well man.

Lunch with Guani at the Ritz Hotel. Guani confessed that his government gave him no instructions at all in reference to the High Commission, except that he might attend. Moreover, it did not compensate him for his expenses. He hinted about the possibility of reimbursement from the High Commission, but I gave him no encouragement. He suggested that some of the meetings at any rate should be in Paris. In principle I agreed with this.

He expressed the personal view that on certain bases Uruguay might welcome further Jewish migration. He said he would like to talk to Louis Oungre about this. I agreed to ask Oungre to get in touch with him. This I did.

Brief conference with Mme. Vavaseur at Dr. Kahn's office. She showed me

16. To make use of the Jordan valley and Hula region as a source of electricity. Devised by Pinhas Rutenberg, Russian-born engineer and founder of the Palestine Electric Corporation.

17. Probably the South American regional branch or affiliate of the ICA (Jewish Colonization Association).

a list of those receiving allowances from her committee in Paris, and expressed great anxiety that funds be made available to continue this work.

Attended a meeting of the re-training committee. After listening to some of the reports, I went off with Edouard Oungre to see the HICEM office and to hear his account of the HICEM work. On the technical side of caring for the actual transport of immigrants, his office seems well organized and competently run.

A little after six I went to the meeting of the National Committee in Rothschild's office. What a method of conducting a meeting! Baron Robert insists on spending much of the time haranguing his colleagues as though they were at a town meeting. The question of colonization in southern France again came up and was vehemently attacked. Baron Rothschild told with much pleasure of Lady Davis's report of my appeal for the French Committee in New York, and of my attack on the over-emphasis in some English and American quarters on "re-construction." Professor Oualid asked the same question which has been asked me in nearly every center where I have been: "What will London and New York do with the large funds they are raising? Why not give more to Paris?"[18]

Had a pleasant and friendly chat with Sylvain Levi, who now seems fully reconciled.

Left the committee in excellent spirits.

Hurried back to the hotel to finish packing, for a last minute conference with Bentwich, and dictation to Miss Sawyer. Then a bite to eat with her while she lectured me on my occasional too casual manner of dealing with non-Americans; in particular, she told me of Mme. Bentwich's displeasure at my failing to have her invited to the Rothschild dinner. I humbly agreed to reform.

As proof of my good intentions, I wrote a note of apology to Mrs. Bentwich on the train. Then in a fashion which I have learned from the Rockefellers, I felt that whatever wrong I had done had been completely righted and forgot about it.

Geneva, Thursday, April 12, 1934

Arrived in Geneva at eight o'clock. Chatted for a moment with Edouard Oungre at the station, and then went to the Bellevue.

18. Norman Bentwich described the situation in France in the early months of 1934: "The French Government which, with occasional lapses of hardness, is generally more liberal than others to those seeking asylum, placed at the disposal of the refugees disused barracks on the outskirts of Paris. I was to find dealing with the French Civil Service involved and embarrassing. The departmentalism . . . was more baffling than the departmentalism in Whitehall; and the constant changing of the personnel at the Quai d'Orsay was another difficulty. Each month we were apt to find another official with whom to start from scratch. I would go to see Senator Bérenger at the Luxembourg Palace of the Senate, and obtain his blessing; but it was a different matter to get anything done in the Bureaux in days of unrest and constant change of cabinets." The problem was compounded by French fear of a fascist movement, which during February 1934 had created serious disturbances. Norman Bentwich, *A Wanderer between Two Worlds* (London: Kegan Paul, Trench, Trubner & Co., 1941), 238.

Tried to see Hugh Wilson, but he was absorbed in disarmament and Leticia[19] discussions.

Long chat with Kotschnig. He told me of his unfinished book, which will need two or three months' work before Christmas, of the Des Moines offer of $3,000 for five months, and of his lack of interest in the Fisk proposal. The more he talked, the more I felt that probably a part-time arrangement would be best all around. We tentatively agreed on this, but it was left to the next day for final decision.

Dictated to Miss Berg letters to Adams, Warburg, etc. I am afraid I showed my irritation at her slowness.

I neglected to mention that while I was out of the hotel in Paris, Adams telephoned a message from Sir William Beveridge to the effect that the latter did not see the necessity of Kotschnig's appointment.

Conference with Prentiss Gilbert. He outlined in a way which showed a complete understanding of the League in theory and in practice, of what it might become in the event that the European political situation—disarmament, etc.—remained so adverse or became worse. He saw the League becoming a purely, but nonetheless essential, technical institution. On the other hand, if political developments became more favorable, it might regain considerable political influence.

He called my special attention to an apparent inconsistency in Wurfbain's practice of addressing official communications sometimes through Gilbert's office, sometimes directly to Washington. Gilbert pointed out that the practice should be one thing or the other consistently.

He added that if we sent all formal communications through Geneva, he would have a complete record and would be in a position from time to time, if we wished him to do so, to communicate informally to the departments, even by telegraph at the government's expense, material which we would prefer not to send officially. I said I would take the matter up with Wurfbain.

Lunch with Miss Ginsberg. She gave me a detailed estimate of her needs. I agreed to send a cable to Mildred, urging her to ask Herbert Swope's cooperation in raising a special emergency fund of $15,000. I said also that I would speak to the Nobel Institute people about the firm project. Later, I said I would consider asking Cecil to write the letter which was suggested by Rosenberg, through a cable received that day from Mildred, which had crossed the one sent by us. As to Kotschnig, Miss Ginsberg agreed to cooperate. She expressed the view that Demuth[20] and Kahn (Ernst), both being Germans, had arranged to cooperate more closely than they were willing to do with her. She quoted Demuth as having said at a conference attended by Bentwich, that since his committee was not recognized by the High Commissioner, they

19. Leticia, town on the Colombian-Peruvian border, subject of dispute in a border war. The League of Nations mediated and awarded it to Colombia in June 1934.

20. Dr. Demuth of the Notgemeinschaft deutscher Wissenschaftler im Ausland (Association for Emergency Aid for German Scholars Abroad).

would not have to recognize the High Commission. She also stressed, as had Kotschnig, the desirability of the High Commissioner having a special fund with which to help out in specially critical situations, and to be used as a form of sanctions.

....

I should have mentioned above that Miss Ginsberg was the first of the whole series of my friends to tell me of the reports current in Geneva that I am exploiting my position for my own financial profit, and that indeed, charges of crookedness are being made.

Attended the Wurfbain reception at the Richmond. Chatted with the bride and groom and with the parents. The bride, when animated, is very attractive.

Up to the Secretariat and chatted for a little while with Brown of the U.P., Sharkey of the A.P., Streit, and Arthur Sweetser. The latter I only had time to begin the discussion about our work. He intimated that there were criticisms of inactivity, nothing having been heard of us in Geneva since the ball had been kicked off in December, and he intimated that more serious rumors were afloat. He attempted to arrange for me to see the Secretary General, but the latter was absorbed in the Leticia controversy and was leaving for Rome the next day, so my conference had to be put off. In any event, the Secretary General indicated that he doubted if he could be of much use.

Chodzko took me aside to explain that from his point of view, the High Commission must be made permanent and enlarged. The League had always refused to meet the Jewish question fairly. Unless there is an international body in existence, governmental in character, to act as a safety valve, inevitably the rising tide of anti-Semitism, which obsesses the youth in all central and eastern Europe, will precipitate tragedies of ominous proportions. In Poland this is a grave danger once Pilsudski ceases to be there to defend the Jews. His thesis could not have been presented more forcibly or with more evidence of complete sincerity.

Incidentally, Chodzko said that if I really wanted him to be in London, it would be desirable for me to speak to the officials in the Polish Foreign Office about it. I said I would very gladly do this. Impressed and moved by Chodzko's statement, I sent off a letter to Felix Warburg about it.[21]

Worked until late with Miss Berg, and then had supper with Mrs. Askew. The latter unburdened herself about the Geneva atmosphere. She said that persons had told her of my iniquities and of the frequent references to financial exploitation or worse. I thanked her for her frankness and expressed the hope that

21. McDonald added, "In Poland only the strong arm of Pilsudski holds in check the fanatical hatred of the anti-Jewish youth—and Pilsudski is 66 years old. . . . In Rumania, Hungary, and of course in Austria similar currents are evident. . . . He warned that unless there is some such governmental organization to act as a safety valve . . . grave developments for the countries of Europe and for their Jewish populations may ensue. . . ." McDonald to Warburg, April 13, 1934, McDonald Papers, Columbia, Special File, Felix Warburg.

any answer that needed to be made would be made at London, though I doubted whether any direct reply would be made to these reports.

Friday, April 13, 1934

Conference with Kotschnig. We agreed that he would join the staff on a three months' basis, the financial compensation to be that which he is now receiving from the ISS, that is approximately 1,400 Swiss francs a month. In addition, he is, of course, to have traveling expenses on the basis fixed in the financial regulations, and the necessary secretarial help. He is to begin work on April 15, and to have ready as complete a report as is possible of the different intellectual committees before the meeting of the Advisory Council. I said I would give him a general letter of introduction and would write to the heads of the various committees asking their cooperation.

Conference with Malcolm Davis. I urged him to come to London to study our whole publicity problem and to cooperate with us there, and possibly to continue to represent us in some capacity in Geneva. He was interested, but thought that his previous engagements would prevent his accepting.

Then he and I went to Arthur's office. He, having invited me to dinner after I had previously arranged an engagement, had graciously consented to come down to the office as early as ten o'clock in order to see me before I had to leave for Vienna at 11:30. Without any preliminaries, I told him and Davis that I, of course, knew of the reports prevalent in Geneva, that while I thought that they had to be taken into account, they were in fact based on grossly exaggerated rumors, and they ignored completely the large program which interested me most. I admitted that on the publicity side we probably had been mistaken, perhaps even negligent. Arthur asked me about the budget. I told him of my salary, which he looked up and found was the same as that of one of the under-secretaries of the League. I told them that I was making a contribution of a substantial portion of my salary, but that I was not saying anything about this publicly, but might do so later. I urged Arthur to try to persuade Davis to come to London. There was no time for a full discussion, but I left with the impression that both Arthur and Davis would help where they can.

Miss Ginsberg and Kotschnig took me to the station for last minute conferences. But before I left Arthur's office, I dictated two cables, a longer one to May and a shorter one to Strauss, asking for further aid in meeting the situation created by the Geneva small-town information service.

On the train had a long and interesting chat with Roehm, the Russian press representative in Geneva. He thinks the Disarmament Conference is doomed, that it is nonsense to expect Russia to join the League, and that the League may therefore degenerate into a purely technical body.[22]

At Zurich, where I arrived about four o'clock, I was met at the station and had a chance to chat for about twenty minutes with Demuth. He seemed

22. The Soviet Union did join the League in 1934 and remained a member until 1940.

pleased at Kotschnig's appointment, offered complete cooperation, appreciated my comment on the success of his committee in Istanbul, and said he would be glad to come to London, but must have a formal letter of invitation in order to assure him of his visa. I left him with the impression of a sincere and sorely tried man.

Vienna, Saturday, April 14, 1934

Arrived in Vienna about nine o'clock in the morning. Went at once to the Hotel Regina, where I met Bentwich. The first interview was with the representative of the JTA. Then followed a delegation from the Jewish community, headed by Dr. Friedman. I was depressed, as had been Bentwich, by the evident timidity of the representatives of the Jewish community, by their fear lest they antagonize further the Dollfuss regime, and thus bring down on their heads worse than had already happened to them. One could not have had a better proof of Jewish insecurity in Austria. They even objected to my saying to the Viennese officials that I, of course, hoped and was confident that in Austria there would be no repetition of the anti-Semitic excesses of the Nazis.[23]

Conference with Hornbostel of the Foreign Office about certain general considerations. I was restrained, however, by Friedman's presence from saying anything definite about Austria's Jewish attitude.

Then to see a technical official, a Dr. (?) Schlage, about passports, etc. I left this conference in Bentwich's hands in order to go to see Klieforth and the American Legation.

Klieforth, who is charged by Judge Mack's daughter as being anti-Semitic, gave no indication of such view. On the contrary, he said he was influencing the regime by indicating an unusual interest in any reports of anti-Semitic meetings or anti-Semitic publications; that he had been instrumental, through these methods, of having a number of meetings discontinued. Starhemberg,[24] whom he knows well personally, told him that earlier he had shared fully Hitler's anti-Jewish views, but that recently he had become convinced that it was a great mistake for Austria to follow the German example.

On the attitude of the Catholic clergy Klieforth was especially interesting. The older clergy are a strongly anti-Semitic, while the cardinal[25] and the more

23. According to Bentwich's memorandum of the meeting, the Austrian relief committee was facing increasing needs despite the fact that only a few refugees were currently arriving from Germany. They had been supporting eight hundred persons, but the numbers were increasing because many of the other refugees had now become destitute. Only Austrian citizens could work or attend Austrian training programs. The committee wanted to set up its own training programs if they could get money from the JDC and the British Central Fund. Notes of the meetings with relief committees in Vienna, and with the Austrian Foreign Office, April 14, 1934. Copy in McDonald Papers, USHMM.

24. Ernst Rüdiger von Starhemberg. Austrian, participant in Hitler's Beer Hall Putsch of 1923. Head of the Austrian Heimwehr, a semi-fascist militia. Helped to suppress the Social Democrats in February 1934 and later, a minister in the Schuschnigg government.

25. Theodor Cardinal Innitzer, archbishop of Vienna.

ultramontane clergy hold out against such extremes. Indeed, the cardinal has gone out of his way to express friendship for the Jews. Nonetheless, there are always possibilities of worse conditions for the Jews.

As to the Dollfuss attack on the Socialists, Klieforth thought this was unnecessary, that the general strike would have been ineffective, but that the extremists in Dollfuss's own ranks forced the issue. Klieforth expressed great pleasure at the coming of Messersmith. I am inclined to doubt the sincerity, however, for Messersmith will be much more independent than a political appointee is likely to be.

Lunch at the house of Gunther, the correspondent of the *Chicago Daily News*. Others present besides Mrs. Gunther and myself were the Bentwiches and a young Englishman studying on a Carnegie or Rockefeller grant. The talk was mostly about political conditions in Austria. Gunther, formerly a great admirer of Dollfuss, now feels that he is the head of a government which commands the enthusiastic support of not more than 5 percent of the population. Someone described the situation as being a series of concentric circles, each being made up of the private or official armies of the various factions. They thought that the Socialists are not finished, but the Nazis, while they missed their opportunity in February, which indeed they perhaps could not have taken because it would have involved direct support of their chief enemies, the Socialists, were biding their time and would grow. Meantime, Starhemberg and the Heimwehr were not satisfied. Indeed, the situation seemed to me so complex that I several times lost myself during the discussion.

Over to see Mrs. Micheles and her daughter. Was received like the prodigal son. Miss Micheles has an offer from one of the women executives in the motion picture industry to be her secretary in the States, but she is uncertain about her visa. I suggested that she write her sister fully and ask her or her husband to report on the exact situation and the Washington viewpoint. I said I would be glad to speak to the authorities in Washington if that would be helpful, or to the American authorities in Vienna.

Tea with the Brunswicks—Judge Mack's daughter and her artistic husband. We gossiped about conditions at home and in Vienna. They are both 100 percent Jews and critical of the borderline variety. Both of them and Mrs. Bentwich saw Bentwich and me off on the train, Mrs. Bentwich meantime having generously forgiven me my Rothschild slight.

Long tiresome trip to Prague, enlivened somewhat by Bentwich's account of Palestinian [Zionist] politics. Greeted on arrival in Prague at about 11:30 by representatives of the press, to whom I gave a brief interview.

Prague, Sunday, April 15, 1934

Was met early in the morning by a representative of the Czech Foreign Office, who came to bring the compliments of his chiefs; his name was Dr. Fisa.

At 10:30 there was a committee meeting with the representatives of all five committees—the Jewish, the Social Democratic, the Salda, the Trade Union, and a fifth. Mr. Bentwich's memorandum summarizes the results of the meeting.[26] In general, we were much encouraged by the close cooperation of the Jewish and non-Jewish bodies, and by the extent to which the non-Jewish refugees are cared for by Jewish leadership.

Lunch with Kose,[27] whom I had known in the States. He is now in the Department of Agriculture and a vice president of the American Institute.

After lunch Kose, Dr. Klatscher, Bentwich, and I went with Mrs. Lowenbach to see her commune about an hour outside the city. It was an inspiring example of what can be done with very little. An old hunting palace was being utilized to house fifty or sixty members of families. They were being provided for at a very small cost, and the children had the full run of a beautiful park. I was much attracted by a young child of about thirteen, Elloise Kaspar, whose mother, I think, was being sent off to the hospital that day to be examined for tuberculosis.

Did some work with a stenographer at the hotel, and then out to dinner with the Lowenbachs at a local club. Had a chance after dinner to chat with Paul Hertz, and got the impression that he would tend to be less critical of the work of the High Commission after we had discussed the matter more fully.

Monday, April 16, 1934

After work with a stenographer, Bentwich and I went to the Palace for a 10:30 appointment with Benes.[28] He was most cordial. He appreciated my interest in an endeavor to correct a misinterpretation of his recent statement about the Anschluss. Then I expressed my admiration of the work done by the relief committees in Czechoslovakia, of the helpfulness of the government, and the organization, on the initiative of the committee, of a national group. I said that I would welcome Mme. Smolkova,[29] as a representative of the National Committee, at the meeting of the Advisory Council. I raised six questions with the minister: passports, stateless refugees, permits to work, retraining, the place of the Red Cross, and the press. Benes's answer to each of these is given in full in

26. The committees each raise their funds, but these can only be used for relief. It was suggested that it would be better if the relief work could be combined under the auspices of the Red Cross headed by Miss Masaryk (daughter of the co-founder and first president of Czechoslovakia). There were no jobs, but half the money for retraining could be raised in the community if the rest could come from overseas. Notes of the meeting with the representatives of the National Committee of C.S., Sunday, April 15, 1934. Copy in McDonald Papers, USHMM.

27. Dr. Jaroslav Kose, active in American-Czech trade relations, later head of American-Czech Chamber of Commerce.

28. Eduard Benes, one of the co-founders of Czechoslovakia, foreign minister and elected president in 1935. Chairman of the Security Committee of the League of Nations and president of the League Assembly, September 1935.

29. Marie Smolkova, secretary of the Czech National Committee for Refugees. Bentwich reported in his autobiography that she carried on until 1939, when she was imprisoned by the Nazis. After two months she was released but "died broken-hearted" in London soon after. Norman Bentwich, *My 77 Years* (Philadelphia: Jewish Publication Society, 1961), 135.

Bentwich's notes on the interview.[30] There was one general consideration, however, which I should note here, which is Benes's emphasis upon the difficult position in which Czechoslovakia finds itself—an island of parliamentarianism surrounded by a sea of dictatorships. This makes the refugee situation in the country and the government's treatment of the individuals much more serious than would otherwise be the case. Each of the neighboring governments looks upon Czechslovakia as a provocation to revolt within its own territories.

Incidentally, from Benes and from Kose the day previous, and from other Czechs, I got a more vivid sense of the conflicting points of view between Czechoslovakia and Poland. The Czechoslovakian interpretation is that Poland is feeling its oats, and is determined to be recognized as a great power and to treat Czechoslovakia as an inferior.

Talked to Miss Masaryk on the telephone. She said she would cooperate and receive funds from Dr. Kahn as president of the Red Cross.

Stopped on the way back to the hotel to see the Polish counselor and to tell him of our plans to visit Poland.

Interviews with the *Prager Presse,* and with the *New York Times,* and with a group of Jewish journalists.

Lunch with Dr. K. Krofta, the assistant minister to Benes, out at the restaurant located on the hill parallel with the Palace. Others present were members of the committees. Krofta talked quite frankly during lunch about Polish relations.

After lunch Bentwich and I met with the secretaries of the relief committees. They were all themselves refugees. Dr. Grossmann[31] seemed to be the leader. We talked about a number of technical questions; Bentwich reports on these in his memorandum.[32] The secretaries stressed the danger of the stateless becoming criminals if no way was found for them to be dealt with as others are dealt with. They also wished the High Commissioner to intervene to protect them against attacks from the Czech press.

Long talk with Dr. Novak, who is now in the Foreign Office in Prague.

An elaborate dinner, given for Bentwich and me, by Dr. Popper on behalf of the B'nai B'rith. Much to drink and eat. Then Bentwich and I each had to make a speech. My English was on this occasion, as on several others, much more appreciated than Bentwich's flowing style. On later occasions Bentwich

30. Benes promised to look into the special problems of the stateless refugees, to see if there could be any liberalization of work permits, but he stressed that the economic and political situation was worse than a year ago. He would support the issue of stamps to raise money for refugees if other countries did likewise. Notes of interview with Dr. Benes, April 16, 1934. Copy in McDonald Papers, USHMM.

31. Kurt R. Grossmann, born in Berlin, secretary general of the German League for Human Rights during the Weimar Republic, an early emigrant to Czechoslovakia in 1933. Came to the United States in 1939, where he published frequently on topics related to Jewish refugees.

32. They stressed their dwindling resources and need for money to help with emigration. McDonald stressed that funds from overseas were limited and any money for relief and maintenance must be found locally. Note of a meeting in Prague on April 16, 1934, with secretaries of the relief committees. Copy in McDonald Papers, USHMM.

often spoke in German, which he handles satisfactorily. Mme. Smolkova, who sat at my right, gave me the "lowdown" on the different personalities present, and saved me from what she said would have been a very serious mistake if I had spoken of Dr. Margolies before I spoke of Dr. Popper. After these two I was free to speak of Councillor Dux and of Dr. Kohn, both helpful on the committee.

Warsaw, Tuesday, April 17, 1934

Last minute preparations. Out to the flying field by eleven. We took off at 11:20 promptly and had a very smooth flight. The landscape afforded constant interest, as the Polish villages were replaced after we crossed the low mountain, by the industrial centers and villages of Upper Silesia and then again by the villages and fields of Poland. I shared the pilot's map with a very attractive young American, Erik Hofman, the representative of the Wasp and Hornet airplane manufacturers. After two hours of flight the pilot showed us a notice to the effect that we would arrive in Warsaw at two o'clock, fifty minutes early, because of a strong following wind. Thus, we did in two hours and forty minutes what took at least fifteen hours by train.

I should not neglect to record that the chargé at the American Legation, who had rather high-hatted me when I tried to reach him on Sunday, made up for this beautifully by having the United States' courier, who was travelling by train, take my heavy bag on to Warsaw ahead of me.

At first we were surprised on landing not to be met by a delegation, but just as we were about to climb in a bus to go to town, we were told that the bus would have to wait until the delegation had arrived. Bentwich rather impatiently wanted them to telephone to tell the delegation not to come, but I told him that this would never do. Anyhow, they had already started. So I urged the company to send off the bus with the other passengers and leave us.

Then came the first of several photographers, followed shortly thereafter by the delegation. This was made up of Professor Schorr,[33] the chief Reform rabbi, Rabbi Levine, the head of the Agudas, Gottlieb, Rosemarin, Turkow, the secretary of the committee, Scheskin, a smooth young engineer who prides himself on being the consul general of Honduras, and perhaps one or two others.

Professor Schorr insisted on making me a very nice carefully prepared speech of welcome in English, which I, failing to sense the full importance of the occasion, satisfied myself by bowing my thanks. Anyhow, it didn't matter; I had enough speeches to make later.

Three of the members of the committee then took us to the hotel for lunch about three o'clock. This was hardly finished before we had to meet the members of the executive committee at tea. Bentwich and I went over with them a number of questions which Bentwich summarizes in his memorandum.

33. Moses Schorr, distinguished biblical scholar and professor at the University of Warsaw, as well as chief rabbi of the Reform movement.

All the members of the committee stressed the undesirability of repatriating the Polish refugees, and gave what seemed to us compelling reasons for this view.[34]

An hour or so later Bentwich and I met the full committee, some twenty-one persons, at their office. This group represented every fractional shade of Jewish opinion in Poland. I made a general statement on the work of the High Commission; Bentwich supplemented it. Then we hoped for a technical discussion of problems in Poland. But we soon learned that we did not know our Poles; they were in no mood for a technical discussion. Instead, Gottlieb, Rosemarin, and most energetically of all, Rabbi Rubenstein, the Mizrachi leader from Vilna, launched a formidable oratorical attack on the United States, the British government, the Palestine administration et al. for not doing more. Bentwich, who was set to interpret Rubinstein's Hebrew speech (the other two talks had been in German and were not interpreted), was too good an Englishman to be able to refrain from interrupting his interpretation by replying to the rabbi's attacks on the British administration of Palestine.

Another member of the committee, speaking in French, continued the attack. Only Rabbi Levine, speaking in German, and with true Viennese *Gemütlichkeit,* made a conciliatory speech.

I, in my best FPA manner, listened as well as I could to all the noise of the battle raging around me and decided that I would make a brief second speech at the end in an attempt to pour oil on the troubled waters. So, addressing myself to each of the individuals, one after another, who had spoken, and replying briefly to certain points they had made, but recognizing essential elements of justice in their attitude, I managed to end the oratory. But out of it all came very little help for the actual situation in Poland. But for me, it was very educational.

Shenkin then took me to the Ariada, a very attractive restaurant, where two of his friends, the two Mrs. Sigmunds, and he and I danced for a while. We were joined by Jabotinsky,[35] the redoubtable Revisionist leader, who interrupted the dancing by setting forth in brilliant and pungent phrases, which bit like acid, his estimates of Weizmann and other Jewish leaders opposed to the Revisionist cause. I was so interested in Jabotinsky as a man, and so anxious to hear more at first hand about Revisionism, that I asked him to lunch with me the next day. Then home and to bed.

34. The committee explained that the so-called "Poles" had never lived in Poland and couldn't even speak Polish. Last year one-half of the total relief funds had come from the JDC and the English Central Fund, but now the Warsaw committees were at the end of their resources. Note of a meeting on Tuesday afternoon, April 17, with the heads of the refugee committee: Dr. Gottlieb, Rabbi Lewin, Prof. Schorr, Mr. Turkow. Copy in McDonald Papers, USHMM.

35. Vladimir Zeev Jabotinsky, Russian-born founder of Revisionist Zionism, which advocated an independent Jewish state on both sides of the Jordan River and a non-Socialist economy in Palestine. Traveled across Europe in the 1920s and 1930s urging Jews to leave before they fell victim to a great catastrophe. Mentor of Menachem Begin and spiritual ancestor of Israel's Likud Party.

Wednesday, April 18, 1934

Over to the American Embassy. The ambassador was away, so I chatted with Mr. Neilson, one of the secretaries.

Then to the Foreign Office, to meet the minister (Mr. Szembek) who is the assistant to the foreign minister. We discussed some technical matters, which discussion Bentwich continued later with some of the other officials. In our interview the same Polish view was stressed as had been stressed by the members of the Jewish committee—the undesirability, even the impossibility, of accepting the repatriation of the Polish refugees in France or elsewhere. We got the impression that the Poles had made the French understand that there was no use in insisting on such repatriation. And in the present temper of the Poles, feeling as cocky as they do, they are not likely to yield to French argumentation on this point.

Back to the hotel to find forty or fifty journalists waiting to receive me. The committee had arranged for tea, so we all sat down, and while drinking tea I expounded on the work of the High Commission and its relations to Poland. Fortunately, my talk was interpreted currently, paragraph by paragraph, by the very intelligent correspondent of the *New York Times,* Szapiro.[36] After I had spoken for about half an hour, there were a number of questions, most of which I could not answer because they dealt too definitely with specific government policies, or in other ways would have required me to give replies that would have been embarrassing.

The interview was scarcely over before it was time to have luncheon with Jabotinsky. I also asked Bentwich to be present. I told the Revisionist leader that I would be grateful if he would tell me as fully as he could the philosophy that underlies his program, his plan of action, etc. This he did with the precision and clarity which makes him a marked man. He was less satisfactory in his answer to my question as to how he meets the argument that his program is impracticable. He then launched into a rather theoretical discussion to the effect that no other program had any elements of practicability. As to the Arab opposition, that cannot be smoothed away. The British government must be induced to aid in the creation of a Jewish majority. Only so can, according to Jabotinsky, the essential ideal of Zionism, a Jewish political state, be achieved.

Throughout the discussion I made no comments except as might tend to draw Jabotinsky out. Whatever elements of unrealism there are in his program, he is essentially realistic on one basic point of view: it is that only through a change in the point of view of the British government can the larger aims of the extreme political Zionists be achieved. He, therefore, is concentrating his efforts on converting the British authorities to his views. Now as to his method of conversion, there will be of course the sharpest division of opinion. Controversy, however, in which I am not called upon to take sides.

36. Jerzy Szapiro, *Times* correspondent in Warsaw, 1933–1939.

My two talks with Jabotinsky deeply impressed me with the honesty, the extraordinary mentality, and the courage of the man. In some respects he is strikingly like Weizmann, from whom of course he differs completely on political issues. I would not attempt to judge between the two men, but Jabotinsky has one quality which is not notable in Dr. Weizmann—that is, generosity towards the personalities and the personal lives of those with whom he radically disagrees on public issues.

After lunch Bentwich and I met with a group of the refugees themselves. They are dissatisfied with the committees who represent them and wish to appeal to us directly. Their talks of need were discouraging, because one could not avoid the feeling that in Poland, more than anywhere else in Europe, much that needs to be done will have to be left undone.

Bentwich and I hurried off from the refugees to a tea at Dr. Schorr's house. It is located inside the enclosure formed by the buildings associated with the Temple.[37] There were present the members of the committee and their wives. Even the most Orthodox of the rabbis sat down at table with the women.

We returned to the hotel in time for a conference with two of the Agudas leaders, the two Rabbis Levine. They emphasized again the appeals that had been made to Bentwich and me in Lausanne, Paris, and London, and to me in New York, for Agudas representation on the Advisory Council. It was clear in this conference, as in the earlier ones, that Agudas's interest in such representation is primarily a matter of prestige. And at the end I remained unconvinced that if we invited Agudas, we could resist inviting the Mizrachi, the Revisionists, the Laborites, and how many other sectarian or sectional interest I cannot tell. However, we promised the Agudas leaders that we would consider the matter again before the meeting of the Governing Body next month.

Bentwich and I went directly from this conference to a high tea arranged by the committee for us at the Europaischer Hotel. There the leaders of the community and we partook of much tea and many rich pastries, for which I managed to substitute some sandwiches because I knew there would be no dinner, the Poles having the Russian habit of dining sometime during the middle of the afternoon and then having tea the rest of the afternoon and night. Jabotinsky, who had been invited to come to the tea and to make a speech, had generously declined to come, because he knew that it would be embarrassing for me to appear on the same platform with him—indeed, I had told him at lunch that this would be impossible—and because he knew that if he came and remained silent, his silence would be interpreted as unfriendly to me. I made a brief speech, which was translated into Polish by Professor Anglestein.

37. Temple, the Tlomacka Street or "Great" Synagogue built in 1878, with a Reform congregation. Blown up by Jürgen Stroop on Heinrich Himmler's order on May 16, 1943, following suppression of the Warsaw Ghetto uprising.

Thursday, April 19, 1934

Fairly early appointment with Zaleski,[38] formerly foreign minister and now the head of the newly organized Polish committee for refugee intellectuals. Their work has just begun. They hope that the Rockefeller Foundation would be willing to supplement funds that they might raise.

The rest of the day until lunch time was given over to visits by Bentwich and me to the Jewish quarters in the city and to two villages outside of town. The impressions made on us by these trips will never be forgotten. The unbelievable poverty in the city itself, the worst of things offered for sale, portions of meat which at home would invariably be discarded, shoddy and wretched cloth and shoes, were eloquent proof of the wretchedness of the people. We entered one or two hovels where whole families lived and worked in what was only a small room, with one exit. As we walked along, we began to be recognized, and the word soon passed up and down the section as to who we were. It was with a sense of real humility, almost of futility, that we went on, realizing that these people looked to us for help, which at the very best could come in only a tiny measure from any efforts we might make. Moreover, I could not refrain from picturing to myself what these people would be like if only they were free to be themselves, the children who, except for the accidents of their birth, might have had the same opportunities as our own.

In the first small village to which we went, largely Jewish, we saw the same evidence of terrible poverty, but lightened somewhat by the open space of the country. We visited one of the traditional Agudas schools where an old man was teaching seven or eight boys the Hebrew prayers. We had to stoop to enter; it was a tiny, bare space, with a single table and one or two chairs. A single book and a strap as prominently in evidence as the book on the table. I could be no judge, but Bentwich told me that the old man was teaching wretchedly. Bentwich was more depressed than I had seen him in all our trips by this relic of medieval teaching. The old man told us what a tiny pittance he received, but I dare say it was all that the parents could afford.

In the larger village we went through the market, visited the headquarters of the Halutz,[39] and also a cooperative bank. There we were shown proudly the records, on which were indicated the amounts of money lent by the JDC. In one of the narrow streets we got caught in a crowd which by that time had become so thick, when the news of our presence had gotten around, that we had difficulty getting out. But we were not permitted to leave until we had been shown the chief art treasure of the community, a colored crayon sketch of Palestine, with pictures of Weizmann and Sokolow.

How piteously these people look to Palestine! It is for them the solace now and the hope for the future. I can now begin to understand the powerful popular appeal which Weizmann, Jabotinsky, and other Zionist leaders, no matter

38. August Zaleski, foreign minister 1926–1932 and later, of the Polish government in exile.
39. Zionist youth movement.

how much they may differ as to methods, make to the masses of the Polish and Eastern Jews.

On our return to the city we asked Professor Schorr why the Warsaw Jews did not send out young people as missionaries to set up modern schools for the poor Jewish children. His answer was, "You try to modernize that school to which you refer in the tiny village and see what happens." This merely reinforced the sad truth which was borne in upon us more and more in Poland, the almost infinite divisions which are felt with much intensity by, in many cases, different members of a single family.

Immediately after we returned to the hotel, we went over to the Europaischer for a luncheon given us by the Foreign Office. What contrast with what we had just seen! The meal was elaborate, the hors d'oeuvres better than one would have at any restaurant in Western Europe, and the rest of the food equally good. The representative of the Foreign Office, a man whom I had known many years in Geneva as host, was a perfect Western gentleman. I could not refrain from telling him something of what we had seen, and of emphasizing the point that Poland has everything to gain by showing the world, by example, that it is not going to follow the Nazi example in its treatment of the Jews. I hardly dared to refer more pointedly to Poland's reputation on this issue.

We also talked for a while at lunch about Polish-German relations. I received again the same impression as earlier, that Poland's treaty with Germany was made figuratively with its tongue in its cheek. I reminded the Foreign Office official again of our anxiety to have Dr. Chodzko, the Polish representative, at the meeting of the Governing Body. He assured me that we would.

Called on the Swedish minister, and later on the Danish minister, to inform them officially of our visits to their countries and to ask them to be kind enough to notify their Foreign Offices.

Tea with Scheskin and his friends.

Brief conference with Natuminsky, the correspondent of the International News Service.

Turkow joined us at dinner, and then off to the train for Berlin.

[JGM's telegram to the FPA: "EVERYWHERE PARIS VIENNA PRAGUE WARSAW OVERWHELMING PROOF IMPERATIVE NEED CORPORATION GENEROUS SCALE STOP DYNAMIC SITUATION DEMANDS ACTION STOP WISH YOUR COLLEAGUES COULD SEE PRESENT TRAGEDY AND SENSE DANGER CATASTROPHE."[40]]

Berlin, Friday, April 20, 1934

Arrived in Berlin at 9:25. Went to the Kaiserhof.

Stopped at Irving Sherman's apartment on my way to the Embassy. He had

40. McDonald to FPA, April 18, 1934. Copy in McDonald Papers, USHMM.

little to say that was new, but offered to put Bentwich in contact with Wilfrid Israel and some of the other members of the community. It seemed undesirable that I should get in touch with these until I knew more about the attitude of the government.

Over to the Embassy. Mrs. Levine called Dieckhoff's office, and was told that he was very sorry he was so tied up that he could not see me, but suggested that I talk with one of the legal experts in the Foreign Office.

After thinking the matter over, I decided not to accept this suggestion. Instead, I asked Bentwich if he would mind seeing the technical man in the Foreign Office, even if doing so might involve the risk of a personal slight. He said he would be glad to go. So this was arranged.

I then instructed Bentwich to say to the legal expert that I wished him to tell Mr. Dieckhoff personally that I did not accept Dieckhoff's excuse, that I did not think he was too busy to see me, that I wish him to know that this was the last opportunity for the Foreign Office to talk with me prior to the meeting of our Governing Body, to which conference the President of the United States' personal friend, Mr. Raymond B. Fosdick, was coming as the U.S.'s official representative.

Then I talked to Mr. White,[41] the chargé d'affaires. He suggested that he might call up Dieckhoff and inquire about the situation. I thanked him, but said I would prefer to wait until I had Bentwich's report.

Then I went to Messersmith's house to see him. He was in bed, recovering from the grippe, but was well enough to talk to me with great cogency and emphasis for more than an hour. What he had to say in substance was: The economic situation worsens steadily. The regime is driven desperately to increase its exports without jeopardizing its currency. In this endeavor help from America in the form of a commodity loan is vital, but such help at this time would be a betrayal of every interest of the United States and of peace in the world. This regime recognizes only force, and only when it is faced with the choice of destruction or yielding is there any chance that it will substantially moderate its Jewish policy. The *New York Times* article of March 28 suggesting that, because of present economic pressure the attitude was moderating towards the Jews, is sheer nonsense. On the contrary, the new forms of controls and monopolies proposed or in effect for certain raw materials will inevitably be used to further hamper Jewish enterprise. A crisis is approaching in Germany which will test this regime, and may even during the course of the winter effect a change. Under these circumstances, aid from the United States in the form of a loan would be tantamount to denying the most elementary American principles. However, Germany has been violating outrageously its promises in the Treaty of 1924 to treat American business in Germany fairly, and at the same time in its attitude towards the interest and amortization payments on its foreign obligations is flaunting its determination to disregard its financial obligation.

The differences among the leaders in the party are real, but not sufficient in

41. John Campbell White, counselor of the American Embassy, Berlin, 1933–1935.

themselves to effect the overthrow of the regime. That might come through a military coup d'etat, or through the slower process of gradual disillusionment of large sections of the population. Already the industrialists and business generally have been facing extraordinary taxation, and there is the prospect of much more radical measures to come. The left wing of the party has not played its last card. The future, therefore, for the regime is dark, but this for the first time gives hope for Germany and the world.

Met Bentwich at lunch. He reported that the Foreign Office man, by inference, confirmed my impression that Dieckhoff's attitude was a mere excuse. We were joined at lunch by Woods of the *Chicago Daily News,* but he had little to say that was new.

Visited with Birchall. He has the same views of the situation as Messersmith. As to Ivy Lee's relation to the regime, he expresses the positive conviction that this distinguished publicist is advising on publicity policies and that for financial remuneration of very large proportion. His personal talk with Lee merely confirmed these impressions on this point.

Called Mr. White at the Embassy. He had already spoken to Dieckhoff. The latter said in substance, "Of course it had been merely a personal wish on my part, I should have been delighted to see McDonald. But there has been nothing new since the foreign minister and I saw him last February; moreover, since we can discuss only technical matters with him, it is better that I not see him, and that he talk to the technical person."

That message explains itself.

Saw Bentwich off to the train for Denmark. Then, having nothing else to do after eight o'clock, and not daring or feeling that it was unwise to call up my Jewish friends, I went alone to a most delightful concert of German songs by the French-Canadian singer, Graveure. It was a very beautiful performance. But again, and this shows how impossible for one to get away from this job, I could not resist the thoughts which came to me as I listened to these beautiful human songs and noted the German audience's appreciation of them, that those are the same folk who persecute the Jews.

Saturday, April 21, 1934

Over to see Sherman at 9:30. He was later during the day to see some of my friends with whom it was undesirable for me to get in contact. We agreed on a method by which he could communicate with me conveniently after I left Germany.

Back to the Embassy to see White and to get from him a clearer statement, if possible, of what Dieckhoff had said. White was frightened when I said that in view of the general attitude I might have to raise publicly in London the issue of the German government's policy. He was nervous lest he be involved. I assured him that I would not mention him in any public way, but that I might, in talking to the President or the Department of State, tell of his cooperation. This, of course, he agreed to.

Had nearly an hour with Geist, the extremely competent and fearless consul under Messersmith. He agrees with the latter's analysis of the economic situation, but does not think it will unseat the regime. He thinks there is no possibility of a coup d'état. Hitler, he is convinced, after [Geist's] spending four days on a bicycle and on foot in remote villages of the country, continues to be regarded as a god and as an ideal with which there can be no quarrel. But the policy of the Hitler regime is frequently criticized, usually the faultfinder attributing the fault to someone other than Hitler. Geist thinks, as does Messersmith, that the new forms of controls and monopolies will be used to whip the Jews. The future is dark economically for Germany, but the darker it becomes, the sooner there may be fundamental modifications. He reiterated Messersmith's views about an American loan. He agreed to send to me before the meeting of the Governing Body some information I was very anxious to have about refugee property. As I was leaving, Geist stressed again the tragedy that would be involved in any commodity loan at this time to the Reich.

Conference with Lochner of the A.P. He gave the same interpretation as the others of the growing economic crisis in the Reich. He stressed, too, the personal differences between the leaders, but he shared Geist's view, rather than Messersmith's, that is, he does not think these differences or the economic crisis are sufficient to precipitate a change in the regime. Within the party, too, there is considerable dissent. Moreover, the bureaucracy, weakened by the infiltration of party leaders, is functioning much less efficiently than in the old days. As to the Jews, conditions do not improve, but may under the stress of worsened economic developments become more acute. I have never seen Lochner so bitter in his attitude towards the regime. This is the more significant because the Nazis have obviously for some time been playing up to him because of his position as head of the A.P. in Germany and as president of the Foreign Press Association.

Lunch with Sherman. He told me of his talks with my friends whom I felt I could not see.

Out to the flying field. We took off at 3:25 for Copenhagen. It was a beautiful flight. We arrived in the Danish capital at five o'clock. What a contrast between one hour and thirty-five minutes and the time Bentwich took on the train—about thirteen hours!

Bentwich and Mrs. Melchior met me at the flying field. We went directly to the Palace Hotel, where almost immediately we had to dress for dinner.

The dinner was given by Professor Bohr,[42] the distinguished scientist, to whom had been assigned in recognition of his distinguished services, a beautiful house for his use during life. Strangely enough, it was inside the ground of one of the large breweries and had been given to the state by the brewer. About thirty-six people were present. Besides the host and hostess, Bentwich and I were the English minister and his wife, the Swedish minister and his wife, Mrs.

42. Professor Niels Bohr, Nobel Prize winner and nuclear physicist.

Ruth Bryan Owen,[43] Professor Franck,[44] formerly from Göttingen, and a number of other professors and scientists. Following Danish tradition the meal was long. Afterwards I had a talk with Professor Franck and Professor Bohr about the problems of the refugee intellectuals. About midnight when I thought the party surely would break up, we were served with sandwiches and additional things to drink. Then Mrs. Owen "insisted" on carrying me off to see the night life of Copenhagen. I was terribly tired, but could find no appropriate language to decline. Fortunately, we found most of the orchestras tired too, so I was back to the hotel and in bed by one.

Copenhagen, Sunday, April 22, 1934

Meeting during the morning with the representatives of the various Danish committees. There, as in Prague, the Jewish and non-Jewish groups appear to be working together very harmoniously. The results of the conference Bentwich has summarized in a memorandum.[45]

Then out to lunch with members of the committee. Then for a drive along the sound and through the beautiful beech forest.

At three o'clock Bentwich and I conferred with the foreign minister. His responses were generally satisfactory. How simple these Danish folk are! The residence of the foreign minister was very modest.

Over to the American Legation for tea with Mrs. Owen and members of her staff. From all accounts she has been brilliantly successful. Nor was this surprising in view of her personality and exceptional intelligence. However, she did shock Bentwich a little, as did her thirteen-year-old daughter.

Took the seven o'clock train for Stockholm via Malmo. Just before ten o'-clock in Malmo, when the train was just about to leave the station and I had prepared myself for bed, my compartment was "rushed" by some newspaper men, who insisted on an interview. So, stretched out on my upper berth, I did the best I could.

Stockholm, Monday, April 23, 1934

Up much too early, because my compartment companion insisted that Stockholm time was one hour in advance of Danish time, which it is not.

Met at the Stockholm station by a representative of the Foreign Office, Mr.

43. Ruth Bryan Owen, daughter of William Jennings Bryan. First woman to be chief American diplomat in a country. Named minister to Denmark in 1933 and served until 1936.

44. Professor James Franck, a Nobel Prize winner in 1925 and hero of the 1914 war. Had given up his chair at Göttingen because he was not prepared to be the sole Jew exempted from the Nazi ban.

45. The chairman explained that the Jewish community was small, about six thousand, and that they had raised a large sum to assist the 1,600 refugees in Denmark. Emigration was the only real solution, but in the meantime the government was trying to be helpful in as many individual cases as possible with work permits, extensions of stay, and so forth. Notes of a meeting with the representatives of the Danish government departments, Saturday April 21, by N. B. Copy in McDonald Papers, USHMM.

Johansonn, Mme. Thulin, and the chief rabbi, and the omnipresent photographers. There was no time for brushing up, so I had to have breakfast with the Foreign Office representative, being photographed again in the process. The Swedes are much too American for one's comfort in this respect!

Conference with Mr. Bauer, head of the committee of intellectuals.

Long discussion with Mr. Steinhardt,[46] the American minister. I found him intensely interested in the German situation and well informed. However, as a nephew of Samuel Untermyer, he has I think felt a little the desirability of leaning over backwards to be fair. Moreover, his many talks with the members of the German Legation, who have spoken to him "with complete frankness," have given him a too favorable a picture of conditions within the Reich. Nonetheless, he is an excellent representative and a charming person.

The foreign minister and his wife gave a luncheon for me at the official residence—much more elaborate than the residence of the minister in Copenhagen. Besides the host and myself were representatives of all the departments concerned with the refugees. As a result, I had an excellent opportunity to discuss with each of them problems with which they deal.

....

After the luncheon I conferred with Dr. Sohlman of the Nobel Institute about the possibility of their sponsoring the film which Miss Ginsberg hopes might produce funds for her committee. Dr. Sohlman said that while they could not sponsor such a film, they would be glad to cooperate.

Press conference at the hotel with half a dozen journalists. I stressed with them the point which the governments everywhere were anxious to have emphasized—that is, that the main job of the High Commission is to help to send the refugees overseas, or at any rate, out of the countries immediately neighboring on Germany. It is important to strike this note because even in Sweden where there are so few refugees, the government is attacked for favoring them.

Immediately after this conference there was another with the representatives of the various committees. The statement by the chief rabbi was particularly interesting. Relatively a newcomer in Sweden, he has already won a high place for himself.

At six o'clock tea with the Steinhardts at their magnificent home, built by a Swede who had become excessively rich through associations with Krueger.[47] Miss Willis, one of the few American secretaries in any legation, was also present. Most of our talk was about the foreign service, and particularly the tendency of so many career men, as now in the Embassy in Berlin, to play up weakly to

46. Laurence A. Steinhardt, minister to Sweden since 1933, later ambassador to the Soviet Union, Czechoslovakia, and Turkey.

47. Ivan Krueger, of Krueger & Toll, billionaire industrialist who had controlled a vast match monopoly. Went bankrupt and committed suicide in 1932.

the government to which they are accredited, rather than to stand up firmly for American rights and the American point of view.

Dinner alone with Schäffer,[48] formerly under-secretary of the treasury in Berlin. In some ways he seems to me the most intelligent German outside of the Reich in economic matters. His point of view might be summarized: The economic situation is bad and will steadily become worse. The regime is caught in the dilemma of being forced to sacrifice the Mark or else to sacrifice the hope of enlarging the foreign trade. Accepting either of these alternatives might be disastrous. Therefore, before making this choice the regime will almost certainly resort either to what will amount to a forced loan, thus making a further serious inroad on capital, or will seize by decree the foreign securities now held within Germany. Through either or both of these measures the decision about devaluation of the Mark might be postponed but only postponed. There is, of course, always the possibility that the steady increase of world trade in general may help Germany materially, but it is unlikely that this help will be sufficient to avoid an ultimate reckoning.

It is unlikely that the refusal to pay interest on foreign securities will be extended to the Dawes loan because Schacht himself underwrote that. But the scrip regime is likely to be extended to the Young loan.

In the political sphere Schäffer expects an agreement on a disarmament convention, and that the Reich will return to Geneva. At that time one might hope to bring pressure effectively in reference to the Jewish issue. Meantime, he deprecated any definite break on my part with the Reich on the issue of their failing to cooperate. Instead, he urged that one threaten such a break, but hold in reserve the actual breach.

He does not think the differences among the leaders in the Reich, though serious, are sufficient to bring about an open clash or to endanger the regime.

He shared my view that our friend Scheffer,[49] who has now become the editor of the *Tageblatt* could under the circumstances, since there was nothing else for him to do, hardly have refused to accept this post. The role of the German journalist is extremely difficult at the best.

Schäffer and I continued our talk until it was time for me to take the ten o'clock train for Malmö.

Tuesday, April 24, 1934

Reached Malmö a little after half past seven. There was just time for a bite of breakfast, when at eight we took the bus to the flying field. We took off promptly at 8:30, were at Copenhagen at 8:45, and then took off again at once

48. Hans Schäffer, former member of the German Democratic Party, Jewish, now living in exile in Stockholm.

49. Paul Scheffer, editor-in-chief of the *Berliner Tageblatt.* Remained until December 1936, though anti-Nazi.

for London. The flight over Denmark, Germany, and Holland was interesting, but as the hours wore on, and the air became more bumpy, and I more sensitive, I began to wish most anxiously for the sight of Amsterdam. Because of head winds we arrived there about fifteen minutes late, at quarter past twelve Dutch time, after four hours and a quarter in the air. After a hurried bit of lunch, we changed planes and took off one more in a Dutch plane; this time the flight was smoother, and we arrived in Croydon at four o'clock English summer time, and I was at the hotel about half past five and delighted with the thought that not for another ten days at any rate would I have to consider travel by air, rail, or boat.

London, Wednesday, April 25, 1934

Except for one or two engagements, worked all day with Miss Sawyer.

Barnet of the [London] *Jewish Chronicle* called and wished me to amplify a statement attributed to me in Poland to the effect that it is not enough to consider merely the refugee problem; one must consider the question of Jewish emigration as a whole. I replied that at this juncture I had nothing more to say.

Lunch with Bernhard Kahn. We compared notes about the situation in the different countries which I had visited. I found that his knowledge of all of the countries was intimate. He agreed to prepare for me a new set of figures on the actual situation of refugees, numbers etc., in the different countries. He pointed out what is, of course, one of the great difficulties in any public statement, that much of what has been accomplished or is being undertaken cannot be discussed publicly, either because the governments concerned would be offended, or because they might feel constrained to withdraw concessions made in practice but never recognized in principle officially. We agreed to meet again within a day or so.

In the late afternoon Wurfbain and Miss Berg came in from Lausanne, at the same time that Bentwich came from his house, where he had been working on the reports of the organizations. Then followed four hours and a half of conference about our plans for the meetings. After Bentwich left, we continued to work until after ten—much too late for a decent dinner.

Thursday, April 26, 1934

Delighted to receive word that Mr. May was going to arrive, with Mrs. May, at two, having gotten off at Plymouth.

Mrs. Lazarus called, and we arranged for engagements with Wilfrid Israel.

Felix Frankfurter's secretary telephoned from Oxford that she had been unable to give my message to him yesterday in town, that he had gotten home too late last night to telephone, and had left this morning for class. That she wondered if I would dictate the message to her. I said I preferred not to. She then added that Frankfurter was busy all day and was going off for the weekend tomorrow, that he would not be able to call me before. She wondered if I would write him. I said that I was afraid what I had to discuss with him must be done personally, so that I would wait until he found it convenient to telephone me, and that I would be in London until the middle of next week

I should have included in my account of last Tuesday the substance of my transatlantic telephone talk with Felix Warburg. I outlined briefly the situation I had found in Germany, and urged the danger of the loan being talked about there. He explained why there was some hesitation about inviting Louis Oungre, and these reasons seemed to me sufficient. I said I would raise the question informally with Sir Osmond and Sir Leonard if and when the appropriate occasion arose. Warburg thought there was no possibility of the commodity loan. He urged me to get in touch with John D. Rockefeller, Jr., when he is on this side, and to discuss with Dr. Weizmann before he sails the possibilities of emigration centers. He also suggested that I check and see that Sir Max Bonn[50] might be induced to unite his efforts with those of the American corporation, rather than proceeding independently. Warburg told me that Sherrill was my enemy because of my failure to invite his son. I explained that the reason for the father's anxiety was to end an affair of his son in Washington.[51] I told Warburg a little more about Sir Philip's attitude on Trans-Jordan, and also of Sir Philip's willingness to talk with complete frankness to Warburg the next time the latter was on this side. In a matter of this sort Sir Philip is vastly more significant than the prime minister. I was glad to hear from Warburg more about the corporation, and sent word through him to Lewis Strauss of ICA's payment to the High Commission.

Continuing Thursday, April 26: Just before lunch Wilfrid Israel came in, and we had a brief talk, which we resumed that night after dinner.

Lunch alone, in order to have a few minutes free to think through my statement for the afternoon tea.

Conference with Mr. May and other members of the staff until the arrival of Cecil.

Cecil had three matters which he wished to raise with me.

(1) About a Countess Dohna, formerly of the German League of Nations Union, now a refugee, and until the last few weeks the recipient of help from Miss Ginsberg's committee. She has written to Cecil to say that she had heard from some of her friends that the reason Miss Ginsberg is unable to continue her grant is that the High Commission has taken the wind out of the sails of Miss Ginsberg's committee and made it impossible for her to

50. Sir Max Julius Bonn, banker and director of the Bank of London and South America, Brazilian Trust and Loan, and Herbert Wagg and Company.

51. The unpleasantness had arisen when retired General Charles H. Sherrill (later in the year appointed ambassador to Turkey) had asked Felix Warburg to endorse the appointment of his son, Gibbs, to the staff of the High Commission at a nominal retainer. McDonald had no place and no money for a position and replied, "Cable me confidentially whether you feel strongly about young Sherrill. Personally I doubt the wisdom arbitrarily creating post to serve Sherrill family purposes." Warburg replied that he had no interest, but that McDonald had made an enemy of the general, as he felt the position had been promised his son.

continue to raise funds. I explained to Lord Cecil my special efforts on behalf of Miss Ginsberg's committee. I then asked Lord Cecil whether he would care to join Miss Ginsberg in an appeal to the States for funds. He said he wouldn't mind, but I doubted whether it would be helpful.

(2) A Mr. Kussfult (?)[52] had approached him for help to complete a study of the arms traffic. Lord Cecil said that he didn't see how he could deal with individual cases like that. I agreed, and asked him to tell Mr. Kussfult to see me after our meetings, and that I might be able to help him to get a special grant to complete his study.

(3) Allan Wells wished Lord Cecil's support for a project to send a journalist through the refugee centers with a view to writing a series of human interest stories which would make easier the raising of funds. The two men suggested Wickham-Steed[53] and Nicolson;[54] neither one seemed ideal for this purpose. It was left that Cecil would ask Allan Wells to see me after our meeting.

Then I explained to Lord Cecil in detail the response from Germany last week. After we had discussed the matter fully, he advised me to see Baron von Hoetsch to explain to the ambassador fully the dilemma that I am in, the Reich unwilling or unable to cooperate, and I impelled to make a report to this effect to the Governing Body and to the world. What, under these circumstances, would the ambassador advise?

I did not commit myself to the acceptance of this suggestion, but I shall probably see Hoetsch over the weekend.

At five Cecil and I went up to where Bentwich and I were having tea party for a number of the leaders here. Among those present were: Sir Osmond d'Avigdor-Goldsmid, Charles Roden Buxton, Sir Robert Waley-Cohen, Anthony de Rothschild, James de Rothschild, Ernest Franklin, Professor C. S. Gibson, Reverend Dr. J. H. Herz, Dr. Bernhard Kahn, Neville Laski, Frank Lazarus, Sir Andrew Mcfadyen, Lionel Montagu, Leonard Montefiore, Louis Oungre, Otto Schiff, and Wickham-Steed—and Mr. May, Mrs. Bentwich, Mr. Wurfbain, Dr. Kotschnig, and Miss Sawyer.

I spoke briefly giving my impressions, particularly of the situation in Austria, Czechslovakia, Poland, and Germany. Mr. Bentwich followed by giving his summary, expressing the imperative and urgent need of facing the whole problem of Eastern Jewry.

In the discussion period Wickham-Steed emphasized the increasing militarization of Germany and the greater degree of anti-Semitism there. Professor Gibson underlined the same points. McFadyen questioned what I said about the economic conditions in Germany probably intensifying the danger for the Jews.

52. More likely Hussfelt.
53. Henry Wickham-Steed, journalist, editor of *Review of Reviews.*
54. Harold Nicolson, writer, diplomat, and politician. Elected as Labour MP in 1935.

He argued that, on the contrary, economic necessities might make the Reich have a fuller appreciation of the Jews. Nothing I have heard elsewhere supports this optimistic conclusion. Moreover, I pointed out that the new Devisen regulations would inevitably increase the burden on the refugee committees out of Germany by reducing the amounts available from Germany to individual refugees. Buxton raised questions about our method of dealing with the stateless refugees. Cecil asked what possibilities of settlement there were outside of Palestine, because to his mind, important though Palestine is, there must be other places to which considerable numbers of refugees can go. I then called upon Oungre and Dr. Kahn. The former stressed the necessity of a considerable measure of world economic recovery as a condition precedent to successful agrarian colonization. Dr. Kahn said it was a mistake to assume that so-called "vacant" countries are the most likely places to send immigrants; very often, the partially settled areas could absorb much larger numbers. Neville Laski asked if it was not true that there were unmistakable evidences of a rising dissent in Germany. I replied that this, for the first time, since the Nazis came into power, seemed to me to be the case. The question was whether this would effect any change in regime; despite Messersmith's belief that it would, I doubt it. Cecil closed the discussion by saying in effect, "Irrespective of what present conditions are in Germany, we will all make a serious mistake if we count on economic distress unseating the Nazis. We must go on with our work preparing for worse things, rather than assuming that conditions within Germany will improve." I assented cordially to this point of view.

After tea there was a chance for a brief exchange of views, and by that time it was the dinner hour.

Dined with the Mays and Miss Sawyer. General discussion about things at home and problems here.

At 8:30 Wilfrid Israel and his cousin joined me and Mr. May in my room. Later, the other two men left, and Israel and I continued our talk until after eleven o'clock. Israel gives the appearance of feeling more and more strongly the strain under which he has been living and working. He is sure that the economic stress in the Reich leading to a larger and larger measure of regimentation of the economic life will adversely affect the Jews. Moreover, the extremists within the Party are already seeking to line up the auxiliary organizations of the peasants, of the women, of the workers, and of other groups to make effective in practice the Aryan clause in the economic sphere as well as in the professional, and increasingly they are succeeding. He showed me a circular announcing a new weekly anti-Semitic magazine, managed by Streicher.[55] This announcement promises that the new publication will unfold the horrors of ritual murders, etc, etc. Apparently, every atrocity tale of the last 1500 years is to be revitalized for the edi-

55. Julius Streicher, Nazi Gauleiter of Franconia, 1933–1940, editor of the vicious anti-Semitic newspaper *Der Stürmer.* Convicted at the International Military Tribunal at Nuremberg and executed in 1946.

fication of the German people. So far there has been nothing current in Germany so violent as this promises to be. Moreover, within the area which he controls Streicher promises to eradicate the Jews altogether. Israel feels that a new crisis is approaching, and that one cannot safely ignore the possibility of another panicky exodus. In this connection he asked me if there was anything I could do to induce the governments bordering on the Reich to prepare for such a possibility, and to refrain under those circumstance from doing what some of them now feel inclined to do, that is, close their frontiers. I promised to consider it, but pointed out that there might be a disadvantage in raising this hypothetical question, because it might, by raising the fears of the governments, cause them to take a sterner attitude toward the refugees they now actually have within their borders.

Israel sees signs of group evacuation by Jews from the smaller towns. This is a new development. He pointed out, too, that the return of a certain number of the refugees to Germany is no real proof that conditions are better.

Israel told me of the relations between his group and the [German] officials. Obviously hereto, nothing has changed for the better during the past months. On no single issue has the regime been willing to talk to them officially.

He sees the possibility of an organized effort to force Jews to carry propaganda abroad that all is well and also to act as the spearheads of a widespread organized effort to recover foreign trade.

I told him I hoped very much that he could return for the meetings next week; that I was anxious that he should have a chance to talk with Raymond Fosdick; that perhaps he might so interest the latter as to induce him to go into Germany. I arranged to let him know where Fosdick was staying by communicating through a mutual friend.

I asked him about Lola Hahn, and he said she was very tired; that the boy [her son] was able to move about, but would almost certainly always be a cripple.

It was with a heavy heart that I said good-night to him.

Friday, April 27, 1934

In conference all the morning about plans for the meetings. Agreed on the outlines for the sessions of the Advisory Council, and also for the Governing Body, the latter subject to Cecil's approval after they had worked it out more fully.

Felix Frankfurter, in answer to my call to him yesterday, telephoned me from Oxford. I told him of my anxiety that no opportunity should be missed to discourage any chance of a commodity loan to the Reich. He made a suggestion which I am going to follow, as to a direct means of presenting this problem to FDR. We tentatively agreed that I would come up to Oxford for a least a few hours the weekend after our meetings.

Mr. Puniansky, formerly of the JTA and now editor of the *Jewish Post,* called to ask what I had to say about a program to settle five million Jews in Portuguese East Africa—a project with which the names of Cecil, Simon, and myself had been connected. I told him emphatically that I knew nothing of it, and would certainly make no comment, though not for publication I was willing to add that I considered it a fantastic idea [as in fantasy].

Lunch with Herbert May. Together we agreed on a number of points including the way we should handle our financial statements at the Governing Body meeting, the treatment of Sherrill if he continues to spread the tales that I had promised and failed to carry out an arrangement with his son. Indeed, the more I think of it, it is possible that the General's tale about wishing to free his son from a flirtation in Washington was camouflage to be able to hide his great desire to be able to say that his son's position with me gave him a position of authority on which he might be able to capitalize in Germany. Anyhow, I would rather have his enmity than to be in a position where he could trade on his relationship with me.

Out to tea with Dr. Weizmann. He, I understand, is not at all well. However, when I saw him, he seemed to me not to be more tired than each time I have met him recently.

Nearly our whole time together, about an hour, was given over to his enthusiastic and contagious explanation of his program for consolidating the debt of his organizations in Palestine. As a result, [after] a series of five nearly all-night meetings, he has induced the settlers to agree to a reconsideration of their contracts, shortening the time to twenty years and increasing the interest rate to three percent. On the basis of these new contracts he has every expectation of securing a loan here which will enable him to refund the existing obligations at a much more favorable rate. In this strengthened financial position he expects soon to be able to begin work on the Hula swamp region, that to be followed up by developments along the Jordan valley.

I, of course, am not at all technically qualified to estimate the probabilities of the success of this program, but as he explained it, it seemed realizable. At any rate, he and I have made a date to meet in Haifa in October, he is to show me around for two days (I to be incognito, with what sort of disguise I don't know!), and I am to spend the night in the chemical institute.[56] It is a tempting prospect. Certainly, I must get to Palestine this fall if it is at all possible.

We had a brief discussion about the situation of the [Hebrew] University. But we were both so absorbed in his large schemes for development that university problems, serious though they doubtless are, seemed relatively secondary.

Then I asked him about his plans to go to the States. He said he was still uncertain, but I am confident that he will sail next week.

Conference with Dr. Michael and his two associates from Paris. They seemed to feel that if only they were represented on the Advisory Council, some magic way would be opened for them to be placed in positions. I sought to dis-

56. Refers to the Daniel Sieff Research Institute in Rehovoth, Palestine, founded by Weizmann in 1934. Became the Weizmann Institute of Science in 1949. Weizmann had a house on the grounds and was subsequently buried there.

courage such expectations. They also seemed to think it was merely a question of inducing the governments to give permission to practice, whereas I argued that the real stumbling block[s] are the medical associations. I asked them to present their plans more fully to Kotschnig.

Worked in preparation for the meeting.

Saturday, April 28, 1934

Staff conference in the morning.

Conference with Sir William Beveridge. He seemed to feel better about Kotschnig's appointment when I explained the latter's relationships in the States.

Lunch at Anthony de Rothschild's with Otto Schiff. I was amused by the evident difference of opinion between the Rothschilds in England and in France as to the movie of the family.[57] Baron Robert is violently opposed to it, while Mrs. Anthony is organizing a fête in connection with it through which she hopes to make substantial amounts for the refugee work.

Over to the Park Lane for tea with Rosen, Kahn,[58] and Schweitzer. Rosen did most of the talking about the following:

(1) Biro-Bidjan—he is less absolutely opposed to it than before, but still holds it is only possible for real pioneers. The Russian president was more enthusiastic about it than Litvinov.
(2) He thinks the region in Central Siberia near Kazan (?) is more hospitable.
(3) There are still possibilities in Crimea if these are developed.[59]
(4) Also, there are possibilities for professional people in Russia.
(5) He and all the others agreed that the Angola and Ecuador proposals as reported in the press were fantastic [as in fantasy].

Worked late on my speech.

Sunday, April 29, 1934

Staff conference including May. Made further plans for the meeting.

Professor Speyer called from downstairs and was infuriated when Miss Berg did not recognize his voice, but was placated after we had talked for awhile upstairs. He repeated that I must not cut my schedule in Brussels too fine.

Lunched with Professor and Mrs. Brodetzky. We had a very agreeable visit. They were quite disarmed by my sympathy for the eastern Jews and my willingness to tell the western Jews that they are in the same boat with the others.

57. The movie was Daryl F. Zanuck's *House of Rothschild* (1934), directed by Alfred L. Werner, starring Robert Young, Loretta Young, George Arliss, and Boris Karloff. Set mostly in the Napoleonic period, the theme is anti-Semitism, with Napoleon cast as a kind of Hitler. The portrait of the Rothschilds was generally flattering, the film was a hit, and it was nominated for best picture.

58. Ernest Kahn, German-Jewish assistant to Otto Schiff.

59. The Russian Crimean plan proposed the settlement of Jewish families, three thousand Russian refugees and five to six hundred German refugees. By 1936 only a few doctors had been settled.

Over to the Laskis at eight o'clock for a very nice buffet supper. I was dog-tired when I went, and more so as the evening wore on. Chatted with many members of the Advisory Council. I was particularly interested in the case of Mrs. Boss and her husband, and promised to write Madariaga about the situation in Morocco. About eleven o'clock went home with the Mays, terribly tired.

Monday, April 30, 1934

Advisory Council in the morning. Carrying out the program we had agreed on in staff conference, I blocked out the plans of organization and major activities during the two days, then outlined my report to the Governing Body. I recognized the criticisms which had been made of the High Commission in many quarters, made no pledge, but asked for a measure of tolerance and understanding, indicating at the same time that I had been the recipient of bitter criticisms from various organizations and individuals about many of the other organizations and leaders. I referred also to the absurd story in the *Daily Herald* about Angola and told of my denial, which I had issued to the press before the meeting.

On the whole, the opening meeting went well. The designations of chairmen and rapporteurs for the two commissions were well received. There was some criticism from Gottschalk about inadequate documentation in advance of the meeting, but nothing serious.

At five o'clock went to see von Hoesch. I told him of what had happened in Berlin and of my desire that the German authorities should indicate before the meeting of the Governing Body whether they intended that our relationships in the future should be conducted through a secondary, technical official. I said, "It would be just as absurd for me to ask your butler where I am to sit at dinner tonight before you have decided to invite me, as it is for us to discuss with a technical expert major questions before policy on them has been determined by higher officials." He did not deny the validity of this analogy and said that he would telegraph Berlin and ask for a reply. Throughout the conference I made no appeal, but indicated that I was merely asking for [information].

13. May 1934: Emigration Options?

London, Tuesday, May 1, 1934

Woke up with a sore throat. Decided to go to the committee meetings for a few minutes, but first went to see the doctor. He urged me to stay in bed and gave me some dope. So I arranged to have Mr. May and André Wurfbain keep my engagements during the day with the high commissioner for Canada, the counselor of the Turkish Embassy, and the high commissioner for South Africa, while Miss Sawyer went to see Cecil.

After a few minutes at Burlington House came back to the hotel and went to bed for the day, hoping to be able to carry on the next day. The most interesting item during the afternoon was Miss Sawyer's report of her talk with Cecil and the latter's concern about finances, the activities of Walter Adams through Austen Chamberlain, etc. Fortunately, through the help of Mr. May we had already worked out the financial statement in such shape that Cecil seemed to be more nearly satisfied, and certainly we would be able to satisfy the Governing Body completely.

. . . .

Wednesday, May 2, 1934

Over with May to the meeting of the Governing Body. The members of the G. B. were slow in arriving, so I had a chance to chat with each one a little while before we began. Cecil, however, arrived just on time, and with his usual desire to begin at once, he insisted that we get under way even though the French ambassador had not arrived.

He accepted all of our suggestions about the formal actions to be taken at the private session, the naming of the finance committee, etc. As a result, we were ready for the public meeting a few minutes after eleven. Fortunately, the public was just about sizable enough to fill the room comfortably.

Cecil called on me to give my report. It was not until I was nearly half through that I began to feel confident that my voice would hold out. After I had concluded, there were some brief remarks by two or three members of the Governing Body, and the meeting was over.

I lunched alone, anxious to have a minute for a nap afterwards.

The afternoon meeting, a joint session of the Advisory Committee and the Governing Board, began at 3:30. First was the report of the academic committee. It evoked little discussion. . . .

The real discussion began with the report of the other committee. Schevenels made a very effective and stirring plea for prompt action; then Louis Oungre as chairman was called upon to explain the possibilities of settlement. Playing up to his audience, he developed grandiose programs almost at command, to the intense annoyance of Dr. B. Kahn and others.[1] There was considerable discussion about the allocation of certificates [for immigration or settlement], the French insisting that there should be a larger proportion for the refugees. Bustamante[2] took issue with the reports that an autonomous Jewish community was to be set up in Ecuador. He insisted that the South Americans are all extremely jealous of any suggestion that they are not fully sovereign states, or that they are willing to bargain away any portion of their sovereignty.

On the whole, the meeting went well. It adjourned about six o'clock.

Stopped at the doctor's on the way back, and then gave Barnett a brief interview for the *Jewish Chronicle.* Told Kunstler that I would meet his principals in Brussels, conferred with Dr. Röttgen and two other doctors about the possibility of the German doctors then in England being allowed to practice. They expressed the view that there would be no serious opposition from the British medical association. I told them that I was sure that was the first point to be assured of.

Late staff conference.

Thursday, May 3, 1934

Governing Body meeting at 11:30. Bentwich had ready for Lord Cecil an itemized statistical statement which seemed to me rather imaginary, but was probably the best that could be done. Most of the morning session was given over to long explanations by different governmental representatives as to their particular attitude on passports. It all seemed rather narrow.

About one o'clock I received word that the German Embassy had had a reply from Berlin, and that it would be given to me if I came over there. So I left before the end of the meeting. Meantime, it had become evident that we could not finish that day, and we tentatively agreed upon a brief session Friday morning, to end with a brief public meeting.

Over to the German Embassy. Received by Prince von Bismarck. He translated in my presence, or rather paraphrased, the contents of a note received from Berlin. According to his account, regret was expressed that Dieckhoff had not been able to see me, but it was added that a decision had been made that these

1. McDonald explained to Felix Warburg, "Dr. Kahn and Mr. Oungre disagree completely as to the makeup of the refugees in France. The former insists that not more than a tiny percentage are available for agricultural settlements, while the latter told the Governing Body that perhaps 25 percent were available for that purpose. Moreover, Dr. Kahn insists that the bulk of the refugees now in France must remain there, but this is a contention which causes every Frenchman with whom I have talked to foam at the mouth when it is mentioned. So strong, in fact, is the French feeling that no one has dared to speak frankly in the public meetings of the Advisory Council or in the private meetings of the Governing Body." McDonald to Felix Warburg, May 5, 1934. Copy in McDonald Papers, USHMM.

2. Antonio Sanchez de Bustamante, Uruguay.

matters were to be handled through Barandon.[3] We would be able to submit through him any considerations we might care to urge, so long as we did not infringe on the zone of matters involving domestic legislation or national policy. Already we had come near that zone in our communications in reference to property, denationalization, and the granting of doctors degrees to Jewish students who had finished their work.

I thanked him for the message, and said that I would report it to the Governing Body.

Lunch with Herbert May, André Wurfbain, and Olive Sawyer.

At 3:30 the Governing Body meeting. The discussion of the morning was continued. Then I reported on the German message. There followed an interesting general discussion. There was a consensus of opinion that one ought to keep the door open as long as possible, but that sooner or later a more direct and public effort would have to be made. Fosdick suggested the possibility of the British government taking the initiative; Cecil thought this unlikely. After there had been considerable talk, Cecil seemed to express the general feeling when he said that he favored my preparing, if necessary, as complete a record as possible, this to be presented to the members of the Governing Board before further action being taken on it.

Friday, May 4, 1934

Governing Body at 10:30. We were not able to finish at the time announced, because technical matters caused delay. At the end of the private session Cecil made a rather pessimistic statement about the work done and urged greater consideration to constructive proposals. I gave my cordial assent. Then, as we were breaking up to go into the public meeting, Cecil turned to me and said that he hoped I understood that he was not at all criticizing me in what he had said.

The public session was very brief. Cecil made his statement. This was followed by an unexpected statement of appreciation of the work of the High Commission's staff by the French representative. As this was being read and translated, I asked Norman Bentwich whether I should reply. He said yes, so I asked Cecil's permission. What I said was, therefore, wholly extemporaneous.

After goodbyes all around with individual members of the Governing Body and with such members of the Advisory Committee as had remained, I walked off with Raymond Fosdick. He seemed to have been really impressed by the sessions. He thought that he might be able to sail with us on the *Rex*.

In the afternoon, staff conference.

At five o'clock to see Geoffrey Dawson at the *Times*. He was completely contemptuous of the *Daily Herald*'s Angola story, and indeed, of the *Herald* itself. Then after a general discussion about Germany and our work I asked him about the article by Cecil for the editorial page. He said he would be glad to have it. . . .

3. Geheimrat Paul Barandon, German Foreign Office legal section.

[The next day McDonald wrote to Warburg about the meetings and concluded:

"This letter may sound to you rather pessimistic or worse. If so, it is perhaps a reflection of a rather tired individual who, having crossed the hurdles of the recent meetings, is somewhat depressed by the apparent lack of basis for a real program. There is so much shadow boxing on the part of some of the organizational leaders, that one wonders how they ever accomplished anything."

He did, however, admit in the same letter

that "the more I hear of vague and always indefinite talks about possibilities of immigration to other parts of the world, the more I appreciate the value of Palestine. At any rate, there you have something more than beautiful sounding words which, when analyzed, so often mean nothing."][4]

....

Saturday, May 5, 1934

Staff conference in the morning.

At 1:45 left for Oxford.

At the Frankfurters' met Mrs. Francis Hirst,[5] to whom Frankfurter was very anxious that I should talk frankly about the German situation. This I did. She is said to be an intimate of Sir John Simon.

Then followed much talk about Germany. Mrs. Frankfurter expressed the most bitter feeling. Both of them also expressed absolute contempt for the attitude of Walter Lippmann[6] on this issue. Frankfurter said that he had, following up my telephone call to him, written FDR along the same lines as I had.

....

[On May 3 McDonald wrote:

My Dear Mr. President:

When I was in Germany a few days ago I was struck by the extent to which official efforts are being made to create the impression that the economic situation there, which becomes steadily worse, is about to be relieved by financial help from the United States Government. This is expected, it is said, through the form of an American governmental loan, the proceeds from which are to be used for the purchase of American commodities—cotton, copper, etc., especially needed in Germany now. (I cannot believe that there is any probability of such a loan.)

4. McDonald to Warburg, May 5, 1934. Copy in McDonald Papers, USHMM.

5. Mrs. Francis Hirst, Helena Cobden, wife of Francis Wrigley Hirst, a financial historian and severe critic of the League.

6. Lippmann's biographer wrote that he showed surprising insensitivity to the human dimension of the Nazi threat, especially as it concerned the Jews. Roland Steel, *Walter Lippmann and the American Century* (Boston: Little, Brown, 1980), 330.

It is frequently said these days in dispatches from Germany that the regime there is moderating its attitude towards the Jews and in other respects. I do not believe that there is any justification whatsoever for these reports. They seem to be designed to create a certain impression abroad, but to have no relationship whatsoever to the actualities of the situation within Germany. On the contrary, there are substantial indications that the notorious Aryan paragraph, hitherto applied chiefly to official and professional circles, may be extended not only as it has already been in practice, but also in theory, to the economic field. In addition, the news in this morning's paper of the establishment of a "revolutionary tribunal" for the trial of political offenses is a significant straw in the wind.

. . . I remain convinced that the regime, unless materially modified, is inconsistent with the peace of Europe.

Under all these circumstances, I cannot refrain from expressing to you my strong personal opinion that any American governmental financial aid at this time to the Reich would be a grave mistake. . . .

Very respectfully yours,
James G. McDonald[7]]

Sunday, May 6, 1934

. . . .

At six began a long conference with Dr. Bonn,[8] Bentwich, May, and Wurfbain also present. Bonn was sure one would be nowhere by soft methods (in dealing with the Germans); the only question was what would be the most effective hard methods. He thought that something perhaps might be done through private letters by FDR to the American ambassador, and similar communication from Downing Street. If this failed, then one would have to go further. He felt it was important that whatever was done should be kept within the framework of the diplomatic amenities, thus making it easier for the regular Foreign Office people to get something done.

. . . .

Monday, May 7, 1934

Conference at Woburn House with Dr. Edie on behalf of the committee of the Anglo-HICEM for German doctors. He wished me to take some initiative with the Home Office to secure permission for those doctors now in England to remain and practice there. I told him that I thought it would be a mistake for me to do that now; that first, he and his colleagues should do everything that they could with the British Medical Association, and afterwards, if it were felt that I would be useful, I would be glad to do anything possible.

7. McDonald to FDR, May 3, 1934, McDonald Papers, Columbia, Special File: Franklin D. Roosevelt.

8. Moritz Bonn, professor at the London School of Economics.

Then attended the meeting of the Anglo-HICEM. Otto Schiff spoke first, but not in a way to create much confidence, as to the work of his committee. I then explained about my visit to Canada. It was agreed that the suggested lists would be prepared, at first not too long, and that I would be asked to forward them to the prime minister. I agreed.

Then I explained briefly the relaxations in the American immigration regulations, and ended by declaring that all of us, including the large organizations and the Anglo-HICEM, must do more than we have done on the constructive side. I quoted Cecil to this effect, deliberately giving the same emphasis he had given.

Conference with Sir Robert Waley-Cohen. He outlined what he considered to be the four fields in which cooperation between the American corporation and the British groups could be best undertaken during the early periods. All of these center in Palestine, but his emphasis on that area should not be taken as meaning that he and his colleagues preclude cooperation elsewhere. His suggestions were

(1) Housing. He feels that the housing situation in Palestine is such that there is urgent need for extensive building operations. These he would undertake through a new operating corporation, the funds for which would be made available by the American and British groups in proportions to be decided later;
(2) Water. The need for the development of additional water supplies is evident. This, too, should be undertaken by a separate corporation, to be financed as suggested above;
(3) Public utilities. He feels that unless a development of ports, electric communications, and other forms of public utilities is taken over and pressed by private interests, these facilities will always lag far behind the actual necessities. It is improbable that a small colonial government would, of its own initiative, ever move rapidly enough or with sufficient understanding of the potentialities of the future to enable the territory to grow as it should. Hence, he proposes a separate company to deal with these matters and to be financed as above;
(4) In addition to the three specific suggestions, he would like to see the Americans and the British cooperate in making available additional funds for the existing financing organizations in Palestine.

He feels that these things can be done best if the American and the British groups, each organized separately, would come together on specific projects. He did not say so, but I am sure he thinks, and I certainly share the view, that it would be very difficult, perhaps impossible, to set up a satisfactory single Anglo-American corporation to deal with all these matters. The Americans and the British will cooperate better on definite undertakings than in general.

Back to the hotel, clearing up last odds and ends, and took the two o'clock train for Brussels. When we boarded the ship at Dover, I was not much surprised to find Louis Oungre on board. We chatted most of the way over. He told me of his work during the war, his frequent crossings [of the Atlantic], talked interestingly of many subjects, but took occasion to knock Dr. Bernhard Kahn by suggesting that the latter had never been himself since his flight from Germany, and that it would have been much better had he remained; that in Paris there was really very little he could do, whereas in Berlin he would have been safe and by now would have become the veritable center of all the Jewish relief work for central Europe. I declined to assent to all these conclusions, because by that time I had had too many reasons to be suspicious of Oungre.

. . . .

Brussels, Tuesday, May 8, 1934

Talked on the telephone to Ambassador Morris.[9] He invited me for dinner that night, telling me that General Sherrill was staying with him. I hesitated about accepting, confessing to Morris the difference of opinion that had arisen between the General and myself. But finally, I decided that I should not run away, and called back the ambassador and accepted.

Conference with Kunstler and his two principals, Dr. Rosenstein and Dr. Lippman. They outlined in detail their plans and urged me to name a special subcommittee of the Governing Body to deal with this proposal. I said I could not do that; if they would send me detailed data, I would inquire of the Rockefeller medical people in New York, first, as to the feasibility of the project, and second, as to the probability of its being financed.

. . . .

Then for a pleasant walk through the park, past the palace and other public buildings, to an engagement with Gottschalk at the Foreign Office. This was, as before, with the technical official dealing with passports. It appeared from our conference that the Belgian reply had been for the record, and that in practice they were much more conciliatory. At least, Gottschalk insisted that his committee was able to get from the government anything which was reasonable.

Just before six I appeared at Speyer's house for tea. Instead of the magnificent gathering I had been led to expect, I found twenty to thirty persons, none of them bearing the outward marks of distinguished elegance. I was introduced to only two or three, when we adjourned to the neighboring room for the meeting. I spoke for about fifteen minutes, Speyer summarized my remarks briefly in French, then Gottschalk spoke extremely well. After that we had tea and informal talk.

Among the persons I met and remember best was a Mr. Paul Oppenheim, the nephew of Mrs. Felix Warburg. It was his father and mother who commit-

9. Dave Hennan Morris, U.S. ambassador to Belgium.

ted suicide because of the humiliation of the Nazi regime.[10] He seemed to me to bear the marks of a terrifying experience. He expressed the warmest feeling towards F. W.

. . . .

Paris, Wednesday, May 9, 1934

Nine o'clock train for Paris. Arrived at the Continental in time for lunch with Miss Sawyer, who had gone on the night before.

At four o'clock over to the Quai d'Orsay [Foreign Office] to see Léger. He received me promptly. . . . I launched into a long story of our relations with Germany, telling him in detail from the beginning. He listened with intense interest. At the conclusion I asked him what he would advise. In summary his views were: One must, of course, seek to keep the door open as long as possible, but there is no likelihood of real German cooperation. It is impossible that they should wish really to help; even if some of the leaders desired, they would not be permitted to do so. One ought, therefore, [to] prepare for the inevitable break. It is important that the record be as impressive as possible; therefore, it should be prepared carefully and submitted first to governmental representatives on the Governing Body.

As I was leaving, we chatted for a little while about the general European political situation. Léger insisted that the stiff line taken by France in its recent note[11] had really cleared the air, for now Germany knew where France stood. There is no possibility of success in the Disarmament Conference; it will dissolve. Then after a year or two, when conditions have become even more grave and the burden of competitive armaments heavier, a new attempt will be made.

At five we began the first of a series of conferences with L. O. [Oungre], Dr. B. K. [Kahn], N. B. [Bentwich], et al. N. B. and I stressed the necessity of a more specific program being worked out by the large private organizations. N. B. in particular wished to have specific schemes formulated on the basis of an analysis of the personnel of the refugees, these schemes then to be submitted formally to the potential immigrant countries. L. O. and K. argued the impossibility of carrying through this program.

Then followed more than an hour of give and take. At the end, it was decided that the next session would include the French. I called up Baron Robert, and it was arranged that we should meet at his house on Thursday at eleven.

At 6:30 I had a conference with Kotschnig. He blocked out his activities until the middle of July, and promised to send me a memorandum for the American group supporting the new arrangement and urging an appropriation

10. Moritz and Käthie Oppenheim, an elderly couple who had given extensive gifts to German science, grew increasingly despondent after the Nazi takeover of power and after their son Paul emigrated to Brussels. On June 9, 1933, they committed suicide in Frankfurt.

11. France refused to acquiesce in Germany's rearmament and was highly critical of Anthony Eden's talks with Hitler on the subject. On April 17 France had rejected further negotiations.

to the A. A. C. for the carrying on of their master file. The more I see of Kotschnig, the better I think of him. . . .

Thursday, May 10, 1934

Conference at Baron Robert's [de Rothschild]. Present were besides the host, myself, Bentwich, Oungre, Kotschnig, Helbronner.

The first half of the discussion was given over to the discussion of the situation in France. The French seemed more reasonable than on previous occasions, recognizing the necessity of permitting the bulk of the refugees to remain in the country until they can be cared for elsewhere, and the desirability of providing the facilities for that end. Helbronner admitted that perhaps he had gone too far in his statement in London about the sorts of immigrants which should be admitted to Palestine. But he added that he had been so outraged by the talk of the Zionists—that they would receive only the pick of the immigrants—that he had gone further than he had intended.

The second half of the discussion was given over to the elaboration of plans, mostly by Oungre, of what could be done in the South American countries. Some of these schemes seemed more or less made to the order of his inquirers and without any very substantial basis.

Then quite out of the blue, with seemingly no provocation, Baron Robert began to talk about the necessity of complete frankness. He recounted how he had told Dreyfus what was being said of him, and that the latter had urged him to be brutally frank. So in that temper he turned on me, saying in effect: It is the general talk that the High Commissioner is a charming person, nice to have at dinner, etc., but that so far his accomplishments have been absolutely nil. Then with appropriate gestures he elaborated on this, even going so far as to mimic some of my attitudes. I listened as calmly as I could, telling him indeed to go ahead and have it out. Then I turned on him and said that in any estimate of my work certain factors must be taken into consideration:

(1) That I had undertaken to try to help a people who were a drag on the market; that the Jews were at the moment unpopular everywhere, and that this condition obviously did not simplify one's task;
(2) Moreover, the Jewish leaders themselves had with very rare exceptions filled my ears from the beginning with tales of the weaknesses or worse of other Jewish leaders; that as a result, the first two or three months of our work was given over to trying to establish some measure of peace, not to speak of confidence, among the Jewish organizations themselves;
(3) That the task of finding funds, made much more difficult by civil war within the Jewish ranks, had occupied weeks of my time. I illustrated this by conditions at home, during my recent stay;
(4) That in any event I didn't really give a damn of what the continental view was of my accomplishments so long as I was able to satisfy my own conscience and my friends at home; and that I had no intention of making a

European career and that such future as I might have would be in the States; that I had foreseen this from the beginning, had therefore insisted on setting up my organization on a basis which would justify itself to Americans irrespective of what the French or other continentals thought, and that I intended to go on along this line;

(5) I spoke briefly of the inevitable misunderstandings which would arise because in the nature of the case one could not publish such small gains as he might make from the governments.

After I had had my say, Baron Robert was very kindly, and the meeting adjourned on the constructive note which he sounded, his promise to try to get the Argentine, Brazil, and Uruguayan representatives together with us before I left Paris. Incidentally, Oungre and particularly Helbronner had come to my defense during Baron Robert's attack. The attitude at least of Helbronner was, I am confident, sincere. He spoke quite warmly of the favorable impression he had gathered of my work from the London meeting. But after it was all over, I was not at all sure whether Baron Robert's attack had merely been one of his characteristic outbursts or had been designed for a specific purpose. In any case, I had a measure of satisfaction in having refrained from making the obvious reply, that is, to repeat some of the attacks made to me on the work of the [French] National Committee. Complete frankness is a much over-rated virtue in human relationships.

Also on this day (U.S.) Assistant Secretary of State Wilbur J. Carr responded to McDonald's previous inquiries (February 6 and April 4) regarding identifying documents needed for refugees to enter the United States. Carr wrote that American consuls were authorized to accept a substitute travel document, such as a Nansen Certificate, if a passport could not be obtained. But "if an alien is in his own country and travel documents are required for exit, the consul will have to inform the alien that he should obtain permission from his government to leave the country.

Aliens entering the United States temporarily are not permitted to accept employment and those admitted in a special status (student, treaty alien) are required to maintain that status, or are subject to deportation; qualified aliens are not prohibited from accepting employment, but it should be mentioned, however, that it would be difficult under present conditions for aliens to find work in the United States."

Aliens who became public charges, Carr continued, were excludable, and aliens unable to satisfy consuls that they would not become public charges could not receive immigration visas.[12] *In short, despite the efforts of McDonald, Chamberlain, and many others, relatively little had changed in the State Department's interpretation of immigration regulations.*

12. McDonald Papers, Columbia, High Commission File 1.

Friday, May 11, 1934

. . . .

Then to the American Embassy. Chatted with Ambassador Straus.[13] He had been receiving from Messersmith and others what seemed to be too optimistic accounts of the probability of a change in the German regime. I told him so. . . . He asked me to come to dinner Sunday night, but I told him I was leaving before then, so he suggested that I call up his brother, Percy, who was staying at his house.

Pleasant and interesting chat with Julius Simon,[14] who was on his way to the States. He agreed completely with the view Bentwich and I had expressed to Rosenberg about Trans-Jordan. He has confidence in the possibility of developments in the Gaza area, but added that much more money is needed if the economic absorptive capacity of Palestine is to be sufficiently enlarged to permit the admission of large numbers of refugees.

To the American Embassy for a pleasant chat with Percy and Mrs. Straus and with Mrs. Jesse Straus in their attractive, but very noisy garden.

Back to the hotel in time to have tea with members of the staff and Miss Gertrude Baer of the Women's International League for Peace and Freedom. She began by telling me some of the things which were being said about our work. I told her she needn't bother, because there was nothing new that she could add. Then she brought up a number of specific points about the stateless, passports, etc. all of which we had been working on for months. She is a nice person.

At 7:30 in my rooms began more than an hour's conference with Bernhard.[15] Bentwich and Wurfbain were also present. At the end, I think our guest had a fairer idea of what we had been attempting to do, but he was a little amusing when he insisted that he had to attack me in order to prod the governments to do something. He promised faithfully to regard our interview as private and in no sense for publication.

. . . .

Saturday, May 12, 1934

At 12:00 Herbert May, Norman Bentwich, and I went to Baron Robert's for the conference with the ambassador of Brazil, the minister of Uruguay, and the first secretary of the Argentine Embassy, the ambassador being in London. Others present besides the host were Louis Oungre, Helbronner, Jacques Lyon,[16] and Senator Bérenger. I was asked to open the discussion. I did so by ad-

13. Jesse Straus, U.S. ambassador to France.

14. Jules Simon, German-born economist and founder of the Palestine Economic Corporation.

15. Georg Bernhard of the *Pariser Tageblatt.* Formerly chief editor of the *Vossische Zeitung,* a convinced German Democrat who had gone into exile.

16. Jacques Lyon, French Foreign Office.

dressing myself to the South Americans. I first urged them to follow the example of Uruguay and join the Governing Body. We were anxious to have them because of the prestige they would bring, because of their knowledge of conditions in their part of the world, and because they would then know better what we are doing. Then I spoke of the desirability from their own self-interest to consider sympathetically the question of receiving larger numbers of the refugees. I stressed how the United States had been built up by refugees, and transformed from a country dependent wholly on its production of raw materials to one with a fairly rounded national economy. I said that I thought the stupidity of the Nazis offered to South America the unique opportunity to supplement their native talents with the brains and technical skill of the German Jews.

Then Oungre, very effectively and persuasively, sketched the possibilities of immigration in each of the three countries. He showed a detailed knowledge of each, and suggested specific ways in which the immigrants could be employed without conflicting with existing national interests. He pledged on behalf of the organizations that none of the immigrants would become public charges, and expressed the hope that ICA and related groups could be given a quasi-monopoly of immigration for a trial period of six months for a limited number of families.

Then followed a general discussion, the French behaving very much better than at the previous conference. The diplomatic representatives promised to inform their governments of what we had said, and I promised to supply them with a formal statement at once.

. . . .

After lunch Senator Bérenger and I had a good talk. He said, "Now you have done something, but have you done enough?" Presently we were joined by Baron Rothschild, Helbronner, Oungre, Lyons, and at the very end by Herbert May. The discussion was of two sorts: first the work being done in France; it was during this that Oungre committed what seemed to me an unpardonable act of disloyalty. In his unmeasured desire to ingratiate himself always more completely in the good graces and the confidence of the French, he made a scarcely veiled attack on Dr. Bernhard Kahn; quite without excuse, he told as an illustration of the potentially dangerous form of German penetration, what Dr. Kahn had said to us two days previous in great confidence, as to the way in which he had gotten around the refusal of the authorities to give him *permits de travail* (work permits) for five German engineers—refugees—needed by a radio factory which had been bought, reorganized by another refugee, and which was then employing 200 French workmen. His method had been to organize the engineers in a cooperative, thus avoiding the necessities of the *permits de travail.* In fact, their work is carried on within the factory. Oungre went so far as to turn to Lyon and say, "Now, from the legal point of view here is a question for you to consider." I was so shocked by this attack on a colleague and on the work in which Oungre should be as much interested as Dr. Kahn that I was henceforth willing to believe anything which Dr. Kahn or anyone else would say to me about the slippery qualities of Oungre. I now realize better than before what Dr. Kahn had meant when two days earlier he checked Oungre in his talk about ICA giving a guarantee, and asked him point blank; "Do you mean ICA?" Oungre had replied, "Well, of course, in these matters we always work with the JDC."

The other part of the group discussion centered on the possibility of France making a token payment. I urged strongly that this be done. Bérenger thought it a possibility.

....

Supper with the Mays, Bentwich, and Miss Sawyer. We had to rush away early to catch the Rome Express.

Rome, Sunday, May 13, 1934

Arrived in Rome on time, a few minutes after seven in the evening. Were received at the Hotel Excelsior like a celebrity. Had worked for some hours on the train and was very tired, but since the broadcast was to take place before 2:00 and the rehearsal shortly after midnight, I decided not to go to bed. Anyhow, I had been somewhat cheered up by being mistaken for my own secretary on arrival, and by a cable from Popkin saying that he liked my talk, which had been finished just before leaving Paris and there turned over to the representative of the Jewish Telegraphic Agency for cabling to the States.

The broadcast itself was very much like a broadcast anywhere.

The occasion of the broadcast was the opening of the United Jewish Appeal at a gala dinner at the Commodore Hotel in New York City to raise money for the refugees. The broadcast was direct to the hotel dining room, hence the 2:00 A.M. hour in Rome. Most of McDonald's speech consisted of stories of people he had encountered in his ten-day trip to Central Europe the previous month. He told of talking to the young wife of a doctor specializing in skin diseases. She herself had been given temporary shelter for herself and her child but the doctor was in Paris waiting with diminishing hope for an opening overseas. "The eyes of that young mother as she told me her story and asked my help, mirrored haunting anxiety. 'I am willing,' she said, 'to go anywhere, to do anything; but my husband must find an opportunity to practice. This endless waiting, this associating day after day with other men also waiting for a chance to exercise their profession—this is more than he can bear.'"

[Within the last few days there has been throughout Germany a nationwide distribution of a special issue of a virulent anti-Semitic publication. That paper (*Der Stürmer*) outdoing itself, features, as if true, the most grotesquely cruel and absurd charges that have been made against the Jewish people during 1500 years. Shocking, lurid illustrations depicting beastly scenes heighten the awfulness of the printed word. Incitement to unreasoning violence could hardly go further."]

In conclusion, he warned that, as bad as the situation currently was, it was only getting worse, worse for the Jews within Germany and more difficult for the refugees in the surrounding countries. The Germans were boasting that the world was no longer interested in the refugees, so McDonald appealed to his audience to prove by their generous contributions that this was not true.[17]

....

Tuesday, May 15, 1934

Over to see Ambassador Long. I gave him a detailed account of our work, and particularly our relations with Germany. I added that since I was to see Suvich[18] and Mussolini and Pacelli, I felt I ought to let him know exactly what I was about. He seemed to appreciate this frankness. I then asked him about Italian-German relations, especially in relation to Austria, reminding him of what he had told me last fall to the effect that Italy would not permit, even if force were required to prevent it, the Anschluss [the takeover of Austria by Germany]. Long said that is undoubtedly was the Italian attitude, that a few months previous they had mobilized a large number of men on the frontier prepared to march, and that a preliminary mobilization order had been issued for the troops in the north of Italy. He said that Suvich had given the word which had precipitated the counter-revolution of February, with its attack on the Socialists. I would have been much interested to hear more, but just then the word came from Miss Sawyer that Pacelli would see me between twelve and one, so I had to leave.

At the Vatican I had no difficulty getting through the series of Swiss guards and into the ante-room of the cardinal secretary of state. But there I was stuck, while two distinguished prelates, one of them a German cardinal, one after the other absorbed nearly forty-five minutes of Pacelli's time. Finally, however, I was ushered in, and greeted this time with considerably less aloofness and caution than on my first visit. I explained that since I had seen him I had taken on my new responsibilities, which I had in no sense expected to do last August.[19] I told of our relations with Germany, and of the apparent increasing economic difficulties within the Reich. Pacelli listened with obvious interest. He then talked about the Concordat (German-Vatican agreement), stressing its importance as a legal basis for the Church's position, even if violated. Time and again he returned to the point that the local [Nazi] leaders are out of

17. Transcript of broadcast (dated May 13, 1934), McDonald Papers, USHMM.
18. Fulvio Suvich, Mussolini's deputy secretary for foreign affairs.
19. See McDonald's diary entry of August 24, 1933 (chap. 4).

hand, that the mass movement of the party is beyond the control of the central authorities. Nor did he disagree with my view that the swing of this last movement is decidedly towards the left, with the effect of diminishing the authority of the conservatives such as Schacht, Schmitt, and von Krosigk, and increasing that of the extremists. He spoke with particular emphasis of Rosenberg's new book as a pagan attack on all of Christianity. I, in turn, emphasized the community of interest between the Jews and the Catholics in the face of a common enemy.

There were no indications from him that he wished to terminate the interview, but I, still hopeful of seeing Suvich before lunch, felt I had to go after about twenty minutes' talk. On the way out Pacelli underlined that everything which he had said was, of course, private and not for publication.

. . . . . .

At quarter of four the representatives of the Jewish community came—Rabbi Sacerdoti, an elegant worldly figure, Mr. di Leon Ravenna, and Orvieto. We carried on a discussion for a half an hour or more, in a mixture of English, French, and Italian. I was surprised to be told that there exists a strong cleavage between the Zionists and the non-Zionists, and that the latter are insisting that the former be eliminated from important offices, because they are not sufficiently nationalistic in the Italian sense. In other words, the effort is being made to be spoken of simply as Italians of Hebrew religion, rather than as Jews. The opinion was expressed that Suvich or Mussolini would speak about this, but in fact neither of them did. As we were concluding our talk, the suggestion was made that they would like to see me again after my conferences with the Italian officials, so I made an engagement for 9:30 that evening.

Meantime, Mrs. Kuhn (Simon, of Cincinnati), whom I had run into in the hotel lobby that morning, had joined our conference. When I met her first, I tried to persuade her to send some money to Miss Ginsberg, whom she knows. She said no, the cost of living in Italy was too high, and she wanted to save what she had for the care of the German children who are going to be put up in her house in Cincinnati. Later, however, she said she would confer with Miss Ginsberg with reference to the possibility of making a special gift to bring the Baroness Dohna or someone of that sort on Miss G.'s list, to the University of Cincinnati.

Suvich, who looks like a junior clerk, listened attentively to my story of our relations with Germany. He then said that he assumed that the best course would be to work with the regime as long as possible, and then, if necessary, make a public statement to the Governing Body and to the public. He suggested also that I might, in a communication meant for Germany but addressed to the League Council, from whom I had my appointment, declare in effect that if better cooperation from Germany were not forthcoming, I would have to resign. My answer to that suggestion was that nothing would please the Germans better than for me to resign. He saw this and replied that perhaps one should not go quite that far. It was agreed that any statement which I might prepare would be submitted to Majoni.

Met Majoni and went with him to have tea in the Pincian gardens and watch the sunset the second time, and at seven o'clock we were in the ante-room of Mussolini.

We were received a few minutes later, in a room fully as large as that in which I had seen Mussolini six years earlier. The present palace, Venezia, is richer in architecture and works of art than his earlier official headquarters. Majoni and I marched together across the length of the huge room, while Mussolini in riding clothes came to meet us. He was cordial and quite informal, joking with Majoni about the improvement which he noticed in him since his marriage.

We then sat down at Mussolini's desk, I directly in front of him. I began the conference by telling Mussolini how much the world looked to him to save the peace of Europe now that it was evident that the United States could not play a leading role. He was not displeased by my remark, and replied by stating some of the elements in the problem, such as the relations between France and Germany, France and Italy, the situation of Austria, etc. But nothing he said gave any clue as to his policy or intentions.

Then I told him the story of our relations with Germany and asked him point blank what he would do if he were in my situation. In reply, he rolled his eyes and remained eloquently silent. I then went on to talk about conditions in Germany, the economic crisis, the tendency of the local leaders to get out of hand—at this he nodded knowingly, full of his own experiences in the past with insubordination of that sort. I told of the new issue of the *Stürmer*,[20] which he said he had already seen, and telling his colleague Majoni of it with graphic gestures; he apparently shares the common feeling that this sort of thing is a reversion to medievalism.

I told him how much the world noted with approval the contrast between his treatment of the Jews and that of the Nazis. In this connection I emphasized the damage, direct and indirect, which is being done in the United States and elsewhere to the interests of Germany as a result of their anti-Semitic attitude. He listened cannily to all of this, as though he were weighing the significance of it for himself. At the end of about half an hour he rose and walked with us across the room. I was struck by his evident splendid health. He had just come in from riding, looked in the pink of condition, and in excellent humor.

Just before the interview Majoni showed me the text in French of the statement which he was including in his report on the London meeting about the mention of the Matteotti Fund. I told him that I approved the text.

20. Its headline was "The Jewish Murder Plot against non-Jewish Humanity Is Uncovered." The illustration depicted the blood libel, the medieval legend that Jews murdered Christian children to use their blood in ceremonies. It showed two Jews with revolting features collecting the blood flowing from two cherubic Christian children who had just been murdered.

. . . .

Out for a brief walk alone, and returned to the hotel at 9:30 to meet three members of the Jewish community. I told them very little of what either Suvich or Mussolini had said, but more of what I had said, in particular my statements to Mussolini about the importance to Italy of the world's good opinion of his treatment of the Jews. They were much too grateful, leaving me with the impression that they are not completely secure themselves.

. . . .

Wednesday, May 16, 1934

Packed and took the ten o'clock train for Naples.

. . . .

At sea, the *Rex,* Friday, May 18, 1934

The weather continued beautiful. We reached Gibraltar on schedule at eight o'clock at night. [John D.] Rockefeller[, Jr.,] and I happened to meet on the top deck, and we chatted for a long time as we were entering the harbor. The talk covered a wide range, jumping back and forth from the scene around us to such topics as the League, which he considers nearly dead. He has refused to go to Geneva, thinks that if war is avoided it will not be through the League; sectarianism is a curse; he wonders how the churches of the future will be supported since the young people are losing interest. This subject had arisen out of my talk about the conflict between the church and the Nazis. He recognized that the Catholic Church has a stronger hold over its young than the Protestants, but he doubted whether this showed itself in any improved morality.

. . . .

Sunday, May 20, 1934

Joined the Rockefellers in their room at tea. The first half of our talk was about the children, the merits and demerits of Lincoln School,[21] etc. Then Mrs. asked me if I was glad I had taken up my present work, and had I left the FPA? I said the answer in both cases was yes, but that I was continuing my interest in the FPA, which under Buell's leadership was going clearly ahead. I then talked about my work, conditions in Germany, finding much more sympathetic understanding from her than from him. His only comment when I told, as illustrative of the horror felt by many Jews, of the suicide of the uncle and aunt of Mrs. Felix Warburg,[22] was, "What good could they do by that?" Mrs. said, "Sometimes when I wake up at night I wonder what can be done with the Jews." I asked her why she was so much interested, and she replied that perhaps it was because of

21. The Lincoln School was in the forefront of the progressive education movement. The Rockefeller children and McDonald's elder daughter, Janet, had attended this school in New York City.

22. Moritz and Käthie Oppenheim—see note 10.

her close acquaintance with Mrs. Felix Warburg and Edward Warburg. The latter had explained to her that his parents could not carry out the program of large endowment for the new Museum of Modern Art,[23] because they felt compelled to give to the German situation. I then undertook to try to explain what probably motivated the Warburgs. I took this excuse to point out that it was so difficult to find non-Jewish money that probably the Warburgs thought they must concentrate.

. . . .

Tuesday, Wednesday, Thursday, May 22–24, 1934

Weather continued pleasant Tuesday and Wednesday. We arrived at Ambrose[24] promptly at five o'clock Thursday morning and docked at nine. Chatted with John D. as we were docking. It was a great relief to see Bobby looking so well.

New York, Thursday, May 24, 1934

Mr. Felix Warburg had kindly come to the boat. We arranged to meet at his house and drive down together to the meeting at Ittleson's office.

. . . .

At Ittleson's office there were perhaps twenty men, including besides the host, Warburg and myself, Henry Morgenthau, James Speyer, Frederick Warburg, Paul Warburg [sons of Felix], David Heyman, Mr. Halley, Gilbert Kahn,[25] Arthur Lehman, Jimmy Rosenberg, et al.

Ittleson made a brief statement, as did Felix, and then I was called upon. I spoke for about thirty to thirty-five minutes. Then followed Ittleson's direct appeal. The result was subscriptions totalling $230,000, including $50,000 from the Felix Warburgs. I was disappointed in Morgenthau's paltry $5,000, Arthur Lehman's $7,000 and Speyer's $5,000. But on the whole, those who had organized the meeting seemed to think that it was fairly successful.

Stopped with Ruth at Warburg's for supper. Others present were a relative from California, interested in the motion pictures, and Dr. Magnes.[26] I talked with the latter about his relations to the Rockefellers, particularly in connection with the university. He said that he had been frequently in touch with the Rockefeller representatives in Paris, and here in New York; that they had agreed on a basis of 50/50 support for three distinguished professors at the university, but that they had not gone further than that.

23. Mrs. Rockefeller—Abby Rockefeller—was one of the founders of the Museum of Modern Art (1929).

24. Ambrose Lightship, the entrance to New York harbor.

25. Gilbert Wolff Kahn, partner at Kuhn Loeb and Company and the son of Otto Kahn.

26. Judah Magnes, former rabbi of New York's Temple Emanu-El, Warburg's temple. He moved to Palestine and in 1935 became president of the Hebrew University in Jerusalem.

Dr. Magnes seemed very tired. Later, Mrs. Warburg told me that he should have an operation now, but because of his wife's objection he was postponing it until he returned to Jerusalem. Apparently, Mrs. Warburg is much disturbed by the clash between Dr. Weizmann and Dr. Magnes.[27] Her dearest friends seem always to be getting into terrible rows with one another, because of basic conflicts of view.

After dinner stayed long enough to listen to the broadcast of Dr. Magnes's address at a Jewish meeting at Claridge's Hotel. It was an effective statement.

....

Monday, May 28, 1934

....

Lunch with Chamberlain and Fosdick. . . . Fosdick felt that the value of his visit to London was to show the interest of Washington in the problem. He felt that he had not been able to make any personal contribution, but that the other was worthwhile. He was kind enough to say that he thought I had handled the meeting excellently. As to the Rockefellers, he led me to feel that the door was still open [for a contribution to the expenses of the High Commission], and that it would be advantageous for us to discuss it further.

Miss Shimer of the Commonwealth Fund came in. We had a long session. She evidently was a little disturbed by the lack of accomplishment of the Christian Committee. I therefore urged that it would be most desirable if a large grant could be made for use among the non-Jewish refugees and to be allocated directly by a committee headed by Cecil. She was interested in my estimate of the amount spent on the refugees to date and the very small proportion which had come from Christian sources. On the whole, her attitude was not unencouraging.

Washington, Tuesday, May 29, 1934

At 10:30 in to see Moffat. He was particularly interested to have me tell him in detail the story of our relations with Germany. Before I had finished it was time to go to see Phillips, so it was arranged that I would come back and continue my talk with Moffat.

Moffat wrote that McDonald "has been able to make no headway in bridging the gap between the German Government and the Commission for German Refugees[,] and a policy has been adopted in Berlin that any discussion on an oral basis should be directed to a junior member of the legal staff. He has been telling the Jews in America that far more is at stake than a mere local persecution of the Jews. He claims that Germany has a definite policy to set the clock back and return the Jew to the Ghetto from

27. Beginning in 1930 Weizmann attacked Magnes because of his support for a bi-national (Jewish-Arab) state in Palestine.

which he had little by little arisen in the course of a 100 years [sic]. On the whole, he had little to offer[,] although he had talked with Léger, Suvich, Mussolini, and others.[28]

Phillips asked me to tell him the whole story. As Fosdick indicated to me, Phillips does not pretend to follow this particular problem in detail. When I had finished my story of our relations with Germany, I asked Phillips what he would do. He said that obviously the only thing is publicity.

Phillips wrote, "James G. McDonald, commissioner appointed to care for German refugees, called this morning and gave me interesting impressions. He has reached pretty much of a deadlock with the German government and is no longer received by high officials. He reports that comparatively few German Jews are leaving Germany, small numbers of refugees are returning to Germany, which about balances the situation. If, however, the German Government swings more to the left, there will presumably be a further anti-Semitic drive which will start up once more the movement away from Germany. McDonald's committee is working first on finding countries where the refugees can remain, second, on providing them with proper papers, 'conduit de voyage,' third, on raising money, most of which must come from the United States and from England."

If McDonald said that comparatively few German Jews were leaving, it could only have been in the context that there were great difficulties in getting out and in finding places of refuge. Phillips's comment seems to reflect his hope that there was no longer a problem for the United States to deal with—particularly in the form of increased German-Jewish immigration.[29]

Returning to Moffat, I concluded my story. He indicated an attitude similar to that of Phillips, but did not express it so definitely.

Then in to see Feis. I told him I wanted to know about the reported project for a German loan or credit. He told me this story in strict confidence. Several months ago when the President had talked to Luther in very straight language, he had said in passing, "Of course, anything that can be done to improve trade relations between the two countries is desirable." On the basis of this report which Luther apparently exaggerated, Berlin immediately decided that they would send a commission to arrange some special trade agreements. Dodd notified Washington to this effect. Immediately there were departmental conferences, in which was made clear the failure of Germany to live up to present obligations, the inadvisability of undertaking new relations with the Reich, etc. As

28. Moffat Journal, vol. 34, Moffat Papers, May 29–30, 1934, call number MS Am 1407, Houghton Library, Harvard University. By permission of the Houghton Library, Harvard University.

29. Phillips Diary, Box 2, Phillips Papers, entry of May 29, 1934, call number bMS Am 2232, Houghton Library, Harvard University. By permission of Houghton Library, Harvard University.

a result, Dodd was notified in such language that the proposed German commission idea was dropped.

Meantime Peck, as Phillips had indicated to me earlier, anxious to get rid of certain surpluses particularly large in such commodities as lard, would like to see either a credit to enable Germany to buy, or some form of barter exchange. However, any such arrangement would be contingent upon State Department approval, which would not be granted.

In to see Carr. He was most cordial. He asked me if, on the basis of my experiences with foreign offices abroad, I had any suggestions for improvement of the State Department. I told him that my experiences were too narrowly limited to certain individuals in the foreign offices with whom I had to deal, for me to have any general points of view, that, therefore, I was afraid I would have to leave that to Stone. Carr spoke of Stone with enthusiasm.

I took occasion to tell Carr about the Montreal situation and the case of Freudenberg. He said he would welcome from Chamberlain full data on these and any other cases of complaint. He thought this was no more than fair, both to the officers in the field and to the complainant.

He agreed that Chamberlain's appointment had been excellent, much better than Houghton's would have been, that Chamberlain and Judge Mack and I were very useful in helping the department to maintain friendly and cordial relations with the Jewish groups.

I should have noted the other day that Fosdick told me that Honoré and Bronet, both men of large standing in France, were of the opinion that I am too pro-German to be effective in my present work. Fosdick had done what he could to disabuse them, saying that he was sure the French Foreign Office itself would not share their view. I asked Fosdick if I should take this matter up with the French ambassador, whom I know very well. Fosdick thought this would be placing too much emphasis on it, but that I ought to see Honoré soon after my return to Paris.

. . . .

After lunch conferred with Colonel MacCormack at the [Cosmos] Club. I first asked him if the Labor bond regulations had been issued. He said not, that he doubted in some ways whether they would be issued, or perhaps they would not be necessary in view of the State Department's new interpretation of the regulations, and perhaps they might be undesirable because of opening the doors too wide. He said Judge Mack had made his report.

Then he went on to indicate that he saw no reason why special efforts should be made to relieve France and other countries which had received the refugees, of their burdens, implying that special concessions should be made only to persons wishing to leave Germany. I took exception to this viewpoint. He then suggested that perhaps I would prepare a program of admissions of the refugees for submission to him and to the Department of State. "Of course," he said "we would not agree to accept your recommendations, but we would be glad to have them." I did not make a definite promise to supply this material, for I wished first to talk the whole matter over with Chamberlain.

I spoke about the Montreal case, and he said that it was absolutely against the rules of the Department of Labor to make any personal recommendations to the consuls; that, therefore, his legal adviser had been wrong in giving the card to the applicant.

Then over to the State Department, where I remained until time for the meeting of the trustees of the Twentieth Century Fund. This began at something after four o'clock, and lasted until after ten. Several times during the meeting I was surprised at Newton D. Baker's conservatism, or at any rate, he seemed to look upon the New Deal as dangerous trifling with fundamental American principles.

. . . .

14. June 1934: Turn for the Worse

New York, Friday, June 1, 1934

Lunch at the *Times*. Besides Arthur Sulzberger and myself there were present James, Ogden, Mr. Ochs, Wiley,[1] and Hamilton Fish Armstrong.[2] The talk was nearly all about conditions in Germany. Armstrong and I were in complete agreement on our impressions. Mr. Ochs seemed deeply stirred by what we were saying. Gradually during the past months the terribleness of the Nazis had begun to tell on him, so much so that as we were leaving he said quietly, but in a tragic tone, "This is all interesting for you who are students," but for him, though he did not say so, it constituted a disillusionment that was making the closing years of his life utterly sad.[3]

. . . .

Tea with Mrs. [Otto] Kahn. She was absolutely hard about her relations to the Jewish problem, exclaiming that she had no more responsibility there than if they were negroes or any other unfortunate people in distress. We also talked about our house in the country.[4] She had evidently forgotten her statement some years ago that she would take it off our hands when we were finished with it, and I did not have the courage to remind her of her commitment. Indeed, when she is in one of her hard moods, it is very difficult to talk with her.

. . . .

Pittsburgh, Sunday, June 3, 1934

Reached East Liberty Station about nine o'clock. Was met there by Leo Lehman, Dreyfus, Rosenbloom, and a fourth member of the Jewish community. Breakfast at the Westmoreland Country Club, during which time I had been instructed to drive hard at the difficult Mr. Dreyfus. This I did.

. . . .

1. Rollo Ogden, editorial writer; Louis Wiley, business manager.

2. Hamilton Fish Armstrong, editor of *Foreign Affairs,* leading U.S. quarterly review of foreign policy.

3. By the summer of 1933 Ochs's agitation about Hitler had ripened into a full-blown depression. "I personally, feel helpless and almost hopeless," he wrote a man who had sent him a survey of conditions in Germany. Ochs never fully recovered and died on April 8, 1935. Susan E. Tifft and Alex S. Jones, *The Trust: The Private and Powerful Family behind the "New York Times"* (Boston: Little Brown & Co., 1999), 156.

4. McDonald had a little prefab summer house on the Kahn estate on Long Island. The estate contained a great French chateau, elaborate gardens, a farm, a golf course, and so forth.

Something was said during the meal [with forty or fifty leading businessmen] of the possibility of transfer of a large number of Marks by Mr. Dreyfus and one of his associates, the former husband of the second Mrs. May, another Mr. Lehman.

Rushed from this luncheon about four o'clock to a meeting of the workers of the Tristate area at the YMHA.[5] It was an excellent audience, primarily Palestinian [i.e., pro-Zionist].

Time for a few minutes' rest before dressing for the dinner at the club. . . . The chairman was excellent. He made much use of Jimmie Rosenberg's name and letters, and then after I spoke, he began his plea for funds. They were all delighted to raise nearly $70,000, instead of the $40,000 which they had fixed for their minimum for the opening night. Despite all the efforts directed at him, Mr. Dreyfus stuck to his beggarly contribution of $2,000, while all around him people were doubling or quadrupling theirs. Despite this particular failure there was enthusiastic feeling of success. Everyone was most cordial in the expressions of appreciation to me. . . .

McDonald spent June 4 on similar fundraising efforts in Philadelphia.

. . . .

Tuesday, June 5, 1934

. . . .

Lunch at Ittleson's office with him and young Edward Norman.[6] The latter is a bumptious, conceited young man, but with a real Jewish interest, with ample leisure, substantial means of his own, and the only son of a very rich father. Therefore, Ittleson and I, though we drove him hard to do something concrete in connection with the present drive, we [*sic*] also held out the hope that he might be one of the great leaders in large enterprises. Norman knows a good deal about Palestine, but is still anti-Weizmann, overstressing the importance of the Mack-Brandeis factional issues. On the whole, I think Ittleson and I made a good beginning. Incidentally, I was again impressed by Ittleson's penetrating intelligence, driving straight to the heart of a difficult problem.

Then down to see Samuel Untermyer. He received me at once. I, not waiting for him to begin to talk, went at him directly about the need for his support of the United Appeal. I explained in detail why funds were needed, and that just in proportion as his own efforts [boycott] succeeded there would inevitably be a larger immediate need in Germany on the part of the Jewish community. Finally, the old boy said, "I am really impressed by what you tell me, and I shall do something."

5. Young Men's Hebrew Association.

6. Edward Norman, later director of the Palestine Economic Corporation and on the board of the Friends of the Hebrew University.

He told me that Colonel House, Dodd, and he were engaged in a kind of triangular flirtation with a view to finding a formula which would enable the authorities [in Germany] to moderate their policy in return for lightening of the boycott. I said I had no faith in such an effort. He agreed it would be difficult for the Jews to accept favors if the other persecuted groups were not included. I agreed, but more important seemed to be the unlikelihood that the regime could make real terms or that these would be kept if made. Untermyer seemed to agree.

....

Thursday, June 7, 1934

Rabbi Lazaron[7] came in to tell me his plans to go to Germany, of Luther's promise to put him in touch with important personalities, and of his own hope that he might do something to bring about a degree of moderation on the part of the Nazi regime. I told him I wished him every success, but I had not the slightest confidence in the practical character of his mission. I was sure he would learn much; that would be all.

Mr. John Simons came to tell me about his project for South West Africa, but he has taken no account of the political difficulties, nor of the opposition to another autonomous Jewish community. Some of the letters he had had commenting on his project were interesting, but on the whole, I remained unconvinced that it offers an opportunity for large-scale colonization.

....

Friday, June 8, 1934

Luncheon of the Jewish press. Besides the representatives of the papers were present Chamberlain, Hyman, Popkin, Goldwasser, Nathan Straus, and myself. Long discussion about the proper method for handling the news about the coming of the refugee children.[8] Finally, there was a general agreement to play it down.

Then followed a discussion of various aspects of our work. At the end, it seemed to all of us that the meeting had been worthwhile and should be repeated whenever I am at home.

Saturday, June 9, 1934

Undersecretary of State William Phillips noted in his diary: "Professor Joseph E. Chamberlain dropped in to ask to send instructions to our Ambassador in Berlin to cooperate with his British colleagues in requesting the German government to listen to

7. Rabbi Morris S. Lazaron of Baltimore, known for his work to promote better understanding among Protestants, Catholics, and Jews, a member of the National Conference of Christians and Jews. One of the founders, in 1943, of the anti-Zionist American Council of Judaism.

8. German Jewish Children's Aid, Inc., planned to bring over children under fifteen years of age and place them in American homes. Each child would be individually approved for an immigrant visa under the quota.

James G. McDonald's plea on behalf of German Jewish refugees. It appears that the German government is allowing these refugees from Germany to bring out very little money with them and, furthermore, that all property they leave behind is ultimately seized. This means that the refugees who are admitted to foreign countries become a burden on their new communities. . . . We have sent such an instruction to Berlin today."[9]

. . . .

Then over to Felix Warburg's. Found the house overrun with preparations for the ballet. Mrs. Warburg greeted me with the words that my wife had not replied to her invitation. While Bobby watched the rehearsal, Felix and I talked. He stressed again the importance of a constructive, comprehensive program as essential for the development of the corporation's plans. Any program, he said, even if it is unworkable, would be better than none. He evidently appreciated what I had been doing in the United Appeal, but expressed the view that this was really their work, and that in any case what could be done during the next few months would not be sufficient to justify my delay in returning abroad. He thought the situation different now from when I had sailed before. I did not take the time to rehearse all the reasons why it was impossible then for me to delay further.

However, after the talk I felt sure that I should not postpone my return beyond the twentieth, particularly since Warburg thought the Zionist invitation to the meeting at Atlantic City of no consequence.

Home late for supper. Then to the high school play [*A Man Who Came to Dinner*]. Janet was very much better than I expected. Her poise was good, and her expression of feeling excellent for a youngster. Nearly all the children did well. The boy who took the leading role was especially good.

. . . .

Tuesday, June 12, 1934

Talked to Alexander Smith about the work being done in Turkey now. His colleague there is leaving Turkey now and is expected to be crossing the Atlantic for New York about the time I would be reaching England. Smith offered to suggest that his associate stop off to see me in London, but I hesitated to accept this. Smith confirmed the public impression that the Turks have become very nationalistic in their economic attitude, and that therefore the chances of their accepting a number of refugees were slight.[10]

Talked to Louis Wiley on the phone. He said he had written a note to the President following my lunch at the *Times* a few days earlier. If anything more needed to be done, he thought that Moley was the best lead. I put in a call for

9. Phillips Diary, June 9, 1934, call number bMS Am 2232, Houghton Library, Harvard University. By permission of the Houghton Library, Harvard University.

10. Beginning in 1933 Turkey admitted a small number of Jewish and anti-Nazi academics.

Moley, but he was said to be out of town. Miss Sawyer followed this up two or three times later, but finally got only the suggestion that I put what I wanted to say in a memorandum. In other words, if I hoped to have Moley as one who will be helpful, I must get myself out of the memorandum class as far as he is concerned.

Lunch with Ralph Straus at Macy's. The only other person present besides Ralph and myself was Beardsley Rummel. For the first time, I had a real chance to get a detailed impression of Rummel. Our talk covered a wide range. I was surprised to find how liberal, even radical, Rummel is in his fundamental philosophies. He was speaking of the absurdity that anyone should have to pay for health or for legal protection, which, according to him, should be as free as elementary education. He and Ralph agreed that the old order is changing and deserves to change, even to the extent of a quasi-communistic regime.

As I was leaving, Ralph walked with me to the elevator. The subject of Ivy Lee came up. I remarked that I was a little surprised that Percy had allowed himself to be persuaded that Ivy was innocent of the charges of Nazi propaganda. Ralph then replied in great confidence that Ivy Lee was no longer retained by Macy's; that they could take no chance with a Jewish boycott; that they had felt something of the sort earlier. He wished me to keep this news, however, strictly to myself.

In the afternoon Professor Grant of Haverford College came in to tell me of the menace which he considered was being created in Palestine by the Jewish invasion. Because of years of archaeological work there he claimed to understand intimately the mind of the Arab peasant. This is such as to make certain an explosion sooner or later. The more he spoke, the more I sensed a latent fanaticism in him. But why he came to me was not quite clear. I promised to read the material he left with me, and to return it to him.

Despite a terrific downpour I found a fairly good crowd at the Commodore meeting arranged by Ashworth's committee.[11] Leiper[12] spoke briefly, Fosdick [Raymond] introduced me in very laudatory terms, but spoke only a little of the work itself.

I was very tired and did not feel that I did well. But in the question period I was made angry by one or two persons inquiring whether I had taken measures to see to it that the Aryan refugees could return to Germany, or that no more would be expelled. My reply was that we had no special mandate to discriminate in favor of the Aryans, nor did I think that we would be justified in doing so, either on the basis of ethics or expediency. At the end Mrs. Rabbi Wise came up to me and said that she was so stirred by my whole approach to the whole problem that she was going to send a small check for non-Jewish refugees. Fosdick, in closing the meeting, again referred in very laudatory terms to me and partic-

11. The American Christian Committee for Refugees.

12. Henry Smith Leiper, executive secretary of the department of relations with churches abroad of the Federal Council of Churches of Christ in America, 1930–1945.

ularly to my work in London, but also again failed to say very much about the refugee problem itself.[13]

. . . .

Wednesday, June 13, 1934

. . . .

Jacob Schwarz, former businessman, came in with a dossier of material about Panama. It seems quite complete, and is supported by Panamanian authorities, but I suspect that it smacks of a land deal on a grandiose scale. Moreover, my faith in Schwarz was severely shaken when he solemnly suggested that the whole thing could by financed by inducing 2,000,000 Jews each to contribute $100 a year. However, I promised to go through the material, submit it to the Anglo-HICEM, and to write him again.

. . . .

We arrived there [at the JDC meeting] while the meeting was in progress. I slipped into the rear and sat down between Felix Warburg and Mr. Bamberger. Hyman was in the process of giving his report [which was followed by another report by Rosen]. . . .

As I was leaving, Mr. Baerwald, the chairman, called on me, though the treasurer was at that moment in the midst of his report. Speaking from where I sat, I agreed with two of the chief points Rosen had made about the refugee situation: first, as to the extreme need in Germany, and second, that on the whole, even within Germany the Jews were better off than as refugees. I then paid a tribute to the JDC and its invaluable help in my task. . . .

Ruth and I arrived at the Eisner's[14] in time for dinner. Others there were ten or twelve of their younger friends. During dinner I had an interesting chat with [Sidney J.] Weinberg of Goldman Sachs, and one of the chief advisers of the President. He told me that Deane was making a great success in NRA; that everybody liked him, that he was having more and more influence, and was going to be offered a very important job in the near future. I was delighted to hear this.

. . . .

As we were talking, Sam Untermyer came in. Weinberg spoke very critically and even caustically of Untermyer's boycott activities. Later, however, when he talked to Untermyer privately he, according to Untermyer's report to me, agreed about the boycott.

13. Before leaving the States the next week, McDonald wrote a letter to a list of well-to-do Christians with whom he was acquainted, appealing for money for Christian refugees.

14. Mark Eisner, lawyer, New York City legislator, president of the Association of Jewish Education.

After dinner about fifty additional people came in, most of them of the Westchester Jewish group. I spoke for about a half an hour or forty-five minutes, aiming much of my talk at Untermyer, who sat nearly in front of me. When I had finished, he was called upon. He spoke for only a minute or two, saying that he did not wish to enter into any controversy with me, that he was much impressed by what I had said, that he wished to limit himself to an expression of appreciation of what I was endeavoring to do. Later, during the money-raising period he made a contribution of $2,000.

Thursday, June 14, 1934

Talked to Chamberlain about the possibility of the State Department going along with the British in their support of our memorandum to Berlin on social insurance.[15] He raised some questions which he said he would have to look up. I said that I hoped the Department would approach it as a matter of principle and not as from a technical point of view. It was agreed that I would call him from Fosdick's office, where I was going after lunch.

In to see Fosdick at his new office. It faces the north and the west on the fifty-sixth floor, and has I think the most beautiful view I have seen in New York. I asked him first about his attitude towards Washington and Berlin. He said he thought the Department ought to support our memorandum. He then called up Chamberlain and talked to him at length. Apparently, Chamberlain is having various items looked up and will communicate with me in a day or two.

I then asked him about John D. [Rockefeller], Jr., and the High Commission [contribution]. He said that he could not get to first base on this proposition, but that he thought I should see John III. So I called up John who said to come right in. Before I left, Fosdick outlined to me the basis on which he thought the approach could be made.

John's office is not as attractive as Fosdick's. It faces south, with a view of the whole midtown and lower town section of the bay. After we had exchanged personal remarks about our families, I launched into a full length account of the need for non-Jewish funds. I said that I had spoken to his father about the problem on the boat but had of course not spoken of money. John replied that his father had deeply appreciated this. I then went on as though I were making a direct appeal. John listened well, and was I think really stirred.

After half an hour or forty-five minutes, he said, "I think it would be a mistake for me to take the matter up directly with father. He dislikes having projects presented in the abstract, but prefers to have them as definite as possible. Therefore, it would be better if I, following up the lead which Packard[16] had

15. A request that refugees be enabled to receive the social insurance to which they were entitled and which they would have received if they had remained in Germany. The British Foreign Office had just authorized Ambassador Phipps "at his discretion" and "unofficially" to ask the German Foreign Office if the United States would do likewise.

16. Arthur W. Packard, head of the Rockefeller Foundation.

given me last winter, sent him a full memorandum of developments since. John thought it would be better if I did not make a direct appeal. I replied that I would prefer to have it on an indirect basis, because I did not wish to put his father in a position of having to refuse, and I did not wish to put myself in the position of being refused. One gentleman to another, as it were. I told John however, that my failure to make a high-pressure salesman statement would not be held against me. He said he was sure that his father would be relieved at a different approach.

. . . .

Friday, June 15, 1934

Up to see Mr. Packard. I told him of my talk with Fosdick and John III. He asked me a number of specific questions, such as the amount of money to be raised by the Jews, the amount already raised, list of the larger contributors. Would a contribution from John D., Jr., meet his whole obligation, etc. etc? It was a very satisfactory conference. I promised to get a memorandum to him before I sailed.

Mrs. Kahn called to ask what we would take for our house in the country if her superintendent had a chance to sell it. I told her that though it cost us much more, we would be willing to take $1,000 for the whole thing, including the furnishings. She told me that she had made a contribution to the JDC through Mrs. Felix Warburg, and she wanted it to be used for my work.

Dinner at Felix Warburg's. Besides Mr. and Mrs. and Ruth and I there were Paul, Eric, [sons], Mrs. Borg, Justice Cardozo,[17] and a woman who may have been his wife,[18] Dr. and Mrs. Adler. Later, Edward [another son] came in for a little while.

Before dinner I chatted with Felix Warburg about my Rockefeller talk. I told him of my tentative arrangement with Packard that if John D., Jr., made a contribution, he would suggest that the fund be expanded along the lines indicated in the conference between Packard and me. Warburg then made a suggestion which seemed to be preferable, that is, that John D., Jr., transmit his contribution to JDC without reservations, that he, Warburg would then return the whole of it to the Cecil committee (for Christian refugees) with an appropriate note. I said I was sure that this would seem even better to the Rockefellers.

After dinner Edward and I talked. He thinks economic conditions are not as unfavorable as they are sometimes reported to be in Germany. But he thinks there are fundamental clashes among the leaders, that the Reichswehr has retained its independence, that there is, therefore, still a possibility of a coup representing the conservatives and the Army. Meantime, the differences between the left and the right within the party are accentuated.

. . . .

17. Benjamin Cardozo, appointed associate justice of the U.S. Supreme Court in 1932.
18. Cardozo never married.

Saturday, June 16, 1934

Lunch with Baerwald. He agreed with my point of view about the desirability of securing an executive for the corporation soon. He thinks Goldwasser would be excellent. He then outlined to me a plan to increase the portfolio of the corporation very substantially by transferring to it certain funds or other assets from the Agro-Joint, JDC, the AMICA, the foundation, and possibly from ICA itself. I thought the scheme was a little bit of a juggling act, and he himself said that it was an attempt to make money serve two functions, but that he thought it sound. The chief obstacles would be ICA and Henry Ittleson. The latter might question whether some of these assets were real enough to justify his putting up his portion of the funds.

On the whole, I enjoyed my talk with Baerwald more than any previous one, and got a better impression of the man.

Monday, June 18, 1934

McDonald spoke at a luncheon, a meeting in Brooklyn at 4:30, a broadcast before dinner and at a meeting after dinner. Day's final entry: "Home very tired."

Tuesday, June 19, 1934

. . . .

Spoke to Moffat on the telephone. Explained why I was unable to come to Washington, and that Chamberlain would made a detailed statement about our request for support of the property memorandum.

I urged that the Department consider the matter on the broad lines of principle, rather than on technical detail. He said that offhand, he thought they would be able to do it, that certainly they would approach it from the point of view I urged. In general, then my talk with him was thoroughly satisfactory.

I called up Raymond Fosdick to tell him that we had gotten off our memorandum to John D., Jr., and that I hoped we would not be penalized because it was not couched in a high-pressure salesman style. He assured me that that would be all right. But so far as the substance of our appeal was concerned, he ventured no opinion as to the likelihood of its success. He merely said that we would certainly have made our record clear. I thought this unsatisfactory, but there was nothing I could do.

Up to Mr Gaisman's[19] house for dinner. During nearly the entire meal he talked very interestingly about his relations with the Gillette people, the way in which he happened to develop the Probak blade and razor, his offer to sell it to the Gillette company, their double crossing, his revenge, the resulting loss of more than $100,000,000 to the Gillette people. He also talked fully about his

19. Henry Jacques Gaisman, inventor, chairman of the board of Gillette Safety Razor Co., 1930–1938.

relations with Liebman, his breach with the latter, the prolonged lawsuit and the eventual elimination of the Liebman crowd. He insisted that C. J. was unwilling to compromise, was unsympathetic to his basic idea of sharing the profits with the employees, etc. I did not get the impression that he was bitter towards C. J., but that he regrets the breach in an old friendship.

After supper we got around to the subject of Germany. I told him of the urgent needs. He said that he sometimes thought that many people did not give as much as they might to the JDC because of the feeling that they would be asked a little later to aid some other group working for the same general purpose. He had given $1,000 to the University in Exile. On the whole, I felt that he had not yet learned to give in large figures. He spoke of persons like Baruch as having large riches, but doubted whether they had given as much as he, $5,000, to the JDC. He said this as if that were a really large amount. In passing, I explained that I might have to make special appeals to a very few persons for purposes which the JDC might not feel justified in supporting as fully as I wished.

As I left, he was extremely cordial, and urged me to come back any time. I learned from the chauffeur who took me home that his employer was very abstemious, rarely goes to town nowadays, lives an extremely quiet life, and is 64 years old.

Home and packed in the midst of Janet's reception for her high school gang, while Bobby, failing to go to sleep as she ought to do, lay awake.

Wednesday, June 20, 1934

Up early. Charles Liebman called. I went over with him my recommendations about the corporations. He agreed. He thought that large contributions from Guggenheims or the Blumenthals or Baruch would have to wait on a specific program. We also talked about Gaisman. C. J. said that conversation is not the best way to approach Gaisman, that a letter would be better, for Gaisman is slow in his thought and very deliberate in action. I ventured to tell Liebman that I thought Gaisman regretted the breach and showed no animosity.

Mrs. Deane came over and took the family down [to the boat], while I drove down with the luggage. Bobby was looked after by Lytleton [the Deanes' ten-year-old son] and Janet by a group of her friends.

Ruth, Janet, and Bobby and a friend and classmate of Janet's, Henrietta Simpson, went with McDonald on this summer trip to Europe.

***Manhattan*, at sea, June 20–26, 1934**

Pleasant weather, voyage uneventful. Met and chatted briefly with Dr. Cohn, who said the Kotschnig memorandum supplied exactly the material which the American committee had intended that Bagster-Collins should secure; that it was of great value to know what the load is going to be. Miss LeHand stopped me one day, and we chatted for a little while. Several talks with

Kaltenborn.[20] . . . Also met Vincent Astor.[21] He said that he had been anxious to meet me because Mrs. Mary Rumsey had spoken to him so often about me. We had no chance however to talk, because I had come up to the party to ask Miss LeHand to dance.

On arrival at Plymouth there were hours to wait before we finally took the train a little after nine, arriving at the Grosvenor House about two the next morning.

London, Thursday, June 28, 1934

. . . .

Just before midnight Ruth and I arrived at the Weizmanns for their reception. Dr. and Mrs. Weizmann were cordial. Met many former associates. Chatted with Otto Schiff, who said that he is certain that all the mass colonization projects are futile, that we must have a long talk about this; Mrs. Ernest Schiff talked to Ruth and me about the children; Sir Osmond asked me how the drive was going in America, and I told him, and he felt that on the basis of this they could get on; otherwise, he seemed, as he had in his letter, to be very pessimistic about the financial situation.

Had a long chat with Simon Marks and his wife. He said that for the moment he was more or less out of Jewish things because of his absorption with a special commission studying the butter and egg trade in Britain. His wife is planning a trip to the west and South Sea islands. He seemed pleased at my report of my references to him in the States. Chatted with Lord Melchett and met his wife, a youngish faded blond. Melchett was as enthusiastic as ever about Palestine; said he would send me a copy of his remarks of the debate in the Lords the previous day.

. . . .

As we were leaving chatted again with Weizmann, he said he had heard from the States that I had been an excellent publicity agent for the Zionist cause, and that the drive was going satisfactorily.

Home just before two o'clock.

Friday, June 29, 1934

. . . .

In the afternoon tea with the family at Lionel Cohen's. Interesting chat there with the distinguished international lawyer, V. Idelson,[22] a Russian Jew

20. H. V. Kaltenborn, leading radio commentator who had spent considerable time in Germany.

21. Vincent Astor, an American member of the Astor family. Owner of *Newsweek*.

22. Vladimir Robert Idelson, practicing in London as an expert on Russian and international law, English barrister since 1928.

who has had an extraordinary career in this country. It was he who put together the Anglo-Persian oil agreement. He knows his Germany and France intimately. I should like to see more of him. . . . Not much opportunity to talk with the Cohens, but enough to get the impression that he is very anti-French, at least so far as putting additional English money for relief into France.

Dinner with Ruth and the girls at [the] Bentwiches. Interesting talk with Nevinson,[23] and afterward with Vernon of the Colonial Office about Tanganyika. He thinks it, rather than Honduras, which he considers impossible, or Kenya, which has too many problems already, offers a chance for settlement. The government there apparently is anxious to set off some Jewish Germans against some of the Nazi Germans now in the territory. It was left that he would try to arrange for an interview for us with the vice-governor, who is now in London.

Saturday, June 30, 1934

. . . .

As we were leaving the Franklins[24] after tea, we heard an announcement on the radio that von Schleicher had been shot and Röhm arrested.[25] The rest of that day nothing was of any interest to me except to try to find the latest news from the front. So much depends on developments there, not merely affecting our own work directly, but influencing much wider issues.

Ernst Röhm, head of the SA, epitomized the potentially disruptive forces within the Nazi Party. A brawler, a well-known homosexual, and an activist contemptuous of the old elites, Röhm became an obstacle—even a threat—to Nazi efforts to generate broad public support and to build up Germany's military strength (since the regular army felt jeopardized by Röhm's large paramilitary organization).

Rivalries within the Nazi movement helped to bring about a dramatic rupture. Heinrich Himmler, head of the SS, and Hermann Göring both saw Röhm and his men as threats to their organizations and ambitions; they helped to persuade Hitler that Röhm was plotting to overthrow him. They also spread rumors that the SA was planning to take over the army or supplant it. Hitler finally decided to strike against Röhm, one of his oldest comrades. On June 30, 1934, a strike by selected squads of Himmler's SS murdered more than eighty SA officials, as well as other assorted political enemies of Hitler, including former chancellor (and re-

23. Probably Henry Woodd Nevinson, writer and journalist for the London *Daily Chronicle* and the *Manchester Guardian.* Campaigner against continuing slavery in Portuguese Angola.

24. Mr. and Mrs. Ernest Franklin, parents of Mrs. Helen Bentwich. Both Mr. and Mrs. Franklin were active in social and philanthropic works. He was treasurer of the Jewish Board of Guardians and other charitable boards and she, the sister of Lady Samuel, had founded a Jewish infant welfare center in London.

25. Ernst Röhm, see inserted commentary in this entry.

tired general) Schleicher. The event has often been called the Röhm Putsch (based on the false Nazi cover story that Röhm was planning a coup) or the "night of the long knives." The killings should have destroyed any illusions that the Nazi regime might become more moderate or might, following its revolution, reestablish the rule of law.

15. July 1934: Visit to the Saar

London, Sunday, July 1, 1934

. . . .

Afterwards with the family to tea at Sir Leonard Cohen's in the country near Rickmansworth. Lady Cohen unfortunately was not very well. Nonetheless, she won the hearts of the youngsters. Sir Leonard and I talked for about an hour and a half. He told me in confidence that he would have to resign from ICA and gave me his personal opinion of the other members of the Board as possible successors. Under present circumstances it cannot be a German. Philippson is hardly sufficiently interested, but out of honor to his father he might be named as a stop-gap. Gottschalk is too conceited and ambitious. The French members are either too old or too new. Montefiore has not the qualities. So it would seem that it falls to Sir Osmond [d'Avigdor-Goldsmid], who, though not as forceful as he might be, is unselfishly interested and able. Speaking of Oungre, Sir Leonard referred to him as a man utterly trustworthy, who never had any thought of himself and no personal axes to grind. I remained silent.

With Ruth out to dinner at Sir Osmond's. Others present besides ourselves and the hosts were Mr. and Mrs. Lionel Cohen and Professor and Mrs. Goodhart. After dinner and the inevitable talk about conditions in Germany we came to the question of money for relief and settlement. To my surprise, I found that Lionel Cohen felt that probably nothing more could be done next year, and that nothing at all should be done for the French. Sir Osmond spoke of his anxiety, and we arranged to go over the figures at his office the next day with a view to an appeal to the States.

Monday, July 2, 1934

Conference at d'Avigdor-Goldsmid's office. Sir Osmond showed me copies of correspondence with Felix Warburg, and later we went over the Allocations Committee's budget in detail. He showed me a letter from Lionel de Rothschild in which the latter criticized the Allocation Committee sharply for lack of prudence in failing to set up a reserve for 1935 and 1936 for the care of refugees within Great Britain. Moreover, Rothschild expressed the positive conviction that no more money could be raised after this year and that he and his brother could not be associated with another appeal. The whole tone of the letter was critical and like an ultimatum. No wonder Sir Osmond resented it.

Sir Osmond thought that it would be possible to raise enough money next year, perhaps £25,000, to care for the refugees in this country, but he doubted if more could be done.

In reply, I pointed out that in that event I should almost certainly have to plan to wind up the affairs of the High Commission by the end of the year, irrespective of the need of the refugees; that it would be extremely difficult to raise the funds necessary in the United States if British Jewry were unwilling to share the responsibility; that I would, therefore, be in a position where I would have to explain to the Governing Body and through them to the governments and to the public that the care of the refugees who were predominantly Jewish could not be pressed forward because funds for such work were not available; that, of course, I would not make an attack on the Jewish communities for failure to supply the funds, for I feel that Christians have an equal or even greater responsibility, but the moral that would be drawn by non-Jews would certainly be that the Jewish communities had not been willing to care for their own; that, moreover, this attitude would be an easy justification to governments for any disinclination they might have in the future to help the Jews. I concluded by asking Sir Osmond whether he thought the leaders of British Jewry were ready to incur this responsibility. He did not give me a positive reply.

Then over to see General Asquith, who is president of the Parana Plantations in Brazil, on whose land the Assyrians (refugees) had been expected to be settled by the League Committee under the direction of the Nansen Office.[1] He explained to us the recent moves in the Brazilian Constituent Assembly which blocked the carrying out of the Assyrian proposal, but said that since this was a quota arrangement on the basis of existing national groups in Brazil, it would not adversely affect a German immigration. We then discussed technical aspects of settlement, but when we learned that settlers in that area must be on the land in time to sow their crops before September, it was evident that nothing could be done there until the winter. It was left that we would communicate with the General after our present intensive survey of the refugee situation is completed.

To the office of Ernest Franklin at Samuel Montagu & Co. I asked Franklin his frank views as to the prospects for raising further relief funds next year in this country and capital funds for settlement this year. To both questions he gave discouragingly negative replies. When I pressed him as to whether he would like to assume responsibility for the failure of an international effort on behalf of Jewish refugees, he simply fell back on the statement that he didn't think additional money could be raised.

Then led by a messenger through the mazes of the financial district, where

1. The Assyrians were an ancient Christian sect (mostly Nestorians) who lived under the Turks and were persecuted by the Muslims. During World War I they fought on the Allied side against the Turks in the hope that they would be given an independent state. Instead, most of their land became part of Iraq, and they were driven from their villages. Thousands ended up in southern Russia and others were scattered in countries around the world, including the United States. The League tried to find homes for them.

I was to have lunch at New Court. There were only four or five people present, including Lionel and Anthony de Rothschild. During the lunch we discussed the German situation, and apparently, I would have been allowed to leave without any reference to the problem of finances for the refugees had I not myself taken the initiative. I, of course, had been forewarned about Lionel's attitude. He began by saying, "Now that the Allocation Committee has already squandered this year's collections, we may be facing a serious situation next year." I took exception to his use of the word "squander," telling him that I had just had an opportunity to examine the budget drawn up by the Allocation Committee, that it seemed to me a wise use of the funds available, except, as I added half jokingly, turning to Otto Schiff, it might be that too large a sum, £25,000, had been allocated for the refugee work within Great Britain. (As a matter of fact, the Schiff Committee is now spending at the rate of about £3,000 a month.) Lionel then withdrew the word "squandered," but insisted that no money could be raised next year for work outside England, and that only with great difficulty would they be able to raise the £25,000 needed for this purpose; that he had given a personal pledge to a number of people from whom he had secured large subscriptions that they would not be asked again; that many of these had given under covenant by which their payments are made over a period of seven years. These obviously would not give again. I then put up to him the same question I had raised earlier in the morning, as to Jewish responsibility. He passed it off by saying that I should discuss the matter further with his brother Anthony, who, after all, was more interested. With this he left Otto Schiff and Anthony de Rothschild and I together. No further progress was made.

Then to Woburn House.[2] . . . Chatted . . . with Otto Schiff. I told (him) that I thought his letter of the day before to Bentwich was the sort that one would be justified in writing only to someone guilty of murder or worse; that I was sure he was mistaken on all the counts, at least so far as those involved any desire on Bentwich's part to interfere with the governmental authorities in the Home Office; that I thought he ought to remember that Bentwich is one of the most unselfish, hardworking, and intelligent Jews in the world. Schiff admitted that perhaps he had been a little strong, but stood his ground. I said the whole matter would have to be talked out.

Out to tea with Bentwich. He was much depressed by the difficulties of the job, and especially by Schiff's sharp attack on him. I cannot understand why men flare out at one another in writing.

Out to dinner with the family to Sir Robert Waley-Cohen's. Present besides ourselves and the host were Mr. and Mrs. Bentwich, Rutenberg, young Sebag-Montefiore,[3] and a cousin of Sir Robert.

2. A building designed to house various Jewish organizations and committees, most importantly, the Board of Deputies of British Jews.

3. Geoffery Sebag-Montefiore, son of Edmund Sebag-Montefiore, former member of the London Stock Exchange who died in 1929.

Rutenberg and I immediately fell into conversation about the German situation, and continued it for nearly an hour after dinner. He is convinced that Bolshevism is coming in the Reich; that nothing can stop it; that the world faces the prospect of a unified Russian-German Communism. Whether one accepts his analysis or not, Rutenberg's interpretation of specific aspects of the recent weekend were most suggestive, and he knows his Germany well.

During dinner Lady Waley-Cohen and I talked mostly about the children and the advantages of being brought up without most of the luxuries.

After dinner when Rutenberg and I had finished our talk and the whole company was assembled, Bentwich and I asked Sir Robert what were the prospects for additional financing of refugee work from England next year. Sir Robert then launched into a long disquisition on his favorite thesis that the larger springs of Jewish charity in England had been dried up by the formation of the Allocation Committee through which the Palestinians [Zionists] exercised a dominant control, thus relegating to the rear the traditional leaders and discouraging them from active support. Though there is, of course, something in this, Sir Robert exaggerates it out of all its true proportions, as Bentwich and I told him. In any case, as we emphasized, he and his colleagues and others of the old leaders, could at any time reassume that leadership by heading a movement to provide ample funds. To this Sir Robert retorted that it was not easy to correct a mistake of the sort that had been made.

Later, he told me privately that no progress whatever had been made with the corporation idea on this side, there had not been a meeting for months, and no funds were in sight. He hoped within a few weeks or months to have made available for work in Palestine perhaps 200,000 pounds sterling. This would be through the Palestine Corporation and perhaps in cooperation with the Palestine Economic Corporation.

Home late.

I forgot in my account of last Sunday to tell of an intensely interesting conference I had with V. Idelson, a prominent Russian international lawyer here. He is intimately acquainted with Germany, had recently sat at dinner next to Brüning, where the latter had talked with apparent great indiscretion about the imminence of a reaction in Germany with the resulting overthrow of the present regime. Idelson had gained the impression that Dr. Brüning was in this country sounding out public and government opinion with a view to the impending changes.

Idelson's interpretation of the weekend's events was that it was the beginning of a palace revolution which would bring into effective power Thyssen,[4] Krupp von Bohlen,[5] et al.; that von Papen was closely associated with this group;

4. Fritz Thyssen, iron and coal industrialist who was an early financial supporter of the Nazi Party. Subsequently broke with Hitler. During World War II spent time in a concentration camp.

5. Gustav Krupp von Bohlen und Halbach, chairman of the heavy industrial conglomerate Friedrich Krupp A.G., 1909–1941.

that the destruction of the left radical leaders of the SA had discredited the whole movement, and left Hitler a prisoner of the right.[6]

I was so impressed by Idelson's erudition and knowledge that even if his detailed analysis should prove inaccurate, I hope to talk to him often.

Tuesday, July 3, 1934

Over to the Embassy to see Ambassador Bingham. He says that British opinion is outraged by the weekend happenings.

Lunched with Professor Bonn. Most of our talk naturally was about the events of the weekend. Bonn thinks that though the regime has fundamentally discredited itself, nothing much more may happen in the near future. On the other hand, the regime has no real chance of success, because it has no means of meeting the economic crisis. It has made the great mistake of trying at the same time to carry on an aggressive foreign policy, to repudiate its debts, and effect a revolution. Any one or two of these might have been accomplished perhaps, but not all three of them.

Over to Montefiore's house for a conference with Leonard Montefiore and his father. The latter is a fine type of Jewish philosophic mind. Unfortunately, it seemed that we had to spend most of our time talking about money and the probability of another Jewish appeal here next year. Their views were that something, but not much, could be done. I hope later to go back and have a talk again with the old man.

As I was leaving Montefiore's, Leonard gave me the Sunday issue of the *Frankfurter Zeitung*. It contained an extraordinarily lurid account of the weekend events; much of it seemed to me very dubious propaganda within Germany.

Sir Philip Cunliffe-Lister received me at his office. There were present one of his associates, Dugdale, and a second whose name I do not remember. After chatting first about the weekend events, Sir Philip expressing vehement disapproval of the Göring actions, we got around to Palestine. Sir Philip told me of the new batch of 500 certificates that were going to be made available for those specially trained as artisans, 200 of these for Germany, and a large part of the remainder for refugees outside.

In this general connection he elaborated a thesis that it would be possible to grant a larger number of certificates if one could be sure that precisely the type of people who are needed would be included by the [Jewish] Agency in the group to whom certificates are allotted. He said he had the impression that Agency politics sometimes had more to do with the allocation of the certificates than the economic requirements within Palestine or the special aptitudes of the immigrants. Therefore, he thought that there might be a system by which permission would be granted for X certificates in general, plus an additional portion Y if these latter were to be filled by people required for specific enterprises such

6. This interpretation was completely inaccurate.

as might be launched by the Palestine Corporation or the Palestine Economic Corporation or other responsible private interests.

We spoke about Trans-Jordania, about the emir's[7] present visit in London, where, according to Sir Philip, he is devoting himself wholly to meeting old friends and to pleasure, that he is receiving no suggestions whatsoever as to Jewish settlement. At this point one of Sir Philip's associates who apparently has the emir more or less in charge said, "If anyone were approaching the emir on business, I should be sure to know it." Sir Philip then repeated the statement he had made to me earlier that Jewish developments beyond the Jordan must wait upon the Jewish success in convincing the Arabs that cooperation is not only possible, but mutually advantageous.

As I was preparing to leave, there was some talk about my proposed visit to Palestine, which Sir Philip welcomed. Then we laughingly referred to the danger of an American remaining too long in England. I pointed out that it is almost impossible for an American to resist the insidious charm of the Britishers and cited the examples of the effect on recent American ambassadors. Sir Philip said that he hoped I would remain long enough to succumb also.

In my resumé of my talk with the Montefiores above, I forgot to mention the very important fact that Leonard confirmed the report I had heard earlier that ICA was contemplating the expenditure of an additional £30,000 on the international work for the refugees. This, he thought, would take up part of the slack left by the failure of the British to have another drive.

With the family to the theater as guests of Neville and Mrs. Laski. The play, *Libel,* was interesting. Laski called my attention to some recent editorials praising the position of Jews in this country. He attacked the position of Sir Robert Waley-Cohen and what he termed the latter's "excuses for inaction and for penuriousness." He, like nearly everyone else here, feels that the recent Nazi coup has disclosed the terrorism which is the basis of the regime, and has therefore fundamentally and irreparably weakened it. He would like sometime to come to the States on a speaking tour before Jewish groups.

....

Wednesday, July 4, 1934

Instead of firecrackers and a holiday, I began the morning by attending the opening of the meeting of the experts' committee organized by Kotschnig to attempt to formulate a comprehensive program for all the intellectual refugees. Dr. Cohn was elected chairman. Present were representatives from nearly all the interested countries, and from all the more important groups. The meetings are to continue for two days.

....

7. Abdullah ibn Hussein, ruler (emir) of Trans-Jordan, appointed by the British when they were given the territory as a mandate in 1921.

An hour's conference with Cecil at his house in the afternoon. I covered with him a very long agenda. He first went over the draft of our letter to Geheimrat Barandon in reference to pensions, social insurance and tangible property.[8] . . . He shares my view that there is now a chance that our negotiations with Germany, which heretofore have been more or less shadow-boxing, may possibly become more or less realistic. I then reported to him the financial progress in Great Britain and the United States. He was anxious to know how soon comprehensive schemes of settlement would be ready. I explained to him that most of the experts in these matters were very skeptical of such schemes, but we were pressing them very vigorously, and we hoped that out of the Immigration Committee meeting the middle of the month might come a group of projects which would expedite fundraising in the United States and possibly here in England.

We talked about the meeting on the next day of the representatives of the Christian communities. Cecil, in looking over the list of acceptances, commented, "They are all excellent persons, but hardly a sou among them." I explained that it was not expected that they themselves would give money, but that they would seek to induce the English and the free churches to set aside a day for a nation-wide appeal. Lord Cecil said he would be glad to serve on the special allocation committee which I had mentioned in my talks to the Rockefellers and in my personal appeal letters at home.[9]

. . . .

We then discussed the situation in general. I confessed to him my concern about the future, particularly because of the uncertainly as to available funds for settlement purposes, and also because of the doubts of the technicians about the programs which had been so far proposed. In any event it seemed to me, however, that within the next two months we should know whether or not the work could profitably be carried forward beyond the end of this year, or whether we should have to plan to wind up the High Commission, confessing frankly that we could not complete the job. He agreed with this analysis.

During the course of the talk he told me of a chat the day before with the German ambassador, who sought to show that the men who had been shot, including von Schleicher, were very dangerous and that they could not have been dealt with in any other way.

. . . .

Thursday, July 5, 1934

Over to the Colonial Office at the office of Mr. Vernon, where Bentwich and I had a conference with Vernon, two other members of the Colonial Office,

8. One of the High Commissioner's jobs was to see if he could convince the German government to allow refugees to take out some of these assets.

9. The joint drive by various Jewish organizations required an allocation committee to determine the distribution of funds raised. See McDonald's entry of March 23, 1934.

and Jardine, vice-governor of Tanganyika. The latter convinced Bentwich and me that, except for a few doctors and dentists, there are no opportunities whatsoever for refugee settlers. The territorial administration is very much opposed to developing poor whites, and there are no opportunities for settlers to become anything else in view of the competition of the natives and more particularly the Indians, on the land and in the trades. He promised, however, that he would offer facilities for a few doctors and dentists on an experimental basis. We are passing this data on to Anglo-HICEM and HICEM. But regretfully, we seem forced to rule the East African territories out of consideration, that is, not only Tanganyika, but Kenya, East Africa, and probably the Portuguese territories in that neighborhood. But at any rate, it is something to know where you stand.

Attended the experts' committee dealing with intellectuals. Under Dr. Cohn's chairmanship and on the basis of Dr. Kotschnig's preparation, real progress seemed to be being made.

Lunch with Cohn and Kotschnig; the latter was terribly upset by the news of the shooting of one of his best German friends in Munich yesterday. This leader of the student work there was taken out from his home under arrest and was found the next day with five bullet wounds in his body. According to Kotschnig's informant, who had just today come from Munich, the terror there has been widespread.

Conference with Mr. te Water, the South African high commissioner. We first exchanged views about the German situation. He feels that Hitler has maintained his strength and will continue to direct the nationalist movement.

As to membership on the High Commission, it is quite impossible for South Africa to accept. Moreover, there is a growing problem of anti-Semitism in South Africa, where already the Jews number 4.28 percent of the total white population. That is a larger percentage than in any of the countries, save perhaps Poland and Hungary.

I then inquired about South West Africa. His reply was absolutely categorical that there was no chance whatsoever for such a scheme as that which Simon in his recent memorandum envisaged. It is unthinkable that the Union government would consent to any large-scale Jewish colonization in that area, much less the establishment of an autonomous or even semi-autonomous Jewish community such as Simon envisaged. If the latter had only bothered to make this inquiry first, he would have been saved the trouble of making his study.

The meeting to consider ways and means of finding additional non-Jewish money for the refugees was held at the Society of the Antiquaries under the auspices of Lord Cecil.

. . . .

The subject was fairly well examined, but again I was discouragingly struck by the tendency of several of the Christian spokesmen, including the chairman himself, to limit the appeal to the non-Jewish refugees solely. Indeed, some of them went further and would have assumed responsibility [only] for the churchmen in good standing. Nonetheless, helpful suggestions were made, which can be followed up advantageously. Among these was one which may lead to my broadcasting over the BBC. Cecil again emphasized the necessity for definite programs and specific statements of needs and resources. I promised him these within a few weeks.

Tea with Miss Ginsberg. Two basic difficulties, however, remained (in addition to fundraising) in connection with Miss Ginsberg's work: first, there is the question as to the extent to which maintenance grants should continue to be extended to persons in the professional group unless it is reasonably certain that they are going to be able to find permanent places in their professions; second, there is the technical difficulty that grows out of the conflicting interpretations of HICEM and of Miss Ginsberg as to which organization should be responsible for submitting candidates for places. Kotschnig hoped that this conflict could be compromised, if not definitely settled. This would be easier were it not for the personalities involved. But this could be said of almost everything else in this work.

Dinner with Demuth of the Notgemeinschaft [deutscher Wissenschaftler im Ausland].[10] Much of our talk was about the meaning of the last weekend's events. He is confident that the [Nazi] regime has been fundamentally weakened, but that only a beginning has yet been made. He doubts that there was any carefully worked-out plot. He had himself been shown lists of shadow cabinets and even pages of names of new functionaries, but all of this seemed to him so extraordinarily amateurish as to be doomed to failure. He had nothing to do with it. Von Papen he considers a man of second-rate ability, always inclined to intrigue, but never really understanding the forces moving about him. The Reichswehr is probably divided in its attitude towards Hitler, but is unquestionably much stronger than before recent events. There is no real confidence now as between Hitler and Göring and Goebbels; there will be further internal developments among these leaders. Meantime, the economic condition of the Reich must become worse and worse unless it manages to secure a foreign loan or raw materials. The supplies of cotton copper, wool, etc. are very low. In this connection the recent financial settlement between the Reichsbank and the British Treasury is important, since there is at least the slight possibility that it might be used as the basis for a British loan. This would be a tragedy; it would mean that the Reich was again strengthened to the point where it might consider ultimately new military adventures. Without these funds the new revolution which has begun would gradually work itself out to a logical conclusion, leaving in all likelihood the new control in Germany in the hands of persons much more peaceful than those now in charge.

Demuth asked about the present status of the passport question; he seemed pleased that we could report substantial progress. He was enthusiastic too about Kotschnig's work.

10. Roughly, Association for Emergency Aid for German Scholars (Abroad).

As we walked in the park after dinner, he talked of Jäckh, expressed doubt as to whether the latter did not still have some vague relations with the present regime. As Demuth put it, Jäckh is never happy unless he feels that he is in the ante-chamber. Certainly I should not trust Jäckh's judgment; he has been consistently wrong for several years in his analysis of German conditions.

Friday, July 6, 1934

Conference at Otto Schiff's office, Bentwich also present. Fortunately, I was a little late in arriving, so that Schiff and Bentwich had had a quarter of an hour alone. As a result, they appeared to have composed all of their personal differences and were in excellent humor; the whole trouble had arisen out of a misunderstanding.

. . . .

Lunch with Sir Max Bonn and Bentwich. After we had chatted about the German situation, I asked Sir Max what he thought about the prospect for additional funds this year and the next year in England. This led him into an elaborate statement which, with interruptions, lasted for more than an hour. He did not, he said, follow up the Van den Porten report, because to have done so would have put into Palestine money which otherwise will be available for more direct work on behalf of the refugees. Moreover, Palestine will care for itself; there are already large sums of money in Palestine which can be made available for development there as soon as some financial leader on the spot sets up an organization commanding the confidence of those with funds. . . . Moreover, large funds are constantly being made available from outside for purely Palestinian purposes. These will continue to be made available, because the Palestinians see only Palestine. Then too, Sir Robert Waley-Cohen will probably manage to get the Sieff crowd to make substantial subscriptions to the stock of the Palestine Corporation. "Of course, within six months they will have a deadly quarrel, but they may be able to work together."

Sir Max emphasized the view that it had been disadvantageous to have the appeals in this country made in an omnibus manner. This had been necessary, but had resulted in much criticism because each group felt that its particular interest had been slighted. This, in turn, had tended to lessen the subscriptions.

Despite the past, however, he felt that substantial new funds could be found from the Jewish community here if two conditions could be met: one, that a fairly definite end of the problem could be envisaged; second, if equally definite schemes to achieve that end could be presented. These, however, would have to be of a business nature, 3 or 3½ percent debentures, so that the subscriber might feel that though he would not himself get his money back, his grandson might have something; and anyway he would not have to pay a portion to the Treasury.

On the whole, Bentwich and I get the impression that Sir Max would be willing [to] support actively a financial effort if a program satisfactory to him could be worked out. Moreover, though he is in no sense a sentimentalist, he nonetheless has a deep feeling of responsibility and is willing to do his utmost to meet it.

Over to Woburn House to see Sir Osmond [d'Avigdor-Goldsmid]. We again went over the figures of allocations by the British Central Fund and the needs on the continent. I was impressed anew that Sir Osmond is doing his utmost to help in other countries. Of course, even he shares the view of most of his colleagues that they should do the least they decently can in France. The attitude of the French leaders has alienated practically the whole community here. It was left that I would talk again with Sir Osmond after my conferences with Kahn and Oungre in Paris.

....

Sunday, July 8, 1934

[Boat and train to Paris.]

On the boat met Professor Moritz Bonn. As was natural, we discussed again the German developments. He is convinced that the Schleicher murder was the result of a private feud with Göring; that it had no real political significance. Meantime, the regime is substantially weakened and faces a serious economic prospect, especially if no foreign loans are forthcoming. Bonn recognized that there were two general possibilities: first, that envisaged by Idelson, the "palace revolution" with the control left in the hands of the large industrialists and the Junkers through the Reichswehr (army); and the other, which Bonn thinks more likely, a substantial enough swing to the left to result in great unrest and possibly civil war. Meantime, as Demuth pointed out to me some days ago, Bonn agreed that what the liberals and democrats should do in Germany is to wait until both extremes have shown their ineptitude. He recognized, however, that such a waiting policy required great restraint.

Arrived at the Continental [Hotel] just before midnight.

Paris, Monday, July 9, 1934

Began my long conference with Herbert May a little after eight o'clock and continued until lunch time.

I should remind the French when they become critical of what they call the High Commissioner's interference when he approaches the French government, that they themselves have been most insistent that the H. C. should deal with the governments "as an equal."

....

May and I started out for a little walk before lunch and ran into Lewis[11] of the United Mine Workers. We discussed with him the best method of securing [American] trade union interest in the trade union refugees, but he had no sug-

11. John L. Lewis, head of United Mine Workers, powerful American labor leader, who in 1935 formed the Congress of Industrial Organizations.

gestions except that we approach the A. F. of L., and he felt it would be a mistake for him to be brought into the matter personally.

Chatted with Mr. and Mrs. Elsas. The brother of the former was at one time mayor of Berlin.[12] He reports Hitler as temporarily strengthened because of the feeling that Hitler was prepared to sacrifice even his friends for the nation's safety.

Lunch with Dr. Kahn. In our discussion of Louis Oungre Kahn said what I believe to be a very true thing, "You take him too seriously. I have dealt with him for twelve years and always in the end have had my way. There is no need to worry about his shiftings."

. . . .

Kahn insisted that there are still possibilities of land settlement in France; the material is available among the refugees, and Baron de Rothschild has given some indication that despite Helbronner's defiance, something may be done with the French government.

As to land settlement under primitive conditions, unless there is an elaborate organization for following up, failure is certain. Nansen, against Kahn's advice, insisted on such projects, and they all failed. Even ICA with a capital of $40,000,000 has settled only 4,000 families in forty years.

We talked about the forthcoming London meeting. He was not very optimistic, but was fully prepared to cooperate. The more and more I see of him, the better I like him.

After a brief siesta May and I continued our talk with Kahn at his office. This time we spent two hours going over the financial situation in each of the countries concerned.

(1) First, France. The liquidation committee has about concluded its work with the first 1,200 and will have approximately 100,000 francs left out of the 3,000,000. Now they are facing the problem of the next list of from 500 to 1,000 individuals presented by the Deutscher Kommission. These are persons who, having eaten up their savings, are now dependent. . . . The question is how funds are to be secured for the liquidation of these. Furthermore, there are perhaps 3,000 others who may become dependent. In addition there are 6,000 or 7,000 who have sufficient means. The hundred or so helpless double zeros must be taken care of by the French charitable institutions. For each of these the JDC and others offer a small lump sum to the institution. If it doesn't consider this sufficient, then it is apt to get nothing. The above figures do not include the non-Jewish refugees. As to the Nazi refugees, Kahn doubts whether there are as many as 1,200 all together.

12. Professor Fritz Elsas, deputy mayor of Berlin, 1931–1933. A Jew who was married to an "Aryan," Elsas was implicated in the July 20, 1944, plot to assassinate Hitler and overthrow the Nazi regime. Executed in January 1945.

(2) Belgium. In Brussels there are about 200 refugees, most of them fit to emigrate. In Antwerp, which is an eastern Jewish town,[13] the refugees are mostly eastern Jews. These are being taken care of in eastern fashion, that is, secretively.

(3) Holland. There are from 350 to 400 being cared for, at a cost of $5,000 a week. Toward this amount the JDC contributes $6,000 a month. The need, therefore, is for $10,000 or more a month additional. The cost of retraining is about $40,000 a year, not including board. This is provided one-fourth by the Belgium Committee, one-half JDC, and one-fourth the Dutch.

(4) Spain. In Madrid there are about 120 Jewish refugees, some 40 in need. In Barcelona between 200 and 300. There is room for an additional 200 or 300 if those there can be liquidated.

(5) Poland. Four to five thousand repatriates (people who had been living and working in Germany for years and were thrown out). The JDC has given nearly $150,000 for work in Poland. In general, the JDC refuses to consider the repatriated Poles as refugees. Incidentally, in this connection Kahn reminded me that in France it is absolutely impossible for a Polish refugee to receive a *carte de travail* [working permit], because if, according to the terms of the reciprocity treaty between the two countries, a Pole works for six months in France, he then has a legal claim on the French unemployment benefits.

(6) Czechoslovakia. 3,000 to 5,000 refugees. Kahn had recently sent 25,000 Kr. to Miss Masaryk. Beginning this fall JDC has pledged itself to match Czech money raised, up to 230,000 Kr. for re-training activities. Within the last few weeks JDC has advanced something for relief. This amount is later to be credited for re-training purposes.

(7) The Saar. Only a small group of refugees. The JDC and British Central Fund have each contributed 15,000 francs.

(8) Austria. Some hundreds of refugees, perhaps not more than 300. In various forms JDC has made available nearly $40,000, but little or none of this for refugee work directly. Kahn refuses to interpret the refugees there as refugees.

(9) Switzerland, Sweden, and Denmark he thought called for no special comment, and, I judge, JDC is not doing anything there.

Kahn recognized that in certain countries, as for example Holland, where, as he put it, "the local committee would be ashamed to ask the JDC for more," [some] might feel that they had a claim on the High Commission. It is this sort of situation which is most embarrassing.

Told Kahn I would try to arrange the meeting for Paris if possible, but he agreed to attend even if it was held in London.

Over to de Rothschild's with Herbert May. Others present besides our-

13. The Jews in Antwerp were mostly Polish Hasidic and ultra-Orthodox.

selves and Baron Robert were Helbronner, Jacques Lyon, and Lambert.[14] Much of the same ground was plowed over again and again as on previous occasions. Lambert amplified in beautiful and nearly endless French the thesis of the French government, which had again been outlined to him that afternoon, that France was not a country of colonization, etc. etc. etc. What was new, however, in his tirade this time, was his charge that Rosen, if not Kahn, knew perfectly well that their programs of land settlement would fail with the refugees, and that they intended to bring in Eastern European Jews, and this was even more intolerable than to settle colonies with the refugees. I denied that there could be any justice in such suggestions, but I don't think I convinced any one. Jacques Lyon tried not very successfully two or three times to stem the tide of Helbronner's righteous oratory. Indeed, Lyon succeeded to the extent of getting a half-hearted admission from Helbronner that separate small farms might be leased and used to settle some of the refugees.

We then talked about the situation in Brazil, and Baron Robert had the Brazilian ambassador called up and arranged for me to see the latter the next morning.

. . . .

Many other subjects were brought up, but the one that interested the French most was the need of their committee of savants [intellectuals]. They felt that there was no way to raise the $600,000 that had been raised last year, and that I should find it. They wanted to know what Kotschnig had been doing and were not satisfied with my report. In the midst of this discussion I took occasion to tell them that at the very time I was being torn limb from limb by the Paris meeting, I was delivering four addresses in a single day on behalf of the joint appeal. I specifically referred to Oungre as among the critics, and said that while he spoke of the High Commissioner "sitting on the money of the corporation," I had heard the same thing said about Oungre and ICA in eight or ten countries.

Helbronner told me with much satisfaction that Bérenger had designated him to represent France on the Governing Body until he, Bérenger, returned from his vacation in September.

As we were leaving, Baron Robert asked if I would care to come and dine with him the next night. I could only say yes.

Then May and I walked home alone and a little later had a quiet dinner in a garden of the Elysée.

Tuesday, July 10, 1934

Meeting with the Quakers and the Entr'aide, Harvey, Mme. Jean Braun, and an American Quaker recently arrived. They told a convincing tale of how

14. Raul R. Lambert, editor of the *Universe Israélite,* a leader in the Franco-Jewish establishment, secretary general of the French National Committee to Aid German Refugees, worked with ICA under Louis Oungre.

they could for very little money per head place from 100 to 150 people, and that without creating any of the difficulties which were blocking the Kahn-Rosen more ambitious plan. I told them of the efforts to get funds, and that they would certainly receive their portion of what was available.

Over with May to see the Brazilian ambassador. He was most cordial, assured us that the new exclusion law[15] would not affect persons who had already received their visas, and expressed the hope that adjustments through administrative measures could be made which would avoid serious restrictions on German immigration. He pledged himself to do everything he could towards this end.

....

Out to lunch with May and the two Oungres. There followed three hours of talk, back and forth and all around a number of subjects. As to Louis Oungre's statement at the Paris meeting, he pretended that he did not understand about the nature of the corporation and its inability to supply relief funds, and that he was merely trying to phrase what was in the minds of the heads of the different committees, that if there was money available, it should be used. I did not question his good faith, but simply said that such a proposal applied equally well to ICA, and added what I had heard about his reposing on ICA's funds.

Both the Oungres insisted that there is no substantial agricultural material among the Jews, either among the refugees or in Germany. As L. Oungre said, "Is it not disgraceful that ICA has not been able during this crisis to place a single Jew on its lands: Would we not have avoided this slur if we could have found the material?"

As to industrial schemes, time and again he tried to argue that one must know exactly what funds are available before he proposes schemes, but finally agreed to present various projects at the meeting in London. I think he will be helpful.

Speaking of ICA, he said that Sir Osmond [d'Avigdor-Goldsmid] would be made the new chairman; that there is no other person really available. This fits in exactly with what Helbronner was to tell me later.

One of the projects which L. Oungre leaned towards and which sounds promising is the organization of a substantial loan bank. This should be studied further.

As we were finishing, Mowrer and Taylor of the *Chicago Tribune* and Mrs. Taylor came along. I introduced them to the Oungres. Louis Oungre asked Mowrer how he spelled his name, and when he was told he bowed with the most flattering humility and said, "You are a prophet; you have the power of divination; I have read your book once, twice, three times; I have it on my desk constantly." Mowrer blushed.

....

15. The restrictive immigration law of May 1934. See McDonald's diary entry of March 14, 1935 (chap. 23), where the Brazilian minister of labor explained this law in considerable detail.

Alone over to de Rothschild's for dinner. I felt a little like an innocent lamb going into the lion's den. Others besides the host and myself were the indispensable Helbronner and Lambert. We had a delightful dinner out of doors, but there was no opportunity for small talk. At once I had to outline the progress of the corporation and of the joint drive. Then followed talk of this and that, while the Rothschild dog devoured the lower part of one of the legs of my trousers. When I displayed my injury to the Baron, he was at first incredulous, then apologetic, but all he did was to punish the dog. Then Helbronner launched into an inquiry about the need for the intellectuals. I stated the situation, then had the brilliant idea that Baron de Rothschild be set on some of the rich visiting Americans. He seized the suggestion. I wrote a letter at once to Arthur Sachs,[16] and he wrote another, and I promised to send the addresses of Blum and perhaps others. I also promised Cohn's address and schedule in Paris, so that they might talk to him about the intellectuals. So the evening ended pleasantly. But I mustn't forget to recall that Rothschild suggested that if only I would make Louis Oungre my agent and use the ICA with its vast knowledge and experience, wonders could be accomplished. He added that Bérenger was so impressed by Oungre, as were other French officials, that Oungre could have what he wanted, whatsoever that might be.

Home alone and to bed.

London, Wednesday, July 11, 1934

8:20 A.M. train for London. Quiet crossing. Arrived in London only a few minutes late, and was at the hotel by four.

Conference with Bentwich, and then over to Sir Robert Waley-Cohen's meeting at Woburn House. Others present besides Sir Robert, Bentwich, and myself, were Sir Osmond d'Avigdor-Goldsmid and Sacher. Out of the talk emerged two specific suggestions: one, the employment of Kauffmann[17] at once to begin the study of specific industrial projects; I said that I would undertake to do this either through the High Commission or the American corporation. Incidentally, it is significant that no one took exception to Sir Robert's rather slighting remark when he asked, "What does Oungre know about industry?" Second, the employment by the English group of another industrial engineer to put on paper specific projects for the distressed areas in England.

At the end, Bentwich raised the question of funds for the non-Jewish refugees. Sir Osmond and Sacher both indicated positive lack of interest, but Sir Robert and I emphasized the importance, if possible, of making the corporation efforts non-sectarian. Sacher said yes, but only if the non-Jews put in their money.

16. Arthur Sachs, member of the banking firm of Goldman, Sachs & Co., art collector, married his second wife, a Frenchwoman, in 1930. He had been on the Board of the FPA in 1928–1929.

17. Dr. Robert Kauffmann, German, formerly of Allgemeine Elekrizitäts-Gesellschaft, a member of the Liquidation Commission of the French National Committee.

As we walked away, Bentwich for the first time seemed encouraged about settlement projects.

Home and discouraged not to find my family, and so ate a bite alone.

Thursday, July 12, 1934

Conference with Malcolm MacDonald[18] [in] reference [to] his trip to the [British] Dominions. Surprised to learn he was contemplating only a visit to Australia and New Zealand. He said he would be glad to speak of the refugee problem to Dominion officials and suggested I write him a letter as a memorandum. He doubted, however, that there would be opportunity for many there, because his department was just completing a study in reference to emigration of British subjects. This would show complete failure to open those areas. He said I might tell Cecil in confidence of this result, but he did not wish any public reference to it until the formal publication.

. . . .

Long distance telephone call with Wurfbain, who reported a cable from Chamberlain to the effect that the [State] Department had authorized Dodd to use his discretion joining British Ambassador urging Reich to talk over personally point raised of property, pensions, and social insurance memorandum.

On July 9 Chamberlain had met with Moffat, who wrote:

"We agreed to send a telegram to Ambassador Dodd authorizing him to join with the British Ambassador in Berlin, who[,] it is understood[,] received similar instructions in supporting the proposal of James G. McDonald that he be enabled to negotiate with an authorized representative of the Reich on a series of problems . . . the limit of 50 Marks a month which may be transferred for living expenses, the refusal of the Germans to let refugees take out any of their capital, the claims of former functionaries to pensions and insurance which they have already paid up, et. cetera. We told Mr. Dodd that if the Germans replied that this was a purely domestic matter, he might counter by saying that these refugees were German citizens who in one way or another were becoming public charges in foreign countries, which gave us the right to intercede."[19]

. . . .

18. Malcolm John MacDonald, British colonial secretary, secretary for the dominions, 1935–1939.

19. Moffat Journal, vol. 34, Moffat Papers, July 9, 1934, call number MS Am 1407, Houghton Library, Harvard University. By permission of the Houghton Library, Harvard University. In answer to McDonald's subsequent request, Dodd wrote that he had seen Phipps and they had decided that they should delay any approach, and an informal talk with von Bülow convinced him "that for the present at least nothing is to be done." Letter from Dodd to JGM sent via air mail to London and then to the U.S. Embassy in Paris. Dated July 23, 1 P.M. Copies to Bentwich, HLM, Chamberlain, and AW. Copy in McDonald Papers, USHMM. Nothing was ever done.

Friday, July 13, 1934

Lunch with Otto Nathan at the Piccadilly Grill. He told me that he had just come back from three or four weeks of conferences with refugees and people in and out of Germany whom he had met in Switzerland, the Saar, and Paris. His views of the German situation were interesting, but need not be recounted here, particularly since they are not supported by most of the other persons with whom I have talked. He seems to me to exaggerate the adverse effect upon Hitler's position of the recent events.

Nathan did interest me in his account of the prevailing criticisms of the High Commission. He suggested the desirability of my spending some days in London and Paris thrashing out these matters with the refugee representatives. I told him that I would be glad to do so. He also outlined a program which he had been evolving since his talks with the refugees. This is a plan to raise by popular subscription funds to be used for loan purposes. He is confident that if such an issue were floated by responsible bankers in at least four or five important centers, millions could be secured. This could then be lent to the refugees for constructive purposes. One form of guarantee he envisioned as supplied by contributions from the refugees in work of approximately 2 percent of their income, this to be used to help service the bonds.

....

Sunday, July 15, 1934

Took Bobby to join the Ernest Schiff children in the Park.

Conference before lunch with Otto Schiff. We talked about Nathan's loan plan, which he was inclined to favor. We also made out a tentative schedule of expenses for the project of a study of economic conditions in Czechoslovakia, Yugoslavia, Turkey, Albania, Spain, and Portugal, to be made by Kauffmann and perhaps also by Major Macindoe. This suggestion had been agreed upon a day or two earlier at a conference between Sir Osmond and Sir Robert Waley-Cohen, at which the latter said they would undertake to see what could be done by a study of the distressed areas of England, this latter to be financed from English sources, the former by the American corporation. Following that suggestion I had written to Felix Warburg to ask if the American group would put up a minimum of $10,000.

....

Lunch with the family as Schiff's guests at Claridge's. Then all out to Sir Robert Waley-Cohen's for tea, tennis, and swimming, after we had picked up Bobby and Rachel Schiff.

In addition to playing croquet with Bobby and Rachel, I talked with Japhet, a cousin or nephew of the London Japhet,[20] now a banker in Palestine; formerly he was in Frankfurt. He is very optimistic about Palestine but doubts if there is

20. Jacob Japhet, German banker who established S. Japhet & Company in Jerusalem in 1933.

available much capital in the country itself for major developments. He said of course there are millions of pounds unemployed, but most of these have to be kept too liquid to serve for long-time investment purposes.

Pleasant visit with the Waley-Cohens and with several of their thirty or forty guests, and home about seven. Bobby and Rachel had become close friends.

Monday, July 16, 1934

Lunch for the Dr. Adlers and the Kuhns[21] and Kuhn's mother at the Royal Palace. It was a pleasant visit, and there were some amusing talk about Mrs. Felix Warburg's carrying on the Schiff tradition of superiority to the Rothschilds. The Schiffs had predated the Rothschilds in the ancestral house in Frankfurt.

. . . .

Tuesday, July 17, 1934

To the tailor to have repaired the ravages of Baron Robert's dog.

Down with Nathan to Schiff's office. . . . Nathan explained his scheme. Schiff thought the purposes to which the fund would be put were good, but doubted that securities could be issued on a business basis unless, as I suggested as a possibility, the original members of the American corporation were prepared to make their securities junior to those to be issued to the public. Short of that, he doubted if there could be a public issue. He had no faith at all in Nathan's idea of servicing the bonds by payments from the refugees in work.

Lunch with Kauffmann and Adams at the Royal Palace. Kauffmann, at my suggestion, took considerable time in giving us his impressions of the German situation in the light of the events of June 30. He doubted that Hitler was less popular; perhaps even the contrary. Of course, fundamental weaknesses were disclosed, but it would be a mistake to assume that there had been within Germany any reaction against Hitler. There had been a swing to the right, but it was unlikely that the Reichswehr would intervene in the near future to effect a decisive solution. The army was not inclined to be political, and Schleicher's experience[22] intensified its non-political character. It would incline to remain aloof and maintain public order but not seek to act as a Praetorian guard. Meantime, economic conditions were bad and will undoubtedly become worse and worse. Out of these will grow popular discontent and disillusionment, but the result, instead of being a decisive one, is more apt to be prolonged economic and even armed conflict within the Reich. Kauffmann anticipates a long period of unsettlement and possibly something like chaos. He does not feel that under these circumstances one can anticipate the return of any considerable number of the refugees, for economic pressure will make such return difficult, indeed, may even

21. Fritz Kuhn, son of Abraham Kuhn, founder of Kuhn Loeb investment banking firm.

22. Schleicher had been active politically even before he became chancellor and a rival to Hitler; then, on June 30, 1934, he was among those murdered by SS squads.

increase the flow of immigrants, while a regime which is controlled by the reactionaries and big industrialists, the Junkers and the Reichswehr, all groups that have fathered anti-Semitism, cannot be expected to put the Jews back on a status comparable to that under the republic.

In the light of this analysis I was all the more surprised by what Otto Schiff had told me earlier about Mildred Wertheimer's suggestion that the time had come to help the Reich economically. Mildred Wertheimer is an incorrigible German.

....

Wurfbain arrived in the middle of the afternoon. With him, went to pick up Bobby and then to Mrs. Bentwich's cocktail party. Met a number of acquaintances there. Was particularly interested in my talk with Newman, Nathan's friend at the London School of Economics. I only regretted that I did not have an opportunity to talk with him longer, for I wished to get his reaction on Nathan's talk to me the day or two previous, when he had elaborated the thesis that all of our formal exchanges with the German government were useless or worse. Nathan contended that in proportion as we managed in inveigle the German authorities into a general discussion of principle about property, pensions, and social insurance, we would jeopardize the efforts of individual refugees to secure redress under these three heads. He did except social insurance, where perhaps we might do something. But in general, he strongly opposed pressing along the line we had begun.

I had asked Kauffmann about Nathan's view on this point. He did not go nearly so far.

Wednesday, July 18, 1934

Conference with Dr. Forell and his friend, Mr. Simpson. Forell is, according to his statement, the one non-Aryan Christian pastor out of Germany. He now holds a pulpit among the Jews in Vienna under a Swedish missionary board for the Jews. He denounced Sir Leon Levison as unreliable or worse. The latter's figures about the numbers of non-Aryan pastors in Germany were fantastic; there were not hundreds, only 35. But Dr. Forell stressed that the condition of the non-Aryan Christians in Germany was worse than that of the Jews, for they lacked comparable defensive organizations. He estimated these at nearly 200,000. I explained that I had no direct concern with conditions inside of Germany. He wished, he said, to keep in touch with me and also, I gather, to secure if possible some sort of sponsorship. I was favorably impressed by his evident honesty, and suggested that he and Simpson talk further with Bentwich. I also suggested that he might, if his missionary board would release him and if the Americans would welcome his coming, go to the States and make his appeal there directly. His English is rudimentary, but could in some weeks be made serviceable.

With Bentwich over to Japhet's office at 60 London Wall. I liked Japhet, a man of 78, a Jewish scholar and the head of the firm. I explained the Nathan idea and asked Japhet's impression as to its practicability from the financial point of view. He thought it possible only if, as I had discussed earlier with Schiff, the insiders were prepared to make their securities secondary to a public flotation. Moreover, in general, he doubted the possibility of securing funds on an investment basis and was inclined to hold that one would have to continue to raise money as before by one after another of special efforts.

We asked Japhet about the Turkish financing scheme. He said that the area in question was desirable and that there were large possibilities for Jews, provided they could be given security against unsettlement or being preyed upon by their neighbors or by officials. Such guarantee could, he felt, be supplied only if the Turkish government itself were prepared to guarantee any loan which was issued in connection with the Anatolia project. This guarantee he emphasized as a sine qua non. He read us a copy of his letter to Walford, which showed that he had not committed himself to anything. He spoke of Walford as "still a visionary, as he had been for 50 years, but an honest man."

Lunch with Bernhard Kahn at the Park Lane. We discussed the Nathan loan scheme. Kahn raised the usual difficulties—that it would be not really an investment scheme, because it would be impossible to organize cooperatives, and on any other basis the human material was not such as to offer prospects of repayment; and most basic of all, the French government must change its attitude, making settlement in France of more than half of the refugees possible.

It was at this point that I reminded Kahn that just because of his distinguished record over twenty years and the resulting high esteem in which he is held in the States, it is not enough for him to outline the difficulties on the basis of past experience; but it is imperative, if a job is to go forward, that he evolve something workable. He replied that the foundation[23] probably would cooperate, but that he thought it would be necessary to have French funds first, and that the ICA part of the foundation might wish to limit the latter's responsibilities and place upon the Americans the bulk of the financing.

As Kahn and I were leaving, we stopped for a moment to chat with the Adlers, who were lunching with Leonard Montefiore. Dr. Adler was much concerned about a particular physician whose distress had been called to his attention—a man who had been offered an unpaid position at one of the hospitals in New York and whose wife hoped to get a job sufficient to support the family until the doctor had found a remunerative post. But there was the question of transportation costs and of some sort of guarantee. I promised to send Dr. Adler the name and address of Dr. Sachs, the head of the emergency committee dealing with physicians in New York.

. . . .

23. Probably the Baron de Hirsch Foundation, which funded the ICA.

Tea at Lionel Cohen's. Chatted with Mr. Idelson, who said he had no occasion to change his estimate of the German situation given to me on the first day of July. He still thinks only a beginning has been made of what will be terrible developments in Germany.

Thursday, July 19, 1934

Meeting of the special committee on emigration at Woburn House. Those present were the two Oungres, Dr. Bernard Kahn, Gottschalk, Otto Schiff, and later Perlzweig for the [Jewish] Agency, O'Connor for the Catholics, Miss Pye of the Quakers, Schevenals, Norman Bentwich, André Wurfbain, and fortunately very late, Rawson.[24] Otto Nathan attended as a visitor, also Kauffmann, and Miss Thompson and Olive Sawyer were in and out. A full resumé of the meeting has been prepared by Wurfbain, so I will simply comment here on my general impressions.

The morning went slowly, and left us at lunch time discouraged. Then after a more discouraging lunch, we returned to what seemed at first an hour or more of futile discussion of figures, led by Gottschalk. But at the end something tangible did emerge. During the last hour or hour and a half, there were a number of constructive suggestions, and the meeting adjourned with the feeling of a job satisfactorily done.

....

Friday, July 20, 1934

....

Just after lunch a German refugee, Seidler, a Capt. Borchard, and Mrs. Omerod[25] came to talk about land settlement in Southern Rhodesia. It quickly became apparent that Seidler was a romanticist and Borchard a crack-brained violent imperialist who insisted that England rule the world. Mrs. Omerod, as she heard the latter talk, became more and more apologetic. She and I agreed after the others had left that there was nothing that could possibly come of these scheme.

Conference with Bentwich at Sir Wyndham Deedes's office at the National Council of Social Service. He is an extraordinarily charming man, and obviously deeply interested in the Christian responsibility for the refugee problem. He asked searching questions as to the needs, as to whom we had appealed to, and then suggested that he would discuss the matter further with [the Anglican bishop] Chichester and with [the archbishops of] York and with Canterbury and perhaps arrange for me to see the latter. I told him that I would be glad to

24. E. L. Rawson. A couple of months earlier he had reported at a meeting of the German Jewish Emigration Council in London on the "dissatisfaction at the lack of initiative and poor efforts of the High Commissioner." Haim Genizi, *American Apathy: The Plight of Christian Refugees from Nazism* (Ramat Gan: Bar-Ilan University Press, 1983), 46.

25. Mary Omerod of the Society of Friends, the liaison in London with Marie Ginsberg's committee.

make a special trip any time to see His Grace. It was left that he was to receive a new, brief memorandum from Bentwich, which he could show to the churchmen.

Press conference at the Woburn House. There was only a small group, some seven or eight, but representing some of the larger papers and agencies. Finished just in time for the meeting with Sir Robert Waley-Cohen's group.

Beside Sir Robert there was present only Sir Osmond, Otto Schiff, and Nathan, Bentwich, Wurfbain, and myself. I reported my negotiations with Kauffmann (Turkish study). Sir Robert reported that the man he hoped to do the study in England was not available, and that he would have to look else where. I then summarized the conclusions of the previous day's meeting. This was followed by a discussion of Nathan's plan. Sir Robert seized on this and seemed to think that one could be satisfied by setting up a small loan kassa[26] in France, and then waiting five or six months to see how it worked, before doing the next thing. Bentwich became vividly impatient at this development, and I supported his contention that one must not be satisfied with such a piecemeal effort, but must try to attack the problem as a whole. There was then some discussion as to the possibility of finding the funds for such a task. I pleaded with Sir Robert and Sir Osmond that it was their job to help in finding the way. But beyond Sir Osmond's promise to write to Oungre about the foundation's cooperation in the loan kassa, nothing tangible issued.

Dinner with Dr. Nathan and three of his friends, Dr. Ernst Kahn, Dr. Stern, and Kurt Battsek. Stern is economic adviser to Sir Henry Strakosh;[27] Battsek was formerly Berlin representative of German Chambers of Commerce. All the men agreed that irrespective of any likely developments within the Reich, there would continue to be a steady emigration from Germany, especially of the younger people. There was no agreement, however, as to what the numbers would be. Kahn estimated these at fewer than did his colleagues on the theory that the total Jewish population in Germany is now not much larger than 450,000, and that the number of young people leaving school each year is not more than 5,000. Meantime, the birthrate continues to diminish and the number of marriages to decrease.

Saturday, July 21, 1934

Trip to Paris with the family, enlivened by Bobby's loss of her cap in the channel. The McDonalds and Olive Sawyer had dinner at Le Doyen and views of Paris at its best in the evening.

26. More than seven hundred cooperative loan banks were established in Eastern Europe between 1924 and 1931, subsidized by JDC and ICA. They made low-interest and no-interest loans to Jewish small businessmen and tradesmen. Often local wealthy Jews contributed to the *kassas*, which benefited over one million people in Poland alone between the wars.

27. Sir Henry Strakosh, Austrian-born banker, gold and diamond merchant in South Africa.

Paris, Sunday, July 22, 1934

Dinner with Nathan and Breitscheid in my room. Was amazed by Breitscheid's pessimism about Germany and Germany's future. He seemed to feel that there was no possibility of a return of the Social Democrats to power; that on the contrary, conditions would probably become worse and worse until something like chaos prevailed. He spoke in tones of unmeasured contempt of the German people, who were willing to follow so abjectly the Hitler leadership and who, despite the events of June 30, showed no inclination to turn away from Hitler. In this connection he referred scathingly to Schacht, von Neurath, et al.

Breitscheid was anxious that the High Commission should set up a register of the refugees in the chief centers. He said this would be of great use in distinguishing the real refugees from those who are in effect profiteering on the refugees. It would be valuable to the French government in simplifying the task of supplying essential papers. He thought it would not involve creating a large bureau. I made no commitment.

During the course of the evening there was an opportunity to explain fully what the High Commission had undertaken to do, and its successes and failures. This seemed to give Dr. Breitscheid a clearer impression and to leave him in a much more sympathetic mood. But he left seemingly as dejected as he had been when he arrived.

Monday, July 23, 1934

Conference with Hugo Simon,[28] chairman of the Deutsche Kommission. The following is Otto Nathan's summary of the conference[29] (I personally was very favorably impressed with Simon, who is obviously a man of wide business experience and thoroughly reliable.):

"Is very glad to have the opportunity of making Mr. McDonald's acquaintance and of discussing refugees' problems with him. Hopes that cooperation will be possible in future.

Very pessimistic view on political situation in Germany. Changes may occur every day. Disintegration of Germany very likely. No great hope that many refugees can and wish to return.

The "Deutsche Kommission" has not made it its task to secure *cartes de travail,* etc. It will help to settle people for constructive work, but it has almost no money at its disposal, and the French are not willing to raise money. Kommission has given in some cases money on a loan basis to refugees. He thinks very highly of developing a scheme of loans. He has not too much faith that refugees will help each other, but he thinks that it is worthwhile to try.

Communication and talks with political leaders essential. He himself, has discussed problem with Herr Marin (from the right) and will continue to do so.

28. Hugo Simon, former colleague of Foreign Minister Walter Rathenau and a German diplomat, dismissed in September 1933.

29. Nathan's summary is included in McDonald's diary.

He is very bitter in his remarks on French Jews, but adds nothing new to what has been said before."

Conference with Bernhard Kahn, who outlined the conditions under which he thought the loan program could be worked out, provided the foundation part of the partnership would be brought into line. The difficulty there would be the English members and Louis Oungre, who would be inclined to say that the Americans should put up the money and the foundation supply the experience. Kahn told me again of the lack of human material among the refugees for cooperatives, the inevitability of larger losses, and the necessity of fuller French cooperation if there was to be any success.

It was at this point that I again loquated on the point that the Americans and I expected more from him than summaries of the difficulties, and what could not be done. He took it in good part. He then replied that, of course, the immigration figures and program worked out in London were nothing more or less than forced emigration, that if they could not be carried out, which they could not be, they would relieve Belgium, Holland, and the other countries of their Jewish refugees, but that the Jewish organizations would simply have transferred the problem from Europe to the immigration countries. Therefore, it was no solution. Besides the money could not possibly be found anywhere in the world—except if all the Jewish organizations decided to make a final effort and exhausted their resources it might be done, but he would never recommend it. The basis of the problem lies in France, and continued efforts must be made to bring the French to face the realities. He thought this could be done perhaps by approaching high officials directly. (Incidentally, Louis Oungre the next day said to me that this would be the one method of ensuring defeat.)

Kahn said that if you want a productive scheme, it can be worked out for Brazil, or the Argentine; but you must first know that you have the money to swing it. If one could go to the governments of either of those countries with several millions of dollars available and plans for the development of certain industries, he could get then not paltry concessions, such as are being asked for now, but a large-scale opening. Moreover, if it were known that such undertakings were on foot, the Jewish material to carry them out would come forward. But not from among the refugees. Only a small portion of the refugees could be fitted in, even into such a scheme.

I explained to Kahn that unless it were possible to formulate schemes which gave promise of success by making available sufficient funds, I was prepared to recommend the liquidation of the High Commission; that it was evident that many of my efforts had not been directly concerned with the refugees but rather with somewhat extraneous Jewish matters; that from the first I had been weakened by the fact that there were no groups, nor for that matter individuals, to which I could turn who were wholly interested in the refugees. I had had to choose, therefore, at the very beginning, between attempting to set up something new or using the existing institutions. Even now Olive Sawyer would from time to time remind me that my job was not to settle Jewish problems but to care for the refugees. After eight or nine months' experience I am still of the opinion that my decision to use the Jewish organizations was wise, not because this has functioned 100 percent, but because otherwise it would probably have been impossible to build any adequate machinery at all. In short, however, unless I could make definite programs for the refugees, I would not feel justified in continuing, no matter how much it might seem to some of my friends that the High Commission could serve the Jewish cause.

Kahn replied that he thought that the High Commission would exist for many years; that he hoped I would remain in Europe indefinitely; that if and where there was a real change of regime in Germany, the High Commission would be invaluable as a negotiating instrument, and without it he did not see how such negotiations could be carried on.

Out to supper with the family and to the Comedie Français with Janet and Henrietta to see the *Voyage de M. Perrichon*. The youngsters were hugely delighted with it. Afterwards, they watched a rather unattractive part of the world go by as we had ices at the Café de la Paix.

Tuesday, July 24, 1934

Long and satisfactory conference with Georg Bernhard. It seemed to me that Bernhard was in a much more reasonable frame of mind than when we had met before; certainly he was much less belligerent. The following is Otto Nathan's summary of that discussion:

"Political development in Germany likely to lead through a period of catastrophes and chaos during which new anti-Jewish persecution to be feared. New emigration very likely among people who were, so far, politically on the right. Such an emigration may make things in France still more difficult because these people are the real 'boches.' Repatriation of *older* Jewish refugees not unlikely once political regime has entirely changed. Bulk of refugees will stay abroad. Young intellectual Jews will leave Germany for many years to come.

Of 30,000 (maximum) refugees in France, about one-third not real refugees. It would not have been difficult to get those people who are really refugees to work in France if French authorities and particularly the French Jewish community had understood [the] problem better and had had more good will. It would have been very wise for France, which lacks people, to add these refugees who are partly very well trained, well educated, and valuable persons to her population. Attitude of French Jews will probably not change before a scandal has occurred. They have no understanding of the problem and do not realize that they are creating, in the long run, just what they want to avoid—anti-Semitism. France, which has a long liberal tradition in dealing with refugees, cannot afford to let these people starve or to expel them actually from the country.

Bernhard holds that French Jews can be convinced only by non-Jews. He hopes that the authority and reputation of Mr. McDonald may help much in dealing with them. Furthermore, he would find it advisable to discuss the problem with a few outstanding political leaders, particularly with Herriot, Bérenger, and Marin.[30] He also mentions Mr. Mandel,[31] previously secretary to M. Clemenceau. Mr. Mandel adheres politically to the right and is himself Jewish."

As we were finishing our discussion, we were jointed by Fritz Wolff, secretary of the Deutsche Kommission. He urged the imperative necessity of attending to the immediate needs of the refugees in Paris. I suggested that some money might be secured by following up on Americans visiting in Paris. Bernhard thought well of this. Below is Nathan's summary of the conference:

"More necessary than anything else is to get '*cartes de séjour*' and '*cartes de travail.*' The Comité National has so little money at its disposal that every day many refugees have to be sent away without any relief at all. Unless we succeed in getting some more money for these purposes, he does not know what will happen. Danger exists that some refugees may become criminals. Mr. Wolff is very reluctant to discuss plans for *constructive* help, since his attention seems entirely absorbed by the *urgent* need for the daily life of the refugees. No plan for future help could, in his opinion, do much to relieve the *actual* terrible situation."

Geheimrat von Gerlach,[32] well-known German pacifist, came to see me. We talked mostly, however, about the need of his wife to secure a *carte d'identité et de voyage* for a year, instead of the one for a six-months' period which she now has. This seemed to me relatively unimportant, and I was disappointed that he had so little to say that was new.

Lunch with Louis Oungre and Ruth at the Ritz. Oungre began by outlining at length in his most crisp and authoritative style the general problems of loan kassa. Later, in a memorandum he sent with a note dated July 29, he put in writing the six reasons why it is not possible to develop loan kassas among the refugees of the sort which have been so successfully developed in the east.

After summarizing all of the difficulties, he then suggested that ways might be found through which the risk of losing 90 percent of the capital could be materially reduced. The chief of these would be to interest responsible local persons to take stock in the loan kassas. In this and in other ways he seemed to feel that a beginning could be made through the joint efforts of the foundation and the corporation.

We then talked about the possibility of changing the attitude of the French government towards the refugees remaining in France. I said to him that he, of course, must recognize that a large proportion of the refugees must be taken care of where they are. He assented. I continued, "You have established for yourself a unique position of confidence with the French authorities, Bérenger et al. You

30. Louis Marin, leader of the Republican Federation, the leading conservative party in France.

31. Georges Mandel (born Louis George Rothschild), in 1934 minister of posts. Arrested by the Laval government in 1940 and sent to Buchenwald. Sent back from Buchenwald to Paris, he was murdered by the *Milice* on July 7, 1944, in the forest of Fontainbleau.

32. Helmut von Gerlach, journalist, politician, and author. Involved in the German League for Human Rights.

can do more than anyone else to bring them to face unpleasant realities. Will you be willing to do it?" His answer was yes, qualified by various conditions, the most important of which were that nothing more must be said of land settlement, efforts to send people abroad must continue unabated, and the bad news must be broken gradually, that is, concession should be secured at first in retail, rather than wholesale, manner. I asked him whether any good could come from following the advice of some of the leading refugees that I should intervene directly with the higher French authorities, rather than through the national committee. He was sure this would be fatal, for no matter how convincing I might be with one of the ministers, the latter inevitably would check with Bérenger or Helbronner, and if these had not previously been convinced, the latter situation would be worse than if nothing had been attempted. Much as I disliked to do so, I felt compelled to confess that he was right.

Then Oungre launched into his favorite topic, that is, his program for developing the Hula swamps.[33] The Zionists, according to him, have paid an absurd price for the concession, many times more than they need to have paid, but they will not be able to get the money to carry on the development. ICA and the corporation could do it. He had had a large idea in opening up Argentina and had carried it through; similarly with Brazil. Now he wanted to do the same in Palestine. It could be done with £1,000,000, and would care for 2,000 families. That would be something worthwhile. He begged me to keep this closely confidential, though he has discussed it, I am sure, with many other persons. He again said that Weizmann had only had the idea of the Hula development after hearing his (L.O.'s) program.

. . . .

Wednesday, July 25, 1934

With Ruth and Otto Nathan to the rue de la Durance. Was shown around by Lambert, Fritz Wolff, and some of the other members of the staff. It was distressing to see the approximately 150 or 200 persons waiting vainly for relief—women with babies in their arms, or with small children, stood about obviously desperately anxious to be helped even a little. As I was leaving one of the offices to pass through the main waiting room, word having gotten around as to who I was, I was surrounded by about 75 or 100 of the refugees. Several of them tried to talk at the same time. Lambert would have drawn me away, but I said that I would like to hear what they had to say. So one after another, three or four of them spoke, while the crowd listened quietly. It was the familiar story of hunger, inability to pay rent, the end of all their resources, and the [French] National Committee unable to help. One of them attacked the functionaries of the National Committee, excepting however from this denunciation Lambert and

33. North of the Sea of Galilee in Palestine. In December 1934 the Hula concession was turned over to a Jewish group for drainage. Some land was reserved for Arabs.

Wolff. When they had finished, I made a brief statement in English, which was excellently translated by Nathan. I expressed my sympathy with their needs, recognized the importance of prompt relief, explained that the High Commission had no funds for that purpose, and promised that I would move at once to try to secure immediate funds. I could not refrain from dropping a hundred franc note into the open purse of one of the mothers who was carrying a month or six-weeks old baby in her arms. The look of incredulity mixed with joy was such that I could scarcely bear it.

Before I left I had another conference with Lambert, Wolff, and the other functionnaires. They did not need to deepen the impression I had already received by their appeal. I agreed that if Wolff, on behalf of the German Commission would undertake to raise half of the amount which they all said would be needed before the first of October, I would ask New York by cable to supply the other half. Lambert expressed the view that not one additional sou could be raised from the French community during that time; but Wolff thought something could be gotten from the German community and from the visiting Americans.

Just in time to go off with Nathan to the station to take the train for Saarbrücken. There was no opportunity for lunch, so we bought baskets of indifferent supplies and ate them on the train.

Under the Treaty of Versailles the coal-rich Saar region was placed under French administration, under the supervision of the League of Nations, for fifteen years, with the French having the right to its coal resources. Then its population was to decide through a plebiscite, scheduled in January 1935, whether to rejoin Germany, join France, or keep the existing situation. McDonald was anticipating (correctly) that the vote would result in a victory for Germany and in another outflow of refugees.

For an hour or more Nathan and I discussed what he should say to the Americans on his arrival there [in the United States]. I told him I knew that Felix Warburg and others there would be interested in his impressions of the German situation and his loan plan. . . . I hoped, however, that he would emphasize as strongly as possible his view that the High Commission is seriously weakened by: (1) the lack of independent funds, and (2) (perhaps even more important) the lack of any organizations which are really dependent upon it or which are wholly devoted to the cause of the refugees. It is obvious that some phases of these considerations could be more emphatically put forth by him than by me. I agreed with his concern lest, if the new loan project were to be carried out by the foundation and the ICA, it would move with discouraging slowness, would narrowly interpret its functions, and would in no way render the High Commission any more independent than it is at present.

. . . .

After a bite to eat, off with Nathan to the home of Dr. Weiler. Others present besides the host and Nathan and I were W. Sollmann,[34] chief editor of the *Deutsche Freiheit,* and Dr. Steinthan, secretary of all Jewish organizations.

As we arrived at about nine o'clock, we were greeted with the startling news just heard over the radio that Dollfuss had been seriously wounded and that a revolt was under way in Vienna. Naturally, there was little talk of refugees until we had had a chance to exchange views about the grim significance of these happenings. They all agreed that they foreboded grave developments.

About 10:00 our talk was interrupted by Mrs. Weiler's coming in to say that she had Vienna on the radio and that Fey[35] was talking. We all went into the next room and sat around in almost agonizing suspense, while the minister of defense recounted the events of the afternoon and evening. So incredible seemed the account given that the various listeners could not agree as to just what Fey meant. It seemed impossible that, while the Chancellor was being held prisoner and gravely wounded, there should be negotiations lasting for hours in which the German minister intervened for the safe conduct of the rebels to the German frontier. Shortly before eleven o'clock Fey's place on the radio was taken by Schuschnigg,[36] who had been named as acting chancellor by the President. He continuing Fey's tale, gradually led up to the dramatic climax: "Dollfuss is dead." Then he concluded with a stirring appeal to the Austrian people for unity and devotion to the ideals for which Dollfuss had died.

When this fact was announced, there were gasps of horror from the listeners. We returned to the other room, but had little heart for continuing our refugee discussion, for it seemed to everyone that the Hitler regime had received its heaviest blow, and that the repercussion would be far-reaching.

The whole atmosphere of our conference was tense; each of the persons present, except Nathan and I, were in real danger of assassination and knew it. As for me, I should not have been surprised at any moment to have seen a bomb come hurtling through the window. And as we said goodnight and were leaving, I felt that someone from the dark might pick us off in the light of the open door. But nothing happened.

The members of McDonald's group in Saarbrücken had reason to be fearful—they were in territory that had been (and would again soon be) part of Germany, whereas Austria was an independent state.

The July 25, 1934, Nazi coup in Austria had been preceded by a wave of terror-

34. Wilhelm Sollmann, German Social Democratic Party journalist and official, tortured by Nazis in March 1933. Fled to the Saar, where he became editor of the anti-Nazi daily *Deutsche Freiheit.* In 1936 went to England, from where he was able to emigrate to the United States.

35. Emil Fey, minister without portfolio in the Austrian government. Special commissioner for Emergency Measures for the Defense of the State against its Enemies. He had previously been vice-chancellor.

36. Dr. Kurt von Schuschnigg, Austrian minister of education. On July 30 he became prime minister and minister of defense, education, and justice.

ism designed to pressure Chancellor Dollfuss into installing Nazi ministers in his government. When this effort failed, SS conspirators, working with at least one diplomat in the German Legation and with Theo Habicht, decided to mount an armed takeover. The Austrian army and the militia known as the Heimwehr remained loyal to the government, and the SS plot to kidnap the Austrian president failed. Despite the murder of Chancellor Dollfuss, the coup collapsed. The segment of the radio report about the German minister in Vienna intervening to help the rebels escape to the German frontier was accurate.

The extent to which Hitler had foreknowledge of this plot is still disputed among historians. At the very least, he knew of coup preparations and did nothing to discourage them—though he may have been fed inaccurate information about the need for a coup. Once it failed, Hitler dissociated himself from the effort, and Habicht was dismissed from his position of party inspector for Austria.[37]

The notion that the Nazi failure in Austria would be a heavy blow to the Nazi regime in Germany proved to be an illusion. And Hitler only deferred his desire to take over Austria.

Otto Nathan's summary of the conference is given below:

"All four were agreed that the situation at the Saar is extremely difficult and dangerous. A putsch such as that which had just happened at Vienna was held likely almost any day. In that case, no military or police force would be available to defend 'lawful' government. According to high authority, among [the] Saar police force, only six officers are held entirely trustworthy in case of a putsch.

Many refugees came through the Saar. The number varies much because of newcomers who first stay in the Saar and depart as soon as they find a place to go. The number has varied in the last year or so between 1,000 and 2,000. At this moment, well over 1,000. Only very few have settled down for good. No prospect that more will do so, since they are unable to receive permit to work or permit to settle down. In case of the Saar going back to Germany, about 50,000 people would have to leave the territory. The situation is not at all comparable with the situation in Germany when Hitler came to power. Because of enormous German propaganda, for which large funds have been put to the disposal of Nazi propagandists, and because of far-reaching espionage, almost everybody who is not pro-Nazi is known and would have to leave. It is supposed that half of the Jewish population (2,000 to 2,500) would have to go.

Furthermore 10,000 Socialists and 10,000 Communists who are all known by name. In addition, at least 10,000 Catholics and about 5,000 liberals, intellectuals, etc."[38]

37. Bruce F. Pauley, *Hitler and the Forgotten Nazis: A History of Austrian National Socialism* (Chapel Hill: University of North Carolina Press, 1981), 128–137.

38. Nathan's summary is included in McDonald's diary.

. . . .

Over to see Mr. Knox[39] at his office in the home of the former ranking official of the Saar. He greeted me very cordially, but was obviously absorbed by the developments of the day before in Austria. He too thought they would have serious effects in Germany and the Saar. We talked for a little while about the refugees, but nothing important was said. He and his colleague doubted if the numbers of refugees from the Saar, in the event of the return of the territory to Germany, would be nearly so large as Weiler had estimated. There would be thousands, but not nearly 50,000.

More interesting was Knox in his talk about political conditions in the Saar. He is in a position of responsibility, but without real power. For example, the Saar police is more than 90 percent disloyal. Only the day before the chief of police had been attacked because of his loyalty to Knox. Illustrative of this same situation was Knox's statement that he wished that morning to telephone to Paris to a friend of his at the Austrian Legation about the developments in Vienna; but he dared not do so because even his own minister of posts could not assure him of a connection with Paris which would not be listened in to by Nazi representatives. Knox is fearful of a Nazi putsch in the Saar. He is certain this would take place if the date of the voting were postponed or if there seemed a likelihood that the voting would be adverse to Germany. And against such a putsch he, Knox, could do nothing. Nor in his judgment was it likely that the French would intervene. Nor could the League take effective action.

Just in time to meet Nathan for a brief talk at the station, where I took the train for Basle.

. . . .

Took the seven o'clock train for Lausanne, where I was met very kindly by Wurfbain about eleven o'clock, and went directly to the Hotel Windsor to join my family. [They had left Paris with Miss Sawyer on the twenty-sixth.]

[On July 27 McDonald cabled Warburg:

HUNDREDS INCLUDING CHILDREN VERGE STARVATION PARIS MINIMUM NEED TEN THOUSAND DOLLARS EACH AUGUST SEPTEMBER STOP DEUTSCHE KOMMISSION UNDERTAKES RAISE HALF IF OTHER SUPPLIED NEW YORK STOP CONVINCED SITUATION REQUIRES EXCEPTIONAL CONCESSION and the same day wrote to him, "The events since I last saw you and my intimate contacts with refugee leaders during the last few days have left me with a nearly oppres-

39. Geoffrey C. Knox, president of the Governing Commission of the Saar, set up by the League of Nations.

sive sense of tragic difficulty. But part of these may be mere physical and mental weariness. At any rate, I hope to approach the problem refreshed eight days hence after a week's vacation."

A letter of July 28 to James Rosenberg was in the same mood:

"The events of the last month cast shadows before them which make me extremely anxious about the future. What has happened is only too accurate an indication of the temper and ruthlessness of those in authority. How under these circumstances, Jewish leaders of intelligence dare plan as though the worst is over, is beyond my comprehension."

Another letter of the same date to Baerwald added:

"It is . . . vitally important that the Jewish leaders at home, who seemed to feel when I talked with them a few months ago, that I was an alarmist and seeking to prey upon their fears, should be made to see now that their fellow-religionists in the whole of central Europe are greatly in danger."[40]]

Tuesday, July 31, through Saturday, August 4, 1934

The McDonalds all had a week's vacation, less than ideal because of bad weather. But at least for JG, it was a break from days of end-to-end conferences and meetings. JG and Ruth returned to Lausanne on Sunday August 5. Janet and Henrietta stayed at their pension until September 1. Bobby stayed at her camp until September 11. Sixty years later her vivid memory of the stay is good food, crisp air, and, most of all, the acute misery of homesickness.

40. JDC Archives, High Commission File 2, 1934.

16. August 1934: The League Keeps Its Distance

On August 5 McDonald and his wife left for Lausanne, where he began to catch up on work and to make plans with Herbert May and others. He took the afternoon train to Paris on Wednesday, August 8.

Paris, Thursday, August 9, 1934

Got in touch with Oungre promptly. He agreed to meet with me and Bandeiro de Mello[1] at twelve o'clock.

Dr. Rosen came to the hotel at 10:30 and with him Dr. Kahn, though I had said to the latter over the telephone a little earlier all I had to say and had not suggested that he come with Rosen.

The only message which Rosen had, or at any rate the only one which he gave me in Kahn's presence, was that he was going back to Russia to try to work out a basis by which certain Jews from Poland could be allowed to come to Russia for agricultural purposes, more or less experimentally. They would not be asked to become Russian citizens until after they had had an opportunity to live there a considerable period. This project would be financed through funds supplied by the Russian government in return for Russian bonds delivered up by the Agro-Joint.[2] Rosen stressed that this proposal would not affect the refugee situation, but that it was relieving the Jewish pressure in Poland. He said that the whole matter was extremely confidential and that I should speak about it to no one. When I asked him what about the religious question, he belittled this by saying that he did not think that religion mattered for a very large number of the Jews in Poland, and that in the Jewish colonies in Russia there were, after all, considerable opportunities for religious association.

The balance of our time was given over to talk mostly by Dr. Kahn. He

1. Brazilian ambassador to France.

2. On the initiative of Felix Warburg, and by agreement between Joseph Rosen of JDC and the Soviet government in 1922, agricultural colonies for Jews were founded on 1.5 million acres in several areas of the Soviet Union: Crimea, Zaporozje, Cherson, Odessa, Caucasia, and White Russia. Some were Zionist colonies settled by people who saw the Crimea as a stepping-stone to Palestine. There were 128 such colonies by 1928, containing fourteen thousand families. During the 1920s the colonies were governed as semi-autonomous Jewish districts, and the Soviet government contributed five hundred thousand rubles a year for their maintenance. The American Society for Jewish Rural Settlement contributed money as well, as did the philanthropist Julius Rosenwald (of Sears Roebuck), who gave $5 million. The program was curtailed in 1933 and ended in 1938.

showed me his letter to Baron de Rothschild in reference to making funds available for the immediate needs in Paris. The plan outlined seemed to me very complicated, but he said it would be clear when I had Baron de Rothschild's reply. Dr. Kahn thought that the plan would be put into effect almost at once. When Rosen asked Kahn what would happen after that, the latter replied that he did not know. Rosen insisted that the only solution would be on the land in France for many of the refugees. I then told him of a suspicion in the minds of the French officials as to his motives. He was much surprised.

Speaking of Louis Oungre, Dr. Kahn said that more might be expected from him now in the way of an independent attitude towards the French government, because in the last few weeks he had received his promotion in the Legion d'Honneur, that he had been working on this for months, and had been, therefore, quite unwilling to risk alienating the authorities.

At twelve o'clock Louis Oungre and I met and then had our conference with Bandeiro De Mello. Oungre did most of the speaking, presenting clearly our desires in reference to Brazil. De Mello listened intently and then replied in a very encouraging way. He said that the Assyrians had been excluded because reports had begun to circulate and had been capitalized in the nationalist press to the effect that there were bandits in considerable numbers among these refugees.[3] He seemed to think that so far as the German refugees were concerned, the recent legislation would not be a serious bar. It was left that we would present him with two memoranda setting out our desires.

. . . .

[After the conference] we talked also about [a] possible change of office. Oungre strongly recommended London as against Paris. In the French capital one would be much too near the bulk of the refugees and the French National Committee. If I had large amounts of money, then I would be king in Paris, but not having money, I would be used simply as a means of getting money and would be overwhelmed by communications from Baron de Rothschild.

Tried to reach Mowrer for lunch, but he was out of town, so had a bite alone and after speaking to three or four friends at the Ritz, gave myself the luxury of

3. When the British mandate over Iraq ended in 1931, the League of Nations suggested that Brazil accept a large number of Assyrian Christians, who feared Moslem rule. The plan was fought by a coalition of nativist organizations and newspapers in Brazil and was ultimately rejected. The campaign against the admission of Assyrians was closely linked to the suggestion that Jewish refugees be allowed to settle in Brazil. An editorial in the *Jornal de Comercio* of Rio was of the following opinion: "The threat that hovers over Brazil of an invasion of the inhabitants of Iraq, which England wished to place in Parana, was a signal of alarm that awakened our people . . . we refer in particular to the Japanese and the Jews, who for good reasons are undesirable immigrants rejected today by all nations that are in need of foreign labor. Now the Jews: Although not fit for the racial formation of Brazil, they continue to disembark at Brazilian ports, filling our cities with parasites, intermediaries, secondhand buyers, installment peddlers, and dishonest elements in commercial circles. . . . Let us have sufficient courage to repel the Japanese, the Jews, and other undesirable elements. . . ." Jeffrey Lesser, *Welcoming the Undesirables: Brazil and the Jewish Question* (Berkeley: University of California Press, 1995), 68–70.

an hour at the Louvre before taking the four o'clock train for London, where I arrived at the Grosvenor House at eleven o'clock.

London, Friday, August 10, 1934

To the Dorchester House at 10:30 to see Bernard Flexner and stayed with him until quarter past twelve. He seemed very well, as did Mary, with whom I spoke for a moment. She appeared really very chic.

Our conference began after the polite preliminaries by a rather lengthy statement by me as to my difficulties with the governments, the private organizations, and the fundraising groups. Flexner listened attentively and at the end burst out with a vigorous declaration.

He had opposed from the first Felix Warburg's and the others' coming to London. It was bound to raise false hopes. One could not deal with the English in that way. They wanted only American money and the opportunity to manage it. The Americans must first set up their own organization and then deal with the British on specific projects.

At the moment there was little hopeful in the English situation, for no one was prepared to do anything except Sir Osmond. Sir Robert Waley-Cohen had a scheme to capitalize the Palestine Economic Corporation and to sell securities in the City; that is all, and Flexner would not for a moment hear of this. He had managed to iron out the controversy about the financing of the Potash Co., but that was his only specific accomplishment.

It was up to the Americans to push the corporation through promptly or quit talking about it. They should then offer to cooperate with the British on each of the projects Sir Osmond had in mind, though none of them were very important: the distressed areas, the study in Europe, the loan kassa in France—but it would be important to have the Americans indicate that they were prepared to match the British and on projects which the latter favored.

More important would be, Flexner considered, the Hula project. He is, therefore, working for the setting up of a syndicate to study that problem scientifically. This would involve an expenditure of about £5,000 to be made up by the corporation, ICA, AMICA, the cement interests in Palestine, and one or two other sources. I asked him about the existing option. He exclaimed that it had been purchased at an absurd price, many times too high, and that it must be allowed to lapse. The final syndicate would, of course, compensate the Zionists for their loss in their initial payments. The latter, too, must be brought in, both to the study syndicate and to the larger organization, to do the work.

Then returning to my problem, Flexner said that Felix Warburg had called him up to say that he had read the minutes of the June 18 Paris meeting and was shocked by them. Flexner said he would like to read them. Warburg warned him that he would be made very angry. After he had read them, he met Warburg and some others and told them, "I think the critics in Paris were right. They were kicking at you through McDonald. The fact is we let Jim McDonald down. We have promised things that we have never performed. That's all there is to it." Warburg and Baerwald were shocked and surprised.

Flexner was emphatic that it had been a mistake to draw me into the financial appeals at all. It was up to the Jews to raise the money as they had done in the past. Moreover, it is a hopeless task to try to make real peace among the organizations. They can with great pain and labor be brought to cooperate on specific projects, but beyond that nothing could be done. I should not waste my energies in such endeavors.

On the contrary, the High Commissioner has an important mission to perform in its relation to governments. These efforts should be intensified, and by concentrating on them, one could accomplish more.

Flexner and I did not talk about the academic situation. He said he had heard a great deal from Cohn about it, and would discuss it with him later. He again, however, expressed his admiration for Kotschnig's work and thought there should be no expenditures by the JDC or others on this side of the field except after the approval of Kotschnig. He had taken the initiative in a specific instance of this sort by telling Kahn that he thought the latter should check with Kotschnig.

Flexner expressed himself almost violently about Dr. Kahn—that he is a tired man, full of nerves and blind spots, sadly needing a prolonged vacation, etc. I attempted to defend Dr. Kahn, saying that I had had the same impression eight months ago, but I felt it less now.

As I was leaving, Flexner said he hoped that I had not made the trip expressly to see him, but he seemed genuinely pleased that I had come. On the way out I had a chance to say goodbye to Mary.

Back at the hotel I got Cecil on the telephone up in Lancashire, where he was on vacation with friends. He said he was sorry that he could not come to Lausanne during the Assembly, and suggested that we have the Governing Body without him. I told him that I much preferred not to do this, and that we would, therefore, probably postpone the meeting until October and have it in London. He said this would, of course, be most satisfactory to him.

I took occasion to talk to him a little about the possibility of changing the office to London. He thought that Lausanne offered no advantages, even from the point of view of the League connection. He would be pleased to see us in London.

Just time to have a bite of lunch and take the two o'clock train for Lausanne, where I arrived Saturday morning.

Lausanne, Saturday, August 11, 1934

. . . .

Pleasant visits with the children. Janet, learning about European girls and parents, has come to feel that having American parents is a great advantage. Her comments on the restraint exercised by European parents were very amusing.

. . . .

Monday, August 13, 1934

Over to meet Herbert May and out to lunch at Coppet with the Johnsons. During lunch there was pleasant talk, much of it led by Mrs. Johnson, an Irish girl. After lunch Johnson, May, and I and Dr. Cohn talked for more than an hour. Johnson told of his Brazilian experiences, where he was for two months, of his faith in the Parana region, and his conviction that Oungre is wrong in insisting that only trained agriculturists can succeed there. His estimate of the cost of emigration per family of the Assyrians was only £50. I questioned him as to whether this included transportation and setting them up on the soil. He insisted that all these items were included. As to the closing of the doors, this he attributed to anti-Japanese feeling. In answer to my question as to other possible openings, he had nothing definite to reply. He and his colleagues are looking. Inquiries had been made in Australia without success, and the chances in Canada were not too promising.

He was not encouraging on the possibility of receiving financial support from the governments. In the past his organization had received very large direct governmental subsidies, but latterly it was more and more difficult to secure these, even on a smaller scale. There might still be a chance to do this, for example in the case of France, as part of a definite program for evacuating X number of refugees.

In answer to my question as to whether he knew of any special reason why the Jewish organizations should have opposed the suggestion that this work be put under his office, he replied that he had no difficulty with them, but presumed that they did not wish to be a minority group, as they would be of necessity in his organization. Moreover, he had had a difference of opinion with Louis Oungre, the latter claiming that ICA should be the predominant representative of the Jewish interests on the Nansen Committee Advisory Council. This Johnson had refused to grant, insisting that ICA should have only one representative, while the other Jewish bodies, such as the Delegations Juives, also had one representative.

After we left the Mays, Johnson and I exchanged views about the Geneva tendency to gossip. He, I think, appreciated my sympathy.

I left the conference with the feeling that Johnson had been very unjustly attacked, but that his [*sic,* he] had perhaps fed the flames of Geneva gossip. Johnson, by the way, continues technically a member of the Secretariat of the League, lent to the Nansen Office. I think we can count upon friendly cooperation from him.

. . . .

Tuesday, August 14, 1934

Busy in the office most of the day. . . . Talked to Edward Warburg[4] on the telephone. Arranged to meet his uncle in Zurich the next day.

4. Edward Warburg, the youngest son of Felix Warburg, financial backer of the new American Ballet.

Worked until eleven with Miss Sawyer on a new draft of the letter to Felix Warburg.

Zurich, Wednesday, August 15, 1934

At the office until time to take the 11:53 train to Zurich.

In the following diary entry, McDonald was being super-cautious, not willing to put in even the initials of the man he came to see, Max Warburg. Earlier in the year Warburg had thought it unwise to see him in Berlin. But Warburg had come to Zurich for meetings of the Board of Governors of the Hebrew University and of the Jewish Agency executive.

Went directly to the Dolder [Hotel]. Had a couple of hours; very pleasant chat with Lola Hahn, her senior [her father Max Warburg] not having yet returned from the meetings in town. There was little that was new in her accounts of the situation [in Germany], except her insistence that there is a growing amount of discontent evidenced among the workers, who now no longer hesitate to express their dissatisfaction. But she anticipates no changes in the near future which might reasonably be expected to minimize the nature or scope of the problem [of the Jews].

Later we were joined by Edward, who seemed quite worn by his three days of conferences, but he retained a lively sense of humor. We talked, among other subjects, about the situation in Paris. Edward said, "But you know Baron Robert de Rothschild is not quite balanced. Moreover, he has unusual personal habits."

About a quarter past seven we went out for a walk. No positive opinion was expressed about future developments. No one can tell whether or not depreciation is in the offing. Economic conditions are difficult, and a citizen ought, if possible, help to find the means for purchase of materials but not in any sense as a quid pro quo for unrelated questions. [Increased trade with Germany in exchange for lessening of restrictions on Jews or allowing them to take some of their assets with them.] It would be a mistake to mix the two. Two days before the purification process[5] one had been asked by the man second in nominal authority[6] what terms would be required for real cooperation. The answer was merely recognition. There was surprise at the moderation of this condition. The initiative had been taken, it is believed, with the knowledge of the superior. More might have come of it, except for later events which naturally relegated such matters to the rear. Personally business is better, but there is always a lack of individual security. But one can do nothing about that. It is necessary to do one's duty and let the rest care for itself. Meantime, the group as a whole has been made more worthy by the trial through which it has gone. That is something.

5. A euphemism for the so-called Röhm Putsch of June 30, 1934.

6. This reference is unclear. Probably, the number two man in the Reichsbank. In August 1934 Schacht also became minister of economics. Possibly, however, a reference to Hermann Göring.

Meantime too, there is a steady leakage [Jews leaving] directed to various parts of the world. It is conceivable that this might continue until a half or more [of the German-Jewish population] has been emptied.

At dinner there was general talk and afterwards I read my draft letter [to Felix Warburg]. My chief auditor [Max], however, was very tired, and I am afraid did not take it all in. Nonetheless, in the discussion that followed, he made clear that it might be misunderstood and would in any case be discouraging. Various suggestions were made, which, for the most part, I could not accept. The general effect of them was to cause me later completely to rewrite the letter.

Thursday, August 16, 1934

Three of us met at breakfast. The senior [Max], having read my draft, said that in view of its contents, he could not suggest any practicable change. We had a pleasant visit, and he went off while Lola and I walked slowly downtown and chatted until time for me to take the train.[7]

The trip back seemed long. I decided not to break the journey at Bern, because I was anxious to reach the office and dictate a new draft of the letter, having decided that it was too defeatist and too much like an ultimatum.[8]

[In the letter to Felix Warburg, McDonald set forth three main difficulties: (1) the negative attitude of the governments, which have sought to use the High Commission to rid themselves of their refugees; (2) the private organizations, none of which has refugees as their primary concern and which blame the High Commission when they fail to meet expectations; and (3) the shortage of funds, for which the High Commission is blamed. In a personal note attached to the letter, he added:

"I am deeply troubled by the situation. My own position sometimes seems unbearable. But I have no intention to surrender. Only a failure of the essential supplies for the work itself could drive me to confess to the world that I had been mistaken in my faith that in a great crisis a way could be found, through the generosity of Jew and Christian. I still have hope that faith will be justified."[9]]

Worked again until eleven with Miss Sawyer in order to get off a new draft to Bentwich.

7. In view of the close friendship and what McDonald viewed as Warburg's unwavering support, it seems strange that Dodd should report in his diary only about a week earlier: "I was glad to speak frankly with such a man [Max Warburg]. Before leaving he indicated that he doubted the wisdom of James McDonald's activity in his position at Lausanne. That has been my attitude from the beginning. Warburg suggested that [Rabbi Morris] Lazaron, living quietly in Berlin, might do more with the German Government than McDonald and I agree with him. Any man who would take a big salary for such a service, all from people who give the money for relief of suffering followers, is not apt to appeal strongly to other givers, and McDonald has shown so much self-esteem on different occasions." Entry of August 9, 1934, *Ambassador Dodd's Diary,* 145–146. On Dodd's attitudes and judgment, see the conclusion of this volume.

8. The letter appended here.

9. McDonald to Felix Warburg, August 16, 1934. Copy in McDonald Papers, USHMM.

Lausanne, Friday, August 17, 1934

Talked with Nahum Goldmann on the telephone and explained that I would be unable to accept his invitation [to the Comité des Delegations Juives meeting, already being referred to as the World Jewish Congress], that I did not expect to be in Geneva. He said that he did not think our work was going to come up before the conference formally. He expected to speak of it in a commendatory way and would let me know if in one of the committees any occasion arose for a particular explanation or defense. He told me where Rabbi Wise was staying, and I arranged to get in touch with the latter that afternoon.

....

André Wurfbain kindly offered to take me to Glion, where we had tea with Rabbi and Mrs. Wise. We had about forty minutes together. It consisted mostly of rapid-fire questions by Wise, which I answered as well as I could in the scant periods which were allowed me. I got the impression that Wise thought the funds were coming in at home slowly for two reasons: one, the amount asked for was too small, and therefore persons cut down their contributions proportionately; and second, the "whispers" about the corporation had caused many people to hold back, feeling that they would be asked again for a large amount. There is doubtless a measure of truth in both these contentions. I agreed with Wise that, as someone had put it to me the day or two previous, one might have to wait for the first pogrom to unloosen the purses of Jewish and other charity.

I had to hurry off to catch my train, but I left with the feeling that Wise was friendly and would not attack. Mrs. Wise is even more friendly. Incidentally, they told me that there was a difficulty at home about the admission of the children,[10] that, for reasons which neither of them could quite be sure, the permission for indefinite stay had been withdrawn. The decision had been taken to limit any given entrants to a year, to be renewable as a matter of course, but naturally on this basis one group of officials could not bind their successors. Hence, the whole plan was jeopardized. Wise did not think that this action would have been taken by the Department of Labor unless Frances Perkins had assented. He wondered whether the State Department were behind this.

Six o'clock train from Terratet. The ride up from Bex to Villars was slow but extremely beautiful. The mountains were at their very best. No chance to see the children that night, but Ruth and I had a late dinner.

Saturday, August 18, 1934

Visits with the children and a long walk with Ruth up towards Betthaye. Back in time for supper at the most beautiful period of the evening.

Two lively sets of tennis with Janet, and then a long visit with Bobby in the afternoon with the girls (Janet & Henrietta) later. To bed early.

10. This comment referred to the plan to bring 250 German-Jewish children to the United States.

Monday, August 20, 1934

Up at six, but too late to get the full effect of the early sunrise, which is so like the most beautiful effects of the sunset. 7:11 train for Bex, then at about 8:30 took the omnibus for Lausanne, arriving at 9:56, but the interval having been happily shortened to no time by an Edgar Wallace thriller, *The Three Just Men.*[11]

Lunch with Dr. and Mrs. Adler. I began at once by summarizing the situation as I saw it, much as I had in my letter to Felix Warburg. Dr. Adler listened well. Then after some discussion of various points I had made, he told me with what I think was real frankness the impressions he had gained in London of our work. In substance, this was that I had been mistaken in throwing myself into financial appeals or in seeking to make peace among the Jewish organizations. Neither of these was really my job, and in neither of them could I hope to have any considerable measure of success. Instead, I would inevitably dissipate my energies and lose the opportunity to do worthwhile things in a third direction. This direction he said was in the relations with governments. I should be dealing with the official bodies, find openings for X thousands of refugees, then make an estimate of the costs, and put these proposals up to the private organizations. My responsibility would then be ended. I replied that I had put forward this as the more likely of three possibilities in my letter to Felix Warburg.

Dr. Adler also said that he had been greatly disappointed at the initial statement last winter to the effect that the governments would neither give any money [n]or would they who had no refugees take any. He thought that on the first point an opportunity had been missed, that more might have been done, that Chamberlain might have gotten something from the United States. I ventured to disagree, suggesting that the governments were not sufficiently interested, and that to have strongly insisted on this point might have jeopardized the whole institution.

Towards the end of our more than two hours' discussion I told Dr. Adler that I hoped he would talk over with Felix Warburg what we had said, but that he would also make clear how untenable would be my position in my dealings with governments if, at the same time, I could not be sure that what I had called the substantive work would go forward, through the organizations having made available to them the requisite funds. He saw this point and admitted too that the funds in sight from the Americans were quite inadequate. He also agreed that the American tendency to bargain was unjustified, at least in so far as the French were concerned. On the whole, it was a useful conference.

Tuesday, August 21, 1934

Kotschnig returned to the office, and he, André Wurfbain, and I spent an hour or more discussing the general intellectual problem, and at the end agreed on a basis of an appeal to the Rockefeller Foundation for money for a central

11. A 1930s Sherlock Holmes.

fund to which contributions could be made to help keep the essential organizations functioning.

Over to the Mays for dinner at Coppet. . . . After we had discussed most of the technical items on our sort of agenda, Mrs. May said she would like to ask a question which might have nothing to do with what we had been discussing. Then she proceeded quite gently but firmly to question whether the work to date had been worth the effort put on it, whether the difficulty was merely or primarily the difficulties with the private organizations, and the lack of funds, or whether other obstacles, perhaps a wrong approach or lack of adequate drive. . . . May and I made the best defense and explanation we could, but I am not sure it was adequate.

. . . .

Thursday, August 23, 1934

In to the Secretariat to see Ben Gerig. He told me that there had been no favorable replies to the thirteen or so letters sent out to governments asking for the admission of the Assyrians.

. . . .

Saw Avenol promptly at eleven, and remained with him until nearly twelve. I began by giving him a very complete picture of the organizational development since last fall and summarized what had been done. Then, expressing our appreciation for the excellent cooperation of individual members of the Secretariat, I asked him whether the language used in the Assembly report on the work of the League during the past year referring to the High Commission was an accurate statement of the relation between the High Commission and the League. He got the text, read it, and said, "Yes, this is exact." I told him that I had assumed that this was the case, but that I was glad to have his confirmation, because I was frequently under fire from individuals and organizations with which I worked who charged that I had not sufficiently developed the possibilities of the League relationship. From what followed in our discussion on this point, it was indubitably clear [that]:

(1) The High Commission is an autonomous body;
(2) The Secretariat will resist any attempt to change that status in the direction of closer relationship to the League;
(3) It would be futile and would create bad feeling if any attempt were made at this Assembly to secure League funds for our work or to have passed any declarations in reference to it or to the policies of Germany affecting the Jews or others who are being discriminated against;
(4) There will be no objection to any personal activities by members of our staff in the way of utilizing the Assembly as a means of getting at a large number of governmental representatives to explain to them what has been

done, or to ask their cooperation in securing from their own governments larger measures of help;

(5) The Secretary General expressed doubt as to the possibility of securing funds from any of the individual governments. In particular, he doubted whether the French government would be willing to present any such project to the Chamber;

(6) The Secretary General asserted that the feeling aroused by Germany's attitude toward the Jews and the others had substantially died down during the past twelve months; that, therefore, at this Assembly it would be impossible not only to secure any strengthening of the High Commission's mandate, but probably even any expression of approval of its purposes. On the contrary, he felt that anti-Semitism had grown quite generally since the last Assembly, and that, therefore, it was much better to keep the High Commission as it is, rather than to risk losing it by trying for more. The Secretary General's language indicated that he, even more strongly than I, feels that the High Commission is an organization which would inevitably be weakened if the governments that make it up are pressed too hard to do what for political or other reasons they may be reluctant to do. In other words, it is dangerous to assume that the governments are vitally interested in the success of the High Commission. They must, therefore, be treated with great discretion, rather than as if the High Commission were essential to them;

(7) As to the attitude of France, the Secretary General disavowed any intimate knowledge, but he understood there was danger of anti-Semitism there if too much were done in placing refugees in employment. Senator Bérenger had spoken of the High Commission as an English institution, serving primarily English purposes, and of scant use to France;

(8) On the question of the Saar, the Secretary General thought that France could not close its doors to the refugees from there, for these would be considered not so much as Germans as "inhabitants of the Saar";

(9) As to the change of office, the Secretary General evinced no great interest, but he certainly did not urge us to remain near Geneva;

(10) As to the High Commission's relations with Germany, Avenol expressed no views, but one could get the impression that he was thinking always of the possible return of the Reich to Geneva [Germany returning to membership in the League];

(11) There would be no objection to our circulation among interested members of the Assembly of a statement of our work, provided only this were not a "League circularization."

On the whole, I left with the feeling that Avenol is interested in our work, that he will be willing to help where he can personally, but that under no circumstances would he be willing himself or that any of his colleagues should risk the slightest jeopardy to the League's relations with Germany in order to help us.

. . . .

Met Tirana in the Secretariat. He thought he might be able to get away even during the Assembly, for he was now engaged in technical work. He thought it desirable that I should first sound out the Secretary General, and if the latter were favorable to his going, we ought to notify the Albanian authorities at least two or three weeks before we were planning to arrive. It had been Herbert May's idea, and in this he seemed to share Olive Sawyer's view, unless one got it from the other, that I should go to Yugoslavia and Albania before the meeting of the Governing Body.

Long conference with Manley Hudson.[12] He asked me a number of questions about the paper he is now writing on questions raised by the admission of the United States to the [International] Labor Office. I then asked him whether he thought we would be justified in following up the invitation from the Japs and reported to have been expressed by Sugimura[13] that refugees come to Manchukuo. Hudson thought that we should do this only if the Chinese were willing, for in the eyes of the world we remained a League institution. I asked him too about the possibility of caring for the Nazi refugees in Yugoslavia. He said yes. As to the Saar, he thought many critical questions would be presented by the plebiscite, but he did not think the Council had exhausted its powers to make provisions for the security of life and property of those who would otherwise be jeopardized when the region returns to Germany.

Manley then asked me what I was planning to do. I replied that I intended that this work should not go on longer than next summer or the fall of 1935, that I was anxious not to seem to be perpetuating an institution for its own sake. He thought this wise, and then asked me whether I would consider a professorship of international relations at Harvard. I replied that I thought Buell would be better for that, but he did not agree. I said I would be interested, because I had decided not to return to organizational work, and would, therefore, if I had the opportunities, prefer to choose between something such as he had suggested with its greater freedom, and larger portion of time for intellectual work, and something of a commercial or remunerative nature. He deprecated the latter.

. . . .

Then for a long conference with Georg Bernhard at the International Club. He told me that there was a bitter dispute in Paris as to whether the recently accumulated fund of 300,000 francs was to be used for immediate relief or for liquidation of list No. 2. He confirmed too the danger of a split between the National Comité and the refugees, though I was not quite certain whether he referred to the Deutsche Kommission or to the newly organized committee representing the rank and file of the German refugees.

12. Manley O. Hudson, who had been at Harvard with McDonald and on the FPA Board in 1918. Bemis Professor of international law at Harvard, member of the Permanent Court of Arbitration, 1933–1945, appointed judge on the World Court in 1936.

13. Yotaro Sugimura. Had been undersecretary of the League of Nations but resigned when Japan withdrew from the League. In 1935 became Japanese ambassador to Italy.

He then urged more rapid action and particularly a quota system for allocating the refugees among the countries. He had an even less practical idea that the nations should lay a special tax on the Jews in order to find the funds to care for the refugees. It was quite new to him when I explained that this would be wholly impossible in the United States and in several of the western European countries.

. . . .

Paris, Monday, August 27, 1934

Lunch with Olive Sawyer and then took the afternoon train to Paris. Long talk with Appleget[14] of the Rockefeller Foundation, who was on the train.

Appleget was seemingly surprised that Mr. John D. Rockefeller, Jr., had not contributed to the refugee work independently of the foundation. I told him of our efforts, and got the impression that he was sympathetic, but received no more tangible help. Appleget said that he did not understand how John D., Jr., had gotten involved in Radio City; it would be necessary to build one or two additional large buildings in order to carry the very high cost of the land. Nelson [Rockefeller], with his keen sense of humor, takes everything much more calmly than John III, who is so very serious.

Tuesday, August 28, 1934

[James] Rosenberg joined me at the hotel about half past eleven. I began by giving him a general picture. Then it seemed better to let him read my letter to Felix Warburg, for as he said, Felix would undoubtedly have shown it to him. Meantime, a phone message came from the JDC office, through whom I had telephoned to Léger's secretary, that Léger would see me at 5:15 that afternoon.

Rosenberg thought my letter was sound, except on the vital point of making the continuation of the High Commission dependent on large funds being made available for relief and settlement. He at first argued that he could not see what I meant. Then later, he strenuously insisted that it would be a mistake to stand on this. He argued that though of course such funds were highly desirable, much useful work could be done by the Commission itself even if the funds were not available; that to make the matter conditional might invite withdrawal by the governments. Moreover, that from my personal point of view it would be a serious mistake to discontinue the work at the end of this year. Rosenberg did not seem to want to say that the High Commission was useful for Jewish purposes and ought to be continued to that end even if the relief and the emigration work could not be pressed forward. Again and again he returned to the thesis that I should not consider myself a relief agent, that I should not be bothered by the criticisms of this or that Jewish organization, that I should hold myself proudly as an equal dealing with governments, that the efforts on behalf of *cartes*

14. Thomas Baird Appleget, administrator at Brown University and from 1929 vice president of the Rockefeller Foundation.

de travail, titres d'identité, etc., were in themselves most worthwhile. He wondered whether I had always in these respects made as much of my position as I might have done.

We went out to lunch together and continued our talk. Apparently stimulated by Léger's prompt making of an appointment for me, Rosenberg developed at length a suggested line of approach with the French authorities: the High Commission is an agency of potential helpfulness to France; the latter's position in the world vis-à-vis Germany, as compared with two or three years ago, presents extraordinarily favorable contrast; then the world regarded France as militaristic and Germany as justly aggrieved; now note the change. France has a vital interest maintaining present favorable opinion of the world, which has resulted in part from its attitude—its hospitality—toward the refugees. France can show this continued interest in the exiles by a gesture of helpfulness towards the High Commission, by a cordial speech through its delegate at the next Governing Board meeting, and through a contribution to the administrative expenses. In these ways France could again designate its world leadership. In short, instead of approaching the French as if one were asking a favor, one should suggest to them the opportunity to serve their own national interest.

. . . .

As we talked, it occurred to me that I might say to Léger, in effect, that from the point of view of French national interest, it is unwise for the authorities to be guided always by the views of the more cautious leaders of the French Jewish community, that these latter, though of course good patriots, were so nervous about the possibility of increasing anti-Semitism that unknowingly they might mistake their own group interest for the national interest. Rosenberg thought this could be said.

Finished lunch just in time to go to the American Embassy to keep my appointment with Jesse Straus. He looked very well and was friendly as usual. After exchanging family greetings, he asked me a number of questions about the Saar and about Germany. He appeared to feel that the plebiscite results were still in doubt, and that conditions might be expected to moderate in Germany. He doubted whether the High Commission could profit much by special efforts at publicity. This inevitably brought in the name of Ivy Lee. I explained my special interest in Ivy Lee's relations to Germany because of his confidential relations with John D. Rockefeller, Jr. Straus said that he had gotten the impression, though he might be mistaken, that Lee had admitted to Percy Straus recently that he had been or was associated with the German government. But in any case, he no longer had any connection with Macy's. This discussion led inevitably to the question of anti-Semitism, and what Straus feared was its increase in the States. He then expressed a doubt about the wisdom of intensive efforts to find substantial funds for relief and emigration, because with the great needs at home these efforts might be criticized. I pointed out that the $2,000,000 raised during the year in the whole of the United States were but a tiny fraction of what would be needed in the States in a single city like New York for a single day. He said that Dean Dunham[15] had recently expressed concern about rising anti-Semitism in Boston and had suggested a conference with Percy Straus and Felix Warburg about it. I expressed something like contempt for Dunham's views, but Straus defended him, even when I pointed out that Dunham's intense economic nationalism went completely counter to his dogmas about freedom of trade. To this, Straus replied that perhaps you would have to reach the latter through the nationalist phase.

All in all, Straus seemed to me a rather timid person, and I was tempted later to write him a note simply to say that complete assimilationism had not saved the German Jews. He asked me to be sure to let him know well in advance the next time my family and I were to be in Paris, because he wished to have us at the house.

Back to the hotel just before Bentwich called. I had a brief talk with him before going over to Léger's office. He agreed that it would be best for me to go alone, and he did not dissent from my view that I might raise the point about the attitude of the more extreme of the French Jewish leaders.

Léger kept me waiting only a few minutes. After a few preliminaries I launched into the substance of my talk. I said that I knew that there were criticisms in a number of directions as to the activities of the High Commission, that some of the French authorities were said to feel that we were too much an English organization, whereas I knew that the British felt that we were too much an American affair. He said that it was perhaps true that Senator Bérenger was a little disappointed at the results and was less interested. I then developed the point of view of France's national interest in the refugee problem; I pointed out the contrast in the way the world regards France now as compared with a few years earlier. I said that this was true not merely in Jewish circles, but in liberal and labor and democratic groups everywhere, and that this at the moment was of inestimable value to the French. I cited the attitude of the American Federation of Labor on the governmental debts and militarism some time ago and its attitude now on the boycott.[16] I added that I was afraid the French authorities did not always realize the larger aspects of this problem, that because of the difficulties about *cartes de travail,* etc., they would be inclined to feel that the refugees were a bother rather than a substantial asset. Then with discretion, but nonetheless clearly, I pointed out that some of the Jewish advisers of the French authorities, though undoubtedly patriotic Frenchmen, were so concerned with the possible rise of anti-Semitism that they, without meaning to do so, would ignore what is the real national interest of France in this problem in order, as they would think, to protect their group position. It was at this point that Léger took out a large memorandum pad and began to make notes. Encouraged by his reaction, for he seemed to understand at once my point of view, I went on to argue

15. Wallace Dunham, dean of the Harvard Business School.
16. On October 11, 1933, the AFL joined the boycott against Germany.

that France should show its leadership in this matter by contributing to the administrative expenses of the High Commission. A little earlier, Léger, referring to one of the advisers of Bérenger and having in mind Helbronner, could not at once recall the latter's name. Léger continued to take notes as I spoke about the possibility of a contribution, and asked me what would be a reasonable amount. I spoke of a couple of hundred thousand French francs. He asked me what would be the situation if the other countries did not follow the French lead. I replied, and here again following Rosenberg's suggestion, that if the other countries also contributed, then France could be said to have shown the way, and if they did not follow, the French interest in the refugees would be even more clearly marked. Léger said something about the difficulty of finding funds for this purpose, but did not indicate at all that it would be impossible. On the contrary, that he would present the whole matter to his minister on the latter's return to Paris in a day or two.

I asked Léger about the Saar. I mentioned the various estimates I had received there in the event of the return of the territory to Germany. I think, but I am not sure, that Léger gave his own estimate of 20,000.[17] In any case, what is very important, he said categorically that France would of course receive the refugees and treat them as Frenchmen, for most of them would have become refugees because of their activity in France's interest. This definite statement confirming what Avenol had suggested seemed to me conclusive.

As I was leaving, Léger spoke very cordially of the work of the High Commission, said that he, from many persons, had heard my own interpretation of the work and my methods of carrying it out spoken of favorably. He even went so far as to speak of my "nobility of conception," etc.

Back to the hotel, where I found Bentwich having tea with Dr. and Mrs. Adler. Laughingly I told Dr. Adler that I had to make a confession, that he had been nearer right than I about the possibilities of governmental action or at any rate, that Léger had indicated that Dr. Adler's idea was not impossible. Dr. Adler was not displeased.

After dinner Bentwich and I met with Rosenberg and Dr. Adler at the Meurice. Rosenberg was delighted with my report of the Quai d'Orsay interview. His quick mind then leaped to other steps, many of which seemed to the rest of us hazardous or quite false. The discussion for a time centered on methods to be used in following up my afternoon initiative. It was agreed finally that there should be an *aide mémoire,* but Bentwich and I doubted the wisdom of my trying to see Léger again. Rosenberg suggested that I could now proceed to see the heads of the other states, saying that the French were considering action favorably, etc. I at once pointed out that would be fatal to try to bargain like this, that the only questions could be first, as to whether I should take up the matter at all with the other governments until I had heard from the French, and if I did, whether I would mention that I had already spoken to the French. After a long

17. Twenty thousand inhabitants might flee if Germany took control.

discussion it seemed best to leave the specific suggestion with the French alone, meantime, however, building up with the other governments, if possible, a favorable atmosphere.

We talked too about the proposed visits to Yugoslavia and Albania. Everybody agreed that under the present circumstances it would be a mistake to take the time off during the Assembly to go so far afield, that in any event the main job between now and the next meeting of the Governing Body is to build solidly our relations with the chief governments on the Governing Body. Rosenberg felt that this should be done through contacts with the permanent under-secretaries of foreign affairs or with the foreign ministers, and that I would have to do it personally. Indeed, Rosenberg doubted whether I should consider at all even later a trip to South America on the theory that one ought to have the governments come to us. He admitted that this would happen only in the event that a very large fund were available for investment in such country. Nonetheless, Rosenberg very strongly deprecated the idea of my becoming a salesman. Throughout the evening Rosenberg, thinking out loud and talking with continued emphasis, was a constant wonder to Bentwich, who later said to me, "Why you know J.R. thinks oratorically." Indeed, during much of the quadrilateral conference I had to remind Rosenberg that Bentwich was there, for he, without meaning to do so, would lecture me as if I were the only auditor.

Wednesday, August 29, 1934

. . . .

Lunch with Mrs. Moorhead,[18] Ann (her daughter), young Jones, and Dorothy Leet[19] at the American University Women's Club. I liked Miss Leet. She told me a disturbing tale of threats by members of the Right parties to copy Hitler's exclusion of the Jews from political positions when they came into power. I said I would like to talk with her again.

Over to the JDC to try to dictate my *aide mémoire.* Ran into Horace Kallen there and together with Bentwich and Schweitzer, listened to Kallen's brilliant but erratic talk. I must say that I sympathize with Schweitzer's comment, when Kallen had left, that it is difficult to be tolerant of so much of so many words and words.

. . . .

18. Mrs. Helen Howell Moorhead, FPA Board member.

19. Dorothy Flagg Leet, director of Columbia University's Reed Hall Paris campus and advocate of cultural cooperation with the French between the wars, as well as a leader in education for women. National secretary of the FPA from 1938 to 1946.

Thursday, August 30, 1934

Dictated my *aide mémoire* for Léger. Submitted it to Bentwich and sent it off by messenger. I used a stenographer associated with some private firm having offices in the hotel. She was not French, nor English, but very effective. Since I had to hurry off to lunch after finishing the dictation, I left her to make the corrected copies. When I came back, I gathered up I thought all of the missing copies, but later when I checked over them, I found that one of the uncorrected copies was missing. So I sent for her, and she gave it back to me. Later, I wondered whether she had kept it for any purpose, but if so, she disguised her feelings extremely well. Anyhow, she seemed so pleased at receiving 30 francs for the two hours' work that I doubt if she is anything more than she pretended to be.

....

Through good fortune when I telephoned Mowrer's office just before lunch, I found Dorothy Thompson[20] there and arranged for the three of us to lunch together. Before that, however, I went to see the exhibit of the Artisanat with Messrs. Chandel and Khaskaline. I was much impressed and gladly agreed to write them a letter about their work. As they showed me the results of the training and indicated their own eager enthusiasm, I felt that here was something that needed every possible support.

....

Lunch with Mowrer and Dorothy Thompson. The latter denied that she was jubilant at being expelled from Germany, but evidently she was not depressed. She told, and Mowrer confirmed what she said, that the Austrian Legation in Germany had been fired upon from both sides during the abortive putsch. Thompson thinks it is a great mistake to assume, as do most people, that in Germany the Reichswehr is likely to combine with the large landowners and Junkers against the present regime. She thinks more likely the Reichswehr will remain non-political, maintaining order under any regime. Moreover, the divisions in Germany now are rather age divisions than class or occupational. There is no Junker under fifty years of age.

Later we were joined by a very interesting Hungarian liberal, who spoke with extreme pessimism about Austria. He said that there are three armies being maintained by the state, that during the recent putsch the regime did not dare to trust the regular army, that the only stable social influence had been destroyed when the Socialists were broken, that unless France or some other country came to the financial assistance of Austria, prospects for the winter were very dark indeed.

20. One of the most influential women in America between the wars, Thompson, a prominent journalist and political commentator, was the Berlin bureau chief for the *New York Post*. In 1934 she was expelled from Germany (the first journalist to be expelled) because of her strong opposition to Hitler and the Nazi regime. In 1928 she married the writer Sinclair Lewis.

After lunch just time to send off the *aide mémoire* to Léger and catch the afternoon train for Lausanne.

. . . .

Friday, August 31, 1934

. . . Went to Geneva for lunch and to get Ruth. Then worked late with Olive Sawyer completing the press statement for the next week. . . .

17. September 1934: The Climate in Geneva

Geneva, Saturday, September 1, 1934

To Villars with Ruth and Miss Sawyer. We left immediately after lunch—Ruth, the children (Janet and Henrietta), and I—for Italy via the Simplon (Pass). It was a lovely trip until we reached the pass, when it began to rain, and at the very top the rain was mixed with snow. The rear tires of our rented Chevrolet with very little tread gave me an uneasy feeling, as the car tended to skid a little as we turned the hairpin curves going up. At the very top I hesitated about going on, but the trip down was much easier, and as we reached Italy, the weather cleared and we had some brilliant views.

Spent the night in Domodossola. The girls were thrilled with this old Italian town.

Sunday, September 2, 1934

Drove through the lake region, stopping for a little while at Stresa which is unusually beautiful, and then on to Milan, where we arrived at the Rosa Hotel a little after three o'clock. The girls spent the rest of the day sightseeing.

. . . .

Geneva, Wednesday, September 5, 1934

Visited with Bobby, said goodbye to the girls' hosts, and started for Geneva a little after twelve o'clock, via France.

Reached Geneva a little after three, deposited the girls at the Mattison apartment, where they are to pay 9½ francs a day pension, and then to the Bellevue.

The press conference amazed me by the attendance. There were forty-five journalists present, including representatives of the Associated Press, the United Press, the *New York [Herald] Tribune,* the London *Times,* [London] *Morning Post,* [London] *Daily Telegram, Labour Herald,* Havas Agency, Reuter's et al., and, of course, the representatives of the Jewish press. I explained at the beginning that much of the mimeographed material was background, but that some of the newer items were included in the first two pages. I called the special attention of the American correspondents to the portion in reference to the corporation, pointing out to them that the full text could be secured in New York.

There were a number of questions asked by different correspondents. These referred mostly to passports, relations with Germany, the countries to which the refugees might go, the question of whether the Jews had contributed as much as they ought to, the reasons for moving to London, etc. I answered all of these, except in reference to the Jewish contributions. To that, I replied that it was hardly appropriate for me to say whether the Jews had done their duty or not, but that I could not refrain from pointing out that, in proportion, the Jews had done infinitely more than the Christians.

Tea with David Woodward, now of Reuter's, and members of the staff. Woodward told of the criticisms, which had been very marked, of the budget of the High Commission's staff, and we talked about ways of meeting these attacks. It was agreed that probably it would have been unwise to have referred to the matter at the large press conference, but that during the subsequent days in Geneva I might well talk frankly to a number of the leaders of the press including Sharkey, Whitaker, Ferguson, the head of Reuter's, and the correspondents of the *Times,* the *Manchester Guardian,* Streit, and a few others.

Thursday, September 6, 1934

. . . .

Lunch with Ruth and Dr. Goldmann. The latter told me that the reservation in his group's [Comité des Delegations Juives—World Jewish Congress] resolution about the work of the High Commission referred to the desirability of its having been kept [remaining] a League institution.

As to the Saar, Goldmann said that Manley Hudson and Beckain had prepared briefs for Goldmann's group to be presented to the Council, supporting the thesis that the Council has the right and the duty to make special provisions for the protection of minorities before turning the regime over to Germany. Goldmann told me that he was expecting to see Barthou[1] on Monday. I urged him to emphasize with Barthou France's national interest in the refugee problem, and to point out how this transcended any group interest. Goldmann said he would do so.

. . . .

Ruth and I went to the International Club for the marine dance. Janet and Henrietta also came. Tirana asked me what were the plans for Albania. I told him I would be unable to go during the Assembly, but that I would like to talk to him later about it.

. . . .

Sharkey called me on the telephone to say that he had received a cable from New York asking about an interview of mine which the A. P. had not covered. I said that I had given out nothing since the Wednesday meeting and that his man had been there. He replied that they had sent something, but that he would like to have something new onto which the A. P. could tie the statement about

1. Jean Louis Barthou, French foreign minister, February–October 1934.

the corporation. So after thinking the matter over for a few minutes, I told him that he might use a statement to the effect that, in view of the recent declaration of Hess and other party leaders, it was now clear that there were no prospects of an early amelioration of the situation of the Jews in Germany, that, therefore, one must anticipate the continuance of the exodus; hence the necessity for the proposed corporation. Sharkey said this was satisfactory. . . .

Friday, September 7, 1934

Met at the Secretariat Kommerzienrat [commercial adviser] Dr. Hermann Röchling.[2] He and two other persons were standing in front of the building, and he recognized me, though it had been several years since Miss Wertheimer and I had talked with him. He said that there could be no doubt about the plebiscite vote, that it would be 99 percent for Germany. I asked him about the anti-Nazi demonstrations the other day. He replied that there could not have been more than 8,000 or 10,000 people there. As to the number of refugees following the return of the territory to Germany, he insisted that there were not more than forty or fifty. I told him that I was anxious to get all sides of the picture, and it was left that we would meet again.

. . . .

Brief conference with Miss Ginsberg, who said that Liechtenstein had accepted the stamp project,[3] and that now it was only a question of the final agreement by the Swiss authority. She hoped for my cooperation in bringing the stamps to the attention of the public if and when they were finally issued in the name of her committee. Some people anticipated more than a million francs income for the committee, but she said she dared not anticipate more than 300,000.

. . . .

Saturday, September 8, 1934

. . . .

Then to the Secretariat, where the Council had just adjourned. I shook hands with Madariaga and with Avenol, who were walking out together; chatted with Borberg, who said that his government had just sent him the detailed statement in answer to our inquiries, that he was having it translated and would send it along in a few days. We talked about the situation in the Saar. He doubts that there can be really effective guarantees and anticipates a considerable number of refugees. As to the situation in Germany, he thinks there is a considerable undercurrent of unrest and dissatisfaction.

. . . .

2. Hermann Röchling, major German steel executive and chairman of the Reich Association Iron. Assisted financially the German takeover of the Saar in 1935.

3. A fundraiser for her committee for refugee professionals.

Goldmann and a group of Jewish journalists said that the Jewish rights were being protected in Upper Silesia, and that they thought if similar guarantees could be imposed in the Saar, they would be effective.

. . . .

Lunched with Ruth at Whitaker's. Madame Tabouis[4] was the center of discussion and, as always, intensely interesting. She was more pessimistic than I have ever seen her before. She was bitter about the Poles, declaring that Beck[5] had been insulting when talking to Barthou on Friday. She feels that the Poles are completely out of hand and working with the Germans. Moreover, within France she anticipates serious domestic disturbances culminating in riots, and possibly even civil war following the expected dissolution of the Chamber at the end of October. The left groups, the Communists and the Socialists, having formed a solid front, the groups to the right are tending to do the same, while the middle groups continue to be more and more ineffective.

As to the negotiations with Russia, she explained what was taking place—that an invitation signed by some thirty countries was being prepared, that to this Litvinov would reply, accepting it in lieu of a formal League invitation, [to join], and that then action would be taken promptly in both the Council and the Assembly. One possible hitch was the attitude of Argentina in the Council, but as a last resort it was understood that President Roosevelt had agreed to intervene at Buenos Aires to prevent a negative vote. Poland had consented to vote for admission, but only after carrying on direct negotiations with Moscow.

I tried to interest Madame Tabouis in the problem of the refugees, but she pooh-poohed the idea that France had any stake in the solution of this question. She contemptuously said, "Throw them into the Seine, or start a plague amongst them."

Sunday, September 9, 1934

. . . .

In the evening Ruth and I went to dinner at the Blakes. Others there were Mrs. J. Makohin . . . and her nephew, young Bolton, son of a congressman from near Cleveland. It was a pleasant party, with fried chicken and wonderful waffles. In the general talk after dinner when we got onto the subject of Russia, Mrs. Makohin showed extraordinary knowledge of conditions in the Ukraine and an intense violent hatred of the Bolsheviks. She said that the Jews have themselves to blame for there not being more support for them as against the Nazis, because they, throughout the world, had never protested against the Bolshevik atrocities, which had caused millions and millions of political murders

4. Genevieve Tabouis, journalist, author, and later member of the French resistance. Niece of French diplomats Paul and Jules Cambon. Wife of Robert Tabouis, administrator of Radio Luxembourg.

5. Colonel Jozef Beck, Polish foreign minister, 1932–1939.

and immeasurably greater suffering than had resulted from the Nazi regime. She then attacked with bitterness, and on the basis of evident detailed knowledge, the Agro-Joint colonization program in southern Russia. She claimed that tens of thousands of peasants had been dispossessed to make place for the Jewish settlers, and, as a result, there exists in that area latent anti-Semitism of such virulence that it only awaits the opportunity to burst over the heads of the Jews. She declares that unless the Jews take special measures to prevent it, there will be bloodshed on a large scale in the region of the colonies.

Mrs. Makohin insisted that she was herself in no sense anti-Semitic, but as she became more and more stirred by her own words, she disclosed what seemed to me a fundamental anti-Jewish attitude involving, despite her large contacts with Russian affairs, ignorance of important factors there. For example, she declared that the Jews had been and were the dominant influence in the Soviet Union; that the leading Communists everywhere are Jews; that Jewish high finance, despite its apparent opposition to Communism, works hand in glove with the Communist leaders. She ended by telling me that if I really wanted to be of service to the Jews, I would warn the leaders of the tragic dangers inherent in the Anglo-Joint policy and in the Jews' relations in general with the Soviet regime.

I refused to be overwhelmed by her eloquence, pointing out that the Jewish leaders who had carried through the Agro-Joint project were men of the highest ethical standards, that they were extremely proud of what they had done, that she exaggerated grossly the influence of the Jews either in bringing about the Bolshevik revolution or at present in Soviet circles, that she similarly exaggerated the power of Jewish finance either in London or Paris or New York, and that in the same way she enlarged out of all true proportion the influence of the Jewish press. But I am afraid that I made no more impression on her than she made on me.

Monday, September 10, 1934

Went to the opening of the Assembly with the girls and Ruth. Had excellent seats for them in the diplomatic gallery. The proceedings were, as always on the opening morning, purely formal, but were interesting for any one who had not seen them before.

Chatted for a moment with De Valera and introduced the family to him.

Tuesday, September 11, 1934

Up with Janet to Villars to get Bobby. She was glad to leave but would have been satisfied to stay. She was the picture of health. The mademoiselle in charge said that Bobby had been a perfect child, and that she would be welcome to come back at any time.

. . . .

Wednesday, September 12, 1934

During the morning occupied in seeing the family off [to the United States].

Miss Sawyer, Kotschnig, and I had gone to the Bavaria after dinner. While sitting there with the Mowrers and Sauerwein,[6] we saw Sandler,[7] president of the Assembly, walk into the place and, seemingly unable to find a seat or anyone whom he knew, walk out again and wander aimlessly along the quai and across the bridge. Miss Sawyer, Kotschnig, and I started home, passed Sandler standing alone, when my two companions insisted that I return and pick up Sandler. This I agreed to do after Olive Sawyer confirmed my reluctant impression that Sandler had been my host at luncheon in Stockholm during the spring. I returned, spoke to Sandler, who remembered at once our Stockholm meeting. We walked back to the Bavaria and talked until twelve o'clock. Mostly he spoke about the program of his party in Sweden, the progress being made there along the lines of the Roosevelt program. I took occasion to speak of the refugees, our hopes of additional intellectuals being received in Sweden, etc. He seemed sympathetic.

Thursday, September 13, 1934

To the Assembly in the morning. Listened to Beck's denunciation of the minority treaties affecting Poland.[8] Never have I seen such a hostile reception to the remarks of a foreign minister in the Assembly. Afterwards there was animated buzzing in the corridors. . . . Everyone I met expressed great concern. There was talk of Poland's withdrawal from the League. Others put it that Poland was moving towards its fourth dismemberment.[9]

Lunch with Jäckh. He told me in detail of his interview with Hitler a year ago last spring. It had been arranged by Hitler's secretary, an old friend of J's. It lasted an hour and resulted in Hitler's writing letters to Goebbels, asking that the latter deal with Jäckh in a reasonable manner in liquidating the Hochschule, and another letter to Rosenberg of the same general purport that the latter should deal with Jäckh in a reasonable spirit in liquidating another work in which Jäckh was interested. Jäckh said that he hoped to return to Germany on his way back to London in order to secure, if possible, special permission from

6. Jules S. Sauerwein, foreign correspondent for *Le Matin, Paris Soir,* and the *New York Times* Paris bureau. Had a reputation as a Nazi and Vichy sympathizer. See Laurel Leff, *Buried by the Times: The Holocaust and America's Most Important Newspaper* (Cambridge: Cambridge University Press, 2005), 143–145.

7. Richard J. Sandler, Swedish foreign minister, newly elected Assembly president, with particular interest in German-Jewish refugees.

8. Irked by continuing League of Nations protection of minorities within Poland, Foreign Minister Beck proposed instead an international conference to create a universal minorities system; he threatened to stop cooperation with the League on minority investigations. See Carole Fink, *Defending the Rights of Others: The Great Powers, the Jews, and International Minority Protection, 1878–1938* (Cambridge: Cambridge University Press, 2004), 340.

9. The state of Poland was partitioned (and ultimately eliminated) by more powerful neighbors three times in the second half of the eighteenth century.

Schacht to send abroad his savings. He is an old friend of Dr. Schacht and hopes for his favor. After that, he never expects again to return to Germany during this regime.

In this connection I told Jäckh of my 1914 articles in defense of Germany.[10] Jäckh replied that he had now begun to doubt his lifelong faith in his own people. He had begun to wonder whether perhaps, after all, there was not something in the German Volk which made them dangerously different from other people; was there not some weakness, some tendency towards brutality, some willingness to follow leadership, no matter how it might violate fundamental ethical principles . . . ?

On the whole, I was glad that we had had such a good talk, for it seemed to me to remove any ground for the unkindly feelings I had had towards Jäckh. I was the more impressed by him this time, because he did not express any visionary hopes for the return of a regime in Germany which he could support.

As we were finishing lunch, Mrs. Habicht came along and joined us. She looked very thin.[11] We had a pleasant chat about this and that. Most of the time, however, Jäckh developed his thesis about fundamental weaknesses of the German people disclosed by their support of the present regime, and particularly by their failure to be shocked by the events of June 30 [1934]. Pete [Mrs. Habicht], no matter what may have been her own feelings, for she must have been much influenced by her husband's pro-Nazi proclivities, did not venture to disagree with Jäckh.

. . . .

Ran into Blake at the Regence on my way to Miss Bartlett's cocktail party. I asked him more about the Makochins. He then told me something which he pledged me not to disclose to a single person, so I am precluded from dictating it to Olive Sawyer. However, it tended to give added importance to what Mrs. Makohin said, and added weight to her grim predictions that there was serious danger for the Jews in south Russia, should the opportunity come for the peasants to have their way.

Friday, September 14, 1934

Over to the Assembly. Arriving during the long and rather uninteresting speech of the Chinese minister to London. The Assembly was not much more interested in it than I. Everybody was waiting for Simon and Barthou. The former spoke for not more than five minutes. His whole manner, while outwardly courteous, was that of a schoolmaster reprimanding a not too important and wayward pupil. The substance of his remarks seemed to me wholly admirable.

Barthou, a much more nervous temperament, was less cool and detached in his manner, but equally the schoolmaster.

10. See chapter 1.

11. For the reasons why Mrs. Habicht may have been haggard, see the second inserted commentary in the July 25, 1934, entry.

Then followed Aloisi,[12] whose statement was so worded as to permit anyone to place any interpretation upon it.

During these various speeches I watched closely Colonel Beck and his colleagues. His attitude was that of the defiant pupil who knew that he was being taken to task, but showed no signs of repentance.

Simon and Barthou were received with applause, but not the enthusiastic plaudits customary in the good old days when Briand and the others made their pleas for high moral principles. The present atmosphere does not permit of such luxuries.

In the lobby afterwards Beck was left severely alone except for a few sycophantic hangers-on.

I met Sir John and told him that I thought his had been an admirable speech. He replied that one could not really permit the Poles to get away with their statement; it was absurd to assume that Polish obligation was contingent upon a similar obligation being assumed by Britain in reference to India, etc. The gossip in the corridors gave general approval to the reproofs to Poland, but there were many questions as to what Poland would do.

Lunch with Kotschnig and Pobereszki.[13] . . . After setting forth his views about the present international situation, Pobereszki said that he thought the High Commission should provide for more frequent statements to the press, particularly here at Geneva during the dead season. He thought that there would have been larger notice taken of the statement made on September 5 if it could have come somewhat earlier. By that time there was too much already going out from Geneva about the opening of the Assembly. He thought too that it would be helpful if I came into personal contact with political leaders in the different countries. Here in Switzerland, for example, he suggested it would be helpful to get in touch with members of the Radical Party who might influence Bern. I thought him a very intelligent, well informed journalist.

Mrs. Olmsted and Dorothy Detzer[14] came to see me to ask what I thought of the project of the W.I.L. to send a delegation to Germany to try to induce the regime there to end the concentration camps for women. I told them that I could see no harm in their mission and that I could not believe they would accomplish much, but that the trip would be educational for them.

Talked with Herbert May before the general staff conference. He disagreed strongly with Pobereszki's suggestion about getting in touch with political leaders. He thought this could accomplish little and would be more likely to do harm, by being misunderstood by the governmental authorities.

. . . .

12. Baron Pompeo Aloisi, Italian foreign minister, president of the League Saar Conference.

13. Michael Pobereszki, later Pobers, a writer and journalist who covered the League for *Le Jour* of Paris. Involved, with Kotschnig, in the International Student Service.

14. Dorothy Detzer, executive secretary and most influential member of the Women's International League for Peace and Freedom, a group that combined progressivism, pacifism, and feminism and was active in arms control issues.

Sunday, September 16, 1934

. . . .

Then over to the residence of Professor G. Ferrero. . .[15] An hour and a half with him and his family. Ferrero analyzed the political situation. He thinks that the Poles are engaged in a long-range conspiracy with the Germans for the dismemberment of western Russia and the Ukraine. He cited a number of indications to this effect. He doubts if war is imminent, because the Germans are in no position to hope to win. The moral deterioration within the Reich, he feels, is proceeding apace.

. . . .

Had a long talk with Sarah Wambaugh about the situation in the Saar. She feels that developments for the plebiscite are proceeding satisfactorily. She feels, however, that there is a danger of forceful action from the groups of the left if they feel that they can in no other way secure protection for their rights against the attacks of the German extremists.

. . . .

Monday, September 17, 1934

Over at ten o'clock to see Dr. Rajchmann[16] of the Secretariat. . . . As to the situation in China, Dr. Rajchman said there was no possibility now of work for additional German doctors from the refugees, and for not more than a very few dentists. He gave the following reasons: the Nazi influence at present is very strong in high Chinese circles; the Chinese medical association is opposed; and conditions in the interior are excessively difficult, virtually impossible. In short, there are almost no openings in China.

On leaving, I asked Dr. Rajchmann whether the Chinese were going to be retained in the Council. He seemed doubtful because, as he said, both the French and the British had refused to instruct their clientele to vote for the re-eligibility.

At the Assembly the center of interest was the vote on the Chinese seat. The decision was adverse by a large majority, while Spain was declared re-eligible. This result was deplored in the corridors as coming out of unworthy intrigue which was interpreted in various ways. The British were annoyed by the Chinese, the Russians are anxious to have Turkey on the Council; perhaps even agreement to this was part of the price of Russian admission. Some of the Balkan states also wished to have Turkey in for reasons of their own. It perhaps was also a concession to Japan and certainly will be interpreted as a victory for Tokyo and as a large step towards the recognition of the Japanese status in Manchukuo. The incongruity of this action was the more marked in the light of

15. Professor of international relations at the University of Geneva. An Italian exile.

16. Dr. Louis W. Rajchmann, director of the League's health section, previously technical reconstruction agent in China for the League's China Committee.

the re-election of Spain, which means that both Spain and Portugal are on the Council, while there is no representative at all from the whole of Asia, except Turkey, which is at least half a European power. In other words, none of the principles urged against China's re-election were any less valid against Spain's re-election. Nor does the personal popularity of Madariaga explain this inconsistency. It was another example of the low state to which the Assembly has fallen. As the Chinese chief delegate said to Whitaker and me after the session, the loss is more the League's than China's.

....

Tuesday, September 18, 1934

With Wurfbain to see de Graeff at the Bergues. We first discussed the situation in Holland. We reported about the extent of the press criticisms without associating ourselves with these. De Graeff refused to admit that there was any justification for these charges, and said that almost no one had been expelled, but that it was true that foreign musicians and other foreign employees working in Holland were being asked to leave at the expiration of their existing contracts. He did not indicate how general this practice is; he justified it on the grounds of the very large degree of unemployment and the past very liberal policy of the Dutch.

Our second topic dealt with my suggestion that the Dutch take the initiative in referring to our work in the Second Committee and that they consider also making a contribution to the administrative expenses. On the second point, de Graeff was quite flat in the negative. He said there was no possibility whatsoever of any Dutch contribution. It was not in the budget, he would not recommend that it be added or provided for in any other way, or rather, he suggested that there was no other way.

But as to action in the Second Committee, he was much more encouraging. He indicated certain difficulties, but said that he would talk to François about it, and left us with the impression that on the whole he was favorable. As we were leaving, I told him that I had an engagement to speak at the formal opening of the special training school in Holland, and that I hoped then to be able to do something to correct the widespread impression about the attitude of the Dutch government.

....

With Bentwich to see Eden[17] at the Beau-Rivage. He was friendly, referring to the discussions which had been had in the League committee when my name was proposed for my present post. I then told him of the problem facing us, and of our anxiety to have some indication of continued governmental sup-

17. Anthony Eden, British delegate to the League, in December 1934 appointed Lord Privy Seal, served as foreign secretary under both Chamberlain and Churchill, and from 1955 to 1957, as prime minister. In the period before 1938 he considered Mussolini a greater menace than Hitler and thought it was possible to reach agreement with Nazi Germany.

port and some direct governmental contribution. He listened with close attention. On the first point he said that he thought something could be done; that he would be glad to support the Dutch initiative if the latter took it, and that he would be glad to speak to the French that very evening.

As to the contributions, however, he was more dubious. He asked what would be involved. I told him that we estimated the budget for the nine months' period in 1935 at not more than £10,000; that I had suggested to the French a contribution of about £2,000 and that it would not be courteous to suggest anything less from the British. Eden laughed and said he wouldn't mind if it were made smaller. He said he would speak to the representative of the Treasury about it.

. . . .

Over to the Assembly early. . . . The proceedings to allow the Russians to enter the League went along according to schedule, but it was 7:20 before the credentials committee had reported. Meantime, the room had become more and more suffocating. Finally at 7:25 Litvinov was called to the platform to make his speech. It was interesting that among the first people to shake hands with him when he came in were the representatives of Rumania, Persia, Turkey, and Poland, all of which countries are under certain conceivable circumstances directly menaced by the Soviets. On the way to the tribune Litvinov shook hands with Barthou, as well he might. The speech lasted from 7:25 until nearly eight o'clock. It was a clear and forcible statement, but not easy to follow because of Litvinov's accent.

During the translation Koo[18] introduced me to Mrs. Litvinov in the lobby. We chatted together for perhaps a quarter of an hour. She was an English secretary, and is very proud of her husband and of his English style, for which she takes full credit. She implied that she was responsible for several of his best phrases.

. . . .

Wednesday, September 19, 1934

. . . .

Forty-minute conference with [Canadian Prime Minister] Bennett at the de la Paix. We first spoke about the possibility of some League statement on the work of the High Commission. Bennett knew little about it, but listened attentively, then glanced through our Report of Progress, and said definitely that he would favor the bringing up of a resolution in the Second Committee, that as chairman he would hold it in order. He suggested that we draft such a statement, and have it presented and supported during the closing period of the Second Committee at the time when he would ask whether there was any other business.

18. Wellington Koo, Chinese minister.

We then turned to the situation in Canada. As he glanced through my letters to himself and to his secretary and noted that they had never been answered, his conscience seemed to prick him, for he was very apologetic and full of explanations.[19] On the constructive side, however, he was not very helpful. He went through the list of suggested immigrants, said that there might be a place for a few ladies' tailors or for butchers, but he doubted the eligibility of the rest. Their regulations were now very exacting, not permitting entrance unless in the case of close relatives or people with jobs practically assured and jobs which would not displace others. Moreover, each of these cases had to be passed as an individual matter by order in council. Such suggestions were being more and more closely scrutinized in order to resist local political influence; also one had to be a little careful about the local Jewish committees dealing with immigration, for they were sometimes inclined to cut a sharp corner.

I explained to him the tendency on this side to speak of Canada as a land of potential immigration, and to criticize the High Commission for failure to achieve greater results in opening the doors there. He said that as soon as he returned to Canada, he would write me at length and in a very clear and positive way about the situation there.

I was amused by his parting remark. We had been speaking about the low state to which the Assembly had fallen, he having said that he had never known a time when political bickering and trading was so evident. Then turning to me he said, "It's a relief to see your fine sensitive face in these surroundings."

. . . .

Met Wurfbain at Fotitch's office. . . . We then discussed the situation in Yugoslavia. Fotitch said that he would inquire from his government as to the various points I had raised and as to whether from my viewpoint it would be worthwhile to visit Belgrade. . . .

In Yugoslavia [according to Fotitch] there is no anti-Jewish feeling, save possibly in the northwest, the former Austrian provinces.

We chatted about conditions in Germany, Nazi racial theories, etc. Fotitch was most cordial, and I left with the feeling that we had made a good beginning. . . .

Worked with Olive Sawyer until two o'clock and then took the 2:24 train to Bern.

Rothmund received us at once, answered in detail our questions about passports, read us the three or four-page confidential instructions just being sent to the various cantons in connection with the new *titre d'identité.* He remained adamant on his definition of a political refugee,[20] and insisted that it was only for this class of exiles and strictly limited at that the [Swiss] federal government could intervene to require a canton to permit a refugee to remain. Also, he re-

19. See also McDonald's diary entry of March 20, 1934.
20. That is, he refused to consider Jews persecuted as Jews to be political refugees.

fused to yield on the question of not considering as a political refugee anyone coming from a country other than that of his national origin. In this connection we spoke of the case of the journalist who had raised the issue at our press conference. It appears that he will probably be allowed to stay.

At the close of our talk Rothmund spoke of the [Swiss] Jewish community as being very moderate in its view and very cooperative, but repeated the usual comments about the eastern Jews, and the danger of anti-Semitism if there is not care. He also said that Professor Oltramare had told him on September 3, when they had met at Coppet, where Rothmund was on a vacation, that either I was planning to use the press to criticize the Swiss policy on passports, or was recommending such action to the organizations.

Rothmund was evidently relieved when I assured him that I had never seen Professor Oltramare until the day before, i.e., September 18. Rothmund took us to the train and said that he had expectations of being in London.

On the way back André Wurfbain made some helpful suggestions about future policy, and he agreed to write a full memorandum at his early convenience about the whole passport situation in Switzerland.

....

Thursday, September 20, 1934

....

Spoke to Ben Gerig about procedure. He said it would, of course, be possible to have something sent forward from the Second Committee to the Assembly, and to be acted upon there as a resolution, recommendation or "voeu." But he seemed to think it would be better to limit action in the Second Committee to a series of statements.

Ran into Norman Bentwich talking with Pelt. The latter was most emphatic that the chairman would rule out of order any suggestion of a discussion of our work; he seemed so excited about it that I regretted that it had been brought up with him, and asked him if he would be good enough to forget that the point had been raised.

....

Started to walk for lunch at Habichts and met Sir Arthur Willert[21] on the quai. He said that he understood that we were asking his delegation (British) for something. I explained what it was, and he gave me the impression that it would be done. Speaking of Cecil, I having said that I got the impression that the latter was not too happy about the attitude of the present government on some problems, Sir Arthur replied that Cecil was never satisfied with the government, even when he was a part of it.

21. Sir Arthur Willert, British delegate to the League, 1929–1934, and Geneva Disarmament Conference, 1932–1934; 1935 head of the Ministry of Information Office southern region.

At Habichts besides the hosts were Countess Apponyi and the Eckstrands. For me, it was a dull party. I enjoyed talking to Mrs. Habicht, and he too was pleasant, but the only subject discussed at the table was that of double nationality, suggested by the fact that Mrs. Habicht retains her American nationality and is also Swiss. I tried to indicate three times that it was much more important to find some nationality for the tens of thousands of people without any than to worry as to whether Mrs. Habicht would be loyal to Switzerland or to the United States. There was no response, however, except a little later, when Habicht brought up the subject of the refugees directly, the Eckstrands and the Countess showed their underlying anti-Semitic prejudices.

. . . .

After the staff conference went to see [Osten] Undén, the Swedish minister without portfolio, former minister for foreign affairs. He listened sympathetically to my suggestion about additional intellectual refugees for Sweden, as had Sandler. He also said that he saw no reason why statements about the High Commission should not be made in the Second Committee, and that he would consult his associates and expected that they would support the initiative if taken there.

. . . .

Friday, September 21, 1934

Conference with Benes at 9:15. We first talked about the work of the High Commission and the League's relation to it. He had no doubt whatever that it was all right for us to have the issue raised in the Second Committee. The Czech delegate would be instructed to support any initiative taken.

As to the financial contribution to the administrative costs of the High Commission, Czechoslovakia would follow the lead of the others. I expressed my gratitude, and then asked if Benes would take a few minutes to give me his interpretation of the present Assembly and the situation which it reflects.

He replied that we were in a second era of the League. No longer, as in the days of Briand, Stresemann et al., were attempts being made to build a new world. Instead, now he and his colleagues were attempting to save this one. They were seeking to erect barriers against catastrophe, that is, war. They are seeking to maintain the status quo, and without saying so, he indicated, to maintain Germany in a position where it could not endanger the League. Incidentally he spoke with what for him was feeling about the emergence during this Assembly of a fourth great power—Poland.

I told Benes of the general feeling of discouragement because of the lack of idealism or hope expressed at this Assembly, and suggested that he take occasion before the end to strike this desired note. He said he might. In answer to my question he said that the President was much better, and that they hoped his progress might be continued.

Conference with Mowinckel, prime minister and minister for foreign affairs of Norway. He agreed to support the initiative in the Second Committee and was sympathetic to what I said about our plans for the intellectual refugees in the northern countries.

. . . .

Met Aubert [French representative in the Sixth Committee] in the lobby of the disarmament building. He said that here had been a hitch about bringing up our matter in the Second Committee, where Haas [the secretary] said it would be out of order. On inquiry, it became evident that the British or Bennett had spoken in terms of a resolution, which, of course, would be much more difficult for the Secretariat to accept. I told Aubert that we had decided that a resolution would be impracticable, that a series of statements would be sufficient.

Aubert then suggested that the Rapport of the Sixth Committee dealing with the Nansen refugees should be amended to include a brief paragraph to the effect that, though the High Commission had been set up as an autonomous body, the League was not disinterested and was following its work. I pointed out that though this would be a very weak statement, it would probably arouse unyielding opposition from the Secretariat as being objectionable to Germany. Aubert said that it was intended merely as a peg on which to hang the desired statements. I told him I did not think it would work. He replied that the French would accept our judgment as to tactics, and I was to let him know whether the matter would come up in the Sixth [minorities] or the Second Committee [technical issues].

Ran into Harrison Brown in the lobby. In a manner unusual for me, I, without the slightest preliminary, said that I had been surprised that he had on the basis of completely inaccurate data led his Chicago committee to send me a telegram not of inquiry but of sharp and preemptory reprimand about passports. He denied that he had seen the text of the telegram, but admitted that he had suggested the need for some such action. He explained that just before he had sailed, a couple of persons had come to him to tell him that the passport situation was wholly unsatisfactory, and in fact nothing was being done. He did not contend that this information was sufficient for the sort of action he had induced. We then left it at that and went on to other matters. . . .

On the way to see Contilo [Argentine ambassador] at the Bergues I stopped in at the de la Paix, found that the Canadian luncheon had broken up, crashed the barriers, and talked for a moment to Bennett. He said yes, there had been objections from Haas, but that he was going to proceed anyway, and he would handle the matter so that the statements made "would have the force of a resolution." Knowing his record for firmness, I had not the slightest doubt that he would carry through. This was a great relief.

Met Wurfbain at the Bergues, and together we saw Contilo.

The Argentine ambassador doubted whether his country would reconsider its attitude towards the Governing Body, but that he would submit to Buenos Aires a memorandum on the subject. We assured him, though I am not sure we convinced him, that membership on the Governing Body would not involve obligations to take refugees.

As to immigration possibilities and as to whether it would be worthwhile for me to consider a trip to Argentina, he suggested that before he could answer that it would be desirable to have a memorandum as to the basis on which such immigration might be projected. He, on his own initiative, suggested that so far as plans generally with Argentina are concerned, they might most advantageously be pressed either from Washington or with the cooperation of the United States authorities. I am not sure whether he said this because of existing exceptionally good relations between Washington and Buenos Aires, or because Wilson's introduction of me had led him to conclude that the United States was officially interested. At any rate, I disabused him of any such possible misunderstanding. We said that we would send him the desired memorandum.

Found Chodzko here at the Bellevue. He was much disturbed at the prospect of the question coming up in the Sixth Committee. He said he would not like to speak there, that Madariaga was very "formuliste," referring evidently to Madariaga's action in ruling a portion of Chodzko's statement two days earlier as out of order. I said that we hoped the question would be considered in the Second Committee, and that he would speak.

....

Over to the Secretariat to continue inquiries in reference to action in the Sixth Committee. The French, represented by Aubert and the English by Skelton,[22] went into a huddle before the meeting, but seemed uncertain of their action.

....

Staff conference. Decided to press for action in the Second Committee, and we allocated the different countries among the staff members.

In the evening to the Derso-Kelen dance at the International Club. It was a really charming affair.

Saturday, September 22, 1934

Much telephoning to members of various delegations with a view to getting the desired action in the Second Committee, but even when the meeting began, we were not quite sure whether the French or the English would take the initiative. Meantime, however, we had gotten assurances from the following countries of support: Yugoslavia, Canada, Great Britain, Norway, Sweden, Czechoslovakia, France, Portugal, Belgium, the Dutch (under certain circumstances), and Poland.

As soon as the consideration of the main report had been concluded, Ben-

22. Oscar Douglas Skelton, undersecretary of state for external affairs and Canada since 1925.

nett made a brief statement about the High Commission and opened the way for the British. Shakespeare[23] spoke very well, following a good deal of Bentwich's memorandum. Dr. Vasconcellos then followed on behalf of Portugal; Mr. Basdevant, on behalf of France, then associated himself with the remarks of the British delegate, noting that though large help had been received from abroad, France herself had made considerable sacrifices. He put the number of refugees still in France at 25,000 to 30,000. When Bentwich later inquired about this estimate from Fouques-Duparc, he was told that it had been checked with Paris by telephone the night before. Dr. Chodzko, as representing Poland and as a member of the Governing Body, spoke in support of the work. Mr. Van Lanschot of Holland, recalling the Dutch initiative, associated himself with the British and French remarks. The representatives of Czechoslovakia and Sweden then spoke in similar vein, the former recalling the fact that large numbers of the refugees had been received in Czechoslovakia. Norway followed in the same line, and Mr. Bennett on behalf of Canada, closed the discussion with words of great encouragement.[24] So ended the first battle to get recognition from the Assembly, despite the well-intentioned, but from our point of view, misguided efforts of the Secretariat to keep the whole subject out of the discussion.

However, at the last moment, no attempt was made by the Secretary of the Second Committee to block the discussion. Indeed, I am not sure that the Secretary General was really displeased, but I have not yet found out.

In the lobby later a number of the newspaper men spoke to me encouragingly. I thanked Chodzko and Fouques-Duparc when I met them. The former said that I should have been present in the room to receive personally the congratulations of the Second Committee, but I retained my view that it was better not to have appeared.

Met Eden, thanked him for the manner and substance of the British initiative. He said, "Well, I suppose you will not now ask us for anything more" (half jokingly). He then added that the answer about finance is negative. His Treasury expert had said it would not be possible, because to do so would require a bill, and that this would be impracticable. To this Bentwich, who was present said, "We'll draft you a bill"—and it was left at that.

The comments of most of the press men whom I met were friendly.

....

[Nahum] Goldmann told of the interesting situation of Lüdecke, who is now in the States offering to sell to Rabbi Wise and Mr. Deutsch his documen-

23. Geoffrey H. Shakespeare, British delegate. Member of the National Liberal Party and a junior minister. In thanking the High Commissioner, the Governing Body, and private organizations, he said, "In spite of the world depression, it had proved possible to do useful work without drawing on public funds." Journal of the 15th session of the League of Nations, 2nd Committee meeting of September 22, 1934, McDonald Papers, USHMM.

24. Bennett said "that, as no draft resolution had been submitted, the Committee did not need to take a vote but, in unanimously congratulating the High Commissioner and his colleagues on the results so far obtained, the Committee had indicated the great importance it attached to this problem." Journal of the 15th session, September 22, McDonald Papers, USHMM.

tary and other material, which, according to Lüdecke, would constitute a heavy indictment of the Nazi regime. My immediate reaction was to tell Goldmann to warn his American friends to have nothing to do with Lüdecke, but Goldmann seemed to feel that they could deal with him unofficially. I was not convinced.

. . . .

Sunday, September 23, 1934

Worked all morning with Olive Sawyer, though she was beginning to feel a little rocky.

We lunched together, and were joined by Derso, but I had to hurry back to keep an appointment with Birchall. We spent an hour or so on the interview I gave him, and then he entertained Olive Sawyer and me with nearly another hour's account of his life. The next day when I saw him he told me that there would be a column and a half in the *Times* of that day.

Birchall described the interview: "Although it was Sunday, Mr. McDonald's sitting room, which is also his workroom, was littered with papers on which he had obviously been at work. Before the interview was finished, a secretary entered to take up with him 'some work which must be got out today.' It was plain that the job . . . is no sinecure." The article then lays out the refugee situation as McDonald saw it.[25]

. . . .

Monday, September 24, 1934

. . . Lunch with Guani, joined later by Herbert May. Guani agreed to preside at the opening meeting of the session in London on November 1, and he again raised the point about it being impossible for him to come to frequent meetings in London, because his government supplied him with no funds for such propose.

Long conference with Dr. Ruppin.[26] He outlined what he considered to be the essential program for evacuating up to 20,000 young Jews from Germany during each of the next ten years. He thought that this plan should be worked out and announced by me, the basis being approximately 10,000 a year to Palestine and the balance to be divided between the United States and Argentina and Brazil. I agreed with the desirability of such an evacuation, but expressed doubt as to my being able to lead in the plan because of my direct obligation to the refugees outside of Germany and because of our expectation of not continuing beyond October 1, 1935. He did not reply to the latter point, assuming perhaps that the tentative plan need not be carried through. As to the first point, he ar-

25. *New York Times,* September 24, 1934, p. 12; see also September 22, 1934, p. 12.

26. Dr. Arthur Ruppin, the first director in 1903 of the Palestine office of the Anglo-Palestine Company, which was designed, through loans, purchase of land, and other economic incentives, to create employment opportunities in Palestine for thousands of new immigrants.

gued that in effect these young Jews were refugees and would in fact become refugees unless they were evacuated.

Ruppin thought that the Agency could handle the Palestine quota, ICA should be induced to care for the South American portion, and that for the United States should be left to me. In answer to my statement, he said that he was confident that ICA would not need to involve itself more than partially in the Hula scheme and would be free to carry on in South America. I judged that his views about Louis Oungre are not very different from my own.

. . . .

Tuesday, September 25, 1934

With André Wurfbain to see Caballero, the permanent representative of Colombia at the League. He explained that there are very few Jews at present in Colombia, that there was no feeling against them, but he could not be sure what would be the attitude if there were to be any considerable increase. Indeed, on this and on other points he could give us very little information, but suggested that we submit to him a memorandum for transmission to Bogota. We chatted for a little while about Inman,[27] whom Caballero said he knew very well when he was minister of education.

Ran into Knox in the corridor of the disarmament building. We walked up and down together and he told me about the discussions here on the Saar. He said that nothing had been done. The Italians were holding up any action on the various points he had raised as a means of pressure on the French. It was all a case of bargaining. He did not put it quite as strongly as someone did a little later who called it blackmail. In particular, nothing had been settled on his suggestions about physical or intangible property of individuals who might be endangered by the change of regime, nor had anything been done about the protection of the investments made during the period that the Saar was administered by the League. And to cap the climax, the Swiss had now decided not to allow the recruiting of the police to supervise the plebiscite.

In general, as I have watched Knox in the corridors, it has seemed to me that he is as much of an outsider in the League as I am. Our office was sacrificed at the demand of Germany. Now the Saar administration is being made a football of politics between France and Italy. No wonder the president of the Governing Commission feels annoyed and discouraged.

. . . .

Lunch with Malcolm Davis. We talked about conditions at home and also about the state of the League. We were in general agreement on both. He gave

27. Samuel Guy Inman, specialist in Latin American affairs, founder and secretary of the Committee on Cooperation with Latin America, 1915–1939. McDonald had known him when they were both on the Mexican committee of the League of Free Nations Association in 1919.

me the impression that there ought to be a reorganization of the American representation here at Geneva, and he thought this would necessarily involve the elimination of Prentiss Gilbert. As to the League, he was inclined to interpret it as passing through a series of normal stages. I told him I thought it was rather that the League was reflecting now, as always, the state of Europe, and since the nations were struggling almost frantically to avoid drifting into war and in this process are bargaining back and forth, so the League has become merely the center for these dickerings.

Professor Quidde[28] came for tea. His is a pathetic story. Exiled only because he is a pacifist and now hard put to keep body and soul together, he said that the Wilhelmstrasse [German Foreign Office] were very friendly to him, but that this was no avail against the firmness of the [Nazi] party. The Foreign Office had said that nothing would create a better impression abroad than for the government to invite him to return, but nothing happened. He is dependent upon chance honoraria from an occasional article, but many of his articles are accepted and then not paid for, as recently with the *Journal de Geneve* and as in the case of a talk over the Swiss wireless. I said that I would get in touch with him again before I left.

. . . .

Wednesday, September 26, 1934

Worked with Miss Sawyer until after eleven, and then over to the Secretariat. Chatted with Pobereszki, who outlined what he termed the Italian intrigue by which the Saar was being used in an attempt to force the French to give Italy a free hand in Austria. He thought it would not succeed. . . . Asked Ben Gerig if he would inquire as to whether the Secretary General was annoyed by the action of the Second Committee last Saturday.

With André Wurfbain and his wife to the Bergues for the luncheon of the Oxford Group.[29] I sat between Mr. Hicks, a young Englishman, and a Miss Bert, a Swiss of Basle. The speaking consisted of brief statements by eight or ten persons, many of them young, concluding with a brief statement by Buchman. Hambro opened by a vigorous attack on the evasion, duplicity, and crass materialism of the Assembly. The following speakers each emphasized, in one way or another, the importance of a spiritual readjustment of the individual. It was a really impressive occasion.

. . . .

28. Ludwig Quidde, historian and writer, one of the founders of the German peace movement in imperial Germany, once tried for lèse-majesté. Left Germany to live in Geneva during the Nazi consolidation of power.

29. The Oxford Group, later known as Moral Re-Armament (MRA), believed that by creating a more moral and spiritual society, they could bring about greater democracy and international justice. The group, started in the 1920s, drew upon the ideas of the American Frank Buchman.

Thursday, September 27, 1934

. . . .

Lunch at the Mays. The only other guest was Chodzko. Talked during the lunch about Madariaga, who, it appears, was defeated in his candidacy for the Chaco committee.[30] Chodzko expressed strongly his view that Madariaga was losing ground by taking himself too seriously. As to the policy of the Polish government, Chodzko said it was absolutely essential that in self-respect the Poles show France that they could not indefinitely be treated as a mere appendage. Locarno, the Four-Power Pact, and now more recently the Eastern Locarno—all had been brought to an advanced stage before Warsaw was consulted.

I left early in order to go home to bed. Later, Herbert May reported that Chodzko had spoken to him at some length about the work of the High Commission. In Chodzko's opinion, it would be a great mistake to consider liquidating the High Commission. It constitutes the only governmental basis for the consideration of problems of Jewish emigration. He thought it important that I should see more of the leaders of eastern Jewry and not appear to be too closely associated with rich, western Jews. There was a third point which I have forgotten.

After resting most of the afternoon, felt much refreshed and ready to go to the concert of the Busch quartet. To the Mays for dinner with Mlle. Chavchavadze. The concert was lovely.

Friday, September 28, 1934

Mr. Brunschweig, a Jewish Genevese businessman, came at nine to apologize for the non-appearance of the representatives of the Schweizer Israelitische Gemeindebund.[31] He then proceeded to tell me of the work of the different Jewish communities in Switzerland, and of the virtual impossibility for them to carry on unaided. I gave him little encouragement as to assistance from England or the United States, but told him that I would take up the matter with Sir Osmond and Dr. Kahn if he would outline his case in a memorandum. He said he would do this.

. . . .

Saturday, September 29, 1934

Dinner at the Mays with the Abrahams and the Prentiss Gilberts. After fifteen or twenty minutes of, for me, quite dull talk about difficulties with the movers (both the Abrahams and the Gilberts were changing their flats), Mrs. May and I had some amusing exchanges about mutual friends. After dinner there was a long and illuminating discussion between Gilbert and Abraham, lis-

30. League committee set up to mediate the dispute between Paraguay and Chile over the Chaco area.

31. Federation of Swiss Jewish Communities.

tened in on by May and me, as to the responsibility for the failure of the League to work more effectively in the Chaco controversy. Abraham began by saying that the root of the difficulty was the uncertainty of the attitude of the United States. This Gilbert took issue with, and sustained his contention by a detailed recital of the step by step developments in the controversy. He does have a most impressively clear and detailed knowledge of the U.S.'s League relationships. From the long discussion there seemed to me to emerge the truth that the failure lies in the unwillingness of Brazil, Argentina, and Chile to work together. Unlike the Letitia dispute, these three powers are more concerned with a peculiar national interest than with the peace of the continent. It was also agreed that, of course, if the United States were a member of the League, it could be more effective in its cooperation, for outside of the institution, it cannot legally commit itself to being bound by covenant obligations, and therefore is estopped from formal participation in a official League inquiry which might result in a report to the Council, which in turn might call for action binding on the League members. Nonetheless, as I said at the end of the talk, it seemed to me that the failure was due as much to lack of downright and powerful leadership, as well in the United States and Geneva, as in South America. This was partially admitted, but Prentiss Gilbert made the significant point that the United States could not take a strong line in view of the present fixed policy of the administration of refraining from announcing a definite policy in a Latin American dispute unless and until the Latin American states themselves had reached essential agreement, and the United States could then join in, rather than seem to impose its will.

Sunday, September 30, 1934

....

Arrived in Paris at the Continental a little after eleven.

18. October 1934: Criticism Is Easy

Paris, Monday, October 1, 1934

Spent most of the morning with Dr. Kahn going over with him most of the aspects of our problem.

(1) Czechoslovakia. He repeated in detail what he had said to me on the telephone. So far as the Jewish committee is concerned, the JDC stands pledged to give Kronen for Kronen 230,000 Krs. In addition 100,000 Kr. for loan kassas, and an additional sum many times this size for other Jewish work in Czechoslovakia . . . ;

(2) The future of the High Commission. He felt that it should be continued. It is impossible to estimate accurately its accomplishments, because these, in the nature of the case, must be largely intangible;

. . . .

(3) The loan kassa in Paris. The funds to start this are available from the foundation, but Dr. Kahn is opposed to their utilization unless and until the French community has made available an initial sum. Otherwise, the French Jews on the loan committee would have no interest in seeing to it that the loans were loans and not disguised gifts.

. . . .

Lunch at the Rothschild bank. Besides Baron de Rothschild and myself only his son, just returned from the States, was present. It was for the most part a pleasant social affair, with chatting about people at home and on this side. However, we did discuss the problem of setting up a loan kassa in Paris, and Dr. Kahn's desire that there should be an initial French subscription. The Baron saw great difficulties in the way, but finally said that he would get in touch with Kahn promptly.

After lunch we were joined by Lambert. He and Baron de Rothschild insisted that it was a mistake to assume that the representatives of the French National Committee did not press their government vigorously in such matters as *carte de travail.* I argued that if the French government could be made to see the overwhelming national interest involved in maintaining its reputation for hospitality towards the refugees, the technical questions involving only a few thousand Germans would be much more easily solved. Lambert and Baron de Rothschild seemed somewhat convinced.

. . . .

Louis Oungre . . . came to see me about four o'clock. Miss Sawyer went down to meet him, and reported that he was apparently somewhat annoyed that I had come on a Jewish holiday and failed to give him fuller notice. However, when I came down a few minutes later, he was amiable enough. We talked about

(1) The date of the Advisory Council meeting. He seemed to think it should have been arranged to follow immediately after the ICA meetings in London the middle of October. I merely reminded him that we had had to choose the date in consultation with Cecil and taking into account as far as we could the probable desires of the governmental representatives;
(2) The problem of finding funds for the continuation of immigration. Oungre was emphatic that ICA could not carry the burden alone. He even doubted if they could continue for the rest of the year. He asked what of the corporation—how soon would it be in a position to help?;
(3) My possible visit to Argentina and Brazil. Oungre seemed to think this would be a good idea, but doubted if he could get away to go along. However, ICA's representatives would be at my disposal.

. . . .

As Oungre was leaving, he asked me point-blank whether he had ever intrigued against me or the High Commission, indicating that there had been a report to that effect. I answered him with a categorical no.

It was arranged that we would meet again before his ICA conferences.

Speaking on the telephone to Dr. Kahn, he told me that he had just heard that Robert Kauffmann had committed suicide, and that his widow had returned to Germany to collect the insurance, said to be about 400,000 Marks.[1] This utterly unexpected news was a shock.

Supper with Mrs. Wurfbain and Miss Sawyer and then to see Wallace Beery in *Viva Villa.*

Tuesday, October 2, 1934

. . . .

A nearly all-day trip from Paris to Amsterdam with Dr. Kahn and Miss Sawyer. En route talked for several hours with Dr. Kahn covering again many old points. One of the new subjects was that of the period for which I should plan to continue the office of the High Commission. Dr. Kahn thought it would be a serious mistake and would be misunderstood and would discourage interested persons if I announced that I thought the work could be wound up in the first nine months of 1935. If desired, the budget could be made for that shorter period, but leaving the tenure of office indefinite. He then made the extremely

1. This information turned out to be completely wrong.

interesting suggestion that if, for any reason, I might wish not to spend so much time abroad after the first of October, it conceivably could be arranged for me to continue as High Commissioner as did Nansen after the Nansen Office was set up; on such a basis I might have to come to Europe only a couple of months in the summer and perhaps a month in the winter, while the office was carried on by someone else.

. . . .

So to bed after midnight, in the noisiest room I have slept in for months, but had the best night's sleep.

Amsterdam, Wednesday, October 3, 1934

Breakfast with my friend [Max Warburg]. He talked very freely. His account of conditions [in Germany] was much the same as that he had given me in another place a year before.[2] But this time there was even more of vehement passionate denunciation of what seems to him to be tantamount to a regime of anti-Christ. It is headed straight for chaos, but its leaders are prepared to threaten and even to carry out the threat to pull down the whole of Europe with their own structure. There is no possibility of really carrying the Ersatz [substitute-synthetic materials] program through to the point where the national economy can be made independent of foreign raw materials. In the Saar the Catholic vote will be decisive against Germany. There can be no question but that Hitler and those about him are preparing as rapidly as possible for war. They are more ready now than is commonly believed. However, the events of June 30 [the so-called Röhm Putsch] have materially reduced the numbers of missions of young men prepared to die. All Christendom is in danger. There is no truth in any of the present government leaders. They are utterly unscrupulous, false, and unreliable.

. . . .

Then off with a group of the Dutch community to Werkdorp Wieringermeer.[3] It was an interesting journey, particularly through the newly made country and to the great dike. We lunched near the school. There I met Mrs. Sigmund Warburg and her brother and Kreutzberger.

The ceremony at the school was run off promptly. Mr. Van der Bergh presided, the speeches were all short, and there were no separate introductions.

After the meeting and during the course of the visit to the farm I spoke at some length with François about the situation of the Poles who were threatened with expulsion from Holland. He assured me that not many were leaving; indeed, that unless in any specific case they could secure the assent of the Polish

2. See McDonald's diary entry of November 21, 1933.
3. A training farm for young Jewish refugees on land reclaimed from the Zuyder Zee.

government to receive an individual, there was no effective means by which he could be expelled. François is expecting to come to the London meeting.

Called upon to lift a lever which released the pile driver, thus beginning the foundation of the new building, I performed the operation so quickly that the newspaper photographers were disgusted.

....

With Mr. Kahn and also with others I talked during the day about the effects of the new decrees prohibiting the employment of persons below the age of twenty-five. This has two sides, that affecting those in employment, and that affecting those who would enter employment. As to the first, it is not clear how it will affect the Jews, but as to the second, it is commonly assumed that it means the virtual exclusion of young Jews from employment.

....

9:25 train for the Hook of Holland.

London, Thursday, October 4, 1934

After what for me was a broken night, we reached Harwich before six o'clock and took the train at seven for London.[4] Went to the Russell Hotel. All my plans for a very easy day to make up for the bad night were made impossible by the archbishop of Canterbury's[5] suggesting that the date for lunch on the fifth be changed to lunch on this day. His Grace had been commanded to appear at luncheon at the Palace in connection with the meeting of the Privy Council to assent to the marriage of Prince George. There was nothing for me to do but assent to the change.

After an hour or so with Bentwich I went to Lambeth Palace. Chatted with Canon Don[6] for a few minutes and was then shown into the office of the archbishop. I began my story at once by telling him of the suicide of Kauffmann, and then went on to give other illustrations of the effect of the regime on Christians with any Jewish blood or married to Jews, even though the latter had become Christians. I seemed to give to him a more acute sense of the tragedy for these folk. Moreover, he assented to my general thesis that the very fundamentals of Christianity are involved. He was interested in Pacelli's reaction, but doubted whether the Romanists would move affirmatively. He said in any event you can never tell what they will do.

After we had talked for about twenty minutes, he said the question is, of course, what can we do about it. He told me something of the many pleas that come to him from all parts of the world, but put forward particularly his com-

4. In October the High Commission office was moved from Lausanne to London to be nearer the English organizations that were taking the lead. There was no longer any point in being near the League.

5. Cosmo Gordon Lang, archbishop of Canterbury 1928–1942.

6. The Reverend Dr. Alan C. Don, canon of Canterbury Cathedral.

mitment to the Assyrians as the chief obstacle to his taking a leading role in this effort to raise the sum which I suggested, £50,000. I argued a little that the Assyrians were the logical charge of His Majesty's Government. This was assented to, but apparently the commitment to undertake an effort from private sources had already been made. Finally the archbishop said that as a first step he would be willing, if I wished it, to have a conference of those interested at Lambeth Palace. Whether he would himself take the initiative in issuing the invitations was not quite clear. The details I was to work out with Canon Don.

At lunch besides the archbishop and Canon Don were the bishop of British Guiana, the bishop of Alaska, and two others who, being more menial than the bishops, were not introduced to me. On our way in to lunch the bishop of British Guiana said, "You know, the Jews in Jerusalem do not like the idea of their fellows being converted, and for such converts they cease to feel responsibility." This was said as if it reflected upon the Jews.

During lunch I talked first with Canon Don, whose views about Christian responsibility are the same as mine. Then with the bishop from British Guiana about conditions in his diocese. On this he was interesting. He sharply took issue with Blake, whom he had known very well there for many years. Nonetheless, the bishop doubted if the Assyrians would go to his territory, and didn't quite see what they would do if they did go there.

During the latter part of the lunch the conversation became general, centering on conditions in Germany. I did most of the talking, seeking to drive home my thesis about the responsibility of the Church. I was listened to attentively, and I think some impression was made, but at the very end the archbishop put the same questions which are so frequently put to me: "But isn't it true that the excesses of the Jews themselves under the Republic are responsible for the excesses of the Nazis towards the Jews, at least in part?"

After lunch I chatted with Canon Don, who arranged that I would get in touch with him again just as soon as our lists of possible guests was ready. The more I see of him, the better I like him.

Sir Osmond came in at 3:15 and stayed for an hour and a half. We began by my presenting the general picture to him much as I had to Felix Warburg in my August letter. He listened and made brief notes. When I had finished, he asked me if I had always had loyal cooperation from Louis Oungre. I told him of my talk with Oungre in Paris, and then detailed the incident at Baron de Rothschild's house which had caused me to report in New York that Oungre was disloyal to Dr. Kahn. In this connection I said to Sir Osmond, "I have the highest regard for Oungre's intelligence, for his ability to present his point of view cogently, but that I thought he had a weakness which showed itself in his desire to play up to his environment. It was this desire to ingratiate himself even further with the French officials, rather than any wish to hurt Dr. Kahn, that had led Oungre to say what he had in Paris."

Sir Osmond listened closely and then said, "You may be quite sure that henceforth there will be no question of any disloyalty towards you. If, as is expected, I am made the head of ICA, Louis Oungre will reflect my views, and on my support you can count confidently." In reply, I told Sir Osmond what was nothing more than the truth, that I looked upon him as the sort of firm support on which I could count unquestionably in this country as I did on Felix Warburg at home; that without a few such secure points from which to operate, my task would be utterly hopeless.

We then passed on to the question of funds. I explained my feeling that it would not be enough to have the resources merely for our office, that the substantive work must be provided for. He said there would, of course, be some funds, but how much he could not tell. Plans here are still unmade, but he, for the moment, is more concerned for the immediate question of finding the means to continue the immigration program beyond the fifteenth of this month. Where could the money come from? ICA could not bear the whole burden. If the Zionists relieved the British Central Fund of its commitment for £27,000 to them, then these would be available for emigration and other purposes. He asked not quite seriously whether I would be willing to suggest to Dr. Weizmann that he relinquish this amount. I replied that I could not, of course, do that, but I would be glad to talk to Dr. Weizmann about the general situation and to inquire whether out of the American Zionist funds some provision might not be made to help on emigration to Palestine.

At the end of our talk Sir Osmond said he was very anxious to continue it, and he asked me to spend the night at Somerhill Saturday and to play golf Sunday morning. I was delighted to accept.

. . . .

Friday, October 5, 1934

Norman Bentwich and I went over to see Sir Wyndham Deedes.[7] I told him of the talk with the archbishop and of the latter's offer. Sir Wyndham thought this was a good opportunity and agreed that we should do our utmost to utilize it effectively. He said that he would send us a list of the names of persons prominent in the Church who might be interested. He agreed that it would be a mistake to make this a conference of organizational officials. He will take up the matter also with the archbishop of York with whom he is spending two days next week. It is important also to communicate with the bishop of Chichester. Sir Wyndham will be a help. His views on the basis for Christian responsibility are broader than those of the archbishop.

Back at the hotel ran into Weizmann and Miss May, his secretary, downstairs. I said jokingly to Dr. Weizmann that Bentwich and I were plotting a conspiracy against him, and I should like to tell him about it soon. He said he would speak to Mrs. Weizmann and arrange for me to come to the house.

7. Brigadier General Sir Wyndham Henry Deedes, head of the National Council of Social Services. Had been chief intelligence officer (under T. E. Lawrence) of the Palestine Expeditionary Force in World War I, worked with the Arabs revolting against the Ottoman Empire. Also the chief secretary of the Government of Palestine, 1920–1923.

Otto Schiff came in for tea. We chatted about things at home, from where he had just returned. The Warburgs are all well, but the corporation shows slight signs of help. As to conditions here, he too was uncertain about funds for another year, and is worried about immigration resources.

. . . .

Saturday, October 6, 1934

Out to Sir Osmond's place, Somerhill, in time for dinner. . . .

Sir Osmond assented to my view that Jewry everywhere has a vital stake in the preservation of the principal of the equality of rights for the Jews in Germany. But he shared my pessimism that perhaps only a pogrom within Germany would arouse conservative Jewry elsewhere to the danger and cause them to act accordingly.

. . . .

He favored strongly my proposed visit to South America with a view to securing, if possible, a new basis for the admission over a period of years of a definite number of Jewish immigrants. I told him of my long talks with Oungre . . . and of Oungre's suggestions about the establishment of new industries with corporation funds. Sir Osmond thought attempts on these grand scales would be costly and wasteful. He was enthusiastic, however, about a loan organization in these countries which would help individuals to set up machines and perhaps thus to lay the basis for larger industries later. . . .

As we were getting ready to go to bed, Sir Osmond returned again to his central interest, the immigration funds. . . . He asked me if I would be willing to say in effect to Felix Warburg, "If I, the High Commissioner, can induce ICA to carry on unaided the immigration financing for the rest of the year, would there be a chance that the JDC or other American funds would aid in carrying this burden in 1935": . . . I said that I would think the whole thing through, and probably cable Warburg about this. . . .

Sunday, October 7, 1934

Breakfast with Sir Osmond in the best English style of self-help from the two side-boards with beautiful silver service.

Eighteen holes of golf on the course within the park. I was above my game and had a wonderful time.

They suggested that I stay for dinner and the night, but I could not do more than remain for an hour or two after Sir Osmond had left. I was glad of the opportunity this gave me to get better acquainted with Lady Goldsmid. We talked about our families. She expressed her thorough disapproval of primogeniture, told how Sir Osmond had as nephew inherited Somerhill, despite the fact that the previous holder had had eight daughters. She showed me the whole house, the view from the roof, and the gardens. It is a beautiful early seventeenth-century place in perfect condition. Earlier, Sir Osmond had told me as we were playing golf about his relations with his numerous tenants, and of the many activities carried on the estate.

I took the three o'clock train back to London. . . .

Monday, October 8, 1934

Leonard Montefiore came in. We talked about the possibilities of inducing the Treasury to make a grant to the High Commission. He was skeptical but made suggestions as to procedure. I asked him what he thought were the prospects for the joint drive next year. He said the women were anxious, and that he personally favored it even if it had to be carried out without the Rothschilds. He repeated what Bentwich had told me of Dr. Weizmann's suggestion that it would be better for the Zionists not to be tied up again in such an arrangement. As to ICA, Montefiore seemed to take the same view about further development in South America as had Sir Osmond. He is not himself enthusiastic about Hula, for it costs too much in proportion to what it supplies in the way of labor opportunities. I asked him if he would help us with our governmental contacts and in other ways after Bentwich left. He said he would be very glad to do whatever he could.

. . . .

Ran into Dr. Weizmann in the barber shop. He said that Sir Osmond had hinted at the conspiracy to which I had referred a day or two before. I said that I doubted if Sir Osmond was referring to exactly the same conspiracy, that, of course, I could not suggest any change in the British Central Fund obligations, but that I did wonder whether from the American Zionist portion of the drive something might not be done for immigration expenses to Palestine. Dr. Weizmann said that it was still uncertain what was to come from the States, but that he had written to Jerusalem to inquire whether something might be done.

As to the possibility of a joint effort here, Dr. Weizmann said he was opposed to it because he didn't believe in being married to a corpse. I told him of the possibility of my visit to South America, and that I wanted to come to Palestine, but at the moment I could not justify it on any ground of need. He said it would at least help me to see what is going on. Apropos of funds from the States, I confessed my disappointment about the corporation to date, and agreed that unless it soon made funds available it might be fairly said that it had hindered, rather than advanced, the work during the year.

. . . .

Tuesday, October 9, 1934

Busy during most of the day with Bentwich and Miss Sawyer. In the late afternoon Dov Hos, a labor representative from Tel-Aviv came to talk to me about three matters:

(1) Iraq. He reports that anti-Semitism is growing apace there. Jewish papers are being banned, and attacks being made upon Jewish individuals. There are about 100,000 Jews in the midst of an Arab community of some millions. I told him that, of course, Iraq was far removed from my jurisdiction, but that I was interested in what he had to tell me and that if the opportunity arose, I should inquire about it from Vansittart and from Sir Philip Cunliffe-Lister;
(2) The situation of the Jewish socialist Zionists in Russia. According to Hos, these individuals numbering several hundred are discriminated against and through special regulations are deprived of almost any possibility of leaving Russia to go to Palestine. Special visa regulations and travel requirements made necessary £150 to £200 per person for transportation to Palestine. This obviously is prohibitive. Here again, I told him that I had no right to raise questions in regard to Russia. But when he told me that he knew Frankfurter, I suggested that he write to the latter, who might be able to induce the State Department to instruct the American ambassador informally to raise this question with the Russian authorities. I myself, if and when I see the Russian ambassador in London, would, if there were an occasion, make a similar inquiry;
(3) The labor shortage in Palestine. Hos explained how, owing to the shortage of Jewish labor, Jewish workmen were being tempted from the land to the towns and in the towns were being tempted from one job to another by the offer of higher pay. The results were very bad. It endangered the labor movement; it brought a large percentage of Arab labor onto the land, thus going counter to one of the basic principles of Zionism—that there should be Jewish labor on the land; and, moreover, the body of floating Arab labor, induced to come into the country by these conditions, constitutes at once a menace to the health of the community, because they live in an extremely unsanitary way and supply inflammable material which might be ready fuel in case of any disturbance of the peace. The High Commissioner tends to urge the [Jewish] Agency to give a larger proportion of certificates to German refugees, but heretofore has been unwilling to increase the total number of certificates to the extent that conditions warrant. It is imperative that the schedule be increased so that Jewish workmen will not be more and more replaced by Arabs, not only on the land but on the railroads, the public works in Haifa, and elsewhere. In this case too, I said to Hos that it was obvious that I had no right to intervene. I would, however, keep what he said in mind when next I had an opportunity to speak to Sir Philip or to Wauchope.[8]

8. General Sir Arthur Wauchope, high commissioner in Palestine since the end of 1931.

Wednesday, October 10, 1934

In view of the shocking news of the assassination of the Yugoslav King and Barthou,[9] I decided not to press to see the French ambassador today, but instead sent him a formal note of condolence.

Spent nearly two hours with Lord Cecil going over the agenda for the next meeting and discussing many phases of our work in detail. . . . One should include also statements about probable future immigration. In this connection one could refer to the Saar, but without going into the political aspects of that problem. As to the future scope of our work, he felt strongly that I should indicate, if not publicly at least then in a private meeting, my feeling that there should be a definite terminus for the office. He put it, "You cannot continue an emergency organization indefinitely." He recognized that there might be need for a similar organization to deal with Jewish immigration or related matters, but he was sure that this should not be our body, but another organization directly under the League auspices. He doubted that the League would be willing to re-adopt us.

I explained that, so far as the budget of the office is concerned, we would this year spend about a third less than was authorized, and the next year less than this year; that we would probably prepare our budget for a ten months' period, thus giving us time to reconsider our position or to liquidate the office after the next Assembly. I told him of the prospect for funds from Jewish sources in England and the United States. We then talked about the possibility of Christian funds. When I reminded him of the percentage of non-Jews as about 20 percent, whereas the amount of non-Jewish money was less than 5 percent, he said he did not think that was a proper way to approach the matter. But instead of following this up by suggesting that the Christians have a responsibility for all refugees, he said, "The only thing I am sure about in this matter of finance is that the Jews are unwilling to look after any except the Jews. Lord Reading said to me definitely that he and his fellow Jews could not concern themselves with other than their co-religionists." I ventured to say that I thought this was very reasonable. Lord Cecil didn't argue the point, but it was evident that he did not share my view. However, he is to see the archbishop on Friday at the latter's request, [and] will urge him to issue the invitation for Lambeth Palace, and in other ways support our plea.

Lord Cecil thought that my proposed visit to the South American countries would be worthwhile only if there were a reasonable prospect of success, and that this would be likely only if I had some specific project or definite basis to suggest. When I explained to him what the ICA group and I had in mind, he seemed to think that that might work, but he again returned to his idea of group settlement and questioned whether there might not be a possi-

9. On October 9 King Alexander of Yugoslavia was assassinated in Marseilles by a Croat extremist with a forged passport. The assassin wounded French Foreign Minister Louis Barthou, who was accompanying the king on his visit to France. Barthou died needlessly due to the lack of prompt medical attention. The assassin himself was killed.

bility for this in British Guiana. He is a member of the committee charged with trying to find funds for the Assyrians. He admitted, however, that there seemed to him to be little material among the refugees for this sort of group settlement.

Lord Cecil read with much interest my memorandum for Léger on the possibility of governmental contributions to the High Commission. He doubted if the British government would do this unless others took the lead. He said it would be no use to see Sir John Simon and not worthwhile to see the prime minister. One must move through Vansittart and the permanent people in the Foreign Office.

In reference to what I might say about Germany, Lord Cecil thought that it was important to be stiff. Moreover, he would be willing if it seemed desirable, to raise some of the same points in the House of Lords. He was sure that one never got anywhere with the Germans by a policy of gentleness.

....

Thursday, October 11, 1934

Much of the morning spent with the members of the Committee of G.R.A.F.[10] Those present besides myself and Wells[11] and his secretary were Mrs. Dugdale,[12] who acted as chairman, Dr. Fox, Miss Bracey,[13] Mrs. Gould, Miss Ogilvie, and Sir Carl Knudsen, treasurer, and Mrs. Omerod.

He asked me first to explain what the present status of the negotiations with the archbishop were. Then followed a general discussion which centered on the question of ways which their group could help. Miss Bracey said that undoubtedly there was need for the archbishop's leadership, and she hoped that definite plans would be worked out to be presented to the Lambeth group. Miss Gould asked if it was meant to create a new organization. I replied that my ideas as to that were not at all fixed, but I hoped it would be possible to use the G.R.A.F. as the executive. Dr. Fox said he hoped that the Lambeth meeting would not be limited merely to church laymen—that humanitarians outside the churches should also be included. He stressed too the need for definite plans. At the end of the discussion on this phase Sir Carl suggested that his group should perpetuate itself until after the Lambeth conference, and that it should until then and afterwards, if it were decided to carry on, serve the general cause in any way which seemed most effective.

Miss Bracey brought up the problem created by the new transfer regulations. She said that a number of schools would be deprived of a considerable income which heretofore had been available from Germany to pay the tuition of

10. German Refugee Assistance Funding, aiding Christian refugees.

11. Alan M. Wells, executive secretary of G.R.A.F.

12. The Honorable Mrs. Blanche Dugdale, niece of Lord Balfour, cousin of Lord Cecil, and intimately associated with Weizmann in the original Balfour Declaration negotiations. Important member both of the Royal Institute of International Affairs and the League of Nations Union.

13. Bertha Bracey, Society of Friends.

German children. On a monthly basis these sums were Kent £550, Holland £330, Litchfield £135, Hazelmere £150. In addition, numerous individuals would now become dependent. She asked what could be done.

In reply, I explained the plan which the Jewish group here was considering, but had to admit that it might not be available for other groups or individuals. Miss Bracey, pointing to the text of the German regulations, expressed the doubt whether any formal system of clearing would be legal. She feared that to ask individuals in Germany to pay what they had been accustomed to pay outside now into a central fund in Germany in order that funds from the outside which otherwise would have gone into Germany may be available to care for the needs of those dependent upon receipts from Germany, would be to put those persons within Germany at the mercy of the secret police.

The problem of the Catholic refugees and the attitude of the Catholic authorities was brought up by Mrs. Omerod. I expressed the view that there was not likely to be any formal cooperation from the Catholic authorities. This was admitted, but Mrs. Omerod asked why should not Cardinal Bourne here in London be asked to find a way of providing for the Catholic refugees, instead of allowing them to be dependent on the non-Catholic committees. I said I would be glad to put this up to the Cardinal, and to make a similar representation to the Cardinal in Paris.

Mrs. Omerod to me privately expressed her great concern lest Woburn House be closed to [non-Jewish] refugees. In this event she said she would have to discontinue her work altogether, for otherwise her house would be simply overrun. I suggested that she write to Schiff expressing her great appreciation of all that he had done during the last year and a half, but deploring any proposal to discontinue the work at Woburn House.

. . . .

In general, it was the feeling of the group that the Lambeth conference offered the last hope of marshalling Christian forces in this country for any substantial drive. They recognized that their own resources had been exhausted and that the possibility of opening up new avenues by them was not in the least hopeful. Hence they are anxious to cooperate in every way that offers itself.

Lunch at the Noel Bakers with Bentwich. We gossiped during the lunch about the state of the world, which Baker thinks is nearly desperate, owing in considerable part to the unwillingness of His Majesty's Government to take any affirmative line. Baker is sure that England could save the situation, and that if the Labour people come in in time, they will do it.

As to funds for the refugees, Baker himself is unable to help. He suggests, however, that we approach Henderson and, if Henderson advises it, then also the general secretary of the British trade union federation when he returns from the States. It would be useful also to see Gillies of the Labour Party. Baker thought that one could use effectively the argument that if the Labour Party forced Marley to withdraw from his Committee in Aid of the Victims of Fascism, then the Labour Party would be obligated itself to do something for the socialists and trade union refugees.

Baker was much interested in our account of our relations with Marley. Baker thinks there is no chance that Harold Laski or other intellectuals would withdraw from the party on this issue. Baker thinks that while Marley is naive, there is something more in his attitude than naiveté; he is really nearly a Communist. Bentwich and I said that if Baker would write us a letter of inquiry, we would reply setting out in detail our relations with Lord Marley.

Talked with Wurfbain on the telephone, he speaking from Paris. He reported that Lambert had said that Helbronner had been named by the French as governmental representative. I agreed with him that it would be desirable for him to inquire again about this from Fouques-Duparc, but I urged that he move warily, for it would not do to be put in the position of opposing a fait accompli.

Amsterdam, Friday, October 12, 1934

Busy with this and that until just time to get the airplane bus from Victoria Station. The flight to Amsterdam was very fast—only an hour and twenty-five minutes—and uneventful.

I called Rosa Manus[14] and arranged to spend the evening with her. . . . I asked Miss Manus to read the letters from the Red Help Committee [Rote Hilfe, a Communist organization] and the Committee of the Victims of Hitlerism [Fascism], and we then discussed at length what might be done. . . .

In general, Miss Manus was inclined to be a little critical of the large Jewish committee on the ground that they were too exclusively Jewish, and therefore failing to include in their care borderline cases. She recognized, however, the excellency of the work done.

She told me of her own committee and the clubhouse which they had organized and were maintaining on a non-denominational basis.

While we were talking, an old Jewish lady, Frau Paula Gallineck, came to see me on behalf of her son, Dr. Alfred Gallineck. Her story, so like hundreds of others about which one hears, was that of a Jewish family uprooted by the Hitler regime and the beginning of a career of a brilliant young doctor ended—at least so far as Germany is concerned. The father is ailing; the son had just reached the point when he would have been able to care for the family. He is a specialist in neurological research and was about to be named to an important post in the hospital in Frankfurt. However, despite an exceptional record and the support of his professors, he was forced to give up his post.

The mother explained that she had come to see me without the knowledge of her son. She was most anxious that something might be found for him, if not in Holland, then in one of the neighboring countries so that he would not have

14. Rosette Susanna Manus, prominent Dutch feminist, founder of the International Archive for Women. Died in Ravensbrück in 1943.

to go as far afield as America. As she put it, "His father is failing and he is our only son." I told her that I would be glad to see him if he would come early the next day. Her gratitude for this small basis for hope was touching.

Saturday, October 13, 1934

After the usual delicious Dutch breakfast, began my series of conferences. The first was with Stokvis. . . . He told me a good deal about the situation of these refugees in Holland, and of the reasons which made the present government so unwilling to be more generous. The present regime in Holland is not only conservative, but has a distinctly religious tone. Moreover, though the officials in the Foreign Office are inclined to be liberal, they have little influence on the Ministries of Justice and of Police, which deal directly with the refugees.

At quarter of ten Dr. Gallineck[15] came. He is attractive in appearance with a pleasing personality. He explained that while perhaps he might be able to stay in Holland, it would require at least five years' more work before he could practice, and that even at the end permission might be refused. He said of course his father and mother were anxious to have him stay in Europe, but that he saw little hope for himself on the continent, and not much more in England. Could I therefore hold out more hope in America? I explained to him in general the situation in the States, and suggested specifically that since he was a friend of Dr. Einstein, that he write to Otto Nathan giving the details of his situation and ask the latter to get in touch with Miss Razovsky and with Dr. Sachs. He was so grateful that I felt conscience-stricken, for I could have no confidence that my suggestion, though it was the best I could do, would really help him. But that applies to so many other similar situations, when individual refugees appeal to me, that one becomes almost helpless.

A few minutes after ten Dr. Cohen arrived. He told me first of the serious illness of Mrs. Van Tyn, who, overstrained by her continuous work for a year and a half as a director of the large refugee committee, had suffered a temporary but complete breakdown following the opening of the farm at Wieringen the week before. For a few days they despaired of her life. She is now better.

I asked Dr. Cohen if he would read the two long letters in reference to the political refugees. After he had done so, he suggested that he would be glad to make personal inquiries about each case, and where the facts seemed to warrant such action, he would bring up the matter in a personal interview with François in the Foreign Office. Almost none of these cases, he said, could be handled officially because nearly all of them involved a refugee who is either a Communist or accused of communism by the German authorities. These have no standing with the Dutch police and are liable to be expelled if the attention of the police is called to them. Quite frankly I inquired of Dr. Cohen if he thought the political refugee committees would be willing to have him act in this way. Fortu-

15. Dr. Alfred Gallinek, emigrated to New York and became a prominent psychiatrist, as well as an expert on the psychology of the Middle Ages.

nately, at this moment we were joined by Professor D. Van Embden, who said that he would gladly ask the heads of those committees. Later during the day he reported to me that the answer was affirmative, so I promised to send Dr. Cohen copies of the letters immediately on my return to London. Meantime, I explained to both Dr. Cohen and to Dr. Van Embden that we would continue to press the Dutch authorities to be as liberal in their interpretation of the existing regulations affecting the political refugees as possible. But here again, I gave this promise with the less enthusiasm, because I had no reason to feel that our intercessions with The Hague would be effective.

Indeed, such events as the assassinations at Marseilles a few days earlier serve not only as an excuse, but do in fact give to a certain degree added reason for the intolerant attitude of governmental authorities towards the radical political refugees. Because of the excesses of a few, the whole group is penalized. The extent to which this may be true I was to learn a few days later in my first conferences with French officials after the Marseilles tragedy.

Dr. Cohen and I talked about the relations between his large Jewish committee and the other work being done on behalf of the refugees in Holland. I told him that certain of the other groups were inclined to criticize his committee on the ground that they were monopolizing the financial resources, and, by their elaborate publicity in connection with Wieringen, were making it difficult for such efforts as that of the Halutz or of the Quakers at Ommen to secure the essential support. To this, Dr. Cohen replied that it was not his fault if the other committees had kept their lights under cover. Moreover, the proceeds of that night's meeting were not to be restricted to Wieringen, but were to be available for all the phases of Jewish work in Holland. This seemed to me a conclusive answer.

. . . .

Professor Van Embden, who teaches economics in the University of Amsterdam, explained interestingly the situation of the political refugees, and the practices of the German [*sic,* should be Dutch] government towards them. Rarely do these officials literally expel a refugee. Their practice is to take them to Sittard, a small town in Lemberg, very near both the Belgian and the German frontiers. There the refugees are left, presumably with a parting word from the police that they must leave the country, it being no concern to the police whether they go to Germany or Belgium. In the first case they risk re-arrest and imprisonment; in the second case they risk a new expulsion.

An additional factor which worsens the conditions of the political refugees is the power exercised by the local authorities to expel. There is a movement on foot to withdraw this power, and limit it to the federal authorities, but it seemed to be unlikely to succeed.

Three representatives of the Vereeniging tot Vakopleiding van Palestina-Pioniers, the Dutch Halutz, came to tell me of their needs. The spokesmen were R. Cohen (a brother of Dr. Cohen), Dr. R. Polak, and E. Visser. Miss Hururtz is the secretary. When they were announced, Dr. Cohen asked me whether he should remain, but asked it in such a way that it left me free to tell him that I thought perhaps it would be better if he left, thus leaving the others an opportunity to speak more frankly about the larger committee. He agreed.

The Haluz representatives said that they did not wish to complain about the larger committee, but that they were fearful of being undercut by it. They then explained the nature of their work, placing young men and women on Dutch farms and training them there for life in Palestine, and all of this on a much more economical basis than was possible at Wieringen. Theirs was a membership organization, had been carrying on its operations for nearly twenty years, had established close and friendly cooperation with the farmers, received workers from all parts of Europe, now had more than 100 on the farms, and could have twice as many if the money were available. They raised particularly the question of more [Palestine] certificates for women. They hoped that I might be able to speak to Wauchope or Sir Philip Cunliffe-Lister about this. I said I would do so informally, when the occasion offered. They urged me to come and see their work. I said I would like to do so when I next came to Holland.

A little after twelve I went with Miss Rosa Manus to her club for refugees. There we first met four or five members of her committee, each of whom told me of a different phase of the club work, the library, the canteen, etc. etc. We then walked through the building. In the largest room used for a canteen and general recreation center there were already gathered a dozen or two refugees. One of them came up to me and explained that he was without any adequate papers; he had gone to the German Consulate to ask for a passport, had been given one good for only three days, and only for return to Germany. This, of course, was of no use, for he felt he did not dare go back to Germany. Another refugee showed me his card from the Dutch police. It was a sort of identification paper, requiring him to report once a month. He wished to have a passport instead, but had been unable to secure it.

On the whole, the club impressed me very favorably. It offers at nominal cost a place for meetings, and must do much to maintain the morale of the refugees.

Nonetheless, Miss Manus and her colleagues were frank to admit that many of those who were in their charge were unwilling to do any work at all unless they could work at the job for which they were trained. In other words, they could not get any volunteer workers to do painting or repairing or fitting up of the club. Instead able-bodied men would sit around and play cards or talk by the hour. Those who were willing to do manual work had mostly gone to Wieringen.

Back to the hotel in time for lunch with Herbert May. He asked me if I had any messages, that he was telephoning the next day, and could transmit anything that I requested. I told him I wished to have further data on the workings of the new [Nazi] decrees about the employment of young people below the age of twenty-five, and also about the most recent of the transfer regulations which affect so adversely the situation of the children and many of the adult refugees. His own opinion of the situation in Germany was that while economic conditions were progressively worse, they would not be bad enough during the winter to endanger the regime. He said, as had several others, that there was an increasing anti-German feeling in Holland.

At 1:30 Mr. and Mrs. Harold Beenhower came to take me to play golf. He is Dutch, a representative of an American banking house. She is an American. On the way out he talked about Dr. Schacht and the German practices in reference to international payments. According to him, none of the clearing arrangements are working—the Germans manipulating their imports and exports in such a way as to destroy any balance which might be available for such payments. To his mind, Dr. Schacht never had any intention of paying. He talked also about our friends in banking circles in Germany.

The course, which lay along the sea amidst the dunes which gave it a most hilly appearance, was beautifully planned and in excellent condition. The weather too was perfection—warm with no wind. And even more extraordinary, my game was not too bad. At times I had as many as four good drives in succession. Even my iron shots were passable. It seems that the less I play, the better I do it.

Back to the hotel a little after six, and late for my appointment with Miss P. She was waiting for me downstairs, and I asked her to come up to the room. While we had a cup of tea, she told me the first installment of her story. Her father and mother, both Jews, felt forced to leave Germany after Hitler came in. They went to San Francisco. There her mother became seriously ill and returned to Germany, where she died three months ago. The girl had left Germany several months previous. She had come to Amsterdam; her papers in perfect order, she was able to find work as an instructor of athletics for girls. This gave her sufficient [means] to keep herself, but six months ago she met a young man, a fellow refugee, just after he reached Amsterdam. That was the beginning of the second, and much more troubled, chapter in her personal life. But this account had to be postponed, because I was due to go out to dinner in a quarter of an hour and had to dress first. Therefore, we arranged to meet after the evening meeting, she to bring her friend with her.

At quarter of seven went out with Dr. Cohen and Mr. Asscher to the Carlton Hotel, where we joined Mr. Van den Bergh, Judge Visser, Mr. Cohen, and the man whose Dutch name translated into English is Goldsmith. Asscher was in good spirits. He told me about working from early in the morning until midnight for many months on the program which he had been asked by the Dutch government to formulate for the Dutch diamond industry. It was just getting under way, and promised to be a success, for they hoped to undersell their competitors in many parts of the world.

. . . .

During the meal I talked with the man at my right about Miss P. and her friend. He has known her almost from the beginning, when she came to Holland, for one of her relatives had called his attention to her and one of her mother's requests just before she died was that he maintain his interest in her. She and her friend had been at his house for dinner the night before. He knew their story in detail, had spoken to the chief of the local police about it; the latter had said it was a very difficult case because of the young man's Communist connections earlier, and because he was without any visible means of support, and, of course, also because he was without any papers whatsoever. It might be necessary to appeal to the Ministry of Justice at The Hague in the event the chief of police felt he could not himself take the responsibility for making an exception to the general rule. I said that I was sorry that there was no chance for me to go to The Hague. My neighbor then said that perhaps if he explained to the chief of police my personal interest in this case, that might be sufficient. In any event, he would let me know.

There was general talk about the new difficulties created by the latest transfer regulations. They said that they did not see how the farm at Wieringen could carry on if all the income from Germany were cut off.

Asscher was, as I thought, foolishly optimistic that there might be such a change in Germany in the next few months as would change fundamentally the Jewish situation. . . .

After dinner we went directly to the conservatory, where we found three hundred to three hundred and fifty people gathered. Asscher was chairman. I was asked to speak first. I talked for about thirty-five minutes, pleading for the Dutch to continue to show the world that the Jewish community in Holland, in proportion to its numbers and resources, could be more generous than any other community.

After my talk there was a tea, during which I had a chance to talk with a number of persons. One of the rabbis thanked me much more than I deserved for what I am trying to do. This same group of Portuguese Dutch Jews whom I had met the week previous at Wieringen told me of their appreciation. . . .

There was an opportunity during the tea to chat for a little while with Mr. Eitje, the member of the committee whose specialty is to arrange for passports for the refugees. He said that 150 had been issued by the Dutch government, but all of these for persons who were preparing to leave Holland. I then asked him what about the friend of Miss P.—would he talk to the man who had interested himself in their case, and then tell me what he thought could be done? This he did, and later told me that he thought the case peculiarly difficult, but he would do what he could.

. . . .

Back to the hotel in Asscher's car, at 11:30—just one hour late for my appointment with Miss P. and her friend.

The three of us walked over to a nearby café and talked over our drinks in low tones of voice, for the place was crowded. What a contrast there was between my two companions, weighted down with the tragic uncertainly of their future, and our neighbors, carefree enjoying their beer or coffee, and unconscious that they were living in a country whose type of freedom is becoming less and less the rule in Europe.

During the course of an hour and a half I eked out from the talk of my two young companions the second chapter of their story. He, a scene painter, had been until the spring of 1933 an enrolled member of the Communist Party in Germany. But a month or so after he had withdrawn, his house was searched, illegal newspapers—Communist and others—were found; he was arrested, sent to a concentration camp, and there confined for six months, during which he, like most of the others who would not tell on their former colleagues, suffered ill-treatment. He insisted, however, that the German authorities have not been able to find proof that he had been a member of the Communist Party, and therefore, their records would not have this charge against him. He had been released as a part of a wider amnesty move, but fearful of re-arrest at any time and unable to secure legal permission to leave, he had left the country illegally and without papers. He had come to Amsterdam, met Miss P., they had fallen in love, and that had been his only occupation since.

I told them of my talks during and after dinner, of my feeling that there was at least a fair chance that his position might be regularized without an appeal to The Hague, but towards this end it was very important that he should, if possible, make clear that he had ceased to be a Communist before his arrest; that I would be willing to intervene with the authorities later if it became clear that such action was necessary and offered a prospect of success.

Then she asked about the possibility of going abroad, having heard that it was easier to secure a passport if one were leaving Holland. I confirmed her impression on this score, but asked her where she thought he could go. She suggested Great Britain or the United States. I pointed out some of the technical difficulties, and that, in addition, it would mean their separation. She replied, "not at all, for I shall go with him." I asked her what about her job; she said that didn't matter, she would be able to get another job, much more quickly than he would be able to find work, and that they could in this way get on. And so they might, but it will be a hard job convincing either the British or the American authorities, who unfortunately are not moved by the kinds of considerations which are actuating these two youngsters. The girl is 26, and the boy 25.

Finally, at one o'clock, when there seemed to be nothing more that could be said that would give any cheer or be of any use, the three of us walked out together to find the weather changed into a cold rain. I asked where she lived. She said a half an hour away by trolley. He said that he would take her home in a taxi. I immediately had visions of his spending two or three desperately needed guilders, so we went together to the hotel, and against their protests, I gave the driver something extra, and they drove off together.

As I went to bed, I was struck by one fact in a long and busy day. It had been two women—the mother of Dr. Gallinger and Miss P.—who had taken the initiative on behalf of the men who needed help.

Amsterdam-London, Sunday, October 14, 1934

Breakfast with Mr. Ariens Kappers, president of the school committee of the Quaker institution at Ommen. He told me of their need for additional funds, especially now that new transfer restrictions would deprive them of more than £300 per month. He did not see how they could carry on unless some clearing arrangement could be made for this sum. I told him of what was being planned by the British Central Fund in this regard, and suggested that he communicate with Miss Bracey of the Friends Committee in London to inquire from her whether some similar arrangement could be worked out. He urged me to come and see the school, and as I had said to Haluz, I said to him that I hoped I might do so later.

An hour's conference with Dr. V. and his wife. He thinks the Saar will return to Germany. He disagrees with those Jewish leaders who would use the Saar as a lever against the Hitler regime; that, he thinks, would only make matters worse.

As to the problem of transfers, he is confident there will be no abatement of the recent restrictions. He told me of personal experiences with the Devisen authorities which seem to show conclusively that no concessions will be made, but rather that severer restrictions may be expected.

Economic conditions are undoubtedly bad in the Reich. The Ersatz program is futile; indeed, as was pointed out to me the day before, Dr. Schacht's talks about Ersatz to frighten Germany's creditors has [*sic*] the effect of frightening even more the prospective purchasers of German goods. Instances were cited to me of large orders which had been countermanded or goods returned because of the fear or the knowledge that substitute materials had been used in the manufacture. This applied particularly to textiles, automobiles, tires, etc.

My general impression of Dr. V. is that of a brilliant, perhaps predominantly self-seeking, lawyer. He is undoubtedly 100 percent German, but I should not be willing to accept the charge made against him that he plays fast and loose with the members of his own community in order to retain for himself a special position with the regime. I should like to talk with him more at length.

While Dr. V. and I were talking, the old man who had spoken to me the night before came to keep his appointment. By that time I should have been ready to leave for the airport, so I invited him to come up to my room and talk to me while I packed. His is the story of the refugee made worse by old age. An engineer and an inventor who had lived for twenty or more years in the States and had accumulated there a substantial fortune, he went back to Germany during the war. Then came the Hitler regime. He is now short of funds, though on the verge of completing a new process for making carbons of letters without carbon paper. He needs money to go on, and thinks that he could find this in England if he could secure permission to enter. I knew nothing to say to him that would be of any help, so I fell back on the too frequently used resort of asking him to write me the details to London. I didn't hold out more than a tiny bit of encouragement. But even that I am afraid cannot be made effective.

To the airport to take the 12:15 plane to London, only to find that there would be a delay of two hours because the connecting plane from Malmo had been forced down by a shortage of petrol, the result of fighting head winds for five hours. While waiting, had lunch and worked on my notes, and took off at 2:15 arriving in London two hours and a quarter later. The return trip taking forty minutes longer than the one to Amsterdam the previous Friday.

At the hotel I found the Wurfbains and Olive Sawyer, so we had tea together.

....

Out to supper with K. S. During the meal Helbronner and Louis Oungre passed us. I chatted with them for a few minutes, first offering my sympathy to Helbronner for the Marseilles tragedy [in which Foreign Minister Barthou was assassinated together with Yugoslavia's King Alexander I]. He told me that he had been talking with Barthou just a day or two before. He added that as perhaps I knew, he had been named as the official representative of the French government on the High Commission Governing Body. I made some acknowledgment, more incoherent than enthusiastic.

To see the film *The Unfinished Symphony,* but was more amused by an unannounced detective film which preceded the feature.

London, Monday, October 15, 1934

Dr. Kahn came in. He left with me a memorandum on the situation in Prague. He told me of the discussions at the meetings the day previous, the references to the High Commission were all friendly enough. It was not formally discussed, but some reference was made to the budget, and it was indicated that the Americans and the ICA would share as before; but nothing was said about the British Central Fund, though Schiff and another representative was present. There was discussion also, though again rather in passing, of the proposal for a Paris loan kassa. The important thing which was said was a categoric statement by Helbronner that the French wanted no such institution in Paris. The implication was clear that he was speaking not merely for the French Jewish community, but also for the French government. If this latter point proves on inquiry to be exact, then the prospects for an amelioration of the situation in France are gloomy, for as Dr. Kahn says, one cannot set up a loan kassa against the will of those who must help administer it, and through whom regulations making for success must be provided. Moreover, unless something of this sort can be done within France, there will be increased and probably insuperable difficulties in securing funds outside for emigration—the only objective which, according to Helbronner, interests the French.

Telephoned Dr. Don at Lambeth, and fixed a definite date for the archbishop's conference—5:30 in the afternoon of October 30. I did not definitely say that the archbishop was committed to sending the invitations himself, but left the way open for that interpretation.

In the afternoon acted as chairman of the meeting at Friends' House of some experts on the question of group settlement. Sir Geoffrey of the Dominions Office, commonly credited with being the chief author of that office's recent report on group settlement, made the chief statement, outlining the general principles which should be taken into account in group settlement. Then followed a discussion participated in by Miss Bracey and Miss Pye of the Friends, Jeffries also of the Friends, Bentwich and a representative of the Parana Company [in Brazil]. From the talk emerged the general conclusion that it would be preferable to send small groups of settlers into the Parana area, where they could fuse with the existing German settlements there, rather than attempt to establish themselves in wholly new areas. The Quakers said that there should be made a more careful inquiry as to the numbers of refugees available to go under leadership to such communities, and that at the same time endeavors should be made to find the funds. They themselves could not be responsible for raising the money, but they would be glad to participate in the attempt which they felt should be a part of the program for the Lambeth conference.

Then to see the French ambassador. After general talk about the situation created by the Marseilles assassination I repeated, perhaps with some added emphasis, the arguments which I had made to Léger in reference to the national interest of France in the refugee problem and the alternative in case the French government did not see fit to cooperate by making it possible to settle a certain number of the refugees in France. The ambassador recognized something of the national interest, but took exception to the suggestion that if France did not act, it would be left to bear the burden alone. He said, "That, of course, is an argument equivalent to a threat which could not be admitted in the discussion." I, of course, replied that no threat was intended, but I was merely stating the situation as it had been presented to me time and again by the Jewish leaders in the United States and Great Britain. He countered by stressing the difficulty of the French position, particularly following the Marseilles assassinations. He had had no word as to the decision of the French government as to a contribution to the High Commission. He then recited the difficulties. I told him that I hoped there might be an answer before the Governing Body meeting.

We talked about Helbronner as the governmental representative. I explained the possibility of confusion between his two roles, intimated that his views as a French Jew might not be the same as those of the French government. The ambassador replied that he thought perhaps the Jews were more identical than I had believed; that, of course, there was a possibility of confusion in the two roles, and that it would be preferable if Helbronner resigned from the Advisory Council.

Before leaving, we talked about the political situation, Germany's need for credits, the attitude of Washington, my own attitude, etc. I told him of my experience with Dr. Schacht in Washington. I left with the feeling that he, as well as Léger, would consider the High Commission a useful institution, even though they might insist on policies which would render its work more difficult.

Alone to see Jack Buchanan in a rather amusing musical comedy, but I was only entertained intermittently.

Tuesday, October 16, 1934

Walter Adams came in to report on his trip to Portugal. The specific results were rather scant, though encouraging as far as they go. There are possibilities of three or four intellectuals being accepted there. . . .

Conference with Sir Leonard Cohen at his house. We talked first about the situation in France. Then he at some length inquired why nothing had been done to follow up the memoranda on South America supplied by Oungre. He seemed to feel that I would be hurt by his bluntness. I made it clear that quite the contrary was the case. I gave my interpretation of my relations with Louis Oungre during recent months, and then explained my present plan to go to South America. Sir Leonard thought this an excellent idea, and that the ICA would cooperate.

As I was leaving, he said he hoped that now that he was no longer officially at the head of things I would not quit coming to see him. I assured him that I would come as before. At the very beginning of our talk I was touched by a message that had been sent by him that morning, inquiring about Barbara.

With Bentwich to Transport House to see the trade union officials—Middleton and Smith. They were much more receptive to our suggestion that labor make another effort on behalf of the socialist and trade union refugees than we expected. They are bringing the matter up at a conference next Tuesday, and made various suggestions for the meeting at Lambeth Palace. Middleton thought it desirable that there be a week set aside during which the churches and labor could make an appeal, if not together, then on the same basis. It was left that Bentwich should supply them with additional data, and they would inform us of the action of their group.

Wednesday, October 17, 1934

. . . .

Lunch with Kurt Battsek.[16] He talked very interestingly about the effects of the Devisen regulations; said they would affect some 600 refugees in England alone, and would involve an amount of about £9,000 a month; that to effect a clearing arrangement would require the formal consent of the German government which the representatives of German Jewry would undertake to try to secure in the next few days. He said that the three German representatives—Kreutzberger,[17] Hirsch, and Borchardt—had arrived the day before with ten Marks apiece in their pockets; that a few days ago a German businessman had

16. Kurt Battsek, of the Experts' Committee, newcomer to settlement possibilities.

17. Max Kreutzberger, director of the Zentralfahrstelle der deutchen Juden, a social worker and community leader. In 1955 he became the first director of the Leo Baeck Institute in New York City.

been refused more than ten Marks despite his statement that he was coming to sell goods in England. The reply to him was that he could borrow from his customers. Nonetheless, Devisen is still available for Germans who wish to buy dollar bonds.

Schiff is now interested in the possibility of a campaign to place 500 children in English homes. I warned Battsek of the possibility of not being able to get the children, even if the women's campaign were diverted in that direction. Nothing has yet been settled about a new drive here.

Battsek knows Koch-Weser[18] very well and understands that the latter is happy in the Parana. Battsek had just written yesterday to Koch-Weser, asking him about the possibilities of German immigration to that area.

....

On the way out from lunch met Dr. Hirsch, who was lunching with Mr. and Mrs. Robert Kauffmann. The latter, I had learned a few days ago, had not committed suicide, as Bernhard Kahn had reported to me on our way to Amsterdam.

Tea with Nahum Goldmann. Chatted about various aspects of the Jewish political situation. He was shocked by Helbronner's appointment; said that though the Alliance was growing closer to his group, he was inclined to think that his people ought to lead a fight against the French Jewish official position and try to persuade the French government to take a different line. I judge that his associate Ballock, who is now the owner of the two most powerful financial journals in Paris and who has on his paid contributors' list such men as Laval, Tardieu, Bérenger et al., is a really influential man whom I should see—probably more influential than Asscher's brother. In Amsterdam the latter had said if I would let him know when I was going to Paris, his brother would arrange everything for me.

I neglected in summarizing my Dutch conversation to say that Professor Van Embden had suggested a possible solution for the political refugees who at present, or at least those who are accused of communism or of other subversive political activities, are shunted back and forth hopelessly across various frontiers. He thought the Dutch government might, for example, establish a sort of internment camp where these refugees would be maintained by the state until the present period in Germany ended and permitted their return. Professor Cohen thought there was something in the idea, as did Miss Rose Manus.

Dinner with Robert Kauffmann. Our talk, which lasted nearly four hours, ranged over a wide field, and was by no means concentrated on Portugal.

(1) He amplified his Portuguese report by stressing the great willingness of the Portuguese community to help in the settlement of Jewish refugees and of

18. Erich Koch-Weser, member of the German Democratic Party, as well as vice-chancellor, interior minister, justice minister at various times during the Weimar Republic. Went into exile after the Nazi takeover. Settled in Parana, Brazil, 1933.

their ability to do so, but he thought that over a period not more than sixty or seventy families could find opportunities there.

(2) He thinks the refugees are returning to Germany now in larger numbers than are coming out. The new transfer regulations will hasten this return process. He doubts if there are nearly as many refugees in France as the French claim. All of them have been required to leave the border *départments* and go to the interior. He has a friend who, for example, had a business in Metz and was required to move to Paris, continues his work in Metz by leaving for Paris each Friday night and returning each Monday morning. His evasion of the regulations is doubtless known to the police, but he is tolerated.

(3) Economically, conditions in Germany are not so bad. In several industries there is even a sort of boom. The Mark is not in danger, for in an authoritarian state the currency can be controlled almost indefinitely. Similarly, a considerable measure of economic discontent, etc. may exist without even shaking the regime.

(4) Fundamentally Hitlerism, at least in that aspect of it which consists in its dictatorship, is but one manifestation of a new age. Other signs are Lenin and Communism, Mussolini and Fascism, and in varying degrees other forms of dictatorships or semi-dictatorships, even, in a sense, the New Deal. It is too early to tell what will be the ultimate outcome of these manifestations. The old regimes are shaken by forces which they neither understand nor can control. The new regimes are experimental, but can not be exorcised away through denunciation. No one can tell how long the transition period will last. The world, including even the United States, may be in for many years of severe crisis, involving perhaps deprivation for tens of millions before new forces are successfully harnessed and made to serve mankind.

(5) The attitude of French bureaucracy and of the French Jewish community is creating violent hatred among the refugees in France and making out of the refugees centers of anti French propaganda wherever they go. It is even being said in refugee circles that they will welcome an opportunity to be in the front line in the next German attack on France. I suggested that in part the attitude of the French might be explained by the *bei uns* [in our country] proclivities of the refugees, but Kauffmann retorted by saying that of course many of the refugees were young and had not learned to remain silent, but they could not help contrasting the courteous way in which they are treated by the 100 percent Nazi consular officials in Paris with the contemptuous attitude of the French officials in the prefecture of the police.

(6) Schacht—whom Dr. Kauffmann knows well—he characterized essentially a peasant, with the latter's narrowness of mind, pig-headedness, and sly cunning. He had known Schacht as a young man, and they had been associated in certain political activities, and he had followed Schacht's development closely throughout. He had a strong position with Hitler, because Hitler knows nothing of economics and thinks that others must, and that Schacht

is the best informed of all. Schacht uses Hitler's ignorance and dependence on him to force from the Führer concessions from time to time.

(7) The present French unwillingness to accept German settlers seems all the stranger to Dr. Kauffmann in view of the fact that, repeatedly through the centuries, the French have been tolerant in their reception of foreigners, and invariably within a generation or two these have become completely French. So would the German Jews if given an opportunity.

(8) Dr. Kauffmann's personal plans are to remain in England for five or six or more weeks, and then, if he does not find anything which fits his needs, he hopes to go to the States after the turn of the year.

About midnight said good bye to Dr. Kauffmann and went to bed.

Thursday, October 18, 1934

Conference with Dr. Kreutzberger.

(1) He left me a memorandum explaining the situation of re-training in different countries, and summing up the request which he had to make to me about Latvia, Lithuania, France, and Czechoslovakia.

(2) The difficulty of transfers was not so serious from his point of view unless the British group, failing to work out a satisfactory clearing arrangement, refused to send funds into the Reich. He and his colleagues were to approach the official in the Wirtschaftsministerium [Economics Ministry] promptly. However, he saw no great hardship in the enforced return of students or even of children who were being educated abroad. There are too many Jewish professionals now. Of course, life outside is more pleasant. He admitted that the transfer difficulty would be serious upon adults dependent upon German funds and unable to return.

(3) He had little that was new on the workings of the new law about the employment of young people under the age of twenty-five. It was too early to tell how these will affect the Jews.

(4) He placed a very low estimate on the number of refugees in France, not more than 5,000.

(5) He is doubtful if there will be a drive in England next year.

(6) He said he hoped I would come to Germany, but it would, of course, be impossible for him or his colleagues to see me there. They had not gotten beyond the situation of nearly a year ago when they asked for permission to come to Lausanne and were refused. It was agreed, however, that I would let L. [Lola Hahn?] know when I was to be in Prague, that she might meet me there.

(7) He confirmed what Miss Sawyer had reported to the effect that it was not permitted for a refugee outside to use his own funds in Germany freely in the care of relatives or otherwise.

. . . .

To the Foreign Office for an half hour's conference with Sargent. I outlined the situation of the High Commission. He seemed sympathetic on the question of a contribution, suggested that if I would supply him with an *aide mémoire,* he would take it up promptly, and will I think urge it strongly.[19]

We then talked about the Saar. He thinks that there will be a substantial German majority: that the territory will return to the Reich, and the mines with it; that there is no basis in the treaty for the retention of property as a pledge for the payment of the mines; that the French would not be supported if they insisted on such a questionable interpretation; that the time for a preventive war had passed; there is no real support for it in France. I asked him whether he supposed the League action would be fairly prompt after the date of the plebiscite. He said that this would be clearer after a special meeting of the Council in November, but he supposed there would be no unnecessary delay.

Half-jestingly, as I was leaving, I quoted Dr. Kauffmann, without mentioning the name, to the effect that it was discouraging that within twenty years England should have forgotten the lessons of 1914 when, had Sir Edward Grey let Germany know that Great Britain would not remain neutral, there would have been no war. Sargent gave me no real answer.

. . . .

Dinner with Bentwich at the home of Sir Arthur Wauchope. We were the only guests. Talked before and during dinner about music, Bach, American politics, and not until about ten o'clock did we get down to Palestinian [Zionist] or Jewish affairs.

(1) Wauchope outlined at some length the problem of emigration, indicated that he felt that a rise in the number of immigrants from 4,000 to 40,000 within the period of his administration was as much as could be reasonably expected, but hinted that for next year they might calculate on a total immigration of 50,000. Nonetheless, he expressed considerable anxiety lest there be a period of acute indigestion in case the present boom conditions suffered any considerable slump. Moreover, he is a little troubled by the possibility of workers who have been brought in for specific jobs, such as electrification or cement works, not being absorbed later in other activities. He recognized that perhaps his Scotch character made him more cautious than others might be, but he was anxious not to leave to his successor a problem created by a policy based on excessive optimism now.

After he had talked some time on this subject, he turned to me and

19. The Foreign Office rejected the idea, saying it "raised a fundamental question of principle in which . . . we can not compromise." Sargent to McDonald, October 29, 1934, National Archives (United Kingdom), FO 371/17701, C 7043/23/18.

asked me point blank: "What do you think I ought to allow as a total for immigration? I have talked with all of the interested parties, Jewish and non-Jewish, but it seems to me that your view being that of a person who approaches the problem from a quite new angle, would be of value to me." This direct request was a little embarrassing. I replied, "It would be presumptuous for me to give a categorical reply, for obviously my knowledge of conditions in Palestine is not sufficient on which to base a judgment. Moreover, I am not a disinterested party, for naturally I should like to have as many of the refugees go to Palestine as possible. However, it does seem to me that the probabilities are that since Palestine has thus far been able to make striking progress despite adverse world conditions, it will be able to continue as conditions elsewhere gradually improve. In addition, I hope that you will in your policy show that Palestine has not fallen victim to the nearly universal feeling that human material is a liability and not an asset. For surely it remains true now fundamentally as in the past, that suitable immigration, bringing with it not only capital in the ordinary sense, but the more valuable intangible capital of human energy, tends to create wealth and new opportunities for additional immigrants. Especially should this [should be, this should] be true in Palestine, where the immigrants bring with them the idealism and moral fervor which is such a definite asset." Along these general lines I tried to emphasize the importance and the probable soundness of a liberal policy.

(2) After swearing us to complete secrecy, Wauchope said that the [Jewish] Agency in Palestine, though its representatives there did not put it boldly, were opposed to certificates being granted to the refugees. Their argument is that the various refugee committees are not as careful in their choice of immigrants as they ought to be, are inclined on the contrary to get rid of undesirables. To what extent did I think this charge was justified? Wauchope continued that he naturally was anxious to do as much for the refugees as possible, but that he must make the welfare of Palestine his primary consideration. He indicated that Dr. Weizmann did not share the view of the Agency executives in Jerusalem.

I said that I was not particularly surprised at the attitude of the Zionist officials, but I was very doubtful that there was any substantial basis for their charge. Moreover, I was under the impression that the Agency authorities checked the choice of immigrants from among the refugees. Bentwich did not seem to think this was the case. In view of the difference of opinion between Bentwich and myself as to the facts of procedure, we were not in a very strong position to urge the claims of the refugees.

Nonetheless, I am sure that the point raised is important, and that we cannot allow the refugees to be discriminated against and, if necessary, we should ourselves head up some checking agency which would remove any ground for suspicion that the local committees were sending undesirables, and thus making it easier for the Zionist authorities in Jerusalem to urge that the allotment for the refugees be cut down still lower.

(3) Women among the immigrants. I told Wauchope of the views expressed in Holland and elsewhere that more of the labor certificates should be allocated to single women. He indicated that he would be willing to do this, but that the Agency authorities did not favor it. Bentwich admitted that this latter attitude in part probably grew out of the fact that there was a good deal of fictitious certification about marriages in order to bring the women in.
(4) The labor schedule. Bentwich argued that the actual needs in the country called for an enlargement of this schedule. Wauchope replied that he would willingly enlarge it, but he would have to cut somewhere else, for he did not wish to have the total immigration above a certain figure. Bentwich suggested that the need for additional laborers was so important to meet the economic situation and also to maintain a proper balance of Jews on the land and in the trades, as compared with sedentary occupations, that he would favor increasing the cash requirement for the so-called "capitalist immigrants" if that were necessary to enable Wauchope to bring in more laborers. I, not feeling myself sufficiently informed, refrained from expressing any definite view.
(5) We did not discuss directly or indirectly Trans-Jordan.
(6) As we were leaving, I said to Wauchope that I hoped the next time we met it might be in Palestine, that thus far I had not gone out because I had not been able to find reasons sufficient to justify my taking the time off, for I did not see what I could do there. Then I added half jokingly, "Of course, I should be delighted to come if there was any hope that I might there do something of a spectacular nature to increase the number of immigrants or in other ways aid the refugees." Wauchope quick as a flash shot back, "Well, don't attempt anything of that sort." We laughed about the matter, but from the exchange one could deduce that I would be welcome, but that the occasion of my visit should not be utilized either directly or indirectly to try to secure changes in the attitude of the government. I should, therefore, have to go technically on a personal visit and eschew while there any activities which would be justifiably interpreted as political. This seemed to be also Bentwich's interpretation as we discussed the matter on our way home.

I liked Wauchope. I had not realized before that he was an old soldier who had made a name for himself as the head of the Inter-Allied Armament Control Commission in Germany. He is skeptical of the possibility of Germany's rearming with heavy guns. His interests are very wide and his devotion to Palestine deep, while his sympathy for the Jewish aspirations there is marked. Incidentally, I should perhaps have noted above that when we were discussing the question of the total number of immigrants, he said that political considerations were not influencing his decision at all.

Friday, October 19, 1934

Talked on the telephone with Sir Robert Waley-Cohen. He made only one suggestion in reference to the Lambeth Palace conference, but said that he might send me other names after he had conferred with some of the people in the City. I doubted it.

Geoffrey Pyke[20] came to the office to explain to me his plan to set up an institute for research on the question of anti-Semitism. He showed me the text of six or seven letters to appear successively in the *Times,* the first by himself, the second by a distinguished list of scientists, the third by a similar list of public men, the fourth by a similar list of Jews, the fifth by men of affairs in the City, a sixth if I were willing by myself. As he outlined his plan, I was more and more taken with it.

I told him that if he would draft a letter, I should be glad to consider signing it. Moreover, if he would communicate with me again before I sailed for New York, I would be glad to see whether it would be practicable for me to raise with Fosdick and Dr. Day the question of the Rockefeller participation and possibly also a similar question to Keppel. I told him that I thought an absolute essential, however, would be to limit the Jewish funds to 50 percent and not to proceed more rapidly than equal funds could be found from non-Jewish sources; that perhaps the best procedure would be to try for a relatively small sum, perhaps £10,000, to set up an international committee of distinguished scientists through whom the plans for the research could be worked out. He agreed to this, but doubted whether it would be necessary to limit the Jewish funds, provided that the auspices for the research were those that he desired, that is, comparable to those of the Royal Society.

Lunch with Melchett at Imperial Chemicals House. After informal talks about many subjects, we got down to the problem of next year. Melchett asked what I planned to do. I told him in some detail, stressing my idea of the allocation of an approximate 20,000 of German immigrants, refugees and others, half to Palestine, somewhat less than a quarter to North America, and most of the balance to South America, and of my tentative plan to try to work out a basis with Argentina and Brazil. He enthusiastically favored this whole program, and was impressed, as was Sir Osmond, by Herbert May's approach to the immigration question. He thought that the only practicable basis.

As to financial prospects for next year, Melchett, after telling me about the difficulties he as chairman of the drive had experienced, said that he doubted if such an effort could be repeated. He favored, therefore, a different approach. Having whipped up the enthusiasm of the Jewish community twice by pointing to the horrors of the Hitler regime and the possibilities of its spread, the appeal on that basis was exhausted; they should turn now and picture a new heaven—that is, make an enthusiastic Zionist appeal. He favored allocating from such

20. Eccentric British-Jewish inventor, who, after becoming rich in the stock market, became involved in anti-Nazi causes. In 1940 he invented Pykrete, a sawdust and ice mixture that was seriously considered by Churchill and Mountbatten as an "unsinkable" material for building warships. He was later involved in Operation Plough, an attempt to destroy Norwegian industry to prevent its use by the Germans.

funds as much money as could be properly set aside for training in Germany or outside of immigrants to Palestine, the cost of their transportation, their setting up in the country, and, of course, a contribution towards the upkeep of the office of the High Commission. Incidentally, I had told him that I hoped that my part of the work might be finished during this next year. He replied that he would consider this a great loss, for there were so few people who were willing to approach the problem as I did.

We spoke briefly of Trans-Jordan, but as something for the future. On the whole, I was satisfied with the interview, and inclined to agree with him that an enthusiastic Zionist drive might give as much to the work for the refugees as could be secured in any other way. Incidentally, this shifted basis might enable the Rothschilds to save their face and still head a new effort.

Long conference with Dr. Don at Lambeth Palace about the details for the meeting there on the thirtieth.

We agreed on the list to be submitted to the archbishop, and also on the draft of a letter. Dr. Don doubted if it would be helpful to have representatives of the Jewish community at the conference, which was to concern itself with the needs of the Christian refugees. He thought that some of the members of the conference might speak more freely if there were only Christians present.

. . . .

Saturday, October 20, 1934

Extremely interesting conference at the hotel with Mr. Fritz Stern.[21] His father had organized the alcohol industry of Germany, and had established important branch activities in Holland, France, Spain, and elsewhere. They had also an office equipment business. But when the Hitler regime made it impossible for governmental or municipal purchasers to buy from Jewish firms, it was made clear that they must withdraw from the office business, and later from their other affairs in Germany. They did this promptly, and were enabled to transfer much of their capital, and are continuing the business successfully outside.

Stern, according to Dr. Kahn, gives generously to refugee needs. He told me of his cooperation with Hugo Simon of the Deutsche Kommission, and of his closer work with Baron de Guenzburg,[22] Alfred, who is more active, and his brother Pierre, who is also deeply interested. These are Russian Jews, who have made for themselves very influential positions in France and do not belong to the "Rothschild clique." He would be glad to have me meet them, for he knows that they would welcome an opportunity to be helpful.

Stern suggested the desirability of a Paris office of the High Commission to keep in closer touch with the refugees and to act as a liaison with the governmental authorities. This he thinks the more important in view of the virtual

21. Fritz Stern of the Syndicat d'Etude.

22. Russian-Jewish family of bankers and philanthropists from St. Petersburg, ennobled by the tsar in 1871. The family maintained a residence in Paris, where they moved permanently after the revolution of 1917 and where Pierre and Alfred were noted industrialists.

closing down of the National Committee. I replied that I had slowly come to this view, that I thought of asking Kotschnig to remain there, that at any rate, I should like to talk with him and his friends further about it. In this connection he indicated that the members of the Deutsche Kommission felt disappointed not having [a] closer relationship with me.

He said he would like to attend in a listener's capacity the Advisory Council meeting. I told him I would invite him. He said he would like also if possible to attend the preceding Sunday's meeting arranged by Laski. I promised to call up Laski about it.

I told Stern about my tentative South American plans, and asked him if he could find someone in Paris with an adequate knowledge of languages who might go along. He raised the question whether I would be free to get away to South America, for he anticipates serious trouble, possibly war, after the turn of the year. In any case, he thought we ought to consider the possibility of making provisions against the internment of refugees and the sequestration of their property by the countries in which they are now resident. He thinks Göring is so unstable that he might, against the will of more moderate influences in Germany, precipitate a crisis.

In Vienna, he says, there is a doctor Eugenia Swartzwald, who is doing wonderful work for the refugees.

At present in France and elsewhere, refugees not allowed to work are being driven toward criminal activities to support their families.

I was much impressed by Stern.

Called Laski as I had promised. He saw difficulties in issuing the invitation, but said he would consider it.

Lunch with members of the staff. Worked with Miss Sawyer until time to take the train to Tonbridge. Had pleasant chats with the two Goldsmid boys, Harry and the young Guardsman,[23] before dinner.

. . . .

Sunday, October 21, 1934

Sir Osmond, because of his sprained ankle, was unable to play golf, so Harry and I played. It was an interesting and close match. After lunch for a walk through only a small part of the grounds with Harry. Everywhere in the woods one saw dozens and dozens of pheasants being bred for the shooting. Between tea time and dinner Lady Goldsmid, Harry, and I badgered Sir Osmond about British foreign policy, for he is the very embodiment of what seemed to me to be typical British qualities.

At dinner I was alone with the family. Afterwards we talked about Jewish and refugee matters:

23. The Goldsmids's younger son, apparently a member of the Royal Household Guard.

(1) The attack on ICA in the *Jewish Chronicle.* Sir Osmond has written the draft of a brief reply, but expects that Sir Leonard will urge him not to send it. I explained something of the widespread feeling that the resources of the ICA should be disclosed; otherwise, it is very difficult to answer unjust criticisms, but he was not convinced;
(2) At the last ICA meeting provisions had been made for a contribution to the High Commission for the first six months of 1935; assurances to this effect had been given to New York, and presumably at the December meeting of ICA a further grant would be made if New York wished to complete the pledges for the budget year;
(3) A long discussion about Helbronner, his attitude towards the situation in France, the loan kassa, his dual representative capacity, etc. Sir Osmond did not assent to my criticisms, but was not at all loath to hear them. As to the loan kassa, someone is coming from America now to discuss these matters;
(4) Sir Osmond was disturbed when he learned that Helbronner was planning to ask Louis Oungre to act as a technical adviser. I said that when Louis Oungre had raised this question with me, I had replied that any governmental representative might bring a technical adviser of his own choice. Sir Osmond saw possibilities of conflict of loyalties, and wrote Helbronner about a number of other matters and incidentally asked if he were naming a technical adviser, but without in any way bringing me into the picture;

. . . .

(10) As to the perpetuation of the High Commission in a modified form under League auspices to deal with Jewish migration problems, he was doubtful, chiefly on the ground that it would tend to indicate that there should be a sort of extraterritoriality for Jews, which he, as an ardent Englishman, could never admit;
(11) Sunday evening before dinner Lady Goldsmid and Harry and I had a stimulating discussion about British politics and the possibilities of fascism here. He is a very bright and discriminating student, very different from his younger brother, who is more the sporting, squire type.

. . . .

Monday, October 22, 1934

Breakfast with Sir Osmond and Harry, and into town with the latter. Before leaving Sir Osmond said that he hoped our talk would have beneficial results.

Called Dr. Don at Lambeth Palace to ask him if he would take up personally with the archbishop the possibility of reconsidering the decision of the other day not to include representatives of the Jewish community at the Lambeth meeting on the thirtieth. Don said he would ask the archbishop, though it might involve some delay, because he had already received the latter's OK for the long list which we together had agreed on. Personally, however, I am still of the opinion that Bentwich is mistaken in his feeling that it would be preferable to have others than members of the Christian community present at what is to be a meeting concerned with the Christian refugees. My view would be different did I not know how the archbishop and Cecil feel.

Tea with the Norman Davises at Claridge's. Before the others arrived, Mrs. Davis and I had a lovely time exchanging information about our families. Later came Mrs. Bullard, Mary Agnes Hamilton,[24] and finally Norman Davis. The talk wandered over a wide field. It seemed to me that Davis was less optimistic than usual about prospects of disarmament or even of avoiding war, though he reiterated that there was no prospect of war in the near future, because no one was ready for it, or rather, because the one country which might want it was not ready. He said that Hitler had performed a useful function by tearing the sheep's clothing off the wolf.

Conference with the bishop of Chichester at the Athenaeum. We went over together a partial list of those invited to Lambeth Palace. He indicated the two or three from whom one might reasonably expect the largest measure of work. He promised, furthermore, that he would go over the whole list carefully with Dr. Don and indicate to the latter which persons he thought it would be desirable to attempt to organize into a committee for action. I asked him how he thought the most effective appeal could be made to the group that would be there. He outlined to me how he would approach it were he delivering a sermon on it.

I asked the bishop whether his representative at last Saturday's church conference in Germany would be back in this country this week, and would be available to come to the meeting. He replied that he would be back, but that he thought it undesirable to ask him to speak, because for him to do so would be to inject a new element into the discussion not too closely related to the subject of the refugees, and thus distract attention from the main purpose of the meeting. Since this was the view also of Don, I did not press the matter further.

As to the bishop's attendance at the meeting, he recognized that, as chairman of the Life and Work [Committee], he had a special status, but he was presiding himself at another meeting at the same time and doubted if he could get away, but he promised to speak to the archbishop later that evening about it.

Up late, but accomplished very little.

Tuesday, October 23, 1934

Fritz Stern telephoned to ask whether Laski had said he might come to the meeting on Sunday. I replied that I had asked, but had had no answer. I assured him that he would be welcome on Monday and Tuesday, irrespective of Laski's decision about Sunday.

Stern said that he had already inquired about a person who might be useful to me on my projected trip to Argentina. He knew of a young Argentinean who

24. Mary Agnes Hamilton, Labour MP, 1929–1931, governor of the British Broadcasting System, author, including a biography of Ramsay MacDonald.

had been in Germany for some years and who speaks fluently German, French, Spanish, and Portuguese. I said I should like to meet him.

Called Miss Bracey and asked her if she could have Paula Kurgass, who had made a recent study of the situation in Paris for the Friends, come to London at our expense to help brief me for our meetings on that particular subject. It is necessary that we have some one who can supply specific data to check that presented by the official representatives.

To the German Embassy at 12:30 to see von Hoctsch. The ambassador, as always, was cordial. We chatted about the vacation he had had and the one I had missed. I remarked that one of the hardships of the present situation was that I could not use the *Europa* or the *Bremen* on my frequent trips back and forth to the States. He asked me why, but he didn't expect a reply, and I gave him none.

I handed him a copy of Bentwich's last letter to Barandon. He read it slowly. Then he said, "I, of course, understand the three points which you make in it. What would you like me to do?" I replied that on this occasion, unlike when I came to see him a few months before, we were not discussing the general approach to the problem, but rather a group of specific issues; that, therefore, it would not be necessary for me to amplify our position. I merely wished to express the hope that there would be a reply before the meeting of our Governing Body, and also to let him know that I expected to pass through Germany early in November on my way to Prague and to the Baltic States; that I planned to call upon some friends in Berlin, including the American ambassador, but that so long as the German government maintained its present interpretation of our relationships, I would not expect to see German officials.

The ambassador explained, as I knew he would, the transfer difficulties; declared that Schacht would not budge from his position that no more Devisen should be made available for use outside the country than came in from day to day; that this had been applied so rigidly recently that for a couple of weeks there were no funds for the expenses of the Embassy; that, therefore, it would be very difficult to made an exception in the cases of the refugee students and others who had been dependent upon funds coming from Germany.

We chatted about the French political situation. I asked him if he thought Laval would carry on or break with the Barthou policy. He doubted that the new foreign minister would have the originality or the pertinacity to strike out on a new line. He cited the latter's failure in Washington as an example of Laval's unwillingness to go counter to his own public opinion. I asked whether he thought that Léger was a great influence in the shaping of French policy. He replied that in his mind Massigli[25] was the real forming influence. The latter, a Protestant, cold and brilliantly well-informed, was the most important figure in French foreign affairs. Of course, the ambassador protested Germany's peaceful intentions

25. René Massigli, League of Nations expert at the French Foreign Office, a principal opponent of appeasement of Germany. Ambassador to Turkey 1939–1940, later ambassador to Great Britain. Commissioner for Foreign Affairs on De Gaulle's National Committee in London during the war.

and asserted that nothing would be easier than for France to be assured on this point. I did not assent.

Directly to New Court. Chatted with Anthony and Lionel de Rothschild for a little while in their office before the others came to lunch. I asked Lionel who is the man in the picture above the mantle, and he said it was his grandfather, Lionel, and that he was said to resemble him. The picture shows marked spiritual qualities, which I could not in the least see in the present Lionel, so wracking my conscience I replied, "There is something of a resemblance in the eyes and the forehead, but then you know it is difficult for us to see spiritual qualities in people we know."

At lunch we were joined by Sir Isidor Salmon, Lionel Cohen, and Otto Schiff. During most of the meal we talked about this and that, and there was a good deal of conversation between two persons and only intermittently general talk. As time passed, I became a little fearful lest nothing real be said about the subject which interests me. Therefore at a moment of pause in the talk I said, "Well, what do you think the Jewish community of Great Britain will do next year?"

I expected an explosion from Lionel to the effect that nothing could be done, but I was pleasantly surprised. He did not outburst at all. A little earlier something had been said about Helbronner. I characterized his attitude vigorously and said that to him, a German Jew should be gotten rid of even if he had to be thrown in the Seine. Lionel Rothschild retorted that he felt much the same way about it, though he himself was a German Jew, but he said this with a laugh.

Mrs. Sieff and other members of the women's committee had come to New Court a few days earlier to discuss the possibility of a separate women's drive. Melchett, the Rothschilds, and the other men were all determined to block the women, but as might have been expected, the women won them over on condition that there should not be any conflict between their effort and what might be done later. Since then they had arranged for a large public meeting with Smuts[26] as the chief speaker, and are hoping to sell tickets at ten guineas each. This the men were inclined to think of as a breach of faith, and as undercutting a larger effort later, but nothing could be done about it.

I asked the group what they thought of Melchett's plan for a glorified Palestinian [Zionist] appeal which would provide for German needs. The prevailing view was that Melchett would not be able to get the Palestinians to agree to this, and some felt that if they did agree, it would be very difficult to carry through the arrangement. Melchett, they thought, exaggerates his influence.

At this point Lionel Rothschild, supported by Lionel Cohen, stressed the importance of creating a situation where local Jewish charities would again have

26. Jan Christian Smuts, leader of the Nationalist Party in South Africa. As a member of the British War Cabinet, played an important role in the decision to issue the Balfour Declaration of November 2, 1917. In 1939 became prime minister of South Africa.

a chance. Otto Schiff tended to support this view, but not so wholeheartedly as to preclude his also favoring another German drive.

I then made a plea for action again by the British community on two grounds—one, of the acute need, two, that for the British not to do so would discourage Jewish communities everywhere and would have a particularly adverse effect in the United States.

At this point Lionel de Rothschild appealed to Sir Isidor, who had not said much during the discussion. He very quietly (for him) said that he thought that something must be done, and that though, as had been pointed out by others, probably a smaller amount than last year would be raised, yet the effort should be made. This statement seemed to have a considerable effect on the whole group, and especially on Lionel de Rothschild.

This gave me an opportunity to outline briefly my idea as to how 15,000 to 20,000 Germans from Germany or from among the refugees could be cared for for a year, half to Palestine and the other half divided between North America and South America: and that towards this end I was considering a visit to Argentina and Brazil. Otto Schiff spoke up and supported this idea on the ground that one could not effect a new arrangement with these countries except on the spot; he had been told emphatically by the Brazilian ambassador here that a recommendation concerning immigration coming from here would probably do more harm than good. I had earlier pointed out that Sir Osmond, Sir Leonard, and Louis Oungre all favored this démarche.

Finally Lionel de Rothschild, to my great relief, said that under these circumstances probably they could next year do somewhat more than raise the amount necessary to care for "Otto Schiff's refugees." They could probably get something for my work as well. That, coming from him, was indeed a concession.

Otto Schiff and I walked away together. We had exactly the same thought. The luncheon had been a great success. Lionel de Rothschild's bark was going to prove to be worse than his bite, and he would be ready to go along. And just as we were congratulating each other, we were joined by Lionel Cohen, who up till today noon, had himself been rather of the intransigent school, and he seemed now inclined to go along.

. . . .

Wednesday, October 24, 1934

Called Laski, who agreed to the invitation to Stern, and I said I would go out that evening for supper.

Over to the office of the *Church Times,* to see Sidney Dark. He is intensely interested in the problem of the refugees, particularly the Jewish refugees. He checked over the list of invitations for the Lambeth conference, made some additional suggestions, and in other ways showed his anxiety to be helpful. On the whole, however, he was not very optimistic.

Over to see Scott Lidgett at the Congregational Central Office Building.

He was even less encouraging than Sidney Dark. He made a number of suggestions, but was not hopeful that any of them would be fruitful.

My conference with the two churchmen left me more lacking in optimism than ever about the Christian response to any refugee appeal.

. . . .

Dinner with Laski at his house. It was a family party, with only himself and wife and the two girls. The older one, down from Oxford for her nineteenth birthday, is an amazingly brilliant but a little over-sensitive child. She speaks fairly well on many subjects, and appears to have a temperament much like her father's

After dinner Laski and I talked about many subjects, including

(1) His projected trip to America. I outlined what could be done in the time. He seemed to grow in his desire to go;
(2) The Sacher and Sieff group. He recognized their generosity, but insisted that they act as though their extra contributions relieved them from any personal responsibility to share in the social community. Mrs. Sieff particularly is a climber, spending large sums in ostentatious entertainment, to which are invited chiefly non-Jews who, after having enjoyed the lavish cabarets, etc., leave, many of them with an increased feeling of anti-Semitism. Moreover, this group does not maintain in its business the same high standards in matters of wages and hours as do the people associated with Isidor Salmon;
(3) His brother, Harold, who takes no interest in Jewish affairs, but devotes himself wholly to his profession and to the Labour Party, where he plays the leading intellectual role. He is intolerant, even arrogant, without that filial respect for his father which Neville Laski always feels. I could now begin to understand why the father had such an evident preference for his older son;
(4) The Sephardi. We were speaking of the pride of Spanish Jews and their position as the aristocracy, when Mrs. Laski reminded me that she was Portuguese, and as her husband told me later, preferred to be spoken of as a Sephardic.

Our talk went on until nearly eleven o'clock.

Thursday, October 25, 1934

Worked all day on my report.

To dinner as Bentwich's guest at the Palladin Club at the Criterion restaurant. There were present about fifty-five to sixty men, nearly all of them either expert in or especially interested in Palestine. Wauchope was the guest of honor.

Other guests included Ronald Storrs,[27] the first military governor of Jerusalem, Mr. Montague Bell, the editor of the *Middle Asia,* or something of that sort, Colonel Meinertzhagen.[28] And among the members were Lord Melchett, Ben-Gurion of the Palestine Agency, Sacher, Brodetzky, Friedman of New York, Edwin Samuel, et al. It was a good dinner, and during the course of it I chatted with Bell, but more with Sacher. With the latter the chief points raised were

(1) He thought there would be a joint drive next year only if the non-Zionists were prepared to go out on a large-ish drive. It would not be worthwhile to combine for a small amount. He thought there was a chance that the others might agree. I told him of the promising reaction from New Court, but he doubted if there would be any effective help from that direction;
(2) He and Friedman asked me why the drive in America had gone so relatively badly. I explained it in terms of the depression, the delay in getting the drive under way, and the relative failure of the Zionists to pull their full weight in the boat.

Bentwich as chairman began the proceedings by rising and saying, "Gentlemen, I give you the toast to the King." We all rose with our glasses, crying "to the King." Then we sat down and Bentwich said, "Now you may smoke." Bentwich spoke very well, chiefly about Wauchope, but making friendly remarks about the other guests.

Wauchope was called upon. He spoke for six minutes without referring directly to the general topic of the evening, "Jew and Arab Relations." He nonetheless gave a clear picture of certain of the essential purposes he has been pursuing in Palestine.

Then followed Ronald Storrs, who spoke for twenty-six minutes, giving as he had been told to do he said, the Arab point of view, but towards the end making certain suggestions of his own. He seemed to me to speak out of great knowledge and with real sympathy for both sides.

Lord Melchett spoke for eighteen minutes, well, but a little circulatory. Nonetheless, as a real Jew and Zionist.

Then came the bête noire of the evening, Montague Bell, who in a paper which he read, seemed to me to express a number of unpleasant truths about the Jewish authorities in Palestine in such a way as to make them peculiarly offensive to his listeners and even to me. The worst result of his talk was to divert

27. General Sir Ronald Henry Amherst Storrs (1881–1955), famed colonial administrator, instigator (with T. E. Lawrence) of the Arab revolt during World War I, military and civil governor of Jerusalem and Judea, 1917–1926. Ordered all buildings in Jerusalem to be faced with local stone, a practice that survives to this day. As McDonald commented in this entry, had sympathy for Jews and Arabs in Palestine.

28. Colonel Richard Meinertzhagen, British soldier, adventurer, and intelligence agent during World War I. Known for his ferocious "Christian Zionism" (support of the Zionist cause), he carried out covert missions in Nazi Germany and the USSR during World War II as well.

most of the discussion that followed into a general defense of Zionism, rather than an analysis of Arab-Jewish relations.

I then spoke for seven minutes. I was tempted to reply to some of Bell's attacks, but restraining myself, made only two points: first, our obligation to Palestine for taking so many of the German refugees, and second our obligation for the support which the Palestinians had given.

Ben-Gurion spoke for twelve minutes, outlining his faith in the ultimate victory of Zionism with millions of Jews in the Palestine area. Laski followed for 17 minutes. He spoke extremely well, but with many too many parenthetical clauses, all of which he kept in perfect order, but which together ate up the time to such an extent that he could have made his points just as effectively in one-third as many minutes.

Sacher spoke for sixteen minutes and a half, giving a general defense of Palestinian [Zionist] administration, and doing it extremely well.

Colonel Meinertzhagen, in a four-minute talk, managed to be maladroit and offensive, referring in the same sentence to his admiration for Hitler and for Jabotinsky, and declaring his conviction that none of the Zionists really believed anything they were saying about the Arabs. He was not an unqualified success.

Bentwich then called on Brodetzky to close the discussion in a few minutes, but he spoke more than fifteen, I thought very well.

As the meeting broke up, I chatted with Wauchope and told him that if I came out to Palestine, it would be solely on a personal visit to educate myself. He expressed a warm desire to welcome me. He was not the less cordial because of my disavowal of any political aims in the projected visit.

. . . .

Home late, but to sleep better than I had for weeks.

Friday, October 26, 1934

. . . .

Talked on the telephone with de Margerie of the French Embassy, following up the conversation with him of the night before. The results of the discussions were the following:

(1) It would be undesirable to suggest to the Governing Body a memorandum to be submitted to the special Council of the League on the subject of the Saar. To do so would be to indicate that the game had been given up. It might also look as though one were using the Saar as an instrument of propaganda. In any case, it would not impress the Germans. I agreed.
(2) There would be no objection to the statement which I proposed to make in reference to the non-cooperation of a certain power [Germany].

(3) On the question of the French contribution [for the administrative expenses of the High Commission], he had been unable to get in touch with Léger.
(4) It was felt that it would be undesirable for me to press for an answer now in writing as to whether I could count on the verbal assurance which Léger had given me in August to the effect that the French would receive the Saar refugees and permit them to become French citizens. The situation had become much more difficult following the murders at Marseilles. It was now very necessary to guard against any public exaggerations.

Lunch with Wurfbain and Remusat. The latter talked fluently and at length about the work of his Catholic Committee, about which I had never heard. According to him, his group had never been refused an application for a *carte de travail* or other paper. Of course, they were careful about whom they interceded on behalf of. He told too of the relations between the Catholic group and Marianoff,[29] of the threatened breach because of the unwillingness of one of the young Jewish writers to make certain minor changes in his article for the *Renouveau,* whereas a much more important Catholic writer had completely rewritten his. Marianoff he characterized as a good but weak man. He doubted whether the Cardinal would be able to continue his cooperation in view of the difficulties referred to.

Conference at the office in the late afternoon on the arrival of Kotschnig from the States, who brought relatively good news.

. . . .

At dinner he told us about his efforts at home [in the United States], his successes and failures, his "hearing" before the New York Foundation, Baerwald's timidity, Chamberlain's great activity, Sulzberger's cordiality, Miss Ogden's great helpfulness, his poor opinion of the set-up of the Christian Committee, his conference with Brandt,[30] who had been preparing another letter on the High Commission but had decided to give it up, the general immigration question in the United States and the manufactured affidavits, the need for active work to prevent the refugees becoming dependent, the impossibility of Miss Razovsky's getting away, his desire not to take over Miss Ginsberg's work. Earlier, he had been concerned lest I name Otto Nathan to take Bentwich's place, and was greatly relieved when I told him that Bentwich was only to be on leave of absence, and that his place would not be filled. I was sorry to hear him say that there was some doubt about Nathan's position at Princeton for another year.

29. Dr. Dimitri M. Marianoff, Dr. Einstein's son-in-law, had a review *Renouveau—Association pour des Intérêts Agricoles des Israélites.* The difficulties presumably were based on the grounds of affiliation with communist organizations.

30. George L. Brandt, State Department assistant chief of the Visa Division and later consul at Cologne, influential in the department.

Saturday, October 27, 1934

Conference with Ambassador Bingham at twelve at the Embassy for a half an hour. I outlined to him as fully as there was time the nature of my report, the subjects which would be discussed, and emphasized that at the first public meeting it was quite unlikely that the American representative would feel called upon to make any statement. I urged him very strongly to be present at least at that meeting to give us the moral support and prestige which his personal collaboration would supply. He said that he would not be able to come to the later meetings because of other engagements, but he would try to come Thursday morning, and after that Johnson[31] would represent him.

I then talked with Johnson, who showed me the stack of material he had just received from America.[32] He said he would study it over the weekend, and would be ready to talk with me almost any time I suggested. It was left that I would call him Monday morning. I explained to him why we were so anxious to have the ambassador himself at the first meeting.

....

Then for dinner at Miss Pye's[33] to talk with her and Frau Paula Kurgass. The latter was as interesting as I hoped she would be. She still has the possibility of going back to Germany, her papers being in perfect order, but she may not do so in view of the fact that she was in prison for a time. Her release was effected by Miss Pye through a personal letter addressed to Hitler.

Frau Kurgass talked freely about the situation in France, elaborating on various points in her report, but was unable to supply me with much undiluted data to help me at Lambeth Palace. She promised, however, to prepare some additional illustrative cases.

I told Miss Pye about the attitude of the French toward the loan kassas, and she said she would raise the question in the Advisory Council. Similarly, she is going to press on the matter of the charges which Paula Kurgass reports as being excessive for all of the documents.

We decided that it would be inadvisable for Frau Kurgass to come to the Advisory Council, for her presence there, associated with Miss Pye, might lead to an embarrassing situation for her with the French authorities. She is to remain here, however, as long as she is needed.

Sunday, October 28, 1934

Chatted with Goldmann about the French situation. According to him, Bérenger is still the official French representative on the Governing Body, and that

31. Herschel V. Johnson, counselor at the American Embassy in London.

32. In addition to sending background information the State Department listed what the United States could not or would not do: no special treatment for refugees, no financial aid, no binding commitments. In other words, Johnson could only listen.

33. Edith M. Pye, active in resettlement for Friends Service Committee.

he had suggested that Helbronner be named as his alternate because Helbronner wanted very much to go and because he is "a bright man." However, Goldmann reports that both Fouques-Duparc and Massigli think this designation is a mistake. Helbronner is working closely with Bérenger on constitutional reform.

. . . .

Monday, October 29, 1934

The Advisory Council meeting began rather promptly at 10:35 at the Royal Society. The preliminary greetings had in all cases been friendly and in most instances cordial. Fortunately, Sir Osmond not only was there at the beginning, but had come prepared to do what I was so anxious he should do, strike a friendly and cooperative note in opening the discussion.

As at the previous meeting of the Advisory Council, I, after some preliminary remarks about the desirability of good temper and a willingness to give the other person the benefit of the doubt, sketched the main points in my report to the Governing Body. Only small sections of it, however, did I read. In closing, I put with considerable frankness the situation in which, because of the sharp criticism from organization leaders, from refugee leaders and the refugee press, I found myself. I emphasized that it would be intolerable if one continued to be the subject of attacks from so many quarters, when in the very nature of things it was quite impossible to satisfy to more than a small extent the divergent interests of the governments, the refugees, and the organizations. I explained my desire to liquidate the work as soon as possible, my earlier inclination to fix a definite date, and of my withdrawal of that suggestion at the urging of the heads of various organizations. In short, as I closed, I in effect challenged Helbronner, Gottschalk, Schevenels, Schmolkova, and the Oungres to either withdraw in some measure their criticisms, or to be left in a position of making the work of the High Commission virtually impossible. I tried to do this in reasonably good temper, but without in any sense apologizing.

Kotschnig then presented in a fifteen or twenty-minute talk the substance of the work done on behalf of the intellectuals. As always, he made a good impression.

The general discussion was opened by Sir Osmond. He spoke briefly, but exactly in the line that would do most to rid the conference of the vicious atmosphere that had prevailed in Paris the previous June. It could not have been done better.

After him followed—not in this precise order—Helbronner, Schevenels, Louis Oungre, Schmolkova, and finally Gottschalk. This last combined his apologia with statements which were hardly generous, but on the whole it was an ingenious retreat. The others all spoke in a way which showed that they were willing to withdraw their general charges of failure made against the office. Indeed, all of them took occasion to praise certain phases of our work.

But the honeymoon period was soon over when we got into the subject of permits to work. Helbronner made the usual statement about France having done the limit that was possible, and the need for sending the refugees abroad. Very little was being said on the other side when I more or less forced Kahn to speak. Rather reluctantly but nonetheless firmly, he put the case for the absorption of a certain number of the refugees in the countries where they are. This brought sharp retort from the French. As a result, there was no definite declaration by the Advisory Council on permits to work.

Out to lunch with Louis Oungre and Sir Osmond as Helbronner's guest. This meal was most cordial. I then learned for the first time what was back of the ICA resolution. It was a desire to give a formal and official auspices to the financial conference in New York. It was evidently Louis Oungre's idea and a clever device. They all thought it would be desirable for me to go to Rome for two purposes: (1) in connection with the Saar; (a) to see whether Pacelli could be interested in the question of guarantees; and (b) in that of the refugees; (2) to sound out the possibility of Pacelli's influence being exercised to aid me in my task of opening the doors in South America. They all also agreed that it was desirable to press forward as rapidly as could be the South American project. The other matter we discussed was my trip to Germany. All were skeptical as to substantial results, but thought it worth trying. Sir Osmond, in particular, thought that it was much more important for me to go because of its offering a greater chance of success, than for him to accept the urgent invitation of the central Jewish organizations. Sir Osmond thought that his being a Jew would make it impossible for him to accomplish anything.

At the afternoon meeting there was a prolonged row about a resolution introduced by Mme. Schmolkova calling for additional retraining facilities. The difficulty arose in connection with the phrase "to prepare them for emigration." Kahn objected and said there should be no indication that they must be emigrated. Helbronner insisted on his favorite thesis. In the midst of the discussion, which at that point involved German, French and English, I suggested that we consider only the English draft so as to get on. To this, Helbronner retorted by a long, eloquent defense of French as the language of diplomacy, etc., etc. In reply, I said that we would make French the official language! And henceforth we did as far as we could, conduct the meetings in French, and limit the drafts altogether to the French texts.

The meeting was adjourned fairly early in order to permit me to keep my six o'clock appointment with Cecil. He spoke enthusiastically about my report, did not think that I had gone too far in my German statement. We also talked about plans for the Lambeth meeting the next day.

Tuesday, October 30, 1934

Continuation of the Advisory Council meeting. The emigration and settlement proposals did not require much debate, but the French group did not miss the opportunity to reflect on what they interpreted as being the unnecessary delay.

Miss Pye presented the report which she and Gottschalk had worked out the previous evening, covering (1) the cost of papers (on which there was little debate); (2) *permits de séjour*, on which there was endless discussion ending in its adoption; (3) no expulsion without grave cause and without explanation; (4) no expulsion without the refugee being supplied with a travel paper. Both these latter were also adopted.

Then a series of resolutions drawn up by Louis Oungre were passed without much debate.

At lunch time walked to the Grosvenor House with Herbert May.

The Advisory Council meeting had left for its afternoon session really only the question of the Saar and one or two minor items. Helbronner had insisted that the question of the Saar be discussed, but actually when I had presented the matter there was little that was said that was helpful. The plain fact is that none of the other countries or committees are inclined to volunteer to take any considerable part of the burden.

Finally, the meeting adjourned in time to allow me to get to Lambeth Palace about 4:30. On the whole, it had been a profitable series of sessions. More and more, it was as though the various members actually were acting as advisers to the High Commissioner rather than, as on previous occasions, his enemies or the enemies of other members of the group. Herbert May probably is right in his statement to me the first day that it would not do for me to put anyone else in the chair; that such a substitution would be taken as a reflection upon the members, and might lead to a return of the June 20 spirit. Indeed, the setup of the Advisory Council, if it works as it should, is almost ideal. Of course, in this instance there was the complication of the dual capacity in which Helbronner and Louis Oungre sat; but that was incidental and not an essential part of the organization.

During the day and the day following Kotschnig was presiding over the meetings of his Experts' Committee.

In Dr. Don's office I had a chance to put down in black and white my ideas for the meeting that was to follow presently. Then we had tea with the archbishop. Schevenels was also there. While we were talking together, in blew Lady Asquith[34] with the exclamation, to her old friend the archbishop, "Why did I come?" When told what the subject of the meeting was to be, she said, "Oh yes, Germany; that was the reason. Tell me about it, but I am not going to stay for the meeting. I am tired, and I can't bear speeches." I tried to tell her, and she rudely interrupted and pointed to the one question which she wanted instantly answered. I thought her a horrid shrunken old woman, and my opinion of her was not improved when at the beginning of the meeting, the archbishop, in telling of those who were not present but were interested, said, "Lady Asquith has just been here, but she is too tired to stay for the meeting, but she is full of sympathy."

34. Lady Cynthia Asquith, wife of the Hon. Herbert Asquith, lawyer and writer, secretary to the author J. M. Barrie (1918–1937).

Dr. Don asked me whether I would stay with the archbishop and come in after the crowd had gathered or go with him to meet the guests. I told him I would much prefer to do the latter. So together we received the twenty or twenty-five men and women who came. It was not a very representative or impressive gathering, though it contained a number of men and women of distinction and genuine concern. . . .

The archbishop introduced the subject briefly. Then I spoke as effectively as I could. Cecil followed with a brief and useful statement. But the discussion soon showed that we had more or less missed fire [misfired]. The archbishop, in a note which he wrote me, indicated that he had thought that the meeting would be concerned only with the Hebrew Christians. I replied that it would be very difficult to draw the line. Lady Snowden wanted to know whether we wanted money or help in other forms. I replied, "Money." Indeed, I had at the conclusion of my talk indicated that £50,000 was needed. Then someone else wanted a definite and detailed plan for a final liquidation of the problem. Others asked about the various appeals that had been made or were pending. Adams explained their plans succinctly. Wells, who had come in a half hour late, put briefly the case of the G.R.A.F. I intervened to explain with more frankness than either of the others why the cooperative effort to date had been ineffective, and said that it was my hope that this meeting would result in putting the necessary force behind it. Then followed a number of statements about the need for closer cooperation, for a definite and final plan, etc., etc. And towards the end Cecil reverted to his favorite thesis that, at least in England, one could only hope for satisfactory returns on the basis of a final scheme. Earlier there had been some references to the Saar, the possibility of additional refugees, and the desirability of capitalizing on that situation; and finally, the archbishop, who had been following each statement carefully and making notes, summed up his views that nothing definite could be accomplished at this meeting, but that if a comprehensive program could be drawn up including the Saar refugees, he would consider calling together another and perhaps larger conference at the psychological moment. It was on this rather inconclusive, but not altogether defeatist, note that the meeting adjourned.

After the meeting I talked for a little while with Adams and Wells. The latter thought in view of the inclusive results that G.R.A.F. would vote to dissolve, and I could not feel that that would be a mistake.

Wednesday, October 31, 1934

Conference with Demuth. He told me of the large plans which are opening up in Turkey through which he hoped that a number of the refugees would be placed in key positions in the Turkish administration. He explained that to take full advantage of these opportunities would require certain financing, a portion of which could be done in Turkey itself, but that the other part would require foreign cooperation. But all of this should not be English. He was anxious to meet Otto Schiff, so I called Schiff and made an appointment. And then we talked about Persia. Demuth is postponing his trip there until he has a report on the situation from a German friend of his who is going out soon, or may already be there, to occupy a definite post.

....

19. November 1934: Grand Tour

London, Thursday, November 1, 1934

. . . .

The Governing Body got under way promptly at 10:30. It was on the whole a quite different group, however, from that which had met eleven months ago at Lausanne: Helbronner, instead of Bérenger, for France; Johnson, instead of Chamberlain, for the United States;[1] Casada, instead of Majoni, for Italy; and Guani, instead of Cecil, in the chair. The private meeting was wholly formal: adoption of the agenda, arranging for the public meeting, and appointment of the Finance Committee.

The public meeting was limited to Guani's brief statement and to the reading of my long report. It was not what one would call an inspiring audience—fifteen or twenty members of the press and about as many members of the public. But I had gotten over expecting a large public at these affairs.

The members of the Governing Body seemed genuinely impressed by the scope of the work indicated in the report and also by certain of the generalizations as to the needs of the refugees, but particularly by the German section.[2] The meeting adjourned early in order to give the members an opportunity to read the documents, which were distributed at the end.

Lunch with Sir Osmond at the Carlton Club. He thought that Sacher would be the best representative of the Weizmann group for the New York meeting. I said I would cable to get Felix Warburg's reaction. Sir Osmond and I talked a little about Helbronner and Louis Oungre. He said that I should not worry about them, that he would handle them, that in their conferences with him recently he had asked them what it was they wanted—did they want to weaken the High Commissioner or to help him? Louis Oungre was to be allowed to act as technical adviser for Helbronner only on condition that he was

1. Chamberlain felt he could not miss three weeks of classes to attend the meeting.

2. In this section McDonald detailed the failure of the German government to cooperate in trying to solve the refugees' problems. "In fact, its attitude has progressively aggravated the difficulties of settlement elsewhere. The restrictions on the withdrawal of their own property from Germany by the Emigrants, whether in the form of capital or income, have been steadily intensified." In addition, destitution was increasing because the resources of those formerly able to support themselves were exhausted. Report of the High Commissioner, the Third Meeting of the Governing Body of the High Commission for Refugees (Jewish and Other) Coming from Germany, November 1–2, 1934, McDonald Papers, USHMM.

not representing ICA and that he did not say a word. This had been made definitely clear to him by Sir Osmond. The latter was much pleased with the portions of the report which I showed him. He said that he would stop on his way that afternoon to check the sailings to New York, but he hoped he would not have to leave until after Christmas. The more I see him, the more I am struck by his keenness and his unfailing courtesy.

The afternoon meeting of the Governing Body with Cecil in the chair began well, but soon degenerated into a depressing debate, which consisted mostly of explanations by the different governmental representatives as to why they could not do anything. It began with Miss Pye's very effective presentation of her resolutions. She argued for one after the other, but was not given an opportunity to hear the discussion of the Governing Body on them, Helbronner having made quite clear that he would object to such procedure. As soon as Miss Pye left the room, the debate began.

As to the cost of papers, there was little argument, but on the right to residence there was a hopeless tangle, and in reference to the other items the situation was not much better. Much the same atmosphere continued during the discussion on the retraining resolution. Finally, Cecil leaned over to me and said, "Really, McDonald, in this sort of discussion, I am of no use." When we adjourned a little before seven, Cecil took me aside saying, "My friend, I am going to tell you something which you may not like. I think I really ought to tell my government to name someone else. At this rate we are accomplishing nothing in this committee. We are not helping you, and I am wasting my time." I explained to him that his withdrawal at this time would be a disaster, and he agreed to say nothing about it.

Dinner with Kotschnig. Discussed with him not only the aspects of his own work, but the larger program which I had in mind for him. He did not object to this, but he was far from enthusiastic about my suggestion of the Baltic trip. Nonetheless, he did not say no to that. He was dubious about an office in Paris, both on the grounds of expense and of unnecessary complications with the local groups. He was most anxious that the Ginsberg committee be kept alive, even if he had to turn over to them larger sums from his working budget than he had at first intended.

Friday, November 2, 1934

The Governing Body resumed its meetings with a revised and greatly shortened agenda. The first item—relations with Germany—brought out no special complications. Similarly, the item dealing with emigration was passed without much controversy. But when in this connection I presented two resolutions which were not on the agenda but which had been clearly foreshadowed by my report, the fat was in the fire. The first of my resolutions suggested the extension of the poor relief facilities of the governments to the refugees. Several governmental representatives saw difficulties in this. But Helbronner went much further. He was opposed to it not only for what it suggested, but also because its introduction without formal notice was an evil practice which he wished formally to protest against. There had been too much of this sort of thing. As this kind of thing went on, Cecil finally losing his temper, delivered a sharp rebuff particularly to Helbronner, but also to several of the other governmental representatives who had been pointing only difficulties and indicating no willingness to recommend anything to their governments that might possibly be objected to. Cecil said, "Gentlemen, I think I really ought to say that we are accomplishing nothing at all. If we are going to limit ourselves merely to reporting to our governments, then we are only doing in a clumsy way what could be done better through the regular diplomatic channels. And I must add that if this is to be the practice and the spirit of this body, I shall very seriously have to reconsider my relationship to it." This rebuff had a temporary effect. Helbronner made a conciliatory speech praising Cecil.

But when my second resolution having to do with permits to work was presented, Helbronner was again off to a flying start, protesting against the aspersions on France, which had done its utmost, and against the unjustifiable procedure of last minute resolutions. I replied with some heat that, while I recognized that technically there might be some ground for complaint about the resolutions not having been formulated earlier, they were both clearly indicated in my report; that surely we were not a formal, diplomatic body so much as a group of persons concerned with getting a job done, and that, therefore, we should not be too *protocolaire.* However, I went on, that on the major point I must take a strong line; I could not admit that the High Commissioner could be inhibited from presenting to the Governing Body whatever measures seemed to him would advance the cause of the refugees. On the contrary, that if the Governing Body took the line that there was such limitation, I should have to reconsider my willingness to go on. Indeed, I would have to refuse definitely to attempt to do the job under such impossible circumstances. To this, Helbronner made no rejoinder.

But the show was not over, because Rothmund then took up the challenge. He addressed me directly and asked me point blank what countries I had in mind when in the resolution there was the implication that certain countries were not doing their duty in the matter of permits to work. He then continued by asking why I should have chosen to single out Switzerland as guilty of unjust expulsions without at the same time indicating what work on the constructive side his country was doing. All of this was said in a tone that was sharp and serious.

Cecil, in his very best manner, came to the rescue by saying, "If I were the High Commissioner, I should definitely refuse to answer the question which countries were meant, but of course, I must let the High Commissioner reply for himself." After this remark it was easier for me to decline to answer Rothmund's question. Then as to his other statement, I pointed out to Rothmund and to the Governing Body as a whole that I had been very careful not to criticize specific governments; that my criticism in my report of the three governments was very mild;[3] that, in fact, I was myself criticized in many refugee quarters on the ground that I am an apologist for the governments. In closing, I paid a tribute to what is being done in Switzerland, and accepted Rothmund's suggestion than at an appropriate moment I would in public indicate this appreciation. After the meeting Rothmund came up to me and said that he hoped that I had understood that there was no ill-feeling; he seemed to be in good spirits.

Earlier, when Helbronner was raising the question of the implication being that France was not doing its duty, Cecil, in his delightful manner, pointed out that no country was mentioned, and that he was quite unwilling to assume that England was meant, and that therefore Helbronner should be equally willing to assume that France was not intended.

On the whole, therefore, under Cecil's excellent leadership, we got past the worst crisis, and proceeded to pass without serious debate the ICA resolution in reference to a financial conference; the acceptance of Kotschnig's report which Helbronner praised; the modification of the statutes, leaving only the financial report and the Saar for the afternoon session.

As we were walking out of the room, Helbronner asked me if it might not be desirable to have a meeting in January in connection with the Saar. I was noncommittal.

Before going to lunch, we had an improvised office conference, deciding on the nature of the press release, and Bentwich, May, and I went off to lunch together to decide what should be included. Bentwich worked it out, and had the draft ready by the time the afternoon session convened.

We began with the discussion of the Saar, I stating the problem, the new difficulties which would be created and the lesser resources which would be available. Helbronner then spoke, repeating much of what he had said earlier in private. But no one except Cecil, of the Governing Body, had anything to say. Indeed, it is difficult to see how they could have. It is important, however, to note that Helbronner did say, or so I understood him, that France would receive the refugees, but could not be responsible for keeping them. This then, is a less satisfactory statement than Léger had made to me in August.

Then followed the presentation of the financial statement. I spoke to it briefly, but there was little need for explanation—everything was in such excellent order. Herbert May's work was never shown to better advantage than in the report itself, which required four or five separate votes by the Finance Committee and almost as many by the Governing Body; but Cecil was able to secure all of these within four or five minutes. I had been with the Finance Committee the

3. After singling out conditions created by the German government preventing the transfer of funds abroad to benefit those who had fled or left Germany, McDonald observed that in certain places, particularly Paris and Prague, the situation of refugees was desperate. And he stated that in many countries refugees were given less and less opportunity to find work. The Third Meeting of the Governing Body of the High Commission for Refugees (Jewish and Other) Coming from Germany, November 1–2, 1934, McDonald Papers, USHMM.

previous day and that morning for a few minutes each time; but May had shown them how necessary were all of the proposed votes. So with their unanimous report, the rest was easy.

I took occasion to explain briefly about the plans for the staff, Bentwich's leave of absence, Kotschnig's broader scope, and Wurfbain's continuing function, and my own plans. Cecil then delivered his prepared remarks, and Guani said some well merited words of praise for the chairman, and the meeting was adjourned in an atmosphere of good will generated in part at least by the tea, which was served at just the right moment. Cecil said nothing more about his resignation, and I think we can count on him carrying on.

I should have indicated earlier that Mme. Schmolkova, before she left, told me that my letter and the draft enclosed with it had been of the greatest value to the committee in Prague; that it had arrived just when they were most discouraged, and had given them the spirit to carry on.

I should also have indicated earlier that throughout the four days' sessions of the two bodies it was perfectly evident that Louis Oungre was advising Helbronner to take in every case a more intransigent line than even he would have taken ordinarily. Exception, of course, should be made in this respect for the group of resolutions which Oungre drafted or prepared the basis for as representing the general view of the ICA.

London, Saturday, November 3, 1934

Over to the Home Office to see Mr. Cooper.[4] . . .

Together we then went in to see Captain Crookshank.[5] I talked for a little while about our work, explaining some of the difficulties we had been having with the governments, leading up to the following points:

(1) Our hope that purely technical offences on the part of the refugees would not be held to be sufficient to disqualify them for permission to work or to reside;
(2) That mere technical membership in the Communist Party or an earlier allegiance to such party ought not, if the individual is abstaining from any political activity, be held to be sufficient to disqualify him for residence or work.

Crookshank's answers were fairly satisfactory, though couched in such language as to permit him to reinterpret it to suit later exigencies. He said that they did not in fact allow mere technical infractions or even mere membership in the Communist Party to weigh definitively against other considerations. On the contrary, they tried to decide each case on its merits and to be just, rather than correct.

4. E. N. Cooper, principal at the Home Office.
5. Henry Frederick Comfort Crookshank, parliamentary undersecretary in the Home Office, 1934–1935. Conservative MP 1924–1956.

Back to the hotel to meet the delegation of three Communists on behalf of the International Labor Defense. They had previously presented a memorandum. They wished to urge that I support the following contentions: that Communists should not be discriminated against in reference to *permits de séjour* and *cartes de travail;* that they should be allowed to carry on propaganda against the existing regime in Germany; that they should be permitted all of the privileges of Communists who are citizens of the countries where the refugees are. I pointed out that we were constantly urging the governments not to discriminate in matters of residence or work against individual refugees because of their political opinions. They seemed much pleased with the section from my report on this subject. I told them quite frankly, however, that their second and third desires were beyond our competence, and that while I did not wish to say that their proposals were unjust, that I would have to tell them I was sure they were utterly impracticable. They seemed satisfied. Later, they asked whether we would be willing to intervene in defense of individuals threatened with unjust expulsion. I said that we would welcome information about such cases, and would do in each instance what we could. They also asked to have us send them material as it was issued. This we agreed to do.

Called Sacher on the telephone and explained about the Governing Body resolution, the ICA initiative, our anxiety to have Weizmann representation, our choice of him, and urged him strongly to accept. He asked a number of questions and then put forward the only objection which seemed to be substantial to the effect that Simon Marks would be going over on business in February, and could he not handle the matter then? I told him that that would be too late, and explained why, and urged that Simon Marks' visit would have value as a follow-up. Later, I called back to explain that we had not thought of Simon Marks in the first place because we had assumed that the latter was still absorbed in his Royal Commission.

....

Monday, November 5, 1934

Considerable negotiations over the telephone as to the best method of preparing the way in Rome. Tried Cardinal Bourne, but found that he was ill. Dr. Don suggested that the best method would be through the Foreign Office if they would do it. Called back Sargent the second time, and he said they would, but I should write him a letter setting forth the situation in some detail.

Called Wigram, also of the Foreign Office, in Mr. Perowne's department. He kindly agreed to communicate with the British ambassador in Berlin, telling him of my arrival. Johnson of the American Embassy had already arranged to do the same for Dodd.

....

Tuesday, November 6, 1934

Called Sargent, who said the letter was OK and would be forwarded, and the answer would be sent to our office.

Lunch with Sir Osmond. I reported to him in some detail about the meetings of the Advisory and the Governing Bodies; told him of the crises, but did not accuse Louis Oungre of unfairness, but did underline the essential inconsistency and impropriety of the dual representation; explained the arrangements which had been made for Rome and for Berlin. As to the latter, Sir Osmond was anxious that I should explain his position to the representatives of the community. In reference to New York plans, he is considering seriously the *Washington,* sailing December 28, but is afraid of the American food. He will join in urging Sacher's acceptance. He expects me to prepare the way, so that there will be no overt attacks on ICA or assumptions that the English are coming as beggars. Throughout, he was not only cordial, but extraordinarily friendly.

. . . .

Tea with Dr. Don at Lambeth. He feels that in addition to a plan and the choice of a fitting time for the appeal, there must be a larger degree of coordination than heretofore, so that the Archbishop might have the assurance that a fairly comprehensive job would be done if he were to join in a real national appeal. Then followed nearly an hour's talk about methods of putting this program into effect. Dr. Don recognized that often cooperative efforts, unless they were completely successful, were worse than scattered efforts. He seemed to hope that someone in our office would be able to act as a center for new coordination under some outstanding public man. I told him that though I had almost no time, I would telephone to certain of the persons interested, and write him again.

Called Miss Pye. She favors the dissolution of the GRAF, thinks Wells is a failure, and is preparing a small group to launch an appeal. She is skeptical of the more ambitious efforts suggested by Don's plan. She recognized that we could not be held responsible for the organization of the work in this country. I suggested that Miss Sawyer might be able to follow up on this somewhat after I left.

Farewell chat with Otto Schiff.

McDonald wrote to Warburg on November 6 that he thought it vitally important that someone of his standing challenge an outburst of anti-Semitism by Sir Oswald Mosley. Originally a Conservative M. P. who turned first to Labour and then to independent politics, Mosley founded the British Union of Fascists. He had adherents in the highest social circles, despite his defense of Hitler. On October 28 Mosley had accused Jews of taking over British culture, dominating the mass media, and agitating for war between Britain and Germany.[6]

6. McDonald to Felix Warburg, November 6, 1934. Copy in McDonald Papers, USHMM. *New York Times,* October 29, 1934.

Wednesday, November 7, 1934

Conference at the American Consulate with Mr. Frazer[7] and the man in charge of visas, a Mr. Broy. They both insisted strongly that not only was there no ground for criticism of unfairness in their treatment of the refugees in the matter of visas, but on the contrary, the figures show that they had been much more lenient to this category than to the ordinary applicants because 90 percent of the applications from refugees had been granted, whereas only about 50 percent or 60 percent of the applications from British subjects were granted.[8] They described in some detail the care exercised in the examination of the claims of the refugees, the necessity for such scrutiny, their experience with many applicants who deliberately falsify the record, the likelihood of collusion from persons in the States, and in general, they presented an impressive case.

I made clear that I was not in any sense complaining, but that I had come to talk the situation over, and that in view of their statements I would write to the Jewish organization chiefly concerned with this matter and explain my certitude that the criticisms thus far advanced were unfounded.

Conference with Cecil at his house. We talked about the follow-up on the Lambeth Palace meeting. He agreed emphatically that the money-raising effort in England should not be our responsibility, that we could not take the leadership, nor be primarily concerned with the co-ordination; that at best we could only advise and help. The success, therefore, of the effort would depend upon finding some outstanding personality able and ready to take and maintain the leadership. Lord Cecil was not at all optimistic that such a person could be found.

Discussed our relations with the Germans. He approved my going to Germany and pressing forward there as energetically as possible the points of view expressed at the Governing Body meeting. We talked about the British ambassador, Sir Eric Phipps, and his wife, who is a sister of the wife of Sir Robert Vansittart; though Cecil did not say so directly, I gathered the impression that he thinks Lady Phipps has more brains than her husband and charm equal to that of her more beautiful sister. He said that I might remember him to the Phippses.

We discussed other aspects of our work, but he made no further reference to the possibility of his withdrawal. On the contrary, he spoke cordially of my part and left me with the impression that I could continue to count on his support. I promised to write him fully from or after my visit to Germany.

Having finished up everything with Miss Sawyer and having arranged for her to meet me at the station, I went to the Sieff ten guinea luncheon at the

7. Robert Frazer, U.S. consul general in London.

8. Germans (including Jews) who went to Britain and then applied for visas to immigrate into the United States were counted under the German quota, which was far from filled at this time. Those who were able to get to Britain and possessed some means (or close relatives in the United States) probably could qualify for visas easier than Jews still remaining in Germany, who faced both financial problems and difficulties with paperwork from German authorities. The American consuls had the discretion to decide on each individual case.

Savoy. I saw at once that it had all the earmarks of the usual swanky social function—expensive clothes, furs, and jewels were oppressively in evidence. I spoke to Mrs. Sieff[9] for a moment on entering the reception room, but received from her no indication that I had had anything special to do with the refugee work. She struck me as a cold and rather hard, but probably effective, individual. A little later, I was introduced to the famous Lady Sassoon,[10] but here again there was nothing to suggest that I was anything more than someone who should be honored by meeting such a distinguished person.

Then I chatted with the Lazaruses, the Laskis, and met some of the less grand persons. After some time the luncheon was announced, and we moved en masse towards the dining room. On the way spoke for a little while with Smuts and reminded him of his talk at the FPA.

At the table I was seated to the left of Lady Astor,[11] who was herself immediately to the left of the chairman, Lady Reading, who was presiding in the absence of Mrs. Anthony de Rothschild.

. . . .

Lady Astor confided to me that she has not prepared the least thing for her speech—that she was going to say that she had come much better prepared in heart than in mind; but did I not, after all, believe that there must be something in the Jews themselves which had brought them persecution throughout all the ages: Was it not, therefore, in the final analysis their responsibility? To this thesis I took violent exception. She appealed to Smuts, who in turn appealed to me, but he did add that a basic factor is the fact that the Jews are the only Semitic people spread throughout the western world and taking an active part in all the affairs of the west. This tended to support my contention that the only basic reason for the anti-Semitism is the fact that the Jews are different from the people among whom they live; that if this is a crime, then Lady Astor is right, but not otherwise.

Lady Astor expressed to me her belief that the Catholic Church is nearly the source of all evil; that in all the Catholic countries one sees today marked forms of social and political demoralization; that only Protestantism and especially protesting [*sic,* should be Protestant] England, gives hope for the future. Incidentally, she referred to her firm conviction about Christian Science, charging that the Catholic Church had perverted the scriptures and had forestalled

9. Rebecca Sieff, wife of Israel Sieff and sister of Simon Marks.

10. Sybil Sassoon, daughter of Sir Edward Sassoon and Aline de Rothschild, sister of Sir Phillip Sassoon. Celebrated hostess and beauty, whose portrait was painted by John Singer Sargent, among others. Married the Marquess of Cholmondeley, hereditary Lord High Chamberlain of England.

11. Lady Nancy Langhorne Astor, U.S.-born wife of British politician and publisher Waldorf Astor, first woman to sit in the House of Commons (1919–1945). She took her husband's place when he inherited his father's viscountcy. She was part of the "Cliveden set," which advocated appeasement of Nazi Germany.

the much more rapid development of mankind towards perfection. All of this seemed to me such a mixture of sense and nonsense, science and fantastic illusions that I listened and did not argue.

. . . .

Lady Reading spoke briefly, following her manuscript closely. It was a dignified and impressive statement. Then she called upon General Smuts to make the toast to the resolution of the day. (I have forgotten to tell of the formal toasts earlier, first to the King, and then to the Queen, the Prince of Wales and the other members of the Royal Family. This was followed by the formal announcement: "Now my Ladies and Gentlemen, you may smoke.")

Smuts spoke only moderately well. He seemed to me to have no heart in his appeal, to be more concerned not to hurt German feelings than to stir the compassion of his audience.

Lady Astor began well with one or two touching stories, but like Smuts she lost her way half through her speech, and, as he, finished, I thought, rather lamely.

Then Mrs. Sieff was called upon to conclude the speaking. Hers was rather a grandiloquent appeal, which might have been just as suitable on a number of occasions; but it was well constructed and well delivered.

After this there was a period of badly arranged money-raising before Lady Astor and I slipped out just as the meeting was breaking up.

At no time during the luncheon was there any reference to the work of the High Commission or the High Commissioner, nor did anyone suggest that I speak. It was with considerable difficulty that I refrained from making this suggestion myself, because as the meeting dragged on and as no one seemed to me to be driving straight to the point, and as I was more and more oppressed by the general atmosphere of swank and social snobbery, I wished nothing so much as for the opportunity to say a few rather sharp pointed sentences. But either through timidity or good sense, I refrained from making any move. Instead, I congratulated the women in charge and went off with Lady Astor, who kindly said she would send me to the train in her car.

On the way to the House of Commons Lady Astor and I talked about American politics. She seemed really glad to have a chance to talk about home affairs, and having lost her rather presumptuous air which she had had when discussing the Jewish problem, she was delightful. She suggested that I let her know when I was next in London.

. . . .

Paris, Thursday, November 8, 1934

Kotschnig and I breakfasted together, and at ten o'clock we had the first of our series of meetings. This was with the Deutsche Kommission. The following were present: Hugo Simon, Fritz Stern, Dr. Gronemann, Dr. Bernhard, Dr.

Friedlander, Fritz Wolff. The following is taken from Kotschnig's summary. The most important questions raised were:

(a) Passports and identity papers: Everyone agreed that it was very difficult to obtain identity papers, but there was a disagreement even within the Deutsche Kommission as to the exact character of these difficulties. This proved that it would be one of my first tasks in Paris to find out what the actual situation is;

(b) Dr. Simon and Dr. Bernhard were very anxious that somewhere or other special lists should be established of bona fide emigrants, i.e., only people who had made a declaration that they are emigrants and that they are fully prepared to accept all responsibilities which might arise out of their stay in France, including military service, etc. The main idea behind this proposal is that in case of war, both the refugees appearing in these lists and their capital would be safe, and that they would not be considered as German, which might mean their being herded together in concentration camps and their capital being confiscated. I pointed out that it was next to impossible to establish lists of that kind, as people who were not bona fide emigrants would probably be the first to try and get onto the lists.

(c) Loan fund: The question of a loan fund was again raised, and it was agreed that I should investigate the attitude of the French with regard to such a loan fund, which would serve for the permanent establishment of a certain number of refugees in France. In this connection it was pointed out that every effort should be made to show the advantages to the French of some of the newly established industries;

(d) All of the Germans present insisted on the necessity of a permanent office of the High Commissioner in Paris. They declared themselves satisfied when I explained to them the present arrangement, which meant that, while no permanent office would be established at present, I would spend a good deal of my time in Paris during the coming winter. (We have made arrangements with Dr. Bernard Kahn to let us have some office space at the JDC whenever I am in Paris.)

Immediately after the conference closed, the one with the German press began. Those present were: Dr. Georg Bernhard and Herr Kaiser of the *Pariser Tageblatt,* Herr von Gerlach (Ligue des Droits de L'Homme), Herr Schwarzchild (*Neue Tagebuch*), Herr Philipsbronn (*Freiheit*), and H.H. Swet and L. Chomski of the Jewish press.

I gave them copies of my report and commented on portions of it. I explained that for the purposes of a press interview, I could not at this time go beyond the statements in the report, and that, therefore, I did not wish to be quoted further, but I should be glad if they cared to use any explanations to enable them to interpret better the report itself. There were the usual questions about permits to reside and to work, and concerning the Saar. The discussion was so animated that I had to break it off in order to keep my appointment for luncheon at the Rothschild bank.

At luncheon besides Baron Robert were present Helbronner, Lambert, and Jacques Lyon. My reception was not marked by great cordiality. Baron Robert said that Helbronner had already given a report of the London meeting. During the discussion that followed I asked their judgment on the proposal to list the refugees so that they might in case of war be exempted from the penalties usually imposed upon enemy aliens. The group scoffed at this idea, saying, in effect, that in any event they would all be lumped together, and as someone put it, "You could not in that contingency have Germans walking about the streets unmolested." As to the possibility of a High Commission office in Paris, Baron Robert put the view of the group quite baldly when he said, "Yes, but only if you bring with you £50,000." More helpful was our discussion of the Saar situation. They were all emphatic that I should be present in Geneva at the time of the election. Jacques Lyon promised to find out for me as soon as possible at what date the Council would meet in connection with the election. On the whole, however, the discussion was not friendly—at least not in any genuine sense. They did, however, express interest in my swing around the circle, and the Baron invited them all to meet me at dinner on my return to Paris November 21.

A three o'clock conference with representatives of the Comité pour la Défense des Droits des Israélites en Europe Centrale et Oriental [Committee for the Protection of the Rights of Jews in Central and Eastern Europe]. . . . The following were present: Baron Alfred de Guenzburg, M. Albert Lévy, and M. Leven, the two latter being rather influential members of the Bourse, Dr. Stern and M. Boris Gourevitch, the general secretary of the organization. The main subject of the discussion was the question of the *permis de travail,* for, according to that group, it ought to be given to highly specialized workers who simply cannot be replaced by French workers. M. Gourevitch produced a lengthy memorandum on this subject, on the strength of which they were applying to the Ministry of Labor to obtain 8,000 *cartes de travail.* . . . They wanted me to support their request. I, while obviously sympathetic with the main ideas of the group, reserved my reply until I had had an opportunity of reading the memorandum. Later I talked to Devinat[12] on the telephone, told him that, of course, I agreed in principle with the memorandum, though I could not vouch for every detail of it. I told him the reasons why I did not wish to be quoted publicly in support of it, but that I hoped its principles could be accepted. Still later, when Gourevitch called me on the telephone, I told him that I had followed upon his memorandum in a way which I thought would be satisfactory to him, but I did not say definitely that I had talked to Devinat.

. . . .

12. Paul Devinat, economic expert and chief of staff at the Ministry of Commerce. Later a member of the cabinet in the Daladier, Doumerge, and Flandin governments.

Friday, November 9, 1934

At 9:30 to see Justin Godart[13] at his apartment. We had a very pleasant visit. First, we talked about the Artisanat. He said they were carrying on, though, of course, they needed more money. Then we talked about the official leaders of the Jewish community. He said that he did not share their views, nor was he fearful as were they. From this we drifted into talk about Germany. All in all it was a freest conversation I had had for several weeks.

. . . .

Lunch at Arthur Sachs's. Besides his wife and himself, there was only one other person present, a cousin, who is a doctor in the Pasteur Institute. Arthur was obviously glad to see me; had read my report, and was pleased with it, though a little concerned about my desire to secure rights of residence and of work for the political refugees. He thought this might jeopardize my efforts on behalf of the others.

The new Mrs. Sachs is an ardent royalist, and as such interested me much more than her husband, who remains as sedately matter of fact as ever. I hope to see her again, and if possible, without her husband.

The doctor confirmed what I had heard from other sources, that Barthou had been allowed to bleed to death. His only wound was in his arm, and the blood flow could have been checked by any Boy Scout, but no one had gumption enough to tie a knotted handkerchief tightly about the vein.

At 2:30 met Louis Oungre at the hotel. He showed me a letter from Kahn written to him, arguing against the financial meeting in New York on the ground that you must first have a plan of emigration. It was not a carefully written letter and did not impress me. Kahn ought not permit himself to be inveigled into putting into writing his casual thoughts, particularly in a letter to Louis Oungre.

Oungre stressed the need for funds before I left for South America. I told him that he could be no more emphatic on that than could I. He stressed too the difficulties and the probabilities of failure, and on these two I agreed with him. We also talked about the Saar election. Incidentally, he told me that he had been much disappointed by the failure of his and my démarche with de Mello. I replied that I did not share his disappointment, for I had not expected that a mere memorandum would do the trick.

At four o'clock Schumann came, and together we went to the palace of Cardinal Verdier,[14] where we met de Fresquet. The cardinal was absolutely on time at 4:30. He was very gracious, listened intently to what I and the others had to say about the present refugee situation of the Catholics in Paris, and of the grave possibilities of the numbers of refugees being enlarged many times after

13. Senator Justin Godart, one of the most influential members of the Radical Party, especially interested in the Zionist Movement, president of Agriculture & Artisanat, worked with refugees in the Department of Agriculture and Labor.

14. Jean Cardinal Verdier, archbishop of Paris, 1929–1940.

January 13. De Fresquet outlined his hopes of setting up a real organization in Paris to deal with the problem and asked the cardinal for a letter, which the latter said he would give. But His Eminence had some doubts as to the creation of an entirely new committee, and in particular, he saw disadvantages in its being set up, particularly on behalf of the Germans, for as he said, "You know one must take account of public opinion, and it is not popular to speak of Germans now in France."

The visit undoubtedly had one good result. It strengthened de Fresquet's position with the cardinal, and makes it easier for him to carry on his program.

I had arranged in advance to have my luggage sent to the train by Antoine, and, Schumann guiding me through the underground, we reached the Gare du Nord in ample time for the Nord Express, which left at 6:15 for Berlin.

Berlin, Saturday, November 10, 1934

Arrived in Berlin on time, a little after eight o'clock. Went directly to the Esplanade, which I thought would be more convenient. As a matter of fact, it worked out so, because as soon as I had had time to change, the telephone rang, and I met Lola Hahn. We arranged for a later conference.

Then over to the Embassy. My friend Mrs. Levine was as glad as usual to see me. The ambassador saw me at once. First, however, I arranged through his secretary to accept his invitation for luncheon on Sunday.

Dodd talked quite frankly; said he had spoken to Neurath a couple of times about our problem, that Dieckhoff had recently told him that the situation of the Jews was improving when, within a few days, that statement was completely disproved by new developments. The older persons in the Foreign Office are holding their own,[15] but that is all. Everywhere one senses extreme nervousness about the Saar. Reichswehr troops are said to have been sent west. This was later confirmed to me from another source, but the purpose attributed to the move was not intervention in the Saar, but the forestalling of any overt act by the SR [*sic*, SA].

While I was talking to the ambassador, the secretary came in to report that the date which he had hoped to make for that afternoon at four with Dr. Schacht and which the latter's secretary had tentatively fixed, could not be held. The reason given was Schacht's absorption in other things and his visit over the weekend to Basle. Would I see instead Dr. Dryse, vice-president and second to Schacht? I said yes. A little later I was told that this could not be until Tuesday, because Dr. Dryse was engaged Saturday afternoon and on Monday was celebrating his sixtieth birthday. He suggested Tuesday at 11:30. Though I, of course, realized that this delay might throw out my plans for Prague or Vienna, I unhesitatingly accepted.

Dodd said that he and his son had just come back from a motor trip

15. That is, the Foreign Office senior personnel were holding their own against encroachments by Nazi Party officials into foreign affairs.

through the south; that in many villages as they entered they noticed large placards which read "Jews not wanted here"—or similar legends. He feels that things are not really better, though there is some amelioration in the large cities.

As to the possibility of pressing our case further, he confessed himself uncertain what to do. He urged me to see Phipps promptly to see if he could take any initiative.[16]

Then I went upstairs to talk with White.[17] He had been asked by the ambassador to arrange for me to see Barandon. He talked to Barandon. The latter had given him the impression that there would be no use in a personal conference, and White advised me against trying to make the appointment. I refused flatly to accept his advice—though I agreed that since it might be embarrassing to him, White, I would not ask him to press the matter further. I said I would press it myself, for I had no reason to save Barandon's feelings nor, in a matter of this sort, could I be concerned with my own feelings. It was my business to find out if the Reich had really gotten to the point where they did not wish that even Barandon should see me. This I could only determine by pressing the matter myself, since White of course would not permit me to quote him. Indeed, White's attitude of timid punctiliousness irritated me this time in exactly the same way it had before. He seems to me much more concerned to prove to the Germans that he does not wish to hurt feelings than he is to do his job.

To the British Embassy. Phipps was very cordial. I told him of Cecil's greetings for him and his wife. He had no suggestions to make about the authorities. He said he was waiting for Dodd. His instructions were to support the American ambassador, and he could not take any initiative, but he did ask me to lunch, on the following Monday.

Dropped into the Adlon for lunch with Enderis. He talked quite freely about the German situation; sees no improvement in the Jewish matter, but confirmed the impression I had gotten from other sources that the Reich is counting on the world getting fed up on the refugees and the gradual petering out of interest in them.

In the late afternoon I took a taxi as per instructions and met my friend [Max Warburg] in the woods not far from Potsdam, where he had come in his own car. We went for a long two hour walk, during which time we boxed the compass, talking about various aspects of the situation in Germany, of personalities there, in the west and in Palestine, and of future possibilities of work. Again, I was impressed by his earnestness and self-sacrifice and vision. In all the [German] public schools now there are special lessons in race and similar subjects each Saturday. In this and in other ways Jewish children are subjected to discrimination. The intellectual life remains dark and foreboding. People

16. Dodd's diary confirms this meeting, but contains much less in the way of details. *Ambassador Dodd's Diary,* 188.

17. John Campbell White, counselor of Embassy, 1933–1935.

one knows have not gone to the theater or to the opera or to concerts since the beginning of last year. It is a sort of ghetto life coming back again. Of course, persons who are less sensitive go about more as usual. The community collections from taxes have been higher in proportion than in the past, but the needs are much greater. We spoke of E. [Edward Warburg] and of his being crushed in effect by the too powerful personality of his father [Felix]. My companion protested violently against the Zionist practice of utilizing various devices to bring in women [to Palestine] under the quota. I told him of Bentwich's and my talks with Sir Arthur on the possibility of enlarging the schedule for unmarried women. After our walk we had dinner together and continued our talk, but as a whole it was a sort of informal, confidential, and even intimate conversation, which leaves deep impress, rather than making for clean-cut reporting later.

Sunday, November 11, 1934

Started out late in the morning to visit the Kaiser Friedrich Museum, but ran into a crowd on the lower end of Unter den Linden and finally found myself on the outskirts of what appeared to be a rather funereal Armistice Day celebration in front of the Schloss. Waited vainly for Hitler to appear.

The Dodds for luncheon. Besides the ambassador and his family there was the son of Dr. Stresemann,[18] the nephew of Bernstorff,[19] a distinguished German professor of agriculture and his wife, a former captain of the Marine, and the local manager of the United States Lines, an old graduate of Indiana, and one or two others. It appears that both Bernstoff and Stresemann are handicapped in their careers because of their distinguished relatives. The younger Bernstorff laughingly told the story that his uncle had said that for his nephew's sake, he would not publish his memoirs until after his death. But the nephew quite properly asked: why not wait until after the nephew's death?

The former officer, speaking about Hitler's attitude towards the Jews said, that it was sometimes hard to understand how it was a good policy unless one accepted the view that perhaps in a hundred years it will prove to have been right, but he added regretfully, "That is very hard on us now."

I told Dodd that White seemed to think that I ought not press Barandon for an appointment, but that unless he, the ambassador, urged me not to do so, I would go ahead. Dodd said all right. Mrs. Dodd spoke up saying, "Well, I suppose Mr. White thought it would not be diplomatic." Miss Dodd, with whom I chatted for a little while, told me that Miss Morris, the daughter of the Ameri-

18. Gustav Stresemann, former chancellor and longtime foreign minister in the republic. Largely responsible for Germany's diplomatic gains, such as the Locarno Treaty (1925) and admission to the League of Nations (1926), but still associated, in the minds of the Nazis, with the Versailles settlement and with democratic government.

19. Count Albrecht Bernsdorff, whose uncle had been German ambassador in Washington during World War I. Later was part of the anti-Nazi resistance movement, was imprisoned and shot in Berlin in April 1945, just as the Russians were taking over the city.

can ambassador (to Belgium), was in Berlin. I later called her up, and we arranged to go to the Furtwängler[20] concert together.

Back to the hotel to do some work, and in the evening to the opera, *Carmen*. The place was packed. At the end of the first act I rose to walk out during the intermission, when to my surprise discovered that I was the only person on my feet. I had forgotten to notice that the program indicated that there would be a longer pause at the end of the second act, so not a single German thought to violate the rule.

Monday, November 12, 1934

Over to the Embassy. Sent two telegrams, one to Messersmith [who had been transferred from Berlin to Vienna], telling him that I would arrive there on Wednesday morning, and the other a telegram of congratulations to the President.[21] After carefully checking all the trains, I had discovered that since I could not leave Berlin until Tuesday night, it would be impossible for me to go to Prague and still be certain to reach Rome Friday morning, though I could spend Wednesday in Vienna and still be in Rome in time.

Another conference with Dodd, but only for a short time. He emphasized again that I should try to get something out of Phipps.

Longish conference with Sherman. He insists that there is a marked loss of what he calls "the spirit of the regime." He is certain it will crack somewhere, but how and when is uncertain. It is true that business is better, but much of it is artificially sustained and cannot be continued indefinitely. Moreover, there are sharp differences among the leaders and marked discontent among a large part of the rank and file. Hitler is in constant fear of assassination.

Lunch at the British Embassy. Besides the ambassador and his two lovely children, nine and twelve, there were Mr. and Mrs. Breen of the staff, Mr. and Mrs. Stevens, [he] the governor of the Saar Commission until 1927, Mr. and Mr. Orme Wilson of the American Embassy, Ebbets, and one or two others. Mr. Breen, who is press attaché of the Embassy, was very frank in his criticism of the regime, as, indeed, were nearly all of the others when they spoke of it. Ebbets, whom I was particularly glad to see, minced no words. We were just in the midst of our discussion when Phipps called us to join him and Stevens for a discussion of the Saar. They were all convinced that there would be a large German majority, that the Catholic vote would by no means be solidly for the status quo. Stevens tended to criticize Knox as anti-German, but the others did not agree. They all were of the opinion that it was highly important that the Council should meet as soon after the election as possible. I urged this very strongly, and when Phipps replied that this was for the League to decide, I pointed out to

20. Wilhelm Furtwängler, famed music director of the Berlin Philharmonic Orchestra. A controversial figure. While he assisted some Jewish musicians, he was accused after the war of being a Nazi collaborator who, at least once, conducted in Berlin wearing a Nazi uniform.

21. The congratulations were for the Democratic Party victory in the 1934 congressional elections.

him that it was rather for Great Britain, France, and Italy to agree on a program, and then the League would decide; that the situation was much too delicate to leave to the initiative of League officials.

....

Tea with Sherman. Then over to see Lochner at the Associated Press office. He told an amusing tale of a German who had been asked to appear at the racial office to prove the purity of his Aryan descent. At first, the clerk in charge inclined to make difficulties, but the moment the applicant disclosed his name to be Hitler, instantly the suggestion that he might have Jewish blood was withdrawn, and he was given a certificate of purity. Sometime before, a Jew by the name of Hitler in Warsaw had asked for the privilege of changing his name because he was attacked from both sides.

Lochner thinks the situation is still critical in the Reich, despite the appearances to the contrary.

Stopped for a short time to see Elliot of the *Tribune.* He is less certain that the regime is in danger.

Then with Miss Morris to the Furtwängler concert, and afterwards for a bite of supper at the Eden Hotel.

Tuesday, November 13, 1934

Breakfast with Hillman. He is sure that there is going to be a large German majority in the Saar. After talking about this, Hillman developed his favorite thesis, which is that liberalism through its failures leads inevitably to reaction and to dictatorship. Hence, he is fearful that a Labour victory in England will prepare the way for Mosley.

Over to the Embassy for a few minutes before going to the Reichsbank to meet Mr. Dryse and Dr. Wilhelm. For an account of this interview, see my memorandum about it written after I left Germany.

[Confidential Memorandum, Conversation at the Reichsbank on Nov. 13, 1934 with Dr. Fritz Dreyse and Dr. K. F. Wilhelm.

This meeting was arranged through the American Embassy here after it had tried in vain to make an arrangement for me with Dr. Schacht. The latter excused himself on the ground that he was so excessively busy with his dual responsibilities and on the ground of his visit to Basle over the past week-end.

Dr. Dreyse received me very cordially. I outlined to him the critical situation created for large numbers of the refugees by the recent Devisen restrictions. I emphasized that not only were thousands of innocent people made destitute, but also there was, from the German national viewpoint, another result of real significance: that is the resentment in the neighboring countries because of the new burdens thus placed upon them. Moreover, that it is important for the Reich to remember that the plight of the refugees constitutes a basis for criticism of German policies over a very wide area and that, therefore, I hoped the possibility of making exceptions in connection with the Devisen regulations would be considered not merely from the technical standpoint but from the broader standpoint of national policy.

Dr. Dreyse then called Dr. Wilhelm, the Reichsbank's expert on Devisen. The latter pointed out Germany's nearly desperate plight in reference to Devisen and said flatly that it would be impossible to find Devisen for the purposes I suggested. Dr. Dreyse elaborated this point of view, saying that, at present, there could be no justification for making an exception in order to allow children, students, and other persons to live abroad. They should return to Germany and cease to be a burden on the exchange. He did not elaborate this statement sufficiently for me to be in a position to judge whether there had been any conscious motivation in the minds of the authorities to force the return of refugees. Nor did I argue with him that many of these persons could not return, or if they did return, they would not find any means of making a living or of securing adequate educational or training facilities. To have gone into this matter fully would not have advanced the major purpose of my visit, which was to find out what, if anything, might be expected in the alleviation of existing restrictions.

We then turned to the discussion of the plan suggested in London recently and which in a somewhat varied form had been proposed by the Jewish organizations here to the Reich. This plan would enable the German Jews who have been sending money out of the country to pay those sums into a central fund for relief purposes in Germany, while, at the same time, the British Central Fund or other similar agencies elsewhere would make available Pounds Sterling or other foreign currencies to the refugees or other persons who had previously been the beneficiaries of remittances from Germany. I pointed out, however, that this plan, even if it were agreed to in full, would meet the transfer question only in small part, and that, therefore, I was discussing it not as an alternative to my proposal or the relaxation of the Devisen restrictions for the benefit of the refugees, but rather as a supplementary scheme.

Dr. Dreyse evidently had not heard of the recent proposal of the Jewish group for this sort of clearing arrangement, for he referred back to the plan which Max Warburg had proposed about a year ago. I made clear that I was not discussing that plan but a more limited proposal now pending before the governmental authorities. We then discussed that.

Neither Dr. Dreyse nor Dr. Wilhelm seemed opposed in principle to such an arrangement. At the very outset I had made it absolutely clear to them that this plan would not mean the loss of any Devisen to Germany, because the British and the others who had been sending in funds to Germany were determined not to continue to made such remittances so long as the Devisen regulations were maintained, and that, therefore, Germany would not be the beneficiary of this foreign exchange in any case. Both the officials of the Reichsbank thought there might be some technical difficulties in executing the plan, but that these should not be insurmountable. However, since they had not heard of the proposal from the other German officials to whom it had been made, they did not feel that they could do more than express a general opinion.

Nonetheless, they promised that Dr. Wilhelm would check up on the present status of the negotiations, would study the matter from the point of view of the Reichsbank and would welcome an opportunity to discuss the matter with me again in the near future. I explained that my plans made necessary my leaving for Vienna and Rome tonight, and that there would be no opportunity for me to return to Berlin in the near future. However, I suggested that one of my colleagues, perhaps Mr. Wurfbain, would be passing through Berlin within a week or ten days on his way to the Baltic states and that he would be glad to learn then what would be the attitude of the Reichsbank on this question.

We parted with mutual expressions of good will and of hopes that economic conditions would so change in the next few years so as to eliminate all Devisen restrictions. I should perhaps add that earlier in the discussion, Dr. Dreyse, when laying down his dictum that there could be no exception now to the present drastic Devisen restrictions, had said that perhaps, if economic conditions improved markedly, there would be occasion to reconsider his opinion. But that, of course, was a generalization which helps us not at all just now.]

Lunch with Duranty and Enderis. Out talk was a mixture of foreign affairs and *New York Times* affairs.

Back to the hotel to pack.

Over to the Foreign Office to see Barandon, who had given me an appointment promptly after I had telephoned him. Indeed, he took the trouble of leaving the message in three separate places to be sure I would get it. A full account of that interview is embodied in a memorandum sent to the office a few days later.

[Memorandum of Conference of Mr. McDonald in the Foreign Office on the afternoon of November 13, 1934.

Present, beside myself, were Geheimrat Barandon of the Legal Section, and Legationsrat Roediger and Legationsrat Baer. The latter is a Devisen expert.

This conference was arranged on my personal suggestion to Barandon, despite the intimation which had been given me indirectly the day previous, that he considered a personal talk with me would have no practical result and that, therefore, he would prefer not to see me. Nevertheless, he made the appointment promptly and was cordial enough throughout the talk.

I began by explaining that there were two purposes in my visit: first, to press the point of view expressed in the concluding paragraph of our last letter to the Foreign Office, dated October 11. In that we had said,

> "With regard to the transfer of the property of emigrants, a new difficulty has arisen since I last wrote, on account of the fresh regulation restricting the remittances of income from Germany. This restriction affects not only adult emigrants, but also hundreds of children who are being educated in schools in other countries. It is submitted that some allowance should be made for those Germans who have been driven from their positions in Germany, whether for racial or political reasons, so that they may be able to apply part of their income from property in Germany to their maintenance abroad. It would create an almost intolerable situation if the German government, having taken measures which

> compel some of its citizens to leave the country, should then by its currency legislation render it impossible for those persons to maintain themselves and their families abroad by use of the income of their own property in Germany. Such action would appear to be one of the matters referred to in my letter of July 11 which would directly throw such an exceptional burden upon other governments and philanthropic organizations as to require the High Commissioner to ask for special remedial measures."

Second, to support unofficially but strongly the proposal which had recently been made by the central Jewish organizations at the Reichswirtschaftsministerium [Economics Ministry] for the permission to participate in a sort of clearing arrangement with the Jewish charitable organizations in England and America.

On the first point, there is little that need be recorded here. I elaborated the arguments we had made previously to support the contention that exceptionally favorable treatment in the matter of Devisen should be accorded to those refugees who, through no fault of their own, had had to leave Germany and who could not return.

Barandon replied in general terms, and his colleague Baer more in detail, explaining that the critical Devisen situation made impossible the granting of the exceptions I proposed; that, however, they wished to make clear that in the past there had been no discriminations against the refugees, but on the contrary, many of these had received more favorable treatment than had Germany's commercial creditors.

The second matter took more time. The proposal apparently had not come to the attention of the Foreign Office, or at any rate, no one of the three officials present had heard of it. Barandon was slow to understand that it did not involve in any way the loss of Devisen by Germany, but that it was simply a device to permit the persons who had previously been sending money abroad to pay those sums into a central fund in Berlin, on condition that the groups outside who had been sending money into Germany for Jewish relief purposes should pay to the refugees who had been receiving remittances from Germany sums equivalent to those remittances. I pointed out that this scheme was by its nature limited and would, even if it were permitted to operate freely, care for only a portion of the refugees, but that, nonetheless, it seemed to me well worth trying.

When the program had been made clear, each of the three officials expressed the view that there did not seem to be anything insurmountably difficult in it. They thought, however, that it was a matter for the decision either of the Reichswirtschaftsministerium or of the Reichsbank, rather than of the Foreign Office. However, they were glad to know that the matter was pending and promised to make inquiries in reference to the present state of the negotiations.

Indeed, Barandon heaved an obvious sigh of relief when I told him at the beginning of our talk that I had been to the Reichsbank that morning. Perhaps this was only because he is an official who prefers to take no responsibility if he can avoid it, or it may be indicative of a desire on the part of the Foreign Office to get rid as far as possible of responsibility for carrying on negotiations with our office. However, Barandon admitted that in the future as in the past any formal communications from our office should pass through the Foreign Office, rather than be addressed directly to the Reichsbank or the Reichswirtschaftsministerium. In this connection, however, I emphasized again to him that the proposed clearing arrangement was not something which our office was suggesting, but rather a device which had been worked out by the Jewish organizations, which we were glad to support.

During the latter part of our talk I took occasion to underline strongly the importance from the German national viewpoint of the liquidation as promptly as possible of the refugee problem. I said that there could be no doubt that the continued presence of thousands of refugees, many of them increasingly impoverished, in the states neighboring Germany and elsewhere constituted foci of irritation against Germany, and that this is true even where no direct agitation against the Reich is carried on. All three officials agreed heartily with me that the Reich was suffering abroad because of the refugee situation, and they expressed a keen desire to do what they could to solve the problem. Nonetheless, I left with the impression that we must anticipate very little will come from the Foreign Office on its own initiative.]

Went directly to the Embassy from the Foreign Office for a conference with Dodd. He said he would see what he could do to follow up and for us to keep in touch with him. As I was leaving, he followed me to the door and said, "If I were you I would tell the Jews not to give up the boycott, for these people only understand pressure of one sort or another."

Time to go back to the hotel, pay my bill, get my luggage and go to the train. Before we left Germany, the conductor came around and told me that several of the papers I had purchased at the station would have to be thrown out before I reached the Austrian frontier; they were not permitted there.

Vienna, Wednesday, November 14, 1934

Arrived in Vienna a little after nine, and went directly to the old Bristol. Called up the Legation, spoke to Messersmith, who said that the only time he had been able to arrange for me to see the foreign minister was during the regular diplomatic reception that morning; that he would take me with him and would call within a few minutes. Together we went in his car to the Baldplatz. The entrance was guarded with rows of soldiers, rifles at attention, and pointed bayonets. No chance was being taken on the building being rushed again, as it was the day Dollfuss was assassinated.

While we waited in the reception room, we met a number of other diplomats including the British minister, Sir Walford Selby; the Yugoslav Gjogge Nostasjevia, the Japanese minister, the Rumanian minister,[22] von Papen, and the

22. Raul Bossy, Rumanian ambassador to Austria, 1931–1934, later ambassador to Hungary, Italy, and Germany.

Papal Nuncio. The latter was by far the most ornamental, though Messersmith tells me that he is not nearly so important a person as the Austrian cardinal.

The Rumanian minister, in the little talk I had with him, indicated his anti-Jewish bias. There was no opportunity to talk with von Papen, who came in just long enough to register his name and leave. The Papal Nuncio, as according to protocol, took precedence over everyone else.

However, we did not have to wait very long before we were shown in to see the foreign minister, Baron Berger-Waldenegg. I plunged at once into the subject I wished to speak to him about, the Jewish situation in Austria. I emphasized the disaster which Germany had brought upon itself by its anti-Semitic policy, and expressed the hope that Austria would not make the same mistake. I did this by means of a number of illustrations of the adverse effects on Germany in different parts of the world. Berger-Waldenegg listened closely, then replied with a categorical declaration that there need be no fear whatever on this score, that we could be perfectly sure that Austria would not follow the German policy, that perhaps there had been some danger prior to the time that the Nazi movement was crushed in Austria. Messersmith supported my general statement, saying that, of course, there is a certain degree of anti-Semitism in Austria and underlining the great desirability of its being rigidly repressed.

....

After a nap went to the Legation, where Messersmith had promised me the use of an English secretary. Before beginning my dictation, I chatted with Klieforth. He said that there had been no warning whatsoever just prior to the events of July 25. He said the present regime is far from secure, probably not more than 23 percent of the people supporting it. For the time being, the anti-Semites are not in the saddle. However, despite his apparently frank talk, he left me, as before, rather unconvinced as to his sincerity. He is too much like several of the members in the Berlin Legation—a sort of dignified playboy chiefly concerned to maintain a close social relationship with the society in which he moves.

Dinner alone with the Messersmiths and their nieces. Messersmith told me of a decisive conference between Röhm and Hitler on June 28. At that time the former told the Führer that he must remain with the SA and not swing over to the conservatives. Losing his temper, Röhm said things to Hitler which, never having been said to him before, gave him for the first time a sense of insecurity and created in him a veritable state of panic. This, according to Messersmith, was followed by feverish activity during the next forty-eight hours, culminating in the events of June 30. Hitler, like all weak men, waited until the last moment and then struck out wildly.

I asked Messersmith why were not the conservatives ready to take advantage of this situation. He replied that it had come too early; and Hitler, sensing the danger in the right as well as the left, took advantage of the situation on the left to strike in both directions at the same time.

Most of Messersmith's talk during the same evening was on the Jewish situation in Austria, with which he and the British minister have been concerning themselves deeply for several months. Messersmith is convinced that Schuschnigg is much stronger than he was at first thought to be, and that increasingly, Schuschnigg is taking a stand against the anti-Semites. In illustration of this improving attitude, Messersmith cited the following:

(1) the separate schools; the provision for these is not being repealed, but the promise has been made that it will be interpreted in a fair way, and this is said to be satisfactory to the Jews.
(2) Friedmann,[23] the head of the Jewish community, had recently been put on one of the governmental advisory bodies.
(3) Schuschnigg refused to accept the advice of the anti-Semite lawyers.
(4) The official Nazi leaders with whom the government has been in conversations, do not, with one exception, put anti-Semitism forward as a major plank in their program.

Messersmith complained about the exaggerated reports sent out by the representative of the Jewish Telegraphic Agency. I sympathized with him. Messersmith told me that Laski had done good work in Vienna, and that he thought his memorandum excellent.

Home late.

Thursday, November 15, 1934

Up early to get the 7:50 train for Rome. It was a long, but not uninteresting day journey until we reached the frontier in the late afternoon, and the night was uneventful.

Rome, Friday, November 16, 1934

Arrived at about 8:30 and went directly to the Hotel Excelsior. This time I was very careful to check as to the price of my room, and managed to get a very comfortable one for 45 lira.

After breakfast called Majoni and arranged to see him later in the day.

Then over to the British Embassy to talk with Sir Eric Drummond. I limited our discussion to the question of the return of the High Commission to the League. He thought there was little chance of it. Legally, he didn't see how it could be taken on again, especially in view of the present fixed policy to slough off as rapidly as possible the extraneous activities of the League.

Assuming that he was right, we then discussed the possibility of modifying the organization so that if I remained as High Commissioner, I need not be present in Europe more than occasionally. To this, Sir Eric saw a number of

23. Desider Friedmann, leader of Austrian Jews, appointed in 1934 to the Austrian Council of State. Deported to Theresienstadt in 1943, he died in Auschwitz in 1944.

difficulties; he cited the case of the Nansen Office, which had degenerated sadly when Nansen retired or ceased to be active and Johnson was left in charge. He admitted that the difficulties which had resulted might have been partially the outcome of Johnson's unfortunate personality, and on this point he was quite emphatic, but he added that unless your active executive were really capable of being the High Commissioner, the suggested delegation of authority probably would not be successful. I told him that I thought it might be possible to find such a person, but that, of course, it was too early for us to make a decision.

In to the American Embassy to see Kirk, the chargé.[24] Thought little of him, and was glad that I had almost nothing to take up with him. Wilson was there, but I did not see him.

Cortesi[25] of the *Times* dropped in to see me, but I had nothing to tell him, and said I might have later in the day.

Lunch alone. Talked with Sir Charles Winfield on the phone, and arranged to meet him early the next morning to go to the Vatican.

In the later afternoon Majoni called for me and together we went to see Suvich. Wilson and Kirk were ahead of us. We chatted with them for a moment as they came out. I told Suvich of my concern about adequate guarantees in the Saar to reduce the number of refugees. He expressed doubt as to the possibility of such guarantees being made really effective. On the next question we discussed, the possibility of a meeting of the Council at the time of the election, he was more satisfactory. He admitted the necessity for such action and, I got the impression, will urge it. We then talked about the Syndicat d'Etudes in Paris, and I asked whether their efforts would be welcomed in Italy. We discussed this at some length. Suvich said this was a matter which would have to be taken up with the head of the state, that he would then report the latter's views with Majoni, who would communicate with me. Later, I told Majoni that I would ask the Paris group to supply me with further data, which I would send on to him.

Back to the hotel where Galeazzi came to see me. He was much interested in the setup of the High Commission, wondered why the Vatican was not represented on it, asked me to supply him with further data, and suggested that he would like to raise the question of Vatican membership. He also offered to help me in any way he could at the Vatican. I thanked him and told him of Sir Charles' initiative; he said this was excellent, but that he would call up Pacelli's office nonetheless.

Saturday, November 17, 1934

Over to the British Legation shortly after ten. Chatted with Sir Charles until time to go to the Vatican. We arrived a few minutes before half past, saw

24. Alexander Kirk, counselor of the Embassy, also acting as chargé in the absence of the ambassador.

25. Arnaldo Cortesi, *New York Times* Rome correspondent.

Pacelli's red hat outside the general reception room, knew, therefore, that he was in, but were disappointed to find the Austrian minister and the Austrian minister of education ahead of us in the waiting room. Moreover, before Pacelli began his reception, there came the minister of the Order of the Knights of Malta, a Roman prince, and the minister of Nicaragua, an old Belgian who probably pays the president of Nicaragua a handsome sum to be accredited to the Papal Court. Together we chatted about this and that, and presently, one after another, the two undersecretaries of state came out from Pacelli's office. I met each of them. They seemed to know me, or at least made a good pretense of it. Then the Austrians went in. While they were inside, there arrived the Polish ambassador. Sir Charles' and my hearts sank. The objective of our being early was to secure our audience before the ambassadors began to arrive, for they outranked ministers, and therefore, we might be kept waiting the whole morning.

When the Austrians came out, the Polish ambassador, without the slightest word of apology and without asking us or the other persons present whether they minded if he went ahead, walked in to Pacelli's office. I was morally certain that another ambassador would arrive before the Pole had finished, and so on through the morning. But to Sir Charles' and my great surprise and relief, the Polish ambassador, accompanied by Pacelli, came out within thirty seconds; Pacelli, bowing in our direction said that the Polish ambassador, when informed that a visitor was present, had kindly agreed to waive his prerogative, and would we come in. Later Sir Charles told me that he was fearful that I would not accept; but I had no such thought, and bowing my thanks to the ambassador, Sir Charles and I walked in.

I told Pacelli of my concern about the probability of a very large increase in the number of Catholic refugees after January 13.[26] Incidentally, I told him of de Fresquet's and my visit to Cardinal Vergier and of the need already in Paris for greater Catholic relief. Two or three times during our talk about the Saar we each emphasized that we were dealing only with humanitarian and charitable aspects of the problem, thus making the record quite clear that politics were not involved.

We also talked about my projected trip to South America, which I interpreted as a program for opening up those countries not merely for Jewish, but also for Catholic refugee immigration. I said that I was very anxious to have the benefit which would come in such a large measure if he were willing to lend me his moral support; that the advantages of this would be all the greater in view of the enhanced prestige of the Vatican and the cardinal secretary following the Eucharistic Congress.

Both of these matters I presented in a tentative manner, with the suggestion that I should appreciate the opportunity to come to see His Eminence again immediately after the Saar election or as near that time as I could be in a position to indicate more definitely the probable needs and my own plans. His reply was all that I could hope for. He said with evident cordiality that he would be de-

26. January 13, 1935, the date of the Saar plebiscite.

lighted to see me, and he indicated his active interest in both problems, but without making a definite commitment.

As I left, he talked about a number of other matters just in passing so that I carried away the impression that my position at the Vatican had become such as to possess the possibilities of real usefulness.

Back to the hotel with Sir Charles, who expressed himself as pleased with our reception and anxious to do anything he could for me later. I think he was really impressed by Pacelli's making place for us ahead of the Polish ambassador.

. . . .

Off with Majoni to see Aloisi. He had been for days in constant meetings of his Committee of Three [for Saar Elections] and of his sub-committees. He was cordial, but obviously still a little hurried when we saw him. We talked about the possibility of guarantees. He is not very reassuring, but he did indicate that on a number of matters the Germans and the French were nearer an agreement than they had been. He said that they were taking up the question of the mines within a day or two, but that, despite the progress made, they would not be ready for a special meeting of the Council on the twenty-first as had been planned. He had, therefore, asked for a postponement. One got the impression from him that at last his committee was down to work, but no assurance whatsoever as to the refugee situation, though he did indicate that some of the figures mentioned were probably exaggerations.

On this same day McDonald wrote Sir Osmond d'Avigdor Goldsmid about the Saar situation:

["Immediately after January 13, if, as still seems to me altogether probably, there is a substantial majority vote for the Reich, then will there {there will} be the greatest difficulty in restraining a popular movement in Germany to take over the Saar at once, without waiting for any decision by the {League} Council. . . . As to the probable number of refugees from the Saar, I learned nothing of value in Berlin that was new. It will depend upon what arrangements the Council makes for guarantees and more upon the degree of effective control that the moderates in Berlin will be able to exercise over the extremists in the Saar itself.[27]]

Afterwards chatted for a moment with Lanza d'Ajeta, Aloisi's chef de cabinet. In meeting him, as in meeting everyone else around the Foreign Office, Majoni was invaluable. He explained to me that he had been a member of the personnel committee for a number of years during his 35 years in the Foreign Office, and, therefore, he had come to be acquainted with all the younger men as

27. McDonald to Goldsmid, November 17, 1934, McDonald Papers, Columbia, High Commission Confidential File 2, 1934.

they came in. And he enjoys keeping his acquaintanceships as they seem to enjoy meeting him again.

I promised Majoni I would send him material in reference to the Syndicat d'Etudes. He made me promise that when I came back next time, I would not tie myself up for lunch or dinner in advance without giving him a chance.

Dinner alone, but was joined for a brief conference by Sacerdoti.[28] He showed me a letter that the community had received from the Foreign Office following up our suggestion of a governmental contribution to the High Commission. The Foreign Office had passed on the suggestion to the Jewish community!, indicating that the government had been assured that there would be no financial responsibility on it, and giving the community the opportunity to bear the burden. The community did not intend to do so, but does plan to use the governmental letter as the basis for a new appeal for refugees in Italy. They were delighted to have the letter because it was the first official recognition of this sort they had had since the unfortunate happening some eight months or so ago, when a number of young Jews were involved in an alleged plot against Mussolini. After that, for many months Mussolini refused to receive even Sacerdoti. I carried away from the conference as from my previous talks with Sacerdoti the feeling that he is more worldly than godly.

Rather frantic last minute signing of my letters brought me by Miss Wallace and a brief interview with Eduardo D. Kleinlerer, Rome correspondent of the JTA. Then just time enough to settle my many bills for telegrams, etc., and off to take the ten o'clock train for Geneva.

As we pulled out, I chatted for a little while with Hugh Wilson while he undressed. I think I ought always to talk with him under such circumstances, because he, for the first and last time, was really quite human.

Sunday, November 18, 1934

Pleasant trip through Switzerland, the weather having changed from cold and rain south of the Alps to clear sunlight north of the Pass. Met on the train little Peggy from Bobby's school, on the way back to Villars. Chatted also again for a little while with Wilson. Instead of going on directly to Geneva, stopped off at Lausanne for the late afternoon and the night.

Geneva, Monday, November 19, 1934

. . . .

Over to the Secretariat. First had considerable talk with Whitaker, Carroll of the U.P., Woodward, and later Sharkey and Streit. I gave them a good deal of background material, but very little matter for publication.

28. Angelo Sacerdoti, chief rabbi of Rome since 1912, a Zionist.

Then a long talk with Arthur Sweetser. He was quite definite in his view that there could be no return for us to the League, because even if Germany made its withdrawal definite, there would always be the hope for its return. He didn't think much either of our association with the Nansen Office.

. . . .

Arthur also outlined to me the broad outlines of the plan which he had sketched for the secretary of state to follow through logically on the U.S. relations to the League. Incidentally, he had asked the secretary why his economic reports were not made available through the secretary general of the Economic Conference, who is, of course, Avenol, and thus be given to all the governments promptly in French. The secretary thought it a good idea, but Arthur had the impression that nothing had happened.

. . . .

Telephoned Galeazzi in Rome; told him that I would have the memorandum material sent him, and asked whether he thought it would be possible to have Pacelli send some word to New York, which would enable me to enlist more actively Cardinal Hayes's cooperation. Galeazzi suggested that Mrs. Brady could help there. That I recognized, but I wished to have the other also if possible. He said he would try.

Tuesday, November 20, 1934

Mingled with a number of persons at the Secretariat. Spoke for a moment with Osusky, the Czech ambassador, about the French present attitude towards foreigners. He agreed with me that it was a sort of panic.

Spoke with Litvinov, first about the Governing Body. He said that they could not be associated with it, because they had too many of their own refugees abroad. Asked him about Rosen, whom he did not seem to remember. Then inquired about the willingness of the Soviet authorities to receive Communist refugees. He said certainly; but they must be certain that they are Communists.

A word or two with Malcolm Davis. Then a brief conference with Mrs. Morgan, which I had to break off in order to talk with Mme. Tabouis. She was very despondent, confirming what I had heard from other sources that Laval was very "pro-German," that is, he was giving away everything in connection with the Saar and on other issues too, for the sake of peace. Apparently, his taking the place of Barthou has made a real change in French policy. Tabouis is pessimistic about the Saar, is sure there will be a large German majority and no protection for the French sympathizers. France, to her mind, is in a parlous state.

Lunch at Ginsberg's. She had quite a party, including the librarian, Chodzko, and about eight others. It was a delicious meal, perfectly served.

Late in the afternoon I talked again with Ginsberg. She assured me that she was not concerned really about the obligations in arrears of her committee, that

Portrait photo of James G. McDonald, 1933. USHMM/McDonald Family.

Meeting of the League of Nations General Assembly in Geneva during the 1930s. USHMM/McDonald Family.

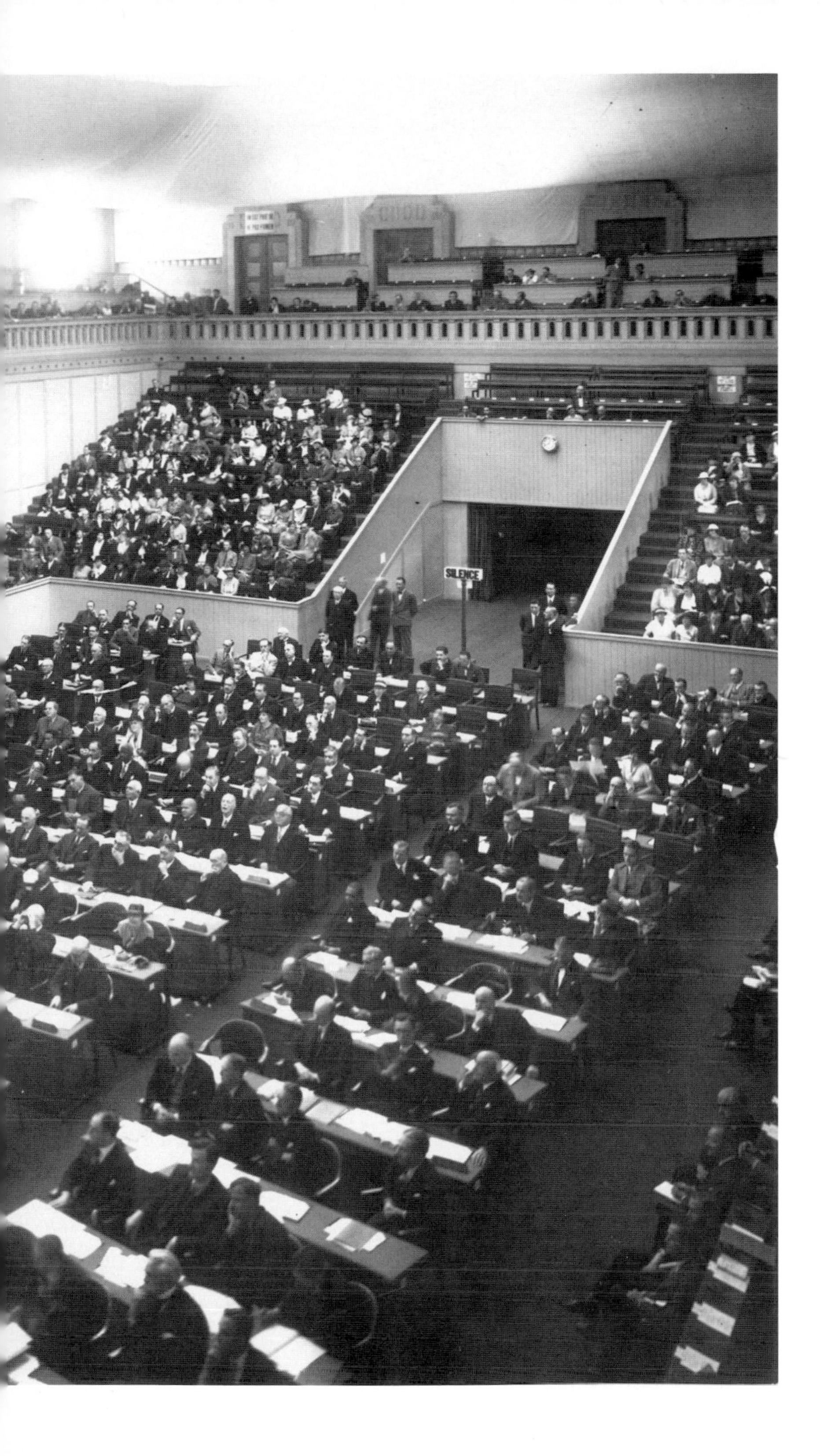
SILENCE

Inscribed 1930s photo of Henry Morgenthau, Sr., former U.S. ambassador to the Ottoman Empire. USHMM/McDonald Family.

McDonald during his Vatican visit for an audience with Cardinal Pacelli, August 14, 1933. USHMM/McDonald Family.

Nazi propaganda employing an early 1920s photo of the directorate of the German banking industry. Entitled "Jews as masters of the money market," it shows Georg Solmssen at the podium. Above him, from left to right, Walther Frisch of the Dresdner Bank, Max Warburg of M. M. Warburg & Co., Otto Bernstein, and Eduard von Eichborn. Front row, seated, Walther Rathenau. USHMM/Marion Davy.

Three leading figures of the American Jewish Joint Distribution Committee in 1933. Left to right, Felix Warburg, JDC chairman 1914–1932; Herbert Lehman, JDC officer and governor of New York 1933–1942; and Paul Baerwald, JDC chairman 1932–1941. Joseph and Miriam Ratner Center for the Study of Conservative Judaism, Jewish Theological Seminary of America.

Viscount Cecil of Chelwood and James G. McDonald attend a meeting of the High Commission in London on May 9, 1934. © AP/Wide World Photos.

James G. McDonald, in his capacity as High Commissioner for Refugees, attends a groundbreaking ceremony for Werkdorp Wieningemeer, a new Dutch village to be built for refugees on land reclaimed from the Zuyder Zee. October 3, 1934. USHMM/ McDonald Family.

"The Jews of Germany Have Been Reduced to the Status of 'Untouchables.' Will We Be Untouchable to Their Sorrow-Laden Appeal?"

THE BULLETIN

OF THE GREATER NEW YORK CAMPAIGN
OF THE UNITED JEWISH APPEAL
OF THE JOINT DISTRIBUTION COMMITTEE AND THE AMERICAN PALESTINE CAMPAIGN

NRA MEMBER U.S. WE DO OUR PART

Vol. I. | FRIDAY, MAY 18, 1934 | No. 1

APPEAL LAUNCHED FOR GERMAN JEWS

RALLYING FORCES OF U. S. JEWS—Felix M. Warburg, National Chairman of the United Jewish Appeal, officially opens $1,200,000 drive as ovation sweeps him into post of chairman of opening dinner. (At right): Mrs. Roger W. Straus, Chairman of the Women's Division, pleading for united support. Under her leadership New York women hope to raise $200,000

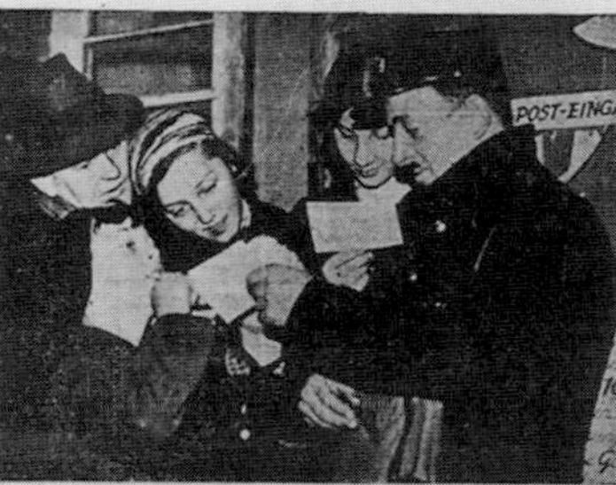

WILL YOU FILL THEIR EN-VE[illegible] by [illegible]s anxiously awaiting [illegible] that will relieve their tragic plight, as thousands of other men, women and children face hunger and want in many corners of Europe—a sorrowful picture, indeed—one that must wring every Jewish heart.

THEY HEAR McDONALD TELL OF REFUGEES' TRIBULATIONS—Rabbi Jonah B. Wise, Dr. Judah L. Magnes, Chancellor of the Hebrew University in Palestine, and Prof. Raymond Moley, who later delivered their own stirring messages, are seen listening as the words of James G. McDonald came from Rome by air to the diners at the campaign opening on Sunday night. (At right)—I. Edwin Goldwasser, one of the three chairmen of the campaign, as he perfected his comprehensive strategy for canvassing the entire city for $1,200,000.

LOCAL DRIVE SEEKS QUOTA OF $1,200,000

The scene is the Hotel Excelsior in Rome. It is three o'clock in the morning. A tall sandy-haired man has just gotten out of bed to speak to America. Seated at a table, he reads into the mike before him a review of a zig-zag march up and down Central Europe on a sad, disheartening mission. Across the Atlantic, 4,000 miles away, in the grand ballroom of the Hotel Commodore [illegible] ner tables eagerly strain, crane to catch the message as his clear-cut, though phonographic voice recites the desperate plight of the Jews in Germany.

As photographers' flash lights boom impertinently, leader after leader of American Jewry rises to face amplifier microphones, stir the audience to piercing realization of the grave responsibility of making possible a fund of $1,200,000 for relief, rehabilitation and settlement of German Jews. On the long board that forms the dais lean the arms of figures like Felix M. Warburg, National Chairman of the United Jewish Appeal, Dr. Judah L. Magnes, Chancellor of the Hebrew University in Jerusalem; Nathan Straus, Jr., one of three chairmen, together with Dr. I. Edwin Goldwasser and Ira M. Younker, of the New York effort; Raymond T. Moley, editor of "Today"; Louis Lipsky, Morris Rothenberg, Rabbi Jonah B. Wise and Paul Baerwald—all co-chairmen of the national campaign; Mrs. Roger W. Straus, chairman of the women's division; Michael Schaap, head of the Trades Council; Arthur Lehman, and Henry Ittleson.

On the way to the ballroom the record audience gathers in an ornate lobby where they pause at more than a dozen tables laden with prospect cards, seating lists, trade groups, information kits. A large staff of evening-gowned stenographers distribute manila envelopes as Boy Scouts from troops 172 and 142 in full uniform with yellow kerchief slung around their necks in cowboy fashion usher guests to their seats. In the East Ballroom an emergency staff of waiters stands in readiness for the overflow crowd which is to hear the proceedings by special loudspeaker hookup. Tables have been planted in every available corner of the ballroom, including the balconade. Remarkable is the systematic plan set up to ac-

(Continued on page [illegible])

GERMAN JEWRY'S FATE IS IN YOUR HANDS

Report of the United Jewish Appeal's May 13, 1934, Hotel Commodore dinner in New York, launching a relief and resettlement fund. More than 2,000 attendees heard McDonald's radiophone address from Rome, describing the plight of German Jews. UJA, the *Bulletin,* May 18, 1934. USHMM/McDonald Family.

THE BULLETIN
OF THE GREATER NEW YORK CAMPAIGN
OF THE UNITED JEWISH APPEAL
OF THE JOINT DISTRIBUTION COMMITTEE AND
AMERICAN PALESTINE CAMPAIGN

Vol. 1 FRIDAY, MAY 18, 1934 No. 1

Why We Must Raise $1,200,000

The battle is on!

The battle to save human lives—Jewish lives; to save the Jews of Germany, wherever they are, from succumbing to outrage; to save Jewish honor from degradation and Jewish values from annihilation by those now in command of the Reich.

It is a battle that must be won for the sake of our self-respect.

We must win this battle on the high plane of a determined effort for the sake of all mankind, for the sake of every human being to worship God in his own way, to enjoy freedom of speech and freedom of action for his legitimate needs and the welfare of his family. It is a battle that we must win.

We must win it, for the sake of the 500,000 Jews in Germany, who are struggling to maintain themselves, to support their wives and children in the face of one of the most atrocious attacks that have ever been made by a government and a dominant political party against a group of people anywhere in the world. We must win it, for the sake of the Jews in Germany, displaced from their positions, deprived of their means of livelihood, who are valiantly struggling to save themselves from the destitution that is deliberately planned for them.

We must win it for the sake of the 50,000 German Jews who are virtually wanderers on the face of the earth, having [illegible] of their fatherland, now bitterly struggling [illegible] sands of Jewish children in Germany who are [illegible] daily in the public schools only because they are Jews, who have been shut out of the higher schools and the colleges, who now face a hopeless future.

[illegible]

Hospital, the Public Education Association, [illegible] Women's Roosevelt Memorial [illegible]ciation, The Women's National Republican Club, and the

parts of Long Island have been organized for the [illegible] Jewish Appeal Campaign, according to Rabbi

Germany who are making such a brave effort to root themselves into the soil of Palestine.

The "big guns" of our battle—which is to raise $1,200,000 in this city in the shortest possible time—were fired at the Hotel Commodore on Sunday night.

From Rome there came over the trans-Atlantic telephone the plea of James G. McDonald, Refugee High Commissioner, on behalf of those who have made their way out of Germany.

We heard the eloquent appeals of the leaders of American Jewry—Felix Warburg, Paul Baerwald, Jonah B. Wise, Louis Lipsky, Morris Rothenberg, Mrs. Roger Straus and Judah L. Magnes. What they told us was a reiteration of what we all already know—but they told it to us in a manner touching our souls and in words that should inspire each and all of us to fight, to work unremittingly until this battle for $1,200,000 for the Jews of Germany from the Jews of New York shall have been won.

If you will take the words of our leaders to your hearts, If you will let the story of German Jewry's tragedy sink deep into your souls, you will need no further urging from us.

Yet, as lieutenants to our leaders in this battle, we nevertheless plead with you to do for the Jews of Germany what you would expect would be done for you if you were in their place.

Courage, determination, and that sympathy which is woven into the warp and woof of Jewish character—these we ask you to exercise.

If you do this, if you will bring this message of Jewish duty to every one of those whom you have undertaken to see on behalf of this cause, we cannot help but succeed.

Chairmen

Greater New York Campaign of the United Jewish Appeal

A CHALLENGE TO THE JEWS OF AMERICA

50,000 Jewish refugees are now living in lands bordering on Germany. In addition, 12,000 have been compelled to return to Poland and other Eastern European lands. Thousands of Jews of Germany, in addition to those who have already settled there, must be helped to establish themselves in Palestine and elsewhere.

refugees, who will:

James G. McDonald, League of Nations' High Commissioner for Refugees Coming from Germany, in a trans-Atlantic telephone message to the opening of the Greater New York Campaign of the United Jewish Appeal, said:

"THE VOELKISCHE BEOBACHTER," the official Nazi organ, recently published an article under the headline—

"KEINE INTERESSE MEHR FUER DIE EMIGRANTEN." (There is no longer any interest in the refugees.)

"This is a challenge for you," Mr. McDonald said, "you can meet it effectively [illegible] the appeals made to you. [illegible]response to

What Is Your Answer To This Challenge . . . ?

Will you let these refugees become a burden on the countries which have given them a haven, with the consequences that such a burden involves? Will you not help them rehabilitate themselves in other lands?

Give Today So That These People May Have the Courage to Want to Live!

I. EDWIN GOLDWASSER,
NATHAN STRAUS, JR.,
IRA M. YOUNKER,
Chairmen Greater New York Campaign
United Jewish Appeal

- -

UNITED JEWISH APPEAL,
Commodore Hotel, New York City.

Herewith is my contribution of $.......... to the $1,200,000 United Jewish Appeal.

Name ....

Address ....

Make Checks Payable to Paul M. Rosenthal, Treasurer
Headquarters Commodore Hotel, 22nd Floor

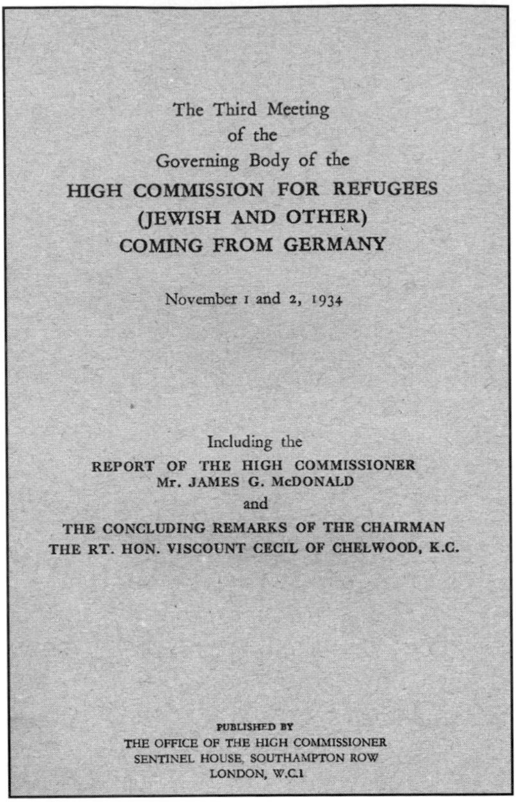

The Third Meeting
of the
Governing Body of the
HIGH COMMISSION FOR REFUGEES
(JEWISH AND OTHER)
COMING FROM GERMANY

November 1 and 2, 1934

Including the
REPORT OF THE HIGH COMMISSIONER
Mr. JAMES G. McDONALD
and
THE CONCLUDING REMARKS OF THE CHAIRMAN
THE RT. HON. VISCOUNT CECIL OF CHELWOOD, K.C.

PUBLISHED BY
THE OFFICE OF THE HIGH COMMISSIONER
SENTINEL HOUSE, SOUTHAMPTON ROW
LONDON, W.C.1

Cover of the report of the third meeting of the High Commission for Refugees, November 1–2, 1934. USHMM/McDonald Family.

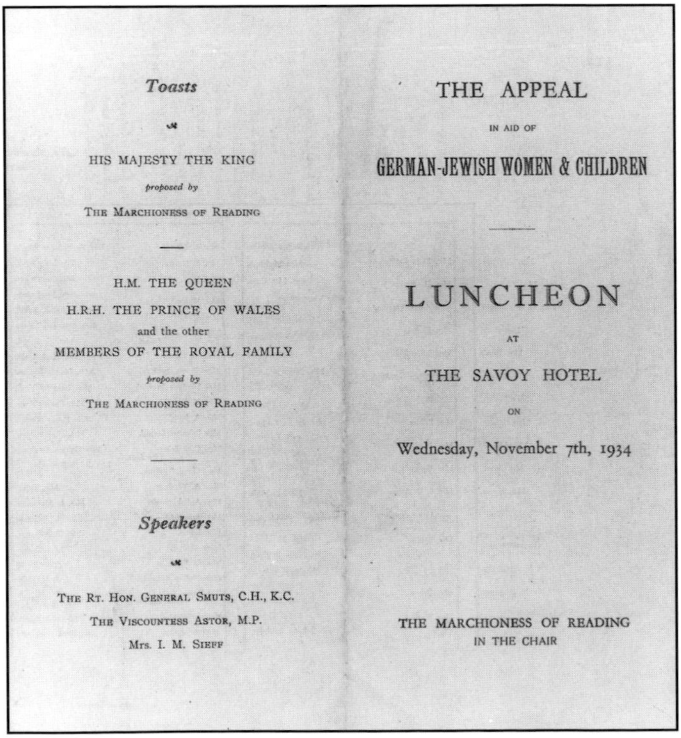

Attended by McDonald, Lady Astor, Jan Christian Smuts, and many prominent British Jews, the November 7, 1934, Savoy Hotel luncheon appealed on behalf of German Jewish refugees. USHMM/McDonald Family.

Toasts

HIS MAJESTY THE KING
proposed by
THE MARCHIONESS OF READING

H.M. THE QUEEN
H.R.H. THE PRINCE OF WALES
and the other
MEMBERS OF THE ROYAL FAMILY
proposed by
THE MARCHIONESS OF READING

Speakers

THE RT. HON. GENERAL SMUTS, C.H., K.C.
THE VISCOUNTESS ASTOR, M.P.
Mrs. I. M. SIEFF

THE APPEAL
IN AID OF
GERMAN-JEWISH WOMEN & CHILDREN

LUNCHEON
AT
THE SAVOY HOTEL
ON
Wednesday, November 7th, 1934

THE MARCHIONESS OF READING
IN THE CHAIR

In New York, McDonald receives the American Hebrew Award for his service on behalf of German-Jewish refugees, January 4, 1935. Philanthropist Felix Warburg (center) and Rabbi Isaac Lardeman (right). UPI.

Miss Richardson.
Mrs. Gillett.
Mrs. Paul Goodman.
Miss Hannah Cohen, O.B.E.
Lady Samuel.
Miss M. Marks.
Violet, Lady Melchett, D.B.E.
Lady Jowitt.
Capt. The Hon. Lionel Montagu, D.S.O.
Mrs. Simon Marks.
The Viscountess Erleigh.
Sir Ernest Oppenheimer.
The Lady Violet Bonham Carter.
Mr. Neville Laski, K.C.
Lady Fitzgerald.
The Very Rev. The Chief Rabbi, Dr. J. H. Hertz.
Lady Simon.
The Countess of Oxford and Asquith.
Mrs. I. M. Sieff (Chairman).
The Rt. Hon. General Smuts, C.H., K.C.

The Ma

Mrs. Auerbach.
Mrs. F. Samuel.
Mrs. C. G. Seligman.
Miss Hertz.
Mrs. Domb.
Mrs. Hyman.
Miss Lazarus.
Miss Herman.
Mrs. Marcus.
Mrs. Monk.
Mrs. Ungar.
Mrs. Woolf.
Daily Telegraph (Representative).
Mr. M. Stephany.
Mr. M. Mitzman.
Mr. L. Rakstansky, LL.B., B.Sc.(Econ.).

B

Mrs. S. L. Lazarus.
Mrs. H. Ansley.
Miss Ailsey Lazarus.
Mrs. Ehrlich.
Mrs. Lillienfeld.
Miss Agnes Goodwin.
Mrs. A. L. Simon.
Mrs. Fellner.
Mrs. Philip Waley.
Miss Gertrude Waley.
Mrs. S. G. Asher.
Miss Grace Ansell.
Mrs. Bloom.
Mrs. Liebster.
Mrs. Delow.
Miss Boyd.

Lady Michaelis.
Miss Michaelis.
Mrs. Gans.
The Viscountess Scarsdale.
Mr. Norman Laski.
Mrs. Alan Selborne.
Mrs. Nove.
Mrs. Norman Laski.
Mrs. Venus.
Mrs. Jules Stein.
Mrs. Simon Rowson.
Dr. Chana Maisel Schochat.
Miss Miriam Moses, J.P.
Mrs. Ephraim Levine.
Mrs. Eichholz.
Mrs. Leo Instone-Gallop.
Mrs. Leon Shalit.
Mrs. H. Hecht.
Mrs. Hilda Brighten.
Mr. Maurice Kentridge.
Mrs. Eugene Bolton.
Captain Metcalfe.
Lady Nathan.
Lady Spielman.

C

Mr. S. Goetze.
Mrs. S. Goetze.
The Hon. Mrs. Leslie Gamage.
Mrs. Richard Raphael.
Mrs. Hastings Brooke.
The Hon. Mrs. Sebag-Montefiore.
Miss A. Hardy.
Miss Rosemary Raphael.
Miss Marjorie Raphael.
Miss Nadine Weisweiller.
Mrs. A. Jessel.
Miss Sylvester Samuel.
Mrs. Cecil Sebag-Montfiore.
Mrs. Claud Spielman.
Miss A. Warburg.
Mrs. A. Benjamin
Mrs. Rosenfeld.
Mrs. Loewi.
Miss Sharpe.
Mrs. R. Eichholz.
Miss Nancy Samuel.
The Times (Representative).
Mrs. Juster.
Mrs. Aronsohn.

Mrs. A. Van den B
The Lady I
Mr. Joe S
Mrs. Joe S
Mrs. E. S
Mrs. Burnett C
Mrs. E. B
Mrs. Noah I
Mrs. Martin Be
Mrs. Isaac Wo
Mrs. George
Mrs. Harry K
Mrs. H. Davi
Miss Clarissa Dav
Mrs. R. G. Edwards M
Mrs.
Mrs. I. Abra
Mrs. R. Sol
Mrs. Fritz A
Mrs. H
Mrs. Rosen
Mr. E. J. L. Ra
Mrs. F
Mr. Silas
Mr. Max F
Mr. Fred Davi

The seating chart for the November 7, 1934, Savoy Hotel luncheon appeal on behalf of German Jewish refugees.

ading

The Viscountess Astor, M.P.
Mr. James McDonald.
The Lady Juliet Duff.
The Countess of Birkenhead.
Commander Oliver Locker-Lampson, M.P.
Lady Sassoon.
The Viscountess Bearsted.
The Lady Emily Lutyens.
Mr. Simon Marks.
Mrs. Corbett Ashby.
Lady d'Avigdor-Goldschmidt.
Mrs. Neville Laski.
Lady Burton.
Mr. Otto Schiff.
Mrs. Weinberg, J.P.
Mr. Robert Solomon, M.C., LL.B.
Mrs. Frank Braham (Organiser).

Melchett.
Golding.
Nelke.
en.
rt Wortley.
Spielman.
o.
el Cohen.
-
les Wolfson.
er Wolfson.
terman.
ray Silverstone.
La Comtesse Ville-Neuf.
st.
D. Eder.
Lockhart.
ell.
Sacher.
or Behar.
or Behar's Guest.
L. Rawson.
Adler, C.B.E., J.P.
Diamond.
Philip Cohen.
rwell.

Mrs. H. Lousada.
Miss A. C. G. Wright.
Mrs. Harris Lebus.
Mrs. George Grumbar.
Lady Salmon.
Mrs. Goldstein.
Lady Prince.
Mrs. A. H. Levy.
Mrs. Klean.
Lady Franklin.
Lady Waley Cohen.
Mrs. Waley Joseph.
Mrs. F. S. Franklin.
Mrs. Jeanette Kohn.
Mrs. Hirsch.
Mr. Frank Braham.
Mrs. Beddington Behrens.
Mrs. Guy.
Mrs. John Goodenday.
Mrs. Walter Payne's Guest.
Miss Wilson.
Mr. Prince Russell.
Lady Colefax.

E

Mrs. M. Epstein.
Mrs. M. Berlin.
Mr. Henry Van den Bergh.
Mrs. L. Elton.
Mrs. Bloch.
Mrs. Freudenberger.
Mrs. Kemble.
Mrs. Snowman.
Mrs. Wolf.
Mrs. L. Lazarus.
Mrs. Froomberg.
Mrs. A. Cohen.
Mrs. Frank Myers.
Mrs. Pauline Sieff.
Mrs. Edward Sieff.
Miss Miriam Sacher.
Mrs. Robert Mayer.
Mme. Conchita Rubenstein.
Mr. Robert Behar.
Mrs. Michael Sieff.
Mrs. Dennis Cohen.
Mrs. Harry Sacher.
Mrs. Harry Sacher's Guest.

Mrs. Asher Feldman.
Mrs. Alvarez.
Mrs. Blumenthal.
Mrs. Balfour.
Mrs. Hoffman.
Mrs. D. H. Aaron.
Mrs. Goldberg.
Mrs. I. Fredman.
Mrs. Lowenstein.
Mrs. Boss Price.
Jewish Telegraph Agency (Representative).
Mrs. Benzion Halper.
Mrs. A. Israel.
Mrs. Kleeman.
Mrs. Frank Lazarus.
Mr. Frank Lazarus.

F

Mrs. Schwab.
Mrs. Schwabacher.
Mrs. Rosenheim.
Mrs. Sussman.
Mrs. Warshaw.
Mrs. Beloff.
Mrs. Trilling.
Mrs. Heineman.
Mrs. David Levi.
Miss Schapiro.
Miss Kessler (Jewish Morning Journal of New York).
Mrs. Gordon West.
Mrs. McEwen.
Miss Slater.
Miss Fletcher (Secretary).
Miss Greaves.

American Jewish leaders and recent German-Jewish émigrés to the United States in April 1935. Seated from left to right are Felix Warburg, Albert Einstein, and Elsa Einstein. Standing (left to right) are unidentified, Morris Rothenberg, and Rabbi Stephen Wise. USHMM/Helen Hamlin.

McDonald's visit to the Vatican (probably 1935). USHMM/McDonald Family.

McDonald's visit to Brazil, April 1935. USHMM/McDonald Family.

if I did not think it necessary to keep Vavasseur,[29] she would sever that connection. She has hopes of sharing in the profits of a stamp to be issued, it is planned, in connection with the Women's International Suffrage Alliance Conference in Istanbul. As to securing funds from members of her own committee, she is unable to make the attempt, but agrees that it would be all right for Kotschnig to see Rappard.

Then she introduced me to Hans Sandelmann, for seven years secretary of the Bureau of the Interparliamentary Union and thus closely associated with Lange; a German citizen, he has been outside of Germany for thirteen years, lived in Argentina four years, speaks Spanish and French perfectly, and recently has made an elaborate tour of South America in connection with his interparliamentary work, and therefore, has a considerable acquaintanceship. He was suggested as a possible colleague on my trip. We chatted for a considerable time. It was finally left that he would, after receiving documentary material about our work, write me a long memorandum outlining his ideas as to methods by which such an inquiry as I had to make might most advantageously be carried out.

My own impressions of the man were rather mixed. He undoubtedly has excellent qualification[s], has a personality of rather flat character, neither impressive nor the reverse. Whether he would have originality and drive or whether he would be pleasant to work with were all question marks.

All of these talks were held in the lobby of the disarmament building while the special Assembly was getting under way. However, I didn't even find the time to go in for a few minutes.

Kotschnig and I hurried off as soon as the Assembly adjourned to keep our appointment with Laval, who had arrived in town that morning.

He was sitting in the lobby of the Bergues when we arrived, talking with another man. He at once recognized me, called me by my name, and asked us to sit down, the other man leaving. Laval referred cordially to our Washington connection. Then I tried to launch into my favorite speech in my best French about France's national interest in making an exception for the refugees, etc. But I was not allowed to more than get started. Laval apparently had made up his mind and wanted to talk to me, rather than to listen.

Laval began what was almost a tirade. France has decided. A recent meeting of a ministerial committee, followed by a cabinet [meeting], had fixed the policy. No more *cartes de travail* to incoming foreigners, no more renewals for people who had come within the last two years, and no new *cartes* for such persons (though on this last point I would not venture to say that he was definite). Moreover, all French employers must reduce the number of foreign employees, no firm might have higher than 20 percent, etc., etc.

Kotschnig tried to support me by pointing out the peculiar difficulties of certain categories of refugees; but he was scarcely listened to.

29. Mme. Vavasseur, in charge of the Paris office of the International Committee for Securing Employment to Professional Workers.

We asked about the Saar. Laval said that, of course, was a political problem, and implied that there might be special exemption for refugees from the Saar, but at the same time indicating that France could not expect to keep such people indefinitely.

In short, much of personal cordiality towards me, but an utterly devastating and demoralizing declaration of French national policy. The talk unfortunately was cut short by the arrival of the French journalists en masse, with whom Laval had an appointment.

Kotschnig and I immediately had a hurried council of war. We decided that we must make desperate efforts to see Herriot the next day in Paris, for as chairman of the inter-departmental committee, he might be helpful. I suggested that Kotschnig get in touch with Mme. Tabouis to help in arranging the Herriot date, and that Kotschnig consider seriously leaving with me on the evening train for Paris. He at once said that he too was inclined to think that it was necessary for him to change all his plans and come with me, but we left that to be decided after eight o'clock, following my interview for which I was overdue, with Benes.

Later, Kotschnig told me that Laval began his interview with the French press by telling them that he had just been seeing the High Commissioner and had been laying down the law to him! Moreover, Laval indicated to the French press that his government is contemplating drastic action towards all the German press, anti-Hitler and [pro-]Hitler, in France.

Benes received me at once, and in his usual friendly way. We talked briefly about the refugee situation in Czechoslovakia. He said that he had no intention of following the French example. He added that any questions that we wished to raise as to re-training or other matters connected with the refugees had best in each instance be taken up first with the Foreign Office.

I then asked Benes if he wouldn't talk with me for a little while about the European situation as he would talk if he were talking with the President of the United States with a view to enlisting the latter's support in the maintenance of peace. Benes settled back and gave me in substance his interpretation. All Europe is obviously rearming because of the fear of war. Probably war can be avoided for another year or eighteen months. During that time several important factors which are now uncertain will have clarified themselves, and one can see better than now whether war is inevitable. Among these factors are: the Saar, the attitude of Poland, the program of Italy, and the aims of Germany once it is rearmed. As to its rearmament, there can be no doubt. It will be fully equipped for war in the spring of 1935.

Europe is divided into camps. The states that want to keep the peace on the basis of the present status quo, including France, Czechoslovakia, Great Britain, Russia, and the Little Entente. But there is a group of bandit powers—Germany, Poland, Hungary, Italy. The policy of the latter is one of blackmail. This would not be so bad if one knew what price Italy really would be satisfied with, but that is never clear. Similarly, the position of Poland becomes more confused.

Each week brings its new crisis and the danger of tragedy. Each time that one danger is averted, preparation must be made to meet the next. Probably they will be met successfully one after another as they arise, but if not, Czechoslovakia is determined to make those who attack it pay dearly.

On the whole, despite the strain and the obvious dangers, the chances favor peace. The United States can help most by indicating its moral support for the peace group of powers.

....

Met Kotschnig at the Bellevue, and together decided definitely that he would go with me to Paris, and we arranged to meet at the ten o'clock train.

Paris, Wednesday, November 21, 1934

Reached Paris on time. Went directly with Kotschnig to the Continental. A little later we were joined by Wurfbain, and we breakfasted together, making plans for the day.

A long talk with Schevenels on the telephone. We discussed the Lambeth Palace meeting, which disappointed him very much. I told him I would use his letter to Kotschnig as the basis for a new appeal to the A. F. of L.

Conference with Baron Guenzburg and A. Cohn. First in reference to the situation in Paris, they were terribly upset by the latest developments. I explained the effort we were going to make during the day, but they had little that was new to offer. We then talked about their plan and their request for funds from America, which I said I would take up with the corporation.[30] And finally the possibility of their considering operating in Italy. Baron Guenzburg agreed to write me a letter which I would forward to Majoni. Again, this group struck me as being excellent in every way.

During our conference there was a telephone call from Louis Oungre. When I answered it, he, in a high state of excitement and in a tone that bordered on the imperialist, told me that he had something very confidential and important to tell me; that I should at once jump into a taxi cab and come to his office. I cut him short by explaining that I was then in conference with a group of persons, that I was waiting on telephone responses to inquiries being made at Herriot's office and at the Foreign Office, and that I could not come then. I suggested that he come to me. He replied, "I am too busy." My reply was that I was sorry, but that I could not go to his office. He asked if I could send someone else. I said that I would be glad to send Wurfbain.

Then, with the excitement worn off a little, he told me briefly what his message was. It was to the effect that he had received very confidential data from Argentina to the effect that the President and other high officials are opposed to any further Jewish immigration at this time. In view of ICA's extraordinary record there in the past, he can only attribute this change to Nazi activities on the spot. In any case, under these circumstances he thinks I should reconsider the possibility of my going.

30. The proposed corporation to invest in refugee resettlement projects.

I thanked him for his information, told him that I would value it highly, that I regarded him as one of the best technical experts in the world, but that as he would recognize I must reserve to myself final decision as to whether or not I undertook the trip; that naturally I could not decide a matter of this sort on the spur of the moment on the basis of his information alone, no matter how important that might be. I added that I would get in touch with him again during the day if I had time. And it was more or less on this note that the conversation ended. Later in the day, I received a long letter from him, setting forth what he had meant to tell me.

Lunch with Baron de Rothschild, Helbronner, and Kotschnig at the bank. The atmosphere was more cordial than when I was last there. I reported on my visits to Berlin, Vienna, and Rome and Geneva. They were chiefly interested in the Berlin and Rome accounts, and most of all in what I had to say about the Vatican.

Then I asked them about the situation in Paris. Their responses indicated that at last they were really afraid that things had gone too far and were out of hand. Helbronner spoke of Lambert's attempt to find out whether there would be an exceptional status for the refugees. Helbronner and Rothschild agreed that if the reported regulations were put into effect, it would make the situation of the refugees impossible; that no money would come in from the outside, either for relief or to aid emigration; that, moreover, one could not hope to secure openings for persons abroad who were literally being thrown out of France. In short, both of them accepted unreservedly and expressed vigorously what might have been called the Kahn viewpoint about a desirable attitude for the French regime. Helbronner, however, did not fail to make some defense for his attitude in London by saying that now I could see that he had merely been expressing the views of the government; that, indeed, in the light of recent developments he had been moderate, instead of intransigent.

Helbronner had meantime made an appointment for the two of us with Léger at four o'clock at the Foreign Office, and I arranged to meet him there. Léger was tied up, but as it turned out this was all to the good, for Helbronner and I then had a long hour and a quarter's conference with Léger's associates, Messrs. Tetreau[31] and Japy, the latter representing the Foreign Office on the inter-ministerial council now formulating the regulations in reference to foreigners.

I began my statement about the French policy and the French national interest. At every point I was aided by Helbronner, who spoke with eloquence and force, arguing sharply against precisely the views which he had maintained so consistently for a year. At the end of an hour the two Foreign Office men agreed that we were absolutely right, that it would be a disaster for France to ignore the

31. Galeazzi S. E. Tetreau, in charge of refugee work in the French Foreign Ministry. He had been the chief secretary of the French government in Syria dealing with Armenian and Assyrian refugees.

political and international implications of the proposed regulations. We then discussed the best means of modifying the present tendencies.

It appeared from their talk that Herriot himself, perhaps because, as Olive Sawyer suggested to me later, of the Gumbel incident,[32] was foremost in his intolerance towards the refugees, though as a matter of fact Japy reported that at the inter-ministerial council, when the regulations had last been discussed, the refugees as such had not been mentioned. It was finally decided that I should write a letter to Herriot and, if possible, deliver it that night, and to send copies to Tetreu and Japy at the Foreign Office. I immediately got in touch with Kotschnig and Wurfbain, who were already at work on a memorandum at Bernard Kahn's office, and told them how to shape their effort. It was indeed amusing to find myself working so closely with Helbronner, to hear the latter insisting that my French was perfect, and to have him support each of my contentions even in detail, and in some cases to go beyond them. As we left together, we parted like lifelong friends.

Over to the American Embassy to have tea with the Strauses. Ambassador Straus came into the drawing room. I explained briefly that we were in the midst of a crisis and asked him if he would do me a favor. I saw at once that he hesitated, thinking that I wanted to involve him in our affair. Indeed, I had more or less mischievously put my request purposely in such a way as to cause him a moment's worry. Then I told him that all I wanted was to borrow his telephone to give my colleagues some further instructions. He said, "Of course you can telephone, but don't say you are speaking from here. Moreover, I completely approve," he added, "of all that the French government is proposing." I replied, "I am not going to argue it with you. I merely want to use your telephone." So in his presence I discussed the matter with the people working at Kahn's office, telling them that the French text had to be ready that night. Later, Straus tried to return to the subject and to discuss it, but I told him that with me it was not an academic matter, and I was not interested to debate it. Nonetheless, Straus insisted on telling me that he so thoroughly approved the French proposals that he had sent examples of the various French *refoulement* (regulations driving out foreigners) and other cards to Roosevelt, telling him that he thought the United States should copy the French procedure in protecting American workmen against foreigners. It would not have been courteous for me to have told Straus what I thought of such action.

Then we had a pleasant visit talking about family matters.

At Kahn's office went over with Bernard Kahn and my two colleagues their memorandum. Then I decided that I would put the whole matter more briefly and pointedly in a rather long covering letter. This I completed and secured the approval of by the others before I had to go off to dinner with Miss Rothbarth,

32. Emil Julius Gumbel, German mathematician, pacifist, and anti-Nazi exile in France. Author of a well-known book on political assassinations by right-wing extremists during the Weimar Republic. He may have alienated French officials through criticism of France's refugee policy. Later emigrated to the United States and worked for the Office of Strategic Services.

half an hour late. Meantime Wurfbain and Kotschnig remained on the job, seeing the two documents through the machines.

Pleasant visit with Miss Rothbarth, who is rather discouraged, as well she might be.

Waited until eleven o'clock for Kotschnig and Wurfbain to return with the final drafts of the letter and memoranda. When they finally arrived, we decided to postpone sending them until the next morning.

Thursday, November 22, 1934

Telephone conversation with Olive Sawyer, who reciprocated by inquiring rather preemptorily where I had been the night before and early that morning when she had been trying to reach me. At her suggestion I called Sir Osmond, told him that I had decided to wait on the *Rex,* and would prepare the way as well as I could for his coming on the third. I also gave an account of Helbronner's extraordinary helpfulness. This pleased Sir Osmond.

Final staff conference, ending with a clear gentlemen's understanding as to division of work between Kotschnig and Wurfbain, and Wurfbain went off to JDC to get and deliver the final texts of the memorandum, I having signed the letters.

Kotschnig took me to the train. While waiting at the station, he suggested that he would follow up with Herriot's *chef de cabinet,* with whom he had so much difficulty the previous day, and attempt to make peace with that official. Kotschnig also decided that it would be well for him to take personally the material to the Foreign Office, for he might in this way meet Tetreau and Japy.

Left feeling confident that between them Wurfbain and Kotschnig will keep things not only in order, but moving.

McDonald sailed from Le Havre, and Miss Sawyer joined him when the vessel docked at Southhampton.

The voyage, SS *Manhattan,* November 22–28, 1934

Friday was a lovely day. Saturday was the reverse, and I regret to record that I showed it. Sunday was beautiful, but Monday was terrible. But the worst was relieved by the news that, despite the bad weather, we probably would dock ahead of record time on Wednesday night.

Tuesday was lovely.

New York, Wednesday, November 28, 1934

Docked late Wednesday night. Met at the pier by Janet and her boy and girl friends,[33] Popkin, Hyman, and Razovsky, the latter two down really to meet the first batch of incoming German children. There was a long wait for the collec-

33. Ruth and Bobby were visiting in Albany, Indiana, with Ruth's parents, J. R. and Kate Stafford.

tion of the luggage, and then, when this was gathered together, there was an even longer wait in the line for a customs official. And then further delay while trying to explain to the customs officer what the printed copies of the report were. He finally allowed them to enter free on the ground that they were an official publication of the High Commission.

Short visit with Janet and her friend; then they went off to Bronxville, and I to the Harvard Club.

Thursday, November 29, 1934

Thanksgiving Day.

Breakfast at Felix Warburg's. Besides him and Mrs. Warburg we were joined by Max Warburg. Our talk covered a very wide range. All were much interested in my report of my visit to Rome. They seemed to feel that in that were inherent important possibilities. Later, Max brought up the question of the boycott. He said that he contemplated issuing a statement urging its discontinuance, and pointing out what he believed to be the very important factor that if one hopes for amelioration of the attitude of the present regime, it will be necessary to help it to avoid extreme economic distress. In no other way can he see any prospect for betterment. Moreover, the only alternative to this regime is chaos, by which I imagine he means a larger degree of radicalism, perhaps even communism. My response was that such a statement would be futile or worse. It could not affect American opinion on the boycott, nor would it be likely to carry conviction in Germany. On the contrary, it might be interpreted there as a mere gesture, and here it would be certain to be bitterly resented.

After breakfast Felix Warburg drove me up to Broyles[34] for Thanksgiving lunch. On the way up we covered six or eight specific items which he had noted down on his dossier. Among these were the question of the budget for the High Commission. He agreed to take the responsibility of seeing that three-fourths of the budget would be allocated among the different Jewish groups. He emphasized his view that it would have been a serious mistake to have fixed a time limit for the discontinuance of the work. As to the personal contribution credited to me on the books of the High Commission, he would speak to Louis Strauss in reference to the last $5,000. He gave his estimate of the work to date, expressing the view that, on the whole, as much had been done as could be expected, and that he felt more confident than some months earlier that we should be able to continue to carry on effectively. In every way he indicated his great appreciation of what I was undertaking.

(According to my calendar I breakfasted again with Felix Warburg on Saturday, Dec. 1, but since this diary is being dictated more than a month later, my memory does not distinguish between the two engagements.)

34. Louise and Jake Broyles, close family friends.

20. December 1934: A Request to the President

New York, Saturday, December 1, 1934

Lunch with Henry Ittleson at his apartment. He, too, was intensely interested in what I had to say to him about Rome. And as to conditions in Germany, he is much more willing now to recognize the truth about the state of the Jews than he used to be. As I left, he told me that I could count upon him to do whatever was within his power.

Up to the school[1] with the Rosenthals. A long talk with Ruutz-Rees. I told her that I recognized Janet's poor preparation, but that I was anxious that she work hard and finish in a year, even with lower grades, than that she should take two years, because I thought she needed the experience of real endeavor. Ruutz-Rees thought there was a chance.

Late to supper with Mildred Wertheimer at the Vassar Club.

Sunday, December 2, 1934

Spent the day with Janet and friends in Bronxville.

Monday, December 3, 1934

. . . .

Lunched with Sulzberger and his colleagues, Mr. Ochs, Ogden, Finley, James, Strunsky, and Adler, at the *Times.*

Took the afternoon train for Schenectady, where I arrived at 6:29 in easy time to deliver my broadcast from the General Electric station at 7:15.

Then took the ten o'clock train for Muncie [Indiana, to visit his mother and bring Ruth and Bobby home].

Tuesday, December 4, 1934

Arrived in Muncie at 10:30. Met by Ruth and Roy [MacCormack, family friend]. Out to Albany. Delighted to see how well Bobby looked. Everybody else was well too.

1. Rosemary Hall. Janet McDonald spent her senior year boarding there. Miss Ruutz-Rees was the head of the school, and the Arthur Rosenthals were family friends, Jane being in Janet's class in Rosemary Hall.

Spoke at the Rotary in Muncie at luncheon, and at the Rotary in Portland that evening.

Wednesday, December 5–Tuesday, December 11, 1934

After a day or two in Albany, spent two days also in Bloomington. Found Mother looking better than I have seen her in many years. Bill's[2] family were also well.

Over the weekend in Albany and Muncie. Took the afternoon train on the eleventh back to New York [with Ruth and Bobby].

During this time Wurfbain had visited Berlin for the High Commission, reporting the results to McDonald. At the Reichsbank he was told it might be possible to canalize private funds from the United States coming to Germany to set them off against German payments abroad. Wurfbain concluded with some general observations: "although the regime is confronted with many difficulties . . . nobody thought that these would prove fatal to the government. Nor was there any reason to expect any amelioration for the situation of the Jews in Germany. Anti-Semitism is not popular with the population, but is being kept up sporadically by the Party. . . . "[3]

Wednesday, December 12, 1934

FPA Board meeting. At the end of the regular business I spoke for a half an hour or so, and then answered questions until nearly ten o'clock. Indeed, I had to hurry over to the Astor to arrive at the National Fund[4] Memorial Session for Baron Edmond [de Rothschild]. Rabbi Wise spoke briefly, preceding me. I spoke for only five minutes, referring to the pioneer work of Baron Edmond, and emphasizing that if the full possibilities of Palestine and the area beyond were ever to be capitalized, it must be on the basis laid down by Baron Edmond—that of genuine cooperation between Jew and Arab. I left immediately afterwards, explaining to the chairman and to Judge Mack that I had to catch a train.

Thursday, December 13, 1934

Took the noonday train home in order to drive up to Smith with Ruth. It was a pleasant drive until in the late evening when it began to snow and there was ice on the roads. But we reached Northampton about 10:30. Dr. Neilson[5] had just been there to see us. I called him, and we arranged to have breakfast together at his house.

2. William McDonald, McDonald's youngest brother.

3. Wurfbain to McDonald, December 10–12, 1934, McDonald Papers, Columbia, High Commission Papers 1.

4. The Jewish National Fund, established by Theodor Herzl in London in 1901 to purchase land for the Jews in Palestine.

5. William Allan Neilson, president of Smith College, 1917–1939.

Friday, December 14, 1934

Breakfast at the Neilsons. Mrs. Neilson, who is German, seems to feel the Nazi regime more keenly than her husband, though he too is deeply stirred.

Spoke at the morning assembly, to about 2,000 girls. Afterwards talked with Neilson for twenty minutes or so. Both he and the dean, as well as the warden, with whom Ruth and I talked later, agreed that it would be better for Janet, if she could possibly make it, to come to college next year, rather than the year after. I got from them the impression that she would have a fair chance of being accepted even if, as I told them would likely be the case, her grades on the boards were low. They said that they were more concerned with what she might do than with what she had done. They urged early registration in order to have a better choice of rooms.

We left about eleven o'clock on our drive to Poughkeepsie. It was a beautiful day, and the scenery along the Berkshire Trail was all that you could ask for. Fortunately, we arrived at Vassar precisely five minutes before three, our engagement with MacCracken[6] being at three o'clock. We talked with him for half an hour or so, and then for a similar period with Miss Thompson. We got from them almost identically the same reaction as from the authorities at Smith. They would prefer to have Janet after a year of hard work, rather than after two years of moderate effort.

Saturday, December 15, 1934

Stopped at Felix Warburg's on my way downtown. I referred to the fact that I had spoken at the National Fund. He said, "If you had asked me I would have advised you against it." I replied: "Yes, I knew that perfectly well. Therefore, I didn't ask you, because I had made up my mind that it was desirable for me to speak."

At the end of our talk Bernard Flexner came in. He referred to the long conference which he, Liebman, and Baerwald had in my office some days earlier, and at which time Liebman and he and I had fixed on a day to spend together. Flexner asked whether we should include Felix Warburg if he could come. To this, I replied half seriously in Felix Warburg's hearing, "Yes, by all means induce him to come, because up till now on financial matters I have been able to get from him only vague generalities." At this, Warburg burst into laughter and said, "I like that—vague generalities." He didn't seem to mind, and I was glad that I had made the point.

Solmssen of the Dresdner Bank and member of the German Trade Delegation came in with Mildred to see me. He said that he wished to talk with me about American public opinion and its attitude towards Germany. He made an argument very similar to that which Mildred Wertheimer had made earlier, to the effect that if one wished moderation, he must help avoid disaster in the Reich. I replied that I knew very little of American opinion, as I had been out of

6. Henry Noble MacCracken, president of Vassar College, 1915–1946.

the country so much; that moreover, on political questions I had no views; but that, nonetheless, I thought that I ought to point out to him that there is a strong body of opinion in the States which normally would be friendly to Germany which now holds the view strongly that the present regime has jeopardized some of the finest values of civilization, and that there can be no real hope of moderation in Germany until after this regime has given way to another. I emphasized that I was not expressing my own view, because I officially had none, but that if he wished to be helpful he would tell his colleagues at home that they need not expect real American cooperation until the occasions for American complaint had been removed.

. . . .

Up to see Mrs. Brady. Told her of my visits with her friend Pacelli. She knows also very well the two undersecretaries of state. I spoke of my desire to see Cardinal Hayes. She said she would call up the cardinal's secretary. I also told her of my great appreciation for the help Galeazzi had given us.

. . . .

Washington, Monday, December 17, 1934

Arrived in Washington early. Went directly to the Cosmos Club.

Breakfast with Fred Howe.[7] He told me with expressions of considerable concern of what he felt to be the increasing anti-Semitism. He referred to complaints in Washington about the undue number of Jewish intellectuals in strategic positions, and also told of bitter complaints from younger doctors at the Physicians and Surgeons Hospital and even at Mt. Sinai in New York.

. . . .

Conference with Colonel MacCormack, commissioner of immigration, in his office in the Department of Labor. Before coming down to Washington I had talked to Professor Chamberlain once or twice on the phone, but I had not had an opportunity to see him except for a moment at the FPA Board meeting. Colonel MacCormack told me in detail of the Washington situation, the probability of legislation further limiting immigration; he expects this to take the form of a reduction of the quotas by 40 percent. This would still leave the German quota approximately 15,000 a year. But even this amount, he thinks, is larger than can safely be utilized to the full. He emphasized the difficulty that was being experienced in absorbing some of the refugees, the tendency for them to congregate in New York, the difficulty of dispersing them throughout the country, despite Razovsky's special efforts in that direction, and finally, he reverted to the theme which I was to hear so often during my stay at home—the increase of anti-Semitism and the danger of its sharp ac-

7. Dr. Frederick Clemson Howe, a consumer advocate in the Agricultural Adjustment Administration and special adviser to Secretary of Agriculture Henry Wallace.

centuation. He referred in this connection to the large number of Jewish intellectuals in Washington, and to the other factors which are commonly referred to as the basis for this discouraging tendency. Not having time to finish our discussion, we arranged for him to lunch with me the next day at the Cosmos Club.

Stone and I went up to the Senate Office Building for lunch with Senator Nye.[8] He looks almost like a boy; in fact, he is barely forty years old. He talked very freely about the work of his arms investigation committee, the opposition they have encountered, and their plans for the future. He was fearful lest the committee recently named by the President to work out legislation "to take the profit out of war," might under such conservative leadership as [Bernard] Baruch[9] and General [Hugh] Johnson, be used to hamstring the arms investigation. Nye was picturesque in his characterizations of the efforts of the Duponts and other large munitions interests to defeat the purposes of his committee. He was encouraged by the extraordinary reception of his investigations not only in the States, but also abroad. He expected that popular support would be such that there would be no doubt of continued Congressional funds for pressing forward the work of the committee. He paid a very high tribute to Stone, saying that he hoped the time would come when his committee would be free to say publicly how much they owed to him.

As we lunched, it was interesting to study the Senatorial types one saw at neighboring tables. Senator [Robert] Wagner [of New York], stocky and intelligent; Senator [William] King [of Utah] debonair and always ready to plead a popular cause; Senator [Hiram] Johnson [of California], looking much younger than I think of him and more like a professor than the redoubtable intransigent isolationist; Senator [George W.] Norris [of Nebraska], benevolent and fatherly in appearance, thus belying the fighting qualities he has displayed throughout a generation in his attacks on the vested power interests.

I was surprised to have Stone and Nye tell me that Norris had become an isolationist, and even jingoistic in his attitude towards Japan. It appears that there is an increasing feeling that war with Japan is inevitable, and even that the sooner the better.

The middle of the afternoon I went to see Moffat of the Western European Division of the State Department. He told me a little about the administration's new neutrality policy. We talked also about the pending barter proposal with Germany, involving about $50,000,000 worth of cotton. He indicated that the department was opposed to this proposal on various grounds, and that he did not think it would be accepted by the President. He seemed interested in my account of our work to date and of conditions in Germany. He said that in his

8. Senator Gerald Nye, Republican of North Dakota. His committee was studying to what extent the U.S. munitions industry had pushed the United States into World War I. William T. Stone had been helping in the research.

9. Bernard Baruch had been chairman of the War Industries Board and economic adviser to the American peace conference delegation after the war.

opinion recent weeks had shown very definite gains for the League, and that on the whole he was more optimistic about the chances of maintaining the peace.

Back to the Cosmos Club to find a telephone message from Miss Scheider, Mrs. Roosevelt's secretary, asking me to dine with the family informally at the White House that evening. I had not asked the President for an appointment; indeed, I had not communicated with him at all, but had merely written Mrs. Roosevelt a note telling her when I expected to be in Washington and that I should be glad to see her if she had a little free time.

. . . .

Dinner at the White House at 7:45. It was a family party, and no one dressed. Among those present in addition to the President and Mrs. Roosevelt and myself were one or two of the in-laws, the secretaries Miss LeHand and Miss Tully, and four or five other members of the President's intimate personal staff.

The talk throughout the meal was of the freest sort, no subject apparently was taboo, and each person seemed to express himself with complete freedom.

Mrs. Roosevelt told jokingly about her recent visit to Philadelphia when she received a medal for something or other. The chairman had explained to her that the medal would have been of gold were it not that the President's regulations made this impossible. To this, the President replied, "They were joking you; there is no prohibition on the use of gold in medals. They didn't wish to give you a gold one anyhow."

It was in this connection that the President turning to me said that he had just signed a letter about me in connection with the award of the American Hebrew Medal to be made in New York on January 3.

The President asked me to tell him about the progress of our work and of conditions in Germany. He showed keen interest in both subjects. He expressed vigorously his opposition to the anti-Semitic policy of the Reich and his feeling, bordering closely on contempt, for Luther and Schacht. I was again struck by the President's memory. He seemed to have clearly in mind points which he and I had discussed about Germany more than a year and a half before when, after my visit to the Reich in April 1933, I had spent the night at the White House. His fundamental opposition to the principles of the Third Reich, which he had shown at the very beginning and had indicated subsequently each time I had talked with him, were obviously as strong as ever.

We talked about a number of aspects of relations with Germany, but no reference whatever was made to the pending proposal for the cotton barter with the Reich. I did not mention it, nor did anyone else. It would have been inappropriate to ask the President's view on it, since everyone knew that his decision would be announced in a day or two.

There was general talk about the increasing development of fascism in Europe and the prevailing menace to democratic and parliamentary governments. I made the point, which I think is absolutely sound, that the President himself, by his willingness to try radical remedies and by his extraordinary capacity for democratic leadership, is doing more than any other single person to vindicate parliamentary procedure by proving that even revolutionary measures can be achieved by orderly processes of democracy.

Then followed amusing talk about the recent election at home. The President said that he was not at all surprised by the overwhelming vote. He and his advisers had calculated the results in advance. He attributed the Republican defeat in considerable part to the utter lack of Republican leadership. He said there was no unity of opinion whatsoever on the Republican side. He told laughingly of a cable received by Jim Farley from James Walker as follows: "Dear Jim: I thought it was an election. It was not. It was a census. Congratulations on the completeness of the returns."

Mrs. Roosevelt, following up on the political discussion, said, "Franklin, are we going into the World Court at this session?" He replied, in effect, that he was studying the question and weighing the possibilities of Senatorial assent. Mrs. Roosevelt pressed him further, saying, "I suppose if we are going in, it must be done early in the session." To this, he replied, "That is what everybody says who is urging action on any particular issue."

I then said half seriously, "I understand that there is a possibility that the United States may go into the League for the same reason that brought in Russia." Someone asked what was the Russian reason, and I gave the obvious answer—fear of Japan. The President, however, made no comment on this subject.

In connection with the subject of dictatorships and democracy, the President told of Ramsay MacDonald's talk to him of the reasons which had prompted MacDonald to break with his Labour colleagues and head the National government. The King had put the matter up to MacDonald as a matter of patriotic duty, emphasizing the danger to Britain and the Empire of a Tory Government at that particular time. When the President had finished his account, I put forward my view that an additional consideration was also Ramsay's love of power, and that, moreover, he had for many years been unwilling to listen to criticism, but was eagerly anxious to have only pleasant things said to him. Mrs. Roosevelt, taking up my line of thought, said, with marked emphasis, "There is nothing worse that can happen to a public man, than to get to the point where he cannot bear criticism, where he wishes only to be flattered and is unwilling to listen to the truth." As she finished, I said, "Well, you know, if a public man selects his family with sufficient wisdom, he never need be in such a position." To this, Mrs. Roosevelt retorted instantly, "But I don't see why you should make such a 'crack' at me." And there was a general laugh around the table.

As the conversation developed during the meal, it seemed to me much too auspicious an occasion to let slip, so I at one point said to the President that if he had a moment or two free at the end of dinner, I should like to talk to him about business. Later, it became evident that there was no need to wait, so I launched into an explanation of the financial problem of our work and of my desire that the United States should contribute to the budget of the office of the High Commission.

I explained that the cost of our office was, of course, only a tiny fraction of the cost of the substantive work. I admitted, too, that the governments were under no obligation to contribute even to this smaller fund. But I emphasized the great moral value there would be in a symbolic contribution by the United States; that already some of the smaller countries had said they would help, and if the United States as a great power would be willing to go along, there would be a good chance of inducing Great Britain, France, and perhaps Italy to follow. I said that I hoped, therefore, the President would be willing to give $10,000 towards the administrative budget.

He listened attentively to all that I had to say, and then replied promptly, "All right." He than turned to Miss LeHand and said, "Please speak to me tomorrow about the matter at the budget conference." I thanked him. After dinner when I was saying goodbye to him, he again referred to the matter in these words, "I shall do the best I can to get the money for you."

During the evening the names of Messersmith and Dodd came into discussion. The President seemed to share my view that Messersmith has been the outstanding American representative abroad in connection with the German matter. I told of the latter's work in Vienna on behalf of the Jews. The President referred with considerable feeling to a recent communication from Messersmith on that subject. As to Ambassador Dodd, I told of his efforts on our behalf in Berlin and of my appreciation for what he tried to do. I did not, however, hide my feeling that some of Dodd's associates were weak, or that even the ambassador himself was so much of a gentleman and a scholar as to find it difficult at first to realize that strong-arm methods are necessary to get results.

The President asked me when I expected to finish my present work. I told him that I hoped to do so before the end of 1935; that, while the job would not be completed perhaps, I did not wish to continue indefinitely abroad. He showed interest in my plans for the South American trip, and will, I think, be willing to help.

As I was saying goodnight, Mrs. Roosevelt said, "Please let me know if you are going to be down in Washington again before you sail."

Tuesday, December 18, 1934

Telephoned to Professor Chamberlain in New York to tell him of the conversation at the White House about a governmental contribution to the High Commission budget. He agreed with my view that it would be well to see the State Department to avoid any possible slip in the execution of the President's desire. Chamberlain expressed the hope that the department would be willing to include this appropriation in the contingent fund and would not insist upon a separate bill to authorize this expenditure.

Called upon Dr. Rowe[10] at the Pan American Union. He offered to do everything possible to expedite my work in South America. He approved the choice of Inman as a colleague on the ground that the latter had intimate personal contacts in all the countries and is looked upon everywhere as an ardent defender of Latin American rights. Rowe said that the Brazilian ambassador, who is very close to the present president, could be of great use to me, and that he would telephone the Brazilian Embassy about my visit. We then discussed other ways in which Dr. Rowe might cooperate. I left feeling sure that there was nothing reasonable that I could ask him to do which he would not undertake.

I arrived at the State Department just in time for my 10:30 appointment with Mr. Phillips, undersecretary of state. As usual, he asked me to tell him of the progress of my work. He listened with close attention. He was particularly interested in our relations with the Reich and my recent visit to Rome. He asked me how long it would be before I finished with the job. I gave him the same answer I had given to the President when he had asked me the identical question.

Phillips wrote up his version, offering a few more details: "James G. McDonald . . . gave me an interesting account of his wanderings; he is about to start on a visit to South America, in an attempt to persuade certain of those countries to admit a small quota of German Jewish refugees. He mentioned the fact that about 20,000 refugees were coming out of Germany annually, that 10,000 were being taken care of in Palestine, which is now booming, but that other parts of the world had to be found for the remaining 10,000; the European countries had exhausted their willingness to receive these émigrés, and where they did receive them the émigrés had the utmost difficulty in receiving permission to work."[11]

Phillips expressed himself strongly about Germany, the impossibility of making any real progress with negotiations there. He was particularly emphatic in his comments on Luther and Schacht; the former cannot be a very effective ambassador. I asked Phillips about the barter negotiations. He said he thought there was no chance that these would go through. They are opposed to the Department's whole program of reciprocal treaties, carrying with them the most-favored-nation treatment. He seemed to think that the President would decide against the proposal.

I did not say anything to Phillips about the President's suggestion of a contribution to the High Commission Budget, preferring to take that up directly with the secretary of state, Hull. I was fearful that Phillips would raise technical objections.

The secretary was very cordial, complimenting me on the work done on behalf of the refugees. We then talked a little while about his general economic program, and also about the barter proposal. I raised the question of a diplo-

10. Dr. Leo S. Rowe, director general of the Pan American Union.

11. Phillips Diary, December 18, 1934, Phillips Papers, call number bMS Am 2232, Houghton Library, Harvard University. By permission of Houghton Library, Harvard University.

matic passport, and he explained that this was never granted except to diplomats actually in the service. I then inquired about special passports. He was not familiar with this, but gave instructions to Mr. McBride to have this issued for me if it were at all possible. He said they would also give me a special letter.

Then I asked him about the President's promise of a contribution. Hull replied that he did not know what the technicalities were, and that, therefore, I had better see Mr. Carr, the assistant secretary of state in charge of departmental, organizational, and financial matters. As I was leaving, I told the secretary that I hoped he would continue to hold aloft the banner of freer trade among the nations.

Mr. Carr received me at once. I told him of my visit to the White House, and of the President's promise. Carr's reply was, "But this is not as easy as the President seems to think." Then followed forty-five minutes of discussion about ways and means of translating the President's wish into an effective contribution. Carr at first seemed to be opposed to the suggestion on principle, and said that he thought the Department had made this clear in its correspondence with Professor Chamberlain when the latter had first raised the question of a contribution last fall.[12] I replied, "No, I think you simply explained the difficulties. And certainly if I had thought that you were opposed as a matter of principle, I should not have gone over your head to the President without speaking to you about it first."

Carr insisted that a special bill authorizing the appropriation would be necessary, because otherwise, a single objection on a point of order would throw out the item from the appropriation bill. He did not seem to think that it could be included in the general contingent item of the Department.

In the midst of our discussion I called up Miss LeHand at the White House, told her that I was with Mr. Carr, and of some of the difficulties he foresaw, and suggested that she clear with him after the matter had been taken up with the director of the budget. She said she would. This conversation seemed to reassure Mr. Carr somewhat.

Then he talked to me at some length about his relations with Mr. Hoover during the war and during the subsequent years. As I was leaving, we referred again to the chief purpose of my visit, and I said, "I am sure, Mr. Carr, that you and the President working together can put this proposal through." He did not demur.

....

In the early afternoon went to the Chilean Embassy. The ambassador is ill, but the chargé, Mr. Cohen, who is Jewish, was most helpful. He told me of the plans of the rector of the University of Chile to come to New York, and of his

12. Chamberlain had discussed the matter with Moffat, head of the State Department's Western Europe Division. Ruling out use of the State Department's emergency fund, Moffat stressed that the American government regarded refugee questions as a matter for private initiative and private funding. See Moffat Journal, October 8, 1934, Houghton Library, Harvard.

desire to find there professors for a new school of economics and also for a school of scientific research. I told him that I would at once communicate with Kotschnig, who would in turn clear with Miss Ginsberg's committee, Demuth's organization in Zurich, and the Academic Assistance Council, with a view to preparing a list of possibilities which the Rector could then discuss with Murrow and other members of the emergency committee in New York.

As to the possibilities of immigration, Cohen was encouraging. He emphasized, however, that whatever effort was made would have to be made on the spot in Valparaiso.

From the Chilean Embassy I went directly to the Peruvian Embassy. The ambassador, Señor Don Manuel de Freyre y Santander, was cordial. He told me he thought there were limited possibilities in his country and that he would be glad to write ahead to the authorities if I would let him know when my plans were definite. I promised that I would communicate with him.

....

In talking to Stone, he suggested that since I had spoken to Drew Pearson that morning about the possibility of my trip to South America, I had better call up Pearson again to make sure that he did not exaggerate in his story my expectations in South America. I got Pearson on the telephone. He was very friendly. Said he understood the situation and would be particularly careful in what he said.

Wednesday, December 19, 1934

Breakfast with Oswald Villard[13] and Fred Howe. Villard, to my surprise, seconded by Howe, was inclined on the whole to blame a part of the prevalence and perhaps increasing anti-Semitism on the manners of the Jews themselves. This, from Villard, was a shock. He added, however, that in Galveston, for example, the chief rabbi[14] was unquestionably the first citizen of the city. On the other hand, he told a story of Ohio University,[15] a small institution near Cincinnati, attended almost exclusively by native Ohio boys and girls. Recently, however, a number of Jewish boys and girls have come there from the east because of the very low cost, and as a result, anti-Semitism was rife. Apparently, the costumes and the manners of these East Side youngsters offended the natives.

Another and more serious example of anti-Semitism which was cited during the breakfast was the resentment of the cotton farmers and their representatives, the Senators of the cotton states, at what they attribute to the Jewish intel-

13. Oswald Villard, born in Germany, editor and owner of the *Nation,* 1918–1932; contributing editor, 1932–1935.

14. No such position existed, but probably a reference to Rabbi Henry Cohen, who served as rabbi from 1888 to 1952. Sometimes referred to as chief rabbi of Texas.

15. This may be a case of mistaken identity. Ohio University is in Athens, Ohio, about 170 miles from Cincinnati. Miami University (Ohio) is located thirty-five miles north of Cincinnati and is small.

lectuals in Washington—the blocking of the cotton barter proposal with Germany. In support of this they cite the probable influence of Morgenthau, secretary of the treasury, Feis, economic adviser of the State Department, Taussig in the Department of Agriculture, and others.

To my surprise, I found two such pacifists as Villard and Howe divided on the question of the attitude of the United States towards Japan.

Miss Shipley of the Passport Division of the [State] Department called me to say that I was going to be given a special passport, and would I supply the necessary data?

At the Argentine Embassy the ambassador, Señor Don Felipe A. Espil, showed keen interest in my project. As the attorney for many years of ICA in Buenos Aires, he is well acquainted with colonization projects in his country and in general with the Jewish situation there. He expressed strongly the opinion that it would not be enough to leave the negotiations with the Argentine government merely with ICA; these should be conducted on a broader basis. Indeed, he was inclined to criticize the ICA settlements on the ground that the settlers did not remain, but moved to the cities.

At first, he suggested that I should address myself to the secretary of agriculture and commerce, using such introductions as he would give me, and also letters from Baring Brothers in London or their representatives, Morgan & Co., in the States. But when I told him of my talks with Pacelli, Espil was enthusiastic in his expectations that if Pacelli would help me, I could directly through the President of Argentina accomplish much more than in any other way. The President had recently received the highest order in the gift of the Pope and was very proud of it. Moreover, the recent Eucharistic Congress had affected a veritable religious revival in Argentina, so that Pacelli's position is at the very highest.

The ambassador added that of course if President Roosevelt would aid me directly, that would be extremely valuable also. The reputation of FDR is very high, not so much because of the administration's friendly words towards Latin America or even its friendly policies towards Cuba and Mexico, but because of the extreme interest of the Argentineans in the New Deal. In other words, they judge FDR more by what he does at home than by what he says about Latin America.

Conditions are improving in Argentina, so that there are better prospects of effecting some immigration arrangement.

As to the attitude of Germans in Argentina, some are Nazis and some are opposed, but he anticipates no opposition from them to my proposal.

Inman, he thinks, would be an excellent colleague. The ambassador added that he would be glad to help me in any possible way, and he asked me to let him know again definitely when I was planning to leave for the south.

The Brazilian ambassador, Oswaldo Aranha, had misunderstood my telephone message, and thought I had come merely to pay a courtesy call. When he learned of the purpose of my visit, he asked me to come back that afternoon, late. This wrecked my hopes of getting the Congressional Limited and thus arriving in New York in time to be with my family that night. But there was nothing to do but accept.

The Uruguayan minister, J. Richling, who, as I learned later to be [*sic,* was] of German descent, proved to be the one South American diplomat who was not cordial or cooperative. He was, indeed, almost hostile. He began by criticizing sharply the work of ICA in Argentina and Brazil. He offered little hope of success in Uruguay and made no promises of cooperation. I attribute this attitude rather to his background than to conditions in Uruguay itself.

Over to the State Department, to make arrangements with Miss Shipley for my special passport.

Called upon Dr. Don Miguel Paz Baroana, Honduras minister. He, contrary to what I had been told in New York, was completely discouraging as to the possibility of intellectual refugees finding places in Honduras.

Lunch with Herbert Feis. Chatted about family matters, and then about the proposed cotton barter. He said that it had been defeated. In connection with the promise of the President to contribute to the High Commission budget, Feis said that he could help with the director of the budget's office if necessary, but he would rather not do anything with the State Department itself. On the whole, Feis is rather pessimistic about economic conditions in Germany.

At three o'clock I went to see Capitan Colon Eloy Alfaro, minister of Ecuador. He thought there were possibilities in his country, and would be glad to communicate with his government whenever I suggested it.

Then I went to what proved to be a very important conference with the Brazilian ambassador. He was very cordial, and said that he would give me as much time as I needed. I explained the tentative program which I had thought of presenting to his government. He replied that this should be easily acceptable. I told him of the failure of the move which Louis Oungre and I had made through a memorandum sent by a member of the Department of Labor. The ambassador replied, "That is of no importance; it was probably dealt with by functionnaires who know nothing of the subject. This time I will put you directly in touch with the President, who is a very close friend of mine. You then take up the matter with him, and do not bother about functionnaires who do things in a routine fashion."

The ambassador then launched into an enthusiastic account of the vast possibilities of his country, its present program of industrialization, and the large plans for the near future. To show me the need for immigration, he read me portions of a long personal letter from the President, in which the latter pointed out that there was need for 20,000 to 30,000 workers in the coffee area alone. He sees Brazil as a second United States, requiring, as did the United States, the labor and technical skill of millions of immigrants.

I asked him whether the new constitution would not interfere with immigration. He said, "Not at all; that it was designed to keep out the Japanese and the Assyrians"; I need not be concerned about it.

Thus throughout the talk of nearly an hour, he showed a real desire to help cut through technical or diplomatic red tape, and to aid in making my visit a success. Nor is he a man who makes promises lightly. He is not a career diplomat, but one of the most powerful figures in present-day Brazil. He is said to have had more to do than anyone else in placing the present President in office.[16] Naturally therefore I was delighted with the interview.

Having missed the train which I wished to take, I decided to have lunch with Ernest Lindley[17] before taking the six o'clock for New York. Unfortunately, he was rather late, so there was little time to talk.

To my surprise, Mrs. Roosevelt was in the same Pullman car as I. She had missed the Congressional because of attending Mrs. Rumsey's Washington funeral. I spoke to her for a moment, remarking how well the President had looked to me the other night. She replied, "Well you got what you wanted, didn't you?" I answered, "Yes, thanks to you."

Then I proceeded to tell her what Mr. Carr had said, that the matter was not as simple as the President had thought. She commented: "That's just what Mr. Carr would say,"—showing that she knew Mr. Carr.

Arrived too late in New York to go home. Spent the night at the Harvard Club.

Thursday, December 20, 1934

Chatted with Jimmie Rosenberg on the telephone, telling him about Washington. He was delighted with the news about the President, but reminded me of my promise to see Rabbi Wise and to use my influence with him not to press his plans for the World Jewish Congress. I said I would see Rabbi Wise, but made no promise about how far I would go with him.

....

In the afternoon, long conference with Dr. Inman at which we practically committed ourselves to the South American trip, but certain details were left for later consideration.

Friday, December 21, 1934

Memorandum for the Secretary of State:

Should we not ask Congress for the $10,000 for the Jewish Refugee organization of which Mr. McDonald is the Commissioner appointed by the League? FDR[18]

16. In 1937 Aranha became foreign minister.

17. Ernest Lindley, chancellor of the University of Kansas, member of the Board of Trustees of the Carnegie Foundation.

18. This memo from the president led to an exchange of further memos, but no action. Official File 1395, Political Refugees (European), 1934–1940, Franklin D. Roosevelt Library, Hyde Park.

Conference with Joseph Hyman at the office. He brought me up to date on a number of JDC matters.

Then at eleven o'clock over to Charlie Liebman's for the conference with him and Bernard Flexner. To my disappointment, the latter had been called downtown on an emergency assignment, and had gone, despite his firm promise to save three hours during this day. Liebman and I then spent the time together, I urging him as strongly as I could to press forward the corporation plans until they took real tangible shape. He said he would do everything in his power.

At two o'clock Flexner appeared, shortly before I had to leave, but he had little to add on the corporation matter. He did urge me strongly, however, to see Zemurray,[19] the president of the United Fruit Company. Unfortunately, we found that he is in New Orleans and will not return before I must leave.

Conference with Lewis Strauss. He said that he did not remember Felix Warburg asking him to provide the additional $5,000 which I had spoken to Warburg about. Nonetheless, he said he would do it if he could, and that before the first of the year. As to the balance on his own pledge, that would certainly be available. Moreover, he wished me to know that he was at my command so far as his resources and ability went.

Then home for the Christmas weekend.

Saturday, December 22, 1934

Getting ready for Christmas.

To lunch at Mr. Gaisman's with Ruth and Bobby. At the meal there was talk about this and that, and afterwards all of us took long naps. From four o'clock until nearly supper time Gaisman and I talked. I stressed the continued need for help on the other side, and the grave danger to Jews everywhere if the Hitler ideology became prevalent. He elaborated at length his conviction that all of these disturbances in the world are the result of nature's law of one beast devouring another. Repeatedly he came back to that theme.

Sunday, December 23, 1934

Lunch at the Lewisohns, with Sam and Margery (her mother was in bed), and Mr. and Mrs. McCormick, he the new commissioner of correction.

Mr. and Mrs. Inman came over during the evening. He and I completed our plans, going so far even as to arrange the itinerary. The more we talked, the better pleased I was that he would be able to go. It was left, however, that the final word on the plans would be given either just before I sailed or by cable at the earliest possible moment from Europe. In general, it was agreed that he would fly, while the rest of us would go by boat.

19. Samuel Zemurray, Bessarabian-born Jewish immigrant to the United States, who, in 1930, took control of the United Fruit Company.

Monday, December 24, 1934

Family Christmas dinner with the Bairds and the Fosters [old friends from Indiana, now living also in New York].

Tuesday, December 25, 1934

Christmas Day. Quiet day mostly at home. In the afternoon we came in to the Morgenthaus, only to find that they had gone south. Then stopped at the Stotthoffs [close family friends] and out to Westchester to spend part of the evening with friends.

Wednesday, December 26, 1934

Called Miss LeHand's office to inquire about the state of Mr. Roosevelt's promise. Miss Tully answered, saying that Miss LeHand was away on vacation, that she herself did not know what had happened, but would inquire and let us know.

Mr. Baerwald came in. We spoke first about the High Commission budget. He confirmed the impression I had gotten from Felix Warburg that the JDC would press the others for collaboration to the point of finding three quarters of the budget. It is expected that this time the [Jewish] Agency will also contribute. Joseph Hyman had told me that they had nearly succeeded in getting this agreement.[20]

I showed Baerwald the material about the stamp proposal from Kotschnig and Ginsberg. He at once said that he would favor advancing the full $5,000, provided there was a promise of repayment from the proceeds of the stamp sale, and that he would like also to put up to Ginsberg through Kotschnig without involving me, the possibility of an additional repayment. He was to telegraph Kotschnig at once.

Thursday, December 27, 1934

. . . .

Up to Felix Warburg's residence for a conference with Dr. Kahn, Dr. Rosen, and Dr. Hexter.[21] Unfortunately, F. W. was called out in the midst of the discussion to attend a partners' meeting just before Jimmie Rosenberg arrived. The discussion broke itself up into the following heads:

(1) France. Kahn reported that Flandin,[22] who had asked to see him, had been much more friendly than might have been expected. When Kahn spoke of

20. In February the JDC accountant received a report on the administrative costs of the High Commission: $10,000 granted by the American Palestine Campaign, $5,000 more if collections permit (they did not), $35,000 granted by JDC for 1935, less $5,000 if extra from Palestine campaign. Confusing?

21. J. K. Hexter, member of the board of the JDC from Dallas.

22. Pierre Etienne Flandin, prime minister of France, November 8, 1934–May 31, 1935. Conservative. Briefly foreign minister in 1940 under the Vichy regime.

the necessity of keeping a proportion of the refugees for the time being, Flandin had replied, "We want to keep them." Similarly Jacquier, the minister of labor, had been more friendly than was anticipated. How these statements could be squared with Laval's attitude is not clear to me. Rosen interjected a somewhat controversial note by declaring that the whole situation in France would today be different if we had all overridden the National Committee's opposition and had already planted some few hundreds of refugees on the soil. These would now be a convincing illustration of what could be done. I was not convinced that Rosen's program could have been carried out; at any rate, it is now over the dam;

(2) The Near East. Hexter urged that Rosen should accompany him during the summer to study the relative value of prospects in Cyprus, Rhodes, and Syria. Rosen demurred on the ground that if he were critical, it would be set down as prejudice, and on the further ground that while he will not take a second place to anyone in judging the Russian situation, he has no special qualifications for estimating possibilities in the Near East. The matter was left undecided;

(3) Russia. Rosen has become almost an enthusiastic convert to Biro-Bidjan. He thinks it offers enormous possibilities for pioneer settlements—that is, for Jews from Poland and other Eastern parts of Europe, and only incidentally and for but a few German refugees. The great advantage he sees in Biro-Bidjan, as compared with other areas for mass settlement, is the government's willingness not only to give the land, but to make the basic improvements—drainage, roads, etc. When pressed by me when I cited Litvinov's coldness to any such proposal, Rosen admitted that Kalinin[23] is the driving force favoring this project. He further admitted that in the back of the Russians' minds is a political and military purpose—a desire to populate that region as a defense in case of conflict with Japan. Nonetheless, he insisted that it offers outside of Palestine the only great place of refuge for Polish Jews.

Rosenberg, who apparently has been thinking this matter through with great care, shares Rosen's view as to the possibilities, but feels that it can be done safely only on a non-sectarian basis. He thinks it would be very dangerous for the Jews as such to be associated with a large project in Communist Russia. Therefore, he would like to see it undertaken at the invitation of the Russian government, addressed to me as the representative of an international organization. Only then, and provided there is considerable non-Jewish funds, will he favor it. Meantime, he is going to work towards the formulation of a scheme on these lines and towards having Kalinin issue me the invitation. He asked me to make my other plans so that I would be free to go to Russia in September with

23. Mikhail Ivanovich Kalinin, president of the Soviet Union.

Rosen. I told him that so far as I could now see, I would be free to do so. Warburg was not in on this part of the discussion, so I do not know his views.

. . . .

Friday, December 28, 1934

Conference with Vladeck at the office. He told me that he had sent $5,000 to Schevenels recently and in all had sent about $19,000. A considerable portion of this, however, was not for relief, but for work within Germany. He told me of the general defense fund which had been provided for at the last meeting of the A. F. of L., and his expectation that a full $50,000 would be raised from this source eventually. He asked if I would write letters to Green, Dubinsky, Lewis, and Sidney Hillman.[24] I said I would. He asked also if I would speak at an early dinner meeting of the trade union officials, Friday the fourth. I hesitated a moment, for this would be my last night before sailing, but since it was the only time available I accepted.

Lunch with John Rockefeller III. He asked me about the progress of my work. I told him of developments since we had last met. . . . Later, during the lunch John told me something of his views about the National Recovery Act. He is far from enthusiastic. He sees dangers and few tangible gains. I am afraid his conservative surroundings are not permitting him to hear the liberal side.

As we were separating, he said that he hoped that I would continue to call him up whenever I came back so that we might lunch together, for he was much interested in keeping in touch with my work.

Having met General Harbord[25] when we entered the club, I hunted up the Harbord party after I said good-bye to John. They were just leaving their table. I was delighted to see Mrs. Harbord again. With them was General Pershing.[26] On the way out I talked with Harbord for a few minutes. He is his old conservative self. I also talked with Pershing. He thinks Germany is rearming and is determined sooner or later to attack France. He looked better than when I last saw him.

Rabbi Wise came in during the afternoon. He talked about many subjects, but I did not directly bring up with him the topic which Jimmie Rosenberg was so anxious that I should stress, that is, the undesirability of continuing the propaganda in the United States on behalf of the World Jewish Congress. Nonetheless, we did approach that general subject, and I was able to emphasize with Wise the danger at home of increasing anti-Semitism and the possibility of its intensification if there were any ground for charging divided allegiance.

. . . .

24. William Green, president of the A.F. of L.; David Dubinsky, International Ladies Garment Workers Union; Sidney Hillman, President of the Amalgamated Clothing Workers of America.

25. General James Guthrie Harbord, U.S. Army, chairman of the board of RCA, 1930–1947.

26. General John Joseph Pershing, commander of the American Expeditionary Forces in Europe during World War I.

Up to Mr. May's to tea. Then to dinner with Jerome Hess[27] and his mother. After dinner I went to the Hotel Pennsylvania to receive the Pi Lambda Phi award, while Ruth and the Hesses stayed at home. I reached the hotel promptly at nine, just when coffee was being served. Arthur Garfield Hays[28] presided, or rather made the presentation. I replied in a brief statement about academic freedom, etc. It was a group of only about 80 or 100 younger college graduates, mostly Jewish. Their reception was very generous.

Saturday, December 29, 1934

The luncheon attributed to a week or so earlier with Gaisman was in fact held on this day. Inman came over at night, and we made our plans for the South America trip (also recorded earlier).

Sunday, December 30, 1934

In the afternoon to tea at Mrs. Rita Morgenthau's. Met a number of old friends. . . . Had a longish talk with Arthur Lehman. He said that what I had to say to him about Rome was the first encouraging sign he had seen since the difficulty broke in Germany. It was evident from the attitude of nearly everyone I met, and they were mostly Jewish, that even on the part of those individuals who do not help in the work, there is a feeling of very real appreciation for what is being undertaken.

Monday, December 31, 1934

Disturbed at not having found the extra $5,000 with which to complete my pledge before the closing of the books at the end of the year, I called Lewis Strauss, who said that he would get in touch with Baerwald. Strauss called me back, said that Baerwald had agreed to advance the funds from the JDC, that perhaps Strauss would repay the JDC, but this was not a pledge. Strauss would do what he did last year, provided he could get the help from a certain individual who was now on his way to California.

. . . .

In the late afternoon attended a meeting of Razovsky's committee. Dr. Baehr[29] gave a report of his committee, indicating that unless they could receive larger funds from the joint drive, they might have to make their own appeal. Razovsky spoke of the work of attempting to place the refugees outside of New York; Warren[30] emphasized the necessity for his group to have larger support if

27. Jerome Hess, lawyer, counsel to Hardin, Hess, Eder, and Rashap, active in the FPA and in international law.

28. Arthur Garfield Hays, trial attorney and longtime defender of unpopular causes as general counsel for the American Civil Liberties Union. Took part in the Scopes trial of 1925 and Sacco-Vanzetti trial of 1927.

29. Dr. George Baehr, secretary of the Executive Emergency Committee in Aid of Displaced Foreign Physicians.

30. George Warren, head of International Migration Service, after 1938 general secretary of President Roosevelt's Advisory Committee on Political Refugees.

they are to continue to do as much as they have done for the refugees. Speaking of the situation in France, Warren said that a member of the Chamber of Deputies, Fatou from Aix en Provence, was working on a project to give a large number of *cartes de travail* to refugees.

Stopped at Mr. Ittleson's house on the way up home, and having arrived so late, stayed for an early supper. Ittleson and I were in general agreement about the German situation and the future of the Jews there. He was much interested in Herbert May's study, but doubted if it would vindicate Max Warburg's thesis that the Jews should be helped to remain in Germany, rather than that they should be encouraged to leave. Ittleson said, "Where the truth is in this matter will depend on what are the currents of history, for one can succeed only if he moves with the prevailing trends, and not against them."

Towards the end of our conversation the names of Bernard Baruch and Herbert Swope came up. Turning to Ittleson, I said, "These two buddies of yours are bad Jews." He was stirred to an impetuous and heated reply, insisting that I was wholly wrong, that I underestimated the part they played, and that I must never say this again. We thrashed the matter out for a few minutes, and I could tell that Mrs. Ittleson was rather sympathetic to my view. Towards the end I said, "Can you ever show me an instance where either of them has been willing to make a real sacrifice for the Jews or to associate himself with an unpopular cause?" Ittleson had no reply, except to say that Baruch would give him money whenever he asked for it, though for Jewish purposes he wished it given anonymously, and moreover, Baruch doubtless preferred to maintain his position so that he could remain the adviser to those in high places and thus be enabled to work more effectively. Something of the same attitude, he said, would apply to Herbert Swope. My parting remark was that I hoped he was right, because each of these men could, if they would, really play an important role.

Perhaps I should note that during our talk Ittleson denounced the proposal to have another joint drive this year, and said that he had announced that he would have nothing to do with it if it were put on that basis. His reasoning seemed to be faulty, and I told him so. But he would not admit that he was wrong. As Felix Warburg said to me when I described the incident, "Ittleson has gotten rich too fast and is too unyielding in his attitudes."

21. January 1935: The Catholic Connection

Tuesday, January 1, 1935

. . . .

Dinner alone with Samuel Untermyer at his apartment. He told me of the progress in his campaign [boycott of German goods]; his tale of how Macy's had been brought into line was extremely amusing and illustrative both of the ruthless adroitness of Untermyer and the vulnerability of the heads of the store. He admitted that Percy Straus was more ready to assume some responsibility for Jewish matters than Jesse Straus, but he doubted that in either case the motivation was other than self-interest. Indeed, he had had more difficulty with their store than with the non-Jewish ones. Now he is planning a drive on Jewish importers, many of whom continue to trade as before. He is also planning to work on the A. F. of L. with a view to making their contribution something more than mere resolutions. As he talked, I could not but admire the pertinacity and the intelligence of the old man. He would, indeed, be a dangerous enemy. His tale of how he had caused dissensions in the ranks of the German societies is proof of this. He has not lost any of his contempt for [Congressman Samuel] Dickstein, whom he looks upon as a dangerous fool. He still regrets that he did not go into Dickstein's constituency at the last election, and defeat him. I then told him about some of our recent work. He thought there were great possibilities in the conversations in Italy. He understands, of course, that all of this matter is in the strictest sense confidential.

We chatted for a little while about Charlie Sherrill, whom Untermyer regards as highly as do I.[1] Untermyer thinks there is still a possibility of transferring the Olympic Games from Berlin, particularly now that Mulhooney has become the head of the American group.

. . . .

1. That is, they both disliked him intensely. "Sherrill pressured the Germans into promising to abide by all Olympic statutes and to guarantee the equal rights of German Jewish athletes . . . [but] publicly ignored all indications that the Germans were failing to honor their pledges." Stephen R. Wenn, "A Tale of Two Diplomats: George S. Messersmith & Charles H. Sherrill on Proposed American Participation in the 1936 Olympics," *Journal of Sports History* 16, no. 1 (Spring 1989): 1–17.

. . . .

Cardinal Hayes[2] received me promptly. I told him in some detail of my three conferences with Cardinal Pacelli and then launched into an analysis of the German situation, with a view to making clear the common stake of the Jews and the Catholics. His Eminence listened attentively, but made no comment during the first quarter of an hour or so.

I then suggested the desirability of Catholic cooperation in the United States in the care of the refugees and also in the project for a corporation to find the funds for emigration and settlement. In reply, he did not take exception to my major thesis about the danger to the Catholics in Germany, though he appeared not to have realized how real the peril is. He talked of the difficulty of finding any funds for other than strictly parish purposes, that even within his own diocese there were important needs which could not be met. I explained that I did not have in mind at all any popular appeal, but rather, that two or three of the leading Catholic laymen might be interested in the sort of cooperation I had outlined. I mentioned specifically George McDonald.[3]

The cardinal said that he had just been talking with George McDonald the day before, that the latter was called upon for innumerable charitable purposes, and he asked whether I had seen McDonald.

I replied that I had not, and intimated that unless the cardinal were willing to support my plea to McDonald, there was little prospect of success. His Eminence finally said that if I would leave a copy of my report, he would send it to George McDonald and tell him about our talk, so that if I returned in February, there might be an opportunity to see McDonald.

It was about this point that the cardinal said that he had had word from Pacelli about my visit. Indeed, I was convinced from the way he spoke of it that the engagement was made for my morning conference only after word had come from the Vatican.

We then went on to discuss various problems of the Church in Mexico, Russia, and elsewhere. The cardinal expressed the view confidently that in the long run the state could not hope to prevail against the Church. He told me of the address he had made on the occasion of a dinner for Cardinal Mercier, when the latter had visited the United States. He had taken Cardinal Mercier as the living embodiment of the uncrushable spirit of the Church.[4]

As I was leaving, he said that he would of course report to Cardinal Pacelli on our talk. He added, "Of course, if there is to be effective cooperation from the

2. Cardinal Patrick Hayes, archbishop of the Diocese of New York since 1919.

3. George McDonald, papal marquis, noted philanthropist, chairman of the executive committee of the Citizens Committee on Unemployment. He had been asked to be vice-chairman of the American Christian Committee but had turned it down, presumably because the Catholic Church had decided not to participate. (No relation to J. G. McDonald.)

4. Desire Desideratus Mercier, archbishop of Brussels-Mechelen. His passive resistance to the Germans during World War I inspired the Belgians to fight on.

Church in the States, it would be necessary for Rome to indicate definitely its desires, and these instructions should come not merely to the cardinal in New York, but to all four of the cardinals. Only then could they move as an organization."

On the whole, I left with the impression that the cardinal had been genuinely interested and, to a certain extent, disturbed by what I had told him, that he would make an initial approach to George McDonald, but that any further action would be dependent upon further instructions from Rome.

Walking down Fifth Avenue on the way back to the office, I saw Mr. Root[5] get out of a car and enter an office building. I followed him in, introduced myself to him in the elevator, and we had a considerable chat before he entered the office to keep his appointment. We talked about the World Court, which he considers as essential as ever but which, as he put it, is one of those institutions which you can support today or tomorrow, and thus there is a tendency to delay final action. He expressed fundamental pessimism about Germany, indicating that he thought the danger of war comes from that direction.

At the office telephoned to Samuel Untermyer telling him the substance of my talk at Madison Avenue and making clear that decisive cooperation would depend on further instructions from Rome, indicating that I was going to move towards that end.

Lunch at Macy's with Percy and Ralph Straus. As we were waiting for lunch, I told them both of Jesse Straus's attitude on the question of the foreigners in France and of his recommendations to President Roosevelt. They were not surprised that he felt as he did about the French situation, but evidently had not thought that he would urge a similar policy at home.

At lunch in addition to talking rather fully about the German situation, I urged Percy to press for action by the corporation on the particular points I had recommended in my letter. He said he saw no reason why the matter could not go forward promptly and would communicate with Liebman.

We talked of the boycott, Percy staying that he was not opposed to individual action, but he did think it a mistake to organize a large-scale public movement.

. . . .

Tried vainly to get Miss LeHand on the telephone. The response was that she was either out or could not speak. I judged that her office had not yet gotten the material I wished in reference to the contribution to the High Commission budget, so I left word that I would call the next day.

. . . .

5. Elihu Root, lawyer, statesman, secretary of state under Theodore Roosevelt, senator who helped plan the World Court.

Conference with Mr. Bamberger and Mrs. Fuld at the Madison Hotel. As always, they seemed deeply stirred by the German situation and were very generous in their references to my part in the work on behalf of the refugees. . . .

Thursday, January 3, 1935

. . . .

Lewis Strauss called me on the phone to say that he was being criticized for the small contribution which the records showed he was making to the JDC, and he wondered if I could not say something that evening which would indicate that he was doing something special for me. At first, I thought I couldn't do it, and then told him while on the air I would make no personal references, I would be able to speak of him along with certain other individuals in an informal talk afterwards.

Got Miss Tully on the telephone at the White House. She read to me a letter from the director of the budget in which he pointed out that if the item for $10,000 were included in the appropriation bill without previous legislative authorization, it would undoubtedly be thrown out on the first point of order raised against it. Therefore, she said that the Department of State was drafting a special bill. At this point, I told her of Chamberlain's suggestion that this amount might be included in the department's contingent fund, thus avoiding the necessity for a special bill. I explained that, of course, I was anxious not to interfere with whatever plans the department might have, but I thought it desirable that she should know of this other possibility. She said that she would prepare a memorandum and put it before the President, and ask him which procedure he preferred. In closing, I told her that Professor Chamberlain would be available to follow up on this matter if it were desired, that he would be available at any time that she wished to reach him, and also of his relations to the Department. She noted his name and address.

. . . .

Erich Warburg joined me at the Rosenthals while I was dressing. He anticipates a series of "bloodbaths" in the Reich comparable to June 30 [1934]. He thinks the [Nazi] regime is less stable, but he sees no clear alternative. On the whole, he appears to be inclined to think that one ought to support the regime economically, though how real his desire on that point is I am not sure.

As I finished dressing, I suddenly discovered with horror that I had not included a collar. I was already late, but the chauffeur managed after ten minutes or so to find me a collar that would do, and I arrived at the Temple Emanuel about half past seven. Fortunately, Mr. Brown was also late, and we were able to go in together.

During dinner I chatted with Felix Warburg, told him a little of my conference at Madison Avenue [with Cardinal Hayes], and urged that Jewish leaders should broaden their defense of tolerance. He had no time to think the thing through and simply gave me his first reaction, which was that Jews had enough troubles of their own.

The program of the evening was a little hectic because, as nearly always, more had been planned than could be gotten through in the time [allowed].[6] Felix Warburg condensed his speech to ten minutes, delivering it during a part of the meal. Then there were three songs by Mr. Schorr, and fortunately the chairman, despite the evident desire of the audience for encores, insisted that the program proceed. Then followed a fifteen-minute speech by one of the heads of the philanthropic organizations. He did not stir the audience much.

At 9:30, when we went on the air—WJZ and associated stations—Judge Tulley was first introduced, and after referring very briefly to the refugee work, launched into an attack on the Mexican government for its attitude of intolerance towards the Catholics. This was looked upon by some as a gratuitous misuse of the occasion, but personally I was glad to see it.

Then Felix Warburg introduced George Gordon Battle.[7] The latter, with heroic self-sacrifice after reading three letters—from the President, Governor Lehman, and Professor Einstein—scrapped the whole of his own speech and introduced me precisely at the moment when I was due to go on the air. The result was that I was enabled to give my talk exactly as I had written it, and so the occasion became very like one of my regular broadcasts from the studio. It seemed well received.

During the applause I asked Felix Warburg if I might speak informally for a few minutes. This I did for about ten minutes, making a plea for more generous American Jewish support.

Afterwards there was a half an hour or more of Movietone and other photographing, in which Landman, Felix Warburg, George Gordon Battle, and I participated.

Warburg called upon Neville Laski to do what in England would have been called "move a vote of thanks." This Laski did extremely well.

I should have noted a day or two earlier my tea visit with Mrs. Otto H. Kahn at her new apartment. She seemed to me much less embittered by the suggestion that she is involved in the German situation, but I doubt if she is yet ready to make any substantial contribution towards the refugees.

Friday, January 4, 1935

Mrs. Sundheim from Philadelphia came in to talk about her project for the sale of art objects on behalf of the refugees. She said that a number of artistic people, including Stokowski[8] in Philadelphia, had volunteered to contribute

6. The occasion was the presentation to McDonald of the American Hebrew Medal in recognition of his service for the promotion of better understanding among Christians and Jews.

7. George Gordon Battle, lawyer with Battle, Levy, Fowler, and Neaman.

8. Leopold Stokowski, famed London-born conductor of the Philadelphia (1912–1941) and London Symphony orchestras, who was still performing when he died at age ninety-five in 1977.

things for the sale. She wished the proceeds to be used for non-sectarian purposes and wanted a letter from me in supporting the proposal. I said I would write it to her.

Talked to Rosenberg on the telephone. He told me to look up Alfred Knopf on the boat. Then he launched into a long discourse on his plans for Biro-Bidjan. It will require some months before his program is ready; meantime, it should be spoken of nowhere. He was working towards a formal invitation from Kalinin to me and to Rosen for September. He had high hopes of finding financial support from the Rosenwalds and General Electric.

He asked me repeatedly if there was anything else I wished to say to him about any of my personal wishes, and if at any time anything occurred to me, to let him know.

Spoke to Lewis Strauss on the phone. He said he had already heard from six or eight people about what I had said the night previous. He was evidently delighted and will, I think, be prepared to carry through again this year as last.

Tea with Mrs. Warburg. She said she had been really stirred by my talk of the night before, but that Max Warburg had thought [that] for me, who must continue to work with Germany, my formal talk was too stiff. He liked my informal remarks better.

....

Stopped at the office to pick up my attaché bag, and was nearly a half hour late to the Vladeck dinner of the trade unionists at the Advertising Club, but it didn't matter because Dubinsky and one or two others were even later. During dinner I talked with Dubinsky and his colleague of the needle workers union and learned that they are in a flourishing condition, with a large campaign fund. I made as strong a plea as I could for immediate and generous support of Schevenels' committees. Vladeck explained what had been done and his hopes that more funds would be available very soon. He said that he would write to Schevenels and make clear to the latter that I had been doing my utmost to stir the unions to action. Dubinsky said that they would help now or in the very near future, and would try to do more later. The New York representative of the A. F. of L. also said he would do what he could.

Home on the train, which reached Bronxville at 9:13, anxious to pack and to get to bed, when, to my surprise and disgust, I met the two prospective renters of our house, who had been asked by Ruth to come out and get acquainted. But it was not as bad as it might have been, for I was able to do some packing while Ruth and they visited. Both she and I were favorably impressed and were inclined to sublet to them, but it was left that the final decision would be made a little later.

Saturday, January 5, 1935

Down to the SS *Rex* by a little after eleven.

....

The voyage, Saturday, January 5–Sunday, January 13, 1935

It was like most other voyages. The weather mostly nice, but only on the first Sunday were we able to swim until we reached the Mediterranean.

....

Stupidly caught some kind of a throat irritation just before reaching Gibraltar, and was annoyed by it the rest of the trip.

....

Landed at Villefranche early Sunday. Again it was a beautiful day, but I spent it largely in bed at the Hotel Luxembourg.

Night train for Geneva.

Geneva, Monday, January 14, 1935

Reached the Bellevue a little late, just before eleven o'clock. Immediately began a long series of conferences with Wurfbain, Kotschnig, and Olive Sawyer, interrupted by a visit from Dr. Olivier, who examined my throat and pronounced it a form of irritation and prescribed various mild remedies.

Indoors all day.

Our discussions turned on the question of what action we could take in view of the imminent announcement of the result of the Saar voting. Kotschnig was emphatic for vigorous action to secure responsibility for the refugees from the Saar through specific authorization by the Council, combined with definite offers of assistance from the chief countries that might be expected to receive certain of the refugees or provide some funds.

Tuesday, January 15, 1935

Conference with Kotschnig and Ginsberg. Decided to sign cable to Joint [Distribution Committee] asking for prompt action on loan of $5,000 and agreeing on Ginsberg's behalf to repayment plus further payment under certain conditions.

Just before lunch Demuth, whom we had asked to come over, arrived. For nearly a half an hour he talked very freely about his visit to Pacelli. I was especially interested in the reaction which he got that His Eminence was fearful of any North American influence which might tend to strengthen Protestantism or radicalism (in Latin America). Pacelli is anxious to maintain Catholic solidarity of those countries and to protect them against demoralizing influences. Apparently, he does not consider that the Jews are a danger. It was impossible to tell from Demuth's report to what extent if any Pacelli's comments along these lines were related to my proposed South American trip. Nonetheless, it was clear that my chances of success would be increased if I were able to enlist the active cooperation of the Catholics, and perhaps even add a Catholic member to the staff for the South American trip.

Conference at tea with members of the staff in a vain effort to agree on a line of policy in the light of the overwhelming German victory in the Saar. As a matter of record, I might perhaps merely indicate here that on Monday night the last thing I said to Wurfbain before he left me was that I should not be surprised if the German majority were 90 percent.[9] I had been much impressed by the news item a day or two earlier that Cardinal Faulhaber had offered his prayers for the return of the Saar to the Fatherland.

At five o'clock Kotschnig and I went to see Massigli at the Bergues. He received us cordially. I told him of the difficulties we were facing because of the uncertainties of what the French policy would be towards refugees from the Saar. We emphasized our feeling that there should be acceptance by the Council of the principle of international responsibility, but that if this were to be helpful, it would have to be much more than formal words. (A detailed memorandum dictated after this interview should be read in this connection.) However, I should point out here that the net result of the conference was to indicate that the French were going to accept, for the time being at any rate, the bulk of the refugees, that they were going to try to get the principle of international responsibility accepted, and that, meantime, they preferred, for reasons of policy affecting Germany or because of other considerations, that we should not take any initiative in the matter or assume that the refugees fell within our province.

At 6:30 Dr. Demuth returned, and we continued our discussion of the morning. He amplified further his impressions of the situation in Rome. He thinks that Pacelli, while of course very important, is by no means the only personality that must be taken into account. He referred particularly to the "Black Pope" [the head of the Jesuits] and the "Red Pope" [the head of the Society for the Propagation of the Faith]. Neither of these is enthusiastic about Pacelli. Demuth thought it desirable, if possible, that I should get in touch with both these centers. I said I would be glad to consider it, but that I felt that I must be careful to keep my situation unconfused and must deal directly with Pacelli, and only move elsewhere if he approved. Dr. Demuth thought I should see Dr. Kaas[10] in Rome, who is said to be more or less in charge of German relations with the Vatican, or rather of Vatican relations with Germany, and in that position is also said to have stood for a very mild policy such as that which is associated with the Pope himself and with Pacelli, as against the stronger policy said to have been urged by the head of the Jesuits, who takes the view that this is a pagan regime, and the sooner it is attacked the better.

As to a possible colleague on my South American trip, Dr. Demuth volunteered to write to Kaas to ask him whether he knew of a young Catholic who would fit my needs, but all this without mentioning my name. . . .

9. The Germans won 90.8 percent of the vote.

10. Ludwig Kaas, Catholic priest born in Trier who became a leader of the German Center Party (member of the Reichstag 1920–1933). In 1925 was appointed secretary to the then papal nuncio in Germany, Bishop Eugenio Pacelli. Kaas played a role in the negotiations preceding the Concordat between Nazi Germany and the Vatican.

We agreed that in South America, so far as the academic work is concerned, I would try to build on what Demuth had done and to lay a broader basis for the continuation of these efforts from this side.

. . . .

Wednesday, January 16, 1935

Kotschnig and I went to see M. Augusto Biancheri Chiappori,[11] who was asked by Aloisi to see us on behalf of the [Saar] Committee of Three. A long memorandum dictated after this interview gives the details. But here I should record that, as with Massigli the night before, I explained our concern about the uncertainty of responsibility for the refugees from the Saar, our willingness to help, but our anxiety that there should be an acceptance of international responsibility and a provision of adequate resources, as well as, if that were practicable, some form of quota to be accepted by the different countries. In his response Biancheri made it quite clear that the refugees from the Saar did not fall within our province; that, moreover, for us to take any definite line in reference to these refugees might make more difficult the work of the Committee of Three in securing from Germany the largest possible measure of guarantees for those who had voted against a return of the territory. In short, his position was on this point similar to that of Massigli; only it was stronger.

Stayed indoors the rest of the day, while Wurfbain and Kotschnig continued to make inquiries around the Secretariat. Nothing more definite was learned from the French or from other interested parties, so that we continued to be left in the position of considerable uncertainty, not only as to what was going to happen to the refugees, but even as to what we could say in answer to inquiries made to us by representatives of the press and others, who not unnaturally continued to assume that the refugees from the Saar were refugees from Germany and therefore our responsibility.

. . . .

Thursday, January 17, 1935

. . . .

In the afternoon attended my first meeting of the Council, or rather chatted in the lobby with correspondents and others. Among those I met were Sharkey, Streit, Whitaker, the U.P. man, the JTA representative, who said that he had been criticized by his office for not having had stories from Geneva last November of my possible trip to South America. . . . Also had a chance to talk with Knox. He told me that the German member of his committee and Mr. Hoffman were anxious to see us. He belittled the rather alarmist stories about the numbers of refugees.

11. Augusto Biancheri Chiappori, Italian diplomat and cabinet minister, in 1933–1934 general director of the international organizations section of the Foreign Office.

Waited around the Council until after seven, and since there seemed no assurance that the Committee of Three would report that evening, I came home and worked with Olive Sawyer late, and we therefore missed the final action about the Saar.[12]

Friday, January 18, 1935

. . . .

Kotschnig saw Kossmann, the German member of the Saar Governing Commission, and then he and I some hours later had a full dress conference with all the members of the commission. The proceedings of this discussion are recorded in a detailed memorandum. I should note, however, that here again the same attitude predominated as in the talks with Massigli and Biancheri. There are two categories of refugees; with those of the Saar we have no responsibility, and it is important that we should not press the point. The conference lasted for about an hour and was extremely illuminating, but not helpful for us.

Ginsberg called me up to say that she had heard indirectly from Litvinov that the question of the refugees was to be put on the Council agenda. This, as we learned later, was merely the result of the French initiative and did not indicate anything as to what action would finally be taken.

. . . .

Supper alone.

Saturday, January 19, 1935

Spent the morning at the Secretariat, most of the time in the lobby outside the Council meeting. Met Kotschnig, who gave me the text of the French memorandum. It followed the general lines we had expected. He told me, too, of the press conference the day before which Laval had had with the French. When asked whether the High Commission would be used as the agency to handle the Saar refugees and he had indicated that he doubted this, he was asked why. His answer was, "It was a mater of efficiency." Later, this was explained as meaning that because of the High Commission being detached from the League, it would not be efficient for it to undertake this responsibility. This news Kotschnig had had from Pobereszki of the *Journal des Nations.*

I held up Benes in the lobby, told him of the present situation of uncertainty about the handling of the refugees from the Saar. He said he thought the distinction between the refugees from the Saar and the refugees from Germany was fantastic and without real meaning; nor did he feel that there was any sense in maintaining the fiction that the High Commission had no relations with the

12. The committee voted to transfer all of the Saar to Germany under the conditions of the Versailles Treaty and set March 1 for the takeover. Baron Popeo Aloisi was appointed to head the committee to work out details. What the committee had not decided by February 15 would be referred to the League Council for reconciliation.

League. He said he would speak to Avenol and find out what the Secretary General had in mind.

Talked again with Knox, who said that he understood the French were bringing the matter up before the Council, but he did not know what would be done. He repeated his statement that he thought the reports of exodus from the Saar were exaggerated.

Spoke to one of the members of the British delegation as to Council action on the refugees. He said that he did not know what was being proposed, but that he would get in touch with the French and find out.

I talked with Madariaga. He at first seemed to think ours was the logical agency to handle the new refugees, but when I pointed out the French desire to emphasize international responsibility and particularly the responsibility of the League, he said at once that he did not see how he could be mixed up with it on that basis.

Chatted for a moment with Vasconcellos, the Portuguese representative. He thought that the distinction[s] being urged as between the two classes of refugees, and between the High Commission and the League, were essentially artificial.

Earlier in the morning I had asked Arthur Sweetser if he could not find out what was in the mind of the Secretary General. He promised to try. Later, he took me aside and reported what he had learned from the Secretary General's chef de cabinet. It was what had been indicated before: that the Council would adopt a resolution referring the matter to the rapporteur for refugees, the Mexican representative, who would in conference with the Committee of Three, study the matter, report at the May meeting of the Council. That Council would be unable to appropriate funds, so the matter would go over to the September Assembly. Meantime, the French would assume responsibility for the Saar refugees, with the expectation of presenting to the Assembly a bill for the financial outlay.

My comment on this was that the refugees were not a form of merchandise which could be stored away for six or eight months, but Sweetser had nothing more to offer.

....

The afternoon and evening spent at the Secretariat. Ran into Prince van Löwenstein[13] and his brother. I asked them where were all their status quo voters.[14] They replied that there were a thousand reasons and no reasons to explain what had happened. But there seemed to me little reason for pressing this conversation.

13. Prince Hubertus zu Löwenstein. His citizenship had been declared forfeit by the Nazi government in November 1934.

14. The Löwensteins had apparently predicted that voters in the Saar plebiscite would choose to keep the status quo (French administration).

Conference with Captain Walters about the refugees. He refused to see that the League had any responsibility, and he was sure that no money could be voted by the Council, and he felt confident that none would be voted by the Assembly. He indicated what I assume is the view of Avenol, that the League is anxious to avoid any talk of refugees as far as it can be done, and certainly to avoid irritating Germany by assuming responsibility for them or by re-establishing connections with us.

Took advantage of meeting Osusky to point out to him the gratuitous attack in the *Journal des Nations* that morning, where the writer of the leading article said in so many words that because the McDonald committee had not been able to solve the problem of the refugees in its care, its efficiency would not be increased by being given additional responsibility, and therefore, some other provision for the Saar people would be made. I said to Osusky that, while, of course, he had nothing to do with this, the paper was commonly spoken of as a Little Entente organ. Osusky replied that he had not seen the article, but that he would interest himself in it.

Chatted with Arthur Sweetser and with Rappard about Madariaga. They both agreed that, while he is one of the most international of all the men accredited to the League, he nonetheless frequently makes difficulties by rather gratuitous comments on subjects that had better not be spoken of in public meetings, and that, in any case, he speaks much too much for his own usefulness.

....

Dinner with Anne O'Hare McCormick and Olive Sawyer at the Coq d'Or. Mrs. McCormick reported that Benes is now much more optimistic than when she last saw him, that he has reversed his position about Mussolini completely. This must be a complete reversal if, as she now reports, he now is enthusiastic about Mussolini. For comparison, my interview with Benes last November.

....

Monday, January 21, 1935

....

Lunch with Arthur Sweetser. We talked about

(1) Representation of the United States in Geneva. Sweetser says that the appointment of Rice[15] by Mrs. [Frances] Perkins makes not the third, but the fourth American representative in Geneva, the others being Gilbert, Wil-

15. William Gorham Rice, Jr., appointed permanent liaison delegate of the U.S. Department of Labor to the International Labor Office.

son, and on occasions the chargé from Bern. Sweetser told me a number of instances illustrating the confusion resulting from this situation, which is made worse because of Gilbert's tendency to interpret every incident in the light of a general persecution complex;

(2) Sweetser is worried about the proposed World Court reservation, but I could not share his concern, for it seemed to me the only possible basis of American adherence, and one which in practice is not at all likely to cause difficulties;

(3) The Rockefeller attitude towards the League is, from the point of view of further financial support, not encouraging. Sweetser had gotten the same impression from John D., Jr., that I had. Similarly, he had gotten the impression that, while John III is still interested in the League and friendly, he is extremely conservative on most other matters;

(4) Sweetser feels sure the League will not assume any new obligations towards the refugees; that, on the contrary, every effort will be made to avoid irritating the Germans. He, therefore, does not anticipate any affirmative action at the May meeting of the Council, and in any case, no money could actually be voted until the September Assembly, and not to become available until the first of next year;

(5) Sweetser's own plans are to remain in Geneva unless something much more attractive than he has reasons to expect turns up at home.

In the afternoon finished the draft of the statement to the press, eliminating from it all those parts of the first draft which could be interpreted as critical of the attitude of the French, the Committee of Three, or the Governing Commission. Arranged for translation through Kotschnig and for distribution by seven that evening. Our assumption that the League action would consist merely in taking notice of the French *aide mémoire* and referring the matter for study to the refugee rapporteur in conference with the Committee of Three was borne out by the brief handling of the matter at the afternoon Council meeting, so there was no necessity to change our release.

Spent from about five o'clock until after the Council adjourned at seven in brief conferences with the journalists. Among those whom I talked to in explanation of our release were Sharkey, Carroll, Whitaker, Streit, Woodward, the representative of the *Berliner Tageblatt,* Gerig, who told me that it would have been possible for me to have distributed some of the copies of the release through him.

I had a longish talk with Piccard, who read to me a communication from the Friends' representatives in the Saar which was based on a complete misunderstanding of the situation in Geneva. I explained frankly what the facts were, and Piccard said he would communicate them to his colleagues.

....

Tuesday, January 22, 1935

Finished up at the hotel the draft of a long communication to the members of the Advisory Council.

....

Olive Sawyer and Kotschnig saw me off on the 12:50 train for Rome.

....

Rome, Wednesday, January 23, 1935

Arrived at the Hotel Excelsior a little after nine. Then after breakfast had a visit from Galeazzi. To him I explained rather fully the things I wanted to say to His Eminence and why, but since I said most of these to Pacelli the next day and will record them as of that date, I need not do so here. As always, Galeazzi was not only cordial and anxious to help, but extremely understanding of exactly what was involved in my proposal. He said that the cardinal had been a little uncertain as to what he would be able to do, and that he wished to know more of my proposal before he saw me. Galeazzi said that he would try to arrange the appointment for Wednesday if I had to leave that night, but I told him that I was in no such hurry and would be glad to stay over until the next day or even until Friday if necessary. Galeazzi said I would know definitely that afternoon.

In the middle of the afternoon I received word that the audience would be the next morning, and somewhat later, that the time would be 9:45. Meantime, Senator Majoni had invited me to lunch on Thursday, which meant that I could not take the Rome Express on Thursday and might as well remain over until Friday noon.

....

Thursday, January 24, 1935

Over to the Vatican at 9:30, fifteen minutes before my appointment. Knowing my way around now better than formerly, I nodded familiarly to the rather grand personage who presides over the outer ante-room, and he, seeming to remember my rather generous tip the last time I was there, ushered me into His Eminence's office promptly at the appointed time.

I began by pointing out that in view of the Saar election, there would be very few Catholic refugees as emigrants to South America, and that since the large proportion of the Protestants were radicals or Communists and therefore not admissible, nearly the whole of the emigration would be Jewish. I expressed the hope that, nonetheless, he would be willing to aid me in my task of opening up those countries to such immigration, in return for aid which Jewish leaders in Washington and elsewhere would give in ameliorating the intolerance of the Mexican regime towards the Catholic Church. It would, of course, be understood that such support could only be of such a nature as not to involve any form of intervention in the affairs of Mexico, but rather, by means of influence on the various governments having relations with Mexico, the importance could be made clear to the Mexican authorities of moderating its intense radical statism.

From this point I developed the thesis that fundamentally the Catholics and Jews are in much the same way endangered by authoritarian-totalitarian statism. The danger is more evident in the case of the Jews, particularly when the racial element is injected into the controversy. But, in essence, the Catholic Church is just as inconsistent with the claims of statism as is any Jewish organization. This becomes evident when, as the cardinal himself had pointed out earlier, one is dealing with a state-supported form of neo-paganism such as threatens in Germany.

The position of the Catholic Church in South America is not endangered by Protestantism, for this takes root only with extreme difficulty in Catholic countries; the danger grows out of the sort of radical state conceptions such as those now prevalent in Mexico. There statism, combined with a radicalism of an extreme sort, threatens not merely the old political and financial power of the Church, but its religious basis as well.

Then I pointed out the influence which might be exerted by certain persons and groups in the United States with a view to moderating the extreme anti-Catholic attitude of the Mexican government. The details on this point seemed to interest His Eminence particularly, though throughout he had followed my analysis with the closest attention.

He said that he would have to study the matter, that he would not be able to give his answer at once, but would let me know what he could do. I asked him whether his reply would be sent directly or through Galeazzi. He replied that it would be through the latter. Before making this response, he had asked me what I wanted. I told him that I hoped for his general support in South America, which might be expressed by word from him to the ranking ecclesiastics and perhaps by direct communications to certain of the ranking governmental officials, particularly the President of Argentina.

It seemed to me evident from Pacelli's attitude that he not only wanted to think the matter over and to consult with one or more of his colleagues, but that he wished to wait to see whether reports from his own people in the States bore out my interpretation of the possibilities.

The next day I learned that Pacelli had called up Galeazzi shortly after my interview and had said that he would have to consult the Pope on the matter which I had broached. This is confirmation of the importance which he attaches to the matter, and also of the actual interest of the Holy Father in these matters.

In my talk with Pacelli I did not, contrary to Demuth's and Kotschnig's suggestions, raise the question of my seeing Dr. Kaas or the heads of the Jesuit Order and of the Society for the Propagation of the Faith. It seemed to me quite clear that it would be better if I did not run any risk of confusing the situation by seeming to work through several sources at the same time. There would have been danger in this under any circumstances, but especially if, as Demuth reported, the "Black and Red Popes" are not too friendly with Pacelli.

Back to the hotel. Most of the afternoon in bed.

. . . .

Waited for the telephone call. The call came through a little after ten o'-clock. The connection was not too good, but sufficient. Felix Warburg talked first; I explained to him my conference of the morning and my anxiety that something should be begun promptly. Then Jimmy Rosenberg came on the wire, and I suggested specifically that he go to Washington to see the Apostolic Delegate.

He was very responsive and will, I think, carry through.

. . . .

After my talk I went downstairs and dropped into conversation with Mrs. Marx, whom I had noticed with her husband, the European representative of Universal Pictures. . . . Mrs. Marx, who had previously been married to a Christian, is intensely bitter about the situation in Germany. She says she will never return, even if the regime were to change, because much of the worst qualities of the present order would remain. She amplified what her husband had said to me earlier about his chief's plan [Carl Laemmle, the head of Universal Pictures] to make a epoch picture entitled *Intolerance.* He would like to show, without singling out Germany, how throughout the ages intolerance has been unprofitable, taking scenes from Spain, Russia, Germany, etc. One difficulty which blocks the way is that all of Laemmle's family remain in Germany, and he is fearful of jeopardizing them.

Later, as I was thinking this matter over, it occurred to me that this film might be a mistake from quite a different point of view. It would be certain to arouse resentment not only among the Catholic hierarchy, but also among the rank and file of Catholics. Therefore, it would work definitely against my program of Jewish-Catholic cooperation.

. . . .

Friday, January 25, 1935

The only engagement of importance was that with Galeazzi at his home on Salustiana, within four or five minutes of the hotel. It was a huge place, four or five stories, filled with furniture and pictures and bric-a-brac of many periods, but the whole not making a very livable establishment. I found him in bed, suffering from a kidney attack. This was not new, but on the other hand, not serious.

He told me first that Pacelli had called him up soon after my interview. I then told Galeazzi more in detail of what might be expected from New York, of my telephone conversation, and of the danger as I saw it to the Church from the Mexican situation. He, on his part, talked with equal frankness. It was left that he would see His Eminence as soon as possible, and would continue to serve as the medium of communication between Pacelli and myself. The more I see of

Galeazzi, the more fully I am convinced that he has a deep personal interest in this matter, is admirably placed to be useful, and is wholly trustworthy.

The Rome Express, leaving at twelve o'clock. It was a long but not unpleasant trip; though traveling second class, I had a compartment to myself. I must confess, however, that I dreaded leaving the sun and comparative warmth of Rome to go back to the cold and rain and fog of Paris and London.

Paris, Saturday, January 26, 1935

Arrived in Paris at the hotel about ten o'clock. Olive Sawyer was already there, having come up from Geneva the day previously. Herbert May and Mrs. May had arrived the night before from the States.

Was fortunate in getting Schevenels on the telephone because he was leaving that day, and there was no chance to see him. I told him of my efforts with Vladeck, Lewis, Green, and the Jewish socialist trade unions. He seemed fairly satisfied that a considerable amount would be forthcoming from the States, though not all of it by any means for German refugees. Indeed, most of the funds being raised are for the general purpose of protecting the interests of trade unionists in Germany and other fascist countries, and only the smaller part is for relief.

As to the English situation, Schevenels was not optimistic that any considerable amount would be raised. I told him that when I got back to England, I would get in touch with trade union officials, including Citrine.[16]

Meantime, since he did not have time to come to the hotel, I arranged to send him the number of small checks amounting to $58 which had come in in response to my radio talk and which, it seemed to me, could more appropriately be used by his committee than by any other single group, and there did not seem to be enough to be divided.

....

In the late afternoon Dr. Kahn came in. He told me that the JDC had, pending the inauguration of the new drive, arranged for the expenditure during the first three months of 1935 of $90,000 in Germany, $40,000 [of this] for emigration purposes, and [another] $30,000 in the refugee countries. These amounts were still somewhat adjustable, depending on what other groups did. He added, "Of course, you need have no worry whatsoever about the budget of the Commission."

I thanked him for this assurance, but reminded him of the gravity of the need for immediate relief, and of the difficult position I would be in—indeed, this position might become impossible—were there not funds to meet the necessities of the moment. Here again, as so often before, he inclined to be reassuring, but without being definite.

16. Walter McLennan Citrine, later first Baron Wembley, general secretary of the Trades Union Congress.

A long conference from 6 until 7:30 with the representatives of the Friends—Dr. Joan Fry, Mr. Harvey, and Frau Kurgass. To my surprise, the burden of their talk was this time not so much the need for funds as it was the absolutely imperative need for modifications of the French policy in reference to papers. They told again with a wealth of detail of the tragedy of hundreds of individuals unable to secure permission to work, unable to leave France. They admitted, of course, that the bulk of these people were not actually expelled, but contended that, nonetheless, even those who were allowed by tacit consent to remain lived in such a state of uncertainty as to be unable to have any hope of establishing themselves.

In response to these statements, I explained fully the various attempts which had been made with the French government, told of the earnest activities now of Helbronner at the Quai d'Orsay, and of our own efforts there. They admitted that perhaps as a result of these activities, the refugees had been saved from the adoption of the drastic policy which had been threatened in the middle of November, but they contended that this was a negative, and not a positive, gain. To this analysis I could not in honesty disagree.

We then talked about the Saar. I gave them the explanation which had previously been embodied in a circular letter to members of the Advisory Council.[17] They seemed satisfied. Dr. Fry was particularly emphatic that it would be a mistake for the Friends to make work for themselves by intervening on behalf of these refugees unless this were necessary. She intended to take this line with her colleagues in London and could not understand the meaning of the clipping in the *Times,* which indicated that the English Friends were going to make a special effort for the Saar refugees. I told them that Dr. Kotschnig would be available soon to give them a first-hand account of the situation in Strasbourg and the Saar. Later, I learned that one explanation of the utterly discouraging account which the Friends gave of their experience in the matter of papers might be that the cases in whose behalf they had intervened were largely of persons on whose behalf previous interventions by the Comité National had failed. In other words, theirs were what might be called desperate cases. But even if this is true, it explains and does not solve the problem.

Sunday, January 27, 1935

....

Shortly after we returned to the hotel, Kotschnig appeared at four o'clock, and the rest of the day was taken up with his account and his preparation of his memoranda on his experiences in Strasbourg, Saarbrücken, Forbach, and Lux-

17. "Germany had never liked the setting up of an institution specifically for the purpose of dealing with German refugees and my activities had not endeared me to the Reich and Party authorities." Confidential Memo, Office of the High Commissioner for Refugees . . . , January 22, 1935, McDonald Papers, USHMM.

embourg. He dictated to Olive Sawyer until late that night. His report showed intense activity on his part, and, I think, very good judgment.

Monday, January 28, 1935

Conference with the members of the Syndicat d'Etude. . . . Besides Baron Alfred de Guenzburg were present his two colleagues, Fritz Stern and Dr. Arthur Kahn.

We began by my report on the response received from the Italian authorities to the effect that they would welcome direct inquiries by members of the Syndicat as to the possibilities of investment in industrial activities there, and their assurance that there would be no difficulty in the matter of permissions to employ a considerable proportion of German workers.

The members of the Syndicat were pleased to receive this report, and said that they would have to confer with their colleagues, because to accept the Italian invitation would be to go beyond their initial expectations, and that they would then follow up directly with the Italian authorities if it seemed possible for them to go ahead.

The second subject discussed was the perennial one of *cartes de travail.* Guenzburg gave an account of the conferences with the small group which included Dr. Kahn with Flandin and Jacquier. I was surprised to hear that Bernard Kahn was a member of that group, because I had understood both from what Felix Warburg had said to me and from what Kahn had said to me in the States that he had refused to be a member of the group and had seen these two officials alone—and only after they had both indicated that they would be glad to see him. In any event, Baron Guenzburg's account of these conferences was essentially the same as Kahn's account of his conferences with these officials. Guenzburg said that Kahn had made a great impression when he told the officials flatly that, while every effort would be made to emigrate refugees from France, no country would accept a refugee on whose passport had been written "undesirable." Both Jacquier and Flandin seemed sympathetic and to understand the reasonableness and the need for more liberal action. Why then the paucity of results?

The explanation given was in brief that Regnier and Herriot were obdurate. It was reported that Gourevitch had received an encouraging reception from the *chef de cabinet* of Herriot, but this account did not impress me. On the contrary, it seems clear that Herriot, reacting to what he feels to be popular opinion, is maintaining an intensely narrow stand and is carrying Regnier with him, who in turn, of course, reflects his views through the Sureté Generale.

. . . .

Finally we talked about Syria. They said that there was nothing for us to do at the moment; that the matter was being considered by the French authorities both in Paris and in Syria; that there were real possibilities, but the settlements must be only partially by German Jews, by non-Zionists, and must not be on the

Palestine border. These statements were confirmatory of what I had heard earlier about the French authorities here [being fearful] of German or Zionist influence in Syria.

As the group left, they were warm in their expression of appreciation of what I was attempting to do to help them.

Then followed a conference with two representatives of the Agriculture et Artisanat. These were the same two young men who had shown me their exhibit when I was previously in Paris. They were now concerned with the need for retraining among the Saar refugees. They were prepared to put their facilities at the disposal of the refugees, but required the authorization of the French government, and funds.

I explained to them our situation in reference to the Saar refugees, the limitation of our responsibility to those from Germany who were concentrated in Strasbourg, and our impression that there were among these only a relatively small number of younger Jewish persons suitable for retraining. I urged that the first step would be to learn more about the program of the French government and to inquire how many persons really need the facilities of the Artisanat. They then wanted to know that, if these inquiries were made and the need were evident, could we help them find the money? Regretfully, I was forced to give them the same answer as earlier, that is, that I would be delighted to give them the fullest extent possible our moral support, but that we could not assume any definite financial obligation. They said this would be helpful, though, of course, they were disappointed not to have more.

Lunch with Olive Sawyer at Dr. Kahn's apartment. It is a large place on what appears to be a new street just back of the Quai d'Orsay. As Dr. Kahn showed us around, it was nearly pathetic the way he, speaking of his huge pieces of furniture and his pictures, etc., kept saying "These are Berlin"—as though Berlin for him were still, despite everything, the ideal. And in reality, I think he still feels that, though as he told me, he does not at all share Max Warburg's view that there is any probability of a fundamental change in the attitude towards the Jews under this regime.

....

Tuesday, January 29, 1935

....

Went directly from the meeting with Louis Oungre to Baron Robert's house. Arrived there just a few minutes before Helbronner, Lambert, Oualid, and the Baron himself arrived. Because of my appointment at 7:30 with the doctor, there was time only for a brief discussion of Oungre's plans and mine for South America and a fuller account by me of the recent conversations at the Vatican. These interested the group intensely. They all spoke of them with real respect. They felt that they contained interesting possibilities and that I should pursue them further.

....

Wednesday, January 30, 1935

At eleven o'clock with Kotschnig and Helbronner to the Quai d'Orsay for an appointment with Tetreau. A full account of this interview is in Kotschnig's memorandum; but here I should report that after a brief statement by me as to our desire to know what the attitude of the French government was to be in response to our memorandum, Helbronner made a most vigorous attack on the French administration for its policy of *refoulements* [expulsions] and refusal to give *cartes de travail.* He was especially emphatic on the former issue. He could not have put the case more effectively. He too had been unable to see Herriot, and made clear his feeling that those responsible for the present policy of aloofness and xenophobia were doing France great harm. Tetreau seemed to agree.

On the matter of the Saar, Tetreau said that the refugees at Strasbourg were to be assimilated, so far as the French were concerned, with the refugees more properly speaking from the Saar itself. I am not sure, however, that on this point Tetreau was speaking with authority.

Helbronner emphasized my trip to South America and that of Oungre as a means of opening ways to relieve France of some of the refugees.

As we were leaving, Helbronner asked that I tell Tetreau about my talks at the Vatican. I did so briefly, but Helbronner amplified the account on the basis of what I had said the night before. He said that these were of great importance and of significance for French policy.

After we left, I told Helbronner that he was an admirable advocate. So he was.

. . . .

After lunch Oungre and I discussed plans for South America. He seemed genuinely anxious that I should carry through my program, and to regret only that I was not able to go as early as the ninth. We agreed on what should be my major objective, that is, the removal of political obstacles to immigration and laying a basis for the admission of individuals or small groups with industrial possibilities, rather than any program of providing for large-scale industrial enterprises.

. . . .

At six o'clock to the meeting of the National Committee at Baron Robert's office. In addition to some brief talk about the situation in France, the main discussion centered on my report of my Rome talk. Here again, as the night before, each of the members of the group was keenly interested and anxious that I should carry the negotiations further.

Indeed, the attitude was so unusually favorable, that I took advantage of it to press for French cooperation at once in the carrying out of the loan kassa as Kahn desired. Baron Robert had nothing or almost nothing to say. Helbronner refrained from opposing. Stern showed so much interest that I urged him to follow the matter up. Later, Lambert told me that the Committee had voted to leave the negotiation with Kahn to Stern.

On my return to the hotel I telephoned Kahn and told him of the developments, which he agreed was probably encouraging.

....

Thursday, January 31, 1935

Overslept and only awakened at 9:15 by the telephone message that de Fresquet was downstairs. Managed to see him fairly promptly. He showed me a list of the members of his newly organized committee. It seemed thoroughly representative, but he was not sure that it was going to be very active. He asked if I had spoken specifically to Pacelli, and I had to confess that I had not done anything on this matter beyond my move some months ago.

I asked de Fresquet about priests among the refugees. His information was rather indefinite, but he had heard of one or two.

De Fresquet had hardly left when Lambert came. He reported on the action of the National Committee in reference to the loan kassa, and added, "You know, of course, that Louis Oungre has not been very warm on this project." But he seemed to think that it might go forward now.

We then talked about Rawitscher. Lambert told me that the grounds for suspicion were Rawitscher's coming from Italy, his possession of a substantial amount of money, his being introduced by an Italian who is looked upon with suspicion by the French authorities. Lambert is sure the man is honest, but equally sure that these considerations have been sufficient to make the police authorities take an unchangeable attitude.

....

Soon after Lambert left there arrived a Dr. Bramson, president of ORT,[18] and his colleague Lvovitch Millerand. Bramson expressed his keen regret that ORT had not been included on the Advisory Council and his anxiety to keep in touch with us. I promised that Kotschnig would communicate with him the next time he was in Paris.

They then explained their desire to establish a certain number of German families from the Saar on the land in France. They told of their success in this respect earlier, but at the same time admitted that they were having difficulty now in preventing the *refoulement* of some of their earlier settlers.

I explained to them fully our relations to the Saar refugees, and pointed out to them the difficulties—even the dangers—of trying to bring in new settlers until the present wave of xenophobia had passed. They seemed to incline to agree, but I am not sure that really they do.

Conference with Jesse Straus at the Embassy. He told me of his troubles with scores of his countrymen trying to get him to support their claims for Legion d'Honneur or in other ways to use him for publicity purposes. His impres-

18. Society for the Promotion of Crafts and Agriculture among the Jews of Russia, founded in 1880 in St. Petersburg, Russia, by a group of wealthy Jews in order to teach vocational skills to Jews.

sions of the German situation were that the regime is weaker, with increasing tension between the SS and the Reichswehr.

I told him of my Rome talks. His first reaction, which was so typical of him, was to ask whether there wasn't a danger that if the Jews drew closer to the Catholics, this might jeopardize their relations with the Protestants. But he seemed to be less fearful when I had explained more fully, and even to be favorable. Throughout he was most friendly and kept me a considerable time over the half hour.

Two o'clock train for Brussels, leaving Miss Sawyer to take the later train for London.

Reached Brussels to find a note from Speyer fixing the dinner for eight, but telling me that Gottschalk was engaged. This, and the fact that Jules Philippson had not returned, wrecked my plans to get away to London the next day.

At Speyer's there was only Mr. and Mrs. The talk covered a wide range, but after dinner I elaborated my theory of the Vatican possibilities. Speyer, whom I learned only the next day is a violent anti-clerical, especially in reference to the Catholics, and even more or less in Jewish religious matters, nonetheless agreed that the South American-Mexican suggestion was well worth trying. He characterized it as a brilliant diplomatic maneuver. But he remained wholly skeptical about the possibilities of developing this rapprochement in Europe.

. . . .

22. February 1935: A Diplomatic Maneuver

Brussels, Friday, February 1, 1935

Lunch with Gottschalk and Mrs. at their house.

Gottschalk told me at length about the Antwerp situation: how it had been confused by divergent counsels there; of his refusal to take charge until they submitted definite lists; of their finally doing so; and of his hope that the 400 or 500 refugees there could be disposed of as follows—Poles back to Poland, a certain number of other Jews to Palestine, a few being permitted to remain permanently in the country, but the others having only temporary permits pending the opening of South America.

He added that if I were not going to South America, he would not know how to argue with his government that they should postpone expulsions of certain of these refugees. His explanation that one of the difficulties in Antwerp[1] was the refusal of the local burgomaster to carry out orders from Brussels, he being much more radical than the national government.

Gottschalk listened closely to my report of the Rome talks, was apparently impressed by them; at any rate, he offered no criticism. On the whole, I think his attitude is much less critical now than earlier.

Conference with Jules Philippson at the latter's office at tea-time. He was particularly impressed by my report of my visit to Rome. He minimized Speyer's skepticism and attacked the latter for his intense anti-clericalism. Incidentally, he also attacked the Zionists and all of the left-wing Jews. He offered, however, to be of any help he could in the Mexican matter, particularly if the Catholics took the initiative. Under those circumstances, he felt that the Consistoire could formally cooperate.

I left him with the impression that he could really be counted upon.

During the middle of the day I called on Ambassador Morris and found him somewhat indisposed physically, but nonetheless glad to see me. He seemed really annoyed that I had failed to do as he had suggested the last time I was there, that is, let him know when I was coming back, and stay at the Embassy.

Had a much longer talk with the daughter, who, for me, was intensely interesting in her account of her German impressions after three months in a Ger-

1. Belgian police carried out raids against undocumented aliens (including Jewish refugees) in December 1934 in an attempt to expel them from the country.

man family, where she had excellent opportunities for associations with young Nazis. She summed up her attitude as being pro-German, but anti-Nazi. She said that Löwenstein's book, which she read only after she came out of Germany, gave her the best picture of what young Germans, as they talked to her, indicated that they felt, that she had found anywhere. So I made a deal with her by which I promised to read Löwenstein's book if she would read Edgar Mowrer's.[2]

In the light of Miss Morris's keen intelligence and rather philosophical approach to the problem, I was amused later by Mrs. Gottschalk's report that, while the young lady was much admired for her looks and her charm, the general opinion was that she was too logical for a woman. Indeed, Mrs. Gottschalk added her own view that it was dangerous for a young woman to be so frankly intellectual, and that she ought to hide that more; otherwise the young men would quite be frightened away.

. . . .

London, Saturday, February 2, 1935

Took the 9:14 train for London, via Ostend. Reached London weary and wanting only to sleep. . . .

Telephoned to Lady Goldsmid's house and was told that she probably would call me back, that he [her husband] had had a relapse ten days before, but was now much better.

Sunday, February 3, 1935

. . . .

Worked a part of the afternoon; then over to Sir Osmond's at 6:15. Was met by Lady Goldsmid, who explained his condition to me and chatted with me until he came down about ten minutes of seven. He seemed very weak, but otherwise looked fairly well. He listened closely to me for nearly forty minutes. I told him first of Oungre's and my South American plans and of my feeling that the conference which he wanted with the New York people need not wait my return. This seemed to please him. He said that he might be able to get off to meet Warburg in the south on February 20, but I don't think there is a chance.

We spoke of the High Commission budget. He said he had heard from Warburg, and that he was confident the budget would be cared for, and indicated that there would be another joint drive here and that the British Central Fund would make its contribution.

I told him of my action in Paris about the loan kassa, my anxiety that the thing should go forward, and Lambert's report that Louis Oungre was not

2. The books mentioned in the exchange between McDonald and Miss Morris were *Tragödie eines Volkes: Deutschland 1918–1934* (1934) [Tragedy of a Nation: Germany 1918–1934], by Prince Hubertus zu Löwenstein, founder of the German Academy in Exile, and *Germany Puts the Clock Back* (1933), by Edgar Mowrer, Paris correspondent for the *Chicago Daily News*.

warm on the subject. Sir Osmond replied that he knew this very well, but, nonetheless, he himself wanted the thing to come into being, even if it would involve a loss of as much as fifty percent of the capital.

I outlined my South American plans as I had discussed them with Oungre. Sir Osmond agreed most emphatically that it was wrong to talk about large-scale enterprises to be financed in South America: first, because the human material is not available; second, because of the inevitable losses. He agreed completely that my program of removing the political obstacles and helping to finance individuals was right. He said that he was prepared to cooperate financially on that basis.

Then followed my usual story about the Rome talk. He, like the others, was much interested and approved my going ahead.

....

Tuesday, February 5, 1935

More than an hour's conference with Lord Cecil. I outlined the present situation to him, and explained why it seemed necessary to have a meeting of the Permanent Committee in order to take stock, and to envisage, if possible, a procedure by which we could gradually work towards the liquidation of our office by the end of the year, and a transfer of such of our duties as still remained to some other organization, preferably associated with the League.

He expressed the view that while a great deal of useful work had been done and was being done by the office of the High Commission, he felt strongly that the Governing Body as at present organized on an autonomous basis and with its present personnel, was useless; that it could only serve if it were related more closely to the League. He said that he had written to this effect to Sir John Simon some months ago; that he had received reply which indicated that His Majesty's Government could not favor a move to bring the High Commission nearer the League because to do so would irritate Germany, and what was a lesser consideration, might seem to imply that the government was prepared to assume a financial obligation. To this statement Lord Cecil had replied in what he characterized a "perhaps too sharp a tone." In effect, he had said, "There is no use in courting Germany; that is the best way to defeat your purpose. Even more than with the United States, it is a mistaken policy to continually make clear that the League is waiting on Germany's cooperation. The thing to do is to go ahead and do what is necessary, and Germany would be more willing to come along. Moreover, it was a great mistake to treat the problem of the refugees as though it were a mere matter of charity. It is a question of humanity, but it is also a political question, because unless solved, the refugees everywhere constitute foci of irritation. To remove such irritation should be a major purpose of the government, since the basic task of the Foreign Office is to maintain peace."

To this letter Lord Cecil had had no reply. He intended in the House of Lords tomorrow to make a statement somewhat along these lines, but couched more diplomatically than had been his letter to the foreign minister. He then asked me if I saw any objection to his plan to make such a statement. I replied that I did not, so long as it did not give the impression that would be discouraging. He said that he intended to make a clear distinction between the work of the office and the uselessness of the Governing Body. I then suggested that he might also refer to the fact that, in addition to the old problem of the Nansen refugees and the more recent one of the German refugees, there are still more recent refugees, such as those from Spain, and that, therefore, it might be reasonable to suggest that the League study anew its relationship to the refugee problem as a whole. Parenthetically, I added that, of course, as he knew, the general tendency in Geneva now was to restrict, not enlarge, the League's humanitarian and other so-called "periphery" activities. To this, Cecil snorted in reply, "That's nonsense," and added that he himself had passed through the stage of thinking that the League ought to limit itself more to strictly international questions in a narrower sense, but he had now decided that it couldn't be done.

We talked about the Saar very briefly.

In general, I got the impression that Cecil would be prepared to carry on, at least through the next meeting of the Governing Body, which would be held normally after my return from South America, and even beyond that if we then saw a logical period to wind up.

....

Lunch with Otto Schiff at the Savoy. . . . Then he spoke to me about Sir Arnold Wilson,[3] a British ex-governor, who had recently been lecturing in Germany, and who felt that, except for the Jewish program, there had been substantial gains in the new regime.

....

In view of the hesitating and rather unsatisfactory cable from Felix Warburg about my suggestion from Rome, began seriously to consider the possibility of returning to New York for three days before going to South America.

....

Lord Marley came to the hotel at nine, and we talked until after ten. As usual, he was quite general in his statements and inaccurate in his statistics, but filled with the best intentions. He does not plan to attack the government in the question period in the House of Lords tomorrow, but rather to raise the issue of the government's attitude [towards the High Commission] with a view, if possible, of modifying it in a more favorable sense.[4] I gave him certain statistics from memory, and brought him up to date on the situation in a number of coun-

3. Sir Arnold Talbot Wilson, soldier, explorer, author. Former British civil administrator in Mesopotamia and political representative in the Persian Gulf. Conservative MP after 1933.

4. Speaking for the government, Lord Strathcona was non-committal, avoiding any suggestion of a more active role. As Lord Cecil wrote to McDonald, "We really got nothing at all out of the Government. Strathcona, who spoke for them, knew nothing whatever about the subject." Cecil to McDonald, February 7, 1935. Copy in McDonald Papers, USHMM.

tries and the problem of the Saar. He is really chiefly interested in a large loan which, he says, is being arranged through a committee of Jewish bankers in Paris and by committees in London and New York for the purpose of establishing certain industries in Russia which would employ a definite proportion of refugee workmen. The Russian government would also supply funds. But I did not get the impression that this plan was anywhere near realization.

He expressed himself as highly amused at Rosen's change of front about Biro-Bidjan. I don't blame him.

Wednesday February 6, 1935

Worked most of the morning on material for Cecil in connection with the discussion in the House of Lords that afternoon on the refugee situation.

Lunch at New Court with Anthony and Lionel de Rothschild and two of their horticulturist friends.

After a delicious lunch and much general talk about the flowers and plants and weather, the Rothschilds asked me if I had anything special to say to them. I replied that there were two matters. First, I hope they would give me their support in my South American trip, particularly in Brazil. They said that, of course, they would give me letters to their representative in Rio and help me to get introductions from the Baring Brothers in Argentina. Second, I talked with them about the Vatican conversations. These appeared to impress them. Lionel said that here in England the Jews and the Catholics had often worked together, that an insurance company with which his firm was associated did most of the underwriting for the Catholic churches in this country. He would I think be glad to help here with the Catholics if the occasion arose.

Immediately after lunch I went over to see Mr. Evelyn Baring,[5] who said he would give me a letter to their representative in Buenos Aires, Mrs. Roberts, but that the really important man in all Argentina was a Mr. Hirsch, the head of the largest grain-dealing firm, and actively interested in manufacturing in Argentina. He considers him to be an extraordinary man and one who, if he wished to do so, could be of the greatest possible assistance. Mr. Baring said he would be glad to give me a letter to Hirsch, but that first he wished to find out if a letter from someone else, perhaps from Anthony de Rothschild, would not be better.

. . . .

Thursday, February 7, 1935

Spoke to Sargent of the Foreign Office on the telephone. I asked him whether the department had seriously studied the question of the refugee problem in general and the possibility of integrating it all under the League. He said

5. Evelyn Baring, one of the younger members of Baring Brothers investment house. Later first Baron Howick of Glendale, who had the misfortune to be Governor of Kenya during the "Mau Mau" uprisings, 1952–1959. His father, Lord Cromer, the great imperial proconsul, was the founder of modern Egypt.

they had not so far as he knew. I asked then if I might come to talk with him about it before the meeting of our Governing Body. He said that he would be very glad to see me, but that he was going to be away over the weekend, and that perhaps it would be better if I saw Mr. Perowne.[6] I said I would call up the latter.

Leonard Montefiore came in. He told me of the initial efforts on the new drive, and of the expectations that perhaps less than half of last year's total would be raised. The Rothschilds were contributing £5,000. He was much interested in my account of my visits to Rome.

....

Friday, February 8, 1935

Breakfast with Erich [Warburg] at Brown's. His account of internal conditions [in Germany] underlined the steady swing to the right, with an increasing power in the military. Dr. Schacht now approaches an economic dictatorship, but his [Erich's] most startling information was of a personal health sort. I shall watch with close attention to see whether developments of the next few weeks support his suggestion.[7]

....

Down to the City to see George E. Korn of the firm of Walter Gibbs, important in Chile. He was very friendly, said he would give me letters of introduction to their agents; but he is frankly skeptical about the possibility of any success in Chile. There is still a considerable amount of unemployment there, which is cared for only by heavy governmental expenditure.

....

Monday, February 11, 1935

Saw Sir Philip Cunliffe-Lister at the Colonial Office. He was most friendly, and when he learned that he had a committee meeting at eleven, and was thus forced to cut short his talk with me, he was extremely apologetic. We had time, however, to discuss briefly the situation in Palestine, the prospects of Trans-Jordan being opened, (on this point he continues to speak much as he did a year ago, the time is not ripe in his view).

....

Then I went over to the Transport House for my conference with Citrine and Middleton. I was much impressed by the former's driving energy. He au-

6. Victor Perowne, British Foreign Office.

7. This vague reference may refer to inaccurate rumors that Hitler was suffering from cancer of the throat. About a year later, American Minister (in Austria) George S. Messersmith wrote about an unnamed well-placed friend in Germany who confirmed that Hitler's throat problem was non-malignant, but that his mental and physical condition were giving his circle considerable concern. Messersmith to Dunn, February 8, 1936, Messersmith Papers, Item 649, University of Delaware Library, Newark, Delaware.

thorized the sending of an additional £1,000 to Schevenels's committee, and evidently intends to do as much more as is possible. All funds, however, now being raised, are not exclusively for German refugees, but for the victims of fascism in several countries. However, the larger portion of the money goes for political, rather than relief, purposes.

Lunch with Helbronner at the Carlton. He was very full of the message which Léger had asked him to give to me, to the effect that from the information received from the chiefs of missions in Latin America there were only slight prospects of success in Brazil or Argentina, but in Paraguay there is an active demand for immigrants, and a considerable need for them in Ecuador, Colombia, Venezuela, and Nicaragua. I thanked him for these suggestions, but told him that it would not be possible for me to start in with Central America or the West Coast because of the plans which Louis Oungre and I had worked out for Argentina and Brazil. However, I would take advantage of the French information just as far as possible.

Helbronner then told me of a meeting of the inter-ministerial conference which he had attended as the representative of the Foreign Office. He had there presented as forcibly as he could the need for differentiation between the refugees and the bulk of foreigners in France. Herriot, in reply, had admitted this distinction, but refused to admit that the right of asylum carried with it the right to work. To this, Helbronner says that he had argued earlier that the right of asylum without the right to work equalled the right to die. Nonetheless, Herriot was not shaken and insisted that there could be no additional *cartes de travail.*

As to the Saar refugees, Helbronner said that plans had been made to care for 40,000, but that "less than 15,000" had come. How much less he didn't indicate. He added that the German refugees from the Saar were to be treated exactly like the Saarlanders themselves. His categorical statement on this point shows that Tetreau's remark to the same effect, which had seemed to me and Kotschnig rather casual a few days earlier, had, in fact, represented a predetermined policy.

....

Bentwich and I then went to the Foreign Office for our conference with Strang and Perowne. I put strongly the case for the need of leadership in effecting an integration of the refugee activities under the League. Strang promised that it would be studied, and that he and his colleagues would keep in touch with Bentwich.

....

Conference with Dr. Weizmann at Sacher's house. Most of the talk was Weizmann's analysis of the situation in Palestine, particularly of the conditions which to his mind threatened a form of moral deterioration. We talked also of Trans-Jordan, of our recent visits to Sir Philip, and of the inevitability of an overflow across the Jordan.

As to my flirtations in Rome, I found Dr. Weizmann more sympathetic than I expected he would be.

I was amused during our talk by an incident that occurred. Mrs. Weizmann came into the room, having just returned from town. She greeted me cordially and then asked her husband if she might bring in someone else. He told her very decisively no, so she took her friend into another room. Dr. Weizmann was just in the midst of outlining his conception of the future of Palestine, and he did not want to be interrupted.

Dinner for the Laskis and the Bentwiches at the Russell. It was a pleasant party, Laski strangely silent. When he did talk, he spoke mostly about his American experiences and was most generous in his praise of my statement at the American Hebrew dinner. He said he wanted nothing so much as to go back to America.

Bentwich talked a little about Palestine, telling us of Sir Robert Waley-Cohen's accident, and of the moral pressure which forced Sir Robert to have his wife buried there.

Since everybody was very tired, and I had promised the Bentwiches that the dinner would not be late, we broke up about 10:30.

Tuesday, February 12, 1935

The meeting of the Permanent Committee began promptly at 10:30 with Cecil, Helbronner, François, and Silvercruys[8] present. There was not much discussion on any of the topics. Helbronner talked longer than any other member of the Committee. Cecil asked a number of questions. The Belgian representative said hardly a word, François was as usual rather non-committal, but definitely skeptical as to the possibility of the refugee work going back to the League. The financial recommendations were all approved, except the one about the auditor's report, which the committee felt they could not approve but should pass on to the Governing Body.

In short, the meeting served more to ratify what had been done, or rather to give an occasion for putting it on record and for outlining future plans, than for any affirmative suggestions. My colleagues were inclined to think that I allowed the meeting to be rushed, but I did not see any advantage whatsoever in prolonging the discussion into the afternoon, and therefore did not try to do so.

Cecil asked me to lunch with him at the Travellers Club. We did not talk refugee matters, but gossiped about politics, the future of the prime minister, Cecil's work in the League of Nations Union, etc.

....

8. Franz Sylvercruys, Belgian president of the Court of Cassation. Baron Sylvercruys from 1929 on, he had a special interest in the guardianship of children.

Wednesday, February 13, 1935

Spoke to Sir Osmond on the telephone. He indicated that ICA would probably make up another £500 and, if necessary, something additional if this were necessitated by the South American trip.

With Wurfbain to Lambeth Palace to see Dr. Don. I outlined the situation in view of the failure of the Saar to present a startling appeal for Christians and suggested that the necessity for a travel fund for about 1,000 of the Christian refugees might meet the Archbishop's conditions for a plan which would be complete within its scope and be limited primarily to Christians. Dr. Don thought that this proposal offered the best opportunity of securing the Archbishop's active support. It was left that if I were able to report that there were openings in South America, the office would present a memorandum of the expense involved and ask the Archbishop for his cooperation in finding the approximately £25,000 needed.

Bentwich and I lunched with Rich of the *Jewish Chronicle* and his colleague Gilbert. I told of my talks in Rome. Rich was skeptical of the value of any (what he called) "political deals," insisting that the Jews' only chance of success was to pitch their case on the moral plane, to work with Catholics in common causes, but not to make such cooperation contingent on a definite quid pro quo. I replied that I thought he exaggerated the element of political bargaining in my suggestion.

Gilbert, who seems in some respects less inclined to be dogmatic than Rich, was much interested in the problem of anti-Semitism and the possibility of its development in the United States.

Final office conference. Packing and to the boat train by eight.

....

The voyage, February 13–20, 1935

We got away from Southampton shortly after midnight, and had pleasant weather until we left Cobh about ten o'clock on the night of the fourteenth. Then began four days of almost continuous pitching. The result was that two-thirds of the passengers were laid low. As we approached New York, the weather became much better.

The trip was notable because of the opportunity for association with Babe Ruth and other notables, including Clive Brook.[9]

....

New York, Wednesday, February 20, 1935

Docked shortly after four. Met at the dock by Ruth and Bobby. Quickly through the customs and to the office for a few minutes.

Then to the meeting at the Harmonie Club, which had been arranged by Dr. Adler. Those present included Dr. Adler, Rosenberg, Lewis Strauss,

9. British actor who starred in dozens of films, including the 1932 *Sherlock Holmes.*

William Rosenwald,[10] Stroock,[11] Arthur Sulzberger, Frederick Warburg,[12] Paul Baerwald, Joseph Hyman, Rothenberg, Judge Lehman, Bernard Flexner, and Cavert.

At the request of the chairman I explained rather at length my idea of possible cooperation in the Mexican situation, with a view to making more likely Vatican support for my ventures in South America. Cavert's presence required me to broaden the basis of my explanation.

When I had finished, I was asked whether I was recommending any specific action. I replied that I did not know the situation here at home well enough to do that, but that I would be much interested in a discussion of the points of view of those present. Earlier, I had outlined not only my talks in Rome, but also my conversations with Jewish leaders in Paris, Brussels, and London following my Rome visit.

Under Adler's direction, but with frequent and lengthy interruptions by Jimmy Rosenberg and occasionally by others, I was told of the various forms of cooperation in the past between the Jews and Catholics, notably at the Peace Conference, in the organization of the Palestine Mandate, and most of all so far as importance in America is concerned, in the fight against the Oregon school law which would have prohibited parochial schools. Louis Marshall had been one of the chief proponents in that legal battle.

Then coming down to date, I was told of the statement published some months ago signed by Catholic, Protestant, and Jewish religious leaders protesting against state intolerance. I was also shown a draft of a new statement to be signed by laymen dealing with the same subject. Though Mexico is not directly pointed to, the moral is plain.

It appears also that Judge Manton, on behalf of the Catholics, has worked out an elaborate legal brief which, if the Vatican approves, it is suggested will be presented to the League of Nations.[13] It is hoped that two Catholic countries, perhaps Argentina and Ireland, would take the initiative at Geneva.

The central idea in this brief is that the Mexican attitude toward the Church is of such a nature that it endangers the good relations between Mexico and other nations, and is, therefore, violative of Article XII of the Covenant.

It was admitted during the discussion that, of course, this proposal raises many very difficult questions of international law, not to speak of those of a political nature. I did not express the doubts which I felt, particularly on the political aspects of the proposal. As it was explained, I could anticipate the active op-

10. William Rosenwald, co-chairman of the United Jewish Appeal, younger son of philanthropist Julius Rosenwald.

11. Solomon Stroock, partner in the influential law firm of Stroock, Stroock, and Lavan, founded in 1876. President of the American Jewish Committee, and chairman of the Board of Directors of the Jewish Theological Seminary.

12. Frederick Warburg, eldest son of Felix Warburg, member Kuhn Loeb, representing his father.

13. Martin T. Manton, senior judge of the U.S. Court of Appeals for the Second Circuit. He proposed that the World Court intervene in the dispute between Mexico and the Catholic Church.

position which the Secretariat of the League, as well as many of the chief countries, would have towards any such scheme.

Rosenberg and others have been and are continuing to confer with Judge Manton. They are considering the possibility of preparing a similar brief on the German situation as it affects Jews, particularly if the Vatican decides to go forward with the Manton proposal and if it appears that there will be substantial support for it.

During the course of the informal discussion after the meeting had more or less broken up, Rosenberg whispered to me that there was on foot [*sic*, afoot] a project to send a delegation of three—a Jew, a Catholic, a Protestant—to investigate the religious situation in Mexico. The personnel suggested was Buell, Rosenberg, and a Catholic, possibly Michael Williams. Rosenberg would have told me more about it, but there was no opportunity then. He pledged me to complete secrecy.

I remained at the club to have dinner with Adler, William Rosenwald, Paul Baerwald, and Joseph Hyman.

I took advantage of the dinner to bring up the question of Bentwich's possible visit to the States. To my surprise, I found considerable hesitation and at first, even some opposition. Baerwald, as always, was inclined to oppose a new idea. He seemed fearful that Bentwich would stress Palestine excessively. Moreover, he repeated tales of Zionist opposition to Bentwich. It was pointed out, however, that this was Revisionist [right-wing Zionist] opposition and could be ignored; and as to the other point, Bentwich certainly would not ignore the non-Zionist phases of the work. Someone suggested that Bentwich might not be useful in some of the larger centers and that he might not wish to speak in the smaller ones. I said that I was sure that he would do whatever was suggested, that he was the most selfless of men. Adler joined me in stressing Bentwich's distinction as a Jewish leader, the desirability of having someone from abroad, and particularly someone so closely associated with the High Commission as Bentwich was. As the discussion proceeded, Baerwald weakened in his opposition, and Hyman became more cordial. But no definite decision was reached. It was left that Baerwald and Hyman would come to see me on Saturday morning. I, in the meantime, planned to talk directly with the official Zionist leaders.

It is difficult to get Jewish agreement on anything which has to do with Jewish personalities!

William Rosenwald asked me if I could use some letters of introduction in South America. I told him I would be delighted to have them. He said that, though he would sign them, they would be really from his wife, who is very much better known in South America than he. Her father is a distinguished French portrait painter popular in South America. William R. also asked me if I could use a briefcase.[14] I told him that one was always useful. He said he would send it to the office before I sailed.

14. This seems to be a euphemism for expense money.

We gossiped as a group for a little while about Neville Laski and his trip. Everybody seemed delighted with N. L.

....

I should have noted above that during the few minutes at the office I telephoned the office of the Apostolic Delegate at Washington and learned that he was out of town. The secretary promised to telephone or telegraph me the next day in reference to an appointment for Friday. Later the Apostolic Delegate told me that he had actually been in New York on the night of the twentieth, but that he was so tied up with engagements that he could not suggest seeing me there.

I learned that it would be impossible to see Cardinal Hayes, because he, and I assume also George McDonald, were in Bermuda.

Thursday, February 21, 1935

Long talk on the telephone with Professor Chamberlain. He agreed that it would be well for me to write the President, formally withdrawing my request for a contribution to the budget of the High Commission. Professor Chamberlain felt that there would be great difficulties in getting a special bill through Congress, that the President had actually forgotten that he had promised to take the initiative and not wait on the other governments, and that though this was a misunderstanding, it would be no use to try to correct it. To do so would only irritate FDR and accomplish nothing. I agreed.

However, I later called the President's office on the telephone to explain that I was withdrawing the request and why.

I told Professor Chamberlain of the proposed date for the next meeting of the Governing Body. He was pleased that it would be as late as the middle of July and said that it would be possible for him to attend.

I told him also of the feeling of the Permanent Committee in reference to a return to Geneva. He felt that this was the most desirable course, but was, as I am, skeptical of its practicability. He agreed, too, that it would be desirable to work towards the liquidation of our organization in its present form by the end of the year.

We then talked about the matters which I had raised with him in my personal letter as to my own future. He said there had been no opportunity yet to discuss these matters with his colleagues, that he would do so at the earliest opportunity, and communicate with me. On the whole, I got the impression that he was not optimistic about the prospects at Columbia.

Lunch at the *New York Times* office. Present were, besides myself, Sulzberger, Mr. Ochs, Mr. James, Mr. Rollo Ogden, and Dr. Finley.

Mr. Ochs continues to be in almost unbelievable depths of despondency. Everything is going to the devil. He even thinks that Hitler is growing stronger all the time. I challenged him that when I saw him again in June, he would admit that he had been wrong at least on this point. Later Arthur Sulzberger told me how difficult it is in the office because of Ochs's black pessimism. The doctors say this is a physical thing, which will after a time pass if Mr. Ochs survives the three or four years which is the allotted time for such moods. He has been in this state now for about two years.

. . . .

Murrow came in to report to me briefly [on the] prospects for intellectual refugees. He thinks it improbable that the Rockefellers will do more than supply another approximately $200,000 necessary to carry the present beneficiaries for another term until they can be finally placed. His committee expected to be able to raise a comparable sum.

I asked him what this limitation meant so far as the larger plans that Kotschnig had for endowments and so on. He said that he thought this meant that they were not at all practicable. The Rockefellers hold the view that most of the men of great distinction or exceptional qualities have been placed, and that the others fall into the general category of needy. Murrow does not share this view, but does not think it can be changed.

I asked him if he would send me for use in South America a copy of the material which had been prepared for the University of Santiago. He said he would.

. . . .

Washington, Friday, February 22, 1935

While I was at breakfast at the Cosmos Club, Stone called me to say that the U.P. man was anxious to see me, and that he thought it desirable for me to see him. So later during the morning I gave him a non-sensational talk.

. . . .

I found the Apostolic Delegate[15] a shortish, rather plump man, who gave the appearance of listening closely, rather than a man who would be prepared to take responsibility. I told him of my visits to Rome, of my concern about the situation in Germany with its effect not only upon Jews but upon Catholics and Evangelicals, and of my feeling that there was developing elsewhere a form of totalitarian statism which was a threat to religious liberty, and which, if successful, would be a menace to Catholicism throughout Latin America. He let me go on at considerable length without interruption. Then he asked some rather pointed questions: first, as to the connection between Mexico and South America; second, as to what specifically I had in mind, as to cooperation in the States; but at this same time he disavowed that he had anything to do with the Mexican situation, which he said was handled by the papal nuncio to Mexico,[16] who

15. Apostolic Delegate to Washington, Bishop Amletto Giovanni Cicognani (served 1933–1959), later named a cardinal and Vatican secretary of state under Pope John XXIII.

16. Papal nuncio to Mexico Archbishop Leopoldo Ruiz y Flores lived in exile in San Antonio, Texas, rather than Mexico City, from 1932 as a result of the conflict between the anticlerical Mexican government and the Catholic Church.

is now in San Antonio. I replied that San Antonio was rather a disadvantageous point from which to deal with a matter which had such international implications. Third, he asked what it was specifically that I expected from Pacelli.

In reply to these various questions I was as definite as was possible under the circumstances. I recognized that he could not himself take action, but I expressed the hope that he would give a report to Pacelli of his impressions of my visit, and I trusted that his report would increase the likelihood that His Eminence would support along the lines I had suggested to him my efforts in South America. The Apostolic Delegate replied that he certainly would send a full report, and I got the impression that it would be a sympathetic one.

We talked a little about the Borah resolution,[17] of which I frankly expressed my opinion that it was a strategic mistake, stirring up as it inevitably did active opposition and giving apparent ground for the feeling that a movement somewhat like that initiated by Senator Fall fifteen or sixteen years ago was being undertaken; that, moreover, there was slight chance of its being approved in the Senate because of the administration's determination not to intervene in the affairs of the Latin American states.

The Manton brief was mentioned, but I got no light as to whether or not it is likely to receive Vatican support.

As I was leaving, I ran into Father Burke, who was just coming into the building. We chatted for a moment. He revealed to me that the Borah resolution had been drafted by the Knights of Columbus. He pointed out what I should have recognized, that there has not yet been in the United States any single Catholic leadership on the Mexican matter; on the contrary, there has been a diversity of counsel and a confusion of leadership. This perhaps made more difficult than I had realized the carrying out of my suggestion to the Apostolic Delegate that there be set up an informal committee of three—Catholic, Protestant and Jewish—to consider ways of cooperation.

My conference with Constantine McGuire[18] was all too short, though it lasted nearly an hour. After a few minutes of reminiscence about our old Harvard friends, we soon launched into the problem which concerns us both. I found, as I expected, that he was intimately informed, not only of conditions in Mexico, but of the inner political situation among the members of the Catholic hierarchy in the United States. The two most important members from the point of view of the Vatican are, in his view, [Cardinal] Hayes in New York and the Archbishop of Cincinnati, the Most Rev. John T. McNicholas, O.P.D.D.[19]

17. Senator William E. Borah had introduced a resolution asking the Senate to protest the Mexican anti-religious campaign.

18. Boston-born lawyer and economist, expert on Latin America, founder of the Georgetown School of Foreign Service. An influential Catholic layman with close ties to the Vatican, whom McDonald had known since his Harvard days.

19. John T. McNicholas, Irish-born, archbishop of Cincinnati from 1925 to 1950 and leading theologian and authority on canon law. Probably the most influential Catholic educator in America.

Constantine was absolutely of my view about the significance of the Mexican situation and the importance of attempting to influence it along the lines which I had indicated. He said that he would be delighted to help in any way he could. I told him that he perhaps would hear from some of my Jewish friends in New York.

. . . .

I hurried off to get the one o'clock train back to New York. On the way had a pleasant visit with Charles Kellogg.

I should have indicated that on Wednesday night I had a long telephone conversation with Cavert. . . . He said that he was personally sympathetic with the view I had expressed at the Harmonie Club; that, however, there was considerable difference of opinion among Protestant leaders as to the actual effect of Mexican religious policy.

. . . .

On the whole, therefore, it is apparent that the Federal Council is not yet ready to join in any common movement. Nonetheless, they will be glad to keep in touch with the Catholics and the Jews on this issue.

Back to Bronxville in time for supper at the Robinsons. They had very considerately invited John and Edna, and we had a nice party. After dinner, while Leland was showing movies, I packed.

About 10:30 Lewis Strauss came over, and we talked for a considerable time. First, I reported to him on my Washington visit and asked him to communicate with the other members of the group that had been at the Harmonie Club. In this connection I was delighted to learn that he not only knows Constantine McGuire, but has been associated with him rather intimately. He shared my view that the latter would be an excellent person to work with.

Second, we talked of the corporation, and Strauss promised that, though he had never been brought into that project, to make it his business to see if it could not be pressed forward, so that I could learn in the near future more of its prospects and in the hope that it might be in a position to support a program in South America. He agreed with me that unless the corporation could be induced to take action, its net effect would have been adverse, and that it was high time that there be a definite decision. We talked about personalities, and he recognized the desirability of an additional driving force.

Third, he said that his personal fund was available now and could be called upon at any time; that, indeed, it was so arranged that in the case of his death, it would still be available for me for the purpose designated.

Fourth, I then told him briefly of the talk at Rosenberg's house in the fall of 1933, before I agreed to accept my present responsibility, and of Felix Warburg's assent to James N. Rosenberg's statement that there would not need to be at any time any concern about personal finance. I told him also of my talk later with

Felix Warburg at his office at which the matter was made more definite in terms of figures. Lewis Strauss understood at once what was involved, and said that he would see to it that the matter was then discussed. He could make no promises any more than he had done with his own personal fund, but he would see what [rest of line at bottom of page omitted].

New York, Saturday, February 23, 1935

To the office about ten. Found Olive Sawyer about ready to sail.

Popkin telephoned and wanted to know whether it would be possible for me to do a record that morning if it could be arranged without any delay. I told him that the time was extremely short, that I had hardly a minute to spare, but I would do my best.

Called Rothenberg. Found, as I thought I would, that he was enthusiastic about the possibility of Bentwich's coming.

Conference with Hyman and Baerwald. We talked first about Norman Bentwich, and as I explained my point of view about it, Paul Baerwald said he saw no objection. Hyman agreed, but added that he thought it desirable to talk with the chairman of the Campaign Committee before a definite decision was taken; that he would do that on Monday and wireless me promptly. Therefore, I had good reason to assume that the matter was settled, except as a matter of form. Nonetheless, I thought it better not to cable Bentwich until all doubt had been removed.

. . . .

Telephoned the White House and got Paula Tulley on the telephone. Both Miss LeHand and Grace Tulley had gone off with the President for the weekend. I told Miss Tulley my reasons for withdrawing my request for funds, and asked her if she would not please discuss with Miss LeHand the possibility of the President's taking some personal initiative which would help me in my South American visit. I suggested the possibility of a personal letter from FDR. She seemed to understand exactly what I had in mind and to be sympathetic, so I decided to leave it at that.

A hectic few minutes' conference with Mildred Wertheimer. Told her the gossip about A. H. [Hitler?] This seemed to satisfy her better than a much longer talk on less exciting matters would have done.

Rushed off with Popkin and his associate to the recording room of the broadcasting record people. On the way up read over the material which Popkin had found among my previous talks. He had used the major portions of my Syracuse broadcast and had interpolated a special paragraph meant for Pittsburgh. Despite my extreme weariness and the lack of an opportunity to read the thing over out loud, I insisted that there was no time for rehearsal, as indeed there literally was not. Therefore, I was recorded at once and fortunately made only two or three minor slips, which the woman in charge said would make the record sound more like a regular broadcast and less like an electrical transcription.

Lunch with Janet and Henrietta. Stopped at Rogers & Peet to pick up some tropical clothing, and back to the office a little before two to go to the boat with Miss Gelber [FPA staff member], Miss Sawyer having gone down earlier with the luggage and her mother.

. . . .

At the dock talked with Edna about the care of Bobby[20] and gave her instructions in case of emergency.

I should have indicated that on Friday night I spoke to Henry Ittleson on the telephone at Palm Beach. . . . He seemed to have so much difficulty understanding me that the rest of the conversation was conducted through Mrs. Ittleson. I explained about my recent visit to Rome, the reactions from the Jewish leaders in Paris, Brussels, and London, and my desire to get his views. He expressed strongly his approval of the line I had taken, and his hope that I would continue to explore the possibilities in those directions.

20. While J. G. and Ruth McDonald were in South America, Bobby went to stay with her aunt and uncle, Edna and John Grice, in Indiana.

23. March 1935: Brazil

The voyage, the *Western Prince,* Saturday, February 23–Thursday, March 7, 1935

It was a pleasant and uneventful voyage. After the first few days the weather was quiet and increasingly warm—so warm in fact as to discourage anything except leisurely outdoor activities, the most popular of which was swimming. The Neptune ceremony [crossing the equator] was amusing.

. . . .

We arrived in Rio the night before we were normally expected. We were not met at the dock by Dr. Inman. Instead, two Brazilian press men met me on board, and at the dock three or four others, mostly representatives of American papers, wanted interviews. I took the line that I had nothing substantial to say at the moment, but would communicate with them if and when I did. Among the newspapermen was a Mr. Garcia, the representative of the *New York Times,* and a Mr. Taves of the U.P., a very young man who said I had done a great service to him when he was trying to get his first job.

. . . .

The next day the McDonalds met up with Samuel Guy Inman, who had arranged to travel with them. Inman's particular interest was in finding places for the so-called refugee intellectuals—scholars and scientists.

Rio de Janeiro, Friday, March 8, 1935

. . . .

Had for lunch with the staff and Ruth a Mr. Fine, representative of the U.P. He was interesting and, up to a point, well informed, but not very helpful in reply to our more technical questions. He thinks that the 2 percent law in the constitution was a means of checking the coming of the Japanese. He told about the gradual process of returning to constitutionalism, the series of elections which had been held, most of them without disturbances, in the different states, with a view to reestablishing regular state governments, . . . the skill of Vargas in placating his enemies, as, for example, the most formidable group of all in Sao Paulo, the president's adroitness in maintaining the balance of power among many elements of factionalism and personalism. He told of the agitation of the

Society,[1] of which one of the most influential members is Felix Pacheco,[2] publisher of the *Journal do Commercia,* which probably had more to do than any other group in securing the enactment of the immigration restriction movement. Moreover, it appears that Pacheco, a scholarly and cultured gentleman with French leanings, may be one of the men whom it will be most important that I should try to placate because of his potential opposition to our project. This Society conducted its agitation primarily against the Japanese.

. . . .

McDonald met with Sir Henry Lynch, senior partner in Davidson, Pullen & Co. Long connected with the Rothschilds, Lynch also held a very powerful position in Brazil, with close ties to the Ministry of Finance, the Foreign Office, and the president.

Sir Henry received me at once on my arrival at his office. I was surprised to find that this was not a bank, but apparently an importing house. I found him sitting in the front part of a rather oldish building on the second floor in his shirtsleeves. He apologized for this, but in view of the weather no apology was necessary, and I was glad to follow his example.

He told me that he had heard directly from the Rothschilds about my coming, and that, moreover, in talking to the British ambassador a few days ago, the latter had mentioned that the British Foreign Office had notified him of my arrival.

We at once plunged into the heart of the problem. I told him that Aranha in Washington had said that one should deal only with Vargas.[3] Sir Henry agreed that this probably was good advice, or at any rate, that without the president, nothing definite could be done. I said, however, that, of course, I should have to pay my first visit to the foreign minister, but that in the meantime, I was very anxious to learn whether in fact the Brazilian ambassador had kept his word about communicating directly with the president.

After we had discussed the problem a little further, Sir Henry offered, if I wished him to do so, to see the foreign minister on Monday, tell him of my arrival, and learn as much as possible about the lay of the land. I had to decide on the spur of the moment whether or not to accept this offer. I was afraid that Sir Henry might be a little offended if I declined. Moreover, it seemed to me that I probably could not have a better approach. Sir Henry had earlier explained that he had been able last summer, at the request of Anthony de Rothschild, to se-

1. Sociedad de Amigos de Alberto Torres. Founded in Rio in 1932 by fifty intellectuals, diplomats, and politicians and named in memory of Torres (1865–1917). An economic and cultural nationalist association opposed to "unassimilable immigrants and foreign minorities." Lobbied successfully against Jews and Japanese and was very influential.

2. Owner and publisher of the most important morning newspaper in Rio.

3. Getúlio Dornelles Vargas, president of Brazil 1930–1945. As he could not constitutionally succeed himself, he had become dictator 1937–1945 and then again a constitutional president, 1950–1954.

cure from the Brazilian authorities the extension of the period for the admission of refugees, particularly from France and Belgium, simply through the exchange of a few telegrams. In connection with this he had gone directly to the foreign minister, and, I think he said, also to the president. In any case he had been not only interested, but successfully active. Moreover, I assumed that he would naturally wish to help to make my mission a success. So I gladly accepted his offer to intervene with the foreign minister.

Then followed some talk about the attitude of the president on immigration. Sir Henry said that he thought Vargas personally was opposed to all immigration except agricultural workers or settlers; that, however, this did not necessarily preclude the president's assent to an exceptional regime if there were compensatory advantages. He thought that the governmental authorities were inclined to exaggerate the danger of any considerable unemployment in Brazil. He himself thought there was no unemployment now that mattered, nor was there likely to be; but he was not sure that the process of steady return to constitutionalism would be continued. There were a number of indications to the contrary.

Sir Henry then began to quiz me on the kind of immigrants that were available. I replied that there had been two general points of view about the possibilities for the refugees in Brazil—the one, that expressed at first by Louis Oungre, involving the setting up of certain large and needed industries with large capital and employing a considerable number of refugees. This plan I thought admirable as a means of losing much money quickly. Sir Henry agreed.

The second plan was the one I was working on, to remove the artificial restrictions to the entrance of a limited number of immigrants who might reasonably hope to be fitted into the economic life of the country, and to be aided during the early stages by funds made available chiefly from New York and London. I cited to him the analogy of the United States. He thought this was the only practicable basis.

It was at this point that he asked me about the agricultural proportion of the immigrants and told me of Vargas's preference. I frankly replied that there were few agriculturists, and that I could see no use in my pretending the contrary. He then asked about the political complexion of the refugees, stressing the present tendency to be extremely suspicious of communism or even radicalism. He asked if we could give guarantees as to these points in reference to our immigrants. It was a little difficult for me to give any completely satisfactory reply.

. . . .

Saturday, March 9, 1935

Went to the bank, and then with Dr. Inman to the American Embassy. Mr. Gordon, the chargé d'affaires, received us promptly. We chatted for five or ten minutes about conditions in Germany and about our working together there during the early spring of 1933. Gordon shared my views about the attitude of the present counsellor of the American Embassy in Berlin [John Campbell White].

Gordon agreed that the Brazilian government at the present time is probably particularly anxious to secure a favorable attitude from the British, the American, and the French governments, and that this desire could be capitalized [on] in connection with my negotiations. He was not very helpful, however, in technical matters of immigration regulations, nor was he willing to speak frankly in giving me his estimates of various political leaders.

....

In the late afternoon Frank M. Garcia, correspondent of the *New York Times,* came in for a long informing talk. He is a Puerto Rican-born American who has lived in Brazil for many years. He began by telling me of the methods by which Vargas manages to eliminate dangerous political opponents, chiefly by putting them in high, but exposed, positions where they either become involved or are discredited. His stories of the relationships of Vargas with the minister of war and the latter's young brother, now involved in an attack on one of the state governments, the head of the secret police, the governor of Rio Grande do Sul, and Monsieur Costa, minister of finance, sounded like a melodrama. Nonetheless, the record disclosed Getúlio Vargas's extraordinary capacity for political management.

On the subject of the possibility of inducing Vargas to make an exceptional immigration arrangement, Garcia feared that the president might be deterred by the minority in the Chamber made up of the group of 50 representing employers, employees, workmen, manufacturers, intelligentsia, and government employees. These are all inclined to be extremely nationalistic. Similarly, the Integralistas,[4] the Brazilian fascists, with their slogan "Country, Church and Home"—are quick to attack the government for any concessions to foreigners.

Nonetheless, if some of the state governors, notably Flores Acuha of Rio Grande do Sul, should take the initiative in asking for additional immigration, this would have an important effect upon the president. I pointed out that one difficulty there is that, of course, the fact that this governor would be interested primarily, and perhaps solely, in agricultural immigrants.

Theoretically, the law of last May still applies, which rigidly limits immigration. The Japanese, who are continuing to come in, are portions of an earlier unfilled quota. The interdepartmental commission designated to find a basis for the application for the two percent law of the constitution, have not yet finished their work. The initiator of that law in the constitution was Miguel Ceuto, very

4. Integralistas. Founded on January 3, 1933, the Ação Integralista Brasileira (AIB) was the largest group with an anti-Semitic agenda in Brazil. It was fascist in orientation, with popular roots among the army, the middle classes, and people of German and Italian descent in southern Brazil. Anti-liberal, anti-capitalist, anti-Communist and openly anti-Jewish, the AIB claimed 180,000 adherents by 1934. It was disbanded by Vargas in 1938 after it attempted a coup.

prominent in the Alberto de Torres. He, like Pacheco, was violently anti-Japanese. Garcia thought it would be most helpful if, by a visit to Pacheco, Dr. Inman and I were able to forestall a vigorous attack by G's [*sic,* should be C's for Ceuto's] followers.

. . . .

Sunday, March 10, 1935

. . . .

Out for a drive along the gorgeous Copacabana beach, tea at the Copacabana Palace, and finally capped the afternoon riding up the two telepheriques[5] to the top of the Sugar Loaf just in time for a magnificent view of the mountains and the bay at sunset and later to see the city lit up.

The lighting of the boulevards along the amazingly symmetrically-shaped series of bays that constitute the vast harbor illustrated what can be done in improving a great natural site if only public authorities have the intelligence to do it. As we drove home, we could only deplore the failure of other cities such as New York or Pittsburgh or Boston, to preserve similarly their natural beauties.

. . . .

Monday, March 11, 1935

Telephoned Mr. Miner at the Consulate about Mr. Diamant as I promised. I was told that Mr. Miner and the Consul General Lee had both definitely made up their mind not to issue the visa, but instead to do what is rare, issue a definite refusal. They were doing this on the ground that Diamant, being a hunchback and liable to become unable to care for himself, might become a public charge. His affidavits of support did not seem to the American authorities sufficient. Against these contentions I could make no effective reply. It was left that I would try to come and see Mr. Miner and Mr. Lee to talk again about Diamant, but also to talk with the consul general about economic and other conditions here.

Over to the French Embassy with Dr. Inman. . . . The chargé, M. Gueyrend, like the officials at the American Embassy, began by telling us about the new constitution and other immigration restrictions, as though we knew nothing at all about these. When we got down to details, he apparently was not better informed than the others had been. Indeed, so far as the attitude of the French government is concerned, he naturally knew much less about that than did we who had been working with the Quai d'Orsay for so long a time.

As to action here, M. Gueyrend was of the common opinion that everything depended upon Vargas. And when, by telephoning to the Foreign Office, we learned that the foreign minister, because of illness, had not yet come back to

5. Cable cars.

town from Sao Paulo and might not return for some days, Gueyrend thought that it would be best for us to get in touch with M. Pimentil Brandao, secretary general of the Ministry of Foreign Affairs, with a view to making a definite date with the president. I immediately telephoned Cabot[6] to ask him if he would arrange this. He replied that he would first have to consult Gordon and would call us back.

My plea to M. Gueyrend was that France had as large an interest as anyone else, or in some respects larger, in getting permission for the refugees to come to Brazil; that I knew of the keen interest of the Quai d'Orsay in this matter; that they would be delighted if the Embassy here were able to help toward that end; and that, therefore, I trusted that he would, after thinking the matter through, agree to cooperate with me closely in order that the Brazilian authorities might realize the advantage of concessions on their part in order to give satisfaction in Paris, where, as at the moment also in London and in New York, the Brazilians are anxious to create a favorable impression because of pending financial negotiations.

Gueyrend listened attentively to my reasoning, but in the best diplomatic tradition he refused to commit himself. Dr. Inman had definitely the impression that Gueyrend would not act effectively unless he heard directly from Paris.

Back to the hotel. Cabled the office, asking them to get Helbronner to induce the Quai d'Orsay to move.

Lunch with staff and Dr. Wilson, second in command of the Rockefeller Yellow Fever work here in Brazil. He told interestingly of the activities of his staff throughout the whole of the country, saying that, while they had definitely defeated yellow fever in the cities, they will had a great deal to learn about it in the jungle where, for example in Goyer, there rage from time to time epidemics even now, and the authorities do not know what the carriers are.

Dr. Wilson, in answer to Dr. Inman's questions, gave a list of the research institutions here which might be interested in receiving one or more refugee workers. Then Dr. Inman pressed Dr. Wilson on the question of the Rockefeller group here using a certain number of the refugees. Dr. Wilson replied that if there were refugees in Rio who came to the Rockefeller office, there might be opportunities for them, but that because of various conditions, it would be impossible for the Rockefeller people to invite refugee doctors or other workers. Among these conditions are the facts that the work is paid for by government money, that there is always a group of doctors ready to criticize the Rockefeller work, and that, therefore, the employment by a group of foreigners would be particularly open to criticism. In short, Dr. Wilson closed the door except on the condition indicated at the beginning. In other respects, however, he was extremely helpful in the detailed information which he supplied.

. . . .

6. John Moore Cabot, secretary of the U.S. Embassy.

. . . .

Joined Dr. Inman and Dr. Vollmer of the Evangelical Hospital downstairs. The latter made many suggestions about governmental institutions where medical or other research persons might be employed. He was also helpful in his suggestion of personalities influential in political circles here. He named Dr. Herbert Moses of *El Globo* and the president of the Press Association. Even more influential, it appears, is the president's dentist, who, in addition to occupying that important post, is the Presbyterian pastor in his suburban church and is the Presbyter for the local Presbyterian region. He works from early in the morning until late in the evening at his profession, and yet has time for all his outside activities. He, of course, knows Dr. Inman, who will get in touch with him directly. . . .

Left about eleven o'clock for our drive to Petropolis,[7]—Ruth, Dr. Inman, and I.

. . . .

The trip up was rather hot and tiresome, but coming down we were thrilled by the panorama of mountains range after range, which gave the effect of being much higher than they really are. From a point near Petropolis we had a comprehensive view of the whole of Rio and the bay, including the surrounding mountains. Petropolis itself is a pretty village, located in a valley towards the top of the mountain, with many flowers and some attractive gardens.

At 3:45 I went to see Sir William Seeds at the charming and luxurious British Embassy. He was quick to tell Dr. Inman and me what we had heard once or twice(!) before from the diplomats, about the impossibility of success in our mission. Sir William evidenced strong feeling on the question because, as we soon learned, it had been he and the Spanish ambassador, together with the Swiss chargé, who had negotiated what they thought was a binding agreement with the Brazilians to admit the Assyrians. Sir William waxed eloquent in his denunciation of the Amigos de Alberto Torres, who had led the attack against the Assyrian proposal. He said that they were utterly unreasonable, and that the Swiss diplomat had vainly tried to placate them. Sir William also denounced the Brazilian press for chauvinism and unreliability.

Moreover, he argued that since the restriction measures were in the constitution and not merely a law, it would be more difficult, if not impossible, to secure an exceptional treatment. He didn't take much stock in our hope that the president would be willing to override technical difficulties, nor was he optimistic about the helpfulness of Ambassador Aranha, who "is inclined to open

7. Named after Emperor Dom Pedro II, the unofficial summer capital and the capital of Rio province from 1894 to 1902. It was never federal Brazil's capital.

his mouth and let it say what it will"—a man who gambles and drinks like a gentleman, but is not very restrained in his promises.

The only factors in the situation which seemed to Sir William encouraging were first, that a number of the refugees had already come, which he did not know, second, that none of these had become public charges or involved with the police. He also thought the financial guarantees helpful. But everything considered, had we taken the advice implicit in his words, we would have canceled our engagement and gone home.

Then over with Dr. Inman and Ruth to the palace of the president. We had to wait only ten or fifteen minutes while Vargas was finishing with one of the Latin American diplomats, when we were ushered into his office.

He greeted us in a friendly manner. Dr. Inman opened the conversation by a diplomatic approach, reminding Vargas of their earlier meeting and of the sending of the volume *America Revolucionaria.*[8]

I made a brief statement in English, in which I emphasized the following points:

(1) The admiration in Paris, London and New York for the progress being made by the present Brazilian regime;
(2) My personal view that Brazil in its potentialities ranks as one of the four great empires, along with the United States, the British Empire, and Russia;
(3) My hope that it would be possible for him to support a program of the admission of approximately five hundred individuals, or 125 to 150 families per month, on condition that these people would be guaranteed against becoming public charges and would be supplied with the funds essential for integrating them in the economic life of the country. Among these possible immigrants were some agriculturists, but most of them were technicians, artisans, workmen, businessmen, etc.;
(4) My conviction that if Brazil were willing to make this move, such action would be viewed with the greatest favor, not only in the diplomatic centers—Paris, London, and Washington—but also in the business and financial circles of those countries. After each point Dr. Inman translated and in some instances amplified and strengthened what I had said.

The president replied, outlining the history of immigration in Brazil, especially the German, in the three southern states. (He himself being a native of Rio Grande do Sul.) He said that the German immigration had given good results, and there were now practically a million Germans or descendants of Germans; as a result of this, Brazil is well disposed toward such immigration. He then went on to explain about the new constitution adopted last year [July 14, 1934], which limits immigration to two percent of the number of any nation ar-

8. *America Revolucionaria,* by Samuel Guy Inman, was published in Madrid in 1933.

riving previous to the adoption of this doctrine. The government has appointed a commission to work out the exact quota for each nation, the commission now being at work on this question. The president said that he was seeing the minister of labor [Magalhães Agamemnon], under whose department questions of immigration come, tomorrow, and that he would instruct the secretary to work out a quota for these refugees along the lines which we had suggested. He made no objections whatever to receiving a certain number of the refugees.

Following this, we discussed a few general matters, reporting to the president the good work that Ambassador Aranha is doing in Washington, and the good impressions in the outside world caused by the president's administration.

Earlier in the talk Vargas asked if there were a number of Jews among the refugees. I replied that most of them were Jews. Vargas gave no indication that this mattered.

I was particularly interested to notice that in speaking about a quota for the refugees, he did not make any specific reference to a quota for Germans. Dr. Inman got the impression that the president intended to convey the impression that the refugee quota would be independent of a quota for German immigrants. I hope this impression is correct, but I was a little fearful that, since the president had been talking about Germans earlier, he might have meant to carry that idea over into his discussion of the quota. At any rate, when we see the minister of labor, as the president suggested we do on Thursday, we should be able to determine more definitely what is meant. The president, taking note of what we had said, told us that he would speak to the minister of labor, who was coming up the next day. On the whole we felt satisfied with our interview.

Wednesday, March 13, 1935

. . . .

After lunch Dr. Inman and I were taken to see the minister of education, Gustavo Copanema. He is a young politician of not much more than thirty-five, from Minas Gerais. He spoke fluently in reply to our inquiries about the possibilities of certain number of the intellectuals being received in this country. But there was little that was definite. He explained that the Federal Ministry of Education was new, having been established only about four years ago, that it had little authority, that the states and the Federal District were really responsible for education, and that, therefore, appeal would have to be made to them.

. . . .

After dinner Mr. Frederico Dahne sent his card, and he and our group talked for about half an hour. He is representing here Governor Acunha of Rio Grande do Sul in an effort to get the federal government to permit the immigration of a number of Japanese laborers. We asked him whether he hoped to be able to avoid the prohibition of the constitution. He said he would be able to arrange that, but did not indicate how. . . . He spoke with decided definiteness about the Jewish colonies, Quatro Irmaos and Philippson,[9] as failures. He declared that most of the original settlers had promptly gone to nearby villages or towns, deserting their lands or sub-leasing them on whatever terms could be secured. He is pessimistic about the possibilities of Jewish settlement on the land, declaring that most of the settlers inevitably tend to become traders or shopkeepers.

....

Thursday, March 14, 1935

Dr. Inman and I went with Dr. Anisio Teixeira, superintendent of schools in the Federal District, to see the technical director of education—Dr. Theodoro Ramos.

Dr. Ramos was very pessimistic about the chances of doing more than had been done. He thought there were no possibilities at all in Minas Gerais or in Rio Grande do Sul. In the latter, according to him, the state army is eating up the resources of the state, and the authorities are forced to call upon the federal government for aid. Similarly, he doubted that the research institutions would be able to take men. In short, he was completely defeatist, except as to the possibility of a professor of physics in Sao Paulo, and the project of Dr. Teixeira in the Federal District. As to the Sao Paulo possibility, he declined to give us the name of a person through whom we should deal, but did mention the names of three of the German professors there, suggesting that we should get in touch with them.

....

Beginning on the next page [paragraph here] is Dr. Inman's summary of the interview [with Minister of Labor Magalhães Agamemnon]. I should like to add that I had the impression that the minister was quite sincere in his implied desire to work out an exceptional arrangement, if that were at all possible. But unless the president makes clear that he desires that such an exception be made, it is extremely doubtful that any initiative in this direction will be taken by the Ministry of Labor.

....

Magalhães Agamemnon: As soon as we told the minister about our visit to the president and the latter's promise to ask the minister to fix a quota for the refugees, the minister came to the point immediately. He said that this quota would be 10 percent of the number fixed for the Germans, the latter number being 3,090 per year. He went on the explain that a commission had been appointed with headquarters in the Ministry of Labor, to work out the quotas for

9. Quatro Irmaos and Philippson were two of three agricultural colonies founded in Rio Grande du Sul by the Jewish Colonization Association between 1904 and 1924. The third was the Hirsch colony. In 1935, 104 Jewish families lived in Quatro Irmaos, outnumbered five to one by non-Jews.

the various nations, according to the constitution, this being 2 percent of the immigrants entering from each country during the last fifty years. When we expressed surprise that the German quota was not larger, he pointed out that during the last twenty or thirty years there had not been a large German immigration, many of them having come to Brazil more than fifty years ago. The figures which he showed us on a printed sheet were temporary for the use of the commission itself, and not for publication. The Italians had the largest number, with over one million immigrants, giving them a quota of a few more than 20,000 a year.

When we told the minister that a number of the Jewish refugees were not German citizens, but were simply living in Germany at the time and therefore might be classed under other quotas, he replied that they had made their decision to classify them as Germans, and any other way of figuring the matter would be too complicated.

It was difficult to argue with the minister, for he said that he had a constitution to obey, and also could be called before Congress at any time for interrogation as he was also subject to severe criticism by the extreme nationalists, especially the Sociedad de Amigos de Alberto Torres (a society about which we are hearing a great deal, since it assumes the responsibility, self-appointed, to watch over the interests of the country relating to immigration.) The minister said that he was opposed to this clause in the constitution, and fought it with all his might; but he was unable to stem the nationalistic tide because of the opposition to the Japanese. The latter are splendid laborers, and as for himself, he would like to see many of them introduced into the country to assist the agricultural problem; but they refuse to identify themselves with the life of the country and are, therefore, not acceptable. Brazil is in tremendous need of agricultural laborers. Sao Paulo needs 40,000 per year, Rio Grande do Sul a similar number, and a number of other states need various thousands annually. As a matter of fact, the minister said while he was being pressed on one side by ultranationalists like the Alberto Torres Society, on the other side the governors of the other states were putting tremendous pressure on him to bring in agricultural immigrants. The difficulty is that Brazil can get no immigration from countries that have any large quotas. Mussolini allows no Italians to come; there are practically no applications from the Hitler government; in fact, Brazil can secure no agriculturists outside of the Japanese. It is easily seen, then, why the refugees that would be admitted must be agriculturists.

In answer to the claim by us that Brazil would need industrialists to develop her great land just as the United States had needed them, the minister explained at considerable length that Brazil did not want to over-emphasize industrialism. There had been some tendency toward this recently, but they were learning from the United States and other over-industrialized countries that agriculture and manufacturing must be kept in parallel developments, with neither one overbalancing the other. Brazil has, as a matter of fact, without saying anything about it, a "planned society," in the sense that the Ministry of Labor is studying scientifically and practically controlling the balance of the economic and the agricultural. This is the biggest job of the Ministry of Labor.

We returned again to the matter of allowing at least this small quota proposed to be industrialists, rather than agriculturists, when the minister again explained the great need of Brazil for agriculturists. In turn, we showed him that we were here on a special job which was given to us because of the great humanitarian need. We were naturally not interested in permanent questions of immigration, and we must appeal to him as a representative of one of the great countries of the world to take its share in solving this injustice to a large group of people. We explained something of why we had taken this temporary work ourselves, and why we believed that Brazil could not eliminate the question by a pure appeal to her own material needs through the years. The minister warmed up a bit, and said that he realized that they ought to take their share of these responsibilities. We left him in good humor, after half an hour's talk, with a promise that we could come to see him later after we had further discussed the question with others.

Both Dr. Inman and I were so flabbergasted by the definiteness of the minister's rejection of our proposal that we decided to go see Mr. H. H. Lichtwardt, general secretary of the YMCA here. Dr. Inman values his judgment highly, and thought that perhaps Lichtwardt would be able to have some suggestions for us. We had tea together, in the large YMCA building, but Lichtwardt was not fruitful in [his] ideas.

....

Friday, March 15, 1935

Up at sunrise with Dr. Inman to go to the nearby beach. It was a glorious morning. Already there was a considerable crowd on the beach and in the water, the colors ranging all the way from the blackest Africa with primitive countenances to the quite indecent white skins of the Nordics.

In the late morning started out to keep some appointments, but was waylaid in the lobby by a refugee, Siegfried Samuel, and his young wife and their interpreter and friend, Ricardo van Ehnert. The story seems too terrible to be true. The first part of it, Samuel's flight from Berlin to Belgium, is familiar. He is a scenario writer. He wished to go to Spain, but the Belgian committee sent him to Brazil because it was cheaper. At that time it was no longer possible to secure immigration visas for Brazil, so the committee sent him as a tourist, but with only a tiny bit of money in his pocket. When the *Oceana* reached quarantine, someone representing the Rio committee came on board, and when Samuel explained that he was without funds, he was advised not to say anything about it because if he did, he would not be allowed to land, and in any case the local committee would look after him. He landed, but when he went to the HICEM committee, Dr. Raffalovich[10] told him that they could have nothing to do with

10. Rabbi Isiah Raffalovitch, head of ICA operations in Brazil from 1923.

him because he had smuggled himself in. Later, the Paris committee sent ten contos to care for a group of ten refugees, but this money had not been turned over to them; instead, Dr. Raffalovich was using part of it on his trip to Palestine.

This story, so shocking in its nature, caused me to thrash the matter out further with the group. I promised to make inquiries to see whether someone in the Jewish community would interest himself in their case and telephone Ehnert before eleven the next day.

Lunch with Mr. S. Steckine, *chefe de publicidade* and associated with the *Gazeta Israelita.* I picked his brains about members of the Jewish community. He explained that the richer and more influential Jews had been so largely assimilated that they had hardly recognized themselves as Jews and had kept away from the community as a whole until the Hitler movement startled them into a sense of their danger. Herbert Moses[11] had since then appeared at synagogue and declared himself a Jew. Steckine also stressed the divisions between eastern and western Jews, and the tendency of the western, German, and Portuguese Jews to wish not to be associated with the eastern Jews.

I told Steckine about the refugees who had been to see me in the morning, and he promised to inquire about them and to report to me.

Immediately after lunch I went to see Sir Henry Lynch, while Dr. Inman kept an appointment with the minister of agriculture. Sir Henry had been seeing the minister of foreign affairs that morning and had discussed with him my mission, saying among other things that, of course, it would not be practicable to include the German refugees in the German quota. He put this on the ground that to do so would be to place the refugees at the mercy of hostile German officials. The foreign minister had said, "Of course that is right." Sir Henry had also told of the interest of his people, the Rothschilds, in the success of my mission and explained how other groups and governments would also be grateful for Brazilian cooperation. Sir Henry told me of the background of the foreign minister, his important financial and economic relationships, his strong position with the president, and the probability that his recommendation would be preferred over against that of the minister of labor. Sir Henry thought that if we could not succeed in getting the refugees outside of the quota, then the percentage of the quota might be enlarged, or at the worst, one could accept the smaller amount with the expectation of being able to wangle something larger later, for that was the way things were done very often here in Brazil.

I was very grateful to Sir Henry and asked him if I might get in touch with him again after I had seen the foreign minister. He invited me and my wife to come to his house that night after dinner, and sent me off in his car to my next appointment.

Bandeiro de Mello[12] does not have his office in the same building with the

11. Herbert Moses, Jewish co-owner of the newspaper *O Globo.*
12. Bandeiro de Mello, worked in the Ministry of Labor.

minister of labor, but in a quite different section of the town. He received me promptly, and we had a long and satisfactory talk. This made me feel that Sir Henry had greatly undervalued de Mello when he had told me a short time before that the latter was merely a functionnaire of little importance.

As to the previous memorandum which Louis Oungre had submitted, that, said de Mello, had been handled in the Ministry of Labor without his having been permitted to influence the decision in reference to it. His chief (the minister of labor) is a narrow-minded man who has never been abroad, and who is very subject to nationalist influences. Moreover, he is probably sympathetic with many of the views of the exclusionists.

However, de Mello is much more optimistic about the minister of foreign affairs, whom he holds in much the same high esteem as does Sir Henry. De Mello felt that we had a very good chance with the foreign minister,[13] and that with that support, the president might be willing to go against the judgment of the minister of labor.

De Mello talked a good deal about some property near the Duzentos Club particularly suitable for immigrants, but neither Dr. Inman nor I could quite see the connection. De Mello feels that the Amigos de Alberto Torres and the Integralistas and the other extreme nationalists reached their height of power when they secured the enactment of the two percent provision of the constitution; that since then they have grown weaker and must continue to do so, because the country is starved for labor. (I did not learn until the next day that Bandiero de Mello is himself one of the largest coffee planters in Sao Paulo).

With Dr. Inman to the Foreign Office, but having arrived half an hour before time, we walked in the neighboring park and admired the strange trees and the stranger animals.

When we returned to the Foreign Office, I had my first experience in being kept waiting by a Brazilian official. But this was not much more than half an hour, a wait not unlike that which one must frequently endure at home or in Europe.

The foreign minister, José Carlos de Macedo Soares, received us in the large room dedicated to the memory of Rio Branco.[14] He was assisted in the interview by Luis G. de Amaral. I made my plea in English, supplemented occasionally by translations by Dr. Inman or by Amaral. I put the case on two grounds, one economic and the other humanitarian. The first was that the refugees would help Brazil because of their quality and because of being aided to integrate themselves, and because they would be carefully selected, excluding, as the minister emphasized would be necessary, Communists.

The second view was that a great wrong had been committed against our

13. José Carlos de Macedo Soares, who "lacked influence even among the diplomatic corps he ostensibly commanded." Jeffrey Lesser, *Welcoming the Undesirables: Brazil and the Jewish Question* (Berkeley: University of California Press, 1995), 74.

14. José Maria da Silva Paranhos, Baron of Rio Branco, famed Brazilian diplomat who advocated resolving disputes by peaceful means. He negotiated the dispute between Brazil and Bolivia over the Acre territory in 1903. Foreign minister, 1902–1912.

common humanity, and the world looked the Brazil to share responsibility of making new homes possible for the victims. I emphasized the interest of London, Paris, New York, and Washington in Brazil's acceptance of our proposal, and the good effect which that would have on world opinion. The minister made no objection to the figures I mentioned, of 500 individuals or 125 families a month; instead, said that, in principle, he was favorable to the idea and would take it up with the president at his next regular conference with him on Tuesday. He then got a sheet of paper and began to take some notes, but since I was quick to see that he had not understood in every respect what I had said, I offered to submit a brief memorandum to his colleague for the minister's use in presenting the matter to the president. This was welcome.

It should be noted that throughout our interview we stressed the fact that most of the refugees would be Jews, and only some of them would be agriculturists.

....

We left much more encouraged than we had left the Ministry of Labor two days before.

....

After dinner Ruth, Dr. Inman, and I went out to Sir Henry's house. He has a magnificent place with elaborate grounds in front of the house, and in the back these reach up to the top of the adjoining mountain. We listened first to the Imperial broadcast of news from London, and chatted about this and that; but it was too good an opportunity to miss, so I took occasion to tell him of the interview with the foreign minister. He agreed that this was encouraging. I then asked him whether he thought we ought to ask for the full 500 a month, even if we were not sure that that number were available or could be financed, or whether we should ask for less. He favored asking for the larger number, on the assumption that the chances of getting it were not less and that the immigration could be financed of as many as were available to come.

....

Saturday, March 16, 1935

....

Before I left to go to the Bank, Steckine came in and told me his impressions of Ehnert and Siegfried Samuel. He is suspicious of the former and thinks that he may have a special interest in securing money for Samuel in order perhaps to pay himself for some earlier loan. At any rate, Ehnert's account of his own position was not clear. As to Samuel, Steckine is sure that he is not a professional scenario writer as he told me, but instead a cook who feels that he has the ability to write. Certainly he is over-wrought, extremely nervous, and at first was quite unwilling to consider accepting Steckine's advice that he give up his hope of finding three contos to repay his debts, or larger amounts to engage in farming, and that he satisfy himself with securing a job for himself and his wife, which would enable them to live while adjusting themselves in Brazil. If he were willing to accept this advice, Steckine said it would be possible to find the amounts needed to keep the family going for the present. Meyer had reported that he had secured three or four places for Samuel, but the latter had given them all up.

In view of this report, I told Steckine that I thought his judgment probably was sound, and asked him to have Augusto (our Portuguese boy) telephone and give the message that I accepted Steckine's view and that I suggested that they keep in touch with him.

....

. . . I got Sir Henry on the telephone and asked him whether he thought it would be desirable to have our proposal to the foreign minister supported formally by the representatives of the United States, Great Britain, and France. He said by all means. Immediately I got in touch with Gordon, asked him if he had instructions which would permit him to support our memorandum. He replied definitely in the negative, that since I was not acting as an American citizen but as an international official, this would not be possible. I told him of our government's membership on the Governing Body, but he said that his instructions definitely limited him. I then asked him if I wished to cable to the Department of State to ask for their more direct help, should I do it myself and would be object? He said he would have no objection at all, but that he thought it better that I do it myself than through his office.[15]

I called up the French chargé, asked him if he had instructions which would permit him to support our memorandum. He replied that he had had no instructions yet, except in reference to Oungre, but that he had written by airmail to inquire.

A half an hour or so later, when by mistake I got the French chargé on the phone, I took advantage of the mistake to ask him whether he would object, since he had received no definite instructions from the Quai d'Orsay, if I cabled direct to Léger to ask the latter to give instructions, since I was sure that France was deeply concerned in getting rid of some thousands of the refugees. At this, Gueyuend to my surprise said, in effect, "I hope that you would not give the impression that I had refused to be helpful." I said of course not. He then replied in effect, "Though I have not received specific instructions, I am sure that my government hopes that your mission will be a success, and I could therefore support your program at the Foreign Office if you wished me to do so, without waiting

15. Wilson, head of the Latin American section of the State Department, told Inman that instructions would be sent to U.S. officials to "render every possible service to the Commission." In fact, the circular notifying the diplomatic representatives of their forthcoming visit asked them to extend courtesies, "bearing in mind, however, that they do not represent the United States." Secretary of State to American Diplomatic Representatives in South America, February 12, 1935, National Archives (United States), Record Group 59, Central Decimal File 548.D 1/208.

for more direct word from Paris." I said that this would be splendid, and asked if I might come to see him at 10:30 on Monday to bring him up to date so that he might the better communicate with the Foreign Office.

Then in order to complete the trio, I got the British Embassy at Petropolis on the telephone, and spoke to the ambassador's secretary. I explained briefly the results of our visits to the president, the secretary of labor, and the minister of foreign affairs, and my desire to have the ambassador's support of our program with the foreign minister. The secretary asked me to wait while he consulted the ambassador, and after a few minutes brought back the word that the latter's instructions did not permit him to do what I requested, particularly since the persons involved were not British subjects. I then asked the secretary if he would inquire of the ambassador if the latter had any objection to my communicating directly with the Foreign Office to ask for their support. After a time a reply was delivered by the secretary that the ambassador had no personal objection, but that he doubted the success of my appeal to the Foreign Office in London. I gave the secretary some additional data on the present situation, but did not ask for comment from the ambassador.

. . . .

Sunday, March 17, 1935

I had been feeling under par for several days, partly, I thought, because of the excessive heat and the difficulty of sleeping. But just as I was finishing the memorandum, I realized that I was grippy and sent for Dr. Pyles. Meantime, I went to bed, took aspirin, and had lost my fever when the doctor arrived late that night. Unfortunately, however, during the whole of the next week I was up and down, and forced to cancel most of my engagements.

Monday, March 18, 1935

Miss Sawyer kept my appointment at the French Embassy that morning with M. Gueyrend. He said that in view of the written instructions each chargé in Rio had received from the Foreign Office asking them to ask for personal interviews with the foreign minister only on the most urgent business, and in view of the fact that he had had a personal interview only a few days before, he did not feel that he could ask for another that day; but that he would go that afternoon to see the secretary-general of the Foreign Office and tell him that the French government was interested in the matter. Thus, apparently we got as much from him as we would have had we cabled again to the Quai d'Orsay, and this time succeeded in getting specific instructions.

Spent most of the day in bed. . . .

Inman spent the morning getting the memorandum put into Portuguese. In the afternoon he presented it to Amaral at the Foreign Office, but received the impression that the latter was not especially interested in it.

. . . .

Tuesday, March 19, 1935

A long helpful conference with Mr. Ralph Olsburgh, representative in this country for more than two decades of the Imperial Chemical interests. He is very well informed, unusually intelligent and straightforward. He, of course, has excellent connections. . . . The only sort of industries which Olsburgh thought the country offered prospects to the refugees were small specialties, such as lead pencil, toys, etc. For these, which had prospect of making money, it would be possible to find Brazilian financing. According to Olsburgh, there is a large amount of Brazilian money ready for investment.

. . . .

Among the types of immigrants who would have the best chance of immediate success in this country are engineers, technicians, and specialists. While it is true that the Brazilians feel that they have enough engineering skill, nearly all the larger concerns already established and those that may be established need the full quota allowed under the law of foreign technical employees. For laborers or merchants, on the other hand, success here will be very difficult—for the former because of the low standard of pay and living, and for the latter because of the keen opposition of the Brazilians and the difficulty of adjustments in the country.

. . . .

The representatives of the Sociedade Beneficente Israelita came in with Steckine. In addition to the president, Dr. Nathan Bronstein, there was a Mr. Israel Dines, and a third man. Our discussion was mostly about the methods which have been used heretofore in caring for the refugee immigrants.

. . . .

My visitors complained sharply of the tendency of some of the immigrants to waste the three contos which were given to them to meet the immigration requirements. There was a long discussion as to how this abuse could be corrected. As a matter of fact, the law now requires that this amount shall not be spent within the first three months, but through subterfuges this restriction has been evaded. The group felt that if these funds could be either pooled or at any rate supervised by a local committee, they would be much more advantageous for the refugees themselves.

. . . .

I took advantage of the presence of the group to inquire about the cases of the individual refugees who had been to see me here in Rio. According to their account:

(1) The Mrs. Cohn whom Miss Sawyer has interviewed a couple of times has had associations here which are said to have been dubious, but this aside, her

chief difficulty appears to have been her husband, whose actions have jeopardized the success of her pension;

(2) Siegfried Samuel, they said, was a man who had had a number of jobs, none of which he was willing to keep; that his wife was a pitiful person, but that he was so unreliable that there was little hope of placing him advantageously. This story and other accounts which I have had from Steckine about Samuel, convinced me that his story that he is a writer and that he has been unjustly deprived of three to six contos, is a pure fabrication.

. . . .

Wednesday, March 20, 1935

In bed until the late afternoon. . . .

Dinner with the staff and Dr. Teixeira. . . .

Teixeira was very interesting on many topics. He characterized the government of Vargas as a "government by omission." Nothing, he said, "is ever decided definitely if a decision can be postponed. Forces are allowed to work themselves out. Men are balanced over against one another, and thus gradually the more dangerous or more influential ones eliminate themselves. For example, there are only two men who were important in the revolution of 1930 still in power. In the present conflict in the various states, Vargas tends to remain aloof, allowing the conflicting elements to settle their own strife. I got the impression from Teixeira that, while he did not expect it, he would not be surprised if there were a political upheaval soon.

Dr. Teixeira was both interesting and amusing in his talk about education and children and life and God. Trained by the Jesuits for membership in their order, his later training at Teachers' College had completely set him adrift from his early motive.

Thursday, March 21, 1935

Was very much impressed by the delegation of the Jewish community which called on me. Included in it were Captain Levi Cardozo, Mr. Herman Rinder, Mr. Joseph Löwi, and Mr. Fineberg.

Mr Löwi, who is giving all of his time to individual work with the refugees, though, of course, under the Brazilian law he is not allowed to practice medicine, would from time to time break into the discussion to describe one or another particularly pathetic case of refugees who had not been absorbed or cared for.

His Brazilian colleagues admitted that there had been and was still perhaps the lack of adequate organization, but that this could and would be remedied.

This led to a long discussion on the present status of the Jewish community in Brazil. It is divided on grounds of origin, on religious differences, and by the sharply differing degrees of assimilation. However, I got the impression that if, as these men want, there could be a certain degree of leadership from the outside and financial support from abroad, the community could be built up so as to encourage a very considerable immigration and be enabled to help the body of newcomers to find their way here. As a matter of fact, the group seemed struck by my picture of the possibilities of this community becoming one of the great Jewish communities of the world, with the advice and help of London and New York. They said that they hoped that I would put this point of view to a group of leaders later.

They are, of course, worried by Integralism, even though for the time being they had made peace with the leaders of that movement. However, one of the most important Brazilian writers active in the Integralist movement has refused to accept the judgment of his colleagues about withdrawing or minimizing their anti-Semitism, and continues to attack Jews. I emphasized to them that they could not be sure of avoiding this danger by refusing to recognize themselves as Jews; that the experience of German Jewry was proof of this.

. . . .

In the middle of the afternoon Sir Henry Lynch called. He said that he had been to see the president the previous day and had talked to the latter at some length about our proposal, but, of course, without specifically mentioning our memorandum. He had been preceded that day by the minister of labor and was followed by the minister of foreign affairs, who had also seen the president the day previous. Sir Henry argued with the president that the country would be benefited by granting the desired permission; the president had replied by citing the constitutional difficulties, to this Sir Henry had answered that there were usually ways to get around technical restrictions if there was a sufficient will to do so. Vargas responded that, as I understood Sir Henry to say, he had named a committee to study our proposal. Sir Henry did not know the personalities on the committee, and did not feel that he had the means of inquiring, but suggested that if I found out, I should let him know.

Friday, March 22, 1935

Again not feeling so very well, with an eye badly inflamed, decided to stay in bed.

Olive Sawyer, at my request, went to see Bandeiro de Mello to find out if he knew anything about the committee said to have been named to study our proposal. I perhaps made a mistake instructing her to be rather frank with de Mello and to let him know that we had heard that the committee was to be named. Her account of the interview follows:

At McDonald's suggestion, I told Bandeiro de Mello that McDonald had learned that the foreign minister had seen the president on Tuesday, that the minister of labor had seen him on Wednesday, following which the foreign minister had seen the president again (although we did not, of course, know that our proposal had been discussed at that interview); and that following these McDonald had learned that the president was to appoint a committee to study the proposal.

. . . .

[Bandeiro de Mello made an inquiry and then] . . . said that the minister of labor was to name the committee, that it had in fact not been named as yet, that the minister was busy this morning, having gone to the boat to meet the minister of finance. . . .

. . . .

Bandeiro de Mello was cordial to me . . . [and promised that McDonald would be asked to expose his views to the committee]. But I did not gather that he was playing McDonald's game in the matter of our proposal, but was rather working with the minister of labor.

. . . .

Steckine came in late in the day. I asked him his opinion of the grotesque article in the *Noticaes* to the effect that we were seeking to bring in 4,000 doctors, pharmacists, etc. He belittled the importance of the paper, said that it was in this matter probably influenced by the Integralistas or at any rate by the obdurate leader of that group, who, unlike his colleagues, had refused to discontinue the anti-Semitic agitation.

. . . .

Sunday, March 24, 1935

Worked with Miss Sawyer for a little while before going off with Ruth to lunch with Louis Oungre and his family at the Copacabana. It was very gay at the hotel, and the beach was extraordinarily beautiful, and I was envious of those who were well enough to enjoy it.

After much friendly talk about families and our recent trips, etc., Oungre launched into a business discussion which lasted, despite my desire to get back to bed, until nearly half past three.

I was terribly sorry to hear of the death of Lady Leonard Cohen. Oungre also said that he doubted whether Sir Osmond was as well as he had hoped he would be, because the last meeting of the ICA, which had been scheduled to be held in Paris, had in fact been held in London.

. . . .

[We discussed] . . . my plans for returning to the States, to Europe, and the meeting of our Governing Body. Oungre argued with cogency that it was vitally important that this time, if the corporation were faced with the kind of specific constructive schemes they had said they wanted, they should be forced to make good on their implied promises. If this were to be done, it was important that I should remain in the States until the corporation had in fact come into being; that it was much more important to accomplish this than to have a meeting of the Governing Body earlier. From my point of view and from that of the work, it would be much more valuable to present to a meeting of the Governing Body, even as late as August, concrete results, rather than negative or indefinite results earlier. I could not effectively disagree with these contentions.

Oungre then told me at length about his experiences in Argentina. On the whole, he is less pessimistic than had been his colleagues. It is true that there is a movement of anti-Semitism, but it is not so dangerous as to cause Oungre to recommend discontinuing efforts to place additional Jews there. On the contrary, after long sessions with the president, the minister of foreign affairs, and particularly the minister of agriculture, who is the key man with complete control of all immigration matters, he had worked out and presented a definite program. His memorandum on this he would give me. It had been presented just the day before he left, and would be followed up by his office. He had gone so far as to name a specific amount which ICA would be prepared to place on deposit in Argentina as a guarantee that the Jewish immigrants would not become public charges.

He had been careful, he said, to explain that his work was complementary to, and not in conflict with or duplicating, mine. His was to work out specific programs and to find the financial basis for these, while mine was more directly political, to secure the necessary assent for the desired immigration. He had prepared the way for me, but in no sense had attempted to do my work.

As to Brazil, he had an open mind, would read my material with interest, and would spend the next three weeks in making studies along the lines which he had instructed his staff here to prepare the data for, when he was in Rio on his way south. He said that the loss of Dr. Raffalovich was very heavy, that one of his problems would be to decide on a reorganization of the ICA office here. I told him of Dr. Löwi, and he said he would be glad to see him. He felt that he would be able to follow up on what we had done in Brazil, to support our initiative with the authorities and to work out specific suggestions for presentation to the corporation, once the government grants the essential permission.

We talked about publicity. He said that even the very small notices of my arrival here had been played up in a hostile sense by the anti-Semitic papers of Buenos Aires, that though *La Prensa* did not share this campaign, it was a movement which had to be taken seriously. As to the article in the *Noticaes* here, that, he said, was the result of German money. In Argentina, certainly, German influence was used strongly against the Jews and any increase in their number through immigration. Success in this respect is easier now in Argentina because of the intense prevailing nationalism, which has led the authorities to issue instructions to the consuls abroad that no immigration is to be admitted, not even agricultural immigrants.

I told Oungre of Rabinovich's article. He characterized him with a long unpleasant word beginning with b.

....

Promptly at ten minutes of nine the Jewish group came for me. When I found that Mr. Rinder was taking his daughter, I suggested that Ruth go also.

The meeting was held in the attractive synagogue and social center of the Spanish Moroccan Jews. This building is an excellent example of what can be done by a small determined group. I was told that it had been built practically by six men; the president, who was at the meeting, had been chiefly responsible. In other words, it appears that this handful of earnest Jews had done more than the much larger sections of Jews who had been more indifferent.

. . . .

Tuesday, March 26, 1935

Conference with Dr. Paul Rapaport at his office in the Rua Alfandega. He is carefully groomed, almost dapper in appearance, but quick and ready to talk. We spoke in French. He told me first of his relations to the community. He recognizes himself as a Jew, but has never been active in Jewish affairs. However, he knew a great deal about ICA, having acted as its attorney. He told me of his newspaper connections. He, with Chateaubriand, own[s] eighteen papers in different parts of the country. . . .

We talked about the Integralistas. Rapaport does not consider that they constitute a permanent danger. The Brazilians cannot be seduced by talk of race purity, and if they are given a sufficient standard of living, they will not be obsessed by Integralistas theories. He then told me of how, some months ago, the Jewish leaders had gotten in touch with the Integralistas leaders and had induced the latter to discontinue their anti-Jewish propaganda gradually. There had been a payment of a "very small" amount of money. Since then the attacks had almost ceased.

. . . .

Rapaport outlined his plan for bringing refugees into the country—a plan that he had urged upon ICA earlier. It is that the refugees should be brought in as agricultural laborers, placed on the fazenda not too far from the cities, and then left free to do other things if, as would be expected, many of them did not fit on the soil. He justified this procedure on the ground that nearly any Jew willing to work could find opportunities once he is in the country. I did not commit myself as to this plan.

I agreed to send him for his confidential information a copy of our memorandum, and we planned to meet again.

. . . .

Bertie Levi, representative of the Wilson Packers in Sao Paulo, and very active in the Jewish community there and one of the chief executives in their relief work, lunched with us. He outlined what had been done during the past two years. He estimated that Sao Paulo had raised and spent on the refugees nearly as much as Rio. Three hundred about [about three hundred] had been placed in Sao Paulo, and he did not think that many more than twice that number had come to Brazil altogether. He complained of the non-cooperative attitude of

Rio, the tendency here to issue orders, and, in general, to treat Sao Paulo as a provincial city. He recognized the abilities of Dr. Raffalovich, but felt that he had become too old and ill, and throughout had failed to recognize the necessity of a broader, all-Brazilian basis for the work.

As to the future, Levi felt that a very large number of refugees could be absorbed, . . . [given proper organization, funding, and facilities for temporary placement].

In short, Levi was an optimist in the best Paulista fashion. He scoffed at the idea that there need be a program involving an expenditure of anything approximating the $5,000 or $10,000 per family which Oungre had suggested.

. . . .

After dinner Inman and I talked with Mr. Olsburgh and his friend from Sao Paulo, the latter giving an account of his visit the previous evening at dinner with the foreign minister. It appears that Macedo Soares said that he was sympathetic to our proposal, that the difficulties lay chiefly in the attitude of Magalhães Agamemnon, that, however, conditions were such that it would be advisable for me to remain for the present. He was not so definite about the attitude of Vargas. The president, however, was not opposed, but was not yet prepared to override opposition. The suggestion which was reported that a certain person might advantageously go abroad was amusing and also illustrative of a favorite method here of dealing with difficult persons. The Greeks had a short word to describe it.

Inman and I were most enthusiastic in our expressions of thanks, as we ought to have been.

Wednesday, March 27, 1935

Called up Louis Oungre and asked him if he could stop in on his way to his office. When he came, he was at first inclined to express fear that there was danger in having asked the support of the three embassies for our proposal. I told him that I had not done it until after consulting Sir Henry. This seemed to reassure him. He also feared that it might be impossible to get the permission for the admission of non-agricultural workers, and that possibly our memorandum might have been phrased differently. I argued that any other statement would have been too far from the truth, and that I thought it preferable to ask for more rather than for less at the beginning, because one could always reduce his program, whereas it might be difficult to enlarge it. He assented unless, as he said, by pressing for the larger program, one spoiled the chances of success with a smaller one.

Louis Oungre then told me that he was thinking of a program which would involve bringing in a large number of people technically as agriculturists, with a view to organizing combined agriculture and industry and also to permitting a certain number to drift into the towns. The first program he thought desirable except for the item of expense. He estimated that it might cost as much as

$5,000 a family. Later in our talk, he spoke of the cost being $1,000,000 for a hundred families. However, he agreed with me that this was utterly impossible as a basis for any considerable immigration.

Inman and I went to see Sir Henry. We reported to him the present situation. He said he was leaving in a short time, within the hour, for Petropolis, and might go up with the finance minister. If he did, he would speak to the latter if there were an appropriate occasion; but in any event, he would speak to him later, and we could be sure of the finance minister's support.

We asked Sir Henry about the suggestion of utilizing Dr. Sebastian Sampaio.[16] He thought him a rather unimportant person.

. . . .

Dr. Paul Rapaport came to see Inman and me in the middle of the afternoon. We talked at length, but nothing much emerged from the discussion, except his suggestion that we utilize Sampaio. The latter, he said, could, if he would, let us know within two or three days whether we had any chance of success. He had easy and constant access to Vargas and to the ministers of foreign affairs and finance. At our suggestion Rapaport said that he himself would speak to the foreign minister.

The French chargé d'affaires, Gueyrend, who said that he had now received definite instructions to assist me in every way, asked if there was anything further that he could do. I thanked him but made no additional suggestions at the moment.

. . . .

Thursday, March 28, 1935

. . . .

Over to the Foreign Office, where I found Inman in conference with the much-talked-of Sampaio. Our conference, which went on for fifteen or twenty minutes—Inman had already been there half an hour—was interrupted constantly by telephone calls or by incoming secretaries. Mr. Gordon called and wanted something which Sampaio felt he could not give him until he had received Gordon's request in writing. The Japanese chargé came in person, and so for the whole period there were constant interruptions and a not very satisfactory atmosphere for our plea.

Nonetheless, I managed to explain briefly our history and what we wanted. Sampaio, with one eye on the telephone, listened; but his reaction was not all that we could have hoped for. He at once began to tell of the difficulties, partic-

16. Dr. Sebastian Sampaio, formerly consul general in New York, now the head of the commercial section of the Foreign Office and recently returned with the financial mission from abroad and now spoken of as a possible secretary to the president. He had been suggested as a key man, an introduction had been offered, but it turned out that he was one of Inman's oldest and most intimate friends. He, however, feared that the entrance of German Jews would hurt negotiations with Nazi Germany for a new commercial treaty. Lesser, *Welcoming the Undesirables,* 74.

ularly after we had admitted that the bulk of the people were not agriculturists. He spoke of the constitution and the political situation almost in the same way as the minister of labor. Finally, however, he agreed that he would inquire of the minister of foreign affairs and learn for us how the land lies.

Despite the promise, however, Inman and I left rather discouraged, not so much by the difficulties which Sampaio had outlined, as by the latter's indifferent or even hostile personal attitude. This was illustrated by his remark, when I had said that the political and financial circles in Paris, London, New York, and Washington had expressed their interest in our proposal, "Yes, I know, but we are also negotiating a commercial treaty with Germany. That cancels out the considerations you have urged, so we can forget them."

His attitude was the more discouraging because of his long personal association in New York with Inman.

Mr. Levi of Sao Paulo came in. He reported a very satisfactory conference with Louis Oungre, said they had agreed in every respect on future procedure. To me, he then elaborated his plan for training of refugees here, his belief that each Jewish community, no matter how small, could be induced to take one additional family, and how by sending immigrants as tourists first class, many could be placed if, instead of giving them the three contos, these and larger sums were placed at the disposal of the various committees. It would, of course, be necessary to get permission of the government for this. He was scornful of Oungre's suggestion that any sum comparable to $5,000 or $10,000 per family would be needed.

. . . .

After dinner Inman and I had a long talk with Mr. Dahne. He said that he had cleared up in the foreign minister's mind a number of points which were troubling Macedo Soares, particularly that we were not seeking to bring in 25,000 but only 500 a month over a period of two years, and that there would be no danger of the immigrants becoming public charges. Dahne feels that the foreign minister is coming to the point where he may be willing to urge the president to override the minister of labor. At the moment our program is being studied by the regular interdepartmental committee concerned with immigration; the representative of the Foreign Office [is] on this committee, and an important man is Vaz de Mello. Two others are Dr. Dulphe Pinheiro Machado and Dr. Oliveira Vianna.[17] The latter is one of the most brilliant intellectuals in Brazil and the leading authority on colonization and race. He is active in the Alberto Torres as the representative of Agamemnon. Inman knows his works very well.

We thanked our friend from Rio Grand do Sul and asked him if he would

17. Francisco Jose de Oliveira Vianna, Brazilian sociologist and social theorist, minister of education under Vargas, who accepted the concept of racial hierarchy, scientism, and eugenics and argued that European immigration would counteract African fertility and cause *embranquecimento* or "whitening" of the Brazilian population.

be able to introduce us to Vaz de Mello. He said he would take us there the next day.

After our meeting with Dahne Inman and I were taken for a gay walk along the quay by the ladies. En route, suddenly became obsessed with the idea that Inman must remain in Brazil to finish up, even if this required that I carry on without him until we reached the west coast. He was not wildly enthusiastic but will play the game.

Friday, March 29, 1935

Sir Henry called to say that he had not in fact ridden up with the finance minister the other day to Petropolis, but had another opportunity to talk with him fully.

Arthur de Souza Costa is increasingly favorable, but had said that Agamemnon Magalhães remained firm in opposition, and that the latter's legal adviser is the head of the Amigos de Alberto Torres. Sir Henry had also talked again to the president, who showed greater sympathy. All in all, it looked as though the thing was going forward. Meantime, Sir William had gone as far in his statement to the Foreign Office as his instructions would permit. I thanked Sir Henry, and we agreed to exchange information as soon as there were new developments.

Called Oungre on the phone. He said

(1) That he had been to the French Embassy, that the latter had received full instructions to aid me, etc.;
(2) That he had been talking to a prominent businessman in the city whom I knew, who felt that the successful conclusion of our matter might require another two months; that, in the meantime, he, Oungre, had presented a tentative program somewhat differing from mine, but consistent with it. He was sorry he did not have a copy, but because of its consistency with my program, that did not matter;
(3) Rapaport and he were anxious to discuss with Sampaio our project, together with Inman and me. I told him of Sampaio's reaction yesterday, and that I thought it best to wait until we had had his first report.

....

After lunch [met with] Dr. Hans Röttgen, formerly of the NEDA [Netherlands Development Office] and more recently of the Hospital at Quatro Irmaos. He had been forced out through some difficulty with the autonomous governing body of the hospital, but he had not come to speak about that.

There are now only sixty Jewish colonists and three hundred non-Jewish colonists of the vast territory of 100,000 hectares [Quatros Irmaos]. Moreover, many of the Jewish colonists work much less well than the others. The director, Eisenbert, a Canadian Jew, is an excellent man, and is coming to see Oungre in a day or two. It would be well for me to talk with him.

Life in the country is very pleasant and very cheap. One conto a month is more than enough to live on. He and his wife live well, had two horses and could not spend more than 300 milreis. A servant boy received 40 milreis a month (about $2.70). His horse cost him $10. A dozen eggs 4 cents. There are great opportunities in this and similar areas for German refugee doctors, because in many of them there are no doctors at all, and the local authorities are willing to wink at the lack of technical requirements having been fulfilled. The Catholic bishop in that neighborhood urges Röttgen to return to work in a mission station.

Röttgen cannot understand why the Brazilian authorities are unwilling to waive the technical requirements for the doctors who are here. He himself had the support of the Governor of Rio Grande do Sul in a special plea to the minister of education for an exemption, but it has been rejected. I told him that it was impossible to move in this matter publicly because of the intense nationalists, but that efforts were being made which we hoped might have good results.

. . . .

Dr. Frederico Dahne was waiting for me at the Foreign Office when I arrived there promptly at the time fixed, 5:30. Before going to the office of Dr. Vaz de Mello,[18] Dahne and I had some time together. I took advantage of this to ask him more about his own work in Rio Grande do Sul. He is the descendent of English and German parents who came to South Brazil. Now thoroughly a Brazilian, he plays a leading role politically and industrially in his state. He is a contractor, building roads, bridges, railways, etc. I was interested to learn that, at present, he finds that Poland is the best market for [buying] steel, Norway and Sweden for cement, the United States for road machinery and certain other types of machinery, while he buys very little in central or western Europe. On his present political mission here in Rio to secure special permission to bring in a large number of Japanese laborers, he has been occupied since the first of the year and now finds that he must remain until into May.

Dr. Inman joined us before Dr. Vaz de Mello was ready.

. . . .

After Dahne introduced us to Dr. Vaz de Mello, he left us, and Dr. Vaz de Mello showed the two of us into his spacious office overlooking the beautiful patio of the Foreign Office with its pond and magnificent royal palms.

Just as we were settling down for our conference, Dr. Sebastian Sampaio came in to speak to Dr. Vaz de Mello. Dr. Sampaio told us that he expected to have some information for us within a day or two. (This referred to the request which Inman and I had made to Sampaio when we saw the latter the day before. He had promised to find out for us from the minister of foreign affairs, with whom he is closely associated, the present status of our program.)

18. Dr. Ildeu Vaz de Mello, chief of the Passport Division of the Office of Foreign Affairs.

I began our talk with Dr. Vaz de Mello by explaining our mission. He interrupted me to say that he, as a member of the interdepartmental committee concerned with immigration, had just received some papers dealing with our request, but he was unable to find them, because the papers he showed us concerned a request for the admission of Russian refugees.

I then continued my explanation, in the course of it handing him a copy of our memorandum, with the suggestion that he take the time then to read it. But he said he preferred to study it later if I would leave it with him, which I did gladly. He said that he would have it mimeographed and send copies to his colleagues on the interdepartmental committee.

He then launched into a long enthusiastic account of the possibilities of Brazil for immigration. He cited with approval the statement of Humboldt that in the future the Amazon would be the center of world civilization. Indeed, he talked much as had Ambassador Oswaldo Aranha when I conferred with the latter in Washington last year. According to the views of these men, Brazil has made only a slight beginning. It is capable of containing hundreds of millions of people. Therefore, the policy embodied in the constitution, of rigid restriction of immigration, is absurd, all the more because of Brazil's obvious need for European blood to strengthen the population here, which is so largely Negro or Indian. So enthusiastic indeed was Dr. Vaz de Mello in his glowing account of the future of Brazil that we had some difficulty returning to the specific matter in hand.

He showed us not the small printed tabulation of the proposed quotas which the minister of labor had let us see a couple of weeks earlier, but the full detailed working sheet of the interdepartmental committee, and also his private sheet on which he had made his personal notations of corrections. We noted that the only large quota is that of the Italians, 28,000 plus. The German quota is 3,088. The Japanese quota is about 3,000. The total immigration permitted under the quotas is 80,000 plus.

Analyzing these figures, Dr. Vaz de Mello characterized them as even more absurd than they appear to be on their face, for, as he pointed out, the large Italian quota will not be filled, perhaps not even as much as a fourth of it. Similarly, other quotas will not be taken up. He estimated that, in fact, only about 40,000 immigrants a year would enter under the quotas. He pointed out, however, that this offered a potential advantage to us, because we could argue that our refugees would be given additional facilities to make up for the 40,000 quota permissions which were not being taken up. As he discussed these possibilities, Dr. de Mello outlined schematically the program which he thinks we should follow. In a supplementary memorandum we should indicate as definitely as possible the four following points:

(1) The quantity and rate of our proposed immigration. This should be shown both in absolute and relative terms;
(2) We should indicate clearly what are the nationalities of the refugees—how many are Germans, how many Polish, and particularly how many are state-

less; for these latter a special arrangement might be made, because, juridically speaking, they do not fall under the quota at all. The quota speaks of nationalities; therefore, those without nationality could enter irrespective of the quotas. (What a brilliant idea! This was the first encouraging word I had heard about the stateless in a year and a half of study about their problem.) While we were discussing this, Dr. Vaz de Mello read the paragraph on the stateless in my November report last year and expressed approval of it. Dr. Vaz de Mello said we should also indicate the number of Jews, though these, of course, could not constitute a nationality and, unlike the stateless, could not be considered outside the quotas;

(3) The financial resources available should be indicated as definitely as possible, and under two heads;

  (a) The funds available for transportation, disembarkation, and to meet the legal requirements for admission.

  (b) The funds available to enable immigrants to settle themselves on the land as *proprietors* or in business.

  Dr. Vaz de Mello emphasized that those coming in with funds to purchase land would not have to be listed, or rather, would not have to be considered as immigrants, and therefore, would not be restricted by the quotas;

(4) There should be precise indications of the professions, the capacities, the training of the refugees seeking admission. Of course, distinguished scientists who might be invited to specific posts would not be considered as immigrants or as bound by the quotas.

After outlining this procedure, Dr. Vaz de Mello in strict confidence told us that he was preparing to urge upon his colleagues on the immigration committee an interpretation of the law which would result in the classification of persons as immigrants only those above the age of 14; that is, basing his idea on a decree still in force which, interpreting the word "immigrant," speaks of persons coming to Brazil to earn their livelihood by their own labors in agriculture or in business. Obviously, children below the working age would not fall into this category. He anticipates that his interpretation may be something of a bombshell. (I could not be as confident as he that his interpretation would be accepted.)

Dr. Vaz de Mello then spoke of the personalities on the inter-ministerial committee, and emphasized the importance of Dr. Oliveira Vianna. (It appears that a part of our work will be to follow up with the other members of the committee.) In addition to mimeographing and distributing to his fellow committeemen, Dr. Vaz de Mello said he would also distribute copies of my last published report if I would supply them to him. (They were sent the next morning.)

During the course of his talk Vaz de Mello frequently spoke of Brazil's unfailing willingness to participate in any great humanitarian movement. He confirmed what had been told us by others of the importance of keeping this aspect of our work always in the foreground.

After our long discussion I asked Dr. Vaz de Mello whether he would recommend that the detailed program which he had outlined should be presented by us as a follow-up, or perhaps if Mr. Oungre were willing, by Louis Oungre as the representative of ICA, the body which normally would have most to do with carrying out such a program.

To my surprise, Vaz de Mello answered emphatically in the negative in reference to the follow-up being carried through by ICA. He said it would be a great mistake to turn the matter now into a purely Jewish proposal or one which was predominantly Jewish.

Dr. Vaz de Mello agreed that we ought to see the foreign minister again, and promised to arrange for an appointment.

Then Vaz de Mello took nearly twenty minutes to show us all of the rooms of the really magnificent palace which houses the Foreign Office. (How civilized these Brazilians really are as compared with so many of our cold, perfunctory Anglo-Saxon officials!)

....

Saturday, March 30, 1935

Everybody up early and on our way to the Gavea Golf Club at 7:30. Inman and I teed off about 8:15. We were accompanied the first nine holes by Ruth and Miss Sawyer. It is an extraordinary course, particularly the first nine holes, which wind up and down and in and through the foothills, with the mountains nearby and the greens and tees offering many magnificent views of the sea. The golf itself was indifferent.

After lunch we took the famous Tijuca drive, ending it by going up Corcovada by the cog railway. From the Christ monument there one has one of the truly great views of the world—the whole city and the adjacent country and the harbor spread out before one. Home in time for dinner, tired but satisfied.

....

Sunday, March 31, 1935

....

In the late afternoon Louis Oungre and his family came over. But it was not a social call, because Oungre and we had so many things to talk about that for nearly two hours we thrashed out our common problem.

We began by an analysis of the memorandum of Inman's and my interview with Vaz de Mello. . . . Oungre was much intrigued by Vaz de Mello's interpretation that the stateless would fall outside the quotas. He agreed that this would be excellent for us, but was inclined to express doubt as to whether in fact other difficulties would not be raised about the stateless which would prevent their easy entrance. . . .

We spent much time in discussion of the third point, in reference to financial resources. Oungre at first suggested that we indicate a definite sum for the item 3a, that is, for transportation, etc. But he admitted that the difficulty in fixing such an amount would be that the authorities might cut the numbers to be admitted down to match the funds indicated as immediately available. It seemed better, therefore, to stick to our general statement that adequate funds would be available for the purposes indicated, and for as many immigrants as are to be admitted.

....

... [Oungre and I had] a long discussion of the legal situation as it affects agricultural immigrants. He argued that in reality, until the quotas have been announced and regulations putting them into effect have been enunciated, the constitutional provisions do not apply, and instead the law of May is still applicable. Under its terms agriculturalists or immigrants who have contracted for agricultural services are admitted without any requirement other than a contract to engage in agricultural work. Oungre, however, pointed out that in section (c) under III of Article 2, there is that phrase "qualified for agricultural work." Does this mean that the immigrants must have been agriculturists or merely that they are over twelve years of age and under 60, as indicated in (c)? Oungre pointed out that this is really a vital question, because very few of the refugees have been agriculturists, but many of them might be "made into agriculturists." Indeed, it is precisely along this line that he is working out programs for both Argentina and Brazil. I expressed my opinion that surely the law would be interpreted to mean those who were coming for agricultural purposes. But Oungre pointed out that in Argentina exactly the same phrase had been interpreted in the narrow sense to mean those who had been trained in agriculture. In order to clear up this point in Brazil, Oungre had asked informally the opinion of an expert in the Department of Justice ... [getting the response that the broader interpretation will probably hold], but it will be some time before he receives a definitive answer.

This led us on to a more general discussion of the division of work here in Brazil as between Oungre and ourselves. He said that he was contemplating raising with the governmental authorities in his capacity as director of ICA, that is, as director of a great colonization society, the question whether, if he bought lands and contracted to bring over x number of agriculturalists, would the government bind itself contractually to permit him to do so? These negotiations would be for agriculturalists and without necessarily speaking of the refugees. In other words, his efforts then would supplement ours on behalf of urban or non-agricultural immigrants.

This program seemed excellent to me. Then arose the question of procedure.

....

In the matter of finance, the only definite figure that Oungre mentioned was $100,000, which he said might be indicated as being guaranteed by the foundation for loan kassas. The expenses of transportation, etc. would have to be made up from ICA and the Joint. The money for large-scale investment would have to be forthcoming on a basis of definite plans, from ICA and the New York group. It was with a view to preparing such plans that Oungre was concentrating here, as he had in Argentina. He hoped to present these plans at the special meeting of his board on the fourth of May, and if they were there approved, to present them later in New York. His estimate this time of what it would cost to settle a family on a combined agricultural and small industrial basis was 25 contos, or about $1,750.

....

I reported on Sampaio's comment the other day when I told him of the interest of the American and the French and the British government in the success of our mission. His indication that the interest of these governments would be counterbalanced by Brazil's desire to complete a commercial treaty with Germany showed that Sampaio was, to put it mildly, realistic. Oungre agreed that so far as his suggestion that he, Dr. Rapaport, and we should go and see Sampaio together sometime, it had better wait until we had had the answer Sampaio had promised me in reply to our initial inquiry.

In answer to Oungre's question as to how long I intended to remain in Brazil, I told him that I now felt that I ought not to leave until about the middle of the month—that I was concerned not only to remain as long as possible in order to get a definite reply on our immediate proposal, but also that I wanted to know as much as I could about the situation here because of my conviction that, irrespective of our immediate success or failure, Brazil offered, in my view, in the long run, next to Palestine, the greatest opportunities in the world for Jewish immigration. Oungre questioned whether this was true immediately, but was inclined to agree from the long-range point of view.

....

Oungre talked about a campaign for distributing immigrants, but said that he had not yet written out a memorandum on this.

This conference was very satisfactory, indicating as it did at the end practically complete agreement as between Oungre and ourselves on both the essential objectives to be aimed at and the methods of attaining these.

24. April 1935: South American Survey

Rio de Janeiro, Monday, April 1, 1935

. . . .

Helpful conference with Bandeiro de Mello at his office. He was interested to receive from me the details of the development of our work. He agreed that Vaz de Mello would be cooperative, but he doubted the latter's ability to be decisively helpful. He said that Dulphe Pinherio Machado, director of de D. N. do Povoamento[1] (Ministere de l'Agriculture), who was also on the general immigration committee, was intensely anti-Semitic, and we must therefore expect him to oppose us. On the other hand, Oliviera Vianna would be on our side. But he especially urged me to see Dr. Walter Niemeyer, whom he characterized as the minister of labor's right-hand man. He is of German descent, with some Jewish blood, sympathetic, broad-visioned, and should be able to influence the minister. De Mello called up Dr. Niemeyer and later gave me a letter of introduction, after fixing an appointment for the next day at noon for myself and Inman. De Mello then repeated in part what he had told me earlier of the reasons why he personally, because of a number of difficulties with his chief, the minister, could not be personally directly useful to us. He declared that the revolution, as is usual, had stirred up the dregs of society, and as a result, a number of new men with little vision or experience had risen to places of authority. By implication, he numbered Magalhães among these.

. . . .

Walked through part of the poorer section of the city, on my way to keep an appointment with Inman and Dr. de Mello Franco, at the latter's fine office in the Rex building, one of the new skyscraper edifices, the pride of the Brazilians. Inman and Franco did most of the talking, though from time to time Franco addressed himself to me in French. He is a brilliant linguist, speaking at least four languages with equal facility. The talk ranged over a great many subjects and throughout illustrated Inman's intimate acquaintanceship with Franco and with a great variety of Latin American problems.

On our particular question, Franco expressed complete sympathy, read our memorandum, and praised it highly, and asked us what we wished him to do. We suggested that he speak to the minister of foreign affairs. He said he would

1. National Rural Settlement Office of the Brazilian Ministry of Agriculture.

do this the next day, but if it were impossible to do so, he would leave a message through a young man close to the minister.

It was a little amusing to note that Franco brought into the conversation his candidacy for the Nobel Peace Prize, and told with evident pleasure of Titulesco's support of this candidacy.[2]

After supper had a debauch of nearly an hour of reading accumulated *New York Times*es. What a mess affairs at home seem to be drifting into!

Tuesday, April 2, 1935

Got Sir Henry Lynch on the telephone. Told him that we felt our negotiations were approaching a climax, and asked if it would be possible for him soon to speak to the minister of finance. He replied that though he had seen the minister repeatedly, there had as yet been no appropriate opportunity. He hoped that there might be such an occasion today, and if so he would seize it.

Sir Henry asked if I had noticed in the paper about the conference at the Foreign Office yesterday attended by the minister of labor, the minister of foreign affairs, and four or five others of that department, including Ildeu Vaz de Mello, Chefe dos Services de Passaportes, on the general subject of immigration. Fortunately, Dr. Inman had already seen it. Sir Henry assumed that this had to do with our problem. I could only say that I hoped so.

Called Oungre to tell him that Inman and I were seeing Niemeyer and to report also on other aspects of my interview with Bandeiro de Mello. Incidentally, I asked Oungre if he thought it would be desirable to bring Dr. Koch-Weser to Rio to confer with the latter about his agricultural and industrial experiences during the last year and a half in the Roland colony. Oungre replied that he did not think it would be necessary to bring Koch-Weser here for information about colonization, because he, Oungre, had been studying the matter during the past week.

Inman and I arrived at the Ministry of Labor promptly at twelve and were shown at once into the same large room where, two weeks earlier, we had been received by the minister of labor. Dr. Niemeyer was holding a staff conference with seven or eight of his colleagues at a long table in another corner of the room. That conference continued for about 40 minutes, while Inman and I compared notes about the state of the world.

When Dr. Niemeyer joined us, he apologized for the delay, and we plunged at once into our subject. Dr. Inman spoke in Spanish, carrying the bulk of the conversation. He presented out program in broad lines, stressing its humanitarian aspects, the relative small number of immigrants we were asking permission for in proportion to the size and possibilities of Brazil, the interest of the work

2. De Mello Franco was nominated for the Nobel Peace Prize in 1935 for mediating the conflict between Colombia and Peru. Nicolai Titulescu, foreign minister of Romania (1927–1928, 1932–1936) was among the many who nominated him.

in Brazil's action, and our anxiety that we might have an early and favorable response.

Dr. Niemeyer at once showed his sympathy by admitting the desirability of approaching the humanitarian viewpoint, rather than the narrow technical one, by telling us of his children's experiences in German and French schools alongside of Jewish children, the lack in Brazil of racial prejudice, and the great need for workers. He himself is a Paulista [from Sao Paulo], and is sympathetic with the desire there for large immigration. Indeed, he went so far as to indicate that Japanese immigration here does not present the same danger as in the United States, because the Japanese become Brazilians and fit readily into the economic life of the country, instead of competing with Brazilian farmers.

Dr. Niemeyer asked us what the immigrants would do here, and what provisions would be made for them. Inman explained in detail the program with Oungre had mapped out for the dispersement of the newcomers throughout Brazil, and the financial provisions which would be made. This seemed to carry weight with Dr. Niemeyer.

Then at my suggestion Inman appealed to Dr. Niemeyer for his personal advice as to how we could further our program. In making this statement, Inman was careful not to indicate any resentment at the attitude of the minister, but at the same time to make clear to Dr. Niemeyer that we hoped he would use his influence with Magalhães to modify the latter's intransigency. I have never seen a case better put. Dr. Niemeyer replied that he would discuss the matter with the minister, that he was in principle completely favorable to our proposal, and he further suggested that whatever influence he could bring to bear from the governors of the various states, particularly from Minas Gerais and Rio Grande do Sul, would be useful. Incidentally, he said that the conference at the Foreign Office yesterday afternoon had not had to do with our matter, but with the question of the Japanese. He indicated further that no special committee had been named. He seemed so much on our side and so interested that, as we left, I gave him a copy of our memorandum to the foreign minister, for his personal information.

Back to the hotel for a very late lunch, for here in Brazil the functionnaires who must have their lunch before they come to work, pay no attention to the ordinary midday meal hour. Nor for that matter, apparently, to the ordinary evening meal hour.

Was greeted at the hotel by Olive Sawyer with a message from Olsburgh that his friend in Sao Paulo had heard from the minister of foreign affairs that our project had been referred back to the minister of labor for decision by him. This, at first, seemed quite a blow, but it does not necessarily change the situation, since in any case we must depend for success upon active intervention in our favor by the president.

. . . As soon as I had returned to my room, Sir Henry was on the telephone to tell me that he had talked with the minister of finance, that the latter was prepared to support our proposal and would speak to the president about it this very day at Petropolis.

. . . .

Wednesday, April 3, 1935

Ruth and Inman and I were out at the Gavea Golf Course by quarter of eight. It was a lovely morning, without sun. Through the courtesy of Mr. Olsburgh I had a new set of clubs, but as was to have been expected, I failed to do them justice.

Back to the hotel before noon.

In the late afternoon Inman and I had another long and helpful interview with Vaz de Mello at the Foreign Office. He said nothing at all about our affair having been turned over altogether to the minister of labor. On the contrary, Vaz de Mello's continued intense interest in the project seems to indicate that his chief is still an important factor in the ultimate decision.

As at our previous interview, Vaz de Mello outlined seriatim a program which he thought would be helpful for us to follow. It was in substance that we should, as far as possible, make our request as definite as might be. Therefore, we should indicate in some detail the exact numbers that might be expected, and also the quality of the prospective newcomers, classifying them as artisans, technicians, professionals, etc. . . .

On the question of finance, Vaz de Mello suggested that each unmarried immigrant should have five contos, each small family the same amount, but a family of six or eight proportionately more. These sums should either be in the hands of the immigrants themselves, or it is possible that they might be pooled in a central fund held in Brazil.

. . . .

Throughout, Vaz de Mello also emphasized that it would, of course, be understood that a really careful selection of immigrants would be made, so that Brazil would not be penalized for its generosity. Moreover, he felt that there should be set up machinery for the distribution of the immigrants throughout Brazil. Towards this end he assumed that the High Commission would be a continuing body, maintaining its responsibility in the choice of immigrants and having its official representative in Brazil to cooperate with the ministries of Labor and of Foreign Affairs in the locating of the refugees here. We, of course, could not give any assurance about the continuance of the High Commission, but we did reassure him as fully as we could in the matter of choice of immigrants and the distribution in Brazil.

Vaz de Mello gave us a long explanation of the Brazilian lack of racial prejudice and the significance of this liberal attitude. According to him, Brazil's misfortune in being made up of so many different races is being turned into its advantage. The set policy of all Brazilian governments to work for the amalgamation of all the Brazilian peoples will create eventually a Brazilian race and at the same time destroy any possibility of serious sectionalism. Brazil is potentially a really imperial and formidable world power.

We asked Vaz de Mello what he would advise as to the immediate strategy on our part. He agreed that we should press vigorously for action. In reference to our forthcoming visit to the minister of foreign affairs, he suggested that we might point out that we had come to Brazil first, and that if we went away empty-handed, we could not expect the smaller and less importance South American countries to aid us. But if, on the contrary, Brazil, consistent with its traditional policy, were generous, we could use this example with real effectiveness everywhere else on this continent.

Vaz de Mello thought it would be important for us to see the cardinal. His own chief would be influenced by the attitude of the ranking Brazilian ecclesiastic. When I said that I had been four times in touch with Pacelli, Vaz de Mello indicated that that connection should be capitalized [on].

. . . .

Thursday, April 4, 1935

Dr. Hans Röttgen, who is now living at the Jardim Hotel, Marechal Floriano, came again to see met to report his experiences since we had last talked. He was obviously depressed.

. . . .

I inquired whether he would be willing to accept the very modest pay, about ¾ of a conto, which the Rockefeller people pay their young medical research men. He said he would. I then called up Dr. Wilson and arranged for Dr. Röttgen to visit him at the Rockefeller office. Röttgen left buoyed up by the hope that he might find something to do.

. . . .

Before dinner I went to see [the French] Ambassador Souza-Dantas, who had arrived only a day or two before from Paris with his wife. We chatted downstairs at the Palace Hotel. He was very cordial, read our memorandum, said it was excellent, and agreed to speak to the foreign minister about it. But he did not think he could speak to the president or to Agamemnon. He said that for him to speak to the latter might be misunderstood by the minister of foreign affairs.

Ruth and I went to dinner as guests of Mr. & Mrs. Ralph Olsburgh. Among the guests were Sir and Lady Montague Burton. . . .

Most of my talk was with Sir Montague. We chatted for half an hour or so before dinner, during most of the meal, and afterwards for a considerable time before we began to play bridge. His views and mine about Bentwich are identical. He spoke of the latter's complete unselfishness and his refusal to use unworthy means to defend himself even when these are used against him.

Sir Montague was interesting in his analysis of anti-Semitism. He denied that there is any such thing as a distinctive form of anti-Jewish prejudice. He thinks that it is the same thing as nationalist prejudices as against a German or a Frenchman. The differences he attributes to the fact that the Jews do not have a state of their own. This theory helps to account for his Zionism.

He is an ardent admirer of Weizmann, particularly of the latter's personality and devotion to the Zionist cause. But he recognizes that Dr. Weizmann, when he is in the political arena, becomes covered with the same sort of mud as the other politicians—Jewish or otherwise. Therefore Sir Montague feels that Weizmann ought to remain aloof from active Zionist politics. But he does not think he will.

....

About ICA Sir Montague spoke with sympathy but discrimination. He thinks that Sir Leonard lived too much aloof, and allowed the institution to get into a bureaucratic rut, and to become more and more aloof from the Jewish masses and Jewish problems. He agreed with me that Sir Osmond would avoid many of these mistakes.

As to the Rothschilds in London, Sir Montague was only mildly critical, holding that they are not ungenerous, but that they have become so assimilated that they no longer feel intensely their Jewish obligations. He shared my enthusiasm for Simon Marks and the newer group of English Jews.

As a bridge player Sir Montague is keen and yet friendly. I much enjoyed watching him as we played until late in the night. His charm of manner is illustrated by his expression when the hostess asked him if he liked to play bridge. He said, "Yes, if I may have the pleasure of playing with Mr. McDonald." His fine manners stand out all the more prominently because of his marked accent, which seems a strange mixture of continental Russian or German and Scotch.

Friday, April 5, 1935

....

Oungre stopped by to give me an account of his interview the day before with Agamemnon. He had gone with the general director of the Ginley (?) interests. Agamemnon had listened for a quarter of an hour while Oungre exposed his plan; but the response was quite uncompromising. He said that Mr. McDonald had said that there were no agriculturists (Oungre underlined this statement of Agamemnon and added that this was very serious. I can almost see him some weeks hence in Paris implying that my alleged statement in this regard had prejudiced the whole enterprise.) I replied that I had not made such a statement, but had admitted, as I was forced to do by the facts, that there was only a small portion of agriculturists.

Agamemnon continued that no urban immigration whatsoever would be allowed, that no stateless could come in, and that even those who came for agricultural purposes would be deported if they returned to the cities. (Later I was told from a number of sources that this threat in reference to deportation would not in fact be carried out and need not be taken seriously). The only concession which Oungre reported was Agamemnon's declaration that in order to be classified as an agricultural immigrant one need not have been an agriculturist, but merely declare his intention to become such.

Agamemnon's attitude was based on the law and the constitution, but Oungre got the same impression we had received—that it would be extremely difficult to budge him. It was apparent that all of Oungre's elaborate maneuvers to influence Agamemnon indirectly through the possibilities of large land purchases from the Ginley or other interests had failed.

....

With Inman to the Foreign Office for our second visit with the minister of foreign affairs. At the beginning of the interview Inman presented an autographed copy of his book. The minister in turn presented us both with copies of his. Then Inman began to re-state our case, when the foreign minister called in Vaz de Mello, suggesting that the latter outline to us the position of the secretary of labor. But Inman, not giving Vaz de Mello an opportunity, went ahead arguing our point. In the course of his talk I reminded him to tell the minister of my relations with the Vatican. This he did, but stumbling a little in his use of such words as His Eminence, His Holiness, etc.—words that do not come naturally from the mouth of a good evangelical missionary. Anyhow, Soares was impressed and replied that he personally was wholly in sympathy with our proposal, that he would bring up the matter again to the minister of labor, and let us know the result. He was noncommittal in answer to our suggestion that perhaps we should see the president again.

Following this interview we went back to Vaz de Mello's office. He said, "You see, the minister knows nothing of the details, and has left the whole matter to me. If you wish me to do so, I will draft for you wholly in my personal capacity a memorandum in the form in which it could be most advantageously be presented to the minister of labor. I will have it ready for you on Monday."

Down to the boat with Inman to see off the Burtons. We had a very nice visit. Inman was much impressed by Sir Montague's intense interest in the possibility of utilizing the refugee scholars in the new Rio University.

....

Saturday, April 6, 1935

....

In the late afternoon Inman and I went to see Felix Pacheco at the office of the *Journal do Commercio.* He received Inman with the greatest cordiality, presented him with two of his books inscribed to his illustrious and distinguished friend, etc. Then followed talk about Latin American affairs, political and otherwise. Finally, Pacheco himself brought up the subject of our mission. He expressed horror at the Nazi program and humanitarian sympathy for the refugees, but explained at considerable length why it was not possible for Brazil to make exceptions in their favor. I did not argue the matter with him, particularly because it seemed to me that there was no chance of convincing him and that all we could hope to accomplish was to leave him in a friendly mood and thus have an additional guarantee against any deliberate attack from his paper.

. . . .

Sunday, April 7, 1935

In the evening interesting talk with Olsburgh about his difficulties in attempting to get two of his men off the *Blue Star* liner that had come in that morning. He had found himself quite lost between the maritime police authorities and the immigration officials in the Labor Office. In vain, he had appealed to one and then the other, and finally to Machedo, the head of the Immigration Section under Agamemnon. Later, he was to learn that Machedo, whom I had heard spoken of earlier as very anti-Jewish and as one of the most obstructionist persons around Agamemnon, was, as he put it, "thoroughly unreliable."

Monday, April 8, 1935

Lunch with Mr. Coates of the Rotary International, whose headquarters are in Montevidéo. He talked at length about the situation in Uruguay, confirmed the report of unemployment, though he belittled the actual number out of work, saying that this had been reduced by facilitating the return of foreigners to Europe. There are no places, he feels, for any workers from abroad and practically none for foreign intellectuals. He expressed in the very best Rotaryese his deep sympathy for the refugees, his horror at the Nazi program, but Uruguay could not be used for the refugees. On the contrary, everyone in Uruguay who was not born there was now being required to revalidate his citizenship. Even Coates himself is being forced to do this after forty years of residence there. All of this was rather depressing, following as it did the earlier discussion of Rotarian ideas and Coates activities in Rotarian conferences on two continents.

. . . .

On the way over to the cardinal's palace I explained to Mr. Lynch [Sir Henry's brother who was accompanying McDonald], my relations with the Vatican, and my hopes from the cardinal. We were kept waiting only a few minutes before we were ushered into the presence of the Cardinal D. Sabastiao Leme.[3] He received us graciously. Mr. Lynch told him of my mission, and then we

3. Sabastiao Leme da Silveira Cintra, archbishop of Rio de Janeiro. A friend of President Vargas. McDonald wrote to Sir Osmond that the cardinal was "the ranking Brazilian ecclesiastic and a strong personality, popular with the government and the people." Letter of April 6, 1935. Copy in McDonald Papers, USHMM.

talked for a while about conditions in Germany. He said that he was well acquainted with affairs there.

In response, the cardinal said that we had arrived in Brazil at an historic epoch. The country was going through a transition from revolutionary to constitutional forms that would in the future be written down as a very significant development in the history of Brazil. He expressed complete sympathy with our proposal, said that it was not a question of Jew or Gentile but one of common humanity. Therefore, we could count upon his support. He asked whether the refugees would be distributed throughout Brazil. We assured him that they would be.

Then I asked him if he would speak to the foreign minister, or rather he, I think, volunteered to do so. In any event, I followed that up by asking if he would also speak to Agamemnon. This he said he could not do. In the same way he replied that because of other circumstances, he could not grant my request that he speak to the president. He suggested that there were certain difficulties that prevented his doing so at this particular moment.

Then the talk turned on Agamemnon. We asked the cardinal what he would suggest as the best method of reaching the latter. I also inquired whether Padre Arruda Camara would be useful in that connection. His eminence replied in the negative, giving us an account of the interesting and patriotic career of this young priest, but saying that Camara was too young to have influence on Agamemnon.

We then asked who could be useful. After thinking it through, the cardinal, who is himself from Pernambuco, said that no one could do so much as Lima Cavalcanti, governor of Pernambuco. But who could influence the governor? The answer was Pedro Ernesto.[4] The cardinal added that of course these suggestions must not be attributed to him. Earlier, he had said that we should not be too discouraged by Agamemnon's position, because everything in Brazil is in a state of transition, and to this rule Agamemnon was not immune.

As we were leaving, I told the cardinal that I hoped to see Pacelli in the summer and that I would take occasion then to report to the latter the sympathetic and helpful reception which I had had.

On the way back to the hotel Mr. Lynch expressed himself as very pleased with the interview.

Fortunately shortly thereafter, Anisio Teixeira came in, primarily to talk to Dr. Inman about the intellectuals, but I took occasion to tell him of the general situation and of my talk that afternoon with the cardinal, asking him if he would not help us with Pedro Ernesto. He replied that he would be delighted to do so, and that circumstances were such as to facilitate his task. He then told me that he was going to Pernambuco the next day with Pedro Ernesto to attend the inauguration of the new governor, that Agamemnon was also going, but on a

4. Pedro Ernesto do Rogo Batista, physician, close friend, and comrade in arms of Vargas during the revolution of 1930.

different boat; on the way up he would speak to Ernesto and then during the days that all of them were living en famille at the governor's palace, there would be an excellent opportunity to discuss the matter with Agamemnon. Teixeira also promised to telegraph me if there were any unusual developments.

....

Then Inman and Teixiera talked about the new university. The new rector, Alfranio Peixoto, is sailing on May 8 and will make contracts with certain of the German professors. As Teixiera was looking over the complete list of professors, he exclaimed that this was the best proof of Nazi barbarism.

While we were talking, Louis Oungre came in to see me. I introduced him to Teixiera. Oungre talked about the new university and did not miss the opportunity to urge rather crudely Teixeira to include at least one French professor. Inman rather resented this and Oungre's prolonged discussion, but was relieved later when Teixiera showed that he felt that Oungre's concern about French influence was rather out of place.

....

Oungre reported that the German ambassador had been active at the Foreign Office, urging that Brazil accept the interpretation that the German quota be reserved only for good Germans—that is, either Aryans or persons from Germany or elsewhere approved by the Reich.

As he was leaving, Oungre warned me about Argentina, said that there, unlike Brazil, there were active organs of anti-Semitism, hence the necessity of my being extremely cautious, remaining entirely incognito, eschewing the press, and, he added, rather significantly, the Jewish community also. There is, I imagine, more back of this latter suggestion than is apparent on the surface.

Tuesday, April 9, 1935

Conference in the morning with Paulo Carneiro, secretary of agriculture in Pernambuco. He outlined to Inman and me ambitious plans for the rebuilding of agriculture in his state, and his desire for immigration. I expressed interest in his program and then showed the possibility of substantial capital investment from London and New York in Brazil. But I emphasized that there was no possibility of these funds being available anywhere in Brazil unless the opposition of his fellow-countryman Agamemnon could somehow be overcome. He recognized the reasonableness of this limitation, said that he would be glad to do what he could with Agamemnon directly and indirectly through Lima Cavalcanti.

....

Then with Inman over to the Uruguayan Embassy. Ambassador Blanco was surprisingly cool; even Inman could not warm him up. I thought this a bad omen. He agreed, however, to let the authorities in Uruguay know of our coming, but was not particularly encouraging about our seeing the president.

....

Wednesday, April 10, 1935

Inman and I over to the Argentine Embassy, where we were kept waiting about fifty minutes by the ambassador, Ramon Carcano. When he appeared, he looked as though he had just gotten up. By that time we only had a few minutes; therefore, after an exchange of compliments and after receiving his promise to notify his government of our coming to Buenos Aires, we left.

....

Conference with Inman and Oungre at the hotel. Inman had an opportunity to ask Oungre about the latter's policy of immigration on the west coast and in Paraguay, Santo Domingo, and Central America. Oungre explained that since they had machinery for the reception and initial care of immigrants only in Brazil, Argentina, and Chile, they had not favored immigration elsewhere, but that he was open to conviction that, in view of the increasing restrictions of these three countries, efforts should be made elsewhere. He was not very satisfactory about Santo Domingo, limited himself for the most part to asking questions and not committing himself to a visit there. Similarly, in reference to the other countries, he was not prepared to assume any definite obligation.

....

The middle of the afternoon Inman and I went for what we hoped would be a final conference with Vaz de Mello. He received us as cordially as ever, but at once dashed our hopes that the memorandum which he had promised ten days before would be ready. He explained that it had not been possible for him in the midst of all his other duties to concentrate on our task. Moreover, he wanted to clear up with us an important point that only the stateless had any chance of being admitted, since only they could be interpreted as falling outside the quota. Therefore, before he could proceed he would have to receive from us fuller data of the percentage of stateless. He went on to explain that stateless could be interpreted in the broadest sense as all refugees who, for one reason or another, do not have valid national passports.

I tried to argue with him that it would be very difficult for me to ask for concessions merely for the stateless, that it would be unjust to the others and would be giving away half our case; that, besides, it was extremely difficult to fix a figure for the stateless, etc., etc. But I did not succeed in shaking him.

....

Earlier Vaz de Mello, Teixeira Leite, and McDonald went over the draft prepared by Oungre. Vaz de Mello made some changes, limiting it to the stateless and agriculturalists. He insisted that in this revised form Oungre's memorandum should be submitted, along with McDonald's new draft for the minister of labor.

Finally, I agreed to cable Europe for the data about the stateless to supply him with it as soon as possible in the hope that Vaz de Mello would be able to have his draft ready for us that week. Then we left, I, at least, very low in spirits because I did not then see how we could really meet Vaz de Mello's conditions.

. . . .

McDonald had not been consulted by Oungre about his memorandum or about the method of presentation. He went at once to see Oungre and told him of his meeting with Vaz de Mello.

I told him of Vaz de Mello's insistence on the stateless and of the other aspects of our talk. Then Oungre, glancing [*sic,* glanced] through the latter part of his memorandum and noting [*sic,* noted] there changes which Vaz de Mello had made in reference to stateless and, as Oungre said, "in other vital respects" (though on this point I am in no position to check because Oungre never let me see the original of his draft).

Then Oungre proceeded to argue that he would not be able to submit this memorandum at all, that to do so would be to weaken, not strengthen, my initiative. I told him that I thought this was a very serious decision to take, and that he and Leite probably could agree on a form which would be satisfactory to Vaz de Mello. But for reasons which did not seem to me wholly clear and which I felt Oungre did not fully explain, he became more and more emphatic that he could not submit, or rather have submitted, this memorandum.

. . . .

I repeated to him that I was most anxious that it should not be interpreted that I had caused him to withdraw the memorandum or that I had ever been a party to it, for such an impression would certainly alienate Leite and might jeopardize my relations with Vaz de Mello. Oungre said that he would make that clear.

. . . .

I left the conference troubled by the feeling of not knowing precisely why Oungre had so suddenly changed his mind.

Fortunately, the Cabots couldn't come to dinner, for I was in no mood to entertain.

Thursday, April 11, 1935

During the evening previous and early this morning I had made up my mind that instead of waiting for Vaz de Mello to take the initiative in a new form of memorandum, I would submit to him a draft, gotten up in as formal and legalistic a manner as I could devise, with Miss Sawyer's help. Spent the morning in an intensive drive to get a new draft, which was practically finished before lunch.

The previous evening Miss Sawyer and I had, after painful study and balancing of conscientious scruples, drafted cables to the office and Mr. May asking for data on the stateless, phrased in such a way as to give them the impression what we needed.

....

Oungre called up and asked me to join him and Teixeira-Leite in a conference at the Copacabana. I was there from about seven until 8:30.

....

Oungre explained at length to Leite his reasons for withdrawing the memorandum and emphasized that I had not been responsible for that decision. Leite was obviously very much upset.

Leite proceeded to argue, using the authority of Vaz de Mello, that not only would immigrants be limited to the stateless, but also to those coming for agriculture; that additional ones were not at all possible. This argument both frightened and angered me, for I felt that Leite, in his anxiety to sell land, was putting into Vaz de Mello's mouth arguments that the latter had not himself felt, or, at any rate, arguments which Vaz de Mello had not urged on me the day before, that is, particularly the limitation to agriculturists.

I replied to Leite that, so far as I was concerned, these dual limitations destroyed all hope of any successful negotiations; that, moreover, even those persons interested in colonization would not invest money in Brazil unless a certain proportion of the immigrants were to be urban, and that therefore the interests wishing to sell land were really defeating themselves by encouraging a strict limitation to agriculturists.

Leite countered by suggesting a certain percentage, 10 percent or 20 percent of those allowed to come in, might be urban. I argued that any such percentage principle would be self-defeating.

The talk went on and on, but not much that was new was added.

....

Before Leite left, I had whispered to Oungre to ask if he did not think it possible or desirable to agree with Leite on some form of memorandum. But Oungre remained adamant.

After Leite left, Oungre walked out with me and begged me to keep him informed by cable of what happened in Brazil and in Argentina so that he might be informed before the meeting of his board and also so that "he might be able to prove that we two are working together in closest harmony."

....

Friday, April 12, 1935

Down to the *Massilia* with Ruth to see the Oungres off. In our final talk Oungre again emphasized his desire that I keep him closely informed. I could not avoid the impression that he was leaving not only depressed by the failure of his own and up to date of my démarche but also with a certain degree of anxiety about facing his board with empty hands. He showed me at the boat a sentence from a cable received that morning from Argentina, which stated that the agricultural minister had rejected his request, but added that through personal connections some individuals might be allowed to enter.

. . . .

At 1:30 Teixeira Leite called me on the phone to say that it was impossible for Vaz de Mello to see me this afternoon, but that an appointment had been fixed for three o'clock the next day, and that he, Leite, would come by for me.

This news was a real blow, because I had written the previous evening to Vaz de Mello expressing the hope that he could see me on Friday, telling him that I was suggesting a new draft of the memorandum Friday morning. The news meant that there was no possibility of finishing up our memorandum for the minister of labor before sailing on the fifteenth for a couple of weeks in the south. In other words, not only would I have to return to Brazil, which I had already reconciled myself to, but we would probably not be able to utilize the period of absence by having our memorandum considered.[5]

. . . .

Saturday, April 13, 1935

. . . .

At three o'clock Teixeira Leite came for me, and we went together to Vaz de Mello's office.

. . . .

Vaz de Mello began by giving me the Portuguese text of our memorandum, telling me that he thought it excellent. He was delighted that we had the data about the stateless and that the cabled reports indicated 40–50 percent. He felt, however, that in certain particulars the memorandum needed to be amplified so as to make it more likely to bring success. Moreover, it would be necessary to indicate that we were asking for admission only of the stateless, and therefore, he felt that I should eliminate the reference to the German nationals and the Polish nationals. Moreover, and here he was from my point of view at his worst, I should indicate that all of those coming were coming for agricultural purposes. They need not have been agriculturists, nor need all of them remain on the land.

5. McDonald had planned to visit Chile but had to change that program also, and Dr. Inman went alone to the west coast.

Nonetheless, there should be an indication of specific financial guarantees for each individual immigrant at the rate of approximately 5 contos per person, or for a small family and proportionately more for a large family. The individual on presenting himself for a visa should have a check drawn to the credit of the Bank of Brazil for these amounts—these to be credited to the immigrant and re-payable to him after he had purchased property or property had been purchased for him and he had been settled in the country.

Each of these points was bad enough in itself, but cumulatively they seemed to me to spell complete defeat, but I did not think that I dared to say so. I argued that I could not limit my appeal to the stateless because my responsibility was much broader. Vaz de Mello replied that I had done everything that I could for the others, and that now there was no use spoiling the chance of the stateless by including reference to those with nationality. I half-heartedly assented.

Second, as to the agriculturists, I argued that this was extremely difficult, and I did not agree to it. However, I did not feel that I could afford to come to the breaking point on it, so left the matter rather indefinite.

Third, as to the guarantees, I recognized that there should be such, but did not discuss in detail the specific guarantees Vaz de Mello suggested. I thought it better to leave this until I had seen his revision of my memorandum.

Then I asked him when he could have his revision ready. He at first suggested that he would work on it Sunday when he would be undisturbed, but when I asked if I could have it Sunday afternoon or Monday morning, he said it could not possibly be ready so soon, that it was a matter of great importance that required thinking through and could not be hurried. My further appeal that I wanted to submit the memorandum before I left for the south, and that I hoped to sail Monday afternoon, met with the response that this would be impossible, that since Brazil is the most important place for me, why should I hurry, that I could not hope to succeed in the south if I had not previously succeeded in Brazil.

Checked at every turn, I finally suggested that I would go south for a short time, and then submit the memorandum immediately upon my return if Vaz de Mello were sure that his revision would be ready by then. He agreed that this would be best, but I was not convinced that there would not be further delay on my return. However, I did all I could to protect against this by urging Blake to press the matter forward and by making clear to Leite that this must be done.

But I must record that throughout the conference Vaz de Mello kept insisting that there ought to be something from Oungre before my memorandum is submitted, and Leite at the very last moment said, "Now be sure to get something from Oungre." It is even possible that they will not cooperate in enabling me to submit my memorandum unless and until they have had something from Oungre.

What a prospect! With the Foreign Office insisting on action from ICA and Oungre insisting that there must be an answer to my démarche first.

. . . .

Sunday, April 14, 1935

Up early and repaid by the most flaming sunrise of our experience.

The trip [by train] to Sao Paulo was from seven a.m. until a little after seven that evening, was interesting and pleasant. There was no dust. Ruth got a new impression of how some people live, as we looked into the adobe huts of one room, dirt floors, no chimney, no windows, and yet many healthy looking children and mothers suffering less from nervous strain than the neurotic ladies of Park Avenue.[6]

. . . .

Monday, April 15, 1935

Dr. Lorch took me over to the office of Dr. Rocha Lima [of the Biological Institution]. We had a pleasant visit. I presented him with the list [of refugee intellectuals] and with Dr. Inman's compliments, but little new was learned. He is prepared to employ a chemist and a plant expert if the money can be found for these two places, but I got the impression that he himself will do nothing to secure the funds. It was suggested that when I saw the governor this need might be indicated to the latter.

Dr. and Mr. Lorch lunched with us. We were later joined by Dr. Mindlin, who was to take us out to Butantan.[7]

At Butantan we had half and hour to 45 minutes with Dr. Afranio Amaral.[8] Out talk was divided into two parts—one, the question of the refugee intellectuals. He studied the Sao Paulo committee [for refugees] and said, "It's all right. We have a majority. Three will work and two will do nothing. We are all friends, and we will stir the lazy ones into action." He thought it important that I should intimate to Mesquita that Azevedo would be willing to do the real secretarial work, for, as Amaral put it, "Mesquita has the French mentality; he is interested in generalities, philosophical and political, but he will not carry anything through. I have arranged for a conference at Mesquita's office tomorrow night at which we will invite Azevedo. The three of us will plan the work." The intimation was clear that nothing was to be expected from Dr. Ramos, who at the moment is under something of a cloud. As to Dr. Rocha Lima, Amaral, who in a sense runs a rival institution (the Butantan has come to be much more important than the Biological Institution), said that Lima would not do anything effective, that he has used up his increased budget by taking on a number of unnecessary veterinaries, and that he will not obstruct but must be pushed.

Furthermore, Amaral said that unless the committee were very active, nothing much would be done, that he had warned Dr. Inman about this. He pledged

6. The State of Sao Paulo in 1932 had fought against the federal government in the revolution. The city of Sao Paulo has been described as the Chicago or New York of Brazil. "Rio for good times, Sao Paulo for business."

7. A snake farm celebrated for its production of antitoxin serums.

8. Dr. Afranio do Amaral, renowned herpetologist and tropical disease expert at Rio and Harvard universities.

himself definitely to do his part of the work, but the rest would depend upon Azevedo. It is important not to forget the Brazilian scientists' opposition to the foreigner. This is a grave mistake, but a natural one.

. . . .

However, I left with the impression of an extraordinary personality, an unusual combination of a scientist and a tremendous organizer. Inman had not exaggerated in these respects. Dr. Amaral is not modest, but he is evidently one of the great men of our times.

Back to the hotel with Dr. Mindlin, Ruth having stopped off with Mrs. Mindlin at their house. We learned from Dr. Mindlin's son, who had been told to go off to make the other appointments, that the governor was unavailable because of the funeral that afternoon of the son of Machado, the most important political leader of the state. Nonetheless, I called at the governor's palace and left my card.

Then with Dr. Mindlin and his son José to the office of Dr. Azevedo. I left him his lists, and we talked about the organization of the work in Sao Paulo. I told him that I was going to suggest to Mesquita that he, Azevedo, do the work of the committee. He said he would be willing to and would, and would talk the whole matter over the next evening with Mindlin and Amaral.

Azevedo looked through the list with great interest and then expressed rather pessimistic views as to the prospects in Sao Paulo. There are, he said, already a large number of foreign professors in the university; need exists, it is true, for additional ones, particularly in his work and in the technical institutions, but no money is available. Besides, it should be remembered that neither Amaral nor Rocha Lima nor he could name new professors or research men; this could only be done by the secretary of education. To this, Mindlin replied that, of course, technically that is true, but what the secretary of education does depends upon what you and the other men recommend to him.

. . . .

Then the three of us, Dr. Mindlin, José and I, went to see Dr. Julio Mesquita Filho. He seemed to me at once to be the man I had expected to meet, a rather intense, intellectual and idealist. He, like all the others I had met, spoke of Inman highly, and then we drifted into general talk about the state of Europe, the dangers of Nazism to the intellectual life, the menace to France, etc., etc. He is intensely anti-German, declaring that the initial mistake was made at the end of the war when the advice of Foch and Clemenceau was rejected and the Allied troops did not march to Berlin, for only so would the Germans have known that they were defeated. Now it will all have to be done over again. He has been in Rome recently and told me with gusto of his talks then with Mussolini and the latter's advisers, when he had warned them against their sympathy for the rising power of Germany. Now he would be able to say he had told them so.

After a time we got down to our subject. I showed him the lists, which he said he would study, agreeing that they were in themselves the best indication of the terribleness of the Nazi regime.

. . . .

Finally, I said to Dr. Filho that in addition to the problem of the intellectuals there was the general problem of immigration and explained to him briefly the actual situation. Then I asked him to go to his brother-in-law, the governor, and to urge the latter to appeal strongly to Rio, to Vargas, and if possible directly to Agamemnon for a more liberal policy. Filho said that he would be delighted to do this, but that before he did he would like to know more exactly what we were asking. I told him in general terms and then promised to send him a copy of our draft memorandum. This, he said, would be exactly what he needed, and that after studying it, he would take it up with Oliviera.

When we returned to the hotel, we found Horacio Lafer[9] in the lobby and Mr. and Mrs. Levi upstairs.

. . . .

Lafer, Mindlin, Levi, and I then had more than a half an hour of rather tense and frank talk. There was a tacit conspiracy to put pressure on Dr. Filho to use his influence effectively. In the course of the time Mindlin and Levi were almost sharp with Filho, but he, defending himself on the ground that he was prepared to do everything possible, argued that it was practically a helpless situation. He cited what Agamemnon had said to him at the time of the Assyrian démarche: "The British and other foreign representatives have been pressing hard, but I will not yield to that or any other pressure." And as Filho continued, "Agamemnon is a very stubborn, a very difficult man. Nor do I think that Garcio Vargas will bring pressure upon him. The president dislikes doing this on any minister. He is even less likely to do it on Agamemnon."

The talk then turned on the possibility of enlisting actively the support of Luiz Cavalcanti [the governor of Pernambuco]. Here I thought Filho realistic when he said, "The governor's influence may be exerted in one of two ways: he may simply say to Agamemnon that he wished that the latter would consider the possibility of acceding to our request; that would mean nothing. Only if Cavalcanti said to Agamemnon, now this must be done, and intimated that if it were not done he would turn against Agamemnon, would tangible results be obtained." And, Filho added, "I do not think the governor will speak to Agamemnon in this way."

His friends asked Filho if he would not take an airplane and fly to Pernambuco and talk to the governor directly. He declined. He did agree, however, that as soon as the party had returned from the north, he would talk to the newly elected Senator Sa, and to other friends of Agamemnon, and directly to

9. Jewish founder of the first major Brazilian industrial syndicate (FIESP), elected to parliament, 1934, finance minister under Vargas, and later foreign minister of Brazil.

Agamemnon, putting the case as strongly as possible. Beyond this he could not go.

This whole discussion left me with the discouraged sense that Filho, like so many others of his kind in similar position, would not really make a daring move; I did not believe him for a moment when he said, "of course, if I were secretary of labor, I would do what you wanted."

There was just time for us to have a bite of supper when, about half past eight, the Mindlins came to take us to the small temple up on the seventh floor of an office building, where the evening meeting was to be held. Dr. Mindlin spoke briefly in introduction; then I talked for perhaps half an hour to forty-five minutes. Dr. Mindlin's older son translated excellently as I went along. I felt a much more sympathetic atmosphere than in Rio.

....

Tuesday, April 16, 1935

I spent about an hour with Consul General Foster talking about the service and some common friends preliminary to my appeal to him on behalf of Dr. Alfons Salinger, now working temporarily with Dr. Lorch and said to be one of the most brilliant young scientists out of Germany. One of the head men at Mt. Sinai [Hospital in New York] is so anxious to have Salinger come to the States that he has agreed to put up a guarantee of $10,000. Foster listened sympathetically and I think will be as generous in his interpretation of the regulations as possible.

....

A group of our newly made friends came to see us off, and they really seemed as though we had known them a long time. They could not have been a greater contrast between the warm hearted and completely interested attitude of the Sao Paulo community and the surprising stand-offish attitude of the community in Rio. Though Olive Sawyer and I discussed several times the latter situation, I was not satisfied with any explanation which either she or I could suggest.

We had a pleasant drive down. Until one came to the Serra there was nothing spectacular in the drive; but when you reached the mountain, it was as though it fell off absolutely precipitously. You looked down upon Santos and the surrounding lowlands from a distance of eight or ten miles as though you were in an airplane. The road down must be driven with care. I was interested the explanation of the work being done by the electric light people in planning a huge reservoir which, built in the Serra, catches the almost continuous rains. The water is then guided down the precipice in huge pipes, about a meter in diameter, to the power plants at the foot. The power is then sent back to Sao Paulo.

....

The voyage on the SS *Highland Princess*, April 16–19, 1935

Pleasant but uneventful trip.

....

On the whole we liked the boat, despite indifferent food. It is so much cleaner and better run than was the *Western Prince.*

Montevidéo, Uruguay, April 19, 1935

We arrived in Montevidéo early Good Friday morning. Spent until lunch time seeing the town. The most interesting parts were the beaches and the well known Gaucho monument, which is so like our traditional conception of the covered wagon—a strikingly beautiful yet realistic treatment in bronze. I noted that of the small shops that were open, many of them seemed to be managed by Jews. In this natural indifference to the Catholic holidays one can imagine one source of anti-Semitism.

Buenos Aircs, Saturday, April 20, 1935

Arrived in Buenos Aires early after a quiet crossing of the river [Rio de la Plata]. Was met on thc boat by representatives of the English press, thc *Herald* and the *Standard.* I had made up my mind that it would be a mistake to try to dodge the press, as Oungre had urged, and that instead I should meet them frankly and try to induce them to present our case in such a way as not to give alarmist and misleading impressions.

....

In the late afternoon the representative of the *Nacion,* Angel Pizarro Lastra, came for an interview. He talked to me as much as I talked to him. He has been in the diplomatic service, speaks several languages, and is willing to discuss frankly the political situation here.

....

Mr. John H. White, representative of the [*New York*] *Times,* came to offer his services. He had received Sulzberger's letter. We talked about the political situation. He agreed that, despite the tendency here in certain quarters toward anti-Semitism, it would have been a mistake for me to attempt to avoid the press. He promised to send me a brief Who's Who on the members of the cabinet and to put me in touch, if I wished, with *La Prensa* and *La Nacion.* He stressed that it was important to see them both, if possible the same day, because each one was very jealous of the other.

....

Worked late with Miss Sawyer, sending out a large number of letters of introduction in the expectation that I should be able to get started full speed Monday morning.

....

Sunday, April 21, 1935

Was startled by Miss Sawyer's announcement that Inman had returned from Paraguay. . . . [10] It was a great relief to have him back, because we need every day we can possibly save for Argentina.

. . . .

In the late afternoon at the hotel a delegation representing the Jewish community came to call on me. It was made up of engineer Alberto Klein . . . , J. B. Eddis, . . . and S. Rabinowich. The latter is president of the central Jewish organization which disguises its general activities under the name "The Committee against Anti-Semitism." Engineer Klein had been to Montevidéo and is apparently one of the moderate well-balanced and highly respected leaders of the community. Eddis is a rich mine and land-owner, the man who began the production of cement in Argentina, a freelance, unwilling to assume organizational responsibility and inclined to be critical.

After getting acquainted, we talked in general terms about the situation of the community and the tendency towards anti-Semitism. They listed for me the following papers as anti-Semitic: *Crisol* and *Criterio*—both Catholic papers, the former a weekly and the latter fortnightly or monthly—*Bandera Argentine, La Fronda, La Voz Nacionalista.*

These are fascist or nationalist papers, markedly anti-Semitic, but none of them carrying great weight. Mr. Eddis said that the editor of the *Argentinische Tageblatt,* Dr. Aleman, the foremost critic of Hitlerism, is a man of great courage and of influence. He was anxious that I should meet him. . . . All the men agreed that the leading papers, such as the *Nacion* and the *Prensa,* were not only not anti-Semitic, but, on the contrary, had protested vigorously against the attacks of the fascists on German [*sic,* Jewish] shops, etc.[11]

The talk turned inevitably on the work of the ICA. Eddis, as I was to learn later, has a rather violent prejudice against ICA and attacked it and the directors as being aloof from the community and inclined in a bureaucratic manner to run everything from on high, or at any rate, from Paris. He thought that a great opportunity was missed by not setting up a local committee which would be representative of the Jewish and Argentinean interests, and through which ICA would cease to be looked upon as a foreign institution. He had talked for more than two hours to Oungre and had told him "many homely truths," but he had no faith that anything would be changed. Klein and Rabinowich were inclined to disagree with the harsher strictures of Eddis.

. . . .

10. Inman had gone at the invitation of President Ayala to receive a civilian decoration. This also enabled him to look into possibilities for exiled professors and scientists.

11. This probably refers to the events of *La Semana Tragica* (tragic week), which began on January 7, 1919, and led to the only pogrom in Latin American history. Right-wing "White guards," policemen, and vigilantes attacked Jewish stores and arrested many Jews as "Bolsheviks" in Buenos Aires, Rosario, and other Argentine cities during a national general strike by workers.

I sensed from this group at once the advantage of disregarding Louis Oungre's advice that I should avoid the Jewish community. They evidently were delighted that I was willing, as, of course, I ought to have been, to talk with them so frankly and to indicate my intention of learning everything I could from them and their colleagues.

....

Monday, April 22, 1935

Visit from Dr. Luis I. Berkman, a prominent young lawyer very active in Jewish communal work. During the hour that he was here we more or less boxed the compass in our discussion of Jewish and related problems. He impressed me as moderate and clear-headed. He was enthusiastic about Dr. Inman because of the latter's helpfulness to the Jewish group at the Montevidéo conference. Unlike Eddis, he was ready to admit the great achievements of ICA in Argentina, but was inclined to be somewhat critical because of what he considered to be too much absentee direction and too little integration of the ICA administration with the life of the community.[12] He explained the present status of the anti-Semitic agitation and told me of the attacks which had been made upon me in the more extreme of the anti-Jewish press, attacks which threatened forcible demonstration on my landing in Buenos Aires.

....

... [I went to the British Embassy and] found the British ambassador typing on an old-fashioned machine in his office. He is more the bluff businessman than the career diplomatist. He started, however, on the same note as had Sir William Seeds in Rio—that he could offer me no hope. He then developed the thesis that the regime here is fixed for the time being in its exclusionist policy, that there is almost nothing he could do, because he did not have instructions to take the initiative, but merely to be of assistance to me informally; that in any event, the Argentineans were beginning to feel that they could manage their own affairs, despite the fact that "we made this country." He agreed with the views that had been expressed to us by others about the minister of agriculture, Luis F. Duhau. But he told me that there was a probability that Duhau would be named as the president of the new Central Bank. He said that Duhau was very ambitious, and that from our point of view it would doubtless be an advantage if Duhau centered his activities in other fields than his present department.

A conference with Nathan Gesang, an ex-president of the Zionist Federation, a lawyer, who has maintained his interest in agriculture. He was extremely

12. ICA began operations in Argentina in 1889 by purchasing land in Santa Fe and established the agricultural colony of Moisesville, the first of many in the provinces of Santa Fe, Entre Rios, La Pampa, and Buenos Aires. 1930 was the peak of ICA settlement, with more than twenty thousand Jewish colonists farming over five hundred thousand hectares. During the 1930s several hundred German Jews settled in the colonies as well.

critical of the ICA organization and present work. He recognized that during the early decades an excellent task had been accomplished, but he insisted that recently nothing had been done to change the practices and principles which had become outworn. It is no longer creative either in developing new techniques in its old colonies or in establishing new colonies. Moreover, it had bought much of its land at such high prices that now it would be more economical for prospective colonization programs to secure their lands from other sources, as land is very cheap and new settlers could be established much more economically than estimated by the ICA authorities. It is a great mistake to leave the initiative in these matters to ICA. If properly organized, colonies could be made self-supporting and even to pay interest after a year or two. I listened to all of this criticism without comment, except to assure Gesang that the highest authorities of ICA were anxious to do their best.

After lunch with Inman, over to the American Embassy to see Mr. Cox.[13] Never have I sat through a more vacuous conference. Cox, though one hundred percent courteous, fenced with us as though we were itinerant tourists infringing upon his precious time. He did not know whether Lamas[14] was in town or when he would arrive nor did he seem very definite that he would be able to present us. He only became emphatic when he indicated that there was no possibility of doing anything to help us see the president. His lack of knowledge of affairs in this part of the world was shown by his confusion in reference to the Assyrian emigration to Brazil, and the fact that he seemed not to have read the morning paper about that same subject. When we left, both Inman and I burst into laughter at the solemn seriousness of the first secretary about nothing at all. We had learned much more from any one of the persons we had seen previously than we had from this American representative. If he does not show more initiative in informing his own government, I am sorry for the State Department.[15]

. . . .

Tuesday, April 23, 1935

Dr. Nissenson of the Federation Zionista came with his secretary. Most of the talk was his critcism of the various activities of ICA. . . . He charged that the ICA administration was not adapting itself to new conditions, that the local administration is too bureaucratic, and much too dependent upon Paris; that, therefore, a new orientation is needed which would enable ICA to do now the same sort of pioneer creative work it had done in the earlier decades. But if ICA would not do it, then it could be done on a purely business basis, because land is now available much cheaper than at the prices paid by ICA, and properly orga-

13. Cox, chargé d'affaires and first secretary of the U.S. Embassy.

14. Lamas, Argentinian foreign minister.

15. On May 10 Cox sent a despatch to the State Department explaining that he had made an appointment for McDonald to see the foreign minister. Cox, pointing out that McDonald did not represent the United States, asked for further instructions about requesting an audience with the president. Cox to secretary of state, May 10, 1935, National Archives (United States), Record Group 59, Central Decimal File, 548.D 1/228.

nized colonization schemes could be made to pay small interest after one or two years.

Interview with the correspondent of *Critica.* With him, as with all the other newspapermen, I emphasized the smallness of the immigration we proposed to bring in at present, and sought to show that it was only a part of a large problem; that, therefore, it was not exclusively Jewish.

Inman and I had an extremely interesting conversation with Dr. Carlos Alfredo Tornquist, to whom I had a letter of introduction from Dr. Rowe. The Tornquist firm had been, until its recent difficulties, more or less the J. P. Morgan of Argentina. Dr. Tornquist was more than courteous. He opened up at once and gave us some of our most realistic impressions of the political situation here. He agreed completely with what Dr. Alemann had told me the previous evening as to the importance of Dr. Paul Prebisch, the sort of sub-secretary of both the Ministries of Agriculture and Finance. He told us also that Miguel Angelo Carcano, son of the Argentinean ambassador to Brazil, may be Duhau's successor if the latter becomes the president of the new Central Bank. Another person in that department of great importance is Carlos Brebbia, formerly in the diplomatic service in Rome and there associated also with the Institute of Agriculture. He, as well as some of his colleagues, is said to be rather fascist and perhaps anti-Jewish. Dr. Tornquist was emphatic that no one could be so helpful as Mr. Alfredo Hirsch. As to Carcano, Dr. Tornquist suggested that he might be largely influenced by his Irish wife. Another personality of importance is Czerny. Dr. Tornquist felt that the influence of the archbishop would be very significant, with the president as well as with Duhau.

Dr. Tornquist, who has intimate contacts in Germany and elsewhere in Europe, values highly these relationships and asked to be remembered to his friend Max Warburg.

. . . .

After lunch a long conference with Dr. Isaac Weisburd, the president of the most important Jewish society in the city, and Dr. Berkman. I had asked particularly to see Mr. Weisburd, because I had been told that he had a definite program for Jewish immigration. However, as he developed it, I was rather disappointed, because it seemed to consist primarily in an effort to enlarge, through the active participation of Alfredo Hirsch and others, the guarantee fund which might be available to assure the Argentine authorities that immigrants would not become public charges. . . .

Since I was to see Alfredo Hirsch next, I took occasion to ask Mr. Weisburd and Berkman what line they thought I ought to take with Hirsch. Their advice was very definite but, it seemed to me, unsound. It was that I should endeavor to induce Hirsch to say that I might use his name when speaking to the government and to say that he would be with ICA and with others a guarantor for the financial soundness of the proposed immigration. My Jewish friends, who had been much disappointed by Hirsch's relative lack of interest in communal matters, seemed to feel that I should use this occasion to tie him in definitely on a financial basis. Quite soundly, they reasoned that his support would be very influential with the government; but I was unconvinced that I should follow their advice, because I felt in the first place that if I began on that line, Hirsch would refuse, or perhaps even resent it; and that, moreover, a quite different approach would offer a much better chance of eventually securing not only Hirsch's general interest, but his definite financial support.

Then over to Bunge and Bern for the long anticipated interview with the formidable Alfredo Hirsch. Inman went with me. Even the atmosphere of the outer office reflected the dominant personality inside. However, we were kept waiting only a few minutes.

As I saw Mr. Hirsch for the first time, I was again struck, as so often in the past, by the fact that observers almost invariably give a distorted picture of the people they seek to describe. It is true that Hirsch must walk with two canes, but aside from that, he is in no sense a physical cripple and would not strike one as being physically peculiar. His face is that of a powerful personality with a brilliant mind, and is thoroughly Jewish.

I began my talk rather brusquely by saying, "Mr. Hirsch, I was told in Europe, both in London and Paris, that you are the most powerful single individual in Argentina and can do more than anyone else to help us."

Then I outlined briefly what we hoped to accomplish. He was inclined to underestimate the task on behalf of the intellectuals, but perhaps because we did not take the time to canvass it thoroughly. On the larger problem of securing some amelioration of the immigration regulations, he was much more interested.

He began by saying that there was a special situation here now which would make it impossible for him to try to help us. That indeed, he would be from a certain point of view the very worst person to move directly with the government. To illustrate this, he told us, after pledging us most seriously not to repeat it, one of the most moving personal tales that I have ever heard. My colleague, Dr. Inman, sat throughout the narration (he told me later) as if he had been watching the unfolding of a tragic drama, which only a great dramatist could adequately have portrayed. I shared his impressions.

McDonald wrote a summary of the story as an insert. It follows here in double brackets.

[[A short period ago at the specific request of the president, he had put his name for membership in the X club [probably the Jockey Club] and had been rejected by the votes of the F. group, determined that, as a Jew, he should not be admitted.

When this action came to the attention of [the] president, he talked with our friend and asked him as a personal favor to allow his name to be resubmitted by the minister of war. After considerable hesitation he had consented.

A short time thereafter a friend of his whom he had known intimately for thirty years came to him privately and asked him to withdraw, saying that he was speaking for the F. group, who were determined that an assent should not be given. This despite the fact that they knew perfectly well that his candidacy was the result of the initiative of [the] president. In coming as a friend and asking the withdrawal, he was really doing a personal favor, because in this way a decisive issue could be avoided and a scandal averted.

Instead of giving a definite reply, our friend [Hirsch] wrote a note to [the] president, telling him of the situation and suggesting that, in order that matters might be easier for him, the withdrawal be agreed to. The latter sent his aide to say that he wished that our friend should not withdraw, that he personally would fight the issue through.

And there the matter rests at this time.

This brief summary gives no sense of the emotional stir which the telling of this story evoked in the teller and in those who listened. All the more, as he, speaking of his great position, his great power, the vast contributions he had made to the material development of the country, his lack of personal enemies, for he insisted that, despite his prominence, he had no personal enemies, and despite his complete association with this country, he could be made the object of this kind of attack. "And what am I to do, for I am a Jew."]]

How mistaken are those members of the community here and visitors like Oungre, who have gotten the impression that Hirsch is detached from this problem! He is detached only in the sense that he is not prepared to accept the community's view as to his duties. Of course, too, the fact that his children have been converted and have "married out" tends to separate him from the community. Nonetheless, I am persuaded that there are possibilities that he may yet be the most powerful factor in an ultimate solution of the problem of opening the immigration doors.

Following his personal story we continued our discussion of the difficulties ahead of us. It was not until I mentioned the possibility of seeing the archbishop that he showed any hopefulness. He said, "That is a brilliant idea." And became more enthusiastic about it, as I told him of my visits to the Vatican. I asked him who could put me in touch best with His Eminence. He promised that he would think it over and let me know the next day.

Then I asked him about seeing the president. He said that he was not sure he was officially in town, but he would find out, and at once went to the telephone but was unable to get the definite information. However, he said he might have it for us that evening or the next day. He did not hesitate to act for us.

Then we talked about conditions in Germany. I told him of the present practice of arresting the refugees who returned and of the developments which seem to me to indicate an ultimate declaration of a second-class citizenship, and also of the activities of German authorities throughout the world attempting to check our work on behalf of the refugees.

As we left, he showed that he was willing to continue our discussion and to help us further.

At the hotel I found the representative of the Jewish daily waiting for me, *Diario Israelita.* After a brief interview I received the executive committee of the Zionist Federation. This included Nathan Gesang, Isaac Kaplan (the president), and Samuel Rabinovich and Marcus Rosovsky (also presidents), Moises Slinin, José Lutzky, Jaime Epstein, Manuel Trope.

After a very generous statement of welcome by the president we talked for a time about Zionist affairs here, in Palestine, and the prospects for the next presidency. Most of these men were of course Weizmannites, but some of them admitted a secret admiration for Jabotinsky.

The most interesting part of the discussion, however, was that led by Mr. Kaplan, who is the active president of the Fraternidad Agraria, the union of cooperative societies in the ICA colonies. This is not controlled by ICA, but is an autonomous body. It acts both as a purchasing and as a selling agent for the colonies. It has been used as a model by the government in its plans for agricultural cooperatives. Moreover, the president of the National Bank has said that never once, even in the most difficult times, has there been a loss from loans to these cooperatives, and that this cannot be said of any other cooperatives in the republic.

. . . .

I asked to be excused from this conference at about eight o'clock, because I was then very tired and had to face the prospect of several hours more of conferences that evening.

. . . .

At engineer Klein's house, where I arrived about half past nine, I found gathered leaders of the community . . . ,[16] a very representative group.

The discussion was opened by my summary statement of some of my experiences during the last year and a half and my concluding appeal that the Jewish community here in Argentina follow the example of the relatively small Spanish

16. Samuel Rabinovich, president of the Central Committee of Jewish Societies,
Simon Mirelman, a member of the Central Committee on the board of the hospital,
Louis I Berkman, secretary of the Central Committee and formerly on the board of the B'nai B'rith, of the asylum and other institutions,
Jacobo Bendahan, president of the B'nai B'rith and formerly president of the Jewish Congregation,
J. B. Eddis, ex-president of B'nai B'rith and formerly of the Jewish Congregation,
Dr. N. Rapaport, president of the Hebrew Society and director of the Jewish Hospital,
Dr. Lén Dujovne, a member of several Jewish boards,
Dr. Natan Gesang, former president of the Zionist Organization,
Isaac Starkmeth, director ICA,
Ing. Simon Weil, director ICA,
Isaac Weisburd, president of the Chevrah Keduscha and of the Jewish Chamber of Commerce,
Alberto Hazen, president of the Safaradi Jewish Community,
Adolfo Hirsch, president of the Hilfsverein der Deutsche Juden,
Dr. Isaac Garcia, ex-president of B'nai B'rith and Jewish Congregation.

and German-Jewish groups in the States forty or fifty years ago, when they encouraged the large flow of immigration from central and eastern Europe. I offered to answer questions in reference to our work or conditions in Germany, but suggested that our major purpose of the evening was to get their reactions to my central proposal and to receive their specific suggestions as to methods which I should follow in advancing our purpose here. The discussion which followed was closely limited to these technical points. Dr. Garcia argued that one door is already wide open and only needs to be utilized—the door of colonization. He urged, too, that there should be an active campaign of publicity to advance the cause. He insisted that to bring about further colonization no changes were necessary in the legal regulations.

To this, Starkmeth replied that theoretically this was true, but that in practice it was not so; that, moreover, the refugees were not primarily agriculturists. But as to my major point, the attitude of the community, Starkmeth, after expressing generously the community's thanks to me, said that I could be sure that Argentine Jewry would unqualifiedly do its part to make a larger immigration possible.

Dr. Rapaport supported this general statement of Starkmeth's.

Mr. Hirsch, after referring to the work of his particular committee, said that he thought the only lever that could be effectively used was the archbishop; that Pinedo, the minister of finance, was also a key man. In reply to Starkmeth's suggestion that there were no agriculturalists among the refugees, said that young people could successfully be adapted.

Mr. Glucksman, who is one of the most wealthy of the active Jewish leaders, said he was sure the means could be found to care for all of the immigrants who would be allowed to come.

Mr. Weil tended to support Mr. Garcia's view, arguing that the immigrants need not to have been agriculturists, but only coming for agriculture. He said that there is a vast space available at extraordinarily cheap prices.

Starkmeth replied that it was not true that it would be sufficient for immigrants to be intended for agriculture—they must be able to prove to the consul that they are agriculturists. This is the point which Oungre had emphasized to me as being so discouraging in the Argentinean situation.

During the discussion of this point it was brought out that in fact there is nothing whatsoever in the constitution to justify an exclusionist policy; that on the contrary, the constitution speaks of Argentina being open unreservedly to any one who wants to come and work here. Moreover, the basic immigration law is not in any sense an exclusionist one. In fact, the whole system of restrictions rests on a series of decrees which were restated and harmonized in the decree [left blank].

. . . . . .

Rabinovich spoke of the large influence of Dr. Inman in political circles here, and of the advantage of preliminary work before a formal approach to the governmental authorities was made.

After the discussion had continued for more than two hours and a half, it was summarized by one of the members as follows:

"The Argentine community is absolutely prepared to play its part. Up till now no Jewish immigrant has been allowed to become a public charge. The Jewish cooperatives are indications of what can be done. One should urge upon the government the necessity of immigration as a means of providing consumers for the surplus production of basic materials. In these ways one could make a convincing case for the opening of the doors."

....

About midnight Mrs. Klein invited us all to have supper.

....

Wednesday, April 24, 1935

Dr. Browning, secretary of Inman's committee, called. He thinks that Paraguay will eventually be destroyed by the superior forces of Bolivia.[17] He is skeptical of any support for our project from the archbishop, for he says that the Church is definitely opposed to Jewish immigration, as indicated by some of the Catholic organs. He had been surprised by the outburst of Catholic enthusiasm on the occasion of the visit of Pacelli, but he felt that that had now died down.

An extremely interesting talk with young Frederick Waisnau of the *Mundo Israelita.* He recalled to me that he had been the young man chosen by the refugees to speak for them at the rue Durance about a year ago, when I went to the headquarters of the Comité National there to see the work on behalf of the refugees in Paris. Some of the tales he told me of what had gone on while he was in Paris, particularly the brutal actions of some of the lesser functionnaires of the National Committee, were shocking and disheartening. For example, the tale of a mother calling with her child at the committee headquarters and asking for money to buy bread and being refused brusquely, she then insisting that her husband was desperately ill and that she must have help. The reply of the functionnaire was, "When your husband dies, bring us the death certificate and we will help you."

Weisnau was lavish in his praise of the attitude of the members of the committee at Woburn House [London] as contrasted with that of the functionnaires in Paris. He spoke of Rawson and the others as sympathetic and extraordinarily helpful, for they really sought to understand each individual case.

Then I asked him about the work of the Jewish committees here in receiving and aiding the immigrants. He was far from enthusiastic. He said that Adolfo Hirsch of the Hilfsverein meant well and was energetic in raising funds, but the actual work was unsatisfactorily done.

17. Reference is to the Chaco War (1932–1935) over the 100,000-square-mile Chaco Boreal territory between Paraguay and Bolivia. At the peace negotiations Paraguay was awarded most of the territory.

I asked him why he had left Germany. He replied that he had been a medical student when the Nazis came in. He saw his career blocked and left. Now he expects to build a different career here.

....

Back to the hotel to receive a telephone call from Alfredo Hirsch, saying that the archbishop would receive me that afternoon and that he was sending his man and a friend of the archbishop to take me over. I said that I was ready to go at once.

Presently Francisco A. Leguizamon, a lawyer and the man from Hirsch's office, came for me. I had to decide quickly whether or not to ask Inman to go along. There were obvious advantages in doing so because of his intimate knowledge of Spanish, but a danger also because of his association here with Protestant activities. I decided to risk it and asked him to go along.

As we were entering the Episcopal Palace, we learned that the man who was to introduce us thought we were Germans. We paused in the portals long enough to straighten him out on that point and to make clear to him our mission and to emphasize particularly my previous connections with Pacelli. This last heartened him.

When we reached the ante-room, I explained to the archbishop's secretary again who we were and my previous visits to the Vatican. We were kept waiting only a few minutes, and then were shown into the presence of the archbishop.[18]

He received us in a friendly manner, and our conversation continued for well over half an hour. I began by explaining in French my relations to the cardinal secretary of state, my impressions of the dangers to the Church in Germany, stressing the point of view that the attack there is not on the Jews alone or even primarily but upon all religions; that, therefore, the Church was facing perhaps the most serious danger since Luther. And to illustrate this I told the story of Goebbels's ambition to make the Nuremberg Party Congress the Eucharistic Congress of the Third Reich.

After this rather prolonged introduction, which seemed to make just the impression I desired, I turned to Inman and asked him to explain in Spanish more about our specific mission. This he did. Then the archbishop began to ask certain questions as to who the people were who would come, were they radicals or communists etc. We assured him on all these points.

It was in this connection that he launched into a statement about the proselytizing tendencies of certain North American Protestant groups here, which he deplored greatly and which he said were opposed by the Argentine people. Inman's face must have been a study.

But more important was the archbishop's categorical statement that the Church was not opposed to Jewish immigration; that, on the contrary, the Jews

18. Santiago Luis Copello, named archbishop of Buenos Aires in 1932 and cardinal (and primate of Argentina) in 1935.

as well as the Protestants, should be faithful to their own religions, that the Church had often been strengthened by Jews who had become Christians, and, of course, Christ and the Apostles had been Jews, and that here in Argentina the Jews had often helped the Church and converts had frequently given great strength. When the archbishop spoke of the founder of Christianity as a Jew, I reminded him that of course the Nazi theorists deny this. He laughed and said, "Of course that is natural, with their pagan ideology."

I took occasion to tell him of my interviews with Brüning at the beginning of the Nazi regime and of the latter's fear for the Church. Inman supplemented what I had to say by telling of the experiences of professors married to converted Jewesses, who were given the alternative of divorce or resignation.

. . . .

We explained in detail what we hoped to secure here from the government. The archbishop indicated that he not only would not oppose, but would favor such concessions. I had told him of the attitude of the cardinal in Rio. Then I asked him if he would be willing to speak to the president along these lines.

In replying, he said that the president was a very just, very equitable man; that he saw him from time to time, and that on the next occasion he would speak to him of this matter.

I did not ask him to speak to the minister of agriculture, for I feared that that might be a mistake.

As we were leaving and I was expressing my thanks for his cooperative attitude, I told him that I would be sure to express to Pacelli when I next saw him our appreciation of His Eminence's willingness to support our efforts.

As we left, our two companions expressed their satisfaction with the interview. I think, indeed, that Hirsch's man probably gave him an enthusiastic report.

Then we discussed the question of the engagement with the president. It was left that Hirsch's man and Leguizamon should go over to the Executive Offices at once to inquire.

Inman and I went back to the hotel. We could not refrain from amused comment on the scene when His Eminence was criticizing militant Protestantism, though, of course, as a matter of fact, Inman has not himself been a militant or interested in that kind of Protestant activity in Latin America for many years.

. . . Over to the *Prensa.*

. . . .

The owner of the paper, Dr. Ezequiel P. Paz, the son of the founder, is a charming man, but like most Argentineans, he can never forget the problem of Argentinean meat. We listened, therefore, attentively and patiently while he talked for five or ten minutes on the inevitability of the United States needing Argentine meat as soon as headway is made at home against unemployment.

After we had explained our mission, he expressed his cordial sympathy and put his services at our disposal, and I think he really meant it.

In order that the story might be presented in the *Prensa,* he sent for one of the writers, Enrique Lipschutz, who had come to Argentina as a Jewish immigrant more than forty years ago.

Needless to say, he listened sympathetically to my story and promised to write it up as I suggested he do.

....

Thursday, April 25, 1935

....

Then to the office of J. Saslavsky, head of the firm of Luis Dreyfus y Cia., the next largest grain dealer after Bunge and Born. Saslavsky was critical of Mr. Oungre's mission on the following grounds: (1) he had burnt over the ground before my coming, and having been rejected, made my task more difficult; (2) Oungre's effort had been made on too economical and secretive a basis; the latter was not only a functionnaire but what was worse, a "French functionnaire"; the work here needed a different approach. Moreover, Oungre's talk of a guarantee of $200,000 was not such as to impress Pinedo, the minister of finance; (3) to be successful the immigration approach would have to be on a much broader basis than Oungre had suggested. It must be more than Jewish.

This last point was amplified by Saslavsky in an extremely suggestive way. He argued that the time has [come and] gone for successful development of Jewish immigration as such. The ICA had done an extraordinary task, but it was not fitting itself to the new day. The time is ripe for the organization of a large concern on a purely commercial basis for the introduction into Argentina of tens of thousands of immigrants, a fixed proportion of which might be Jews. Now is exactly the time for this effort because, with the organization of the new national bank and the financial machinery for the liquidation of frozen domestic assets, excellent land in many parts of the republic must be disposed of at bargain prices—prices much lower than the ICA lands. If a syndicate headed by London and New York Jews and supported by Jews in Argentina were organized, it could almost dictate its own terms to the government, provided only Pinedo and the other authorities were convinced that real capital was behind the proposal. As to local support, Saslavsky felt sure that this was the kind of a proposal which Alfredo Hirsch not only would support, but might even take the initiative in organizing.

I was the more impressed by this presentation of Saslavsky, because it was based on the same fundamental thesis as that which had been advanced by Dr. Alemann a few nights before at Mr. Eddis's house. It was, in a word, that it would be easier to secure the admission of 100,000 immigrants, including 10,000 Jews, than to secure permission for the entrance of 1,000 Jews alone. In short, that to try to solve the Jewish problem alone is to court defeat.

Of course, in estimating the soundness of the views of Saslavsky on this point, one must remember that he, while a Jew, cannot bring himself to be interested wholly or merely in Jewish affairs from the communal point of view. In this he is like Alfredo Hirsch.

Saslavsky thought that the best approach to the government here is through the British ambassador. He agreed, of course, that the influence of the archbishop could be very great. The key man, however, he thinks, is Pinedo, an extraordinarily intelligent and discriminating leader. Duhau is, of course, also important, but in that department perhaps the sub-secretary of agriculture, Carlos Brebbia, is perhaps a more serious obstacle to our success, for he is fascist in inclination and possibly anti-Semitic. But one must not forget that the president himself, though he does not usually choose to intervene in matters which concern specific departments, is a man of great intelligence and capable of decisive action. Therefore, one's approach perhaps should be directly to the president. As to Saavedra Lamas, the minister of foreign affairs, he is not likely in a matter of this sort, to have great influence.

At the end Saslavsky disclosed to me his own personal attitude towards Judaism—an attitude quite common among the most successful Jews financially, but it is not an attitude which is likely ever to make an appeal to the really religious Jews. However, it tends to justify Weizmann's theory that Judaism can only hope to be perpetuated through the "saving" remnants.

Saslavsky recognized Alfredo Hirsch as the financial leader in Argentina and gave me the impression that he would be prepared to follow in any program which Hirsch worked out or supported. Indeed, he said that Hirsch's interest was such as to make him the logical director of such an enterprise. Saslavsky said he hoped I would see him again before I left.

. . . .

After the conference [at the Instituto Cultural Argentino Norte-Americano], accompanied by Dr. Nelson and another official of the Institute, Inman and I paid our formal visit to *La Nacion*. . . . We had a long talk with one of the editors, Mr. Antakoletz, a Jew who already knew much of our work, had read my report, and was extremely well informed about conditions in Germany. The whole group of Argentines were unanimous in their condemnation of the German regime as barbarous. As the talk developed, the thought occurred to me again the extent to which Germany is provoking enmity in every part of the world.

. . . .

During dinner I took full advantage of my place next to Prebisch to talk to him throughout the meal. We discussed conditions in Germany, the development of our work (this giving me a chance to make clear to him the limited nature of our proposals here).

Though critical of a large-scale immigration, he seemed sympathetic to our smaller proposal. He told me that though technically he is the head of the economics department of the National Bank, he has in fact been assigned for some time to the government, and has been in close relations with the departments of Agriculture and of Finance.

After dinner for more than an hour the talk centered about Prebisch. He outlined and defended vigorously his central thesis that for the time being, Argentina is not a field for large-scale colonization. A Dr. Weil who was present, a member of the grain firm by that name, argued that the country needed 100,000 immigrants to develop its resources and to begin to build up an economy which would make the country less dependent on the export market. Prebisch admitted that as a long range program this might be desirable, but insisted that, at present, it was purely academic to urge it. He argued that unless and until the rest of the world, particularly the United States and Europe, changed their importation policies and began again to enable Argentina to export, this country cannot accept Europe's exports of human beings—nor for that matter any considerable amount of European or American export of capital. On this latter point he contended that much of Argentina's present financial difficulty from the point of view of exchange arises out of its excessive borrowings in 1926 and 1927.

Throughout his argumentation Prebisch showed himself to be a devoted advocate of the principles of free exchange in every field, but in practice he insisted that until the rest of the world returned to sanity in these respects, Argentina must keep its doors almost complete closed to the income of immigrants or capital. He denied, however, that he and his colleagues had faith and were practicing the principles of a planned economy. He said that they could not know enough to do this.

He elaborated a point that he had made to me during the meal—one which weakens greatly the larger program which Saslavsky had outlined to me the day previous—that is, that the lands now being turned over to the new liquidation organization by the banks which had had to foreclose and then were unable to dispose of the properties, would not be available for settlement by immigrants from abroad. He said that these lands, except in very small part, were already occupied by Argentine farmers who had previously been tenants, but now would be given an opportunity to become peasant proprietors through easy terms spread over a period of twenty-five or thirty years. Moreover, these farmers experienced in Argentine conditions and in the use of machinery are in a much better position to succeed than would European immigrants be. He cited as proof of this last contention the situation of a group of Danish agriculturalists just south of Buenos Aires who, though well trained in Danish methods, had not been able to establish as high a standard of living for themselves as was maintained by their surrounding neighbors, Argentines of Italian or other extraction.

Inman argued that until the country was much more thickly occupied than at present, it would be impossible to supply to the farmers the essential facilities—schools, doctors, hospitals, etc.—which would induce [*sic*] to that higher standard of living essential if the provinces are to absorb a substantially larger part of their own production and of the industrial production of the cities. He implied that Prebisch was taking only the short-range view and ignoring the basic necessity for filling up the vacant areas. Prebisch admitted the desirability of this development, but contended that it could not be done in a year or two, and that until world conditions changed, the admission of large numbers of people would only make matters worse. Meantime, he said, the movement was under way to send to the country as fast as possible surplus population of Buenos Aires.

Dr. Dang argued that, instead of making land available to tenants for purchase on long terms, they should be allowed to rent it at nominal terms, thus discouraging them from becoming speculators in land. I replied that it seemed to me unreal to assume that the owner or the prospective owner of 80 or 100 acres would become a speculator, or so rich that he would not have to expend most of his income to maintain his family.

Everybody agreed that what Argentina needs is more domestic consumption, a higher standard of living for the masses with all that that would mean in the utilization of agricultural and industrial production. But throughout, Prebisch stuck to his contention that this end could not be advanced at present by the encouragement of immigration or the investment of capital.

He admitted, of course, that individuals who came to the country with a small capital of their own should be welcome. But if they had had to borrow this capital with the expectation of repaying it abroad, he would not recognize their coming as desirable. This, of course, had an obvious direct relation to our suggestion that the refugees be advanced funds or that the groups in New York and London invest substantial amounts in the country. Unless Saslavsky was entirely mistaken about Pinedo, the minister of finance does not share Prebisch's tendency to resist the incoming of capital.

....

During the latter part of the evening the talk returned to the narrower subject of Dr. Inman's and my task here. I disavowed any immediate interest in the large-scale immigration proposal which had been suggested to me the day previous by Saslavsky. I was anxious that Prebisch should not confuse that with our much more modest immediate objective. He did discriminate and said that he thought some hundreds a month, totaling during a period four or five thousand, would be possible. Earlier, when we had been talking at dinner, he said he would be glad to arrange for me to meet Dr. Brebbia, the undersecretary of agriculture, who, he said, was the key person in this problem. I got the impression that he not only would do this, but would do it in such a way as to give us a favorable start with the department.

Friday, April 26, 1935

Bernardo Meyer-Pellegrini, a friend of the Rosenwalds, called in the morning. It is his brother who is so active in politics. Unfortunately, he is now abroad. Bernardo recently lost his entire fortune, and for a time, as he told me, was so shocked by the betrayal of a friend that he could not speak. Even now, he shows the marks of the blow. He said that he was an intimate friend of Duhau and offered to help in that direction. But I felt that I ought not to accept his suggestion—at least not immediately. It was left, therefore, that I was to be free to call upon him at any time when he could help. He said that I should telephone him at his house in the morning before nine o'clock.

Dr. Hugo Salomon, the friend of Rosenwald's, a distinguished specialist on metabolism who, immediately after the war sensing the danger of fascist developments in Europe, prepared to come to Argentina, where he has been for many years, came to see Inman and me. Unfortunately, he was unable to make many suggestions to us about places for intellectuals. Instead, he repeated what we were to hear so often later, the conditions which make practically impossible the admission not only of doctors and lawyers, but of intellectuals of any sort.

. . . .

At the Foreign Office Dr. Inman ran into some friends of his, whom he had known at Montevidéo or earlier. They greeted him with great cordiality, spoke of knowing his books, etc. But when we were shown into the office of the secretary of the minister, our reception there confused us. The secretary did not seem to know that we were supposed to have an appointment with the minister, and so, for fifteen minutes or more, he and we carried on a verbal fencing match, we making clear to him our mission, and he apparently trying to make up his mind as to whether he would suggest to the minister that we be admitted. When he finally went out to inquire, Inman and I joined in vigorous denunciations of the stupidity or weakness of the American Embassy in not having acted more effectively in arranging the conference.

Finally, however, we were shown into Dr. Carlos Saavedra Lamas's office. He and Inman greeted one another with cordial expressions of friendship and mutual admiration. I presented my letter from Dr. Rowe. Then, after Inman had delivered his personal message from the secretary of state, we got down to the subject of our mission. Here Saavedras Lamas was not very satisfactory. He seemed to prefer to talk about the great advantages of immigration to Paraguay. For President Ayala he expressed high praise and for the richness of the latter's country [Paraguay]. All of this seemed to me, however, as little more than diplomatic stalling.

Saavedras Lamas did, however, speak about the possibilities of immigration as soon as the liquidation organization was in a position to dispose of its lands. But here he talked, it seemed to me, without much knowledge, and in any event he reiterated that the time was not quite ripe for the utilization of these lands. However, he said he would discuss the matter with his colleagues, but this did not convince me that he would move effectively.

As we were leaving, I seized the opportunity to tell him that I had heard his name mentioned in connection with the Nobel Peace Prize abroad. He smiled with pleasure, but modestly said that the Nobel Peace Prize which he wished was to succeed in ending the Chaco war. I whispered to Inman to ask about an interview with the president. He did so, but Saavedras Lamas's reply was noncommittal. In this again there was an indication of how we had been disadvantaged by the Embassy's weakness.

....

[Minister of Agriculture] Brebbia was cordial enough when I was shown in. I told him that I knew of his work in Rome, in the diplomatic service, and in the Institute of Agriculture. He said that he had in all spent nearly 20 years abroad, and, as he later underlined significantly, "I have been in Europe so much that it is no longer a fetish for me."

As I had planned, I began by telling him that I was not there to try to "sell him" a definite program, but rather, to confer with him and to ask his help in solving the problem which faced us. I explained that we were concerned with a limited immigration and that there would be definite guarantees against the newcomers becoming public charges. He at once asked just how would such guarantees be given. I replied that if it were deemed necessary, it might be possible to create an Argentine corporation for that purpose (this suggestion Dr. Berkman and I had discussed earlier).

Brebbia soon indicated that he and his colleagues were formulating a program for their country which they wished to carry out without interference from abroad. I told him that I sympathized heartily with this objective and that I admired the devotion which he, Prebisch, and others were giving to this cause. But I asked if he did not agree that Argentina in the long run needed more people. He said yes, but we must make sure to protect and to develop the Argentine race. The way he put this made me feel that the reports I had had about his tendency towards extreme nationalism, perhaps influenced a little by Nazism, had not been exaggerated.

He suggested that if I would submit a memorandum, he and his colleagues would study it and would be able to give me an answer within perhaps three days. I said that I wished to have the benefit of his counsel before I submitted a formal memorandum and asked him if he would be able to go over with me on Monday a draft. He said that he was too busy to do so on Monday, but asked that I submit the draft then, and said that he would confer with me on Wednesday. I reminded him that that was a holiday; he replied, "All the better; one will be less interrupted." It was on this note that I left.

Saturday, April 27, 1935

I should perhaps report that when Inman and I had a bite of supper with Ruth and Olive Sawyer the night previous, we were rather discouraged, Inman even more than I, because he had not been able to get a real hold in his efforts on behalf of the intellectuals. I therefore more or less insisted that he join Mr. Clark and me on Saturday at golf.

. . . .

At lunch [at Dr. Berkman's apartment] for the first time I heard a rather frank discussion of the question of social anti-Semitism in Buenos Aires. It appears that in the more exclusive social clubs there is either a rigid exclusion or an increasing tendency in that direction. I was interested in the fact that apparently no one had heard of the incident of the Yacht Club [*sic,* Jockey Club?].

Then out to the Tigre with Dr. Berkman and some of his friends—the Kleins and a Mr. Asscher and one or two others. It was a long drive out in the confusing and disquieting traffic of the city, but worthwhile when it was finished. The winding channel through the mazes of islands inhabited and uninhabited made a beautiful picture, especially at sunset time and in the dark. It is Buenos Aires's one natural resort.

After tea drove back with Dr. Berkman, who told me of evidences of anti-Semitism in the exclusion of the young Jewish candidates from the police and recently in a medical school examination. He insisted, however, that these attitudes were not natural, that they were purely the result of German influence, and would, he hoped, die out with the decline of the prestige of that influence. He reminded me too that the growing influence of the Socialists might serve as an antidote.

Sunday, April 28, 1935

Worked during the morning with Olive Sawyer.

Family luncheon at the Eddis's. The talk ranged over many subjects, including some of Mr. Eddis's favorite topics, such as the possibilities of Argentina, etc. I was increasingly impressed by his thoroughness, his driving qualities, and his good Jewishness.

. . . .

Then with the rest of the Eddis family to the ballet at the Colon Theater. I have never seen a more magnificent theater. It is modeled on the Scala of Milan and would compare more than favorably with the Metropolitan. Most of the ballets were interesting.

Afterwards to tea at the "Paris," the rendezvous of the smart set at tea-time.

Monday, April 29, 1935

. . . .

At 10:30 I went over to the apartment of Schwelm. . . . [19] He seemed to me more bloated and affected by drink than when I met him first in London. But

19. Don Adolpho Julio Schwelm, a German-English Argentine who promoted European emigration and colonization of Misiones Province in Argentina, where he founded the city of El Dorado.

he was just as intelligent and as interesting on his favorite subject of Eldorado and colonization in general.

He was extremely critical of the ICA administration, claimed that they lacked entirely in any after-care, and for that matter, so did all the other colonization programs except his own. He told me of a specific proposal he had made to Max Warburg in reference to a possible settlement of 2,000 persons. I suggested that he send me a copy. He said that Warburg had been favorably impressed, but had replied that the matter had to be handled by Oungre and me. I left with a felling that Schwelm is brilliant, but that I cannot follow up on his proposal, and that he cannot be useful in our project here in Buenos Aires.

Luncheon with Inman at the home of Dr. Edouardo Krapf, Dr. Demuth's correspondent here. It was a disheartening story that he and his wife told. She is an Argentinean, the niece of Alfredo Hirsch; he has Argentine citizenship, though he left Germany only a year and a half or so ago. He is a brilliant neurologist, a specialty in which there are almost no practitioners in this country. Incidentally, he speaks Spanish perfectly. Despite all of these factors and despite also the fact that his wife's uncle has exerted every influence he could, it has not been possible to find a place in a hospital or to secure permission for Dr. Krapf to practice. No wonder he is discouraged about the possibility of placing other intellectuals.

I was interested in one condition which I had not realized, which makes the placing of intellectuals more difficult in this country. This is the tendency of professional men to hold six or even eight different posts in different fields. For example, a professor must be very conscientious and strong-willed not to accept an additional post if it becomes available, even if he has no particular qualification for the job. What a system!

I fell in love with the five-year old daughter of the house, who, when she was introduced to me and I spoke to her in English, quickly pulled herself together, and instead of replying in Spanish, used with perfect correctness a few of the English words which she was just beginning to learn. Later, the two of us and her mother visited together in the nursery. She told her mother that Mr. McDonald was so nice that she would like to meet Mrs. McDonald also.

Over with Inman to see Prebisch at the Ministry of Agriculture. At lunch Krapf, Inman, and I had discussed the question of a memorandum for the Argentine authorities. Krapf and Inman were strongly of the opinion that it would be a mistake to present a formal request, which would require a formal answer. They insisted that this would be to invite a refusal for two reasons: one, officials always hesitate to commit themselves in writing whenever there is the possibility of an attack; (2) in this case there is more than the probability of an attack, because the nationalists and the anti-Semites are only waiting to criticize any obvious concession. I was persuaded by these arguments.

In the conference with Prebisch I told him of my talk with Brebbia and of the latter's suggestion of a memorandum. I then asked Prebisch whether he thought it would be better to keep the whole thing on an informal plane. He was sure it would be. He then read the draft of my memorandum, thought that it was much too formal, and agreed with Inman that something more in the nature of a letter would be better. He seemed to feel that it might be possible on this basis to get a kind of gentleman's agreement which would accomplish the same purpose as a formal assent without involving the risks of the latter.

....

Inman and I were taken by Mr. Ewing to the House of the People, the Socialist headquarters, where we met and talked with several of the most important Socialist leaders, including Dr. Gimenez, who has been most active in fighting the white-slave traffic and in advancing social legislation; Dickmann, the official leader, a vigorous and discriminating man; Repetto, one of the intellectual leaders; Solari, and two or three others. The talk was partly about conditions in Germany, of which they showed intimate knowledge, but more about our work here, for the success of which they expressed sympathy and a willingness to help politically. Unfortunately, since the present regime is an extremely conservative one, and in some respects perhaps even an unconstitutional one, I did not think it wise to ask for definite action by the Socialists at this time.

Had to hurry with Ewing via the subway to reach Alfredo Hirsch's office by 6:30. I found him at his desk, engrossed in the study of many balance sheets, the totals of which seemed to run into hundreds of thousands, or millions, of pesos. But he settled back, and we talked for about forty-five minutes. I told him of my interviews since we had last met, particularly of those with Prebisch and with Brebbia. He thought that this had been the best way to move. I added that I had been disappointed that an appointment with the president had not yet been made. He called in his man Markus to inquire why the delay. The latter explained that the president's secretary had assumed that we had been received the day our cards had been presented, immediately following our reception at the archbishop's palace. Hirsch instructed Markus to move as energetically as possible.

The name of Dr. Ernesto F. Alemann came up. This was the occasion of Hirsch's expression of wondering admiration that Alemann, as a businessman, dared to continue to fight the Nazis so openly and without the least sign of compromise. Hirsch said, "He is a terrible fighter." It was easily seen that Hirsch, with all his tens of millions and his business interests dominating the grain trade in Argentina and in many parts of South America and reaching to every part of the world, was himself unwilling to risk any part of his business by a similar attitude.

Our talk reverted inevitably to conditions in Germany and their effect upon the international situation. Hirsch hopes that the Reich will be involved in such a way as to lead to the overthrow of the present regime, for he is of the opinion that only so can the present tendency for Nazism to spread be checked. Again, he showed his interest in the possibility of the Church and the Jewish leaders working more closely together. He was delighted that the views I had expressed to the archbishop about the danger to the Church had been strikingly vindicated by the events in Germany during the past week. He would, I think, be interested in the proposal which I had raised tentatively with some of the leaders in Europe. But I did not feel that I could broach this subject now, particularly that I could not ask his financial support until after canvassing the local situation here much more thoroughly. I had decided that it would be impossible to get from him a large amount for more direct refugee purposes.

Hirsch became so interested in our discussion that he followed me to the door, and even said that he would see me downstairs. This, from a man who is accustomed to give orders, was indicative of how much he is stirred.

It remains to be seen whether Hirsch's substantial response will in any wise match his intellectual and emotional reaction.

Back to the hotel late and too tired to go out to the dinner, which Mr. Ewing had arranged and to which he had invited Inman and me to meet eight or ten literary men and to hear the discussion of local and national problems. Instead, Ruth, who had not been feeling very well, and I had a bit of supper downstairs.

Tuesday, April 30, 1935

Lunch as the guest of Pedro Weil on the top floor of Buenos Aires's chief skyscraper. This building is one of the Hirsch properties. . . .

Our talk was mostly about conditions in Germany. However, I had a chance to become better acquainted with Pedro Weil. He is, at the age of thirty-two or thirty-three, the senior partner in the second largest grain firm in this country. He is much more a member of the community than Hirsch in every way. He invited me to visit his *estancia* [country estate or ranch] in the state of Santa Fe, which he says is the richest part of the country. I told him I should like to do it—and would have done so had it been possible for him to go with me, for this would have given us a chance for long talks together. He, however, had to see his mother off on the boat the following Saturday, so I decided to postpone my weekend in the country. But I left the luncheon with the feeling that Pedro Weil was a man to be counted upon.

Inman has recently been telling me disquieting reports to the effect that the leaders of the American colony, when they learned of our visit, had met together to decide whether or not we should be officially received; that with the approval of the Consul General Warren,[20] they had decided in the negative. At first, I could not take this report seriously, but Inman, knowing Americans abroad in

20. Avra M. Warren, American consul general in Buenos Aires, 1932–1935. McDonald's difficulties with Warren here (and further, in chap. 25) are telling in light of Warren's subsequent actions. In May 1939, as chief of the State Department's Visa Division, Warren instructed American diplomats in Havana not to press the Cuban government to admit the passengers of the SS *St. Louis*. In November 1939, following an inspection tour of American consulates in Europe, Warren instructed consuls to toughen visa requirements and to sharply reduce the number of visas to those (by then desperately) seeking to enter the United States. Richard Breitman and Alan M. Kraut, *American Refugee Policy*, 65–66, 71–72, 119.

Latin America better than I, went directly to Warren about it. He learned there that this report was true, that Warren had approved this action on the ground that we were not officially representing the United States, that the United States was not a member of the League, that our mission concerned a controversial issue here where there are conflicting interests of the Jews and anti-Jews, the pro and the anti-Nazis, etc. Inman took a strong line and insisted that he would not tolerate this kind of sabotage and intended to report it in Washington.

Furthermore, Inman told me that there had been protests to Dr. Enrique Gil following the reception for me at the Argentine-North American Cultural Association.

With these reports in the forefront of my mind, it was not difficult to imagine with what feelings I attended the cocktail party for the American community given by Mr. and Mrs. Ascher Reese, the head of the General Electric interests here, at the Plaza Hotel. The host is a New Zealander and his wife an Argentinean, but at least half of the group were American. I was much interested in Mr. Warren's reaction when, as I was talking with Mr. Reese, Warren came up. Mr. Reese introduced us, Warren and I shook hands, and then he, without saying a word, or certainly nothing more than how do you do, turned his back and walked away. I thought he looked as though he were embarrassed.

After the party the Clarks and Ruth and I went off to an excellent dinner at the Jockey Club.

25. May 1935: Regret and Relief

Buenos Aires, Wednesday, May 1, 1935

Mr. Isidoro Weil called for Inman and me at about eight to play golf at the Olivos course. It is not a bad course, but nowhere to be compared with San Andreas. My golf was very bad.

Lunch at the Weil home, we having picked up Ruth on the way back from the golf course. Mrs. Weil is a charming and vivacious woman, and we had a jolly time.

On the way to Weil's we happened to pass in the street the automobile of Alfredo Hirsch, in which he was returning from his morning at the office, though this was a national holiday. He called at the Weils and invited us all over for tea. So after a welcome nap, while the others went out for a drive, we all went to the palatial home of Alfredo Hirsch.

After tea Mr. Hirsch undertook to show us his treasures. First, he took Inman and me to see his unique pre-Maya beautifully painted and preserved clay Indian head. Then we examined rare, early sixteenth-century Bibles and original editions of many notable books. Later, he took us upstairs and opened his safe to show us, among other extraordinarily valuable books, a beautifully preserved first edition of Las Casas.[1] Inman was thrilled as I have never seen him before by the opportunity to handle these precious books. Throughout these examinations the daughter, who was with us, showed as much interest and as deep a knowledge of everything as did her father. He said to me, with a show of feeling, that it was only his daughter who was interested; his boys didn't care for these things.

Then Hirsch showed us his Jesuit and Bolivian dining room. In the walls have been fitted some of the finest woodwork, doors, and paneling of the Jesuit period in the missions and in Paraguay. Many fine examples of Bolivian silver, plaques, and other forms were about the room, also pictures which fitted into the general colonial Jesuit style.

From there to the large music room with its Aeolian organ and its many pictures, including a large one of the Rembrandt period. Everything was in excellent taste and showed that the selections had been made by someone who really understood and appreciated what he was buying.

1. Bartolomé de Las Casas (1484–1566), Spanish priest who was the first to be ordained in the New World and became a staunch defender of native people in the Americas, defending their human rights before the Spanish monarchs. His most famous work was *The Destruction of the Indies,* a work highly critical of Hernando Cortes's expedition of conquest.

There was an amusing incident which needs no comment. Inman and I were admiring an early Renaissance marble Virgin and Child. Hirsch told us the story of his purchase of it. He had tried to buy it from a Viennese connoisseur, but they could not agree on the price. Later, the owner got into trouble through some shady dealings with a view to recovering unjustly from the insurance company. He was arrested, put in jail, and ultimately his objets d'art were sold by the court at a public auction, and Hirsch succeeded in getting his Madonna and Child at 500 florins less than he had originally offered for it. The glee which he showed in this successful business transaction was as marked as his appreciation of the beauty of the object itself.

. . . .

Thursday, May 2, 1935

. . . .

Over to see Mr. Roberts of Long, Roberts, and Co., to whom I had a letter from Baring Brothers. I should have seen him earlier, because he is, in a sense, the opposite number here to Sir Henry Lynch in Rio. . . .

Mr. Roberts, though interested to a degree, showed that he was not really concerned with the problem and was not putting his mind intensively on it. But he said that he would be glad to see me at any time if later I wished him to help further.

Mr. Roberts explained to me that he was born in this country and had been associated with it always. He, of course, knows intimately all of the people in the government, and though he is probably a British citizen, he has most of the advantages of being an Argentine. I learned later that he is one of the new directors of the new bank. What an advantage the British have through men like Roberts and Sir Henry over Americans in their business relations in these countries!

At the American Embassy I was at once shown in to see Mr. Cox. I told him without preliminaries that I had come to him on an unpleasant mission, to talk to him about two situations, the first of which probably did not concern him personally.

Then I told him of the action of the leaders of the American community, including Warren, and of the protest to the Cultural Society. I said that I considered the attitude of Mr. Warren utterly unjustifiable, that the least he could have done would have been to remain neutral. I added that I intended to report this matter to the authorities in the Department of State, and also to tell it in higher quarters if the opportunity arose. I suggested that Mr. Cox tell Mr. Warren of my intention so that he might have an opportunity if he wished to do so, of reporting on the matter himself to the department. Incidentally, I said that I knew of the attitude of some of the members of the community toward Dr. Inman, but that I unqualifiedly supported him and that I intended to tell the authorities in Washington that I thought he, better than any American I knew, was fitted by knowledge of the South American countries and intimate sympathy for their aspirations to serve the United States in this continent.

To all of this Cox listened, but without comment, except to say that he was sorry "that I was having my little troubles."

My second point was the unsatisfactory nature of our reception at the Foreign Office and of my impression that the appointment had not been made definitely with the foreign minister, but with the Foreign Office in a more general way. Mr. Cox was categorical in his statement that he had made the appointment himself for the foreign minister himself, and had done this at the very time when Mr. Hinkle was telling me of it at the meeting at the Cultural Society. I replied that I was delighted to know this, and that I accepted unqualifiedly his statement on the point.[2]

I then raised the point that Cox had not shown the slightest willingness to try to get us the interview with the president. He replied that he had said that he thought he could not do so. I pointed out to him, however, that he had said quite definitely when Inman and I had seen him first, that "he could not ask for an audience with the president." He read me a portion of his instructions, which said that we were not to be considered as representing the United States. I replied that we had never made any such pretensions. Cox implied that he would require special instructions to ask for an audience with the president, but I pressed him on the point, and he admitted that this was not the case.

Finally, I said that I intended to go to the British ambassador and to ask for his help. If he felt that he could not ask for the audience, that I would have to choose between cabling to Cecil to ask him to ask for special instructions, or to cable to the State Department asking for the same thing. I promised I would call Cox back after I had talked with the British ambassador. Cox said that this was a satisfactory arrangement, but he kept repeating that he did not see why I should expect the American ambassador to move, rather than the British ambassador, since I was not acting as an American official, but as an international one. And to my further disgust, his last words were that he was so sorry I was having my troubles. What a weakling to represent the United States!

....

Took a taxi to the Ministry of Agriculture, where I arrived about twenty-five minutes of three. I met Brebbia's secretary at the entrance, and we walked together to Brebbia's office. There I had to wait for fifteen or twenty minutes. Preceding me into Brebbia's inner office was an attractive-looking young man

2. Cox wrote that McDonald complained that he had again been kept waiting by the foreign minister, implying that the Embassy was to blame. He reported further that the British Foreign Office had given the British ambassador permission to arrange a meeting with the president, but so far he did not feel he could do so. Cox to secretary of state, May 10, 1935, National Archives, Record Group 59, Central Decimal File, 548.D 1/228.

whom I was later to meet—Guillermo Salazar Altamira. Brebbia presented him as the director of immigration and left us together for a little while. We talked in French. He apparently had read our memorandum.

When Brebbia came back, he said that he had been through the memorandum and thought that it would be best if I discussed further the technical details with Altamira. Then if we two could not reach complete agreement, I should come back to see him again. I explained to him that I felt it better if we could work out a kind of gentleman's agreement, rather than to ask for a formal exception in favor of the refugees. Brebbia did not commit himself, but I thought he liked the idea.

....

Friday, May 3, 1935

Mr. Aldolfo Hirsch and the secretary of the Hilfsverein, Lilli Kellermann, came to talk to me about the situation from the point of view of their society. . . . I began to ask them questions about the technical problem of immigration. Hirsch was inclined to say that, in reality, there were no serious obstacles, because anyone could come in first class. But Kellermann pointed out that since there was only one line which offered a very low first-class rate, and that had a capacity of only fifteen or twenty persons a month—the Holland-South American Line—something more was needed. . . .

I should have reported that yesterday afternoon, while I was sitting downstairs, two young Jewish girls who had heard me speak at the Instituto Cultural Argentina-Norte Americana came up to speak to me. There followed one of the most interesting discussions I have listened to since reaching this country. I asked the girls about anti-Semitism here (Miss Marie Hauberman acted as spokesman for herself and her colleague, Eugenia Oiring). They were waiting in connection with the tea which was being held that afternoon on behalf of the Jewish Hospital. Miss Hauberman said that there was an increasing amount of anti-Semitism, evidenced particularly in the universities and affecting most the young men seeking or entering professional careers. She cited a number of examples of brilliant young Jewish students who were penalized by their professors in favor of sons of good Argentine families, even though these latter boys following the tradition of the Argentine aristocracy, had worked almost not at all, assuming that their names would see them through. As a result, many young Jewish people were changing their names, and in other ways also seeking to hide their origin.

Then Miss Hauberman launched into an attack on Alfredo Hirsch. She said that she could understand the cowardice of those who had to make their way, but that he, the richest man, except perhaps one, in the country, with great business connections throughout the continent, should be fearful to recognize himself as a Jew was something utterly inexcusable. Think, she said, "what a source of strength he could be to the whole community if, as a good Jew, he stood out as our banner leader." "But what can you expect from the rank and file, from the poor, from those who must make their way, if they see the great become renegades."

Miss Hauberman said she herself was not old enough to be religious, but that surely the temple was the bond and symbol of unity, the source from which all the great values of civilization had come. Therefore, it was her duty and that of her young colleague to respect and support the temple until they became old enough to feel the religious spirit. But Alfredo Hirsch did nothing for the temple, and very little for the other charities—only 4,000 pesos a year for the Hilfsverein.

Then she told of the organization of the Civic Legion of young Jewish persons to defend the temples against the vandal attacks of the anti-Semites, with their tar and smoke bombs. The young people were organized into groups and stood guard inside and outside the temple on every feast day. More and more of them were joining this organization.

As she talked, I could see in Miss Hauberman the born leader. She spoke with such eloquence born of deep conviction. It is this sort of instinctive loyalty and courage which will, I suspect, defeat, as it must have defeated in the past, the plans of the timid assimilationists among the Jews, who would solve their problems by disappearing as a people. Miss Hauberman's attitude is the more remarkable, because she said emphatically that neither she nor her friend were Zionists, but on the contrary, they were good Argentines with enough work to do here without concerning themselves about Palestine.

Indeed, in the demands which the young Jews made to the Argentine government for the protection of the temples, they insisted that, as good Argentines, they had as complete a right to be protected as any other citizen; but they had added that if they were not protected, they would protect themselves. Miss Hauberman promised to write out for me a statement about the work among the young people.

At eleven o'clock I went in to see the British ambassador. He asked me how I was getting on. I replied that from a technical point of view not too badly, but from the political point of view less satisfactorily. Then I told him of my talks with Brebbia, Prebisch, et al. He thought these satisfactory, and agreed that the idea of a gentlemen's agreement is probably the best way out.

Then, after telling him why Cox felt that he could not ask for an interview for me with the president, I asked the British ambassador if he would do so. He said that he thought perhaps it would be best if he telegraphed asking for permission to do so, since his instructions were so general as not to be clear. He said he would telegraph that day and hoped to have a reply Saturday or at the latest Monday. He warned me, however, that there might be a further delay of three or four days, because he himself had had to wait three days the last time he had asked for an interview for himself. He doubted whether it would be possible for him to go with me.

As I was leaving, we chatted about Cecil, Balfour, Simon, Eden, and other figures in British foreign policy. I was only sorry that I had not gone to the

British ambassador in the first instance to ask for his aid, rather than the American chargé.

In the later afternoon Dr. Starkmeth and Mr. Weil, on my invitation, came to see me. We had nearly an hour and a half together, all on the subject of the technical difficulties in the way of immigration. The explanation consisted mostly of a monologue by Dr. Starkmeth, who spoke without giving Weil more than one or two opportunities to express his views. At the end, rather reluctantly, Starkmeth agreed to prepare for me a memorandum outlining the points he had made. Therefore, here I discuss them only briefly. The first and major difficulty was or is financial. In addition to the cost of the passport—five gold pesos—the three other essential documents cost ten pesos each for each child over fifteen years of age. The passage, except on the one line, is at first-class rates prohibitive. Unless the immigrants come first class, if they are not agriculturists, they must have a job in advance. Indeed, the employer must ask specifically for such and such a person, and may be required to prove that it is impossible to find in Argentina someone to do the work required. There are, of course, various categories of exceptions to these restrictive measures, but most of these do not apply to the refugees. For example, the exceptions include artists, those who were formerly resident in the country, and certain other groups. The chief exception, and the one of interest to the refugees, is that on behalf of the agriculturists; but these must have a definite contract with a landowner or with a colonization society, or must prove that they own property, or have the funds with which to buy [it]. Starkmeth insisted that the Argentine authorities have left the way open for individual consuls to require proof that the agricultural immigrant not only intends to work on the soil, but that he has been a trained agriculturist. This would obviously be impossible for more than a very few of the refugees to do. This is one of the points on which they suggested that I particularly try to secure from the government a more generous interpretation.

Another general class exempted from the restrictive measures is, of course, those individuals who possess 1,500 pesos cash.

Starkmeth indicated that the government had refused categorically Oungre's request for the elimination of the thirty peso requirement for documents. Starkmeth thought that the refusal to make this concession to the ICA—when it had been made to Schwelm's organization and perhaps to others—was an evidence of anti-Semitism.

Starkmeth urged that we try to get the government to pledge itself to treat the *carte d'identité et de voyage* as it would treat a passport. He said that it does not do so now; that indeed, many of the consuls refused to accept the *carte d'identité et de voyage* at all for visa purposes. He hoped also that the consuls would be given instructions not to require definite documents of good conduct from the refugees, because it was impossible for many of them to secure these.

It appears from what Dr. Starkmeth and Mr. Weil said, and also from what one could read between the lines, that Oungre had received very little satisfaction from either President Justo or from Duhau, the minister of agriculture. The former appears to have taken the line that this was a matter for the minister of agriculture and that, therefore, he could not concern himself with it. Duhau, in turn, had indicated that he was opposed to immigration in general, even for the farm, as well as for the cities, and that he was certainly not prepared to make any exceptions in favor of the Jews.

The official reply to Oungre's memorandum consisted of a blunt rejection by Duhau, which was based upon a technical opinion prepared by Zalazar Altamira for Brebbia. Altamira is credited with having said that—or at least having indicated—that he had been ordered to reach certain conclusions. This impression was given when Dr. Starkmeth had asked him how he could write an opinion which was so contrary to the views which he had expressed in a speech only a few years before, on the occasion of the twenty-fifth anniversary of the death of Baron Hirsch.

Dr. Starkmeth seemed convinced that the present regime is definitely anti-Semitic, and that we are not likely to receive a sympathetic hearing from Justo, Duhau, or Brebbia. Nonetheless, he said he thought that there was a better chance of receiving something by the informal approach, rather than by repeating the direct official effort made by Oungre.

As I was walking out with Starkmeth and Weil, we met Adolfo Hirsch and Arturo Löwensberg, who had come to continue our talk of the morning. They had brought with them, at my request, Miss Kellermann. Then for more than an hour they talked to me with frankness and a certain bitterness about the situation here. They started by saying that it had been impossible to tell Oungre anything unpleasant about the work of ICA or its personnel, because without exception, Starkmeth had always been with Oungre. On various occasions Oungre had been invited without Starkmeth, but each time Starkmeth came. They spoke of Starkmeth as a man who twenty-five years ago had doubtless done good work organizing here the colonization of Polish and Russian Jews, but who now as an old man was utterly unfit to handle German Jews under the changed circumstances of today. He knew only one method, and he was unwilling to learn any other—nor, indeed, would he admit that there was anything which he did not know. Weil, on the other hand, was much more pliable, much more open-minded, but Starkmeth never gave him an opportunity. The local community could get on with Weil, but not with Starkmeth.

Hirsch was skeptical about the possibility of cooperating with ICA in any large-scale program of settlement unless it were done on traditional ICA lines, and these are not the least adapted to the new immigrants or to the changed economic conditions in Argentina. ICA lands are fit for the most part only for grain or for other crops of which there are already an abundance; but ICA is almost certain to oppose the purchase of other lands, such as are suggested in Rio Negro. Anyhow, money from the outside, to be used in cooperation with ICA's funds, is apt to be used for ICA purposes if the ICA organization is in charge.

Hirsch and Löwenberg, as well as Miss Kellermann, were bitter in their declarations that nearly all of what I had heard a week or so ago at engineer

Klein's house, as to what the local community would do in supplying ample funds for the care and settlement of hundreds of new refugees, was only "words, words, and nothing more." Not one of the persons there was prepared to give substantially, and certainly not Eddis. Only the Hilfsverein, with its modest budget, was working for the refugees, and it was having the greatest difficulty finding the money to carry on its present very limited program. Therefore, it was absurd for the so-called community leaders to give me the impression that two or three hundred new immigrants a month could be provided for here easily from local resources.

Actually, about 1,300 refugees had come to the country, or at any rate, about that number had been handled directly or indirectly by the Hilfsverein. This had taxed their resources. They had found that it required about £25 per person to be sure to be able to integrate them in the life of the country. At this rate they felt that they would be able to care for 150–250 a month, but only with these ample funds. Starkmeth had criticized this amount as excessive, though Oungre had at first been inclined to think it reasonable. In this connection they bitterly denounced Starkmeth as a man who was still satisfied to deal with immigrants on the basis by which he would give them 20 pesos and then throw them out on the street if they came back for more, having been unable to do with that amount. They lumped Starkmeth and Alfredo Hirsch together, saying that the latter had, when he gave his last 4,000 pesos ($1,000) to the Hilfsverein, said, "This is all I will do." When asked what would happen with the persons not taken care of, he had said, "Throw them out."

....

In this conference, as in the morning conference with the Hilfsverein representatives, the question was raised of the tendency of the committees abroad to dump undesirables among the other refugees abroad. I had to confess that I could not deny that in practice I was afraid the committees did do this sometimes. Moreover, I frankly confessed that I sympathized with the local communities here and in Sao Paulo and Rio in their protests that their judgment must be taken into account in the choice of immigrants, since theirs must be the final responsibility for the settlement of these persons. It is easy enough for persons like Helbronner, Gottschalk, and Edouard Oungre to talk about the immediate necessity of getting people out of Paris or Antwerp, but it is no solution to transfer the problem to the cities here by sending individuals who can not make their way and who, in addition to becoming a burden on the local communities, increase the tendency towards anti-Semitism.

Adolfo Hirsch then sketched briefly a project which he had discussed, he said, for nine hours with Louis Oungre. He is to give me a fuller memorandum later. In substance, it is a plan for the development of fruit and vegetable industries in the Rio Negro area. It would utilize the services of a very large number of refugees on the land, in the canning and related industries, and in the merchandizing chain store shops in Buenos Aires.

Though Oungre was reported to be interested, Hirsch has no faith that ICA would cooperate in such an enterprise: first, because it would mean the putting of money into lands other than those of the ICA; second, because the local management of ICA here are unfit for this enterprise and would oppose it; and third, because the ICA central management is not adapted for this kind of new enterprise in Argentina. I told them that I did not agree to these pessimistic conclusions, that I hoped, therefore, they would present their program to me more in detail and give me an opportunity to discuss it in New York and London. The only figures they gave me were extremely tentative, an investment of 1,200,000 pesos (approximately $300,000). Oungre had suggested that eighty percent of such an amount might be found outside of the country if the other twenty percent could be found here. Hochschild[3] has said that he would invest five percent of such a sum or as much as Alfredo Hirsch would put in. In view of the fact that I was to see Hochschild that very evening, I was delighted to have this matter called to my attention.

Because of these prolonged afternoon conferences Inman and I were late reaching Dr. Alemann's house for dinner. At the Alemanns were, in addition to the hosts and Inman and I, Mr. Hochschild, Mr. Alemann's sister, Hochschild's associate, and perhaps one other. During dinner the talk was mostly about Hitler and Hitlerism; but after dinner the talk drifted to South America, and for the first half hour or so Hochschild told of the situation in Bolivia and of the prospects for peace. He thinks that both countries are anxious to end the fighting and are now looking for a way out.

I asked Hochschild about Adolfo Hirsch's plans. He said that he did not know the details, but that he had confidence in him and hoped the program would go forward. Then I asked him whether he thought I or someone else could induce Alfredo Hirsch to participate. His first reply was in the negative; then, when I indicated to him something of my previous talk with Hirsch, Hochschild said that probably I could succeed with him, particularly if I could associate his name and the enterprise with those of important leaders in London and New York with whom Alfredo would like to come in closer contact.

I asked Hochschild about J. B. Eddis. The reply was more bald than some I had received previously, and tended to increase my uncertainty as to the extent to which Eddis could really be useful.

Hochschild drove Inman and me home. Everything Hochschild said—and even more his manner—gave me the impression of great reserve strength. Moreover, I saw in him nothing of a tendency to dodge his responsibility as a great Jewish industrialist. I only wish that Alfredo Hirsch felt the same way.

The next day Inman went alone to the west coast to look into possible opportunities for placing refugee intellectuals. Over the next six weeks he also visited Chile,

3. Moritz ("Mauricio") Hochschild, influential German-born, Jewish metal trader with extensive mining interests in Bolivia, Chile, and Peru, especially in tin.

Peru, Ecuador, Colombia, Panama, Costa Rica, Nicaragua, Honduras, Guatemala, and Mexico.

Saturday, May 4, 1935

. . . Golf on the San Isidro course, with Mr. Alvarez of Westinghouse. It was a lovely day, a good course, but the golf was bad.

After tea back to the hotel in time for my conference with Mr. J. Saslavsky. Mr. Saslavsky and I talked quite frankly about the problem here and about personalities. I listened with the greater respect to his views, because he is universally respected not only as an extremely successful business man, but as a public-spirited citizen who, though his children have all married out, has himself remained willing always to help in community affairs. He has never forgotten his very humble Russian-Jewish origin.

. . . .

Saslavsky was much interested in what I had to tell him of the Adolfo Hirsch scheme. He thought it sounded reasonable and said he would participate. He thought perhaps I might persuade Alfredo Hirsch to do so also. As to Eddis, he expressed skepticism. In general, he said that one must not exaggerate possibilities from the financial point of view of the community. There were a few rich men, but most of these were not the active ones in community affairs; that, in fact, the community was having or had had great difficulty in meeting its obligations to the temple, and that these and the charitable obligations about exhausted the available resources. I was particularly interested in this view, because it so strikingly confirmed what Adolfo Hirsch had told me.

. . . .

Sunday, May 5, 1935

Mr. Neyer called for me at 6:15, and we drove out to San Andreas. It was an overcast, cold, and unpleasant day, but I had some of my best golf—a 42 coming in, with two 250 yard drives, so the world looked very bright.

To the sanitarium in the late afternoon.[4] Dr. Solomon came in, and we talked for more than an hour. He didn't seem to care to talk shop, or at least not his shop, so we talked about my work. He told an extremely interesting tale of his practicing in this country for three years without a license, and of the attempts to oust him, and of his eventually being admitted after he had passed all of the examinations, and had during the previous three years had a practice that reached towards a million pesos.

. . . .

When I was asking Solomon about his relations with President Justo and Duhau, he said that though he knew them both well, he feared that he had ex-

4. Ruth had not been feeling well and had been invited to spend a few days at Dr. Solomon's sanitarium. She suffered from migraine headaches.

hausted his possibilities of asking their help on behalf of refugees, because he had so frequently appealed to them in the past. He suggested, however, that Alberto Justo, a nephew of the president, whom he knew very well, might be induced to use his influence with the president. Alberto is said to be one of the liberalizing influences on the president, because Alberto feels that the Socialists should be encouraged, rather than denounced, for they remain, after all, a constitutional party.

. . . .

Monday, May 6, 1935

Lunch with A. L. Bradford [United Press] and his Argentine colleague, Richardo Diaz Herrera. I was much interested in Herrera's interpretation of the Nationalist movement in Argentina. He denied that it springs in any sense from the Nazi or fascist movement, except that some of the more extreme groups here like to ape the German or Italian models. Fundamentally, the Nationalist movement is a sign of coming of age—the natural and proper reaction of a country which had been so largely dependent upon foreign capital and enterprise and had found itself suddenly deserted in the crisis of 1928–30.[5] It is not at all anti-Jewish, nor aimed at any other particular foreign group. Rather, it is a desire to develop the potentialities of the Argentines to run their own affairs, with the cooperation (but no longer in any sense under the tutelage) of the foreigner. Herrera thought that the anti-Semitic and other extremist movements here were weak and would remain unimportant. Moreover, in the probable event of the return to power of the radicals, the Nazi manifestations would be severely repressed and liberalism gain proportionately. I should like to see more of Herrera, because he seems so typical of the 100 percent but reasonable Argentine.

At four o'clock I went with Miss Kellermann of the Hilfsverein to what I hope is the first of a series of technical conferences with Guillermo Salazar Altamira, the director of the Immigration Department. He received me at once, and in a most cordial spirit.

I began by making a brief statement to the effect that I had not come to present a specific formula to the Argentine authorities, but rather to ask their cooperation and advice on the solution of a great humanitarian problem. I pointed out that I was not representing any private group or interest, but was speaking on behalf of the High Commission named by the League; and that, though I was not presenting a formal proposal, I was nonetheless making an official démarche.

I handed to Altamira copies of the High Commission's statutes and its recommendations in reference to travel papers.

Then I suggested that perhaps Altamira and his colleague might be inter-

5. The crisis of 1928–1930 refers to the crash of 1928, which ended Argentine prosperity, and the military takeover of the government in 1930, which forced out President Hipolito Yrigoyen. This was the first military coup in the history of a country that had been stable since 1862 and (more or less) democratic since 1912.

ested in the procedural concession which had been made by the United States government in favor of the refugees. I pointed out that though there had been no changes in the law or in the regulations, admission of the refugees had been made substantially easier.

He began his reply by saying that the general purpose of the immigration regulations was two-fold: first, to forestall the coming of indigents; second, to encourage immigration to the country and to discourage that to the cities, because it is realized that Argentina has a fully developed head (Buenos Aires), but a very weak, thin body (the rest of the country).

He declared that it would be impossible to change the regulations formally in behalf of any special group. Much as the authorities might wish to make such changes in favor of the refugees, it would be impossible to do so, because the regulations must be maintained intact to protect the country against undesirables (in this connection he referred to the desire of the French in Syria to send many undesirable Syrians and Assyrians to Argentina). Nonetheless, it would, he thought, be practicable, to so change the spirit of the interpretation of the regulations and the practice in the application of the regulations as to make easier the admission of refugees, and that it was from this point of view that he thought we could most advantageously discuss the matter. (This fitted in so nicely to what I had assumed after many conferences here must be the only practicable procedure that I was delighted to have Altamira take this line.)

Incidentally, he denied vigorously that in the application of the regulations there was any discrimination against Jewish immigrants. There was, he recognized, certain vociferous groups [*sic*] who were now agitating along anti-Semitic lines, but they did not control the policy of the government. Nonetheless—and this was significant—the agitations of these extremists merely confirmed what he had said about the impossibility of the government's making a formal exception or openly modifying the regulation in favor of the refugees.

Then he began to read portions of the regulations, and we discussed a number of points seriatim:

a) the question of accepting the *carte d'identité et de voyage* as a substitute for a German passport for visa purposes. On this he was not completely satisfactory, but indicated that in practice the consuls might be instructed to visa these documents, but I must make this matter clearer in our subsequent talks;

b) the requirement of a certificate of good conduct weighs very heavily with the Argentine authorities. I argued that in practice it is frequently impossible for the refugees to secure this certificate from the German authorities, and that to insist upon it in every case is to work undue hardship. Altamira recognized that this might be the case and said that it might be possible to encourage the individual consuls to be more liberal in granting the visa when they are convinced that this particular certificate cannot be obtained.

In this connection Altamira read the following extract from Article XVII of the regulations:

"The Consular officers who are specially authorized to this effect can extend under the responsibility of the Consul, conditional permits for landing to those persons who owing to the plainly justified fortuitous reasons, do not possess complete documentation . . . or in special cases not foreseen. . . ."

Altamira added smilingly, "It probably seems to you as though this article were drafted precisely to meet the case of the refugees." I agreed that it seemed so.

Then he suggested this possible procedure: might it not be practicable for the Argentine government itself, after a number of refugees had been admitted provisionally without their certificates of good conduct, to submit officially to the German government a list of such refugees, with the request that the Berlin authorities indicate if against any of these persons there was a criminal record. In case such records were disclosed, the refugees against whom these were indicated would be subject to deportation.

This whole idea was new to me, so I hesitated to give a definite opinion, either as to the desirability or the probable practicability of the procedure, but I indicated my interest in it and my feeling that something of this sort might be useful. Altamira and I will talk about it further. It was only one of many points which Altamira made during our conference which convinced me that he was not speaking on his own responsibility, but was speaking on behalf of Brebbia as well;

c) The problem of agricultural immigrants. On this matter we talked at length. First, I brought up the question of the thirty pesos gold required from each agricultural immigrant for the three necessary certificates. I asked if it was not true that at least in the case of the Schwelm concession in Eldorado, this requirement had been waived. He said that it had been, but that in other cases, unlike in Eldorado, the concession had worked badly. I replied that I, of course, knew of the unfortunate experience which the government had had in the notorious Zuckerman concession.

I asked him why the plea of ICA to be relieved of this burden had not been granted. He replied that it had been refused because the plea on this point had been coupled with the unacceptable proposal in reference to the admission of a considerable number of immigrants on an unrestricted basis, or, at any rate, on a basis so indefinite as to preclude its acceptance. From this I gathered that if ICA were to make a formal application for a special concession on the matter of the 30 gold pesos, it would be granted. Certainly Altamira said that it would be granted to any responsible newly organized colonization society which could prove its responsibility and which specifically asked that these fees be waived.

Altamira said that it would be possible to instruct the consuls to interpret Article IV paragraph (a) the words "rural destination" in the broadest and most generous way. There would be no requirement, for example, that the refugee claiming to have a rural destination, prove that he is a trained agriculturist. It is sufficient that the purpose be proved. Moreover, it will not be necessary that such an immigrant actually work on the soil; it will be sufficient that he is employed in any enterprise connected with agriculture—such, for example, as merchandising the product or any other indirect association with the land. To illustrate how broad his interpretation was, Altamira said that a watchmaker going to one of the provincial towns could be interpreted as an agriculturist! In other words, he evidently meant to indicate that the authorities are prepared to interpret as agriculturists any one who is prepared to go beyond Buenos Aires.

Certainly if a large-scale agricultural and industrial project could be worked out in this country, there would be no difficulty whatsoever in the light of Altamira's interpretation in bringing in as many refugees as might be required or as might be utilized in such an undertaking.

Incidentally, Altamira said that the 2500 peso basis of admission was applicable not merely to agriculturists, but to others.

Speaking of the possible application of these interpretative concessions, Altamira said that, of course, not all of the consuls could be trusted to put them into effect. In particular, the phrase "under the responsibility of the consul" in Article XVII and elsewhere in the regulations, placing as it does nominally at least so much discretion in the hands of the individual consul and at the same time might be interpreted as making him liable for mistakes, makes it necessary that only a few consulates, for example where there are consuls general, should be entrusted with the discretion implicit in Article XVII and in the suggested concessions.

This did not seem to me a serious matter, because there are sufficient of these offices in western Europe, according to Altamira, to serve as visa offices for our purposes.

I asked Altamira whether this phrase about the consuls' personal responsibility did not tend to make the individual consuls lean over backwards for fear that they would be penalized for having made an exception in favor of an immigrant if such person later proved to be undesirable. He replied that this idea of responsibility was not strictly interpreted; that it was meant merely to preclude the possibility of careless action by the consuls or favoritism on their part. He did not think that it really dissuaded the consuls from using their discretion in favor of an applicant.

As I indicated above in connection with one particular point, Altamira was so definite throughout all of his talk in connection with all of his suggested concessions that he must have been speaking with the knowledge and approval of his immediate superior, the undersecretary of agriculture, Brebbia. The importance of this is obvious.

Moreover, his whole tone was that of a man anxious to go as far as he possibly could to meet in practice our needs. He seemed, as had Brebbia earlier, relieved and, as it were, liberated by my decision not to require a formal written answer from his department or from the minister of agriculture.

As I was leaving, he said, "I assume that I am to have the pleasure of other conferences with you." I assured him that I would be greatly pleased with this and would communicate with him very soon.

As we walked out together, Miss Kellermann said, "On the basis of these interpretations there would be few difficulties." Earlier, on our way to the office she had quite bluntly said that she and the members of her group were convinced that the ICA committees in Europe had in the past been seeking to send only the persons considered by the Belgian and French governments as least desirable there.

After a hurried bite of supper, over to the sanitarium. Found Ruth in most cheerful spirits.

We were joined by Mrs. Solomon, who came to thank me for my flowers. She talked interestingly about the reasons which had caused the doctor to emigrate from Vienna. Apparently, it was not only or perhaps not even primarily his anticipation of possible growing anti-Semitism, but also the fact that he was being required to pay over 60 percent of his income to the state. They were laughed at when they told their colleagues that they were coming to Argentina. Recently, however, several of these doctors have tried to come themselves, but had not been encouraged by the authorities in Argentina.

Late in the evening Dr. Solomon came up to say that his very good friend, Professor Alfredo Manes, perhaps the world's most distinguished authority on the science of insurance, was coming somewhat later, and would I come down. I found Manes a typical German combination of business and academic characteristics, but at the moment showing more a refugee psychology than of anything else. Technically he is not a refugee, because his wife remains in Germany, and he is free to come and go. However, he had been forced out of the university and out of his more important position which he had created for himself as the head of a worldwide organization with branches in dozens of countries, studying current problems of insurance. So far as his university post was concerned, he had been temporarily reinstated, and then had been allowed to resign, thus, as he put it, "saving his honor." However, what appeared to hurt him most was illustrated by this statement: "Of course they will not allow me to print, and I cannot live without publishing my articles and books."

It appears that following a series of lectures he gave in Buenos Aires last year for an organization of insurance companies, he had been invited as a guest professor at the university for this semester, and had received a promise of sufficient compensation from the insurance companies to cover his expenses. Now, however, he finds that the insurance companies have gotten into trouble and wish to reduce materially their commitments. Moreover, the dean of one of the schools in the university had that morning treated him with extreme rudeness, not even asking him to sit down, and telling him that the university had no funds with which to print the announcement of his lectures; that he would have to do this at his own expense, and that, therefore, nothing had been done to announce his coming. Never had be been treated in such a way.

Conditions for the Jews in Germany are becoming worse. This he attributed in part to the constant attacks of the Jewish press on the outside; if he had his way, these would cease altogether. But Dr. Solomon shared my view that the program within Germany would be much the same, because the attacks outside are merely used as an excuse. During this discussion the name of Dr. Alemann was raised by me as someone who might possibly be of help to Dr. Manes. but the latter in a startled tone said, "Please do not say a word to Dr. Alemann about me, for if I were in the slightest way connected with him, it would be fatal for my situation in Germany."

This led Dr. Solomon to say that he thought Alemann was an extremist not only in his anti-Nazi views, but also in his anti-religious attitude. To illustrate the latter he said that Dr. Alemann, despite the universal interest in the Eucharistic Congress, had refused to say a word about it [in his newspaper].

I promised Dr. Manes to speak to one or two persons here about his situation, among them Saslavsky.

Home late.

Tuesday, May 7, 1935

I called the British Embassy, and was told that the ambassador was asking for my audience with the president.

I then called the American Embassy and left word for Cox of this fact.

At the ICA office Dr. Starkmeth introduced me to two of his colleagues, and the three of us, together with Mr. Weil, conferred on the results of my interview with Altamira. One of the men translated rapidly my memorandum into French. During the course of the reading Dr. Starkmeth could at times scarcely restrain his impatience, for from time to time he would explain, "That is untrue; that is wrong; or that gives a false impression." I urged him to wait until the reading had finished to discuss the matter as a whole.

The reactions of the group may be summarized as follows:

If, which they doubted, Altamira were frank and honest in his suggestions to me, then a great gain had been made. They agreed that Altamira could not have been speaking on his own responsibility merely, but must have spoken with the knowledge and consent of Brebbia. They recognized that it might be that the governmental authorities had decided in practice to be more lenient in their interpretation of the regulations, but they remained skeptical on this point.

In particular, they declared that Altamira's statement about the ICA and the thirty gold pesos was completely inaccurate; that, in fact, Oungre had asked for this concession separately from anything else, and that it had been refused. Therefore, it was not correct to say that the refusal this time was because of the request being included with that for the admission of 300 persons a month.

They emphatically asserted also that there is a discrimination against Jews in the matter of visas and in other immigration questions. They felt that in his declaration on this point, Altamira was probably merely following instructions to put the best case he could before me as a representative of the League of Nations.

But after something of the warmth of feeling and worn itself off, the group agreed that if I could, in fact, get the government to change its practice on two points—the thirty pesos and the interpretation of "an agricultural destination"—a great victory would have been won.

I disavowed any feeling of confidence that I would be able to make good on all the points suggested in the Altamira interview, but I said that I would continue as energetically as possible to carry forward what all of them seemed to agree was an encouraging beginning. It was agreed that I would communicate with them again as soon as I had anything new to report.

....

Mauricio Hochschild came in, and we talked for more than an hour. My initial impression of great strength and reserve was not lessened. First, he told me of his recent talk with Alfredo Hirsch and his suggestion to Hirsch that he take on three hundred refugees in his various enterprises if he, Hochschild, would take on one hundred. Hochschild had already taken on several, and had found some of the lawyers to make excellent business men. But Hirsch refused flatly and said that he would not take even ten. He argued that he would have to consider the views of his partners, but, in fact, he probably is not interested.

Then Hochschild asked Hirsch if he would join him in an agreement that each gave 1,000 pesos a month to the Hilfsverein. Hirsch said he would have to think about it, even though, as Hochschild told him, that amount could mean nothing to him. Hochschild is going to give his irrespective of Hirsch's decision.

Hochschild said that he had admired greatly Adolfo Hirsch's work in the Hilfsverein, but that he and his colleagues in that work did not have a sufficient vision to meet the present crisis. What was needed was something on a larger scale. Therefore he had proposed to Saslavsky that the latter work out a program by which 5,000 young people from Germany could be brought to this country and gradually placed in business and other enterprises in different parts of the country. He thought this could be done without causing new difficulties here. In answer to my question about the governmental regulations, he said it would only be necessary to bring them out first class, and that there were a number of lines on which this could be done for about 700 Marks.

This enterprise, however, Hochschild was sure, must be kept separate from ICA control. He said this not because of any particular criticism of ICA personnel, but because ICA has been concerned with and is particularly fitted to deal with eastern Polish and Russian Jews and makes a mess of dealing with German Jews. He insists that the two kinds of Jews must be dealt with by separate organizations.

Then we discussed the Adolfo Hirsch project. He confirmed that he really believed that this scheme could be worked out on a satisfactory basis, and that he was prepared to put in five percent of the $1,200,000 pesos which was wanted. He felt that at the suggested figure of £25[6] a head, this organization could place in Argentina satisfactorily from forty to fifty families a month, and that this cost was not excessive. I asked him if a concrete program had been

6. £25 was the sum that each immigrant was required to bring in.

worked out, and he said he would ask Adolfo Hirsch to present it to me within a day or two.

But he reiterated again his feeling that this could be only in a euphemistic sense an investment.

Indeed, he elaborated with much cogency and conviction his view that it is really absurd to expect to find real investments as the means through which to help the refugees. Nor did he think it right that rich Jews in New York, London, or Paris should sit on their money while their co-religionists disintegrated, waiting until sound investments could be devised through which the rich man's money could be made available for the poor people's needs.

I was so impressed by his statement of the case that I said I hoped he would be willing to put it so to some of the men in New York and in England. He replied that he would be delighted to do so whenever the opportunity occurred. He only regretted that because of business and family engagements, he could not be with me in New York during the conferences with the ICA authorities, but he would put himself at my disposal when we were together in London or Paris.

As to possible cooperation with the Catholics, he doubted if any general basis of working together could be devised, but he recognized the advantage of ad hoc cooperation and hoped I would continue to work along this line.

As he was leaving, he again paid his respects in violent language to Alfredo Hirsch, condemning in unqualified terms the latter's cowardliness.

....

Just before nine Saslavsky called for me to take me to dinner at his house. On the way to dinner I asked if he had heard of the proposed Catholic settlement scheme in Argentina. He said he had not.

It was rather a sizable party. In addition to Mr. and Mr. Saslavsky, Brebbia, and myself, there were present or came in after dinner two sons-in-law and some daughters, Mr. and Mr. Levi (a partner), and some others.

During dinner there was general talk, but I had an opportunity to drive home with Brebbia the Nazi conception of the master race and the position where this view left the Italian and other Latin peoples. After dinner for a couple of hours there was a discussion about the economic situation in the Argentine, the needs and possibilities of immigrations, etc., etc. It was much less helpful to me than a similar discussion some evenings earlier at Alemann's house, when Prebisch had been the center. Brebbia, unlike Prebisch, is reserved, cautious, and much more the functionnaire. Besides, his mind is nothing like so original or free as that of Prebisch.

Throughout the evening Brebbia tended to limit himself to technical points or to negative views.

He argued that the country could not now absorb any except agricultural immigrants, that so long as the rest of the world maintained its policy of restricting its purchases of Argentine goods,[7] even agricultural immigration must be restricted.

Alemann returned a number of times to his favorite thesis that Argentina ought to encourage group immigration from Switzerland, Denmark, and the other Scandinavian countries, particularly of younger people who would bring their own capital in small amounts. Brebbia retorted at once that they could have nothing to do with any government-organized or government-supported immigration; that he was through with immigration which would involve the running into his office every week or so of the consuls or diplomatic representatives of the countries from which the immigrants came. Alemann replied that this might be an important consideration if the immigrants were coming from large and powerful countries, but he could see no serious harm in a visit to Brebbia's office of the consul of the Swiss Republic or the visit of a similar official from Denmark.

This then gave me an opportunity to point out that the one group of immigrants on whose behalf Brebbia need never worry about receiving visits from foreign consuls or diplomats was the German refugees. There was a general laugh from the group at this point.

I tried to argue during the course of Brebbia's declarations against immigration that Argentina could not expect to increase the standard of living of its people, and thereby absorb an increasing portion of its produce, unless the present system of extremely low-scale workers on the land who live in a most primitive fashion were replaced to some extent at any rate by settlers who would gradually demand and consume much more. Brebbia was inclined to agree with this, but to say that time was not yet for this development; that one could not suddenly turn back the hands of the clock and replace the latifundia by peasant proprietorships. But I am not really sure that he got my point.

At another juncture in the discussion I tried to argue that there must be opportunities in a great country like Argentina for energetic young men other than on the land itself. Brebbia's reply was, "But where? In what precise positions or industries?"

To this question I replied, I am afraid rather sharply, somewhat as follows: How can any set of officials or any other group of men tell in advance precisely what any immigrant or group of immigrants can accomplish, or how they can integrate themselves in the life of a community? Would any one have imagined that, when Saslavsky came to the Argentine thirty or forty years ago, a poor

7. The worldwide Great Depression had major effects upon Argentina. Exports dropped by 40 percent, foreign investment dried up, and unemployment and inflation skyrocketed, the last because a widening trade deficit forced the government to borrow heavily. Much of the Argentine economy revolved around the British market for beef, but the British government reduced beef imports in order to protect beef producers within the Empire. The Roca-Runciman Treaty of 1933 guaranteed Argentina a fixed share of the chilled beef market in Britain, but only in exchange for trade concessions for British goods in Argentina. Other countries also raised tariffs on Argentine goods as a result.

Russian immigrant, that he would be today the second most powerful grain dealer in the country? Or for that matter, who could have known when Brebbia's own father came to Argentina a generation ago that his son would be occupying a key position in the government today. And similarly in our own country, had the bureaucrats a generation or more ago decided that they were competent to exclude immigration on the ground that the country could not absorb newcomers or that the newcomers could not exactly indicate what they would do after their arrival, then I—and hundreds of thousands of people like me in the States—would never have been permitted to play our part there, because our fathers would have been excluded.

My general argumentation was not badly received, but I doubted if it really carried conviction to Brebbia. Anyhow, I was much annoyed when at this juncture Levi and also one of the Saslavsky's sons-in-law, an attractive but rather fresh young man, both energetically supported Brebbia's view that there was danger in urban immigration.

At one point when Brebbia and I were talking together alone, I tried to get him to agree that the Argentine authorities ought to give their consuls in Europe a large degree of discretion in the matter of visaing *cartes d'identité* and in determining whether or not a refugee applicant for a visa might be given it even if he did not supply his certificate of good conduct. Brebbia replied that they would make up their own minds here in Buenos Aires on this question. But I pointed out that only the man on the spot in Europe could see the applicant, and that only he, therefore, was in a position to have a judgment whether the applicant was telling the truth when he said that he could not secure his certificate of good conduct.

Brebbia seemed for a moment convinced on this point, but later I was to learn that he had not been convinced at all, or at any rate, if he were convinced, he was not willing to break with the bureaucratic tradition and take the lead in urging a new policy.

....

Late in the evening I had an opportunity to talk with Brebbia alone about the situation of the Catholics in Germany. This interested Brebbia obviously. I asked him what would be his attitude if, when I returned next time to the Argentine, I came as much on behalf of the Catholics as on behalf of the Jews. He did not reply directly, but I know that his attitude would be very different, that the possibility of Catholic refugees had already modified his attitude towards my mission.

Brebbia said that he thought I ought to see the president and that he would speak to the latter's secretary about it. He said he would also arrange for me to meet his chief, Dr. Duhau, the minister of agriculture.

It was just about one o'clock when I got home.

Wednesday, May 8, 1935

This was a day relatively free of engagements.

Lunched with Mr. Eddis after having visited him in his office at 461 Cangallo, where he showed me the maps and pictures of his ranch and examples of the products of his mines. We lunched at Cath & Chaves. Nearly the whole time was given over to his account of the factors, for which he blamed his wife, which were now culminating in the engagement of his daughter to a Catholic and an Argentine. It was, he insisted, the influence of her mother and her refusal to put the girl in Jewish schools or to encourage her in having Jewish company, that they now found themselves faced with this, from his point of view, tragic prospect.

As he talked, I felt that much of his present foresight was hindsight, that in fact he had not been nearly as anxious years ago as he now thought he had been, to see to it that his daughter was given a Jewish upbringing. Moreover, I was inclined to doubt that he would carry out his drastic threats of leaving Argentina with his capital in order that he might thereby deprive his prospective son-in-law of the certainty which Argentine law gives a son-in-law of a share in the father-in-law's estate.

Thursday, May 9, 1935

....

Lunch at the Savoy Hotel, as the guest of Ewing, with Dr. Jimenez, a Socialist leader in social and humanitarian activities. . . . Dr. Jimenez indicated that the Socialists were interested in the success of my efforts and would be glad to help where they could. But because of the present political alignment with the reactionaries and conservatives in power, the Socialists have little opportunity to help.

....

At 6:15 I went to Alfredo Hirsch's office for another conference. I told him of the difficulties in securing an appointment with the president, particularly of the latter's insistence that it was not enough for the British ambassador to ask for an interview for me; it was necessary that he accompany me. Hirsch's comment was that he personally had been convinced from the beginning when it was evident that there would be difficulties, that Justo did not want to see me, that he preferred not to be mixed up directly in this matter. The reasons which had been urged for delay had really been excuses.

When I told him that we were discussing the possibility of a gentlemen's agreement with the Argentine officials, he laughed rather cynically and told me the story of his talk with Duhau sometime previously. It was at the time when there was question as to whether or not Argentina would live up literally to the gentlemen's agreement it had made about withholding a portion of its wheat supply from the world market. The American ambassador had been trying for weeks to get a definite answer from Duhau but in vain. Finally, one day Duhau, in talking to Hirsch, said, "Of course we are going to sell; why not? The promise not to do so is, after all, not written. It is only a gentlemen's agreement."

Hirsch laughingly said, "I hope your gentlemen's agreement will be more effective. But don't you ever under any circumstances quote me about this story."

Then changing the subject, I asked Hirsch for £10,000 suggesting that it would be the greatest possible encouragement on the other side if he were willing to match what the Rothschilds and others in London and Warburg in New York were doing.

Without batting an eye, Hirsch said he could do nothing of the sort; he was giving so much in Argentina, where his first responsibility was, that he could not give outside. He said, for example, that he was giving 5,000 pesos to the Hilfsverein. I replied that I was not speaking of 5,000 pesos but of £10,000. This merely evoked more exclamations about the constant calls on him for money. I was tempted to tell him the story of the man who complained of his wife's extravagance because of her persistent requests for money, when as a matter of fact he never gave her any. I did get in during this part of the talk some reference to the fact that the shroud has no pockets, but I cannot flatter myself that I fazed Hirsch in the least.

Then I asked him about the possibility of putting some of his intelligence to work on the task of organizing the settlement of a large number of refugees in the Argentine. He said that Hochschild had just been talking to him about the possibility of employing some hundreds of refugees in his business, but how could he do this, how could he serve on a committee, much less head a committee, when his is not a Jewish firm, and the bulk of the capital is Christian, when they have important business connections in Hamburg and Berlin? What would the German minister think of him? They would lose their German business if he became associated, or rather if the firm were associated, with a Jewish cause.

Then, to prove his high and disinterested morality he told how during the war he had been put on the blacklist by the Allies and subjected to various indignities through the fact he had maintained the strictest neutrality. One could only do his duty, and if he were maligned for this, he would have the satisfaction of knowing that he was really above reproach.

We then talked about the possibility of cooperation with the Vatican. He insisted that there might be possibilities of ad hoc cooperation, but that there could be no general agreement. The Jews would be willing, but the Vatican would not be, even when faced, as at present, by the danger of the development of a national church in Mexico. Despite this threat to the Church, Hirsch felt confident that it is gaining in the world as a whole. Then he told me what, of course, I knew very well, of the Church's insistence that in mixed marriages the children must be Catholic. Though this had, of course, been brought home to him in his own case because of the marriage within the next few months of his son to a Catholic girl, his interpretation of it was that the Church, like a hard-headed business man, was successfully driving a hard bargain. And he could only admire the Church for it.

He saw me to the door as usual, as we parted. But as I walked back to the hotel, I kept saying to myself, what is the use of being the most powerful industrialist in Argentina, or perhaps in South America, if you remain as cowardly as a mouse, or rather, if in proportion as you enlarge your material interests, you lose the last vestige of your moral freedom.

Friday, May 10, 1935

Final conference with Zalazar Altamira at his office at eleven. We began by some minutes of friendly gossip about ages, etc. of some of Altamira's associates—Prebisch, Pinero,[8] Brebbia, Duhau, et al.

Then I spoke about the Catholic element of the refugee problem and the interest which it seemed to have for Brebbia. Altamira said that it was good to keep this in mind.

I next tried to tie him down on the question of authority to the consuls to visa *cartes d'identité et de voyage* without asking in each case for authority from Buenos Aires. He said he thought this could increasingly be worked out in practice, but that it would be difficult to give a general undertaking to that effect.

Similarly, I pressed him again on the question of authorizing the consuls to grant visas even when a certificate of good conduct is lacking, without having to ask for authorization in each case. Here again Altamira gave much the same answer. It is an answer which would be satisfactory if it really meant what he seemed to imply.

In connection with the requirement of a certificate of good conduct I pointed out and Altamira agreed that so far as subversive elements are concerned, these would always be able to secure forged documents, that in fact the only persons who were penalized by the present practice of the Argentine authorities were those who were honest and really unable to secure the certificate, but without connections which would enable them to secure forged documents.

I asked specifically once more whether ICA would have a reasonable chance of being relieved from the requirement of depositing thirty gold pesos for each agricultural immigrant if the organization once more formally made the request for this exemption. He said that he thought there was a very good chance of success if this request were made quite independently of connection with any other matter.

In general, he said he thought it desirable that we should act on the principle of a gentlemen's agreement, nothing in writing, nothing formal, but with the understanding that the Argentine authorities would in practice facilitate the admission of refugees. In other words, it would be a gentlemen's agreement.

Finally, Altamira suggested that this agreement should be for a trial period, to see how it would work for three months or something of that sort. I agreed that this would be best.

We parted with mutual expressions of high regard, and I with a feeling that a good deal had been accomplished with Altamira.

8. Federico Pinero, minister of finance.

I went directly to the Casa Rosada, where I was to meet Alemann for my appointment with Pinero, the minister of finance. While we were waiting for a quarter of an hour or so, Alemann and I chatted about Pinero's career and the brilliant part he had played in the reorganization of Argentine finance.

When we were shown into the large magnificent office of Pinero, I was struck by his tired and unshaven appearance. There is nothing about him of the Beau Brummel.

I began by expressing my admiration for what I had heard of his accomplishments in the financial field. I told him that some of the most highly placed foreigners in Buenos Aires, whose interests had been in a sense adversely affected by his exchange regulations, had nonetheless personally expressed to me their opinion that had they been in Pinero's position, they would have done the same; that they regarded his management as extremely able, and from Argentine's point of view, thoroughly justified. This acknowledgment seemed to please him.

My second preliminary was to disclaim any intention of laying down a definite program which I would expect the Argentine authorities to approve. On the contrary, I had come to ask their advice in the solution of a world problem. I recognized that they were engaged in a gigantic task of reorienting the economic and financial affairs of their country and that in these matters advice from a European or a North American would be presumptuous.

I also explained that we were concerned not merely with Jews, but also with Protestants and Catholics. Apparently, it was particularly important to do this in this office, because as Alemann explained to me in our talk afterwards, his brother, who is in that ministry, had overheard Pinero's secretary talking about me as the "importer of Jews."

Then I briefly summarized the various points on which I hoped the Argentine authorities would be willing in practice to apply an interpretation favorable to the admission of the refugees.

Pinero's response was throughout most satisfactory and encouraging. He agreed that the method I suggested was the right one, that it should be a matter of interpretation, rather than a formal agreement, and he seemed to see no substantial reason why the practice of favorable interpretation, to which I referred, should not be adopted. He at once saw the absurdity of the restrictions in reference to the certificate of conduct, because he recognized that the dangerous subversive element could always secure forged papers.

He said emphatically that Argentina needs immigration, even on a fairly large scale; but he was opposed to group settlement on a national basis such as Alemann suggested. And without my suggesting anything about the Jewish colonies, Pinero called attention to them in Entre Rios, saying that they were no good—that they were not successful. I did not press this point with him, because by then we were short of time.

However, he seemed so sympathetic to my general appeal on behalf of more liberal procedure for the admission of refugees that I ventured to tell him of the difficulties I had been encountering in trying to see Justo. Pinero said at once that the president ought to see me, and that during a conference he was having with him that afternoon he would speak to him about the matter. I expressed my cordial appreciation of this willingness to help.

I left him with the feeling that here was a man of broad caliber and not merely sympathetic, but able and willing to be of substantial assistance.

Walked with Alemann down the Mayo 25 [Avenido 25 de Mayo] to Pedro Weil's office. Alemann said he was delighted with the conference and that he was sure Pinero would do what he could.

Young Weil was waiting for me in his office at the top of the skyscraper.

I asked him first about the fruit plantation and preserving project of Adolfo Hirsch. He was warm in his praise of Hirsch's good intentions and sincerity, but was skeptical about the proposition being a business one. To his mind, there were too many elements of uncertainty—the weather, the possibility of oversupplying the market, etc. Nonetheless, it would be worth trying.

I asked him what he thought Pinero meant by his critical remarks in reference to the Jewish colonies in Entre Rios. Weil then told me of the wave of speculative expansion which the colonists had gone in for during the years just before 1929, aided and abetted by the large grain operators like Alfredo Hirsch, and even by [the] Weil brothers. The result was the present years of serious depression. He said that Rothmann, whom I had met the other day when I was lunching with Jimenez and Ewing, was one of the operators who had lost heavily and had been seriously discredited.

According to Weil, Argentina needs and can absorb almost any number of young unattached men without families, preferably those with technical training and prepared to work hard and to live simply. For the best of these there will be many chances to rise. Technicians of all sorts are needed; experts in the operation of diesel motors, etc., etc. He himself needed some of these at once. But there was no room at all for the commercial class, especially not for the petty businessman. These would only clutter up the cities and help to give the Jews a bad name.

I asked him about Eddis. He said he did not know much about him, but there was something which was not quite clean at the beginning of the latter's career.

Then we drifted into talk about the Jewish communities. P. Weil, himself largely assimilated, was utterly pessimistic about the possibilities of reconciling the conflicting and warring Jewish groups. And I left with the impression that personally he would make little sacrifice toward that end, though he was most warm in his expression of appreciation to me for my part in the present work and generous in his offer of cooperation.

Barely time for lunch before the hour had arrived for the appointment with the archbishop. Luguizamon was again late, so I decided not to wait on him, but went over to the palace alone. At first I was rather dismayed, because the secretary whom I knew was not present, and the other secretary in the outer office was anything but cordial. He spoke nothing but Spanish and had little patience with my endeavors to make myself understood. Moreover, two anterooms were crowded with people waiting to be received.

Fortunately, as I hoped, the archbishop's personal secretary soon appeared, recognized me, and told me that His Eminence would see me in just a moment. Presently he took me around past the two ante-rooms, and I was shown in.

I reminded the archbishop of my previous talk, pointed out to what extent the sad events of the past two weeks had only too fully vindicated my pessimistic estimates of the attitude of the Nazis toward the Church. I was surprised when he told me that he had not time to read his papers carefully and had not been fully informed of these developments.

McDonald's comment about the sad events of the past two weeks referred to a stepped up Nazi campaign against the Catholic Church, during which priests, monks, and nuns were accused of violating German regulations regarding transfer of funds out of the country.

Some were charged with helping to smuggle Jewish capital out, which was a way of calling attention both to the wealth ascribed to Jews and that of the Catholic Church. The real goal was to stimulate anti-Catholic feeling among the German people. The first "trial," concluded on May 16 convicted a nun and imposed a large fine and a jail sentence of five years.[9]

I asked him what would be his attitude in the event of any considerable Catholic refugee migration. He said he would welcome all the refugees, but naturally more especially the Catholics. I inquired whether he would approve the setting up of a special committee to care for these newcomers. He replied that that would not be necessary, because two existing committees now functioning in connection with two of the German parishes could serve. He suggested that I discuss this matter further with the parish priests in these two churches. (Unfortunately, I did not have time to follow up this suggestion.) As I left, the archbishop expressed, as he had earlier, the most cordial approval of my work.

Then I went directly to the office of Dr. Duhau, the secretary of agriculture. As I was waiting for the minister who had not yet arrived, I chatted with a couple of his secretaries in Spanish, and later talked with his English-speaking assistant. When Duhau passed through the ante-room, everybody stood at attention. This was not surprising, for he is a man of a rather elegant and self-assertive type, who would be expected to have people stand around.

My reception, when I began my talk with him, was rather cool. I at once disclaimed any intention of laying down any definite plans, but rather of asking his cooperation. I then outlined briefly the substance of my talks with Zalazar Altamira, and expressed the hope that Duhau would agree with the plan for a gentlemen's agreement. But he was not prepared to assent without many qualifications.

9. J. S. Conway, *The Nazi Persecution of the Churches, 1933–45* (New York: Basic Books, 1968), 125.

He said that the regulations were meant to protect the interests of Argentina. When I pointed out that we were here concerned with only a small number of possible immigrants, he replied, "Yes, that is what each person says who is asking for exceptional treatment, and if one granted all these exceptions, the total of newcomers would be very large, and they might wake up to find Argentina a crowded country."

Feeling defeated by my direct approach, I then brought in the Catholic theme. As I told Duhau of Pacelli's attitude, of the danger to the Church in Germany, of the interest indicated by the cardinal in Rio and the archbishop in Buenos Aires and as I gave illustrations of present Nazi practices, Duhau became more and more interested and lost more and more of his coldly formal manner. He expressed himself as shocked and horrified, but he doubted if there could be any effective resistance to the Nazi attacks.

Finally, I pleaded with him on behalf of the refugees on the ground of humanity. He said that, of course, touches us in a weak spot, for Argentina is always sensitive to the call of humanity. But despite this generalization, the most I could get from him at the very end when I expressed the hope that he would pass on the word to Brebbia and Zalazar Altamira of approval for the gentlemen's agreement idea, was that he would study it.

Moreover, he was noncommittal when I expressed the hope that if I came back to Argentina, I might have the pleasure of another conference with him.

So I left rather discouraged.

At the hotel, where I met on my return Dr. Browning, Mr. Ewing, and Dr. Saralegui for the first meeting of the intellectuals' committee, we were joined for a little while by Arthur Lehman. He was in town on the *Franconia* cruise. He listened with interest to the discussion of our group. As he left, he asked me how many of the members were Jews. I told him none. He expressed wonder that they would interest themselves in this question.

At the committee meeting I reported that Pinero had told me that afternoon that he thought there might be possibilities for places for some of the intellectuals in his department or in the new bank which was being organized under the management of Prebisch.

....

By the time the committee meeting broke up, it was eight o'clock. I had been in almost continuous conference during the day and felt terribly tired. So after supper, together Ruth, Miss Sawyer and I decided to go to an early movie only to discover that the feature picture did not begin until after eleven. So despite our good intentions, we did not get back to the hotel until one o'clock.

Saturday, May 11, 1935

Called up Alemann and asked if he could have prepared for me three or four typewritten pages of extracts from recent news items illustrating the attitude of the Nazis toward the Church.

Long conference with Adolfo Hirsch. He told me at length about the situation of the community, the tendency of the richer people to give very little, and yet to feel that they had thereby done their duty. For example, the Hilfsverein had only some twenty donors who gave more than 20 pesos. I was shocked when he told me the actual amounts given by some rather rich people.

I checked with him on the criticism which I had heard to the effect that it [the Hilfsverein] limited its activities to the German-speaking immigrants. Hirsch explained that in a sense this was true, because they were anxious to limit their work to the refugees and not to deal with immigrants in general. On the other hand, he declared that they did not interpret German-speaking in the narrow sense, and that any immigrant who had been in Germany for some time and could therefore speak a little German was considered eligible for help. I could see, however, from the way he put it, that there might easily be ground for criticism by the eastern—Russian or Polish or Rumanian—Jews. Hirsch illustrated in a somewhat different way the same fundamental point of view which Schwarzschild had represented so strikingly—the desire of the German Jews to help their fellow German Jews, rather than Jews generally.

Hirsch complained that the ICA was continuing to send families, though few in number, to Buenos Aires without consulting the local committee or without providing funds for the settlement of the refugees. He deplored the sending of families because of the extreme difficulties of placing them. On the other hand, he confirmed what so many persons had told me, that there were always places for young people—that is, single men. There was almost no limit, provided money were available to the number of these who could be placed.

Dr. Browning told me that he had heard it said that the reason the *Prensa* had not supported our project editorially was that the *Critica* had had a feature story about our work before the *Prensa* was visited. I explained that we had not called upon the *Critica,* but they had sent someone to see me, that, in fact, about the same time there appeared a considerable article in the *Prensa.* I thanked him for his information, but suggested that a more real reason for the attitude of the *Prensa* lay in the fact that they had not so long ago attacked the government vigorously on the ground that it was too lenient in immigration matters and had argued that Argentina should not make itself a dumping ground for refugees. Certainly, the elder Paz had been as cordial as one could expect when Inman and I called on him.

About half past nine Ruth, Miss Sawyer, and I went to dinner at the Eddis's. They had invited about twenty or twenty-five persons, including a number of [their daughter] Violet's friends. One of these was her fiancé. It was an amusing evening, with an elaborate buffet supper, dancing and music. It was difficult to get away. Actually, we had not begun to eat until about 10:30, and when we started home after one, we were accused of breaking up the party. However, in the best Argentine fashion it lasted until nearly four.

Sunday, May 12, 1935

Out to the country with Mr. Levi and Saslavsky to play golf at Rondeleigh. We were able to play only eleven holes, because it was a considerable trip out, and we were expected at a picnic which was given at Saslavsky's weekend country place and attended by all the members of his firm.

On the way out Saslavsky told us how deeply stirred he had been by the list of expelled professors. He had not believed such barbarism possible.

Levi said that their experience had been that Brebbia was very suspicious and always went contrary to the views of the large exporters, because he suspected them of ulterior motives. Therefore, he, Levi, had deliberately differed with me on the question of the desirability of immigration when we were discussing this at Saslavsky's house the other night in order that Brebbia might not feel that the meeting had been "rigged."

We arrived at Saslavsky's weekend house after the other guests had begun to eat. What a feast it was! It was typically Argentinean—meats of many sorts roasted on the open fire, and vegetables and foods of other sorts. A family reunion in Indiana might have supplied a greater variety of food other than meat, but it could not have supplied more ample quantities.

The Levis drove us back fairly early in order that we might have a little rest before our tea party. Arrived at the hotel. Was shocked to find that Miss Sawyer had been laid up all day and would be unable to attend the party for which she had made all the arrangements. The party was held in the roof room of the City Hotel and was, I think, a great success.

During the tea I had a chance to talk for a little while with Dr. Solomon and took the occasion to present a number of persons to him. Alemann repeated his offers of help in any way possible in following up my work here. Selzer helped to entertain some of the younger people, and also met a number of others who were interested in him. I was surprised but glad that Zalazar Altamira came with his wife. But the sensation of the afternoon was the arrival of Mrs. Alfredo Hirsch and her daughter. I did not realize that this was such a triumph until several members of the Jewish community told me that not in years had any member of the Alfredo Hirsch family been at a Jewish party. Mrs. Hirsch said that her husband was very sorry he could not come, that he was taking a series of treatments for his rheumatism. The daughter seemed glad to meet a number of the other guests.

Since it had been arranged that there would be tables and chairs for everyone, even though there were just under one hundred guests, nearly everyone stayed until after six o'clock, and the party did not really break up until after seven. The number of people who came was the best proof of the interest of the Jewish community in my endeavors.

Though I was very tired, I could not get out of the dinner which I had promised to attend at the Plaza as the guest of ICA. Starkmeth and Weil had invited Adolfo Hirsch and two or three others. I was interested during dinner in the account which Starkmeth gave me of his career before and since his coming to Argentina. He is a real personality, but one might still question whether he has not outgrown his usefulness in the Argentine situation.

We all talked about the developments during my three weeks in the country and agreed that, while we could not be sure of the extent to which the so-called gentlemen's agreement would actually be carried out, it would be best to assume that it would be and to act accordingly. Towards the end of the dinner Starkmeth graciously offered a toast in honor of my "great accomplishments" in the good cause while in the Argentine.

Back to the hotel late.

Monday, May 13, 1935

A committee representing the central organization, made of Bergman, Adolfo Hirsch, and one or two others. They were anxious to get from me a full statement of the situation to date. I then summarized for them the points which I had discussed and, I thought, agreed on with Zalazar Altmira as follows: the thirty gold pesos; the *cartes d'identité et de voyage;* the certificate of good conduct; the question of agricultural destination; and the general policy of proceeding by interpretation on the basis of a gentlemen's agreement. I also indicated the possibility of certain consulates being chosen as those to whom greater discretion might be given.

Then we discussed the situation in Argentina. I said that I would strongly urge that their point of view be taken account of in the selection of immigrants to be sent, and that I would insist that money from abroad should be made available for the settlement of these immigrants.

They were anxious to know through whom they should keep in touch. Bergman asked about the American Jewish Congress. I explained that this was primarily a political body and had little or nothing to do with the refugees. I emphasized that, as a practical matter, they must continue to work with ICA, that to attempt to do otherwise would be futile, that our office could not take the place of HICEM or ICA, nor could we improvise comparable machinery. I recognized the difficulties of these relationships in the past, but told them quite frankly that I felt that they would have to work out a modus operandi.

I added that now that I had spent time in Argentina and knew first-hand of the situation, I would not hesitate to speak strongly to Sir Osmond and others concerned in support of what I felt to be the essentially correct attitude of the Buenos Aires committees, and that I was confident to have more influence than formerly. This assurance seemed to relieve their minds.

....

At Brebbia's office in the Ministry of Agriculture at two o'clock. I had to wait about a quarter of an hour before he was free. First of all, I thanked him for his kindness in arranging the interview with Duhau and told him of my talks with Pinero and the archbishop. I elaborated somewhat on the threat to the Church.

Then I tried to tie him down to the points which I had understood Zalazar Altamira had agreed to. But before raising the specific questions, I asked his advice as to whether I ought to write an informal personal letter summarizing my interpretation of the conversations. He said that undoubtedly this would be helpful. I replied that I was anxious, however, not to put the matter in such a form as would require a formal reply or might lead to a formal dissent. He said in his rather bureaucratic tone, "We would not hesitate to make any corrections that might be necessary in our reply." The way he said this seemed to me to indicate that he would be punctilious in his examination of my statement, and would be inclined to take exception to any point which might conceivably cause him embarrassment later if he did not object to it at the time.

Disturbed by this fear, I told him that I was unsure whether under the circumstances I ought to write a letter at all. I suggested that perhaps I might write something that afternoon yet, and send it over to him by messenger, and then telephone him from Montevidéo to inquire if the text were satisfactory. If it were, I would submit it formally; if it were not, I would be free to make changes. He thought this a satisfactory procedure.

Then I began my talk of specific points by assuming that the whole arrangement would be a gentlemen's agreement. This phrase seemed to stir Brebbia into reverting to his natural bureaucratic type, for he said, "Among gentlemen, what is the difference between a gentlemen's agreement and a convention?" I replied that, of course, in essence there was no difference, but from the political point of view the informal arrangement might have advantages. He assented, but without enthusiasm. This was the beginning of my disillusionment.

I sought to confirm from him Altamira's suggestion that ICA would be granted exemption from the thirty peso requirement if it applied again for this without connecting this appeal with any other issue. Brebbia said, "Yes, that method of application would increase the favorable chances," but he was far from being as definite or as encouraging as Altamira had been.

The same applies to the point about *cartes d'identité et de voyage*. Yes, they would be inclined to be more lenient in this respect, but there could be nothing definite, and he gave the impression that the consuls would have to get express authorization in each case.

Similarly, in the matter of the certificate of good conduct, he recognized the force of my arguments, but in practice it probably would not be possible for the consuls to take the initiative.

Indeed, on the general question of consular responsibility he was completely unsatisfactory. He said as a matter of fact, no consul will take the responsibility of making an exceptional ruling on the points above. His assumption in this regard was so definite that it shocked me, but I could not question the accuracy of his views.

Then I tried to argue with him on the desirability of giving the consuls in certain centers to be selected exceptional authority, and thus freeing them from the threat implicit in the existing regulations. I called his specific attention to

Article XVII of the regulations, and suggested as had Altamira that this might have been drafted with the refugees specifically in mind. But Brebbia was not impressed. He proceeded to tell the story of the difficulties that had been created by previous attempts to give to certain consuls greater authority than to others. This had meant, in practice, that the bulk of the immigrants would come from certain ports; this led to constant protests from the shipping companies which did not serve these parts, and by the diplomatic representatives on behalf of those companies. The Argentine authorities had, therefore, found it impossible to continue this practice and would be unwilling to try it again in the case of the refugees. This seemed so flat and definite that I could not understand how Altamira in good faith was able to suggest to me the possibility which Brebbia now rejected categorically.

Then Brebbia, as if seeking to excuse himself for his utterly negative attitude, asked me if I had yet seen Justo. I explained that I had not and the reasons therefore. Brebbia's comment was, "That is too bad, because the rest of us are bound by the regulations, but if he had suggested a degree of liberality, it would have been much easier for us to have met your wishes." I could not tell whether this was a mere perfunctory passing of responsibility, or whether it expressed a genuine view. I was inclined to believe the former.

Some minutes we then chatted about the future. I expressed the hope that we might meet again soon, either in London or Paris, or New York. He said he hoped it would be abroad, because here in Buenos Aires he had no time at all to himself.

As I was leaving, he said with evident sincerity, "Do feel free to cable me or write me at any time about any difficulty which may arise. I am completely at your orders." This last phrase which is on the lips of every Argentine loses some of its force by constant reiteration.

Back to the hotel, where I told Miss Sawyer of the demoralizing interview with Brebbia. We then discussed the possibility of a memorandum, but I decided not to try to dictate it until after I had had a few minutes' nap. Then I worked for an hour or so, but was so dissatisfied with the result that I hesitated to send it. It was extremely difficult to say anything definite in the light of Brebbia's analysis, and to write a memorandum which was merely generalities promised little value. My draft was so negative in its character that it tended to reduce the results of the conversations to a list of the things which had not been granted. After Miss Sawyer and I talked it over, I decided not to send it.

Saslavsky came in to say goodbye and to report on his conversations with Justo that afternoon. He had not gone to the president specifically to talk about the problem of refugees, but he had been kept waiting so long that he said he would not have stayed at all had it not been for his promise to me to bring up the refugee matter to Justo.

According to Saslavsky, Justo knew all about my mission. He said he had been waiting for the British ambassador to bring me. Salslavsky had then taken the line that it was better that I had not seen Justo, because had I done so there would inevitably have been publicity about it, and the German minister would have followed me at the Casa Rosada and might have made it more difficult for Justo to adopt in practice a helpful attitude. I am not sure that this was a wise line for Saslavsky to take, but it probably did no harm, for by that time there was no longer any chance of my seeing the president this trip in any case.

Saslavsky reported that he had disabused Justo's mind of any impression that the latter might have had that Oungre's mission and mine were identical. The president had recalled that someone—he did not remember definitely who it had been—had been to talk to him about immigration. Saslavsky stressed that Oungre's mission was practical, though not commercial, but that mine was on the higher plane of humanity. Justo said that he recognized this distinction.

Saslavsky then explained that I was not asking for formal changes, but for changes in spirit and in interpretation of the regulations and in their application. According to Saslavsky, Justo replied at this point in these words, "That is exactly my idea; that is my point of view." In other words, he seemed completely sympathetic.

Not having been present at the interview, I do not know quite how to interpret this remark of the president, but it is certainly encouraging. And there can be no doubt that if I could give an increasing Catholic slant to the problem, the chances of success would be enlarged.

Saslavsky and I agreed that it would be desirable to have someone close to the president go over with him a list of the refugee professors. Saslavsky did not think he should do this, but thought that probably it could be arranged. I should write Saslavsky and Ewing about it.

When Saslavsky left, he pledged his support in every way that he could be useful. He should be a real source of strength. If only Alfredo Hirsch were the same type of man, the story in Argentina would be very different.

. . . .

Then over to the *Nacion,* where I chatted for a few minutes with Alberto Gerschunoff.[10] He said that he was sure that the most important work I could possibly perform would be to direct my efforts towards securing from the Vatican a general statement denouncing anti-Semitism as un-Christian and uncivilized. Gerschunoff is an impressive individual.

The Eddises came to say goodbye, and I am sorry to have to record that I was by that time—it was then after half past eight—so late that I was perhaps discourteous to them, after they had done so much for us.

Down to the boat alone shortly before nine. Actually we did not sail until nine or ten o'clock Uruguay time. A delegation came to see me off—Berkman, Klein, and one other.

10. Alberto Gershunoff, sometimes referred to as the father of Jewish–Latin American literature. His most famous novel was *Los Gauchos Judios de Las Pampas* [Jewish Cowboys of the Pampas], published in 1910, which is based on his early experiences in Entre Rios.

I left Argentina with mixed feelings of having made the best efforts I was capable of, but still painfully conscious that at several points—notably in the efforts to see the president—I had made mistakes of tactics. Even more disquieting was the memory of the devastating bureaucratic conversation of Brebbia as illustrated in his refusal to commit himself to anything that afternoon.

On the other hand, it was quite clear that my task had been made much more difficult by the fact that every one assumed it to be merely a Jewish problem and my inability to show on the basis of concrete data that it was in considerable part a Catholic problem as well. Experience with a great variety of officials had proved that while the government might not be influenced directly by advice or suggestions from the hierarchy, it would be immeasurably more ready to make concessions if these were not subject to the attack that they had been made in favor of Jews, but instead had been made in behalf of refugees of which a considerable part are Catholics.

Moreover, I was convinced that it was worthwhile to attempt to follow my original hunch about Catholic-Jewish cooperation and to follow it at the Vatican itself. The skeptics may be right in their assumption that there can be no agreement in principle, but there are undoubtedly are possibilities of mutual support in specific instances. In addition, you have the important possibility such as that which was emphasized by the editor at the *Nacion*.

Nonetheless, despite the strength of the Jewish community in the Argentine and the willingness of many of them to help, I doubt if it would be wise to encourage any large influx of Jews. The situation in these respects is almost completely a reverse of that in Brazil, where there are infinite possibilities, but in Rio itself no community worth the name on which to build.

Commenting on the McDonald mission, historian Haim Avni wrote: "the High Commissioner left Buenos Aires with little more than a "gentleman's agreement," as he called it. The main reason was the vociferously anti-Semitic propaganda being disseminated in Argentina, and a chief culprit was the unofficial but highly influential organ of the Catholic Church, Criterio, *edited by Gustavo Franceschi. While McDonald was in Buenos Aires, Franceschi called upon Congress "to reform the immigration laws and sacrifice liberalism on the altar of necessity to keep the Republic from losing its distinctiveness." In his talks with the archbishop, McDonald had been assured of the Jews right to settle in Argentina. This, however, was not the view expressed in* Criterio, *which clearly enjoyed Church backing.*[11]

Montevidéo, Uruguay, Tuesday, May 14, 1935

After a quiet, restful night, the boat docked at about 7:30. I was met by Mr. Harriman of the American Legation. He did not, however, go to the hotel with

11. Haim Avni, *Argentina and the Jews: A History of Jewish Immigration* (Tuscaloosa: University of Alabama Press, 2002), 134–135.

me because he was also meeting the American minister, Mr. Lay, who was arriving at exactly the same time on the *American Legion,* which was docking a few minutes after we had tied up. Harriman told me, however, that I was invited to a luncheon at the La Nata Hotel. I went on to the Parque Hotel. It has a beautiful site, but is old fashioned, and because all of the bathrooms open onto the corridors, its prevailing odor is strongly reminiscent of Venice!

On arrival I found a note from Mr. Hugo Baruch, the directing person and the president of the *Sociedad de Protección a los Immigrantes Israelitas.* This society is not a large one. It has only modest headquarters and a small budget, but I should judge does its work excellently. Certainly no one could have been more helpful than was Mr. Baruch.

I called him up as soon as I had had breakfast, and he came to see me at nine and stayed until after eleven. This long talk gave me an opportunity to box the compass, not only on Jewish affairs in Uruguay, but also on the general economic situation as well. As to the latter, he confirmed the impression, which I had received from other sources, to the effect that the country has not only not yet emerged from the crisis [the depression], but is probably continuing to suffer more and more. He said that Uruguay was much worse off than either Brazil or Argentina, owing probably to its complete dependence upon its export of meat and to the fact that it had undergone an unusually extravagant expansion during the latter years of the new economic era. Baruch concluded, therefore, that the opportunities for immigration were necessarily restricted at the present time, but he felt that something could be done if sufficient money were available to enable the newcomers to establish themselves. He emphasized that only when the money was available could he and his associates assume responsibility for caring for the immigrants.

He described in some detail the technical regulations affecting immigration. As in Brazil and Argentina, the officials talk always about the need for agricultural immigrants and in principle are opposed to the coming of other than agriculturists. Agriculturists are admitted freely if they can show that they have a contract to work or have arranged to settle themselves. Artisans also are admitted, provided they can prove to have a contract for employment. Less easy would be the admission of commercial persons without a certain capital.

In general, anyone having six or seven hundred pesos (Uruguayan) (about $400) is admitted without question. It is to be noted, however, that this is not per family, but per person. There does not appear to be the distinction between first and third class passengers applying for admission as in Argentina.

On the whole, Baruch feels that the government is friendly to Jewish immigration. Moreover, the officials are notoriously easy-going and are not likely to raise difficulties unnecessarily. He feels that if there were set up in Uruguay an institution with a considerable capital, it would be possible to secure from the government an exemption from the requirement of the six-seven hundred pesos per person. In other words, if there were a guarantee against such immigrants being public charges. But—and he repeated this many times—"without money we can do nothing."

We then talked about the possibilities in Uruguay for intellectuals. Baruch was not encouraging, but he suggested that it would be helpful to see Dr. Alfredo Navarro, vice president of the republic and president of the Senate, and also the minister of public instruction. In addition, he named Dr. Azevedo Blanco, minister of public health, and Dr. Caviglia,[12] a prominent businessman interested in intellectual matters.

We then drifted into a general talk about the position of the Jews in Uruguay and the problem of the Jews generally created by the Nazi movement. In Montevidéo, as elsewhere in South America, the Jewish community is of fairly recent date and is predominantly eastern European, with only a small minority of German or Sephardic Jews. This creates a special problem in the matter of immigration, and also from the point of view of active interest in German Jews as such. Moreover, most of the Uruguayan colony is poor; there are only a few members of moderate means, and with one or two exceptions, these tend to lose their interest in communal affairs in just about the proportion as they gain in worldly goods. Baruch himself must be one of the exceptions. I should judge that he is a man of only moderate resources, for he drives a pre-war Fiat which you would not be able to present as a gift to an American workman; but he commands great respect in the community.

Not accepting Baruch's pessimistic estimate of the possibilities for intellectuals, I asked him if he would be good enough to try to arrange for me to see a number of the men in the university, and also some of the persons he had named. He promised to do his best.

Lunch at La Nata with a group of the American community. I assumed that the lunch had been arranged for the new minister, Mr. Lay. Also present were the three members from the States of the American delegation to the Pan American Commercial Congress—two of these from the State Department. In addition to these guests and myself there was Mr. Dominian and about twelve or fourteen American businessmen. They were younger than many I had seen in Rio or in Argentina, and I liked them on the whole better. The community all together numbers only sixty or eighty persons, including women and children.

During the meal I managed to induce some of my neighbors to talk about economic conditions in the country. Without exception, they agreed with the pessimistic estimate of Mr. Baruch. They insisted that the bottom had not yet been reached.

We also gossiped a little about the makeup of the present government, the quasi-dictatorship of Terra,[13] who is so typical of Uruguay, a provincial country

12. Dr. Buenaventura Caviglia Campora, distinguished etymologist.

13. Gabriel Terra of the Colorado Party. Elected president in 1931, assumed dictatorial powers in 1933 in cooperation with Luis Alberto de Herrera of the Blanco Party. The two men ruled jointly in a mild dictatorship. The arrangement was made legal in the 1934 constitution, which curtailed individual liberties in Uruguay.

gentleman in his manner and outlook, though he has been a lawyer and a politician most of his life. Apparently, he is a rather easy-going dictator.

At three forty-five Mr. Dominian came to the hotel. As chargé for some time, he was extremely well informed; evidently too, he has excellent relations with the Uruguayan authorities, for he was able to tell me that the president had consented to see me the next morning at ten o'clock at his private residence.

I asked Mr. Dominian who could probably help most in getting on with my work on behalf of the intellectuals. He suggested that Felipe A. Connor, an old friend of Inman's and the secretary of the YMCA for many years in Montevidéo and, during recent years, the secretary of the South American Federation of YMCA's, knew everyone and would probably be glad to help. Dominian called up Connor, who came to see me at five.

Mr. Connor and I continued the general discussion of possibilities in Uruguay. So far as intellectuals are concerned, he thought that Dr. Eduardo Monteverde, a prominent mathematician, and Dr. Carlos José Montenear, the head of an educational institute, would be interested. Particularly, however, he felt that his colleague, Hugo Grassi, secretary of the YMCA with American training, would be useful. Grassi has a unique position in Montevidéo, because among the members of the classes at the Y or on the board are many dozens of the most influential men of the town. In this respect Mr. Conner said Grassi is a most exceptional Y secretary.

Because I had to follow matters up promptly, I asked Mr. Connor if he would call up Mr. Grassi to inquire if I could talk with him this evening. It was arranged for me to meet Grassi with Connor and some of the younger intellectuals at the YMCA for supper. Apparently, the YMCA is a club much frequented by the younger professors, as well as by many businessmen.

At six o'clock Mr. Baruch returned to report that he had arranged for a number of interviews on the afternoon of Wednesday. We then went out for a long walk along the beach, following the magnificent new boulevard which reaches from our hotel a full twelve kilometers to the extreme end of the summer colony. This elaborate public work is only one of several in Montevidéo which was made possible by the reckless lending by American bankers before 1929. It is also an evidence of the Uruguayan quality, which is shared by the Brazilians and the Argentineans, of grandeur in the decoration of their capitals.

Baruch was interesting in his estimates of the European situation, about which he is very pessimistic, and in his analysis of his own people.

As to the latter, he concluded that they tend to exaggerate in themselves the bad, as well as the good, qualities of other folk among whom they live.

At 7:45 I met Grassi and Connor at the YMCA. We were joined by Antonio Lucas and by some other younger men. They all showed the liveliest interest in the problem of the intellectuals. As they looked through the lists, they could not repress expressions of horror at the expulsion of men of such distinction on racial or religious grounds. They all indicated their willingness to help in any possible way. It was agreed that Dr. Francisco Pucci, a prominent dentist with contacts in all sorts of circles, should be included in any committee that might be set up. Mr. Clementi Estable, professor in the school of medicine, was also mentioned. Alberto C. Estrada offered to do what he could to put me in touch with Dr. Navarro. Our discussion lasted for nearly two hours.

Wednesday, May 15, 1935

Mr. Dominian came for me about 9:30. We chatted about various men in the diplomatic or consular service—Cox of Buenos Aires, White of Berlin, and Messersmith. Dominian belongs to the school of Messersmith, rather than to the group of the other two.

Dominian said that he had asked for my interview with the president not on any official ground, nor even because the United States is a member of the official Governing Body, for this he did not know, but only because as a "distinguished American," I had asked for the interview. This, he said, was the usual practice and did not require personal and individual authorization from the department. All of this was illuminating in the light of the attitude of Cox in Buenos Aires.

We reached the president's residence promptly at ten. Armed guards and plain clothes men who could be mistaken for nothing but detectives, were on hand at all the doors and gates. While waiting in the drawing room, Dominian and I chatted with the uniformed aide of the president. Dominian took advantage of this occasion to not only explain my mission, but also to point out that the United States had taken the initiative in seeing to it that Uruguay was invited to be a member of the Peace Commission on the Chaco. That was good diplomacy.

The president, as he came in, struck me as more of a rancher and a countryman than a politician or a diplomat. Dominian briefly explained my mission, and I then first expressed my thanks and that of the Governing Body for the participation of Uruguay and for the excellent services rendered by Mr. Guani. I also stressed that Guani, because of his many personal connections in Paris, Brussels, London, and in Geneva, has been able to do more for Uruguay, much more, than a diplomat ordinarily could. I had the impression that the president knew little of Guani, but that he was pleased to have this report.

I then said that we had nothing special to ask for from the government, but that I wished to explain briefly the problem of the intellectuals. This did not seem to have the least interest for Dr. Terra, for as I finished, he turned to me and looked me full in the face (I was sitting facing the light so that he had a much better chance to observe me than I had to observe him) and said, "What other mission have you?" I replied that I had none other. He answered, "But you look like you were a superior person." His tone and what he said afterwards showed clearly that he could not understand why I should be interested in the refugees as a whole or in the intellectuals. He himself has doubtless been in the business of creating a certain number of refugees, though in keeping with South American traditions, his dictatorship has been mild.

From this conference I went directly to the office of the Jewish Immigration Society, where I spent an hour and a half with Mr. Baruch and his colleagues and perhaps twenty of the men members of the Jewish community.

With Estrada I went to the home of Dr. Navarro in one of the attractive suburbs. I only learned later that he has one of the show gardens of the town, so I missed the opportunity to see it. His library, however, in which we waited for a quarter of an hour or so until his arrival, was also interesting. He is a well known Francophile, with not only strong pro-French sympathies, but with a cultured taste for French literature and art. The room showed these qualities.

We talked in French, first about the general effects of the Nazi intolerance on the intellectual world. His views would satisfy an extreme person. Then I asked him about the possibilities for intellectual refugees in Uruguay. He expressed the keenest interest, but was emphatically pessimistic. I had been forewarned on one of the reasons for his pessimism. A distinguished surgeon, he has recently gone into politics, and as a politician, he is more reactionary than the dictator. He waxed eloquent in his denunciation of the university, of which he formerly was such a distinguished part. Indeed, he had been so popular with the students that they have set aside one day a year which the called "Navarro Day." Now, however, he is at open war with them.

His attitude is illustrated by the following summary of his statement:

"The university is honeycombed with communism. The students have more authority than the professors. There are regular soviets. The government should make a clean sweep of these insidious, subversive elements. I have urged the president to do so, but he says that nothing will induce him to have another row with the university. (There had been student strikes recently, during which the students had taken over the university buildings.)

"Because of the differences between the government and the university, no suggestion from governmental headquarters would be welcomed by the students or the faculty. Therefore, nothing could be done by me. Moreover, there are so many factions within the university that what one professor supports, another will oppose. In short, there is nothing to do."

Later, I was told that the report of communism, etc. was a gross exaggeration, that the fact was that the university was the one center of opposition to the Terra regime which had not succumbed.

But in any event, it was clear that either Navarro could not or would not be of any material help at this time.

This strengthened my growing feeling that if we were to have a committee that would be effective in Montevidéo, it would have to be made up of the younger people and not, as in Rio or Buenos Aires, of more or less distinguished educators and others of that ilk.

. . . .

Immediately after lunch I met Mr. Baruch, who took me over to the university to meet Milies, with whom we were to see a number of the deans. Since the dean of medicine had not arrived, we went across the street to see the dean of chemistry and pharmacy, Dr. Pedro Pulluffo. We were told that he was next door in the building which was being constructed for his school. Presently he joined us and showed much more than casual interest in our suggestions. He not only sympathized with the plight of the refugees and expressed horror at the expulsion of these distinguished men; he also said that he needed and hoped to employ three or four of them. We studied the list together, and it was left that he was to be given a copy as soon as an additional one was available. He said he would be delighted to have Dr. Milies and the other members of the committee keep in touch with him. Of course, reference was made to the inevitable problem of money, of which there is apparently an even greater shortage in Uruguay than in most other parts of the world.

Then we returned to the Medical School, where we were at once received by the dean, Dr. Hector Rossello. He also indicated interest, but I did not have the feeling that it was as deep as that of his colleague across the street. Nonetheless, he said that if he could have a list of the men in biology and related sciences, he would study it and make suggestions to the next meeting of his governing body. The choice, however, of any of these would depend upon his receiving additional funds, because, at the moment, the resources of his school are exhausted. He, like so many other educationalists with whom I talked in various countries of South America, emphasized the fact that many of their professors were unpaid.

This naturally increases the difficulty of finding the means to engage foreigners who would in the nature of the case have to receive salaries sufficient to live on.

This question of salary came up later that evening when I was meeting with some of the members of the continuation committee. They seemed to feel that salaries comparable to those which were being paid to professors in Sao Paulo would be too large for Montevidéo. They felt that about two hundred pesos would be the normal amount a month, though they admitted that it would be difficult for a married man to live on this. Nonetheless, they insisted that the cost of living was cheaper in Montevidéo than in Sao Paulo. I had no opportunity to test this view.

From the Medical School we went to the office of the minister of education, Dr. Martin Echegoyen.[14] He has the reputation of being the one liberal in the Terra government. It appears that his record in the past has been so excellent and his personality is so attractive that even the liberals and radicals forgive him for his present associations.

He received us with great cordiality, indicated a deep personal interest in the plight of the refugee intellectuals and in the principles which were involved in the Nazi program of expulsion. On the other hand, he gave us such a gloomy

14. Martin Echegoyen, eventually became president of Uruguay, 1959–1960.

picture of the financial situation of the country, its increasing deficit, arrears in salaries, intense difficulties in maintaining the present educational status, that we could not but feel that the prospects for more than a very few new men were negligible. As he was telling of the drastic financial difficulties, I said, "But it appears that the authorities can afford the luxury of tearing down considerable sections of the city in order to build magnificent new avenues." I referred to the work which is being pushed intensively on the avenue which is to reach from the Plaza Independencia (?) down to the elaborate Congress building. Except for the Champs Elysée and the main street in Leningrad, I do not recall, save perhaps the Avenida Alvear in Buenos Aires, a street in the heart of a city as wide as this one. It appears that the engineers insisted that it must have this extraordinary width in order that the whole of the Congressional building might show from the end of the street. Dr. Echegoyen's reply was that this extravagant development was being put through by the municipality and not by the national authorities.

The net result of our visit to the minister of education was not encouraging. Nonetheless, I received the definite impression that he is a man not only willing, but anxious to do whatever may be within his power.

By the time we had finished this conference we were already late for our meeting with the dean of the School of Engineering, which is in a distant part of the city next to the port. Fortunately, just as we were entering the building we met someone going out, and we asked him for directions to the office of the dean. He replied, "I am the dean." Though we knew that he was going off to a meeting for which he was overdue, he insisted that we come back to his office and talk. Very briefly we explained about the intellectuals in general and told him of the number of men in his field, or rather showed him the list [of those] who were available. And in the most business-like fashion, he went through the list, indicated the type of men that he would like to have, and said that as soon as he had a list for himself, he would study it carefully and would discuss with the members of the committee the question as to whether he would communicate directly with the men or do it through the committee. What was even more encouraging about this man is the fact that he has the money with which to engage additional men.

Mr. Baruch, Dr. Milies, and I then went back to the YMCA, where we met Grassi and Connor. Then for about half an hour we discussed the plans of setting up a continuation committee. They agreed that here it would be better to have a group of young men. After considerable urging, Grassi said he would be willing to act as correspondent, though he was already very busy. We then agreed on the other members of the committee as follows:

Dr. Antonio Lucas, a young professor in the Medical School;
Alberto C. Estrada, a young law student with important connections in more conservative circles;

Dr. Francisco Pucci, the leading dentist of the town, and with the same wide connections which distinguished dentists appear to have in Latin America.

. . . .

There was then just time to go back to the hotel to pack and to return for a bite of supper with Mr. Connor. He talked interestingly about his work in different parts of South America and of Grassi's unusual position in Montevidéo. The latter's influence in many circles is an illustration of the great incidental value of the YMCA when it is properly led. Incidentally, I was amused at Connor's tale of negotiations with the Montevidéo authorities in connection with the project of cutting off a substantial corner of the YMCA's beautiful new building in order to add an extra and absolutely unnecessary thirty meters to the width of the new avenue.

I arrived at the dock at nine o'clock when the *Almanzora* was due to appear. She was a little late, and this allowed the French boat, the *Florida,* to come into the basin first. . . . Anyhow, it was nearly eleven o'clock before I was able to go on board. Found Ruth and Miss Sawyer refreshed after their "vacation" across the river.

Thursday and Friday, May 16 and 17, 1935

On board SS *Almanzora* en route to Santos, Brazil.

Saturday, May 18, 1935

A very busy morning before we reached Santos. It was our last opportunity to get mail off promptly—or so we thought at the time—for Montevidéo, and also the last chance to catch the airmail for Europe. We were occupied, therefore, right up to the time of docking.

. . . .

Then followed a comedy of errors and of red tape in getting through the Santos customs. Never have I seen anything to equal it in any part of the world. I was taking off only a small suitcase and our two attaché cases. Against my will, all except the one attaché bag was taken from me by one of the porters, and I discovered later put in a railroad wagon, where the other luggage coming off at that port was put. My friends and I went to the custom house, but found that despite all our talk about an engagement with the governor, it was impossible to get my two bags until the crowd of ten or fifteen men had much later pushed down the wagon to the customs house, but that was not the end. We then had to fill out a paper certifying as to what luggage we had, display our passport, secure a special examiner, and finally, after about half an hour we were excused. What would happen if there had been more than four or five passengers I dislike to contemplate. It is evident that Santos has devised a perfect scheme for solving the unemployment problem!

I went up to Sao Paulo, while Ruth and Miss Sawyer remained on board. . . . [they were meeting McDonald in Rio two days later.]

The trip up the Sierra was exciting. The narrow road, the need for speed, and the astonishingly beautiful view of Santos and the islands. It was very much like an airplane view. The weather changed rapidly, and it was cool and pleasant by the time we reached the plateau. The dust, however, after we left the concrete road which ended at the top of the Sierra, was often so thick that you could hardly see through it. There is no pavement from the Sierra until you reach the suburb of Sao Paulo itself.

With no opportunity to wash up, for we were already late, we went directly to the Government House in the center of the town to see the governor. He is an attractive-appearing man, keen and intelligent. It was at once evident that he knew about the purpose of our visit, not only in general but in some detail. Julio Mosquita had, as he had promised, talked to his brother-in-law.

After discussing the situation of the intellectuals, on whose behalf Dr. Armando de Salles Oliveira showed a special concern, for he is a man of genuine intellectual interests, he said that he would support the efforts of the heads of different schools and research institutions to secure the services of some of these men. This is encouraging, because upon the governor more than anyone else depends the possibility of the money being made available.

We then talked about the immigration situation in general, and especially the attitude of Magalhães Agamemnon. The governor expressed the usual Paulista view strongly in favor of immigration, and then asking me again if it really was true that Agamemnon had said what I reported him to have said. The governor promised to talk to the minister of labor, and he made this promise in such a way as to leave no doubt that he meant it.

Later, I was told by a number of persons that Oliveira is not only very strong in his own state, but that unless there are unexpected developments, he should be Getúlio Vargas's successor.

From the governor's office we went directly to that of the secretary of education and public health, Dr. Cantidio de Moura Compos. Here our talk was again satisfactory, but less so, chiefly because the secretary was much more formal and gave less evidence of genuine concern. Nonetheless, he promised his support.

Then we went directly to the office of the secretary of agriculture. There had been a change in this office since I was in Sao Paulo four or five weeks before. The present secretary is Dr. Luiz Piza Sobrinho. Unlike the previous incumbent, he is not a dirt farmer, but more of an intellectual type. His attitude was definitely encouraging. He knew the problem, was interested in it, and anxious to procure the services of specialized technicians for his department. Two or three times he said that he would support any proposal which Rocha Lima would make. Moreover, he would call together the experts at the head of the various divisions of his office and ask them for suggestions. It was evident that he too had been talked to by men well informed on our problem.

When we had finished this third interview, it was late in the afternoon, for all three men had been induced by Dr. Mendlin to come to their offices especially to permit me to meet them. We went to the hotel. . . .

At the urgent advice of Dr. Mendlin I arranged to see representatives of the press before supper. Dr. Lorch and Dr. Mindlin were present during the talk, the latter acting as interpreter and the former doing his best to curb the enthusiasm of his colleague.

After informal supper at the Lorches' house the two doctors and I went to the office of the *O Estado de Sao Paulo* to meet the owner, Dr. Julio de Mesquita Filho. While waiting on him, we had a long talk with one of the most intelligent Brazilians I have met, Adolpho Santos Filho. He is a mulatto from Bahia, a former student of engineering at MIT, now employed in the Light and Power, but working for funds on the *Estado.* He is said to be one of the rich men of his country. His years in the States have given him a critical attitude about things Brazilian, which is very rare in the young intellectuals. He was caustically critical of the assumption of his fellow intellectuals that they did not need anything from abroad. He criticized them for their indifference and laziness, for their lack of initiative and originality, and insisted that not until these were replaced by others of a more affirmative sort, would the country progress.

We had about decided that Mesquita would not come that evening, for it was then well after eleven o'clock and I had written him a note, when he appeared. He was apologetic for being late and cordial as before. I thanked him for his initiative with his brother-in-law and told him how satisfactory the talk with the governor had been. He was glad to hear it.

Then we launched into a talk about the situation abroad. Always an ardent Francophile, he was bitterly critical of Germany and also concerned about the action of Italy in Abyssinia [invasion and later occupation]. He knows Italy well, having lived there for a time when he was a political refugee after the 1932 Paulista revolution.[15] Despite the fact that he continues to have Nitti as one of his foreign correspondents, he has many friends in Italy and deplores what he considers the rash adventure of Mussolini in Africa. I tried to draw the moral that the worse conditions become in Europe, the more important it is for us to look to the new world and especially to Brazil for hope on behalf of oppressed peoples. He agreed, and is of the opinion that the present exclusionist polities of his government would in the not distant future be replaced by a much more liberal attitude.

After we had said goodbye and I had walked out, Dr. Mindlin remained behind for a little while, as he told me later, drove in on Mesquito the necessity for action. Dr. Mindlin and I then, over cups of chocolate, discussed the owner of the *Estado.* This paper, when managed by the elder Mesquita, was not only the

15. Paulista revolution, a conservative insurgency, the so-called "constitutionalist revolt" against Vargas in July 1932. An abortive attempt by the Paulista coffee planters to retake control of the government.

most powerful journal in Brazil, but was an institution in which really centered the intellectual and, in a sense, the commercial life of the state of Sao Paulo. To a certain extent, that influence has continued. But according to Dr. Mendlin, Mesquita Filho is only a shadow of his great father. He has neither the business acumen nor the intellectual depth nor the commanding personality, nor, for that matter, is he as good a business and newspaper man. Nonetheless, Dr. Mindlin agreed that Mesquito Filho and his group are still the most important influences in the state.

Sunday, May 19, 1935

A cold rainy morning and the prospects anything but encouraging for golf. Nonetheless, I drove out to the course with Mr. A. Bertie Levi, where I practiced for an hour or so in the rain. The net result was a couple of blisters and a torn finger. I never will learn to have gumption enough to wear gloves or adhesive tape when using the same club for many shots.

On the way back Levi told me that he hoped that if there were to be more refugees coming to Sao Paulo, his committee might know of it well in advance so that they might not be caught napping. He recognized Mindlin as the dynamic leader of the community, with great influence among the people in authority, but he insisted that the actual work of placing refugees in new jobs depended upon his committee, and that the most successful single man in these endeavors was Wissmann, who, with his broad business connections, was able to be most effective. I promised to keep him informed.

We stopped at his house, which is quite new, to see it and his wife and her daughter. The house is in no sense Brazilian, but might have come from Indianapolis or Milwaukee. Only the beautiful floors and the exceptionally successful dining room with its beautiful woodwork and built in massive furniture, showed what one could do with the woods of Brazil.

....

Lunch with the Consul General Foster and his wife. As I was saying goodbye, Foster told me that he had about decided to give a visa to the young doctor protégé of Dr. Lorch, Dr. Alfons Salinger, on whose behalf I had appealed to Foster when I was previously in Sao Paulo.

While I was paying my bill, [Fritz] Kreisler[16] came into the lobby carrying his violin and accompanied by two women who apparently had called to walk with him to the concert hall in the municipal theater just across the street. It was amusing to see the struggle which Kreisler had to put up to prevent one of the women taking his violin away from him in order to have the privilege of carrying it.

16. Fritz Kreisler, Austrian violinist and composer, one of the great violinists of the twentieth century. Left Berlin for France in 1938 and settled in the United States in 1943. Of Jewish descent, married to an American citizen.

At the theatre I was astonished to find the hall only a third to a half full. The explanation given me was that this was a third concert which had not been announced in advance. But I could not avoid the impression that Sao Paulo is not as devoted to music as it is to business. It was a glorious concert.

After the concert we picked up my bags at the hotel and went to the Lorches' home. We were early enough to walk through the gardens. These must cover many acres, for in one direction they reach for several hundred meters. Dr. Lorch told me regretfully that the taxes on this huge place in the heart of the city were becoming burdensome. His wife, a daughter of the original Klabin, had inherited this place. The house is not quite as large in proportion as the grounds.

During tea Drs. Lorch, Mindlin, and a politician friend of theirs, Dr. Antonie Augusto de Covelle, and I discussed our general problem of immigration. Dr. Covelle talked extremely well for nearly an hour. In particular, he stressed, as had the cardinal archbishop in Rio, that Brazil is at the moment in a state of flux, the political situation is changing, the exclusionist tendency is likely to wane, the personality of Agamemnon cannot continue indefinitely to determine the national policy, and that, therefore, one should not be discouraged by present obstacles. Covelle said that one ought to begin to work in the states for the influence of the governors and of state opinion must in the end be decisive upon Rio. I admitted this, but pointed out that this would be not a matter of a few weeks, but of many months, and that the need of the refugees for a place to go was immediate.

Then we talked about the doctors who are in Brazil. Mindlin thought that Covelle could be induced to take a special responsibility in this matter. Dr. Covelle, however, was pessimistic, saying that the constitution, the law, the administrative decisions, and the firm attitude of the medical association, all were opposed to any concessions. He would, however, consider what he could do.

. . . .

Immediately after the meal we had to hurry to the station. Never before had I noted how bad the streets of Sao Paulo are. The goodbyes made me feel that I was leaving real friends. . . .

At nine promptly Brazil's best known train, the Southern Cruiser, pulled out of the station. After investigating my stateroom, I was walking forward in the train to the lounge when I ran into Kreisler standing up at the door of his compartment talking with his manager, Mr. Charles Foley. I stopped to tell Kreisler how much I had enjoyed his concert; then for a considerable time we talked about Germany and the European situation. Kreisler is not, I am convinced, pro-Nazi, as he is so frequently said to be. He has lived in Germany for thirty years, his wife prefers it there, and he has never broken with the regime, but he was extremely critical in his talk. He scoffed at the race theories of the Nazis, declared that Goebbels, a fanatic type, is extremely dangerous, but that Göring, who loves wine, food and things of the flesh, is a much more human creature and therefore less harmful, indeed, rather attractive personally. What interested me most in Kreisler's analysis of the German situation was not his point of view that the failure of the Allies to be generous following the peace had ruined the republic (though this of course is a view with which I agree), but rather his definite assertion that he was convinced that the Nazi leaders are determined to eradicate from the whole of the German youth all religious loyalties of the old fashioned sort—Protestant or Catholic. He said this following our talk about the attacks on the Evangelicals and on the Catholics.

Later, as I was leaving the lounge where Kreisler and his entourage had come for a bite of supper, I noticed as I passed the latter's stateroom, his precious violin lying there quite unguarded. I could not resist the thought of what sensation would be caused if someone picked it up and walked off at the little station where we were at the moment stopping.

Rio, Monday, May 20, 1935

....

At eleven o'clock Dr. Leitchie of ICA came to see me. He reported on developments in reference to their démarche during the weeks since I had gone south. Following the receipt of Louis Oungre's telegram instructing him to make a formal representation to the Brazilian authorities on behalf of the ICA, he had prepared a memorandum and had submitted it to Vaz de Mello. The latter had made a number of suggestions as to phraseology, and some that were more substantial, particularly dealing with the type and amount of guarantees expected from ICA on behalf of each individual immigrant, three contos for each adult and two contos for each child above the age of twelve. Leitchie said this was, of course, a point on which there would have to be further discussion, because he felt that in view of ICA's general guarantee, it was unjust to require also the specific guarantees in each individual case. This matter was now awaiting a report from Paris. But there was another reason for delay: Vaz de Mello was insisting that Leitchie secure from Paris a formal certification to the effect that he is authorized to sign on behalf of ICA. He had telegraphed for this, but had not yet received by airmail the necessary authorization.

I read the text of the draft of ICA's proposed statement. It followed closely the lines of the statement prepared earlier for submission by Teixeira Leite.

Then Leitchie and I exchanged views on the actual Brazilian situation. He shared my pessimism about the possibility of favorable action at the present time. He, like I, is uncertain as to whether Vaz de Mello is deliberately inviting delay, or is motivated wholly by a desire to help. In any event, we were both sure that we must continue to work with him; to have a break in that quarter would unnecessarily jeopardize every effort with the Brazilian authorities. For after all, Vaz de Mello stands at a post where he could, if he wanted to, at almost any time check any program which might be worked out against his judgment with higher officials.

On the whole, I got a favorable impression of the new head of the ICA Rio office. He seems intelligent and discriminating. Whether he could be guilty of the sort of unscrupulous action which Röttgen attributes to him, I am in no position to judge. In any event, he is not likely to risk taking any considerable initiative without the explicit authorization of the Paris office. We agreed that we would keep each other informed of developments during my stay.

In the middle of the day the wife of Dr. Röttgen came to see me. Her tale was distressing in the extreme. When she reached Rio, she had found her husband with but four milreis in his pocket. Since then they had been living as the guests of Mr. Peper at a modest pension. She herself was ready and anxious to work and hoped to secure a position in a German pharmaceutical office. But she was worried about her husband, who, being of a tense nature, found the enforced idleness with no opportunity at all to work and with diminishing prospects of finding such opportunity, terribly demoralizing. For herself, she had no real concern; it was only about him that she worried.

Then she told me more about the situation at Quatro Irmaos. They had been forced to turn over their household effects without payment and were certain to have to take a heavy loss. Then there was much more about the attitude of Leitchie and Louis Oungre.

I told her that I would speak to Anisio Teixeira, with whom I was lunching that day, in the hopes that he might be able to find something for her husband. I would also, if Dr. Röttgen wished, speak again to the Rockefeller people.

Lunch with Dr. Anisio Teixeira. He was in rather a subdued mood. He seemed less optimistic about his university than he had been. Some hitch seemed to have occurred about finding adequate funds. He was to meet Dr. Pedro Ernesto Batista[17] and some others of the municipal officials that afternoon at four to clear the matter up. . . .

Teixeira spoke now about four or five professors. I hope that he will not have to reduce to this extent his contracts.

I asked Teixeira about his conversations in Pernambuco. He said that Pedro Ernesto and he had had long talks with the governor of Pernambuco and Agamemnon, but that they had not been able to shake Agamemnon's opposition to urban immigration. The latter insisted that, under present circumstances, to admit city workers would be to invite the development of an urban proletariat. Reading between the lines of what Teixeira said, I received the even more discouraging impression that neither Pedro Ernesto [n]or the governor of Pernambuco had been willing really to go to the bat with Agamemnon. Apparently, therefore, Sir Henry's friend's efforts in Pernambuco with the governor had not been fruitful.

On the way over to Sir Henry's office, where Teixeira drove me in his car,

17. Pedro Ernesto Batista played a key role in the revolution of 1930 and was rewarded with the mayoralty of the Federal District. A radical educational reformer, he secularized Brazilian education. Under pressure from Catholic nationalists, he was imprisoned by Vargas in 1936.

we had further talk, but mostly about personal matters. Teixeira is such a charming and deeply sincere individual that he quickly draws one into serious and revealing personal talks.

I reported to Sir Henry the situation to date. He, for the first time, was frankly pessimistic. I told him of the efforts from Sao Paulo to arrange for me to see the president ad interim quickly. Sir Henry called up the presidential palace, learned that the telegram from Sao Paulo had not been received, and himself suggested to the secretary in charge that he would be glad if the president could receive me before I had to leave.

....

After dinner, Ruth and I went with the Olsburghs to the Municipal Theater to see the English Players in Pygmalion. . . . I was interested to get from Olsburgh the latest news about the difficulty he had had with the immigration authorities in securing the admission of the two young engineers for his company in Brazil. Despite the fact that, as the representative of Imperial Chemicals, he has a close position with the government, it had taken days to secure the release of these two young men from the steamer. Finally, it had been the police, rather than the immigration authorities, who had opened the door.

From what Olsburgh said and from what I heard from others, the head of the immigration department, Dr. Dulphe Pinheiro Machado, is a confirmed exclusionist. He is a Malthusian and is not influenced by anti-Jewish prejudices in his views on immigration. He and Gustavo Barbossa, one of the leaders of the Integralistas who refuses to live up to the truce on the Jewish question, are two of the most important personalities blocking the way. In this connection, Dr. Paulo Rapaport emphasized, when I was talking with him, that it is a mistake to assume that Agamemnon alone is the obstacle to greater freedom in immigration. Previous secretaries of labor have been similarly influenced by Machado and others.

Tuesday, May 21, 1935

....

. . . [I went to] my engagement with Edmund Lynch [brother of Sir Henry] and the bishop of Valença (the archbishop was out of town).

We talked for the most part about the school the bishop wished to develop at Valença. It had already been formally authorized by the state, and the buildings were available, and also the equipment. He would prefer to turn it over to a teaching order from Germany or elsewhere, whose coming would be approved by Pacelli. . . .

We then spoke about Catholic refugees in general. The bishop and Lynch were both positive that there would be no difficulty whatsoever in the admission of any number of such refugees who might desire to come. I asked specifically about legal obstacles, and they assured me positively that there would be no trouble. They added that they can also secure admission of individual Catholic missionaries or groups of Catholic missionaries who might wish to work in Brazil.

Mr. Harry M. Fineberg, at my suggestion, came to the hotel to accompany me to the presidential palace and to act as interpreter, because I had been mistakenly informed that Don Carlos spoke only Portuguese. Before we left the hotel, Fineberg told me a good deal about the situation of the community in Rio. He said there was no unity, and even worse, no leadership or willingness to take responsibility by those in a position to wield influence and command respect in the city as a whole. These men, almost without exception, refused to do anything. They were hiding their heads in the sand in the false hope that they would be able to avoid dangers which had struck their fellows elsewhere. Throughout, he spoke with marked feeling and considerable bitterness.

At the palace, while we were waiting for the president, Fineberg told me more about his own personal situation. He is one of the oldest members of the community and had done much to build up the institutions, Zionist and others, such as there were. But recently he had resigned from all the committees in anticipation of the marriage of his daughter, who had become engaged to a young Catholic boy. Since that event had taken place, he had felt more or less estranged from the community. As he talked, he seemed to me a strange mixture of Jewish nationalist, for he is an ardent Zionist, but with no religious convictions; on the contrary, perhaps because of his early extremely strict bring-up, he is anti-religious. Yet despite his marked Jewishness, he is in a sense a defeatist, because of his assumption that the fewer Jewish children are born, the fewer Jews there will be to suffer in the world. From this point of view, he rather welcomed his daughter's marrying out.

Antonio Carlos (Senhor Presidente ad interim Dr. Antonio Carlos[18]) spoke very good French, so we used that language, except when Carlos and Fineberg talked together. He received us cordially, and immediately after I made my statement, he said of course that Brazil needs immigration; "it is absurd to assume the contrary." I told him that we had been encouraged by the attitude of all the officials except Agamemnon Magalhães. He promised to speak to Agamemnon the next day, and said that he thought he would have word for us before I sailed on Thursday.

We also talked about the intellectuals, but since I had nothing definite to ask for there, the discussion was brief. Carlos expressed his intense dislike of the racist theories of the Nazis, and his wonder that such nonsensical ideas could be seriously entertained.

Then went directly to the Kreisler concert at the Municipal Theater, for which performance Charles Foley, Kreisler's manager, had kindly given us seats. . . .

That evening about nine o'clock Mr. Herman Rinder came, somewhat in

18. Antonio Carlos de Andrada, former governor of Minas Gerais and Vargas ally in 1930.

advance of the two other members of his group. I told Rinder with considerable frankness my surprise that I had received so little help from the community in Rio, that I had not realized how inactive the group here had been until in Sao Paulo and in Buenos Aires I had occasion to see how extremely helpful those communities were. I said that after the first two weeks in Rio there might have been no community at all so far as my experience went, whereas both in Sao Paulo and in Buenos Aires everything possible was done to assist me. Rinder, in explanation, said there was no unity and that only a few of the men, Horacio Lafer and Rapaport, for example, were willing to and were able to help with the authorities. I replied that I had been deeply disappointed by Lafer's timidity and his utter defeatism, and that, so far as Rapaport is concerned, his two suggestions to me had proved of no value, and that after making these, Rapaport had not offered to be of further service.

About this time Rapaport arrived, so we went upstairs to my sitting room, where we could talk more freely. Presently we were joined by Captain Cardias. The group asked me what results had been obtained. I summarized the situation, leaving them all to understand that I felt disappointed at the support they had given me. In reply, the general view was expressed that at the moment the community leaders were fearful of the Integralist developments, permitting one to draw the conclusion that they were therefore unusually timid. Rapaport said that he would have offered to do more had he not felt from the beginning that my mission was certain at this time to be unsuccessful. Had he felt otherwise, he would have put himself completely at my disposal. I did not labor the obvious moral that the surest way to be defeated is to act on the assumption that you are going to be defeated. Rapaport continued that the tide at the moment was against us, but that there were excellent reasons to believe that presently there would be a reversal, and that then much might be done. He was polite enough to add that, from the psychological point of view, my visit had been of great value to the community.

I saw the group downstairs and out to the street, but the parting was rather a depressing one.

Wednesday, May 22, 1935

. . . .

Back to the hotel in time to meet S. Steckine of the *A Gazeta Israelita.* I asked him to stay during lunch. He was full of talk about the interminable dissensions, personal animosities and feuds, among different sections and individuals of the community. . . . Steckine told me of a number of instances where he had himself asked influential members of the community why they had not replied to letters that I had written to them. A typical answer was that if they replied to my letter or came to see me, they would feel obliged to take a certain responsibility, and this they were not prepared to do. All of Steckine's account merely confirmed and helped to explain my own opinion of the community.

Lessa and I went during the middle of the afternoon to call on the minister of education. Lessa was anxious to get the minister to authorize Alfranio Peixote, now in Europe to contract at least tentatively a number of professors for the federal institutions while at the same time he was doing this for the municipal university. The minister's response was disappointing. He indicated in very general terms that there was a need for a number of experts in several fields, but he did not say that he was willing or ready to have Alfranio move in this matter. On the contrary, he said that he thought that he would have to go to Europe himself, not only on this question, but on a number of others. He had no definite plans, but he might do this after a few months. This was discouraging in view of the always changing political situation in the capital.

As we walked out and were comparing notes about the weak position of the minister, Lessa, who himself must have a certain amount of Negro blood, said, "While, of course, I could not prove it by any scientific measurements, I have strongly the opinion that in many cases the pure whites are weaker than those of mixed blood. It does not appear that unadulterated whites work so effectively in the tropics."

Teixeira-Leite came for me promptly to go to the Foreign Office. On the way over I gathered from him that there had been no important developments from his side since I had last seen him.

Vaz de Mello was waiting for us, having, as he said, hurried back almost breathlessly from the port where he had taken some papers for one of the ministers bound for Europe.

Vaz de Mello told us that he had worked out a formula which he thought had nine out of ten chances of being accepted by the government shortly after the return of the president. There would then be a meeting of the interministerial committee on which are represented the departments of Foreign Affairs, of Labor and of the others concerned; that he would then submit his formula and was confident of its approval. He was unwilling to show it to me, because he said it must first be discussed with his own chief and with the interdepartmental group.

However, from what he said about it, and he talked at considerable length, I was given the impression that so far as it concerned our proposal, it followed the general lines of my second draft memorandum, with particular reference to the stateless. I regretted, however, to hear Vaz de Mello go off on a long tangent about his development of a new scheme of control of immigration, or rather, of immigrant workers. He told us with great gusto that, after studying fundamentally the systems of all the countries, he had now worked out a plan which was simplicity itself and which would be to the benefit of the immigrant as well as the employer. Under his scheme if it is adopted, it will be necessary for both the employer and foreign worker to secure a card from the Labor Office permitting the former to engage the latter and the latter to take employment. The card will indicate definitely what kind of employment is being allowed. If, for example, for agricultural work, then should the worker leave the land he would be unable to secure permission to work in the city. In this way he would be forced to stay on the land until such time as he might become a Brazilian citizen, when he would be free to choose his occupation without restriction. Vaz de Mello insisted that this scheme would work very simply, that there would be no red tape about securing the necessary permissions, and that in practice it would be a great benefit to all.

My conscience did not permit me to say that I welcomed such a program, but since I did not dare to criticize it openly, I remained silent. Teixeire-Leite, however, was nearly rhapsodical in his praise.

. . . .

Finally we managed to get back to our subject. Vaz de Mello deplored my leaving, said that he was sure that if I only remained until the president came back, things would be fixed up. Moreover, during the interval I could go off to Minas Gerais, his native state, and there in the most marvelous climate in the world, on the cool plateau, I could hunt and fish and live with the simple folk of the country and refresh my soul and body. All of this was very touching, but I insisted that my engagements in New York the beginning of June required my sailing the next day. Moreover, I knew perfectly well that the president and the foreign minister would not be back before the middle, perhaps the last of June, and that during the weeks immediately following there would be so many other and more important matters to be attended to that the poor refugees would have to wait, probably until July, for a final decision. Under these circumstances, there was nothing for me to do but to stick firmly by my decision.

Then the suggestion was made that perhaps it would be possible for me to designate a representative who might continue the conversations. Vaz de Mello welcomed this, provided I could find a Brazilian and provided also I were willing to give him—he at first said full powers—but later did not require this. I said I would study the matter closely that evening and the next day, and would let him know. He suggested that if I chose a representative, it would be well for me to bring him to the Foreign Office so that the two might meet and have a preliminary talk. It was left that way, and after reiterated expressions of admiration, we parted, Teixeira-Leite taking me back to the hotel.

. . . .

Back at the hotel, I called up Sir Henry and asked his advice about a possible representative. He had no helpful suggestions. Then Olive Sawyer and I debated the possibility of asking Rapaport to serve. I finally decided to send him a telegram saying that I wanted very much to see him the next morning. It was then late for dinner, and afterwards we began to pack.

Thursday, May 23, 1935

Mr. Meyer came to see me this morning at nine. I reported to him the results of the conversations the day previous with Vaz de Mello, and that I was considering inviting Rapaport to represent me. Before I mentioned the name of

Rapaport, Meyer said that obviously the only person who could represent me would be Dr. Leitchie. I explained that this would be difficult both from my point of view and from the point of view of the ICA. The ICA proposal and mine, though closely related, were different, and it would seem ought to be handled by different persons. Moreover, it was very doubtful if Louis Oungre would wish to have Leitchie formally representing me. Meyer agreed.

But then he raised the question as to whether I ought not first consult Oungre about the choice of Rapaport. He said that he had the impression that when Oungre was last here he and Rapaport had had a not too friendly conversation. He would not say anything definite, but indicated that there had been some difference between the two.

I thanked him for his suggestion, said I could not promise to accept it, though I would think it over carefully. In any case, however, I said I would tell Oungre that he had made the suggestion to me. This seemed to put Meyer's mind at rest. I could not tell whether he was making doubly sure, or whether he really thought Oungre might wish to have an opportunity to object.

At ten Röttgen came in again. While he was there, I called up Soper, or rather, Wilson told me that he thought Soper would be able to receive Röttgen on Monday morning early, but Wilson could not, of course, commit himself as to whether Soper would consider it possible to give Röttgen an opportunity to work if the funds were found outside.

I also, while Röttgen was there, put in a call for Afranio Amaral, but was unable to get him at once. I therefore asked Röttgen to come back about one and had him stay for lunch. Just before he arrived the call to Butantan was put through. I explained to Amaral Röttgen's qualifications, but Amaral said he needed someone more closely specialized in his field. Then I brought up the names of a number of other people, and Amaral said he would be glad to consider them.

I reported to Röttgen the disappointing results of my talk with Amaral. I explained that there seemed to me only the two possibilities, the one through Teixeira and the other the Rockefeller. I promised to write both Teixeira and Soper.

In my letter to Soper I told him that I had made arrangements through Mr. Peper that an amount sufficient for the subsistence of Röttgen would be provided monthly for a minimum period of six months if the Rockefellers would find a place for him to work, and that the money would be provided through Peper directly or would be supplied through Peper to the institute, whichever Dr. Soper might prefer.

Late that day after we had gone on board, Peper came down to the boat. I showed him my letter to Soper and added that I would make myself personally responsible for a conto a month for the period of six months, provided the Rockefeller arrangement went through. I then turned over to Peper all of my milreis, which totaled $600. It was arranged that Peper would give me the names of friends in New York and in London through whom I could make the requisite payments in dollars or pounds to his credit, thus avoiding the necessity of transfer and the losses incident thereto.

After we had finished this discussion, Peper brought up the question of Röttgen's relation to ICA. He said that he personally would not feel so badly about what ICA had done if only Oungre had not refused flatly to see Röttgen. He added that Asscher and other members of the Dutch committee and, of course, Schevenels knew about this situation, and that the latter was bitter about it. Moreover, he said that there were some persons who wanted to make use of the ICA letter of guarantee to the Brazilian consul.

I said most emphatically to Peper that, because of my official relations with ICA, it would be absolutely necessary that during the whole period Röttgen was receiving any subvention from me there must be no utilization of Röttgen's situation as a basis for an ICA attack. I added that such an attack would in no case do any good, because everybody admitted that whatever might be Röttgen's moral claim, he did not have a legal hold on ICA for the return of the six contos. Under these circumstances, it would be futile for him to permit himself to be used. Peper gave me absolute assurance that he would see that Röttgen did not give himself over for this purpose.

Moreover, Mr. Peper said that if there was anything else that he could possibly do, that I could count upon him absolutely. I arranged with him to repeat cables in case any reached me after our departure from Rio.

During the middle of the morning I got Rapaport on the telephone and arranged to go directly to his office. Meantime Miss Sawyer and I drafted a cable to Oungre indicating that I was contemplating naming Rapaport and would probably do so unless Oungre strongly advised the contrary. We indicated in the cable the necessity for an immediate reply.

I was favorably impressed by Rapaport in my brief talk with him. He said that he would be glad to serve for me if I finally decided to ask him to do so. We arranged to meet again that afternoon.

At 4:30 Rapaport came to the hotel. We discussed fairly fully the actual situation. He, in the meantime, had read the drafts of our two memoranda, the one which had been submitted formally to the Ministry of Foreign Affairs, and the other which had not been submitted to the Ministry of Labor. He said he would be glad to help out partly because of the nature of the work and partly because it was something of a sporting proposition, giving him, in addition, an opportunity to follow affairs closely with the authorities. I asked him categorically what financial arrangement if any he would require, and he said definitely that this was not a business matter, that he could not accept any honorarium and agreed when I said that it would then be a "labor of love." He suggested merely that it would be well if I wrote to Vaz de Mello, indicating that he had been named and if I would write to him. We then parted agreeing to meet at the Foreign Office at 5:30.

When I reached the Foreign Office at 5:30, Rapaport was already chatting with Vaz de Mello. Later, I learned that they had not known each other before, because Rapaport had to explain to Vaz de Mello that though he is of Viennese origin, he has been a naturalized citizen of Brazil for twelve years and is a professor at the law school. This seemed to relieve Vaz de Mello's mind.

We had little time at Vaz de Mello' office, because I was under the impression then that I would have to be at the boat at shortly after six, not having been informed that the sailing had been delayed until eight o'clock. Probably it would have made little difference had I stayed longer, because Vaz de Mello was not willing to show us the draft of his own memorandum, and in his talk with us so far as I was concerned, merely covering again old ground. He explained to Rapaport his point of view about the stateless and his new proposal for control, Rapaport was rather non-committal. Afterwards, he spoke of Vaz de Mello as a "confusionist"—a man whose mind is so free that he gets his essential ideas all mixed up. Rapaport added that probably we would be able to take advantage of this tendency of Vaz de Mello, because very often if you work closely with that kind of a man, who usually, despite his many words, never understands the heart of a problem, you could secure concessions which otherwise would not be granted. Rapaport shared my view that we must work through the Foreign Office.

During part of our talk Vaz de Mello dropped into Portuguese, but I insisted that he speak French, putting it on the ground half jokingly that his French is better than his Portuguese. Certainly he does speak French with great fluency and is proud of his facility. As we were saying goodbye, there were many exchanges of expressions of mutual regard, and Vaz de Mello gave his opinion that the chances of success were excellent.

Rapaport took me to the boat. I left feeling that he is a good choice, and if he wishes to do so, he can do as much as anyone to whom the mission might have been entrusted.

During the day I went into Sir Henry's office. . . . I told Sir Henry that I would welcome an opportunity to tell his colleagues in New Court of his great helpfulness to me. He said that he was always anxious to be of service.

Incidentally, it might be recorded, both because it puts the case perfectly and because it shows Rapaport's keenness of mind, his summing up of Sir Henry's relationship to our affair. According to Rapaport, in the old days when Brazil was paying its public debt and there were no serious issues outstanding between the foreign governments or bankers and the Brazilians, Sir Henry would have been free to put his whole force into my case. But now he had to reserve at least 95 percent of his prestige and influence for his own work, chiefly at the moment in connection with the unfreezing process of the foreign-owned credits. Therefore, he could only use the marginal portion of his prestige on my behalf and could therefore open doors for me, but could not himself enter the doors and himself gain for me my objectives.

The situation could not have been more neatly put.

At the boat Fineberg and Steckine chatted about conditions in the colony, offered their unqualified services, Fineberg, in particular, saying that he was preparing and was going to print at his own expense in the Jewish paper a series of articles on the community.

. . . .

Just before sailing I wrote Rinder a note, telling him that I was leaving in somewhat more cheerful mood than I had been when I talked with him, because I now had the assurance of Rapaport's support.

I left Brazil after my nearly six weeks there during the two stays, with mixed feelings of regret and of relief—regret that because of fundamental conditions we were not strong enough to secure a successful issue for our mission, but relief that for the time being at any rate the period of waiting had ended. There was some solace in the thought that perhaps what I had learned of conditions might be useful either in the same connection later, or in other connections.

The voyage, on SS *American Legion,* Thursday, May 23–Thursday, June 6, 1935

On the first day out, Friday, I violated my fixed policy and yielded to Miss Sawyer to the extent of agreeing to work for some hours.

The second day this unusual procedure was continued, with the result that a considerable amount of back work was caught up.

. . . We enjoyed Trinidad, though it was hot and not too inviting. The most interesting "sight" for us was the Botanical Gardens.

Bermuda was a welcome break in the trip, though by that time I had really gotten into the midst of my report and almost begrudged the time necessary to visit the island.

We docked in Brooklyn about 1:30 in the afternoon of June 6.

26. June 1935: Downsizing

New York, Thursday, June 6, 1935

Met at the dock by Mr. Warburg, Popkin, and Leland Robinson, who had brought down Janet. She looked wonderfully well. It was most considerate of him to have given the day to bring her in from school.

Warburg and I chatted about the results of the trip. I was able naturally to give him only highlights during our stay on the dock and our drive up to the FPA office. He looked rather well.

After settling down or beginning to settle down at the office, I left in the middle of the afternoon to meet Ruth and Janet and Robinson at Stothoffs.[1]

Went directly to the Robinsons where we are staying.

Friday, June 7, 1935

. . . .

Lunch at Felix Warburg's office. Present besides Warburg and myself were William Rosenwald, James Rosenberg, Sol Stroock, Joseph Hyman, Paul Baerwald, Mr. Liebman.

Before lunch I talked with Rosenwald about mutual acquaintances in Buenos Aires. We were in complete agreement about Alfredo Hirsch.

During and following the luncheon I summarized my experiences in South America. Afterwards there were a number of questions.

Incidentally, I said that I felt that the corporation had been a mistake, or at any rate that the idea of helping the refugees on an investment basis was extremely difficult to carry out in practice and perhaps altogether impracticable. Exception was taken to this by Warburg and one or two others. . . . At the end, young Rosenwald said that he thought that, under the circumstances, everything had been done that could be done.

Paul Baerwald asked me to go over to his office with him; he evidently had something on his mind. He told me of his plan to induce Sir Osmond to recognize for ICA a larger responsibility in the German situation than heretofore. He spoke of the determination of the German members of the ICA board to bring this matter up on the basis of the will of Baron de Hirsch.[2] He felt that this was

1. Mr. and Mr. Stewart Stothoff, close family friends whose son George was a classmate of Janet's at Lincoln School.

2. Baron Maurice de Hirsch, great Jewish philanthropist who in the 1890s spent vast sums to resettle several thousand Russian Jews in Argentina.

a matter which only Felix Warburg could effectively bring to the attention of Sir Osmond. I agreed.

....

Monday, June 10, 1935

Called up Michael Williams and asked him in reference to seeing the Cardinal [Hayes]. He suggested that I should write directly, rather than attempt to use any personal influence. This I did, but up to the time of my sailing more than two weeks later, I had not had a reply.

Lunch at the *New York Times.* Present besides my host, Mr. Sulzberger, and myself were Ogden, Adler, James, Merz, and Finley, and perhaps Strunsky. After the luncheon exchange of views, Sulzberger asked me to return to his office.

Before we had gone in to lunch, in order to avoid any embarrassment, I had said to Sulzberger that Herbert May had sent me a copy of his letter to Sulzberger in reference to the possibility of my being asked to join the *Times.* Sulzberger then suggested that we adjourn that discussion until after lunch, when we would have more time.

Sulzberger began by saying that when the suggestion was first made to him, nothing occurred to him as then possible. In the meantime, however, he had given the matter considerable thought, and there had begun to outline itself in his mind a position which he thought might interest me and which might be of real value to the *Times.* As he saw it, thinking out loud, it would consist of three parts:

(a) A certain amount of writing in the field which I was most competent to handle, presumably European affairs;

(b) The spokesman of the *Times* at public functions of importance, where it might seem that the paper should be represented. He emphasized that he, as president, ought to hold himself as had Mr. Ochs; that Mr. James, because of his administrative duties, could not get away; that Mr. Adler, while he might speak on certain technical subjects, had neither the time nor the preparation and personality for a general spokesman.

Referring to Dr. Finley, Sulzberger said that my work in the field would be a little like his, but that he hoped I might bring back more from my meetings than Dr. Finley did. The latter rarely had any suggestions of value for the paper on the basis of his outside contacts. Mr. Wiley, on the other hand, had capitalized on his connections, but Sulzberger would not expect me to do as Wiley had done, because one can never be another person;

(c) As he was speaking, Sulzberger said that it had occurred to him that in my role as the outside representative of the *Times,* since that would involve enlarging constantly my connections with various leaders of various movements, industries, etc., I might well help to develop a new policy in reference to letters to the editors. For example, what he said he had in mind was that I should be in a position to know who were the responsible and best informed spokesmen on various problems and then try to get from them letters to the *Times* promptly when an important event occurred in a particular field.

When he had finished his outline, I expressed my appreciation of his consideration of me in these connections, indicated my interest, but did not assume that I had been offered a position. Nor did I then raise any question about hours or salary. Instead, I merely asked about the degree to which I would be free to express either editorially or orally personal opinions. To this point he gave a definite answer which he elaborated in subsequent interviews. It was that in both these respects, since I would be a representative of the *Times,* I would be expected to keep within the four corners of the program of the paper.

He elaborated on this point and illustrated his meaning by speaking of the FPA as representing the type of objective approach and factual emphasis which is exactly what he had in mind. He had watched the FPA for a number of years and my part in it, and from the *Times'* point of view, he would have favored creating the FPA if it had not already existed.

At the end, it was left that we would both think the matter over and meet again in a week or so.

I should add that there was one other point which I had raised. This concerned the amount of time one would have for reading. To this, Sulzberger's answer was, I presume necessarily, indefinite; but he indicated that one must expect a position on the *Times* to be in the fullest sense of the word, a full-time job.

Tuesday, June 11, 1935

. . . .

Caught an early train out to the country. Over to see Janet. Then to supper and an all-evening talk with Jimmy Rosenberg.

In his usual way, Rosenberg laid out with great elaborateness the background of his argumentation to the effect that I should, as a final act when leaving my present work, present to the League in a form later to be agreed upon, a statement about the rights of religious and racial minorities which would be a sort of "bill of rights." The two of us were alone. It was a beautiful evening, and in the half darkness while I listened, Rosenberg sketched for nearly an hour the background and fundamentals of his thesis. . . .

I accepted in principle the desirability of my making this final gesture. I expressed doubt that a sufficient basis could be found for a formal request for an advisory opinion. I agreed, however, that there might well be the opportunity to make the sort of statement which might be heard and, in a measure, influence opinion in many parts of the world. I added, however, that I was unwilling at this stage to commit myself definitely either as to the principle or as to its application. Rosenberg said that he would think less of me than he does if I had not made those reservations.

We then discussed Rosenberg's further program of making available the services of Professor Janowsky, who has written a very good book on the origin and the meaning of the minority treaties and who is planning a year in Geneva to continue those studies;[3] and of Fagan, whom Rosenberg thought could be made available by the American Jewish Committee. I said that I would be delighted to meet Janowsky and Morris Cohen,[4] with whom he is associated, and that I had been most favorably impressed by Fagan's memorandum. I suggested, therefore, that these three and Rosenberg and I should lunch together in the near future, and that after that I would give a definite answer as to the two men.

....

Wednesday, June 12, 1935

....

Luncheon at Warburg's office for Sir Osmond, who, with Louis Oungre, had arrived the day previous. Those present besides the host and two visitors and myself included Rosenberg, Baerwald, Stroock, Hyman, Adler, Strauss, Frederick Warburg, Liebman, Bernard Flexner, et al. Before luncheon I presented Sir Osmond with a copy of my ad interim report which, with much labor, had been worked into some sort of shape during the first days after my return.

I spoke briefly of my South American experience. Then each person at the table who had recently come spoke for a short time.

....

At a quarter of five I went to the meeting of a group of prospective large givers in the Pershing Square building, presided over by Arthur Lehman. I made as strong a plea as I could. Warburg did the same. But the responses when they came did not, to my mind, indicate that we had materially increased the gifts over what would have been given.

....

Thursday, June 13, 1935

....

Luncheon with Lipsky and Rothenberg and two or three of their colleagues. Much of our talk was about Palestine and Trans-Jordan. One of the men also brought up the question of the desirability of the joint drives. His colleagues did not share his doubts, nor did I.

I was more favorably impressed with Lipsky this time than previously. He seemed less hard and unyielding. He expressed keen appreciation of my incidental work in removing prejudices among the Jews against Zionism.

3. Oscar I. Janowsky, author of *Jews and Minority Rights, 1898–1919* (New York: Columbia University Press, 1933).

4. Morris R. Cohen, professor of philosophy, City College of New York.

Friday, June 14, 1935

Morning conference at the Harmonie Club. Among those present were Sir Osmond and Louis Oungre, Felix Warburg, Baerwald, Hyman, Dr. Kahn, Alexander Kahn, Rabbi Jonah Wise, a number of other representatives of the JDC, the two Germans—Dr. Hirsch and Kreutzberger—Dr. Adler, and during the early part of the session, the Bernstein brothers of HICEM.

The meeting began with a statement by one of the Bernsteins on the work of HICEM. During the period from April 1933 to May 1935 11,000 refugees had been helped at a cost of approximately $300,000. He estimated the numbers of Jewish refugees eligible for emigration overseas at about 2,500–1,200 in Paris and 400 in Antwerp. The total, including non-Jews, he estimated at about 6,000.

In connection with possible emigration I raised the question of the French government reducing in effect the first-class boats to South America. Oungre said he did not think this was possible. Warburg whispered to me that he thought it might be and that I should not give it up.

Then Bernstein sketched the possibilities in various countries; but this seemed to me of little value, except for his estimate of 600 certificates for Palestine, which would cover 800 people.

Kreutzberger doubted whether there were more than 1,000 among the refugees ready for emigration. He urged better preparation and better selection.

Jonah Wise asked how do the refugees fare in the country of refuge? Oungre replied, admitted that in the rush of last year there had not been as careful selection as was desirable. He told the usual story of people wasting their three contos, but gave the impression that ICA was doing everything that could be done in South America.

I intervened in the discussion at this point to stress the importance of not sending undesirables, and of taking fuller account of the views of the local organizations, and of supporting such organizations more effectively.

Dr. Kahn with his usual precision then blocked out what he called a two-year plan for the emigration of 2,500 persons. In the first year 1,200 to 1,500 at a cost of $180,000, the second year 1,000 to 1,200 at a cost of $120,000. This total of $300,000 would not cover the cost of retraining, and I think would not include either the amount needed for settling the individuals in the country.

Oungre interposed to emphasize that it would be a great mistake for me publicly to speak about the need of support from New York and London for the local committees in South America, because these committees could be maintained by the local communities.

After this the meeting was turned over to the Germans, who presented their long range program. . . . Dr. Hirsch's appeal, which began with his assumption that the Baron Hirsch will obligated the trustees to do more for Germany, stirred Sir Osmond to reply. He pointed out that the primary purpose of the founder had been to aid Russian Jews, but that by stretching their authority, the trustees had gone far afield. He said that there were two funds, only one of which was free from rigorous restrictions and from which they were allowed to spend capital or for purposes from which there could be no expectation of return. He assured us, however, that he was determined that ICA would do its maximum.

Then he outlined what the organization was committed to. This included £13,000 to assure the continuation of the HICEM emigration work for the next six months; an experimental colonization project in Brazil; [and] certain expenditures in Poland.

....

Sir Osmond said it was difficult for his organization to commit themselves beyond the six months' period.

Jonah Wise spoke of the JDC as a continuing organization with a program over many years. He thought that they could expect to raise, year after year, about what they had been raising.

Paul Baerwald was not so optimistic.

Warburg praised Sir Osmond's statement, but pointed out that there was no provision for retraining and that there was still a deficiency in the amount available for emigration.

I took this occasion to emphasize that it was only the leadership of Sir Osmond that in my opinion had been sufficient to overcome the inertia and the opposition of certain leaders in England to a second drive this year.

Lunch with John D. [Rockefeller] III in the new restaurant on the roof of the RCA building. John talked about the Roosevelt program, expressing the rather common opinion that FDR is attempting to do too much. John also stressed that the President is failing to utilize the experience of leaders in industry and finance.

....

Saturday, June 15, 1935

Golf in the afternoon at the Century Club with Charles Liebman and one of his friends. I had to leave before the end of the eighteen holes in order to attend the meeting at Percy Straus's house.

There I found Sir Osmond, Louis Oungre, Felix Warburg, and Paul Baerwald. Charles Liebman did not appear. The talk was all about the ICA's scheme to settle on an experimental basis twenty families in Brazil. The idea was to have them produce milk and cheese and other crops particularly suitable for immediate consumption in the neighboring cities. As usual, Oungre talked with marked precision and a degree of eloquence, but throughout it all to my mind there was an element of unreality. The purpose of the exposition was to enlist the support of the corporation, if not on a 50/50, then on some basis, in this enterprise.

Afterwards, I chatted for a little while with Percy Straus. He had not been convinced by Oungre perhaps in part because of his previous experience with Oungre, which had left him skeptical of the latter's schemes and suspicious of his eloquence.

Ruth and I took the ten o'clock train for Atlantic City, arriving there very late that night.

Atlantic City, Sunday, June 16, 1935

Unable to play golf because by the time I had called Judge Lewis, it was too late. Instead, therefore, had a long walk with the judge before lunch with him and his family.

The convention of the B'rith Sholom[5] was held in the ballroom of the magnificent new amphitheater. Perhaps there were 3,000 or 4,000 people present, but they hardly filled half of this smaller room. The mayor, a Jew, made a stirring speech of welcome to the delegates. Judge Lewis, as the acting high potentate, delivered an interesting address, and my talk ended the session. After dinner with the Lewises and a walk along the beach, we went to bed early because of the necessity of having an early start the next day.

New York, Monday, June 17, 1935

Back to New York just in time for a little work at the office before going out to Mrs. Felix Warburg's for the luncheon meeting there. My brother Lee[6] and Ruth went with me. At the meeting the presence of so many sleek, elegantly dressed, and bejeweled ladies as usual led me to be somewhat more brutal in my presentation than ordinarily I am. I did not stay to see the results, but I was later told that the returns had been satisfactory.

Three or four days before I had learned through the governor's secretary in Albany that the date with the President[7] had been fixed for Tuesday the eighteenth. This was extremely inconvenient, because that day was wholly booked up with appointments ranging in importance from one with the dentist to my luncheon for Sir Osmond. But after consulting State, it seemed to me that I had no choice but to accept the date fixed. Hence took the five o'clock for Washington, arriving at the Cosmos Club a little after nine.

Washington, Tuesday, June 18, 1935

Breakfast with Chamberlain. We planned what we would say to the President. Then over at the FPA office I dictated the statement. After considerable effort I got in touch with Cornelius Jacoby, the consul for Luxembourg and arranged for him to meet us at the White House office.

Chamberlain and I went to see Moffat, who called in Dunn, his successor.[8] We discussed the general situation and were again assured that the United States would welcome a move to put the whole refugee problem back under the League. Of course, this is no very great concession on our part, because the

5. Brith Sholom, Jewish fraternal and service organization founded in Philadelphia in 1905.

6. Joseph Lee McDonald, economics professor at Dartmouth College.

7. To present FDR with the first issue of Luxembourg stamps being sold under the auspices of Marie Ginsberg's committee for the benefit of refugee scholars.

8. James Clement Dunn, chief of the State Department's Western European Division.

United States would not necessarily be involved in such procedure, though as Olive Sawyer pointed out, that possibility ought to be studied.

Met for a few minutes with Chamberlain and Mr. Simmons, the head of the Visa Division.

Long conference with Phillips. He seemed really anxious to get my picture of the South American situation as it affects our problem. I told him in some detail the attitude of the consul general and of Cox in the Argentine. His only comment was that it was absurd for the consul general to have involved himself in the policy of the American group towards us.

Shortly after twelve we were shown into the President's office, obviously being sandwiched in between other and longer interviews. The photographers were there en masse. Earlier that morning I had checked with the President's secretary and learned that there would be no talking, that this would involve too much loss of time, and that we would have to satisfy ourselves with the photographers.

As I led the way into the office, I was given another illustration of the President's personality. Before I could reach his desk he had waved a greeting and called out, "Glad to see you, Mac." Then followed the presentation of the others, some informal talk about the stamps, while the photographers busied themselves. Before we left, I told the President the story of the confusion between the baby carriage and the machine gun manufacturing plants in Germany. He seemed to like it and countered by his story in reference to Luxembourg, in which he seems to be interested. Before we left I asked McIntyre[9] about my giving to the press copies of the statement I had prepared to read to the President. He looked it over, handed it to the President, saying that it was innocuous, and got the latter's consent. Outside, we were met by the press, and I gave them copies of the statement.

Lunch with Constantine McGuire. He outlined a plan which I think has possibilities. He starts with the assumption that Germany can only be influenced in its attitude towards the Jews and the Catholics by manifestations of adverse public opinion abroad. He suggested that the plight of the intellectuals be called to the attention of each of the groups in the United States which are represented among the refugees by considerable numbers of their professions. For example, he would send to all of the members of the bar association, the medical associations, etc., a letter signed by a group of officials of the different learned and professional societies, enclosing a list of the intellectual refugees. It might be suggested in the letter that each recipient consider in what way he or his group could aid these exiles. McGuire suggested that he would be willing to outline this plan in a letter to me, but more than that, he would be glad to interest the executives of some of the learned societies, and if necessary he might find some of the funds needed from Catholic sources.

9. Marvin McIntyre, presidential appointment secretary. McIntyre had previously had doubts as to the suitability of the President receiving the stamps. He asked Phillips, who vouched for the character of those involved and recommended going ahead. McIntyre to Phillips, May 23, 1935, President's Personal File 2569, Franklin D. Roosevelt Presidential Library, Hyde Park, N.Y.

I told him that I felt that there were possibilities in this program, but that because I was going away so soon, it would be impossible for me to do more than call it to the attention of some of the individuals and groups in New York, who might themselves be able to follow up.

Later, it occurred to me that the Luxembourg stamps would be one item to be called to the attention of all the members of the professional societies, and that these would not only serve as an excuse in part for the letter, but also might be sold on a larger scale because of such circularization.

Two o'clock train for New York.

New York, Wednesday, June 19, 1935

. . . .

To the dentist at eleven and to lunch with Percy and Ralph Straus. Again, as always in my talks with them, I sensed the fundamental conflict between their Jewish background and the assimilationist tendencies. Ralph again recognized the vulnerable position of their business from two points of view, the anti-Semitic or the ultra-Jewish. As to a contribution towards the United Jewish Appeal, Percy reaffirmed his policy of limiting himself to the corporation.

. . . .

To the broadcasting station, where I delivered my talk in my very best manner, blissfully ignorant of the fact that at least in the whole metropolitan area and where Olive Sawyer was in Massachusetts, it was impossible to hear me because of the cannonade-like static.

Before going back to the Harvard Club, I made my first visit to the [Radio City] Music Hall. The picture "Becky Sharp" amused me because of her spirited acting and interested me because of the new color technique. I was not, however, too much impressed by the multitudinous Roxy-ettes [Rockettes].

Thursday, June 20, 1935

Luncheon conference at the Lawyer's Club. Besides Rosenberg and myself were present Chamberlain, Janowsky, Morris Cohen, and Fagan. It was a rather thorough discussion of the central problem. At the end there was general agreement that Janowsky and Fagan would work under my direction along lines which I would indicate, and that prior to my utilization of the results of their labors, they were not to publish it in any form without my specific consent. Janowsky is going to Palestine, but expects to be back in Geneva in early August. Fagan is going there for his vacation the middle of the summer, and will, if he secures permission from the AJC, remain for several months. It was made perfectly clear, however, that I was still reserving judgment on the major question of issuing the statement for which Janowsky's and Fagan's work was to be preparatory.

On the way uptown I stopped in to see Frank Altschul. He is concerned about anti-Semitism, showed interest in my work, but was adamant against any contribution to the FPA. He said, "I am not interested in it, I doubt if it is accomplishing anything, and earlier I was interested in you, not the organization."

....

Friday, June 21, 1935

Long conference with Smolar[10] of the Jewish Telegraphic Agency. He told me of an undercurrent of criticism in the Yiddish press of our work. He was skeptical of the Vatican flirtation. I like him and think that he is unusually intelligent and discriminating.

....

Luncheon with Felix Warburg and Jimmy Rosenberg at the former's office. Most of the talk was given over to the proposed statement to be issued by me. Warburg was not as enthusiastic about it as Rosenberg, but felt that it should be done.

....

. . . Conference with Rabbi Wise, Deutsch and myself. The talk covered a considerable range—possibilities in South America, in Palestine and Trans-Jordan, the necessity for larger funds. On this latter point Wise suggested that only through a conference called by a group of such men as Felix Warburg, Albert Lasker, et al., could American Jewry be made to see its own danger and be led to supply the missions needed for the crisis. Deutsch was so stirred that he said he would gladly give months of his time to this. He said he would see Warburg soon.

Another conference with Sulzberger at the latter's office. We more or less began from where we had left off. He amplified somewhat more fully his conception of the possible job. I asked a number of questions, but the main point in the discussion was that of salary. Sulzberger asked me what I had been receiving. I told him. He said this was rather on the top side of what he had had in mind as a beginning salary—$10,000–$12,000. It would be difficult to meet my minimum figure and impossible to meet my higher figure, because an existing salary scale was involved, and it would be impossible to ignore that. However, he said he would get the figures and study the possibilities in the light of these. I said that there was no hurry, that I would be back in New York the following Friday after my return from the west, and if he were free we could then talk again. He said he would be glad to do this, because he assumed that I would like to know something definite before I sailed. I said that naturally I would be pleased if I could.

At Bronxville I stopped with Ruth and Mrs. Robinson to see Leland, who was still in the hospital. I told them the story of my interview with Sulzberger.

10. Boris Smolar, reporter and editor-in-chief of the Jewish Telegraphic Agency.

Leland, turning to Ruth, said, "Of course, you would be willing to accept the lower figure if that were the means of keeping your husband at home." She replied, "I would not." This was not quite as bad as it sounded, because what she meant was that she did not feel it was right that an organization like the *Times* should, as she put it, haggle about terms.

....

Sunday, June 23, 1935

Up early, and on the road [to Indiana] just before eight o'clock. We spent the night at Greensburg, just south of Pittsburgh.

Monday, June 24, 1935

Again up early, and on the road before seven, covering seventy miles before breakfast. We reached Richmond [Indiana] before three o'clock. We were delighted to find Bobby so well. We were to learn later, however, that we should not openly concern ourselves so much about her health. That evening when Edna went into her room, Bobby said, "I don't think my family are much interested in me; they seem only interested in my health."

On Tuesday, June 25 J. G., Ruth, and Bobby went to Bloomington to visit J. G.'s mother and brother Bill. Wednesday they drove to Albany, where Ruth's parents, Jim and Kate Stafford, lived and where Ruth and Bobby stayed for the summer. On Thursday McDonald took the train back to New York.

New York, Friday, June 28, 1935

....

Inman and I had nearly an hour with Dr. [Albert] Einstein. We were met at Dr. Bulkley's office by Mr. Einstein's son-in-law, Marianoff, who tells me that he is returning to Paris in July, but is coming back to the States to stay later in the summer.

Our talk with Einstein covered a considerable range, but it was mostly about the situation of the intellectuals. He agreed most cordially with the point of view that many of these men will have to readjust themselves to new vocations, and that the sooner they recognize this necessity, the better. I urged him to emphasize this sometime in a public statement. He was much interested in Inman's account of the possibilities in South America, but held out no hope that he would be able to make a swing around the circle of those countries with Inman, as the latter urged him to do.

I told Dr. Einstein that I did not think there were possibilities in the Belgian Congo at all comparable to those suggested in the letter which he had forwarded to me.

Dr. Einstein asked what was the system by which individual refugees learned of the possibilities for settlement. I explained.

Einstein is very pessimistic about the situation in Germany, and is most of all depressed by the lack of resistance from the intellectuals.

Again, I was impressed by Einstein's versatility of interests, but also by the difficulty of making him follow through on a single subject.

In McDonald's third conference with Sulzberger, he was offered a salary at the New York Times of $13,200 a year, no contract: "each person is on a month to month basis, technically, though as you know actually people remain indefinitely." The hours would be seven to seven with some flexibility for editorial persons and one night a week to take turns making up the editorial page. There could be no acceptance of honoraria. McDonald promised to let Sulzberger know before the end of summer and agreed with his request that he should not come to the Times directly from the High Commission nor announce his prospective connection before resigning.

Saturday, June 29, 1935

Hectic last minute calls and conferences.

The embarkation was more hectic than usual, because of the mad scramble of the passengers and their friends.

While waiting for the boat to pull out, chatted with Dr. Wise. He tells me that Weizmann wants to be president of the [Hebrew] university and head of the Zionist Congress.

. . . .

On board SS *Ile de France,* Sunday, June 30, 1935

Worked most of the day. Met Count Pierre de Louisse, a secretary in the French Embassy in Washington. He deplored the failure of his government to make concessions to Germany in sufficient time and on a sufficient scale to gain any real advantage from it.

27. July 1935: Liquidation Plans

The voyage, June 30–July 4, 1935

Had Waldman[1] of the American Jewish Committee for lunch with the Seligmans and Olive Sawyer. We first discussed the McGuire proposal. The consensus of opinion was that the chances of securing any considerable number of posts for refugees by this method were slight, but that nonetheless, it was worth doing. . . . I am asking Waldman if he will be good enough to follow up with McGuire. I should call this proposal to the attention also of Razovsky and ask Waldman to confer with her.

At more length we talked about the Fagan memorandum and the proposed statement to be issued by me.

. . . .

On the substance of the matter Seligman was skeptical of our being able to build up a legal case for an Advisory Opinion [from the League]. But he considered the chances worth the rough investigation. He is far from enthusiastic about the Fagan memorandum. He told me afterward that he thought it was sloppy, and that, therefore, any work that Fagan did I should have checked by Hudson and perhaps others.

Seligman's chief doubt on the legal side centered on the point of the Germans' assurance in an exchange of notes at the Peace Conference that they would treat their minorities on a basis of equality. He was not sure that this assurance was binding legally, or if it were, that it would apply to the Jews in Germany.

. . . .

Several interesting talks with the Neilsons. I need only note, however, the president's statement that he had gone over Janet's record with the committee on admissions, and had told them that he wished her to be admitted unless in the light of her record in the board examinations they felt that this would be disastrous. This and what else he told me convinced me that her chances are good.

Lunch with Leo Simon at our table. He outlined at length the present status of the [French] Syrian colonization proposal.[2] The group with which he is

1. Morris Waldman, Hungarian-born rabbi and social worker. Executive secretary of the American Jewish Committee, 1928–1945. Although opposed to a Jewish boycott of Nazi Germany, worked to depict Nazism as a threat not only to Jews but to universal ideals of human rights.

2. Syria was at this time a French mandate under the League.

associated is relying primarily on the influence of Senator Justin Godart and Paul Devinat,[3] both of whom are members of the committee. According to Simon, both these men are much interested and the latter particularly influential. I cannot but be skeptical of this, knowing Devinat as well as I do. Simon mentioned a number of other French personalities as also interested. However, I shall talk with Devinat about these before I set down anything about them.

My impression from Simon's long talk was that the French were still marking time in reference to this proposal, and that there is slight chance of anything being done in time to help the German refugees. This is the more likely to be the case because of the French insistence that there be no settlements near the Palestine frontier and the resulting lack of interest, or possibly even opposition, on the part of the Zionists to the diversion of any considerable amount of money to Syrian development proposals.

July 4 was notable because we passed the *Normandie* at lunch time. She was only about a quarter of a mile away—a beautiful sight, but not making a full impression of size.

Dinner with Rabbi and Mrs. Wise and Mrs. Simons. The talk was for the most part about persons, rather than technical Jewish affairs.

That afternoon Rabbi Wise and I spoke in the tourist section to some hundreds of younger persons from the tourist and third class. I outlined our efforts on behalf of the refugees and was rather pessimistic. Rabbi Wise spoke about conditions in Germany. There followed a period of rather pointless discussion. The young man who opened it, having nothing serious to disagree with in either of the preceding talks, went off on left-wing tangents which had no relation to what had been said before.

London, Friday, July 5, 1935

Up early and breakfast by six. The tender left at seven. . . .

The train left at 8:10 and we were in London about half past twelve. Wurfbain met us, and we were ready to work by the middle of the afternoon.

. . . .

Saturday, July 6, 1935

Worked all day at the office. Kotschnig arrived just after lunch.

. . . .

Monday, July 8, 1935

Worked at the office during the morning.

Lunch with Bentwich at Lincoln's Inn, where we again had the good fortune to meet Idelson. He was as brilliant as ever. We promised to call him in reference to lunch just as soon as the Governing Body meetings are over. He had

3. French politicians of the Radical Socialist Party who served in various cabinets during the 1920s and 1930s. Sympathetic to the League and refugees.

an interesting suggestion about my end-of-the-year statement to the effect that there might be a splendid basis for it supplied by legislation in the Reich during the next month or two. I anticipate a fuller talk with him on this and related topic.

In the late afternoon general staff conference about liquidation scheme, as well as plans for the Governing Body meeting.

. . . .

Tuesday, July 9, 1935

General conference with Cecil in the afternoon. We went over all the plans—or at least most of them—in connection with the Governing Body meeting and the proposed liquidation scheme. . . . He also agreed that resolutions would be prepared thanking the Latin American states for their cordial reception to Inman and myself, and also appreciation for Sweden and Norway. . . . He agreed that the Swedish money should not be returned, but favored its use in connection with the project for non-Jewish refugees.

He read through carefully the first five pages of my draft report. Emphatically he agreed that I should take the line I proposed to do in the way beginning. He said that it was highly important that I should strike that note. He agreed too that we should work towards a definite liquidation date at the end of the year, but said that we might have to reconsider that date if the Assembly failed to take any action. Nonetheless, he felt, as I did, that it would be better to have any work that was to be carried on in the hands of existing organizations, rather than to set up a continuation committee of the High Commission.

He expressed definite views about personalities on the staff. Wurfbain he found much too routine and bureaucratic; Kotschnig he was enthusiastic about—even more so than about Bentwich. He said that if he were choosing an executive to carry on under the new High Commission, he would select Kotschnig.

. . . .

Cecil felt that it might be possible to have the final liquidation meeting of the High Commission towards the end of the Assembly in Geneva, but recognized that it was too early to fix a time.

Outlined briefly the ideas underlying the proposal for a final statement by me at the end of the year, to be addressed to the Secretary General of the League by Cecil and me. In principle, he approved the idea and said he would participate. He felt, however, that it is impossible now to be sure that the political atmosphere in November would be such as to make such a statement desirable. He approved, however, the idea of utilizing and directing the activities of Janowsky and Fagan.

Cecil apologized for having to leave at four o'clock to see a personal friend received in the House of Lords at 4:15. He invited me to go along. I gladly accepted, because I had not previously been in the House of Lords or witnessed this quaint ceremony, the origin of which is lost in the dim past.

I should have included in the above a report that Cecil had advised strongly against turning over to the members of the Governing Body my report on Argentina and Brazil. He said that one certainly could not trust material the least bit confidential, and which was therefore salable, in the hands of certain diplomats. He then told the story of advice which had been given to him as a young man that he should never expect a confidence to be kept by certain diplomats, because these were always anxious to gain more income by selling secrets, and the higher their positions, the more valuable their secret information, the returns from the sale of which enabled them to improve progressively the quality of their successive mistresses. He added that, of course, this might be merely a British libel, but that anyhow in practice he had found confidences frequently abused.

From the House of Lords I went to Sir Osmond's house, where we had an hour and a quarter or so together. His mind seemed to me as clear as ever, and physically he seemed to be stronger than when I last saw him in the States. However, Lady Goldsmid, as I was leaving, expressed to me her lively concern about him.

. . . .

We discussed at length the question of winding up our organization and the possible reorganization under the League.

. . . .

As to the results of his New York visit, Sir Osmond thought that it had been worthwhile in clearing the air, but he was disappointed in not having gotten more money, but he recognized that "the poor devils do not have it."

I brought up the question of ICA renewing for the last two months of the year, its contribution to the High Commission on a pro rata basis for the first ten months. He said he would take it up with his colleagues on Sunday, and I got the impression that he would urge it.

As to ICA's general obligations, he said that he was making it a matter of confidence that his colleagues approve the commitment which he had made in the States, that is, to supply the funds necessary for the transportation and (I assume, though he did not definitely say so) the settlement of all the Jews in the refugee countries whose papers are in order and who have opportunities to go abroad. "If my colleagues do not support me in this, I will resign." Further, he said that he would like to have ICA take a similar obligation in reference to Jews who were able to leave Germany. He was less confident, however, that he could secure assent to this. But in any event, the obligations could be taken only for a six months period, because beyond that there could be no assurance as to what funds would be available.

I told him in some detail the story of my relations with Röttgen and my commitment to supply a conto a month for six months. I explained how this related to ICA, but did not directly or impliedly criticize Oungre. Sir Osmond was obviously much interested in the story, said that he had only heard that some doctor associated with Quatros Irmaos had left his post. He said that he thought I ought to be recompensed for my outlay. I told him that I had not mentioned the matter for that purpose, and I did not expect compensation. . . .

Just before Lady Goldsmid came in, I told Sir Osmond about Rabbi Wise's comment on Weizmann and the latter's theory of salvation through the remnants. Sir Osmond's comment was, "How much you have learned about Jewish affairs during the years you have been on this job!" The Wise story was this: I was telling him on the boat of my letter to Weizmann on the way up from South America, in which I had written the latter that now after nearly two years of work in Jewish affairs, I had come more nearly to understand what he had meant when he had spoken to me in November 1933, of his faith that the Jews could only be saved through "the remnants" who had remained faithful; the majority was always falling away. Stephen Wise's comment was, "It was not Weizmann who said that, it was Isaiah, and Weizmann has not forgiven Isaiah for thinking of it first, any more than he has ever forgiven Herzl for having the idea of the national home before he, Chaim Weizmann, had it." And yet it was in this same conversation that Rabbi Wise deplored at length the divisive tendencies among the Jews!

Wednesday, July 10, 1935

Talked with Hexter about my possible visit to Palestine. He agreed that November and the first half of December were, except for the absence of wild flowers, the most attractive time of the year. Incidentally, it has the advantage over the spring of avoiding the plague of tourists.

. . . .

Schoen and his wife came in to see me. He had noticeably become more nervous and overwrought since I had seen him last. Both in his eyes and in those of his wife was that look of terrible fear and insecurity which I have come to know so well in the eyes of refugees who have reached the end of their resources and see no future. He told me first of his plans to go to Russia, where he hopes to secure a position in the Stalin broadcasting station. . . . He also told me of his plan to work out with a Viennese a project for an opera company of English singers. He wanted to know if I would write a letter to the authorities giving him a good character reference and thus aiding him to get permission to work. He was anxious, however, that I should not emphasize that he was in desperate need. . . . I said I would do this when he sent me a copy of his letter.

We then talked about possibilities in America. I called up Bate of the NBC. The latter talked at length about what he had undertaken to do for Schoen, and agreed that if the latter would call him up towards the end of the month, he would ask Royal, the NBC program manager, to see Schoen.

Finally, and reluctantly, the Schoens asked whether I was in a position to help them find some additional funds, saying that the £50 given them some months ago was nearly exhausted. I said that I would speak to Kotschnig and to the friends and asked him to call me later.

....

Thursday, July 11, 1935

Lunch at New Court. Food, as always, above reproach. Besides Lionel and Anthony and myself were present Mr. Goslin, the British government's broker in the purchase and sale of governmental securities, Robert de Rothschild's son, who had been in the States, a third man by the name of Stephenson, and Robert Waley-Cohen.

Talk as always was mixed, rambling all the way from serious discussion about economics and politics in Brazil, the Argentine, and Chile, and economic conditions in Germany, Italy, and the States, to Anthony's comment about his horses and Lionel's showing us pictures of his chrysanthemums. Sir Robert made the interesting comment that the Royal Dutch Shell tankers were unable now to reach any of the docks on the Red Sea or around the shoulder because every available inch of space was piled high with Italian war "materiel."[4] Everywhere there was complete confusion.

As to Germany, Sir Robert thought that conditions were getting worse, because the Reich is forced to pay higher prices for everything it buys, since the sellers must accept payment for the most part in goods. Inevitably, he maintains, there is a drastic depression of the domestic living standards. This conclusion the others did not wholly accept. There was a consensus of opinion, however, that the economic situation in Italy is very bad. As to local politics, the group seemed to feel sure that Labour would make substantial gains but they hoped that because of the lack of outstanding leaders the Conservatives would be retained in power. Morrison seemed to them the most promising of the Labour leaders.

As I was leaving, Anthony told me to get in touch with him at any time if there was anything he could do.

....

Friday, July 12, 1935

....

In the afternoon Mr. Prendergast, the American representative on the Governing Body, came in to talk about the forthcoming meeting. I urged that he re-

4. Refers to the staging and preparations by the Italian military for an attack on Ethiopia, which was launched from Eritrea and Italian Somaliland on October 3.

frain from "making the record," and thus avoid the difficulty brought about by Johnson at the last meeting. He said he would be more than willing.

Saturday, July 13, 1935

Spoke at the beginning of the Experts' Committee meeting at the Russell.

....

Worked late at the office in getting out the draft of my report, which had occupied most of my time during the previous days.

Sunday, July 14, 1935

....

I had Dr. Bernard Kahn as my guest at the Park Lane. He was inclined to emphasize the dangers of reorganization of refugee work under the League. He feared that the Germans would be swamped by the mass of Russians and other refugees, and that the governments, if given an excuse, might make additional refugees. On this last point, he seemed chiefly concerned lest Rumania, where there are thousands of Jews who are really stateless but who thus far have been treated as Rumanians, might be formally denationalized. I urged him to present these considerations at the Advisory Council meeting the next day.

Monday, July 15, 1935

Advisory Council meeting all day. It was more peaceful than might have been expected. Adams was present during the morning, but made no criticism. Schevenels, the Dutch, and even Helbronner, spoke of the work as having been as well done as circumstances permit—the former two being quite generous in their praise.

....

After the meeting I talked with the Dutch about their situation, and was more than ever convinced that it is a tragedy not to have the aid from the outside which is so desperately needed. I raised the question of the possibility of my visiting Wieringen, but nothing definite was decided.

Tuesday, July 16, 1935

....

In the afternoon, conference with Dr. Wischnitzer of the Immigrant Aid Society of Berlin. His tale was discouraging. He gave the impression that it would still not be desirable for the Jewish organizational heads to see me in Berlin.

A bite of supper and then to the theater with Jane Rosenthal to see "Jill Darling."[5]

Wednesday, July 17, 1935

The Governing Body all day. The private session was brief, but in addition to the routine items—adopting the agenda, naming the finance committee, and approving the public meeting—there was time enough for nearly a quarter of an hour of confidential report by me on certain aspects of the South American situation, notably the intense nationalism now prevalent, the activity of German officials and the effect of German influences, and the attitude of the Church.

Public meeting as usual consisted of a brief statement by Cecil, and my report.[6] I have rarely been as tired in trying to read a report, but managed to get through the 43 minutes without, I hope, too many indications of weariness.

The report recommended liquidation of the High Commission and transfer of responsibility for refugees to the League itself. McDonald also stated that there were more than 80,000 Jewish refugees from Germany: that 27,000 of them had settled in Palestine, 6,000 in the United States, 3,000 in South America, 800 in other countries, 18,000 had been repatriated to countries of Central and Eastern Europe, while 27,000 were still refugees in Europe "without political security." McDonald estimated that $10 million had been raised over the two years for the relief and rehabilitation of the refugees, American Jews having contributed $3 million of this sum, British Jews $2.5 million.[7]

We then went into private session and got through a lot of work before we broke up at lunch. Indeed, all of the items on the agenda which were to be treated seriously—except that of reorganization—had been dealt with before 1:30.

The afternoon session practically was given over to the problem of reorganization and liquidation. Again, as so often in the past, Cecil showed his skill as chairman by getting things through in the minimum of time and by maintaining always his complete command of the situation. Also, his sense of humor never fails him, particularly as shown in his notes to me.

As we were breaking up, I spoke to the Swedish delegate, who said he would inquire at Stockholm about the desirability of my visit there before the Assembly. The Dane said he would do the same at Copenhagen. Cecil and I had our pictures taken by Miss Sawyer's little black box. I was quite touched by Cecil's parting greeting, when, as on some recent occasions, he called me "My darling."

5. Jane Rosenthal, daughter of Mrs. Arthur Rosenthal, friend of and the same age as Janet McDonald.

6. The full text in the *New York Times,* July 18, 1935, p. 1; the *Times* also ran an editorial endorsing the transfer of responsibility.

7. *American Jewish Yearbook* (1934–1935), 185–187.

Helbronner was friendly enough at the close and said he would look forward to seeing me at Geneva. Bustamante, Guani's alternate, remained, I am afraid, to the end a little hurt by my perhaps maladroit reference at the private meeting that morning to his country, when I spoke of the economic situation not improving there.[8]

. . . .

Thursday, July 18, 1935

Conference with Leonard Montefiore. With complete frankness I told him of my estimate of the present Jewish situation, particularly in the light of Sir Osmond's illness. I stressed too my feeling that there is no justification really for the British community holding in reserve a substantial amount for next year, while at the same time such situations as that in Holland exist. He did not dissent from my views, but did not hold out much hope that anything effective could be done either to forestall the danger I saw, or to cause the British group to relinquish its hold on the reserve fund for next year.

Visit to the consul general, but since the specific matter which I was to discuss with him had already been taken up by Miss Razovsky, I did not mention it.

In the afternoon a long conference with Mr. Maisky, Russian ambassador. I explained to him fully about the reorganization plan and expressed the wish to discuss it with the people in Moscow. He raised the question whether I wished to go officially or as a privileged tourist. In the first case it would need a special statement from the authorities in Moscow to the effect that they were prepared to entertain such negotiations. I at once said that that was unnecessary, and that I would go as a tourist technically. The visa, he said, could be arranged through the Intourist. He was cordial, but gave me no indication as to what he thought the attitude of his government might be.

. . . .

Conference with Weizmann at his office. He expressed his great pleasure at receiving my letter from South America. He urged me to come to Palestine, but not before the fifteenth of November, about the time he was arriving. His house would not be ready, but he would welcome me in his temporary quarters. He again expressed his grave concern at the psychological conditions in Palestine. The material development he is quite confident about, but he is troubled by other factors.

. . . .

8. Chamberlain could not attend the meeting. He had to go to California because his brother was seriously ill. Instead, a staff member from the embassy in London represented the United States.

Friday, July 19, 1935

. . . .

Conference with Dr. Don. I explained to him our plan to use the Swedish money for preparing the technical data for a non-Jewish settlement. Promised that within a few days he would have a memorandum on the number and estimated cost of settling the Christian refugees, and by the end of the summer an engineer's report on the definite project, probably in Colombia.

He told me that Johnson had been to see him about the Saar refugees, but he had held out little hope of the archbishop's being able to help because of his prior commitment to the Assyrians and his secondary commitment to us.

Lunch with Mr. Rich of the [*Jewish*] *Chronicle*. . . .

He was much interested in my telling about the Jewish communities in South America, and in my estimate of the situation in this country. He encouraged me to outline a program for the British community, but I limited myself to a single point—that it seemed to me that the community should envisage the refugee problem and other Jewish needs on the continent as of considerable duration and not for one or two years only. I told him too what I thought about the British reserve fund. We also talked frankly about Sir Osmond's position.

I left him with the feeling that he at least would be friendly in the estimate of our work.

Interview by Barnett of the *Chronicle.*

In answer to the Jewish Telegraphic Agency question, I told them that our report from Brazil was that the announcement of a special concession to 5,000 refugees was unfounded.

In the late afternoon, conference with Sir Leonard Cohen. As always, he was very friendly to me personally, but he did not disguise his feeling that the High Commission had been of little use, his conception of it being formed largely on the basis of data supplied by Louis Oungre.

. . . .

Sunday, July 21, 1935

In the afternoon drove over to see the Bishop of Chichester, and gave him an account much like that I had given Dr. Don. . . . He will, I think, as in the past, be ready to help with the archbishop.

. . . .

Monday, July 22, 1935

Promised Schoen on the telephone to urge Schiff to use his good offices to secure an extension of his residence permit.

I said I would try to arrange for some additional funds. Later, I did this through the Friends.

. . . .

Wurfbain and I went to see the Norwegian chargé. His government has as yet had very little response to its initiative. He will welcome further suggestions from us, and will pass on to us news as he receives it. The government would welcome a visit to Oslo, especially late in August or late in September.

Painful interview with Mrs. Markstein, allegedly the adopted daughter of Einstein, and Professor S. Herschdorfer, who has taken on the formidable task of caring for her and her son, who, she says, looks so much like Einstein. All I could promise was to write to Professor Fay of the National Institute for Research in Dairying, where Professor Herschdorfer hopes to secure a post.

....

Tuesday, July 23, 1935

....

Conference with the German ambassador at 7:45. He was sympathetic to my suggestion about reorganization and expressed himself as personally favorable. On the second point, that of a possible new transfer arrangement, he was completely pessimistic. As to special visa and *laisser passer*, he said he would be delighted to have that. He promised to send on to the Wilhelmstrasse documents I took for him, and to tell them of my desire to talk with someone in the Foreign Office and in the Reichsbank. I told him I expected to be there about the twentieth or so.

....

Wednesday, July 24, 1935

Conference with Cecil. He felt he could not go to Geneva unless the government asked him or unless there were some other special thing for him to do. He could not hang around the lobbies. He agreed to sign the letters of thanks to the South American and other governments, but thought that our draft should be made a little more cordial. He reported that Johnson was now raising technical difficulties, having come to the conclusion that his elimination might be a part of the price of reorganization. Lord Cecil is heading a delegation today to Sir Samuel Hoare[9] to take up a number of matters of foreign policy which will include the refugees, because he is sure that Hoare's support is essential to get the British government to act; and this government's action is essential to bring the French into line and thus, to give the necessary support to the Norwegian initiative. Helbronner had said that he had an official statement from the French government, which he was asked to give Cecil, to the effect that the latter would support any program supported by the British.

Cecil saw no objection to the letter to Mrs. FDR.[10]

9. Sir Samuel Hoare, British foreign secretary after Sir John Simon, 1935. Believed in the need for collective security.

10. See italicized insert into July 31, 1935.

We agreed that immediately after the Assembly we would consult together to consider what action was necessary to call a meeting of the Permanent Committee for the consideration of the next steps.

In the afternoon to the country.

Thursday, July 25, 1935

Back from the country on the early morning train. Conference with Waldman at the office. He told me of the information he had had from confidential sources of grave new dangers in Germany.

Eleven o'clock train for Brussels. Four o'clock Ostend; six o'clock Brussels.

....

Brussels, Friday, July 26, 1935

Long conference with Majoni. He said that the question of Italy's attitude towards the reorganization of refugee work under the League had been discussed at the Foreign Office. They had reached the conclusion that they would not oppose unless Germany were still opposed. Otherwise, there was no reason for Italian opposition. I told him of my forthcoming visit to Berlin, and he asked me if I would write him when I knew more of the German attitude.

We then talked for a little while about Italy and Abyssinia. Majoni said it would be very easy for Great Britain to solve the problem; it need merely give Kenya to Italy. Mme. Majoni rather pathetically said, "Why is England against us?"

Afternoon train to Paris, where I arrived at 5:45. I had previously telegraphed to Bernard Kahn to try to have Georg Bernhard at the JDC office. He was there. We talked together for a couple of hours—first of our plans, and then of the German situation. Bernhard told of the significant case of a large department store in Berlin refusing to take down the anti-Jewish signs, though requested to do so by representatives of the government and of the Reichsbank. Finally, the fire brigade came and took them down. The point was that trade had increased steadily despite, or possibly because of, the sign.

Bernhard insists that for the first time he feels there is danger of real disturbances. Not until a few weeks previous had he ever felt the discontent was sufficient to be a danger. He went so far as to see the possibility of communism. Meantime, the threat to the Jews becomes worse. Bernhard also paid his respects to the French Jews.

Kahn dined with me and we talked about his Russian plans until time for me to go to the train.

....

Geneva, Saturday, July 27, 1935

Arrived in Geneva on time. Met at the station by the Mays' car, and out to their house for lunch.

....

Sunday, July 28, 1935

. . . .

Dinner with the family and Cohns. Afterward, Cohn developed at some length the thesis that I should make my final statement in the form of a classic oration, delivered to some Assembly, and broadcast, restating fundamental ideals. He thought that the occasion offered me one of those opportunities that come very rarely for a really historical presentation. May supported these views.

After the family had gone to bed, I had a delightful walk in the garden alone.

. . . .

Tuesday, July 30, 1935

. . . .

Talked with Gilbert. He was anxious to have all of our material, which I promised to send him. He said that he would be following events at the Assembly, and was glad to know that our government had indicated that it would approve of reorganization under the League.

To [Harold Beresford] Butler's office, for a half an hour's talk. He said that the man was the all-important factor in any successful reorganization scheme. He was frankly critical of the League and its timidity under the Avenol regime. He said that his office was prepared to make a fight for their enlarged budget on the basis of their activities.

. . . .

Lunch with Sweetser and Gerig. Arthur surprised me by telling me that he had read my report and had felt that I owed the League a great debt because of the opportunity it had given me for enlarging my field of activities and for deepening my understanding of international relations.

. . . .

Wednesday, July 31, 1935

Spent the morning in the League corridors, chatting with newspaper men about the forthcoming Council. But I had decided that nothing much would happen and to leave that day for my holidays.

. . . .

A week earlier McDonald had summed up the situation in an extended letter to Eleanor Roosevelt.

[Dear Mrs. Roosevelt,

I wish I might have now an opportunity to sit down and talk with you. Not since my visit to Germany in March and April, 1933 about which I told you and the President on my return home—have I had as deep a sense of impending tragedy as now. Unless present tendencies are sharply reversed, the world will be faced in the near future with the problem of another great exodus of refugees from Germany. And in that event the percentage of non-Jews will be higher than in the first exodus. That problem would be literally overwhelming, and would fall—as the problem of the refugees so far has fallen—upon the countries of refuge and upon the generosity of the citizens of those countries.

It is my conviction that the party leaders in the Reich have set for themselves a program of forcing gradually the Jews from Germany by creating conditions there which make life unbearable. That, many of us closely in touch with German affairs, have feared for some time. The news of the last few weeks brings confirmation.

There is also another phase of the Reich's program, even broader in its scope. This is the determination, openly avowed in high party quarters, to establish a State church, loyalty to which, particularly of the children and younger people, would take priority over loyalty to any one of the established religions—Catholic, Protestant, or Jewish.

This extreme form of statism must have repercussions far beyond the German frontier.

Under these circumstances I wonder how long the Governments of the world can continue to act on the assumption that everything which is taking place in Germany, and the threat implicit in present developments, are matters purely of German domestic concern? Is that not merely to evade for a time an issue which must sooner or later be faced? And is not the refusal to face it now giving aid and comfort to the extremist forces in the Reich?

In short, I am raising a question whether the time has not come when, in harmony with other precedents in American history, the American Government should take the initiative in protesting against the prevailing violations of elementary civil and religious rights in Germany. Such a protest would, I anticipate, evoke enthusiastic and grateful response from millions of Americans.

Very sincerely yours,
James G. McDonald

Handwritten notation: Please give Miss LeHand for the President and tell her Mrs. R says it is important.

Eleanor Roosevelt to James G. McDonald, August 1, 1935
Dear Mr. McDonald,
I have your letter of July 24, and am sending it at once to the President.[11]]

11. Official File 198A, Franklin D. Roosevelt Presidential Library, Hyde Park, N.Y.

Conclusion

Richard Breitman

An early supporter of the League of Nations, James G. McDonald discovered the moral and political failings of the League in dealing with Nazi Germany. This bitter lesson contributed to his decision to resign as League of Nations High Commissioner for Refugees at the end of 1935. But he had other, lesser disappointments as well.

McDonald had originally hoped to become American ambassador to Germany. An ambassador represents his country and his president, not primarily his own convictions. President Roosevelt likely sensed McDonald's leanings—to speak out against Nazi persecution and discrimination—after their meeting on May 1, 1933. Although FDR had difficulty filling the post of ambassador,[1] he avoided sending McDonald to Berlin. The United States was then too weak economically and militarily—too preoccupied with recovery from the Great Depression—for an interventionist role in European affairs. McDonald, however, went repeatedly to Germany, first for the Foreign Policy Association and for himself, later as League High Commissioner.

McDonald's contacts in Nazi circles—men such as Putzi Hanfstaengl—knew of his past sympathy for Germany. Other Nazis simply looked at his tall frame and fair hair and viewed him as one of them. They wanted him as American ambassador for the most superficial reasons, and he would have sorely disappointed them if his wish and theirs had been granted. He certainly alienated them through his efforts as an advocate for refugees and German Jews considering emigration.

One popular historian, John V. H. Dippel, has claimed that if Jews wanted to leave Germany in 1933 and after, "they found doors abroad relatively open to them. Around the world, the severe economic impact of the depression was abating and with it, the pressures to keep out job-seeking immigrants."[2] In contrast, Herbert Strauss's detailed scholarly study of German-Jewish emigration to

1. See Robert Dallek, *Democrat and Diplomat: The Life of William E. Dodd* (New York: Oxford, 1968), 187–190.

2. John V. H. Dippel, *Bound Upon a Wheel of Fire: Why So Many German Jews Made the Tragic Decision to Remain in Nazi Germany* (New York: Basic Books, 1996), 113.

places throughout the world, published well before Dippel's work, emphasized the obstacles and, for most, the extraordinary efforts necessary for them to find permanent places of settlement.[3]

Six decades after the end of the Holocaust, scholars and the public continue to ask why no one "moved Heaven and earth" to prevent it or mitigate it. In his diary James G. McDonald compiled a very detailed record of what he and his allies tried to do before Nazi persecution of Jews and others reached the level of the Holocaust. He supplied compelling evidence that much of the world was closed to Jews trying to emigrate. While Nazi policies toward German Jews were still in flux during 1933–1935, McDonald nonetheless felt that many of the Jews were doomed if they could not find ways and means to emigrate.

McDonald tried to act on four levels—international, with national governments, with non-governmental organizations, and, more than occasionally, in aid of specific individuals. If he failed much more often than he succeeded, his diary shows how he tried, and quite often, the reasons for his failures. His entries supply wonderful, detailed information about differences of policy and personality among supporters of humanitarian action and about the level of opposition to it—particularly among government officials.

Chapters 5 through 8 and 16 and 17 covered the proceedings of the League of Nations in such detail that comment here seems almost superfluous. Both the League hierarchy and a good number of national delegates to the League were so fearful of further offending Germany (which withdrew from the League in October 1933) that McDonald's commission received little or no League support—and no League funding whatsoever. Secretary General Joseph Avenol was apparently hoping that Germany might return to membership in the League, so that he was unwilling to take the slightest risk in backing the High Commission.[4] None of that stopped various participants and observers in Geneva from criticizing McDonald for inefficiency or self-enrichment at the expense of refugees.

In the course of his efforts in Geneva and elsewhere, McDonald obtained direct access to foreign statesmen and elicited candid statements both about refugee problems and international relations generally. On November 19, 1934, for example, Pierre Laval—later to become French premier under the Vichy regime—unleashed a revealing tirade against foreigners in his country; Eduard Benes, then foreign minister of Czechoslovakia, then sketched out concisely his largely accurate diagnosis of European affairs as disrupted by bandit nations and predicted that war could not long be avoided. Benes perceived that attempts to placate potential aggressors would not succeed. (Other diplomats and statesmen, still plagued by memories of World War I, wanted to believe that major

3. Herbert A. Strauss, "Jewish Emigration from Germany: Nazi Policies and Jewish Responses (I)," *Leo Baeck Institute Yearbook* 25 (1980): especially 339.

4. See McDonald's diary entry of August 23, 1934.

war could be avoided—all the more reason not to offend Germany.) Laval and Benes, each in different ways, could only have reinforced McDonald's feeling that he needed to find answers soon for Jews seeking havens.

Taking into account the range of views he heard at Geneva and elsewhere and adding his own direct observations, McDonald triangulated his own course based on his expectation of escalating persecution within Germany and future war. He had no illusions about Hitler's regime disappearing as a result of internal dissent or opposition from the military or the business elite—its base of support was too broad. Others raised the prospect of Hitler's disappearance or eclipse, but apart from gossip about Hitler's health, McDonald did not buy into this notion. He was also skeptical of projections that Germany's economic difficulties might bring Hitler's regime down.

What scope remained for a humanitarian advocate? The Nazi regime's utter immobility was not at first obvious to McDonald, who hoped to "build a bridge" from Lausanne, where the High Commission was based, to Berlin.[5] McDonald repeatedly visited Germany to try one method after another to facilitate Jewish emigration, but, with one exception discussed below, got only negative responses or no response whatsoever. The reasons are not obvious even today.

One of the best historians of Nazi anti-Jewish policies in the 1930s, Francis Nicosia, wrote in 2005 that, prior to the Final Solution, Nazi Germany had no comprehensive policy beyond promotion of Jewish emigration.[6] For the years 1933–1935 Nicosia's statement rests largely on one instance of official Nazi support for Jewish emigration—the Transfer Agreement (Haavara) worked out between Nazi Germany and the Jewish Agency for Palestine.[7] This arrangement allowed emigrants to Palestine to salvage some of their abandoned German assets through credits redeemable at banks in Palestine. The export and sale of German goods to Palestine supplied funding to pay off the credits. Nazi Germany confiscated most of the emigrants' assets and managed to raise its exports in the process. During the period 1933–1936 more German Jews emigrated to Palestine than anywhere else.[8]

McDonald did not comment explicitly about this Haavara agreement in his diary (although he personally lobbied British officials to allow more Jews to enter Palestine). But he was well aware that most American and British government officials, as did McDonald himself, opposed economic measures that would reward or assist Nazi Germany. When McDonald's associate Mildred Wertheimer suggested in July 1934 that it might be time to change this view, he termed her an incorrigible German![9] Whether or not they supported the movement to boycott

5. See, for example, McDonald's diary entry of November 16, 1933.

6. Francis R. Nicosia, "Jewish Farmers in Hitler's Germany: Zionist Occupational Retraining and Nazi 'Jewish Policy,'" *Holocaust and Genocide Studies* 19, no. 3 (2005): 366.

7. See Francis R. Nicosia, *Zionism in National Socialist Jewish Policy in Germany, 1933–39* (Chicago: University of Chicago Press, 1978).

8. Strauss, "Jewish Emigration from Germany: Nazi Policies and Jewish Responses (II)," *Leo Baeck Institute Yearbook* 26 (1981): 345.

9. See McDonald's diary entry of July 17, 1934.

German goods, American Jewish leaders almost unanimously opposed increased American economic ties with Germany. Emigration of Jews from Germany to Western countries needed different arrangements or forms of assistance.

During late 1933 and 1934 McDonald repeatedly sought to sell German officials on one arms-length transaction. If Germany would use blocked German Jewish assets for relief purposes in the country, funds raised outside Germany, which might otherwise be sent into Germany for relief, could be devoted to finding places of settlement and extracting substantial numbers of German Jews. But even without McDonald's unacceptable kicker—Germany would have to refrain from persecuting those Jews who remained—these suggestions did not elicit interest beyond Foreign Minister von Neurath. The non-Nazi foreign minister carried little weight on foreign policy, let alone on the Jewish question. At best, Neurath could raise this possibility with more powerful figures, who showed utterly no interest in the notion of planned, orderly emigration in cooperation with the League High Commissioner. McDonald tried to do everything he could think of to help German Jews emigrate, and responsible German officials would hardly meet with him, let alone consider his ideas seriously.

In March 1934 American Ambassador William Dodd described McDonald's mission to Hitler directly. He did so awkwardly—in such a fashion that it was easy for the Chancellor to reject the whole idea as pointless.[10] Still, Hitler's reaction was revealing. The notion of foreign and international involvement in Germany's treatment of Jews hit such a nerve that, even if there were practical economic benefits for Germany, Hitler had no interest in them.

Dodd, too, kept a diary, a version of which was published by his son and daughter in 1941, a year after Dodd's death. Its availability in published form (the original was never made available) generated a certain amount of interest among scholars later. For example, it was used extensively (although not uncritically) by Dodd's biographer, Robert Dallek. McDonald's diary, meanwhile, remained unknown, a small part of it used only by his daughter, Barbara McDonald Stewart, in her Columbia dissertation and subsequent book.[11] Although many of McDonald's papers have long been available, relatively few scholars have written substantially about his efforts.[12]

McDonald's reading of conditions in Germany differed radically from that of Dodd. In his diary McDonald commented that Dodd saw an early moderation of the Nazi regime,[13] confirming other sources showing how the ambassa

10. See inserted commentary in diary entry of March 7, 1934.

11. Barbara McDonald Stewart, *United States Government Policy on Refugees from Nazism, 1933–1940* (New York: Garland, 1982).

12. The most detailed coverage is by Haim Genizi, *American Apathy: The Plight of Christian Refugees from Nazism* (Ramat Gan: Bar-Ilan University Press, 1983); "James G. McDonald and the Roosevelt Administration, 1933–45," *Bar-Ilan Studies* 1 (2000): 285–306; "James G. McDonald: High Commisioner for Refugees, 1933–35," *Wiener Library Bulletin* 30 (1977): 40–52. See also Jeffrey Lesser, *Welcoming the Undesirables: Brazil and the Jewish Question* (Berkeley: University of California Press, 1995). Both authors used McDonald's papers at Columbia; this diary was not then available.

13. See chapter 4, entry of August 12, 1933.

dor translated his anti-Nazi views into practice. He thought he knew the limits of appropriate criticism: others transcended them. Dodd questioned the wisdom of the external Jewish-led boycott of German goods, worrying that a Communist revolution might upset Hitler, German Jews, and "not a few of the rest of us . . . if German industry is stalled by America joining a British boycott! . . . [Actually, American Jews were in the forefront of the boycott action.] You can see, therefore, how I must react to the urge for immediate action on the Jewish issue—much as I abhor much that is being done."[14]

Upon appointing Dodd and after telling him that he wanted an American liberal in Berlin as a standing example, FDR likely also told him that Nazi Germany was treating German Jews shamefully and that American Jews were most upset about this situation, but that it was not a governmental matter. Nonetheless, Dodd should try to use his personal influence to ameliorate the situation.[15]

Dodd was given to symbolic gestures of disapproval of the Nazi regime. In a speech before the American Chamber of Commerce in Berlin he criticized arbitrary and minority governments throughout history. Dodd also declined an invitation to attend the Nuremberg Party Rally.[16] But such actions did not get him far even with the more conservative elements in the government, such as Foreign Minister Neurath, in which Dodd placed too much hope. Other American diplomats in Berlin perceived more of the reality.

Consul Raymond Geist, when pressed by a superior in the State Department, said that Dodd's rare visits to Nazi authorities "had no effect because he does not have the force of character necessary. . . . The only kind of person who can deal successfully with the Nazi Government is a man of intelligence and force who is willing to assume a dictatorial attitude with the Government and insist upon his demands being met. Mr. Dodd is unable to do this."[17] After a while, Dodd ceased even to make much effort to influence the German government. Moreover, he frowned on subordinates visiting Nazi officials too, leading one frustrated State Department official to comment in his diary: "what in the world is the use of having an ambassador who refuses to speak to the government to which he is accredited?"[18]

When the Nazi government prepared to expel Edgar Ansel Mowrer, one of the most critical American journalists in Berlin, Dodd refused to support Consul General George Messersmith and Mowrer himself, both of whom wished to

14. Quoted in Dallek, *Democrat and Diplomat,* 201; other material, 198–201. Yet Dodd also told McDonald to "tell the Jews not to give up the boycott, for these people [the Nazis] only understand pressure of one sort or another." McDonald's diary entry of November 13, 1934. On Dodd's inconsistency, see below.

15. *Ambassador Dodd's Diary,* 4–6. Dallek, *Democrat and Diplomat,* 192, 373–375, gives a slightly more positive cast on these instructions than Dodd's diary itself.

16. Dallek, *Democrat and Diplomat,* 210–211; Phillip Metcalfe, *1933* (Sag Harbor, N.Y.: Permanent Press, 1988), 140–141.

17. Assistant Secretary of State Wilbur J. Carr's memorandum of conversation with Raymond Geist, June 5, 1935, Carr Papers, Box 12, Library of Congress.

18. William Phillips Diary, December 29, 1935, Houghton Library, Harvard University.

contest the expulsion, despite death threats against Mowrer and the stationing of police outside his home. Dodd described Mowrer as just as vehement, in his own way, as the Nazis: Mowrer's early departure was in the interest of everyone. Mowrer obviously did not agree: he never forgave Dodd for his failure to defend an American citizen or the rights of a free press.[19]

Dodd's own private actions undercut his stated opposition to Nazi persecution of the Jews. He actually took advantage of the vulnerable situation of one Berlin Jewish family to obtain suitable, well-located housing at a cheap rent. In mid-1935 Assistant Secretary of State Wilbur Carr obtained a detailed account.

> Mr. Geist stated that when the Ambassador came to Berlin[,] it was at a time when the unfavorable Nazi attitude toward Jews was at its heighth [*sic*]. The Ambassador succeeded in renting the house of a well-to-do Jew [Frederick Warburg] for a mere nominal rent of 600 marks a month. . . . The only reason he [Dodd] obtained the house at that rent was because it was the desire of the owner to have the property protected through the occupancy of it by the American Ambassador. The lease was for one year only, expiring last August [1934]. The attitude of the Nazi Government toward the landlord having undergone a marked change, the landlord sought to get his house back. The Ambassador and Mrs. Dodd did not wish to move. Mr. Geist was given the task of persuading the landlord to give a new lease. . . . [Geist tried to find alternative residences, but could not prevail upon Ambassador Dodd. Geist] finally persuaded him [Warburg] to grant the Ambassador another lease for a thousand marks a month. Mrs. Dodd refused to pay it. . . . [The landlord finally signed] a lease for 800 marks a month . . . [and agreed] to put at the disposal of the Ambassador certain articles of furniture and rooms theretofore reserved for the exclusive use of the landlord. . . . Mr. Geist says that Mr. and Mrs. Dodd's conduct in connection with this whole matter has almost resulted in scandal in Berlin.

Martha Dodd's (Dodd's daughter) social relationship with Secret Police Chief Rudolf Diels, a married man, only made the situation worse, according to Geist.[20]

Matching but dissonant diary entries of February 7, 1934, by McDonald and Dodd (see chap. 10) about their conversation undercut the reliability of Dodd's notations. Dodd misunderstood or misrecorded the source and the amount of the funds McDonald had raised—just as he had earlier mistakenly thought that British Jews were driving the movement to boycott German goods. Dodd made light of McDonald's difficulties in trying to bring about German Jewish emigration. (He later expressed his personal disdain for McDonald,[21]

19. Jesse H. Stiller, *George S. Messersmith, Diplomat of Democracy* (Chapel Hill: University of North Carolina Press, 1987), 42–43; *Ambassador Dodd's Diary,* 24; Dallek, *Democrat and Diplomat,* 201–202.

20. Assistant Secretary of State Wilbur J. Carr's memorandum, June 5, 1935, Carr Papers, Box 12, Library of Congress.

21. See chapter 16, diary entry of August 17, 1934, note 8.

probably misattributing to Max Warburg his own view.) On matters of fact, Dodd was sloppy; on matters of judgment, he was wild and inconsistent.[22] He gave McDonald little help in pressing German officials for what small and few concessions might have been obtainable.

McDonald dealt with at least two very different categories of victims of Nazi persecution. Some Jews and many political opponents of the Nazis dropped everything and simply fled Germany in 1933. They ended up in France, Belgium, the Netherlands, Britain, Czechoslovakia, and, in smaller numbers, elsewhere. Jewish refugees who made it to Britain were relatively well supported by Jewish charitable organizations; elsewhere, for example, in France, the economic position of these refugees was generally dire—worse than that of Jews still in Germany. Paradoxically, McDonald was under greater pressure to find settlement options for refugees who were already outside Germany in temporary havens than to extricate Jews from the Nazi grasp. (In fact, Jews in Germany were technically outside his mandate.) Both French government officials and French Jewish leaders strove to move Jewish refugees out, not to take in more. A third potential category—Jews in Poland and other Eastern European countries threatened by rising right-wing and anti-Semitic movements, either on their own initiative or following the German example—was so large that McDonald could do little but take note of the scope of this problem. He talked at times about the need for a far-reaching, even worldwide, program to combat anti-Semitism, but American Jewish leaders were reluctant to go this route.[23]

McDonald had some sense of the potential catastrophe for Jews remaining in Germany. On March 29, 1933, he had heard his old acquaintance Putzi Hanfstaengl declare that Germany could deal with 600,000 Jews in a single night. He must have feared or sensed the worst, for he subsequently predicted to Walter Lippmann that the first consequence of a possible Polish attack on Germany would be a slaughter of German Jews.[24] The theory behind this remark was that the Nazis viewed Jews as so corrosive that they would have to be excised in time of war.

On April 8, 1933, McDonald met with Hitler and heard him expound on the Jewish threat. In taking on the Jews, Hitler claimed, Germany was fighting in the interest of the world, "etc." Perhaps the most revealing thing about this diary entry is that he did not record everything Hitler said. Was it because he had heard the same thing before—from Hanfstaengl, from Lüdecke, from Daitz (among those recorded in the diary)? Or, more likely, was it because McDonald was using a German stenographer and not at all sure about how much he should write down? (He had been made aware that cables and telephone conversations were tapped.) After he returned to the United States, McDonald repeated to a

22. Messersmith's biographer Stiller notes that Dodd once wrote a bitter and irrational letter to the State Department, both denying and regretting having endorsed Messersmith for promotion. Stiller, *Diplomat of Democracy,* 42.

23. See McDonald's diary entry of January 1, 1934.

24. McDonald's diary entry of May 16, 1933.

small audience what may have been Hitler's acrid conclusion: "The world does not know how to get rid of the Jews. I will show them."[25]

Hitler's reported comment left many options open. There were, of course, possibilities of letting Jews leave and of forcing them out. But Hitler's assumption that the world would benefit from the elimination of Jews also suggested the most extreme interpretation, which later materialized. Both contemporary sources and McDonald's recollections indicate that in 1933 he recognized the worst case.[26]

Since the 1960s scholars have done a great deal of research to try to determine how and when Nazi Germany reached a policy of genocide. Opinion has abandoned the older notion that Hitler was always and irrevocably committed to destroy Jews wherever he could reach: that given Hitler in power, a Holocaust was inevitable.[27] Recent scholarship has emphasized that within Nazi Germany experiments, uncertainties, pressures from below and responses from above, and disagreements among rival agencies, rather than any concerted plan, escalated the persecution of Jews over time. In the need to consolidate and maximize power and sensitive to potential economic damage, Hitler often sided with more conservative elements in the early years of his rule, pursuing discriminatory laws, rather than allow party extremists to strike out wildly or violently against Jews.[28]

After the first months of violence and initiatives from below, Hitler imposed some restraints, avoiding steps that might inflict immediate damage to the economy. (Many private Jewish banks survived into 1938.) The April 1, 1933, experiment—an officially sanctioned public boycott of Jewish businesses—was not repeated. But in a myriad of other ways (as McDonald's sources noted), the regime moved steadily to separate Jews from German society. In historian Saul Friedländer's terms, Nazism was a political religion in which anti-Semitism played a central role, even had a redemptive quality. Hitler's tendency to see the battle with Jewry in terms of perdition or redemption blocked upper-level efforts at pragmatic arrangements for emigration.[29] Government bureau-

25. See inserted commentary in McDonald's diary entry of April 8, 1933.

26. After serving as ambassador to Israel, McDonald published a book about his mission there; he and his publisher included (in a short section about the author) the fact that Hitler had disclosed to McDonald "his purpose to destroy German Jewry." James G. McDonald, *My Mission in Israel 1948–1951* (New York: Simon and Schuster, 1951), 304.

27. Lucy S. Dawidowicz, *The War Against the Jews: 1933–1945* (New York: Bantam, 1986, orig. 1975); Gerald Fleming, *Hitler and the Final Solution* (Berkeley: University of California Press, 1987).

28. Saul S. Friedländer, *Nazi Germany and the Jews*, vol. I, *The Years of Persecution, 1933–1939* (New York: HarperCollins, 1997), 116.

29. Friedländer, *Nazi Germany and the Jews,* 72, 87, 99–100. Even later, when the regime sought to move Jews out of the country shortly before Germany went to war, Nazi desires to seize all Jewish assets and to inflict punishment still got in the way of emigration, if to a lesser extent. If there was any strategy behind what amounted to chaotic forced Jewish emigration in late 1930s, it may be that Hitler and others expected that foreign countries would be less inclined to complain about Nazi persecution of remaining German Jews. But some of what happened may well reflect differences among agencies and rival Nazi officials.

crats and Nazi Party chieftains pursued their own agendas not in a vacuum, but in light of Hitler's virulent views. From 1933 on, Nazi officials really wanted "punishment" of German Jews. McDonald recorded in his diary how his friends among German Jews—particularly Max and Erich Warburg, Lola Hahn, Wilfrid Israel, and others—perceived over time an increasingly dire future.

Unable to ease the path of Jews out of Germany, McDonald turned increasingly to exploring potential sites of permanent settlement and raising enough money so that immigrants—Jewish and non-Jewish—might be considered assets, rather than objects of suspicion or worse. His fundraising strategy among Jewish circles involved bringing Zionist and non-Zionist leaders and organizations together to work for common goals—a difficult and frequently frustrating task. Chaim Weizmann, the most prestigious figure among Jews worldwide, was emotionally opposed to expenditure of resources anywhere other than in Palestine and concerned about fundraising efforts that might siphon off potential financing for Palestine. Hoping to see half a million Jews in Palestine before his death,[30] he expressed caustic sentiments about assimilationist German Jews. Felix Warburg, the most generous among Jewish philanthropists, was skeptical of Palestine's absorptive capacity and supported multiple approaches elsewhere. Conservative non-Zionist Jewish leaders in Britain, men such as Lionel and Anthony de Rothschild and Sir Robert Waley-Cohen, gave at best grudging support to the High Commission and consistently underestimated the scope and duration of the problem faced by Jews in Germany. Louis Oungre, head of the Jewish Colonization Association (ICA), had the most practical experience with resettlement but was oriented toward removing refugees from France and bolstering existing ICA ventures. Baron Robert de Rothschild saw German Jews more as Germans than as Jews and worried about the number of them already in France.

It was too much for McDonald to keep these men and others, such as Stephen Wise and Julian Mack of the American Jewish Congress—Zionists, but with differences of policy and personality from Weizmann—on the same course. (His diary represents a wonderful source on attitudes and interactions among Jewish elites in various countries.) The most he accomplished was to keep them occasionally from undercutting each other—and himself. Nonetheless, McDonald's joint fundraising campaign for German Jewish Aid was the direct ancestor of the United Jewish Appeal.

One of his purposes was to establish a corporation—formally called the Refugee Economic Corporation—that could invest substantial funds in new or existing enterprises—in Palestine, in African countries, or in South America. Such enterprises would then arrange to employ substantial numbers of refugees, allowing for their admission to the country or territory. The corporation might or might not have yielded some return for donor/investors. McDonald did not

30. See McDonald's diary entry of January 29, 1934.

invent this notion: it was the brainchild of Charles Liebman, James Rosenberg, and perhaps others.[31] But he was asked to claim responsibility for it, which he did. He kept raising the corporation idea with potential large donors, if not particularly successfully or exclusively, until his resignation at the end of 1935. The Refugee Economic Corporation came into being, but it did not have far-reaching effects.

McDonald also pursued an ecumenical strategy, consistently describing Nazi persecution in broad terms so that others noticed the suffering of non-Jews (including those Christians whom the Nazis considered Jews). Nazi efforts to coordinate the Evangelical Church and to persecute some officials of the Catholic Church made McDonald's strategy more palatable, for it was easier to arouse broad sympathy for victims of religious persecution than for Communists or Social Democrats.

McDonald was far from unique in recognizing that Nazi Germany posed a threat to Western civilized values—and ultimately to Western civilization itself. But some of those who, during the 1930s and early 1940s, depicted Nazism as a universal problem refused to recognize that Jews were a particular Nazi target—or that special measures to help them might be justified.[32] McDonald's approach was broad without in any way underestimating the threat to German Jews—and to a lesser extent, the Jews in other parts of Europe threatened by right-wing extremist movements.

Still, McDonald's strategy held substantial risks. Jewish leaders and organizations undoubtedly thought (and one or two said) that they had enough troubles of their own to deal with. On the other hand, some Christians were not terribly interested in Jewish causes. Even as liberal a Protestant body as the Federal Council of Churches in the United States wanted to craft a fundraising appeal so that it emphasized only the need of non-Jewish refugees. This was not at all what McDonald wanted—he knew very well that the large majority of those most in need were Jews—and he was ready to drop the idea of working with the Federal Council if it pursued this line.[33]

McDonald sold American Jewish leaders and Jewish organizations on the wisdom of challenging anti-Catholic persecution in Mexico as a means of earning credit with the Catholic Church. Having developed an asset, McDonald used it where it might do much good: in an extraordinary private discussion with Cardinal Pacelli, he used the prospect of further Jewish influence in Washington and pressure against the anticlerical Mexican government to enlist Vatican support for his upcoming efforts in South America.[34] Through the aid of

31. See McDonald's diary entry of December 25, 1933.

32. See Tony Kushner, *The Holocaust and the Liberal Imagination: A Social and Cultural History* (London: Blackwell, 1994).

33. McDonald to Ogden, personal and confidential, December 3, 1933. Copy in McDonald Papers, USHMM.

34. See McDonald's diary entry of January 24, 1935.

Enrico Galeazzi (a highly influential individual little covered in historical works on the Vatican), McDonald learned that Pacelli brought the matter to the attention of Pope Pius XI.

Whatever the Vatican did or did not do in response, in March and April 1935 McDonald received friendly treatment from Sabastiao Cardinal Leme in Rio de Janeiro and the archbishop of Buenos Aires. Their reception stood in marked contrast to the behavior of American and British diplomats, which ranged from frigidity to polite indifference toward the High Commissioner during his South American visit. Still, no one on the outside among the South Americans showed much willingness to join with McDonald in heavy lobbying with high government officials on behalf of Jewish refugees. (Some German Catholics were admitted to Brazil as a result of McDonald's efforts.[35]) McDonald's one nominal ally in South America, Louis Oungre, pursued a different strategy—looking for opportunities for large enterprises that would employ many refugee-immigrants. Oungre and his organization, however, were not in good standing with Brazilian and Argentinean government officials—or even with most Jewish communal leaders. Whether out of some kind of organizational self-interest or personal contrariness, Oungre frequently undercut McDonald's own efforts aimed at creating entry for foreign Jews into existing Brazilian and Argentinean enterprises and institutions.

McDonald did not need additional handicaps. The political and economic climate in Brazil and Argentina was laden with anti-Semitism. In Argentina, even the president's support could not gain Alfredo Hirsch, one of the wealthiest men in the country, admission to membership in the Jockey Club in Buenos Aires. Brazil was somewhat more tolerant and certainly needed settlers. Brazilian law and government officials, however, gave preference to trained farmers, and most of the relatively small numbers of Jews trained for farming were sent to Palestine. But scarcity of Jews trained for agriculture was only the tip of the problem. As Brazilian economic conditions eased after the Great Depression, growing desire for ethnic homogeneity and fear of Jewish connections with communism—and new anti-Semitic organizations—created new barriers to Jewish immigrants. Even where government officials were not themselves anti-Semitic, they took account of the political climate.

Though suggesting that McDonald's ancestors must have been Irish immigrants to the United States (otherwise, why would McDonald interest himself in such issues!), Brazilian President Getúlio Vargas listened politely to McDonald's plea for the annual admission of approximately six thousand refugees, most of whom would be Jewish, with outside financial guarantees that they would not become public charges. He seemed to be receptive. But, apart from the placement of small numbers of refugee scholars and intellectuals in Brazil, nothing much happened. In mid-1937 Getúlio Vargas personally authorized a new se-

35. Lesser, *Welcoming the Undesirables,* 72.

cret immigration circular that sharply restricted Jewish immigration specifically.[36]

Brazil and Argentina were important litmus tests for the prevalence of anti-Semitism. Even though they had experienced severe problems during the Depression, both countries had plenty of land and, in the long run, needed immigrants—as most government officials and private businessmen recognized in conversations with McDonald. In Europe (and in the United States) the case for taking in refugees and immigrants was much more debatable, which meant that, at the time, it was harder to determine when, where, and how much anti-Semitism played a role among those who opposed measures on behalf of refugees.

McDonald did not go out of his way to label people as anti-Semites. Still, he recorded numerous comments by influential figures in various countries, and some of the remarks were revealing. Heinrich Rothmund, head of the Police Section of the Federal Ministry of Justice and Police in Switzerland, insisted on a definition of political refugee that excluded German Jews. Despite some nominally positive comments about Swiss Jews as "cooperative," Rothmund warned about the danger of eastern Jews entering Switzerland and raising the level of anti-Semitism.[37] (Those who were themselves anti-Semitic certainly recognized what would strengthen their case.) Nor was it an accident that Rothmund directly challenged McDonald at a subsequent meeting of the Governing Body of the High Commission.[38] There is additional evidence of Rothmund's anti-Semitism,[39] but even without it, Rothmund's comments and behavior recorded in McDonald's diary suggest it. Archbishop of Canterbury William Cosmo Gordon Lang, in the course of declining to assist in fundraising, was even less ambiguous, asking rhetorically, "But isn't it true that the excesses of the Jews themselves under the Republic are responsible for the excesses of the Nazis towards the Jews, at least in part?"[40] On another occasion, when McDonald did not have to be diplomatic, he responded to charges that there was some reason for Jews always being persecuted with "it is because the Christians are not Christian."[41]

36. Lesser, *Welcoming the Undesirables,* 52–94. Lesser had access to the McDonald Papers at Columbia, but not to this diary. His verdict was that McDonald was overly optimistic about what he might accomplish and placed too much hope on the state governments. As a result, and given the hostile climate, he produced very limited short-term results, but exerted an influence that contributed later to opening of Brazil to new immigration. McDonald's diary supplies some evidence to support Lesser's view that initially, he was overoptimistic (Lesser uses the term "naively," but he quickly learned of the many difficulties in Brazil and even more in Argentina. Continuation of his efforts reflected more persistence than naiveté.)

37. McDonald's diary entry of September 19, 1934.

38. See McDonald's diary entry of November 2, 1934.

39. See Alfred A. Hässler, *The Lifeboat Is Full: Switzerland and the Refugees, 1933–1945,* tr. Charles Lam Markmann (New York: Funk & Wagnalls, 1969), 10, 30–53.

40. See McDonald's diary entry of October 4, 1934.

41. See McDonald's diary entry of January 11, 1934.

Some U.S. government officials expressed unflattering views of potential immigrants. A. Dana Hodgdon, an official in the Visa Division of the State Department, "in some of his talk showed a spirit which I [McDonald] resented. It was as if a person by applying for a visa thereby automatically stamped himself as undesirable." McDonald sensed that Hodgdon's views were shared by others in the Visa Division.[42] Again, McDonald usually avoided giving a label to this behavior, but his diary allows us to see it for what it was.

McDonald ran into similar attitudes in the Canadian government. Frederick Charles Blair in the Immigration Branch of the Department of Mines and Resources believed that Jews were involved in illicit liquor or narcotics traffic. It was not coincidental that Prime Minister R. B. Bennett, after first inviting McDonald to submit lists of refugees seeking haven, changed his mind and determined that none could be admitted.[43]

Beyond anti-Semitism, reasons for opposition to immigration in many parts of the world were numerous in the 1930s. Most countries were slow to recover from the Depression; few societies were so resilient and self-confident that they could greet newcomers with equanimity, and everywhere politicians worried primarily about their constituents, not outsiders. If war was a threat, foreigners—even those persecuted by Nazi Germany—were perceived as a security risk. Of course, few individuals in the 1930s had McDonald's perception of imminent danger to Jews on a very broad scale. Those who were not well disposed toward Jews could find ways to ignore what was at the time "simply" persecution of a group that might or might not be partly responsible for its own troubles. What did the situation of German Jews or Jewish refugees have to do with them?

Some philanthropists and members of the American elite distinguished sharply between worthy and unworthy causes. John D. Rockefeller, Jr., supported the placement of refugee scholars in academic positions in the United States, but despite repeated efforts by McDonald and others, and despite his own friendly ties to McDonald, Rockefeller did not contribute even a token amount to the proposed Refugee Economic Corporation or to the expenses of the High Commission. Mrs. Rockefeller once said to McDonald, "Sometimes when I wake up at night I wonder what can be done with the Jews."[44] (McDonald did term John D. Rockefeller III "instinctively rather anti-Semitic."[45]) Edward A. Filene, who was Jewish, could not see why this was a particularly important matter. President Lowell of Harvard University wasn't interested in German refugees and could not meet with McDonald.[46] Oswald Villard, owner and editor of the leftist magazine the *Nation,* blamed at least part of the preva-

42. McDonald's diary entry of January 15, 1934. See also inserted commentary in diary entry of December 30, 1933.

43. McDonald's diary entry of March 20, 1934; Irving Abella and Harold Troper, *None Is Too Many: Canada and the Jews of Europe 1933–1948* (New York: Random House, 1983), 6–7.

44. McDonald's diary entry of May 21, 1934.

45. McDonald's diary entry of October 26, 1933.

46. McDonald's diary entry of March 21, 1934.

lence of anti-Semitism in the United States on the manners of the Jews themselves.[47] McDonald's contacts with a wide range of influential Americans—Jews and non-Jews—supply a window on elite attitudes toward Jews and Jewish causes during the mid-1930s.

McDonald hoped to loosen American immigration policy and regulations. He was less involved in lobbying efforts in Washington than was Columbia professor Joseph Chamberlain or Judge Julian Mack. Still, through McDonald's repeated contacts with high State Department officials, Commissioner of Immigration and Naturalization Daniel MacCormack, and others, he collected enough information that his diary, supplemented by other primary sources, can illuminate some unresolved or controversial issues in the historiography of American refugee policy.

On September 9–10, 1933, Jay Pierrepont Moffat wrote of his efforts to dissuade Secretary of State Hull from indicating support for resettling Jews:

> I then showed him a draft which Green and I had prepared for use either by the President or himself if necessary in which the Jewish question, or rather religious and cultural persecution, was brought up in a way which we felt would get the message over but could not give offense. The Secretary then asked if I would see if we could work out some sort of a statement approving the settling of Jews in other parts of the world than Germany. I urged him against such a course on the ground that it would be illogical for us to urge that when we were unwilling to admit more than a small percentage under our quota law. He replied that it might be possible to make up a selective list and admit those who had no Communistic tendency. Again I urged him against such a course, partly because it would reverse the policy for which we have fought for twelve years and partly because any German Jew who could give proof that he would not become a public charge may enter now as the quota for Germany is far from filled. Congressman Sabath had evidently made a strong impression the day before and I am much concerned over the trend of the Secretary's mind on this point.[48]

The policy "for which we have fought for twelve years" was the first immigration quota law (1921), transcended by the Johnson-Reed Act of 1924, followed by President Hoover's instruction of September 1930, tightening enforcement of the clause barring those "likely to become a public charge." Moffat opposed the slightest relaxation of these measures to benefit German Jews, and he regarded American support for resettling Jews elsewhere as a potential wedge to loosen restrictions in the United States. These comments suggest why Moffat, Undersecretary of State William Phillips, and Assistant Secretary of State Wilbur Carr consistently showed little interest in McDonald's mission—and did nothing to help him.[49] Their commitment to immigration restriction had direct bearing upon lack of American government support for McDonald's efforts.

47. McDonald's diary entry of December 19, 1934.

48. Moffat Journal, vol. 34, Moffat Papers, September 9 and 11, 1933 [*sic*], Houghton Library, Harvard University.

49. See also McDonald's diary entry of March 5, 1934, and notes 5–7.

Although sometimes misled, McDonald sensed more than occasionally that the State Department was not particularly helpful. He tried to work around it, with countervailing forces in government and immigration experts outside it. His diary adds significantly to available information in scholarly literature about the views and the role of Commissioner of Immigration and Naturalization Daniel MacCormack. MacCormack at first supported the use of bonds as guarantees that some refugees would not become public charges—and as a way of getting around consuls' use of the public charge provision as grounds for rejecting visa applicants from Germany. Later, however, MacCormack became concerned about increasing anti-Semitic sentiment in the United States and adverse congressional reaction to rising immigration. (To be fair, McDonald's diary contains independent evidence of rising anti-Semitism.[50]) MacCormack shied away from any public announcement about the bonding procedure, and then he convinced himself that the consuls in Germany had eased up on issuing visas. In any case, he, too, was concerned that use of labor bonds might open the doors to America too wide. MacCormack ultimately concluded that the tolerable annual limit for immigrants from Germany was below fifteen thousand. Thus, the Labor Department never pushed its advantage over the State Department to allow the use of public charge bonds.[51]

McDonald's diary supplies the first conclusive evidence that President Roosevelt was directly involved in the plan to use public charge bonds to do "what was necessary" in admitting refugees. At the same time, however, McDonald recorded FDR's own concerns about adverse congressional reaction to, and publicity about, an influx of refugees.[52] Similar concerns surfaced a year later, when McDonald, bypassing State Department officials, asked the President for $10,000 in government funds—to show official American support for the High Commission just before he set off to South America. Again, FDR's first reaction was to approve; then he became concerned about possible criticism and asked whether he needed congressional approval, which caused the initiative to bog down. Eventually, McDonald withdrew his request.[53]

In this diary President Roosevelt is not the indifferent figure depicted in some of the scholarly literature about America and the Holocaust.[54] He was clearly more sympathetic to McDonald and his cause than anyone in the State Department, or even than MacCormack, but as politician and statesman, he felt severely constrained by the climate in Congress and, to an extent, in the country at large. In addition, apart from Eleanor Roosevelt, there was no one around

50. See, for example, McDonald's diary entry of December 17, 1934.

51. See McDonald's diary entries of December 30, 1933; January 15, 1934; March 7, 1934; March 27, 1934; May 29, 1934; and December 17, 1934. For the literature, Breitman/Kraut, *American Refugee Policy,* 18–24.

52. See McDonald's diary entry of January 16, 1934.

53. See McDonald's diary entries of December 17–19, 21, 1934

54. David S. Wyman, *Paper Walls: America and the Refugee Crisis, 1938–1941* (Amherst: University of Massachusetts Press, 1968); *The Abandonment of the Jews: America and the Holocaust, 1941–1945* (New York: Pantheon, 1984).

him willing to follow up on McDonald's suggestions with regard to Jewish refugees. McDonald's initiatives, despite attracting the President's interest, usually came to naught.

In three of the four conversations McDonald had with Roosevelt during 1932–1935 McDonald was able to elicit FDR's view of the world and the threats to peace. President Roosevelt clearly recognized both a German problem and a Japanese problem, and he understood that there was some prospect of a major war. If he had any remedy at all in these early years of his administration, based on the remarks McDonald recorded, it was to persuade others to recognize clearly where the sources of trouble lay. For him, drawing sharp lines against potential enemies took precedence over trying to reverse or limit the damages they were already causing. After Felix Frankfurter passed on to Roosevelt McDonald's forecast of what might develop in Germany, the President responded that he was very interested, but that he did not see what he could do about it.[55]

McDonald's talks with Roosevelt are but one example of many rich nuggets of historical information found in this period of his diary. McDonald's three talks with Cardinal Pacelli, the future Pope Pius XII, supply new insights into his personality and political strategy. Pacelli's defense of the Concordat and his initial unwillingness to be of help to German Jews and refugees, both recorded by McDonald, will give supporters and opponents more evidence to grapple with in the debate about how the cardinal and future pope viewed Nazi Germany.[56] The mystery of what Pacelli did or did not do in response to McDonald's requests lies in Vatican archives. McDonald communicated with Albert Einstein and Edward R. Murrow on refugee matters and with Chaim Weizmann (frequently) and Vladimir Jabotinsky (once) on a broad range of issues: his diary entries may interest and perhaps influence future biographers of these men and others.

Volume I of McDonald's diary ends at the point where he had accomplished what he thought he could as High Commissioner and had taken steps to wind up his role. He wanted to manage his formal resignation in such a way that it drew attention to the cause and perhaps weakened opposition to it. That process of maneuver—what might be called the end game—in a further segment of his diary has been left for volume 2. Drawing upon McDonald's papers, other private collections, and government records, the second volume of this series will also cover McDonald's return to refugee diplomacy in 1938–1939 as chairman of the President's Advisory Committee on Political Refugees. It will show that some of McDonald's early failed initiatives bore fruit later.

McDonald's meticulous reporting of day-to-day events—a few small victories and many great disappointments—will certainly enrich future discussions of Western policies and Jewish reactions before the Holocaust. And his call for a broad campaign against anti-Semitism across the world resonates into the twenty-first century. In that sense, his efforts were not in vain.

55. See McDonald's diary entry of January 24, 1934.
56. See McDonald's diary entry of August 24, 1933.

INDEX

Page numbers for text boxes are shown in italics. Abbreviations used in the index are as follows: FDR (Franklin D. Roosevelt), HCR (High Commission for Refugees), JGM (James G. McDonald).

Abyssinia, 787
Academic Assistance Council, 330, 334, 340
Adams, Walter, 270n43
Addams, Jane, 249n16
Adler, Cyrus, 101, 101n12, 127n8, 456, 463
Adler, Julius Ochs, 140n5
AEG. *See* Allgemeine Elektrizitäts-Gesellschaft (AEG)
AFL. *See* American Federation of Labor (AFL)
Agamemnon, Magalhães, 641–42, 655, 665, 670–72, 674, 682–83, 754
agricultural settlements: in Argentina, 686n12, 691, 698–99, 713–15, 719–20, 724–26, 731; industrial-agricultural balance in Brazil, 642–43, 655–56, 670–71, 679, 754; Jewish lack of experience for, 429; Philippson (Brazil), 641, 641n9; primitive-condition settlements, 426; Quatro Irmaos (Brazil), 640–41, 641n9, 658–59, 754, 780; in Soviet Union, 80, 448, 448n2, 471. *See also* Biro-Bidjan settlement region (Soviet Union); Parana Plantations (Brazilian refugee employment organization)
Agudath Israel, 285, 308, 363
Akron disaster, 44
Albania, 459, 464
Aldrich, Winthrop, 79, 79n21, 82–83, 85
Alemann, Ernesto F., 688, 696, 704, 715, 722, 725, 730
Alexander I of Yugoslavia, 498, 498n9, 503
Allgemeine Elektrizitäts-Gesellschaft (AEG), 37n58
Alliance Universelle Israelite, 153, 164, 220, 277
Allocation Committee, 349, 415–16, 418
Aloisi, Baron Pampeo, 474n12, 562
Altamira, Guillermo Salazar, 709–10, 713, 717–20, 722, 729, 737–38
Altschul, Frank, 75–76, 75n10, 772–73
Amaral, Afranio do, 679–81, 679n8
American Christian Committee, 304, 320
American Federation of Labor (AFL), 462, 462n16, 589
American Jewish Committee, 6–7, 27, 66, 128, 170–71
American Jewish Congress: Deutsch affiliation with, 66n26; HCR and, 93, 117, 190; mentioned, 139; Sulzberger opposition to, 139; support for boycott of German goods, 31; Weizmann conflicts with, 798; Wise as leader of, 58n5
American Jewish Joint Distribution Committee (JDC): central committee financing and, 333–35; Feilchenfeld and, 236; Felix Warburg role in, 55–56; financial contributions to, 411; French refugees and, 158, 253; HCR and, 77, 128, 170–71, 190, 332; joint drive, 316, 316n16, 329–30, 608; loans to Warsaw Halutz, 364; Russian settlements and, 448n2; Zionists and, 298, 299–300, 303–304

American Palestine Committee (APC), 306, 306n37
American Society for Jewish Farm Settlement in Russia, 55
AMICA, 351
Amtorg, 336, 336n31
Anglo-American Committee of Inquiry on Palestine, 2
Anglo-HICEM: overview, 158n36; African immigration and, 421–22; Edouard Oungre on, 158–59; HCR and, 217; immigration committee, 283–84; Kahn on, 348; program for German doctors, 384; Schiff on, 170, 343
Angola, 378, 379
anti-German sentiment, 4
anti-Semitism: acceptance in German society, 375–76; in Argentina, 689–91, 702, 710, 717, 740, 800–801; in Austria, 558; in Brazil, 635, 635n4, 651, 653, 800–801; in Canada, 326; as Christian issue (humanization), 73, 76, 140n7, 152, 253, 416, 436; German-Jewish War Veterans denial of, 327; in Iraq, 497; JGM approach to, 6, 68, 73, 241, 801; Lady Astor views, 544–45; Mosley outburst of, 542; Mussolini and, 395–96; observance of Christian holidays and, 684; proposed Pyke research institute on, 518; refugee resettlement and, 140–41, 241, 258n26, 714, 802; *Der Stürmer,* 375–76, 392–93, 395, 395n20; Town Hall address and, 66–67, 73, 75–76, 139; in Uruguay, 684; in the U.S., 461–62, 575–76, 582–83, 802–803; U.S. Christian action against, 243–44. *See also* race theory of Nazis
APC. *See* American Palestine Committee (APC)
Appleget, Thomas Baird, 460, 460n14
Aranha, Oswaldo, 583–84, 633, 638–39, 660
Argentina: agricultural settlements, 686–87, 686n12, 691, 692–93, 713–15, 719–20, 724–26, 731; anti-Semitism in, 689–91, 702–703, 710, 717, 740, 800–801; Committee against Anti-Semitism, 685; immigration policy, 686, 692, 698, 701, 712, 718–20, 722–23, 729, 737–38; JGM immigration efforts in, 522–23, 606, 619, 703–704, 736, 800–801, 801n36; Nationalist movement in, 717, 717n5; Oungre refugee employment organization, 442, 653, 800; *La Semana Tragica* (tragic week), 685, 685n11; settlement proposals for, 390, 439, 481–82, 525, 583, 621, 696–98, 723–24, 736–37, 737
Ashworth, Robert A., 301n21
Asquith, Herbert, Earl of Oxford and Asquith, 279n1
Asquith, Lady Cynthia, 533n34
Asscher, Abraham, 180n60, 183
assimilationism: Cecil view of, 201; Erich Warburg and, 54, 74; ineffectiveness for German Jews, 462; JGM on, 711; Siegmund Warburg and, 54; Straus brothers and, 772
Assyrians: overview, 416n1; Archbishop Lang on, 492–93; Argentina policy for, 718; in Brazil, 416, 449, 449n3, 452, 584, 638; lack of success in securing relief for, 457
Astor, Lady Nancy, 544–45, 544n11
Atherton, Ray, 268n40
Australia, 245, 452
Austria: blockage of refugee emigration from, 347; coup of 1934, 444–45, 465, 558; Czech opposition to relief efforts in, 343; dangers to Jews in, 152, 356, 558; Dollfuss comments on, 115–16; Italian opposition to Anschluss, 393; as Nazi concern, 81, 82; political tendencies in, 312; refugee budget review, 427; restrictions on refugees in, 356n23
Avenol, Joseph: biographical sketch, 84n33; discussion of HCR structure, 457–58; feelings for Germany, 148n18; High Commissioner nomination and, 129, 133, 150–51; position on Nazi Jewish policy, 86; position on refugees, 84–85, 87, 123–24, 791
Avni, Haim, 740
Azevedo, Dr., 679–81

Baeck, Leo, 187, 187n68, 191
Baehr, George, 245n11, 590, 590n29

Baerwald, Paul: biographical sketch, 24n6; discussion of Refugee Corporation, 410; on ICA efforts for German refugees, 764–65; meetings with JGM, 7, 100, 101; mentioned, 24, 126; Zionist Organization view of, 235
Baker, Newton D., 63, 63n20, 401
Baker, Noel, 500–501
Baldwin, Roger N., 301, 301n27
Balfour Declaration, 223n26
Bamberger, Louis, 254n21
Bank for International Settlements (BIS), 50, 84, 334
banking: assets of refugees and, 141–42; coerced financing of Nazi interests, 36; Devisen foreign exchange regulations, 511–12, 523, 553–57; German economic status, 33–34, 49, 82; German manipulation of international payments, 505. *See also* economy; Transfer Agreement (Haavara)
Barandon, Paul, 382, 382n3, 551, 555–57
Barbossa, Gustova, 755
Baring, Evelyn, 619, 619n5
Baron de Hirsch Fund, 303n28
Barrett, Halsey V., 8
Barrett, Janet McDonald (daughter), 5, 8
Barthou, Jean Louis, 468, 468n1, 498, 498n9, 503, 510, 548
Baruch, Bernard, 19, 19n41, 576, 576n9, 591
Baruch, Hugo, 741
Bastion refugee quarters (Paris), 219, 219n23
Batista, Pedro Ernesto, 673–74, 673n4, 754
Battle, George Gordon, 596, 596n7
Battsek, Kurt, 511, 511n16
Bauer, Gustav, 15n23
Bauzin, Lucien, 53, 53n92
Beck, Jozef, 470, 470n5, 472, 472n8, 474
Becker, Benjamin, 249n14
Beery, Wallace, 124
Belgium: expulsion of refugees, 615, 615n1; HICEM refugee support in, 768; occupation of Rhineland, 83, 83n30; refugee policy of, 121, 185–87, 427; support for League, 105; World War I role, 4
Bell, George Kennedy (Bishop of Chichester), 177n55
Bell, Montague, 527
Benes, Eduard: biographical sketch, 358n28; analysis of European affairs, 791–92; on chief League goals, 480; on the Czech relief effort, 566; High Commissioner nomination and, 150; meeting with JGM, 358, 359n30, 603; mentioned, 94
Ben-Gurion, David, 528
Bennett, R. B., 324–25, 802
Bentwich, Norman: biographical sketch, 93n49, *144;* Christian appeal on behalf of refugees and, 178; criticized in Schiff letter, 417; as Deputy High Commissioner, 145–46, 146n15, 184, 187; on the Dutch refugee proposal, 108–10; HCR proposal and, 107, 113, 117, 143, 145; JGM meetings with, 99–100, 100–101, 104, 169; as League refugee contact, 93; mentioned, 106, 169, 669; visit to U.S., 625, 630; visit to Warsaw Jewish quarters, 364–65; Zionists relationship with, 228, 625
Bérenger, Henri: biographical sketch, 122n3; as Governing Body representative, 194; League address critical of Germans, 123; on League refugee negotiations, 122; press leak on HCR budget, 211–12
Berg, Marie Louise, 159, 159n38
Berger-Waldenegg, Baron, 558
Bergmann, Carl, 36, 82
Berkman, Luis I., 686
Berle, Adolph A., 19, 19n39
Berliner Tageblatt, 36
Bernhard, Georg, 390n15, 440, 459–60, 787
Bernsdorff, Count Albrecht, 551, 551n19
Bertling, Karl-Otto, 26, 26n21, 82
Beveridge, Sir William, 270n42
Bieler, Jean Henri, 192, 192n81
Billikopf, Jacob, 244n9
Bingham, Robert W., 100, 100n9
Birchall, Frederick T.: biographical sketch, 28n33; coverage of Hitler address, 70n43; Hanfstaengl on, 28; Jewish position of, 99; mentioned, 36; *New York Times* article on JGM, 484
Biro-Bidjan settlement region (Soviet Union), 225–29, 225n32, 308, 336, 348, 378, 588, 597

BIS. *See* Bank for International Settlements (BIS)
Bismarck, Prince Otto von, 343–44, 343n6, 381–82
Blair, Frederick Charles, 324, 324n23, 802
Blanco, Azevedo, 742
Blomberg, Werner von, 43, 43n68, 48
Bohr, Niels, 368, 368n42
Bok, Curtis, 342, 342n3
Bolivia, 487–88, 487n30, 693, 693n17, 701
Bolshevism, 418, 470
Bonn, Sir Max, 373, 373n50, 424
Bonn, Moritz, 384, 384n8, 419, 425
Bonnet, Henri, 124n5
Borah, William E., 65, 65n24, 628, 628n17
Borberg, William, 193, 193n82, 203
Boston Herald, 59
Bouton, S. Miles, 35–36, 35n54, 81
Bowman, Isaiah, 79
boycott (international boycott of German goods): AFL support for, 462, 462n16; American Jewish Congress support for, 31; Dodd on, 557, 794n14, 795; economic impact of, 104–105, 366, 368, 374–75; Erich Warburg opposition to, 55; FDR position on, 31; Max Warburg opposition to, 55, 571; Messersmith on, 187; Proskauer approach to, 68; Untermyer support for, 403–404, 407–408; Wertheimer reassessment of, 792–93; Wise support for, 58n5. *See also* economy
Bracey, Bertha, 499–500, 499n13, 523
Bradford, A. L., 717
Brady, Mrs. Nicholas F., 89, 89n41
Brandao, Pimentil, 637
Brandeis, Louis D., 129, 129n13, 313
Brandt, George L., 529n30
Brandt, Karl, 332n26
Brazil: anti-immigration sentiment in, 632–33; anti-Semitism in, 635, 635n4, 640, 651, 653, 800–801; Assyrians in, 416, 449, 449n3, 452; exclusion law of 1934, 429, 429n15, 632, 639–40, 651, 663, 752; Germans in, 639–40, 641–42, 660, 674, 800; industrial-agricultural labor balance, 642–43, 655–56, 670–71, 679, 754; Italians in, 642, 660; Japaneses in, 429, 632–33, 635–36, 640–42, 659–60; JGM immigration efforts in, 621, 634, 645–46, 647, 800–801, 801n36; Parana Plantations (Oungre refugee employment organization), 416, 442, 449, 449n3, 452, 510, 800; Paulista revolution, 750, 750n15; as seed site for funding, 439; settlement proposals for, 390, 525, 584, 654–79, 753–54, 769; Siegfried Samuel story, 643–44, 646–47, 650
Brebbia, Carlos, 697, 699, 701, 709–10, 722, 724–26, 735–38, 740
Breitscheid, Rudolf, 12, 12n16, 14, 98, 160, 438
Brinkmann, Rudolph, 79, 79n19
British Central Fund, 190, 425, 494, 554
British Guiana, 498–99
Brodetsky, Selig, 189, 189n76
Brown, Harrison, 481
Broyles, Louise and Jake, 255n23
Brüning, Heinrich: biographical sketch, 17n26; bishops' peace with Hitler and, 30; Concordat and, 83, 91; as enabler of Nazi power, 38; JGM interview with, 82, 92, 695; mentioned, 81; Nazi overthrow predicted by, 418–19; Nazi treatment of, 17
Brunschweig, Mme., 164
Bücher, Hermann, 37
Budish, J. M., 336
Buell, Raymond Leslie, 19, 19n36, 71–72, 72n47
Bullitt, William C., 264
Bülow, Bernhard Wilhelm von, 12, 12n10, 15, 17, 48, 50, 52
Burton, Sir Montague, 344, 344n8, 669–70
Bustamante, Antonio Sanchez de, 381, 381n2
Butler, Harold Baresford, 106, 106n23, 116, 121
Butler, Nicholas Murray: biographical sketch, 25n17; Carnegie Endowment and, 328; discussions of German conditions, 54, 57, 65, 125; German ambassadorship and, 57, 58, 69; mentioned, 25, 50
Buxton, Charles Roden, 174

Cabot, John Moore, 637
Cadogan, Alexander, 124, 124n4
Camara, Arruda, 673
Canada: anti-Semitism in Quebec, 326; immigration regulations, 478; JGM efforts in, 304, 312, 324–25; Johnson efforts in, 452; refugee list proposal, 324–25, 325n24, 326–27, 400–401, 802
Carcano, Miguel Angelo, 688
Cardozo, Benjamin, 409, 409n17
Carlos de Andrada, Antonio, 756, 756n18
Carnegie Corporation, 301–302, 301n24, 328
Carneiro, Paulo, 674
Carr, Wilbur J.: anti-immigration views, 314n11, 803; on Dodd's Berlin accommodations, 795; JGM conference with, 313–14; meeting with JGM, 400; proposed U.S. contribution to HCR and, 581; on substitute travel documents, 389
Carter, Edward Clark, 51, 51n83
Las Casas, Bartolomé de, 707, 707n1
Catholics: anti-Catholic prejudice, 544–45, 596, 605–606, 624–25, 628–29; anti-Semitism of, 356–57, 740; bishops' peace with Hitler, 30; Cardinal Faulhaber praise for Saar plebiscite, 599; Catholic Committee, 529; Concordat, 83, 90, 393–94; German racial theory and, 40; Jewish-Catholic cooperation, 33–34, 75, 125, 593–94, 595–96, 624–25, 704–705, 799–800; JGM South American trip and, 598–600, 704–705, 726, 728, 730; Latin American immigration policy and, 726, 728, 732–33, 740, 755–56; loyalties of Saar Catholics, 552, 561–62, 605; in Mexico, 596, 605–606, 624–25, 628–29, 728; Nazi suppression of, 593, 726, 732–33, 753; Nuremberg Party Congress and, 694; provision for Catholic refugees, 500, 548–49. *See also* Center Party (Germany)
Cavert, Samuel McCrae, 135, 135n28, 138
Caviglia Campora, Buenaventura, 742, 742n12
Cecil, Lady Robert, 168
Cecil, Lord Robert, Viscount of Chelwood: as Advisory chairman candidate, 166, 194, 201; biographical sketch, 107n28, *167;* efforts on refugee property, 421; as Governing Body representative, 148, 148n19, 171, 537; on HCR liquidation, 778–79, 786–87; as High Commissioner candidate, 111, 122, 143; meetings with JGM, 373–74, 499, 617–18; mentioned, 107; support for English and French representation, 278; view of Zionism vs. assimilation, 201
Center Party (Germany), 30, 90–91. *See also* Catholics
Ceuto, Miguel, 635–36
Chaco dispute, 487–88, 487n30, 693, 693n17, 701, 744
Chamberlain, Joseph P.: biographical sketch, 77n15; Carr on, 400; FPA relationship with, 5; as Governing Body representative, 150, 180, 183; mentioned, 125; pro-immigration efforts, *13,* 803; proposal to establish HCR, 77; proposed U.S. contribution to HCR and, 579, 581, 581n12, 626; on the situation in Paris, 220; support for anti-property-seizure directive, 404–405, 431, 431n19
Chiappori, Augusto Biancheri, 600
Children's Aid Society (OSE), 225, 225n31
Chile, 487–88, 487n30, 582, 620
China, 475
Chodzko, Withold, 203, 203n6, 354, 365, 487
Christian Committee for German Refugees, 342
Christians: Anglican support for HCR, 434, 494; anti-Semitism as Christian issue, 73, 76, 140n7, 152, 243–44, 253, 436; Christian appeal on behalf of refugees, 178; fundraising efforts with, 342, 422–23, 498; German treatment of converted Jews, 492; Hebrew Christians, 222; JGM "Christian Responsibility Toward German Refugees" broadcast, 256n24; Lambeth conference, 522, 525; Nazi suppression of, 753; non-

Christians (*continued*)
Aryan Christians, 434; relief as "political" issue, 257. *See also* Catholics; Federal Council of Churches; non-Jewish refugees
Cicognani, Amletto Giovanni, Bishop, 627–28, 627n15
Citrine, Walter McLennan, 608, 608n16, 620–21
Clemenceau, Benjamin, 62, 681
Close, Ralph W., 312–13
Cohen, David, 180n59, 272, 502–504
Cohen, Joseph L., 173, 173n49
Cohen, Sir Leonard: biographical sketch, 170n47; HCR and, 153, 170–71; resignation from ICA, 415; on South American settlements, 511; on Soviet Union representation, 227
Cohen, Sir Lionel, 524–25
Cohen, Morris R., 767, 767n4
Cohen, Sir Robert Waley: assessment of conditions in Germany, 798; on British-U.S. cooperation, 385; Laski critical of, 420; on Nathan refugee loan plan, 437; Palestine Corporation and, 424, 450; on the world moral appeal, 272–73; on Zionist domination of Allocation Committee, 418
Cohn, Alfred E., 253, 330, 340, 411, 420, 567
Colombia, 485, 621, 785
Comité d'Entr'aide Europeanne, 219–20, 428–29
Comité des Délégations Juives, 117, 190, 190n77, 192–93, 206–208, 459
Comité pour la Défense des Droits des Israélites en Europe Central et Oriental (Committee for the Protection of the Rights of Jews in Central and Eastern Europe), 547
Commert, Pierre, 103, 103n18
Committee in Aid of German Scholars, 245–46
Committee on Intellectual Cooperation. *See* International Institute on Intellectual Cooperation
Commonwealth Fund, 245, 398
Communists: alleged Jewish association with, 15n23, 471, 588; Biro-Bidjan settlement region and, 225n32; Madison Square Garden meeting, 309, 309n3, 341; Matteotti Fund and, 348; Nazis and, 10, 23, 30, 507; treatment of Communist refugees, 108, 502, 505–506, 540–41, 564, 645
Concordat, 83, 90, 95, 393–94
Connor, Filipe A., 743
Copanema, Gustavo, 640
Copello, Santiago Luis (Archbishop of Buenos Aires), 694, 694n18, 697, 731–32
Cosgrave, William Thomas, 103, 103n16
Coudenhove-Kalergi, Richard, 121–22, 121n2
Coudert, Frederick René, 69, 69n37, 159
Covelle, Antonie Augusto de, 752
Cox (chargé d'affaires, U.S. Embassy, Argentina), 687, 687n13, 708–709, 709n2
Cox, James M., 63, 63n19
Crimea settlement, 378, 378n59, 448n2
Criterio (Argentine newspaper), 740
Crookshank, Henry Frederick, 540, 540n5
Cudahay (Cudahy), R. J., 75, 75n9
Cunliffe-Lister, Sir Philip: on Arab-Jewish relations, 420; biographical sketch, 152n24; on French refugees, 232; mentioned, 620; on Palestine, 152, 223–24; on professional certificates for refugees, 419–20; on Trans-Jordania, 345–46
Cyprus, 588
Czechoslovakia: Czech National Committee as relief channel, 349; JDC contributions to, 489; opposition to Austrian relief effort, 343; refugee problem and, 105–106, 427; relief effort in, 86–89, 357–59, 358n26, 359n30, 566

Dachau Concentration Camp, 96, 97–98
Dahne, Frederico, 640, 657, 659
Daitz, Werner, 38, 40, 796
d'Ajeta, Lanza, 562
Daladier, Edouard, 52, 52n86, 110
Dallek, Robert, 793
Daniel Sieff Research Institute, 377n56
Dark, Sidney, 525
d'Avigdor-Goldsmid, Lady, 495–96
d'Avigdor-Goldsmid, Sir Osmond E.: on

the Allocation Committee budget, 415–16; biographical sketch, 174n50; as HCR contact, 153, 174–75; as ICA chairman, 429, 764–65, 769, 779–80; meetings with JGM, 495–96, 520–21, 616–17; Saar refugees and, 562; on support for French refugees, 425
Davis, Malcolm W., 106, 106n25, 157, 191, 191n79
Davis, Norman H.: biographical sketch, 48n74; meeting with Hitler, 5s2; meetings with JGM, 103, 112; mentioned, 48–49, 109; negotiation techniques of, 119
Dawes, Charles, 11n7
Dawson, George Geoffrey, 382
de Becker Remy, Mme., 184, 184n66, 185–86
de Valera, Éamon, 102–103, 103n17
Dean, Vera Michaelis, 132, 132n23
Deane, Albert Lyle, 25–26, 26n18, 407
Deedes, Sir Wyndham, 436, 494, 494n7
Demuth, Fritz, 353n20, 423, 598, 599, 606
Denmark, 91, 105, 369n45, 427
Derso, Alois, 114, 114n38, 116, 119
Detzer, Dorothy, 474n14
Deutsch, Bernard S., 66, 66n26, 68, 131, 139
Deutsche Allgemeine Zeitung, 46
Deutsche Kommission, 438, 545–47
Devinat, Paul, 547, 547n12, 777, 777n3
Devisen, foreign exchange regulations, 511–12, 523, 553–57
Dickstein, Samuel, 264, 592
Dieckhoff, Hans Heinrich von: assessment of Nazi regime, 81; biographical sketch, 12n8; on the Foreign Office, 42–43; JGM meeting of 1934, 290–93; mentioned, 12, 48; on Nazi persecution of Jews, 43; opposition to League relief efforts, 93, 94, 109, 113; refusal to meet with JGM, 366, 367, 379, 381–82; on the rise of Nazi power, 46; support for JGM ambassadorship, 71
Diederick, Anna (mother), 2
Diels, Rudolf, 795
Diernet, Pierre, 163
Dippel, John V. H., 790–91
Disarmament Conference: economic pressures on Germany and, 371; German withdrawal from, 126, 126n7, 151; Henderson on, 110, 199; Hull on, 129; importance to France, 61, 115, 122; Nazi aggression and, 109–10; Roehm on, 121; Streit on, 84; Woodward on, 107
Dodd, Martha, 795
Dodd, William E.: assessment of Nazi moderation, 79; authorization on anti-property-seizure actions, 431, 431n19; on the boycott of German goods, 557; on conditions in Germany, 187; FDR on, 579; German ambassador appointment, 73, 82, 794–95; HCR and, 191, 195; Hitler discussion about JGM, 317–18, 339; JGM call of 1934, 338; JGM meetings of 1934, 293–94, 551–52; on JGM's Jewish relief efforts, 93, 94, 454n7, 795–96; relations with Nazis, 793–95
Dollfuss, Engelbert: attack on Socialists, 357; biographical sketch, 91n46; blockage of refugee emigration, 347; League Assembly address on refugees, 114; mentioned, 91–92; murder or, 444–45; Wertheimer-JGM meeting with, 115–16
Dominian, Leon, 742–44
Don, Alan C., 492–93, 492n6, 522, 541–42, 623
Dowdecker, Neal, 81
Dowling, Victor J., 68, 68n36
Doyle, Michael Francis, 315, 315n14
Draper, Arthur, 75
Dreyfus, Pierre, 160n41
Dreyse, Fritz, 553–55
Dubinsky, David, 589, 589n24, 597
Duca, Ion, 238, 238n46
Dugdale, Mrs. Blanche, 499n12
Dugdale, Sir Thomas Lionel, 223, 223n26
Duggan, Stephen P., 137, 137n37
Duhau, Luis F., 686, 697, 712–13, 716, 727–28, 732–33
Dulles, Allen, 118, 118n42
Dulles, John Foster, 5, 33, 33n46, 48, 52
Dunham, Wallace, 462n15
Dunn, James Clement, 770, 770n8
Dupont, Pierre Samuel, III, 248n13

Dupuy, Jean, 106
Duranty, Walter, 79, 79n23, 80

Echegoyen, Martin, 746–47, 746n14
Eckener, Hugo, 42, 42n64, 44
Economic Conference, 84
economy: effect of German economic isolation, 104–105, 366, 368, 374–75; loan kassas, 437, 437n26, 441, 489, 509, 612–13; Messersmith on Nazi economic motives, 366–67; Nazi discrimination against U.S. firms, 49; Nazi economic moderation, 85; Nazi unemployment figures, 94–95; Papen economic proposals, 11, 12, 14; Schäffer discussion of German economy, 371, 371n48; U.S. proposed loan to Germany, 366, 368, 376, 383–84, 399–400. *See also* banking; boycott (international boycott of German goods)
Ecuador, 378, 381, 584, 621
Eddis, J. B., 685, 714, 727, 731
Eden, Anthony, 476–77, 476n17
Ehnert, Ricardo van, 643, 646–47
Eichelberger, Clark M., 106, 106n26
Einstein, Albert: approach to relief efforts, 246, 247; on intellectual refugees, 774–75; JGM contact with, 226, 805; as pacifist, 123; as U.S. refugee committee candidate, 302–303; visa delay incident, 35
Eisner, Mark, 407n14
Elliot, Charles, 11n4, 38
Elsas, Fritz, 426n12
Enabling Act (Germany), 26
Enderis, Guido, 28, 28n32, 36, 550
Entre Rios (Argentina), 730
Espil, Felipe A., 583
Estable, Clementi, 744
Estrada, Alberto C., 744–45, 747
Evian Conference, 2

La Farge, John, 243n7
Farley, James, 64, 64n21, 230–31
Faulhaber, Michael von (Cardinal), 304, 304n32, 316, 599
Federal Council of Churches, 24, 140–43, 178, 178n56, 246, 799. *See also* Christians
Federation of Jewish Charities, 55
Feilchenfeld, Ernst: as advocate for refugees, *13;* biographical sketch, 77n14; JDC and, 236; JGM relationship with, 252; mentioned, 125, 130–31, 138; proposal to establish HCR, 77, 107
Feis, Herbert, 25, 25n14, 399–400
Ferrero, G., 475n15
Ferriere, Mlle., 192
Fey, Emil, 444n35
Field, Frederick Vanderbilt, 266n37
Filene, Edward A.: biographical sketch, 67n33; meeting with JGM, 67; mentioned, 199, 316; unconcern for refugees, 328–29, 330, 802
Filho, Julio Mesquita, 681
Fineberg, Harry M., 756
Finley, John H., 79, 79n24, 140
Flandin, Pierre Etienne, 587
Fleischmann, Raoul, 237
Fleishhacker, Herbert, 308n1
Flexner, Bernard, 233n37, 320, 450, 574, 586
Foch, Ferdinand, 681
Foreign Office (Germany): Bouton on Nazi control of, 35–36; Dieckhoff on, 42–43; establishment of Nazi Foreign Office, 36; on JGM ambassadorship nomination, 71; Lüdecke predicted housecleaning in, 50; Mowrer concern for future of, 45
Foreign Policy Association (FPA): Eleanor Roosevelt relationship with, 5, 59n9; High Commissioner nomination and, 77–78, 135–36; interest of Germans in, 46; JGM and, 26–29, 39, 790; Lamont contribution to, 139; Max Jordan support for, 137; "Our Monetary Policy" meeting, 248; Schacht view of, 12; Stone-JGM refugee relief efforts, 92–93; Sulzberger on, 766; Vera Micheles Dean address to, 132; Wertheimer role in, *13*
Forell, Dr., 434
Fosdick, Harry Emerson, 6, 57n3, 58, 137, 319
Fosdick, Raymond D.: biographical sketch, 57n3; discussion of Rockefeller refugee contribution, 241–42, 398, 410; Governing Body involvement, 150, 310–11, 315, 317, 321; High Commissioner nomination

and, 126–28, 132, 134, 136; mentioned, 57, 65
Four-Power Pact, 52
FPA. *See* Foreign Policy Association (FPA)
France. S*ee also* Paris
general: anti-immigration sentiment, 441–42, 458, 564, 791, 796; HCR relationship, 278, 425, 451, 461; Monteaux orchestral performance, 42; Nazi view of French racial characteristics, 40
foreign relations: concern for border closure by, 376; disarmament negotiations and, 118–19, 122, 387, 387n11; FDR on French security, 61; foreign policy of 1933, 103–104, 106; Franco-Polish alliance suggestion, 62, 69, 105; German military buildup and, 15, 17; Herriot debts-and-disarmament mission, 52; Marseilles assassination, 468, 468n1, 498, 498n9, 503, 510, 548; occupation of Rhineland, 83, 83n30; policy on Germany, 110, 566
refugees: Bentwich on, 352n18; budget for, 426; capacity for, 146, 158, 161, 218, 232, 381, 381n1, 426, 428, 440; danger of impostors, 440; danger of southern France colonization, 350, 352; economic dependency of, 348; French Jews' view of, 156–57, 161, 165–66, 440, 461, 513; Laval policy on, 566–69, 587–88; *permits de travail* (work permits), 164, 391, 438, 489, 565, 590, 609, 612, 621; population, 483, 513, 514; *refoulement* (expulsion) of refugees, 612, 613; repatriation of Polish refugees in France, 218, 360n34, 361, 362; Saar refugees, 529, 539, 566, 599, 611, 613, 621
Franceschi, Gustavo, 740
Franck, James, 369, 369n44
Franco, Dr. de Mello, 665–66, 666n2
François-Poncet, André, 17, 17n25, 42, 95
Frankfurter, Felix, 5, 67, 230–31, 805
Frankfurter Zeitung, 71
Franklin, Ernest, 413n24, 416
Fraternidad Agraria (union of cooperative colonies, Argentina), 691
Frazer, Robert, 100, 100n11, 543, 543n7
French National Committee to Aid German Refugees, 160n40, 161, 209–10
Freyre y Santander, Manuel de, 582
Frick, Wilhelm, 23
Friedheim, William, 104–105
Friedländer, Saul, 797
Friedmann, Desider, 559, 559n23
Friends' Service Committee, 317
Funder, Friedrich, 91–92
Furtwängler, Wilhelm, 552n20

Gaedecke, Miss, 44, 50, 80, 81, 94
Gaisman, Henry Jacques, 410–11, 410n19
Galeazzi, Enrico: biographical sketch, 89n40; on the Concordat, 91; mentioned, 89, 564; Vatican support for refugees and, 605–608, 799–800
Gallinek, Alfred, 502, 502n15
Garcia, Frank M., 635
Garcia, Isaac, 691n16, 692
Geist, Raymond, 294, 368, 794–95
Gerig, Ben, 105, 105n20, 111, 113–14
Gerlach, Helmut von, 440, 440n32
German ambassadorship (U.S.), 29, 54, 57–63, 57n2, 67, 69, 71, 73, 790
German Broadcasting Company, 36
German Christian movement, 77, 77n12
German General Electric. *See* Allgemeine Elektrizitäts-Gesellschaft (AEG)
German Jews. *See also* Germany; Jews; purification; refugees
general: demographic estimates of, 437; denial of anti-Semitism, 327; *Frontsoldaten* Jews, 78, 78n18; German Jewish Aid, 798; nationalistic character of, 156–57; support for Hitler, 35
international relations: direct aid from relief organizations, 228, 235, 289; effect of German economic isolation, 104–105, 366, 368, 374–75; German-Jewish emigration, 241n3, 301, 301n23, 790–92; Haavara (Transfer Agreement), 792; Pacelli discussion of, 91, 91n45; relief efforts for youths, 246, 302, 313, 349; representation on HCR, 177, 180–81, 183; Ruppin plan for evacuation of, 484; Weizmann disdain for, 171–72, 177

living conditions: conditions of 1933, 27, 30, 31, 32, 35; conditions of 1934, 366–68, 375–76, 398–99; conditions of 1935, 721–22, 787, 788–89; Moffat concern for, 25; Wilfrid Israel accounts of, 176–77, 269, 798
Nazi actions against: Dachau Concentration Camp, 97–98; decree of second-class citizenship, 176, 176n54, 182, 187, 194, 201, 221, 229–30; discrimination by residential tenure, 182; expulsion from small villages, 549–50; Nazi boycott of businesses of, 26–28, 33, 43, 44, 787; Nazi suppression of property rights of, 226, 229, 404–405, 431, 431n19, 795, 797; Nazis enabled by divisions among, 78; Restoration of the Professional Civil Service law and, 44; treason laws and, 176, 187
German Press Association, 46
German Refugee Assistance Fund (GRAF), 499, 534, 542
Germany. *See also* German Jews; Hitler, Adolf; Nazi Regime
general: election of 1932, 22; Enabling Act, 26; Nazi state church proposal, 77, 77n12; Nazi theory of racial nationalism, 40; Papen economic program, 11, 12, 14, 19; parliamentary elections of 1933, 23; Reichstag fire, *16,* 23, 28; Restoration of the Professional Civil Service law, 44; use of emergency powers, 10, 12, 23
assessment of conditions in: Baeck, 187; Bernhard, 440; Breitscheid, 438; Dodd, 187, 549–50; Enderis, 550; Felix Warburg, 54; Frederick Warburg, 57; Geist, 368; Goldman, 47; Hirsch, 187; James Warburg, 65, 65n23; Jesse Straus, 613–14; Kauffmann, 513; Max Warburg, 550–51; Melchior, 32, 187; Messersmith, 187, 366–67; Wilfrid Israel, 375–76
international relations: Anglo-German Commercial Treaty of 1924, 366; Austrian Anschluss, 393; disarmament negotiations and, 118–19; "dismemberment of Germany" plan, 68; Dutch refugee proposal and, 108–109, 117, 123; HCR and, 187, 191, 193–95, 199, 200–202, 205, 216, 226; JGM relationship with, 260, 366, 367, 379, 782; Polish-German Treaty of 1934, 41, 264, 350, 350n15, 365; preparations for war, 15, 17, 491, 566, 791–92; suppression of Prussian state, 12, 12n12; violence against Americans in Germany, 81; withdrawal from League, 126, 126n7, 151
Gershunoff, Alberto, 739, 739n10
Gesang, Nathan, 686
Gil, Enrique, 706
Gilbert, Prentiss: biographical sketch, 51n80; on German-HCR relations, 193; meetings with JGM, 113–14, 150, 487–88; mentioned, 51, 110; reorganization of U.S. League representation and, 486, 488; State Department report on HCR, 154, 156
Gimbel, Berrnard, 140, 140n6, 240
Ginsberg, Marie: discussion of HCR, 154; Luxembourg stamp project of, 770–72, 770n7; mentioned, 84, 85, 149, 349, 353–54; on the repatriation of Polish refugees in France, 218
Glick, David, 243, 243n5
Godart, Justin, 548, 548n13, 777
Goebbels, Paul Joseph: biographical sketch, 29n36; attendance at League Assembly, 110, 113, 114–15; Hanfstaengl disputes with, *16;* Kreisler on, 752; meeting with Rappard, 119; mentioned, 98; Nuremberg Party Congress ambitions, 694; temperament of, 114–15, 119
Gold, Shalom, 324n22
Goldman, Henry: assessment of relief proposals, 246; biographical sketch, 23n2; on conditions in Germany, 47; on FDR New Deal programs, 252; on German anti-Semitism, 23; mentioned, 139
Goldmann, Nahum, 92, 92n47, 154–55, 192–93
Goldsmidt, Alfons, 332
Goldwyn, Samuel, 53, 53n93
Goodhart, Arthur Lehman, 175, 175n52
Gordon, George, 27, 27n22, 29, 31, 39
Göring, Hermann: biographical sketch, 27n24; on the "bloodless" revolu-

tion, 49; Hanfstaengl relationship with, *16;* Kreisler on, 752–53; mentioned, 27, 37, 42, 94, 98; Reichstag fire and, 28, 30; Röhm and, 413; on U.S. public opinion, 49n78
Gottschalk, Max, 185, 186
Gourevitch, M., 547
GRAF. *See* German Refugee Assistance Fund (GRAF)
Grassi, Hugo, 743, 747–48
Great Britain
general: Balfour Declaration, 223n26; concern about Japanese aggression, 61; memorandum on social insurance in Germany, 408, 408n15; Nazi view of as natural ally, 41; Passfield White Paper, 56, 223n26; proposed loan to Germany, 423; refugee population, 515–16; refugee problem and, 121, 146, 234; support for French refugee relief, 115, 451; support for Palestine in, 196, 197n84, 234, 362, 424; Woburn House (London), 500, 693
High Commission for Refugees: British Jews importance to, 416; British representatives, 195–96, 197n84, 226; Christmas fundraising appeal in, 193–94; financial contributions by, 476–77, 784; representation on Governing Body, 278; response to JGM appointment, 135
Great Depression: Canadian P.M. Bennett on the NRA, 325; discussion of New Deal programs, 252, 325, 401; effect on Argentina, 725n7; European effects of NRA, 300; Industrial Recovery Bill, 75; rise of Nazism and, 10; worldwide reception of refugees and, 790–91
Greece, 142
Green, Jerome, 108, 108n29
Green, William, 589, 589n24
Grossmann, Kurt, 359, 359n31
Guani, Alberto, 203, 203n7, 351, 744
Guenzburg, Baron de, 519n22, 567, 610
Gueyrend, M. (Chargé of the French Embassy, Brazil), 636–37, 656
Guggenheim, Harry F., 333, 333n28
Guggenheim Foundation, 305
Gumbel, Emil Julius, 569, 569n32
Guthrie, William D., 57, 57n4
Guyana. *See* British Guiana

Haavara (Transfer Agreement), 792
Habicht, Elizabeth, 112, 112n36
Habicht, Theo, 112–13, 112n36, 445
Hadassah, 326
Hahn, Lola: biographical sketch, 79n20; on the collection of statistical data, 271–72; concern for German Jews, 176–77, 273, 798; on German discontent with the Reich, 453; strained appearance of, 79
Hammarskjold, Hjalmar, 116, 116n41
Hammerstein-Equord, Kurt von, 82
Hanfstaengl, Ernst "Putzi," 790; on the *Akron* tragedy, 44; arrangement of Hitler meeting, 47–48; arrangement of von Bittenfeld meeting, 34; biographical sketch, *16;* disdain for Lüdecke, 39, 41; disdain for Rosenberg, 41; on Hitler and the Jews, 15; mentioned, 12; nonconciliatory stance of, 38; threats against Jews expressed by, 27–29, 796; as translator for Hitler, 52
Harbord, James Guthrie, 589, 589n25
Hard, William, 249, 249n15
Harkness, Edward H., 319n19, 342
Harvey, M. Mallon, 219–20
Hauberman, Marie, 710–11
Hayes, Carleton J. H., 319n18
Hayes, Patrick J. (Cardinal), 593–94, 593n2, 595
Hays, Arthur Garfield, 590, 590n28
Hearst, William Randolph, 20, 20n45
Hebrew Christians, 222
Hebrew Immigrant Aid Society (HIAS), 158n36, 217, 255–56
Heineman, Dannie, 272n45
Helbronner, Jacques: as Advisory Council member, 510; anti-immigration views, 426, 428, 524; biographical sketch, 350n14; on Laval refugee policy, 568–69; opposition to loan kassas, 509; on the screening of Palestine settlers, 388; on settlements in southern France, 350; on South American settlements, 621, 637
Hellman, Mrs. Maurice, 73, 73n3
Henderson, Arthur, 110, 110n32, 199, 199n2

Herrera, Richardo Diaz, 717
Herriot, Edouard: anti-immigration views, 569; biographical sketch, 17n27, 51n85; debts-and-disarmaments mission, 51–52; FPA speaking invitation, 53; on Franco-Polish action against Germany, 62; mentioned, 17, 59
Hertz, Paul: biographical sketch, 14n19, 149n23; on direct aid to German Jews, 228; mentioned, 14, 149; on socialist representation in HCR, 192
Herwarth von Bittenfeld, Hans Wolfgang, 34, 34n47
Herzl, Theodor, 780
Hess, Jerome, 135, 135n32, 590, 590n27
Hexter, J. K., 587–88, 587n21
Heyman, David, 137, 138, 237, 237n44, 265–66, 333–34
HIAS. *See* Hebrew Immigrant Aid Society (HIAS)
HICEM, 421–22, 768–69. *See also* Anglo-HICEM
High Commission for Refugees. *See also* League of Nations
  overview: Avenol overview, 147–49, 457–58; JGM overview, 141–43, 276–77, 443; Oungre overview, 350–51; relationship with governments, 454, 460–61, 463–64
  administration: Allocation Committee, 349, 415–16, 418; Bentwich as Deputy High Commissioner, 145–46, 146n15; budget, 174, 175, 195, 196, 211–13, 215, 571; Governing Body, 140, 142, 143, 148, 148n17, 157–58, 190n78, 203, 203n8, 536; Hoover considered as High Commissioner, 88–89, 111; JGM as Refugee Commissioner, 1, 125–26, 133, 150, 790; Permanent Committee membership, 209; publicity, 338, 355, 474–75; salaries of staff members, 215, 278; Wertheimer role in, *13;* Wurfbain role in, 188
  Advisory Council: Alliance representation on, 220; Cecil as chairman candidate, 194, 201; Ittleson as candidate, 184; Kahn as JDC representative, 332; Laski as candidate, 175–76; proposed Agudas representation, 363; resolutions on travel papers, 533; Rosenberg as candidate, 184; Second International and, 192; Trade Union International and, 192
  financial support: Brandeis advice on, 313; British government contributions, 476–77, 499; Carnegie Corporation grant, 300–301, 301n24, 328; Felix Warburg support, 55–56, 244; Friends' Service Committee, 317; fundraising events, 397, 403; ICA contributions, 227, 333, 494; Ittleson contributions, 7, 244, 313; JDC support, 590; Jewish individuals, 164, 244; Jewish organizations, 189, 439–40; joint drive, 316, 316n16, 496, 527, 591, 616; League initial contribution, 155–56; Liechtenstein stamp project, 469, 469n3; proposed U.S. contribution, 579, 585, 585n18, 595, 626, 630; Rabbi Wise assessment of, 455; Rockefeller Jr. contributions, 118, 121, 122, 126, 136, 136n33, 305–306, 309, 321; worldwide appeal proposal, 171, 172
  historical events of: JGM opening address, 200, 203, 203n9; location of offices of, 180, 449, 492n4; Nansen Committee establishment, 77n16; opening conference, 201, 203–205, 209–14; proposal of 1933 to establish HCR, 77, 107, 110–11, 125; proposed liquidation of, 487, 489, 490–91, 498, 521, 531, 571, 617, 778–79, 783–89
  mission: criticisms of inactivity of, 332, 332n26, 354, 388–89, 432; German rejection of intervention on refugees, 113–14; governmental (non-affiliated) character of, 147–48, 152–53, 154–55, 156, 157–58, 163, 166, 195; Hitler comments on, 317–18; League recognition of, 480–83, 483n24, 559–60, 617; refugee property as concern, 193, 226, 229; relationship with German government, 187, 191, 193–95, 199, 200–202, 205, 216, 226, 282–83, 290–93, 468–69, 617; representation of intellectuals, 330, 334–36, 348,

420, 428, 451; representation of Jewish organizations, 136, 206–209, 281, 284, 439–40; Sino-Japanese solution as model for, 105; State Department disinvolvement in, 132–33
Hilfsverein (Argentina), 710, 714, 723, 734
Hillman, Sidney, 589, 589n24
Himmler, Heinrich, 28n27, 96, 96n1, 413
Hindenburg, Paul von: boycott curtailed by, 43, 44; election of 1932 and, 10, 22; erosion of power of, 33–34, 36, 42; Professional Civil Service law and, 44; Reichstag fire emergency decree issued by, 23; Reichswehr loyalty to, 45
Hirsch, Adolfo, 691n16, 692, 693–94, 710–11, 713–16, 723–24, 736
Hirsch, Alfredo, 688–90, 694, 696–97, 704–705, 707–708, 710–11, 714–15, 723–24, 727–29, 735, 800
Hirsch, Baron Maurice de, 303n28, 764–65, 764n2
Hirsch, Otto, 181, 181n63, 187, 279n50, 768–69
Hirst, Mrs. Francis, 383, 383n5
Hitler, Adolf: alleged illness of, 620, 620n7; appointment as German chancellor, 22; Baron Rothermere defense of, 279; "conciliatory" speech of 1933, 70n43, 81; disarmament negotiations and, 109–10; Dodd discussion about JGM, 317–18; Dodd negotiation of Jewish relief with, 793; Hanfstaengl and, *16,* 27, 27n25; HCR and, 216; intransigent race theory of, 34, 85–86, 797, 797n29; Jewish support for, 35; JGM analysis of, 76; JGM-Hitler meeting, 47–48, 58, 65n23, 796–97, 797n26; Knickerbocker on, 79–80; management of Reichswehr, 45; *Mein Kampf* (1925–26), 10, 40n62; Melchett on, 278–79, 286; personality and leadership qualities, 1, 14, 96, 98, 792; Röhm Putsch and, 558; "The world does not know how to get rid of the Jews." comment, 48, 58, 796–97, 797n26; von Bismarck on, 344. *See also* race theory of Nazis
Hoare, Sir Samuel, 786, 786n9
Hochschild, Moritz "Mauricio," 715, 715n3, 723–24, 728
Hodgdon, A. Dana, 259, 262, 802
Hoetsch, Leopold Gustav Alexander von: biographical sketch, 282n4; discussion of Dieckhoff controversy, 379; on the *Herald* account of JGM in Berlin, 296–97; review of JGM earlier meeting, 343–44; on transfer regulations, 523
Holland: alleged expulsion of refugees, 476, 491–92, 503; Haluz settlement, 503–504; League refugee proposal, 105–106, 108–109, 117, 123; Ommen settlement, 503, 508; proposed camp for political refugees, 512; relief support in, 272, 427, 502, 782, 784; Werkdorp Wieringemeer, 491, 502–503
Holmes, John Haynes, 58, 58n5
Honduras, 413, 584
Hoover, Calvin, 32, 32n45
Hoover, Herbert: Cudahay criticism of, 75; election of 1932, 21; as High Commissioner candidate, 88–89, 111, 122, 123; immigration quota directive, 235–36, 803; policy on Japan, 12n9
Hos, Dov, 496–97
Houghton, Alanson B., 140, 140n4, 150
House, Edward M., 21, 58n8, 59, 320
House of Rothschild, 378, 378n57
Howe, Frederick C., 575, 575n7, 582
Howe, Louis, 60, 60n12, 64
Hudson, Manley O., 85, 459, 459n12
Hugenberg, Alfred, 30, 30n40, 35, 41, 85–89
Hull, Cordell: at Economic Conference, 84; FDR message to Hitler and, 62n17; High Commissioner nomination and, 129, 132–33; on the importance of free trade, 70; position on resettlement, 803; proposed U.S. contribution to HCR and, 581; statement of 1933 on religious persecution, 101
Hungary, 152
Hussein, Abdullah ibn, 420, 420n7
Hyman, Joseph C.: discussion of Governing Body, 183–84; discussion of JDC-Zionist negotiations, 298, 299–300; as French liaison for

Hyman, Joseph C. (*continued*)
HCR, 175; on German-HCR relations, 200; mentioned, 143; report of Weizmann comments, 164–65

ICA. *See* Jewish Colonization Association (ICA)
Idelson, Vladimir Robert, 412–13, 412n22, 418–19, 425
ILO. *See* International Labor Organization (ILO)
Industrial Recovery Bill, 75
Inman, Samuel Guy, 485n27, 580, 632, 636–41, 643, 645, 657–58, 671, 673–74, 694, 703–706
Integralistas (Brazilian fascists), 635, 635n4, 645, 651–52, 654, 755
intellectual/professional refugees. *See also* refugees
general: Academic Assistance Council, 334, 340; Central Information Bureau for placement, 278n47; French committee of savants, 428; Kotschnig as representative of, 334–36, 348, 355, 420, 451; plan to engage Germans on, 771–72; responsibility for placement of, 423; Rockefeller view of, 627, 637
locations: Argentina, 703, 721–22; Brazil, 641, 649, 650, 659, 749, 752, 758–59; France, 428; Palestine, 419–20; Sweden, 480; Uruguay, 741, 743, 745–47; U.S., 435
types: artisans, 419–20; economists and business scholars, 721–22; engineers, 649, 747; medical doctors, 435, 501–502, 637, 650, 659, 703, 721, 752; natural sciences, 641, 746
International Institute on Intellectual Cooperation, 124, 124n5
International Labor Organization (ILO), 116, 459
Iraq, 416n1, 449n3, 497
Irwin, Edward Frederick Lindley Wood Lord, 331
Isaacs, Gerald Rufus, Viscount Erleigh, 266n38
Isaacs, Rufus Daniel, 1st Marquis of Reading, 88, 88n38
Israel, 2
Israel, Wilfrid, 176–77, 176n53, 269, 271–72, 798
Italian Chamber of Commerce, 83
Italy: Breckinridge Long on Italian dictatorship, 93; capacity for accepting refugees, 209; disarmament negotiations and, 118; HCR liquidation and, 787; JGM meeting with ambassador from, 45–46; Leticia dispute, 354, 488; Mussolini relations with Italian Jews, 563; opposition to Austrian Anschluss, 393; preparations for war, 781, 781n4; role in refugee relief, 86–89, 117; Zionism in, 394. *See also* Mussolini, Benito; Pacelli, Eugenio (Cardinal)
Ittleson, Henry: approach to relief efforts, 247, 591; biographical sketch, 67n31; on FDR New Deal programs, 252; HCR and, 7, 139, 184, 244, 313; mentioned, 143, 339–40; on the Town Hall address, 67, 139

Jabotinsky, Vladimir, 361–63, 361n35, 805
Jäckh, Ernst, 46, 46n71, 49, 424, 472–73
Jaffe, Rebecca, 139, 140
James, Edwin L., 235n41
Janowsky, Oscar I., 766–67, 767n3
Japan: attack on China, 12n9; disarmament negotiations and, 118, 121; FDR on Japanese aggression, 61; Manchukuo and, 475; naval rivalry with U.S., 117; Sino-Japanese dispute, 86, 86n35, 105; Tanaka Memorial, 61, 61n15
Japhet, Jacob, 432n20, 435
JDC. *See* American Jewish Joint Distribution Committee (JDC)
Jesuits, 599, 606
Jewish Agency, 56, 316, 316n16, 329–30, 496, 527, 591, 767
Jewish Chronicle, 521
Jewish Colonization Association (ICA): AMICA, 351; in Argentina, 685–88, 686n12, 691, 703, 713–15, 719, 723, 736; attack in *Jewish Chronicle,* 521; Biro-Bidjan settlement study and, 225, 227, 228–29; in Brazil, 753; British fund-raising and, 146, 420; Burton on, 670; Cohen resignation, 415; d'Avigdor-Goldsmid view of, 779–80; HCR and, 136, 171, 174, 185–86, 190, 226–27, 284,

521; Louis Oungre and, 429, 662–64, 798; Percy Strauss on, 331; South American settlement negotiations and, 583
Jewish Daily Forward. See *Vorwaerts*
Jewish Refugee Committee, 100n10
Jewish Telegraphic Agency: JGM interview with, 138; leaked story on JGM-British government difficulties and, 197n84, 198, 266, 271; permission sought for *Vorwaerts* story, 337; report on filled German visa quota, 301, 301n23
Jewish War Veterans, 327
Jews: French Jews' view of refugees, 440; German treatment of Christian converts, 492; Hanfstaengl on, 15; Jewish-Catholic cooperation, 75, 593–94, 595–96, 624, 624–25, 704–705, 799–800; JGM relief initiatives for, 233, 235–36, 793, 795–96, 798, 798–99; Melchett Jewish Hitler thesis, 286; overview of political divisions, 207; persecution in European nations, 796; racial Judaism thesis, 182; responsibility for violence against, 47–48, 493; Sephardic Jews, 526; support appeal to "borderline" Jews, 248, 323, 323n21. *See also* German Jews; Zionism
Johnson, Alvin, 154, 154n29
Johnson, Herschel V., 530, 530n31
Johnson, Samuel Hugh, 19, 19n40
Johnson, T. F., 84, 88, 88n37, 452, 559–60
Joint Distribution Committee, 6–7
joint drive, 316, 316n16, 329–30, 496, 527, 591, 767
Joint Foreign Committee, 99–100
Jordan. *See* Trans-Jordania
Jordan, Max, 30, 33, 83, 137
Journal des Nations, 603
Jung, Leo, 308n2
Junkers, 75, 78–79, 425, 465
Justo, Alberto, 717
Justo, Augustín P., 709, 709n2, 711, 716–17, 738–39

Kaas, Ludwig, 599, 599n10, 606
Kahn, Arthur, 610, 611
Kahn, Bernhard: biographical sketch, 35n52; comments on HCR, 372, 489, 490–91; comments on refugee relief, 146–47, 426–27, 438–39, 768; criticism of, 94, 200; departure from Germany, 35; as French liaison for HCR, 171, 173–74, 175, 195–96; as JDC representative, 332, 608; Lambert and, 428; Louis Oungre and, 147, 386, 391–92, 426, 493, 548; meetings with JGM, 348–49, 439–40, 489; on the "vacant countries" settlement thesis, 375
Kahn, Ernest, 378n58
Kahn, Mrs. Otto, 132, 132n22, 402, 409, 596
Kalinin, Michi Ivanovich, 588, 588n23
Kallen, Horace, 140–41, 140n8
Kann, Jacobus H., 182–83, 182n64
Kappers, Ariens, 508
kassas, 437, 437n26, 441, 489, 509, 612–13, 616–17
Kastl, Ludwig, 12, 12n15
Kauffmann, Robert, 430, 430n17, 433, 489, 512–14
Kelen, Emery, 114, 114n38, 116, 119
Kellermann, Lilli, 710–11, 713, 717, 721
Kellogg, Paul U., 5, 66, 66n28
Kenya, 413, 787
Keppel, Frederick Paul, 301, 301n26, 328
Ketchum, Patricia Sugrue, 8
Kiep, Otto Karl: biographical sketch, 28n29; decline of power of, 50, 81; Hanfstaengl threats against, 28; mentioned, 74; Nazi opposition to, 36
Klein, Alberto, 685
Klieforth, Alfred W.: biographical sketch, 42n66; concern for Schlessinger, 45; on Hindenburg, 42, 44; mentioned, 91; opposition to anti-Semitism in Austria, 356
Knickerbocker, Hubert R.: biographical sketch, 11n6; anger at lack of refugee support, 79; appeal to JGM for help for Jewish friends, 43; Hanfstaengl threats against, 28; mentioned, 11, 38; on Nazi atrocities, 32, 45; on Schlessinger, 45, 46
Knox, Geoffrey C., 446, 446n39, 600
Koch-Weser, Erich, 512n18, 666
Kohler, Max, 139, 334, 334n30
Kohn, Hans, 137, 137n36
Kose, Jaroslav, 358, 358n27

Kotschnig, Walter: biographical sketch, 255n22; Cecil on, 778; Deutsche Kommission meeting, 545–47; as HCR intellectual representative, 334–36, 340, 348, 353–55, 420, 428, 451; Laval meeting, 566; mentioned, 456; report on trip to U.S., 529
Krapf, Edouardo, 703
Kreisler, Fritz, 751–52, 751n16, 756
Kreutzberger, Max, 511n17, 514
Krno, Ivan, 147–49, 147n16, 194
Krosigk, Lutz Graf Schwerin von, 48
Krupp von Bohlen und Halbach, Gustav, 418–19
Kuh, Frederick, 271n44
Kuhn, Mrs. Simon, 394
Kurgass, Paula, 523, 530

Laemmle, Carl, 607
Lafer, Horacio, 682, 682n9, 757
Lamas, Carlos Saavedra, 697, 700–701
Lambert, Raul R., 428, 428n14, 613
Lambeth conference, 522, 525
Lamont, Thomas W., 26, 26n19, 139
Landau, Jacob, 266, 266n36, 301, 301n23, 337n33
Lang, William Cosmo Gordon (Archbishop of Canterbury), 178, 492–93, 492n5, 801
Lange, Christian L., 111–12, 111n35, 114, 122
Lasker, Albert, 238n45, 249–50
Laski, Harold, 526
Laski, Neville J.: biographical sketch, 92n48; as Advisory Board candidate, 175–76, 269, 273; on illegal immigration in Palestine, 346; JGM meetings on refugees, 92, 93, 99–101, 104, 526; JGM relationship with, 168n45, 220, 221n24; on the Nazi Regime, 420
Lastra, Angel Pizarro, 684
Laval, Pierre, 52, 52n87, 523, 564, 565–66, 791–92
Lawrence, Dave, 137
Lazaron, Morris S., 404, 404n7
Leach, Agnes Brown (Mrs. Henry Goddard Leach), 138, 138n1
League of Free Nations Association, 5
League of Nations: Assyrian diaspora and, 416, 416n1; avoidance of war as chief goal, 480; campaign for U.S. membership in, 5, 249, 578; Dutch refugee proposal, 105–106, 108–10, 117, 123–24; FDR view of, 20; Germany withdrawal from, 70n43, 126, 126n7, 151; HCR recognition by, 480–83, 483n24, 559–60, 617; JGM views on, 21, 85–89, 790–91; Madariaga on, 52; position on Nazi Jewish policy, 86; position on refugees, 87, 604, 618; Saar region jurisdiction, 443; Sino-Japanese dispute, 86, 86n35, 105; Swedish resolution on civil liberties, 117. *See also* High Commission for Refugees
Lebanon, 214, 214n16, 224
Lee, Ivy: biographical sketch, 257n25; as Nazi propagandist, 263–64, 367, 406; Rockefeller relationship with, 461
Leet, Dorothy Flagg, 464n19
Leffingwell, Russell C., 301, 301n25
Léger. *See* Saint-Léger, Alexis
Leguizamon, Francisco A., 694
LeHand, Marguerite "Missy," 130, 130n14
Lehman, Arthur, 240n2, 733
Lehman, Herbert H., 67, 67n32
Lehman, Irving, 240n1
Leiper, Henry Smith, 243n8, 406n12
Leitchie, Dr., 753–54, 759–60
Leme, D. Sabastiao (Cardinal), 672–73, 672n3, 800
Lesser, Jeffrey, 801n36
Lester, Sean, 188, 188n70
Leverkuehn, Paul, 82, 82n29
Levi, A. Bertie, 654–55, 657
Levi, Sylvain, 153, 153n25, 164
Levison, Sir Leon, 222, 222n25, 343, 434
Lewis, John L., 425–26, 425n11
Lewisohn, Sam and Margaret, 131, 131n18
Ley, Robert, 116
Lichtwardt, H. H., 643
Lidgett, Scott, 525–26
Liebman, Charles J.: biographical sketch, 100n7; corporation strategy of, 231, 237, 411, 586, 799; on France as settlement site, 158; Gaisman relationship with, 411; JGM conversation on refugees, 100; mentioned, 94, 100, 101, 135

Liechtenstein, 469, 469n3
Lilienthal, David E., 131, 131n19
Lima, Rocha, 679, 749
Lindsay, Sir Ronald, 53n95
Lippmann, Walter: Einstein visa delay incident and, 35, 35n50; Hanfstaengl and, 39, 796; Luther interest in, 38; opinion on German ambassadorship, 69; view of German Jews, 383, 383n6
Lipschutz, Enrique, 696
Lipsky, Louis, 235n42, 248
Little Forum, 333, 333n29
Litvinov, Maxim, 217, 217n22, 564, 588
Lobkowicz, Prince, 202
Lochner, Louis, 96, 368
London Daily Herald, 296–97, 379, 382
London Refugee Conference, 173, 240, 274–79
Long, Breckinridge, 89, 89n42, 93, 393
Louis Ferdinand, Prince of Prussia, 80
Lowell, Abbott Lawrence, 327, 802
Löwensberg, Arturo, 713
Löwenstein, Hubertus, Prince zu, 602, 602nn13,14, 616, 616n2
Löwi, Joseph, 650, 653
Lucas, Antonio, 743, 747
Lüdecke, Kurt: arrangement of Goebbels interview, 36; documentary material on Nazis, 483–84; on German racial purity, 35, 40; Hanfstaengl association with, *16;* on loyalty to Hitler, 49–50; nonconciliatory stance of, 38; threats against Jews expressed by, 796
Ludwig, Emil, 143, 143n11
Lusitania, 4–5
Luther, Hans: biographical sketch, 12n13; disclosure of intercepted cable, 38, 39; as FDR intermediary to Hitler, 62, 65, 69; on the German financial outlook, 19; mentioned, 12, 42, 70, 74; on refugee property protections, 260–61; view of Nazis as conciliatory, 37–38
Lutheran Church, 58
Luxembourg, 770–72, 770n7
Lynch, Edmund, 755
Lynch, Sir Henry Joseph, 633–34, 644, 646, 651, 666, 755, 759, 762
Lyon, Jacques, 390n16, 428
MacCormack, Daniel D., 258n27, 259–60, 400, 803–804
MacDonald, Carlisle, 53, 53n94
MacDonald, James Ramsay: biographical sketch, 53n95; disarmament negotiations and, 110; FDR and, 578; Franco-Polish alliance and, 62; mentioned, 53, 59
MacDonald, Malcolm, 430, 430n18
MacFadyen settlement, 289
Machado, Dulphe Pinheiro, 657, 665, 755
Mack, Julian: biographical sketch, 138n2; on Jewish settlements, 798; on the JGM relief proposal, 233; pro-immigration lobbying efforts, 138, 803; reinterpretation of immigration laws, 238
Mackensen, August von, 18, 18n33
Madariaga, Salvador de: biographical sketch, 52n88; Chaco committee defeat, 487–88, 487n30; comments on Saar refugees, 602; on disarmament, 52; High Commissioner nomination and, 111–12, 150; mentioned, 107, 603
Magnes, Judah, 397, 397n26
Maisky, Ivan, 270n41
Majoni, G. C., 209, 395, 562–63, 787
Makohin, Mrs. J., 470–71, 473
Malaya, 289
Malot, M. J., 185–86
Manchukuo, 459, 475
Mandel, Georges, 440n31
Manes, Alfredo, 721–22
Manton, Martin T., 624–25, 624n13, 628
Manus, Rosette, 501, 501n14, 504
Marianoff, Dimitri M., 529n29
Marin, Louis, 440n30
Markel, Lester, 332n27, 338
Marks, Lord Simon: biographical sketch, 189n73; considered for Permanent Committee, 288; importance of Palestine to, 273, 287; mentioned, 412; as Weizmann associate, 189
Marley, Dudley Leigh Aman Lord, 225n29
Marley, Lord, 347–48, 501, 618–19
Marriner, Theodore, 104, 104n19
Marshall, Louis, 153, 153n28
Masaryk, Jan, 94
Masaryk, Miss, 358–59, 358n26

Mason, Max, 242n4
Matteotti Fund, 308, 309, 347, 395
May, Herbert L.: biographical sketch, 54n1; HCR counselor, 156; High Commissioner nomination and, 77–78, 133; on liquidating the HCR, 487–88; meetings with JGM, 338, 377; mentioned, 54, 72, 83–84, 147; press leak on HCR budget, 211–12; proposals on refugees, 85
May, Mrs. Herbert L., 149, 149n21
McAdoo, William G., 20, 20n45, 103
McCormick, Anne O'Hare, 59, 59n10
McDonald, George, 593–94, 593n3
McDonald, James G.
addresses: American Jewish Congress (1933), 68; Astor address (1934), 329; B'rith Sholom (1935), 770; Chautauqua Summer Program (1933), 76; Cosmopolitan Club (New York, 1933), 24n5; course lectures, 5; Federal Council of Churches (1933), 134–35, 140–43; FPA research conference (1933), 59; High Commission opening address (1933), 200, 203, 203n9; James Rosenberg home (1934), 322–23, 323n21; Lawyers Club, New York, remarks to Jewish leaders (1933), 233; Lewisohn party (New York, 1934), 241; Liebman dinner address (1934), 254; list of mid-1933 addresses, 73; Lutheran Church headquarters (1933), 58; National Conference on the Cause and Cure of War, short address (1934), 263; National Peace Conference (1933), 132; New Court comments (London, 1934), 286–89; radio broadcasts, 22, 22n1, 71, 101, 101n14, 105, 255, 256n24, 630; Rhode Island Bar Association (Providence, 1933), 23n3; Town Hall (1933), 66–67, 73, 75–76, 139; Town Hall Club Distinguished Service Medal address (1934), 251, 251n17; Town Hall, "The Crisis in Geneva" (1934), 243; Twentieth Century Club (Pittsburgh, 1933), 23; United Jewish Appeal broadcast, 392–93; Young Men's Hebrew Association (Mt. Vernon, N.Y., 1933), 133
biographical highlights: American Hebrew Medal award, 577, 596, 596n6; Barbara "Bobby" McDonald illness, 290, 290n11, 297–98, 332, 337; closing on Bronxville house, 102n15; discussion of career with Felix Warburg, 73–74; financial situation, 6–7, 74, 127, 136, 139, 285, 341, 629–30; FPA chairmanship, 5; High Commissioner for Refugees, 77–78, 125, 133, 215; Indiana University affiliation, 3, 5; League of Nations affiliation, 5–7; meeting with Hitler, 47–48, 58, 65n23, 796–97, 797n26; meetings with FDR, 20–21, 60–64, 263–64, 267–68, 577–79, 790; meetings with Pacelli, 90–91, 93, 393–94, 532, 541, 561–62, 583, 605–608, 799–800; professional positions, 2; upbringing, 2–4
political views: approach to anti-Semitism, 6, 68, 241, 253, 801; on German-Jewish emigration, 791–92, 795–96; Jewish relief efforts by, 793, 795–96, 798–99; on the persecution of non-Jews, 799; support for Jewish settlements, 798; U.S. pro-immigration lobbying efforts, 802–803
writings: diary compilation, 1–2, 8–9, 793; dissertation, 3; *German "Atrocities" and International Law* (1914), 4, 260, 473; *My Mission in Israel 1948–1951* (1951), 8, 797n26
McDonald, Joseph L. (brother), 770, 770n6
McDonald, Kenneth (father), 2
McDonald, Ruth (wife), 3
McFadyen, Sir Andrew, 374–75
McGarrah, Gates W., 50–51, 51n79
McGuire, Constantine, 628–29, 628n18, 771–72
McIntyre, Marvin, 771, 771n9
McNicholas, John T., 628, 628n19
McReynolds, Samuel, 60
Meinertzhagen, Richard, 527n28, 528
Melchett, Lord: biographical sketch, 278n48; on the corporation proposal, 278–79; Hitler theory of, 286; on Palestine, 412, 518–19, 524
Melchior, Carl: biographical sketch, 14n18; on conditions in Germany,

32, 187; death of, 238; mentioned, 14; position on Nazi violence, 27, 181
Mello, Bandeiro de, 449, 644–45, 644n12, 651–52, 665
Mello, Ildeu Vaz de, 657–58, 659–63, 659n18, 668–69, 671, 675–79, 753, 758–62
Mendelssohn-Bartholdy, Albrecht, 24, 24n4
Mercier, Desire Desideratus, 593, 593n4
Mercier, Mme. Ernest Mercier, 159, 159n39
Merz, Charles, 71, 71n45
Mesquita Filho, Julio de, 750–51
Messersmith, George: analysis of German situation in 1933, 31; assistance with Nathan visa, 46; on conditions in Austria, 558–59; on conditions in Germany, 94, 187, 366–67; Dodd opinion of, 796n22; Einstein visa delay incident and, 34–35; FDR on, 579; mentioned, 42; on Nazi economic nationalism, 49; on Nazi purification initiative, 37, 94; proposal of German monarchy, 80; protest over Mowrer expulsion, 794–95; on U.S. protest at Nazi treatment of Jews, 49n78
Mexico: Apostolic Delegate on, 627–28; Catholic Church in, 596, 605–606, 624–25, 628–29, 728; Pacelli discussion of, 91, 799
Meyer, André, 136
Meyer, Eugene, 73
Meyer, Julius T., 66
Meyer-Pellegrini, Bernardo, 700, 759–60
Miller, Douglas P., 11n5
Miller, Ludwig, 77n12
Millis, Walter, 69
Mindlin, Jose E., 750–51
Mize, Stephen, 8
Moffat, Jay Pierrepont: anti-immigration views, 803; biographical sketch, 25n13; on divisions among Jews, 258n26; draft of FDR/Hull statement on religious persecution, 101; on the German barter proposal, 576–77; High Commissioner nomination and, 128–29, 129n12; meetings with JGM, 64–65, 398–99; mentioned, 25; view of HCR accomplishments, 311n7
Moisesville colony (Argentina), 686n12
Moley, Raymond, 20, 20n43, 25, 38, 60, 125
Monteaux, Pierre, 42, 42n65
Montefiore, Leonard G.: biographical sketch, 99n6; on the British reserve fund, 784; High Commissioner proposal and, 113; JGM meeting with, 99–100; on the joint drive, 496; mentioned, 104, 106, 111, 419
Montenear, Carlos José, 743
Monteverde, Eduardo, 743
Montoux, Paul, 156–57
Moore, Hugh, 317
Moore, R. Walton, 311n8
Moorhead, Helen Howell, 115, 464n18
Moral Re-Armament (MRA), 486
Morgenthau, Henry, Jr., 60, 60n13
Morgenthau, Henry, Sr., 21, 21n47, 24, 57–58, 140, 244, 258
Morley, Felix, 261
Morocco, 348
Morris, Dave Hennan, 386, 386n9
Morris, Ira Nelson, 29, 29n35, 615–16
Morrow, Elizabeth Cutter, 342, 342n4
Moses, Herbert, 644, 644n11
Mosley, Oswald, 542
Mosquita, Julio, 749
Motta, Giuseppe, 188–89, 188n71
Mottistone, John Edward Bernard Seely Baron, 286, 286n7
Mowrer, Edgar: biographical sketch, 17n28; expulsion of by Nazis, 794–95; *Germany Puts the Clock Back* (1933), 616; Hanfstaengl threats against, 28; JGM association with, 17; mentioned, 38, 81; on Nazi atrocities, 30, 45
Mowrer, Paul Scott, 52
Mozambique. *See* Portuguese East Africa
Muhlstein, Anatole, 349n13
Munich Picture Gallery, 98
Murrow, Edward R., 245n12, 627, 805
Mussolini, Benito: as check on Nazis, 33–34, 89, 89n43, 393, 395; disarmament negotiations and, 110; JGM meeting of 1934, 395; mentioned, 83; refugee stance as model for Germans, 114; relationship with Italian Jews, 563

Namibia. *See* South West Africa
Nansen, Fridtjof, 77n16
Nansen Committee: agricultural settlement experiment of, 426; dissimilarity to HCR, 142; Nansen passports as model, 180, 389; Nansen retirement and, 559–60; refugee problem and, 84, 88, 105, 122; relationship with Jewish organizations, 452
Nathan, Otto: appeal for help with visa, 46; biographical sketch, 12n11; description of Austrian coup, 445; mentioned, 12, 14; refugee loan plan of, 432–33, 435, 437, 437n26, 439, 443, 546; reports of Nazi atrocities, 35; resignation of, 31–32
Nation, The, 802
National Broadcasting Corporation, 244, 246
National Civil Service Reform League, 5
National Committee. *See* French National Committee to Aid German Refugees
National Conference on the Cause and Cure of War, 263
National Council of Jewish Women, 244–45
National Peace Conference, 132
National People's Party (Germany), 22, 23, 30
National Recovery Administration (NRA). *See* Great Depression; Roosevelt, Franklin D.
National Socialist German Workers' Party. *See* Nazi Regime
Navarro, Alfredo, 742, 745
Nazi Regime: Aryan paragraph, 384; "bloodless" Nazi revolution, 49; boycott of Jewish businesses, 26–28, 33, 43, 44, 787; Dodd relations with Nazis, 793–94; election of 1932, 22; establishment of Party Foreign Office, 36; German discontent with, 269, 294, 368, 375, 453, 552; interception of cables and telephone calls by, 38, 39; Jewish expulsion policy, 792, 797n29; League intervention on refugees and, 87, 93, 94, 109, 113–14, 117; Lüdecke material on, 483–84; moderation of economic policies, 85; Nazi views of JGM, 790; opposition to emigration of youths, 349; "palace revolution" rumors, 418–19, 425; party rallies of, 11, 98–99, 794; peace-from-dictatorship argument for, 112–13; persecution of non-Jews, 507, 799; propaganda effectiveness, 263; Reichstag fire and, 23; repatriation policy, 291; resentment of Versailles and, 70, 78, 110, 132, 168; rise to power of, 10, 33, 38; Röhm Putsch, 413–14, 421, 423, 425, 433, 491, 558; Soviet Union treaty with Nazis, 1; support by German intellectuals, 32; support by German Jews, 35; support by middle-class, 43–44, 50; supposed moderation following Hitler speech, 79–80; as utopian dictatorship, 513. *See also* Germany; Hitler, Adolf; purification; race theory of Nazis
NBC. *See* National Broadcasting Corporation
Neilson, William Allan, 573n5, 574
Neurath, Baron Constantine von: attendance at League Assembly, 110, 114; biographical sketch, 15n24; decline of power of, 48, 50, 81, 96–97; disarmament negotiations and, 110, 119; establishment of Nazi Foreign Office and, 36; JGM meeting of 1934, 290–93, 317, 339; mentioned, 18, 52, 94; Nazi opposition to, 44; position on Jewish refugees, 97, 109, 117, 793
Nevinson, Henry Woodd, 413n23
New Deal. *See* Great Depression; Roosevelt, Franklin D.
New Republic, 55
New School for Social Research, 51n84
New York Daily Herald, 224
New York Foundation, 137, 138, 237, 247
New York Herald Tribune: article on Dutch refugee proposal, 119, 121, 124, 132; German ambassadorship and, 69; Stowe as Paris bureau head, 53n89; U.S. policy shift on League article, 105
New York Times: article on Nazi moderation, 366; Astor address article, 332, 338; Birchall article on JGM, 484; concern about perceived Jewish associations, 71; coverage of 1933

Hitler address, 70n43; coverage of HCR founding, 208–209; coverage of HCR liquidation, 783, 783n6; JGM as writer for, 2, 765–66, 773–74, 775; JGM interview of 1933, 230, 230n35; publication of Nazi atrocities, 58
New Yorker, 237
Nicaragua, 621
Nicolson, Harold, 374, 374n54
Nicosia, Francis, 792
Niebuhr, Reinhold, 304n31
Niemeyer, Walter, 665, 666–67
Nobel Institute, 353, 370
non-Jewish refugees: Fosdick on, 319; fundraising and, 422–23, 430; Jewish support for, 498; non-Aryan Christians, 434; Paris non-Jewish organizations, 193; persecution of non-Jews, 178n56, 753, 799; population of, 195, 230n35; relief efforts for, 342–43; Woburn House accommodation of, 500. *See also* refugees
Norlin, George, 32, 50
Norman, Edward, 403, 403n6
Norway, 105, 786
Nossig, Alfred, 196
NRA (National Recovery Administration). *See* Great Depression; Roosevelt, Franklin D.
Nuremberg Party Rally, 98–99, 794
Nye, Gerald, 576, 576n8

Ochs, Adolph, 71, 71n44, 402, 402n3, 626–27
Ogden, Esther G.: biographical sketch, 24n10; High Commissioner nomination and, 77, 134; JGM diary letters of 1933, 103–20, 161–66; mentioned, 24, 140
Olendorf, Dr., 183
Olsburgh, Ralph, 649, 755
Omerod, Mary, 436n25
Ommen settlement (Holland), 503, 508
Oppenheim, Moritz and Käthie, 55, 387n10, 396
Oppenheim, Paul, 386–87
ORT. *See* Society for Trades and Agricultural Labor (ORT)
OSE. *See* Children's Aid Society (OSE)
Osusky, Stephen, 105, 105n21, 111–12, 603
Oualid, William, 136, 153, 164
Oungre, Edouard, 147, 158–59, 170
Oungre, Louis: biographical sketch, 133n25; on the Argentine rejection of refugees, 567–68, 653, 712–15; Argentine settlements and, 713, 714–15; assessment of HCR, 350–51; Brazilian refugee corporation and, 416, 442, 449, 449n3, 452, 634, 652, 800; Brazilian settlements and, 584, 645, 658, 662–64, 666–67, 670–71, 675–77, 753–54, 760–61, 769; d'Avigdor-Goldsmid on, 493–94; on French attitude toward refugees, 441–42; as HCR contact, 153, 169, 430; on Jewish settlements, 798; JMG South American trip and, 612; Kahn relationship with, 147, 386, 391–92, 426, 493, 548; on loan kassas, 441, 616–17; mentioned, 331, 540; settlement strategy of, 800; Sir Leonard Cohen on, 415
Owen, Ruth Bryan, 369, 369n43
Oxford Group, 486

Pacelli, Eugenio (Cardinal): biographical sketch, 90n44; Demuth visit with, 598, 599; Galeazzi relationship with, 89n40; JGM meeting of 1933, 90–91, 93, 799–800; JGM meeting of 1934 (May), 393–94; JGM meeting of 1934 (November), 532, 541, 561–62, 583; JGM meeting of 1935, 605–608; JGM meeting with Cardinal Hayes and, 593–94; position on Jewish refugees, 805
Pacheco, Felix, 632–33, 633n2, 671–72
Packard, Arthur W., 315, 315n15, 408–409, 408n16
Paderewski, Ignace Jan, 196n83
Palestine. *See also* Jews; Zionism
general: Balfour Declaration, 223n26; British HCR representation, 196, 197n84; British-U.S. cooperation, 385; Comité des Delegations Juives, 190n77; Haavara (Transfer Agreement), 792; HCR jurisdiction, 145, 152, 172, 173n48, 234; Palladin Club conference, 526–28; Passfield White Paper, 56, 223n26; refugee fundraising efforts, 424, 524; Relief

Palestine (*continued*)
Corporation, 273–74, 287; salvation-through-remnants approach, 270, 326, 780
settlements: diversification of settlements, 228; Gaza region, 390; Hula swamp settlement, 346, 351, 377, 442, 442n33, 450, 496; Jordan valley settlement, 377; proposed binational state, 398n27
settlers: Arab-Jewish relations, 224, 228, 345–46, 406, 420; Eastern European immigrants, 364–65; illegal immigration, 346; labor shortage, 497; Oungre employment proposal, 442; Palestine Economic Corporation, 55, 418, 419–20; screening of immigrants, 388, 516; women's role, 551
views of: Bentwich, *144;* Brandeis, 129; Felix Warburg, 56, 798; JGM, 223–24, 234, 273, 275–76, 383; Norman, 403; Weizmann, 213–14, 270, 273–74, 275–76, 784, 798
Panama, 407
Papen, Franz von: biographical sketch, 11n3; mentioned, 18, 81; negotiation of Hitler chancellorship, 22; Papen economic proposals, 11, 12, 14; strategy for controlling Nazis, 35, 38; support for Concordat, 91; supposed Nazi overthrow and, 418–19, 423
Paraguay: Chaco dispute, 487–88, 487n30, 693, 693n17, 701; demand for refugees in, 621, 700
Parana Plantations (Brazilian refugee employment organization), 416, 442, 449, 449n3, 452, 510, 800
Paranhos, José Maria da Silva, 645, 645n14
Paris: Bastion refugee quarters, 219, 219n23, 256n24; dispute over disbursement of relief funds, 459; HICEM refugee support in, 768; Kahn refugee plan for, 448–49; loan kassas for, 489, 509; Paris non-Jewish organizations, 193; Paris refugee arrangements, 164, 173–74, 175, 238, 244–45, 253; refugee conditions in, 442, 446, 693. *See also* France
Parkes, James, 134, 134n27, 143, 147, 198, 215
Parsons, Geoffrey, 69
Passfield White Paper, 56, 223n26, 306n37
Pasvolsky, Leo, 51, 51n81
Patenotre, Raymond, 52
Patterson, Richard, 137
Paz, Ezequiel P., 695–96
Pearson, Drew, 74, 74n5, 582
Peel Commission, 56
Peixote, Alfranio, 757–58
Pell, Herbert C., 48, 48n75
Pelt, Adrianus, 108–10, 108n30, 121
Perkins, Frances, 455
permits de séjour (residency permits), 441, 533, 541
permits de travail (work permits): in Brazil, 758–59; Catholic Committee success with, 529; Central Information Bureau for placement, 278n47; as crime prevention device, 441; designation of type of work on, 758–59; discrimination against Communists and, 541; in France, 164, 391, 438, 489, 547, 565, 590, 591, 609, 612, 621; HCR role with, 460–61; for highly skilled workers, 547; Rothmund on, 538–39; Syndicat d'Etude discussion of, 610
Perowne, Victor, 620, 620n6
Pershing, John Joseph, 589, 589n26
Peterson, Elizabeth. *See* Habicht, Elizabeth
Philippson (Brazilian Jewish settlement), 640–41, 641n9
Phillippson, Jules, 184, 184n65, 185–86, 188, 227, 615
Phillips, William: biographical sketch, 25n12; anti-immigration views, 259, 803; discussion of Governing Body representation, 140, 310–11; FDR message to Hitler and, 62n17; on the High Commissioner nomination, 128, 129n12; JGM meetings with, 64, 310–11; on JGM South American trip, 580; mentioned, 25, 139; on publicity to expose Nazi atrocities, 399; view of HCR accomplishments, 311n6
Phipps, Sir Eric, 543, 550
Pickett, Clarence, 300, 300n20, 313

Pilsudski, Joseph, 152, 354n21
Pinedo, Frederico, 697
Pinero, Federico, 729, 729n8, 730
Pittman, Key, 60, 65, 65n25
Pius XI (Pope), 800, 805
Pius XII (Pope). *See* Pacelli, Eugenio (Cardinal)
Piza Sobrinho, Luiz, 749
Pobereszki, Michael (later Pobers), 474n13
Poland: anti-Semitism in, 152, 354n21, 796; Franco-Polish alliance suggestion, 62, 69; German invasion of, 1, 7; League protection of minorities in, 472, 472n8; Polish Danzig settlement, 85, 85n34; Polish Jews' status in Germany, 78; Polish-German Treaty of 1934, 41, 264, 350, 350n15, 365; refugee budget review, 427; repatriation of Polish refugees in France, 218, 360n34, 361, 362; representation on the Bureau, 269; response of Polish Jews to JGM visit, 360–61; role in refugee relief, 86–89; Russian settlement program and, 448, 448n2; visit to Warsaw Jewish quarters, 364–65
Politis, Nikolaos Sokratis, 121, 121n1
Portugal, 512–13
Portuguese East Africa, 376–77
Prebisch, Paul, 688, 697–99, 703–704
President's Advisory Committee on Political Refugees, 1–2
Prittwitz, Fredrich Wilhelm von, 25, 25n16, 36
Priwin, Hans W., 36
propaganda: German anti-Semitic publications, 375; Ivy Lee involvement with, 263–64, 367; Jewish participation in, 376; JGM writings on, 4; Untermyer concern about, 139; in the U.S., 139, 264
property: Devisen foreign exchange regulations, 511–12, 523, 553–57; Dieckhoff discussion on, 291–92; as German vs. international concern, 431, 431n19; HCR actions, 193, 226, 281; letter to Barandon on, 421; Luther discussion about transfer of, 260–61; Moffat on refugee property, 258n26; Nazi seizure of refugee property, 404–405, 431, 431n19; Nazi suppression of property rights, 536n2, 795, 797; transfer regulations, 382, 472–73, 499–500, 513, 514, 523, 573
Proskauer, Joseph M., 68, 68n35, 127, 233
Prussia, 12, 12n12
Pucci, Francisco, 743–44, 748
purification: of Academy of Medicine, 94; of German Broadcasting Company, 36; of German General Electric, 37; prohibition of intermarriage, 82; theory of racial purity and, 40–41; uncompromising Hitler position on, 85–86; of Warburg business, 79n19. *See also* Nazi Regime; race theory of Nazis
Pye, Edith M., 530, 530n33, 537, 542
Pyke, Geoffrey, 518, 518n20

Quakers: conditions in Paris for, 523; designation as non-political body, 347–48; Friends' Service Committee, 317; HCR fundraising and, 313; Ommen settlement (Holland), 503, 508; relief proposal of, 428–29
Quatro Irmaos (Brazilian settlement), 640–41, 641n9, 658–59, 754, 780
Quidde, Ludwig, 486, 486n28

Rabinowich, Samuel, 685
race theory of Nazis: contempt for Jews and, 35; fear of Jewish rule and, 40; foreign immigration quotas and, 674; Hitler eloquence on, 34; intransigent belief in, 85–86; JGM physical characteristics and, 39, 40; myth of Aryan supremacy, 76; public school lessons in, 550; question of Aryan refugees and, 406n12; redemptive quality of, 797, 797n29; status of Latin peoples in, 724; stories of racial office encounters, 553; treatment of African troops occupying Rhineland, 83, 83n30; treatment of converted Jews, 492. *See also* Hitler, Adolf; Nazi Regime; purification
Raffalovich, Isiah, 643–44, 643n10, 653, 655
Railey, H. H., 106, 106n27, 131, 132
Rajchmann, Louis W., 475, 475n16

Rapaport, N., 691n16, 692
Rapaport, Paulo, 654, 656, 755, 757, 759–63
Rappard, William E.: account of Goebbels meeting, 119; biographical sketch, 110n34; on German-HCR relations, 110, 194, 195; on Madariaga, 603; view of disarmament negotiations, 121
Rawson, E.L., 436n24
Razovsky, Cecilia, 244–45, 244n10, 247
Reading, Lady, 544–45
Reading, Rufus Isaacs Lord, 88, 88n38, 111, 219, 221, 223, 225–26
Reconstruction Finance Corporation (U.S.), 19, 19n35
Reed, Adele Wilcox (Mrs. David Aiken), 14, 14n20, 17, 18, 96
Refugee Economic Corporation: overview, 798–99; announcement at Lewisohn party, 241; board of trustees formation, 321, 330–31; David Cohen support for, 272; discussion with Felix Warburg on, 248; executive position, 410; Felix Warburg on, 337–38; financial support, 267; JGM assessment of, 764; Lewis Strauss on, 629; Liebman role in, 100n7, 231, 237, 316, 799; London Conference resolution, 277; Oungre on, 652; Palestine and, 273–74; presentation to Europeans, 247–48; Rabbi Levy support for, 327; Rosenberg role in, 232, 318, 322, 799; Waley Cohen assessment of, 418; Wilfrid Israel on, 269
refugees. *See also* German Jews; intellectual/professional refugees; non-Jewish refugees; *permits de travail* (work permits); property; Refugee Economic Corporation
  general: ideological differences in relief approaches, 253; JGM relocation plan, 294, 525; policy toward host nations, 400; political refugees, 478–79, 502–503, 512; principle of human capital and, 516; proposed human-interest story on, 374; statistical data on, 271–72
  financial concerns: loan kassas, 437, 437n26, 441, 489, 509, 612–13, 616–17; loan plan of Otto Nathan, 432–33, 435, 437, 437n26, 439, 443, 546; personal effort fundraising strategy, 246; proposed Jewish tax to fund refugees, 460; women's refugee drive, 517, 524
  labor and education: Erich Warburg education fund proposal, 237, 247; industrial settlements, 429, 430; labor bonds for visas, 259, 259n30, 264, 264n34, 335, 400, 804; professional certificates, 419–20, 516–17; retraining facilities, 532, 611
  settlements: conditions in France, 442, 446; refugee "bill of rights," 766; refugee population figures, 195, 230n35, 426–27, 483, 783; unjust refugee expulsions, 503, 533, 538, 612, 613, 615, 615n1; use of national indigent relief facilities, 537–38; "vacant countries" thesis, 375, 714
  travel and immigration: cost of travel papers, 533, 537, 546, 712, 718, 729; German repatriation policy, 291; impostor refugee problem, 440, 546; passport arrangements, 139, 141, 180, 210–11, 277, 281, 291, 481, 546, 712, 718; *permits de séjour* (residency permits), 441, 533, 541; registry proposal for, 438, 546, 547; "stateless" classification, 642, 644, 662, 670, 675–76; visa quotas and documentation, 291, 291n12, 301, 301n22, 543, 543n8
Reichstag fire, *16,* 23, 28, 30
Reichswehr: assessment of loyalty in, 45, 423, 465; Dieckhoff prediction of Nazi influence in, 43; Hammerstein as moderating influence on Nazis, 82; Hanfstaengl on, 28, 29; Junkers as source of Nazi opposition in, 75, 78–79, 425, 465; possibility of intervention against Nazis, 29, 32; Siegmund Warburg on, 29
Respondek, Erwin, 81, 81n28
Rhodes, 588
Rhodesia. *See* Southern Rhodesia
Rice, William Gorham, Jr., 603n15
Richards, Bernard, 139
Richling, J., 584
Ridder, Bernard, 75, 75n6
Rinder, Herman, 756–57

Ritter, Karl, 48, 48n77, 123
Röchling, Hermann, 469, 469n2
Rockefeller, Abby Aldrich, 396–97
Rockefeller, John D., III: High Commissioner nomination and, 134; JGM view of, 134, 245, 309, 802; League refugee funding and, 408–409; mentioned, 589; support for JGM ambassadorship, 58; Sweetser on, 604
Rockefeller, John D., Jr.: FPA relationship with, 5; Hanfstaengl proposal of embassy financing by, 48; League refugee funding and, 118, 121, 122, 126, 136, 136n33, 305–306, 309, 321, 408–409, 460, 627; meeting with JGM, 396; position on Jewish immigration, 802; Sweetser on, 604
Rockefeller Foundation, 241–42, 456–57, 637. *See also* Fosdick, Raymond D.
Röhm, Ernst: biographical sketch, 28n28; confrontation with Hitler, 558; Röhm Putsch (Schleicher murder), 413, 421, 423, 425, 433, 491
Roland colony, 666
Romania, 152, 238, 238n46, 782
Roosevelt, Eleanor: discussion of High Commissioner nomination, 130, 130n15; FPA relationship with, 5, 59n9; JGM letter of 1933, 76; JGM letter of 1935, 788–89; JGM meetings with, 59–60, 64, 577–79, 585; mentioned, 70; support for coal miner relocation, 300; support for JGM, 804–805
Roosevelt, Franklin D.: Argentine esteem for, 583; on the boycott of German goods, 31; disarmament address of 1933, 69, 69n39; discussion of New Deal programs, 252; election of 1932, 19–21, 230–31; on European climate for war, 267–68, 805; FPA relationship with, 5; Frankfurter-JGM discussion of, 230; immigration policy, 264n34, 804–805; JGM meeting of 1932, 20–21; JGM meeting of 1933, 60–64, 790; JGM meeting of 1934 (January), 263–64, 267–68; JGM meeting of 1934 (December), 577–79, 585; JGM South American trip and, 630; Luxembourg stamp photo session, 770–72, 770n7; mentioned, 70; proposed message to Hitler, 62, 62n17; recommendations of Jesse Straus, 594; statement on religious persecution, 101. *See also* German ambassadorship
Roosevelt, Theodore, Jr., 122, 123, 126–28
Root, Elihu, 594, 594n5
Rosen, Joseph A.: biographical sketch, 217n20; discussion of settlement sites, 378; on French refugee policy, 158, 428, 588; Russian settlement program, 448, 588, 619
Rosenberg, Alfred, 36, 36n55, 39, 50, 394
Rosenberg, James N.: biographical sketch, 24n8; advice on French support for HCR, 460–61, 462–64; on the Biro-Bidjan settlement, 597; corporation strategy of, 232, 799; Hanfstaengl disputes with, 16; HCR and, 77, 125, 127, 134n26, 136, 139, 184; Hindenburg assessment of power of, 43; on Jewish-Catholic cooperation, 75; JGM and, 7; mentioned, 24, 32, 100n7; on the refugee "bill of rights," 766–67; Trans-Jordania plan, 322, 345–46; World Jewish Congress and, 585
Rosenthal, Samuel, 336
Rosenwald, Julius, 448n2
Rosenwald, William, 624n10, 625
Ross, Frederick, 99
Rosso, Augusto, 314n12
Rothbarth, Edwin, 347, 347n11
Rothbarth, Margarete, 157, 157n33, 160
Rothenberg, Morris, 233n36, 329
Rothermere, Harold Harmsworth Lord, 279, 279n49
Rothmund, Heinrich: biographical sketch, 189n72; on the definition of refugees, 478–79, 801; as Swiss HCR delegate, 189, 203; on work permits, 538–39
Rothschild, Anthony de, 153, 633–34, 798
Rothschild, Baron Robert de: biographical sketch, 160n40; assistance with South American trip, 619; on conditions in Paris, 220; on French refugee policy, 160–61, 426, 430, 568; as HCR contact, 153; New

Rothschild, Baron Robert de (*cont.*)
Court meeting chair, 286–89; opinion of JGM, 189; on the refugee registry proposal, 547
Rothschild, Baroness Robert de, 179
Rothschild, Lionel de, 153, 415, 417, 524, 798
Röttgen, Hans, 658–59, 669, 754, 760–61
Rousseau, Theodore, 136
Rowe, Leo S., 580, 580n10, 700
Royal, John F., 137
Ruiz y Flores, Leopoldo (Archbishop, Papal Nuncio to Mexico), 627–28, 627n16
Rumania. *See* Romania
Rumbold, Sir Horace, 46, 46n70
Ruppin, Arthur, 484–85, 484n26
Russia. *See* Soviet Union

SA (*Sturmabteilung*, Nazi paramilitary force), 28nn27, 33, 37, 98–99
Saar: briefs asserting right to protect minorities from, 468; inadvisability of Governing Body memorandum on, 528; League action following election, 601n12; placement of refugees from, 458, 463, 485–86, 529, 560–62, 566, 600–603, 609, 609n17, 611, 613, 621; plebiscite vote on statehood, 469, 515, 548, 552–53, 599, 599n9, 602; political fragility in, 445–46; proposal for Christian refugees, 623; refugee budget review, 427, 443; situation of Catholics in, 552, 561–62, 599, 605
Sacerdote, Angelo, 563, 563n28
Sacher, Harry: biographical sketch, 189n75, 296n19; discussion of fundraising, 527; mentioned, 296; on non-Jewish refugees, 430; as Weizmann associate, 189
Sachs, Arthur, 430n16
Saint-Léger, Alexis: advice on Germany, 387; biographical sketch, 157n34; JGM advice on French government (*aide mémoire*), 462–63, 465; JGM observations on, 160; on Laval refugee policy, 568–69
Salinger, Alfons, 683
Salles Oliveira, Armando de, 749
Salm, Fritz, 82
Salmon, Sir Isador, 287n9
Salomon, Hugo, 700
Salz, Siegfried, 42
Sampaio, Sebastian, 656–57, 656n16, 659
Samuel, Siegfried, 643–44, 646–47, 650
Samuel, Sir Herbert, 224n28
Sandelmann, Hans, 565
Sandler, Richard J., 472n7
Santos Filho, Adolpho, 750
Sargent, Sir Orme, G., 166, 166n44, 515, 619–20
Sarnoff, David, 252n20
Saslavsky, J., 696–97, 716, 724, 725–26, 738–39
Sassoon, Sybil, 544, 544n10
Sauerwine, Jules, 472n6
Save the Children Fund, 174
Sawyer, Olive, 143, 162, 651
Schacht, Hjalmar: arrangement of Hitler meeting, 51; Bergmann on, 36; biographical sketch, 12n17; concern for German economy, 83; defense of Nazi policies, 33–34; as FDR intermediary to Hitler, 62, 65, 68–69, 263; financial manipulations of, 505; as Hitler-JGM intermediary, 229–30; JGM confrontation on Hitler, 68–69, 82; Kauffmann on, 513–14; Lüdecke/Daitz on, 41; Luther on, 38; mentioned, 12, 79, 94; moderation of economic policies and, 85
Schäffer, Hans, 371, 371n48
Scheidemann, Philipp, 15n23, 98
Schevenels, Walter, 347n12, 589, 597, 608, 621
Schiff, John, 78, 78n17
Schiff, Otto: biographical sketch, 100n10; on Brazilian colonization, 525; Felix Warburg telegraph on the High Commissioner nomination, 128; HCR and, 174, 222; letter attacking Bentwich, 417; mentioned, 100, 343, 385; on Nathan loan plan, 433; opposition to mass colonization, 412; suggestion on immigration-employment linkage, 268–69; on Weizmann, 169–70
Schleicher, Kurt von: appointment of 1932, 22; biographical sketch, 18n32; dismissal by Hitler, 45; mentioned, 18; shooting of, 413, 421, 422, 423, 425, 433

Schmitt, Kurt, 79, 79n22, 80, 85, 94
Schorr, Moses, 360, 360n33
Schuschnigg, Kurt von, 444n36, 559
Schwartz, Paul, 50, 71, 71n46, 255
Schwarz, Jacob, 407
Schweitzer, David J., 35, 35n51, 136–37, 143
Schwelm, Adolpho Julio, 702–703, 702n19
Scott, James Brown, 315, 315n13, 328
Sebag-Montefiore, Edmund, 417n3
Sebag-Montefiore, Geoffrey, 417n3
Second International, 174, 174n51, 192. *See also* Social Democratic Party
Seeds, Sir William, 638–39
Selby, Sir Walford, 557
Seligman, Eustace, 136, 776
Sephardic Jews, 526
Shakespeare, Geoffrey H., 483, 483n23
Sherman, Irving, 80–81, 80n25, 83, 94, 552
Sherrill, Charles H., 373, 373n51, 377, 386, 592, 592n1
Shotwell, James T., 19, 19n37, 132, 132n20
Sieff, Lord Israel, 189, 189n74
Sieff, Rebecca, 524, 526, 544–45, 544n9
Simon, Fritz, 170
Simon, Hugo, 438–39, 438n28
Simon, John, 114, 114n37, 152, 404, 422
Simon, Jules, 390, 390n14
Simon, Leo, 776–77
Simons, Hugo, 193
Sinclair, Harry F., 53, 53n90
Smith, Al, 230
Smith, Alexander, 405
Smolar, Boris, 773, 773n10
Smuts, Jan, 524, 524n26
Snowden, Viscount, 114, 114n39
Soares, José Carlos de Macedo, 645, 645n13, 655, 657, 671
Social Democratic Party (Austria), 116
Social Democratic Party (Germany), 12, 12n12, 14, 26, 30, 149
Socialists: in Argentina, 702, 704, 727; Austrian suppression of, 357, 393; Madison Square Garden meeting, 309, 309n3, 341; Paris refugee arrangements and, 174, 174n51; suppression of Russian Jewish socialists, 497. *See also* Second International; Social Democratic Party
Sociedad de Amigos de Alberto Torres, 632–33, 635–36, 638, 642, 645, 657
Sociedad de Protección a los Immigrantes Israelitas, 741
Sociedade Beneficente Israelita, 649
Society for the Propagation of the Faith, 599, 606
Society for Trades and Agricultural Labor (ORT), 207, 207n13, 225, 613, 613n18
Society of Friends. *See* Quakers
Society of Friends of True Germany, 125
Sokolow, Nahum, 364
Sollmann, Wilhelm, 444n34
Solmssen, Georg, 574–75
Solomon, Dr., 716, 721–22
South Africa, 277, 312–13, 422
South West Africa, 252, 404
Southern Rhodesia, 435
Souza Costa, Arthur de, 658
Soviet Union: acceptance of Communist refugees, 564; Agro-Joint colonization program, 471; American Society for Jewish Farm Settlement in Russia, 55; Amur region refugee settlement, 217, 217n21; anti-Semitism in, 471, 473; Biro-Bidjan settlement region (Soviet Union), 217, 217n21, 225, 225n32, 227, 228–29, 308, 336, 348, 378, 588, 597; Calvin Hoover on, 32; capacity for accepting refugees, 261; Crimea settlement, 378, 378n59; disarmament negotiations and, 121; Duranty on, 79–80; HCR and, 217–18, 227, 261, 265, 784; Japan hostility with, 117; League membership, 355, 355n22, 470, 477; Nazi treaty with, 1; Pacelli discussion of, 91; Polish refugee settlements in, 448, 448n2; suppression of Jewish socialists, 497
Spain, 91, 105, 427, 475–76
Speyer, James Joseph, 186n67, 320
Speyer, Prof., 136, 614
SS (*Schutzstaffel,* Nazi protective guard): Hanfstaengl on, 28, 29; report on demonstration by, 80, 98–99; Röhm Putsch, 413–14, 421, 423, 425, 433, 491
Stahlhelm: described, 11n1; JGM attendance at demonstration, 17–18; mentioned, 11; Nazi influence in,

Stahlhelm (*continued*)
29; Nazi opinions of, 41; suppression of Jewish membership in, 78
Stallforth, Federico, 53, 53n91
Standard Club, 249
Starhemberg, Ernst Rüdiger von, 356, 356n24
Starkmeth, Isaac, 691n16, 692, 712–14, 722, 735–36
Steckine, S., 644, 646–47, 652, 757
Steinhardt, Laurence, 370n46
Stern, Fritz, 519–20, 519n21
Stern, Sir Frederick, 266n39
Stewart, Barbara McDonald (daughter): book on U.S. policy on Nazi refugees, 793; childhood, 5–6, 7; illness of, 290, 290n11, 297–98, 332, 337; on JGM's diary, 2; mentioned, 405
Stimson, Henry, 12n9
Stokowski, Leopold, 596, 596n8
Stolper, Gustav, 42, 42n67, 136, 256
Stone, William T., 34, 34n49, 92–93, 107
Storrs, Sir Ronald, 527, 527n27
Stowe, Leland, 53, 53n89
Strakosh, Sir Henry, 437n27
Straus, Jesse, 351, 390n13, 461–62, 569, 592, 594, 613–14
Straus, Percy, 330–31, 337, 341, 406, 592
Straus, Ralph, 406
Strauss, Herbert, 790–91
Strauss, Hugh Grant, 251n18
Strauss, Lewis: financial support for JGM, 7, 242, 333, 338, 586; as French liaison for HCR, 171, 175; mentioned, 222, 320; on the relief corporation, 629; support for JDC, 595
Strauss, Richard, 40n61
Strauss, Robert Kenneth, 19, 19n42
Strauss, Roger, 68, 68n34, 127
Streicher, Julius, 98, 375, 375n55
Streit, Clarence K, 84, 84n31, 106, 119, 308
Stresemann, Gustav, 98, 551, 551n18
Strunsky, Simeon, 235, 235n40
Stürmer, Der, 375–76, 392–93, 395, 395n20
Sugimura, Yotataro, 459n13
Sulzberger, Arthur Hays: biographical sketch, 24n7; on JGM *Times* employment, 765–66, 773, 775; mentioned, 24, 71; opposition to American Jewish Congress, 139; on the *Times* publication of Nazi atrocities, 58
Suvich, Fulvio, 393–94, 393n18, 560
Swartzwald, Eugenia, 520
Sweden: Christian refugees and, 785; intellectual refugees and, 480; League resolution on civil liberties, 117; refugee problem and, 105, 370–71, 427
Sweetser, Arthur: as advocate for refugees, *13,* 105; biographical sketch, 51n82; dismay over German situation, 51; on funding for League refugee program, 118, 121; on German-HCR relations, 199; High Commissioner nomination and, 111, 113, 133, 150; meeting with JGM, 603–604; mentioned, 51, 84, 124, 564; role in *Herald* article leak, 132
Switzerland: alleged expulsion of refugees, 538; refugee problem and, 105, 427, 479, 487; temporary refugees in, 347; treatment of political refugees, 801
Swope, Gerard, 39, 39n60, 341
Swope, Herbert: biographical sketch, 29n34; Hanfstaengl on, 29; JGM view of, 591; mentioned, 39, 340–41; support for JGM ambassadorship, 67
Sylvercruys, Franz, 622, 622n8
Syndicat d'Etude, 610–11
Syria: emigration to Argentina from, 718; Hexter visit to, 588; High Commissioner role and, 152; settlement in Palestine and, 224; settlement proposals for, 610–11, 776–77, 776n2
Szapiro, Jerzy, 362, 362n36

Tabouis, Genevieve, 115, 121, 470, 470n4
Tanganyika, 413, 421–22
Teixeira-Leite, Anisio, 641, 650, 673–77, 675–77, 753–55, 760
Terra, Gabriel, 742–44, 742n13
Tetreau, Galeazzi S. E., 568, 612
Thomas, Norman, 306n36
Thompson, Dorothy, 465, 465n20

Thomsen, Hans, 15, 15n22, 47
Thyssen, Fritz, 418–19
Tietz, Ludwig, 81, 81n27, 94, 100, 183
Tilden, Bill, 83
Tillich, Paul, 304n30
Tirana, Rifat, 119, 119n43, 459
Titulescu, Nicolai, 666, 666n2
Today magazine, 341
Tornquist, Carlos Alfredo, 688
Trade Union International, 192
trade unions: AFL boycott support, 462, 462n16; as HICEM non-Jewish group, 284; John L. Lewis conversation, 425–26; Paris refugee arrangements and, 174; relief aid from, 589; as source of resistance to Nazis, 125; support for Schevenels' committees, 597
Transfer Agreement (Haavara), 792
Trans-Jordania: Arab-Jewish relations in, 345; discussion with Cunliffe-Lister on, 345–46; High Commissioner role and, 152; Lord Melchett on, 279; Rosenberg plan for, 322, 390; settlement in Palestine and, 224
Treaty of Locarno, 261, 261n32
Treaty of Versailles, 5; attributed Jewish role in, 15; German dislike for, 70, 78, 110, 132, 168; occupation of Rhineland, 83, 83n30; overview, 15n23; proposed invocation of Article 11, 84, 84n32, 94, 94n51; Saar region jurisdiction and, 443
Tugwell, Rexford G., 19, 19n38
Tulley, Judge, 596
Turkey: acceptance of refugees in, 405, 405n10, 534–35; Anatolia settlement project, 435; Assyrian diaspora and, 416n1; Friends of Turkey dinner, 136; invited into Governing Body, 277; Kahn plan for refugees in, 348
Twentieth Century Fund, 67n33, 214

UNESCO, 124n5
United Jewish Appeal: Felix Warburg role in, 55; German Jewish Aid as predecessor, 798; joint drive, 316, 316n16, 329–30, 496, 527, 591, 767; opening ceremony, 392–93
United States. *See also* German ambassadorship
domestic affairs: elections of 1932, 19–21, 230–31; elections of 1934, 552n21, 578; U.S. anti-Semitism, 461–62, 575–76, 582–83, 802–803
foreign relations: campaign for League membership, 5, 249, 578; disarmament negotiations and, 118, 121; German ambassadorship, 29, 54, 57–63, 57n2, 67, 69, 71, 73, 790; legal restrictions on humanitarian aid, 311n8; position on Mexico-Catholic relations, 628–29; support for France, 115
High Commission for Refugees: Chamberlain as Governing Body representative, 150, 180, 183; Christmas fundraising appeal and, 193–94; disinvolvement in, 132–33; proposed contribution to, 579, 585, 585n18, 595, 626, 630; response to JGM appointment, 135
immigration: Congressional opposition to, 235, 235n43, 314, 335; difficulties with German refugees and, 575–76; labor bonds, 259, 259n30, 264, 264n34, 335, 400, 804; placement of refugees in U.S., 590; plan for German-Jewish children, 455, 455n10; quota laws, 235–36, 238–39, 250, 803; relaxation of regulations, 385; State Department policy, 311, 311n5; statement on refugee relief, 118, 120, 123; substitute travel documents, 389; treatment of visa applicants, 259, 262, 802
policy on Germany: Anglo-German Commercial Treaty of 1924, 366; memorandum on social insurance, 408, 408n15; Nazi propaganda in U.S., 139, 264; Nazi view of U.S. as natural ally, 41; proposed barter agreement, 576–77, 580, 583; proposed loan to Germany, 366, 368, 376, 383–84, 399–400; public opinion of Nazi atrocities, 49n78; public opinion on Nazi atrocities, 574–75; public support for war, 123; suggested trade stance, 453
United States Holocaust Memorial Museum, 8–9
Untermyer, Samuel, 134n26, 139, 403–404, 407–408, 592

Uruguay: Chaco dispute and, 744; immigration policy, 211, 351, 672, 741–42; Jewish community in, 742; JGM visit, 674–75; settlement proposals for, 390, 584, 745–46
Urwick, Lyndall, 199n3
USSR. *See* Soviet Union

van der Lubbe, Marinus, 23, 28
Van Embden, D., 503, 512
Van Kirk, Walter W., 24, 24n9, 140, 140–41
Van Tyn, Gertrude, 180n61, 183, 502
Vansittart, Sir Robert, 53n95, 100, 543
Vargas, Getúlio Dornellas, 632–33, 633n3, 634, 635, 639, 650, 800–801
Vavasseur, Mme. Daniel, 164, 164n43
Venezuela, 621
Verdier, Jean (Cardinal), 548–49, 548n14
Vianna, Oliveira, 657, 657n17, 661, 665
Viereck, George Sylvester, 96–97, 96n2
Villard, Oswald, 582, 582n13, 802
Vladeck, B.C., 337–38, 589, 597
Vorwaerts, 337, 337n32, 341

Wagner, Robert, 75, 75n7
Wainhouse, David W., 139, 139n3
Wald, Lillian D., 5, 70, 70n41
Waldman, Morris, 776, 776n1
Waldo, Richard, 135
Wallace, Henry, 320, 320n20
Walter, Ellery, 66n27
Walters, Frank, 84, 87, 87n36, 603
Wambaugh, Sarah, 119, 119n44, 121
Warburg, Edward, 409, 452n4, 551
Warburg, Erich: analysis of Jewish resistance, 78–79; assessment of Nazi regime, 595; assimilationist tendencies of, 54, 74; biographical sketch, 11n2; concern for German Jews, 798; mentioned, 11, 50; opposition to boycott, 55; proposed education funding for refugees, 237, 247
Warburg, Felix: biographical sketch, 25n11, *55–56;* on the collection of statistical data, 271–72; on conditions in Germany, 54; conversation on the Refugee Corporation, 337–38; on direct aid to German Jews, 228, 289; financial contributions by, 7, 73, 244; FPA relationship with, 5; HCR and, 127–28, 133–34, 238; Jewish organizations relationships and, 27, 208, 235; JGM Dachau account written for, 98; London Refugee Conference, 240; mentioned, 25, 100n7, 107, 126, 132, 135, 140; on Palestine as settlement site, 56, 798; role in fundraising, 240, 409; support for JGM, 7, 67, 73
Warburg, Mrs. Felix, 240, 276
Warburg, Frederick, 57, 135, 624n12, 795
Warburg, James, 60, 60n14, 65, 65n23, 70, 135
Warburg, Max: approach to German Jews, 74, 591, 798; Argentina settlements and, 703; biographical sketch, 55, *181;* as Dachau "betrayer of Germany," 98; discussion of HCR, 180–82; JGM relationship with, 453–54, 454n7; mentioned, 50; opposition to boycott, 55, 571; property transfer plan of, 554–55; on Röhm Putsch, 491; suspected surveillance of, 44
Warburg, Nina Loeb, 70, 70n40
Warburg, Paul, 55
Warburg, Siegmund, 27, 27n23, 29, 31, 54, 80, 94
Wardwell, Allen, 150, 279n2
Warren, Avra M., 705–706, 705n20, 708–709
Warren, Constance, 135, 135n29
Warren, George, 590, 590n30
Washington Post, 73, 261
Wauchope, Sir Arthur, 497n8, 515–17, 527
Weil, Pedro, 705, 712–13, 722, 731
Weil, Simon, 691n16, 692
Weisburd, Isaac, 688
Weisnau, Frederick, 693
Weizmann, Chaim: biographical sketch, 145n13; Burton on, 670; critique of racial Judaism of, 182, 185–86; on direct aid to German Jews, 228; discussion of HCR, 152–54, 164–65, 172, 496; on divisions among Jews, 206–207; Felix Warburg relationship with, 56; German Jewish opinion of, 171–72, 177; on HCR jurisdiction in Palestine, 145, 234; Hyman on, 164–65; Jabotinsky

compared with, 363; JGM relationship with, 165, 172–73, 179, 189, 221n24, 269–70, 805; Julian Mack differences with, 239, 321; on Laski nomination to Board, 269, 273; Palestine as settlement site, 213–14, 224, 270, 273–74, 275–76, 621–22, 798; Polish Jewish opinion of, 364; salvation-through-remnants thesis of, 270, 326, 780; Schiff on, 169–70
Weizmann Institute of Science, 377n56
Welles, Sumner, 70, 70n42
Wells, Alan M., 374, 499n11
Werkdorp Wieringemeer, 491, 502–503
Wertheimer, Mildred: on the 1932 elections, 12; 1933 letter on League action on refugees, 85–89; biographical sketch, *13;* European travels of, 103–106; HCR proposal and, 77, 107, 111, 113–14, 143; meeting with Dollfuss, 115–16; mentioned, 24, 42, 47, 121; on the proposed loan to Germany, 434; reassessment of boycott, 792–93
Whitaker, John T., 105–106, 105n22, 119, 121, 124, 132
White, John Campbell, 94, 366–67, 366n41, 550, 550n17
White, John L., 684
Wickham-Steed, Henry, 374, 374n53
Wiley, Louis, 402n1, 405–406
Wilhelm, Crown Prince of Germany, 18, 18n32
Wilkinson, Ellen, 225n30
Willert, Sir Arthur, 479, 479n21
Williams, Michael, 75, 75n8
Williams, Whiting, 99, 99n5
Wilson (U.S. State Department), 647, 647n15
Wilson, Arnold Talbot, 618, 618n3
Wilson, Dr. (Brazil), 637
Wilson, Hugh R.: biographical sketch, 109n31; on German-HCR relations, 193; High Commissioner nomination and, 129, 150; mentioned, 109, 112; U.S. statement on refugees and, 118, 120, 123
Wilson, Woodrow, 5
Winchell, Walter, 55
Winds of War, The (1971), 1
Wischnitzer, Mark, 202n5, 782
Wise, Jonah B., 233n38, 235, 306, 769
Wise, Stephen S.: biographical sketch, 58n5; on the High Commissioner nomination, 131; on the importance of Felix Warburg, 240; on Jewish settlements, 153, 798; JGM meeting on refugees, 92, 93; Laski letter on, 101; mentioned, 68, 139; reaction to JGM reports from Germany, 48n73, 58; on the Weizmann salvation-through-remnants thesis, 780; World Jewish Congress and, 585, 589
Woburn House (London), 500, 693
Wolff, Fritz, 440
women, 83, 517, 524
work permits. *See permits de travail* (work permits)
World Court, 103, 578, 594, 604
World Jewish Congress, 154–55, 455, 585, 589
World Telegram, 138
World War I, 3–5, 78, 515, 681, 752–53. *See also* Treaty of Versailles
World War II: avoidance of war as chief League goal, 480; German preparations for, 491; invasion of Poland, 1, 7; warnings of imminent conflict, 256, 267–68, 520, 566–67, 805
Wouk, Herman, 1
Wurfbain, André: biographical sketch, 149n20; on HCR staff, 151, 162, 188; JGM relationship with, 194; mentioned, 149, 456; negotiation for property transfer, 573

Young Men's Hebrew Association, 133, 403
Yrigoyen, Hipolito, 717n5
Yugoslavia: acceptance of refugees in, 459; anti-Semitism in, 478; assassination of King Alexander, 498, 498n9, 503, 510; invited into Governing Body, 277; proposed trip to, 464

Zaleski, August, 364, 364n38
Zemurray, Samuel, 586, 586n19
Zimbabwe. *See* Southern Rhodesia
Zionism: anti-Semitism and, 670; in Argentina, 691, 711; British HCR relations and, 195–96, 197n84, 226, 418, 494; Canadian Hadassah presi-

Zionism (*continued*)
dent discussion, 326; Cecil on, 201; in Italy, 394; Jabotinsky on, 362; JDC and, 298, 299–300, 303–304; Kann experiences of, 182–83; Lipsky relief proposals and, 248; negotiations for Jewish relief and, 117, 185–86, 798; overview of political organizations, 207; salvation-through-remnants thesis, 270, 326, 780; Syria settlements and, 777; thesis of Nazi enablement by, 78; Warsaw Halutz headquarters visit, 364. *See also* Jews; Palestine

Zionist Federation (Argentina), 691

Zionist Organization, 117, 235

Richard Breitman is professor of history at American University. He is author of *The Architect of Genocide: Himmler and the Final Solution* and *Official Secrets: What the Nazis Planned, What the British and Americans Knew,* among other works. He is co-author (with Alan Kraut) of *American Refugee Policy and European Jewry, 1933–1954* (Indiana University Press, 1988). He is editor-in-chief of the United States Holocaust Memorial Museum's journal *Holocaust and Genocide Studies.*

Barbara McDonald Stewart received a Ph.D. in history from Columbia University and taught at George Mason University. She is author of *United States Government Policy on Refugees from Nazism, 1933–1940.*

Severin Hochberg, who received his Ph.D. from New York University, is a historian at the Center for Advanced Holocaust Studies at the United States Holocaust Memorial Museum, where he has specialized in refugee issues.